Lecture Notes in Artificial Intelligence   3248

Edited by J. G. Carbonell and J. Siekmann

Subseries of Lecture Notes in Computer Science

Keh-Yih Su   Jun'ichi Tsujii
Jong-Hyeok Lee   Oi Yee Kwong (Eds.)

Natural Language Processing – IJCNLP 2004

First International Joint Conference
Hainan Island, China, March 22-24, 2004
Revised Selected Papers

 Springer

Series Editors

Jaime G. Carbonell, Carnegie Mellon University, Pittsburgh, PA, USA
Jörg Siekmann, University of Saarland, Saarbrücken, Germany

Volume Editors

Keh-Yih Su
Behavior Design Corporation
2F, No.5, Industry E. Rd., IV Science-Based Industrial Park Hsinchu, Taiwan
E-mail: kysu@bdc.com.tw

Jun'ichi Tsujii
University of Tokyo
Faculty of Science and Graduate School of Information Science and Technology
Department of Computer Science
7-3-1 Hongo, Bunkyo-ku, Tokyo 113-0033, Japan
E-mail: tsujii@is.s.u-tokyo.ac.jp

Jong-Hyeok Lee
Pohang University of Science and Technology (POSTECH)
Department of Computer Science and Engineering
San 31 Hyoja-dong, Nam-gu, Pohang 790-784, Republic of Korea
E-mail: jhlee@postech.ac.kr

Oi Yee Kwong
City University of Hong Kong
Language Information Sciences Research Centre
Tat Chee Avenue, Kowloon, Hong Kong
E-mail: rlolivia@cityu.edu.hk

Library of Congress Control Number: 2004117792

CR Subject Classification (1998): I.2.7, I.2, F.4.3, I.7, J.5, H.3, F.2

ISSN 0302-9743
ISBN 3-540-24475-1 Springer Berlin Heidelberg New York

This work is subject to copyright. All rights are reserved, whether the whole or part of the material is concerned, specifically the rights of translation, reprinting, re-use of illustrations, recitation, broadcasting, reproduction on microfilms or in any other way, and storage in data banks. Duplication of this publication or parts thereof is permitted only under the provisions of the German Copyright Law of September 9, 1965, in its current version, and permission for use must always be obtained from Springer. Violations are liable to prosecution under the German Copyright Law.

Springer is a part of Springer Science+Business Media

springeronline.com

© Springer-Verlag Berlin Heidelberg 2005
Printed in Germany

Typesetting: Camera-ready by author, data conversion by Olgun Computergrafik
Printed on acid-free paper   SPIN: 11382423   06/3142   5 4 3 2 1 0

Foreword

IJCNLP 2004 heralded a new era for computational linguistics and natural language processing in Asia, as it coincided with the launching of the Asian Federation of NLP Associations (AFNLP) in Sanya, Hainan, China. This was a timely development for the most populous and linguistically diversified region in the world, and there is little wonder that this conference managed to draw over 200 participants. Following an enthusiastic response to the call for papers from 19 regions and the vigorous and rigorous efforts of the Program Committee Co-chairs, the sizable collection of papers presented at this conference enabled AFNLP to be compared with related organizations such as COLING and ACL, which have been in existence for more than 40 years.

The organizers recognized that it is important for serious attempts to be made to increase and improve efforts in this area all across Asia. Towards this end, and to contribute to a better awareness of topical issues, IJCNLP 2004 included two panels of special interest: (1) Panel on Emerging Asian Language Processing Efforts, and (2) Panel on Multilingual NLP for Public Information Services, which was devoted to the NLP requirements envisioned by the organizers of the 2008 Olympics. There were also two thematic sessions on (a) Natural Language Technology in Mobile Information Retrieval and Text Processing User Interfaces, and (b) Text Mining in Biomedicine. The offerings of this conference were further enriched by tutorials and workshops as well as an Asian Symposium on Natural Language Processing to Overcome Language Barriers, organized as a satellite event by the Institute of Electronics, Information and Communication Engineers (IEICE) and the Communications Research Laboratory (CRL) of Japan.

The publication of the collection of papers from IJCNLP 2004 by Springer in the Lecture Notes in Artificial Intelligence (LNAI) series is a welcome move and further testifies to the standards of the research efforts reported here.

A conference of this size and scope is not possible without the contributions of many individuals. Special thanks must go to the International Advisory Committee (Nicoletta Calzolari, Eva Hajicova, Eduard Hovy, Mark Johnson, Aravind Joshi, Martin Kay, Bente Maegaard, Joseph Mariani, Makoto Nagao, Donia Scott, Hozumi Tanaka, Hans Uszkoreit, Tianshun Yao), and the Organizing Committee. In particular, we are especially grateful to the Program Committee Co-chairs, Keh-Yih Su and Jun'ichi Tsujii; Publicity Chair, Hitoshi Isahara; Satellite Events Chair, Key-Sun Choi; Finance Committee Chair and Vice Chair, Kam-Fai Wong and Tom Lai, who had to deal with a complex "one conference, two currencies" situation and separate budgeting; and the Publication Chair and Vice Chairs, Jong-Hyeok Lee, Olivia Kwong and Sadao Kurohashi. The Local Organizing Committee in Beijing undertook the challenging responsibility for local arrangements in Sanya, and we are grateful to its Chair, Youqi Cao, and its Vice Chair and External Liaison Person, Maosong Sun.

We must also thank Makoto Nagao, the Honorary Chair of the conference, and the three keynote speakers, Ching-Chun Hsieh, Mark Johnson and Hans Uszkoreit.

IJCNLP 2004 must gratefully acknowledge financial sponsorship from a number of sources: the Association for Computational Linguistics (ACL), the Association for Computational Linguistics and Chinese Language Processing (ACLCLP), the Association of Natural Language Processing (ANLP), the Chinese Information Processing Society of China (CIPS), the Korean NLP Society, Microsoft Japan for the workshop "Beyond Shallow Analyses – Formalisms and Statistical Modeling for Deep Analyses," and the Chinese Language Computer Society (CLCS) for the workshop "Named Entity Recognition for Natural Language Processing Applications." Through CIPS, additional contributions were obtained from the National Natural Science Foundation of China, Fujitsu R&D Center Co., Ltd., Institute of Automation, Chinese Academy of Sciences, Microsoft Research Asia, NEC Laboratories, China, Peking University, TRS Information Technology Limited, and Tsinghua University. Without such support this conference would not have been possible. We also wish to thank the Finance Office of the City University of Hong Kong for graciously taking on the responsibility as credit card clearinghouse, and the City University Press and the University Printing Office for advice. Last but not least, to the many unnamed individuals and students in Beijing, Hong Kong, Pusan, Taipei and Tokyo, whose contributions were no less important in making this conference possible, we say thank you.

The Sanya region of Hainan Island has gained considerable prominence in recent years, the latest global event being the Miss World Contest. It is hoped that in future years, reference will be made in NLP circles to AFNLP's IJCNLP in Sanya as a watershed in NLP development.

August 2004   Benjamin K. Tsou
                                                     President, AFNLP

Preface

This book is a collection of selected papers presented at the 1st International Joint Conference on Natural Language Processing (IJCNLP 2004), the flagship conference organized by the Asian Federation of Natural Language Processing Associations (AFNLP) which took place on Hainan Island, China during 22–24 March, 2004.

A total of 211 papers from 19 regions were submitted to the conference. The program committee which consisted of 20 internationally well-respected experts acting as area chairs and organizers of the thematic sessions, selected 66 papers for oral presentation and 35 for poster presentation. Authors were invited to revise their papers to reflect the vigorous and constructive discussions at the conference, and we received 84 revised papers for this volume.

The articles in this volume cover diverse fields in NLP, from theoretical contributions in finite state technology, parsing, discourse modeling, machine learning, etc., to basic NLP technologies of semantic disambiguation, shallow parsing, sentence/text generation, etc., to NLP applications such as machine translation, text mining and information retrieval. We also have articles on topics crucial for Asian language processing, including word segmentation, chunkers, etc. The linguistic diversity in Asia has posed exciting challenges, not only to researchers who believe in the universality of human language and the technologies in computational linguistics, but also to those interested in practical applications of NLP for Asian languages. This volume should give them a good collection of the current and the most advanced results in such research.

At the same time, since the conference attracted contributions from active and respected researchers all over the world, the articles in this volume not only showcase language-specific research output, but also represent the general current achievements in our field, from both the theoretical and technological fronts. In particular, the two thematic sessions, "Text Mining in Biomedicine" and "Natural Language Technology in Mobile Information Retrieval and Text Processing User Interfaces," solicited high-quality contributions on these emerging technological challenges.

We would like to thank the area chairs and the reviewers who carried out professionally rigorous reviews and selection of papers for the conference, as well as the authors who revised their already high-quality papers to reflect the discussion at the conference. Special thanks are also given to Jin-Dong Kim (University of Tokyo) and Christine Günther (Springer) who gave technical and editorial support in the preparation of this volume.

August 2004   Keh-Yih Su,   Jun'ichi Tsujii,
                                                                                           Jong-Hyeok Lee,   Oi Yee Kwong

Conference Co-chairs

Guangnan Ni   Chinese Academy of Engineering, Beijing
Benjamin K. Tsou   City University of Hong Kong, Hong Kong

Program Co-chairs

Keh-Yih Su   Behavior Design Corporation, Hsinchu
Jun'ichi Tsujii   University of Tokyo, Tokyo

Program Committee

John Carroll   Sussex University, Brighton
Keh-Jiann Chen   Academia Sinica, Taipei
Ann Copestake   University of Cambridge, Cambridge
Robert Dale   Macquarie University, Sydney
Chu-Ren Huang   Academia Sinica, Taipei
Chin-Hui Lee   Georgia Institute of Technology, Atlanta
Gary Geunbae Lee   Pohang University of Science and Technology, Pohang
Alessandro Lenci   University of Pisa, Pisa
Dekang Lin   University of Alberta, Alberta
Yuji Matsumoto   NAIST, Nara
Sung Hyon Myaeng   Information and Communications University, Daejeon
Hwee Tou Ng   National University of Singapore, Singapore
Franz Och   ISI-USC, Los Angeles
Manabu Okumura   Tokyo Institute of Technology, Tokyo
Martha Palmer   University of Pennsylvania, Philadelphia
Laurent Romary   LORIA, Paris
Declerck Thierry   DFKI and Saarland University, Saarbruecken
Kenji Yamanishi   NEC, Tokyo
Tiejun Zhao   Harbin Institute of Technology, Harbin
Chengqing Zong   Chinese Academy of Sciences, Beijing

Reviewers

Steven Abney   Pierrette Bouillon   Jason Chang
Hani Abu-Salem   Thorsten Brants   Eugene Charniak
Eneko Agirre   Elizabeth Owen Bratt   Hsin-Hsi Chen
Akiko Aizawa   Paul Buitelaar   John Chen
Collin Baker   Harry Bunt   Hua Cheng
Nuria Bel   Miriam Butt   Colin Cherry
Emily Bender   Jean Caelen   Lee-Feng Chien
Christian Boitet   Nicoletta Calzolari   Tat-Seng Chua
Kalina Bontcheva   Jeongwon Cha   Fabio Ciravegna

Fabio Crestani
Dan Cristea
Dick Crouch
Chris Culy
Hamish Cunningham
Walter Daelemans
Ido Dagan
Jianwu Dang
Jean-Louis Dessalles
Laurence Devillers
Bonnie Dorr
Phil Edmonds
Gregor Erbach
Christiane Fellbaum
Sandiway Fong
Anette Frank
Pascale Fung
Jianfeng Gao
Sheng Gao
Ismael García Varea
Daniel Gildea
Claire Grover
Koiti Hasida
Wen-Lian Hsu
Taiyi Huang
Kentaro Inui
Masato Ishizaki
Donghong Ji
Hongyan Jing
Kristiina Jokinen
Arne Jönsson
Min-Yen Kan
Seungshik Kang
Kyoko Kanzaki
Lauri Karttunen
John Kelleher
Chris Khoo
Genichiro Kikui
Jong-Bok Kim
Jung-Hee Kim
Minkoo Kim
Alistair Knott
Philipp Koehn
Greg Kondrak
Anna Korhonen

Geert-Jan Kruijff
Sadao Kurohashi
Kui-Lam Kwok
Oi Yee Kwong
Tom Lai
Wai Lam
Philippe Langlais
Mirella Lapata
Gianni Lazzari
Gary Geunbae Lee
Jong-Hyeok Lee
Tan Lee
Mun-Kew Leong
Gina-Anne Levow
David Lewis
Haizhou Li
Hang Li
Chin-Yew Lin
Charles X. Ling
Bing Liu
Ting Liu
Robert Luk
Qing Ma
Bernardo Magnini
Robert Malouf
Inderjeet Mani
Daniel Marcu
Stella Markantonatou
Shigeru Masuyama
Yuji Matsumoto
Diana McCarthy
Kathleen McCoy
Paul Mc Kevitt
Helen Meng
Paola Merlo
Robert Moore
Tatsunori Mori
Masaaki Nagata
Chieko Nakabasami
Hwee Tou Ng
Grace Ngai
Jian-Yun Nie
Takashi Ninomiya
Cheng Niu
Tadashi Nomoto

Stephan Oepen
Kemal Oflazer
Miles Osborne
Kyonghee Paik
Patrick Pantel
Jong Park
Seong-Bae Park
John Patrick
Adam Pease
Ted Pedersen
Gerald Penn
Wim Peters
Detlef Prescher
Dragomir Radev
Stefan Riezler
German Rigau
Hae-Chang Rim
Brian Roark
Tetsuya Sakai
Susanne Salmon-Alt
Rajeev Sangal
Anoop Sarkar
Mark Seligman
Melanie Siegel
Jacques Siroux
Virach
  Sornlertlamvanich
Richard Sproat
Suzanne Stevenson
Michael Strube
Tomek Strzalkowski
Jian Su
Eiichiro Sumita
Maosong Sun
Hisami Suzuki
Hideki Tanaka
Hozumi Tanaka
Takaaki Tanaka
Jianhua Tao
Declerck Thierry
Takenobu Tokunaga
Peter Turney
Akira Ushioda
Takehito Utsuro
Antal van den Bosch

Josef van Genabith
Gertjan van Noord
Renata Vieira
Stephan Vogel
Haifeng Wang
Taro Watanabe
David Weir
Fuliang Weng

Jan Wiebe
Andi Wu
Dekai Wu
Lide Wu
Jun Xu
Peng Xu
Bert Xue
Endong Xun

Kenji Yamada
Qiang Yang
Jiangsheng Yu
Min Zhang
Shuwu Zhang
Fang Zheng
Guodong Zhou
Ming Zhou

Table of Contents

Dialogue and Discourse

Fast Reinforcement Learning of Dialogue Policies
Using Stable Function Approximation 1
    Matthias Denecke, Kohji Dohsaka, and Mikio Nakano

Zero Pronoun Resolution Based on Automatically Constructed Case Frames
and Structural Preference of Antecedents 12
    Daisuke Kawahara and Sadao Kurohashi

Improving Noun Phrase Coreference Resolution by Matching Strings 22
    Xiaofeng Yang, Guodong Zhou, Jian Su, and Chew Lim Tan

Combining Labeled and Unlabeled Data
for Learning Cross-Document Structural Relationships 32
    Zhu Zhang and Dragomir Radev

FSA, Parsing Algorithms

Parsing Mixed Constructions in a Type Feature Structure Grammar 42
    Jong-Bok Kim and Jaehyung Yang

Iterative CKY Parsing for Probabilistic Context-Free Grammars 52
    Yoshimasa Tsuruoka and Jun'ichi Tsujii

Information Extraction and Question Answering

Causal Relation Extraction
Using Cue Phrase and Lexical Pair Probabilities 61
    Du-Seong Chang and Key-Sun Choi

A Re-examination of IR Techniques in QA System 71
    Yi Chang, Hongbo Xu, and Shuo Bai

A Novel Pattern Learning Method
for Open Domain Question Answering 81
    Yongping Du, Xuanjing Huang, Xin Li, and Lide Wu

Chinese Named Entity Recognition
Based on Multilevel Linguistic Features 90
    Honglei Guo, Jianmin Jiang, Gang Hu, and Tong Zhang

Information Retrieval

Information Flow Analysis with Chinese Text 100
  Paulo Cheong, Dawei Song, Peter Bruza, and Kam-Fai Wong

Phoneme-Based Transliteration of Foreign Names for OOV Problem 110
  Wei Gao, Kam-Fai Wong, and Wai Lam

Window-Based Method for Information Retrieval 120
  Qianli Jin, Jun Zhao, and Bo Xu

Improving Relevance Feedback in Language Modeling Approach:
Maximum a Posteriori Probability Criterion
and Three-Component Mixture Model 130
  Seung-Hoon Na, In-Su Kang, and Jong-Hyeok Lee

BBS Based Hot Topic Retrieval
Using Back-Propagation Neural Network 139
  Lan You, Yongping Du, Jiayin Ge, Xuanjing Huang, and Lide Wu

How Effective Is Query Expansion for Finding Novel Information? 149
  Min Zhang, Chuan Lin, and Shaoping Ma

Lexical Semantics, Ontology and Linguistic Resources

The Hinoki Treebank. A Treebank for Text Understanding 158
  Francis Bond, Sanae Fujita, Chikara Hashimoto, Kaname Kasahara, Shigeko Nariyama, Eric Nichols, Akira Ohtani, Takaaki Tanaka, and Shigeaki Amano

Building a Parallel Bilingual Syntactically Annotated Corpus 168
  Jan Cuřín, Martin Čmejrek, Jiří Havelka, and Vladislav Kuboň

Acquiring Bilingual Named Entity Translations
from Content-Aligned Corpora 177
  Tadashi Kumano, Hideki Kashioka, Hideki Tanaka, and Takahiro Fukusima

Visual Semantics and Ontology of Eventive Verbs 187
  Minhua Ma and Paul Mc Kevitt

A Persistent Feature-Object Database
for Intelligent Text Archive Systems 197
  Takashi Ninomiya, Jun'ichi Tsujii, and Yusuke Miyao

Machine Translation and Multilinguality

Example-Based Machine Translation
Without Saying Inferable Predicate 206
   Eiji Aramaki, Sadao Kurohashi, Hideki Kashioka, and Hideki Tanaka

Improving Back-Transliteration by Combining Information Sources 216
   Slaven Bilac and Hozumi Tanaka

Bilingual Sentence Alignment
Based on Punctuation Statistics and Lexicon 224
   Thomas C. Chuang, Jian-Cheng Wu, Tracy Lin, Wen-Chie Shei, and Jason S. Chang

Automatic Learning of Parallel Dependency Treelet Pairs 233
   Yuan Ding and Martha Palmer

Practical Translation Pattern Acquisition
from Combined Language Resources 244
   Mihoko Kitamura and Yuji Matsumoto

An English-Hindi Statistical Machine Translation System 254
   Raghavendra Udupa U. and Tanveer A. Faruquie

NLP Software and Application

Robust Speaker Identification System
Based on Wavelet Transform and Gaussian Mixture Model 263
   Wan-Chen Chen, Ching-Tang Hsieh, and Eugene Lai

Selecting Prosody Parameters for Unit Selection Based Chinese TTS 272
   Minghui Dong, Kim-Teng Lua, and Jun Xu

Natural Language Database Access
Using Semi-automatically Constructed Translation Knowledge 280
   In-Su Kang, Jae-Hak J. Bae, and Jong-Hyeok Lee

Korean Stochastic Word-Spacing
with Dynamic Expansion of Candidate Words List 290
   Mi-young Kang, Sung-ja Choi, Ae-sun Yoon, and Hyuk-chul Kwon

You Don't Have to Think Twice if You Carefully Tokenize 299
   Stefan Klatt and Bernd Bohnet

Automatic Genre Detection of Web Documents 310
   Chul Su Lim, Kong Joo Lee, and Gil Chang Kim

Statistical Substring Reduction in Linear Time 320
   Xueqiang Lü, Le Zhang, and Junfeng Hu

Detecting Sentence Boundaries in Japanese Speech Transcriptions
Using a Morphological Analyzer 328
  Sachie Tajima, Hidetsugu Nanba, and Manabu Okumura

Specification Retrieval –
How to Find Attribute-Value Information on the Web 338
  Minoru Yoshida and Hiroshi Nakagawa

Semantic Disambiguation

Conceptual Information-Based Sense Disambiguation 348
  You-Jin Chung, Kyonghi Moon, and Jong-Hyeok Lee

Influence of WSD on Cross-Language Information Retrieval 358
  In-Su Kang, Seung-Hoon Na, and Jong-Hyeok Lee

Resolution of Modifier-Head Relation Gaps
Using Automatically Extracted Metonymic Expressions 367
  Yoji Kiyota, Sadao Kurohashi, and Fuyuko Kido

Word Sense Disambiguation Using Heterogeneous Language Resources ... 377
  Kiyoaki Shirai and Takayuki Tamagaki

Improving Word Sense Disambiguation by Pseudo-samples 386
  Xiaojie Wang and Yuji Matsumoto

Statistical Models and Machine Learning for NLP

Long Distance Dependency in Language Modeling: An Empirical Study .. 396
  Jianfeng Gao and Hisami Suzuki

Word Folding: Taking the Snapshot of Words Instead of the Whole 406
  Jin-Dong Kim and Jun'ichi Tsujii

Bilingual Chunk Alignment Based on Interactional Matching
and Probabilistic Latent Semantic Indexing 416
  Feifan Liu, Qianli Jin, Jun Zhao, and Bo Xu

Learning to Filter Junk E-mail from Positive and Unlabeled Examples . 426
  Karl-Michael Schneider

A Collaborative Ability Measurement for Co-training 436
  Dan Shen, Jie Zhang, Jian Su, Guodong Zhou, and Chew-Lim Tan

Flexible Margin Selection for Reranking with Full Pairwise Samples . 446
  Libin Shen and Aravind K. Joshi

A Comparative Study on the Use of Labeled and Unlabeled Data
for Large Margin Classifiers 456
    Hiroya Takamura and Manabu Okumura

Comparing Entropies Within the Chinese Language 466
    Benjamin K. Tsou, Tom B.Y. Lai, and Ka-po Chow

NTPC: N-Fold Templated Piped Correction 476
    Dekai Wu, Grace Ngai, and Marine Carpuat

A Three Level Cache-Based Adaptive Chinese Language Model 487
    Junlin Zhang, Le Sun, Weimin Qu, Lin Du, and Yufang Sun

Taggers, Chunkers, Shallow Parsers

Using a Smoothing Maximum Entropy Model
for Chinese Nominal Entity Tagging 493
    Jinying Chen, Nianwen Xue, and Martha Palmer

Deterministic Dependency Structure Analyzer for Chinese 500
    Yuchang Cheng, Masayuki Asahara, and Yuji Matsumoto

High Speed Unknown Word Prediction Using Support Vector Machine
for Chinese Text-to-Speech Systems 509
    *Juhong Ha, Yu Zheng, Byeongchang Kim, Gary Geunbae Lee,
and Yoon-Suk Seong*

Syntactic Analysis of Long Sentences Based on S-Clauses 518
    Mi-Young Kim and Jong-Hyeok Lee

Chinese Chunk Identification Using SVMs Plus Sigmoid 527
    Yongmei Tan, Tianshun Yao, Qing Chen, and Jingbo Zhu

Tagging Complex NEs with MaxEnt Models:
Layered Structures Versus Extended Tagset 537
    Deyi Xiong, Hongkui Yu, and Qun Liu

A Nearest-Neighbor Method for Resolving PP-Attachment Ambiguity 545
    Shaojun Zhao and Dekang Lin

Text and Sentence Generation

Detection of Incorrect Case Assignments in Paraphrase Generation 555
    Atsushi Fujita, Kentaro Inui, and Yuji Matsumoto

Building a Pronominalization Model
by Feature Selection and Machine Learning 566
    Ji-Eun Roh and Jong-Hyeok Lee

Text Mining

Categorizing Unknown Text Segments for Information Extraction
Using a Search Result Mining Approach 576
    Chien-Chung Huang, Shui-Lung Chuang, and Lee-Feng Chien

Mining Table Information on the Internet 587
    Sung-won Jung, Gi-deuk Han, and Hyuk-chul Kwon

Collecting Evaluative Expressions for Opinion Extraction 596
    Nozomi Kobayashi, Kentaro Inui, Yuji Matsumoto, Kenji Tateishi, and Toshikazu Fukushima

A Study of Semi-discrete Matrix Decomposition for LSI
in Automated Text Categorization 606
    Wang Qiang, Wang XiaoLong, and Guan Yi

Systematic Construction of Hierarchical Classifier
in SVM-Based Text Categorization 616
    Yongwook Yoon, Changki Lee, and Gary Geunbae Lee

Theories and Formalisms for Morphology, Syntax and Semantics

Implementing the Syntax of Japanese Numeral Classifiers 626
    Emily M. Bender and Melanie Siegel

A Graph Grammar Approach to Map Between Dependency Trees
and Topological Models 636
    Bernd Bohnet

The Automatic Acquisition of Verb Subcategorisations
and Their Impact on the Performance of an HPSG Parser 646
    John Carroll and Alex C. Fang

Chinese Treebanks and Grammar Extraction 655
    Keh-Jiann Chen and Yu-Ming Hsieh

FML-Based SCF Predefinition Learning for Chinese Verbs 664
    Xiwu Han, Tiejun Zhao, and Muyun Yang

Deep Analysis of Modern Greek 674
    Valia Kordoni and Julia Neu

Corpus-Oriented Grammar Development for Acquiring a Head-Driven
Phrase Structure Grammar from the Penn Treebank 684
    Yusuke Miyao, Takashi Ninomiya, and Jun'ichi Tsujii

Word Segmentation

Unsupervised Segmentation of Chinese Corpus Using Accessor Variety ... 694
    Haodi Feng, Kang Chen, Chunyu Kit, and Xiaotie Deng

Chinese Unknown Word Identification Using Class-Based LM 704
    Guohong Fu and Kang-Kwong Luke

An Example-Based Study on Chinese Word Segmentation
Using Critical Fragments 714
    Qinan Hu, Haihua Pan, and Chunyu Kit

The Use of SVM for Chinese New Word Identification 723
    Hongqiao Li, Chang-Ning Huang, Jianfeng Gao, and Xiaozhong Fan

Chinese New Word Finding Using Character-Based Parsing Model 733
    Yao Meng, Hao Yu, and Fumihito Nishino

Thematic Session: Natural Language Technology in Mobile Information Retrieval and Text Processing User Interfaces

Introduction 743
    Michael Kuehn, Mun-Kew Leong, and Kumiko Tanaka-Ishii

Spoken Versus Written Queries for Mobile Information Access:
An Experiment on Mandarin Chinese 745
    Heather Du and Fabio Crestani

An Interactive Proofreading System for Inappropriately Selected Words
on Using Predictive Text Entry 755
    Hideya Iwasaki and Kumiko Tanaka-Ishii

Dit4dah: Predictive Pruning for Morse Code Text Entry 765
    Kumiko Tanaka-Ishii and Ian Frank

Thematic Session: Text Mining in Biomedicine

Introduction 776
    Sophia Ananiadou and Jong C. Park

Unsupervised Event Extraction from Biomedical Literature
Using Co-occurrence Information and Basic Patterns 777
    Hong-woo Chun, Young-sook Hwang, and Hae-Chang Rim

Annotation of Gene Products in the Literature with Gene Ontology Terms
Using Syntactic Dependencies 787
    Jung-jae Kim and Jong C. Park

Mining Biomedical Abstracts: What's in a Term? 797
    Goran Nenadic, Irena Spasic, and Sophia Ananiadou

SVM-Based Biological Named Entity Recognition
Using Minimum Edit-Distance Feature Boosted by Virtual Examples 807
    Eunji Yi, Gary Geunbae Lee, Yu Song, and Soo-Jun Park

Author Index 815

Fast Reinforcement Learning of Dialogue Policies Using Stable Function Approximation

Matthias Denecke, Kohji Dohsaka, and Mikio Nakano

Communication Science Laboratories
Nippon Telegraph and Telephone Corporation
3-1 Morinosato Wakamiya
Atsugi, Kanagawa 243-0198
{denecke,dohsaka,nakano}@atom.brl.ntt.co.jp

Abstract. We propose a method to speed up reinforcement learning of policies for spoken dialogue systems. This is achieved by combining a coarse grained abstract representation of states and actions with learning only in frequently visited states. The value of unsampled states is approximated by a linear interpolation of known states. Experiments show that the proposed method effectively optimizes dialogue strategies for frequently visited dialogue states.

1 Introduction

The application of reinforcement learning to finding optimal dialogue policies holds great potential for the automated design of spoken dialogue systems. The task of designing the dialogue policy is taken over by the computer, directed only by feedback from the user whether the dialogue with the system was experienced as positive or negative (Singh et al [1]).

Nevertheless, there are problems with the existing approaches. One major concern is the size of the state-action space. Since convergence towards an optimal policy slows down as the size of state and action spaces increase, information coded in the state and action spaces need to be balanced against the amount of feedback available.

We propose representations of the state and action spaces that allow for an efficient learning of dialogue policies. This is achieved by partitioning the state and action spaces into coarse grained abstract states and actions. Learning is carried out in the abstract spaces. Consequently, the learned dialogue policies are to some degree *underspecified* with respect to which action is to be taken by the dialogue manager. Additional knowledge is then used to select among the actions proposed by the learned dialogue strategy.

However, the size of the abstract state action space is still too large to learn dialogue policies effectively. To further increase convergence of the learning algorithm, we combine the abstract state and action representations with a function approximation approach to reinforcement learning. We select a sample of frequently visited states and learn the action value function only for this sample. The action value function for states not in the sample set is the weighted average of the action value functions of sampled states, where "similar" dialogue states carry a higher weight than "dissimilar" dialogue states. This approach is an application of stable function approximation in off-line reinforcement learning as described in Gordon [2].

2 Reinforcement Learning in Spoken Dialogue Systems

Levin and Pieraccini [3] suggested that dialogue policies can be designed using *Markov decision processes*. A Markov decision process is defined by its state and action sets $S = \{s_1, \ldots, s_m\}, A = \{a_1, \ldots, a_n\}$, its transition probabilities $P(s'|s,a)$ and reward function $R(s,a)$. The reward function represents the expected value of the reward when applying action a in state s. We identify states and actions by integers between 1 and m, or 1 and n, respectively.

2.1 Reinforcement Learning

Reinforcement learning is the problem faced by an agent that must learn policies through trial and error interaction with its environment. The agent bases its decision at time t on a *value function* $Q_t(s,a)$ which estimates "how good" it is to select action a in state s. Information on the success (or absence thereof) of the actions taken is used to increase (or decrease) $Q_t(s,a)$. This is done in such a way that the value function of successful state-action combination pairs converges to higher values than the value function of unsuccessful ones.

If the state and action spaces are small, the value function can be represented by a two-dimensional table $Q(s,a)$. Updates of the value function can be done on-line (during exploration of the environment) or off-line (after exploration has been terminated). In the off-line case, value iteration (Kaelbling et al. [4]) can be used, where the action value function is updated according to

$$Q_{t+1}(s,a) \leftarrow R(s,a) + \lambda \sum_{s'} P(s' \mid s,a) \max_{a'} Q_t(s',a') \qquad (1)$$

where $P(s' \mid s,a)$ and $R(s,a)$ are the estimated transition and reward models, respectively. It can be shown that the repeated application of (1) converges towards a value function Q^* and that the policy

$$\pi^*(s) = \mathrm{argmax}\,_a Q^*(s,a) \qquad (2)$$

is optimal within a small error bound.

2.2 Learning Dialogue Policies

Learning dialogue policies using reinforcement learning allows a system designer to improve an existing dialogue strategy simply by providing positive or negative feedback on sample dialogues. The application of reinforcement learning to spoken dialogue systems has been previously investigated in Walker et al [5] and Singh et al [1]. In order to come up with a working system for data collection, the initial dialogue policy has been hand-crafted. While users interact with the initial system, the policy state space is explored. Due to the initial hand crafted strategy, the actions of the initial system are sensible, yet not necessarily optimal. At the end of the dialogue, the users provide feedback of -1, 0 or 1, depending on the quality of the dialogue. After data have been collected from the users, the transition probabilities are learned by applying a standard value iteration algorithm using equation (1).

Williams and Young [6] describe a method to bootstrap this initial dialogue strategy from a small corpus using supervised learning methods. Roy et al [7] model the dialogue using a Partially Observable Markov Decision Process.

2.3 Scalability and Data Sparseness Problems

It turns out that for many applications the state and action space is too large relative to the amount of available feedback for the action value function to converge toward something useful. In many tasks, most states encountered will not have been experienced during training. For these reasons, there have been investigations on how to generalize the value function based on a limited subset of states experienced during exploration. This approach is referred to as *function approximation*, since the value function of unknown state action pairs is approximated with the help of previously encountered ones.

However, problems may arise due to the way in which the estimation of the value function and reinforcement learning interact. This is because that an update of the value function is not local to (s, a), but typically affects the estimated value of other state action pairs as well. Therefore, there are cases in which function approximation is unstable.

Gordon [2] proves stable convergence of value iteration with function approximation for a large class of approximators he calls *averagers*. The idea of his work is that the action value function at a given point can be approximated by the weighted average of exact (i.e. not approximated) action value functions at other points. Under certain conditions, convergence is guaranteed.

Other approaches to increasing convergence speed for learning spoken dialogue systems have been explored previously. Scheffler and Young [8] use eligibility traces (see Sutton and Barto [9]) to better distribute the reward information across the state-action space. However, in this work, a reward function is explicitly given by the system designer. In our case, we are interested in learning dialogue strategies without explicitly formulating a reward function.

Goddeau and Pineau [10] achieve a reduction in state space by providing a backup model for states and actions. The many-to-1 mapping from states and actions to backup states and backup actions effectively partitions the state and action space into a smaller state-action space of equivalence classes.

3   Our Approach

In light of the previous discussion, we apply off-line reinforcement learning to dialogue management as follows. We define a set of abstract dialogue states and abstract dialogue actions. We then explore the abstract state action space by selecting actions randomly.

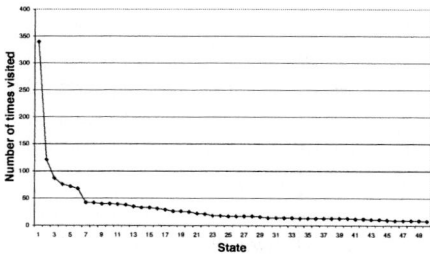

Fig. 1. Distribution of encountered dialogue states during exploration of the state-action space.

We note that the distribution of number of times a given dialogue state is visited during exploration varies greatly. Figure 1 shows the distribution of dialogue states visited during 250 dialogues with 25 different users. Shown are the absolute frequencies for the 50 most often visited dialogue states. There was a total of 972 dialogue states.

Since stable function approximation requires the selection of an adequate subset of states for value iteration, we take advantage of the distribution of state frequencies and select those states that are visited frequently. Following Gordon [2], value iteration is carried out on the subset of states while the value function of unsampled states is approximated. The approximation of unsampled states is done in such a way that the value function for unsampled states resembles the value function of "similar" visited states.

4 Coding of State and Action Spaces

4.1 Coding of the Action Space

Actions in the dialogue manager are specified as rules. A rule r has a list of preconditions $pre(r)$, a list of postconditions $post(r)$ and a list of actions. The semantics of preconditions and postconditions can be paraphrased as: It is sensible to apply an action if the dialogue manager is in a state in which the preconditions hold and the dialogue manager wishes to bring about a state in which the postconditions hold. For example, a slot value can only be confirmed if the slot is filled. Furthermore, the postcondition ensures that an action is not applied twice. For example, if a slot is already filled, the user is not prompted a second time. The use of preconditions and postconditions, if formulated appropriately, always leads to sensible dialogues, but not necessarily to optimal ones.

We view two states in which the sets of meta data annotations of applicable actions are equal as equivalent. This approach gives rise to a two level representation of dialogue and action spaces as illustrated by figure 2. In this example, the abstract action Confirm maps onto the concrete actions Confirm_Dep-Time and Confirm_Dep-Location. After executing of either action, both possible resulting dialogue states map on the same abstract dialogue state shown in the upper right of the figure.

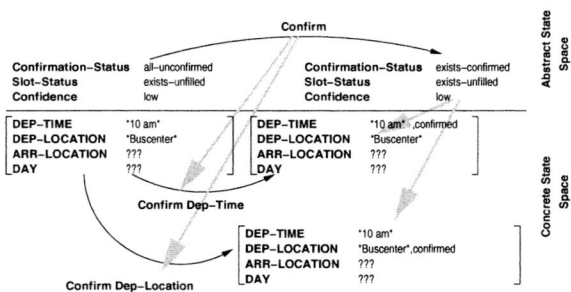

Fig. 2. Two level representations of dialogue state and action spaces.

As in Singh et al [1], we encode actions along the three characteristics *grammar*, *prompt type* and *confirmation*. The grammar feature can take values *restricted* and *unrestricted*. The prompt feature can take the values *open ended* and *directive*. The meaning of these characteristics correspond to those introduced in Singh et al [1]. The confirmation characteristic can take the values *explicit confirmation one*, *explicit confirmation all*, *implicit confirmation previous* and *none*. Table 1 (a) lists possible combinations of the characteristics.

Table 1. (a) Encoding of actions. (b) Organization of the abstract dialogue state space. The total size can be obtained by multiplying the size $\mid V_i \mid$ of the variables V_i.

Action	Conf.	# Slots confirmed	Prompt Type	Grammar
Expl. Conf. 1	explicit	1	directive	restricted
Expl. Conf. all	explicit	all	directive	unrestricted
Prompt, no conf	none	0	directive	restricted
Prompt, no conf	none	0	open ended	unrestricted
Prompt, impl conf 1	implicit	previous	directive	unrestricted

Variable	Possible Values	Size
Confirmation	all unconfirmed, some unconfirmed, all confirmed	3
Length of input	short, intermediate, long, very long	4
Information	no filled, some filled, all filled	3
Min Confidence	low, medium, high	3
Max Confidence	low, medium, high	3
Intention	selected, determined, finalized	3
Total size		972

4.2 Coding of the State Space

In our approach, following Denecke [11], we partition the state space according to the information they contain with respect to action selection. For example, two different dialogue states might necessitate prompting for the value of two different slots. In order to avoid prompting the wrong value, we need to add preconditions to the actions. The complete abstract dialogue state space is shown in Table 1 (b). We note that not all combinations of variable assignments represent sensical dialogue states as not all variables are independent of each other.

We assume that at any time in the dialogue, there is a set of slots to be filled. The set of slots is the union of the slots specified in the active dialogue goals. A slot i is called *needed* if there is a goal currently active (i.e. not deselected) that requires slot i to be filled. Thus, the number of needed slots decreases as more and more goals become deselected. For convenience, we define N_t and F_t the set of needed slots, and filled slots, at time t, respectively. For each slot i, we have predicates $filled_t(i)$ and $confirmed_t(i)$ evaluating to *true* if the ith slot has been filled, or filled and confirmed, respectively. Furthermore, there is a function $prompted_t(i)$ returning the number of times the ith slot has been prompted. Finally, there is a function $confidence_t(i)$ returning $low, medium$ or $high$, depending on the confidence with which the value in the slot has been recognized. If $filled_t(i)$ is $false$, $prompted_t(i)$ is 0 and $confirmed_t(i)$ is undefined.

The variable *Confidence* evaluates to the minimal confidence score of all filled slots, or

$$Confidence_t = \min{}_{i \in N_t(i) \cap F_t(i)} confidence_t(i) \qquad (3)$$

and is set to high at the beginning of the dialogue. Variable *Information* evaluates to $allFilled$, $existsFilled$ or $allUnfilled$ according to

$$Information_t = \begin{cases} allFilled & \forall i : filled_t(i) \\ allUnfilled & \forall i : \neg filled_t(i) \\ existsFilled & otherwise \end{cases} \qquad (4)$$

The variable *Confirmation* is evaluated to $allUnconfirmed$, $existsUnconfirmed$ and $allConfirmed$ along the lines of the evaluation of variable $Information$.

The variable *Intention* represents the degree to which the intention of the user could be determined. In the following, let S denote the information established in the discourse (irrespective of the source of information, i.e. answers to questions or database access). Furthermore, g, g' refer to dialogue goals and $pre(g)$ to the preconditions of goal g.

At the beginning of the dialogue, S does not contain any information, or $S = \bot$. In other words, it is not yet determined which service of the dialogue system the user is going to demand. Formally,

$$\begin{aligned} \exists g, g', g \neq g' : &\ compatible(pre(g), S), \\ &\ compatible(pre(g'), S) \end{aligned} \qquad (5)$$

Additional information established through information seeking questions, database access or invocation of services in the back-end, increases the informational content of S up to the point where there is only one goal g^* whose preconditions are compatible with S. Formally,

$$\begin{aligned} \forall g, g' : &\ compatible(pre(g), S), \\ &\ compatible(pre(g'), S) \\ \Rightarrow &\ g = g' \end{aligned} \qquad (6)$$

Additional interaction between system and user will yield more information until the established information S is at least as specific as the precondition of g^*:

$$\exists g : subsumes(pre(g), S) \qquad (7)$$

Since we assume the preconditions of the goals to be mutually incompatible, there is only one goal whose precondition subsumes S. Conditions (5), (6) and (7) define the values *selected*, *determined* and *finalized*, respectively, of the variable *Intention*.

4.3 Mapping to MDP States

Following the previous section, each abstract dialogue state can be represented as a 6 dimensional vector $s(\mathbf{v}) = \langle v_1, \ldots, v_6 \rangle$ where v_i is the value of the i th variable V_i in the abstract dialogue state. From this representation, we obtain the state of the Markov Decision Process $s(\mathbf{v})$, $1 \leq s(\mathbf{v}) \leq m$ according to

$$s(\mathbf{v}) = \sum_{i}^{6} v_i \prod_{j=1}^{i-1} | V_j | \qquad (8)$$

with the empty product equaling 1. $| V_j |$ denotes the number of values variable V_j can take.

4.4 Distance Between Dialogue States

As mentioned above, we approximate the state-action value function for some abstract dialogue states as a weighted sum of the value of the abstract value function in other states. In order to choose appropriately close states, we need to define a distance function. We define the distance $d(\cdot, \cdot)$ between two abstract dialogue states to be the Euclidean distance between the values of the abstract state variables. The values are assigned integers 0,1,2,3 in the order in which they are displayed in Table 1 (b).

4.5 Stable Function Approximation

In what follows, s, s', s'' and t represent abstract dialogue states obtained via the mapping defined in equation 8, and a, a' and a'' represent abstract actions. Following Gordon [2], the application of the standard Bellman value update operator is replaced with a combined operator $M_A \circ T_M$. T_M is the standard update (see equation 1) for those states s that are frequently visited.

$$Q'(s, a) = R(s, a) + \lambda \sum_{s'} P(s' \mid s, a) \max_{a'} Q(s', a') \qquad (9)$$

Subsequently, the averaging operator M_A determines the Q values for the remaining state action pairs (t, a):

$$Q''(t, a) = \sum_{s'} \sum_{a'} \beta_{tas'a'} Q'(s', a')$$

If t is an exact state we set $\beta_{tas'a'} = 1$ for $t = s$ and $a = a'$, and 0 otherwise. If t is an approximated state, we set $\beta_{tas'a'} = 0$ for $a \neq a'$. For the remaining β, we set $\beta_{tas'a} = N/d(t, s')$, where N is a normalization factor so that $\sum_{s'} \beta_{tas'a} = 1$. Substituting $Q'(t, a)$ for equation 9, we obtain for approximated states t:

$$\begin{aligned} Q''(t, a) &= \sum_{s'} \sum_{a'} \beta_{tas'a'} \left(R(s', a') + \lambda \sum_{s''} P(s'' \mid s', a') \max_{a''} Q(s'', a'') \right) \\ &= \sum_{s'} N/d(t, s') \left(R(s', a) + \lambda \sum_{s''} P(s'' \mid s', a) \max_{a''} Q(s'', a'') \right), \end{aligned}$$

where s' ranges over exact states only. A value backup during value iteration becomes then $Q(t, a) \leftarrow Q''(t, a)$.

5 Application of Stable Function Approximation to Dialogue Processing

We recall that the reinforcement learning algorithm valuates state action combinations in the abstract space while the dialogue manager needs to apply actions in the concrete space (cf. figure 2). The optimal action a^* to be applied in (abstract) state s is determined according to

$$a^* = \operatorname{argmax}_{a \in \mathcal{A}(s)} Q_t(s, a) \qquad (10)$$

where the (abstract) action a is in $\mathcal{A}(s)$ if there is at least one (but potentially more than one) concrete action available whose precondition is satisfied in the concrete dialogue state. If the abstract action a^* represents multiple concrete actions, it is the task of the dialogue manager to choose among the candidates. At this point, system designers can introduce additional domain knowledge (such as to require the dialogue manager to always prompt for arrival information before departure information), or ties may be broken randomly.

When coding the abstract state space, care needs to be taken that all relevant information for abstract action selection is contained in the abstract state space. To illustrate this point, we assume an alternative coding in which the variable $Information$ was missing. Consider two concrete dialogue states s_1 and s_2 in which all but one slots are filled and confirmed. In s_1, the last slot is unfilled. In s_2, the last slot is filled but not confirmed. The sets of applicable (abstract) actions are $InfoSeekQuestion$ and $ConfirmationQuestion$, respectively. Yet, since both concrete dialogue states map onto the same abstract dialogue state, the exploration algorithm cannot select the actions correctly.

On the other hand, the abstract dialogue state resulting from an abstract state transition is not necessarily determined deterministically. Consider two dialogue states s_1 and s_2 with at least three slots. In s_1 all but one slots are filled, in s_2 all but two slots are filled. The dialogue states map onto the same abstract dialogue state, in particular one in which the variable $Information$ has the value $someFilled$. If now, the abstract action $InfoSeekQuestion$ is applied, then the resulting abstract states differ: s_1 maps to an abstract state in which $Information$ is set to $allFilled$ while the variable remains unchanged in s_2.

Since the value function for a concrete state correspond to those for the abstract state that contains the concrete state, value update is always non-local for abstract states that contain more than one concrete state. If the representation of the abstract states is chosen inappropriately, concrete states with dissimilar characteristics may be grouped together in such a way that the value function of the abstract state is not a good representative of the actual value functions for the concrete states. In this case, additional state variables should be used to discriminate between dissimilar concrete states.

6 Evaluation

We implemented a Japanese bus information system. We encoded the abstract state and action spaces as described in the previous sections. For training purposes, we collected a corpus of 500 dialogues from 50 different users. Each user had to fulfill a task consisting of 10 dialogues. The task was presented to the user on paper. After presentation, the user interacted with the system by voice only to acquire the information necessary to complete the task. At the end of the dialogue, user indicate whether the experienced dialogue was good, average or bad.

Reinforcement Learning. The implemented system has 972 different abstract dialogue states and 5 different abstract actions. Of the 972, one third (or 324) were final states, implying that their value function is 0 for all actions. Out of those 972 states, 185 were visited during exploration. Of those, 43 were final states. Among the remaining 142 states, there were 49 states in which, when visited, always the same action was applied. The number of states in which two, three, four or five different actions were applied, is 31, 33, 19 and 10, respectively. Thus, the size of the state-action space spanned by the exploration equals $2^{31} + 3^{33} + 4^{19} + 5^{10}$.

Using the collected dialogues and feedback from the users, we trained an MDP using the procedure outlined above. We selected the 50 most frequently visited states and approximated the value functions in the remaining states as described above.

To determine whether the reinforcement learning algorithm converges, we determine the number of states s in which the optimal action as determined by equation (10) differs from the optimal action in the same state before the current dialogue was presented. The result is shown in figure 3 (a). It can be seen that the learning converges after approximately 125 dialogues.

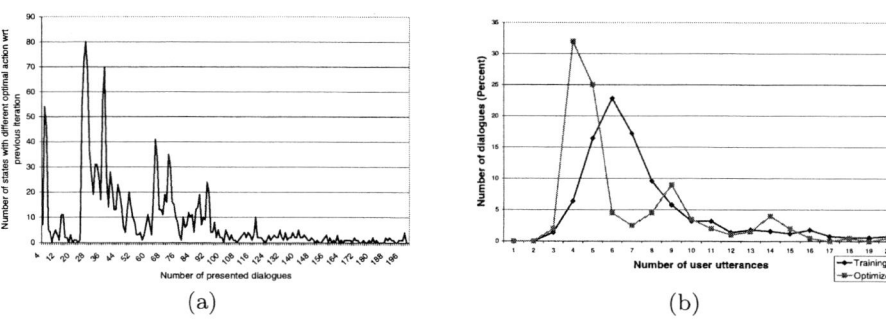

Fig. 3. (a) Shown are the number of dialogue states in which the optimal action differs compared to the previous iteration. A value of 0 means that the MDP behaves exactly as the MDP before the last iteration. (b) Number of dialogues of a given length using the exploratory and the optimized strategy.

Optimized MDP. After training, we collected 200 dialogues with the optimized system, having users perform the same tasks under the same conditions. None of the users of the optimized dialogue system participated in the data collection.

We found that using the optimized system, 188 different states have been visited, 138 of which were intermediate. Out of these 138 states, 31 (22.5 %) were not encountered during training. Task completion rate is 85.5 % (171 dialogues out of 200) compared to 78.6 % (393 dialogues out of 500) in the unoptimized case. 96.5 % (193 dialogues out of 200) came to a proper end with the system giving information, but not necessarily the one the user asked for, compared to 90.8 % (454 out of 500 dialogues) in the unoptimized case.

Figure 3 (b) shows the number of dialogues over the number of user utterances for the exploratory strategy and the optimized strategy. It can be seen that for the unoptimized system, the most often occurring length is 6 user uterances (23 %). In the optimized case, the peak is much more pronounced at about 32 % while the length has been reduced to 4 turns. This is due to the fact that the state-action space for these dialogues is well explored during data collection and many of the involved states are selected for training purposes. However, the optimized dialogue strategy does not show an improvement for lengthier dialogues. This is explained by the fact that as a dialogue get longer, it is more likely to encounter a state that has not participated in the training of the decision process.

7 Discussion

We described a novel method for fast reinforcement learning of dialogue policies. We showed that the proposed method effectively shortens the lengths of frequently visited dialogues. This is despite the fact that the state-action space is considerably larger than in previously reported work. However, the optimized dialogue strategy does not do much for infrequently visited states as these are excluded from training.

There is clearly a trade-off between granularity of the state space and the degree to which the value function is approximated. In one extreme, a small state space would not require any approximation while not representing enough information to adequately learn optimal dialogue strategies. In the other extreme, a detailed space encoding allows for precise learning of optimal dialogue strategies, but only on a relatively small subset of the state space. This leaves open the question whether an adequate state representation can be learned given the distribution of state visits.

Acknowledgements

We would like to thank Shoji Makino and all members of the Dialogue Understanding Research Group for support and helpful discussions. We would also like to thank the anonymous reviewers for their helpful comments.

References

1. S. Singh, D. Litman, M. Kearns, and M. Walker. 2002. Optimizing Dialogue Management with Reinforcement Learning: Experiments with the NJFun System. *Journal of Artificial Intelligence Research*, 16:105–133.

2. Geoffrey J. Gordon. 1995. Stable function approximation in dynamic programming. In *Proceedings of the Twelfth International Conference on Machine Learning.*
3. E. Levin and R. Pieraccini. 1997. A Stochastic Model of Human Computer Interaction for Learning Dialog Strategies. In *Proceedings of Eurospeech, Rhodos, Greece.*
4. L.P. Kaelbling, M.L. Littman, and A.W. Moore. 1996. Reinforcement Learning: A Survey. *Journal of Artificial Intelligence Research*, 4:237–285.
5. M. Walker, J. Fromer, and S. Narayanan. 1998. Learning optimal dialogue strategies: A case study of a spoken dialogue agent for email. In *Proceedings of ACL/COLING 98.*
6. J. D. Williams and S. Young. 2003. Using Wizard-of-Oz Simulations to Bootstrap Reinforcement Learning Based Dialog Management Systems. In *Proceedings of the 4th SIGDIAL Workshop on Discourse and Dialogue.*
7. N. Roy, J. Pineau, and S. Thrun. 2000. Spoken Dialog Management for Robots. In *Proceedings of the 39th Annual Meeting of the Association for Computational Linguistics.*
8. K. Scheffler and S. J. Young. 2001. Corpus-based dialogue simulation for automatic strategy learning and evaluation. In *Proceedings NAACL Workshop on Adaptation in Dialogue Systems*, pages 64–70.
9. R.S. Sutton and A.G. Barto. 1998. *Reinforcement Learning*. MIT Press.
10. D. Goddeau and J. Pineau. 2000. Fast Reinforcement Learning of Dialog Strategies. In *IEEE Conference on Acoustics, Speech and Signal Processing (ICASSP), Istanbul, Turkey.*
11. M. Denecke. 2000. Informational Characterization of Dialogue States. In *Proceedings of the 6th International Conference on Speech and Language Processing, Beijing, China.*

Zero Pronoun Resolution
Based on Automatically Constructed Case Frames and Structural Preference of Antecedents

Daisuke Kawahara and Sadao Kurohashi

University of Tokyo, 7-3-1 Hongo Bunkyo-ku, Tokyo, 113-8656, Japan
{kawahara,kuro}@kc.t.u-tokyo.ac.jp

Abstract. This paper describes a method to detect and resolve zero pronouns in Japanese text. We detect zero pronouns by case analysis based on automatically constructed case frames, and select their appropriate antecedents based on similarity to examples in the case frames. We also introduce structural preference of antecedents to precisely capture the tendency that a zero pronoun has its antecedent in its close position. Experimental results on 100 articles indicated that the precision and recall of zero pronoun detection is 87.1% and 74.8% respectively and the accuracy of antecedent estimation is 61.8%.

1 Introduction

Anaphora resolution is core technology to achieve a breakthrough in natural language applications, such as machine translation, text summarization, and question answering. To resolve anaphoric expressions, the following two clues can be considered:

- Anaphoric expressions and their context have syntactic and semantic constraints to their antecedents.
- Anaphoric expressions are likely to have their antecedents in their close position.

As for the syntactic and semantic constraints, only the coarse constraints have been used so far. For instance, some previous researches used shallow semantic classes, such as human, organization, and object, and considered the agreement between the classes of an anaphor and its antecedent as the semantic constraints (e.g. [1–3]). The reason why only these coarse constraints have been used is that knowledge bases which provide precise selectional restriction have not been available. Recently, wide-coverage case frames have been constructed automatically from large corpora, and provide fine-grained selectional restriction [4]. We employ these case frames for the selectional restriction.

The case frames are also necessary to detect zero pronouns. A case frame has the information about case markers that a verb subcategorizes. By matching an input predicate-argument structure with a case frame, we can recognize case slots that have no correspondence with the input as zero pronouns. Previous work assumed perfect pre-detection of zero pronouns, or detected zero pronouns based on hand-crafted sparse case frames [5]. On the other hand, we utilize the automatically constructed case frames, which enable accurate zero pronoun detection.

The second clue for anaphora resolution, i.e. distance tendency, has been attempted to capture by previous researches (e.g. [6, 3, 5]). They incorporated distance between an anaphor and its antecedent into a feature of machine learning techniques or a parameter of probabilistic models. The biggest problem with these approaches is that they do not consider structures in texts to measure distance, but rather just a flat distance, such as the number of words or sentences. To model the distance tendency precisely, we classify locational relations between zero pronouns and their possible antecedents by considering structures in texts, such as subordinate clauses, main clauses, and embedded sentences. We calculate how likely each location has antecedents using an annotated corpus, and acquire structural preference of antecedents.

In addition to these two devices, we exploit a machine learning technique to consider various features related to the determination of an antecedent, including syntactic constraints, and propose a Japanese zero pronoun resolution system. We concentrate on zero pronouns, because they are much more popular than any other anaphoric expressions in Japanese. This system examines candidates in an increasing order of structural preference of antecedents, and selects as its antecedent the first candidate which is labeled as positive by a machine learner and satisfies the selectional restriction based on the case frames.

2 Zero Pronoun Resolution Based on Case Frames

We employ the automatically constructed case frames [4] for zero pronoun detection and selectional restriction that antecedents must agree. This section firstly outlines the method of constructing the case frames, and then describes the case analysis based on them and the zero pronoun detection using the case analysis results.

2.1 Automatic Construction of Case Frames

The biggest problem in automatic case frame construction is verb sense ambiguity. Verbs which have different meanings should have different case frames, but it is hard to disambiguate verb senses precisely. To deal with this problem, predicate-argument examples which are collected from a large corpus are distinguished by coupling a verb and its closest case component. That is, examples are not distinguished by verbs (e.g. "*tsumu*" (load/accumulate)), but by couples (e.g. "*nimotsu-wo tsumu*" (load baggage) and "*keiken-wo tsumu*" (accumulate experience)).

This process makes separate case frames which have almost the same meaning or usage. For example, "*nimotsu-wo tsumu*" (load baggage) and "*busshi-wo tsumu*" (load supply) are similar, but have separate case frames. To cope with this problem, the case frames are clustered using a similarity measure function. The similarity is calculated using a Japanese thesaurus, and its maximum score is 1.0. The details of this measure are described in [4].

Table 1. Case frame examples.

	CM	examples
youritsu (1) (support)	ga	<agent>, group, party, ⋯
	wo	<agent>, candidate, applicant
	ni	<agent>, district, election, ⋯
youritsu (2) (support)	ga	<agent>
	wo	<agent>, assemblyman, minister, ⋯
	ni	<agent>, candidate, successor, ⋯
⋮	⋮	⋮

We constructed case frames by this procedure from newspaper articles of 20 years (about 21,000,000 sentences). The result consists of 23,000 predicates, and the average number of case frames for a predicate is 14.5. In Table 1, some examples of the resulting case frames are shown.

2.2 Zero Pronoun Resolution Based on the Case Frames

We build a zero pronoun resolution system that utilizes the case frames and the structural preference of antecedents, which is stated in Section 3. The outline of our algorithm is as follows.

1. Parse an input sentence using the Japanese parser, KNP.
2. Process each verb in the sentence from left to right by the following steps.
   2.1. Narrow case frames down to corresponding ones to the verb and its closest case component.
   2.2. Perform the following processes for each case frame of the target verb.
      i. Match each input case component with an appropriate case slot of the case frame. Regard case slots that have no correspondence as zero pronouns.
      ii. Estimate an antecedent of each zero pronoun.
   2.3. Select a case frame which has the highest total score, and output the analysis result for the case frame.

The rest of this section describes the above steps (2.1) and (2.2.i) in detail.

Narrowing Down Case Frames

As stated in Section 2.1, the closest case component plays an important role to determine the usage of a verb. In particular, when the closest case is "*wo*" or "*ni*", this trend is clear-cut. In addition, an expression whose nominative belongs to <agent> (e.g. "<agent> has accomplished"), does not have enough clue to decide its usage, namely a case frame. By considering these aspects, we impose the following conditions on narrowing down case frames.

```
...
(1) Ishihara chiji-ga  saisen-wo mezashite, chijisen-heno rikkouho-wo hyoumei-shita.
    governor reelection aim         gov. election candidacy     announce
    (The governor Ishihara announced his candidacy for reelection to the governor.)
(2) Jimintou-wa           shiji-suru houshin-wo kettei-shitaga, Minsyutou-wa
    Liberal Democratic Party support    policy     decide       Democratic Party

    dokuji  kouho-wo youritsu-suru koto-wo kentou-shiteiru.
    original candidate support    (that)    examine
    (The Liberal Democratic Party decided to support him, but the Democratic
    Party is examining to support its original candidate.)
...
```

Fig. 1. An example article.

- The closest case component exists, and must immediately precede its verb.
- The closest case component and the closest case meet one of the following conditions:
  • The closest case is *"wo"* or *"ni"*.
  • The closest case component does not belong to the semantic marker <agent>.
- A case frame with the closest case exists, and the similarity between the closest case component and examples in the closest case exceeds a threshold.

We choose the case frames whose similarity is the highest. If the above conditions are not satisfied, case frames are not narrowed down, and the subsequent processes are performed for each case frame of the target verb. The similarity used in this process is defined as the best similarity between the closest case component and examples in the case slot.

Let us consider *"youritsu"* (support) in the second sentence of Fig.1. *"youritsu"* has the case frames shown in Table 1. The input expression *"kouho-wo youritsu"* (support a candidate) satisfies the above two conditions, and the case frame *"youritsu (1)"* meets the last condition. Accordingly, this case frame is selected.

Matching Input Case Components with Case Slots in the Case Frame

We match case components of the target verb with case slots in the case frame. When a case component has a case marker, it must be assigned to the case slot with the same case marker. When a case component is a topic marked phrase or a clausal modifiee, which does not have a case marker, it can be assigned to some pre-defined case slots described in [7].

The result of case analysis tells if the zero pronouns exist. That is, vacant case slots in the case frame, which have no correspondence with the input case components, mean zero pronouns. In this paper, we concentrate on three case slots: *"ga"*, *"wo"*, and *"ni"*.

In the case of *"youritsu"* (support) in Fig.1 and the selected case frame *"youritsu (1)"*, *"wo"* case slot has a corresponding case component, but *"ga"* and *"ni"* case slots are vacant. Accordingly, two zero pronouns are identified in *"ga"* and *"ni"* case of *"youritsu"*.

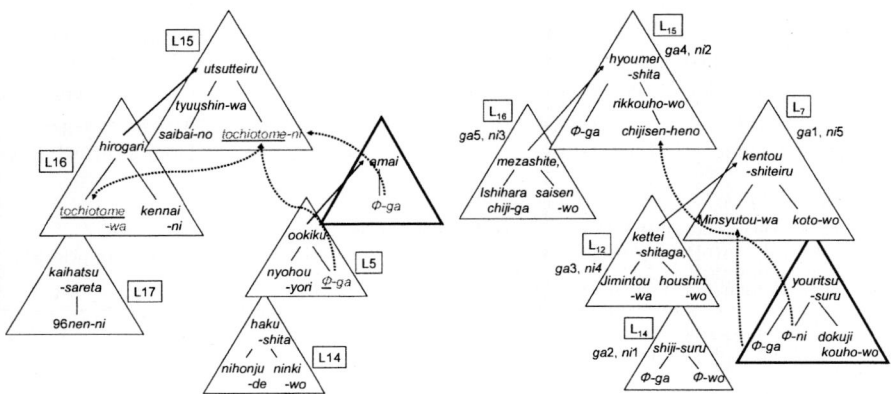

Fig. 2. How to handle antecedents.　　**Fig. 3.** Location classes in case of $V_z = youritsu$.

The procedure for estimating antecedents of detected zero pronouns is described in Section 5.

3 Learning Structural Preference of Antecedents

According to the selectional restriction of the case frames, possible antecedents are restricted to the eligible ones, but more than one possible antecedent still remain in many cases. To narrow down possible antecedents further, we exploit the distance tendency that zero pronouns are likely to have their antecedents in their close position. Previous researches measured the closeness by flat distance, such as the number of words or sentences between zero pronouns and their antecedents, and did not consider structures in texts. To model the distance tendency precisely, we classify locational relations between zero pronouns and their possible antecedents by considering the structures in texts, such as subordinate clauses, main clauses, and embedded sentences. We call the classification of the locational relations **location classes**, and calculate how likely each location class has antecedents based on an annotated corpus. Ordering these likelihoods yields the structural preference of antecedents, which is exploited in our zero pronoun resolution system.

This section describes how to handle antecedents in a training corpus, and then introduces the location classes. Finally, we illustrate how to calculate the structural preference of antecedents, namely the ordering of the location classes.

3.1 Handling Antecedents in the Relevance-Tagged Corpus

We learn the ordering of location classes using "Relevance-tagged Corpus" [8]. This corpus consists of Japanese newspaper articles, and has several types of relevance tags, such as predicate-argument relations, relations between nouns, and coreferences.

Table 2. Location classes of antecedents.

the sentence under consideration	
L_1 : case components of "parent predicate of V_z"	MC
L_2 : case components of "parent predicate of V_z"	
L_3 : case components of "parent predicate of V_z"	MC, P
L_4 : case components of "parent predicate of V_z"	P
L_5 : case components of "child predicate of V_z"	
L_6 : case components of "child predicate of V_z"	P
L_7 : case components of "parent predicate of parent noun phrase of V_z"	MC
L_8 : case components of "parent predicate of parent noun phrase of V_z"	
L_9 : case components of "parent predicate of parent predicate of V_z"	MC
L_{10}: case components of "parent predicate of parent predicate of V_z"	
L_{11}: case components of "predicate of main clause"	MC
L_{12}: case components of "predicate of subordinate clause depending on main clause"	
L_{13}: other noun phrases following V_z	
L_{14}: other noun phrases preceding V_z	
1 sentence before	
L_{15}: case components of "predicate of main clause"	MC
L_{16}: case components of "predicate of subordinate clause depending on main clause"	
L_{17}: other noun phrases	
2 sentences before	
L_{18}: case components of "predicate of main clause"	MC
L_{19}: case components of "predicate of subordinate clause depending on main clause"	
L_{20}: other noun phrases	

We investigated 379 articles, consisting of 3,695 sentences, in the corpus. There are 11,149 predicates, including verbs, adjectives, and noun+copulas. Out of these predicates, 5,530 predicates have zero pronouns, and there are 6,602 zero pronouns in total. Out of these zero pronouns, 4,986 zero pronouns have their antecedents in their articles. The remaining 1,616 zero pronouns have no antecedents in their articles, and in many cases their referents are unspecified people, that are equivalent to general pronouns in English (e.g. "They say that ···").

As to a zero pronoun which has its antecedent in the article, its antecedents are not only the directly annotated one but also indirect ones which are linked by other coreference links. In other words, these indirect antecedents are the entities which corefer to the annotated antecedent, and other zero pronouns which refer to the same referent. We handle them equally to the annotated one, because this treatment is natural to measure the distance between a zero pronoun and its antecedents. For instance, "*amai*" (sweet) in Fig.2 has a zero pronoun in its "*ga*" case, and its antecedent is "*tochiotome*" in the main clause of one sentence before. Since this antecedent "*tochiotome*" is coreferential to "*tochiotome*" in the subordinate clause of one sentence before, we regard the latter also as the antecedent. Besides, "*ookiku*" in the target sentence has a zero pronoun in its "*ga*" case, which refers "*tochiotome*", and we regard this zero pronoun as the antecedent, too.

For learning structural preference of antecedents and building a classifier, stated in the following sections, 279 articles in the corpus are used, and the rest 100 articles are reserved for the experiment.

3.2 Setting Up Location Classes

To model the distance tendency precisely, we introduce **location classes**, which are the classification of locational relations between zero pronouns and their antecedents. Considering subordinate clauses, main clauses, embedded sentences, and so on, we established 20 location classes as described in Table 2. In Table 2, V_z means a predicate that has a zero pronoun. We call a predicate whose case component is an antecedent V_a, which is quoted in Table 2. "MC" means that V_a constitutes the main clause, and "P" means that V_z and V_a are conjunctive.

For example, let us consider "*amai*" (sweet) in Fig.2, which has a zero pronoun for "*ga*". "*utsutte-iru*" (move) is a main clause of one sentence before, and the case components are of "*utsutte-iru*", i.e. "*tyuushin*", "*saibai*", and "*tochiotome*", are located in L_{15}. "*ookiku*" (big) is a child clause of the target verb "*amai*", and the case components of "*ookiku*", i.e. "*nyohou*" and a zero pronoun referring "*tochiotome*", are in L_5.

3.3 Ordering Location Classes

We investigate how each location class is likely to have antecedents using the corpus. We calculate score of location class L as follows:

$$\frac{\text{\# of antecedents in } L}{\text{\# of possible antecedents in } L}$$

For a zero pronoun of "*amai*" in Fig.2, the possible antecedents in L_{15} are "*tyushin*", "*saibai*", and "*tochiotome*". In this case, since "*tochiotome*" is the antecedent, this location class has one antecedent, and three possible antecedents. These numbers are counted through the whole corpus, and the score of the location class is calculated by the above formula.

We then sort these scores and obtain location class order for each case markers of zero pronouns. Fig.3 shows the location class orders for the zero pronouns ("*ga*" and "*ni*") of "*youritsu*" (support). The first location classes for "*ga*" and "*ni*" are L_7 and L_{14}, respectively, and this exemplifies that the location class order of each case marker is different from the other orders. In addition, L_{12} is close to the target zero pronoun in the flat distance, but is not placed high in the location class order.

4 Building a Classifier

We utilize a machine learning technique to consider a lot of factors related to antecedent estimation. We employ a binary classifier to judge if a possible antecedent is eligible for an antecedent. The classifier is trained using the features shown in Table 3.

The classifier is trained using Support Vector Machines (SVM). Training data are created from "Relevance-tagged Corpus". We treat the closest correct antecedent as a positive example and possible antecedents between a zero pronoun and the positive antecedent as negative examples. Zero pronouns that have their closest correct antecedents in more than two sentences before are not used for training. In the case of "*amai*" (sweet) in Fig.2, two "*tochiotome*" in one sentence before and the zero pronoun referring "*tochiotome*" in "*ookiku*" are positive examples, and the other nouns are negative.

Table 3. Feature set for the classifier.

features related to both zero pronoun and possible antecedent
· similarity between possible antecedent and examples of case slot   (0 - 1)
· location class of possible antecedent   ($L_1, \cdots, L_{20}$)
· possible antecedent is located before zero pronoun   (yes, no)
· possible antecedent depends over zero pronoun   (yes, no)
features of possible antecedent
· case marker of possible antecedent   (ga, wo, ni, $\cdots$)
· predicate of possible antecedent is in a noun-modifying clause   (yes, no)
· possible antecedent is in the first sentence of the article   (yes, no)
· possible antecedent depends on main clause   (yes, no)
· possible antecedent is marked by a topic marker   (yes, no)
· possible antecedent belongs to <agent>   (yes, no)
· strength of predicate clause of possible antecedent   (0, 1, $\cdots$, 6)
features of zero pronoun
· case marker of zero pronoun   (ga, wo, ni)
· predicate of zero pronoun is in a noun-modifying clause   (yes, no)
· voice of predicate of zero pronoun   (active, passive, causative)
· type of predicate of zero pronoun   (verb, adjective, noun+copula)
· head of zero pronoun is a verbal noun   (yes, no)
· examples of the corresponding case slot belong to <agent>   (yes, no)

5   Estimation of Antecedents of Zero Pronouns

We estimate antecedents of zero pronouns based on examples in the case frames and the classifier. We examine possible antecedents according to the location class orders, and label them positive/negative using the binary classifier. If a possible antecedent is classified as positive and its similarity to examples in its case slot exceeds a threshold, it is determined as the antecedent. At this moment, the procedure finishes, and further candidates are not tested.

For example, "*youritsu*" (support) in Fig. 3 has zero pronouns in "*ga*" and "*ni*". The ordered possible antecedents for "*ga*" are L_7:"*Minsyutou*", L_{14}: "*Jimintou*"(ϕ *ga*), L_{14}:"*Ishihara chiji*"(ϕ *wo*), $\cdots$. The first candidate "*Minsyutou* (similarity: 0.73)", which is labeled as positive by the classifier, and whose similarity to the case frame examples exceeds the threshold (0.60), is determined as the antecedent.

6   Experiments

We conducted experiments of our zero pronoun resolution system using "Relevance-tagged corpus". To make article length uniform, we used 10 sentences at the beginning of each article. We used the SVM package, TinySVM[1], 2nd-order polynomial kernel. For testing, the system was given 100 articles that have correct dependency structure.

To illustrate the effectiveness of our approach, our experiments are performed under 7 configurations (Fig.4) using three parameters: search strategy, distance measure, and scoring. In Fig.4, ex-7 corresponds to our approach, ex-1 is similar to the approach suggested by [6], and ex-3 is similar to [3]. Experimental results are also shown in Fig.4. The accuracies (F-measure) are calculated by evaluating both detection and antecedent estimation of zero pronouns together. Our

---
[1] http://cl.aist-nara.ac.jp/~taku-ku/software/TinySVM/

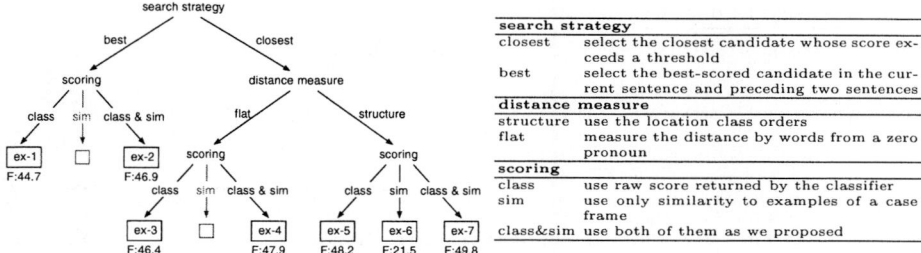

Fig. 4. Configurations of our experiments.

approach (ex-7) achieved 53.9% (496/921) in precision and 46.3% (496/1072) in recall, and outperformed the other methods significantly.

We also evaluated each accuracy of detection and antecedent estimation of zero pronouns under ex-7 setting. For the detection, we attained 87.1% in precision, 74.8% in recall, and 80.5% in F-measure. For the antecedent estimation, the accuracy was 61.8%. We compare our accuracies with [5], whose experiments are similar to ours. They achieved 48.9% in precision, 88.2% in recall, and 62.9% in F-measure for zero pronoun detection, and 54.0% accuracy for antecedent estimation on 30 newspaper articles. It is difficult to directly compare their results with ours due to the difference of the size of the test articles, but our method gave improvements over theirs in F-measure of zero pronoun detection by 17.6% and in accuracy of antecedent estimation by 7.8%. In particular, the significant improvement of zero pronoun detection indicates that the automatically constructed case frames are more effective than hand-crafted case frames which are used by [5].

Some major errors are shown in the following.

Errors caused by analysis limitation

The current system analyzes only predicates, and this means that it only handles some parts of all the relations in an article.

syusyou-wa   Syakaitou-no   ritou   mondai-ni-tsuite, tairyou ritou-niwa
prime minister-TM Socialist Party-of secession problem-about   much secession acc.

itara-nai-tono   mitoushi-wo nobeta.
(not) cause that prospect acc. state

(The prime minister stated his prospect about the secession problem of the Socialist Party that φ would not cause secession of many members.)

In this example, "*itara-nai*" has a zero pronoun of "*ga*". Its antecedent is identified as "*syusyou*" by the system, but the correct antecedent is "*Syakaitou*" (the Socialist Party). This is because "*Syakaitou*" is not included in any case components of the predicates and is not ranked high in the location class order. To cope with this problem, it is necessary to deal with not only predicates but also verbal nouns. When analyzing them in this example, "*ritou*", which is in high rank for "*itara-nai*", has "*Syakaitou*" in its "*ga*" case, and "*itara-nai*" can be analyzed correctly as a result. Like this example, it is necessary to clarify and utilize a lot of relations in sentences, and this will lead to an improvement in the accuracy.

Detection errors of zero pronouns
Our system tends to recognize false zero pronouns.

shireikan-wa,	⋯	Russian-*gun-no*	*sensya*	50*dai-wo*	*hakai-shita-to*	*happyou-shita*.
general-TM		Russian army of	tank	50 acc.	destroy that	announce

(The general announced that ϕ had destroyed 50 tanks of Russian army.)

In this example, since the selected case frame of "*happyou*" (announce) has vacant "*ni*" slot, the system erroneously identifies it as a zero pronoun. This problem is not attributed to case frame errors, but context dependence. That is to say, in this context we do not think of whom the general announced the destruction to. To handle this problem, we need to incorporate context dependent features into the classifier.

7 Conclusion

We have described a Japanese zero pronoun resolution system. This system detects zero pronouns and restricts their possible antecedents based on automatically constructed case frames. To prefer close possible antecedents from a zero pronoun, we also introduced structural preference of antecedents. The experimental results showed that our approach significantly outperformed the previous work and the baseline methods.

References

1. McCarthy, J.F., Lehnert, W.G.: Using decision trees for coreference resolution. In: Proceedings of the 14th International Joint Conference on Artificial Intelligence. (1995) 1050–1055
2. Murata, M., Isahara, H., Nagao, M.: Pronoun resolution in Japanese sentences using surface expressions and examples. In: Proceedings of the ACL'99 Workshop on Coreference and Its Applications. (1999) 39–46
3. Soon, W.M., Ng, H.T., Lim, D.C.Y.: A machine learning approach to coreference resolution of noun phrases. Computational Linguistics **27** (2001) 521–544
4. Kawahara, D., Kurohashi, S.: Fertilization of case frame dictionary for robust Japanese case analysis. In: Proceedings of the 19th International Conference on Computational Linguistics. (2002) 425–431
5. Seki, K., Fujii, A., Ishikawa, T.: A probabilistic method for analyzing Japanese anaphora integrating zero pronoun detection and resolution. In: Proceedings of the 19th International Conference on Computational Linguistics. (2002) 911–917
6. Aone, C., Bennett, S.W.: Evaluating automated and manual acquisition of anaphora resolution strategies. In: Proceedings of the 33rd Annual Meeting of the Association for Computational Linguistics. (1995) 122–129
7. Kurohashi, S., Nagao, M.: A method of case structure analysis for japanese sentences based on examples in case frame dictionary. In: IEICE Transactions on Information and Systems. Volume E77-D No.2. (1994)
8. Kawahara, D., Kurohashi, S., Hasida, K.: Construction of a Japanese relevance-tagged corpus. In: Proceedings of the 3rd International Conference on Language Resources and Evaluation. (2002) 2008–2013

Improving Noun Phrase Coreference Resolution by Matching Strings

Xiaofeng Yang[1,2], Guodong Zhou[1], Jian Su[1], and Chew Lim Tan[2]

[1] Institute for Infocomm Research, 21 Heng Mui Keng Terrace, Singapore, 119613
{xiaofengy,zhougd,sujian}@i2r.a-star.edu.sg
[2] Department of Computer Science, National University of Singapore, Singapore, 117543
{yangxiao,tancl}@comp.nus.edu.sg

Abstract. In this paper we present a noun phrase coreference resolution system which aims to enhance the identification of the coreference realized by string matching. For this purpose, we make two extensions to the standard learn-ing-based resolution framework. First, to improve the recall rate, we introduce an additional set of features to capture the different matching patterns between noun phrases. Second, to improve the precision, we modify the instance selection strategy to allow non-anaphors to be included during training instance generation. The evaluation done on MEDLINE data set shows that the combination of the two extensions provides significant gains in the F-measure.

1 Introduction

Noun phrase coreference resolution is the process of determining whether or not two noun phrases in a document refer to the same entity. In recent years, supervised machine learning approaches have been applied to this problem and achieved reasonable success [1–5].

The previous work has reported that three features contribute most to noun phrase coreference resolution, namely, string match, name alias and apposition. Among them, string match is of the most importance. In the system by Soon et al. [3], for example, simply using head-match feature can achieve a recall as high as 56.4% and 55.2% for MUC-6 [6] and MUC-7 [7] data set, respectively. Indeed, in most of genres, there are large numbers of cases when the coreference between noun phrases is realized by string matching. Therefore, we can expect a good overall performance if high accuracy of string matching can be obtained.

Unfortunately, in contrast to name alias and apposition which are comparatively easy for a shallow system to resolve, the cases of matching of strings are more complicated. The types of the noun phrase modifiers and their matching patterns have considerable influence on coreference determination. For example, two phrases containing different adjective modifiers, such as "the red apple", "the green apple", usually refer to different entities. Also, some special modifiers, such as the superlative adjective or relative clauses, indicate that a noun phrase is a discourse-new description [8] and do not refer to any preceding noun phrase even if they are full-string matched. Therefore, the simple head-string matching or full-string matching check is not sufficient for coreference resolution; the former will lead to a low precision, and the latter may guarantee the precision, but nevertheless with significant loss in recall (over 10% as in Soon et al.'s system).

String matching tasks have been explored by a number of communities including statistics, database and artificial intelligence communities. Various string distance metrics have been proposed to measure the matching degree of noun phrases [9]. However, string matching in coreference resolution task is comparatively complicated in that many contextual factors have to be considered. So far, several researchers have dealt with string matching in coreference resolution by heuristic methods (e.g. [10]) or using similarity features such as Minimum Edit Distance [11] or LCS [12] (See "Related Work" for further discussion).

In this paper, we present a NP coreference resolution system which investigates the coreference realized by string matching. We make two extensions to the standard learning-based approach framework to improve the recall and the precision of the resolution. First, we incorporate a set of features that is supposed to capture the various matching patterns between noun phrases. In calculating the matching degree of strings, we explore several similarity metrics, together with two different weighting schemes. Second, we modify the training instance selection strategy. Traditionally, training instances are formed based on one anaphor and its possible antecedents. However, non-anaphors are also informative in that they can effectively help the anaphoricity determination. In our approach we make use of non-anaphor in generating the training instances, which provides us significant gains in coreference resolution precision. The experimental results show that combination of the above two modifications boost the performance in F-measure compared with the baseline system.

2 Data Corpus

Our coreference resolution system is a component of our information extraction system in biomedical domain. For this purpose, we have built an annotated coreference corpus which consists of 200 MEDLINE[1] documents from GENIA data set[2]. The documents are all from biomedical literature with an average length of 244 words. The distribution of different types of markables is summarized in Table 1.

Table 1. Distribution of different types of markables in the 200 MEDLINE data set.

	Total Number	Percentage
Anaphoric Markables		
Non-pron	3561	29.1%
Pron	131	1%
Non-Anaphoric Markable		
Non-pron	8272	67.6%
Pron	259	2.1%
Total	12223	100%

---

[1] http://www.medstract.org
[2] http://www-tsujii.is.s.u-tokyo.ac.jp/~genia/index.html

To determine the boundary of the noun phrases, and to provide the necessary information for subsequent processes, a pipeline of Nature Language Processing components is applied to an input raw text. Among them, named entity recognition, part-of-speech tagging and text chunking adopt the same Hidden Markov Model (HMM) based engine with error-driven learning capability [13, 14]. The named entity recognition component trained on GENIA corpus [15] can recognizes up to 23 common Biomedical entity types (i.e. Virus, Tissue, RNA, DNA, Protein, etc) with an overall performance of 66.1 F-measure (P=66.5% R=65.7%)

3 The Framework of the Baseline Coreference Resolution System

We built a baseline coreference resolution system which adopts the standard learning-based framework employed in the work by Soon et al. [3].

During training, for each anaphor NP_j in a given text, a positive instance is generated by pairing NP_j with its closest non-pronominal antecedent. A set of negative instances is also formed by NP_j and each of the non-pronominal markables occurring between NP_j and NP_i.

A training instance is associated with a feature vector which, as described in Table 2, consists of 8 features. Here two string match features are tried in the system exclusively, i.e., *FullStrMatch* and *HeadStrMatch*. They represent the tightest and the loosest matching criterion, respectively.

Table 2. Feature set for baseline coreference resolution system.

1.	ante_Type	the type of NP_i (definite np, indefinite np, pronoun, ProperNP...)
2.	ana_Type	the type of NP_j (definite np, indefinite np, pronoun, ProperNP...)
3.	Appositive	1 if NP_i and NP_j are in an appositive structure; else 0
4.	NameAlias	1 if NP_i and NP_j are in an alias of the other; else 0
5.	GenderAgree	1 if NP_i and NP_j agree in gender; else 0
6.	NumAgree	1 if NP_i and NP_j agree in number; else 0
7.	SemanticAgree	1 if NP_i and NP_j agree in semantic class; else 0
8.	HeadStrMatch	1 if NP_i and NP_j contain the same head string; else 0
8'.	FullStrMatch	1 if NP_i and NP_j contain the same string after discarding determiners; else 0

When the training instances are ready, a classifier is learned by C5.0 algorithm [16]. During resolution, each encountered noun phrase, NP_j, is paired in turn with each preceding noun phrase, NP_i, from right to left. Each pair is associated with a feature vector as during training, and then presented to the coreference classifier. The classifier returns a positive or negative result indicating whether or not NP_i is coreferential to NP_j. The process terminates once an antecedent is found for NP_j, or the beginning of the text is reached. In the former case, NP_j is to be linked into the coreferential chain where the antecedent occurs.

4 New String Matching Features

4.1 String Matching Factors

Noun phrases preceded or followed by modifiers are common in numbers of genres. Generally, the modifiers of a noun phrase carry important information for coreference resolution. Two noun phrases with the same head string may probably refer to distinct entities if their modifiers fail to be matched. For example: "activation of T lymphocytes" - "activation of the proenkephalin promoter", "the first candidate" - "the second candidate", "the B cells" - "the Hela cells", and so on.

Also, the presence of some special modifiers, such as superlative adjective or relative clause, indicates that the modified noun phrase is a discourse-new description[3] and do not refer to any previously mentioned entity. For example:

(e1) *She jumps at the slightest noise.*
(e2) *Great changes have taken place in the town where he lived.*

In addition to modifiers, the head of a noun phrase itself provides clues of coreference. Typically, a group of definite noun phrase such as "the morning" and "the fact", refers to time or a larger situation and may not be used as anaphors. In such cases, noun phrases can not be linked together even if their modifiers are all matched well.

In our system, the above factors that influence coreference determination are incorporated in terms of features. Specifically, given a noun phrase, we first extract the information of its head and modifiers. Then, we measure the matching degree of their modifiers and keep the results in the features. We will introduce the detailed processing in the following subsections.

4.2 Noun Phrase Processing

To facilitate matching, for each noun phrase, we keep the information of its head-string, full-string and modifiers into a case structure as shown in Table 3. The value of each attribute is a bagging of word tokens.

During matching modifiers of noun phrases, it is possible that one string is name alias to the other, or two words in the strings are morphological variants to each other. In these cases, even though the modifiers contain different tokens, they can still be well matched. Therefore, in order to improve the recall rate of the resolution, we apply the following three actions to the attribute values of a noun phrase.

1. Expand the attribute values. If an attribute contains an acronym, replace the acronym with its corresponding definition[4].
2. Remove from the attributes values those stop-words, that is, non-informative words, including the prepositions (e.g. "of", "to", "in", etc), the articles (e.g. "a", "an", "the"), and all kinds of punctuation marks (e.g. "[", "]", "-", etc.).

---
[3] Vieira and Poesio [10] gave a detail introduction to the discourse-new description.
[4] In our system we use a heuristic method to extract the acronym list from the documents in collection.

Table 3. Attribute List of a noun phrase, NP_i.

NP_i	
Head	The head of NP_i
EntireNP	The entire string of NP_i
NUM	The number modifier of NP_i
VERB	The nonfinite modifier (*verb+ed*, *verb+ing*) of NP_i
PrepObj	The object of the preposition
ADJ_J	The Adj (normal form) modifier
ADJ_R	The comparative Adj modifier
ADJ_S	The superlative Adj modifier
ProperNP	The proper noun modifier
OtherNP	The normal nominal modifier

3. Stem the remaining words in the attribute values. In most cases, morphological variants of words have similar semantic interpretations and can be considered as equivalent. Currently we just use simple rules to truncate words, e.g. "terminal" is stemmed as "termin".

As an example, suppose the definition of the acronym of "LTR" and "HIV-1" is "long terminal repeat" and "human immunodeficiency virus type 1", respectively. The noun phrase "LTR of HIV-1" will be converted into:

Table 4. An example: Structure of "LTR of HIV-1".

Input NP: LTR of HIV-1
NP.Head = { repeat }
NP.EntireNP = { long termin repeat human immunodeficien virus type 1 }
NP.NUM = { 1 }
NP.PrepOBj = { human immunodeficien virus type 1}
NP.ADJ_J = { long termin }
NP.ProperNP = { human immunodeficien virus type 1}

4.3 Feature Definition

In addition to the features used in the baseline system, we introduce a set of features which aim to capture the matching patterns of the modifiers between noun phrases. All features are listed in Table 5 together with their respective possible values.

Features 9 - 30 record the matching degree, which we will discuss in the next subsection, between the attribute values of two noun phrases. For example, the feature *ante_ana_Prep* is to keep the matching degree of NP_i.PrepObj and NP_j.PrepObj. Note that ante_ana_[attribute] is different from ana_ante_[attribute]; the former is the matching degree of the possible antecedent NP_i against the possible anaphor, NP_j, while the latter is that of NP_j against NP_i. The values may be not equal to each to under some degree metrics.

Table 5. New string matching features of our coreference resolution system.

9. ante_Relative	1 if NP$_i$ is modified by a relative clause; else 0	
10. ante_specialNP	1 if NP$_i$ is a special definite np which acts as a non-anaphor; else 0	
11. ana_Relative	1 if NP$_j$ is modified by a relative clause; else 0	
12. ana_specialNP	1 if NP$_j$ is a special definite np which acts as a non-anaphor; else 0	
13. ante_ana_(EntireNP, Number,	Matching degree of	
~ Verb, Prep, AdjJ, AdjR,	NPi.(EntireNP, ..., CommonNP) against	
21 AdjS, ProperNP, CommonNP)	NPj.(EntireNP, ..., CommonNP)	
22. ana_ante_(EntireNP, Number,	Matching degree of	
~ Verb, Prep, AdjJ, AdjR,	NPj.(EntireNP, ..., CommonNP) against	
30 AdjS, ProperNP, CommonNP)	NPi.(EntireNP, ..., CommonNP)	

4.4 String Similarity Metrics

The matching degree of the attributes is measured in terms of string similarity. Three similarity metrics have been explored in our system:

- **Contain**

$$Contain(S1, S2) = \begin{cases} 1 & : \text{ if S1 is contained in S2} \\ 0 & : \text{ otherwise} \end{cases} \quad (1)$$

The *Contain* metric checks whether the tokens in S1 is completely contained in S2. The intuition behind it is that if a possible anaphor contains less information than a possible antecedent, they are probably coreferential to each other.

- **ContainRatio**

$$ContainRatio(S1, S2) = 100 \times \frac{\sum_{t \in S1 \cap S2} w1_t}{\sum_{t \in S1} w1_t} \quad (2)$$

where $w1_t$ is the weight of token t in S1.
ContainRatio measures the ratio of the number of common tokens between S1 and S2. It provides a smooth variant of function *Contain* in evaluating the degree that one string is contained in the other.

- **COS-Similarity**

$$COS-Similarity(S1, S2) = 100 \times \frac{\sum_{t \in S1 \cap S2} w1_t \times w2_t}{\sqrt{\sum_{t \in S1} w1_t^2} \times \sqrt{\sum_{t \in S2} w2_t^2}} \quad (3)$$

The *COS-similarity* metric is widely used in Information Retrieval systems to calculate the similarity of documents or sentences. Note that for this is a symmetric metric, that is, $COS-Similarity(S1, S2) == COS-Similarity(S2, S1)$. This however does not hold truth on the metrics *Contain* and *ContainRatio*.

4.5 Weighting Schemes

In the metrics *ContainRatio* and *Cos-Similarity*, we use weight to reflect the importance of a token. Two weighting schemes are explored in our study:

- **Binary Scheme.** This simplest scheme assigns weight 1 to a token if the token occurs in the current string, or 0 if otherwise.
- **TFIDF Scheme.** Well known in the information retrieval community, this scheme takes into account the frequency factor of a token throughout all documents. The weight of a token t in a document d can be defined as:

$$w_{dt} = f_{dt} \times \log \frac{N}{df_t} \quad (4)$$

where f_{dt} is the frequency of token t in document d, while N is the number of documents in the date set (e.g., 200 in our system) and df_t is the number of documents containing token t.

5 New Training Instance Selection Strategy

In the traditional learning-based coreference resolution system, the training instances are formed by an anaphor and its possible antecedent. However, non-anaphors are also informative in that they provide important information for anaphoricity determination. As in the example sentence (e1) and (e2) in section 4.1, indefinite noun phrases, or definite noun phrase modified by superlative adjective, give us clues that they are a discourse-new entity and do not refer to any preceding noun phrase, even they match in the full string. However, such information can not be obtained if non-anaphors are absent in the training instances. As a result, the generated classifier would probably fail in the cases of non-anaphors, and thus degrade the precision rate of the resolution.

To improve the ability of anaphoricity determination, in our system we make use of non-anaphors to generate training instances. Specifically, for each non-anaphor NP_j, we

- Search for the first noun phrase NP_i which contains the same head string as NP_j from backwards.
- If such NP_i exists, generate a training instance by pairing NP_i and NP_j. Naturally, the instance is labeled as negative.

6 Results and Discussions

Our approach was evaluated on the MEDLINE data set introduced in Section 2. Five-fold cross-evaluation was done with each bin containing 40 documents from the data set. The performance of different coreference resolution systems was evaluated according to the scoring scheme proposed by Vilain et al. [17].

The first two lines of Table 6 list the performance of the baseline systems described in section 3. Here *HeadStrMatch* is the system using feature 8, i.e. *HeadStrMatch*, while *FullStrMatch* is the system using feature 8', i.e. *FullStrMatch*. The two baselines achieve an F-measure of 60.9% and 58.4%, respectively. *HeadStrMatch*, which performs the loosest matching check, gets a high recall 71.4%, but comparatively low precision 53.1%. By contrast, *FullStrMatch*, which performs the tightest matching check, obtains a high precision (68.5%) at a price of significantly low recall (51.0%).

Table 6. Experimental results on the Medline data set using C5.0 (the *ed systems use *ContainRation* metric with Binary weighting scheme).

	Recall	Precision	F-measure
HeadStrMatch	71.4	53.1	60.9
FullStrMatch	51.0	68.5	58.4
NewFeature*	70.5	63.8	66.9
NonAnaphor+NewFeature*	68.1	**69.7**	**68.9**

The third line of the table summarizes the performance of the system *NewFeature*, which adopts our new string matching features as described in Section 4. Compared with *HeadStrMatch*, *NewFeature* achieves a significant increase of 10.7% in the precision rate with only a small loss (0.9%) in recall. On the other hand, compared with *FullStrMatch*, the recall rate of *NewFeature* improves significantly (about 20%), while the precisions drops only 4.7%. As a whole, our new features produce gains of about 6% and 8.5% in F-measure over *HeadStrMatch* and *FullStrMatch*, respectively.

Results on the modification to the training instance selection strategies are shown in the last line of Table 6. Compared with *NewFeature*, the inclusion of non-anaphors in the training instance generation gives an increase of about 6% in the precision. The precision is even higher than that of *FullStrMatch*. While the recall drops a little (2.4%), we see a further increase of 2% in F-measure. The drop in recall is reasonable since the learned classifiers become stricter in checking non-anaphoric markables. The degrade in recall was also reported by Ng and Cardie [18], where they use a separate anaphoricity determination module to improve the coreference resolution.

In our experiments, we also explore the influence of the three string similarity metrics (i.e., *Contain*, *ContainRatio*, *Cos-Similarity*) and the two weighting schemes (i.e., *Binary* and *TF.IDF*), on the performance of coreference resolution. The results are summarized in Table 7. From the comparisons shown in the table we can find the tradeoffs between the recall and precision when applying different similairty metrics. For example, in the system *NewFeature* (with *Binary* weight), the metric *Cos-Similarity* leads to the highest recall (72.8%), while *ContainRatio* produces the highest precision (63.8%). However, from the overall evaluation, the metric *ContainRatio* outperforms all the other two competitors in the F-measure.

Table 7. Influence of different string similarity metrics and token weighting schemes on the resolution.

Strategy	Similarity Metric	Binary Weight			TFIDF Weight		
		R	P	F	R	P	F
NewFeature	Contain	70.6	61.7	65.8	-	-	-
	ContainRatio	70.5	63.8	67.0	72.1	61.3	66.2
	Cos-Similairty	**72.8**	60.2	65.9	69.3	62.9	65.9
NonAnaphor+NewFeature	Contain	66.5	71.4	68.5	-	-	-
	ContainRatio	68.1	69.7	**68.9**	65.2	69.9	67.4
	Cos-Similairty	66.7	70.0	68.3	63.7	**72.5**	67.8

In comparing the two different weighting schemes, it is interesting to note that the systems using *TF.IDF* does not perform better than those using *Binary* in the F-measure. *TF.IDF* scheme may improve precision, especially for *Cos-Similarity* metric (2.7% higher). Nevertheless, the contribution of the frequency information to precision rate is not significant enough to compensate the loss in recall. We see that the recall drops (over 3.0% for *Cos-Similarity* metric) at the same time (the exception is *NewFeature+ContainRation*, where *TFIDF* gets a higher recall but lower precision than *Binary*). In fact, in determining the coreference relationship between two noun phrases, each token in the modifiers, no matter how many times it occurs throughout the current document and the entire data set, may likely provide an important clue. That is may be why *Binary* weighting scheme seems to be superior to *TF.IDF* scheme.

7 Related Work

Several work has been done on the resolution of coreference realized by string matching. (e.g. [2, 10, 3, 4, 11, 12, 19]). Compared to existing approaches, our approach has the following advantages:

- Our approach can deal with all types of nouns. In contrast, the study by Vieira and Poesio[10] focuses only on definite noun phrases. Also, the conditional model by McCallum and Wellner [19] is mainly for Proper noun coreference resolution.
- Our feature set can capture various matching patterns between noun phrases. In contrast, for the feature MED used by Strube et al. [11] and LCS by Castano et al. [12], the matching is restricted only on the full strings of noun phrases.

Ng and Cardie [18] proposed an anaphoricity determination module to improve the coreference resolution. In their approach, a multiple anaphoricity classifier has to be trained and applied in the coreference resolution. In contrast, the anaphoricity determination function is integrated seamlessly in our coreference classification, attributed to our training instance selection strategy.

8 Conclusion

In the paper we presented a system which aims to address the coreference realized by string matching. We improve the performance of the baseline resolution system in two ways. First, we proposed an extensive feature set to capture the matching information between noun phrase modifiers. To improve the recall rate, techniques such as expansion, stemming, and stopping words removal were applied to the original strings. Different matching degree metrics and weighting schemes have been tried to obtain the feature values. Second, we modified the selection strategy for training instances. Non-anaphors now are also included in the training instance generation. This enhances the anaphoricity identification ability of the classifier, and thus improves the precision.

While the experimental results show that combination of the above two modifications boost the system performance, there is still room for improvement. For example, in calculating the matching degree of two strings, the semantic compatibility between words, e.g., hypernym or synonym, have influence on the string matching. We would like to take this factor into account for our future work.

References

1. Aone, C., Bennett, S.W.: Evaluating automated and manual acquistion of anaphora resolution strategies. In: Proceedings of the 33rd Annual Meeting of the Association for Compuational Linguistics. (1995) 122–129
2. McCarthy, J., Lehnert, Q.: Using decision trees for coreference resolution. In: Proceedings of the 14th International Conference on Artificial Intelligences. (1995) 1050–1055
3. Soon, W., Ng, H., Lim, D.: A machine learning approach to coreference resolution of noun phrases. Computational Linguistics **27** (2001) 521–544
4. Ng, V., Cardie, C.: Improving machine learning approaches to coreference resolution. In: Proceedings of the 40th Annual Meeting of the Association for Computational Linguistics, Philadelphia (2002) 104–111
5. Yang, X., Zhou, G., Su, J., Tan, C.: Coreference resolution using competition learning approach. In: Proceedings of the 41st Annual Meeting of the Association for Computational Linguistics, Japan (2003)
6. MUC-6: Proceedings of the Sixth Message Understanding Conference. Morgan Kaufmann Publishers, San Francisco, CA (1995)
7. MUC-7: Proceedings of the Seventh Message Understanding Conference. Morgan Kaufmann Publishers, San Francisco, CA (1998)
8. Poesio, M., Vieira, R.: A corpus-based investigation of definite description use. Computational Linguistics **24** (1998) 183–261
9. Cohen, W., Ravikumar, P., Fienberg, S.: A comparison of string distance metrics for name-matching tasks. In: Procedings of IJCAI-03 Workshop on Information Integration on the Web. (2003)
10. Vieira, R., Poesio, M.: An empirically based system for processing definite descriptions. Computational Linguistics **27** (2001) 539–592
11. Strube, M., Rapp, S., Muller, C.: The influence of minimum edit distance on reference resolution. In: Proceedings of the Conference on Empirical Methods in Natural Language Processing, Philadelphia (2002) 312–319
12. Castano, J., Zhang, J., Pustejovsky, J.: Anaphora resolution in biomedical literature. In: International Symposium on Reference Resolution, Alicante, Spain (2002)
13. Zhou, G., Su, J.: Error-driven HMM-based chunk tagger with context-dependent lexicon. In: Proceedings of the Joint Conference on Empirical Methods on Natural Language Processing and Very Large Corpus, Hong Kong (2000)
14. Zhou, G., Su, J.: Named Entity recognition using a HMM-based chunk tagger. In: Proceedings of the 40th Annual Meeting of the Association for Computational Linguistics, Philadelphia (2002)
15. Shen, D., Zhang, J., Zhou, G., Su, J., Tan, C.: Effective adaptation of hidden markov model-based named-entity recognizer for biomedical domain. In: Proceedings of ACL03 Workshop on Natural Language Processing in Biomedicine, Japan (2003)
16. Quinlan, J.R.: C4.5: Programs for machine learning. Morgan Kaufmann Publishers, San Francisco, CA (1993)
17. Vilain, M., Burger, J., Aberdeen, J., Connolly, D., Hirschman, L.: A model-theoretic coreference scoring scheme. In: Proceedings of the Sixth Message understanding Conference (MUC-6), San Francisco, CA, Morgan Kaufmann Publishers (1995) 45–52
18. Ng, V., Cardie, C.: Identifying anaphoric and non-anaphoric noun phrases to improve coreference resolution. In: Proceedings of the 19th International Conference on Computational Linguistics (COLING02). (2002)
19. McCallum, A., Wellner, B.: Toward conditional models of identity uncertainty with application to proper noun coreference. In: Procedings of IJCAI-03 Workshop on Information Integration on the Web. (2003) 79–86

Combining Labeled and Unlabeled Data for Learning Cross-Document Structural Relationships

Zhu Zhang and Dragomir Radev

University of Michigan
Ann Arbor, MI 48109, USA
{zhuzhang,radev}@umich.edu

Abstract. Multi-document discourse analysis has emerged with the potential of improving various NLP applications. Based on the newly proposed Cross-document Structure Theory (CST), this paper describes an empirical study that classifies CST relationships between sentence pairs extracted from topically related documents, exploiting both labeled and unlabeled data. We investigate a binary classifier for determining existence of structural relationships and a full classifier using the full taxonomy of relationships. We show that in both cases the exploitation of unlabeled data helps improve the performance of learned classifiers.

1 Introduction

With the proliferation of web-based information resources and related applications, such as information extraction, text summarization, and question answering, computational models for natural language discourse structures have gained increasing attention. Recently, the study of multi-document discourse has emerged, which is different from traditional discourse analysis in that multiple related documents may be written in different styles, use different vocabulary, and reflect inconsistent perspectives.

Inspired by Rhetorical Structure Theory (RST) [1], the notion of Cross-document Structure Theory (CST) was proposed by [2]. The central idea is to posit a set of rhetorical relationships that hold between sentences across topically-related documents. It has been shown that the availability of such information can help multi-document text summarization [3]. It is also conceivable that other NLP- or IR-related applications, such as semantic entity and relation extraction (where semantic relations may instantiate cross document boundaries), and non-factoid question answering (where answer generation may demand "fusing" information from multiple documents), can potentially benefit from the understanding of multi-document discourse structure.

A prerequisite of the applications is to automatically identify CST relations from text. In [4], we explored the possibility of classifying CST relationships by using a strictly supervised machine learning approach, and achieved promising results. In this paper, we try to improve the classification model by leveraging both labeled and unlabeled data.

2 Related Work

Effort has been made to identify RST relationships from text. [5] proposed a first-order formalization of the high-level rhetorical structure of text, and provided a theoretical analysis and an empirical comparison of four algorithms for automatic derivation of text structures. Marcu's knowledge-based approach relied on "cue phrases" in implementing algorithms to discover the valid RST trees for a single document. This is reasonable because of the conventions of writing and the valid assumption that authors tend to write documents using certain rhetorical techniques. However, in the case of multiple documents and cross-document relationships, we cannot expect to encounter a reliable analog to the cue phrase. This is because separate documents, even when they are related to a common topic, are generally not written with an overarching structure in mind. Therefore, when identifying CST relationships, it may pay off to look for deeper-level cues and to pursue statistical approaches instead.

[6] presented a machine learning approach to classifying RST relationships. Only lexical features are used in the naive Bayes classifier, and part-of-speech information is only used for feature selection for comparison purposes. Worth noting is that the authors take advantage of the available linguistic knowledge and exploit various cues in obtaining training data. Doing so is, again, much harder in the cross-document context.

Within the realm of machine learning, there has been growing interest in a family of learning techniques that aim at inducing classifiers by leveraging a small amount of labeled data and a large amount of unlabeled data. Among them is bootstrapping, or weakly supervised learning. It chooses the unlabeled instances with the highest probability of being correctly labeled and uses them to augment labeled training data. Two of the most influential bootstrapping algorithms are the co-training algorithm [7] and Yarowsky algorithm [8]. Recently [9] provided a very cogent comparison of the two with some nice extensions.

Bagging (bootstrap aggregation) predictors [10] is a method for generating multiple versions of a predictor and using them to get an aggregated predictor. The aggregation averages over the versions when predicting a numerical outcome and does a plurality vote when predicting a class. The multiple versions are formed by making bootstrap replicates of the learning set (specifically, the replicates are of the same size as the original data and are generated by sampling with replacement) and using these as new learning sets. Variations of the idea have been explored by [11] and [12].

3 Problem Definition

3.1 Cross-Document Structure Theory

Cross-document Structure Theory (CST) is a functional theory for multi-document discourse structure. It is used to describe cross-document semantic connections, such as "elaboration", "contradiction", and "attribution", among text units of related documents. Instead of assuming deliberate writing, as RST does, CST views topically-related documents as generated by a "collective authorship".

We focus on sentence-level CST relationships in this study. A total of 18 CST relationships are defined in [4]. All relationships are domain-independent.

3.2 Formulation of the Classification Problem

As a first approximation, we cast the CST relationship identification problem in a standard classification framework. Conceptually, given an unordered sentence pair $P(S_1, S_2)$, where sentences S_1 and S_2 are from two different but topically related documents, we are interested in determining the type(s) of CST relationships between them. In this paper, we investigate the following two scenarios:

Binary Classification. Here we are interested in the existence of cross-document relationships regardless of type. If the two sentences are related in any types, the pair is assigned a label "1", otherwise a "0".

Full Classification. In this case we do care about the type(s) of cross-document relationships between the sentence pair. Moreover, it is possible for a single pair to have multiple labels (see section 4 and 5.3 for more details). The class labels are adapted from the CST taxonomy. Therefore, there are 19 possible labels in total (18 CST types plus a special type "no relationship").

4 Experimental Setup and Data Collection

Due to nonexistence of readily available data set, we had to actively collect data and have human judges annotate the CST relationships. As our first attempt, we collected six clusters of related news articles from various sources. The clusters were chosen to be diverse with respect to their topics, the time span across the documents, the cluster size, and the publishers. One cluster was used strictly for corpus development and judge training purposes. It was carefully annotated for CST relationships by the authors in developing the markup scheme and the guidelines to be used by the independent judges to be hired. The other five clusters were annotated by the human judges.

Human annotation is expensive, and it does not always yield ideal results. Human judges often do not agree, due to the inherently ambiguous nature of natural language. The large search space makes the situation even worse. In a ten-document cluster with 20 sentences on average in each document, for example, a human judge will have to examine roughly 18,000 sentence pairs if he or she needs to exhaust all possibilities. This is an incredibly tedious job in any sense, and consequently, it is very difficult for multiple judges to reach reasonable agreement on the annotation. One possible way to alleviate the problem is to exploit the observation that CST relationships are unlikely to exist between sentences that are *lexically* very dissimilar to each other. In other words, certain similarity measures might behave as a useful proxy for finding CST-related sentence pairs. We experimented with a few lexical-level similarity metrics, including Cosine [13], word overlap, longest common subsequence and BLEU [14], and then measured their correlation with CST-relatedness. Using the very carefully annotated *Milan9* as "training" data, we found that word overlap rate 0.12

is the "best" cutoff criterion for selecting sentence pairs, in the sense that it helps minimize selected number of sentence pairs without losing too many CST-related pairs (the recall is 87.5%). We then applied this measure on the other five clusters and selected, from a huge number of possible sentence pairs, a total of 4,931 potentially "interesting" ones for human judges to annotate. This way the judges' workload is significantly reduced. Eight judges were hired; each judge annotated at least one cluster; each cluster was annotated by two judges. The judges were allowed to assign multiple CST types to a single sentence pair, given the inherently ambiguous nature of the problem and the fact that the CST types are sometimes not mutually exclusive.

The more interesting part of the story is that we can get unlabeled data from any other sources virtually for free. The purpose of this study is exactly to explore the possibility of improving CST classifiers by exploiting both labeled and unlabeled data. Specifically, we use a set of 6,000 sentence pairs of arbitrary similarity from another news cluster (*Shuttle10*, which is about the Columbia Shuttle accident in 2003) as unlabeled data in our experiments.

5 Classification Exploiting Labeled and Unlabeled Data

In this section, we discuss the micro-level supervised learning component and the macro-level bootstrapping procedure respectively.

5.1 Underlying Supervised Learning: Algorithm and Features

In [4], we choose to use boosting, specifically AdaBoost [15], for our task. In this study, we build upon the same supervised learning component and investigate the effect of unlabeled data. The basic idea of the boosting algorithm is to find a "strong" hypothesis by combining many "weak" or "base" hypotheses. Moreover, BoosTexter [16], the off-the-shelf implementation of boosting, explicitly supports multi-label classification, which is very convenient for the multi-label full classification scenario in our problem.

Lexical features by themselves are apparently not sufficient for identifying CST relationships between sentences. Therefore, we considered various features at three linguistic levels, the details of which follow. The general idea is to quantify the similarity or distance between two sentences at different levels.

For most sentence pairs, the procedures for computing all features, such as tokenization, part-of-speech (POS) extraction, and head guessing, can directly or indirectly take advantage of the output of the Charniak parser [17]. For the very few sentences on which the parser fails, we used heuristic backoff procedures.

Lexical Features. At this level, we are only interested in the surface tokens. No stemming or stop-word deletion is done. Three features are considered: number of tokens in S_1, in S_2, and in common.

Shallow Syntactic-Level Features. We try to capture the overlap between two sentences with regard to 6 parts of speech: regular noun, proper noun, verb, adjective, adverb, and (cardinal) number, which are considered to convey relatively more substantial information than others. For each x in the 6 POS types, we compute the following counts, which gives us a total of 18 features:

- Number of tokens having POS x in S_1
- Number of tokens having POS x in S_2
- Number of common tokens having POS x

Deeper Syntactic-Level Features. The idea here is to find the most prominent concepts discussed in each sentence pair (by taking advantage of the syntactic structure) and compute their lexical semantic distance More specifically, this is done through the following steps:

1. Find the top level NP (noun phrase) and VP (verb phrase) in S_1 and S_2.
2. Find the head tokens of both NP and VP by using the head rules in [18].
3. Align the heads correspondingly (i.e., NP vs. NP, VP vs. VP).
4. For each head pair, compute lexical semantic distance measures (*lch*, *jcn*, *res*, *lin*, and *hso*) by using the semantic distance toolkit [19].

For each sentence pair, we have two pairs of heads (heads of NPs and heads of VPs). For each head pair, we compute the five semantic distance measures above. Therefore we have a total of 10 features in this group. For example, given the following sentence pair, five distance measures will be computed for word pairs {Bush, President} and {visit, arrive} respectively.

(S1 (S (NP (NNP Bush))(VP (VBZ visits)(NP (NNP China)))(. .)))
(S1 (S (NP (DT The)(NNP President))(VP (VBZ arrives)(PP (IN in)(NP (NNP Beijing))))(. .)))

5.2 Committee-Based Bootstrapping Using Bagging

The central idea of weakly supervised learning is to take advantage of the information hidden in large amount of unlabeled data. In this case specifically, we want to choose the unlabeled data points that have the highest probability of being correctly labeled (by a classifier or a set of classifiers trained on currently available labeled data) and include them into the labeled data set.

We propose a committee-based data augmentation procedure (Algorithm 1) using bagging, which is in spirit very similar to those used in [11] and [12] but with an extra step size parameter, motivated by the following reasons:

- It is conceivable that the classifier performance will not keep improving infinitely with additional unlabeled data. We are interested in finding the best cutoff point.

Algorithm 1 Committee-based data augmentation.

Require: labeled data set L
Require: unlabeled data set U
Require: augmentation step size S
  repeat
    Generate n bootstrap datasets from L using bagging
    Train a committee of n classifiers on the n bootstrap data sets respectively
    Run the committee on U
    Add at most S agreed-upon (by all committee members) data points into L
  until No data points can be added into L

- A more important intuition is to maintain inertia for the augmented data set and the corresponding classifier, instead of introducing too much perturbation at one time. In other words, the number of extra data points added into the labeled set in each iteration should not be very large compared to the size of the seed set.

Once the labeled data set is augmented by Algorithm 1, we experiment with two different strategies:

- Train a single classifier on the augmented data set L, and use it as the final predictor (referred to as the *FinalSingle* strategy).
- Train a set of bagging predictors on the augmented L, and let the committee vote on new data points (referred to as the *FinalBagging* strategy).

5.3 Data Treatment

While he treatment of unlabeled data is relatively trivial (we only need to compute feature vectors for them and assign blank labels correspondingly), proper treatment of the labeled data is crucial, as they are used as "seeds" for the bootstrapping process.

As mentioned in section 4, each document cluster is annotated by two judges, and the judges are allowed to assign multiple labels to a single pair. The judges don't always agree: they may either disagree on whether two sentences are CST-related at all or disagree on the types of CST relationships between them. Instead of asking the judges to resolve the disagreements, we decided to only include the data points on which the two judges at least agree on the existence of CST relationships (regardless of type). $3,942$ out of $4,931$ sentence pairs satisfy this condition ($kappa = 0.53$). This is an important decision based on our understanding of the underlying linguistic phenomenon, instead of technical inability of dealing with noisy data. Since the ability to determine the existence of any CST relationships is important for many potential applications, we want the model to be as clean as possible. On the other hand, once the CST-relatedness is known, it is reasonable for multiple CST relationships to exist between two sentences. Therefore, below is how labels are assigned to data points in the two classification scenarios respectively:

- In the binary classification case, a label "1" is assigned to a pair if it is unanimously believed to be CST-related, and a label "0" if it is unanimously believed to be not related.
- In the full classification case, each sentence pair is assigned the union of the labels given by the two judges if they agree that the two sentences are CST-related, or a label "0" if they agree that the two sentences are not related.

The whole labeled data set is then split into a (seed) training set, a validation set, and a test set by uniform random sampling in the proportion of 6:2:2.

5.4 Evaluation Metrics

For binary classification, besides the standard classification accuracy, we also measure precision, recall, and F-measure.

For full classification, besides class-specific IR metrics, we compute the following aggregate metrics:

- One-accuracy (whether the top-ranked label is among the correct ones)
- Coverage (how far do we have to go down the ranked label list to find all the correct ones)
- Average precision (analogous to non-interpolated average precision for evaluating document ranking performance)

6 Experiments and Results

In presenting the experimental results, we are especially interested in whether the exploitation of unlabeled data can help improve the performance of resultant classifiers. Notice that in both cases, the baseline strategy is to assign the label "0" (i.e., no CST relationship) to all data points, which achieves an accuracy of 75.13% on the test set.

In the experiments, we used the following parameter values: rounds of boosting – 400; number of bags – 10; step size for data augmentation – 200. The same supervised learning component is used across all experiments, for the purpose of fair comparison.

6.1 Binary Classification

By observing the classifier behavior on the validation set, we notice that the performance maximizes with roughly 400 additional unlabeled data points. The actual performance on the final test set is presented in Table 1. As we can see, using unlabeled data does result in significantly improved classifier. A minor note is that the *FinalBagging* strategy gives slightly worse results than *FinalSingle*, although still better than the strictly supervised learner.

Table 1. Performance of binary classifier.

	Accuracy	Precision	Recall	F-measure
Labeled data only	0.8789	0.8278	0.6477	0.7267
Labeled & unlabeled data (*FinalSingle*)	0.8905	0.8699	0.6580	0.7493
Labeled & unlabeled data (*FinalBagging*)	0.8853	0.8562	0.6477	0.7375

6.2 Full Classification

In this scenario, we again find that adding roughly 400 additional unlabeled data points gives the best results on the validation set. The improvement in aggregate performance metrics still consistently holds, except that the *FinalBagging* strategy works better than *FinalSingle* this time (Table 2).

Table 2. Performance of full classifier: aggregate metrics.

	One-Accuracy	Coverage	Average precision
Labeled data only	0.8093	1.1070	0.8729
Labeled & unlabeled data (*FinalSingle*)	0.8157	1.0773	0.8768
Labeled & unlabeled data (*FinalBagging*)	0.8376	1.0721	0.8839

Class-specific results are summarized in Table 3 (Only CST types that occur more than 20 times in the test data are shown; the F-measures of the strictly supervised learner are also presented for comparison purposes). We see mixed results here. With extra unlabeled data, the bootstrapped classifier wins on some CST types and loses on some others. A possible explanation is the sparseness of the seed training data relative to the large number of classes.

Table 3. Full classifier performance on individual CST types.

CST type	Precision	Recall	F-measure	F-measure (supervised)
No relationship	0.8875	0.9605	0.9226	0.9186
Equivalence	0.5000	0.3200	0.3902	0.3429
Subsumption	0.1000	0.0417	0.0588	0.0513
Follow-up	0.4727	0.2889	0.3586	0.3946
Elaboration	0.3125	0.1282	0.1818	0.2478
Description	0.3333	0.1071	0.1622	0.2353
Overlap	0.5263	0.2941	0.3773	0.4324

6.3 Lessons Learned

Experiments in both classification scenarios justified the hypothesis that there is an upper bound on performance of classifiers that incorporate unlabeled data.

The improvement of performance is always followed by a drop. [11] contends that this is because the gains from additional training data are eventually offset by the sample bias in mining the unlabeled data points. On the other hand, this indicates the necessity of further, more focused, human annotation, which gives rise to potential combination of bootstrapping and active learning.

Secondly, the conservative stepwise strategy of augmenting labeled data is very appropriate; aggressive greedy augmentation hurts more than it helps. In the binary classification scenario, for example, the latter strategy would have added over 5,000 data points into the labeled set within 3 iterations, and results in a accuracy of 0.8489 and a F-measure of 0.7073, which is even worse than the strictly supervised learner.

7 Conclusion and Future Work

This paper describes an empirical study that leverages both labeled and unlabeled data to train machine-learned classifiers for cross-document structural relationships. We show that both the binary classifier and the full classifier can be improved by exploiting unlabeled data. From a machine learning theoretical point of view, we were able to show that bagging and boosting, traditionally viewed as competitors, can be combined to generate strong performance.

Looking into the future, on one hand, there is plenty of room for improving the underlying supervised learning performance by designing more sophisticated feature vectors; on the other hand, it is worthwhile investigating meaningful ways of keeping humans in the loop and overcoming the performance bottleneck by focused annotation.

The classification problem studied in this paper is still a somewhat simplified version of the full CST relationship identification problem. Some relationships have directionality, e.g., A following-up B is different from B following-up A. To be able to address issues like this, more intelligence needs to be built into the CST identifier. Another caveat is that the classifiers in the current experiments only look at "local" information within each sentence pair. In some cases, the "global" context plays an important role in determining the CST relationship(s).

In this paper, we have made further attempt to show that automatic identification of CST relationships is feasible. Various NLP- and IR-related applications may expect to see improvements by exploiting cross-document structure.

Acknowledgments

This material is based upon work supported by the National Science Foundation (Washington, DC) under Grant No. 0082884. Any opinions, findings, and conclusions or recommendations expressed in this material are those of the author(s) and do not necessarily reflect the views of the National Science Foundation.

References

1. Mann, W.C., Thompson, S.A.: Rhetorical Structure Theory: towards a functional theory of text organization. Text **8** (1988) 243–281
2. Radev, D.: A common theory of information fusion from multiple text sources, step one: Cross-document structure. In: Proceedings, 1st ACL SIGDIAL Workshop on Discourse and Dialogue, Hong Kong (2000)
3. Zhang, Z., Blair-Goldensohn, S., Radev, D.: Towards CST-enhanced summarization. In: Proceedings of the 18th National Conference on Artificial Intelligence, Edmonton, Alberta (2002)
4. Zhang, Z., Otterbacher, J., Radev, D.: Learning cross-document structural relationships using boosting. In: Proceedings of the 12th International Conference on Information and Knowledge Management CIKM 2003, New Orleans, LA (2003)
5. Marcu, D.: The Rhetorical Parsing, Summarization, and Generation of Natural Language Texts. PhD thesis, Department of Computer Science, University of Toronto (1997)
6. Marcu, D., Echihabi, A.: An unsupervised approach to recognizing discourse relations. In: Proceedings of the 40th Annual Meeting of the Association for Computational Linguistics (ACL). (2002) 368–375
7. Blum, A., Mitchell, T.: Combining labeled and unlabeled data with co-training. In: COLT: Proceedings of the Workshop on Computational Learning Theory, Morgan Kaufmann Publishers. (1998)
8. Yarowsky, D.: Unsupervised word sense disambiguation rivaling supervised methods. In: Proceedings of the 33rd Annual Meeting of the Association for Computational Linguistics (ACL). (1995) 189–196
9. Abney, S.: Bootstrapping. In: Proceedings of the 40th Annual Meeting of the Association for Computational Linguistics (ACL). (2002) 360–367
10. Breiman, L.: Bagging predictors. Machine Learning **24** (1996) 123–140
11. Banko, M., Brill, E.: Scaling to very very large corpora for natural language disambiguation. In: Meeting of the Association for Computational Linguistics. (2001) 26–33
12. Ng, V., Cardie, C.: Weakly supervised natural language learning without redundant views. In: HLT-NAACL 2003: Proceedings of the Main Conference. (2003) 173–180
13. Salton, G., Lesk, M.E.: Computer evaluation of indexing and text processing. Journal of the ACM (JACM) **15** (1968) 8–36
14. Papineni, K., Roukos, S., Ward, T., Zhu, W.J.: Bleu: a method for automatic evaluation of machine translation. In: Proceedings of the 40th Annual Meeting of the Association for Computational Linguistics (ACL). (2002) 311–318
15. Freund, Y., Schapire, R.E.: A decision-theoretic generalization of on-line learning and an application to boosting. Journal of Computer and System Sciences **55** (1997) 119–139
16. Schapire, R.E., Singer, Y.: Boostexter: A boosting-based system for text categorization. Machine Learning **39** (2000) 135–168
17. Charniak, E.: A maximum-entropy-inspired parser. Technical Report CS-99-12, Computer Scicence Department, Brown University (1999)
18. Collins, M.: Head-Driven Statistical Models for Natural Language Parsing. PhD thesis, University of Pennsylvania (1999)
19. Patwardhan, S., Pedersen, T.: distance.pl: Perl program that measures the semantic relatedness of words (version 0.11). http://www.d.umn.edu/~tpederse/distance.html (2002)

Parsing Mixed Constructions in a Type Feature Structure Grammar

Jong-Bok Kim[1] and Jaehyung Yang[2]

[1] School of English, Kyung Hee University, Seoul, Korea 130-701
[2] School of Computer Engineering, Kangnam University, Kyunggi, Korea, 449-702

Abstract. Because of the mixed properties of nominal and verbal properties, Korean gerundive phrases (GPs) posit intriguing issues to both theoretical as well as computational analyses. Various theoretical approaches have been proposed to solve this puzzle, but they all have ended up abandoning or modifying fundamental theory-neutral desiderata such as endocentricity (every phrase has a head), lexicalism (no syntactic rule refers to the word-internal structure), and null licensing (abstract entities are avoided if possible) (cf. Pullum 1991, Malouf 1998). This paper shows that it is possible to analyze and efficiently parse the mixed properties of Korean GPs in a way that maintains the desiderata while avoiding abstract entities. This has been achieved through Korean Phrase Structure Grammar, an extension of HPSG that models human languages as systems of constraints on typed feature structures. The feasibility of the grammar is tested by implementing it into the LKB (Linguistics Knowledge Building) system (cf. Copestake 2002).

1 Mixed Properties of Korean Verbal Gerundive Phrases

Like English, Korean gerundive phrases (GP) display verbal properties internally and nominal properties externally (Chung et al. 2001). It is not difficult to find out that they exhibit verbal properties in terms of the internal syntax. One telling piece of evidence comes from the fact that the gerundive verb inherits the arguments from the lexeme from which it is derived. As shown in (1), the gerundive verb takes the same arguments as the lexeme, a nominative subject and an accusative object[1]:

(1) [John-i   ku chayk-ul/*uy   ilk-ess-um]-i   myenghwak-hata
    John-NOM that book-ACC/*GEN read-PAST-NMLZ-NOM clear-do
    'John's having read the book is clear'

Various other phenomena also show that GPs are internally similar to VPs. The GP can include a sentential adverb as in (2)a; an adverbial element can

---

[1] The paper adopts the following glosses: ACC (accusative), ARG-ST (argument structure), COMP (complementizer), DAT (dative), DECL (declarative), GEN (genitive), HON (honorific), NMLZ (nominalizer), NOM (nominative), NEG (negation), REL (relativizer), SYN (Syntax), SEM (semantics), TOP (Topic), and the like.

modify the gerundive verb as in (2)b; the GP can include the sentential negation marker *an* 'not' as in (2)c; it also can contain the full range of auxiliaries as in (2)d:

(2) a. John-i   **papokathi** ku chayk-ul   ilk-ess-um
       John-NOM foolishly   that book-ACC read-PAST-NMLZ
       'John's having read the book foolishly'
    b. John-i   chayk-ul **ppalli/*ppalun**   ilk-um
       John-NOM book-ACC fast(adv)/*fast(adj) read-NMLZ
       'John's reading books fast.'
    c. John-i   chayk-ul **an**   ilk-um
       John-NOM book-ACC NEG read-NMLZ
       'John's not reading books.'
    d. John-i   chayk-ul ilk-ko   **siph**-um
       John-NOM book-ACC read-COMP want-NMLZ
       'John's wanting to read books'

Whereas the internal syntax of the GP is much like that of a VP, its external syntax is more like that of an NP. The GP can appear in the canonical NP positions such as subject or object as in (3)a or as a postpositional object in (3)b (cf. Yoon 1989).

(3) a. [ai-ka   chayk-ul ilk-um]-i   nollapta
       child-NOM book-ACC read-NMLZ-NOM surprising
       'That child's reading a book is surprising'
    b. [John-i   enehak-ul   kongpwuha-m]-**eytayhay** mollassta
       John-NOM linguistics-ACC study-NMLZ-about   not.know
       '(We) didn't know about John's studying linguistics.'

One thing worth pointing out here is that the GP does not have the full distribution of NPs, either. As demonstrated in (4), the GP cannot serve as the head of a relative clause, implying that the external syntax of the GP is somewhat different from that of a canonical NP.

(4) *John-un [[salam-tul-i __ molulila-ko   sayngkakha-n] [Mary-ka   ilccik
     John-TOP people-PL   not.know-COMP think-REL   Mary-NOM early
     ttenass-um]]-ul alassta.
     left-NMLZ   knew
     '*John knew [Mary's leaving early] that he thought that people wouldn't notice'.

These mixed and complicated properties of GP have provided a challenge to syntactic analyses with a strict version of X-bar theory, in particular, with respect to the theory-neutral desiderata such as endocentricity and lexicalism. This paper shows we can provide an effective and systematic way of capturing these mixed and complicated properties without abandoning these desiderata once we adopt the mechanism of multiple classification of category types with systematic inheritance. The grammar we developed as an application of the constraint-based grammar of HPSG to Korean is called Korean Phrase Structure Grammar (KPSG). We have checked the feasibility of the grammar by implementing it into the LKB (Linguistic Knowledge Building) system.

2 Korean Phrase Structure Grammar

2.1 Basic Picture

The Korean Phrase Structure Grammar, aiming to develop an open source grammar of Korean, consists of grammar rules, inflection rules, lexical rules, type definitions, and lexicon[2]. As in HPSG (Sag et al. 2003), the grammar adopts the mechanism of type hierarchy in which every linguistic sign is typed with appropriate constraints and hierarchically organized. All the linguistic information is thus represented in terms of *sign*. The type *sign* is classified into subtypes as represented in a simplified hierarchy in (5):

(5)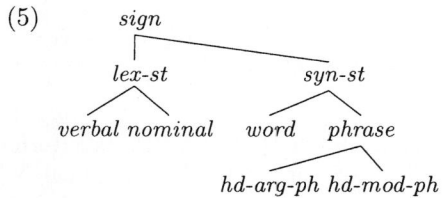

The elements in *lex-st* type, forming the basic components of the lexicon, are built up from lexical processes such as lexical rules and type definitions. Parts of these elements will be realized as *word* to function as syntactic elements. Phrases projected from *word* form basic Korean well-formed phrases such as *hd-arg-ph* (*head-argument-ph*) and *hd-mod-ph* (*head-modifier-ph*). All the syntactic rules in KPSG are either unary or binary. Different from English (and from the Japanese grammar of Siegel and Bender 2002), we assume that Korean adopts the following simplified phrasal well-formed conditions[3]:

(6) Korean X' Syntax:

a. hd-arg-ph:
[ ]->#1,H[ARG-ST <...#1...>]

b. hd-mod-ph:
[ ] -> [MOD #1], H[#1]

c. hd-filler-ph:
[ ] -> #1, H[GAP <#1>]

d. hd-word-ph:
[word] -> [word], H

(6)a means that when a head combines with one of its arguments, the resulting phrase is a well-formed phrase. (6)b allows a head to combine with a phrase that modifies it. (6)c is a constraint for a head to form a phrase (with a missing

---

[2] The space does not allow us to explicate the morphological and semantic system of the KPSG. As for morphology, we integrated MACH (Morphological Analyzer for Contemporary Hangul) developed by Shim and Yang (2002). This system segments words into sequences of morphemes with POS tags and morphological information. As for semantics, we adopted the Minimal Recursion Semantics developed by Copestake et al. (2001).

[3] Of course, further constraints need to be specified on these phrases. For example, the phrase *hd-word-ph* has additional constraints on the argument structure of the head. See Kim and Yang (2004) for details.

gap) with a filler. (6)d basically generates a word level syntactic element by the combination of a head and a word. This condition in (6)d, not found in languages like English, forms various types of complex predicates found in the language (cf. Kim and Yang 2003).

The type *hd-arg-ph* can easily license basic sentence types such as the following:

(7) a. [[pi-ka   [o-ass-ta]]].   'It rained.'
         rain-NOM come-PST-DECL
     b. [John-i   [Mary-eykey [chayk-ul   [cwu-ess-ta]]]].
         John-NOM Mary-DAT   book-ACC give-PST-DECL
         'John gave Mary a book.'

Since the phrase condition (in particular *hd-arg-ph*) allows a head (lexical or phrasal) to combine with one of its syntactic arguments, KPSG generates only binary structures as represented by the brackets.

One welcoming, desirable consequence of this binary approach concerns the sentence internal scrambling, one of the most complicated facts in the SOV type of language. For example, the sentence in (8) with five syntactic elements can induce 24 (4!) different scrambling possibilities, with the head verb fixed in the final position.

(8) [mayil]   [John-i]   [haksayng-tul-eykey] [yenge-lul]   [kaluchi-ess-ta]
     Everyday John-NOM students-PL-DAT   English-ACC teach-PST-DECL
     'John taught English to the students everyday.'

A most effective grammar would no doubt be the one that can capture all such scrambling possibilities within minimal processing load. In KPSG, the conditions on *hd-arg-ph* and *hd-mod-ph* allow us to generate all the word ordering possibilities for cases like (8). The following is one of the three encoded rules for the *hd-arg-ph* in the LKB system[4]:

```
head-arg-rule-1 := hd-arg-ph &
[SYN.ARG-ST #2,
ARGS<#1, syn-str&[SYN.ARG-ST [FIRST #1,
                              REST #2]]>].
```

Such a rule basically licenses a head to combine with only one of its complement(s), resulting in a binary structure. This kind of simple X' syntax is enough to capture the intriguing sentence internal scrambling without positing various movement operations.

2.2 The Structure of Lexicon and Forming Gerundive Verbs

The starting point of structuring the lexicon in the KPSG is parts of speech in the language. Like the traditional literature, the KPSG assumes *verbal*, *nominal*,

---

[4] Since the LKB does not allow a set operation, the LKB implementation requires to write three *head-arg-rules*, depending on which argument in the ARG-ST combines with the head.

adverbial, and *adnominal* as the language's basic categories. These are further subclassified into subtypes. For example, the type *verbal* is taken to have the rather simplified hierarchy given in (9)[5].

(9)
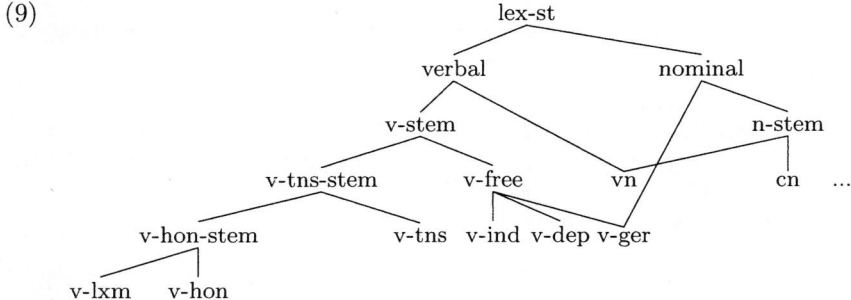

The key point of capturing the mixed properties of GPs comes form the multiple inheritance mechanism in which the type of gerundive verbs (*v-ger*) is declared to be the subtype of both *v-free* and *nominal* as represented here (cf. Kim 1998 and Kim and Yang 2003). One main difference from traditional grammar is the assignment of the HEAD feature POS: It assigns [POS *verb*] not to *verbal* but to the type *v-stem*, a subtype of *verbal*, and [POS *noun*] not to *nominal* but to the type *n-stem*, a subtype of *nominal*: there arises thus no conflict in the inheritance of the POS value on *v-ger*[6].

The KPSG thus differs from standard approaches in that it introduces three related features POS, VERBAL, and NOMINAL. This makes the grammar flexible enough to refer to each of these features when necessary. For example, all [VERBAL +] objects will have non-empty ARG-ST values, only the [POS *noun*] element will serve as the head of a relative clause, all [NOMINAL +] elements could serve as the host of the genitive marker, etc. This system then makes it unnecessary to introduce an additional part of speech such as *gerundive* as Malouf (1998) did for English.

In forming a gerundive verb, the KPSG thus starts from a transitive verb lexeme *ilk-* 'read' given in (10)a and and then forms a *v-tns-stem* with the attachment of the past tense suffix *-ess*. This *v-tns-stem* then combines with the nominalizer suffix *um*, forming the type *v-ger*. In this process, verbal properties (e.g. POS and VERBAL value) are inherited from *v-lxm* and *v-tns-stem*, whereas their nominal properties (e.g. NOMINAL) are incurred from its supertype *nominal*. The gerundive verb *ilk-ess-um* 'read-PST-NMLZ' will thus have at least the lexical information given in (10)b:

---

[5] The lexicon only provides elements for *v-lxm* and all the other type elements are generated from the morpho-syntactic, semantic constraints. See Kim and Yang 2003.

[6] One great advantage of this system is that it can also successfully capture the mixed properties of verbal noun. Notice here that the verbal noun type *vn* is slightly different: In the present system, this type will have [NOMINAL +, VERBAL +], but [POS *noun*]. These feature specifications will predict the facts that verbal nouns are in part nominal and in part verbal though morphologically they are more like nouns unlike gerundive verbs.

(10) a. $\begin{bmatrix} v\text{-}lxm \\ \text{ORTH ilk-} \\ \text{SYN} \begin{bmatrix} \text{HEAD} \begin{bmatrix} \text{POS } verb \\ \text{VERBAL +} \\ \text{NOMINAL } - \end{bmatrix} \end{bmatrix} \\ \text{ARG-ST } \langle \boxed{1}\text{NP}, \boxed{2}\text{NP} \rangle \end{bmatrix}$ b. $\begin{bmatrix} v\text{-}ger \\ \text{ORTH [ilk + ess] + um} \\ \text{SYN} \begin{bmatrix} \text{HEAD} \begin{bmatrix} \text{POS } verb \\ \text{VERBAL +} \\ \text{NOMINAL +} \end{bmatrix} \end{bmatrix} \\ \text{ARG-ST } \langle \boxed{1}\text{NP}, \boxed{2}\text{NP} \rangle \end{bmatrix}$

Such a cross-classification of the type *v-ger*, allowing multiple inheritance, is also reflected in the feature descriptions in the LKB. The following represents a sample source code:

```
v-ger := v-free & n-stem &
[ SYN #syn & [HEAD.MOD <>],
  SEM #sem,
  ARGS <v-tns-stem & [SYN #syn, SEM #sem]>].
```

As observed here, as a subtype of *v-free* and *n-stem*, the type *v-ger* thus inherits the constraints from its supertypes. Being a subtype of *v-free*, it inherits verbal properties from the type *v-free*, selecting arguments and assigning case values to them. Since it is a subtype of *nominal*, *v-ger* would undergo nominal suffixation processes such as case attachment. In addition, the grammar introduces the binary-valued features VERBAL on the type *verbal* and NOMINAL on the type *nominal*, which plays crucial roles in capturing mixed properties as well as various generalizations in the Korean grammar.

2.3 Projecting Gerundive Verbs into Syntax

Once we build up a gerundive verb with rich information that could be relevant in syntax, we then now need to look at how it is projected in syntax. Within the KPSG, the lexical entry in (10)b will be projected into structure like (11):

(11)
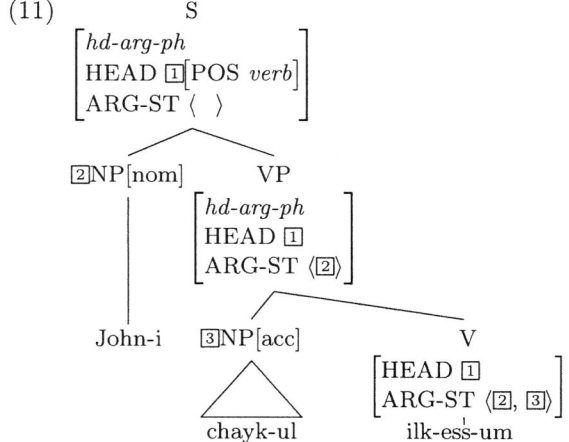

As noted, the gerundive verb *ilk-ess-um* 'read-PST-NMLZ' inherits all the other properties such as argument structure value from the verb lexeme *ilk–* 'read'. This explains why the gerund selects a nominative subject, can be modified by an adverb, allows sentential adverbials within the clause, combines with the sentential negative marker, occurs with an auxiliary verb, and the like. Because the gerundive verb selects the same argument(s) as the verb lexeme it is derived from, the phrase formed by the gerundive and one of its complements will be a well-formed *hd-arg-ph*. This resulting VP combines with the remaining nominative argument, the subject. This is what the top node S in (11) represents, reflecting the internal properties of GPs.

Prevalent are morphological and syntactic phenomena supporting this line of approach. Support for the treatment of the gerundive predicate induces a projection of [POS verb] comes from (a) the presence of a tense and an agreement suffix and (b) the possibility of heading an independent sentence as in (12):

(12) sensayngnim-i chayk-ul **ilk-usi-ess-um.**
teacher-NOM book-ACC read-HON-PAST-NMLZ
'The teacher has read the book.'

The analysis also provides a simple way of capturing relativization and extraction phenomena. Though GPs externally act like noun phrases (because of the NOMINAL feature), they do not serve as the head of a restrictive relative clause as repeated here in (13).

(13) *John-un [[salam-tul-i __ molulila-ko sayngkakha-n] [Mary-ka ilccik
John-TOP people-PL not.know-COMP think-REL Mary-NOM early
ttenass-um]]-ul alassta.
left-NMLZ knew
'*John knew [Mary's leaving early] that he thought that people wouldn't notice'.

As hinted, the only thing the grammar needs to specify is the constraint that a relative clause modifies a phrase projected from the feature [POS *noun*] not the one with [NOMINAL +] as represented in part of the relative clause modifying rule in the LKB description:

```
head-rel-mod-rule := binary &
[ SYN ...
  ARGS < phrase & [ SYN [ HEAD.MOD < #1 & [ SYN.HEAD.POS noun,
                                            SEM.INDEX #2 ] >,
                   ... ] ],
         syn-st & #1 & [ SYN.VAL [ ARG-ST #argst,
                                   GAP <! !> ] ] > ].
```

As indicated in the first element of the ARGS value, the relative clause can modify an element whose head bears [POS *noun*] value here. This will then correctly block any relative clause from modifying a gerundive verb head though it behaves like a nominal element.

It is possible to extract an element from GPs, indicating that the GP behaves more like Ss and less like NPs in terms of the external syntax:

(14) **ku chayk-un**   na-nun [John-i   __ ilkess-um]-ul   mitnunta
    that book-TOP I-TOP John-NOM __ read-NMLZ-ACC believe
    'That book, I believe John read.'

This is unexpected when considering the external status of the GP to be a pure NP. The KPSG, allowing extraction from a sentence level element ([POS *verb*]), takes the GP to be just like a sentence with the positive NOMINAL feature. Nothing thus blocks this extraction.

3 Some Further Consequences

Unlike a clitic or a phrasal approach that treats the nominalizer as a phrasal element or a clitic (cf. Yoon 1989), the present lexical analysis takes it to be a pure suffix, reflecting its morphological properties (cf. Kim 1998). However, examples like (15), in which the nominalizers seem to scope over the two coordinate sentences, seem to devalue such a lexical approach[7].

(15) [[A-ka   sakwa-lul mek-ess]-ko   [B-ka   maykcwu-lul masi-ess]-m]
    A-NOM apple-ACC eat-PST-CONJ B-NOM beer-ACC   drink-PST-NMLZ
    'A ate apples and B drank beer.'

In our analysis, this is also predictable. Since the second GP is also a type of sentence, cases like (15) are coordination of two sentences. There is no category mismatch in our analysis: the second conjunct is different from the first one only in its FORM value.

The present analysis also provides a simple way of dealing with cases where the subject is realized as genitive:

(16) ?[John-uy chayk-ul   ilk-um]
    John-GEN that book-ACC read-NMLZ-NOM
    'John's reading books '

As we can observe, the case value on the subject of the gerundive verb is different from that on the subject of the English gerund. Korean allows only nominative or genitive. The example in (16) differs from the nominative subject GP only in the way that the VP combines with a genitive specifier to form a possessive noun phrase. This case analysis is predicted within a rule-based case theory (cf. Kim 2004) in which the subject of a verbal element with the feature [VERBAL +] gets NOM whereas the specifier of [NOMINAL +] gets GEN. This system then would allow the following four possibilities:

(17) a. [John-i [chayk-ul [ilk-um]]] (ilk-um: [VERBAL +])
    b. [John-uy [chayk-ul ilk-um]] (ilk-um: [VERBAL +, NOMINAL +])
    c. [John-uy [chayk-uy ilk-um]] (ilk-um: [NOMINAL +])
    d. ?[John-i [chayk-uy ilk-um]] (ilk-um: [NOMINAL +, VERBAL +])

---

[7] Treating *um* as an independent lexical or phrasal element brings a serious drawback since this means an element like *v-tns-stem* to appear in syntax. That is, this would allow an element like *mek-ess* 'eat-PST' to freely appear in syntax contrary to the fact that only *v-free* elements can appear in Korean syntax.

As noted in the bracket with what feature is relevant for the case assignment in a sense, we could observe that the enriched information on the gerundive verb *ilk-um* can license GEN to its arguments due to the feature NOMINAL.

4 Testing the Feasibility of the Analysis

The grammar we have built within the typed-feature structure system here, eventually aiming at working with real-world data, has been first implemented into the LKB.

In testing its performance and feasibility, we used the SERI Test Suites '97 after the successful parsing of the self-designed 250 sentences. The SERI Test Suites (Sung and Jang 1997), carefully designed to evaluate the performance of Korean syntactic parsers, consists of total 472 sentences (292 test sentences representing the core phenomena of the language and 180 sentences representing different types of predicate). In terms of lexical entries, it has total 440 lexemes (269 nouns, 125 predicates, 35 adverbs, and 11 determiners) and total 1937 word occurrences.

The present system correctly generated all the lexemes in the test suites and inflected words. In terms of parsing sentences, the grammar (syntactically and semantically) parsed 423 sentences out of total 472[8]. Unfortunately, the test suites do not include any gerundive phrases, which seems to be a serious drawback when considering their frequent usages in real life; we included 50 test sentences for gerundive constructions adopted from the literature on Korean gerundive phrases (e.g. Kim 1998, Lapointe 1993, Yoon 1989) and the Sejong Project Basic Corpus. The present system successfully parsed all these sentences. Another promising indication of the test is that its mean parse (average number of parsed trees) for the total 458 (423 plus 35) sentences is 1.97, controlling spurious ambiguity at a desired level.

As noted here, the test results provide clear evidence that the KPSG, built upon typed feature structure system, offers high performance and can be extended to large scale of data. Since the test suites here include most of the main issues arising in analyzing major Korean constructions, we believe that further tests for designated corpora will surely achieve nearly the same result of high performance too.

5 Conclusion

This paper has shown that it is possible to analyze English and Korean GPs in a way that maintains the lexical integrity principle, captures endocentricity, and avoids empty categories. This has been achieved through the development of

---

[8] Failed 49 sentences are related to the grammar that the current system has not yet written. For example, the SERI Test Suites include examples representing phenomena such as left dislocations of the subject, gapping, and non-subject *pro* drops. It is believed that once we have a finer-grained grammar for these phenomena, the KPSG will be able to parse these remaining sentences.

KPSG, an extension of HPSG, that could reflect the language particular properties. HPSG is a sign-based grammar in which the basic unit of linguistic object *sign* is a structured complexes of linguistic information, represented by *typed feature structure*. The feasibility of the grammar developed has been checked with its implementation into the LKB system. The result of an existing test suite and self-constructed experimental data is quite promising though there still remains an issue of testing it with a large scale of corpora.

Acknowledgements

We are grateful to the three anonymous reviewers for comments and suggestions. We also thank Sae-Youn Cho, Jae-Woong Choe, Chan Chung, and Yongkyoon No for helpful comments. The first author also acknowledges the financial support by the Brian Korea 21 project in the year of 2004.

References

Chung, Chan, Jong-Bok Kim, Byung-Soo Park, and Peter Sells. 2001. Mixed Categories and Multiple Inheritance Hierarchies in English and Korean Gerundive Phrases. *Language Research* 37.4: 763–797.
Copestake, Ann. 2002. *Implementing Typed Feature Structure Grammars*. CSLI Publications.
Kim, Jong-Bok. 1998. Interface between Morphology and Syntax: A Constraint-Based and Lexicalist Approach. *Language and Information* 2: 177-233.
Kim, Jong-Bok and Jaehyung Yang. 2003. Korean Phrase Structure Grammar and Implementing it into the LKB System (In Korean). *Korean Linguistics* 21: 1–41.
Kim, Jong-Bok and Jaehyung Yang. 2004. Projections from Morphology to Syntax in the Korean Resource Grammar: Implementing Typed Feature Structures. In *Lecture Notes in Computer Science* Vol 2945, pp 13-24, Springer-Verlag.
Malouf, Robert. 1998. *Mixed Categories in the Hierarchical Lexicon*. Stanford: CSLI Publications.
Sag, Ivan, Tom Wasow, and Emily Bender. 2003. *Syntactic Theory: A Formal Approach*. Stanford: CSLI Publications.
Shim, Kwangseob and Yang Jaehyung. 2002. MACH: A Supersonic Korean Morphological Analyzer. In *Proceedings of Coling-2002 International Conference*, pp.939-45, Taipei.
Siegel, Melanie and Emily M. Bender. 2002. Efficient Deep Processing of Japanese. In *Proceedings of the 3rd Workshop on Asian Language Resources and International Standardization*. Coling 2002 Post-Conference Workshop. Taipei, Taiwan.
Sung, Won-Kyung and Myung-Gil Jang. 1997. SERI Test Suites '95. In *Proceedings of the Conference on Hanguel and Korean Language Information Processing*.
Lapointe, Steven. 1993. Dual Lexical Categories and the Syntax of Mixed Category Phrases. In A. Kathol & M. Bernstein (eds.), *Proceedings of ESCOL*, 199-210.
Pullum, Geoffrey. 1991. English Nominal Gerund Phrases as Noun Phrases with Verb-Phrase Heads. *Linguistics* 29: 763–799.
Yoon, James. 1989. *A Restrictive Theory of Morphosyntactic Interaction and Its Consequences*. Ph.D. Dissertation. University of Illiniois, Urbana-Champaign.

Iterative CKY Parsing
for Probabilistic Context-Free Grammars

Yoshimasa Tsuruoka[1,2] and Jun'ichi Tsujii[2,1]

[1] CREST, JST (Japan Science and Technology Agency)
Honcho 4-1-8, Kawaguchi-shi, Saitama 332-0012
[2] University of Tokyo
7-3-1 Hongo, Bunkyo-ku, Tokyo 113-0033
{tsuruoka,tsujii}@is.s.u-tokyo.ac.jp

Abstract. This paper presents an iterative CKY parsing algorithm for probabilistic context-free grammars (PCFG). This algorithm enables us to prune unnecessary edges produced during parsing, which results in more efficient parsing. Since pruning is done by using the edge's inside Viterbi probability and the upper-bound of the outside Viterbi probability, this algorithm guarantees to output the exact Viterbi parse, unlike beam-search or best-first strategies. Experimental results using the Penn Treebank II corpus show that the iterative CKY achieved more than 60% reduction of edges compared with the conventional CKY algorithm and the run-time overhead is very small. Our algorithm is general enough to incorporate a more sophisticated estimation function, which should lead to more efficient parsing.

1 Introduction

There are several well-established $O(n^3)$ algorithms for finding the best parse for a sentence using probabilistic context-free grammars (PCFG). However, when the size of the grammar is large, the computational cost of $O(n^3)$ is quite burdensome. For example, the PCFG learned from the Penn Treebank II corpus has around 15,000 rules and the number of edges produced for parsing a 40-word sentence sometimes exceeds one million.

Many research efforts have been devoted to reducing the computational cost of PCFG parsing. One way to prune the edges produced during parsing is to use a beam search strategy, in which only the best n parses are tracked. Roark [1] and Ratnaparkhi [2] applied this technique to PCFG parsing. The advantage of this method is that one can incorporate beam search strategies into existing parsing algorithms without any significant additional processing cost. However, it has a major drawback: the Viterbi (highest probability) parse may be pruned during parsing, so the *optimality* of the output is not guaranteed.

Another way to reduce the number of edges produced is to use best-first or A* search strategies [3–5]. Best-first strategies produce edges that are most likely to lead to a successful parse at each moment. While best-first strategies do not guarantee to output the Viterbi parse, an A* search always outputs the Viterbi parse by making use of an estimation function that gives an upper bound of the score to build a successful parse.

A* parsing is very promising because it can prune unnecessary edges during parsing, while keeping the optimality of the output parse. From an implementation point of view, however, A* parsing has a serious difficulty. It maintains an agenda to keep edges to be processed. The edges in the agenda are properly scored so that an appropriate edge can be retrieved from the agenda at any moment. One of the most efficient ways to implement such an agenda is to use *priority queues*, which requires a computational cost of $O(log(n))$ at each action [6], where n is the number of edges in the agenda. Since the process of retrieving and storing edges is conducted in the innermost loop of the A* algorithm, the cost of $O(log(n))$ makes it difficult to build a fast parser by using the A* algorithm.

In this paper, we propose an alternative way of pruning unnecessary edges while keeping the optimality of the output parse. We call this algorithm *the iterative CKY algorithm*. This algorithm is an extension of the well-established CKY parsing algorithm. It conducts repetitively CKY parsing with a probability threshold until the successful parse is found. It is easy to implement and the runtime overhead is quite small. We verified its effectiveness through experiments using the Penn Treebank II corpus.

This paper is organized as follows. Section 2 explains the iterative CKY parsing algorithm along with its pseudocode. Section 3 presents experimental results using the Penn Treebank II corpus. Section 4 offers some concluding remarks.

2 Iterative CKY Parsing

The CKY algorithm is a well-known $O(n^3)$ algorithm for PCFG parsing [7,8]. It is essentially a bottom-up parser using a dynamic programming table. It fills out the probability table by induction.

The iterative CKY algorithm, which we present in this paper, is an extension of the conventional CKY algorithm. It repetitively conducts CKY parsing with a threshold until the successful parse is found. The threshold allows the parser to prune edges during parsing, which results in efficient parsing. The reason why we need to execute parsing repetitively is that CKY parsing with a threshold does not necessarily return a successful parse[1]. In such cases, we need to relax the threshold and conduct parsing again. When CKY does return a successful parse, it is guaranteed to be optimal.

The details of the algorithm are described in the following section.

2.1 Algorithm

Figure 1 shows the pseudo-code of the entire algorithm of the iterative CKY parsing algorithm. Note that probabilities are expressed in logarithmic form.

---
[1] "Successful" means that the resulting parse contains S at the root of the tree.

```
function iterativeCKY(words, grammar, step)
{
    threshold = 0
    until CKY'() returns success
    {
        CKY'(words, grammar, threshold)
        threshold = threshold - step
    }
}

function CKY'(words, grammar, threshold)
{
    Create and clear π[]

    # diagonal
    for j = 2 to num_words
        for A = 1 to num_nonterminals
            if A → w_i is in grammar then
                π[i, i, A] = log(P(A → w_i))

    # the rest of the matrix
    for j = 2 to num_words
        for i = 1 to num_words-j+1
            for k = 1 to j-1
                for A = 1 to num_nonterminals
                    for B = 1 to num_nonterminals
                        for C = 1 to num_nonterminals
                            α = π[i, k, B] + π[i+k, j-k, C]
                                +log(P(A → BC))
                            if (α > π[i, j, A]) then
                                β = outside(A, i, j)
                                if (α + β ≥ threshold) then
                                    π[i, j, A] = α

    if π[1, num_words, S] has a value then
        return success
    else
        return failure
}
```

Fig. 1. Pseudocode of the iterative CKY parsing algorithm. Probabilities are expressed in logarithmic form. "S" is the non-terminal symbol corresponding to a whole sentence. Outside(...) is the function that returns the upper bound of the outside Viterbi log-probability (see Section 2.2).

The main function **iterativeCKY(...)** repetitively calls the function **CKY'(...)** giving a threshold to it until it returns a successful parse. The threshold starts with zero and is decreased by a predefined *step* at each iteration.

The function **CKY'**(...) is almost the same as the conventional CKY algorithm. The only difference is that it is given a threshold of log-probability and it prunes edges that do not satisfy the condition

$$\alpha_e + \beta_e \geq \text{threshold}, \quad (1)$$

where α_e is the inside Viterbi log-probability[2] of the edge, which is calculated in a bottom-up manner, and β_e is the upper bound of the outside Viterbi log-probability of the edge. Therefore, the sum of α_e and β_e is the highest log-probability among those of all possible successful parse trees that contain the edge. In other words, the sum is the most optimistic estimate. How to calculate β_e is described in Section 2.2.

After filling the dynamic programming table, the algorithm checks whether the non-terminal symbol "S" is in the cell in the upper right corner of the matrix. If it is, it returns *success*; otherwise, it returns *failure*.

It should be noted that if this function returns *success*, the obtained parse is optimal because pruning is done on the most optimistic estimate. The algorithm prunes only the edges that would not lead to a successful parse within the given threshold. The edges needed to build the optimal parse are never pruned.

When this function returns *failure*, it is called again with a relaxed threshold.

It is important that the value of β_e can be computed off-line. Therefore, what we need to do in runtime is just retrieve the information from the precomputed table. The runtime overhead is very small.

It might seem wasteful to iteratively perform CKY parsing until a successful parse is found. Somewhat counterintuitively, however, the waste is not very problematic. Although the first few attempts come to nothing, the total number of edges produced to give a successful parse is smaller than for normal CKY in most cases. Table 1 shows an example of iterative CKY parsing. Each row shows the number of edges and the parsing result. The parser conducted seven iterations until it finally obtained a successful parse. Thus the edges produced during the first six trials were wasted. However, since the number of edges increases exponentially as the threshold decreases in a constant step, the number of the wasted edges is relatively small.

The point is that we do not know the log-probability of the successful parse of a sentence in advance. If we did, setting the threshold to that log-probability would result in maximum pruning, because the tighter the threshold is, the more edges we can prune. In preliminary experiments, we tried to estimate the log-probability of a sentence using its length in order to reduce the number of wasted edges, but we did not have much success. In this paper, therefore, we take the simple strategy of decreasing by a constant step from the threshold at each iteration.

---

[2] In this paper, we use the term "inside (or outside) Viterbi probability" to refer to the probability of the Viterbi parse inside (or outside) an edge. Do not confuse it with the *inside (or outside) probability* which refers to the sum of the probabilities of all possible parses inside (or outside) an edge.

Table 1. Example of log-probability threshold and the number of edges. The log-probability of the sentence is -62.34.

Log-probability threshold	Number of edges	Parse result
0	0	failure
-10	0	failure
-20	0	failure
-30	22	failure
-40	594	failure
-50	4,371	failure
-60	16,080	failure
-70	38,201	success
Total	59,268	
Normal CKY	110,441	success

2.2 Upper Bound of Outside Viterbi Probability

There are many ways to calculate the upper bound of the outside Viterbi probability of the edge, depending on how much contextual information we specify. In this work, we use *context summary estimates* proposed by Klein [5].

Summary	(1, 6, NP)
Most Optimistic Tree	S → PP , NP VP . PP → IN NP NP → DT JJ NN VP → VBD ? [NP] ? ? ? ? ?
Log-Probability	-11.3

Fig. 2. Context summary estimate [5].

Figure 2 shows an example, where the edge is NP. In this case, the *context summary* is that NP has one word on the left and six on the right. The tree is the most optimistic tree, meaning that it has the highest probability among all possible trees that conform to this context summary. This estimate can be calculated efficiently in a recursive manner. For details of how to compute this estimation, see [5].

The estimates for all possible combinations of *lspan* (the number of words on the left), *rspan* (the number of words in the right), and symbols in the grammar are computed in advance. The memory size required for storing this information is

$$\text{(number of symbols)} \times \frac{(\text{max sentence length})^2}{2}. \tag{2}$$

For instance, the number of symbols in the set of binarized rules learned from the Penn Treebank is 12,946. If we parse maximum-40-word sentences, the memory required is about 80 MB (assuming that the size of each entry is 8 bytes).

We can use richer contexts for the upper bound of outside Viterbi probabilities. It is a trade-off between time and space. By using a richer context, we can obtain tighter upper bounds, which lead to more pruning. However, more space is required to store the estimates.

3 Experiment

To evaluate the effectiveness of the proposed algorithm, we conducted experiments using the Penn Treebank II corpus [9], which is a syntactically annotated corpus in English.

3.1 Binarization

Since all rules in the grammar must be either unary or binary in CKY parsing[3], we binarized the rules that have more than two symbols on the right side in the following way.

– Create a new symbol which corresponds to the first two symbols on the right.
– The probability of the newly created rule is 1.0

This process is repeated until no rule has more than two symbols on the right side.

For example, the rule
  NP → DT JJ NN (0.3)
is decomposed into the following two rules.
  NP → X_{DTJJ} NN (0.3)
  X_{DTJJ} → DT JJ (1.0)

The probability distribution over the transformed grammar is equivalent to the original grammar. It is easy to convert a parse tree in the transformed grammar into the parse tree in the original grammar.

3.2 Corpus and Grammar

Following [5], we parsed sentences of length 18-26 in section 22. The grammar used for parsing was learned from section 2 to 21.

We discarded all functional tags attached to non-terminals and traces, which are labeled "-NONE-", in the Treebank. The grammar learned had 14,891 rules in the original form. We binarized them and obtained 27,854 rules.

---

[3] Strictly speaking, the original CKY algorithm requires all the rules to be binary. We used a slightly extended version of the CKY algorithm which can deal with unary rules.

3.3 Step of Threshold Decrease

We first conducted experiments to estimate the optimal step of threshold decrease using a held-out set. The held-out set was created from the first 10% of section 22. The remaining sentences in the section were reserved for the test set.

Figure 3 shows the relationship between the step of threshold decrease and the total number of edges for parsing the held-out set. The best efficiency was achieved when the step was 11. The curve in the figure indicates that the efficiency is not very sensitive to the step when it is around the optimal point.

Figure 4 shows the relationship between the step and the time taken for parsing the held-out set[4]. The best setting was again 11.

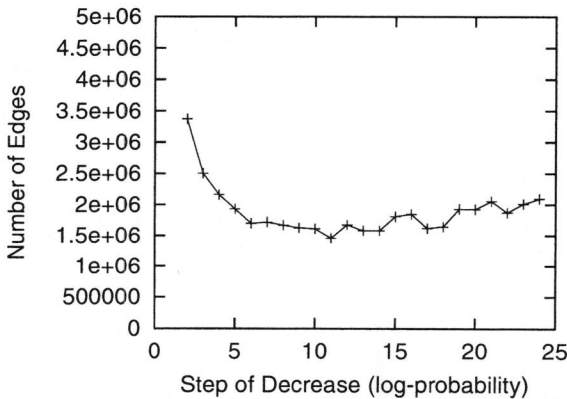

Fig. 3. The step of decrease in log-probability threshold and the total number of edges.

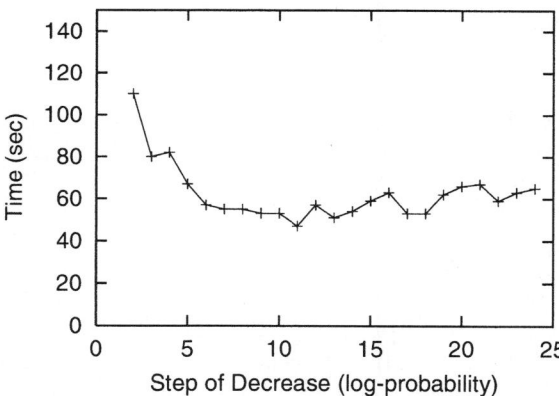

Fig. 4. The step of decrease in log-probability threshold and the total time.

---

[4] The experiments were conducted on a server having a Xeon 3.06 GHz processor and 1 GB of memory.

Table 2. The number of edges produced for parsing first several sentences in the test set.

Sentence length	Normal CKY	Iterative CKY	Ratio
19	68,366	16,343	0.24
19	69,979	4,194	0.06
24	96,185	45,232	0.47
21	110,926	15,220	0.14
23	115,296	85,634	0.74
23	102,797	18,393	0.18
25	165,564	109,002	0.66
20	86,454	21,622	0.25
22	71,797	33,819	0.47
26	127,250	62,834	0.49
⋮	⋮	⋮	⋮

Table 3. Performance on the test set.

	Number of edges	Time (sec)
Normal CKY	45,406,084	1,164
Iterative CKY	17,520,427	613

3.4 Evaluation

We evaluated the efficiency of the parser on the test set. The step of threshold decrease was set to 11, which was determined by using the held-out set as described above.

Table 2 shows the number of edges produced for parsing the first several sentences in the test set. There were a few sentences for which the iterative CKY produced more edges than the normal CKY. In most cases, however, the number of edges produced by the iterative CKY was significantly smaller than that produced by the normal CKY.

Table 3 shows the the total number of edges and the total time required for parsing the entire test set. The number of edges produced by the iterative CKY was 39% of that by the normal CKY. This is a significant reduction in computational cost. As for the parsing time, the iterative CKY is almost twice as fast as the normal CKY. This result indicates that the run-time overhead of iterative CKY is quite small.

3.5 Simulating Ideal Cases

Klein et al. [5] reported more than 80% reduction of edges using the same estimate under the A* search framework. Our reduction ratio is not as good as theirs, probably because our algorithm has to make several attempts that fail and the edges produced during those attempts are wasted.

In this work, we used a simple strategy of decreasing the threshold by a constant step at each iteration. It would be interesting to know how much we can further improve the efficiency by sophisticating the way of giving the threshold to the parser.

Table 4. Simulating ideal cases.

	Number of edges	Time (sec)
Ideal CKY	7,371,359	260

We simulated the ideal cases, where we knew the sentence probability in advance, by giving the parser the threshold that is exactly equal to the sentence log-probability. The number of edges and the total time for parsing the entire test set by the ideal parser are shown in Table 4. The results suggest that developing a method for estimating the probability of a sentence in advance should further improve the efficiency of the iterative CKY.

4 Conclusion

This paper presented an efficient and easy-to-implement iterative CKY parsing algorithm for PCFG. This algorithm enables us to prune unnecessary edges produced during parsing, which results in more efficient parsing. Since the run-time overhead of our algorithm is very small, it runs faster than the conventional CKY algorithm in an actual implementation.

Our algorithm is general enough to incorporate more sophisticated estimates of outside Viterbi probabilities, which should lead to more efficient parsing.

4.1 Future Work

We used the simplest context summary estimate as the upper bound of outside Viterbi probabilities in this paper. Since tighter bounds would lead to more reduction of edges, it is worth investigating the use of other estimation methods.

References

1. Roark, B.: Probabilistic top-down parsing and language modeling. Computational Linguistics **27** (2001) 249–276
2. Ratnaparkhi, A.: Learning to parse natural language with maximum entropy models. Machine Learning **34** (1999) 151–175
3. Charniak, E., Goldwater, S., Johnson, M.: Edge-based best-first chart parsing. In: Proceedings of the Sixth Workshop on Very Large Corpora. (1998)
4. Caraballo, S.A., Charniak, E.: New figures of merit for best-first probabilistic chart parsing. Computational Linguistics **24** (1998) 275–298
5. Klein, D., Manning, C.D.: A* parsing: Fast exact viterbi parse selection. In: Proceedings of the HLT-NAACL. (2003) 119–126
6. Cormen, T.H., Leiserson, C.E., Rivest, R.L., Stein, C.: Introduction to Algorithms. The MIT Press (2001)
7. Ney, H.: Dynamic programming parsing for context-free grammars in continuous speech recognition. IEEE Transactions on Signal Processing **39** (1991) 336–340
8. Jurafsky, D., Martin, J.H.: Speech and Language Processing. Prentice Hall (2000)
9. Marcus, M.P., Santorini, B., Marcinkiewicz, M.A.: Building a large annotated corpus of english: The penn treebank. Computational Linguistics **19** (1994) 313–330

Causal Relation Extraction Using Cue Phrase and Lexical Pair Probabilities

Du-Seong Chang* and Key-Sun Choi

Department of Electrical Engineering & Computer Science, KORTERM, BOLA
Korea Advanced Institute of Science and Technology
373-1, Guseong-dong, Yuseong-gu, Daejeon, 306-701, Korea
dschang@world.kaist.ac.kr, kschoi@cs.kaist.ac.kr

Abstract. This work aims to extract causal relations that exist between two events expressed by noun phrases or sentences. The previous works for the causality made use of causal patterns such as causal verbs. We concentrate on the information obtained from other causal event pairs. If two event pairs share some lexical pairs and one of them is revealed to be causally related, the causal probability of another event pair tends to increase. We introduce the lexical pair probability and the cue phrase probability. These probabilities are learned from raw corpus in unsupervised manner. With these probabilities and the Naive Bayes classifier, we try to resolve the causal relation extraction problem. Our inter-NP causal relation extraction shows the precision of 81.29%, that is 7.05% improvement over the baseline model. The proposed models are also applied to inter-sentence causal relation extraction.

1 Introduction

Causality or *causal relation* refers to 'the relation between a cause and its effect or between regularly correlated events'[1]. Even if not a few questions order to find causality from text, the current Question Answering system cannot respond causal questions. The recent Question-Answering system can produce correct answers to 83.0% of questions (Moldovan et al., [2002]). But the answer accuracy has a wide variation across the question type. Moldovan et al. ([2003]) states the relatively high answer accuracy on questions about the person, the time, the location, and so on. They show very low performance on causal questions. Causal questions are answered with a low precision score of 3.1%. Since there are few causal questions in their test suite of TREC(Text REtrieval Conference), total performance is high in spite of the low performance on causal questions. However, causal questions are very frequently used in an actual question answering. For a web site[2] in which users exchanged questions and answers, there are

---

* This research was supported in part by KISTEP Strategic National R&D Program under contract M1-0107-00-0018 and by KOSEF under contract R21-2003-000-10042-0.
[1] From Merriam-Webster's Online Dictionary.
[2] Naver Knowledge iN, http://kin.naver.com

130,000 causal questions from 950,000 sentence-sized DB. This fact shows that it is necessary to analyze the causal relation for a high performance Question-Answering.

To response the causal question such as (1a), the following problems should be solved. The first problem is *event extraction*, which extracts events from the paragraphs including keyword 'hiccups' of the question. *Event* is defined as 'a phenomenon or occurrence located at a single point in space-time'[3]. The second problem is *causal relation extraction*, which analyzes the causal relation between events. *Causal question answering* is the last one to be solved. It infers the answer to the question. In this paper, we concentrate the causal relation extraction.

(1a) What are hiccups caused by?
(1b) The oral bacteria that cause gum disease appear to be the culprit.

Cue phrase is a word, a phrase, or a word pattern, which connects one event to the other with some relation. The causal relation between events is assumed by the cue phrase. The causal cue phrase is used for connecting the cause and effect events. When events are expressed by noun phrases, the cue phrase connecting events is a verb phrase in general. For example, in (1b), the verb 'cause' is a cue phrase to connect two events expressed by noun phrases, 'the oral bacteria' and 'gum disease'. Several lexical pairs are assumed to lead the causal relation. The lexical pair 'bacteria' and 'disease' is an example of the causal lexical pair. If the term pair 'the oral bacteria' and 'gum disease' is causally related, we can infer that the event pair 'bowel bacteria' and 'bowel disease' is causally related. Causal lexical pairs are learned from cause-effect event pairs. We define *lexical pair probability* as the probability of the lexical pair that is a part of causal event pairs. The pair of concept classes of each event, [B03] and [C23.550.288][4], also lead the causality of event pair. *Conceptual pair probability* is defined as the probability of the conceptual pair that has the causal relation. Cue phrases connecting two events are also considered to have connection probability. We define *cue phrase probability* as the probability of the cue phrase that connects causal event pairs. With these probabilities, we introduce a causal relation classifier based on Naive Bayes classifier. These probabilities are learned from the raw corpus in an unsupervised manner.

In section 2, selected works are compared for the causal relation extraction. Our classification model will be explained in section 3. In this paper, we aim to extract the causal relation that exists between two noun phrases or sentences. In section 4, we evaluate the proposed model for the inter-noun phrase causality extraction, and prove it adaptable to the inter-sentence causality extraction.

---

[3] From The American Heritage Dictionary of the English Language: Fourth Edition, 2000.

[4] They represent [bacteria] and [disease]. These conceptual numbers follow the biomedical ontology (Medical Subject Heading, [2004]).

2   Related Works

Causal relations are expressed with various forms in the literature: between subject and object noun phrases like (2a), between two sentences or phrases as in (2b,c), and in intra-structure of a noun phrase like (2d)[5]. The causal relation also exists between paragraphs that describe events. This relation is a part of rhetorical structure and is out of the focus in this paper. In the examples, each cause event is connected with its effect event by the causative verb ('generate'), causal connectives ('for this reason' or 'that'), or the intra-NP structure. In this paper, we are focusing on the inter-NP and inter-sentence causal relation.

(2a) Earthquakes generate tidal waves.
(2b) The meaning of a word can vary a great deal depending on the context. For this reason, pocket dictionaries have a very limited use.
(2c) The traffic was so heavy that I couldn't arrive on time.
(2d) Disease-causing bacteria

Marcu and Echihabi ([2002]) used the inter-sentence lexical pair probability for discriminating the rhetorical relation between sentences. To distinguish the causal relation from the other rhetorical relations, they used the sentence pairs connected with 'Because of' and 'Thus'. From the selected sentence pairs, causal lexical pairs are automatically collected. They used nouns, verbs, and adverbs only. Non-causal lexical pairs are also collected from randomly selected sentence pairs. With these two kinds of lexical pairs, they compose the Naive Bayes classifier. The sentence pairs are classified to 'causal' or not. The result showed 57% accuracy in the inter-sentence causality extraction. The lexical probability contributes to the causality extraction in part. From their result, we supposed that the lexical pair and other probabilities contribute to the inter-noun phrase causality extraction and the inter-sentence causality extraction. The other supposed probabilities are the cue phrase probability, cue phrase confidence score, and concept pair probability. With these probabilities and the unsupervised learning technique, we try to resolve the causality extraction problem.

Initial works on the causal relation analysis used hand-made causal patterns to find the causality. Khoo et al. ([1988] and [2000]) used the semi-automatic causality pattern learning on the syntactically analyzed corpus. Girju and Moldovan ([2002]) used the inter-noun phrase causal relation to improve the Question-Answering performance. To extract the inter-noun phrase causal relation, they used the cue phrase filter and the dictionary based ranking model. With simple rules reflecting the meaning of head nouns, each noun phrase pair is classified into 5 ordered classes. We call this order the *noun class rank*. The examination regarding classes 1 to 4 as causal relation shows a precision score of 65.5%. Their decision tree classifier learned on the causality-annotated corpus showed a precision of 73.91% (Girju, [2003]). In their works, cue phrases were verbs connecting a subject and an object noun phrase. 60 cue phrases were semi-automatically acquired from WordNet (Miller, [1995]) and corpus.

---

[5] Examples are selected from (Girju and Moldovan, [2002]).

For the supervised learning of causal relation classifier, causality-annotated corpus is required. But the construction of such corpus would take much effort. The supervised method has the limitation to be scaled up. In this paper, we propose new methods using the cue phrase probability and the lexical pair probability. The probabilities are learned from the raw corpus in an unsupervised manner. Proposed models use a large amount of corpus for improving the performance. In case of using the dictionary or WordNet as a basis of causality, the unregistered words in the dictionaries hinders from finding the correct causal relation. In manually annotated test set of section 4, 36.4% of unknown words decrease the performance of baseline systems. We solve this unknown word problem by using the lexical pair probability.

3 Causal Relation Extraction Model

3.1 Causality Candidate Extraction from Dependency Structure

In this works, the result of the event extraction is candidates of the event. After causal relation extraction, each event candidate is assigned to be a cause event, an effect event, or none of both. In the case of inter-noun phrase causality extraction, the event extraction is the noun phrase-chunking problem. For extracting event candidate, the syntactic analyzer is used. As an input of classifier, we use the ternary expression composed of cause-effect event candidates and cue phrases. For inter-noun phrase causal relation extraction, the ternary expression for causality candidates is <cause noun phrase, cue phrase, effect noun phrase>. Causality candidates are extracted from the dependency structure of sentences. We use several modules, which are a noun phrase chunking, a noun reference resolution, an appositive noun phrase analysis, and a cue phrase-filtering module.

Figure 1 is a dependency structure of the sentence (3a). It is the result of the Connexor dependency parser (Tapanainen and Jarvinen, [1997]). Noun phrases and transitive verbs are selected from the dependency tree. Intransitive verbs with a prepositional phrase are also considered. (Some prepositions introducing time and place are not considered.) The relative pronoun is replaced with its antecedent. We try to find the forward references in the boundary of a sentence tree. After the appositive noun phrase analysis is finished, we can find two ternary expressions, (3b,c), from the sentence (3a). These ternary expressions are finally filtered by pre-defined cue phrases. Pre-defined cue phrases are based on 60 causal verbs defined in (Girju et al., [2002]).

(3a) Skin cancer usually appears in adulthood, but it is caused by sun exposure and sunburns that began in childhood.
(3b) <'sun exposure', 'caused by', 'skin cancer'>
(3c) <'sunburn', 'caused by', 'skin cancer>

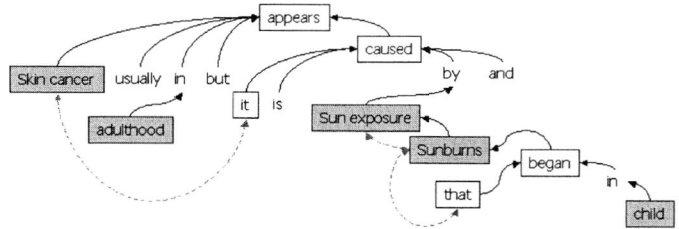

Fig. 1. Dependency structure of sentence (3a).

3.2 Causal Relation Classifier

The causality candidate, the ternary (t_i), is classified to be 'causal (c_1) ' or 'non-causal (c_0)'. To solve this classification problem, we apply Naive Bayes classifier. The class c^* of the ternary t_i is computed as shown in (1).

$$c^* = \arg\max_{c_j} P(c_j|t_i) = \arg\max_{c_j} \frac{P(c_j)P(t_i|c_j)}{P(t_i)} \quad (1)$$

When we consider the cue phrase CP_{t_i} and lexical pairs LP_{t_i}, as causal features of the ternary, $P(t_i|c_j)$ in (1) will be rewritten as (2). We assume these features are independent each other.

$$P(t_i|c_j) = P(CP_{t_i}|c_j) \prod_{k=1}^{|t_i|} P(LP_{t_i k}|c_j) \quad (2)$$

In (2), $P(CP_{t_i}|c_j)$ and $P(LP_{t_i k}|c_j)$ is the cue phrase probability and the lexical pair probability, which are defined in section 1. These probabilities can be learned from the causality-annotated ternary set. But the construction of the causality-annotated ternary set takes time and effort consuming. In this paper, we use the raw corpus rather than the causal relation annotated corpus. To make it possible, EM (Expectation-Maximization) procedure is used with the Naive Bayes classifier. Parameters trained in EM are prior probability $P(c_j)$, cue phrase probability $P(CP_{t_i}|c_j)$, and lexical pair probability $P(LP_{t_i k}|c_j)$. The parameters are smoothed using the Laplace method for the lexical pairs unseen in training data.

The Naive Bayes classifier is bootstrapped from the initial classifier. The training data is the ternary set filtered by cue phrases. There are three training stages. In the initialization stage, we build an initial classifier and initialize Naive Bayes parameters. As an initial classifier, we use the dictionary-based classifier described in section 2.3. It does not need the extra training sequence. The cue phrase confidence score is another available initial classifier. The cue phrase confidence score, $P(c_j|CP_{t_i})$, is defined as the probability of the causal class for the given cue phrase. This confidence score requires relatively small set of annotated corpus rather than the lexical pair probability. After whole training corpus is classified with an initial classifier, highly ranked ternaries are selected as the initial causality-annotated set. From this annotated set, the parameters of Naive Bayes classifier are initialized.

The second training stage is called Expectation step. Whole training corpus, including the annotated part, is classified with the current classifier. The final training stage is called Maximization step. From the newly classified data, parameters are re-estimated. Expectation and Maximization step are repeated while classifier parameters improve.

3.3 Causality Classification Model

The trained classifier can be interleaved with other causal classifiers, which are the dictionary based rank (noun class rank) and the cue phrase confidence score. We propose three classification models. *The classification model CP+LP* uses the cue phrase probability and the lexical pair probability as shown in (3). This uses the noun class rank as a back-off model. If the cue phrase probability and the lexical pair probability, $P(c_j|t_i)$, cannot decide an evident causal class, the noun class rank probability is used. To do this, Discrimination value, $Dist(t_i)$, is introduced as shown in (4). The threshold h is a constant. The noun class rank probability $P(c_j|rank_{t_i})$ is defined as the probability of the causal class for the noun class rank of the given ternary. This probability is learned from the automatically annotated corpus.

$$P_{CP+LP}(c_j|t_i) = \begin{cases} P(c_j|t_i) & \text{if } Dist(t_i) > h \\ P(c_j|rank_{t_i}) & \text{otherwise} \end{cases} \quad (3)$$

$$Dist_{t_i} = \left| \frac{\log P(c_0|t_i) - \log P(c_1|t_i)}{\log P(c_0|t_i) + \log P(c_1|t_i)} \right| \quad (4)$$

The classification model CP+NC+LP uses the cue phrase probability and the lexical pair probability interleaved with the noun class rank probability as shown in (5). The sum of weights, w_{nc} and w_{lp}, must be 1.

$$P_{CP+NC+LP}(c_j|t_i) = w_{nc} \times P(c_j|rank_{t_i}) + w_{lp} \times P(c_j|t_i) \quad (5)$$

The cue phrase confidence score is also learned on the automatically annotated corpus. *The classification model CP+NC+CPC+LP* uses the cue phrase probability and the lexical pair probability interleaved with the noun class rank and the cue phrase confidence score as shown in (6). The sum of weights, w_{nc}, w_{cpc}, and w_{lp}, must be 1.

$$P_{CP+NC+CPC+LP}(c_j|t_i) = w_{nc} \times P(c_j|rank_{t_i}) + w_{cpc} \times P(c_j|CP_{t_i}) + w_{lp} \times P(c_j|t_i) \quad (6)$$

Figure 2 is the structure of proposed causality extraction system. Candidates for the causal event pairs are extracted from the raw corpus through an NP chunking with syntactic analysis. The causality candidate is composed of a pair of events and a cue phrase connecting two events. The causality analysis problem

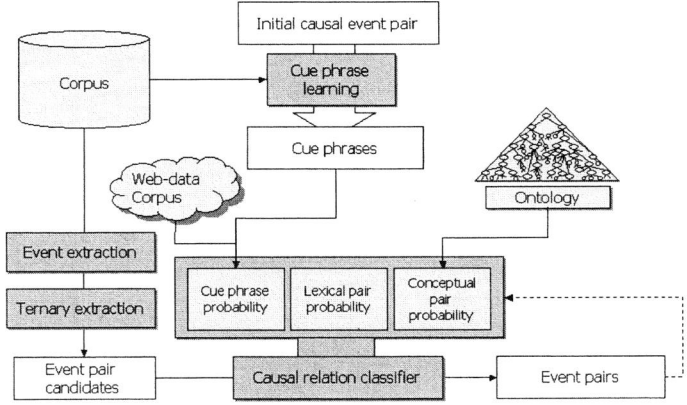

Fig. 2. Proposed causality extraction system.

is redefined as a classification problem to assign the causal class, 'causal' or 'non-causal', to the causality candidates. Causal event pairs are extracted with the cue phrase and lexical pair probabilities. Extracted causal event pairs are used for re-training the classifier.

4 Evaluation

4.1 Inter-NP Causality Extraction

A part of TREC corpus is used for the inter-noun phrase causality extraction. The training corpus is 5 million sentence-sized articles from LA TIMES (1989~1990) and Wall Street Journal (1987~1990). We use two test sets, which are selected from different domains. The first one is from Wall Street Journal articles. The other is from Medline medical encyclopedia of A.D.A.M. Inc. All sentences in test sets include the word 'cancer'. The first one, we call it cTREC, comes from general domain. The other, we call it cADAM, comes from medical domain. Test sets are manually classified with two human annotators, which one is the first author and the other is medical domain expert. They agree the result with 72.8%. A gold standard is made with discussion between annotators.

The cue phrase probability (CP) and the lexical pair probability (LP) are trained on the training set. As an initial classifier for the inter-noun phrase causality extraction, the noun class rank was used. For the parameter initialization, all ternaries were ranked with noun classes. And highly ranked ternaries were selected as a causality-annotated set. As a result, ternaries ranked by 1 to 3 were annotated to 'causal' (c_1), and parts of ternaries ranked by 5 were annotated to 'non-causal' (c_0). Table 1 shows the evaluation result on test sets. The classification model NC follows the model of (Girju and Moldovan, 2002), which uses the cue phrase filter and the noun class rank. The classification model

Table 1. Inter-noun phrase causal relation extraction result.

Classification model	Test set	Precision	Recall	F-value
NC	cTREC	82.88	64.79	72.73
	cADAM	65.17	42.34	51.33
	Total	75.00	53.76	62.63
LP with No EM	cTREC	76.35	79.58	77.93
	cADAM	73.68	51.09	60.34
	Total	75.71	67.03	71.10
CP+LP	cTREC	82.14	80.99	81.56
	cADAM	78.99	79.56	79.27
	Total	80.58	80.29	80.43
CP+NC+LP	cTREC	83.10	83.10	83.10
	cADAM	77.78	76.64	77.21
	Total	80.51	79.93	80.22
CP+NC+CPC+LP	cTREC	83.21	80.28	81.72
	cADAM	79.43	81.75	80.58
	Total	81.29	81.00	81.15

LP with No EM follows the classification model of (Marcu and Echihabi, 2002), which uses the lexical pair probability without EM process. The last three models are proposed models. For the classification model CP+LP, we assign 0 to the value of the threshold h. And for the noun class (NC) weight w_{nc} and the cue phrase confidence score (CPC) weight w_{cpc}, 0.1 is assigned.

Contribution of the cue phrase probability and the lexical pair probability: The proposed model CP+NC+CPC+LP shows the highest precision of 81.29%, which is improved by 7.05% from the baseline model (NC). Actually in all the proposed models, the causality extraction performance is increased. We can say that the cue phrase probability and the lexical pair probability are useful for the causality extraction.

Contribution of the noun class on domains: For the general domain test set (cTREC), the result of the interleaved with the noun class (CP+NC+LP) shows the precision improved by 1.19% from the non-interleaved (CP+LP). However, for the medical domain test set (cADAM), the precision is decreased by 1.53%. It is caused by unknown words in the medical domain test set. Terminologies and pronouns in the specific domain include more unknown words than in the general domain. For the baseline model NC, unknown words of cADAM decreases the performance by 15.1% in the precision and by 11.1% in the recall. We can say that the noun class is useful in general but not in the specific domain.

Contribution of the cue phrase confidence score: The classification model interleaved with the cue phrase confidence score (CP+NC+CPC+ LP) does not show the significant improvement from the non-interleaved model (CP+ NC+LP). It is because the cue phrase probability and the cue phrase confidence score share the same information space.

Robustness of the proposed model: In the proposed model (CP+LP), 37.5% of the unknown word-causing error of the baseline system (NC) is correctly classified. The proposed model does not refer the word sense. It refers only the lexical pair frequency in the corpus. We can say that the proposed model is free from the unknown words.

High performance of the unsupervised learning: The proposed models are learned in an unsupervised manner. It does not require the pre-annotated data. Nevertheless, the performance is relatively high.

4.2 Inter-sentence Causality Extraction in Korean

If events are represented by sentences or verb phrases leading subordinate clause, cue phrase could be conjunctive adverbs or verb endings in Korean. 54 cue phrase patterns are selected by human annotators. The event extraction module marks event boundaries on the dependency structure of sentences. In the inter-sentence causality extraction, an event is 'a predicate and its arguments'. After all event candidates are extracted from the dependency tree of adjacent sentence pairs, they are filtered by cue phrases. The input of the classifier is the ternary expression of <cause sentence, cue phrase, effect sentence>. We use the Korean dependency parser of (Chang and Choi, [2000]). The same classifier described in section 3 is used for the inter-sentence causality extraction. We use the cue phrase confidence score as the initial classifier. To learn this initial classifier, human annotator annotates 970 sentence pairs, which are 5~20 sentence pairs for each cue phrase. The training set is the 2158 document sized medical encyclopedia (HealthChosun [2003], Joins HealthCare [2003]). It contains 30 thousand of ternaries. As a test set, we use 4 documents, which are not included in training data but same domain.

The universality of the proposed model: For the inter-sentence causality extraction, the proposed model (CP+LP) shows a precision of 74.67%, which is increased by 8.87% from the baseline (CPC). As a result, we can say that the proposed model is adaptable for the inter-sentence causal relation extraction.

5 Conclusion

In this paper, causality extraction models are proposed. Proposed models use the cue phrase probability and the lexical pair probability. These probabilities are learned from the raw corpus in unsupervised manner. Proposed models show higher performance than baseline systems. Proposed models use only the raw corpus and do not make a performance decrease by the unknown words. Therefore, the models can be easily adapted to the other domain such as the medical. Proposed models are used not only for the inter-noun phrase causality extraction but also for the inter-sentence causality extraction.

To use the conceptual pair probability, the word sense disambiguation has to be also considered. Proposed models classified the ternaries after filtered by cue phrases. For the fully automatic learning of causality extraction, the cue phrase learning has to be solved. The incremental learning of the cue phrase is in progress. The proposed causality extraction is used for the causal Question Answering. The Question Answering based on causal relation is also going on. The causality extraction can be used for the causal browsing. The causal QA and browser is demonstrated on the web site, http://gensum.kaist.ac.kr/~dschang/ENC/CQA.html

References

[2000] Chang, Du-Seong and Key-Sun Choi, 2000, Unsupervised learning of the dependency grammar using inside and outside probabilities, in *Proceedings of the 12th Hangul and Korean Information Processing* (in Korean)

[2003] Girju, Roxana, 2003, Automatic Detection of Causal Relation for Question Answering, in *Proceeding of Workshop in the 41st Annual Meeting of the Association for Computational Linguistics Conference*

[2002] Girju, Roxana and Dan Moldovan, 2002, Mining Answers for Causation Questions, in *Proceeding of AAAI Symposium on Mining Answers from Texts and Knowledge Bases*

[2003] HealthChosun Medical Library, http://hpsearch.drline.net/dizzo/healthinfo/healthinfo.asp

[2003] Joins HealthCare Medical Encyclopedia, http://healthcare.joins.com/library

[2000] Khoo, Cristopher S.G., Syin Chan, and Yun Niu, 2000, Extracting Causal Knowledge from a Medical Database Using Graphical Patterns, In *Proceedings of The 38th Annual Meeting of the Association for Computational Linguistics*

[1988] Khoo, Cristopher S.G., J. Kornfit, Robert N. Oddy, and Sung Hyon Myaeng, 1998, Automatic Extraction of Cause-Effect Information from Newspaper Text without Knowledge-Based Inferencing, in *Literary and Linguistic Computing*, 13(4), pages 177-186

[2002] Marcu, Daniel and Abdessamad Echihabi, 2002, An Unsupervised Approach to Recognizing Discourse Relations, in *Proceedings of the 40th Annual Meeting of the Association for Computational Linguistics Conference*, Philadelphia, PA

[2004] Medical Subject Heading, 2004, http://www.nlm.nih.gov/mesh

[1995] Miller, G., 1995, WordNet: a Lexical Database, *Communications of the ACM*, 38(11):39-41

[2003] Modovan, Dan I., Marius Pasca, Sanda M. Harabagiu, Mihai. Surdeanu, 2003, Performance Issues and Error Analysis in an Open-Domain Question Answering, *ACM Transactions on Information Systems*, Vol. 21, No. 2, pages 133-154.

[2002] Moldovan, Dan I., Sanda M. Harabagiu, Roxana Girju, Paul Morarescu, Finley Lacatusu, Adrian Novischi, Adriana Badulescu and Orest Bolohan, 2002, LCC Tools for Question Answering, in *Proceedings of the 11th Text Retrieval Conference*, NIST.

[2000] Nigram, Kamal, Andrew K. McCallum, Sebastian Thrun and Tom Mitchell, 2000, Text Classification from Labeled and Unlabeled Documents using EM, *Machine Learning*, 39(2/3) pages 103-134.

[1997] Tapanainen, Pasi and Timo Jarvinen, 1997, A non-projective dependency parser in Proceedings of the 5th Conference on Applied Natural Language Processing, *Association for Computational Linguistics*, pages 64-71.

A Re-examination of IR Techniques in QA System

Yi Chang, Hongbo Xu, and Shuo Bai

Institute of Computing Technology, Chinese Academy of Sciences, Beijing 100080, China
{changyi,hbxu}@software.ict.ac.cn, bai@ncic.ac.cn
http://www.software.ict.ac.cn

Abstract. The performance of Information Retrieval in the Question Answering system is not satisfactory from our experiences in TREC QA Track. In this article, we take a comparative study to re-examine IR techniques on document retrieval and sentence level retrieval respectively. Our study shows: 1) query reformulation should be a necessary step to achieve a better retrieval performance; 2) The techniques for document retrieval are also effective in sentence level retrieval, and single sentence will be the appropriate retrieval granularity.

1 Introduction

Information Retrieval (IR) and Information Extraction (IE) are generally regarded as the two key techniques to Natural Language Question Answering (QA) System that returns exact answers. IE techniques are incorporated to identify the exact answer while IR techniques are used to narrow the search space that IE will process, that is, the output of the IR is the input of IE.

According to TREC QA overview: [11], most current question answering systems rely on document retrieval to provide documents or passages that are likely to contain the answer to a question. Since document-oriented information retrieval techniques are relative mature while IE techniques are still under developing, most of current researches have focused on answer extraction: [5], [8], [9]. There is little detailed investigation into the IR performance which impacts on overall QA system performance. Clarke et al.: [3] proposed a passage retrieval technique based on passage length and term weights. Tellex et al.: [10] make a quantitative evaluation of various passage retrieval algorithms for QA. Monz: [6] compares the effectiveness of some common document retrieval techniques when they were used in QA. Roberts and Gaizauskas: [7] use coverage and answer redundancy to evaluate a variety of passage retrieval approaches with TREC QA questions.

In most of current researches, the granularity for information retrieval in QA is passage or document. What is the potential of IR in QA and what is the most appropriate granularity for retrieval still need to be explored thoroughly.

We have built our QA system based on the cooperation of IE and IR. According to our score and rank on past several TREC conferences, although we are making progress each year, the results are still far from satisfactory. As our recent study shows, IR results in much more loss comparing with IE. Therefore, we re-examine two important questions that have ever been overlooked: 1) whether a question is a good query for retrieval in QA? 2) Whether the techniques for document retrieval are effective on sentence level retrieval?

In this paper, we compare some alternative IR techniques and all our experiments are based on TREC 2003 QA AQUAINT corpus. To make a thorough analysis, we focus on those questions with short, fact-based answers, called Factoid questions in TREC QA.

In Section 2, we describe our system architecture and evaluate the performance of each module. Then in section 3, according to the comparison of four document retrieval methods, we find the reason to limit our retrieval performance. We then present in Section 4 the results of four sentence level retrieval methods and in Section 5 we research different retrieval granularities. Finally, Section 6 summarizes the conclusions.

2 System Description

Our system to answer Factoid questions contains five major modules, namely Question Analyzing Module, Document Retrieval Engine, Sentence Level Retrieval Module, Entity Recognizing Module and Answer Selecting Module. Figure 1 illustrates the architecture.

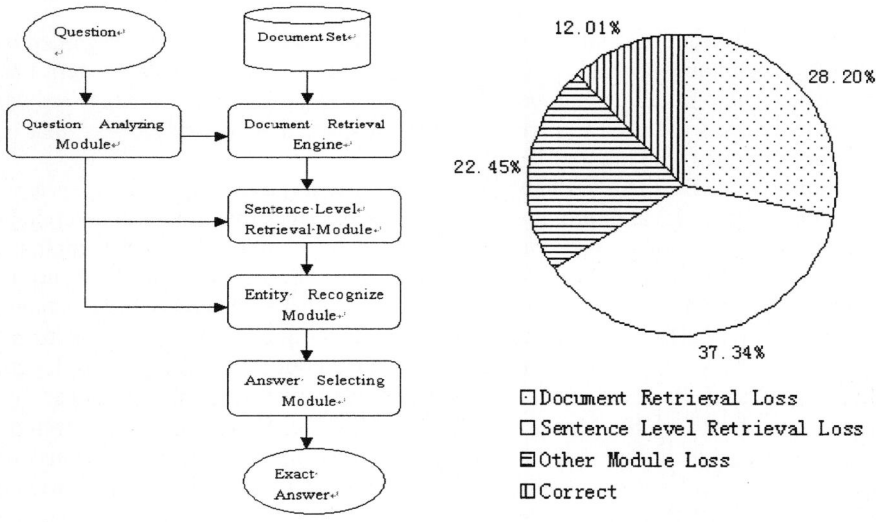

Fig. 1. The Architecture of QA system   **Fig. 2.** Loss Distribution

In this paper, a Bi-sentence means two consecutive sentences and there is no overlapping between two consecutive Bi-sentences; a phrase means a sequence of keywords or one keyword in a question, where a keyword is a word in the question but not in Stop-word list.

To answer each question, Question Analyzing Module makes use of NLP techniques to identify the right type of information that the question requires. Question Analyzing Module also preprocesses the question and makes a query for further retrieval. Document Retrieval Engine use the question to get relevant documents and selects top ranked relevant documents. Since the selected documents contain too much information, Sentence Level Retrieval Module matches the question with the selected relevant documents to get relevant Bi-sentences, and selects top ranked Bi-sentences. Entity Recognizing Module identifies the candidate entities from the selected Bi-sentences, and Answering Selecting Module chooses the answer in a voting method.

In our TREC 2003 runs, we incorporate PRISE and Multilevel retrieval method and we select 50 documents and 20 Bi-sentences. As our recent study shows: among the 383 Factoid questions whose answer is not NIL, there are only 275 questions whose answer could be got from the top 50 relevant documents, while there are only 132 out of 275 questions whose answer could be extracted from the top 20 relevant Bi-sentences. All our statistics are based on the examination of both answer and the corresponding Document ID.

Figure 2 illustrates the loss distribution of each module in our QA system. It is amazing that more than sixty percent of loss is caused by IR while we used to take it for granted that IE is the bottleneck of QA system. So we should re-examine the IR techniques in QA system, and we take account of document retrieval and sentence level retrieval respectively.

3 Document Retrieval Methods

Is a question a good query? If the answer is YES, the retrieval algorithm will determine the performance of document retrieval in QA system. When we implement a document retrieval system with high performance, we could get a satisfactory result. To explore this, we retrieve relevant documents for each question from the AQUAINT document set with four IR systems: PRISE, basic SMART, Enhanced-SMART and Enhanced SMART with pseudo-relevant feedback. In these experiments, we use the question itself as the query for IR system.

PRISE
The NIST PRISE is a full text retrieval system based on TFIDF weighting, which uses fast and space efficient indexing and searching algorithms proposed by Harman: [4]. To facilitate those participants in the TREC QA Track who do not have ready access to a document retrieval system, NIST also publishes a ranked document list retrieved by PRISE, in which the top 1000 ranked documents per question are provided.

Basic SMART
SMART is a well known and effective information retrieval system based on Vector Space Model (VSM), which was invented by Salton in the 1960s. Here we give the experiments with basic SMART and compare its performance with PRISE to make a complete evaluation.

Enhanced-SMART (E-SMART)
According to the study of Xu and Yang: [13], the classical weighting methods used in basic SMART such as Lnc-Ltc do not behave well in TREC. In TREC 2002 Web Track, Yang improved the traditional Lnu-Ltu weighting method. Following the gen-

eral hypothesis that relevance of a document in retrieval is irrelevant to its length, Yang thought over the normalization of the query's length. He found that the length of a query should be emphasized much more, but not weakened according to the hypothesis above. When he added the modified Lnu-Ltu weighting method into the basic SMART system, the performance of document retrieval was greatly improved. In TREC 2002 Web Topic Distillation Task, this method has been proven to be very effective and efficient. Inspired by the success in Web Track, we studied the performance of Enhanced-SMART system in TREC QA Track.

Enhanced-SMART with Pseudo-relevant Feedback (E-SMART-FB)
We think one of the difficulties of IR in QA system is that the number of keywords is too limited in a question. It is natural to expand the query with pseudo-relevant feedback methods. Pseudo-relevant feedback is an effective method to make up for lack of keywords in a query. In our pseudo-relevant feedback, several keywords with the highest term frequency in the top k ranked documents returned by the first retrieval are added into the initial query, and then we make a second retrieval. In the experiments on Web Track after TREC 2002, we correct a bug in SMART feedback component. Our experiments shows that the evaluation performance in Web Topic Distillation Task can outperform that of any other system when we introduce pseudo-relevant feedback into the Enhanced-SMART. We try to explore the potential of document retrieval in TREC QA Track, so we also do experiments in QA document retrieval by Enhanced-SMART with pseudo-relevant feedback.

3.1 Performance Comparison

Figure 3 shows the comparison of four document retrieval methods. X coordinate means the number of documents we select to make statistics. Y coordinate means the number of the questions that could be correctly answered, and here we mean the exact answers of these questions are contained in the selected documents.

According to figure 3, the results of Enhanced-SMART retrieval technique, which proved to be one of the best in TREC Web Track, are almost the same as PRISE; basic SMART performs worst, and the performances of other three methods are similar.

In the figure 3, selecting 100 documents the curve representing the basic SMART reaches its peak performance of 216, and Enhanced-SMART with pseudo-relevant feedback to 291, Enhanced-SMART to 293. PRISE reaches the best result among them: 294 out of 383 questions could be answered correctly, and the accuracy is 76.76%. Since the document retrieval is still the first step in QA system, such kind of performance is far from satisfactory. Selecting more documents could increase the number of potential correct questions, however, it is likely to impair the accuracy of the following step because the documents which are lower relevant to the question probably contain more noise. That the slope of the curve in the figure is becoming shallower illustrates our analysis.

From TREC 2002 QA overview: [11], the best system has a final accuracy of more than 70%, which is close to our document retrieval performance. This shows that there should exist a great increase in our document retrieval. It is well known that the retrieval result is based on two factors: the retrieval algorithm and the query. Since the retrieval algorithm has proved to be very effective, while the results it used in TREC QA document retrieval is much lower than expectation, we think the point is the latter: a question is not equal to a good query.

As our further experiments show, the pseudo-relevant feedback doesn't take effect, which means the simple statistics-based query expansion is not good. We should think thoroughly about the query reformulation, and more effective techniques should be studied, in particular, we can make use of semantic information to reformulate the query. We use the required NE type of a question in IE to find the candidate answer, however we overlook it in IR because the words where most of the required NE types are derived from are Stop-words or unimportant words with too high frequency. We think that utilizing the required NE type would be our next attempt to reformulate the query.

Many query expansion methods have been proposed in QA system, but we used to regard them as optional. However, our experiments show that the reformulation of query should be necessary to get a better IR result.

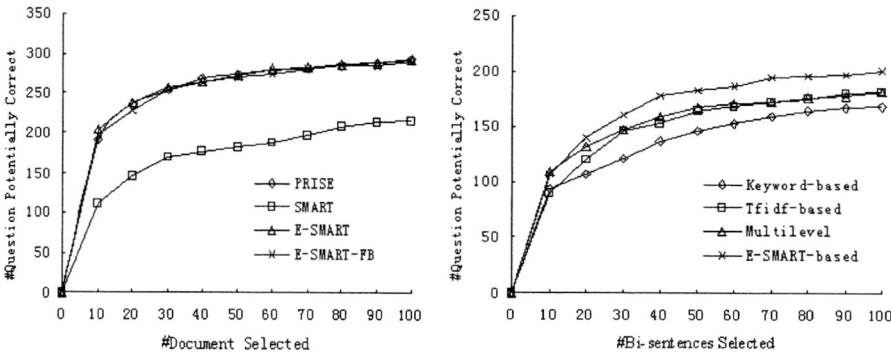

Fig. 3. Document Retrieval Comparison   **Fig. 4.** Sentence Retrieval Comparison

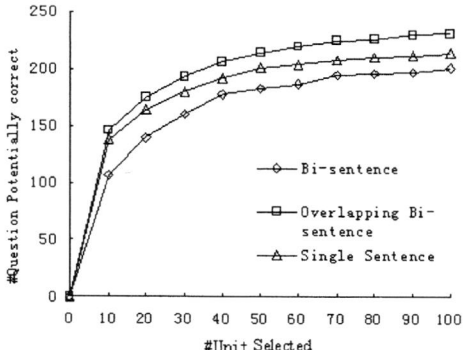

Fig. 5. Retrieval Granularity Comparison

4 Sentence Level Retrieval Methods

According to the conclusion of Allan: [1], finding relevant sentences from the document is difficult based on VSM, we used to think that the techniques for document retrieval are not suitable to sentence level retrieval, so we proposed a Multilevel method in order to get a better retrieval result. We compare the Multilevel Retrieval with the other three methods: Keyword-match Retrieval, TFIDF-based Retrieval and Enhanced-SMART-based Retrieval. We noticed that there are some questions whose answer should be extracted from more than one sentence, so we take two consecutive sentences as the granularity of retrieval, which we called Bi-sentence. To avoid the repetition of information, we define that there is no overlapping sentence between two consecutive Bi-sentences. In following experiments, we retrieve relevant Bi-sentences from the top 50 documents provided by PRISE.

Keyword-Match Retrieval
The algorithm of Xu: [12] is regarded as one of the basic methods to compute the weight of Bi-sentence:

$$weight\_p = \beta \times count\_k /(count\_q + count\_p) \qquad (1)$$

Where $weight\_p$ means the weight of the Bi-sentence, $count\_k$ means the number of matching keywords between the question and the Bi-sentence, $count\_q$ means the number of keywords in the question, $count\_p$ means the number of keywords in the Bi-sentence and β is an experiential parameter. The Bi-sentence with a larger weight has the priority to be retrieved.

TFIDF-Based Retrieval
It is very natural to take the similarity between a question and a Bi-sentence as the weight of the Bi-sentence. We turn the question and the Bi-sentence into vectors with the TFIDF formula. The weight of the Bi-sentence is the inner product between the question vector and the Bi-sentence vector. The Bi-sentences that have larger similarity with the question will be retrieved.

Multilevel Retrieval
Vector Space Model takes a document as a vector with each word an element, and words are independent from each other. It seems that VSM has lost much useful information. Therefore, we want to integrate more information to improve sentence level retrieval. What we think to use first is syntax and semantic information including phase, Chunk, POS and so on, but it is difficult to apply such information in VSM model. So we proposed a Multilevel Retrieval method.

Our method is based on two assumptions: 1) Bi-sentences that can match a phrase which is made up of more than one keyword are more relevant than those only can match separate keywords. 2) Bi-sentences that can match a phase of a question in original form are more relevant than those only can match in stemmed form.

We make use of the Chunk, Pos and Stem information to apply a four-level method to select candidate Bi-sentences. At each level, we define two kinds of sub strings, Compulsory Phrase and Assistant Keyword. Compulsory Phrase is a phrase set in which each element is obligatory to match a Bi-sentence. Assistant Keyword is a keyword set in which each element is optional to match. Those words not belong to the Compulsory Phrase and Stop-word list are regarded as the elements of the Assistant Keyword. We compute the weight of a Bi-sentence as below:

$$weight\_p = \beta \times count\_\alpha / (count\_q + count\_p) \tag{2}$$

Where $count\_a$ means the number of matching Assistant Keyword between the question and the Bi-sentence, and other parameters are the same as those in the equation (1).

At the first level, we take the last Noun Group and the last verb in the last Verb Group as the Compulsory Phrase. And those phrases with initial capital on each word are also regarded as the Compulsory Phrase. At the second level, we move the verb from the Compulsory Phrase to the Assistant Keyword because the verb is not easy to match and we don't fulfill the verb expansion. At the third level, we only leave those phrases composed of successive initial capital words as the Compulsory Phrase. At the last level, the Compulsory Phrase is empty, and all words belong to Assistant Keyword.

All relevant Bi-sentences are ranked by the following rules: the Bi-sentence selected from the higher level has a higher priority, and in the same level, the Bi-sentence with a larger weight has a higher priority. Furthermore, the first level is based on original matching, while the other three levels are based on stemmed matching.

Enhanced-SMART-Based Retrieval

Whether an effective document retrieval technique is still successful in sentence level retrieval? Since the Enhanced-SMART proves to be an effective document retrieval system in Web Track, we attempt to study its performance in a small granularity.

We first construct Bi-sentences from the top ranked 50 documents retrieved by PRISE. Then we take each Bi-sentence as a document, and use Enhanced-SMART to make index on them. Finally we use the question itself as a query to retrieve the Bi-sentences most relevant to the question.

4.1 Performance Comparison

Figure 4 shows the comparison of four sentence level retrieval methods in the granularity of Bi-sentence. The performances of Multilevel Retrieval and TFIDF-based Retrieval are similar, but what surprises us is that our attempt to Enhanced-SMART-based retrieval makes a hit. It defeats Multilevel Retrieval, and gets to a higher performance in sentence level retrieval. Selecting top 100 ranked Bi-sentences, the Enhanced-SMART-based retrieval reaches its peak where answers of 201 questions can be found, while by the Multilevel retrieval, only 181 questions could be right answered.

In fact, Enhanced SMART is a variant of TFIDF weighting method based on VSM model. In its Lnu-Ltu weighting formula, the length of a document and query is considered well. The experiment results show that TFIDF method based on VSM can also achieve a good performance in sentence level retrieval.

Such a result is beyond our original intention. In figure 4, the performance of Multilevel Retrieval is better than keyword-match retrieval and simple TFIDF method. It seems that our expectation about Multilevel Retrieval is reasonable, but Enhanced SMART overthrows our original idea.

A reason for us is that we didn't implement a complete Multilevel method, many factors were ignored during the matching at each level, and we also made no use of some more useful information such as NE type.

We think the limited scale of corpus is another important reason for the unsatisfactory performance of Multilevel Retrieval. At the same time, the algorithm in Multilevel method is still too simple, a better scoring strategy is needed to substitute our simple method.

5 The Granularities of Retrieval

According to the previous section, we learn that the performance of small granularity retrieval such as Bi-sentence is good using the same techniques as document retrieval. However, we want to make it clear what granularity will perform the best and what is the best performance it can achieve.

In our original opinion, there is no repetition of information in Bi-sentences. However, this method would possibly break two highly relevant sentences into two Bi-sentences and the importance of each Bi-sentence would be weakened by the other sentence in it. Furthermore, if the answer should just be extracted from these two sentences, our endeavor to taking two consecutive sentences into account will be in vain.

So we examine another retrieval granularity, overlapping Bi-sentence, that is, every two sentences will construct an overlapping Bi-sentence, and every two consecutive overlapping Bi-sentences have one sentence in common.

The repetition information is what we try to avoid, so we further consider single sentence as our retrieval granularity. That is, we make index on each single sentence to retrieve in the Enhanced SMART.

Figure 5 displays the performance of three granularities of retrieval. Since a Bi-sentence or an overlapping Bi-sentence contains two sentences, we should compare the number of questions that could be correctly answered between m Bi-sentences and $2m$ single sentences. According to the figure 5, Bi-sentence that we used in TREC 2003 QA track performs worst, while the results of the other two granularities are similar: Selecting 50 overlapping Bi-sentences we hit the value of 215 on the represented curve and making a selection of 100 single sentences we get 214; Selecting 100 overlapping Bi-sentences we reach 232 and selecting 200 single sentences we obtain 228.

Comparing with techniques used in our TREC runs, only 132 out of 275 questions could be correctly answered by selecting 20 Bi-sentences, while utilizing the Enhanced-SMART to retrieve 40 single sentences that are equal in data to 20 Bi-sentences for further process, we could at most correctly answer 192 questions. That is an amazing improvement of 45.45% in sentence level retrieval module.

Selecting 200 single sentences, the accuracy of sentence retrieval reaches 82.91%, that is, 228 out of 275 questions could be correctly answered. Using semantic-based query reformulation, we could probably further improve the performance of sentence retrieval. In a word, what we can affirm is that the techniques for document retrieval are also effective in sentence retrieval.

6 Conclusion

Considering document retrieval and sentence retrieval separately, we achieve an acceptable performance on each module, but the overall performance of IR in QA system is still far from satisfactory because of the cumulated loss in document retrieval and sentence retrieval. Using the 50 top ranked documents produced by PRISE and retrieving 200 single sentences from them, the accuracy of document retrieval is 71.80%, and the accuracy of sentence retrieval is 82.91%, while the overall accuracy of IR is the product of the two module's accuracy, that is only 59.53%.

Since the techniques used in document retrieval and sentence retrieval are the same, we suppose that retrieving sentences from the corpus directly will combine two cumulated loss into one and the overall performance might get better. We will fulfill this idea in the next step.

In conclusion, after re-examining the IR techniques in QA system, we get a satisfactory answer to the two questions presented at the beginning of this article, which will greatly enlighten our future research in QA domain:

- A question is not a good query, and query reformulation should be a necessary step to get a better retrieval performance.
- The techniques for document retrieval are also effective in sentence level retrieval, and single sentence will be the propriety retrieval granularity.

References

1. James Allan, Courtney Wade, Alvaro Bolivar. Retrieval and Novelty Detection at the Sentence Level, Proceedings of the 26th Annual International ACM SIGIR Conference on Research and Development in Information Retrieval (2003)
2. Yi Chang, Hongbo Xu, Shuo Bai. TREC 2003 Question Answering Track at CAS-ICT, Proceedings of the 12th Text REtrieval Conference (2003)
3. C.L.A. Clarke, G.V. Cormack, D.I.E. Kisman, T.R. Lynam. Question Answering by Passage Selection (MultiText experiments for TREC-9), Proceedings of the 9th Text REtrieval Conference (2000)
4. Donna Harman, Gerald Candela. A Very Fast Prototype Retrieval System Using Statistical Rankin, SIGIR Forum (1989) 100-110
5. Dan Moldovan, Sanda Harabagiu, Roxana Girju, Paul Morarescu, Finley Lacatusu, Adrian Novischi, Adriana Badulescu and Orest Bolohan. LCC Tools for Question Answering, Proceedings of the 11th Text REtrieval Conference (2002)
6. Christof Monz. Document Retrieval in the Context of Question Answering, Proceedings of the 25th European Conference on IR Research (2003)
7. I. Roberts, R. Gaizauskas. Evaluating Passage Retrieval Approaches for Question Answering, http://www.dcs.shef.ac.uk/research/resmes/papers/CS0306.pdf.
8. Martin M. Soubbotin, Sergei M. Soubbotin. Use of Patterns for Detection of Likely Answer Strings: A Systematic Approach, Proceedings of the 11th Text REtrieval Conference (2002)

9. Rohini Srihari, Wei Li. Information Extraction Supported Question Answer, Proceedings of the 8th Text REtrieval Conference (1999)
10. Stefanie Tellex, Boris Katz, Jimmy Lin, Aaron Fernandes, Gregory Marton. Quantitative Evaluation of Passage Retrieval Algorithms for Question Answering, Proceedings of the 26th annual international ACM SIGIR conference on Research and Development in Information Retrieval (2003)
11. Ellen M. Voorhees. Overview of TREC 2002 Question Answering Track, Proceedings of the 11th Text REtrieval Conference (2002)
12. Hongbo Xu, Hao Zhang, Shuo Bai. ICT Experiments in TREC-11 QA Main Task, Proceedings of the 11th Text REtrieval Conference (2002)
13. Hongbo Xu, Zhifeng Yang, Bin Wang, Bin Liu, Jun Cheng, Yue Liu, Zhe Yang, Xueqi Cheng, Shuo Bai, TREC-11 Experiments at CAS-ICT: Filtering and Web, Proceedings of the 11th Text REtrieval Conference (2002)
14. Yiming Yang, Xin Liu. A re-examination of text categorization methods, Proceedings of the 22nd Annual International ACM SIGIR Conference on Research and Development in Information Retrieval (1999)

A Novel Pattern Learning Method for Open Domain Question Answering

Yongping Du, Xuanjing Huang, Xin Li, and Lide Wu

Department of Computer Science, Fudan University
Shanghai, 200433
{ypdu,xjhuang,lixin,ldwu}@fudan.edu.cn

Abstract. Open Domain Question Answering (QA) represents an advanced application of natural language processing. We develop a novel pattern based method for implementing answer extraction in QA. For each type of question, the corresponding answer patterns can be learned from the Web automatically. Given a new question, these answer patterns can be applied to find the answer. Although many other QA systems have used pattern based method, however, it is noteworthy that our method has been implemented automatically and it can handle the problem other system failed, and satisfactory results have been achieved. Finally, we give a performance analysis of this approach using the TREC-11 question set.

1 Introduction

Question answering has recently received much attention from the natural language processing communities. The Text Retrieval Conference (TREC) Question Answering track provides a large-scale evaluation for open domain question answering systems. The goal of question answering is to retrieve answers to questions rather than documents as most information retrieval systems currently do.

An integrated QA system has three main components as shown in Fig.1. The first is question analysis that determines the answer type and translates natural language questions into queries for the search engine. The second is search module that retrieves relevant documents or snippets from the document collection, which can potentially answer the question. The third component, answer extraction, analyzes these documents or snippets and extracts answers from them. For example, question "What is the largest city in Germany?" is the input of the QA system and the answer "Berlin" is returned as the output.

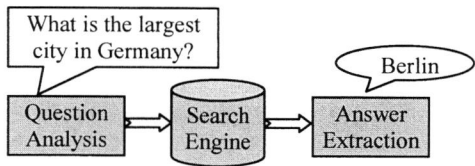

Fig. 1. Architecture of QA System

We develop a novel pattern based method for implementing answer extraction. For each type of question, the corresponding answer patterns can be learned from the Web automatically. Given a new question, these answer patterns can be applied to find the answer.

Many other question answering systems have used pattern based method. ISI [1] and Singapore-MIT Alliance[2] have implemented pattern learning of different question type for QA. For instance, the pattern "in <ANSWER>'s <NAME>" is learned for the question type "LOCATION", where "<NAME>" denotes the question term. A serious limitation of these patterns is that it can handle only one question term in the candidate answer sentence and it can't work for more complex questions that require multiple question terms in the answer sentence. InsightSoft[3] has achieved good performance in TREC but their patterns can't be learned automatically. It is noteworthy that our method has been implemented automatically and it can answer questions that require more than one question term in the candidate answer sentence.

The wealth of information on the Web makes it an attractive resource and many systems have make use of the Web knowledge[4][5][6]. We also take advantage of the variety on Internet for learning different answer patterns which are used for answer extraction in QA. Each answer pattern is consisted of the following three parts:

<Q_Tag>+[ConstString]+<A>

Here, <Q_Tag> stands for the key phrases of question and we will introduce them later. <A> stands for the answer, and any string holding the position will be extracted as the answer. [ConstString] is a sequence of words.

This paper first introduces the question analysis for <Q_Tag> identification in section 2, and then presents the process of learning answer patterns in section 3, following answer extraction with these answer patterns in section 4, finally, we give the performance analysis in section 5.

2 Question Analysis

We define a set of symbols to represent question as illustrated in Table 1, which are the objects or events the question asks about.

The symbol set of Q_Tag includes four kinds of symbol: Q_Focus, Q_NameEntity, Q_Verb and Q_BNP. Here, Q_NameEntity includes different name entity symbols, such as Q_LCN, Q_PRN and so on. It should be pointed that the noun phrases denoted by the symbol Q_BNP don't include the noun phrases which had been denoted by the symbol Q_Focus and Q_NameEntity.

Q_Focus denotes the key words of the question and it contains the following instances:

- the head word of the noun phrase, which is binding with interrogative
  eg: Which *river* runs through Dublin ?
- the "Noun Phrase" of the question whose sentence structure is "Interrogative + be verb+ Noun Phrase+ …"
  eg: What is *the most populous city* in the United States?
- the "ADJ" of the question whose sentence structure is "How+ ADJ+ be Verb(auxiliary verb)+…"
  eg: How *tall* is Mt. Everest ?

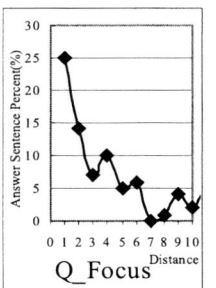 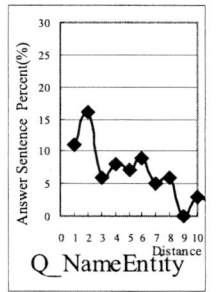 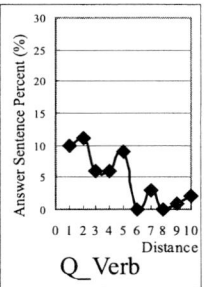 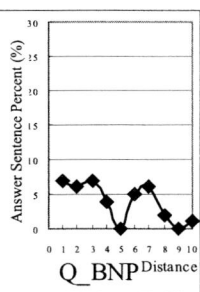

Fig. 2. Distribution of Q_Tag Around Answer

Q_NameEntity, Q_Verb and Q_BNP are analyzed from our Name Entity tagger, Parser and the BNP Chunking tool respectively.

Of all the TREC questions(TREC8-TREC11), we select the answer sentences of 182 questions and these questions contain all the Q_Tag symbols. The distribution of different Q_Tag symbols around the answer in the sentence is shown in Fig.2, and the distance denotes the word count between Q_Tag and the answer. All these Q_Tag symbols are assigned different weights as shown in Table 1, taking into account the possibilities they appear around the answer.

Table 1. Symbol Set of Question

Q_Tag	Description	Example	Weight
Q_Focus	the key word or phrase representing the object that the question asks about	What country is the holy city of Mecca located in?	4
Q_NameEntity (Q_LCN Q_PRN…)	the name entity of the question	What country is the holy city of Mecca located in?	3
Q_Verb (Q_BeVerb Q_DoVerb)	the main verb of the question	What country is the holy city of Mecca located in?	2
Q_BNP	the noun phrase of the question	What country is the holy city of Mecca located in?	1

In our system we adopt a six-class answer type classification, illustrated in Table 2. Currently our system can achieve the precision of 90%, taking 1893 questions of TREC as test data.

Table 2. Answer Type

LCN (Location)	PRN (Person Name)	ORG (Organization)
NUM (Number)	DAT (Date)	BNP (Noun Phrase)

The question pattern (Q_Pattern) is generated from its Q_Tag symbol set, in other words, every element of the question is replaced with its corresponding Q_Tag, and

Table 3. Sample Question Type

Question Type	Question
[LCN] What Q_BeVerb Q_Focus in Q_LCN ?	What is the largest city in Germany? What is the most populous city in the United States?
[DAT] When did Q_LCN Q_DoVerb Q_BNP ?	When did Hawaii become a state ? When did North Carolina enter the union ?
[NUM] What Q_BeVerb Q_Focus of Q_BNP ?	What is the diameter of a golf ball ? What is the melting point of copper ?
[PRN] Who Q_BeVerb Q_Focus of Q_LCN ?	Who is the prime minister of Australia? Who was the first coach of the Cleveland Browns?

then the classification of questions will be built based on the Q_Pattern and the answer type. Sample question types along with corresponding questions are shown in table 3.

Answer patterns can be learned automatically using the <Q_Tag, Answer> pairs as training examples and then used for answer extraction. For instance, answer pattern ", <A> Q_BeVerb Q_Focus in Q_LCN " can be used to answer the question "What is the largest city in Germany?" where "Q_Focus" denotes the question term *"the largest city"* and "Q_LCN" denotes the question term *"Germany"*. The answer "Berlin" can be extracted from the snippet "... , *Berlin is the largest city in Germany* and is developing into a metropolis of sciences, arts, ...".

3 Pattern Learning and Evaluation

We will explain our approach with the sample below.
 Sample question type: [LCN] What Q_BeVerb Q_Focus in Q_LCN ?
 Sample question: What is the largest city in Germany ?
 Where Q_BeVerb=*"is"*, Q_Focus=*"the largest city"*, Q_LCN=*"Germany"*, and Answer=*"Berlin"*.

3.1 Pattern Learning

The answer patterns of each question type are learned by the following algorithm:

1. Constructing Query: "Q_Tag +Answer" is constructed as the query where Q_Tag includes all kinds of Q_Tag except Q_BeVerb. For example, the query of above sample question is: *"the largest city"*+*"Germany"*+ *"Berlin"*.
2. Searching: The query is submitted to the search engine Google, and then the top 100 documents are downloaded.
3. Snippet Selection: The snippets are extracted from the documents for pattern learning, containing 10 words around the answer.
4. Answer Pattern Extraction: Replace the question term in each snippet by the corresponding Q_Tag, and the answer term by the tag <A>. The shortest string containing the Q_Tag and the tag <A> is extracted as the answer pattern. For example, considering the string "...With its 3.4 million inhabitants, *Berlin is the largest*

city in Germany and is developing into a metropolis of sciences, arts, ...", the answer pattern ", <A> Q_BeVerb Q_Focus in Q_LCN " is extracted.
5. Computing the Weight of Each Answer Pattern: It is computed by the following formula considering the weight of the Q_Tag and the distance between different Q_Tag with the answer. ($\alpha=1$, $\beta=0.6$)

$$Weight_P = \alpha \cdot \frac{1}{Distance} + \beta \cdot \sum_{j=1}^{n} \frac{Weight_{Q\_Tag\ j}}{Weight_{Sum}} \quad (1)$$

Here,

$$Dis\tan ce = \frac{\sqrt{d_1^2 + d_2^2 + \cdots + d_n^2}}{n} \quad (2)$$

$$Weight_{Sum} = \sum_{k=1}^{m} Weight_{Q\_Tag\ k} \quad (3)$$

Where, m is the number of Q_Tag contained in the question type, n is the number of the Q_Tag contained in the answer pattern, d_i is the distance between different Q_Tag and the answer, measured by the count of the distinct words. We discard the patterns whose $Weight_P$ is less than a threshold T (T=0.3).

For each question type, it usually have many questions just as shown in Table 3 and we learn answer patterns for all of them. For the sample question above, we obtain following answer patterns:

, <A> Q_BeVerb Q_Focus in
Q_LCN Q_Focus in Q_LCN , <A>
<A> Q_BeVerb Q_Focus
...

3.2 Pattern Evaluation

Among all these answer patterns we have learned, some of them may extract the wrong answer. For the above sample question, answer pattern "<A> Q_BeVerb Q_Focus" can extract candidate answer "*Portland*" from the snippet "*Portland is the largest city* in Oregon. The skyline, seen here across the Willamette River..." However, the correct answer is "Berlin". This wrong answer is due to the fact that this answer pattern lacks the restriction of the question term "Germany"("Q_LCN"). As a rule, more complex answer pattern, i.e. including more question terms, is more valid to extract the correct answer. Thus it is necessary to evaluate these answer patterns.

The approach of answer pattern evaluation is as follows.

1. Query for each answer pattern of the question is formed and submitted to Google, and then the top 100 snippets are downloaded for answer pattern evaluation. The query consists of three parts:

[Head]+[Tail]+[Q_Focus+Q_NameEntity]

Where, [Head] stands for the string before the tag <A> of the answer pattern, and that [Tail] stands for the string after the tag <A> of the answer pattern. The value of them may be NULL, and [Q_Focus] or [Q_NameEntity] will be added into the query only if the [Head] and the [Tail] don't contain the term it represents. For the above answer pattern "<A> Q_BeVerb Q_Focus" and sample question, the query is "is the largest city"+ "Germany". Here, [Head]= NULL, [Tail]= "is the largest city", [Q_Focus]= NULL and [Q_NameEntity] = "Germany"

2. The confidence of each answer pattern is calculated by the formula:

$$Confidence_P = Num_{Correct\_Match} / Num_{Match} \qquad (4)$$

$Num_{Correct\_Match}$ denotes the number of snippets that tag <A> is matched by the correct answer, and Num_{Match} denotes the number of snippets that tag <A> is matched by any word.

3. At last the score of each answer pattern is computed as the formula: (λ=0.7)

$$Score_P = (1 - \lambda) \bullet Weight_P + \lambda \bullet Confidence_P \qquad (5)$$

Answer patterns with higher score lead to choose the answer with greater reliability, and those with lower score can't guarantee the correctness of its response. Some answer patterns along with their evaluation score are shown in Table 4.

The major advantage over other pattern based QA systems is that more than one question term can be included in the answer pattern, such as "Q_Focus in Q_LCN , <A>", containing two question terms "Q_Focus" and "Q_LCN". For longer question it is difficult to decide the unique question term containing the key information of the question, furthermore, the answer pattern containing more question terms is more confident for answer extraction.

Table 4. Sample Answer Pattern

Question Type	Answer Pattern	Score
[LCN]What Q_BeVerb Q_Focus in Q_LCN ?	Q_Focus in Q_LCN Q_BeVerb <A>	1.24
	, <A> Q_BeVerb Q_Focus in Q_LCN	0.98
Sample question:	Q_Focus in Q_LCN , <A>	0.85
What is the largest city in Germany ?	<A> Q_BeVerb Q_Focus	0.72
[DAT]When did Q_LCN Q_DoVerb Q_BNP ?	Q_LCN Q_DoVerb Q_BNP in <A>.	0.98
	Q_DoVerb Q_BNP in <A>, Q_LCN	0.86
Sample question:	in <A>, Q_LCN Q_DoVerb Q_BNP	0.86
When did Hawaii become a state ?	<A>, Q_LCN Q_DoVerb Q_BNP	0.77
[NUM]What Q_BeVerb Q_Focus of Q_BNP ?	Q_Focus of Q_BNP Q_BeVerb <A>,	1.23
	Q_Focus of Q_BNP to <A>.	0.86
Sample question:	Q_BNP Q_BeVerb <A> and	0.84
What is the diameter of a golf ball ?	Q_BNP Q_BeVerb <A>,	0.75
[PRN]Who Q_BeVerb Q_Focus of Q_LCN ?	Q_Focus of Q_LCN <A> Q_BeVerb	1.54
	Q_BeVerb <A>, Q_Focus of Q_LCN	0.98
Sample question:	Q_LCN Q_Focus <A> on	0.91
Who is the prime minister of Australia ?	<A> : Q_Focus of Q_LCN	0.82

4 Answer Extraction

Considering massive amounts of data on Internet, we select Google as the search engine for our question answering system. For each query submitted, Google returns top 100 snippets for answer extraction.

The answer patterns can be used to extract answer to a new question as follows:

(Sample question "What is the most populous city in the United States?" is used for explaining the following algorithm)

1. Identify the Q_Tag of the new question and then generate its Q_Pattern.
   Sample Q_Tag:
   Q_BeVerb="is" Q_Focus="the most populous city" Q_LCN= "the United States"
   Sample Q_Pattern: What Q_BeVerb Q_Focus in Q_LCN ?
2. Determining the question type of the question based on its Q_Pattern and answer type. The corresponding answer patterns of this question type are also selected from the predefined answer patterns.
   Sample question type: [LCN] What Q_BeVerb Q_Focus in Q_LCN ?
   Sample answer pattern: , <A> Q_BeVerb Q_Focus in Q_LCN
3. Replace Q_Tag symbols of each answer pattern with the corresponding question term of the question.
   Sample answer pattern is instantiated as:
   , <A> is the most populous city in the United States
4. For each answer pattern and each snippet returned, select the words matching tag <A> as the candidate answer.
5. Discard the candidate answers which don't satisfy the answer type of the question, using name entity tagger.
6. Sort the remainder candidate answers by their answer pattern's score and their frequency, and the one with the highest score is selected as the final answer.

In this stage, we resolve the problem of answer semantic restriction. As for the sample question, candidate answer "it" is extracted from the snippet "More than seven million people live in New York City, *it is the most populous city in the United States.*", using the answer pattern ", <A> Q_BeVerb Q_Focus in Q_LCN". However, the answer type of this question is "LCN", and this candidate answer doesn't satisfy this restriction then it is discarded.

5 Performance Analysis

We take the data of TREC-9 and TREC-10 as training examples for learning these answer patterns. To evaluate the performance of this approach we have done experiment, using the 500 questions of TREC-11.

The performance of QA system is influenced by the amount of text returned by the search engine. Fig.3 illustrates the impact of the retrieved snippet number, grouped by various interrogatives. The result is measured by the Mean Reciprocal Rank (MRR) score [7], a precision-like measure.

Here, *Num* denotes the maximum number of snippets search engine (Google) returned. The precision gets great improvement when *Num* is increased from 50 to 100 for more relevant snippets are returned, on the other hand, it doesn't increase any more when *Num* is increased to 200. When too many snippets are returned, the actually relevant snippets are submerged in a large amount of text, consequently a very large number of candidate answers are extracted and the system does not always rank the correct answer within the top five. Thus in our system the default maximum number of snippets is set to 100.

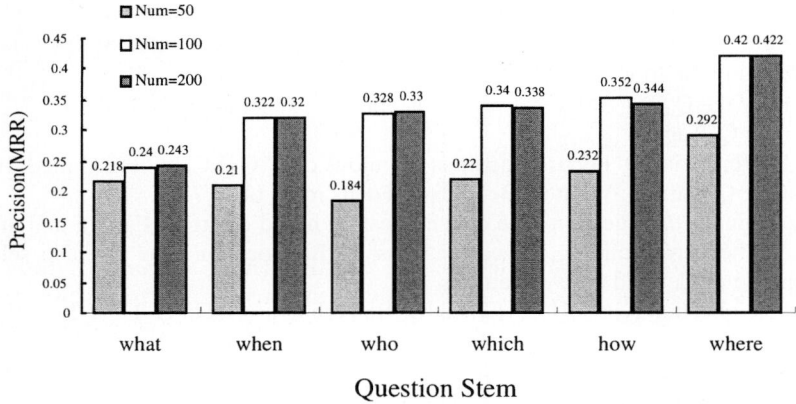

Fig. 3. Impact of maximum number of snippets processed

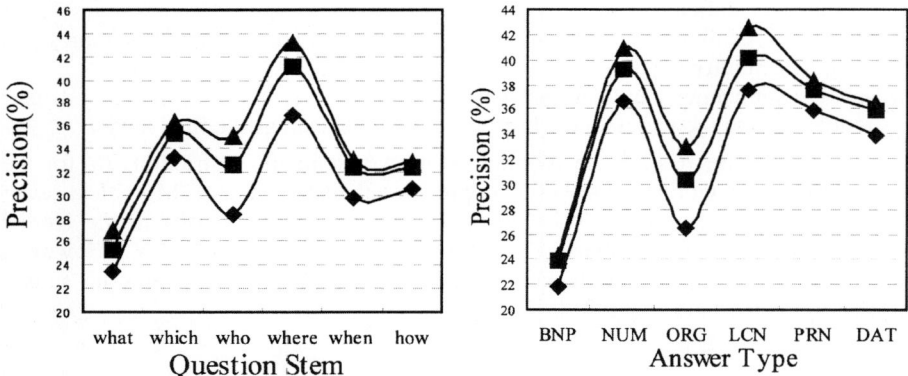

Fig. 4. Percentage of Correct Answer Across Various Question Stems

Fig. 5. Percentage of Correct Answer Across Various Answer Types

For some questions, the system doesn't return correct answer due to the bad ranking of candidate answers, in fact, correct answer has been extracted with the lower score. We analyze the result when different top k answers are considered for evaluation. Fig.4 and Fig.5 illustrate the experiment results across various interrogatives and answer types respectively.

We find a majority of correct answers are contained in the top 10 candidate answers and the performance gets greater improvement compared to the result of only top 1 answer is considered. It shows the shortcoming of our system that we should not only depend on the pattern score for candidate answer ranking but also other factors, such as the relevant degree of snippet to the question.

The overall precision of 500 questions is 0.309 and this result is within the top 1/3 groups in TREC-11 using the precision for evaluation.

6 Conclusion

The design of our QA system is a test for the novel pattern learning technology and the efficiency of this approach depends on the quantity and diversification of answer patterns largely. We take part in the TREC-12 this year and the primary evaluation result shows our result is above the median score of all runs submitted.

Among all these answer patterns what we have learned, some are too specific that they are almost useless for answering the new question. For instance, one of the answer patterns to the question *"What is a shaman?"* is *"Q_Focus was the priest, the <A> and"*, where "Q_Focus" denotes the question term *"a shaman"*. Here, *"the priest"* is related to this question closely and then this answer pattern is almost useless for answering new question. We will eliminate this kind of answer patterns in the future.

At present we only take the data of TREC-9 and TREC-10 as the training examples and that only top 100 documents to each <Q_Tag, Answer> pair query are downloaded for answer pattern learning, thus the number of answer patterns we have learned is restricted on account of the above factors, which influences the performance of our system. But the result is encouraging and we will go on with the development for higher performance. We believe it is an effective approach when more reliable answer patterns are learned.

Acknowledgements

This research was partly supported by NSF(Beijing) under contracts of 69935010 and 60103014, as well as the 863 National High-tech Promotion Project (Beijing) under contracts of 2001AA114120 and 2002AA142090.

References

1. Deepak Ravichandran and Eduard Hovy. 2002. Learning Surface Text Patterns for a Question Answering System. Proceedings of the ACL Conference.
2. Dell Zhang, Wee Sun Lee. 2002. Web based Pattern Mining and Matching Approach to Question Answering. Proceedings of the TREC-11 Conference. NIST, Gaithersburg, MD, 505-512.
3. M.M. Soubbotin. 2001. Patterns of Potential Answer Expressions as Clues to the Right Answer. Proceedings of the TREC-10 Conference. NIST, Gaithersburg, MD, 175-182.
4. Susan Dumais, Michele Banko, Eric Brill, Jimmy Lin, and Andrew Ng. 2002. Web Question Answering: Is More Always Better? Proceedings of the 25th Annual International ACM SIGIR Conference on Research and Development in Information Retrieval, August 2002, Tampere, Finland.
5. E. Brill, J.Lin, M.Banko, S. Dumais, and A. Ng. 2001. Data-Intensive Question Answering. Proceedings of the TREC-10 Conference. NIST, Gaithersburg, MD, 183-189.
6. Cody C. T. Kwok, Oren Etzioni and Daniel S. Weld. May 1-5, 2001. Scaling Question Answering to the Web. Tenth World Wide Web Conference. Hong Kong, China.
7. Voorhees, E. 2001. Overview of the Question Answering Track. Proceedings of the TREC-10 Conference. NIST,Gathersburg, MD, 157-165.

Chinese Named Entity Recognition Based on Multilevel Linguistic Features

Honglei Guo[1], Jianmin Jiang[1], Gang Hu[1], and Tong Zhang[2]

[1] IBM China Research Laboratory, HaoHai Building, No.7, 5th Street, ShangDi, Beijing, P.R.China, 100085
{guohl,jiangjm,hugang}@cn.ibm.com
[2] IBM T.J. Watson Research Center, Yorktown Heights, New York, 10598, USA
tzhang@watson.ibm.com

Abstract. This paper presents a Chinese named entity recognition system that employs the Robust Risk Minimization (RRM) classification method and incorporates the advantages of character-based and word-based models. From experiments on a large-scale corpus, we show that significant performance enhancements can be obtained by integrating various linguistic information (such as Chinese word segmentation, semantic types, part of speech, and named entity triggers) into a basic Chinese character based model. A novel feature weighting mechanism is also employed to obtain more useful cues from most important linguistic features. Moreover, to overcome the limitation of computational resources in building a high-quality named entity recognition system from a large-scale corpus, informative samples are selected by an active learning approach.

1 Introduction

Named entities are phrases that contain names of persons, organizations, locations etc. Named entity (NE) recognition is an important task in many natural language processing applications (e.g. information extraction, machine translation, etc.). There have been a number of conferences aimed at evaluating NE recognition systems, for example, MUC6, MUC7, CoNLL2002, CoNLL2003, ACE (Automatic Content Extraction) evaluations. Recent research on English NE recognition has focused on the machine learning approach [1]. The relevant algorithms include Maximum Entropy (see [2] and [3]), Hidden Markov Model (HMM) (see [3]and [4]), AdaBoost [5], Memory-based learning [6], Support Vector Machine [7], RRM method[8] etc. Most existing approaches for Chinese NE recognition use hand-crafted rules with word (or character) frequency statistics. It is only recently that machine learning based Chinese NE recognition systems have appeared. Some algorithms have been investigated, including HMM (see [9] and [10]), class-based language model (see [10] and [11]), RRM type methods (see [10] and [12]), etc. We can argue that Chinese NE recognition is more difficult than English NE recognition. In Chinese, there is no space to mark word boundaries and no standard definition of words. No external features such as capitalization can help recognize Chinese NEs. Therefore it is difficult to determine the boundary of Chinese NE. It is also difficult to recognize NEs merely by looking at Chinese characters used.

In this paper, we present a RRM based Chinese NE recognition system that integrates the advantages of character-based model and word-based model. In order to capture the linguisitic features of Chinese NEs, we use Chinese characters as the basic token units, and integrate word segmentation information, semantic feature, part of speech, NE triggers etc. In order to overcome the limitation of computational resources (e.g. memory consummation, annotated corpus) in building a high-quality NE recognition system, we select more informative samples based on uncertainty sampling. Meanwhile, a feature weighting mechanism is used to guide the learning algorithm to focus on important linguistic features.

This paper is organized as follows. Section 2 gives a brief overview of the underlying algorithm. Section 3 describes the training and test data. Section 4 presents a Chinese NE recognition model based on multilevel linguistic features and presents experimental results on a large-scale corpus. Section 5 describes a feature weighting mechanism for Chinese NE recognition model. Section 6 discusses a procedure of selecting informative training samples to overcome computational limitations. Finally the conclusion is given in Sect. 7.

2 Robust Risk Minimization Classifier

We can view the NE recognition task as a sequential classification problem. If we use w_i ($i = 0, 1, ..., n$) to denote the sequence of tokenized text, which is the input to the system, then every token w_i should be assigned a class-label t_i. For NE recognition, the class-label sequence $\{t_i\}$ encodes the entity information.

In this paper, we adopt the B-I-O encoding, which we shall explain later.

Our Chinese NE recognition system employs the Robust Risk Minimization (RRM) classification method. The class label value t_i associated with each token w_i is predicted by estimating the conditional probability $P(t_i = c|x_i)$ for every possible class-label value c, where x_i is a feature vector associated with w_i.

We assume that $P(t_i = c|x_i) = P(t_i = c|w_i, \{t_j\}_{j \leq i})$. The feature vector x_i can depend on previously predicted class labels $\{t_j\}_{j \leq i}$, but the dependency is typically assumed to be local. In the RRM method, the above conditional probability model has the following parametric form:

$$P(t_i = c|x_i, t_{i-l}, ..., t_{i-1}) = T(w_c^T x_i + b_c),$$

where $T(y) = \min(1, \max(0, y))$ is the truncation of y into the interval $[0, 1]$. w_c is a linear weight vector and b_c is a constant. Parameters w_c and b_c can be estimated from the training data.

The generalized Winnow method in [13] describes such a method. However, in this paper, we use a different simpler and more efficient procedure. Our experience suggests that the difference is not important as far as accuracy is concerned.

3 Data

IBM China Research Laboratory has created a large-scale annotated Chinese corpus (about 100M Chinese characters). All of the data are news articles selected from several Chinese newspapers (e.g. 2001 and 2002's Beijing Youth Daily, Xinmin Evening News etc.). They cover various domains (e.g. economics, sports, etc.). All the named entities (NEs) in the corpus are annotated manually.

All training and test data used in our experiments are selected from the annotated Chinese corpus. The size of the training data set is 1.05M Chinese characters. The size of the test set is 1.34M Chinese characters.

4 Selection of Linguistic Features in Chinese Named Entity Recognition

It is difficult to achieve language independence in a very high quality NE recognition system because different languages usually require different features. Feature design and integration is very important in the overall system design. In this section, we present a Chinese NE recognition model by integrating the advantages of character-based and word-based models.

In this paper, we focus on recognizing four types of NEs: person (PER), location (LOC), organization (ORG), and miscellaneous NE (MISC) that does not belong to the previous three groups (e.g. products, brands, conferences etc.).

We adopt the B-I-O scheme to encode the entity-information into a sequence of class-labels, so that a single class label is assigned to every token. Each token unit is tagged as either the first token in a NE of type X (B-X tag), or a non-initial token in a NE of type X (I-X tag), or a token outside of any NEs (O tag). For example, the location "Diao4 Yu2 Tai2 Guo2 Bin1 Guan3 (i.e. Diaoyutai State Guesthouse)" is encoded as " Diao4 Yu2 Tai2 (i.e. Diaoyutai)(B-LOC) Guo2 (i.e. State)(I-LOC) Bin1 Guan3 (i.e. Guesthouse)(I-LOC)".

4.1 Integrating the Advantages of Character-Based Model and Word-Based Model

Since both Chinese characters and Chinese words can be used as basic token units in Chinese NE recognition, some researchers have already started to investigate the behavior of the two approaches [10]. However, previous studies didn't incorporate them into one system.

We argue that both have their own advantages. Therefore by integrating them into a single system, we can benefit from both character-based and word-based models. For example, Chinese word segmentation information, which are often useful, are not present in character-based models. On the other hand, although Chinese word information are used in word-based models, in order to achieve high performance, the boundary of the NEs should be aligned with Chinese word units. This is not always achievable.

Therefore for Chinese NE recognition, both character-based models and word-based models have their advantages and disadvantages. Character-based models can avoid problems caused by Chinese word segmentation errors, but cannot effectively capture rich information contained in Chinese words, which are generally regarded as basic linguistic units in the Chinese language. Although word-based models implicitly use larger views to capture useful cues on NE, they are heavily affected by Chinese word segmentation errors. In addition, since there are more words than characters, word-based models are more severely affected by the data sparseness problem, that is, we don't have sufficient data to obtain accurate statistical estimates.

Our method of integrating the character-based and word-based approaches is by creating multilevel linguistic features that incorporate both character-based features and word-based features. In order to achieve this, we use Chinese characters (not Chinese words) as the basic token units, and then map word-based features that are associated with each word into corresponding features of those characters that are contained in the word. In general, we may regard this approach as information integration from linguistic views at different abstraction levels. Although we have so far only studied this idea on the Chinese NE recognition task, we believe that the general concept can be potentially useful for other NLP problems (including English NE recognition) as well.

In our baseline experiments of a character-based Chinese NE recognition model and a word-based model, only some basic linguistic features are employed. These features include the basic token units (Chinese characters in the character-based model or Chinese words in the word-based model), NE hints. The baseline performance difference between the character-based model and the word-based model (see Table 1) also implies that linguistic information beyond the basic linguistic features can significantly affect the quality of Chinese NE recognition.

Table 1. Baseline performances for character-based model and word-based model.

Type	F(%) (Word-based model)	F(%) (Character-based model)
PER	84.80	83.71
LOC	85.87	80.09
ORG	75.50	66.81
MISC	60.14	53.14
Total	80.66	75.53

Therefore we integrate a diverse set of local linguistic features, including word segmentation information, Chinese word patterns, complex lexical linguistic features, external NE hints, aligned at the character level. In our system, local linguistic features of a token unit are derived from the sentence containing this token unit. All special linguistic patterns (e.g. date, time, numeral expression) are encoded into pattern-specific class labels aligned with the token. The features are listed below.

1. Basic token view features:
   Chinese characters in a $-2 \sim 2$ window surrounding the current focused basic token unit.
2. Chinese word segmentation units view window:
   (a) Chinese words in a larger 6-Chinese-word-window (i.e. $i = -3, ..., 3$) surrounding the current focused basic token unit;
   (b) Chinese words where the 5-Chinese-character-window (i.e. $i = -2, ..., 2$) is anchored.
3. Lexical linguistic features: Part of speech features and semantic features.
4. Chinese pattern features where the 5-Chinese-character-window is anchored, including types such as date, time, numeral expression, English word, etc.
5. Relative position of the current Chinese character in the current Chinese word, which indicates this character is the initial or non-initial character in the Chinese word.
6. The previous two predicated tags.
7. The conjunction of the previous tag and the current token unit.

In addition, we also apply external NE hints, including

1. 221 surnames, 517 location suffixes, 8,065 organization suffixes, 5,321 titles, 649 Chinese characters which are frequently used in Chinese names, 461 Chinese characters which are frequently used in translation names. These external hints are used to determine whether a token unit may trigger or terminate a particular NE class. For example, "Jiao4 Shou4" (i.e. "professor") may trigger the NE class person.
2. Gazetteers: 6,160 locations and 1,656 organizations. These gazetteers can help determine potential classes for each token.

Figure 1 illustrates various features and views at the current character c_i, where w_{c_i} denotes the word where c_i is anchored. In the viewing window (we choose a window size of 2) at the current character c_i, each token around c_i is codified with a set of primitive features, together with its relative position to c_i.

$$\rightarrow \text{Tagging} \rightarrow$$

Character		c_{i-2}	c_{i-1}	c_i	c_{i+1}	c_{i+2}	
Word	w_{i-3}	w_{i-2}	w_{i-1}	w_i	w_{i+1}	w_{i+2}	w_{i+3}
Word$_c$		$w_{c_{i-2}}$	$w_{c_{i-1}}$	w_{c_i}	$w_{c_{i+1}}$	$w_{c_{i+2}}$	
POS		p_{i-2}	p_{i-1}	p_i	p_{i+1}	p_{i+2}	
Semantic		s_{i-2}	s_{i-1}	s_i	s_{i+1}	s_{i+2}	
.....							
Tag		t_{i-2}	t_{i-1}	$\boxed{t_i}$			

Fig. 1. Linguistic feature window in Chinese NE recognition.

4.2 Experimental Results

In our evaluation, only NE with correct boundary and correct class label is considered as the correct recognition. The standard F_β measure is defined below. In this paper, we use $F = F_{\beta=1}$.

$$F_\beta = \frac{(\beta^2 + 1) \times \text{Precision} \times \text{Recall}}{\beta^2 \times \text{Precision} + \text{Recall}},$$

where,

$$\text{Precision} = \frac{\text{Number of correct recognized NEs}}{\text{Number of recognized NEs}},$$

and

$$\text{Recall} = \frac{\text{Number of correct recognized NEs}}{\text{Number of correct NEs}}.$$

The experimental results (see Table 2) show that our integration model (processing from right to left) gives a very significant performance enhancement on Chinese NE recognition. Chinese word segmentation information and its surrounding context have a significant impact on performance enhancement, which can give a 5% improvement in F-measure points. Part of speech, semantic information, NE hints also give a slight performance enhancement (see Table 3).

Since a sentence can be processed from left to right or from right to left during training and decoding, we also compared the difference in system performance when processing-order is taken in these two directions. The overall performance when processing is from left to right is lower than that of from right to left (see Table 2). For recognizing persons, the performance of processing from left to right is in fact better. However, for recognizing organizations, locations and miscellaneous named entities, the performance of processing from right to left is better. One reason is that most of the triggers for person names in Chinese are initial characters in person names, while most of the triggers for locations, organizations, miscellaneous named entities are ending characters.

Since Chinese word is the basic linguistic representation unit in Chinese, we have built a word-based model with complex linguistic features. Its F-measure points (PER: 88.17%, LOC: 88.40%, ORG: 77.68%, MISC: 62.68%, All: 83.30%) are lower than the full integration model. Obviously, the disadvantages of word-based models described before have made a negative impact on the performance.

Table 2. Integration model with complex linguistic features (processing from right to left vs. from left to right).

Type	Processing from right to left			Processing from left to right		
	Precision(%)	Recall(%)	F(%)	Precision(%)	Recall(%)	F(%)
PER	91.36	88.42	89.87	92.16	88.10	90.08
LOC	89.48	88.88	89.18	90.33	87.10	88.68
ORG	81.47	77.08	79.22	82.80	74.16	78.24
MISC	74.08	56.76	64.27	69.96	56.20	62.23
Total	86.79	82.49	84.59	87.29	81.00	84.03

Table 3. Performances without using word segmentation information (SEG), part of speech (POS), semantic feature (SEM) or NE hints.

Type	F(%) (with all features)	F(%) (without SEG)	F(%) (without POS)	F(%) (without SEM)	F(%) (without NE hints)
PER	89.87	86.86	89.12	89.65	89.55
LOC	89.18	85.28	88.64	89.16	88.99
ORG	79.22	70.04	78.72	78.92	78.82
MISC	64.27	55.64	63.80	64.57	63.87
Total	84.59	79.38	84.00	84.46	84.28

We have the following observations from the above experimental results:

1. Better Chinese NE recognition model can be obtained by using more complex linguistic features. By integrating character-based and word-based models, we can achieve better performance in Chinese NE recognition than either character-based or word-based models. Chinese word segmentation information and its surrounding context have a significant impact on performance.
2. The performances for PER, LOC and ORG are better than that of MISC. We believe that the main reason for the poor performance of MISC is that there are less common indicative features among various misc NEs which we do not distinguish. In fact, misc NEs can be further divided into thirteen categories, including products, conferences, events, brands, etc. In addition, there are a relatively small number of positive training samples for misc NEs.

5 Feature Weighting in Chinese Named Entity Recognition

Since good features can significantly enhance the performance, we may repeat those good features more times in constructing the input vector to the classifier.

An equivalent method is to employ a feature weighting mechanism that assigns each feature a weight which indicates its importance in NE recognition. For example, if the weight of Chinese word segmentation information is 3 (i.e. weight=3), it means that this feature's value in the input vector will be employed three times. This allows us to bias the learning algorithm so that more relevant feature components have higher influence while less relevant ones have less influence on the system decision. If the features are not weighted (i.e. weight=1), then the effect is to let the algorithm find the relevant ones by itself. By weighting those more important features according to Chinese linguistic knowledge (such as Chinese word segmentation information), performance can be further enhanced (see Table 4). The experiments also indicate that the performance may deteriorate when the weight for a feature is more than a certain threshold.

Table 4. F-measure for weighting word segmentation information.

Type	F(%) (Weight=1)	F(%) (Weight=3)	F(%) (Weight=4)
PER	89.22	89.87	88.75
LOC	88.61	89.18	88.04
ORG	77.91	79.22	76.17
MISC	62.53	64.27	63.00
Total	83.69	84.59	82.91

6 Select Informative Training Samples by the Active Learning Approach

Since only limited external resources are available for recognizing Chinese NEs, we need to use a large number of training data, and let the learning algorithm find relevant classification patterns. In practice, the amount of annotated data is a bottleneck for supervised learning methods. Typically a higher performance system requires more features and a larger number of training data. However, this requires larger system memory and a more efficient training method, which may not be available. Within the limitation of available computational resources, it is thus necessary for us to either limit the number of features or to select more informative data which can be efficiently handled by the training algorithm.

In order to overcome the existing computational limitation, we build our Chinese NE recognition model incrementally using a variant of uncertainty-sampling [14]. The main steps are described as follows.

1. Build an initial recognition model (see Table 5) by training an initial data set which is randomly selected from a larger original candidate data set.
2. Refine the training set by adding more informative samples and removing those redundant samples. In this refinement phase, all the data are annotated by the current recognition model. Each annotation prediction has a confidence score. Lower confidence score usually indicates a wrong annotation prediction. Therefore, we add the top n new samples (e.g. $n=1000$) with lowest confidence scores into the training set. Meanwhile, in order to keep a reasonable size of the training set, the top m old training samples (e.g. $m=500$) with highest confidence scores are removed from the training set.

Table 5. Initial model by training an initial training set.

Type	Precision(%)	Recall(%)	F(%)
PER	86.55	84.44	85.48
LOC	86.70	83.70	85.18
ORG	78.97	67.74	72.92
MISC	60.39	51.08	55.34
Total	82.42	76.56	79.39

3. Retrain a new NE recognition model with the newly refined training set.
4. Repeat Step 2 and Step 3, until the performance doesn't improve any more.

Using this incremental training method, we created a refined high-quality training set (see Table 6) from the larger candidate data set. Since the refined training data consist of highly informative samples, we are able to obtain a better model (see Table 2 in Sect. 4.2).

Table 6. NEs in the original data set, the initial training set, the final refined training set and the test data set.

Type	NEs (the original data set: 9M Chinese characters)	NEs (the initial training set: 1M Chinese characters)	NEs (the refined training set: 1.05M Chinese characters)	NEs (the test data set:1.34M Chinese characters)
PER	77,890	12,575	18,898	11,991
LOC	90,587	12,869	24,862	12,353
ORG	80,446	12,197	22,173	9,820
MISC	22,571	4,691	8,067	1,820
Total	271,494	42,332	74,000	35,192

Our experience with the incremental sample selection strategy suggests as follows. In learning NE recognition models, annotated results with lower confidence scores are more useful than those samples with higher confidence scores. In order to obtain a high-quality Chinese NE recognition model, it is necessary to keep the informative samples. Informative sample-selection is an effective method for overcoming the potential limitation of computational resources, and can alleviate the problem of obtaining a large amount of annotated data.

7 Conclusion

We presented a Chinese NE recognition system which incorporates character-based and word-based models. From experiments performed on a large-scale corpus, our integrated Chinese NE recognition model achieves appreciably better performance than either character-based models or word-based models alone. More generally, our approach can be regarded as a special case of utilizing information from different linguistic levels. We believe that this idea can benefit other NLP tasks, although its effectiveness remains to be carefully investigated.

In our system, the following features have significant impacts on its performance: Chinese characters, word segmentation information and its surrounding context, part of speech. A feature weighting mechanism is also employed to guide the learning algorithm to focus on important linguistic feature components.

In practice, the limitation of available computational resources may become an obstacle. In order to build a high quality NE recognition model, it is necessary to select the most informative training data. We described an incremental data selection mechanism and showed that this method can significantly improve performance.

References

1. Sang, E.F.T.K., Meulder, F.D.: Introduction to the CoNLL-2003 shared task: Language independent named entity recognition. In Daelemans, W., Osborne, M., eds.: Proceedings of CoNLL-2003. (2003) 142-147
2. Borthwick A. :A Maximum Entropy Approach to Named Entity Recognition. New York University. (1999)
3. Klein, D., Smarr, J., Nguyen, H., Manning, C.D.: Named entity recognition with character-level models. In: Proceedings of CoNLL-2003. (2003) 180-183
4. Bikel, D.M., Schwartz, R.L., Weischedel, R.M.: An algorithm that learns what's in a name. Machine Learning **34** (1999) 211-231
5. Carreras, X., Màrquez, L., Padró, L.: A simple named entity extractor using adaboost. In: Proceedings of CoNLL-2003. (2003) 152-155
6. Meulder, F.D., Daelemans, W.: Memory-based named entity recognition using unannotated data. In: Proceedings of CoNLL-2003. (2003) 208-211
7. Isozaki, H., Kazawa, H.: Efficient support vector classifiers for named entity recognition. In: Proceedings of Coling-2002. (2002)
8. Zhang, T., Johnson, D.E.: A Robust Risk Minimization based Named Entity Recognition System. In: Proceedings CoNLL-2003. (2003) 204-207
9. Yu, S., Bai, S., Wu, P.: Description of the kent ridge digital labs system used for muc-7. In: Proceedings of the Seventh Message Understanding Conference (MUC-7). (1998)
10. Jing, H., Florian, R., Luo, X., Zhang, T., Ittycheriah, A.: Howtogetachinesename (entity) : Segmentation and combination issues. In: EMNLP 2003. (2003)
11. Sun, J., Gao, J., Zhang, L., Zhou, M., Huang, C.: Chinese named entity identification using class-based language model. In: Proceedings of Coling-2002. (2002)
12. Jiang, J., Guo, H., Hu, G., Zhang, T.: Chinese named entity recognition by regularized winnow algorithm. In: Proceedings of 20th International Conference on Computer Processing of Oriental Languages. (2003) 50-56
13. Zhang, T., Damerau, F., Johnson, D.E.: Text chunking based on a generalization of Winnow. Journal of Machine Learning Research **2** (2002) 615-637
14. Lewis, D., Catlett, J.: Heterogeneous uncertainty sampling for supervised learning. In: Proceedings of the Eleventh International Conference on Machine Learning. (1994) 148-156

Information Flow Analysis with Chinese Text

Paulo Cheong[1], Dawei Song[1], Peter Bruza[1], and Kam-Fai Wong[2]

[1] CRC for Enterprise Distributed Systems Technology (DSTC)
The University of Queensland
Brisbane, QLD 4072
{pauloc,dsong,bruza}@dstc.edu.au
[2] Department of Systems Engineering and Engineering Management
The Chinese University of Hong Kong
Shatin, N.T., Hong Kong
kfwong@se.cuhk.edu.hk

Abstract. This article investigates the effectiveness of an information inference mechanism on Chinese text. The information inference derives implicit associations via computation of information flow on a high dimensional conceptual space, which is approximated by a cognitively motivated lexical semantic space model, namely Hyperspace Analogue to Language (HAL). A dictionary-based Chinese word segmentation system was used to segment words. To evaluate the Chinese-based information flow model, it is applied to query expansion, in which a set of test queries are expanded automatically via information flow computations and documents are retrieved. Standard recall-precision measures are used to measure performance. Experimental results for TREC-5 Chinese queries and People Daily's corpus suggest that the Chinese information flow model significantly increases average precision, though the increase is not as high as those achieved using English corpus. Nevertheless, there is justification to believe that the HAL-based information flow model, and in turn our psychologistic stance on the next generation of information processing systems, have a promising degree of language independence.

1 Introduction

Humans have the ability to swiftly make reliable judgments about the content of brief text fragments. For example, with the two phrases "welcome to Penguin Books" and "Antarctic Penguin", the term "penguin" within these two phrases is *about* two rather different concepts: the publisher Penguin Books, and the short, black animal living in the ice-cold Antarctic. In situations involving large amounts of incoming electronic information (e.g., defence intelligence), judgments about content (whether by automatic or manual means) are sometimes performed based simply on a title description or brief caption because it is too time consuming, or too computationally expensive to peruse whole documents. The process of making such "aboutness" judgments has been referred to as *informational inference* [9].

An information inference mechanism has been proposed which automatically computes information flow through a high dimensional conceptual space [9]. Each concept is represented as a vector of other concepts in the conceptual space. The information flow is a reflection of how strongly Y is *informationally contained* within X, which discovers the implicit associations between concepts. This is a breakthrough from the explicit term associations via co-occurrence relationships used in traditional information processing systems. For example, "bird" is an information flow derived from "Antarctic Penguin", even if it may never co-occur with "penguin".

The main research focus of the information flow analysis has been placed on cognitive science and logic. Words are represented as vectors in a high dimensional semantic space automatically derived from a text corpus. Information flow computation between vectors is proposed as a means of suggesting potentially interesting implicit associations between concepts. A psychologistic stance has been advocated in building the "semiotic-cognitive information system", which refers to the systems manipulating "meanings", which are motivated from a cognitive perspective. It is believed that the information flow model can possibly be applied to another language, i.e., it is language independent. With the booming growth of Chinese electronic documents on the Internet, there has been a great incentive to develop an effective Chinese Information Retrieval system. Moreover, the research is challenging to conduct because of its complexity in language structure. English and other Western languages share the same characteristics of easily distinguishable words and phrases, but Chinese sentences are structured by characters without distinguishable word boundaries.

The goal of this paper is to investigate the effectiveness of the information flow model in Chinese language. The model is evaluated in form of automatic query expansion. Initial queries are expanded by information flow analysis. The key to effective query expansion is the ability to infer expansion terms relevant to the topic of the query. If the inference mechanism is "unsound", then terms extraneous to the query topic will be introduced causing irrelevant documents to be retrieved. This causes a loss of precision. Therefore, there is a justification that the performance of query expansion via information flow analysis serves as an indicator of the soundness (i.e., compatibility to human judgment) of information flow analysis itself.

2 Information Flow Analysis

2.1 Representing Information in a High Dimensional Conceptual Space

How can information, or concepts, be represented and processed in a full, rich-in-meaning context? From the cognitive science aspect, Gärdenfors proposed a cognitive model on 'conceptual space', which is built upon geometric structures representing concepts and properties [5]. In the conceptual level, information is represented geometrically in terms of a dimensional space.

Recent investigations on lexical semantic space models open a door to realize Gardenfors' conceptual spaces theory. Humans encountering a new concept derive the meaning via an accumulation of experience of the contexts in which the concept appears. The meaning of a word is captured by examining its co-occurrence patterns with other words in the language use (e.g., a corpus of texts). There have been two major classes of semantic space models: document spaces and word spaces. The former represents words as vector spaces of text fragments (e.g. documents, paragraphs, etc) in which they appear. A notable example is the Latent Semantic Analysis (LSA) [6]. The latter represents words as vector spaces of other words, which occur with the target words within a certain distance (e.g., a window size). The weighting scheme can be inversely proportional to the distance between the context and target words.

The Hyper-space Analogue to Language (HAL) model employs this scheme [3,4]. The concepts, which occur in the similar contexts, tend to be similar to each other in meaning. For example, nurse and doctor are similar in semantics to each other, as they always experience the same contexts, i.e., hospital, patients, etc.

The semantic space models have demonstrated cognitive compatibility with human processing. For example, Burgess and Lund showed via cognitive experiments that "human participants were able to use the context neighbourhoods that HAL generates to match words with similar items and to derive the word (or a similar word) from the neighbourhood, thus demonstrating the cognitive compatibility of the representations with human processing" [4].

2.2 Hyperspace Analogue to Language (HAL)

Song and Bruza propose to use the HAL vectors to prime the geometric representations inherent to Gärdenfors' conceptual spaces [2,9].

Given an n-word vocabulary, the HAL space is a $n \times n$ matrix constructed by moving a window of length L over the corpus by one word increment ignoring punctuation, sentence and paragraph boundaries. All words within the window are considered as co-occurring with each other with strengths inversely proportional to the distance between them. After traversing the corpus, an accumulated co-occurrence matrix for all the words in a target vocabulary is produced. It is sometimes useful to identify the so called *quality properties* of a HAL-vector. Quality properties are identified as those dimensions in the HAL vector for c which are above a certain threshold (e.g., above the average weight within that vector). HAL vectors are normalized to unit length before information flow computation. For example, the following is part of the cosine-normalized HAL vector for "*Iran*" computed derived from applying the HAL method, with stop words removed, to the Reuters-21578 collection which consists of Reuters new articles in the mid-late eighties. This example demonstrates how a word is represented as a weighted vector whose dimensions comprise other words. The weights represent the strengths of association between "Iran" and other words seen in the context of the sliding window: the higher the weight of a word, the more it has lexically cooccurred with "Iran" in the same context(s). The dimensions reflect aspects which were relevant to the respective concepts during the mid to late eighties. For example, Iran was involved in a war with Iraq, and president Reagan was involved in an arms scandal involving Iran.

The quality of HAL vectors is influenced by the window size; the longer the window, the higher the chance of representing spurious associations between terms. Lund and Burgess employed a window size of 10 in their experiments [7], while Bruza and Song found the window size of 8 is ideal for the information flow model to achieve the best precision [2]. Accordingly, a window size of 8 will also be used in the Chinese information flow model.

Table 1. HAL vector

Iran	
Dimension	Value
arms	0.64
iraq	0.28
scandal	0.22
gulf	0.18
war	0.18
sales	0.18
attack	0.17
oil	0.16
offensive	0.12
missiles	0.10
reagan	0.09
...	...

More formally, a concept c is a vector representation: $c = <w_{cp_1}, w_{cp_2}, ..., w_{cp_n}>$ where $p_1, p_2, ..., p_n$ are called dimensions of c, n is the dimensionality of the HAL space, and w_{cp_i} denotes the weight of p_i in the vector representation of c. A dimension is termed a property if its weight is greater than zero. A property p_i of a concept c is a termed a *quality property* iff $w_{cp_i} > \partial$, where ∂ is a non-zero threshold value. Let $QP_\partial(c)$ denote the set of quality properties of concept c. $QP_\mu(c)$ will be used to denote the set of quality properties above mean value, and $QP(c)$ is short for $QP_0(c)$.

2.3 Combining Concepts

Our ability to combine concepts and, in particular, to *understand* new combinations of concepts is a remarkable feature of human thinking. Regarding to the context of this paper, combinations of words in document title may represent a single underlying concept, for example, "Gatt (General Agreement on Tariffs & Trade) talks". An important intuition is that one concept can dominate the other within a combination. For example, the term "Gatt" can be considered to dominate the term "talks" because it carries more of the information in the combination.

Song and Bruza [9] have proposed a concept combination heuristic, which is essentially a restricted form of vector addition whereby quality properties shared by both concepts are emphasized, the weights of the properties in the dominant concept are re-scaled higher, and the resulting vector from the combination heuristic is normalized to smooth out variations due to differing number of contexts the respective concepts appear in. The following is a fragment of the vector resulting from the combination of the HAL vectors for "gatt" and "talks" using the above combination heuristic:

gatt ⊕ talks = < agreement: 0.282, agricultural: 0.106, body: 0.117, china: 0.121, council: 0.109, farm: 0.261, gatt: 0.279, member: 0.108, negotiations: 0.108, round: 0.312, rules: 0.134, talks: 0.360, tariffs: 0.114, trade: 0.432, world: 0.114,>

2.4 HAL-Based Information Flow

As HAL vectors are not perfect representations of the associated concepts, a computation is done on how many dimensions of one concept are present in another concept.

Definition HAL-Based Information Flow

$i_1, ..., i_k \vdash j$ iff degree($\oplus c_i \triangleleft c_j) > \lambda$

where c_i denotes the conceptual representation of token i, and λ is a threshold value. ($\oplus c_i$ refers to the combination of the HAL vectors $c_1, ..., c_k$ into a single vector representation representing the combined concept. Details of a concept combination heuristic can be found in [2].

The degree of inclusion is computed in terms of the ratio of intersecting quality properties of c_i and c_j to the number of quality properties in the source c_i:

$$\text{degree}(c_i \triangleleft c_j) = \frac{\sum_{p_l \in (QP_\mu(c_i) \wedge QP(c_j))} w_{c_i p_l}}{\sum_{p_k \in QP_\mu(c_i)} w_{c_i p_k}}$$

The underlying idea of this definition is to make sure that a majority of the most important quality properties of c_i appear in c_j. Note that information flow produces truly inferential character, i.e., concept j need not be a property dimension of c_i. Table 2 shows an example of information flow computation where the weights represent the degree of information flows derived from the combination of "GATT" and "talks".

Table 2. Information flows from "Gatt talks"

Information Flows	Degree
gatt	1.00
trade	0.96
agreement	0.96
world	0.86
negotiations	0.85
talks	0.84
set	0.82
states	0.82
EC	0.81
...	...

2.5 Deriving Query Models via Information Flow

A query model can be derived as an expansion of an initial query. Bruza and Song [2] introduce an "alternative, non-probabilistic approach to query modeling", whereby the strength of information flow is computed between the query Q and the term w. To illustrate this concept, information flow can be viewed as a reflection of how strongly the term w is informationally contained within the query Q. It automatically expands the user's initial query Q with terms related to the query terms in Q yielding a query Q'. The expanded query Q' is then used to return documents to the user.

A query model can be derived from Q, where $Q = (q_1, ..., q_m)$, in the following ways:

- Compute degree($\oplus c_i \subseteq c_t$) for every term t in the vocabulary, where $\oplus c_i$ represents the conceptual combination of the HAL vectors of the individual query terms q_i, $1 \leq i \leq m$ and c_t represents the HAL vector for term t.
- The query model $Q' = <t_1 : f_1, ..., t_k : f_k>$ is comprised of the top k information flows, while f_k indicates the degree to which we can infer t_i can be inferred from Q in terms of underlying HAL space.
- The original query terms are boosted adding weights 1.0 to the above derived query model.

The weight f_i associated with the term t_1 in our query model is not probabilistically motivated. Instead, it indicates the degree to which t_1 can be referred to Q in terms of the underlying HAL space.

In order to determine the dominant concept among the query terms, concepts will be sorted by inverse document frequency multiplied by query term frequency (*qtf*idf*). More specifically, query terms can re ranked according to *qtf*idf*. Assume such a ranking of query terms: $q_1,...,q_m$ ($m > 1$). Terms q_1 and q_2 can be combined using the concept combination heuristic described in [2] to yield the combined concept $q_1 \oplus q_2$, whereby q_1 dominates q_2 (as it is higher in the ranking). The degree of dominance is directly related to the difference between the respective *qtf*idf* scores. The process recurses down the ranking resulting in the composed query "concept" $((..(q_1 \oplus q_2) \oplus q_3) \oplus ...) \oplus q_m)$. This denotes a single vector from which query models can be derived. If there is a single query term ($m =1$), it's corresponding HAL vector is used for query model derivation.

3 Evaluating Chinese Information Flow Analysis via Query Expansion

The effectiveness of information flow analysis with Chinese text can be evaluated in form of query expansion. The structure is depicted as below:

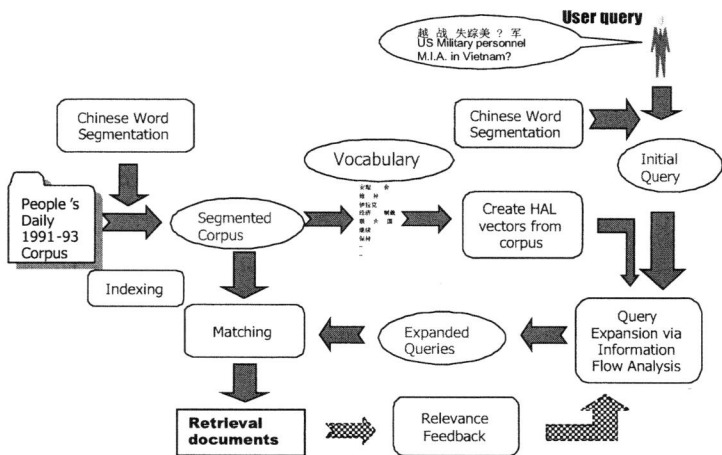

Fig. 1. Structure of the framework

Chinese Word Segmentation. Articles in the corpus will be segmented by the Chinese word segmentation. Queries will also be segmented for matching and further query expansion. The dictionary-based segmentation approach, combined with statistical mechanisms is employed.

Indexing. The segmented documents are indexed by using document term frequency and inverse document frequency (*tf*idf*). More specifically, the Okapi BM25 formula (Robertson et al, 1994) is employed. This generated index is used to match the result of information flow analysis, indicating the relevant documents.

HAL Creation. A HAL space is built from the segmented documents in the corpus.

Query Expansion via Information Flow. The word-segmented query will be expanded with further relating concepts to enrich its meaning. As detailed in Section 2, a query model is derived by from each initial query via HAL-based information flow analysis. The expanded queries will be sent to match the relevant document in the corpus.

Matching. The expanded query is matched against documents indexed by the *tf*idf* approach, while the matching function of dot product is used. The list of retrieved documents will be output to file for evaluation of the system.

Relevance Feedback. This optional module uses the top M ranked retrieved document for pseudo feedback. A sub-HAL space can be created from these documents for a more accurate information flow analysis.

3.1 Experiments

3.1.1 Experimental Setup

Corpus. The corpus of People Daily's 1991-1993 article collection is used in our system, containing 139, 801 news articles with 125 million text characters [10]. A vocabulary of 87, 780 non-stop words is established in the experiments, derived from the word segmented corpus articles. A HAL matrix is generated from the corpus.

Queries. TREC-5 Chinese topics 1-28 [10] are used in the experiments. Since general queries used in search engines are often one to three terms long, we use the topic titles as queries. Long queries may be abstracted from all sections of the topics, i.e. the description, narratives and title. In this set of TREC-5 query topics, after segmentation and stopword elimination, a long query contains 29.5 terms on average, while each query title carries on average 4.64 key terms. With 16% the size of a long query, terms in a short query carry the most straight-forward details about the query.

Two models were proposed and tested in the experiments:

HAL-Based Information Flow Model (IF). This model investigates if information flow analysis benefits to query model derivation. Prior study suggests using top 80 information flows to expand the initial query is best performing.

Information Flow Model with Pseudo Feedback (IF/Pse). This model was implemented by constructing high dimensional context space by using the top fifty documents in response to a query, and thereafter deriving a query model deriving from this local collection.

Baseline

The Okapi BM25 model with parameters ($k1=1.2$, $k2=0.0$, $b=0.75$), which is a well-known probabilistic IR model [8], is used as baseline. Query vectors are produced using query term frequency with query length normalization, which is defined similarly to the BM25's document term frequency with parameter $k3=1000$.

Performance Measures

The performance measures used in the paper include average precision (AvgPr), recall, initial precision (IniPr, i.e. interpolated precision at 0% recall) and R-precision (i.e. precision after R (= number of documents which are relevant to a query) documents have been retrieved). Among them, the Average precision is considered major performance indicator.

3.1.2 Experimental Results
The experimental results are shown as follows:

Table 3. Comparisons of various query models against the baseline model

	Baseline	IF	IF/ Pse
AvgPr	0.2526	0.3047	0.3245
IniPr	0.3357	0.4286	0.4786
Recall	1030/1378	1115/1378	1163/1378
R-Pr	0.2622	0.3195	0.3325

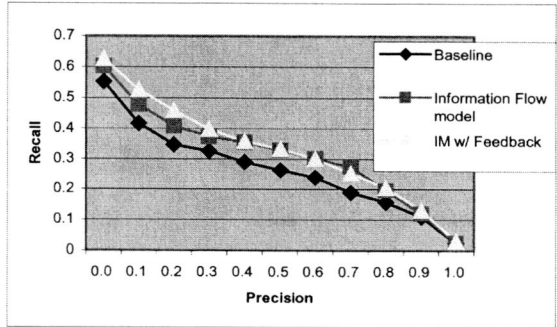

Fig. 2. Precision-recall curves comparing the baseline model with information flow models

In comparison with baseline, the performance gain in the information flow model can be as high as 27.6% with pseudo-feedback. The information flow model without feedback achieved a 20.5 % increase as compared to the baseline model. Both information flow models generate excellent recall results of over 80%, with 80.9% without feedback and 85.1% with feedback.

Comparison with English Information Flow Analysis
The HAL-based information flow model has been successfully applied to automatic query expansion for English document retrieval with encouraging results [2]. It outperforms the BM25, query expansion via pure term co-occurrence, and other two well-regarded language modelling approaches. Results from the experiments reported in this paper suggested that the Chinese information flow model largely increases average precision, though these increases were not as high at those achieved using an English corpus [2]. Table 4 summarizes the performance of English and Chinese information flow models.

The average precision increase of information flow model over baseline model is 21% (Chinese) and 28% (English). English information flow model with pseudo-feedback achieves over 41% better than baseline model, as compared to 28% of Chinese information flow model with pseudo-feedback. It is also worth to mention that the Chinese information flow model generates comparable results to the other Chinese IR systems [11].

Table 4. Comparisons of Average Precisions between English and Chinese Information Flow Model

Topics	Baseline	Information Flow Model	Information Flow Model w/ feedback
AP89 Topics 1-50	0.1824	0.247 (+35%)	0.258 (+42%)
AP89 Topics 101-150	0.210	0.265 (+26%)	0.301 (+43%)
AP89 Topics 151-200	0.249	0.298 (+20%)	0.344 (+38%)
Average of AP89 Topics	0.2138	0.27 (+ 27%)	0.301 (41%)
TREC-5 Chinese Topics	0.2526	0.3047 (+21%)	0.3245 (+28%)

The authors suggest a number of possible reasons for such difference. Firstly, different corpora and query topics may have different characteristics. Secondly, without any delimiters, Chinese word segmentation is difficult to achieve the same result as human judgment. Thirdly, due to the complexity of Chinese, words may have different versions of wordings under different dialects or local slangs, while morphologic ambiguities largely exist in Chinese. In addition, translation of foreign terms can be different with different translators.

4 Conclusion

This paper addresses an information inference mechanism based on information flow computation on a high dimensional conceptual space created by a cognitively motivated semantic space model, namely the Hyperspace Analogue to Language (HAL). A psychologistic stance has been advocated in building the "semiotic-cognitive information system, which refers to the systems manipulating "meanings", which are motivated from a cognitive perspective. This stance is expected to be language independent. To test this hypothesis, we apply the HAL-based information flow analysis to Chinese text and evaluate it via query expansion in information retrieval. Promising results are generated from the experiments, which are satisfactory when compared to similar Chinese IR models. For the TREC-5 queries and People Daily's collection, the information flow model has achieved promising results with Chinese language. An average precision of 28% over baseline model (BM25) has achieved by the Chinese information flow model with pseudo-feedback, and 20% by the model without pseudo-feedback. HAL and information flow are proved to have a high degree of language independency, indicating the HAL-based information flow model and its semiotic and cognitive nature are not bound to languages.

Acknowledgements

The work reported in this paper has been funded in part by the Co-operative Research Centre for Enterprise Distributed Systems Technology (DSTC) through the Australian Federal Government's CRC Programme (Department of Education, Science and Training), and by CUHK under the Strategic Grant Initiative (Project account no: 4410001). The authors would like to thank Zi Huang for her great work and assistance on the Chinese word segmentation system.

References

1. Barwise, J., & Seligman, J. (1997) Information Flow: The Logic of Distributed Systems. Cambridge Tracts in Theoretical Computer Science 44.
2. Bruza, P.D. and Song, D. (2002) Inferring Query Models by Information Flow Analysis. In: Proceedings of the 11th International ACM Conference on Information and Knowledge Management (CIKM 2002) pp.260-269.
3. Burgess, C., & Lund, K. (1997) Parsing Constraints and High-Dimensional Semantic Space. Language and Cognitive Processes, 12, pp.177-210.
4. Burgess, C., Livesay, L., & Lund, K. (1998) Explorations in Context Space: Words, Sentences, Discourse, In Foltz, P.W. (Ed) Quantitative Approaches to Semantic Knowledge Representation. Discourse Processes, 25(2&3), pp. 179-210.
5. Gärdenfors, P. (2000) Conceptual Spaces: The Geometry of Thought. MIT Press.
6. Landauer, T., and Dumais, S. (1997). A Solution to Plato's problem: The latent semantic analysis theory of acquisition, induction, and representation of knowledge. Psychological Review, 104(2), 211-240.
7. Lund, K., & Burgess, C. (1996) Producing High-dimensional Semantic Spaces from Lexical Co-occurrence. Behavior Research Methods, Instruments, & Computers, 28(2), pp. 203-208
8. Robertson, S.E., Walker, S., Spark-Jones, K., Hancock-Beaulieu, M.M., & Gatford, M. (1994) OKAPI at TREC-3. In Proceedings of the 3rd Text Retrieval Conference (TREC-3). pp. 109-126
9. Song, D. and Bruza, P.D. (2003) Towards context-sensitive information inference. Journal of the American Society for Information Science and Technology, Volume 54, Number 4, pp. 321-334.
10. Text Retrieval Conference (TREC), National Institution of Standards and Technology(NIST). http://trec.nist.gov/data/
11. Cheong, P., Song, D., Bruza, P.D., Wong, K.F. (2004) Information Flow Analysis with Chinese Text. In Proceedings of the 1st International Joint Conference on Natural Language Processing (IJCNLP-04). pp. 91-98. *Hainan Island, China, 2004.*

Phoneme-Based Transliteration of Foreign Names for OOV Problem

Wei Gao, Kam-Fai Wong, and Wai Lam

Department of Systems Engineering and Engineering Management,
The Chinese University of Hong Kong, Shatin, N.T., Hong Kong
{wgao,kfwong,wlam}@se.cuhk.edu.hk

Abstract. A proper noun dictionary is never complete rendering name translation from English to Chinese ineffective. One way to solve this problem is not to rely on a dictionary alone but to adopt automatic translation according to pronunciation similarities, i.e. to map phonemes comprising an English name to the phonetic representations of the corresponding Chinese name. This process is called transliteration. We present a statistical transliteration method. An efficient algorithm for aligning phoneme chunks is described. Unlike rule-based approaches, our method is data-driven. Compared to source-channel based statistical approaches, we adopt a direct transliteration model, i.e. the direction of probabilistic estimation conforms to the transliteration direction. We demonstrate comparable performance to source-channel based system.

1 Introduction

In cross language information retrieval (CLIR), query expressed in a source language is used to retrieve information represented in a target language. It involves keyword translation from the source to the target language and document translation in the opposite direction. Proper nouns, i.e. names of people, places, companies, etc., are by far the most frequent targets in queries. Contemporary dictionary-based translation techniques are ineffective as name dictionaries can never be comprehensive. New foreign names appear almost daily; and they become unregistered vocabulary in the dictionary. This brings about the classical Out-Of-Vocabulary (OOV) problem in lexicography. OOV names can worsen the performance of translation and retrieval.

Based on phonology, foreign name can usually be translated, or more appropriately transliterated into its target counterpart in terms of pronunciation similarities between them. Transliteration rules are practically mapping templates between the phonemes of source and target names. Existing rule bases are compiled manually. They are not easy to expand and are mostly non-universal, i.e. they are subjected to the interpretation of individual producers. In Mandarin of China mainland, for instance, the name of "Bin Laden" can be translated as /ben la deng[1]/ (本拉登), /bin la deng/ (宾拉登), /ben la dan/ (本拉丹) and /bin la dan/ (宾拉丹). In Taiwan's Mandarin, similar transliteration confusions exist as well: "Hussein" corresponds to /hai shan/ (海珊), /ha shan/ (哈珊) and /hu sheng/ (胡笙). Chinese dialects further render rule-based approach inefficient. Some popular names of celebrities initially transliterated

---

[1] Mandarin pinyin is used as phonetic representation of Chinese characters throughout this paper. For simplicity, we ignore the four tones in the pinyin system.

by Cantonese are somehow spreading in Mandarin: /lang na du/ (朗拿度), the Cantonese transliteration of "Ronaldo", often appears in Mandarin news media as equivalent to its Mandarin transliteration /luo na er duo/ (罗纳尔多). Thus, rule-based approach has been undermined and an effective data-driven transliteration method is required.

In this paper, we present a statistical method for phoneme-based transliteration of foreign names from English to Chinese. Phonological transformation knowledge is acquired automatically by machine learning from existing source-target name pairs. Unlike source-channel based methods, it starts off with the direct estimation on transliteration model, which is then incorporated with target language model for the post-correction of generated hypotheses. Section 2 summarizes related work, in particular with source-channel model; Section 3 presents our model in detail; Section 4 elaborates the implementation of the model; Section 5 gives experimental results and analysis; Section 6 concludes the paper.

2 Related Work

Virga and Khudanpur [8] described a data-driven transliteration technique based on IBM's source-channel model, which was initially proposed for French-to-English statistical machine translation [3]. The fundamental equation is from Bayes' rule:

$$\hat{C} = \arg\max_{C} p(C \mid E) = \arg\max_{C} p(E \mid C)p(C) = \arg\max_{c_1 c_2 \ldots c_{|C|}} p(e_1^{|E|} \mid c_1^{|C|})p(c_1^{|C|}) \cdot \quad (1)$$

where $E = e_1^{|E|} = e_1 e_2 \ldots e_{|E|}$ denotes a $|E|$-phoneme English name as the observation on channel output, and $C = c_1^{|C|} = c_1 c_2 \ldots c_{|C|}$ represents E's $|C|$-phoneme Chinese translation as the source of channel input. $|E|$ and $|C|$ are the number of sound units they contain. The channel decoder reverses the direction, i.e. to find the most probable pinyin sequence $\hat{C}$ given an observation E, which indirectly maximizes the posterior probability $p(C|E)$ via optimal combination of the *inverted*-transliteration model $p(E|C)$ and the target language model $p(C)$. $p(E|C)$ was trained on name pairs represented by ARPABET symbols at English side and pinyin notations at Chinese side. It proceeded with a standard bootstrapping of IBM's translation model training in GIZA++ [1]: 5 EM iterations of Model-1 followed by 5 of Model-2, 10 of HMM and 10 of Model-4. $p(C)$ was trained on a pinyin vocabulary using tri-gram with Good-Turing smoothing and Katz back-off by CMU-Cambridge Language Modeling Toolkits [4]. Decoding was done by using USC-ISI ReWrite Decoder [5]. Note that the estimation of $p(E|C)$ is in the reversed direction, i.e. from Chinese to English. In fact, this is within the same framework as the generative model for Japanese-to-English backward transliteration proposed by [6]. The method demonstrated pinyin error rates in edit distance by 42.5%~50.8% on different data [8].

3 Our Forward Transliteration Model

3.1 Pitfalls of Source-Channel Model

The source-channel model in Eq-1 has two limitations for our task:

1. It is hard to extend the baseline of transliteration model by introducing additional dependencies [7], such as flexible neighboring or contextual phoneme features;
2. It allows only one target language phoneme to be associated with a contiguous group of source language phonemes, but not vice versa. The example in [8] exposes this limitation (see Fig. 1): /u/ and the second /i/ in the third line have to be looked as "spuriously" produced from dumb sound ε. Under IBM's model, such "inserted" symbols are known as *zero fertility* "words". They are "deleted" by source-channel during training and "reproduced" when decoding by considering inserting one of them before each target symbol of each remaining unaligned source phoneme according to the number of possible *zero fertility* symbols [5]. Although adding *zero fertility* symbols may increase the probability of hypotheses, incorrect transliterations are still abundant as such insertions are frequent. Without the loss of generality, it would be more natural and easier to handle if /f-u/ and /s-i/ were looked as initial-final clusters converted from single English phoneme /F/ and /S/. This is feasible under our direct model.

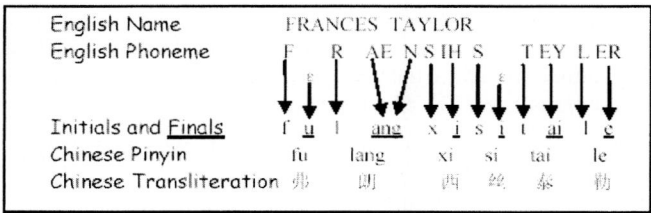

Fig. 1. An example depicting the process of English-to-Chinese transliteration in [8]

3.2 Soundness of Direct Model

We substitute $p(C|E)$ for $p(E|C)$ in Eq-1 so that we have a different forward transliteration method as follows:

$$\hat{C} = \arg\max_{C} p(C|E)p(C) = \arg\max_{c_1 c_2 \ldots c_{|C|}} p(c_1^{|C|} | e_1^{|E|}) p(c_1^{|C|}) \cdot \quad (2)$$

The basic idea is that a direct transliteration model $p(C|E)$ concentrates on producing the most likely transcriptions for a given E, probably with ill-formed pinyin sequences though, and the language model $p(C)$ helps make corrections on the forms, e.g. eliminating illegal pinyin strings and yields better rankings of result syllables. Although Eq-2 is beyond the Bayes' theorem, it is mathematically sound under the more general Maximum Entropy (MaxEnt) principle [2,7]. We explain it briefly for completeness.

MaxEnt is a well-founded framework for directly modeling the posterior probability, where a set of M feature functions $h_m(E, C)$ and their corresponding model parameters λ_m, $m = 1, \ldots, M$, are introduced. The direct transliteration probability is given by:

$$p(C|E) = p_{\lambda_1^M}(C|E) = \frac{\exp\left[\sum_{m=1}^{M} \lambda_m h_m(E,C)\right]}{\sum_{E'} \exp\left[\sum_{m=1}^{M} \lambda_m h_m(E',C)\right]} \cdot \quad (3)$$

[7] suggested we could obtain the target sequence $\hat{C}$ that maximizes the posterior probability by omitting the normalization constant denominator:

$$\hat{C} = \arg\max_{C} p(C \mid E) = \arg\max_{C} \left\{ \exp\left[\sum_{m=1}^{M} \lambda_m h_m(E,C)\right] \right\}. \quad (4)$$

Then we select two feature functions and parameters: $h_1(E, C) = \log p_\theta(C|E)$, $h_2(E, C) = \log p_\gamma(C)$, $\lambda_1 = \lambda_2 = 1$. Thus the Eq-2 maximization obtains in combination of the direct $p_\theta(C|E)$ and $p_\gamma(C)$ with respect to model parameters θ and γ. The optimal parameters are to be estimated individually on parallel training corpus.

We summarize 4 possible general conditions mapping an English phoneme to items in pinyin's vocabulary in accordance with this direct model:

1. An English phoneme maps to an initial or a final, which is the most usual case;
2. An English phoneme maps to an initial-final cluster, e.g. /F/ - /fu/ and /S/ - /si/ in previous example;
3. An English phoneme maps to dumb sound ε, e.g. /S T AE N F ER D/ (Stanford) to /si tan fu/ (斯坦福), where /D/ is omitted in translation;
4. Insert additional pinyin syllables, e.g. /F L OY D/ (Floyd) to /fu luo yi de/ (弗洛伊德), where /yi/ is inserted to cater for the sound /OY/ that has already been mapped to /uo/.

4 Direct Model Training

4.1 Alignment of Phoneme Chunks

We first introduce alignment indicators in a pair of sound sequences. Within total 39 phonemes (24 consonants, 15 vowels) in the English sound inventory and 58 pinyin symbols (23 initials and 35 finals) in Chinese, there are always some indicative sound units (indicators) that help for alignment. For E, they are: all the consonants; vowel at the first position; and the second vowel of two contiguous vowels. In C, accordingly, they are: all the initials; final at the first position; and the second final of two contiguous finals. Note that similar indicators are easily identifiable in other Romanized systems in Chinese. They are independent of alignment model.

We define the following variables: $\tau(S) = $ # *of indicators in sequence S, $t = max\{\tau(E), \tau(C)\}$, and $d = |\tau(E) - \tau(C)|$. We chunk E and C by tagging their indicators and compensate the one with fewer indicators by inserting d dumb sound ε(s) at its $min\{\tau(E), \tau(C)\}$ possible positions ahead of its indicators. ε is practically also an indicator defined for alignment. This ensures that both sequences end up with the same number of indicators. The t chunks separated by indicators in E should align to the corresponding t chunks in C in the same order. They are called *alignment chunks*. There are $\|A\| = \left[P_t^d \right] = \dfrac{t!}{(t-d)!\, d!}$ number of possible alignments at chunk level with respect to different positions of ε.

This method can guarantee each chunk contains two sound units at most. Thus, in a pair of aligned chunks, only three mapping layouts are possible for individual units:

1. e-to-c_1c_2: The alignment would be e-to-c_1c_2 where c_1c_2 is considered as an initial-final cluster;
2. e_1e_2-to-c_1c_2: The alignment would be e_1-to-c_1 and e_2-to-c_2;
3. e_1e_2-to-c: By adding a ε at C side, the alignment would be considered as e_1-to-c and e_2-to-ε or e_1-to-ε and e_2-to-c. In this case, we update $||A|| = ||A|| + 1$.

Fig. 2 shows the alignment chunks (indicators are tagged using '|') between the example pair /AE L B AH K ER K IY/ (Albuquerque) and /a er bo ke er ji/ (阿尔伯克尔基), where 5 alignments are possible at chunk level. But the total possible alignments would be 9 due to the existence of /K ER/ - /er/ in the first 4 alignments.

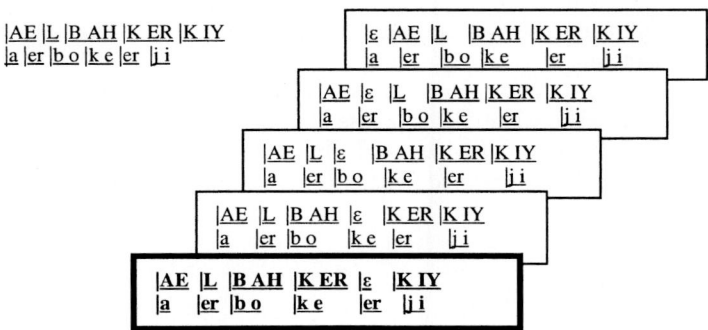

Fig. 2. An example depicting alignments of phoneme chunks between a name pair

4.2 EM Training for Symbol-Mapping Probabilities

We then applied EM training to find the most probable alignment (Viterbi alignment) for each name pair and compute symbol-mapping probabilities. The training goes as follows:

```
1) Initialization: For each name pair, assign equal weights ||A||⁻¹ to
   all alignments based on phoneme chunks.
2) Expectation: For each of the 40 English phonemes, count the instances
   of its different mappings on all alignments produced. Each alignment
   contributes counts in proportion to its own weight. Normalize the
   scores of the pinyin sound units it maps to so that the mapping prob-
   ability sums to 1.
3) Maximization: Re-compute the alignment scores. Each alignment is
   scored with the product of the scores of the symbol-mappings it con-
   tains. Normalize the alignment scores so that each pair's alignments
   scores sum to 1.
4) Repeat step 2-3 until the symbol-mapping probabilities converge, i.e.
   the variation of each probability between two iterations becomes less
   than a specified threshold.
```

Compared to the brutal-force alignment [6], our EM training based on aligned phoneme chunks produces much fewer possible alignments, thus fewer possible mappings for each English phoneme. Mappings crossing chunks are also avoided. Therefore, the symbol-mappings tend to be more accurate. For each pair, the Viterbi alignment is found whose alignment score (weight) approaches to 1 with the iteration.

Dumb sound ε is introduced to both sides of phonetic alphabets during the processing of phoneme chunks. It plays an important role for the case 3 and 4 in Section 3.2. The EM training also calculates the transition probabilities from English phonemes to initial-final clusters. The algorithm identifies these clusters and dynamically appends them to pinyin inventory as additional candidates for transcriptions. This can improve the shortcomings caused by *zero fertility* symbols in source-channel model.

4.3 WFST for Phonetic Transition

We then build a weighted finite state transducer (WFST) based on the symbol-mapping table for the transcription of each English phoneme into its possible pinyin counterparts. Each arc carries the transition labels and transition costs. Fig. 3 shows part of the transducer. Note that the arcs such as [AA:uo|0.904] are split into multiple arcs, i.e. [AA:u|0.904] and [ε:o|0] jointed by intermediate nodes 1, 2,...5,... This is for the following transducer for pinyin syllable segmentation being able to connect with it.

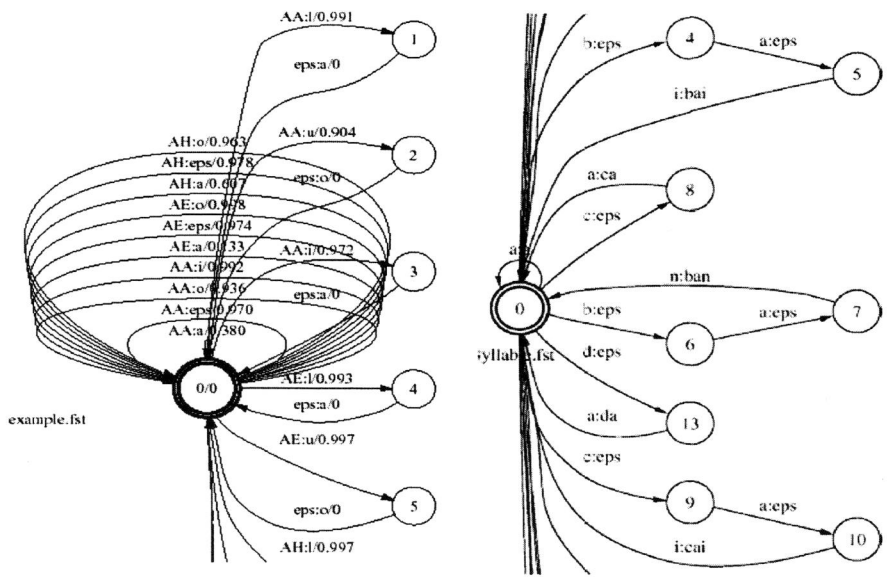

Fig. 3. Part of the WFST[2] based on $p(C|E)$

Fig. 4. Part of the FST for pinyin syllabification

4.4 Issues of Illegal Pinyin Syllables

Many pinyin symbol sequences produced by the transliteration model cannot be syllabified or include illegitimate syllables as the transducer has no knowledge about pinyin's regulations. Actually only 396 of 23*25 possible combinations of initials and finals can constitute legal pinyin syllables. We can easily collect them from our cor-

---

[2] Label "eps" in the figure represents dumb sound ε (epsilon).

pus by using an automatic scanning program. Based on this knowledge, we construct a FST as shown in Fig. 4. It is composed with the previous WFST for sifting out illegal pinyin sequences and segmenting them into syllables.

4.5 Language Model Training and Bi-gram WFSA

A syllable-based bi-gram language model of pinyin is trained using the Chinese part of the same 41,674 instances, on which the transliteration WFST is built. The model $P(C)$ is approximated by counting the frequencies of syllable occurrences in this data set using the equation:

$$p(C) \cong \prod_i p(c_i \mid c_{i-1}) \cong \prod_i \frac{count\ (c_i c_{i-1})}{count\ (c_i)} . \tag{5}$$

where c_i is the pinyin syllable of a Chinese character.

We then implement the bi-gram model using a weighted finite state acceptor (WFSA) with one state for each item in the pinyin syllable vocabulary. Between each pair of states, say x/y, there is a single transition whose label is the syllable y and whose probability is $p(y|x)$. We then add a special final state with transitions leading to it from every other state labeled by ε with probability 1.0. Finally, a start state is added with transitions to every state y with label y and probability $p(y)$.

The WFSA is used to re-rank the pinyin syllable sequences yielded from the composition of the previous two transducers and the search results of k-best path algorithm. Because the search space of the syllables produced by the previous transducers is extremely large, we apply the bi-gram search to only the first few hundred candidates for each English name.

5 Experiments and Evaluation

5.1 Similarity Measurement

Similarity measurement is based on edit distance, which is defined as the minimum number of insertions, deletions and substitutions required for transforming one string to the other. The performance of transliteration is measured by error rate, which is defined as: $e = d(S_1, S_2) / |S_2|$, where S_1 is the machine transliteration and S_2 the standard, $d(S_1, S_2)$ denotes the edit distance between the two transliterations, and $|S_2|$ is the length of S_2.

The process is participated by a bilingual dictionary (LDC's English-Chinese bilingual named entity list beta v.1.0), an English pronunciation dictionary (CMU's pronunciation dictionary) and a Chinese character-pinyin table (LDC's Chinese character table with pinyin). We harvest 46,305 name pairs from the bilingual dictionary, all of which also appear in the pronunciation dictionary with deterministic phonemic representations. We obtain English name pronunciations and their Chinese equivalents by looking up the pronunciation dictionary and the character-pinyin conversion table. In the experiments, 41,674 name pairs are used for training, in which a portion of 4,631 pairs is used for close test, and the remaining 4,631 pairs for open test.

5.2 Experimental Results

Experiment I. Only top-1 machine transliteration of each name is chosen for comparison with the standard translation. We set up six error rate ranges: [0%], (0%~20%], (20%~40%], (40%~60%], (60%~80%] and (80%~100%][3]. We count the number of names whose error rate falls in each range and the accumulative percentages are listed in Table 1.

Table 1. Results of experiment I

Error rate (%)	0	0~20	20~40	40~60	60~80	80~100
Close	12.33%	10.39%	34.36%	28.34%	9.91%	4.67%
Open	10.20%	12.13%	33.58%	29.29%	10.40%	4.40%

Experiment II. The system yields top-50 candidates for each foreign name. We count the number of correct transliterations whose error rate is 0. The accumulative percentage is listed in Table 2. This test evaluates the proportion of instances whose correct transliteration can be found in top-n generated candidates.

Table 2. Results of experiment II

Top n	1	10	20	30	40	50
Close	12.33%	50.32%	59.20%	61.81%	62.98%	63.63%
Open	10.20%	46.56%	54.87%	57.82%	58.84%	59.23%

Experiment III. For comparison with source-channel based system, we implement the work desribed in [8]. We replicate their first traslation system [8] with the only exception that we obtain phoneme sequences of English names via looking up pronunciation dictionary instead of text-to-speech system. We test our system and our implementation of [8]'s system on the aforementioned data set. The averaged error rate of top-1 machine transliterations is shown in Table 3.

Table 3. Transliteration error rates compared to the source-channel based system

Systems	Source-Channel	Ours
Close	33.65%	38.00%
Open	34.85%	38.50%

So far, the transliteration model and the language model are both trained on the same 41,674 instances. To explore the influence of the two components separately, we train our transliteration model on the 4,631 instances for close test and keep the language model intact. We achieve error rate of 42.67% in open test. Then we train the language model on this 4,631 instances and reuse the previous transliteration model. This time, the error rate rises up to 46.78%.

---

[3] (M%~N%] denotes > M% AND ≤ N%.

5.3 Discussions

In experiment I, the possibility of finding correct transliterations in top-1 result candidates is fairly low, evidenced as only 12.33% and 10.20% of test instances end up with correct transliterations. If we consider acceptable transliterations whose error rate is less than 20%, the accumulative percentage would be 22.72% and 22.33% for the close and open test respectively. Two pinyin sequences having 20% edit distance can be exemplified as /ben la deng/ (本拉登) and /ben la dan/ (本拉丹). Hence, machine transliterations with 20% error rate or less can be considered as phonetically equivalent but misspelled.

From experiment II where top-50 transliterations are examined, nearly half of the test instances (50.32% for close test and 46.56% for open test) can have their correct transliterations within top-10 transliteration candidates. We also note the considerable increase on the percentage of correct transliterations if we examine top-20 candidates compared to only top-1. But no apparent improvement is achieved if we further yield more top candidates.

In experiment III, our approach demonstrates comparable performance to source-channel based system, but slightly worse by 4.35% on close test and 3.65% on open test in averaged error rates. The error rates (between 30% and 40%) indicate that the top-1 transliterations from the two systems are generally acceptable. Error rate more than 50% should be unacceptable since two pinyin sequences with 50% difference in edit distance are identified as phonetic representations of nearly different names like /ya li shan da/ (亚力山大) and /ya li shi duo de/ (亚里士多德).

Furthermore, the distinct rise of error to 46.78% indicates that our approach is more sensitive to the language model than to the transliteration model. The paucity of data can affect the search using language model, evidenced by the serious error increase as the language model is trained on sparse data. The reason is that transliteration model only reflects symbol-mapping relationships among phonemes rather than sequences, leaving lots of work to be done by language model. The problem is supposed to be alleviated by improving the transliteration model further.

6 Conclusion and Future Work

We model the statistical transliteration problem as a direct phonetic symbol transcription model plus a language model for post-adjustment. The baseline indicates a comparable performance suggested by source-channel based system. The advantage of direct method is its flexibility for incorporating features with respect to dependencies among surrounding phonemes. We can expand our transliteration model in the future using contextual feature functions within MaxEnt framework [2]. Also, we will improve our language model using tri-gram for a better accuracy or smoothing techniques for overcoming data sparseness.

References

1. Al-Onaizan, Y., Curin, J., Jahr, M., Knight, K., Lafferty, J., Melamed, D., Och, F.J., Purdy, D., Smith, N.A., Yarowsky, D.: Statistical machine translation. Final Report of JHU Workshop (1999).

2. Berger, A.L., Della Pietra, S.A., Della Pietra, V.J.: A maximum entropy approach to natural language processing. Computational Linguistics (1996) 22(1): 39-72.
3. Brown, P.F., Della Pietra, S.A., Della Pietra, V.J., Mercer, R.L.: The mathematics of statistical machine translation: Parameter estimation. Computational Linguistics (1993) 19(2): 263-311.
4. Clarkson, P., Rosenfeld, R.: Statistical language modeling using the CMU-Cambridge toolkit. In Proc. of the 5th European Conf. on Speech Communication and Technology (1997) 2707-2710.
5. Germann, U., Jahr, M, Knight, K., Marcu, D., Yamada, K.: Fast decoding and optimal decoding for machine translation. In Proc. of the 39th Annual Meeting of ACL (2001) 228-235.
6. Knight, K., Graehl, J.: Machine transliteration. In Proc. of the 35th Annual Meeting of ACL (1997) 128-135.
7. Och, F.J., Ney, H.: Discriminative training and maximum entropy models for statistical machine translation. In Proc. of the 40th Annual Meeting of ACL (2002) 295-302.
8. Virga, P., Khudanpur, S.: Transliteration of proper names in cross-lingual information retrieval. In Proc. of the ACL Workshop on Multi-lingual Named Entity Recognition (2003).

Window-Based Method for Information Retrieval

Qianli Jin, Jun Zhao, and Bo Xu

National Laboratory of Pattern Recognition
Institute of Automation, Chinese Academy of Science
Beijing P.O. Box 2728, China, 100080
{qljin,jzhao,bxu}@nlpr.ia.ac.cn

Abstract. In this paper, a series of window-based methods is proposed for information retrieval. Compared with traditional tf-idf model, our approaches are based on two new key notions. The first one is that the closer the query words in a document, the larger the similarity value between the query and the document. And the second one is that some query words, like named entities and baseNP called "Core Words" are much more important than other words, and should have special weights. We implement the above notions by three models. They are Simple Window-based Model, Dynamic Window-based Model and Core Window-based Model. Our models can compute similarities between queries and documents based on the importance and distribution of query words in the documents. TREC data are used to test the algorithms. The experiments indicate that our window-based methods outperform most of the traditional methods, such as tf-idf and Okapi BM25. And the Core Window-based Model is the best and most robust model for various queries.

Keywords: Information Retrieval, Window-based Method, Named Entity

1 Introduction

Information retrieval is recently one of the hotspots in nature language processing. The key algorithm of an IR system is similarity computing between queries and documents. Till now, the most popular algorithm is the inner product of vectors, and the vectors can be built by using weighting technologies, such as binary weight, tf-idf, query expansion, relevant feedback and etc. In other words, most of the existing algorithms are based on vector computing. However, this method usually gets limited precision, because sometimes, a vector can not represent a query properly. For instance, if we have the following query and two documents:

Query: "Can radio waves from radio towers or car phones affect brain cancer occurrence?"

Document A: "John claimed his brain cancer was caused by the wave from his cellular phone. That claim, put forth in a lawsuit, has no basis in accepted scientific fact."

Document B: "I was listening to the radio, when the tower collapsed. I ran several blocks before my brain kicked in, and saw that another wave of people started running towards a police car."

We definitely know that Document A is relevant to the Query, while Document B is not. But if binary word vector model is used, the similarity value between Document B and the query is larger than the one between Document A and the query. We also try some other weighting technologies such as tf-idf, query expansion and etc., but find that in this case, based on vector computing, Document B seems more "relevant" to the query than Document A. Why does this situation appear? Though Document B includes many query words, they appear separately in the different parts of the document. A separate word can hardly represent a clear meaning. Usually, a query consists of several words, which as a whole represents a meaning. Just as the above example, when "phone" and "brain cancer" appear together closely in the same sentence of the document, we have the confidence to say that this document is relevant to the query (as Document A). However, when these query words appear separately in the document, it may be irrelevant to the query (as Document B). So, **the first key notion** of our window-based method is as follows:

> *Query words appearing closely in the document provide more contributions to the similarity value than the ones appearing separately. The closer the query words in a document, the larger the similarity value between the query and the document.*

In the traditional tf-idf method, different query words are given different weights based on inverse document frequency (idf). So, the frequently used words are given smaller weights because of their less importance. Sometimes, it works well. However, in some cases, it is unreasonable. In the example query, "radio wave" and "brain cancer" is much more important than other words, because they represent the main meaning of the query. While other words, like "phone", "affect", are less important. So, we should improve the weighting technology based on the characteristics of the different queries. It's well know that Named Entities and some nouns are most important in all the query words. According to this, we develop **the second key notion** of our window-based method as follows:

> *Some query words, like named entities and baseNP are called "Core Words", while the other words are called "Surrounding Words". "Core Words" are much more important than "Surrounding Words", and should have special status in the retrieval processing (i.e. having larger weights).*

Based on the two key notions expressed above, we develop a series of window-based methods for information retrieval. In the next section, we will express them in mathematic models. And the experiments show that window-based methods outperform the existing vector-based method, such as binary weight, tf-idf, query expansion and etc.

2 Window-Based Method for Information Retrieval

Based on the above two key notions, we developed three window-based models for the application of information retrieval. They are called "Simple Window-based Model", "Dynamic Window-based Model" and "Core-window-based Model", from the simplest model to the most complex one. We implement our first key notion in Model One and Two, and implement our second key notion in Model Three.

2.1 Model One: Simple Window-Based Model

As our first key notion, the closer the query words in a document, the larger the similarity value between the query and the document. So, we introduce a window in the retrieval processing. When the query words co-occur in the window, a larger similarity weight is provided.

First we put all the words of the document into the word sequence orderly, like the Figure 1. Each sub-sequence with d continual words is included in a d-width window. Let N denote the number of the words in the whole sequence, and d denote the width of the window. Then the similarity value (Sim1(Q,D)) between query and document can be represented as follows:

$$Sim1(Q,D) = \sum_{i=1}^{N-d} SWin(i, i+d) \tag{1}$$

$$SWin(i, i+d) = [\sum_{j=i}^{i+d} t_j * idf_j] * [\sum_{j=i}^{i+d} t_j] \tag{2}$$

where SWin(i,i+d) denotes the similarity value between the query and the d-width window from the ith word to (i+d)th word in the whole sequence in the Simple Window-based Model. tj is the binary signal of the jth word in the whole sequence. Here, tj is equal to ONE if the jth word is a query word, otherwise, it is equal to ZERO. And idfj is the inverse document frequency of the jth word in the sequence.

The final similarity value between a query and a document is the sum of the similarity values of all the windows. The similarity value in a single window, represented as Formula 2, consists of two items. The first one $[\sum_{j=i}^{i+d} t_j * idf_j]$ is just like the traditional tf-idf method. And the second one $[\sum_{j=i}^{i+d} t_j]$ provides more weight, when more than one query word appeared in the corresponding window. If there are 3 query words in a window, we will get 3 times of the original tf-idf value. So, the more query words in the window, the larger the final similarity value.

Let's take a look at the above example again. Some tj and idfj values are listed in the Finger 1. The values of idfj are logarithmic inverse document frequencies learned from large corpora, and are listed below.

Word	brain	cancer	radio	tower
idf	2.27	2.13	1.14	2.04
Word	phone	wave	Car	
idf	1.75	1.74	1.25	

Using the traditional tf-idf model, we can get:

Sim(query,document A) = 6.15   Sim(query,document B) = 8.44

That means document B is more relevant. While, by using Simple Window-based Model with the 5-width window, the result will be:

Sim1(query,document A) = 46.08   Sim1(query,document B) = 43.56

That means document A is more relevant to the query. The number of query words in document A is less, but they are closer with each other and closer in meaning with the query. So, our approach is more reasonable compared with tf-idf. Later, the experiments of TREC data also support this conclusion.

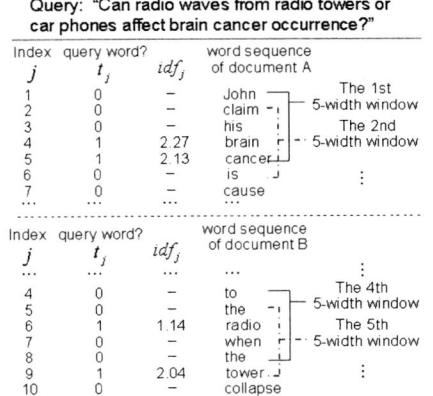

Fig. 1. Example for window-based method   **Fig. 2.** Example for the value of *TightWin*

2.2 Model Two: Dynamic Window-Based Model

In Simple Window-based Model, we give larger weight to the window, which includes more than one query word. But what is the distribution of these query words in the window? They can be separate or conjoint. If these query words in the window are conjoint, they maybe form a phrase. Phrases usually are less ambiguous than words. So, we should give the conjoint query words larger weight than the separate query words in the window. Another problem in Model One is that it is difficult to decide the width of window in real applications. A fixed window width cannot be suitable for all queries. In order to solve the above two problems, Model Two is proposed, which is called Dynamic Window-based Model. In this Model, a dynamic window width called "TightWin" is developed to modify the original fixed window.

Define: TightWin is the smallest window width, which can overlay all the query words in the original window.

In Figure 2, we give several examples about the value of TightWin. If the query words distribute separately in the original window, the value of TightWin is large. And if they are conjoint, the TightWin is small. So, we should give a large weight when TightWin is small.

Let N denote the number of the words in the whole sequence, and d denote the width of the window. Then the similarity values between query and document in Model Two (Sim2(Q,D)) can be represented as follows:

$$Sim\,2(Q,D) = \sum_{i=1}^{N-d} DWin\,(i,i+d) \qquad (3)$$

$$DWin(i, i+d) = SWin(i, i+d) * \left(\frac{[\sum_{j=i}^{i+d} t_j]}{TightWin}\right)^p \qquad (4)$$

$$= [\sum_{j=i}^{i+d} t_j * idf_j] * [\sum_{j=i}^{i+d} t_j] * \left(\frac{[\sum_{j=i}^{i+d} t_j]}{TightWin}\right)^p$$

where DWin(i,i+d) denotes the similarity value between the query and the d-width window from the ith word to (i+d)th word in the whole sequence in Dynamic Window-based Model. tj is the binary signal of the jth word in the whole sequence. Here, tj is equal to ONE if the jth word is a query word, otherwise, it is equal to ZERO. And idfj is the inverse document frequency of the jth word in the sequence.

TightWin is defined above, and p is a parameter, which is larger than zero.

Compared with Model One, Model Two has an additional item $([\sum_{j=i}^{i+d} t_j]/TightWin)^p$, which provide adjustment to the original fixed window. For example, when 3 query words appear conjointly, the value of this item will be $(3/3)^p = 1$. When these 3 query words appear separately in the 5-width window, it will be $(3/5)^p = 0.6^p$, which is less than 1. So, conjoint query words provide more contributions to the final similarity value.

For the example in Figure 1, we can compute the similarity value between query and documents by using Formula (3) and (4) with 5-width window as follows (p=1.0):

Sim2(query, document A) = 46.08 Sim2(query, document B) = 37.20

Comparing the two values, we can make sure that document A is more relevant to the query than document B, because the first value is larger than the second one. Later, the experiments show that Model Two outperforms Model One.

Actually, in our window-based model, similarity value between a query and a document is not only decided by appearance of the query words in the document, but also decided by the distribution of the query words in the document. Model One describes the distribution model of the query words outside the window. And Model Two additionally describes the distribution model inside the window. So, our first key notion is wholly implemented by the first two models.

2.3 Model Three: Core Window-Based Model

In the above two models, when query words appear closely in the document, they will be given larger weight. In some cases, it may bring some problems. Take a look at the above example query again.

"Can radio waves from radio towers or car phones affect brain cancer occurrence?"

When the query words "radio waves" and "brain cancer" appear closely in a document, we can say that this document is most likely relevant to the query. But, when the query words "car phone" and "affect" appear closely in a document, we are not sure whether it is relevant.

So, based our second key notion, we parse the query sentence and classify the query words into two groups. They are "Core Words" and "Surrounding Words" defined as follows.

Define: (1) The query words, which represent the main meaning of the query, such as baseNP and Named Entities, are called "Core Words".
(2) The query words, which are not core words, are called "Surrounding Word".
(3) A window is called "Active Window", if and only if it includes Core Words.

Obviously, Core Words are much more important than Surrounding Word. So, Active Window should have larger weight than the common window.

Let N denote the number of the words in the whole sequence, and d denote the width of the window. Then the similarity value between query and document in Model Three (Sim3(Q,D)) can be represented as follows:

$$Sim3(Q,D) = \sum_{i=1}^{N-d} CWin(i, i+d) \tag{5}$$

$$\begin{aligned} CWin(i, i+d) &= DWin(i, i+d) * [\sum_{j=i}^{i+d} t_j^*] \\ &= [\sum_{j=i}^{i+d} t_j * idf_j] * [\sum_{j=i}^{i+d} t_j] * (\frac{[\sum_{j=i}^{i+d} t_j]}{TightWin})^p * [\sum_{j=i}^{i+d} t_j^*]^m \end{aligned} \tag{6}$$

where CWin(i,i+d) denotes the similarity value between the query and the d-width window from the ith word to (i+d)th word in the whole sequence in Core Window-based Model. tj is the binary signal of the jth word in the whole sequence. Here, tj is equal to ONE if the jth word is a query word, otherwise, it is equal to ZERO. t_j^* is another binary signal of the jth word in the whole sequence for Core Words. t_j^* is equal to ONE if the jth word is a Core Word, otherwise, it is equal to ZERO. And idfj is the inverse document frequency of the jth word in the sequence. TightWin is defined in 2.2, and m is a parameter, which is larger than zero.

Compared with Model Two, Model Three has an additional item $([\sum_{j=i}^{i+d} t_j^*])^m$, which focuses on the Core Words in the window. For example, when 3 core words co-occur in a window, this window is "active" and the value of this item will be 3^m. When these are no Core Words in a window, the window is not active and the value will be zero. So, only the active window has contributions to the final similarity value. The more the core words in the window, the larger the similarity value.

In Figure 3, some examples are given about Core Words and Active Window. For the above example, "radio wave" and "brain cancer" are selected as Core Words. And by using Formula (5) and (6), we can compute the similarity value between the query and documents as follows (m=p=1.0):

Sim3(query, document A) = 72.53 Sim3(query, document B) = 18.48

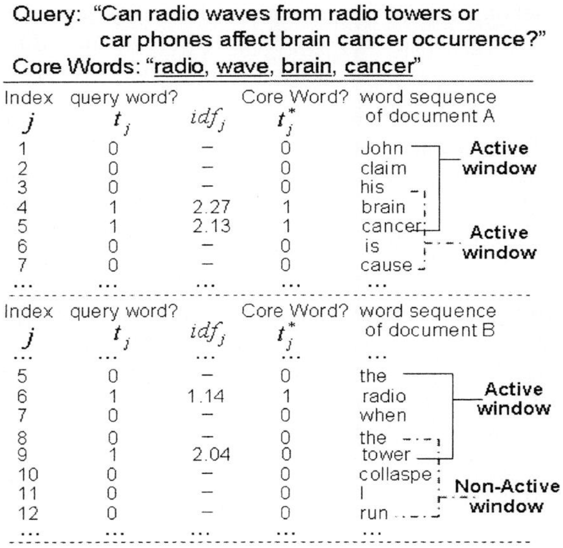

```
Query: "Can radio waves from radio towers or
        car phones affect brain cancer occurrence?"
Core Words: "radio, wave, brain, cancer"
Index  query word?         Core Word?   word sequence
  j        t_j     idf_j      t_j*       of document A
  1         0        -          0        John ──┐
  2         0        -          0        claim  │ Active
  3         0        -          0        his   ─┘ window
  4         1       2.27        1        brain ─┐
  5         1       2.13        1        cancer │ Active
  6         0        -          0        is    ─┘ window
  7         0        -          0        cause
 ...       ...      ...        ...       ...
Index  query word?         Core Word?   word sequence
  j        t_j     idf_j      t_j*       of document B
 ...       ...      ...        ...       ...
  5         0        -          0        the   ─┐
  6         1       1.14        1        radio  │ Active
  7         0        -          0        when  ─┘ window
  8         0        -          0        the   ─┐
  9         1       2.04        0        tower ─┘
 10         0        -          0        collaspe┐
 11         0        -          0        l       │ Non-Active
 12         0        -          0        run    ─┘ window
 ...       ...      ...        ...       ...
```

Fig. 3. Example for Core Words and Active Window

Comparing the two values, the first value is much larger than the second one. It means that Document A is relevant, while Document B is irrelevant. It's quite reasonable. Later, the experiments show that Model Three has the best performance.

Our two key notions are implemented by the above three models step by step, from the simplest one to the most complex one. These models outperform the traditional tf-idf model, because they take care of the relationship between the query words.

3 Experiment Results

TREC (http://trec.nist.gov) Data are used to test the algorithms. There are all together:
(1) 528155 documents with XML format
(2) 200 queries (TREC topic 301-450 and 601-650)

We only use the description section of the TREC topics. They are short queries.

3.1 Overall Accuracy

200 queries are used to retrieve relevant documents from the corpora by using our window-based models. And also we implement several other algorithms to compare with our models, such as tf-idf [1] and (BM25)[2] (k1=1.2, b=0.75, k3=1000).

We use 5-width window and set p=m=1.0. In Model Three, we parse the query sentence automatically and select the baseNP and named entities as core words. The overall result is in Figure 4.

From figure 4, we can see that our models outperform the traditional tf-idf model. And also, Core Window-based Model has the best performance, because in this model, we not only consider the distribution of the query words in the document, but also give larger weights to the more important query words.

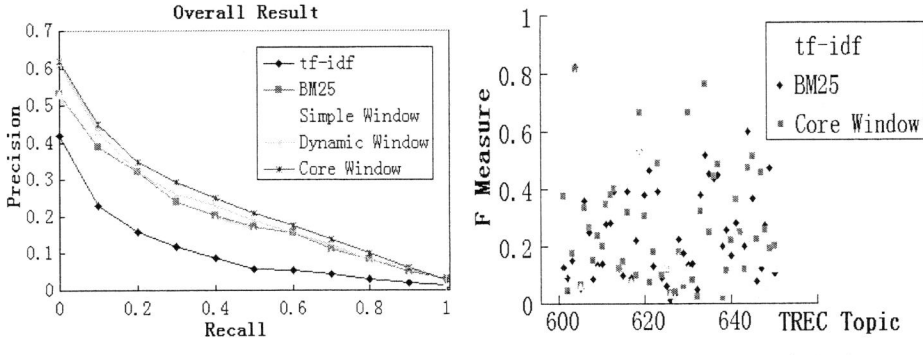

Fig. 4. Overall Accuracy **Fig. 5.** F Measure for Each Topic

Figure 5 shows more details about each query's performance (TREC topic 601-650). In most cases, Core Window-based Model has the best performance, but it has some exceptions. We deeply research the exceptions and find that the automatic baseNP and Named Entity recognition of the query sentence brings the error. Some unimportant words are selected as core words, while really essential words are slipped. When we correct them manually, there will be no exception. So, we believe that window-based methods are robust for most queries.

3.2 Window Width Analysis

Figure 6 shows the performance of Model One and Two with the various window widths. In Figure 6, each curve represents the average F measure of 50 queries. In the top part, we can see that it is difficult to select a fixed optimal window width for different queries in Simple Window-based Model. In Dynamic Window-based Model, four curves have similar shapes and peaks. So, Model Two is much more robust for different queries than Model One. And also, when the width of dynamic window is larger than 7, the performance is quite stable and not sensitive to the window width. It's very important for a real system. In addition, when the window width is set to 2 or 3, our models are very similar to the bi-gram or tri-gram indexing model for information retrieval [8].

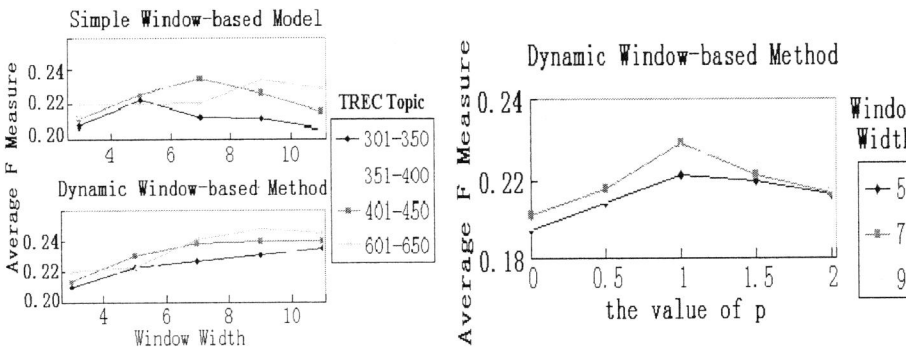

Fig. 6. Average F Measure with Window Width   **Fig. 7.** Parameter Analysis of Model Two

3.3 Parameter Analysis for Dynamic Window

In Dynamic Window-based Model, there is a parameter p. If p is set to zero, Model Two is simplified to Model One. Figure 7 shows how the value of p affects the average F measure of 200 queries with different window widths. We can see that the positions of three curves' peaks are close to each other. It means that we can easily optimize the value of p in Model Two.

3.4 Parameter Analysis for Core Window

In the Core Window-based Model, there are two parameters which will affect the final result. We try to optimize p and m together. The following table shows the average F measure of 200 queries with the variations of p and m.

Table 1. Average F measure

m \ p	0.5	1.0	1.5	2.0
0.5	0.247	0.251	**0.263**	0.248
1.0	0.252	**0.270**	0.254	0.241
1.5	**0.265**	0.260	0.254	0.242
2.0	0.240	0.241	0.237	0.236

It seems that when fitting the requirement of p+m=2.0, the system has the best performance. Actually, Formula 6 consists of two parts: traditional tf-idf part and window-based part. And in the second part, p and m appear as the exponents. So, from the above table, we get a fixed optimal rate for the weights of two parts.

4 Conclusion

In this paper, we propose a series of window-based methods for information retrieval. Our approaches are based on two key notions. One is that the closer the query words in a document, the larger the similarity value between the query and the document. And the other is that some query words, like named entities and baseNP called "Core Words" are much more important than other words, and should have special weights. By implementing the above notions, our three models can compute similarities between queries and documents based on the importance and distribution of query words in the documents. We use TREC data to test the algorithms. The experiments show that window-based methods outperform most of the traditional methods. And the Core Window-based Model is the best and most robust one. In the future, we plan to combine the window-based models with other technologies, such as query expansion and relevant feedback. And also, we are trying to use window-based methods in other applications, such as information extraction and text classification.

Acknowledgements

This work is sponsored by the Natural Sciences Foundation of China under grant No. 60372016, 60121302, and the Scientific Research Foundation for Returned Overseas Chinese Scholars, State Education Ministry.

References

1. Karen Sparck Jones. (1972) A statistical interpretation of term specificity and its application in retrieval. Journal of Documentation, 28:11–21.
2. S.E. Robertson, S.Walker. (1999) Okapi/Keenbow at TREC-8. Text Retrieval Conference, NIST Specail Publication 500-246.
3. Warren R. Greiff. (1998) A theory of term weighting based on exploratory data analysis. In Proceedings of SIGIR-98.
4. Hiemstra, D.(2000) A probabilistic justification for using tf.idf term weighting in information retrieval. International Journal on Digital Libraries 3(2), 131-139, Springer-Verlag, Berlin Heidelberg.
5. Salton, G. And C. Buckley.(1988) Term-weighting approaches in automatic text retrieval. Information Processing & Management 24(5), 513-523.
6. Kenneth W.Church, William A.Gale, (1995) Inverse Document Frequency(IDF): A Measure of Deviations from Poisson. AT&T Bell Laboratories.
7. Fujita, S. (1999) Notes on Phrasal Indexing JSCB Evaluation Experiments at NTCIR AD HOC, in Proceedings of NTCIR-1 workshop.
8. Tokunaga Takenobu, Ogibayasi Hironori, Tanaka Hozumi,(2000). Effectiveness of complex index term in information retrieval. The 6th RIAO Conference. Pp.1322-1331.
9. Kaszkiel et al.(1997) Passage Retrieval Revisited. SIGIR'97.

Improving Relevance Feedback in Language Modeling Approach: Maximum a Posteriori Probability Criterion and Three-Component Mixture Model

Seung-Hoon Na, In-Su Kang, and Jong-Hyeok Lee

Div. of Electrical and Computer Engineering,
Pohang University of Science and Technology (POSTECH),
Advanced Information Technology Research Center (AITrc)
{nsh1979,dbaisk,jhlee}@postech.ac.kr

Abstract. Recently, researchers have tried to extend a language modeling approach to apply relevance feedback. Their approaches can be classified into two categories. One typical approach is the expansion-based feedback that sequentially performs 'term selection' and 'term re-weighting' separately. Another approach is the model-based feedback that focuses on estimating 'query language model', which predicts well users' information need. This paper improves these two approaches of relevance feedback by using *a maximum a posteriori probability criterion*, and *a three-component mixture model*. *A maximum a posteriori probability criterion* is a criterion for selection of good expansion terms from feedback documents. *A three-component mixture model* is the method that eliminates the noise of the query language model by adding a 'document specific topic model'. The experimental results show that our methods increase the precision of relevance feedback for a short length query. In addition, we make some comparative study between several relevance feedbacks in three document collections.

1 Introduction

The basic idea of the language modeling approach to information retrieval, first introduced by [5], is not to explicitly assume relevance information, but to assume individual document models for each document and estimate them. With these document models, documents are ranked by query likelihood where the document models will generate a given query. In spite of its mathematical simplicity, language modeling approaches have shown to perform well empirically showing comparative performance to classical probabilistic models.

The language modeling approach has had difficulty with handling relevance feedback within a well-founded framework. Some researchers have tried to incorporate relevance feedback into the language modeling approach in a principled fashion. Their approaches can be classified into two categories – expansion-based and model-based.

Expansion-based feedback is similar to the typical classical approach that sequentially performs 'term selection' and 'term re-weighting', [1], [5]. At the 'term selection', new query terms are selected from feedback documents, and at the 'term re-weighting', such selected terms are re-weighted according to its significance[1]. In this approach term selection criterion is very important, but it has only been dealt with heuristically so it is not naturally applied to term dependent or more general situations. To this end, we propose maximum a posteriori probability criterion that is more intuitively motivated with a principle fashion and provide tractable methods in more generalized situations.

Another alternative approach is model-based feedback that deals with the problem of estimating a 'query language model' that represents the user's information need [3], [4], [8]. The new expansion query is sampled from this estimated the query language model. Thus, the problem of estimation of the query language model is very important in this approach.

To estimate the query language model, Zhai and Jefferty [8], who organize model-based feedback, assumed that all terms in feedback documents are generated from the two-component mixture model that consists of the query language model and a background collection model. Unfortunately, this assumption have a problem when the feedback documents contain other topics as well as query-relevant topics. If we agree that most documents have multiple topics as well as query-relevant, two-component mixture model may cause the estimated query language model to have some noise. Thus, we use the 'three-component mixture model' that consists of a query language model and a background language model and a 'document specific topic model'. The three-component mixture model will estimate the query language model more correctly.

The remainder of the paper is organized as follows. In Section 2 we review background and previous relevance feedback methods in language modeling. Section 3 and Section 4 describes the maximum a posteriori probability criterion and the three-component mixture model, respectively. Section 5 shows experimental results of the new methods and previous relevance feedback methods. Finally, we offer conclusion and present our research direction.

2 Relevance Feedback Approaches in Language Modeling

The basic idea of language modeling ranks documents in the collection with the query-likelihood that a given query **q** would be observed during repeated random sampling from each document model [1], [5][2].

$$P(\mathbf{q}|\theta_D) = \prod_w P(w|\theta_D)^{c(w;\mathbf{q})} \qquad (1)$$

where $c(w;\mathbf{q})$ is the number of term in given query, D is a given document.

Next, the retrieval problem is reduced to the problem of estimating a unigram language model $P(w|\theta_D)$.

---

[1] In this paper, we assume the viewpoint that term re-weighting in expansion-based approach, more elaborate document models are re-constructed by optimizing unknown smoothing parameters [1].

[2] There is some difference between authors about interpretation of a query. [5] treats a query as a set, while [1] interpreted a query as a sequence of words. In this paper, we adopt the sequence interpretation.

As mentioned in the section 1, previous relevance feedback methods in the language modeling approach have been explored by two distinct approaches: expansion-based, model-based. In the remainder of the section, we will give details on each approach.

2.1 Expansion-Based Feedback

Ponte's method [6], the first heuristic work in expansion-based feedback, used the ratio method that select terms having a high generative probability on top retrieved document models, but a low generative probability on the collection language model.

$$LR(w) = \sum_{D \in \mathcal{R}} \log \frac{P(w|\theta_D)}{P(w|\theta_C)} \qquad (2)$$

Where $\mathcal{R}$ is set of feedback documents, $P(w|\theta_D)$ is the probability of term w given the document model θ_D for D. The ratio method performs in practice well, but is not based on the well-founded framework. The development of a well-designed framework for the term selection (expansion) is one an important issues in this approach.

Zhai and Lafferty [7] mentioned on the 'query modeling role' of smoothing that distinguish the common and non-informative terms in a query different from the 'estimation role'. Hiemstra [1] proposed the term specific smoothing that conceptually connects the query modeling role of smoothing into re-weighting of classical probability model. In term specific smoothing, the importance of query term can be quantified with a separate smoothing parameter λ_i for each term.

2.2 Model-Based Feedback

Zhai and Lafferty [8] introduced a model-based feedback within KL divergence, motivated by Ng's work [4] that generalizes the most language modeling approaches and makes the feedback problem more tractable. Model-based feedback does not re-estimate smoothing parameters, but instead estimates the 'query language model' that is the probability distribution for the number of each terms in a new query to obtain high retrieval performance. The documents are ranked with inverse proportion to KL-divergence between the query language model and the given document language model.

$$D(\theta_Q \| \theta_D) = -\sum_{w} p(w|\theta_Q) \log p(w|\theta_D) + C(\theta_Q) \qquad (3)$$

where $P(w|\theta_Q)$ is the query language model.

3 Maximum Posterior Probability Criterion

One term selection problem is to select 'good' terms for constructing a new query among terms occurring in feedback documents. In the language modeling approach, a query is a sample generated by a specific document model. Thus, the term selection problem is to find a query sample to predict the top document models in an entire query sample space. Here, the query sample space is a set of all possible sequences of vocabulary[3].

To make this problem tractable, imagine that a single specific document model θ_D is given and we want to search the best query sample (with fixed length) to predict well this document model. A reasonable strategy to this problem is to maximize the a posteriori probability of the query sample of the document model.

$$\mathbf{q}^* = \arg\max_{\mathbf{q} \in Q} P(\theta_D \mid \mathbf{q}) \qquad (4)$$

where Q is query sample space. $\mathbf{q}^*$ is the best sample to predict this document model. We call this strategy by *maximum a posteriori criterion*.

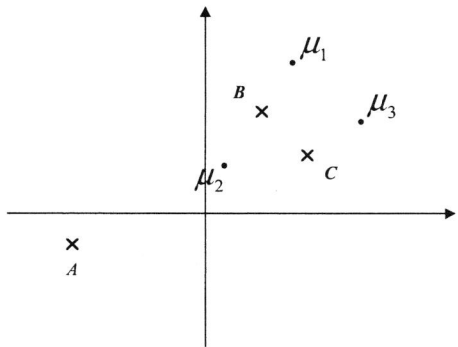

Fig. 1. Imaginary situation for Maximum posterior probability criterion

Figure 1 illustrates this maximum a posteriori criterion, where the problem is simplified to a problem in the two-dimensional real number space. Here, three Gaussian distribution $N(\mu_i, \sigma)$ with the mean μ_i and the variance σ respectively and a sample space { A, B, C } are given. Among the sample space, if we find a sample predicting well of the second Gaussian distribution $N(\mu_2, \sigma)$, we will select sample A, because it maximizes posterior probability on the second Gaussian model. Sample B and C give larger likelihoods than A on the second Gaussian, but they never good samples because their posterior probability for $N(\mu_2, \sigma)$ is not the maximum in this sample space. However, if we use the maximum a posteriori probability criterion, then sample A will be selected.

At this point, we can treat the query selection problem in relevance feedback. To this end, we extend the above maximum a posterior criterion into more generalized criterion that can be applied to the situation that multiple document models $\theta_{D_1}, \theta_{D_2}, \ldots, \theta_{D_m}$ are given. The term expansion problem is to find the best query sample that 'simultaneously' maximizes a posteriori probability for each document model. Clearly, it forces us to combine all posteriori probabilities on each document model with '*and event*'. Thus,

---

[3] In our term selection problem, the query sample space Q is restricted with query size and uniqueness of each query term.

$$\mathbf{q}^* = \arg\max_{\mathbf{q} \in Q} \prod_{i=1}^{m} P(\theta_{D_i} | \mathbf{q}) \tag{5}$$

Also, if we assume term independence, then

$$\prod_i P(\theta_{D_i} | \mathbf{q}) = \prod_i \frac{P(\mathbf{q} | \theta_{D_i}) P(\theta_{D_i})}{P(\mathbf{q})}$$

$$= \prod_i \prod_{w \in q} \frac{P(w | \theta_{D_i}) P(\theta_{D_i})}{P(w)} \tag{6}$$

where $P(w) = \sum_{D \in \mathcal{M}} P(w | \theta_D) P(\theta_D)$, $P(\theta_D) = \frac{1}{|\mathcal{M}|}$, and $\mathcal{M}$ is the set of all existing document model in a given collection.

To maximize (6), we must select terms with rank ordered by the following individual term score.

$$score(w) = \prod_i \frac{P(w | \theta_{D_i}) P(\theta_D)}{P(w)} \tag{7}$$

If we assume uniform prior probability $P(\theta_D)$,. then,

$$score(w) \propto \sum_i \log \frac{P(w | \theta_{D_i})}{\frac{1}{|\mathcal{M}|} \sum_{D \in \mathcal{M}} P(w | \theta_D)} \tag{8}$$

Now, this formula (8) will be used in term sorting for term selection.

4 Three-Component Mixture Model

In model-based feedback, query language model estimation is important, because it play the two roles of re-weighting and term expansion. To estimate a query language model, Zhai and Lafferty [8] suggested the two-component mixture model with the unknown query language model and a background collection language model. For $D \in \mathcal{R}$,

$$P(w | D) = \lambda P(w | \theta_Q) + (1 - \lambda) P(w | \theta_C) \tag{9}$$

However, this two-component mixture model can make the query language model include some irrelevant portions, because the feedback documents have multiple topics. It is difficult to catch this portion of a query language model by using only a collection background model. To build a more accurate query language model, it is necessary to revise this model to eliminate these irrelevant portions.

To this end, we add a single document specific model into the original two-component mixture model. As a result, we obtain the following three-component mixture model.

$$P(w | D) = \lambda_Q P(w | \theta_Q) + \lambda_S p(w | \theta_D^s) + \lambda_C p(w | \theta_C) \tag{10}$$

where $\lambda_Q + \lambda_S + \lambda_C = 1$, and $p(w | \theta_D^s)$ is the non-relevant topic model of the document D.

4.1 Approximation to Document Specific Model

One ad-hoc method is a naive approximation that almost all terms in feedback documents are irrelevant to the query topic.

$$p(w|\theta_D^s) \approx p(w|\hat{\theta}_D) \tag{11}$$

Although this approximation may not inconsistent to the assumption of the relevant feedback, query language modeling can be estimated more carefully. The naïve approximation will bring only highly shared portions in feedback documents into the query language model.

Another alternative method is the mixture approximation using a topic collection language model.

$$p(w|\theta_D^s) \approx \pi p(w|\hat{\theta}_D) + (1-\pi)p(w|\theta_{C_w}) \tag{12}$$

where $p(w|\theta_{C_w})$ is a topic collection language model that is estimated from all documents which include term w.

4.2 Estimation of Query Language Model

To estimate query language model, we use the EM algorithm, which iteratively updates query language model θ_Q to maximize (locally) generative likelihood of feedback documents. Initially, $P(w|\theta_Q^{(0)})$ are set to

$$P(w|\theta_Q^{(0)}) = \frac{\sum_{D \in \mathcal{R}} c(w;D)}{\sum_{D \in \mathcal{R}} \sum_w c(w;D)} \tag{13}$$

where $c(w;D)$ is the count of term w in document D.

Next, we perform the E-step and M-step iteratively.

E-step:

$$P(w \text{ is Rel}|D)^{(k)} = \frac{\lambda_Q p(w|\theta_Q)^{(k)}}{\lambda_Q p(w|\theta_Q)^{(k)} + \lambda_S p(w|\theta_D^s) + \lambda_C p(w|\theta_C)} \tag{14}$$

M-step:

$$p(w|\theta_Q)^{(k+1)} = \frac{\sum_{D \in \mathcal{R}} c(w;D)P(w \text{ is Rel}|D)^{(k)}}{\sum_{D \in \mathcal{R}} \sum_w c(w;D)P(w \text{ is Rel}|D)^{(k)}} \tag{15}$$

where λ_Q and λ_S and λ_C are constants.

5 Experimentation

All feedback methods described in this paper are evaluated in NTCIR3 test collections and topics.

1. KR: Korea Economic Daily (1994)
   66147 number of documents, 30 Topics
2. JA: Mainichi Newspaper (1998-1999)
   220078 number of documents, 42 Topics
3. CH: CIRB010, United Daily News (1998-1999)
   381682 number of documents, 42 Topics

In all experiments, we used four types of query provided by NTCIR 3 task: Title, Description, Concept, All (All: consists of all topic fields). Table 1 describes the average number of query terms for each collection. For indexing, we performed preliminary experimentations on NTCIR-3 test collections using various indexing methods (Morphlogy and word, bi-character). As a result, we found that bi-character indexing units are highly reliable for Korean or other Asian Languages. Our all experiments in this paper are performed using the bi-character indexing unit.

Table 1. The average length of query for each topic and collection

	Title	Desc	Conc	All
KR	5.5	19.4	13.8	109.9
JA	8.5	33.1	18.9	212.3
CH	6.3	20.3	14.3	143.3

Table 2. Relevance feedback methods evaluated in experimentation

Approach	Symbol	Method
Expansion-based	lr	Likelihood ratio method
	lr+	Likelihood ratio method and term specific smoothing
	mpp	Maximum a posteriori probability criterion
	mpp+	Maximum a posteriori probability criterion and term specific smoothing
Model-based	qc	Two-component mixture model
	qdc	Three-component mixture model using naïve approximation

5.1 Relevance Feedback Performance

Table 2 lists the relevance feedback methods evaluated in this experimentation. Three previous methods are marked with 'lr', 'lr+', 'qc'. Here, '+' indicates that the method used the term specific smoothing [1] for term reweighting. And, our methods are marked with 'mpp', 'mpp+','mpp*', 'qdc'.

In expansion-based approaches (lr, lr+, mpp, mpp+), top 15 retrieved documents used as feedback documents, and 50 new query terms are added into the original query. In model-based approaches (qc, qdc), the top 10 retrieved documents are used to estimate the query language model. Table 3 shows the final experimental results of relevance feedback methods in three collections. Free parameters of two-component mixture model and three-component mixture model are set by $\lambda=0.25$ and, $\lambda_D=0.175$, $\lambda_S=0.075$, $\lambda_C=0.75$, respectively. We selected parameters empirically that performed well in our preliminary experimentation.

As shown in Table 3, all relevance feedback methods improve significantly the performance of our initial retrieval results. 'mpp' and 'mpp+' showed a slight improvement over 'lr' and 'lr+' of [6] for title and description and concept, but they sometimes show a lower performance than 'lr' and 'lr+', although the ratio method is almost equal to maximum a posteriori probability criterion when using Jelinek smoothing. Also, the 'qdc' shows a notable improvement over the original approach 'qc', although the approximation method for 'qdc' is *adhoc* naïve approximation that may be dangerous. In KR, CH collection, it does not seem to significantly increase performance, but in JA collection, it improves average performance over the original method more than 1 percent. If we use better model to approximate the document specific model, then the performance can be improved.

Table 3. Average precision of relevance feedback methods for KR and JA collections (above) and CH collection (bottom). The evaluation measure is non-interpolate average precision. Underlined number and bold number indicate that the method improves against the previous method and that the method has best performance in the column of the table, respectively

	KR				JA			
	Title	Desc	Conc	All	Title	Desc	Conc	All
init	0.3090	0.2496	0.3277	0.4203	0.2975	0.2937	0.3169	0.4186
lr	0.3491	0.3524	0.3965	0.4797	0.3506	0.3719	0.3778	0.4615
mpp	0.3508	0.3538	0.4001	**0.4799**	0.3569	0.3746	0.3834	0.4583
lr+	0.3703	0.3603	0.4068	0.4671	0.3729	0.3909	0.3891	**0.4625**
mpp+	0.3721	0.3608	**0.4073**	0.4698	0.3797	0.3922	**0.3920**	0.4561
qc	0.3874	0.3716	0.3795	0.4561	0.3847	0.3835	0.3684	0.4374
qdc	**0.3914**	**0.3779**	0.3859	0.4610	**0.3882**	**0.3956**	0.3816	0.4251

	CH			
	Title	Desc	Conc	All
init	0.2392	0.1997	0.2516	0.3266
lr	0.2953	0.2882	0.3190	**0.3851**
mpp	0.2920	0.2913	0.3223	0.3846
lr+	0.2961	0.2796	0.3124	0.3662
mpp+	0.2914	0.2845	0.3149	0.3641
qc	0.3136	0.3224	0.3220	0.3679
qdc	**0.3155**	**0.3306**	**0.3256**	0.3701

One interesting result is the effect of re-weighting (marked with '+') according to query length. For a short length query like title or concept, re-weighting is highly effective, but for a long length query re-weighting degrades the performance. One possible explanation is that, as the given query is longer, the number of matching terms in the document gives more large impact on performance, while the effect of the term weighting is much weaker. Thus, to perform well for a long query, we may need a method that incorporates the coordination level matching into the current re-weighting scheme.

Another interesting effect is that model-based feedbacks show a superior performance than the expansion-based feedbacks when the initial retrieval performance is relatively low (less than 0.31). This means that the model-based feedback is more robust than the expansion based approach over the initial retrieval performance. This can be explained by the duplication of term weighting in the query language model. The default weight is the likelihood odd between the document language model and the collection language model, and another additional weight is the term distribution from query language model. However, the default weight disappears in term specific re-weighting of the expansion-based approach.

6 Conclusion

In this paper, we proposed two methods to improve relevance feedback in the language modeling approach, and performed comparative experimentations between several relevance feedback methods, including our new methods.

Experimental results are summarized as following. 1) Relevance feedback significantly improved the performance of baseline retrieval results. 2) The new proposed methods in this paper increased the performance of previous methods a bit, but sometimes the improvement is significant. 3) For a short length query, the term specific smoothing had shown to improve significantly retrieval feedback. However, for a long query, it seems to decrease performance. 4) Model-based feedback is more robust over the initial retrieval performances against the expansion-based feedback. By contrast, when the initial retrieval performance had good, expansion-based feedback showed a better performance over than model-based feedback.

Acknowledgements

This work was supported by the KOSEF through the Advanced Information Technology Research Center(AITrc) and by the BK21 Project.

References

1. Hiemstra, D.: Term Specific Smoothing for Language Modeling Approach to Information Retrieval: The Importance of a Query Term. In Proceedings of 25th Annual International ACM SIGIR Conference on Research and Development in Information Retrieval (2002)
2. Lafferty, J. and Zhai, C.: Document Language Models, Query Models, and Risk Minimization for Information Retrieval. In Proceedings of 24th Annual International ACM SIGIR Conference on Research and Development in Information Retrieval (2001)
3. Lavrenko, V. and Croft, B.: Relevance-based language models. In Proceedings of 24th Annual International ACM SIGIR Conference on Research and Development in Information Retrieval (2001)
4. Ng, K.: A Maximum Likelihood Ratio Information Retrieval Model. In TREC-8 Workshop Notebook (1999)
5. Ponte, A. and Croft, J.: A language modeling approach to information retrieval. In Proceedings of 21st Annual International ACM SIGIR Conference on Research and Development in Information Retrieval (1998)
6. Ponte, A.: A language modeling approach to information retrieval. In PhD thesis, Dept. of Computer Science, University of Massachusetts (1998)
7. Zhai, C. and Lafferty, J.: A Study of Smoothing Methods for Language Models Applied to Ad Hoc Information Retrieval. In Proceedings of 24th Annual International ACM SIGIR Conference on Research and Development in Information Retrieval (2001)
8. Zhai, C. and Lafferty, J.: Model-based Feedback in the Language Modeling Approach to Information Retrieval. In Proceedings of the 10th Annual International ACM Conference on Information and Knowledge Management (2002)

BBS Based Hot Topic Retrieval Using Back-Propagation Neural Network

Lan You, Yongping Du, Jiayin Ge, Xuanjing Huang, and Lide Wu

Department of Computer Science, Fudan University, Shanghai, 200433
{lan_you,ypdu,jyge,xjhuang,ldwu}@fudan.edu.cn

Abstract. BBS, often referred to as forum, is a system that offers so much information, where people talk about various topics. Some topics are hot while others are unpopular. It's rather a hard job for a person to find out hot topics in these tons of information. In this paper we introduce a system that automatically retrieves hot topics on BBS. Unlike some topic detection systems, this system not only discovers topics but also judges their hotness. Messages are first clustered into topics based on their lexical similarity. Then a BPNN (Back-Propagation Neural Network) based classification algorithm is used to judge the hotness of topic according to its popularity, its quality as well as its message distribution over time. We have conducted experiments over *Yahoo! Message Board* (Yahoo BBS) and retrieved satisfactory results.

1 Introduction

BBS (Bulletin Board System) is so popular today that thousands of people present their view on various topics there. Some topics are hot while others are unpopular. From these hot topics, we can see what the people are interested in, see their view of some social phenomena or a certain political event. But it's rather a hard job for a person to find out such topics in these tons of information. So we designed a system to automatically retrieve hot topics on BBS. The system allows a terminal user to specify the domain and the time span that he or she is concerned about. And after a few minutes, hot topics during the required time span in that specific domain will be presented in a friendly way.

Some part of our work is similar to topic detection, which is one of the major tasks of TDT [1]. Like some topic detection systems [2][3][4][5], we discover topics using a clustering algorithm. But we can't just stop here. We then use a BPNN (Back-Propagation Neural Network) based classification algorithm [6] to judge the hotness of topics. Each topic is given a hotness score. At last those highly scored topics (i.e. hot topics) will be presented to terminal users.

In section 2.1, we describe the architecture of our system. Section 2.2 and section 2.3 describe our clustering and classification approach for retrieve hot topics. And section 3 presents the results of the experiments we conducted using our BBS based hot topic retrieval system. A conclusion of our work is given in section 4.

Before we take a close look at the system, let's see some concept about BBS.

1.1 Some Definitions for BBS

There are many terms about BBS. A lot of websites have their own definition of these terms. To standardize our research work, we made clear definition for some terms:

- Message: A message is the article that an author writes on a certain subject. There are two kinds of messages: Start message is the first message in a thread; Reply message is the response to a certain message in the thread.
- Thread: A thread is composed of a start message and its reply messages. Messages in one thread mostly talk about a same topic. The structure of a thread can be viewed as a tree, whose root is the start message, and the children of each node (representing a message) are the reply messages to it.
- Message Board: A message board is designed for a certain domain on BBS.
- Author: An author is the person who releases the message.
- Reader: A reader is the person who reads the message.

1.2 Hot Topics on BBS

The key problem to BBS based hot topic retrieval is how to measure the hotness of a topic. We believe that, as an information platform, BBS provides end users with the capability of interactive information exchange. The content and methods of this exchange can be used to measure topic hotness.

We found that a hot topic always has several characteristics as follows:

- Numerous messages: If a topic is discussed by a lot of messages, it is high probably important. Certainly we should consider the quality of these messages.
- Numerous authors: The hotness of a topic is closely related to the number of authors who talk about it.
- Response: If there are a lot of messages talking about one topic in a short time, it is likely to be a hot topic.
- Authority: A message written by a famous author will attract many readers. In addition, the message that is cited from other medium will also probably bring a hot discussion because of its quantity of information.
- Relevance: Of course, we should consider users' interest, too. Among the hundreds of message boards, a user is interested in only a few ones.

2 BBS Based Topic Retrieval System

2.1 System Architecture

We designed the architecture of the BBS based hot topic retrieval system as Fig. 1. First, we analyze the authors and compute their authority. To each thread, we extract its meta data, which includes the number of messages in the thread, the hierarchy of the thread tree, the title of each message, the length of text, and the author and the post time. Then, message filtering will be carried out to remove empty, junk and irrelevant messages. After that, threads are clustered into groups. Threads in the same group are assumed to talk about the same topic. Next, by hotness classification, topics are scored and sorted according to the information acquired from above steps. Finally, those topics with highest score are submitted to user as the hot topics.

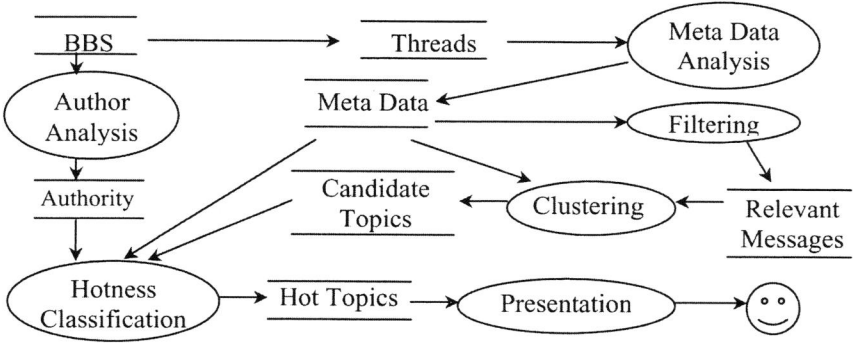

Fig. 1. Architecture of hot topic retrieval

2.2 Thread Clustering

Since messages in one thread mostly talk about the same topic, we cluster threads into groups, each of which represents a topic. We use a two-pass k-means clustering algorithm. In the following subsections, we will depict the algorithm and the selection of terms (features) in VSM.

2.2.1 K-Means Clustering Algorithm Based Approach

This approach consists of two pass of k-means clustering. Before describing the approach, we define the following identifiers: n is the dimension of VSM, m is the number of threads, k is the number of clusters, $X=\{x_i, i=(1,2,...,m)\}$ is the collection of threads, $Y=\{y_j, j=(1,2,...,k)\}$ is the collection of cluster centroids, $C=\{C_j, j=(1,2,...,k)\}$ is the collection of clusters, and N is the maximum iteration.

Here are the basic steps of k-means clustering algorithm:

- Step 1: Select k cluster centroids: $y_1, ..., y_j, ..., y_k$; Let $C_j = \emptyset$, $j=1,2,...,k$
- Step 2: Calculate the similarity of $x_i(i=1,2,...,m)$ to cluster centroid $y_j(j=1,2,...,k)$, then put x_i to the most similar cluster of C_j. That is to say, $C_j=C_j \cup \{i\}$. The similarity is calculated by the following cosine formula:

$$Sim(x_i, y_j) = \frac{\sum_{l=1}^{n} x_{il} * y_{jl}}{\sqrt{(\sum_{l=1}^{n} x_{il}^2)(\sum_{l=1}^{n} y_{jl}^2)}} . \qquad (1)$$

- Step 3: Recalculate cluster centroids: $y_j = (\sum_{i \in C_j} x_i) / m_j$, where m_j is the size of cluster C_j.
- Step 4: If there is little or even no change in cluster centroids, or iteration count reaches N, stop; else goto step 2.

Output of the algorithm is the final clusters and their clustering centroids.

One of the key problems of k-means algorithm is the selection of *k*, which directly decides the number of topics. Because the exact number of topics on BBS is unknown, we estimate *k* as follows:

```
If (ThreadNum <= 10)
      k = ThreadNum/2;
If ((ThreadNum > 10) && (ThreadNum <= 100))
      k = ThreadNum/4;
If ((ThreadNum > 100) && (ThreadNum <= 1000))
      k = ThreadNum/5;
If (ThreadNum>1000)
      k = ThreadNum/8;
```

Here we define "*ThreadNum*" as the number of threads.

Another key problem is the selection of the initial clustering centroids. The basic algorithm selects the clustering centroids randomly when there is no prior knowledge. Since we aim at hot topics, which contain more messages definitely, we select the first *k* threads that have more reply messages as the initial clustering centroids.

Tiny clusters can't become hot topics, so we set a threshold of the minimum size of cluster (number of threads within a topic) as *ThreadNum/2k*. After the first pass of clustering, those tiny clusters with sizes less than the threshold will be thrown away.

Before the second pass of clustering, we compute the within-class similarity (similarity between threads within a cluster) of the rest clusters. Low within-class similarity suggests that threads on different topics may be clustered in one group incorrectly. The size of clusters should be decreased. So we set a threshold σ. If the minimum within-class similarity is less than σ, *k* will be modified as follows:

```
If (ThreadNum <= 10)
      k = ThreadNum/2;
If ((ThreadNum > 10) && (ThreadNum <= 100))
      k = ThreadNum/3;
If ((ThreadNum > 100) && (ThreadNum <= 1000))
      k = ThreadNum/4;
If (ThreadNum > 1000)
      k = ThreadNum/6;
```

After the second pass of clustering, we assume that each cluster can represent a specific topic. Then the results of clustering are candidate topics.

2.2.2 Term Selection and Weighting

During clustering, each thread is represented by a term vector. We will give higher weights to those words that appear in the title or the start message. The weight of $term_k$ given by the TFIDF formula is tf_k*idf_k, where tf_k is the frequency of $term_k$ in the message collection, idf_k is the inversed document frequency of $term_k$, $idf_k=\log(m/m_{tk})$, *m* is the total number of threads, m_{tk} is the number of threads $term_k$ appears.

Vector matrix are established after feature term selection, where the *ith* row in the matrix denotes the *ith* thread (*thread$_i$*), the *jth* column denotes the *jth* term (*term$_j$*), the element of matrix is marked as *Value (i , j)*, which is calculated as follows:

$$Value(i,j) = \begin{cases} 1.5 * tf_{ij} * idf_j, & \text{If term}_j \text{ appears in the title of the start message in thread}_i \\ 1.2 * tf_{ij} * idf_j, & \text{If term}_j \text{ appears in the content of the start message in thread}_i \\ tf_{ij} * idf_j, & \text{otherwise} \end{cases} \quad (2)$$

2.3 Hotness Classification

The hotness of a topic depends on the number of messages, the number of authors, the quality of messages and the authority of authors. Thus, the problem of hotness judgment of a topic can be treated as a problem of classification, where some features can be used to classify topics into hot ones and general ones. In the following part, we will describe the BPNN based classification algorithm and the feature selection.

2.3.1 BPNN Based Classification Algorithm

BPNN is a classical classifier proved to be efficient in many areas. We use a BPNN with one layer of hidden nodes. The activation function taken on hidden nodes is the sigmoid function:

$$\sigma(y) = \frac{1}{1+e^{-y}} . \quad (3)$$

The BPNN we used only has one output node Y. A topic is represented as an n-dimension vector. After feeding it throughout the network, a score is given by the output node for each topic. A threshold is set at the output node Y. Those topics that get a score above the threshold are classified as hot.

2.3.2 Feature Selection

The most important thing of the classification is to select what features to represent a topic. We considered four families of features:

The first family of features reflects topic hotness from the aspects of the number of threads and messages, including:

- *#threads*: the number of threads within a topic
- *#replies*: the number of replies within a topic
- *#relevant replies*: the number of replies that are relevant to the topic

The second family of features reflects topic hotness from the aspect of the number of authors who take part in the discussion, including:

- *#authors*: the number of authors on a topic
- *#relevant authors*: the number of authors whose message are relevant to a topic

The third family of features reflects topic hotness from the aspect of the authority of authors or medias, including:

- *average authority*: the average authority of authors on a topic
- *average author rank*: the average rank of author authority on a topic
- *#other media*: the number of messages that are cited from other media

The fourth family of features reflects topic hotness from aspect of the interval of author time, including:

- *average interval*: the average interval between every two messages in one topic

Features in the same family may have some redundancy. For instance, an author with high rank must have high score of authority. And features from different families may also have some relevance. For example, the more messages in one topic, the more authors. To show the relation between features quantificationally, we analyze the first three families of factors with manually tagging samples of topic hotness (500 topics). Correlation coefficient between every two features is shown in Table 1.

Table 1. Correlation analysis of features

	A	B	C	D	E	F	G	H
A	1.00							
B	0.12	1.00						
C	0.10	0.97	1.00					
D	0.69	0.71	0.67	1.00				
E	0.73	0.64	0.65	0.97	1.00			
F	-0.13	0.42	0.42	0.09	0.06	1.00		
G	0.03	-0.13	-0.13	-0.14	-0.14	-0.41	1.00	
H	0.02	0.20	0.19	0.18	0.15	0.13	0.02	1.00

A:	#threads	B:	#replies
C:	#relevant replies	D:	#author
E:	#relevant authors	F:	Average authority
G:	Average author rank	H:	#other media

The formula for correlation coefficient is:

$$r = \frac{\Sigma(X_1 - \overline{X_1}) \cdot (X_2 - \overline{X_2})}{\sqrt{\Sigma(X_1 - \overline{X_1})^2 \cdot \Sigma(X_2 - \overline{X_2})^2}} \quad . \tag{4}$$

We can see from the table that two pair of features: "*#replies*" and "*#relevant replies*", "*#author*" and "*#relevant authors*" tightly correlate with each other. Their correlations are close to 1. Average authority and average author rank show negative correlation. It's easy to explain these phenomena: the first pair is about the number of messages; the second is about the number of authors; and obviously the higher the rank (the smaller the rank number), the higher the authority score.

At last we omit three features: "*#replies*", "*#author*" and "*average authority*". Thus the number of nodes in the neural net is reduced, and the training data is much more fully utilized.

Because a hot topic always has a lot of message in a relatively shot period, we take interval as the fourth family of feature to the hotness classification. But we cannot directly use *average interval* (that is the average interval between every two messages in a topic). This is because during a topic's lifecycle, discussion is not always hot. Most messages of this topic are posted in a relatively short part of this period.

We observed the top 6 topics with most messages in our experiment data. We can see the messages distribution in Fig. 2. It seems that the distribution of messages is not even, and the hot discussion always lasts 10 percent to 30 percent of the whole lifecycle. So we decided to use interval information as such: Let T to be the hour which has the maximum messages. Then compute the average interval in the period from T_{min} (10 percent of lifecycle before T) to T_{max} (10 percent of lifecycle after T).

$$Average\ in\ terval = \frac{T_{max} - T_{min}}{\#\ of\ messages\ posted\ between\ T_{min}\ and\ T_{max}}. \quad (5)$$

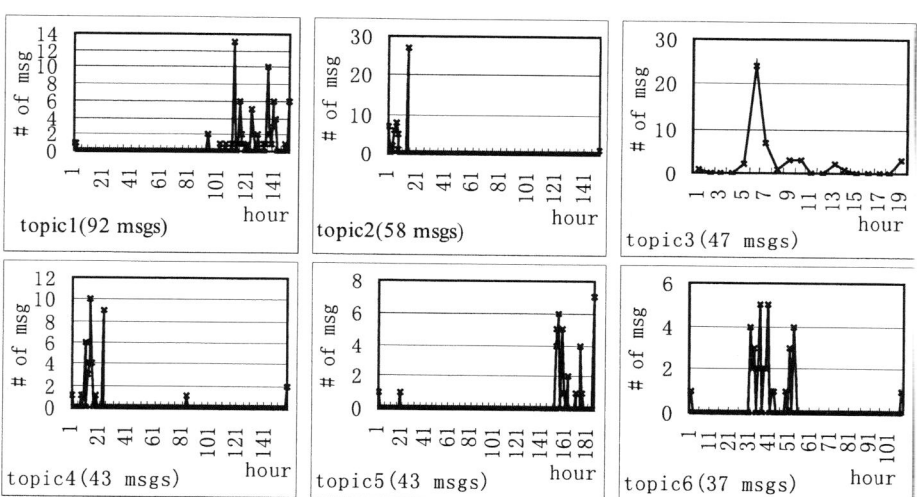

Fig. 2. Lifecycle of topics. The x-axis is the lifecycle of a topic, which is divided by hour. The y-axis is the number of messages

3 Experiments

3.1 Selection of Target BBS

We selected the BBS of Yahoo Finance (http://biz.yahoo.com/co/). It has a relatively complete list of stocks, and a large amount of visitors. It classifies 6877 stocks into 12 groups. Such a lot of data is rather valuable for large scale text processing.

3.2 Evaluation

Since the hot topic retrieval is done in two major processes: thread clustering and hotness classification, the evaluation was given for both clustering and classification.

We don't directly use the evaluation methods of TDT because of the difference between tasks and. So we designed an approach of our own. This approach keeps effectiveness and efficiency while also saves human effort.

3.2.1 Evaluation of Clustering

The purpose of thread clustering is to put similar threads into a cluster. Therefore, the evaluation should be performed by comparing the results of automatic clustering and manual tagging.

Because manual clustering is very time consuming, we took a scheme based on manual relevance assessment between thread pairs instead. From a certain board and a certain time span, select n threads: $thread_1$, $thread_2$, ..., $thread_n$ randomly. System automatically cluster these threads into: C_1, C_2, ..., C_k. Every two threads of $thread_i$ and $thread_j$ make up a thread pair of $p(thread_i, thread_j)$. Select pairs of threads randomly and make sure that some of these pairs consist of threads within the same clusters while others consist of threads from different clusters. Assessors judge the relevance between two threads in one pair. In order not to be biased by the automatic clustering, they aren't told whether or not two threads are in the same cluster beforehand. Therefore, pairs can be classified into two categories of relevant and irrelevant by assessors and the system respectively. If these two kinds of clustering are much consistent, thread clustering is proved to perform quite well.

We selected the threads posted in IBM board during the 10th week and the threads posted in Microsoft board during the 1st week, where 1842 and 2315 messages are posted respectively. These two sets of threads were clustered separately. From the clustering results, we selected 200 pairs of threads randomly. Half of pairs are selected from one cluster while the others are selected from different clusters. Several assessors assessed these thread pairs: the assessors browsed the two threads and determined whether the pair is relevant.

The evaluation results are shown in Table 2. The first and second columns are the numbers of thread pairs that are classified relevant (Rel.) and irrelevant (Irrel.) by the assessors. And the first and second rows are the numbers of thread pairs that are classified relevant (Within a Cluster) and irrelevant (Across Cluster) by the system.

Table 2. Result of clustering

	Rel.	Irrel.	Sum
Within a Cluster	34	66	100
Across Clusters	8	92	100
Total	42	158	200

In the 42 relevant pairs, 34 are clustered into one cluster by the system. And in the 158 irrelevant pairs, 92 are across clusters. Thus, the precision of thread clustering is 0.63. Here accuracy is defined to be the ratio of the number of thread pairs correctly clustered by the system to the total number of thread pairs. When considering relevant pairs, the relevant precision is $34/100 = 0.34$, and the relevant recall is $34/42 = 0.81$.

It can be easily found the relevant recall of thread clustering is higher than the relevant precision, which means that thread clustering tends to put more threads into one cluster. But this kind of error can be compensated during hotness classification.

3.2.2 Evaluation of Hotness Classification

The hotness classification is done on the basis of thread clustering. To evaluate this classification, we also use precision and recall. One problem in the evaluation is how to manually judge the hotness of a topic. The assessors were given not only the context of a topic, but also its statistical information, like number of messages, number of authors, average author rank and message distribution, etc.

When the number of topics increases, the difficulty of evaluation also increases exponentially. So, we can only select an appropriately time span for assessors to evaluate the hotness of topics. Here, "appropriately time span" means that is should be long enough to include the average life cycle of topics. Since most topics exist from several hours to about one hundred of hours, one day to one week are both appropriate. And in some message board one month is also acceptable. Based on this idea, we at last chose messages from IBM, SUN, Microsoft, Dell four boards during 12 specific time span. Clustering was done over them. After thread clustering, 1174 topics are generated, among which 957 (128 hot topics) are randomly chosen as training data and the remaining 217 (18 hot topics) are chosen as test data.

In our experiments, we also tried other classifiers besides BPNN. The alternative classifiers we choose are Perceptron and Naïve Bayes. Like the BPNN classifier, these two classifiers also give each topic a hotness score, and those topics that have a score beyond a specific threshold are classified to be hot ones. Let Y be the output of classifier and T be the threshold. If Y is greater than T, a topic is regarded as hot. When T increases, the precision will increase, while the recall will reduce.

The following figures show the performance of the three classifiers. In Fig. 3, it can be easily found that the performance of Perceptron is the worst, since it is just a simple linear unit. Mostly, BPNN can lead to best performance, but when precision falls between 0.6~0.8, Naïve Bayes classifier performs the best. Fig. 4 presents the precision, recall and F-value of three classifiers when the best performance (highest F-value) is achieved. It can be observed that the F-value of BPNN is the highest and that of Perceptron is the lowest. As a conclusion, both Fig. 3 and 4 shows that the BPNN performs the best and Perceptron performs the worst.

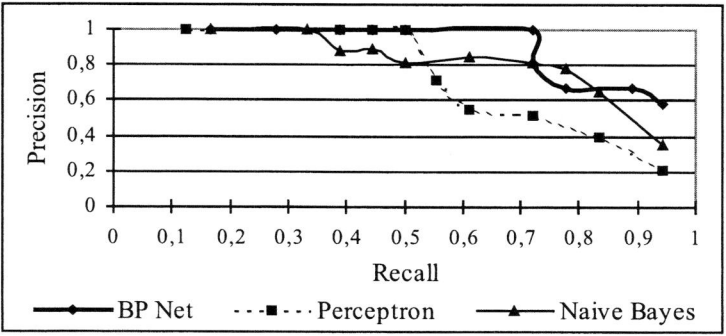

Fig. 3. Precision and Recall of Hotness Classification. The x-axis stands for recall and the y-axis stands for precision

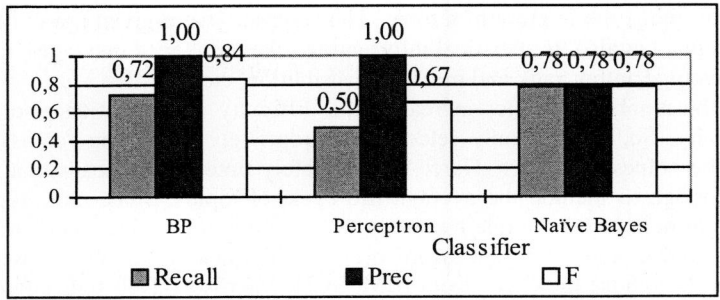

Fig. 4. Best Performance of Three Classifiers

4 Conclusion

We discussed our system for retrieving hot topics on BBS. It is done in two steps: First, we discover topics by clustering threads using a k-means clustering approach. Then, we judge the hotness of a topic by using a BPNN based classification algorithm. And we carefully analyzed the features used for classification. At last the results of our experiments were evaluated for both of the two steps. Our experiments show that our system is practical, and helps to retrieve useful information on BBS.

Acknowledgements

This research was partly supported by FRDC and FLAB, NSF (Beijing) under contracts of 69935010 and 60103014, as well as the 863 National High-tech Promotion Project (Beijing) under contracts of 2001AA114120 and 2002AA142090. We are thankful to Xin Li, Jian Gu, and Lin Zhao for their help in the implementation.

References

1. TDT. Jun. 2003. The 2003 topic detectionand tracking (TDT2003) task definition and evaluation. http://www.nist.gov/speech/tests/tdt/tdt2003/index.htm
2. Frederick Walls, Hubert Jin, Sreenivasa Sista, Richard Schwartz. 1999. Topic Detection in Broadcast News
3. Khoo Khyou Bun, Mitsuru Ishizuka. 2002. Topic Extraction from News Archive Using TF*PDF Algorithm. Proceedings of the 3rd International Conference on Web Information Systems Engineering.
4. Ron Papka, James Allan, and Victor Lavrenko. 1999. UMASS Approaches to Detection and Tracking at TDT2
5. Yiming Yang, Tom Pierce, Jaime Carbonell. 1998. A Study on Retrospective and On-Line Event Detection. In proceedings of SIGIR-98, 21st ACM International Conference on Research and Development in Information Retrieval .
6. Tom M. Mitchell. 1997. Machine Learning. McGraw Hill

How Effective Is Query Expansion for Finding Novel Information? *

Min Zhang, Chuan Lin, and Shaoping Ma

State Key Lab of Intelligent Tech. and Sys., Tsinghua University,
Beijing, 100084, China
{z-m,msp}@tsinghua.edu.cn, lch@mail.lits.tsinghua.edu.cn

Abstract. The task of finding novel information in information retrieval (IR) has been proposed recently and paid more attention to. Compared with techniques in traditional document-level retrieval, query expansion (QE) is dominant in the new task. This paper gives an empirical study on the effectiveness of different QE techniques on finding novel information. The conclusion is drawn according to experiments on two standard test collections of TREC2002 and TREC2003 novelty tracks. Local co-occurrence-based QE approach performs best and makes more than 15% consistent improvement, which enhances both precision and recall in some cases. Proximity-based and dependency-based QE are also effective that both make about 10% progress. Pseudo relevance feedback works better than semantics-based QE and the latter one is not helpful on finding novel information.

1 Introduction

Information retrieval (IR) techniques have become dominant in finding information in people's daily life. Current systems return ranked list of documents as the answer for an informational request. It is most possibly, however, that not whole documents are useful to the user, and lots of redundancy exists.

One approach to provide direct information to users is question-answering. Another one would be to return only relevant AND new sentences (within context) rather than whole documents containing duplicate and extraneous information. The latter one is named finding novel information, which has been paid more attention to recently. TREC (Text REtrieval Conference), which is one of the most famous conferences in IR, proposed a new track named Novelty in 2002.

Being compared to document-level IR, term mismatch problem is more considerable in sentence-level novel information finding because of the short content in sentences. In all of current IR models, information is represented as terms, namely characters, words or phrases. Only if at least one query term appears in a document, the document may be selected. In natural language, however, one

---

* Supported by the Chinese Natural Science Foundation (NO. 60223004, 60321002, 60303005), and partially sponsored by the joint project with IBM China research.

concept can always be expressed using different terms. It leads to term mismatch and the possible missing of useful information.

To solve this term mismatch problem, query expansion (QE) techniques have been proposed. Generally there're three branches of QE approaches. One is to expand query using a global thesaurus which can be constructed according to semantic knowledge [1][2], or learned by statistical relations such as co-occurrence and mutual information [3][4][5][6][7], or got by some syntax-based learning [8][9][10][11] such as dependency-based word similarity [12]. The second kind of QE is to use thesaurus learned by local collection information [11]. And the third one is to expand query by pseudo relevance feedback [13][14].

In traditional IR, the effectiveness of QE technologies is instable. Voorhees [10] tried different weights to expansion terms, even manually selecting terms, but got less than 2% improvement. In the new task of finding novel information, however, how effective are QE-based technologies? This paper makes an empirical study on three kinds of QE approaches for finding novel information, and gives a comparison of their effectiveness.

The remaining part of the paper is constructed as follow: Section 2 describes the global thesaurus-based expansion, including thesauri based on semantics, statistical proximity, and dependency. Section 3 gives a brief introduction to pseudo relevance feedback. Section 4 shows an algorithm of finding novel information with QE based on local co-occurrence. Experiments and analysis are addressed in section 5. Finally the conclusion is drawn.

2 Global Thesaurus-Based Expansion

2.1 Thesaurus Based on Semantics

In this kind of approaches, people construct a thesaurus manually and select terms that have the same or similar semantic meanings. Therefore the noise taken into the thesaurus is relatively less. But the manual classifications of words are always too sensitive or too rough, hence it is difficult to be decided to what extent terms should be added.

Since WordNet [1](http://www.cogsci.princeton.edu/~wn/) is such a semantic thesaurus for English words that is used most widely, it was selected in our study. Totally three kinds of information were observed in experiments: hyponyms (descendants), synonyms and coordinated words. Effects of different levels of hyponyms have been studied.

2.2 Thesaurus Based on Statistical Proximity

Research of using statistical approaches on a large corpus is based on a distribution hypothesis which states that two words are semantically similar to the extent that they share contexts [15].

Dr Dekang Lin has made an in-depth study and provided an online dictionary (http://www.cs.ualberta.ca/~lindek/demos/proxysim.htm) based on statistical proximity on a generally corpus [7], which is one of the best thesauri of this kind of approaches. Hence this thesaurus is used as the representative in our study.

2.3 Thesaurus Based on Dependency

This kind of researches is to combine the statistical and the syntax information. If two terms frequently have same or similar dependencies according to a general corpus, they are taken as similar or having a tight relationship.

In this paper, we use Dr Dekang Lin's online thesaurus based on statistical dependency [12] (http://www.cs.ualberta.ca/~lindek/demos/depsim.htm).

3 Pseudo Relevance Feedback

Pseudo relevance feedback strategies are to expand the query with top n terms extracted from the top m initial retrieved documents after initial search. In the task of finding novel information, each sentence is taken as an individual document. The n terms are chosen based on their similarities to the query [14].

4 Local Thesaurus-Based Expansion

Compared with global thesauri, thesaurus learned from local collection has the advantage that relations between words represents characteristics of retrieving collections directly. Therefore it may be more helpful. Following gives an algorithm of finding novel information with QE based on local co-occurrence (called LCE). It expands terms highly co-occurred with any of query terms in a fixed window size within a sentence in the retrieving collection.

The algorithm is described as following:
Suppose given a user query Q, the set of sentences in the collection is S;
1. Filter all stop-words in sentences in S;
2. To each $q_i \in Q$:
1) Construct a co-occurrence vector T_i:
   $T_i = ((t_{i1}, f_{i1}), (t_{i2}, f_{i2}) \ldots (t_{in}, f_{in}))$,
   where t_{ij} is the jth term co-occurred with q_i in the window (size N),
   f_{ij} is the co-occurrence frequency of t_{ij} and q_i;
2) Normalize co-occurrence frequencies in T_i, and get a new vector T_i':
   $T_i' = ((t_{i1}, f_{i1}'), (t_{i2}, f_{i2}') \ldots (t_{in}, f_{in}'))$, f_{ij}' is the normalized score of f_{ij};
3) Select terms that $f_{i1}' \geq \theta_i (\theta_i \geq 0)$ to expand q_i and forms a new query Q';
3. Find novel information in S using expanded new query Q'.

5 Experiments and Analysis

For finding novel information task, two standard test collections are available: TREC (Text REtrieval Conference)'2002 & TREC'2003 novelty tracks test sets. In each set, there are 50 queries, a collection of supposed relevant documents and a set of identified sentences with relevant and new information (called *qrels*) for each query. The *qrels* are generated by assessors.

The two test sets, referred as novelty 2002 and novelty 2003, respectively, are extremely different from each other. Collection of novelty 2002 is poorly relevant to the given user queries. And that of novelty 2003 can be taken as highly reliable relevant sets of documents for queries. Empirical studies have been performed on both collections.

The results are evaluated in terms of *precision*, *recall* and *F-measure*. Sometimes $P \times R$ is also used as one metric.

$$precision = \frac{\#\ relevant\ (or\ new)\ sentences\ matched}{\#\ sentences\ retrieved}$$

$$recall = \frac{\#\ relevant\ (or\ new)\ sentences\ matched}{\#\ relevant\ (or\ new)\ sentences}$$

Since the task of finding novel information is quite difficult than traditional document-level IR task, the precision and recall are much lower.

5.1 Using Global Thesaurus

Semantics-Based QE. Table 1 and Table 2 show QE effects of using different semantic relations, namely hyponyms, synonyms and coordinates, extracted from WordNet on novelty 2002 and 2003 respectively.

Table 1. Effects of QE using WordNet semantic relations (novelty 2002).

methods	precision	recall	F-measure	$P \times R$
unexpanded	0.20	0.28	0.197	0.064
Hyponyms	0.18	0.32	0.197	0.066
Synset	0.17	0.32	0.195	0.068
Coordinate	0.18	0.29	0.189	0.061

Table 2. Effects of QE using WordNet synonyms and hyponyms (novelty 2003).

methods	precision	recall	F-measure
unexpanded	0.633	0.637	0.552
Hyponyms	*0.618*	*0.680*	*0.569*
Synset	0.625	0.665	0.564

In novelty 2002 experiments, expansion based on synonyms achieves trivial improvement in terms of average $P \times R$ while it does not help in terms of *F-measure*. On novelty 2003 (see Table 2), results are better. A little improvement (+3.1%) of system performance has been obtained using F-measure.

The advantage of using global semantic thesaurus is that the noise taken into the thesaurus is relatively less. But there're two main disadvantages: First, manual classifications of words are always too sensitive or too rough, hence it is difficult to decide how many terms should be expanded. Second, because of the ambiguity of natural language, similarities of terms can not be confirmed without context, and therefore expansion based on a global semantic thesaurus is no longer reliable.

Proximity-Based QE. Table 3 and Table 4 describe the effect of proximity-based QE on both test sets. Encouraging results have been achieved, especially on novelty 2003 collection. By using proximity-based expansion, about 10.1% improvement is obtained in terms of F-measure. Also it is shown that after expansion, precision is decreased while the recall is increased, and the overall improvement is made.

Such statistical proximity-based QE approach changes the semantic similarity to the proximity relation, and hence it avoids some difficulties such as word ambiguity, although the relationships between terms got by this approach do not have clear explanation in natural language understanding.

Table 3. Effects of QE by proximity-based expansion (novelty 2002).

methods	precision	recall	F-measure	$P \times R$
unexpanded	0.20	0.28	0.197	0.064
proximity-based QE	0.19	0.30	0.200	0.066
improvement	-5.0%	+7.1%	+1.5%	+3.1%

Table 4. Effects of QE by proximity-based expansion (novelty 2003).

methods	precision	recall	F-measure
unexpanded	0.633	0.637	0.552
proximity-based QE	0.580	0.831	0.608
improvement	*-8.4%*	*+30.4%*	*+10.1%*

Dependency-Based QE. Experimental results of using dependency-based QE to find novel information is shown in the following Table 5 and Table 6. Results are consistent on both test sets. This approach works a little better than proximity-based QE and gets 11.6% improvement on novelty 2003 in terms of F-measure, although the improvement in novelty 2002 is not so obvious.

As mentioned in section 2.3, dependency-based expansion combines statistical information and syntax information, which is the most important advantage of such approaches. And it explains why this kind of QE performs better than statistical proximity-based QE. But the approach also has shortcomings. Since construct such a thesaurus should use a syntax parser, which is not precise, parsing errors will affect the quality of the thesaurus and therefore hurt the performance of finding novel information.

Table 5. Effects of QE by dependency-based expansion (novelty 2002).

methods	precision	recall	F-measure	$P \times R$
unexpanded	0.20	0.28	0.197	0.064
dependency-based QE	0.19	0.31	0.200	0.067
improvement	-5.0%	+10.7%	+1.5%	+4.7%

Table 6. Effects of QE by proximity-based expansion (novelty 2003).

methods	precision	recall	F-measure
unexpanded	0.633	0.637	0.552
dependency-based QE	0.590	0.827	0.616
improvement	*-6.8%*	*+29.8%*	*+11.6%*

5.2 Using Local Co-occurrence-based QE

Effects of using local co-occurrence-based expansion (LCE) in finding novel information are given in Table 7 and Table 8. Results are extremely good. It enhanced system performance greatly in both test sets. Two points are interesting when it is compared with other expansion techniques:

Firstly, LCE lead to consistent great improvement on both test sets which reach to 15.2% and 14.5% respectively, while other expansion approaches could hardly get much improvement in poorly relevant documents of novelty 2002.

Secondly, on novelty 2002 collection, LCE made consistent great progress in terms of both recall and precision, while other QE-based techniques improved the recall but hurt the precision.

When using LCE, characteristics of the retrieval collection have been taken into account, such as word usage context information, and hence the information provided by local thesaurus is more helpful.

Table 7. QE by local co-occurrence expansion (novelty 2002).

methods	precision	recall	F-measure	$P \times R$
unexpanded	0.20	0.28	0.197	0.064
LCE	0.21	0.34	0.227	0.081
improvement	+5.0%	+21.4%	+15.2%	+26.6%

5.3 Pseudo-relevance Feedback

Table 9 gives the effect of pseudo relevance feedback on novelty 2003. More than 5% improvement has been achieved in all cases. And it shows that when more terms are added, the better performance is achieved.

Table 8. QE by local co-occurrence expansion (novelty 2003).

methods	precision	recall	F-measure
unexpanded	0.633	0.637	0.552
LCE, window = 1	0.557	0.866	0.613
improvement, window = 1	-12.0%	+36.0%	+11.1%
LCE, window = 10	0.536	0.955	0.632
improvement, window = 10	-15.3%	+49.9%	+14.5%

Table 9. Effects of pseudo relevance feedback (to expand top M terms in top 3 documents) (novelty 2003).

methods	precision	recall	F-measure	improvement
unexpanded	0.633	0.637	0.552	–
M=10	0.593	0.716	0.584	+5.8%
M=15	0.590	0.732	0.587	+6.3%
M=100	0.589	0.744	0.594	+7.6%

5.4 Comparisons of Approaches

The overview of effects of QE approaches in finding novel information on novelty 2002 and novelty 2003 is shown in Figure 1 and Figure 2, respectively.

Effects on novelty 2003 are better than that on novelty 2002. But the comparison results of effects of different QE approaches are consistent on both test sets. Local co-occurrence-based QE always performs best and makes more than 15% improvement. QE approaches based on statistical proximity and based on dependency are also helpful, improving system performance for about 10%. Pseudo relevance feedback works better than semantic-based QE and the latter one is not helpful to the task of finding novel information.

6 Conclusion

This paper gives an empirical study on effects of different QE techniques in finding novel information. Three branches of approaches have been studied, namely QE based on global thesaurus, QE based on local co-occurrence information and pseudo relevance feedback. In global thesaurus-based approaches, three thesauri namely semantics, statistical proximity, and dependency, have been observed.

According to experiments on two standard test collections of TREC'2002 and TREC'2003 novelty tracks, following conclusions can be drawn.

Firstly, the effect of QE-based approaches in finding novel information depends on the relevance of original documents collection, which comes from the initial results in traditional document-level retrieval.

Secondly, comparison results of effects of different QE approaches are consistent. (1) local co-occurrence-based expansion(LCE) performs best and made more than 15% consistent improvement in both tests. (2) QE approaches based

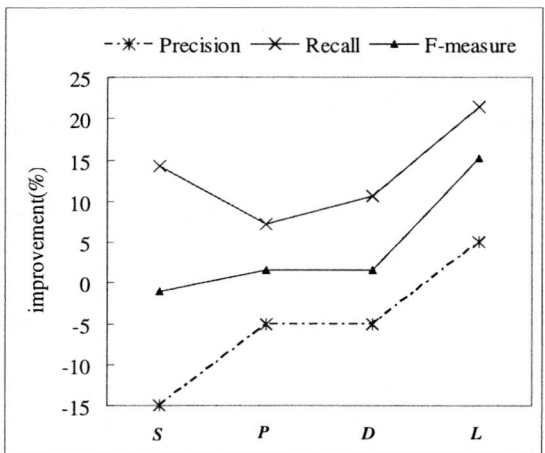

Fig. 1. Comparison of QE approaches (novelty 2002), *S*: Semantic-based QE, *P*: Proximity-based QE, *D*: Dependency-based QE, *L*: Local co-occurrence-based QE.

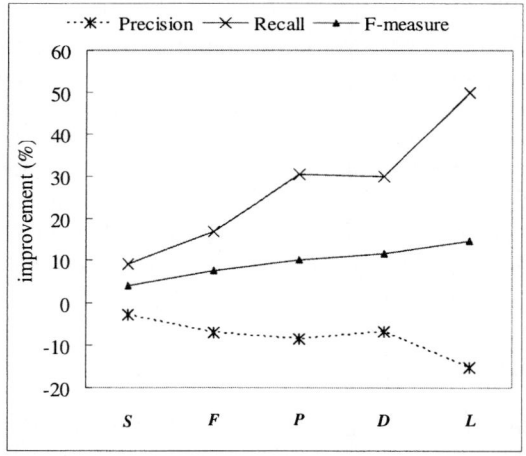

Fig. 2. Comparison of QE approaches (novelty 2003), *S*: Semantic-based QE, *F*: relevance feedback, *P*: Proximity-based QE, *D*: Dependency-based QE, *L*: Local co-occurrence-based QE.

on statistical proximity and based on dependency are both effective to the task, making about 10% enhancement of performances in novelty 2003. And dependency-based QE is a little better. (3) Pseudo relevance feedback works better than semantics-based QE, and improves system performance at about 5%. (4) Semantic-based QE is not helpful on finding novel information.

Thirdly, *LCE* is the only approach that improves system performance in terms of both precision and recall in novelty 2002. Except for that, all QE approaches improve recall but hurt precision as the same time.

In the future, the effects of more QE techniques, especially those most recently proposed ones, will be studied on more test collections. And further analysis will be made.

References

1. Miller G. A., et al.: Introduction to WordNet: An on-line lexical database. International Journal of Lexicography (special issue), (1990) 3(4):235–312
2. Smeaton A. F. and Berrut. C.: Thresholding postings lists, query expansion by word-word distances and POS tagging of Spanish text. In Proceedings of the 4th Text Retrieval Conference (1996)
3. Van Rijbergen.: A theoretical basis for the use of co-occurrence data in information retrieval. Journal of Documentation, (1977) 106–119
4. Crouch, C. J., Yong, B.: Experiments in automatic statistical thesaurus construction. In Proceedings of 15th Int. ACM/SIGIR Conf on R&D in Information Retrieval, Copenhagen, Denmark (1992) 77–87
5. Schutze, H. and Pedersen, J.O.: A cooccurrence-based thesaurus and two applications to information retrieval. In Proceedings of RIAO'94. (1994) 266–274
6. Chen H., et al: Automatic thesaurus generation for an electronic community system. Journal of American Society for Information Science. (1995) 46(3): 175–193
7. Lin D., et al.: Identifying Synonyms among Distributionally Similar Words. In Proceedings of IJCAI-03 (2003)
8. Ruge G.: Experiments on linguistically-based term associations. Information Processing and Management. (1992) 28(3):317–332
9. Grefenstette G.: Explorations in automatic thesaurus discovery. Kluwer Academic Publisher (1994)
10. Voorhees. E. M.: Query Expansion Using Lexical-Semantic Relations. In 17th Annual International ACM SIGIR conference (1994)
11. Xu J. and Croft. W.B.: Query Expansion Using Local and Global Document Analysis. In Proceedings of the 19th Annual International ACM SIGIR Conference. (1996) 4–11
12. Lin D. and Pantel. P.: Concept Discovery from Text. In Proceedings of Conference on Computational Linguistics 2002. Taipei, Taiwan. (2002) 577–583
13. Rocchio. J.: Relevance feedback in information retrieval. The Smart retrieval system experiments in automatic document processing, Prentice-Hall, Englewood Cliffs, NJ. (1971) 313–323
14. Attar R. and Fraenkel A. S.: Local feedback in full-text retrieval systems. Journal of the Association for Computing Machinery. (1977) 24(3): 397–417.
15. Harries Z.S.: Mathematical Structures of Language. New York, Wiley Publisher, (1968)

The Hinoki Treebank.
A Treebank for Text Understanding

Francis Bond[1], Sanae Fujita[1], Chikara Hashimoto[2],
Kaname Kasahara[1], Shigeko Nariyama[3], Eric Nichols[3],
Akira Ohtani[4], Takaaki Tanaka[1], and Shigeaki Amano[1]

[1] NTT Communication Science Laboratories,
Nippon Telegraph and Telephone Corporation
{bond,sanae,kaname,takaaki,amano}@cslab.kecl.ntt.co.jp
[2] Kobe Shoin Women's University
chashi@sils.shoin.ac.jp
[3] Nara Advanced Institute of Science and Technology
{eric-n,shigeko}@is.naist.jp
[4] Osaka Gakuin University
ohtani@utc.osaka-gu.ac.jp

Abstract. In this paper we describe the motivation for and construction of a new Japanese lexical resource: the Hinoki treebank. The treebank is built from dictionary definition sentences, and uses an HPSG grammar to encode the syntactic and semantic information. We then show how this treebank can be used to extract thesaurus information from definition sentences in a language-neutral way using minimal recursion semantics.

1 Introduction

In this paper we describe the construction of a new lexical resource: the Hinoki treebank. We present the motivation for its construction, and a preliminary application. The ultimate goal of our research is natural language understanding – we aim to create a system that can parse text into some useful semantic representation. Ideally this would be such that the output can be used to actually update our semantic models. This is an ambitious goal, and this paper does not present a completed solution, but rather a road-map to the solution, with some progress along the way. The mid-term goal is to build a thesaurus from dictionary definition sentences and use it to enhance a stochastic parse ranking model that combines syntactic and semantic information.

Recently, significant improvements have been made in combining symbolic and statistical approaches to various natural language processing tasks. For example, in parsing, symbolic grammars are being combined with stochastic models (Toutanova et al., 2002). Statistical techniques have also been shown to be useful for word sense disambiguation (Stevenson, 2003). However, to date, there have been no combinations of sense information together with symbolic grammars and statistical models. Klein and Manning (2003) show that much of the gain in statistical parsing using lexicalized models comes from the use of a small set of function words. General relations between words are not so useful, presumably because the data is too sparse: in the Penn treebank normally used to train and test statistical parsers *stocks* and *skyrocket* never appear together. They note that this should motivate the use of similarity and/or class based approaches: the superordinate concepts capital (⊃ *stocks*) and move upward (⊃ *skyrocket*) frequently appear together. However, there has been little success reported on using ontologies with statistical parsers, despite the long history of their succesful use with rule-based systems (Ikehara et al., 1991; Mahesh et al., 1997).

We hypothesize that there are two major reasons for this lack of success. The first reason is that there simply is no single resource that combines syntactic and semantic tagging in a single corpus, so it is impossible to train statistical models using both sources of information. The second is that it is still not clear exactly what kind of semantic information is useful in parsing or how to obtain it.

Our proposed solution to these problems has three phases. In the first phase, we are building a treebank using the Japanese semantic database Lexeed (Kasahara et al., 2004). This is a hand built self-contained lexicon: it consists of headwords and their definitions for the most familiar 28,000 words of Japanese, with all the definitions using only those 28,000 words (and some function words). This set is large enough to include most basic level words and covers over 75% of the common word tokens in a sample of Japanese newspaper text. We then train a statistical model on the treebank and use it to help us induce a thesaurus. In phase two, we will tag the definition sentences with senses and use this information and the thesaurus to build a model that combines syntactic and semantic information. We will also produce a richer ontology – for example extracting qualia structures (Pustejovsky, 1995) and selectional preferences. In phase three, we will look at ways of extending our lexicon and ontology to less familiar words.

In this paper we discuss preliminary results from phase one. In particular, we introduce the construction of the treebank, building the statistical models and inducing the thesaurus. The technologies we are using in phase one are not new, the novelty is in the combination.

In the following section we give more information about Lexeed. Then, in Section 3 we discuss the creation of the treebank: Hinoki. The design is inspired by the Redwoods treebank of English (Oepen et al., 2002) a dynamic treebank closely linked to an HPSG analysis. Hinoki uses the JACY Japanese grammar (Siegel and Bender, 2002).

We describe the use of the Lexeed corpus and the grammar used in the treebank to create a stochastic parse ranker and a thesaurus (§ 4). Finally, we outline in more detail our path to the goal of understanding Japanese (§ 5).

2 The Lexeed Semantic Database of Japanese

The Lexeed Semantic Database of Japanese aims to cover the most common words in Japanese (Kasahara et al., 2004). It was built based on a series of psycholinguistic experiments where words from two existing machine-readable

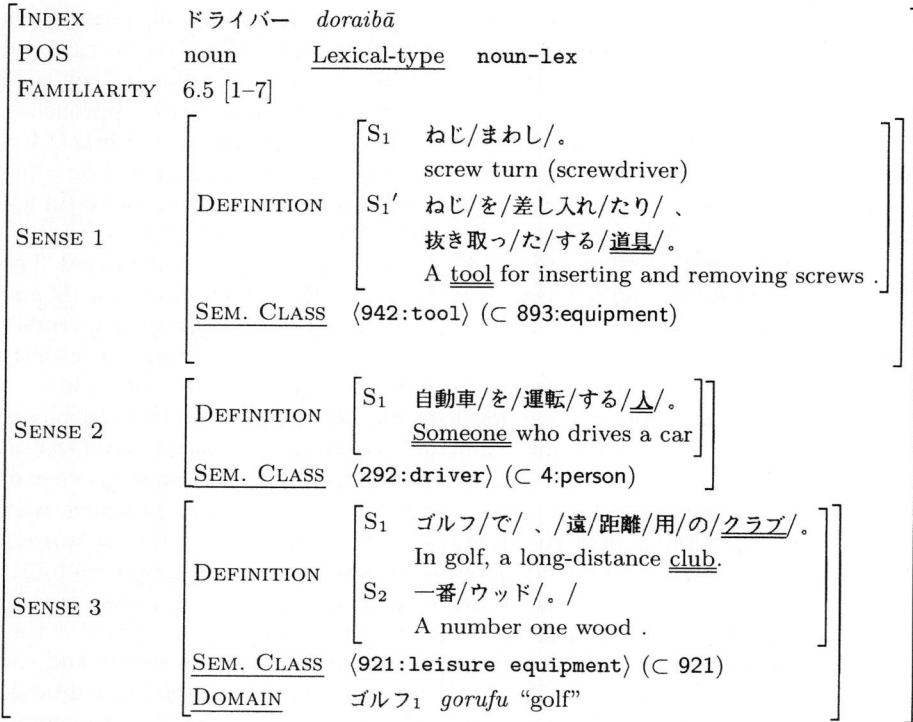

Fig. 1. Entry for the Word *doraibā* "driver" (with English glosses).

dictionaries were presented to subjects and they were asked to rank them on a familiarity scale from one to seven, with seven being the most familiar (Amano and Kondo, 1999).

Lexeed consists of all words with a familiarity greater than or equal to five. There are 28,000 words in all. Many words have multiple senses, there were 46,347 different senses. Definition sentences for these sentences were rewritten by four different analysts to use only the 28,000 familiar words and the best definition chosen by a second set of analysts. In the final configuration, 16,900 different words (60% of all possible words) were actually used in the definition sentences. An example entry for the word ドライバー *doraibā* "driver" is given in Figure 1, with English glosses added. The third sense has two defining sentences. There are 1.7 defining sentences/sense overall.

3 The Hinoki Treebank

The structure of our treebank is based on the Redwoods treebank of English (Oepen et al., 2002). The treebank is built up from the parse output of an HPSG grammar. We chose this structure for several reasons. The most impor-

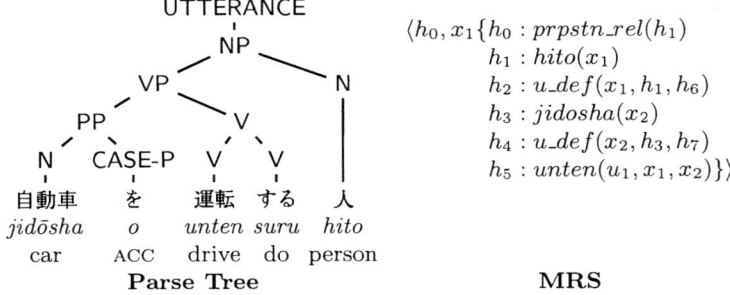

Fig. 2. Parse Tree and Simplified MRS for ドライバー₂ *doraibā* "driver".

tant is that the representation is very rich. The treebank records the complete syntacto-semantic analysis provided by the HPSG grammar, along with an annotator's choice of the most appropriate parse. From this record, all kinds of information can be extracted at various levels of granularity. In particular, traditional syntactic structure (e.g. in the form of labeled trees), dependency relations between words and full meaning representations using minimal recursion semantics (MRS: Copestake et al. (1999)). An example of the labeled tree and MRS views for ドライバー₂ *doraibā* "driver" is given in Figure 2.

Another important reason was the availability of a reasonably robust existing HPSG grammar of Japanese (JACY), and a wide range of open source tools for developing the grammars. We made extensive use of the LKB (Copestake, 2002), a grammar development environment, in order to extend JACY to the domain of defining sentences. We also used the extremely efficient PET parser (Callmeier, 2000), which handles grammars developed using the LKB, to parse large test sets for regression testing, treebanking and finally knowledge acquisition. Most of our development was done within the [incr tsdb()] profiling environment (Oepen and Carroll, 2000). In addition to its well documented facilities for comparing different versions of a grammar (or the same grammar using different parsers), it has facilities for annotating treebanks, updating them and training stochastic models using them. These models can then be used by PET to selectively rank the parser output.

3.1 Creating and Maintaining the Treebank

The construction of the treebank is a two stage process. First, the corpus is parsed (in our case using JACY with the PET parser), and then the annotator selects the correct analysis (or occasionally rejects all analyses). Selection is done through a choice of discriminants. The system selects features that distinguish between different parses, and the annotator selects or rejects the features until only one parse is left. The number of decisions for each sentence is proportional to $\log_2$ of the number of parses, although sometimes a single decision can reduce the number of remaining parses by more or less than half. In general, even a sentence with 5,000 parses only requires around 12 decisions.

Because the disambiguating choices made by the annotators are saved, it is possible to update the treebank when the grammar changes (Oepen et al., 2004). Although the trees depend on the grammar, re-annotation is only necessary in cases where either the parse has become more ambiguous, so new decisions have to be made, or existing rules or lexical items have changed so much that the system cannot reconstruct the parse.

One concern that has been raised with Redwoods style treebanking is the fact that the treebank is tied to a particular implementation of a grammar. The ability to update the treebank alleviates this concern to a large extent. A more serious concern is that it is only possible to annotate those trees that the grammar can parse. Sentences for which no analysis had been implemented in the grammar, or which fail to parse due to processing constraints are left unannotated. This makes grammar coverage an urgent issue. In the next section we discuss how we extended the grammar coverage in order to build the treebank.

3.2 Extending the Grammar

Testing JACY on the full set of 81,000 defining sentences from Lexeed gave a coverage of 39.3%, using the inbuilt unknown word mechanism. This was trivially extended to 46.2% by adding some orthographic variants.

We decided to test JACY's usability by attempting to extend its coverage on the Lexeed defining sentences to over 80% in 4 weeks. Six people were involved in this task; none of whom were involved in the original JACY development. Three of the six had little experience with HPSG.

We expected dictionary definitions to be a relatively easy domain. Barnbrook (2002, p87) showed that for English defining sentences, some eight sentence types covered over 92% of all entries. Japanese defining sentences showed similar regularity. In addition, there is little reference to outside context, and Lexeed has a fixed defining vocabulary.

Because we also wanted to experiment on treebanking in the same timeframe, we restricted ourselves to considering only the first defining sentence for each sense of all words with a familiarity greater than or equal to 6.0. This came to some 10,000 sentences, with an average length of 10.1 words/sentence. Finally, because we wanted to enter full syntactic information for all of the words in Lexeed, we switched off the unknown word processing. This gave us an initial coverage of around 10%.

We were able to bring the coverage to over 80% within the four weeks. The results are shown in Figure 3 which shows both the increase in coverage and change in the number of parser analyses.

The first big increase in coverage (to 55%) came from automatically expanding the lexicon. Tuning the lexicon and rules led to some incremental gains, mainly from relaxing the constraints on some existing rules. We also added some new rules,[1] for example a rule to parse compound verbs. This bought us to over

---

[1] We benefited greatly from some advice from the JACY developers.

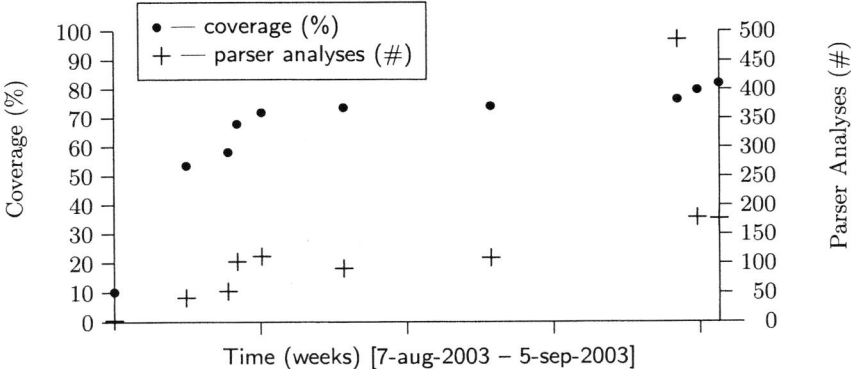

Fig. 3. Evolution of coverage.

70%, at which point we started treebanking. Up to this point, none of the rules we added had been specific to the definition domain.

After two weeks treebanking, we made several small improvements and added a new domain-specific rule for definitions such as ***driver***: *In golf, a long distance club.*. In this case the phrase *in golf* does not modify anything internal to the definition, but is effectively external to it. To handle this, we added a construction which effectively adds a constructionally defined predicate above a noun phrase, if and only if there is an extra adverbial to modify the phrase and the noun phrase is the highest constituent (the root): ***driver***: *In golf, [driver means] a club for ....*. Although the implementation of the construction was specific to Japanese, the idea is not at all language specific, and the resulting semantic representation is language neutral.

Keeping the number of analyses as low as possible is very important from the point of view of building the treebank. All extra ambiguity means more work in selecting the best parse. However, as coverage increases, real ambiguity also increased unavoidably. Occasionally, a rule would cause massive spurious ambiguity. In our first attempt to allow adverbial modification of root noun phrase fragments, we allowed adverbial modification of any noun phrase fragment, which sent the ambiguity skyrocketing to around 500 parses per sentence. The final ambiguity at the end of the four weeks was around 180 parses/sentence. This means that on average each tree requires 7-8 decisions to disambiguate it fully.

3.3 Current Status

We have now treebanked all of the 10,000 sentences with familiarity ≥ 6 which could be parsed (8,000), and over 15,000 of the second and subsequent sentences. Of these sentences, 95% were able to be resolved to one correct parse. Around 5% had no correct parse, mainly due to two errors – one in the construction of the semantic representation for determiners and one in the way coordinate constructions are constructed. The annotator could not settle on a single correct parse for fewer than 1% of the sentences.

All the words in Lexeed's basic vocabulary have been entered in JACY. The current vocabulary size is around 32,000 words. We are now working with the main developers to reduce the average ambiguity and increase the coverage. The handling of numeral classifiers has also been improved (Bender and Siegel, 2004). The extended JACY grammar is available for download from www.dfki.uni-sb. de/~siegel/grammar-download/JACY-grammar.html.

4 Applications

The treebanked data and grammar have been tested in two ways. The first is to train a stochastic model for parse selection. The second is to use the parsed data to extract a thesaurus.

4.1 Stochastic Parse Ranking

Using the treebanked data, we built a stochastic parse ranking model with [incr tsdb()]. The ranker uses a maximum entropy learner to train a PCFG over the parse derivation trees, with the current node as a conditioning feature. The correct parse is selected 61.7% of the time (training on 4,000 sentences and testing on another 1,000; evaluated per sentence). More feature-rich models using parent and grandparent nodes along with semantic features have been proposed and implemented with an English grammar and the Redwoods treebank (Oepen et al., 2002). We intend to include such features, as well as to add our own extensions to train on constituent weight and semantic class.

4.2 Knowledge Acquisition

In addition to our work on the development of a Japanese language HPSG treebank, we are using the the corpus of dictionary definition sentences for knowledge acquisition. Past research in knowledge acquisition from definition sentences in Japanese has primarily dealt with the task of automatically generating hierarchy structures. Tsurumaru et al. (1991) developed a system for automatic thesaurus construction based on information derived from analysis of the terminal clauses of definition sentences. It was successful in classifying hyperonym, hyponym, and synonym relationships; however, it lacked any concrete evaluation of the accuracy of the hierarchies created. More recently Tokunaga et al. (2001) created an ontology from a machine-readable dictionary and combined it with an existing thesaurus.

Our method differs from the aforementioned in two main respects: first, prior research has been limited to nouns, where our method handles all parts of speech; second, we are fully parsing the input, not just using regular expressions.

It is the use of full syntactic analysis with a well defined semantics (Minimal Recursion Semantics, Copestake et al. (1999)) that is the most important.

There are three reasons. The first is that it makes our knowledge acquisition somewhat language independent: if we have a parser that can produce MRS, and a dictionary for that language, the algorithm can easily be ported. The second reason is that we can go on to use the same system to acquire knowledge from non-dictionary sources, which will not be as regular as dictionaries and thus harder to parse using only regular expressions. Third, we can more easily acquire knowledge beyond simple hypernyms, for example, identifying synonyms through common definition patterns as proposed by Tsuchiya et al. (2001).

To extract hypernyms, we parse the first definition sentence for each sense. The parser uses the stochastic parse ranking model learned from the Hinoki treebank, and returns the MRS of the first ranked parse. Currently, 82% of the sentences can be parsed. In most cases, the word with the highest scope in the MRS representation will be the hypernym. For example, for $doraib\bar{a}_1$ the hypernym is 道具 *tool* "dōgu" and for $doraib\bar{a}_2$ the hypernym is 人 *hito* "person" (see Figure 1). Although the actual hypernym is in very different positions in the Japanese and English definition sentences, it takes the highest scope in both their semantic representations.

For some definition sentences (around 20%), further parsing of the semantic representation is necessary. For example, ドライバー$_3$ is defined as ***driver***: *In golf, a long distance club*. In this case *in golf* has the highest scope: the hypernym is the complement of the empty copula. Again, this semantic representation is not language dependent, so we do not have to recreate the knowledge extraction system for new languages. Further, as we expand the scope of the knowledge acquisition the parsing can give us more information: for example that this sense of *driver* is used in the domain of **golf**.

We evaluate the extracted pairs by comparison with an existing thesaurus: the Goi-Taikei (Ikehara et al., 1997). Currently 58.5% of the pairs extracted for nouns are linked to nodes in the Goi-Taikei ontology (Bond et al., 2004). Some examples are given in Table 1. The remaining entries are words whose definition requires more parsing (15%) or those where one or both words could not be found in the Goi-Taikei.

Table 1. Sense Disambiguation using Hypernyms.

Word	Hypernym	Word Node	Hypernym Node
ドライバー$_1$ "driver"	人 "person"	worker	person
ドライバー$_2$	道具 "equipment"	tool	equipment
ドライバー$_3$	クラブ "club"	leisure equipment	leisure equipment

In general, we are extracting pairs with more information than the Goi-Taikei hierarchy of 2,710 classes. In particular, many classes contain a mixture of class names and instance names: 豚肉 *buta niku* "pork" and 肉 *niku* "meat" are in the same class, as are ドラム *percussion instrument* "drum" and 打楽器 *dagakki* "percussion instrument", which we can now distinguish.

5 Conclusion and Further Work

In this paper we have explained the motivation for the construction of a new lexical resource: the Hinoki treebank, and described its initial construction. We have further showed how it can be used to develop a language independent system for acquiring thesauruses from machine-readable dictionaries.

The first step in our path toward developing a system capable of fully understanding Japanese is to treebank all the defining sentences in Lexeed. This means that we must improve the coverage of the grammar, so that we can parse all sentences. When we have completed this task we will retrain our statistical model and use the new grammar to relearn the hypernym relations with higher precision.

In phase two we will add the knowledge of hypernyms into the stochastic model, and look at learning other information from the parsed defining sentences – in particular syntactic lexical-types, semantic association scores, meronyms, synonyms and antonyms.

In phase three, we will use the acquisition models learned in phase two, to extend our model to words not in Lexeed, using definition sentences from machine readable dictionaries or where they appear within normal text. In this way, we can grow an extensible lexicon and thesaurus from Lexeed.

Acknowledgements

We would like to thank Colin Bannard, Timothy Baldwin, Emily Bender, Ulrich Callmeier, Ann Copestake, Dan Flickinger, Stephan Oepen, Yuji Matsumoto and especially Melanie Siegel for their support and encouragement.

References

Shigeaki Amano and Tadahisa Kondo. *Nihongo-no Goi-Tokusei (Lexical properties of Japanese)*. Sanseido, 1999.

Geoff Barnbrook. *Defining Language – A local grammar of definition sentences*. Studies in Corpus Linguistics. John Benjamins, 2002.

Emily M. Bender and Melanie Siegel. Implementing the syntax of Japanese numeral classifiers. In *Proceedings of the IJC-NLP-2004*. Springer-Verlag, 2004. (this volume).

Francis Bond, Eric Nichols, Sanae Fujita, and Takaaki Tanaka. Acquiring an ontology for a fundamental vocabulary. In *COLING 2004*, Geneva, 2004. (to appear).

Ulrich Callmeier. PET - a platform for experimentation with efficient HPSG processing techniques. *Natural Language Engineering*, 6(1):99–108, 2000.

Ann Copestake. *Implementing Typed Feature Structure Grammars*. CSLI Publications, 2002.

Ann Copestake, Dan Flickinger, Carl Pollard, and Ivan A. Sag. Minimal recursion semantics: An introduction.
  (manuscript http://www-csli.stanford.edu/~aac/papers/newmrs.ps), 1999.

Satoru Ikehara, Masahiro Miyazaki, Satoshi Shirai, Akio Yokoo, Hiromi Nakaiwa, Kentaro Ogura, Yoshifumi Ooyama, and Yoshihiko Hayashi. *Goi-Taikei – A Japanese Lexicon*. Iwanami Shoten, Tokyo, 1997. 5 volumes/CDROM.

Satoru Ikehara, Satoshi Shirai, Akio Yokoo, and Hiromi Nakaiwa. Toward an MT system without pre-editing – effects of new methods in **ALT-J/E**–. In *Third Machine Translation Summit: MT Summit III*, pages 101–106, Washington DC, 1991. (http://xxx.lanl.gov/abs/cmp-lg/9510008).

Kaname Kasahara, Hiroshi Sato, Francis Bond, Takaaki Tanaka, Sanae Fujita, Tomoko Kanasugi, and Shigeaki Amano. Construction of a Japanese semantic lexicon: Lexeed. SIG NLC-159, IPSJ, Tokyo, 2004. (in Japanese).

Dan Klein and Christopher D. Manning. Accurate unlexicalized parsing. In Erhard Hinrichs and Dan Roth, editors, *Proceedings of the 41st Annual Meeting of the Association for Computational Linguistics*, pages 423–430, 2003. URL http://www.aclweb.org/anthology/P03-1054.pdf.

Kavi Mahesh, Sergei Nirenburg, Stephen Beale, Evelyne Viegas, Victor Raskin, and Boyan Onyshkevych. Word sense disambiguation: Why statistics when you have these numbers? In *Seventh International Conference on Theoretical and Methodological Issues in Machine Translation: TMI-97*, pages 151–159, Santa Fe, 1997.

Stephan Oepen and John Carroll. Performance profiling for grammar engineering. *Natural Language Engineering*, 6(1):81–97, 2000.

Stephan Oepen, Dan Flickinger, and Francis Bond. Towards holistic grammar engineering and testing – grafting treebank maintenance into the grammar revision cycle. In *Beyond Shallow Analyses – Formalisms and Satitistical Modelling for Deep Analysis (Workshop at IJCNLP-2004)*, Hainan Island, 2004. (http://www-tsujii.is.s.u-tokyo.ac.jp/bsa/).

Stephan Oepen, Dan Flickinger, Kristina Toutanova, and Christoper D. Manning. LinGO redwoods: A rich and dynamic treebank for HPSG. In *Proceedings of The First Workshop on Treebanks and Linguistic Theories (TLT2002)*, Sozopol, Bulgaria, 2002.

James Pustejovsky. *The Generative Lexicon*. MIT Press, Cambridge, MA, 1995.

Melanie Siegel and Emily M. Bender. Efficient deep processing of Japanese. In *Procedings of the 3rd Workshop on Asian Language Resources and International Standardization at the 19th International Conference on Computational Linguistics*, Taipei, 2002.

Mark Stevenson. *Word Sense Disambiguation*. CSLI Publications, 2003.

Takenobu Tokunaga, Yasuhiro Syotu, Hozumi Tanaka, and Kiyoaki Shirai. Integration of heterogeneous language resources: A monolingual dictionary and a thesaurus. In *Proceedings of the 6th Natural Language Processing Pacific Rim Symposium, NLPRS2001*, pages 135–142, Tokyo, 2001.

Kristina Toutanova, Christoper D. Manning, and Stephan Oepen. Parse ranking for a rich HPSG grammar. In *Proceedings of The First Workshop on Treebanks and Linguistic Theories (TLT2002)*, Sozopol, Bulgaria, 2002.

Masatoshi Tsuchiya, Sadao Kurohashi, and Satoshi Sato. Discovery of definition patterns by compressing dictionary sentences. In *Proceedings of the 6th Natural Language Processing Pacific Rim Symposium, NLPRS2001*, pages 411–418, Tokyo, 2001.

Hiroaki Tsurumaru, Katsunori Takesita, Itami Katsuki, Toshihide Yanagawa, and Sho Yoshida. An approach to thesaurus construction from Japanese language dictionary. In *IPSJ SIGNotes Natural Language*, volume 83-16, pages 121–128, 1991. (in Japanese).

Building a Parallel Bilingual Syntactically Annotated Corpus

Jan Cuřín[2], Martin Čmejrek[2], Jiří Havelka[1,2], and Vladislav Kuboň[1]

[1] Institute of Formal and Applied Linguistics, Charles University in Prague
`vk@ufal.mff.cuni.cz`
[2] Center for Computational Linguistics, Charles University in Prague
`{curin,cmejrek,havelka}@ufal.mff.cuni.cz`

Abstract. This paper describes a process of building a bilingual syntactically annotated corpus, the PCEDT (Prague Czech-English Dependency Treebank). The corpus is being created at Charles University, Prague, and the release of this corpus as Linguistic Data Consortium data collection is scheduled for the spring of 2004. The paper discusses important decisions made prior to the start of the project and gives an overview of all kinds of resources included in the PCEDT.

1 Introduction

Probably the most important trend in linguistics in the last decade is the massive use of large natural language corpora in many linguistic fields. The concept of collecting large amounts of written or spoken natural language data has become extremely important for several linguistic research fields.

The majority of large corpora used by linguists are monolingual, although there are several examples of bilingual corpora (e.g. Hansard corpus). The efforts of Czech computational linguists also concentrated in the past on creating large scale monolingual corpora as for example the Czech National Corpus (annotated on morphological level) or Prague Dependency Treebank (PDT). The PDT is annotated on three levels - morphological layer (lowest), analytic layer (middle) - superficial (surface) syntactic annotation, and tectogrammatical layer (highest) - level of linguistic meaning. Dependency trees, representing the sentence structure as concentrated around the verb and its valency, are used for the analytical and tectogrammatical layers of PDT.

Only very few parallel bilingual corpora were available for the Czech-English language pair before the start of our project. A Reader's Digest corpus, which had been used in several smaller projects in the past, was one of the few exceptions. The situation with other language pairs was even worse, no reasonable resources were available at that moment.

2 The Initial Considerations

The experience gained in the process of building the above mentioned corpora indicated that collecting the data is much easier than annotating it. The deeper is the level of annotation, the longer and more expensive is the process of creating it. This fact is even more important for a parallel corpus, where every sentence is annotated twice, independently in each language.

Generally there are two possible strategies for building a parallel corpus. The first one is the parallel annotation of already existing parallel texts, the second one is the translation and annotation of already existing syntactically annotated corpus.

The first approach has from our point of view two major drawbacks. In addition to the obvious problem of double annotation efforts there is also a problem of "relatedness" of parallel texts available. The up-to-now main parallel Czech-English resource, Reader's Digest corpus, contains extremely free translations, which have proved difficult in several machine-learning experiments [1].

The second approach, the human translation of an existing monolingual syntactically annotated corpus into the target language and its subsequent syntactic annotation, not only seems to allow better control over the translation quality and reliability, but also reduces the necessary annotation efforts to annotation of a text in a single language. These initial considerations led to a decision to translate some already existing corpus.

2.1 Choosing the Translation Direction

When the choice of the general strategy had been made it remained to decide what kind of syntactic annotation to use and to choose a source language (and a source corpus, too). There were two natural candidates for the source text, namely the PennTreebank (for English) and the Prague Dependency Treebank (for Czech). The size of both corpora is approximately the same (more than 1 million words), both are syntactically annotated, both contain newspaper data (although PDT not exclusively, it also contains data from other sources). The choice of the PennTreebank as a source corpus was then pragmatically motivated – all the translators were native speakers of Czech and we have supposed that they should be able to provide higher quality of translation when translating into their native language.

2.2 Type of Syntactic Annotation

Another important issue was the choice of the annotation scheme. In fact this is the point where PennTreebank and PDT differ to a greatest extent. The syntactic annotations of the PennTreebank are relatively simple and transparent, they are based on constituent trees coded through a system of brackets accompanied by tags, while PDT is based on dependency trees. More precisely, Penn Treebank (version 3; LDC catalog no. LDC99T42, ISBN: 1- 58563-163-9) comprises the surface syntactic structure, various types of null elements representing underlying positions for wh-movement, passive voice, infinitive constructions etc., and also predicate-argument structure markup.

The PennTreebank annotation of the sentence "*UAL's decision to remain independent company sent share prices tumbling.*" is shown in Figure 1.

```
((S
   (NP-SBJ
     (NP (NNP UAL) (POS 's) )
       (NN decision)
       (S
         (NP-SBJ (-NONE- *) )
         (VP (TO to)
           (VP (VB remain)
             (NP-PRD (DT an) (JJ independent) (NN company) )))))
   (VP (VBD sent)
     (S
       (NP-SBJ (NN share) (NNS prices) )
       (VP (VBG tumbling) )))
   (. .) ))
```

Fig. 1.

Due to the fact that Czech is a language with relatively high degree of word-order freedom its sentences relatively often contain some phenomena (discontinues constituents etc.) which cannot be coded by a simple bracketing system. The annotation scheme of the PDT is therefore more complicated and less transparent than that of the PennTreebank.

The Figure 2 shows the PDT annotation of the first three words in the sentence "*Smlouvy o debetu však KB poskytuje pouze omezenému počtu vybraných klientů.*" [The KB provides debit agreements only to a limited number of selected clients.] Similarly as in the previous case the annotation contains both morphological and syntactic tags.

```
<s id="ln95047:001-p5s4">
    <f cap>Smlouvy
    <l>smlouva
    <t>NNFP4-----A----
    <A>Obj
    <r>1<g>6
    <f>o
    <l>o-1
    <t> RR--6----------
    <A>AuxP
    <r>2<g>1
    <f>debetu
    <l>debet
    <t>NNIS6-----A----
    <A>Atr
    <r>3<g>2
    ...
```

Fig. 2.

3 The Translation Process

In order to achieve maximal quality of the translation we have divided the process of translation of PennTreebank data into several steps.

3.1 Filtering the Tags from the Treebank

Although the CD containing PennTreebank 3 contains not only fully morphologically and syntactically annotated data, but also various other levels of annotation (including text files with the data in the plain text format), we have decided to take as a basis for translation the files containing the fully annotated data (files having the *.mrg* extension in the PennTreebank 3) which will be included in the PCEDT. This decision was motivated by the endeavor to maintain a closest possible relationship between the annotated English and annotated Czech data. We have found several examples where the data in the plain text format were not included in the annotated part of PennTreebank, therefore we have decided to apply simple filters removing all tags and assigning each sentence its unique number consisting of the file name and the sequential number of a sentence in the file, starting from 0. The sentence from the Figure 1 then looks like this:

```
<wsj_1102.mrg:3::>UAL's decision to remain independent company
sent share prices tumbling.
```

3.2 Preparing the Glossary

Due to the fact that the translation of Wall Street Journal texts from PennTreebank is extremely difficult, we have decided to provide the translators with a glossary of most frequent terms. The glossary should help to maintain the consistency of translation even when multiple translators do the job.

Originally we have considered to use a translation tool DejaVu for the extraction of terms, but it turned out that it is not able to handle more than 1 million words of PennTreebank, so we were forced to create our own simple extraction tool in Perl. The extraction tool made a list of frequently cooccurring word sequences of various length. This list of course contained multiple random word sequences, so we have applied manual filtering in order to get a list of real terms. This list was then translated into Czech and distributed to all translators.

3.3 Translation and Revisions

The translators (there were about 20 human translators involved in various stages of translation) were asked to translate each English sentence as a single Czech sentence and to avoid unnecessary stylistic changes of translated sentences. The translations are revised on two levels, linguistic and factual. It turned out that especially the factual revision is extremely difficult due to the nature of source texts. The Wall Street Journal articles are written in a style which is very far from the style of Czech newspaper articles. The text is full of economic slang, it is extremely compact, packed with references to institutions, people, and events which are not generally known outside of Wall Street circles. This is the main reason why the revisions are proceeding slower than we have expected – only about one fifth of translated texts is fully revised at the moment.

4 The Annotation of the PCEDT

As mentioned above, the annotation scheme of PDT has been chosen for the annotation of the PCEDT. Apart from the linguistic reasons for this decision there was very strong technical one – due to the long experience with annotations of the PDT we had at our disposal several skilled annotators involved in annotations of the PDT.

Let us now briefly summarize basic facts about the annotation scheme of PDT (and PCEDT). In PDT, a single-rooted dependency tree is being built for every sentence as a result of the annotation both at the analytical (surface-syntactic) and tectogrammatical (deep syntactic) level. Every item (token) from the morphological layer becomes (exactly) one node in the analytical tree, and no nodes (except for the single "technical" root of the tree) are added. The order of nodes in the original sentence is being preserved in an additional attribute, but non-projective constructions are allowed. Analytical functions, despite being kept in nodes, are in fact names of the dependency relations between a dependent (child) node and its governor (parent) node. Only a single (manually assigned) analytical annotation (dependency tree) is allowed per sentence. There are 24 analytical functions used, such as Sb (Subject), Obj (Object), Adv (Adverbial), Atr (Attribute in noun phrases) etc.

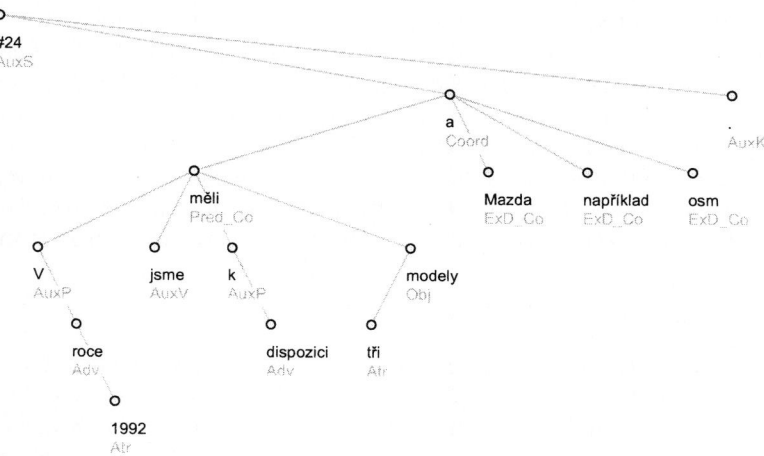

Fig. 3. Analytical annotation of the sentence "*V roce 1992 jsme měli k dispozici tři modely a Mazda například osm.*" [In the year 1992 we had at our disposal three models and Mazda (had) for example eight (models).]

The tectogrammatical level is the most elaborated, complicated but also the most theoretically based layer of syntactico-semantic (or "deep syntactic") representation. The tectogrammatical layer annotation scheme is divided into four sublayers:

- dependencies and functional annotation,
- the topic/focus annotation including reordering according to the deep word order,
- coreference,
- the fully specified tectogrammatical annotation (including the necessary grammatical information).

As an additional data structure we use a syntactic lexicon, mainly capturing the notion of valency. The lexicon is not needed for the interpretation of the tectogrammatical representation itself, but it is helpful when working on the annotation since it defines when a particular node should be created that is missing on the surface. In other words, the notion of (valency-based) elipsis is defined by the dictionary.

The tectogrammatical layer goes beyond the surface structure of the sentence, replacing notions such as "subject" and "object" by notions like "actor", "patient", "addressee" etc. The representation itself still relies upon the language structure itself rather than on world knowledge. The nodes in the tectogrammatical tree are autosemantic words only. Dependencies between nodes represent the relations between the (autosemantic) words in a sentence, for the predicate as well as any other node in the sentence. The dependencies are labeled by functors, which describe the dependency relations. Every node of the tree is furthermore annotated by such a set of grammatical features that enables to fully capture the meaning of the sentence.

See [2] and [3] for details on analytical and tectogrammatical annotations of PDT, respectively.

5 The Annotation Tools Used in PCEDT

While the morphological annotation of the English part is simply taken over from the Penn Treebank, the analytical and tectogrammatical markups of the English part of the corpus are obtained by two in dependent procedures transforming the phrase trees into dependency ones. The Penn Treebank phrase trees had to be automatically transformed into dependency trees: only terminal nodes of the phrase tree are converted to nodes of the dependency tree and the dependency structure is built recursively so that the node representing a head constituent governs the nodes representing its sibling constituents. The transformation procedure is based on rules taking into account the information from the phrase tree (POS, functional markup, traces etc.), resulting into two different structures – analytical and tectogrammatical ones.

The annotation of Czech at the morphological level is an unstructured classification of individual tokens (words and punctuation) of the utterance into morphological classes (morphological tags) and lemmas. The original word forms

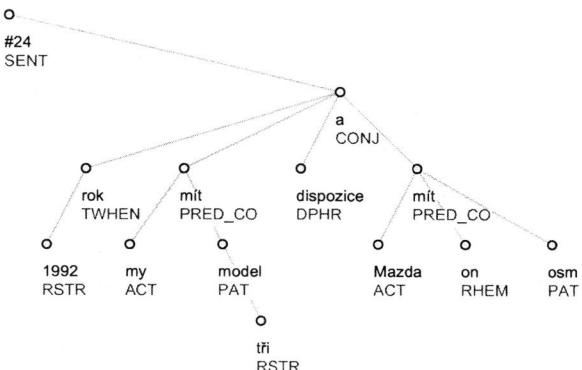

Fig. 4. Tectogrammatical tree for the sentence "*V roce 1992 jsme měli k dispozici tři modely a Mazda například osm.*" [In the year 1992 we had at our disposal three models and Mazda (had) for example eight (models).]

are preserved, too. In fact, every token has gotten its unique ID within the corpus for reference reasons. Sentence boundaries are preserved and/or corrected if found wrong (the errors in original texts contained in the Czech National Corpus have been preserved in the corpus). The number of tags actually appearing in the PDT is about 1100 out of 4,257 theoretically possible. The data has been double annotated fully manually, the annotators selected a correct tag out of a set provided by a module of an automatic morphological analysis (cf. [2]).

The Czech part is automatically annotated by the BH tagging tools [4] on the morphological level. The analytical representation is obtained by a statistical dependency parser for Czech – either Collins parser [5] or Charniak parser [6], both adapted to dependency grammar – and a C4.5 classifier assigning syntactic functions to nodes of the dependency tree. The tectogrammatical markup is a result of an automatic, rule-based transformation of analytical trees according to linguistic rules [7] and a C4.5 classifier assigning tectogrammatical functions [8].

6 Additional Resources Included in PCEDT

For both development testing and evaluation measured by BLEU metrics [9], a test set of about 500 sentences was retranslated back from Czech into English by 4 different translator offices, two of them from the Czech Republic and two of them from the U.S. Figure 5 illustrates the differences between retranslated sentences and an original sentence from the Penn Treebank.

To be able to observe the relationship between the tectogrammatical structure of a Czech sentence and its English translation (without distortions caused by automatic parsing), we have manually annotated on the tectogrammatical level both Czech and English sentences from the test set.

The PCEDT comprises also a translation dictionary, compiled from three different Czech- English manual dictionaries: two of them were downloaded form

Original from PTB: *Kaufman & Broad, a home building company, declined to identify the institutional investors.*

Czech translation: *Kaufman & Broad, firma specializující se na bytovou výstavbu, odmítla institucionální investory jmenovat.*

Reference 1: *Kaufman & Broad, a company specializing in housing development, refused to give the names of their corporate investors.*

Reference 2: *Kaufman & Broad, a firm specializing in apartment building, refused to list institutional investors.*

Reference 3: *Kaufman & Broad, a firm specializing in housing construction, refused to name the institutional investors.*

Reference 4: *Residential construction company Kaufman & Broad refused to name the institutional investors.*

Fig. 5. A sample English sentence from WSJ, its Czech translation, and four reference retranslations.

the Web and one was extracted from Czech and English EuroWordNets. Entry-translation pairs were filtered and weighed taking into account the reliability of the source dictionary, the frequencies of the translations in the English monolingual corpus, and the correspondence of the Czech and English POS tags. Furthermore, by training GIZA++ [10] translation model on the training part of the PCEDT extended by the manual dictionaries, we obtained a probabilistic Czech-English dictionary, more sensitive to the specific domain of financial news.

7 Conclusion

Building a large scale syntactically annotated parallel bilingual corpus is an extremely difficult endeavor, even if both languages are typologically similar and the syntactic annotation is based on similar linguistic tradition. This paper describes a method developed for the situation when both languages are typologically different as well as the data types traditionally used for the description of syntax. We do not think that our method is the only method possible, but nevertheless, we hope that the description of our method may help other researchers to avoid some of our mistakes when developing their own parallel syntactically annotated corpora.

The exploitation of the PCEDT for the stochastic machine translation is only most obvious application of this new parallel bilingual corpus. We hope that after the publication of currently available data (slightly more than one half of the Wall Street Journal section of Penn Treebank has been translated up to now) and especially after the completion of the whole project the PCEDT will prove to be a valuable source of data for various applications.

Acknowledgement

The work described in this paper has been supported by the grant of the MŠMT ČR No. ME642, No. LN00A063, by NSF Grant No. IIS-0121285 and partially supported by the grant of the GAČR No. 405/03/0914.

References

1. Al-Onaizan, Y., Curín, J., Jahr, M., Knight, K., Lafferty, J., Melamed, D., Och, F.J., Purdy, D., Smith, N.A., Yarowsky, D.: The Statistical Machine Translation. Technical report (1999) NLP WS'99 Final Report.
2. Hajič, J., Panevová, J., Buráňová, E., Urešová, Z., Bémová, A., Štěpánek, J., Pajas, P., Kárník, J.: A Manual for Analytic Layer Tagging of the Prague Dependency Treebank, Prague, Czech Republic. (2001)
3. Hajičová, E., Panevová, J., Sgall, P.: A manual for tectogrammatic tagging of the prague dependency treebank. Technical Report TR-2000-09, ÚFAL MFF UK, Prague, Czech Republic (2000)
4. Hajič, J., Hladká, B.: Tagging Inflective Languages: Prediction of Morphological Categories for a Rich, Structured Tagset. In: Proceedings of COLING-ACL Conference, Montreal, Canada (1998) 483–490
5. Hajič, J., Brill, E., Collins, M., Hladká, B., Jones, D., Kuo, C., Ramshaw, L., Schwartz, O., Tillmann, C., Zeman, D.: Core Natural Language Processing Technology Applicable to Multiple Languages. Technical Report Research Note 37, Center for Language and Speech Processing, Johns Hopkins University, Baltimore, MD (1998)
6. Charniak, E.: A Maximum-Entropy-Inspired Parser. Technical Report CS-99-12 (1999)
7. Böhmová, A.: Automatic procedures in tectogrammatical tagging. The Prague Bulletin of Mathematical Linguistics **76** (2001)
8. Žabokrtský, Z., Sgall, P., Džeroski, S.: Machine Learning Approach to Automatic Functor Assignment in the Prague Dependency Treebank. In: Proceedings of LREC 2002. Volume V., Las Palmas de Gran Canaria, Spain (2002) 1513–1520
9. Papineni, K., Roukos, S., Ward, T., Zhu, W.J.: Bleu: a method for automatic evaluation of machine translation. Technical Report RC22176, IBM (2001)
10. Och, F.J., Ney, H.: A Systematic Comparison of Various Statistical Alignment Models. Computational Linguistics **29** (2003) 19–51

Acquiring Bilingual Named Entity Translations from Content-Aligned Corpora

Tadashi Kumano[1], Hideki Kashioka[1], Hideki Tanaka[2], and Takahiro Fukusima[3]

[1] ATR Spoken Language Translation Research Laboratories,
2-2-2, Hikaridai, Keihanna Science City, Kyoto 619-0288, Japan
tadashi.kumano@atr.jp
[2] NHK Science and Technical Research Laboratories,
1-10-11, Kinuta, Setagaya-ku, Tokyo 157-8510, Japan
[3] Otemon Gakuin University, 1-15, Nishiai 2-chome, Ibaraki, Osaka 567-8502, Japan

Abstract. We propose a new method for acquiring bilingual named entity (NE) translations from non-literal, content-aligned corpora. It first recognizes NEs in each of a bilingual document pair using the NE extraction technique, then finds NE groups whose members share the same referent, and finally corresponds between bilingual NE groups. The exhaustive detection of NEs can potentially acquire translation pairs with broad coverage. The correspondences between bilingual NE groups are estimated based on the similarity of the appearance order in each document, and the corresponding performance came up to $F_{(\beta=1)} = 71.0\%$ by using small bilingual dictionary together. The total performance for acquiring bilingual NE pairs through the overall process of extraction, grouping, and corresponding was $F_{(\beta=1)} = 58.8\%$.

1 Introduction

Translating named entities (NEs) correctly is indispensable for correctly conveying information when translating documents including many NEs, such as news articles. NE translations, however, are not listed in conventional dictionaries. It is necessary to retrieve NE translation knowledge from the latest documents.

We aim to extract translation pairs of NEs from bilingual broadcast news articles or newspaper articles with broad coverage. Each bilingual pair of the articles is written to convey the same topic. However, it is not always possible to assign sentential correspondence for them, because they are not literally translated. Furthermore, since NEs do not appear repeatedly, we cannot expect to obtain a statistically sufficient frequency even when we construct a large corpus. Most of the previous studies on acquiring translation pairs from bilingual corpora were not able to fully handle the task of extracting infrequent expression pairs from not-literally-translated bilingual documents.

To achieve our goal, we propose a new method that first extracts NEs from the source and target parts of a bilingual document pair, then finds correspondences between the bilingual NEs. The exhaustive detection of NEs using the (monolingual) NE extraction technique can potentially acquire a translation pair

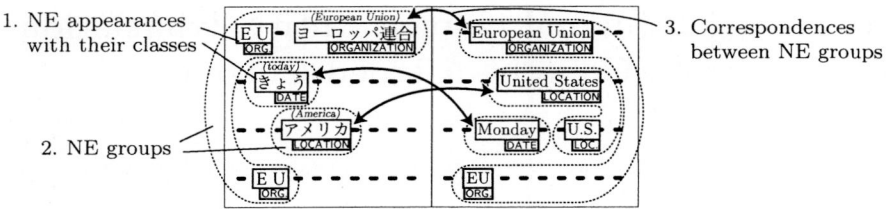

Fig. 1. Representation of NE Translations in a Document Pair.

that appears only once in an entire corpus. The correspondence estimation is based on the similarity of the appearance order in entire documents, therefore sentential alignments between document pairs are not required. We came to the idea of deciding corresponding relations based on the similarity of the appearance order in documents from a prior analysis of an "NHK J-E News Corpus," the Japanese-English broadcast news article pairs with NE tags [1]. The analysis showed that even in a content-aligned corpus, which is not translated literally, when an NE appears in a document, its translation is very likely to appear in the counterpart document, and the appearance order also shows a strong correlation.

In this paper, we will report the preliminary experiment of our proposed method. In Section 2, we will first formulate the task. Then we will introduce our corpus and briefly report the corpus analysis in Section 3. In Section 4, the method will be explained thoroughly. The implementation and performance of each module will be introduced. In Section 5, we will show an evaluation and analysis of an experiment on extracting Japanese-English translation pairs of NEs, having all the modules connected. Related work will be described in Section 6, and finally, we will refer to our future plans in Section 7.

2 Task Definition

When several expressions in a document exist for the same referent, all of them can be translated as the same expression in a counterpart language. It is not always possible to determine the actual translation for each expression from the counterpart document when the document pair is composed of a non-literal translation.

For this reason, we defined the task of acquiring NE translation pairs from not-literally-translated bilingual documents as the extraction of NE group pairs that share the same referent in each of the documents. Specifically, it is formulated by the extraction of the following three kinds of information (Figure 1):

1. NE tokens with their classes (person, organization, etc.) for both of the documents in the pair,
2. NE groups sharing the same referent in each of the documents in the pair,
3. One-to-one correspondences between NE groups of the same class in both documents.

3 Construction and Analysis of Japanese-English Broadcast News Corpus with NE Tags

We have constructed an NE-tagged bilingual corpus called the "NHK J-E News Corpus" [1]. Named entities and some numeral expressions (we simply call all of them 'named entities' or 'NEs') are tagged manually in 2,000 pairs of Japanese-English broadcast news articles by NHK (Japan Broadcast Corporation). The tags are designed so as to express the three kinds of information described in Section 2. The tag assignments conform to the guidelines of the Japanese information extraction workshop IREX [2] NE task not only for the Japanese documents but also for the English documents of the corpus. The classes of NEs are: **ORGANIZATION, PERSON, LOCATION, ARTIFACT, DATE, TIME, MONEY**, and **PERCENT**. The corpus contains 43,420 NE tokens and 22,944 groups for the Japanese, and 28,341 tokens and 18,630 groups for the English.

The facts from our previous analysis of the corpus are summarized as follows:

- The NEs in Japanese are fairly well translated into English in spite of the decrease in article size through the overall translation.
- The more members an NE group has, the more likely it is to be translated.
- The appearance order of NE groups in an article and the order of each translation of the NE groups in the counterpart is fairly strongly correlated. When comparing the order of NE groups belonging to the same NE class, the correlation is much stronger.

4 NE Translation-Pair Extraction Method

As a straightforward implementation to produce the three kinds of information, we sequentially combine the three individual components: *1. NE extraction, 2. Grouping within language,* and *3. Corresponding across languages.*

4.1 NE Extraction

We made an NE extraction program based on Support Vector Machine [3], that follows the method proposed by Yamada et al. [4] by using the chunk annotator YamCha[1]. YamCha classifies every word or morpheme (we call them *chunks* hereafter) into "chunk classes" sequentially from one end of a sentence to the other. In place of the chunk classes defined by Yamada et al., we adopted those by Isozaki et al. [5] like **PERSON-BEGIN, PERSON-MIDDLE, PERSON-END, PERSON-SINGLE**, etc. The specifications are described partly as follows:

Common specifications

- Use of 2nd degree of polynomial kernel, and pair wise method for multi-class
- Next 2 chunks for both directions from the current chunks as the context

---
[1] http://cl.aist-nara.ac.jp/~taku-ku/software/yamcha/

Japanese

- Tokenized and POS tags by the Japanese morphological analyzer ChaSen[2]
- Features of each morpheme: emergence/base form and pronunciation, part of speech, and type of contained letter (Chinese character / *hiragana* / *katakana* / numerical letter / alphabet / other)
- Classified from the end of the sentence to the head

English

- Obtaining POS tags by Charniak's nlparser[3]
- Features of each word: emergence/lowered form, part of speech, initial 1/2/3 letter(s) (lowered), last 1/2/3 letter(s) (lowered), and letter type (exclusive) (all uppercase / all lowercase / capitalized / single uppercase / all numeral / numeral initial / all brackets / all others)
- Classified from the head of the sentence to the end

By using the NHK J-E News Corpus for the training and testing of 10-fold cross validation, the extraction performance is $F = 94.0\%$[4] ($\beta = 1$, hereafter) for Japanese and $F = 92.4\%$ for English. For reference, the performance using Japanese 'CRL NE data,' which was prepared for IREX and is publicly available, for the training and testing of 10-fold cross validation is $F = 86.1\%$[4].

4.2 Grouping Within a Language

The types of coreference between NEs do not vary greatly. Typical coreferences that the grouping process should find are: the full name and only the last name of a person, the full name and the abbreviation of an organization, the date and the week name of a day, and so on.

We unconditionally assign identical NE tokens of the same NE class to a single NE group. In addition, we use a few simple conditions as follows to decide two NE tokens of the same NE class as identical:

Japanese

For named entities (in the narrow sense):
- One is a substring of the other (e.g. "農水省" ≃ "農林水産省" *(Ministry of Agriculture, Forestry and Fisheries of Japan)*).

For numeral expressions:
- Both ones normalized Chinese numerals into Arabic are identical (e.g. "二百三十円" ≃ "二三〇円" *(230 yen)*).

---

[2] http://chasen.aist-nara.ac.jp/
[3] http://www.cs.brown.edu/people/ec/#software
[4] There are some NEs in the hand-tagged data whose boundaries are not consistent with those of the morphemes. We currently remove such NE tags from training and testing data, which may affect the performance.

Table 1. Grouping Performance.

$F_{(\beta=1)}$	Avr.	ORG.	PES.	LOC.	ART.	DAT.	TIM.	MON.	PEC.
Japanese	**58.1%**	55.0%	92.2%	65.0%	35.6%	0.4%	—	—	8.7%
English	**79.0%**	72.1%	97.8%	77.1%	63.6%	9.2%	—	2.1%	47.6%

English

For named entities (in the narrow sense):
- One is the subword of the other (e.g. "George Bush" ≃ "Bush").
- One is the acronym of the other (e.g. "EU" ≃ "European Union").

For numeral expressions:
- One is identical to the other ignoring minor differences in spacing.

We applied the grouping process to the NHK J-E News Corpus with hand-tagged NE token information. The grouping performance was measured by judging whether a given NE token and another NE token belong to the same NE group or not. The result is shown in Table 1.

The overall performance for English is better than that for Japanese. We consider the main reason to be as follows; first, over-groupings are caused in Japanese because an NE token is sometimes a substring of unrelated NEs, second, NEs in non-Japanese or their transliterations sometimes appear in Japanese documents, which cannot be grouped with their coreference by a substring. We suppose that the latter problem can be solved by cooperating with the next process of corresponding across languages. Currently almost all temporal or number expressions are left ungrouped, because more intelligent methods for grouping are needed to find those coreferences.

4.3 Corresponding Across Languages

The corresponding process is formulated as selecting the best set of correspondences out of all possible sets for a document pair. Each possible set consists of one-to-one correspondences between an NE group of a certain NE class in the source document and an NE group of the same NE class in the target document. We will define a correspondence estimator to measure the plausibility of each correspondence set. The estimator has the following features that directly reflect the analysis described in Section 3:

1. The more correspondences the set has, the larger the estimator indicates.
2. The correspondence between NE groups having more members results in a larger value for the estimator.
3. The more that the order between any two NE groups in one of the documents of a pair and the order of those correspondences in the counterpart tend to be the same, the larger is the estimator's indication, especially when the two NE groups belong to the same NE class.

In the following section, we will first propose an estimator as a baseline, then we will make some enhancements.

Baseline Estimator. We define a baseline estimator E_{CO} as a mixture of the token corresponding rate c_t, which reflects the Feature 1. and 2., and the group order preservation rate o_g, which reflects the Feature 3.

$$E_{CO} = \alpha c_t + (1-\alpha)o_g \quad (0 \le \alpha \le 1) \tag{1}$$

Token corresponding rate. This represents the rate for an NE token in one of the documents in a pair to have a corresponding NE token in the counterpart, in other words, the rate that an NE token will be a member of an NE group that has a corresponding NE group in the counterpart.

$$c_t = \sum_{g'_s \in T(G_s)} |g'_s| + \sum_{g'_t \in T(G_t)} |g'_t| \bigg/ \sum_{g_s \in G_s} |g_s| + \sum_{g_t \in G_t} |g_t|, \tag{2}$$

where

G_s (or G_t): set of all NE groups in the source (or target) side,
g_s: an NE group in the source side,
$|g_s|$: the number of members in g_s,
$T(G_s)$: a subset of G_s, each of which has a corresponding NE group in the target side.

Group order preservation rate. Consider two NE groups in one of the documents in a pair, each of which has a corresponding NE group in the counterpart. The preservation of their appearance order is defined such that the order of the first appearing member in each NE group is the same as the order of the first appearing member in each correspondence. The group order preservation rate is now defined as a mixture of the rate of the preservation for selecting two NE groups without considering NE classes, and for selecting two NE groups of the same NE class.

$$o_g = \beta o_{g(any)} + (1-\beta)o_{g(same)} \quad (0 \le \beta \le 1), \tag{3}$$

$$o_{g(any)} = \sum_{g'_{s_1}, g'_{s_2} \in T(G_s)} p(g'_{s_1}, g'_{s_2}, t_t(g'_{s_1}), t_t(g'_{s_2})) \bigg/ {}_{|T(G_s)|}C_2, \tag{4}$$

$$o_{g(same)} = \sum_c \sum_{g''_{s_1}, g''_{s_2} \in T(G_s(c))} p(g''_{s_1}, g''_{s_2}, t_t(g''_{s_1}), t_t(g''_{s_2})) \bigg/ \sum_c {}_{|T(G_s(c))|}C_2, \tag{5}$$

where

$t_t(g_s)$: the corresponding NE group of g_s in the target side,
$p(g_{s_1}, g_{s_2}, t_t(g_{s_1}), t_t(g_{s_2}))$:
  1 $\cdots$ the appearance order between g_{s_1} and g_{s_2} in the source side (defined as the order of the first appearing token in each NE group) and that between $t_t(g_{s_1})$ and $t_t(g_{s_2})$ in the target side are the same,
  0 $\cdots$ not the same,
$|T(G_s)|$: the number of groups in $T(G_s)$,
$G_s(c)$: a subset of G_s, each of which NE class is c.

Some Enhancements

Consideration of order-altering within a sentence. Some local altering of the order often occurs through translations, due to the difference in focus for a fact between the source and target language (for example, the Japanese expression "日米 *(Japan and U.S.)*" might be translated into English as "U.S. and Japan"), or a difference in syntactic structure.

We thus enhanced the definition of function p to reduce penalties of order-altering within a sentence, and then defined the new order preservation rate o'_g by using the enhanced p' in place of p in the o_g:

$$p'(g_{s_1}, g_{s_2}, t_t(g_{s_1}), t_t(g_{s_2})) = \\ p(g_{s_1}, g_{s_2}, t_t(g_{s_1}), t_t(g_{s_2})) \cup s(g_{s_1}, g_{s_2}, t_t(g_{s_1}), t_t(g_{s_2})), \quad (6)$$

where

$s(g_{s_1}, g_{s_2}, t_t(g_{s_1}), t_t(g_{s_2}))$:
1 $\cdots$ the first appearing tokens in both g_{s_1} and g_{s_2} are in the same sentence of the source document, and the first appearing tokens in both $t_t(g_{s_1})$ and $t_t(g_{s_2})$ are also in the same sentence of the target document,
0 $\cdots$ others.

Using existing knowledge for correspondence. Consulting bilingual dictionaries is indeed a great help for corresponding bilingual NEs. Some other knowledge, for example, a rule for transforming a year expressed in a Japanese era into the Christian calendar, or a transliteration technique, can be used in the same way as bilingual dictionaries. We defined a new estimator $E_{CO'H(\mathcal{K})}$ that additionally takes the group corresponding hint $h_g(\mathcal{K})$ into account:

$$E_{CO'H(\mathcal{K})} = \gamma(\alpha c_t + (1-\alpha)o'_g) + (1-\gamma)h_g(\mathcal{K}) \quad (0 \le \alpha, \gamma \le 1), \quad (7)$$

$$h_g(\mathcal{K}) = \sum_{g'_s \in T(G_s)} h(\mathcal{K}, g'_s, t_t(g'_s)) \Big/ |T(G_s)|, \quad (8)$$

where

$h(\mathcal{K}, g_s, t_t(g_s))$:
1 $\cdots$ the knowledge $\mathcal{K}$ (e.g. bilingual dictionary) indicates that a member in g_s and a member in $t_t(g_s)$ are a corresponding pair,
0 $\cdots$ others.

Experiments. We applied the corresponding process to the NHK J-E News Corpus with hand-tagged NE tokens and grouping information, using the estimators proposed above with parameters: $\alpha = \beta = \gamma = 1/2$. Some additional estimators that excluded the consideration of order preservation were also prepared for comparison. Definitions of all the estimators are given again in Table 2. Moreover, the correspondence knowledge used for these experiments and their coverage (the rate for the knowledge to find a corresponding English NE for each appearing Japanese NE token in the test corpus) are as follows:

Table 2. Correspondence Estimators.

$$\begin{aligned}
E_{CO} &= 1/2\, c_t + 1/2\, o_g \\
E_{CO'} &= 1/2\, c_t + 1/2\, o'_g \\
E_{CO'H(dic)} &= 1/2\, (1/2\, c_t + 1/2\, o'_g) + 1/2\, h_g(dic) \\
E_{CO'H(dic+rule)} &= 1/2\, (1/2\, c_t + 1/2\, o'_g) + 1/2\, h_g(dic+rule) \\
E_C &= c_t \\
E_{CH(dic+rule)} &= 1/2\, c_t + 1/2\, h_g(dic+rule)
\end{aligned}$$

Table 3. Cross-language Correspondence Performance ($F_{(\beta=1)}$).

E_{CO}	$E_{CO'}$	$E_{CO'H(dic)}$	$E_{CO'H(dic+rule)}$	E_C	$E_{CH(dic+rule)}$
56.9%	60.5%	69.7%	71.0%	36.6%	52.3%

dic (coverage: 13.6%): existing Japanese-English dictionary

rule (coverage: 2.3%): hand-coded procedural rules for generating English correspondence candidates from Japanese expression: 1. date in Japanese style to English style, 2. the Roman alphabets in Japanese code to ASCII code.

The performance for identifying hand-tagged correspondences for each estimator is shown in Table 3.

We can surely say that the consideration of order preservation plays a main role in estimation. The existing knowledge makes up for the weakness of relying solely on the order preservation.

To achieve higher scores in performance, we would like to make our correspondence estimation model more sophisticated by giving it a better mathematical validity.

5 Overall Evaluation

We conducted an overall experiment by combining the three components for the NHK J-E News Corpus. We used the result of the 10-fold cross validation for evaluating the NE extraction performance as the output of the NE extraction, and for corresponding across languages, we adopted the estimator $E_{CO'H(dic+rule)}$.

The performance for acquiring bilingual NE token pairs is F = 58.8%. We found that one grouping failure could cause a chain of corresponding mistakes, because each NE group that should be combined into one group claims individual NE group in the counterpart document as its correspondence. A failure in NE extraction may also bring the same trouble when it causes the wrong number of NE groups. Balanced production of NE groups between language pair is essentially needed for acquiring NE pairs with higher quality.

6 Related Work

Many methods have been proposed for acquiring translation-pairs from bilingual corpora, however, most of these methods require the bilingual corpora to be aligned in a sentence correspondence, or require literally translated document pairs that make it possible to estimate potential sentence correspondences [6–8]. For those bilingual corpora, we can estimate correspondences by structural evidence, such as the similarities between word positions and sentence structure.

Some methods have also been suggested for "noisy parallel corpora" such as content-aligned corpora, or comparable bilingual corpora in the same content domain. For comparable corpora, some studies have employed a technique that estimates translation pairs based on the similarity of adjacent words cooccurring with target words [9,10]. Aramaki et al. [11] estimated translation pairs by parsed tree matching between sentence corresponding pairs, which were selected according to bilingual dictionaries. These techniques may have problems in coverage. The former can extract translation pairs only from high-frequency words. The coverage of the latter depends on how many sentence corresponding pairs can be found, in other words, how many sentences are translated literally.

Another approach has been proposed, which focuses the extraction targets on NEs. This approach effectively uses the characteristics of NEs, such as capitalization, to locate their occurrences in documents. First, extraction target words are specified with broad coverage in the source language. Then, the counterparts are retrieved in the target language. Moore [12] used a sentence-aligned parallel corpus of English and French for NE translation-pair extraction. After recognizing capitalized English words as NEs, he determined statistically which French word sequences as translations. Some methods have also been proposed to find the translation of NEs in the source language from the target language using transliteration [13,14]. These methods also have problems; the former requires sentence-aligned parallel corpora, and the latter can be applied only to names of persons and places whose pronunciations directly determine the translation.

7 Conclusion

In this paper, we proposed an NE translation pair acquisition method that is able to extract translation knowledge from "content-aligned corpora," such as broadcast news articles and newspaper articles, in which it is difficult to recognize a one-to-one sentence correspondence. Our method uses an NE extraction technique to recognize NEs in the source and target sides, then finds correspondence based on the similarities of the appearance order in each document.

We conducted an experiment of NE translation pair extraction from 2,000 Japanese-English article pairs in an NHK J-E News Corpus. We employed a cross-language correspondence estimation model using a small bilingual dictionary as supplementary correspondence clues, whose corresponding performance came up to $F_{(\beta=1)} = 71.0\%$. The overall performance for acquiring NE pairs was $F_{(\beta=1)} = 58.8\%$. Each component of the current system still has naïve implementation, so we believe that system improvements will raise the performance.

In the current method, errors that occur at an early stage cumulatively cause mistakes in a later stage, as described in Section 5. We would like to improve the system performance by making a global optimization across the stages.

Acknowledgments

This research was supported in part by the National Institute of Information and Communications Technology.

References

1. Kumano, T., Kashioka, H., Tanaka, H., Fukusima, T.: Construction and analysis of Japanese-English broadcast news corpus with named entity tags. In: Proceedings of the ACL 2003 Workshop on Multilingual and Mixed-Language Named Entity Recognition: Combining Statistical and Symbolic Models. (2003) 17–24
2. Sekine, S., Isahara, H.: IREX: IR and IE evaluation project in Japanese. In: Proceedings of the 2nd International Conference on Language Resources and Evaluation (LREC-2000). (2000)
3. Vapnik, V.N.: The Nature of Statistical Learning Theory. Springer (1995)
4. Yamada, H., Kudo, T., Matsumoto, Y.: Japanese named entity extraction using support vector machine. IPSJ Journal **43** (2002) 44–53 (in Japanese).
5. Isozaki, H., Kazawa, H.: Efficient support vector classifiers for named entity recognition. In: Proceedings of the 19th International Conference on Computational Linguistics (COLING-2002). (2002) 390–396
6. Kay, M., Röscheisen, M.: Text-translation alignment. Computational Linguistics **19** (1993) 121–142
7. Utsuro, T., Ikeda, H., Yamane, M., Matsumoto, Y., Nagao, M.: Bilingual text matching using bilingual dictionary and statistics. In: Proceedings of the 32th International Conference on Computational Linguistics (ACL-94). (1994) 1076–1082
8. Haruno, M., Yamazaki, T.: High-performance bilingual text alignment using statistical and dictionary information. In: Proceedings of the 34th International Conference on Computational Linguistics (ACL '96). (1996) 131–138
9. Tanaka, K., Iwasaki, H.: Extraction of lexical translations from non-aligned corpora. In: Proceedings of the 16th International Conference on Computational Linguistics (COLING-96). (1996) 580–585
10. Fung, P., Lo, Y.Y.: Translating unknown words using nonparallel, comparable texts. In: Proceedings of the 17th International Conference on Computational Linguistics and the 36th Annual Meeting of the Association for Computational Linguistics (COLING-ACL '98). (1998) 414–420
11. Aramaki, E., Kurohashi, S., Kashioka, H., Tanaka, H.: Word selection for EBMT based on monolingual similarity and translation confidence. In: Proceedings of the HLT-NAACL 2003 Workshop on Building and Using Parallel Texts: Data Driven Machine Translation and Beyond. (2003) 57–64
12. Moore, R.C.: Learning translations of named-entity phrases from parallel corpora. In: Proceedings of the 10th Conference of the European Chapter of the Association for Computational Linguistics (EACL 03). (2003) 259–266
13. Goto, I., Uratani, N., Ehara, T.: Cross-language information retrieval of proper nouns using context information. In: Proceedings of the 6th Natural Language Processing Pacific Rim Symposium (NLPRS 2001). (2001) 571–578
14. Al-Onazian, Y., Knight, K.: Translating named entities using monolingual and bilingual resources. In: Proceedings of the 40st Annual Meeting of the Association for Computational Linguistics (ACL-02). (2002) 400–408

Visual Semantics and Ontology of Eventive Verbs

Minhua Ma and Paul Mc Kevitt

School of Computing & Intelligent Systems, Faculty of Engineering,
University of Ulster, Derry/Londonderry, BT48 7JL
{m.ma,p.mckevitt}@ulster.ac.uk

Abstract. Various English verb classifications have been analyzed in terms of their syntactic and semantic properties, and conceptual components, such as syntactic valency, lexical semantics, and semantic/syntactic correlations. Here the visual semantics of verbs, particularly their *visual roles*, somatotopic effectors, and level-of-detail, is studied. We introduce the notion of *visual valency* and use it as a primary criterion to recategorize eventive verbs for language visualization (animation) in our intelligent multimodal storytelling system, CONFUCIUS. The visual valency approach is a framework for modelling deeper semantics of verbs. In our ontological system we consider both language and visual modalities since CONFUCIUS is a multimodal system.

1 Introduction

A taxonomic classification of the verb lexicon began with syntax studies such as Syntactic Valency Theory and subcategorization expressed through grammatical codes in the Longman Dictionary of Contemporary English [13]. The classification ground has recently shifted to semantics: lexical semantics [6], conceptual components [9], semantic/syntactic correlations [12], and intrinsic causation-change structures [1]. Here we introduce visual criteria to identify verb classes with visual/semantic correlations.

First, in section 2 the intelligent multimodal storytelling system CONFUCIUS is introduced and its architecture is described. Next, in section 3 we review previous work on ontological categorization of English verbs. Then we introduce the notion of *visual valency* and expound CONFUCIUS' verb taxonomy, which is based on several criteria for visual semantics: number and roles of visual valency, somatotopic effectors, and level-of-detail, in section 4. Finally, section 5 summarizes the work with a discussion of possible future work on evaluation of the classification through language animation, and draws comparisons to related research.

2 Background: CONFUCIUS

We are developing an intelligent multimedia storytelling interpretation and presentation system called CONFUCIUS. It automatically generates 3D animation and speech from natural language input as shown in Figure 1. A prefabricated objects knowledge base on the left hand side includes the graphics library such as characters, props, and animations for basic activities, which is used in *animation generation*. The input stories are parsed by the *surface transformer, media allocatior* and *Natural Language*

Processing (NLP) modules. The natural language processing component uses the Connexor Functional Dependency Grammar parser [10], WordNet [6] and LCS (Lexical Conceptual Structure) database [4]. The current prototype visualizes single sentences which contain action verbs with visual valency of up to three, e.g. *John gave Nancy a book*, *John left the restaurant*.

The outputs of *animation generation*, *Text to Speech* (TTS) and *sound effects* combine at *synchronizing & fusion*, generating a 3D world in VRML. CONFUCIUS employs temporal media such as 3D animation and speech to present stories. Establishing correspondence between language and animation, i.e. language visualization, is the focus of this research. This requires adequate representation and reasoning about the dynamic aspects of the story world, especially about eventive verbs. During the development of animation generation from natural language input in CONFUCIUS, we find that the task of visualizing natural language can shed light on taxonomic classification of the verb lexicon.

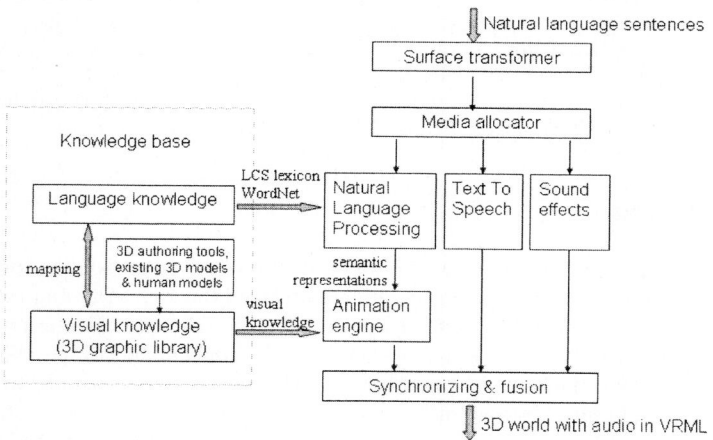

Fig. 1. Architecture of CONFUCIUS

3 Ontological Categories of Verbs

3.1 Syntactic Perspective: Valency and Aspectual Classes

In 1980s, the Longman Dictionary of Contemporary English (LDOCE) was the most comprehensive computational lexicon with a description of grammatical properties of words. It had a very detailed word-class categorization scheme, particularly for verbs. In addition to part-of-speech information LDOCE specifies a subcategorization description in terms of types and numbers of complements for each entry. In LDOCE grammar codes separate verbs into the categories: D (ditransitive), I (intransitive), L (linking verb with complement), T1 (transitive verb with an NP object), T3 (transitive verb with an infinitival clause as object), etc. These grammar codes implicitly express verb subcategorization information including specifications on the syntactic realization of verb complements and argument functional roles.

The notion of valency is borrowed from chemistry to describe a verb's property of requiring certain arguments in a sentence. Valency fillers can be both obligatory (*complements*) and optional (*adjuncts*): the former are central participants in the process denoted by the verb, the latter express the associated temporal, locational, and other circumstances. Verbs can be divided into classes based on their valency.

There are different opinions on the type of a verb's valency fillers. Leech [11] raises the idea of *semantic valency* to operate on a level different from surface syntax. Semantic valency further developed to the theory of thematic roles in terms of which semantic role each complement in a verb's argument structure plays, ranging from Fillmore's [7] case grammar to Jackendoff's [9] Lexical Conceptual Structure (LCS). The term *thematic role* covers a layer in linguistic analysis, which has been known by many other names: theta-role, case role, deep grammatical function, transitivity role, and valency role. The idea is to extend syntactic analysis beyond surface case (nominative, accusative) and surface function (subject, object) into the semantic domain in order to capture the roles of participants. The classic roles are *agent, patient (theme), instrument*, and a set of locational and temporal roles like *source, goal* and *place*.

Having a set of thematic roles for each verb type, Dixon [3] classifies verbs into 50 verb types, each of which has one to five thematic roles that are distinct to that verb type. Systemic Functional Grammar [8] works with 14 thematic roles divided over 5 *process types* (verb types). Some linguists work out a minimal thematic role system of three highly abstract roles (for valency-governed arguments) on the grounds that the valency of verbs never exceeds 3. Dowty [5] assumes that there are only two *thematic proto-roles* for verbal predicates: the *proto-agent* and *proto-patient*. Proto-roles are conceived of as *cluster-concepts* which are determined for each choice of predicate with respect to a given set of semantic properties. Proto-agent involves properties of volition, sentience/perception, causes event, and movement; proto-patient involves change of state, incremental theme, and causally affected by event.

The ontological categories proposed by Vendler [14] are dependent on aspectual classes. Vendler's verb classes (activities, statives, achievements, and accomplishments) emerge from an attempt to characterize a number of patterns in aspectual data. Formal ontologies such as DOLCE (Descriptive Ontology for Linguistic and Cognitive Engineering), SUMO (Suggested Upper Merged Ontology) and CYC all assume the traditional aspectual (temporal) classification for their events (processes).

3.2 Semantic Perspective: WordNet and Dimension of Causation

The verb hierarchical tree in WordNet [6] represents another taxonomic approach based on pure lexical semantics. It reveals the semantic organization of the lexicon in terms of lexical and semantic relations. Table 1 lists the lexicographer files of verbs in WordNet 2.0, which shows the top nodes of the verb trees.

Asher and Lascarides [1] put forward another lexical classification based on the dimension of causal structure. They assume that both causation and change can be specified along the following four dimensions so as to yield a thematic hierarchy such as the one described in the lattice structure in Figure 2.

- *locative*: specifying the causation of motion, e.g. put
- *formal*: specifying the creation and destruction of objects, e.g. build

- *matter*: specifying the causation of changes in shape, size, matter and colour of an object, e.g. paint
- *intentional*: specifying causation and change of the propositional attitudes of individuals, e.g. amuse, persuade

Table 1. WordNet verb files

Lexicographer file	Contents
verb.body	grooming, dressing, bodily care
verb.change	size, temperature change, intensifying
verb.cognition	thinking, judging, analyzing, doubting
verb.communication	telling, asking, ordering, singing
verb.competition	fighting, athletic activities
verb.consumption	eating and drinking
verb.contact	touching, hitting, tying, digging
verb.creation	sewing, baking, painting, performing
verb.emotion	feeling
verb.motion	walking, flying, swimming
verb.perception	seeing, hearing, feeling
verb.possession	buying, selling, owning
verb.social	political/social activities & events
verb.stative	being, having, spatial relations
verb.weather	raining, snowing, thawing, thundering

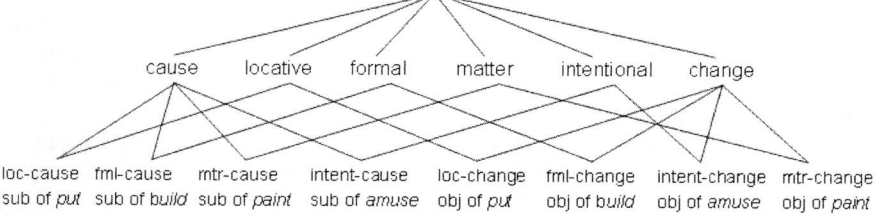

Fig. 2. Dimension of causation-change

3.3 Semantic-Syntactic Correlations: Levin's Verb Classes

Besides purely syntactic and purely semantic methodologies, parallel syntactic-semantic patterns in the English verb lexicon have been explored as well since it is discovered that words with similar meaning, i.e. whose LCSs [9] are identical in terms of specific meaning components, show some tendency toward displaying the same syntactic behavior. Levin's [12] verb classes represent the most comprehensive description in this area. She examines a large number of verbs, classifies them according to their semantic/syntactic correlations, and shows how syntactic patterns systematically accompany the semantic classification.

4 Visual Semantics and Verb Classes

In order to identify the full set of meaning components that figure in the visual representation of verb meaning, the investigation of semantically relevant visual properties and ensuing clustering of verbs into classes needs to be carried out over a large number of verbs. Here we identify three visual factors concerning verb categorization: (1) *visual valency*, (2) somatotopic effectors involved in action execution (visualization) and perception, and (3) level-of-detail of visual infomation. Eventive verbs are categorized according to involved somatotopic effectors, visual semantic roles (e.g. obligatory argument number and classes, humanoid vs. non-humanoid roles), and the level-of-detail they indicate.

Verbs belonging to the same class in our classification are visual "synonyms", i.e. they should be substitutable in the same set of animation keyframes, through not necessarily in exactly the same visualization. Visualization of action verbs could be an effective evaluation of the taxonomy.

4.1 Visual Valency

Visual valency refers to the capacity of a verb to take a specific number and type of *visual arguments* in language visualization (3D animation). We call a valency filler a *visual role*. We distinguish two types of visual roles: human (biped articulated animate entity) and object (inanimate entity), since they require different process in animation generation. Visual valency sometimes overlaps with syntactic and semantic valency. The difference shown in 1-3 is the number of obligatory roles. It is obvious that visual modalities require more obligatory roles than surface grammar or semantics. What is optional in syntax and semantics is obligatory for visual valency.

1) *Neo* pushed *the button*.
   syntactic valency 2, subject and object
   semantic valency 2, agent and theme
   visual valency 2, human and object
2) *Michelle* cut *the cloth (with scissors)*.
   syntactic valency 2, subject, object, optional PP adjunct
   semantic valency 2, agent, theme, optional instrument
   visual valency 3, 1 human and 2 objects, all obligatory
3) *Neo* is reading.
   syntactic valency 1, subject
   semantic valency 1, agent (and optional source)
   visual valency 2, 1 human and 1 object, all obligatory

Therefore, three visual valency verbs subsume both syntactic trivalency verbs such as *give* and syntactic bivalency verbs such as put (with goal), cut (with instrument), butter (with theme, in *butter toast*) and, an intransitive verb may turn up three visual valency, e.g. dig in *he is digging in his garden* involves one human role and two object roles (the instrument and the place).

We classify visual roles into atomic entities and non-atomic entities based on their decomposablility, and further subclassify non-atomic roles into human roles and object roles.

4.2 Somatotopic Factors in Visualization

The second visual factor we consider in our verb taxonomy is somatotopic effectors. Psychology experiments prove that the execution, perception and visualization of action verbs produced by different somatotopic effectors activate distinct parts of the cortex. Moveover, actions that share an effector are in general similar to each other in dimensions other than the identity of the effector. Recent studies [2] investigate how action verbs are processed by language users in visualization and perception, and prove that processing visual and linguistic inputs (i.e. action verbs) associated with particular body parts results in the activation of areas of the cortex involved in performing actions associated with those same effectors.

On these theoretical grounds, we take effectors into account. However, we only distinguish facial expression (including lip movement) and body posture (arm/leg/torso) in our ontological system (Figure 3). Further divisions like distinction between upper/lower arm, hands, and even fingers are possible, but we do not make our taxonomy too fine-grained and reflect every fine visual distinction. Here is an example of using somatotopic effectors to classify action verbs *run, bow, kick, wave, sing, put*:

$$\left\{\begin{array}{l}\text{Facial expression} - \textit{sing, laugh} \\ \text{Body posture} \left\{\begin{array}{l}\text{Leg} - \textit{run, kick} \\ \text{Arm} - \textit{wave, put} \\ \text{Torso} - \textit{bow}\end{array}\right.\end{array}\right.$$

4.3 CONFUCIUS' Verb Taxonomy

The verb categories of CONFUCIUS shown in Figure 3 represent a very minimal and shallow classification based on visual semantics. Here we focus on action verbs. Action verbs are a major part of events involving humanoid performers (agent/experiencer) in animation. They can be classified into five categories: (1) one visual valency verbs with a human role, concerning movement or partial movement of the human role, (2) two visual valency verbs (at least one human role), (3) visual valency ≥ 3 (at least one human role), (4) verbs without distinct visualization when out of context such as trying and helping verbs, (5) high level behaviours or routine events, most of which are political and social activities/events consisting of a sequence of basic actions.

We further categorize the class of one visual valency verbs (2.2.1.1) into 'body posture or movement' (2.2.1.1.1) and 'facial expressions and lip movement' (2.2.1.1.2) according to somatotopic effectors. The animation of class 2.2.1.1.1 usually involves biped kinematics, e.g. walk, jump, swim, and class 2.2.1.1.2 subsumes communication verbs and emotion verbs, and involves multimodal presentation. These verbs require both visual presentation such as lip movement (e.g. *speak, sing*), facial expressions (e.g. *laugh, weep*) and audio presentation such as speech or other communicable sounds.

There are two subcategories under the two visual valency verbs (2.2.1.2) based on which type of roles they require. Class 2.2.1.2.1 requires one human role and one object role. Most transitive verbs (e.g. *throw, eat*) and intransitive verbs with an implicit instrument or locational adjunct (e.g. *sit* on a chair, *trolley*) belong to this class. Verbs in class 2.2.1.2.2, such as *fight* and *chase*, have two human roles.

Class 2.2.1.3 includes verbs with three (or more than three) visual roles, at least one of which is a human role. The subclass 2.2.1.3.1 has two human roles and one (or more) object role. It subsumes ditransitive verbs like *give* and transitive verbs with an implicit instrument/goal/theme (e.g. *kill, bat*). The subclass 2.2.1.3.2 has one human

1. On atomic entities
   1.1. Movement/rotation: change physical location (position or orientation), e.g. bounce, turn
   1.2. Change intrinsic attributes such as shape, size, color, texture, and even visibility, e.g. bend, taper, (dis)appear
   1.3. Visually unobserved change: temperature change, intensifying
2. On non-atomic entities
   2.1. No human role involved
      2.1.1. Two or more individual objects fuse together, e.g. melt (in)
      2.1.2. One objects divides into two or more individual parts
         e.g. break (into pieces), (a piece of paper is) torn (up)
      2.1.3. Change sub-components (their position, size, color, shape etc), e.g. blossom
      2.1.4. Environment events (weather verbs), e.g. snow, rain, thunder, getting dark
   2.2. Human role involved
      2.2.1. Action verbs
         2.2.1.1. One visual valency (the role is a human, (partial) movement)
            2.2.1.1.1. Biped kinematics, e.g. go, walk, jump, swim, climb
               2.2.1.1.1.1. Arm actions, e.g. wave, scratch
               2.2.1.1.1.2. Leg actions, e.g. go, walk, jump
               2.2.1.1.1.3. Torso actions, e.g. bow
               2.2.1.1.1.4. Combined actions
            2.2.1.1.2. Facial expressions and lip movement, e.g. laugh, fear, say, sing, order
         2.2.1.2. Two visual valency (at least one role is human)
            2.2.1.2.1. One human and one object (vt or vi+instrument/source/goal), e.g. trolley (lexicalized instrument)
               2.2.1.2.1.1. Arm actions, e.g. throw, push, open, eat
               2.2.1.2.1.2. Leg actions, e.g. kick
               2.2.1.2.1.3. Torso actions
               2.2.1.2.1.4. Combined actions, e.g. escape (with source), glide (with location)
            2.2.1.2.2. Two humans, e.g. fight, chase, guide
         2.2.1.3. Visual valency ≥ 3 (at least one role is human)
            2.2.1.3.1. Two humans and one object (inc. ditransitive verbs), e.g. give, buy, sell, show
            2.2.1.3.2. One human and 2+ objects (vt + object + implicit instrument/goal/ theme), e.g. cut, write, butter, pocket, dig, cook
         2.2.1.4. Verbs without distinct visualization when out of context
            2.2.1.4.1. trying verbs: try, attempt, succeed, manage
            2.2.1.4.2. helping verbs: help, assist
            2.2.1.4.3. letting verbs: allow, let, permit
            2.2.1.4.4. create/destroy verbs: build, create, assemble, construct, break, destroy
            2.2.1.4.5. verbs whose visualization depends on their objects, e.g. play (harmonica/football), make (the bed/troubles/a phone call), fix (a drink/a lock)
         2.2.1.5. High level behaviours (routine events), political and social activities/events, e.g. interview, eat out (go to restaurant), call (make a telephone call), go shopping
      2.2.2. Non-action verbs
         2.2.2.1. stative verbs (change of state), e.g. die, sleep, wake, become, stand, sit
         2.2.2.2. emotion verbs, e.g. like, disgust, feel
         2.2.2.3. possession verbs, e.g. have, belong
         2.2.2.4. cognition, e.g. decide, believe, doubt, think, remember
         2.2.2.5. perception, e.g. watch, hear, see, feel

Fig. 3. Ontology of events on visual semantics

role and two (or more) object roles. It usually includes transitive verbs with an inanimate object and an implicit instrument/goal/theme, e.g. *cut, write, butter, pocket*. The visual valency of verbs conflating with the instrument/goal/theme of the actions, such as *cut, write, butter, pocket, dig, trolley*, have one more valency than their syntactic valency. For instance, the transitive verb *write* (in *writing a letter*) is a two syntactic valency verb, but its visualization involves three roles, *writer, letter*, and an implicit instrument *pen*, therefore it is a three visual valency verb.

There is a correlation between the visual criteria and lexical semantics of verbs. For instance, consider the intransitive verb *bounce* in the following sentences. It is a one visual valency verb in both 4 and 5 since the PPs following it are optional. The visual role in 4 is an *object*, whereas in 5 it is a *human* role. This difference coincides with their word sense difference (in WordNet).

4) The ball *bounced* over the fence.
   WordNet sense: 01837803. Hypernyms: jump, leap, bound, spring
   CONFUCIUS verb class 1.1
5) The child *bounced* into the room.
   WordNet sense: 01838289. Hypernyms: travel, go, move
   CONFUCIUS verb class 2.2.1.1.1

4.4 Level-of-Detail (LOD) – Basic-Level Verbs and Their Troponyms

The classes from 2.2.1.1.1.1 through 2.2.1.1.1.4 are the most fine-grained categories in Figure 3. They can be further classified based on *Level-of-Detail* (LOD). The term LOD has been widely used in relation to research on levels of detail in 3D geometric models. It means that one may switch between animation levels of varying computation complexity according to some set of predefined rules (e.g. viewer perception).

Let's have a look at the *verbs of motion* in Levin's [12] classes. They subsume two subclasses: *verbs of inherently directed motion* (e.g. *arrive, come, go*) and *verbs of manner of motion* (e.g. *walk, jump, run, trot*). We find that there are actually three subclasses in *verbs of motion*, representing three LODs of visual information as shown in the tree in Figure 4. We call the high level *event level*, the middle level *manner level*, and the low level *troponym level*. The event level includes basic event predicates such as *go* (or *move*), which are *basic-level verbs* for atomic objects. The manner-of-motion level stores the visual information of the manner according to the verb's visual role (either a human or a non-atomic object) in the animation library. Verbs on this level are basic-level verbs for human and non-atomic objects. The troponym level verbs can never be basic-level verbs because they always elaborate the manner of a base verb. Visualization of the troponym level is achieved by modifying animation information (speed, the agent's state, duration of the activity, iteration) of manner level verbs.

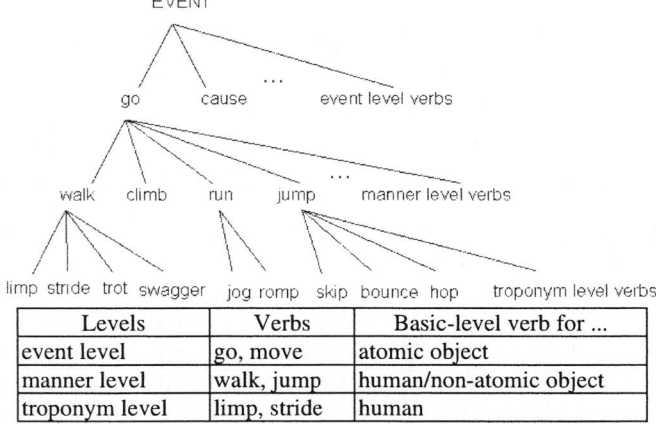

Levels	Verbs	Basic-level verb for ...
event level	go, move	atomic object
manner level	walk, jump	human/non-atomic object
troponym level	limp, stride	human

Fig. 4. Hierarchical tree of verbs of motion

In the following examples, 6a is a LCS-like representation of *John went to the station*. The predicate *go* is on the event level. The means of going, e.g. by car or on foot, is not specified. Since the first argument of *go* is a HUMAN, we cannot just move John from one spot to another without any limb movement, the predicate *go* is not enough for visualization a human role. We need a lexical rule to change the high-level verb to a basic-level verb, i.e. change *go* to *walk*, when its visual role is human (6b), because walking is the default manner of movement for human beings. In 7a the predicate *run* is enough for visualizing the action since it is a basic-level verb for human.

6) John *went* to the station.
    a) [EVENT go ([HUMAN john],[PATH to [OBJ station]])]
    b) [EVENT walk ([HUMAN john],[PATH to [OBJ station]])]
7) John *ran* to the station.
    a) [EVENT run ([HUMAN john],[PATH to [OBJ station]])]

This approach is involved with the visualization processes. The manner-of-motion verbs are stored as key frames of involved joint rotations of human bodies in the animation library, without any displacement of the whole body. Therefore *run* is just *running in place*. The first phase of visualization is finding the action in animation files and instantiating it on the first argument (i.e. the human role) in the LCS-like representation. This phase corresponds to the manner level (run) in the above tree. The next phase is to add position movement of the whole body according to the second argument (PATH). It makes the agent move forward and hence generates a *real* run. This phase corresponds to the event level (go) in the tree.

The structure in Figure 4 is applicable to most troponyms, *cook* and *fry/broil/braise/micro-wave/grill*, for example, express different manners and instruments of cooking.

5 Conclusion

In many ways the work presented in this paper is related to that of Levin [12]. However, our point of departure and the underlying methodology are different. We categorize verbs from the visual semantic perspective since language visualization in CONFUCIUS provides independent criteria for identifying classes of verbs sharing certain aspects of meaning, i.e. semantic/visual correlations. A visual semantic analysis of eventive verbs has revealed some striking influences in a taxonomic verb tree. Various criteria ranging from visual valency, somatotopic effector, to LOD are proposed for classifying verbs from the language visualization perspective. Future research should address evaluation issues using automatic animation generation and psychological experiments.

References

1. Asher, N., Lascarides, A.: Lexical Disambiguation in a Discourse Context. *Journal of Semantics*, 12(1): 69-108, (1995)
2. Bergen, B., Narayan, S., Feldman, J.: Embodied verbal semantics: evidence from an image-verb matching task. *Proceedings of CogSci*, Boston ParkPlaza Hotel, Boston (2003)

3. Dixon, R.M.W.: *A new approach to English Grammar on semantic principles.* Oxford: OUP (1991)
4. Dorr, B. J., Jones, D.: Acquisition of semantic lexicons: using word sense disambiguation to improve precision. Evelyne Viegas (Ed.), *Breadth and Depth of Semantic Lexicons*, Norwell, MA: Kluwer Academic Publishers (1999) 79-98
5. Dowty, D. R.: Thematic proto-roles and argument selection. *Language*, 67(3): 547-619, (1991)
6. Fellbaum, C.: A semantic network of English verbs. *WordNet: An Electronic Lexical Database*, C. Fellbaum (Ed.), Cambridge, MA: MIT Press (1998) 69-104
7. Fillmore, C. J.: The case for case. *Universals in Linguistic Theory*, E. Bach and R. Harms (Eds.), New York: Holt, Rinehart and Winston (1968) 10-88
8. Halliday, M.A.K.: *An Introduction to Functional Grammar.* London: Edward Arnold (1985)
9. Jackendoff, R.: *Semantic Structures.* Current studies in linguistics series. Cambridge, MA: MIT Press (1990)
10. Järvinen, T., Tapanainen, P.: A Dependency Parser for English. Technical Report, No.TR-1, Department of General Linguistics, University of Helsinki (1997)
11. Leech, G.: *Semantics.* Cambridge University Press (1981)
12. Levin, B.: *English verb classes and alternations: a preliminary investigation.* Chicago: The University of Chicago Press (1993)
13. Procter, P.: *Longman dictionary of contemporary English.* London: Longman (1987)
14. Vendler, Z.: *Linguistics and Philosophy.* Ithaca, NY: Cornell University Press (1967)

A Persistent Feature-Object Database for Intelligent Text Archive Systems

Takashi Ninomiya[1,2], Jun'ichi Tsujii[1,2], and Yusuke Miyao[2]

[1] CREST, Japan Science and Technology Agency
Kawaguchi Center Building, 4-1-8, Honcho, Kawaguchi-shi, Saitama
{ninomi,tsujii}@is.s.u-tokyo.ac.jp
[2] Department of Computer Science, University of Tokyo
Hongo 7-3-1, Bunkyo-ku, Tokyo
{ninomi,tsujii,yusuke}@is.s.u-tokyo.ac.jp

Abstract. This paper describes an intelligent text archive system in which typed feature structures are embedded. The aim of the system is to associate feature structures with regions in text, to make indexes for efficient retrieval, to allow users to specify both structure and proximity, and to enable inference on typed feature structures embedded in text. We propose a persistent mechanism for storing typed feature structures and the architecture of the text archive system.

1 Introduction

For the last decade, the main stream of NLP has focussed on studies for practical techniques, such as information retrieval (IR) or information extraction (IE) with widely accessible corpora. For example, the bag-of-words techniques significantly increased IR performance, and studies on IE proved that information can be extracted by matching hand-crafted templates with text. However, these techniques are difficult to use in sophisticated approaches, such as reasoning-based or linguistically-motivated approaches, because the bag-of-words techniques are not inherently structural, and matching templates is not well enough defined to be used for inference procedures. With the increasing importance of knowledge sharing and processing by XML, such as Semantic Web or question and answering (QA), intelligent procedures, like how to express a system of knowledge, how to identify user demands, and where to locate information embedded in text, are required to solve the problem.

The concern of this study is twofold: persistency of database and integration of knowledge management, text archives and NLP. In general, the more complex the framework, the less persistent its database becomes. For example, let us consider data objects in an object-oriented programming language where a class hierarchy is defined, and each object belongs to a class that defines its variables and functions. In such a case, all data become useless when their class definitions change. There are some solutions to this persistency problem, such as versioning. The most effective solution is to separate the data structures and semantics as much as possible, similar to XML or a text database where entries are separated by 'space' and 'new line'.

For integration, we assume that knowledge management includes the handling of heterogeneous, dynamic and structural knowledge sources. They are heterogeneous because they are developed and managed by independent groups, organizers, or persons,

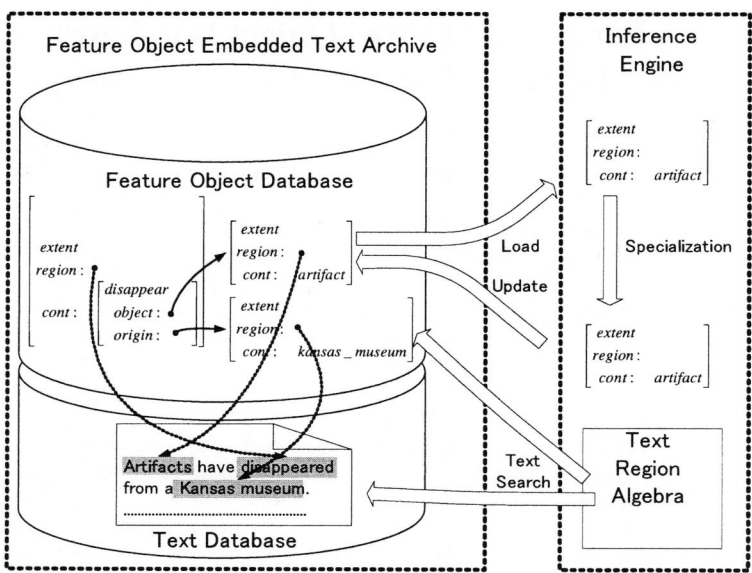

Fig. 1. Overall Foetea architecture.

for different purposes and with different ontologies. They are dynamic because the type of ontology to be used for inference can easily be changed in the process of development and maintenance. Lastly, the knowledge sources should be able to express semantic structural relations like events, anaphora, predicate argument structures, or quasi-logical forms for intelligent IE or QA. We believe that a set of such semantic relations, including syntactic relations, gives more precise and complex text processing than the bag-of-words techniques when they are embedded in text.

In this paper, we introduce an intelligent text archive system, where data structures are persistent, and assigned regions of text, and users can specify both structure and proximity of text, and enable inference over structures embedded in text. We use typed feature structures [1] as the structures, because they are mathematically well-defined, and many linguistically-motivated grammar formalisms [2] are defined by feature structures. With a logic programming language for feature structures [3–5] and indexing scheme for feature structures [6–8], structural relations can efficiently be inferred by deduction, like a deductive database. Users can find feature structures embedded in text by structural specification or proximal specification using region algebra.

2 Feature-Object Embedded Text Archive System (Foetea)

Feature-object embedded text archive (Foetea) is an intelligent text archive system consisting of text, data structures and an inference engine. Figure 1 shows the overall architecture of Foetea. According to management policies, the architecture is separated into the following three layers.

Fig. 2. Text.

Data Representation Layer. The data representation layer consists of a *feature-object database* (explained later). The role of this layer is to represent data structures as labeled directed graphs, without any interpretation of the labels assigned to edges and nodes. Only a few operations, e.g., loading, storing and rewriting of data structures, are allowed.

Text Layer. Regions in the text are annotated with data structures in the data representation layer. This stand-off approach enables us to annotate heterogeneous data structures and over-lapped regions. The role of this layer is to represent text and regions associated with data structures, without any interpretation of regions and text.

Conceptual Layer. In the conceptual layer, data structures and text regions are interpreted and operated. Intuitively, this layer corresponds to the semantics for the data structures. Interpretation and inference of data structures is only allowed in this layer.

This separation makes the data structure persistent because a change in the interpretation of data structures does not impact on the data structures themselves. In general, the size of data structures is supposed to be very large. If the change of interpretation impacts on the data structures, only a small change in the interpretation mechanism will make all the data structures rubbish, or forces us to rewrite all the data structures, one by one.

As a system, Foetea has the following components: *feature-object database* for the data representation layer, *inference module* and *text region algebra module* for the conceptual layer, and *text*, *regions* and *extents* for the text layer.

Feature-Object Database. A *feature-object database* is comprised of a set of feature structures and a set of *associations*. Let Key be a set of keys and Assoc be a set of associations defined in the database. An association is a pair (k, q), where q is a node of a feature structure and k is a *key*, such that k is unique in the set of associations. A *feature object* is a feature structure associated with a *key*. Figure 4 shows an example of a feature-object database. Intuitively, the database is a very large feature structure without a root node, and associations are global variables that represent sub-structures within the feature structure. This means that the database system allows structure-sharing between different feature objects.

Text, Region and Extent. Text is a sequence of character assigned integers starting from zero up to the size of the text. Figure 2 shows an example of the text, "Articles have disappeared". With integers assigned to the text, a *region* is defined by a pair of integers, a starting position and an ending position in the text. In the example, the region $(0, 9)$ corresponds to the character sequence "Artifacts". An extent is a pair

Containment Operators
  Containing: $A \triangleright B = G(\{c | \exists a \in A, b \in B. (a.s < b.s \wedge b.e < a.e \wedge c.s = a.s$
  $\wedge c.e = a.e \wedge c.f = (a.f \triangleright b.f))\})$

  Not Containing: $A \not\triangleright B = G(\{c | \exists a \in A. (c.s = a.s \wedge c.e = a.e \wedge c.f = (a.f \not\triangleright \_)$
  $\wedge \not\exists b \in B. (a.s < b.s \wedge b.e < a.e))\})$

  Contained In: $A \triangleleft B = G(\{c | \exists a \in A, b \in B. (b.s < a.s \wedge a.e < b.e \wedge c.s = a.s$
  $\wedge c.e = a.e \wedge c.f = (a.f \triangleleft b.f))\})$

  Not Contained In: $A \not\triangleleft B = G(\{c | \exists a \in A. (c.s = a.s \wedge c.e = a.e \wedge c.f = (a.f \not\triangleleft \_)$
  $\wedge \not\exists b \in B. (b.s < a.s \wedge a.e < b.e))\})$

Combination Operators
  Both Of: $A \triangle B = G(\{c | c.s = min(a.s, b.s) \wedge c.e = max(a.e, b.e) \wedge c.f = (a.f \triangle b.f)\})$

  One Of: $A \triangledown B = G(\{c | c.s = a.s \wedge c.e = a.e \wedge c.f = (a.f \triangledown \_)\}$
  $\cup \{c | c.s = b.s \wedge c.e = b.e \wedge c.f = (\_\triangledown b.f)\})$

Ordering Operator
  Followed By: $A \diamond B = G(\{c | \exists a \in A, b \in B. (a.e < b.s \wedge c.s = a.s \wedge c.e = b.e$
  $\wedge c.f = (a.f \diamond b.f))\})$

Index Operator
  Index: $I(A) = G(\{c | c \in \texttt{Extent} \wedge \exists k, q, F. ((k, q) \in \texttt{Assoc} \wedge k = c.f$
  $\wedge q$ is the root node of $F \wedge F \sqcup A$ is defined$)\})$

Shortest Matching Operator
  GCL: $G(A) = \{a | a \in A \wedge \not\exists b \in A. (b \neq a \wedge a.s < b.s \wedge b.e < a.e\}$

Fig. 3. Operators of text region algebra.

$\langle r, k \rangle$ where r is a region and k is a key, i.e., a feature structure is associated with a region. Let Extent denote the collection of extents in the database. We write $x.s$ for the start position of $x \in$ Extent, $x.e$ for the ending position of $x \in$ Extent, and $x.f$ for the key associated with $x \in$ Extent.

Inference Engine. We suppose an inference engine is a system supporting a logic programming language for typed feature structures like PROLOG with typed feature structures as its predicate arguments instead of first order terms [3–5]. Users can retrieve feature objects from the feature-object database, specialize or modify them by inference, and insert or update them to the database. Users can also specify extents in the combination, ordering, and containment relations using text region algebra.

Text Region Algebra. Text region algebra [9, 10] is usually used for searches on structured text annotated with tags, e.g., XML documents, to specify both proximity and structure. Text region algebra for tags can be transcribed into that for feature objects. Figure 3 shows the operators of text region algebra for feature objects, that are transcribed from [9]. The difference is that the index operator $I(A)$ retrieves extents that have feature objects unifiable with A. With text region algebra for feature objects, users can specify the relation of the feature objects' position in the text. For example, suppose all paragraphs in the text are annotated with feature objects [**paragraph**], and named entities are annotated by NE taggers. All paragraphs that include both named entities "Mars" and "rover" can be retrieved by a query algebra $I(\,[\textbf{paragraph}])\triangleright(I(\,[\textbf{mars}])\triangle I(\,[\textbf{rover}]))$. Text region algebra enables us to find feature objects that are difficult to find using unifiable relations, but are easily found by specifying containment, combination, and ordering relations.

Figure 4 shows an example of text, extents, associations and feature structures. In the example, syntactic and semantic analysis are annotated by semantic parsing. As Foetea allows structure-sharing between different feature objects, a feature object that represents a coreference in a long distance dependency can be represented. Structure-sharing tagged as 29 represents a coreference of "Investors" and "they".

3 Persistent Database Model for Typed Feature Structures

3.1 Background

Feature Structure

A feature structure is a tuple $F = \langle Q, \bar{q}, \theta, \delta \rangle$, where Q is a set of a feature structure's nodes, $\bar{q}$ is the root node, $\theta(q)$ is a total node typing function that returns the type assigned to q, and $\delta(\pi, q)$ is a partial function that returns a node reached by following path π from q.

Type Constraint

Let $Intro(f)$ be the function that returns the most general type having feature f, and $Approp(f, \sigma)$ be the function that specifies the most general type of value that feature f can have for a node of type σ. A feature structure is said to be *well-typed* if, whenever $\delta(f, q)$ is defined, $Approp(f, \theta(q))$ is defined, and such that $Approp(f, \theta(q)) \sqsubseteq \theta(\delta(f,q))$. A feature structure is called *totally well typed* if it is well-typed and if $q \in Q$ and feature f are such that $Approp(f, \theta(q))$ is defined, then $\delta(f, q)$ is defined. Type constraint is the constraint defined for each type. The idea of type constraint is that a feature structure of type σ must satisfy the constraint defined for σ. Well-typedness and totally well-typedness are also special cases of type constraint.

3.2 Interpretation of Data Structures in Conceptual Layer

Feature structures in the conceptual layer are totally well-typed and may have type constraints, but feature structures in the data representation layer are independent of their interpretation, such as type hierarchy, the order of features, appropriateness of types and features, and any other type constraints. Any inference, such as unification, is not allowed in the data representation layer. The operations allowed by the database are *insertion*, *perfect loading*, *partial loading*, and *update*.

3.3 Operation

Insertion

Given a key $k \in \text{Key}$ and a feature structure G in the conceptual layer, G is inserted to the database without modifying any feature structures in the database. The association (k, q) for some q is rewritten to $(k, \bar{q}')$ where $\bar{q}'$ is the root node of the inserted feature structure.

```
₀Investors₉ ₁₀are₁₃ ₁₄appealing₂₃ ₂₄to₂₆ ₂₇the₃₀ ₃₁Securities₄₁ ₄₂and₄₅ ₄₆Exchange₅₄ ₅₅Commission₆₅.
. . . . . . . . .
₃₅₃They₃₅₇ ₃₅₈make₃₆₂ ₃₆₃the₃₆₆ ₃₆₇argument₃₇₅ ₃₇₆in₃₇₈ ₃₇₉letters₃₈₆ ₃₈₇to₃₈₉ ₃₉₀agency₄₀₆
```

$\text{Extent}_W = \{((0,9), e_1), ((10,13), e_2), ((14,23), e_3), ((24,26), e_4), ((27,30), e_5), ((31,41), e_6),$
$((42,45), e_7), ((46,54), e_8), ((55,65), e_9), ((353,357), e_{10}), ((358,362), e_{11}),$
$((363,366), e_{12}), ((367,375), e_{13}), ((376,378), e_{14}), ((379,386), e_{15}), ((387,389), e_{16}),$
$((390,406), e_{17})\}$

$\text{Extent}_P = \{((27,65), e_{18}), ((24,65), e_{19}), ((14,65), e_{20}), ((10,65), e_{21}), ((0,65), e_{22}),$
$((387,406), e_{23}), ((379,406), e_{24}), ((376,406), e_{25}), ((363,375), e_{26}), ((358,406), e_{27}),$
$((353,406), e_{28})\}$

$\text{Extent} = \text{Extent}_W \cup \text{Extent}_P$

$\text{Assoc} = \{(e_1, \boxed{1}), (e_2, \boxed{2}), (e_3, \boxed{3}), (e_4, \boxed{4}), (e_5, \boxed{5}), (e_6, \boxed{6}), (e_7, \boxed{7}), (e_8, \boxed{8}), (e_9, \boxed{9}), (e_{10}, \boxed{10}), (e_{11}, \boxed{11}),$
$(e_{12}, \boxed{12}), (e_{13}, \boxed{13}), (e_{14}, \boxed{14}), (e_{15}, \boxed{15}), (e_{16}, \boxed{16}), (e_{17}, \boxed{17}), (e_{18}, \boxed{18}), (e_{19}, \boxed{19}), (e_{20}, \boxed{20}), (e_{21}, \boxed{21}),$
$(e_{22}, \boxed{22}), (e_{23}, \boxed{23}), (e_{24}, \boxed{24}), (e_{25}, \boxed{25}), (e_{26}, \boxed{26}), (e_{27}, \boxed{27}), (e_{28}, \boxed{28})\}$

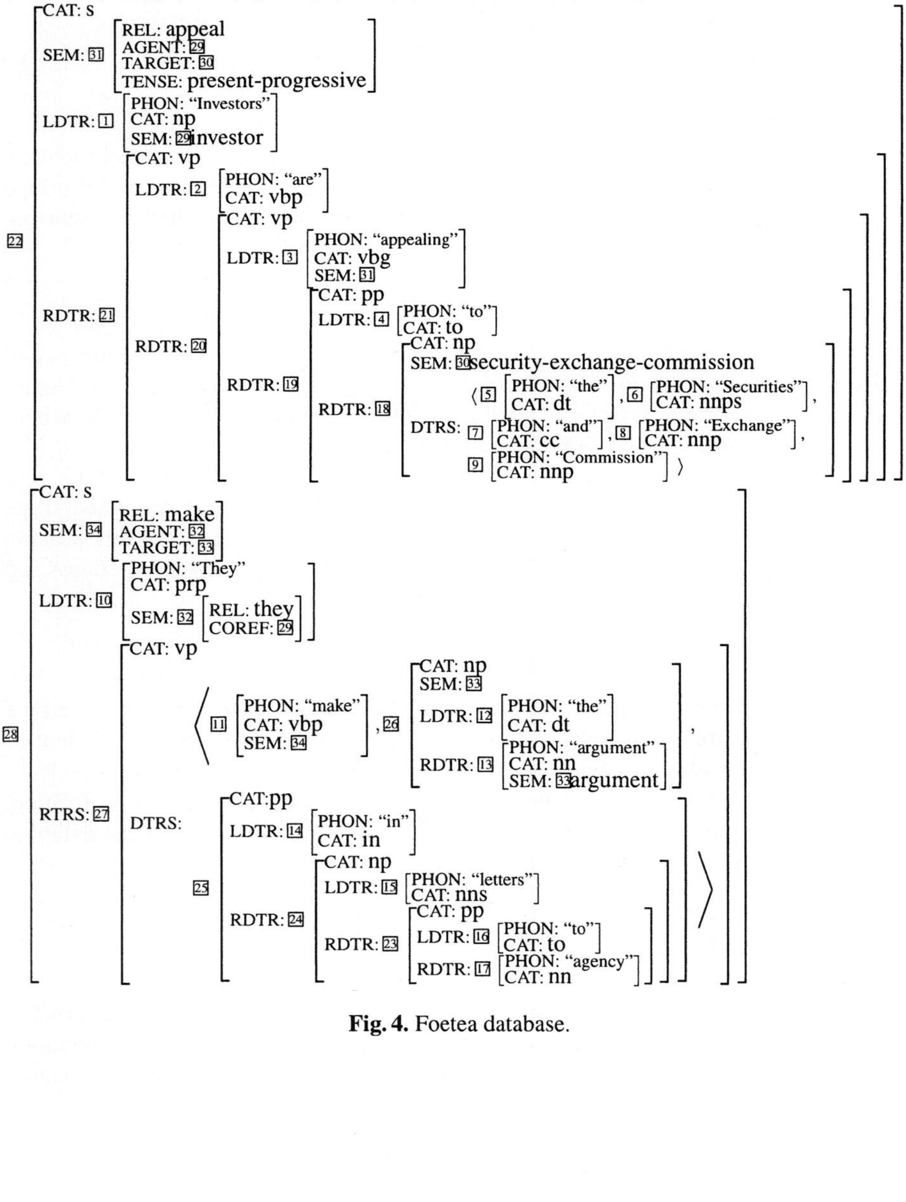

Fig. 4. Foetea database.

Perfect Loading

Let F be a feature structure in the data representation layer. Perfect loading is the operation to calculate the most general feature structure G such that $F \sqsubseteq G$ and G satisfies the type constraints including totally well-typedness. If such a feature structure cannot be interpreted in the conceptual layer, this operation fails. Perfect loading retrieves all information in feature structures in the database if there are no inconsistencies.

Partial Loading

Let F be a feature structure $\langle Q_F, \bar{q}_F, \theta_F, \delta_F \rangle$ in the data representation layer. Partial loading is the operation to calculate the most general feature structure G such that G satisfies the type constraints including totally well-typedness, and $F' \sqsubseteq G$ where F' is a feature structure $\langle Q_F, \bar{q}_F, \theta_F, \delta_{F'} \rangle$ where $\delta_{F'}(f, q) = \delta_F(f, q)$ if $Approp(f, \theta_F(q))$ is defined, otherwise $\delta_{F'}(f, q)$ is undefined. Partial loading retrieves all information of types in F and tries to retrieve the edges of F as possible. For a node q and an edge labeled with feature f such that $\delta(f, q)$ is defined, the edge will not be retrieved if the type assigned to q is prohibited from having feature f. Figure 6 shows an example of feature objects. Suppose 'sem' does not have the feature TENSE:, i.e., $Approp($TENSE:, **sem**$)$ is not defined. Perfect loading fails to retrieve F_1 because **sem** is not unifiable with any type that has the feature TENSE:. On the other hand, partial loading succeeds in retrieving F_1 by ignoring feature TENSE:. The result of the partial loading of F_1 becomes F_3.

Update

Update is a transaction that takes keys $\kappa \subset K$ and a description of the logic programming language. While the transaction is operating, feature structures associated with κ in the database are retrieved into the conceptual layer first. Next, a description of the programming language is executed. If the execution fails, the transaction finishes without changing the database. If it succeeds, the retrieved feature structures are updated to the database, and the transaction finishes.

For simplicity, suppose that only one key $k \in \text{Key}$ is given. Figure 5 shows the process of updating. Let F be a feature structure $\langle Q_F, \bar{q}_F, \theta_F, \delta_F \rangle$ such that there exists an association $(k, \bar{q}_F)$ in the data representation layer. Let $G(= \langle Q_G, \bar{q}_G, \theta_G, \delta_G \rangle)$ be a feature structure acquired by retrieving F from the database. For all $q_F \in Q_F$, $map(q_F, q_G)$ is defined if q_F in F is retrieved. When updating G, G is inserted to the database, and for all q_F and q_G such that $map(q_F, q_G)$, all edges that lead to q_F are rewritten and led to the inserted q_G.

Suppose that we have F_1 and F_2 depicted in Figure 6, and we want to unify the feature structure reached by following AGENT: in F_1 and the feature structure reached by following AGENT:COREF: in F_2. First, F_1 and F_2 are retrieved to the conceptual layer by partial loading, and then they are unified in the conceptual layer. Finally, they are updated to the data representation layer, and the result becomes F'_1 and F'_2.

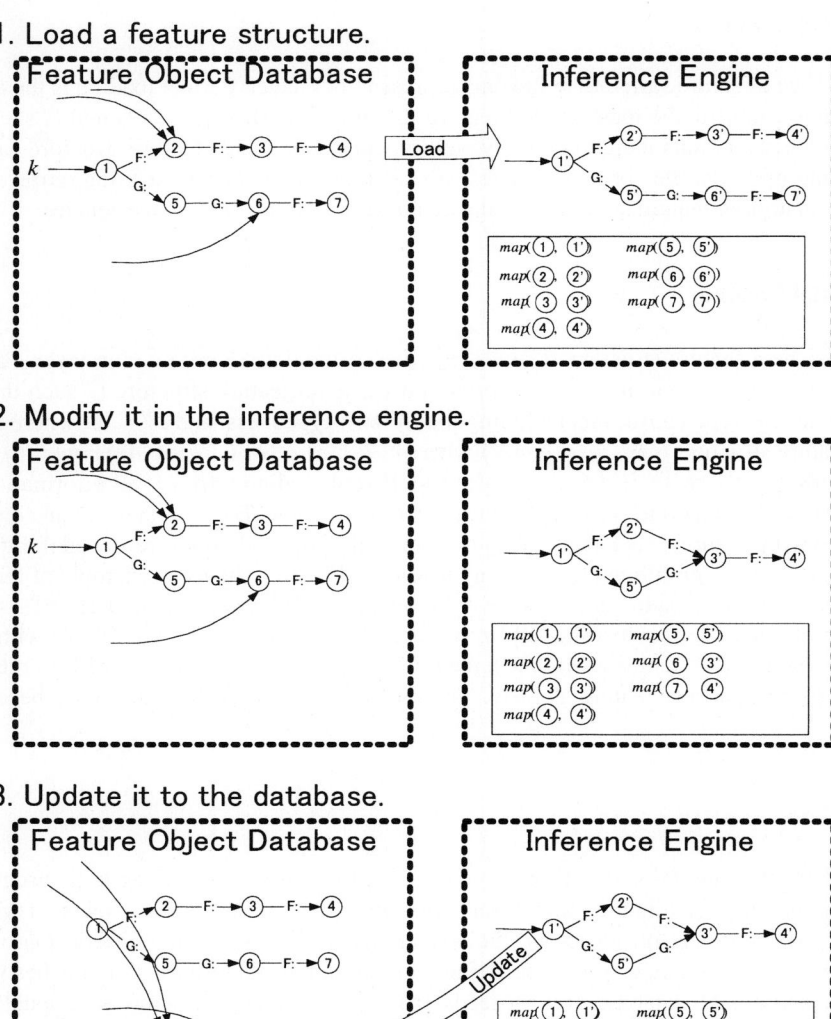

Fig. 5. Updating procedure.

4 Conclusion

We proposed a persistent mechanism for storing typed feature structures and the overall architecture of the text archive system. The aim of the system is to associate typed feature structures with regions in text, to make indexes for efficient retrieval, to allow

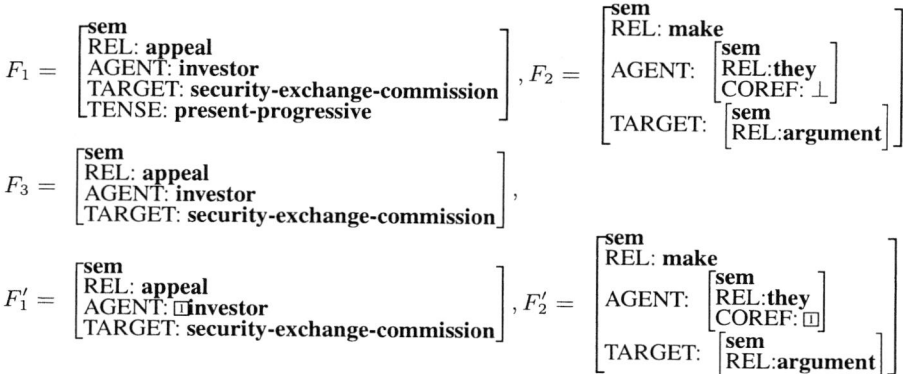

Fig. 6. Feature objects.

users to specify both structure and proximity, and to enable inference on feature structures embedded in the text. This persistent mechanism is achieved by separating the role of the typed feature structures into data representation and interpretation. Feature structures are preserved in the data representation layer that corresponds to data representation, and can be modified in the conceptual layer that corresponds to interpretation. Though only a few operations to feature structures are allowed in the data representation layer, we have exemplified that they are sufficient because modified feature structures in the conceptual layer can be updated, as if they were modified in the data representation layer.

References

1. Carpenter, B.: The Logic of Typed Feature Structures. Cambridge University Press, Cambridge, UK (1992)
2. Sag, I.A., Wasow, T.: Syntactic Theory : A Formal Introduction. CSLI Publications, Stanford, CA (1999)
3. Carpenter, B., Penn, G.: ALE: The attribute logic engine. user's guide (version 3.2.1) (2001)
4. Wintner, S., Francez, N.: Efficient implementation of unification-based grammars. Journal of Language and Computation **1** (1999) 53–92
5. Makino, T., Yoshida, M., Torisawa, K., Tsujii, J.: LiLFeS — towards a practical HPSG parser. In: Proc. of COLING-ACL-1998. (1998) 807–811
6. McCune, W.: Experiments with discrimination-tree indexing and path indexing for term retrieval. Automated Reasoning **18** (1992) 147–167
7. Sekar, R., Ramakrishnan, I.V., Voronkov, A.: Term indexing. In: Handbook of Automated Reasoning. Elsevier Science Publishers (2001) 1853–1964
8. Ninomiya, T., Makino, T., Tsujii, J.: An indexing scheme for typed feature structures. In: Proc. of COLING 2002. (2002) 1248–1252
9. Clarke, C.L.A., Cormack, G.V., Burkowski, F.J.: An algebra for structured text search and a framework for its implementation. The computer Journal **38** (1995) 43–56
10. Jaakkola, J., Kilpeläinen, P.: Nested text-region algebra. Technical Report C-1999-2, Department of Computer Science, University of Helsinki (1999)

Example-Based Machine Translation Without Saying Inferable Predicate

Eiji Aramaki[1], Sadao Kurohashi[1], Hideki Kashioka[2], and Hideki Tanaka[3]

[1] Graduate School of Information Science and Tech. University of Tokyo, Hongo, Bunkyo-ku, Tokyo 113-8656, Japan
{aramaki,kuro}@kc.t.u-tokyo.ac.jp
[2] ATR Spoken Language Translation Research Laboratories, 2-2 Hikaridai, Seika, Soraku, Kyoto 619-0288, Japan
hideki.kashioka@atr.jp
[3] Science and Technical Research Laboratories of NHK, 1-10-11 Kinuta, Setagaya-ku, Tokyo 157-8510, Japan
tanaka.h-ja@nhk.or.jp

Abstract. For natural translations, a human being does not express predicates that are inferable from the context in a target language. This paper proposes a method of machine translation which handles these predicates. First, to investigate how to translate them, we build a corpus in which predicate correspondences are annotated manually. Then, we observe the corpus, and find alignment patterns including these predicates. In our experimental results, the machine translation system using the patterns demonstrated the basic feasibility of our approach.

1 Introduction

With the rapid growth of the Internet, the availability of electronic texts is increasing day by day. View of this, much attention has been given to data-driven machine translation, such as example-based machine translation [1] and statistical machine translation [2]. However, previous studies have mainly focused on parallel translations.

In reality, however, a human being often does not make a perfectly parallel translation. In the following example, T_{human} is a human translation of an input sentence S, and T_{mt} is one of our machine translation system.

S: Canada-de <u>hirakareta</u> tsuusyou-kaigi-de ...
(a trade conference <u>that was held</u> in Canada)
T_{mt}: At a trade conference <u>held</u> in Canada ...
T_{human}: At a trade conference in Canada ...

A machine translation system tends to translate word for word, as shown in T_{mt}. On the other hand, a human being does not explicitly translate the underlined verb phrase (VP) "hirakareta (*be held*)" as shown in T_{human}. The reason why the underlined phrase is not expressed is that a human avoids redundant expressions, and prefers a compact translation without it. We call such a phrase which is not expressed in translation *null-align* phrase in this paper. Besides the fact verb phrases are sometimes null-aligned, the difficulty of VP-alignments has been pointed out [3].

For this reason, in order to investigate how to translate VPs, we built a VP-aligned-corpus with two types of information annotated: (1) for each phrase, whether the phrase is a VP or not, (2) for each VP, where the VP in one language corresponds in the other. In this paper, we analyze the VP-aligned-corpus and suggest a method for achieving appropriate VP translations.

Though the proposed method does not depend on language pairs and translation directions, this paper describes Japanese-English translation.

This paper is organized as follows. The next section presents how to build the VP-aligned-corpus. Section 3 reports several observations of the VP-aligned-corpus. Section 4 describes how to achieve appropriate VP translations. Then, Section 5 reports experimental results, Section 6 describes related works, and Section 7 presents our conclusions.

2 VP-Aligned-Corpus

The VP-aligned-corpus is built using the following method: First, all of the sentence pairs in the corpus are automatically converted into phrasal dependency structures, and their phrasal alignments are estimated. Next, annotators modify the correspondences. In this section, we describe a corpus for the annotation and its annotation process.

2.1 NHK-News-Corpus

To build a VP-aligned-corpus, we need a bilingual corpus consisting of natural translations. We used a bilingual news corpus compiled by the NHK broadcasting service (NHK News Corpus). It consists of about 40,000 Japanese articles (from a five-year period) and English ones which are translations of Japanese articles by humans. The average number of Japanese sentences in one article is 5.2, and that of English sentence is 7.4. Table 1 shows an example of an article pair. In Table 1, the underlined phrases and sentences have no parallel expressions in the other language. A large number of underlined expressions indicates that the Japanese articles are freely translated to be natural as English news.

2.2 Annotation Process

The annotation process consists of the following four steps:

STEP 1: Estimation of Sentence Alignment
We use DP matching for bilingual sentence alignment based on a translation dictionary (two million entries in total). Next, we extract 1-to-1 sentence pairs. For the evaluation data (96 articles), the precision of the sentence alignment was 77.5% [4].

Table 1. NHK-news-corpus.

石川県 (Ishikawa Prefecture) 輪島市で外国の大使や一般の参加者など千人あまりが急な斜面の棚田で田植えを体験する催しが行われました。輪島市白米町には (in Shiroyonemachi) 千枚田と呼ばれる大小 (of all various sizes) 二千百枚の棚田が急な斜面から海に向かって拡がっています。田植え体験は農作業を通して米作りの意義などを考えていこうという (thinking about the significance of the rice crop farming) 地球環境平和財団の呼び掛けで開かれたもので、海外三十四ヵ (34 oversea countries) 国の大使や書記官 (ambassador and secretary)、それに一般の参加者ら合わせておよそ千人が集まりました。田植えに使われた苗は去年の秋、天皇陛下が皇居で収穫された稲から育てたものです。参加者たちは裸足になって水山に足を踏み入れ地元に伝わる田植え歌に合わせて慣れない手つきで (unskillfully) 苗を植えていました。きょうの輪島市は雲が広がったもののまずまずの天気となり、出席された高円宮さまも海からの風に吹かれながら田植えに加わっていました。地球環境平和財団は今年の夏休みに全国の子どもたちを対象に草刈りや生きものの観察会を開く他、秋には稲刈体験を行なう予定にしています。(The weather in Wajima City was not bad. Prince Takamadonomiya joined the rice-planting feeling the wind from the sea. The private Foundation for Global Peace and Environment is planning to organize watching wildlife and mowing events in summer vacation and a harvesting event in autumn.)

Ambassadors and diplomats from 37 countries took part in a rice planting festival on Sunday in small paddies on steep hillsides in Wajima, central Japan. About one-thousand people gathered at the hill, where some two-thousand 100 miniature paddies, called Senmaida, stretch toward the Sea of Japan. The event was organized by the private Foundation for Global Peace and Environment. The rice seedlings are grown from grain harvested by the Emperor at the Imperial Palace in Tokyo last autumn. Barefoot participants waded into the paddies to plant the seedlings by hand while singing a local folk song about the practice of rice planting.

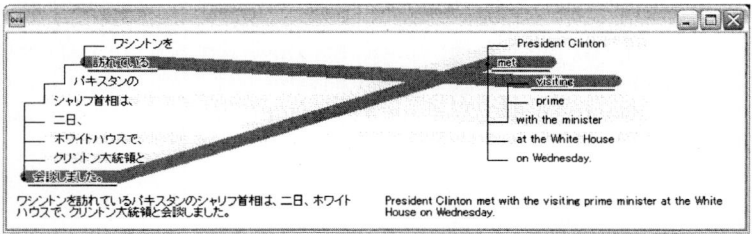

Fig. 1. Annotation Tool.

STEP 2: Conversion to Phrasal Dependency Structures

The phrasal dependency structures of the sentence pairs are estimated by parsers. The English parser [5] returns a word-based phrase structure, which is merged into phrases by the following rules and converted into a dependency structure by deciding head phrases [4].

1. Function words are attached to their following content words.
2. Compound nouns are attached into one phrase.
3. Auxiliary verbs are attached to the main verb.

The Japanese parser KNP [6] outputs the phrasal dependency structure, and that is used as is.

STEP 3: Phrasal Annotation

VPs are annotated in the phrasal dependency structures. We define a VP as a phrase that contains (1) a verb or (2) an adjective that has an argument as its child.

STEP 4: Correspondence Annotation: For each Japanese VP, annotators mark its corresponding phrases in the English sentence. As mentioned be-

Table 2. Classification of VP-correspondences.

Classification (Japanese: English)	#
VP-VP	9779
VP-ϕ	6831
VP-PP, VP-NP	*710*
OTHERS	*316*

* The numbers in *Italic* are estimated automatically because the annotated information tells whether phrases are VPs or not.

fore, Japanese VPs do not always correspond to English VPs. We also allow annotators to mark the phrases that are not VPs (for example, a NP or a PP). In addition, when a Japanese VP has no parallel expressions, annotators mark **VP-ϕ**. In the same way, for each English VP, annotators make the annotations.

We annotated 5,500 sentence pairs. The annotation work was carried out using a GUI tool that can be operated by a mouse. Figure 1 shows the annotation tool and an annotated sentence pair. In this paper, we illustrate a sentence structure by locating its root node at the left as shown in Figure 1.

3 Analysis of a VP-Aligned-Corpus

In a VP-aligned-corpus, Japanese VPs do not always correspond to English VPs literally. We classify and count annotated correspondences from the view point of where Japanese phrases correspond in English (Table 2). As shown in Table 2, since the ratio of correspondences that are not VP-VP is more than 40%, so we cannot consider them as exceptional phenomena.

This section describes the classification.

1. **VP-VP:** A Japanese-VP corresponds to an English-VP.
   We paid little attention to **VP-VP**s in this paper, because these correspondences are estimated by conventional alignment methods.
2. **VP-ϕ:** A Japanese-VP has no parallel expressions in the phrase level.
   VP-ϕs arise for the two reasons: (1) the sentence alignments failed and the Japanese-VP has a parallel expression in another English sentence, or (2) the Japanese-VP occurs in a context that allow it to be null-aligned.
   The latter example, has been already shown in Section 1, is illustrated as follows:

(At a trade conference in Canada ...[1])

---

[1] The expressions in the branket are a part of an English sentence.

Table 3. Judgements of CAPs.

Judgement	#	Classification	#
good	56	P-CONTEXT	21
		C-CONTEXT	16
		PC-CONTEXT	19
bad	24	Parse error	3
		Alignment error	11
		Phrase chunking error	1
		Others	9

* The classifications in the good judgment (P, C, PC-CONTEXT) are mentioned in the next page.

As I mentioned before, "hirakareta (*be held*)" in the above context is redundant to translate. We present a more detailed classification of this type in Section 4.

3. **VP-PP, VP-NP:** A Japanese-VP corresponds to an English-NP or PP.
   A Japanese VP is sometimes translated into a "NP" or a "preposition + NP." The following discussion does not deal with these cases, because they are also estimated by conventional alignment methods.
4. **Others:** A Japanese-VP corresponds to a phrase in another category.
   We paid little attention to this type, because the number of this type is small as shown in Table 2.

4   Learning Null-Aligned Translations

We concentrate **VP-**ϕ in this paper because the amount of it is the highest the other classifications except for **VP-VP**.

The observation of **VP-**ϕ leads to the fact that the surroundings of a **VP-**ϕ are parallel with each other. For example, (1) in the last section is aligned as follows:

We call such an alignment pattern consisting of three Japanese phrases and two English phrases a **Condensed Alignment Pattern** or simply a **CAP** in this paper[2].

The following is an image of a CAP:

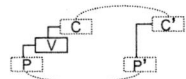

---

[2] There are reverse CAPs consisting of three Japanese phrase and two English phrases in the corpus. However we paid no attention to them because this paper deals with translation in the Japanese-English direction.

Example-Based Machine Translation Without Saying Inferable Predicate

If a null-aligned phrase in a CAP is always inferable and redandant to translate, we can regard CAPs as translation examples, and achieve compact translations using them.

In order to examine the above assumption, we randomly extracted 80 CAPs from the corpus. Then, we manually checked whether null-aligned phrases in CAPs are inferable (good) or not (bad) (Table 3). As a result, except for some errors (alignment errors, parse errors and so on) almost all CAPs are appropriate as translation examples. Therefore, we can use them as translation examples.

However, if we regard an entire CAP as a translation example, it can be used only in the case where it is equal to the input sentence. To cope with this problem, we estimate unnecessary parts of CAPs, and generalize them.

First, we classify the CAPs depending on whether its parent (**P**) or child (**C**) is the unnecessary context.

1. **C-CONTEXT:** only **C** is a necessary context.
   There is a case in which a null-aligned VP tied to its child (**C**) and its parent (**P**) is not a necessary context. In the following example, the Japanese **V** (*take*) performs as only a case-marker for **C** (*spring*).

   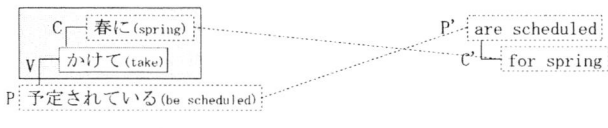

   (...are scheduled for spring...)

   In the above example, both a **V** and a **P** are VPs. On the other hand, in the following example, the **P** is a NP.

   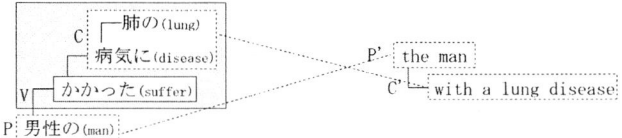

   (The man with a lung disease ...)

   In this example, a **V** is a null-aligned phrase, because it is associated with **C** (*disease*).

   Accordingly, we can see different linguistic phenomena depending on whether the **P** is a VP or not. However, we deal with them uniformly in from the structural view point.

2. **P-CONTEXT:** only **P** is a necessary context.
   In contrast, the following examples are cases in which a **C** and a **P** are tied each other. In this type, we can also see different linguistic phenomena depending on whether the **P** is a VP or not.
   When the **P** is a VP, the **P** and the **V** have similar meanings, because the **P** has the child phrase (**C**) instead of the **V**. In the following, **V** "kisya-kaiken-shi (*have a press conference*)" is a null-aligned phrase, then **P** "say" has **C** "a Pakistani scientist" as its child.

Table 4. Examples of CAP Fragments including "hirakareta (be held)".

CAP Fragments: Ps and V				CAP Fragments: Cs and V			
V	P	P'	Frequency	C	V	C'	Frequency
hirakareta	kaigi	conference	17	kaigi		meeting	5
	kaigou	meeting	2	Canada	hirakareta	Canada	4
	syuukai	gathering	1	Lyon		Lyon	4

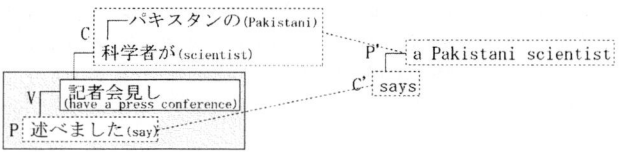

(A Pakistani scientist says ...)

On the other hand, if the **P** is not a VP, the **P** associates with a **V**, and the **V** is a null-aligned phrase. (1') is an example of this type, and is illustrated as follows:

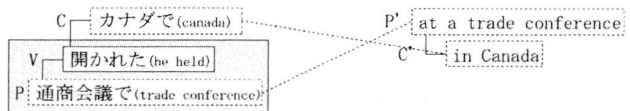

(At a trade conference in Canada ...)

3. **PC-CONTEXT:** Both a **P** and a **C** are necessary contexts.

There is cases in which both a **P** and a **C** are necessary contexts. In such a case, we regard the entire CAP as a translation example. In the following example, both **C** (*each country*) and **P** (*rescue teams*) associate with **V**(*be sent*).

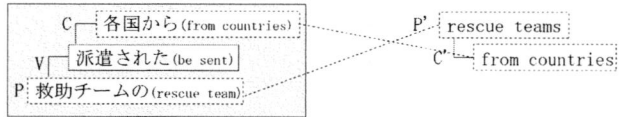

(Rescue teams from countries ...)

4.1 Estimation CAP Context

The classification in the above section is based on subjective judgments and estimations of all the CAP's contexts is difficult and insignificant. However, in the case that a **P** is obviously the context, we can find many CAPs that include **P**, **P'** and **V**. Therefore, we divide a CAP into two CAP-fragments and count their occurrences.

For example, Table 4 shows CAP fragments that include "hirakareta (*be held*)" from the Section 1 example. CAP fragments including "kaigi(*conference*)"

Table 5. Estimated CAP Context.

	# of CAPs
P-CONTEXT	1120
C-CONTEXT	297
PC-CONTEXT	2802

Table 6. BLEU Score.

	Testset(240)	Subset(104)	Subset(14)
BASELINE	24.6	24.7	26.3
CAPMT	24.8	-	29.0
CAPMT+	25.0	25.7	-

* The numbers in brackets in Table 6 are # of sentences.

occur 17 times, and those including "Canada (*Canada*)" occur only 4 times. Therefore, We can decide that "kaigi(*conference*)" is the context that allows "hirakareta (*be held*)" to be a null-aligned phrase.

The algorithm of the context estimation is follows:

1. For a phrase in a CAP, we decide the headword. For a NP, we regard the last noun as the headword. For a VP, we regard the main verb as the headword. Otherwise, we regard the entire phrase as the headword.
2. First, we divide CAP into two fragments as follows:

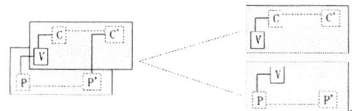

Then, we count their frequencies. Where, the frequency of (**P**,**P'**,**V**) is $freq(P)$, and that of (**C**,**C'**,**V**) is $freq(C)$.
3. After counting, for each CAP, if $(freq(P) > freq(C) \times 2)$, a **P** is the context (P-CONTEXT)[3].
4. On the contrary, if $(freq(C) > freq(P) \times 2)$, a **C** is the context (C-CONTEXT).
5. Otherwise, both a **P** and a **C** are contexts (PC-CONTEXT).

5 Experiments

We evaluated our method from the following two view points: (1)how many CAPs were extracted (2)how much CAPs improved the translation accuracy.

5.1 CAP Extraction

We examined how many CAPs were extracted from our translation examples. The translation examples consist of 52,749 automatically aligned sentence pairs that were extracted from NHK News Corpus. As a result, 4,219 CAPs were extracted in total. It shows that we can extract one CAP from each 12 sentence pairs.

Table 5 shows the ratio of their estimated contexts. As mentioned before, the judgments of the CAP context is too subjective to argue. We evaluated the propriety of context estimation in full translation tasks.

---
[3] This threshold was determined by a preliminary experiment not to deteriorate the accuracy of the system.

Table 7. Translation Examples.

REF	... quake struck areas along northeastern Afghanistan ...
BASELINE	... disaster area of the earthquake occurred in afghanistan northeast ...
CAPMT+	... disaster area of the earthquake in afghanistan northeast ...
REF	An air show in the US state of Maryland on the 14th ...
BASELINE	Air show was held in maryland of the united states on the 14th ...
CAPMT+	Air show in maryland of the united states on the 14th ...
REF	... summit due to be held on the 25th.
BASELINE	... summit meeting conducted on 25th.
CAPMT+	... summit meeting on 25th.

5.2 Full Translation

We evaluated the CAP's improvements in full translation tasks using our Japanese-English translation system [4]. The system produces a translation using translation examples which are the similar to the input sentence.

We compared the following three conditions.

1. *BASELINE*: the EBMT system [4] without CAP translation examples.
2. *CAPMT*: the EBMT system using both *BASELINE*'s translation examples and CAP translation examples which are not estimated their contexts.
3. *CAPMT+*: the EBMT system using both *BASELINE*'s translation examples and CAP translation examples which are estimated their contexts.

We evaluated them using BLEU[7]. BLEU is a score computes the ratio of N-gram for translation results found in reference translations. We used N=3.

We prepared a testset consisting of 240 lead (top) sentences randomly extracted from the NHK-news-corpus, and four references that were made by NHK's professional translators. Some sentences in the testset were translated without CAP translation examples. In such sentences outputs of *CAPMT* and *CAPMT+* are equal to ones of *BASELINE*. Therefore, we also compared translation results in the subsets consisting of translations which are different from *BASELINE*.

The results shown in Table 6, and some translation examples are shown in Table 7. Although the score of *CAPMT+* was almost equal to one of *BASELINE* in the entire testset, it had 1.0% improvement in the subset. In addition, its coverage was high, because its subset consisted of 104 sentences.

In contrast, the *CAPMT*'s subset consisted of only 14 sentences. Therefore, its improvement had little statistical significance.

6 Related Work

The field of data-driven machine translation concentrates mainly on the study of statistical machine translation (SMT) and example-based machine translation (EBMT).

In SMT, a system has to deal with a freely translated corpus in order to estimate the condensed alignment patterns (CAPs) in this paper. Since the corpus in this paper (NHK News Corpus) has a high perplexity (more than 100 in the IBM Model 4), it is a difficult task for the SMT system.

In EBMT, previous researches deal with restricted domains that have fairly high parallelism, such as, software manuals [8], business documents [9], White Papers [10] and so on. In such corpora, the condensed alignment patterns are rare.

7 Conclusion

In this paper, we describe the classification of verb phrase translations, and proposed the method to translate null-aligned verb phrases. On the theoretical side, the proposed method works well, because null-aligned translation examples improved translations in the half testset, as shown in the experimental results. However, for all of the testset, our method did not achieve extensive improvement. One of the reasons is that the amount of condensed alignment patterns is not enough. However we believe this problem will be resolved as the size of the corpus increases, because the News Corpus is increasing day by day.

References

1. Nagao, M.: A framework of a mechanical translation between Japanese and english by analogy principle. In: Artificial and Human Intelligence. (1984) 173–180.
2. Brown, P.F., Pietra, S.A.D., cent J. Della Pietra, V., Mercer, R.L.: The mathematics of statistical machine translation: Parameter estimation. Computational Linguistics **19** (1993)
3. Aramaki, E., Kurohashi, S., Sato, S., Watanabe, H.: Finding translation correspondences from parallel parsed corpus for example-based translation. In: Proceedings of MT Summit VIII. (2001) 27–32
4. Aramaki, E., Kurohashi, S., Kashioka, H., Tanaka, H.: Word selection for ebmt based on monolingual similarity and translation confidence. In: Proceedings of the HLT-NAACL 2003 Workshop on Building and Using Parallel Texts: Data Driven Machine Translation and Beyond. (2003) 57–64
5. Charniak, E.: A maximum-entropy-inspired parser. In: Proceedings of NAACL 2000. (2000) 132–139
6. Kurohashi, S., Nagao, M.: A syntactic analysis method of long Japanese sentences based on the detection of conjunctive structures. Computational Linguistics **20** (1994)
7. Papineni, K., Roukos, S., Ward, T., Zhu, W.J.: Bleu: a method for automatic evaluation of machine translation. In: Proceedings of ACL 2002. (2002) 311–318
8. Menezes, A., Richardson, S.D.: A best-first alignment algorithm for automatic extraction of transfer mappings from bilingual corpora. In: Proceedings of the ACL 2001 Workshop on Data-Driven Methods in Machine Translation. (2001) 39–46
9. Sato, K., Saito, H.: Extracting word sequence correspondences with support vector machine. In: Proceedings of the 19th COLING. (2002) 870–876
10. Watanabe, H., Kurohashi, S., Aramaki, E.: Finding structural correspondences from bilingual parsed corpus for corpus-based translation. In: Proceedings of the 18th COLING. (2000) 906–912

Improving Back-Transliteration by Combining Information Sources

Slaven Bilac and Hozumi Tanaka

Department of Computer Science
Tokyo Institute of Technology, Tokyo
{sbilac,tanaka}@cl.cs.titech.ac.jp

Abstract. Transliterating words and names from one language to another is a frequent and highly productive phenomenon. Transliteration is information loosing since important distinctions are not preserved in the process. Hence, automatically converting transliterated words back into their original form is a real challenge. However, due to wide applicability in MT and CLIR, it is a computationally interesting problem. Previously proposed back-transliteration methods are based either on phoneme modeling or grapheme modeling across languages. In this paper, we propose a new method, combining the two models in order to enhance the back-transliterations of words transliterated in Japanese. Our experiments show that the resulting system outperforms single-model systems.

1 Introduction

With the advent of technology and increased flow of goods and services, it has become quite common to integrate new words from one language to another. Whenever a word is adopted into a new language, pronunciation is adjusted to suit its phonetic inventory. Furthermore, the orthographic form of the word is modified to allow representation in the target language script. This process of acquisition and assimilation of a new word into an existing writing system is referred to as transliteration [1].

Since integration of new words is a very productive process, it often happens that the new pairs are not recorded in machine or human dictionaries. Therefore, it is impossible to rely on the dictionary lookup to find the transliteration pairs. Failure to find a target language equivalent represents a big problem in Machine Translation (MT) where failures in dictionary lookups can cause translation failures. Furthermore, transliteration represents a significant problem in the field of Cross-Language Information Retrieval (CLIR) where the goal is to retrieve all the related documents in two or more languages [2]. In many cases the results would be greatly improved, if the system were able to correctly identify the English equivalent of a Japanese or Korean transliteration and then search for documents based on the original word.

When the source language and the target language use the same (or very similar) alphabet, there are hardly any problems, as the speakers of both languages can easily identify the string. On the other hand, if two languages use very different writing codes, the acquired word undergoes heavy transformation in order to become an acceptable vocabulary entry. For example, the English word *cache* is transliterated in Japanese as キャッシュ "kyasshu"[1].

Although governments provide guidelines on how to transliterate, words commonly appear in several different forms. The wide variety of transliterations can be seen both in Korean [3] and Japanese [1,4]. For example, the English word *interface* has five different transliterations in EDICT Japanese-English dictionary[2]: インターフェース "intaafeesu" インターフェイス "intaafeisu", インタフェース "intafeesu", インタフェイス "intafeisu" and インタフェス "intafesu".

While automatic transliteration in itself is difficult, back-transliteration or transliteration back into the original language is even harder. Increase in difficulty results from the fact that various distinctions, present in the source language, are not preserved when the word is transliterated into the target language. For example, Japanese has only five basic vowels and no /θ/ or /ð/[3] sounds, whereas non-existent sounds are replaced with the closest equivalents. Consequently, the following three English words: *bass,bath* and *bus* are transliterated as バス "basu"[4]. The system trying to obtain a back-transliteration for バス as therefore three valid choices which cannot be disambiguated in the absence of additional contextual transformation.

Transliterated words are normally written in katakana, one of three Japanese writing systems. While other vocabulary (i.e. animal names or onomatopoeic expressions) can also be written in katakana, the fact that something is written in katakana is a good hint that it might be a transliterated foreign word or a name. Thus, unlike Arabic or Korean, where a big part of the back-transliteration problem is identifying candidate transliterations [5,3], in Japanese back-transliteration can be directly applied to any katakana strings absent from the bilingual dictionary.

In this paper we propose a method to improve back-transliteration by combining the information based on pronunciation and spelling. Even though we concentrate on Japanese and English, our method is applicable to other language pairs.

The reminder of this paper is organized as follows: in Section 2 we review previous approaches to (back-)transliteration. In Section 3 we describe the proposed method and outline the implementation details. Finally, Section 4 gives a short evaluation and a discussion or results obtained.

2 Previous Research

Previous approaches to (back-)transliteration can be roughly divided into two groups: grapheme- and phoneme-based. These approaches are also referred to as direct- and pivot-based methods, respectively.

---

[1] We use *italics* to transcribe the English words, while Japanese transliterations (e.g. キャッシュ) are given with romaji in "typewriter" font (e.g. "kyasshu"). The romaji used follows [1], thus closely reflecting English-like pronunciation with long vowels transcribed as "aa" rather than "ā".
[2] ftp://ftp.cc.monash.edu.au/pub/nihongo/
[3] All phonemes given in // are written in IPA symbols.
[4] Here /θ/ is replaced with /s/, and /æ/ is replaced with /a/.

2.1 Grapheme-Based Modelling

In this framework, the English string is not converted into a phonemic representation before its alignment with the transliterated string. Brill et al. [4] propose a noisy channel model for Japanese. This model allows for non-atomic edits: several letters can be replaced by a different letter combination [6]. The input string is broken down into arbitrary substrings, each of which is output independently (and possibly incorrectly). The model is trained to learn edit-probabilities and the best back-transliteration is chosen using a modified edit distance algorithm [7, 8]. This method fails to generate the correct string in cases where English spelling is not reflected in the pronunciation (e.g マイム "maimu" being incorrectly back-transliterated into *maim* instead of *mime*).

For transliteration, Goto et al. [9] propose a maximum entropy based model for Japanese, while Kang and Choi [10] propose a decision tree-based model for Korean.

2.2 Phoneme-Based Modelling

The systems based on phoneme alignment are more numerous. Jeong et al. [3] propose a method using first order HMM model to generate English strings from Korean input. The result is compared with dictionary entries using a variety of string similarity algorithms to find the best match.

For Japanese, Knight and Graehl [1] employ a compositional model combining romaji-to-phoneme, phoneme-to-English and English word probability models into one. The combined structure is treated as a graph, and the top ranking strings are found using the *k-best* path algorithm [11]. A similar model has been applied for Arabic-English back-transliteration [5]. However, this model cannot handle cases where the transliteration reflects the original spelling. For example, *tonya* and *tanya* have different transliterations of "toonya" and "taanya" but the system taking only pronunciation into account is unable to distinguish between the two.

Finally, Oh and Choi [12] propose a system trying to incorporate two different English-to-phoneme models into a single Korean transliteration system: standard English pronunciation and pronunciation closely following the spelling. However, this system uses only the origin of the word (estimated by a match against a finite set of affixes) to decide which model to apply when producing the transliteration.

3 The Combined Model

The systems introduced in the previous section model transliteration based on either phoneme or grapheme level. Nonetheless, even though most of the transliterations are based on the original pronunciation, there is a significant number of words where transliteration corresponds more closely to the spelling of the original. For example the first *e* in *eternal* is transliterated as "e" instead of "i" in エターナル "etaanaru". *phantom* is transliterated as ファントム "fantomu" rather than "fentamu"*. We believe, that we can better account for such behavior by combining the two information sources to maximize the use of the data available.

3.1 Probabilistic Model Specification

Given the Japanese word in romaji (i.e. alphabet)[5], the goal is to produce an English word (phrase) that maximizes the probability $P(E_a|J_a)$. Applying the Bayes' rule and dropping the constant denominator we get $P(J_a|E_a) \times P(E_a)$ where $P(E_a)$ is the source model and $P(J_a|E_a)$ is the noisy channel. We train the channel model as described below, and then reverse it to handle the romaji input.

3.2 Grapheme-Based Model (GM)

In this model the English word is directly rewritten as a Japanese romaji string with probability $P_g(J_a|E_a)$. Here, we follow [4] to arbitrarily break up the E_a string into n parts and output each part independently. Thus, the resulting probability of outputting J_a can be rewritten as in the equation (1).

$$P_g(J_a|E_a) \cong \prod_{i=1}^{n} P_g(J_{a_i}|E_{a_i}) \tag{1}$$

We implement $P_g(J_a|E_a)$ as a weighted Finite State Transducer (WFST) with E_{a_i} as inputs, J_{a_i} as outputs [1, 13] and transition costs as negative logs of probabilities. This WFST is then reversed and the best transliteration is computed as its composition with the source model $P(E_a)$.[6] The resulting WFST is searched for k-best transliterations using the k-best path algorithm. A probability $P_g(E_a|J_a)$ is associated with each path obtained.

3.3 Phoneme-Based Model (PM)

In this model the channel is broken into two stages: a) conversion of the English alphabet into English phonemes with some probability $P(E_p|E_a)$ and b) conversion of the English phonemes into romaji with some probability $P(J_a|E_p)$. Consequently, $P_p(J_a|E_a)$ can be rewritten as equation (2). Rather than manipulating these two distributions separately, we compute their composition to obtain a unique probability distribution $P_p(J_{a_i}|E_{a_i})$.

$$P_p(J_a|E_a) \cong \prod_{i=1}^{n} P(J_{a_i}|E_{p_i}) \times \prod_{i=1}^{n} P(E_{p_i}|E_{a_i}) \tag{2}$$

Consequently all English alphabet strings can be rewritten directly into romaji without requiring their conversion into intermediate phoneme representation. This removes the

---

[5] As stated above, transliterated words are normally written in katakana, potentially inducing an another stage in the model: rewriting romaji characters into katakana $P(J_k|J_a)$. However, katakana characters generally have a unique alphabetic equivalent, thus reducing this distribution to 1. We implement the katakana to romaji conversion as a preprocessing module.

[6] We use the AT&T FSM library (http://www.research.att.com/~mohri/fsm/) for WFST composition.

requirement of having a pronunciation dictionary for the back-transliteration[7]. Furthermore, since both models are dealing with the same unit types, it is possible to directly combine them, allowing for certain parts of the input string to be converted by one and the rest by the other model. We leave this method of combination for future research.

3.4 Combining the Models

After obtaining the back-transliterations $E_{a_{phon}}$ and $E_{a_{graph}}$ with the respective probabilities of $P_p(E_a|J_a)$ and $P_g(E_a|J_a)$, we can assign the final score of a transliteration $S_c(E_a|J_a)$ as in equation (3) where γ and δ are set to maximize the accuracy on the training set[8]. Transliteration with the highest score is selected as the best.

$$S_c(E_a|J_a) = \gamma P_p(E_a|J_a) + \delta P_g(E_a|J_a)$$
$$\text{s.t.} \quad \gamma + \delta = 1 \tag{3}$$

3.5 Training the Models

For the GM, we follow [4] closely to extract the character-string mappings. Since romaji and English alphabet are equivalent character sets, they can be aligned using the non-weighted Levensthein distance. Then, letter-edits are expanded to include up to N edits to the right and to the left. For example for the pair (roo,row) we get: $r \to r$ $o \to o$ $o \to w$. For $N = 1$, edits $ro \to ro$, $roo \to row$, $oo \to ow$ are also added to the set. We collect a complete set of edits $\alpha_g \to \beta_g$ in the training set and assign the probability to each according to equation (4). Throughout, we distinguish edits that appear at the beginning or the end of the word or neither.

$$P(\alpha \to \beta) = \frac{count(\alpha \to \beta)}{count(\alpha)} \tag{4}$$

Given the collection of edits $\alpha_g \to \beta_g$ for each input word J_a we can generate a WFST which contains all possible ways to rewrite the input string.

3.6 Training the Phoneme Model

For the PM, the English phoneme and English alphabet sets are not equivalent, hence the edit-distance algorithm cannot be applied directly to obtain the optimal alignment. Instead we proceed to obtain the best alignment using the EM algorithm [15]. Given the input strings, we generate all possible alignments constrained so that: a) each unit in one string aligns to one or more units in the other string and b) there are no crossing alignment arcs. Here the base unit represents either a letter or a phoneme[9].

After the EM algorithm selects the optimal alignment, we proceed to expand the set of individual alignments with N adjacent units as above to obtain a set of possible rewrites $\alpha_{e_a} \to \beta_{e_p}$. This process is repeated to obtain the set of all possible rewrites of English phonemes into romaji $\alpha_{e_p} \to \beta_{j_a}$.

---

[7] However, the pronunciation dictionary is still necessary for the training.
[8] Parameters are trained using Golden Section Search [14].
[9] The CMU pronouncing dictionary (http://www.speech.cs.cmu.edu/cgi-bin/cmudict) phoneme set is used for a total of 39 phonemes without the tone marks.

Each input α_{e_a} with all its mappings β_{e_p} is converted into a WFST and composed with a WFST encoding the complete set of mappings $\alpha_{e_p} \to \beta_{j_a}$ to obtain the set of all possible rewrites of English alphabet strings α_p into romaji strings β_p based on the PM.

For the case ($N = 0$), the model for mapping romaji to English phonemes is similar to the one described by Knight and Graehl [1]. However, we learn the alignments both for English alphabet to English phoneme strings and English phoneme to romaji strings, add context information and compose the resulting models to get direct mappings from English alphabet to romaji. We will see the benefits of these improvements in the following section.

4 Evaluation

We extracted a collection of about 7000 words in katakana together with the corresponding English translation from the EDICT dictionary. About 10% (714 tokens) of these entries were left out for evaluation. The remaining set was expanded, so that for each katakana word containing a long vowel or a geminate consonant, we add one with these removed. The pronunciations for training the PM were obtained from the CMU pronouncing dictionary. When no pronunciations were available the words were excluded from the training.

Table 1 gives the result of our experiments with 714 EDICT transliterations for the Phoneme Model without context (PM0), the Grapheme Model (GM), the Phoneme Model (PM) and the combined model (COMB). Here, PM0 was trained only on the directly aligning edits ($N=0$), and the remaining models used a context of two units to the left and to the right ($N=2$). The test dictionary contains all words appearing in the English translations in the EDICT dictionary (over 30,000 words). The top-1 and top-10 accuracies are given for two language models (LM): EDICTa where all words have equal probability and EDICTb where probabilities reflect the corpus frequencies from the EDR English corpus [16]. The transliterations were considered correct, if they matched the English translation, letter-for-letter, in a non-case-sensitive manner.

Table 1. Transliteration results for the EDICT test set.

		EDICTa		EDICTb	
	Inputs	Top-1 (%)	Top-10 (%)	Top-1 (%)	Top-10 (%)
PM0	714	281 (39.36)	368 (51.54)	232 (32.49)	365 (51.12)
GM	714	473 (66.25)	595 (83.33)	455 (63.73)	591 (82.77)
PM	714	571 (79.97)	664 (93.00)	484 (67.79)	623 (87.25)
COMB	714	604 (**84.59**)	698 (**97.76**)	504 (**70.59**)	649 (**90.90**)

We can see that the PM yields better results than the GM with the same context window. This justifies the consideration of pronunciation for transliteration, and it shows that our method of mapping English to romaji using pronunciation is effective. Furthermore, we can see that the proposed method (COMB) gives the best performance in all cases.

It might seem surprising that using EDICTb results in reduced accuracy. However, the corpus frequencies bias the model so erroneous transliterations consisting of shorter more frequent words are preferred over longer, correct, but infrequent words. This shows the importance of a good LM from which to select transliterations.

For the second set of experiments we extracted 150 katakana words from the EDR Japanese corpus not in the EDICT dictionary and we used the complete CMU dictionary word set (around 120,000 words) compiled into models CMUa and CMUb, as described above.

Table 2 gives the transliteration results for this test set. We can see a significant overall drop in accuracy. It is partially due to a larger set of words to choose from, hence a more difficult task. Since various spellings with similar pronunciations are contained in the dictionary, corpus frequencies help improve the top-1 accuracy, thus the higher accuracy rates for the CMUb language model. For example, with CMUb *service* is selected rather than *servis* as the top transliteration of "saabisu" in センターサービス "centaasaabisu" *center service*.

Table 2. Transliteration results for the EDR test set.

		CMUa		CMUb	
	Inputs	Top-1 (%)	Top-10 (%)	Top-1 (%)	Top-10 (%)
PM0	150	27 (18.00)	47 (31.33)	20 (13.33)	36 (24.00)
GM	150	49 (32.67)	86 (57.33)	69 (46.00)	96 (64.00)
PM	150	58 (**38.67**)	82 (54.67)	67 (44.67)	91 (60.67)
COMB	150	57 (38.00)	106 (**70.67**)	70 (**46.67**)	107 (**71.33**)

However, a bigger problem is the inability of our system to handle non-English terms (e.g. サハリン "saharin" *Sakhalin*) and abbreviations (e.g. リハビリテーションセンター "rihabiriteeshonsentaa" *rehabilitation center* is abbreviated as リハビリセンター "rihabirisentaa") which make a sizable portion of EDR out-of-vocabulary items. Rather than trying to obtain an English equivalent of these terms, the system would ideally be able to determine the possible origin of the word from the context available (e.g. user query in CLIR) and then apply an adequate language model.

Brill et al. [4] provide no direct evaluation of their transliteration system. Instead, they evaluate the ability of their system to extract English-katakana pairs from non-aligned web query logs. On the other hand, Knight and Graehl [1] give only the accuracy for transliteration of personal names (64% correct, 12% phonetically equivalent) but not for general out-of-vocabulary terms. This makes comparison with our system difficult. Nonetheless, the above experiments show that the combination of the phoneme- and grapheme-based models helps the overall accuracy and coverage. In the future, we would like to explore different ways of combining these models to further increase the positive effect of the combination.

5 Conclusion

Back transliteration is the process of converting transliterated words back into their original form. Previous models used either only phoneme- or only grapheme-based information contained in the transliteration. Instead, we propose a method for improving back-transliteration by combining these two models. We go on to describe how we implemented the models to allow combination and finally, we evaluate the effectiveness of the combined model and point out some deficiencies we hope to address in the future.

Acknowledgements

We would like to thank Taiichi Hashimoto, Michael Zock and three anonymous reviewers on valuable comments and help in writing this paper.

References

1. Knight, K., Graehl, J.: Machine transliteration. Computational Linguistics **24** (1998) 599–612
2. Lin, W.H., Chen, H.H.: Backward machine transliteration by learning phonetic similarity. In: Proc. of the Sixth Conference on Natural Language Learning. (2002) 139–145
3. Jeong, K.S., Myaeng, S.H., Lee, J.S., Choi, K.S.: Automatic identification and back-transliteration of foreign words for information retrieval. Information Processing and Management **35** (1999) 523–540
4. Brill, E., Kacmarcik, G., Brockett, C.: Automatically harvesting katakana-English term pairs from search engine query logs. In: Proc. of the Sixth Natural Language Processing Pacific Rim Symposium, Tokyo, Japan (2001) 393–399
5. Stalls, B.G., Knight, K.: Translating names and technical terms in Arabic text. In: Proc. of the COLING/ACL Workshop on Computational Approaches to Semitic Languages. (1998)
6. Brill, E., Moore, R.C.: An improved error model for noisy channel spelling correction. In: Proceedings of the 38th Annual Meeting of the Association for Computarional Linguistics (ACL 2000), Tokyo, Japan (2000) 286–293
7. Damerau, F.: A technique for computer detection and correction of spelling errors. Communications of the ACM **7** (1964) 659–664
8. Levensthein, V.: Binary codes capable of correcting deletions, insertions, and reversals. Soviet Physics–Doklady **10** (1966) 707–710
9. Goto, I., Kato, N., Uratani, N., Ehara, T.: Transliteration considering context information based on the maximum entropy method. In: Proc. of IXth MT Summit. (2003)
10. Kang, B.J., Choi, K.S.: Automatic transliteration and back-transliteration by decision tree learning. In: Proc. of the 2nd International Conference on Language Resources and Evaluation (LREC 2000). (2000)
11. Eppstein, D.: Finding the k shortest paths. In: In Proc. of the 35th Symposium on the Foundations of Computer Science. (1994) 154–165
12. Oh, J.H., Choi, K.S.: An English-Korean transliteration model using pronunciation and contextual rules. In: Proc. of the 19th International Conference on Computational Linguistics (COLING 2002). (2002) 393–399
13. Pereira, F.C.N., Riley, M.: Speech recognition by composition of weighted finite automata. In Roche, E., Shabes, Y., eds.: Finite-State Language Processing. MIT Press (1997) 431–453
14. Press, W.H., Flannery, B.P., Teukolsky, A., Vetterling, T.: Numeric Recipies in C. 2nd edn. Cambridge University Press (1992)
15. Dempster, A.P., Laird, N.M., Rubin, D.B.: Maximum likelihood from incomplete via the em algorithm. Journal of the Royal Statistical Society **39** (1977) 1–38
16. EDR: EDR Electronic Dictionary Technical Guide. Japan Electronic Dictionary Research Institute, Ltd. (1995) (In Japanese).

Bilingual Sentence Alignment
Based on Punctuation Statistics and Lexicon

Thomas C. Chuang[1], Jian-Cheng Wu[2], Tracy Lin[3],
Wen-Chie Shei[2], and Jason S. Chang[2]

[1] Department of Computer Science, Vanung University
No. 1 Van-Nung Road, Chung-Li, Tao-Yuan, 320
tomchuang@cc.vit.edu.tw
[2] Department of Computer Science, National Tsing Hua University
101, Kuangfu Road, Hsinchu, 300
jschang@cs.nthu.edu.tw
[3] Department of Telecommunication, National Chiao Tung University
1001 University Road, Hsinchu, 300
tracylin@faculty.nctu.edu.tw

Abstract. This paper presents a new method of aligning bilingual parallel texts based on punctuation statistics and lexical information. It is demonstrated that the punctuation statistics prove to be effective means to achieve good results. The task of sentence alignment of bilingual texts written in disparate language pairs like English and Chinese is reportedly more difficult. We examine the feasibility of using punctuations for high accuracy sentence alignment. Encouraging precision rate is demonstrated in aligning sentences in bilingual parallel corpora based solely on punctuation statistics. Improved results were obtained when both punctuation statistics and lexical information were employed. We have experimented with an implementation of the proposed method on the parallel corpora of Sinorama Magazine and Records of the Hong Kong Legislative Council with satisfactory results.

1 Introduction

Recently, there is a renewed interest in using bilingual corpora for building natural language processing systems, including data-driven machine translation (Dolan, Pinkham and Richardson 2002), computer-assisted revision of translation (Jutras 2000) and cross-language information retrieval (Kwok 2001; Gey, Chen, Buckland and Larson 2002; Chen and Gey 2001). For that, it is essential to align bilingual corpora at the sentence level with very high precision (Moore 2002; Chuang, You and Chang 2002, Kueng and Su 2002). With aligned sentences, further analyses such as phrase and word alignment (Ker and Chang 1997; Melamed 1997), bilingual terminology (Déjean, Gaussier and Sadat 2002) and collocation (Wu 2003) extraction can be performed.

Much work has been reported in the literature of computational linguistics describing how to align English-French and English-German sentences. Almost all of these methods are based mainly on sentence lengths. Church and Gale (1991) and Brown et al. (1992) showed that length-based sentence alignment produces surprisingly good results for the language pair of French and English with success rates well over 96%.

However, length-based methods do not perform as well for the alignment of copora that are noisy or written in a disparate language pairs, such as English and Chinese sentences. Wu (1994) indicates that the lengths of English and Chinese texts are not as highly correlated as in French-English task, leading to lower success rate (85-94%) for length based aligners.

Simard, Foster, and Isabelle (1992) proposed using cognates on top of lengths to improve alignment accuracy for noisy texts. According to the Longman Dictionary of Applied-Linguistics (Richards et al., 1985), a cognate is "a word in one language which is similar in form and meaning to a word in another language because both languages are related." Simard, Foster, and Isabelle used an operational definition of cognates, which include digits, alphanumerical symbols, punctuations and alphabetical words that are almost identical and readily recognizable by the computer. However, for disparate language pairs such as Chinese and English without a shared roman alphabet, it is not possible to rely on lexical or punctuation cognates for high-precision sentence alignment. Several other measures of cognateness for close Western language pairs have also been suggested, but none of them are sufficiently reliable or suitable for disparate language pairs. For the English-Chinese task, there are no orthographic, phonetic or semantic cognates in existence, which are readily recognizable by the computer. Therefore, the simple cognate-based approach is not applicable to the Chinese-English task.

The rest of the paper is organized as follows: In Section 2 of this paper, we show how punctuations in two disparate languages like English and Chinese correspond to each other. In Section 3 we define punctuation-based probability functions indicators of mutual translation. In Section 4, we pro-pose a new method to consider the additional lexical information for improved performance of sentence alignment. In Section 5, we describe experiments and evaluation on bilingual sentence alignment. A brief conclusion is provided in Section 6.

2 Punctuations Across Languages

Although the ways different languages around the world use punctuations vary, symbols such as commas and full stops are used in most languages to demarcate writing, while question and exclamation marks are used to indicate interrogation and emphasis. However, these punctuations can often be encoded differently or be used in different ways.

Although the average ratio of the punctuation counts in a text is low (less than 15%), punctuations provide evidence, which makes possible high degree of alignment precision. Our method can easily be generalized to other language pairs since minimal *a priori* linguistic knowledge of punctuations is required.

3 Punctuation and Sentence Alignment

In this section, we will describe how punctuations in two languages can be *soft matched* to measure the likelihood of mutual translation for the task of sentence alignment. We will use an example to illustrate the method next. A formal description follows.

Example 1 shows a Mandarin Chinese sentence and its translation counterpart of two English sentences in a parallel corpus.

(1c) 逐漸的，打鼓不再能滿足他，「打鼓原是我最喜歡的，後來卻變成邊打邊睡，一個月六萬元的死工作」，薛岳表示。

(1e) Over time, drums could no longer satisfy him. "Drumming was at first the thing I loved most, but later it began half drumming, half sleeping, just a job for NT$60,000 a month," says Simon.

If we keep punctuations in the above examples in the original order and strip everything else out, we have eight punctuations from the Mandarin part (1c) and ten punctuations from the English part (1c) as follows:

(2c) ，，「，，」，。

(2e) ，． " ，，， ， " ．

It is not difficult to see that the two punctuation strings match up quite nicely, indicating that the corresponding texts are mutual translations. Roughly, the first two commas in Chinese correspond to the first English comma and period, while Chinese open quote in the third position corresponds to the English open quote also in the third position. The two Chinese commas inside the quotes correspond to two of the four commas within the quotes in English. Two consecutive marks (」，) correspond to (,") forming a 2-2 match. Correspondences like those can be unraveled via a dynamic programming procedure; much like when one is working with sentence alignment.

Based on our observation, the part of the one-to-one punctuation match between two parallel texts, Chinese and English, is well over 50%. It implies that there is still a large discrepancy of the punctuation mappings between Chinese and English. We therefore define a punctuation compatibility factor to account for the variability in punctuation matching. The punctuation compatibility factor γ as an indicator of mutual translation is defined as

$$\gamma = \frac{c}{\max(n,m)} \qquad (1)$$

where n = the number of Chinese punctuations
 m = the number of English punctuations
 c = the number of matching punctuations with prob. value over a certain threshold

We then take the total number of punctuations and the number of punctuations that involved in comparable 1-1 and 2-2 matches as a compatibility indicator of mutual translation of English and Chinese sentences. Results indicated that the average compatibility for pairs of sentences, which are mutual translations, is about 0.67 (with a standard deviation 0.17), while the average compatibility of random pairs of bilingual sentences is 0.34 (with a standard deviation 0.17). Figures 1 shows the compatibility factors of sentence pairs that are mutual translation and otherwise. Overall, compatibility base soft-matching punctuations in ordered comparison indeed provides reliable information to tell the difference between mutual translation and unrelated translation.

In order to perform soft matching of punctuation, we define a probability of the sequence of punctuations $P = p_1 p_2 ... p_i$ in one language (L1) translates to the sequence $Q = \pi_1 \pi_2 ... \pi_j$ of punctuations in another language (L2) as follows:

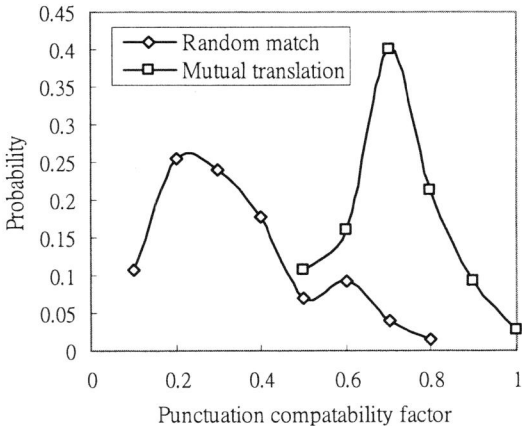

Fig. 1. Compatibility of translation pairs vs. random pairs with max(m,n)=10

$$P(P,Q) = \prod_{k=1,m} P(p_k, \pi_k) P(|p_k|, |\pi_k|) \qquad (2)$$

where $P = p_1 p_2 ... p_i$, $Q = \pi_1 \pi_2 ... \pi_j$
  p_i = 0 to 2 English punctuations,
  π_i = 0 to 2 Chinese punctuations

In order to explore the relationship between the punctuations across from Chinese to English sentences that are mutual translations, we prepared a small set of manually aligned texts and investigated the characteristics and the associated statistics between the punctuations. The information was then used to bootstrap on a larger corpus. An unsupervised EM algorithm is used to optimize the punctuation correspondence between a text and its translation counterpart. The EM algorithm converges quickly after several rounds of training.

There are several frequently used punctuations in Chinese text that are not available in English text. For example, the punctuation "、" and "。". Although these punctuations often correspond to the English punctuations "," and "." respectively, they are not used identically. For instance, one of the uses of "," in English is to introduce a apposition phrase but that does not carry over to any Chinese punctuations. The differences lead to 20-40% discrepancy in correspondence for these two punctuation marks (see Table 1). We also observed that in most cases the links of punctuations do not cross each other much like the situation with sentence alignment. Two implicationns follows from this non-crossing constraint: First, it is possible to use dynamic programming to soft-match punctuations across languages. Secondly, it is possible to achieve sub-sentential alignment based on punctuation alignment. In the rest of the paper we will focus on using punctuations as means for sentence alignment. The Viterbi path of aligning punctuations is determined based on punctuation translation probability and match-type probability. The punctuation correspondences and probabilistic values are shown in Tables 2 and 3.

Unlike the way Simard et al. (1992) handled punctuations as cognates and looked for order-free, hard matches, we soft-matched punctuations and modeled the com-

Table 1. Some of the most frequent punctuation matches and match types

E_{punc}	C_{punc}	P_{type}	Count	Prob.
,	，	1-1	541	0.809874
.	。	1-1	336	0.657528
"	」	1-1	131	0.34203
.	，	1-1	113	0.221133
"	「	1-1	112	0.292423
"	「	1-1	65	0.16971
"	」	1-1	59	0.154044
,	、	1-1	56	0.083832
,	。	1-1	41	0.061377
!	！	1-1	38	0.883508
,"	」，	2-2	6	0.956403
."	」，	2-2	3	0.916449
?"	——	2-2	2	0.611063
.!	…！	2-2	1	0.785235
	，	0-1	229	0.389455
	—	0-1	58	0.098639
	。	0-1	52	0.088435

Table 2. Probability function of punctuation match types(Notice that the number of counts showed in the table is not an integer because the counts were adjusted using the Good Turing Smoothing Method for better results.)

Match Types	Counts	Probability
0-1	588.0005	0.225027
1-0	286.001	0.109452
1-1	1698.076	0.649852
1-2	2.466198	0.000944
2-1	0.965034	0.000369
2-2	37.19216	0.014233

Table 3. The match type probability $P(m_k)$

Match type	1-1	1-0, 0-1	1-2	2-1	1-3	1-4	1-5
Probability	0.65	0.000197	0.0526	0.178	0.066	0.0013	0.00013

compatibility of punctuations across two languages using Binomial distribution. Each punctuation mark appearing in one language either has a translation counterpart of one to two punctuation marks determine by p, a parameter of average rate of having punctuation counterpart. In summary, we differ from Simard's approach in the following interesting ways:

1. We use the cumulative value of Binomial distribution, while Simard et al. used a likelihood ratio.
2. We go beyond direct and hard matching punctuation marks between parallel texts. We allow a punctuation mark in one language to match up with a number of compatible punctuation marks. We use joint probability similar to the phrase translation probability proposed in Marcu and Wong (2002).
3. We take into consideration of intrinsic sequencing of punctuation marks in ordered comparison. The flexible and ordered comparison of punctuation is carried out via dynamic programming.

Following Gale and Church (1993), we align text blocks E and C by optimizing some probability function $P(E, C)$ related to mutual translatability of sentence fragments in E and C. However instead of basing mutual translatability on sentence lengths, we use punctuation compatibility. With that in mind, we define the probability $P(E, C)$ as follows: Given two blocks of text E_i and C_i in E and C, we first strip off non-punctuations therein and find out the maximum number of punctuations n in E_i and C_i. Subsequently, a matching procedure is carried out to find out the number of compatible punctuations r in ordered comparison of punctuations across languages. Therefore we have

$$P(E_i, C_j) = \sum_{k=1}^{t} P(m_k) P(E_{i,k}, C_{j,k})$$

$$= \sum_{k=1}^{t} P(m_k) b(r_k, n_k) \qquad (3)$$

$$= \sum_{k=1}^{t} P(m_k) \binom{n_k}{r_k} p_k^{n_k} (1 - p_K)^{r_k - n_k}$$

Where n_k= the max number of punctuations from the kth English/Chinese segment,
r_k = the number of compatible punctuations in the kth English and Chinese segment,
p_k = the probability of having a punctuation counterpart across from one language to the other,
$P(m_k)$= the match type probability aligning $E_{i,k}$ and $C_{j,k}$.

From the data, we have found that about two thirds of the times, a sentence in one language matches exactly one sentence in the other language (1-1). Additional possibilities for more difficult cases are also considered: 1-0 (including 0-1), and many-1 (including 1-many). Chinese-English parallel corpora are considerably noisier, reflecting from wider possibilities of match types. We use a small set of hand aligned sentence to derived match type probabilities. See Table 3.

4 Lexical Information

In order to see whether some simple method of using lexical information can improve the performance of sentence alignment method. We experimented with incorporating lexical information in the sentence alignment process. We propose to take advantage of corpus-based bilingual lexicon which is the results of word alignment of applying

Competitive Link Algorithm (Melamed 2000). The proposed method of using corpus-based bilingual lexicon is much simpler than the elaborated model proposed by Chen (1993), which is trained on the fly and takes into consideration of the more difficult cases of 1-0 and 0-1 word translations.

In a nutshell, Competitive Linking Algorithm operates on a set of aligned sentences and produces a clean bilingual lexicon based on statistical measures. Word counts and word and translation occurrence counts are used to derive logarithmic likelihood ratio (Dunning 1996) for any given pair of source and target words co-occurring in at least one pair of aligned sentences. For each of the aligned sentences, CLA links word pairs with high LLR valued in a greedy fashion. Under the assumption of one-to-one word correspondence, a word that is part of linked pair is excluded from subsequent consideration and not allowed to link with other words. After the first round, the LLR scores are replaced with lexical translation probabilities that are based on the numbers of linking and co-occurring as two parameters in Binomial distribution. Those probabilistic values are re-estimated repeatedly until there is only slight change from iteration to iteration.

For our purpose, we need to obtain a bilingual lexicon based on CLA, which covers a substantial part of average texts. For that, we utilized the bilingual examples in a learner's dictionary, Longman Dictionary of Contemporary Dictionary of English (Proctor 1988). The dictionary examples were written with a controlled vocabulary of 2,000 most frequent words in English comparable to the General Service List (GSL) put forward by West (1953). GSL is reported to cover about 80% of words in average English text. We ran CLA on bilingual examples in LDOCE and obtained relatively clean bilingual lexicon which cover substantial part of words and their translation equivalents in bilingual texts.

With a "general service" and "clean" bilingual lexicon L at our disposal, we model $P_{lex}(E_k, C_k)$, the probability of mutual translation for a pair of bilingual text segments based on Binomial distribution. Therefore, we have

$$P_{lex}(E_k, C_k) = B(r; n, p) \qquad (5)$$

where $n = $ # instances of L words in E_k
$r = $ # times when an expected translation listed in L is found in C_k
$p = $ average rate of finding a match

The probability of having a translation counter-part for content words in GSL was estimated as $p = 0.670$ with a standard deviation 0.170. For random pairs of bilingual sentences, $p = 0.340$, with a standard deviation 0.167. As with the case of punctuations, there appears to be a marked difference between the two distributions, indicating that indeed matching words across language against the lexicon acquired from bilingual examples in a learner dictionary provides reliable indication of mutual translation for effective sentence alignment.

With consideration of lexical information, the equation of the probability of mutual translation for a pair of bilingual text (E, C) becomes

$$P(E,C) = \prod_{k=1,m} P_{lex}(E_k, C_k) P_{pun}(E_k, C_k) P(|E_k|, |C_k|) \qquad (6)$$

5 Experiments and Evaluation

To explore the relationship between the punctuations between pairs of Chinese and English sentences that are mutual translation, we prepared a small set of 200 pairs of text aligned at the sentence and punctuation levels. We then investigated the characteristics and the associated statistics between the punctuations. We derived estimates for the punctuation translation probability and fertility probabilities from the small hand-tagged data. This seed information was then used for the punctuation translation model on a larger corpus via an unsupervised EM algorithm.

We have experiment an implementation of the proposed punctuation-based method. The experimental results indicate that the punctuation-based approach leads to encouraging sentence alignment precision for a relatively difficult case of HK LEGCO corpus. Adding lexical information on top of punctuations leads to even higher precision rates. See Table 4 for more details.

Table 4. Experimental results of HK LEGCO corpus

Method	#paragraphs	#matches	#correct matches	Precision	Average length
Punctuation only	100	529	332	63%	90.73
Length only	100	389	284	73%	123.74
Punctuation + Lexicon	100	508	425	84%	94.52
Length + Lexicon	100	334	246	74%	144.28
Punctuation + Length	100	476	435	91%	100.94
Punctuation + Length + Lexicon	100	454	437	96%	105.88

6 Conclusion

We developed a very effective sentence alignment method based on punctuations and lexical information. The probability of the match between different punctuation marks between the source and target languages is calculated based on large bilingual corpora. We have experimented with an implementation of the proposed method on the parallel corpus of Chinese-English HK LEGCO corpus. The experimental results show that the punctuation-length-lexicon based approach offers good precision rates approaching 96%.

A number of interesting future directions present themselves. First, alignment at sub-sentential level based on punctuations alignment can be exploited to produce finer-grained bilingual analysis. That will constrain word alignment and provide translation memory and bilingual concordance that are more effective for example-based machine translation (EBMT), computer assisted translation (CAT) and language learning (CALL). Lastly, we plan to apply this method to many different language pairs, such as Japanese-English.

Acknowledgement

We acknowledge the support for this study through grants from National Science Council and Ministry of Education (NSC-2213-E-238 -015, NSC 90-2411-H-007-

033-MC and MOE EX-91-E-FA06-4-4) and from MOEA under the Software Technology for Advanced Network Application Project of the Institute for Information Industry.

References

1. Brown, P. F., J. C. Lai and R. L. Mercer (1991), Aligning sentences in parallel corpora, in 29th Annual Meeting of the Association for Computational Linguistics, Berkeley, CA, USA. pp. 169-176.
2. Chen, Stanley F. (1993), Aligning Sentences in Bilingual Corpora Using Lexical Information. In Proceedings of ACL-93. Columbus OH, 1993.
3. Chuang, T., G.N. You, J.S. Chang (2002), Adaptive Bilingual Sentence Alignment, Lecture Notes in Artificial Intelligence 2499, 21-30.
4. Déjean, Hervé, Éric Gaussier and Fatia Sadat (2002), Bilingual Terminology Extraction: An Approach based on a Multilingual thesaurus Applicable to Comparable Corpora. In Proceedings of the 19th International Conference on Computational Linguistics COLING 2002, pp. 218-224, Taipei, Taiwan, Aug. 24-Sep. 1, 2002
5. Dolan, William B., Jessie Pinkham, Stephen D. Richardson (2002), MSR-MT: The Microsoft Research Machine Translation System. AMTA 2002: 237-239.
6. Gale, William A. & Kenneth W. Church (1991), A program for aligning sentences in bilingual corpus. In Computational Linguistics, vol. 19, pp. 75-102.
7. Gey, Fredric C., Aitao Chen, Michael K. Buckland, Ray R. Larson (2002), Translingual vocabulary mappings for multilingual information access. SIGIR 2002: 455-456.
8. Jutras, J-M 2000. An Automatic Reviser: The TransCheck System, In Proc. of Applied Natural Language Processing, 127-134.
9. Kay, Martin & Martin Röscheisen (1993), Text-Translation Alignment. In Computational Linguistics, 19:1. pp. 121-142.
10. Kueng, T.L. and Keh-Yih Su, 2002. A Robust Cross-Domain Bilingual Sentence Alignment Model, In Proceedings of the 19th International Conference on Computational Linguistics.
11. Kwok, KL. 2001. NTCIR-2 Chinese, Cross-Language Retrieval Experiments Using PIRCS. In Proceedings of the Second NTCIR Workshop Meeting, pp. (5) 14-20, National Institute of Informatics, Japan.
12. Marcu, Daniel, and William Wong. (2002). A Phrase-Based, Joint Probability Model for Statistical Machine Translation, EMNLP.
13. Melamed, I. Dan (2000), Models of Translational Equivalence among Words, Computational Linguistics, 26(2), 221-249.
14. Moore, Robert C. (2002), Fast and Accurate Sentence Alignment of Bilingual Corpora. AMTA 2002: 135-144.
15. Piao, Scott Songlin 2000, Sentence and word alignment between Chinese and English. Ph.D. thesis, Lancaster University.
16. Proctor, P. (1988) Longman English-Chinese Dictionary of Contemporary English. Longman Group (Far East), Hong Kong.
17. Richards, Jack et al. Longman Dictionary of Applied Linguistics, Longman, 1985.
18. Simard, M., G. Foster & P. Isabelle (1992), Using cognates to align sentences in bilingual corpora. In Proceedings of TMI92, Montreal, Canada, pp. 67-81.
19. West, Michael (1953). A General Service List of English Words, Longman, London.
20. Wu, Dekai (1994), Aligning a parallel English-Chinese corpus statistically with lexical criteria. In The Proceedings of the 32nd Annual Meeting of the Association for Computational Linguistics, New Mexico, USA, pp. 80-87.

Automatic Learning of Parallel Dependency Treelet Pairs

Yuan Ding and Martha Palmer

Department of Computer and Information Science,
University of Pennsylvania, Philadelphia, PA 19104
{yding,mpalmer}@linc.cis.upenn.edu

Abstract. Induction of synchronous grammars from empirical data has long been an unsolved problem; despite generative synchronous grammars theoretically suit the machine translation task very well. This fact is mainly due to pervasive structural divergences between languages. This paper presents a statistical approach that learns dependency structure mappings from parallel corpora. The new algorithm automatically learns parallel dependency treelet pairs from loosely matched non-isomorphic dependency trees while keeping computational complexity polynomial in the length of the sentences. A set of heuristics is introduced and specifically optimized for parallel treelet learning purposes using Minimum Error Rate training.

1 Introduction

Statistical approaches to machine translation, pioneered by (Brown et al., 1990, 1993), perform competitively with more traditional interlingua based approaches, mainly due to the ability of leveraging large amounts of parallel corpora. A major criticism of "pure" statistical MT approaches is the lack of syntax or semantics.

In recent years, hybrid approaches, also known as "syntax based statistical machine translation" have begun to emerge. However, up to today, the syntax based statistical MT systems are still outperformed by the state of the art template based statistical MT systems (Och, 2003). We believe that this is due to: (1) pervasive structural divergences between languages, caused by both systematic differences between languages (Dorr, 1994) and the loose translations in real corpora. (2) The lack of well-defined formal syntax systems that can be learnt efficiently from empirical data.

(Wu, 1997) introduced a polynomial-time solution for the alignment problem based on synchronous binary trees. (Alshawi et al., 2000) extended the tree-based approach by representing each production in parallel dependency trees as a finite-state transducer. Both these approaches learn the tree representations directly from parallel sentences, and do not make allowances for non-isomorphic structures. (Yamada and Knight, 2001, 2002) modeled translation as a sequence of tree operations transforming a syntactic tree in one language into a string of the second language.

When researchers try to use syntactic trees in both languages, the problem of non-isomorphism grows when trees in both languages are required to match. (Hajic et al., 2002) allowed limited non-isomorphism in that n-to-m matching of nodes in the two trees is permitted. However, even after extending this model by allowing cloning operations on subtrees, (Gildea, 2003) found that parallel trees over-constrained the alignment problem, and achieved better results with a tree-to-string model using one input tree than with a tree-to-tree model using two.

Most of the above approaches do not define synchronous grammar formalisms or explicitly induce such a grammar from parallel corpora. Grammar theoreticians have proposed various generative synchronous grammar formalisms for MT, e.g. Synchronous CFG or Synchronous Tree Adjoining Grammars (S-TAG) (Shieber and Schabes, 1990). Generative synchronous grammars share many nice mathematical properties similar to their monolingual counterparts. However, due to the inability of learning syntactic structures from large amounts of non-isomorphic tree pairs, induction of a synchronous grammar from parallel corpora is still unsolved.

This motivates us to look for an algorithm that will automatically learn parallel syntactic structures without the unrealistic tree isomorphism assumption.

This paper presents a statistical approach to learning dependency structure mappings from parallel corpora. We first define the synchronous tree partitioning operation on parallel dependency trees. Then we introduce the algorithm, which breaks down the sentence-level parallel dependency trees into phrase-level parallel dependency treelets by a series of synchronous tree partitioning operations. The framework of the algorithm is an extension to the dependency tree word alignment algorithm in (Ding et al., 2003). The algorithm is executed in an iterative fashion, first assumes free word mapping without any constraints and then gradually adds constraints to word level alignments by breaking down the parallel dependency structures into smaller pieces. The major advance of the new algorithm from that of (Ding et al., 2003) is the use of syntactic categories in dependency trees and Minimum Error Rate Training to combine various heuristics with parameters specifically optimized for the treelet learning purpose.

2 Objective

2.1 Why Dependency Structures?

According to (Fox, 2002), dependency representations have the best phrasal cohesion properties across languages. The percentage for head crossings per chance is 12.62% and that of modifier crossings per chance is 9.22%.

At the same time, a grammar based on dependency structures has the advantage of being simple in formalism yet having the formal generative power equivalent to that of CFG. Moreover, dependency structures are inherently lexicalized as each node is one word. In comparison, phrasal structures (Treebank style trees) have two types of nodes, where the lexical items go to the terminals and the word order and phrase scope information goes to the non-terminals.

2.2 Synchronous Partitioning Operation

We introduce this operation by a pseudo-translation example:
- [Source] The girl kissed her kitty cat.
- [Target] The girl gave a kiss to her cat.

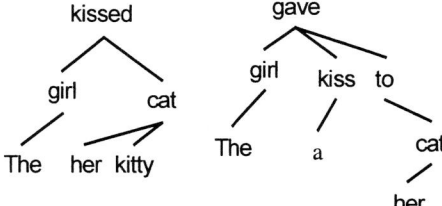

Fig. 1.

If we examine the node mappings in the above two sentences, we will find that almost any tree-transduction operations defined on a single node will fail to generate the target sentence from the source sentence. However, suppose that we find that the two node pairs lexicalized as *"girl"* and *"cat"* on both sides should be aligned, and hence fix the two alignments. We then partition the two dependency trees by splitting the trees at the fixed alignments. This operation is defined as the synchronous partitioning operation, which generates the following dependency graphs: ((e) stands for an empty node). We refer to the three resultant dependency substructures as "treelets". This is to avoid confusion with "subtrees" since treelets don't necessarily go down to every leaf.

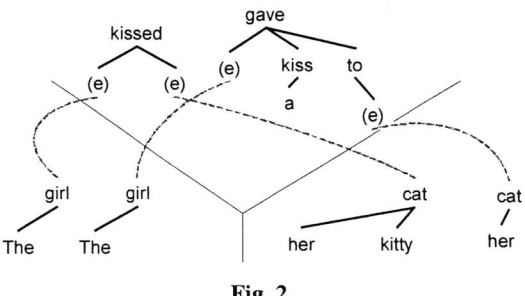

Fig. 2.

If we view each treelet as a single non-devisable unit for any tree-based transduction, (or an "elementary tree" in a tree based grammar sense), the two sentences show isomorphism between treelet derivations.

Ideally, our algorithm should generate such treelet pairs that are as fine-grained as possible, which will finally allow us to generate a synchronous grammar which captures structural variations between languages.

3 The Framework

The iterative framework of the algorithm bootstraps between statistical modelling and parallel tree structures, which is an extension to the dependency tree based word alignment algorithm in (Ding et al., 2003).

Step 0. For each sentence pair e and f, initialize the two trees for e and f as a treelet pair.

Step 1. View each tree as a "bag of words" and train a statistical translation model on all the tree pairs to acquire word-to-word translation probabilities. In our implementation, IBM Model 1 (Brown et al., 1993) is used.

Step 2. For each treelet pair, compute probabilities of the word to word mappings for all NON-ROOT nodes. Then use a heuristic function to select the BEST word pair (e_{i*}, f_{j*}) for the tentative synchronous partitioning operation.

Step 3. If the word mapping (e_{i*}, f_{j*}) selected in Step 2 satisfies certain syntactic constraints, execute the synchronous tree partitioning operation on the treelet pair at the word pair (e_{i*}, f_{j*}). Hence two new treelet pairs are created, and the old treelet pair is replaced.

Step 4. Go back to Step 1.

As the algorithm walks through the iterations, we have an increasing number of treelet pairs, which will finally converge to a maximal set.

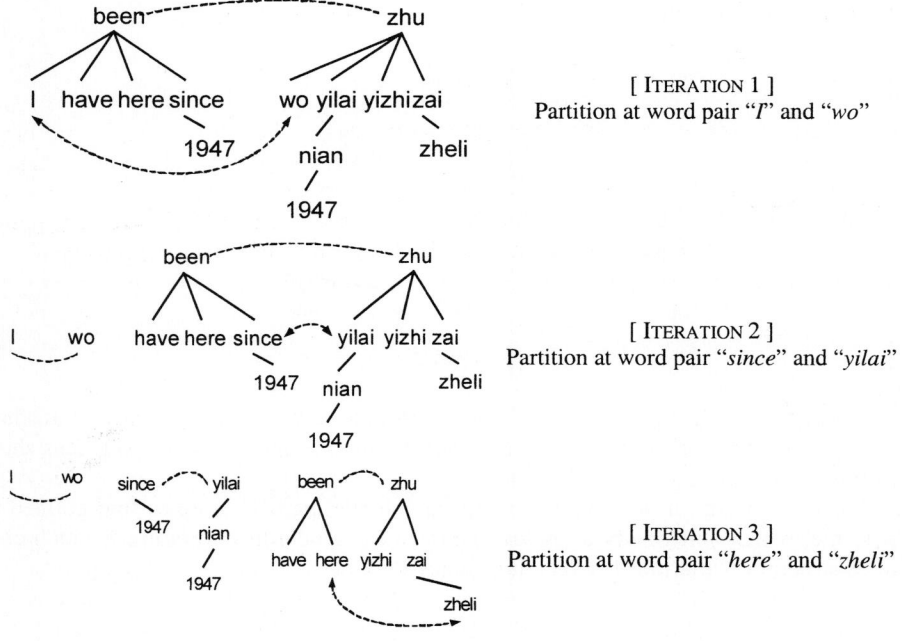

Fig. 3. An Example

In IBM Model 1, the translation probability $P(f \mid e)$ has a unique local maximum, so the result of this algorithm is only dependent on the choice of the heuristic function h. In our implementation, we only pick tentative word pairs that maximize word translation probability. Let $T(h)$ be the time complexity for the heuristic function. Thus we reduce the algorithm time complexity to $O(m \times T(h))$, which is linear to the size of the treelet pair,.

An example of a series of synchronous partitioning of the treelets for three iterations is given below to illustrate the algorithm. (Chinese in romanised form)

- [English] *I have been here since 1947.*
- [Chinese] *Wo 1947 nian yilai yizhi zhu zai zheli.*

Partition Assumption
The correctness of the algorithm relies on the assumption that when a synchronous partitioning operation happens to a pair of nodes, meaning the two nodes are aligned, all their descendents shall align to their descendents. This is however, much weaker than the word level isomorphism assumption. We call this the "partition assumption".

Although violations of such an assumption do occur in data, the hope is, since IBM Model 1 is a bag of words model, if we only have operations above and below such violations, the probability training results will be the same.

4 Syntactic Constraints

4.1 Content Words

For each language, we classify the words into two categories: content words and functional words. We want to constrain all the tentative word pairs used for the synchronous partitioning operation to be a pair of content words.

The content word part-of-speech categories for English and Chinese that we used are given below (POS tags in accordance with Penn English/Chinese Treebanks):

- *[English]* JJ JJR JJS NN NNS NNP NNPS PRP PRP$ VB VBD VBG VBN VBP VBZ WP WP$ CD MD
- *[Chinese]* VV VA VC VE NR NT NN PN JJ CD OD

4.2 Fertility Threshold

Let us suppose we want to create two treelet pairs by fixing the node pair (f_j, e_{a_j}).

We set a fertility threshold to make sure that the resultant treelet pairs have reasonable sizes on both sides. Currently this fertility threshold is set to be 2.0. If any treelet pair resulting from a tentative synchronous partitioning operation has the numbers of the nodes on two sides differing with a ratio larger than the threshold, the tentative synchronous partitioning operation is invalid.

5 Heuristic Functions

The heuristic function in Step 2 takes a tentative node pair (f_j, e_{a_j}) from the two treelets and outputs a certain value which corresponds to the confidence of this labelling. Here we introduce five different heuristic functions.

5.1 Inside-Outside Probability

Suppose we have two trees initially, $T(e)$ and $T(f)$. For each synchronous partitioning operation on word pair (f_j, e_{a_j}), both trees will be partitioned into two treelet pairs. The treelets rooted at the original roots are called the "outside treelets" and the treelets rooted at the node pair used for the synchronous partitioning operation are called the "inside treelets", as shown below:

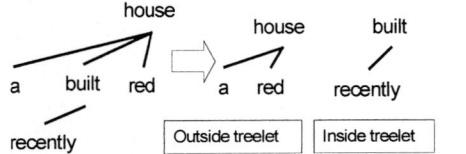

Inside and Outside Treelets Partition "*a recently built red house*" at node "*built*"

Fig. 4.

Here we borrow an idea from PCFG parsing, and call the treelets rooted with e_{a_j} and f_j inside treelets $T_{in}(e, e_{a_j})$ and $T_{in}(f, f_j)$. The other two treelets are called outside treelets $T_{out}(e, e_{a_j})$ and $T_{out}(f, f_j)$. So, we have:

$$P(T(f), (f_j, e_{a_j}) | T(e)) = P(T_{out}(f, f_j) | T_{out}(e, e_{a_j})) \times P(T_{in}(f, f_j) | T_{in}(e, e_{a_j}))$$

The intuition behind this heuristic is that the inside-out side probability is a measure of how well the new treelet pairs created by the tentative word pair (f_j, e_{a_j}) preserve the dependencies. In other words, if the inside-outside probability is large, we expect the nodes in one outside treelet to be aligned to the nodes in the other outside treelet and the same for the nodes in the inside treelets.

We can further decompose this probability. We define the size function to be the number of nodes in a treelet. Let $l_{out} = size(T_{out}(e, e_{a_j}))$, $m_{out} = size(T_{out}(f, f_j))$, $l_{in} = size(T_{in}(e, e_{a_j}))$, $m_{in} = size(T_{in}(f, f_j))$. So:

$$P(T_{out}(f, f_j) | T_{out}(e, e_{a_j})) = \frac{1}{(l_{out}+1)^{m_{out}}} \prod_{f_k \in T_{out}(f, f_j)} \sum_{e_{a_k} \in T_{out}(e, e_{a_j}) \cup \{0\}} t(f_k | e_{a_k})$$

$$P(T_{in}(f, f_j) | T_{in}(e, e_{a_j})) = \frac{1}{(l_{in}+1)^{m_{in}}} \prod_{f_k \in T_{in}(f, f_j)} \sum_{e_{a_k} \in T_{in}(e, e_{a_j}) \cup \{0\}} t(f_k | e_{a_k})$$

The above two probabilities are derived using ideas from IBM Model 1 (Brown, 1993). The first heuristic function is: $h_1(f_j, e_{a_j}) = \log P(T(f), (f_j, e_{a_j})|T(e))$.

5.2 Inside-Outside Penalty

Having defined the inside-outside probability, we now use its opposite. While we want to increase the inside outside probability, we want this penalty to be as small as possible, which is the probability of the inside treelet generated by the outside treelet times that of the outside treelet generated by the inside treelet. So we can define:

$$h_2(f_j, e_{a_j}) = -1 \times (\log P(T_{out}(f, f_j)|T_{in}(e, e_{a_j})) + \log P(T_{in}(f, f_j)|T_{out}(e, e_{a_j})))$$

5.3 Entropy

Since each tentative word pair (f_j, e_{a_j}) satisfies $\arg\max_{e_i \in e} t(f_j|e_i)$, where e is the set of nodes in the English treelet, and $t(f_j|e_i)$ is the probability of e_i being translated to f_j, we have $t(e_i|f_j) = \dfrac{t(f_j|e_i)P(e_i)}{P(f_j)}$. Intuitively, the conditional entropy of the translation probability distribution will serve as a good estimate of the confidence in the chosen word pair. Let $S = \sum_{e_i \in e} t(e_i|f_j)$ and $\hat{e} \in e$:

$$H(\hat{e}|f_j) = \sum_{e_i \in e} -\frac{t(e_i|f_j)}{S} \log(\frac{t(e_i|f_j)}{S}) = \frac{\sum_{e_i \in e} -t(e_i|f_j)\log(t(e_i|f_j))}{S} + \log S$$

The third heuristic function is defined as: $h_3(f_j, e_i) = -1 \times H(\hat{e}|f_j)$

5.4 Word Pair Probability and Syntactic Category Templates

The forth heuristic is simply defined as the word pair translation probability: $h_4 = t(f_j|e_{a_j})$

The dependency trees acquired from automatic parsers already provide us with the syntactic category of each node. Observing this, we collected syntactic category mappings from the automatically aligned results and did a cut off. By doing this we generated a set of likely syntactic category mappings, as we expect such mappings would be observed more often in the parallel corpora.

Hence we can define the fifth heuristic as: $h_5 = \begin{cases} 1 & template\_match \\ 0 & no\_template\_match \end{cases}$

6 Minimum Error Rate Training

We define the total score of the heuristic as a linear combination of all the heuristics introduced in Section 5. $h(f_j, e_{a_j}) = \sum_k \lambda_k h_k(f_j, e_{a_j})$

In order to determine the λ_k for each heuristic function, we use minimum error rate training. The error function is defined as follows: Let (f_j, e_{a_j}) denote the word pair used for a tentative synchronous partitioning operation, which will create two treelet pairs: $(T_{in}(f, f_j), T_{in}(e, e_{a_j}))$ and $(T_{out}(f, f_j), T_{out}(e, e_{a_j}))$.

Define the set of all the possible mappings as: ($\times$ stands for cross-product) $P = Nodes\{T_{in}(f, f_j)\} \times Nodes\{T_{in}(e, e_{a_j})\} \cup Nodes\{T_{out}(f, f_j)\} \times Nodes\{T_{out}(e, e_{a_j})\}$

Define G as the set of word alignment pairs in the gold file, define: $G - P = \{(\hat{e}, \hat{f}) | (\hat{e}, \hat{f}) \in G, (\hat{e}, \hat{f}) \notin P\}$, we have: $Err(f_j, e_{a_j}) = \frac{|G - P|}{|G|}$

If we recall the definition of the "partition assumption" introduced at the end of Section 3, this error measure is exactly the percentage of gold file alignments that violates the partition assumption.

Let the best parameter set $\bar{\lambda}*$ be: $\bar{\lambda}* = \arg\min_{\hat{\lambda}} Err(f', e')$, where $(f', e') = \arg\max_{(f_j, e_{a_j})} h(f_j, e_{a_j})$ We used hill climbing with random restart to search for the best parameter vector in the parameter space.

7 Results

We use an automatic syntactic parser (Bikel, 2002), trained using Penn English/Chinese Treebanks to produce the parallel unaligned syntactic structures. We then used the algorithm in (Xia 2001) to convert the phrasal structure trees into dependency trees. The following table shows the statistics of the datasets we used.

The training set consists of Xinhua newswire data from LDC and the FBIS data. We filtered both datasets to ensure parallel sentence pair quality.

The testing sentences are provided by the courtesy of Microsoft Research, Asia and IBM Research. The sentence pairs are manually aligned at word level.

Table 1.

Dataset	Xinhua	FBIS	Microsoft	IBM
Genre	News	News	Stories	News
Sent#	56263	21003	500	326
Chn W#	1456495	522953	5239	4718
Eng W#	1490498	658478	5476	7184
Type	unaligned	unaligned	aligned	aligned
Usage	training	training	testing	testing

We used part of the testing data as dev test to train the best $\bar{\lambda}*$ given below:

Table 2.

h	1	2	3	4	5
λ	0.1459	0.0343	0.9129	0.4175	0.6546

Note that the trained parameter values in the above table do not reflect the relative weights of different heuristics since different heuristics are not normalized.

The following figure shows the number of parallel dependency treelets learnt from the training set and the cumulative error rate on the testing set as the algorithm goes through 20 iterations. The error rate function is defined in Section 6. Note that as the treelets are getting smaller, the cumulative error rate inevitably increases. Also we see that the number of treelets collected is converging.

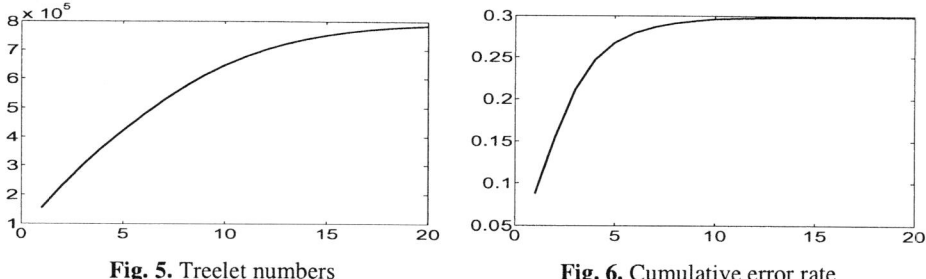

Fig. 5. Treelet numbers   **Fig. 6.** Cumulative error rate

We see that the cumulative error rate is converging to 30%. With a comparison to the findings in (Fox, 2002), which stated that the inherent head crossing in dependencies is around 12.62%, we find this result to be reasonable.

After 20 iterations we collected 784924 treelet pairs from the training set. This means the treelets are converging to an average size of 5.26 words per treelet.

To test the quality of the treelet pairs we used "content word alignment error rate". For each content word, we find its alignment in the corresponding treelet that maximizes the translation probability. Even with such a simple alignment model we can improve alignment results due to the use of more fine-grained treelet pairs.

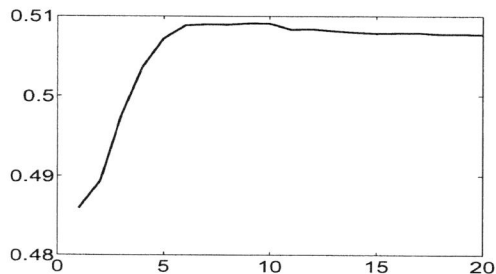

Fig. 7. Content word alignment precision

The algorithm in our previous work (Ding et al., 2003) based on the similar framework showed an overall better performance than IBM Models 1 to 4 in word level alignment tasks.

8 Conclusion and Future Work

In this paper, we show a statistical approach to learning parallel syntactic structures from parallel corpora. The new algorithm introduced in this paper automatically learns parallel dependency treelet pairs from loosely matched non-isomorphic dependency trees. We evaluated the quality of the learnt dependency treelets and results showed that the more fine grained treelets helped content word alignments.

Future work includes inducing a formalized synchronous dependency grammar from the learnt treelets. Ideally, once the synchronous dependency grammar can be induced, it can be used for a machine translation system.

References

1. Hiyan Alshawi, Srinivas Bangalore, and Shona Douglas. 2000. Learning dependency translation models as collections of finite state head transducers. *Computational Linguistics*, 26(1): 45-60.
2. Daniel M. Bikel. 2002. Design of a multi-lingual, parallel-processing statistical parsing engine. In *Proceedings of HLT 2002*.
3. Peter F. Brown, John Cocke, Stephen A. Della Pietra, Vincent J. Della Pietra, Frederick Jelinek, John D. Laferty, Robert L. Mercer, and Paul S. Roossin. 1990. A statistical approach to machine translation. *Computational Linguistics*, 16(2): 79-85, June.
4. Peter F. Brown, Stephen A. Della Pietra, Vincent J. Della Pietra, and Robert L. Mercer. 1993. The mathematics of statistical machine translation: parameter estimation. *Computational Linguistics*, 19(2): 263-311.
5. Michael John Collins. 1999. Head-driven Statistical Models for Natural Language Parsing. Ph.D. thesis, University of Pennsylvania, Philadelphia.
6. Yuan Ding, Daniel Gildea and Martha Palmer. An Algorithm for Word-level Alignment of Parallel Dependency Trees. *Proceedings of the 9th Machine Translation Summit of International Association of Machine Translation*, New Orleans, 2003
7. Bonnie J. Dorr. 1994. Machine translation divergences: A formal description and proposed solution. *Computational Linguistics*, 20(4): 597-633.
8. Heidi J. Fox. 2002. Phrasal cohesion and statistical machine translation. In *Proceedings of EMNLP-02*, pages 304-311
9. Daniel Gildea. 2003. Loosely tree based alignment for machine translation. In *Proceedings of ACL-03*.
10. Jan Hajic, et al. 2002. Natural language generation in the context of machine translation. Summer workshop final report, Center for Language and Speech Processing, Johns Hopkins University, Baltimore.
11. Franz Josef Och. 2003. Minimum Error Rate Training in Statistical Machine Translation. *In Proceedings of ACL-03*.
12. S. M. Shieber and Y. Schabes. 1990. *Synchronous Tree-Adjoining Grammars*, Proceedings of the 13th COLING, pp. 253-258, August 1990.
13. Dekai Wu. 1997. Stochastic inversion transduction grammars and bilingual parsing of parallel corpora. *Computational Linguistics*, 23(3):3-403.

14. Fei Xia. 2001. Automatic grammar generation from two different perspectives. Ph.D. thesis, University of Pennsylvania, Philadelphia.
15. Kenji Yamada and Kevin Knight. 2001. A syntax based statistical translation model. In *Proceedings of ACL-01*, Toulouse, France.
16. Kenji Yamada and Kevin Knight. 2002. A decoder for syntax-based statistical MT. In *Proceedings of ACL-02*, Philadelphia.

Practical Translation Pattern Acquisition from Combined Language Resources

Mihoko Kitamura[1,2] and Yuji Matsumoto[2]

[1] Graduate School of Information Science, Nara Institute of Science and Technology
8916-5 Takayama, Ikoma, Nara, Japan
{mihoko-k,matsu}@is.aist-nara.ac.jp
http://cl.aist-nara.ac.jp/

[2] Corporate Research & Development Center, Oki Electric Industry Co., Ltd.
2-5-7 Honmachi, Chuo-ku, Osaka, Japan

Abstract. Automatic extraction of translation patterns from parallel corpora is an efficient way to automatically develop translation dictionaries, and therefore various approaches have been proposed. This paper presents a practical translation pattern extraction method that greedily extracts translation patterns based on co-occurrence of English and Japanese word sequences, which can also be effectively combined with manual confirmation and linguistic resources, such as chunking information and translation dictionaries. Use of these extra linguistic resources enables it to acquire results of higher precision and broader coverage regardless of the amount of documents.

1 Introduction

Reliably enlarging translation dictionaries is crucial for the improvement of machine translation quality and cross-lingual retrieval performance. Recently, an increasing number of translation dictionaries and translated documents have been computerized in order to improve translation efficiency. Numbers of researchers have been attempting to create translation dictionaries automatically by using these translation dictionaries and documents effectively[1, 2].

We presented before an automatic translation pattern extraction method that greedily extracts pairs of Japanese and English word sequences based on their frequency of co-occurrence in parallel corpora[1]. While this method realized a highly precise extraction of translation patterns only by using a parallel corpus and a morphological analyzer, it also had the weakness that precision has to be maintained by restricting coverage of patterns, because precision and coverage relate inversely.

This paper presents a practical translation pattern extraction method, which is based on that method, combined with manual confirmation and linguistic resources such as chunking information and translation dictionaries. With this method, translation patterns are accurately extracted from corpora as small as 500 sentences.

The next section explains our proposed method. Section 3 presents our experimental results and discusses them, and Section 4 presents related works. Finally Section 5 concludes the paper.

2 Improved Algorithm

In this section, we analyze the problems of our previous method, and describe our improvements.

2.1 Weaknesses of the Basic Algorithm

We analyzed the translation pattern results of the basic algorithm. The analysis showed the following mistakes. A) The correspondence is partly correct. However, the correspondence includes one or more unnecessary words. B) The correspondence is not correct. C) The extraction results contain many ambiguous correspondences.

A) is caused by mistakes in the choice of the extent of word sequences. Correspondences extracted by the basic algorithm often ignore the sentence structure, because arbitrary word sequences are paired. In order to resolve this problem, the improved method uses input sentences already divided in chunks. B) comes from the absence of semantic information. We tackle it by accessing dictionaries and accepting information from a human operator. For C), we introduce an idea of "*divergence sensitivity*" into standard definitions for correlation score.

2.2 Algorithm

The following shows the flow of the process to extract correspondences of Japanese and English word sequences. The changes from the basic algorithm[1] are described in italic. The steps (5)-2 and (5)-3 only apply if a translation dictionary is provided, and the step (5)-4 if a human operator is available.

(1) Japanese and English texts are separately analyzed morphologically *and structurally.*

(2) *For each sentence pair (ES, JS) in (E, J) , the sets EWS and JWS of phrase-like word sequences included in a segment appearing in ES and JS are constructed.* The pair (EWS, JWS) is inserted in the sentence database. The total number of occurrences of each word sequence is also kept separately.

(3) An initial threshold value f_{min} for the minimum number of occurrences is chosen appropriately according to the database.

(4) For every pair of word sequences occurring more than f_{min} times, the total number of bilingual co-occurrences in the database is counted.

(5)-1 For each pair of bilingual word sequences, a correlation score is calculated. The most plausible correspondences are then identified using the similarity values. *The approved correspondences are kept as correspondence candidates, but they are not directly registered in the "Correspondence Dictionary" yet.*

(5)-2 *A correspondence candidate (ews, jws) is registered in the "Correspondence Dictionary" if at least one word of ews and one word of jws are associated in the translation dictionary.*

(5)-3 *Even if the condition of (5)-2 is not satisfied, correspondence candidates that have already been approved twice in the same f_{min} level are registered in the "Correspondence Dictionary".*

(5)-4 *A human operator can also be employed to check that correspondences satisfying the condition of (5)-3 are really correct. Incorrect correspondences are remembered so that they will not be presented twice to the operator.*

(6) For each newly registered correspondence (ews, jws), and each pair (EWS, JWS) in the database such that EWS contains ews and JWS contains jws, all word sequences including ews (resp. jws) are removed from EWS (resp. JWS). The total number of occurrences for each word sequence is updated. The steps (4) through (6) are repeated until no new pair is approved.

(7) The threshold value f_{min} is lowered, and the steps (4) to (7) are repeated until f_{min} reaches a predetermined value f_{end} (e.g. $f_{end}=1$).

Chunking. During the step (1) of our improved algorithm, sentences are not only analyzed morphologically, but also divided into syntactically related non-overlapping segments (chunks). Examples of chunks are noun phrases, verb phrases and preposition phrases. The improved method limits the extraction of word sequences to the sub-sequences of a chunk. It is hoped that this process contributes to the reduction of translation patterns extracted that ignore the sentence structure.

Translation Dictionary. The goal of the basic algorithm was to extract highly accurate correspondences from a parallel corpus without using any linguistic resources. But in practical use, it is important to enhance the quality of extracted correspondences by using efficiently existing linguistic resources. We introduce a mechanism to refer to translation dictionaries during extraction. Yet, we must be cautious that excessive dependence on translation dictionaries should not prevent the extraction of correspondences between unknown words.

In step (5)-2, correspondences that can be related to a dictionary entry are registered first. A pair of word sequences (ews, jws) is related to a dictionary entry (ed, jd) if either $ed \subset ews \land jd \cap jws \neq \emptyset$ or $jd \subset jws \land ed \cap ews \neq \emptyset$, that is if one side of the entry matches a part of one word sequence, and the other side of the entry contains a part of the other word sequence. Functional words like prepositions in English, and particles in Japanese, are ignored.

Next, in step (6), word sequences including one side of these correspondences are excluded from extraction candidates. Only correspondences that do not conflict with such highly probable correspondences may pass this filter, and be extracted in the next pass in step (5)-3.

Though our method uses translation dictionaries to avoid improbable translations, the extraction of correspondences unrelated to any dictionary is only delayed. This allows extracting technical terms and new words that do not exist in translation dictionaries.

Manual Confirmation. The safest approach to determine correct correspondence candidates is still to have a human operator check it manually. This is however a costly process and human intervention should be limited to cases that cannot be evaluated automatically. We limit candidates presented to the operator to those selected in (5)-3, as they are statistically possible, but lack corroboration. Moreover the list to check is sorted in decreasing order of correlation score and in alphabetic order, to speed up the selection of correct correspondences. Correspondences refused once are remembered to avoid querying the operator again.

2.3 Correlation Score of Translation Candidates

Dice Coefficient. In the basic method[1], the correlation score of a translation pair (w_J, w_E) is calculated by the weighted Dice Coefficient defined as

$$sim(w_J, w_E) = \log_2 f_{je} \cdot \frac{2f_{je}}{f_j + f_e}$$

where f_j and f_e are the numbers of occurrences of w_J and w_E in Japanese and English corpora respectively, and f_{je} is the number of co-occurrences of w_J and w_E. By choosing to approve only pairs such that $sim(w_J, w_E) \geq \log_2 f_{min}$, we can ensure that no word sequence occurring less than f_{min} times (i.e. not yet considered at this step) can yield a greater correlation score than $sim(w_J, w_E)$.

Log-Likelihood. As an alternative, we also consider the Log-Likelihood [3, 4], which is another measure for co-occurrence. Supposing f_{all} is the number of sentences included in the parallel corpus, it is defined as

$$sim(w_J, w_E) = \phi(f_{je}) + \phi(f_e - f_{je}) + \phi(f_j - f_{je}) + \phi(f_{all} + f_{je} - f_e - f_j)$$
$$- \phi(f_e) - \phi(f_j) - \phi(f_{all} - f_j) - \phi(f_{all} - f_e) + \phi(f_{all})$$
$$\phi(f) = f \cdot \log f$$

Correspondingly, we should not approve pairs for which the Log-Likelihood is less than $sim(w_J, w_E) \geq \phi(f_{all}) - \phi(f_{all} - f_{min}) - \phi(f_{min})$.

Divergence Sensitive Model. The extraction results of the basic algorithm contain many ambiguous correspondences. In other words, a word sequence in one language may be associated to many word sequences in the other. If the parallel corpus contains many similar sentences, the ambiguity cannot be resolved only by co-occurrence, and the output results in two or more correspondences for one sequence. On the other hand, when the correspondence is one to one, it is more likely that the correspondence is correct.

On these grounds, we define a modified correlation score sensitive to divergence as

$$dsim(w_J, w_E) = \frac{sim(w_J, w_E)}{\log_2(fw_{JE} + fw_{EJ})}$$

where fw_{JE} (resp. fw_{EJ}) is the number of translation patterns of w_J (resp. w_E) under the current f_{min}. The above definition is such that $dsim(w_J, w_E) = sim(w_J, w_E)$ when w_J is in one to one correspondence with w_E, and lower otherwise.

3 Experiments

We used English-Japanese parallel corpora that are automatically generated from comparable corpora of major newspapers, the Yomiuri Shimbun and the Daily Yomiuri[5]. These corpora have in average 24 words per English sentence and 27 words per Japanese sentence. We used respectively Chasen[1] and CaboCha[2] for Japanese morphological and dependency analysis. For English analysis, we use the Charniak parser[3]. The translation dictionary combines the English to Japanese and Japanese to English system dictionaries of the machine translation system we are developing[6], and has 507,110 entries in total.

We evaluate the results by their accuracy and coverage. Accuracy is evaluated according to the following 3 levels. The global accuracy is evaluated as the ratio of the number of OK and OK+NM to all extracted patterns. They are described as "OK(OK+NM)" in tables.

OK: the result can be used as an entry in a translation dictionary.
NM(near miss): at most one spurious word on one side of the correspondence.
NG: otherwise.

The coverage is calculated by the following formula in respectively English and Japanese corpus, and evaluated as the average of the two corpora.

$$coverage(\%) = (1 - \frac{nonextracted\,wnum}{wnum}) \cdot 100$$

The non-extracted words of a sentence are the content words (i.e. words with an independent meaning) that are not included in any extracted correspondence applicable to this sentence. "*nonextracted wnum*" is the total number of non-extracted words for a whole (monolingual) corpus. Respectively "*wnum*" is the total number of content words in a corpus. Additionally we provide another evaluation of coverage, based on the same formula, where the number of words is to be understood as the number of distinct words rather than their total number of occurrences. They are indicated as "total coverage (distinct coverage)" in tables.

---

[1] http://chasen.aist-nara.ac.jp
[2] http://cl.aist-nara.ac.jp/~taku-ku/software/cabocha
[3] http://ftp.cs.brown.edu/pub/nlparser

Table 1. Comparison between the basic algorithm and the proposal methods.

No.		1.	2.	3.	4.	5.	6.	7.	8.
method		basic	chunk	dict	hand	dict			hand
measure		Dice				d-Dice	Log	d-Log	d-Log
$f_{end}=2$	total	3,033	3,057	2,981	2,847	2,455	3,830	2,905	3,527
	accuracy	88(92)	91(94)	95(97)	97(99)	98(99)	94(98)	97(99)	98(100)
	coverage	79(12)	80(15)	80(15)	80(15)	78(13)	83(16)	81(12)	82(13)
$f_{end}=1$	total	16,784	16,276	10,276	7,274	9,957	6,412	6,432	6,250
	ok	6,766	7,293	6,996	6,821	7,040	5,740	5,750	5,993
	nm	434	391	335	221	333	222	231	151
	accuracy	40(42)	44(47)	68(71)	93(96)	70(74)	89(92)	89(92)	96(98)
	coverage	85(16)	86(19)	86(19)	85(19)	86(19)	85(19)	85(19)	85(19)
	time	11h47m	4h15m	4h49m	6h58m[4]	4h44m	1h04m	1h05m	3h03m

3.1 Comparative Experimental Results

Comparison with the basic algorithm. Our first experiment compares between the basic method and improved methods using 8,000 sentences from the above-described parallel corpus. The results are shown in Table 1. All cases use the Dice coefficient. "1." is the basic algorithm, "2." adds chunking, "3." adds a translation dictionary to "2.", and "4." adds human checking to "3."

Experiments with the basic algorithm[1] had been limited to $f_{end} = 2$ in order to obtain good accuracy. Indeed the original method has 88% accuracy then, which is a good enough result, but our method shows up to 97% accuracy under the same conditions, which is close to perfect. If we lower f_{end} to 1, the gap widens, the basic algorithm having only 40% accuracy, while the new method can go up to 93% (with human help).

What is interesting is that in spite of a decrease in the number of extracted correspondences, the coverage does not degrade. All these methods allow ambiguous extraction, all correspondences of identical score being extracted simultaneously. The experimental results show that our method can eliminate improbable correspondences by a filtering based on linguistic resources.

Comparison between correlation measures. In our next experiment we compare the efficiency of various correlation measures. The algorithm is based on chunking+dictionary method(Table 1-3.), but we change the measure. "5." uses "divergence sensitive Dice Coefficient", "6." uses "Log-Likelihood", and "7." uses "divergence sensitive Log-Likelihood". Comparing Dice and Log-Likelihood, the accuracy for $f_{end} = 2$ differs only slightly, but the accuracy for $f_{end} = 1$ differs noticeably. Nevertheless, the coverage of Dice and Log-Likelihood is similar. We can conclude that Log-Likelihood is more effective than Dice when we want to extract in level $f_{end} = 1$.

In both cases we can also see that making the measure divergence-sensitive improves the accuracy of the results. Correct correspondences are increased,

---

[4] It took 1 hour 57 minutes to check candidates manually. We discuss this in section 3.2.

Table 2. Effect of the corpus-size and the corpus-quality.

		1.	2.	3.	4.	5.	6.	7.	8.	9.
type		middle	middle	middle	begin	middle	end	middle	middle	letters
size		500	1,000	4,000	8,000	8,000	8,000	16,000	32,000	9,045
en	wn*1	12,231	24,381	97,720	175,768	193,284	200,707	38,5543	762,018	158,652
	dwn*2	2,451	3,481	6,665	7,687	8,866	9,355	11,641	15,002	2,746
ja	wn*1	14,206	27,818	111,787	209,709	221,119	228,949	441,867	880,525	222,737
	dwn*2	2,893	4,299	8,805	9,853	12,012	13,000	15,938	20,719	3,052
f_{end} = 2	accur	94(96)	96(98)	96(99)	97(99)	96(99)	96(99)	96(99)	96(98)	92(95)
	cover	66(14)	68(13)	73(12)	81(13)	76(12)	75(11)	79(12)	80(12)	92(22)
f_{end} = 1	total	633	1,284	4,048	6,452	6,588	6,676	10,704	17,368	4,631
	ok	550	1,200	3,437	5,764	5,640	5,613	9,186	14,551	3,113
	nm	29	37	200	236	335	351	555	894	271
	accur	87(91)	88(93)	85(90)	89(93)	86(91)	84(89)	89(92)	84(89)	67(73)
	cover	72(18)	73(17)	75(15)	85(19)	81(16)	78(15)	83(16)	84(17)	94(34)
	time	0h01m	0h03m	0h16m	1h06m	4h58m	7h58m	22h36m	52h35m	0h26m

*1: "wn" is total number of words for a whole corpus
*2: "dwn" is total number of distinct words for a whole corpus

and incorrect ones either decrease or are stable. We have also observed that divergence sensitive measures make clearer the correlation between score and accuracy (the result is not shown in this paper). Consequently, we think that divergence sensitiveness is effective in acquiring more acceptable results.

Effect of the size and the quality of corpus. Table 2 shows the effect of changing the corpus-size and the corpus-quality. The "size" indicates the number of sentences used in each case. We used the divergence-sensitive Log-Likelihood measure, like in Table 1-7. Since the sentences in the newspaper corpus[5] are sorted by order of confidence by the sentence alignment program, we selected sub-corpora of each size from the beginning, the middle, and the end of the corpus to see the effects of the quality of the parallel corpus. Additionally, we also used business contract letters[7], which are not treated with an a sentence-alignment program but are aligned by hand. The business contract corpus is a technical document, and contains far fewer distinct words than the newspaper corpus.

Naturally, accuracy is very sensitive to the quality of the corpus, but not to its size. Here we consider "quality" for our own purpose, meaning that the translation is literal, and does not include many similar sentences. The result in Table 2 shows that "begin", which offers the best quality, has the best accuracy, while "letters", which is translated literally but has many similar sentences, has poor accuracy.

More importantly, coverage increases with the size of the corpus without loss of accuracy. The best coverage is obtained for "letters", which has a limited vocabulary and low sparseness, but it is hard to compare with the other corpus, as the total number of patterns extracted is actually lower.

Table 3. Samples of Corresponding Word Sequences.

grade	Japanese	English	Score
OK	中 (center) ・ 東欧 (East Europe) 諸国 (countries)	the CEEs	11.48
	洗練 (refining) する (do) られる (passive)	sophisticated	7.61
	コモ (Como) ン (*unknown-word*) ハウス (house)	the common house	6.62
NM	冷戦 (cold war)	war	48.45
	冷戦 (cold war)	the cold	44.14
	に従って (in accordance with)	in accordance	1.82
NG	米国 (America)	Washington	32.12
	いまだに (still)	have yet	18.52
	休息 (rest) その他 (other) の (of)	other work	6.62

3.2 Discussion

In Table 3, we show examples of translation patterns extracted from the 4th experiment of Table 1, using chunking, dictionary, and manual confirmation. This method can extract interesting correspondences. For example, though the Japanese word sequence "コモ/ン/ハウス" was incorrectly analyzed morphologically[5], it is correctly associated to "the common house" in the final results. The primary cause for near misses is incorrect or restrictive chunking. For example, the Japanese word "冷戦" means "the cold war", but it was incorrectly divided into "the cold" and "war" by chunking. We could recover these divided word sequences by referring to the original parallel sentences.

All examples of NG(error) correspondences are caused by mistaken application of the translation dictionary. The problem can be traced back to our rather lax notion of "related" entry, and to the overly broad coverage of used dictionaries. It would be safer to use a more adapted dictionary, and accept only matching entries. A next best method is to check more extensively for stop words (to be excluded from the lookup process). Alternative methods, like the usage of a monolingual corpus, may help here too.

Our last concern is the workload required by manual confirmation. In the 4th experiment of Table 1, manually checking low-confidence candidates took about 2 hours for one operator. During this check, 1,900 correct correspondences could be extracted out of 5,500 candidates. An average time of 2 seconds by candidate was sufficient to dramatically improve the accuracy. In the 8th experiment of Table 1, the same experiment using Log-Likelihood combined with manual checking also achieved up to 96(98)% accuracy. The ratio of improvement to workload seems high enough to justify this semi-manual approach.

4 Related Works

There are two approaches to automatically extract translation patterns from parallel corpora: one is to look for the translations of a predetermined set of phrases of the source language in the sentences of a parallel corpus, and the other is to extract patterns as exhaustively as possible without such a predetermined set.

---

[5] As an output of the analysis, "コモンハウス" is correct, but it is divided in pieces like "コモ/ン/ハウス".

Moore[8] adopted the former approach, using a hierarchy of 3 learning models, each one refining the accuracy. In order to enhance the accuracy, his method requires sentences to be perfect translations, and uses language-dependent information such as capitalization and punctuation. This method was targeted at extraction of technical terms and proper nouns in computer software manual. It achieves good precision in this case, but the applicability of such an approach to more general contents is questionable. Our method effectively uses dictionaries and statistical information too, and is able to extract many proper nouns, as shown in Table 3.

Al-Onaizan and Kevin[9] belongs also to the first approach. Their method is again geared towards technical terms. They use a large monolingual corpus of data such as Web pages for the target language (English), and transliteration information for the source language (Arabic). Their approach to deal with two languages of different families, by using effectively existing linguistic information, is similar to ours. Some of their ideas could be incorporated into our method. For instance, when manually checking an expression, it could be searched on the Web to confirm whether it is correct, and transliteration of English words into Japanese could be used.

Meanwhile, Melamed[10], Yamamoto and Matsumoto[11], and Yamamoto et al.[2], belong to the second approach.

Our method uses three kinds of information, chunking information, translation dictionaries and manual confirmation, to improve the accuracy of extracted correspondences. Correspondingly, Melamed [10] carefully selects accurate translation pairs by filtering candidates using four kinds of information: translation dictionaries, part of speech, cognate detection and syntactic information. This looks similar to our approach, but the difference is that our method targets extraction of translation candidates consisting of multiple word sequences, while Melamed limits his target to single word correspondences. In that case, the process is not constrained by computing power when using linguistic resources, as there is only a limited number of combinations. When dealing with word sequences of arbitrary length, usage of language resources should be balanced with computational complexity.

The method in Yamamoto and Matsumoto[11] resembles ours in its use of the dependency structure in generating candidate word sequences. On the other hand, the difference with their method is that it aims at extracting structural translation patterns larger than chunks, while we use word chunk information in order to extract small but precise patterns. We plan to use these small patterns to implement structural matching[12], as another way to extract structural patterns.

5 Conclusion

In this paper, we proposed a practical method to extract translation patterns, which can be combined with manual confirmation and linguistic resources, such as word chunk information and translation dictionaries.

When the method was tested with a 8,000 sentence parallel corpus, it achieved 96% accuracy and 85% coverage, to compare to respectively 40% and 85% for the original algorithm. Without manual confirmation, it achieved 89% accuracy and 85% coverage.

Our method requires no language-dependent information such as cognate detection and transliteration; consequently we believe it is applicable to any language pair for which appropriate tools and data are available. One of the reasons that our approach is not automatic but semi-automatic is the prospect that the extraction results can be directly used as bilingual dictionaries in a machine translation system. In the near future, we plan to investigate the quality of a data-driven machine translation system using our extraction results under frameworks for machine translation evaluation such as BLEU [13].

Acknowledgements

This research is supported by a grant from NICT of Japan.

References

1. Kitamura, M., Matsumoto, Y.: Automatic extraction of word sequence correspondences in parallel corpora. In: Proceedings of WVLC4. (1996) 79–87
2. Yamamoto, K., Kudo, T., Tsuboi, Y., Matsumoto, Y.: Learning sequence-to-sequence correspondences from parallel corpora via sequential pattern mining. In: Proceedings of HLT-NAACL 2003. (2003) 73–80
3. Dunning, T.: Accurate methods for statistics of surprise and coincidence. In: Computational Linguistics. Volume 19. (1991) 61–74
4. Matsumoto, Y., Utsuro, T.: Lexical knowledge acquisition. In: Handbook of Natural Language Processing. Marcel Dekker (2000) 563–610
5. Utiyama, M., Isahara, H.: Reliable measures for aligning japanese-english news articles and sentences. In: Proceedings of ACL-2003. (2003) 72–79
6. Kitamura, M., Murata, T.: Practical machine translation system allowing complex patterns. In: Proceedings of MT Summit IX. (2003) 232–239
7. Ishigami, S.: Business Contract Letter Dictionary, E-book Version, No.1 Sale of Goods. IBD Corporation (1992) In Japanese.
8. Moore, R.: Learning translations of named-entity phrases from parallel corpora. In: Proceedings of EACL-2003. (2003) 259–266
9. Al-Onaizan, Y., K., K.: Translating named entities using monolingual and bilingual resources. In: Proceedings of ACL-2002. (2002) 400–408
10. Melamed, I.: Automatic evaluation and uniform filter cascades for inducing n-best translation lexicons. In: Proceedings of WVLC3. (1995) 184–198
11. Yamamoto, K., Matsumoto, Y.: Acquisition of phrase-level bilingual correspondence using dependency structure. In: Proceedings of COLING-2000. (2000) 933–939
12. Kitamura, M., Matsumoto, Y.: A machine translation system based on translation rules acquired from parallel corpora. In: Proceedings of RANLP-95. (1995) 27–44
13. Papineni, K., Roukos, S., Ward, T., W.J., Z.: Bleu: a method for automatic evaluation of machine translation. In: Proceedings of ACL-2002. (2002) 311–318

An English-Hindi Statistical Machine Translation System

Raghavendra Udupa U. and Tanveer A. Faruquie

IBM India Research Lab, New Delhi 110016, India
{uraghave,ftanveer}@in.ibm.com

Abstract. Recently statistical methods for natural language translation have become popular and found reasonable success. In this paper we describe an English-Hindi statistical machine translation system. Our machine translation system is based on IBM Models 1, 2, and 3. We present experimental results on an English-Hindi parallel corpus consisting of 150,000 sentence pairs. We propose two new algorithms for the transfer of fertility parameters from Model 2 to Model 3. Our algorithms have a worst case time complexity of $O(m^3)$ improving on the exponential time algorithm proposed in the classical paper on IBM Models. When the maximum fertility of a word is small, our algorithms are $O(m^2)$ and hence very efficient in practice.

1 Introduction

The explosive growth of Internet and the increasing demand of knowledge based applications and services has resulted in a great interest in the language industry as more and more information and services are now available in multiple languages. This multilinguality has triggered a need for giving the user information and services in a language of his choice. Automatic Machine Translation is the enabling technology which addresses this need and has now become a necessity. Unfortunately, traditional machine translation systems dedicate a considerable period of time on building hand-crafted translation rules, dictionaries and grammars in close consultation with bilingual linguists. As a result these systems are not easily scalable and adaptable.

Statistical Machine Translation provides cost effective and reliable solution to the problems of scalability and adaptability and is reasonably fast and accurate. In statistical machine translation, the system examines large amounts of bilingual text which are translations of each other and learns how the two languages are related. Such a system has now become a reality thanks to the progress made in storage and processing power and the availability of large bilingual corpus. Systems using statistical techniques can be readily trained for a novel language pair. This drastically reduces the deployment time and cost for such systems. They are easier to maintain and readily tunable for specific domain or language usage. Statistical systems can remarkably extend the reach of knowledge and information.

In this paper we describe an English-Hindi statistical translation system based on IBM models and present the results of our experiments with it. The rest of the paper is organized as follows: Section 2 discusses briefly the fundamental equation of statistical machine translation. Section 3 describes the IBM models 2 and 3 and proposes two efficient algorithms for the transfer of fertility parameters from Model 2 to Model 3. Section 4 describes an English-Hindi translation system and results of our experiments.

2 Statistical Machine Translation

Statistical Translation models were invented at IBM [1]. These Models are based on the source-channel paradigm of communication theory. Consider the problem of translating a English sentence e to a Hindi sentence h. We imagine that e was originally conceived in Hindi which when transmitted over the noisy communication channel got corrupted and became an English sentence. The goal is to get back the original Hindi sentence from the English sentence generated by the channel by modeling the noise characteristics of the channel mathematically and determining the parameters of the model experimentally. This can be expressed mathematically as

$$\hat{h} = arg \max_{h} Pr(h|e)$$

By Bayes' Theorem
$Pr(h|e) = Pr(e|h)Pr(h)/Pr(e)$ and therefore,

$$\hat{h} = arg \max_{h} Pr(e|h)Pr(h)$$

The above equation is known as the *Fundamental Equation of Statistical Machine Translation*.

The Fundamental Equation of Statistical Machine Translation shows that if we can determine the probability distributions $Pr(e|h)$ and $Pr(h)$ then translation from one language to another can be treated as a search problem. The computational tasks in a SMT system are therefore:

- Estimating translation model probability $P(e|h)$
- Estimating language model probability $Pr(h)$
- Search for the sentence h maximizing the product $P(e|h)Pr(h)$.

Conceptually, the probability distribution $P(e|h)$ is a table which associates a probability score with every possible pair of English and Hindi sentences (e, h). Similarly, $Pr(h)$ is a table which associates a probability score with every possible Hindi sentence h. It is impractical to construct these tables exactly by examining individual sentence pairs since the number of conceivable sentences in any language is countably infinite. Therefore, the challenge is to construct approximations to the probability distributions $P(e|h)$ and $Pr(h)$ and a practical search strategy that gives an acceptable quality of translation.

3 IBM Translation Models

3.1 Translation Model

The problem of estimating the conditional distribution $P(e|h)$ is known as the translation modeling problem. The conditional distribution $P(e|h)$ is expressed in terms of a set of parameters and these parameters are estimated by a process called *training*. The input to the training process is a corpus of aligned bilingual sentences and the training process is essentially an iterative application of the EM algorithm [5]. The EM algorithm attempts to maximize the likelihood of the set of translations in the training corpus and converges to a local maximum. In the seminal paper [1] Brown et al proposed a series of five translation models of increasing complexity and provided algorithms for estimating the parameters of the models.

IBM Translation Model 2. IBM translation model 2 is a generative model, i.e., it describes how an English sentence e could be stochastically generated given a Hindi sentence h. It works as follows:

- Given a Hindi sentence h of length l, choose the length (m) for the English sentence from a distribution $\epsilon(m|l)$.
- For each position $j = 1, 2, \ldots m$ in the English string, choose a position a_j in the Hindi string from a distribution $a(a_j|j, l, m)$. The mapping $\mathbf{a} = (a_1, a_2, \ldots, a_m)$ is known as alignment between the English sentence e and the Hindi sentence h. An alignment between e and h tells which word of e is associated with which word of h.
- For each $j = 1, 2, \ldots m$ in the English string, choose an English word e_j according to the distribution $t(e_j|h_{a_j})$.

It follows from the generative model that probability of generating $e = e_1 e_2 \ldots e_m$ given $h = h_1 h_2 \ldots h_l$ with alignment $\mathbf{a} = (a_1, a_2, \ldots, a_m)$ is

$$Pr(e, a|h) = \epsilon(m|l) \prod_{j=1}^{m} t(e_j|h_{a_j}) a(a_j|j, m, l).$$

It can be easily seen that a sentence e could be produced from h employing many alignments and therefore, the probability of generating e given h is the sum of the probabilities of generating e given h under all possible alignments a, i.e., $Pr(e|h) = \sum_a Pr(e, a|h)$. Therefore,

$$Pr(e|h) = \epsilon(m|l) \sum_{a_1=0}^{l} \cdots \sum_{a_m=0}^{l} \prod_{j=1}^{m} t(e_j|h_{a_j}) . a(a_j|j, m, l)$$

The above expression can be rewritten as follows:

$$Pr(e|h) = \epsilon(m|l) \prod_{j=1}^{m} \sum_{i=0}^{l} t(e_j|h_i) a(i|j, m, l).$$

IBM model 1 is a special case of model 2 obtained by assuming a uniform distribution for $a(i|j, m, l)$ usually held fixed at $(l+1)^{-1}$.

IBM Translation Model 3. Given a Hindi sentence h of length l IBM Model 3 generates the English sentence e as follows:

- For each Hindi word h_i in position $i = 1, 2, \ldots l$ of the Hindi sentence h, choose the number of words ϕ_i and the corresponding list of English word τ_i that h_i generates according to the distribution $n(\phi_i | e_i)$.
- Choose the number of words ϕ_0 and the list of word τ_0 for the null word according to the probability distribution $n_0(\phi_0 | \sum_{i=1}^{l} \phi_i)$
- Let the length of English sentence be $m = \phi_0 + \sum_{i=1}^{l} \phi_i$.
- For each location $i = 1, 2, \ldots l$ in Hindi sentence and the corresponding location $k = 1, 2, \ldots \phi_i$ choose a English word τ_{ik} according to the distribution $t(\tau_{ik} | e_i)$.
- For each location $i = 1, 2, \ldots l$ in Hindi sentence and the corresponding location $k = 1, 2, \ldots \phi_i$ choose a position π_{ik} from $1, 2, \ldots m$ according to the distribution $d(\pi_{ik} | i, l, m)$.
- If the position has been chosen more than once return failure.
- For each position $k = 1, 2, \ldots \phi_0$ in the fertility of the null word choose a position π_{0k} from the $\phi_0 - k + 1$ positions remaining vacant in $1, 2, \ldots m$ using a uniform distribution.
- The generated English sentence e is the string $e_{\pi_{ik}} = \tau_{ik}$.

It follows that probability of generating $e = e_1 e_2 \ldots e_m$ given $h = h_1 h_2 \ldots h_l$ is

$$Pr(e, a | h) = n_0(\phi_0 | \sum_{i=1}^{l} \phi_i) \cdot \prod_{i=1}^{l} n(\phi_i | e_i) \phi_i! \cdot \prod_{j=1}^{m} t(e_j | h_{a_j}) \cdot \prod_{j : a_j != 0} d(j | a_j, m, l)$$

Fertility Probabilities Transfer. The parameters of Model 3 are estimated by training the model on the parallel corpus iteratively. To begin the training of Model 3 we need to initialize its parameters suitably. A standard practice is to use the estimated parameters of Model 2 to seed Model 3 parameters. Since Model 2 does not employ fertility probabilities explicitly, they need to be estimated using the other parameters. This estimation is known as transfer of fertility probabilities. The classical algorithm for the transfer of fertility probabilities described in [1] is complicated and inefficient. As shown in that paper, the algorithm has exponential time complexity. In this section we describe much simpler and more efficient algorithms for the transfer of fertility probabilities. We first describe an $O(m^3)$ time algorithm and then a much simpler $O(m^3)$ time algorithm.

$O(m^3)$ Time Algorithm. Equation (1.107) in the paper [1] allows us to compute the count $\tilde{c}_{\tilde{\theta}}(\phi | h; \mathbf{e}, \mathbf{h})$ in $O(lm + \phi g(\phi))$ operations where $g(\phi)$ is the number of partitions of ϕ and grows with ϕ as $(4\sqrt{3}\phi))^{-1} \exp(\pi \sqrt{2\phi/3})$. If $|\mathbf{e}| = m, |\mathbf{h}| = l$, and ϕ_{max} is the maximum fertility of any Hindi word, then the number of operations in computing all the fertility counts affected by the sentence pair $(\mathbf{h}, \mathbf{e})$ is $O(ml + l(\sum_{\phi=0}^{\phi_{max}} \phi g(\phi)) + ml\phi_{max} + ml)$, i.e., $O(ml^2 \phi_{max} + l(\sum_{\phi=0}^{\phi_{max}} \phi g(\phi)))$.

We now describe an alternative scheme for computing the fertility counts. We observe that the contribution of the word $h_i = h$ to $\tilde{c}_{\tilde{\theta}}(\phi|h;\mathbf{e},\mathbf{h})$ is equal to the probability that exactly ϕ words in the sentence $\mathbf{e}$ are aligned with h_i. Let this probability be $\tilde{p}_{\tilde{\theta}}(i,\phi|\mathbf{e},\mathbf{h})$. Therefore,

$$\tilde{c}_{\tilde{\theta}}(\phi|h;\mathbf{e},\mathbf{h}) = \sum_{i=1}^{l} \delta(h,h_i)\tilde{p}_{\tilde{\theta}}(i,\phi|\mathbf{e},\mathbf{h}). \tag{1}$$

Now, $\tilde{p}_{\tilde{\theta}}(i,\phi|\mathbf{e},\mathbf{h})$ is the coefficient of x^ϕ in the polynomial:

$$\prod_{j=1}^{m}(x\tilde{p}_{\tilde{\theta}}(i|j,\mathbf{e},\mathbf{h}) + 1 - \tilde{p}_{\tilde{\theta}}(i|j,\mathbf{e},\mathbf{h}))$$

Therefore, $\tilde{c}_{\tilde{\theta}}(\phi|h;\mathbf{e},\mathbf{h})$ is the coefficient of x^ϕ in the polynomial:

$$\sum_{i=1}^{l} \delta(h,h_i) \prod_{j=1}^{m}(x\tilde{p}_{\tilde{\theta}}(i|j,\mathbf{e},\mathbf{h}) + 1 - \tilde{p}_{\tilde{\theta}}(i|j,\mathbf{e},\mathbf{h}))$$

This polynomial is the same as the RHS of Equation (1.115) in the paper [1]. We thus have

$$\sum_{i=1}^{l} \delta(h,h_i) \prod_{j=1}^{m}(x\tilde{p}_{\tilde{\theta}}(i|j,\mathbf{e},\mathbf{h}) + 1 - \tilde{p}_{\tilde{\theta}}(i|j,\mathbf{e},\mathbf{h})) = \sum_{k=0}^{m} c_k x^k$$

with

$$c_k = \tilde{c}_{\tilde{\theta}}(\phi = k|h;\mathbf{e},\text{bfh}).$$

It can be seen that the above equation defines a linear equation for each $x \in R$. Therefore, a set of values $\{\xi_0, \xi_1, \ldots, \xi_m\}$ for x produces a linear system $Ac = b$ where the kth row of A is $[1, \xi_k, \xi_k^2, \ldots, \xi_k^m]$, $c = [c_0, c_1, \ldots, c_m]$, $b = [b_0, b_1, \ldots, b_m]$, and $b_k = \sum_{i=1}^{l} \delta(h,h_i) \prod_{j=1}^{m}(\xi_k \tilde{p}_{\tilde{\theta}}(i|j,\mathbf{e},\mathbf{h}) + 1 - \tilde{p}_{\tilde{\theta}}(i|j,\mathbf{e},\mathbf{h}))$. If the set $\{\xi_0, \xi_1, \ldots, \xi_m\}$ is chosen such that A is invertible, then system $Ac = b$ can be solved using Gaussian Elimination in $O(m^3)$ operations. The number of operations needed by this scheme is $O(m^2 l + m^3)$ since $O(m^2 l)$ operations are needed for computing b and $O(m^3)$ operations are needed to solve the system $Ac = b$. If the maximum fertility of any Hindi word is ϕ_{max}, then $c_k = 0$ for all $k > \phi_{max}$. This also implies that for every i, at most ϕ_{max} of $\tilde{p}_{\tilde{\theta}}(i|j,\mathbf{e},\mathbf{h})$ are non-zero. These non-zero probabilities can be determined in time $O(m)$. Since only ϕ_{max} unknowns have to be determined, the computation of b requires only $O(l(m + \phi_{max}^2))$ operations and solving the linear system requires only $O(\phi_{max}^3)$ operations. Therefore, the total number of operations needed is $O(ml + l\phi_{max}^2 + \phi_{max}^3)$. Since both l and ϕ_{max} are $O(m)$, the algorithm is clearly $O(m^3)$. When ϕ_{max} is small (which is true in practice), the algorithm is $O(m^2)$. Clearly, our scheme has a much better time complexity than the original scheme. The matrix A does not change with the sentence pair $(\mathbf{e}, \mathbf{h})$ as it depends only on ϕ_{max}.

A Simpler $O(m^3)$ Time Algorithm. We now show that fertility parameters can be computed in $O(m^3)$ time using a much simpler algorithm. We observe that if we can compute the coefficients of the polynomial

$$\prod_{j=1}^{m}(x\tilde{p}_{\tilde{\theta}}(i|j,\mathbf{e},\mathbf{h}) + 1 - \tilde{p}_{\tilde{\theta}}(i|j,\mathbf{e},\mathbf{h}))$$

efficiently, then computing the fertility counts (and hence, fertility probabilities) is easy. Let

$$\prod_{j=1}^{m}(x\tilde{p}_{\tilde{\theta}}(i|j,\mathbf{e},\mathbf{h}) + 1 - \tilde{p}_{\tilde{\theta}}(i|j,\mathbf{e},\mathbf{h})) = \sum_{k=0}^{m} \rho_k x^k.$$

The following algorithm computes the coefficients $\rho_k, k = 0, \ldots, m$ in $O(m^2)$ time by successive multiplication of the terms of the polynomial.

- $\eta_0 = 1$;
- for $j = 1$ to m do
  - $\eta_j = 0$;
- end-for
- for $j = 1$ to $m - 1$ do
  - for $k = 0$ to m do
    * $\rho_k = 0$;
  - end-for
  - for $k = 0$ to $j - 1$ do
    * $\rho_{k+1} = \rho_{k+1} + \eta_k \tilde{p}_{\tilde{\theta}}(i|j,\mathbf{e},\mathbf{h})$;
    * $\rho_k = \rho_k + \eta_k(1 - \tilde{p}_{\tilde{\theta}}(i|j,\mathbf{e},\mathbf{h}))$;
  - for $k = 0$ to m do
    * $\eta_k = \rho_k$;
  - end-for
- end-for

If the maximum fertility is ϕ_{max} then the above algorithm can be modified to compute the coefficients in $O(m + \phi_{max}^2)$ time. Since the coefficients are computed for each $i = 1, \ldots, l$, the overall time complexity of the algorithm is $O(ml + l\phi_{max}^2)$. When ϕ_{max} is small, the algorithm has complexity $O(m^2)$.

4 English-Hindi Statistical Translation System

Our English-Hindi machine translation system is based on IBM models 1, 2, and 3. The first two models are used only to seed the training of Model 3. Our corpus has about 150,000 sentence pairs and consists of data from several domains including news, government documents, conversation, and magazine articles. The translation models were trained on this corpus. We first trained the models on 100,000 sentence pairs and then on the complete corpus. This was done to study the effect of corpus size on the performance of the translation system. The Hindi vocabulary had 72,900 words and the English vocabulary had 59,800 words. The trigram Hindi language model was built by training on a Hindi corpus consisting of about 80 million words. The language model had a perplexity of 188.

Hindi is a verb ending, free word order inflectional language. Below we present the best translations generated by our system for a few test inputs along with the corresponding Language Model and Translation model scores. The alignment produced by the decoding algorithm is also shown . The words in the input and output sentences are indexed starting with 0. The first digit represents the word of the output Hindi sentence and the second digit corresponds to the word in input English sentence e.g. 0 1 | 1 0 | 3 2 means that first word in the output sentence aligns with the second word in the input sentence, the second aligns with first, the third aligns with null word and the fourth aligns with third word.

Input English Sentence : Diwali is celebrated in all parts of India
Best Hindi Translation : deepavlee bhart ke sabhee bhagon meN mnaya jata hai
Language Model Score : 21.27
Translation Model Score : 8.36
Total score : 29.64
alignment : 0 0 | 1 7 | 2 6 | 3 4 | 4 5 | 5 3 | 6 2 | 8 1

Second Best Hindi Translation : sabhee bhagon meN mnaya jata hai bhart kee deepavlee
Language Model Score : 23.57
Translation Model Score : 7.55
Total score : 31.13
alignment : 0 4 | 1 5 | 2 3 | 3 2 | 4 1 | 5 7 | 6 6 | 7 0

Input English Sentence : innocent people are killed by terrorists
Best Hindi Translation : AatNkvadee d+vara nir+doSh log mare jate haiN
Language Model Score : 14.86
Translation Model Score : 6.89
Total score : 21.75
alignment : 0 5 | 1 4 | 2 0 | 3 1 | 4 3 | 6 2

Input English Sentence : unemployment is an electoral issue in India
Best Hindi Translation : bhart meN berojgaree Ek cunavee mud+da hai
Language Model Score : 19.77
Translation Model Score : 8.83
Total score : 28.61
alignment : 0 6 | 1 5 | 2 0 | 3 2 | 4 ,3 | 5 4 | 6 1

Table 1 shows the BLEU and NIST scores of our system. The test data consisted of 1032 English sentences (of restricted sentence length).

Table 1. BLEU and NIST scores.

Training corpus size	100 K	150 K
Model	3	3
No. of test sentences	1032	1032
BLEU Score	0.1298	0.1391
NIST Score	4.5186	4.6296

We get a 7.16% improvement in BLEU score and a 2.46% in NIST score as the training corpus size is increased from 100,000 sentences to 150,000 sentences. The test sentences were decoded using the Dynamic programming decoding algorithm [11].

5 Conclusions

We have discussed our English-Hindi Statistical Translation system generated from a modest corpus size of 150,000 sentence pairs and have evaluated its performance using BLEU score and NIST score. We have described two novel and efficient algorithms for fertility parameters transfer.

References

1. Brown, P.F., S.A. Della Pietra, V.J. Della Pietra, and R.L. Mercer.: The mathematics of Statistical Machine Translation: Parameter estimation. Computational linguistics. **19(2)**, (1993), 263-311
2. Berger, A., S. Della Pietra, and V. Della Pietra.: A maximum entropy approach to natural language processing. Computational linguistics. **22(1)**, (1996)
3. Brown, P.F., V.J. Della Pietra, P.V. deSouza, J.C. Lai, and R.L. Mercer.: Class based n-gram models for natural language. Computational linguistics. **18(4)**, (1992)
4. Berger, A., P. Brown, S. Della Pietra, V. Della Pietra, J. Gillette, J. Laffert , R. Mercer, H. Printz, L. Ures.: The Candide system for machine translation. Proceedings of the ARPA Human Language Technology Workshop. (1994)
5. L. E. Baum.: An inequality and associated maximization technique in statistical estimation of probabilistic functions of a Markov process. Inequalities. **3**, (1972), 1-8
6. K. Knight.: Decoding complexity in word replacement translation models. Computational Linguistics. **25(4)**, (1999)
7. F. Jelinek.: A fast sequential decoding algorithm using a stack. IBM Research Journal. **13**, (1969)
8. Brown R. D. Example-based Machine Translation in the Pangloss System. International Conference on Computational Linguistics (COLING-96). (Aug 1996), Copenhagen, Denmark.
9. R.M.K. Sinha, K. Sivaraman, A. Agrawal, R. Jain, R. Srivastava, A. Jain.: ANGLABHARTI: A Multilingual Machine Aided Translation Project on Translation from English to Hindi. IEEE International Conference on Systems, Man and Cybernetics. (1995), Vancouver, Canada.

10. C. Tillman, S. Vogel, H. Ney, and A. Zubiaga.: A DP-based search using monotone alignments in statistical translation. Proc. ACL. (1997)
11. C. Tillman.: Word Re-Odering and Dynamic Programming based Search Algorithm for Statistical Machine Translation. Ph.D. Thesis. (2001)
12. K. Papineni, S. Roukos, T. Ward and W.-J. Zhu.: Bleu : A Method for Automatic Evaluation of Machine Translation. IBM Research Report. (2001) RC22176 (W0109-022)
13. G. Doddington.: Automatic Evaluation of Machine Translation Quality using N-gram Co-occurence Statistics. Human Language Technology: Notebook Proceedings. (2002) 128-132

Robust Speaker Identification System Based on Wavelet Transform and Gaussian Mixture Model

Wan-Chen Chen[1], Ching-Tang Hsieh[2], and Eugene Lai[2]

[1] Dept. of Electronic Engineering, St. John's & St. Mary's Institute of technology, Taipei
`steven@mail.sjsmit.edu.tw`
[2] Dept. of Electrical Engineering, Tamkang University, Taipei
`{hsieh,elai}@ee.tku.edu.tw`

Abstract. This paper presents an effective method for improving the performance of a speaker identification system. Based on the multiresolution property of the wavelet transform, the input speech signal is decomposed into various frequency bands in order not to spread noise distortions over the entire feature space. The linear predictive cepstral coefficients (LPCCs) of each band are calculated. Furthermore, the cepstral mean normalization technique is applied to all computed features. We use feature recombination and likelihood recombination methods to evaluate the task of the text-independent speaker identification. The feature recombination scheme combines the cepstral coefficients of each band to form a single feature vector used to train the Gaussian mixture model (GMM). The likelihood recombination scheme combines the likelihood scores of independent GMM for each band. Experimental results show that both proposed methods outperform the GMM model using full-band LPCCs and mel-frequency cepstral coefficients (MFCCs) in both clean and noisy environments.

1 Introduction

In general, speaker recognition can be divided into two parts: speaker verification and speaker identification. Speaker verification refers to the process of determining whether or not the speech samples belong to some specific speaker. However, in speaker identification, the goal is to determine which one of a group of known voices best matches the input voice sample. Furthermore, in both tasks, the speech can be either text-dependent or text-independent. Text-dependent means that the text used in the test system must be the same as that used in the training system, while text-independent means that no limitation is placed on the text used in the test system. Certainly, the method used to extract and model the speaker-dependent characteristics of a speech signal seriously affects the performance of a speaker recognition system.

Many researches have been done on the task of speech feature extraction. The linear predictive cepstral coefficients (LPCCs) were used because of their simplicity and effectiveness in speaker/speech recognition [1], [2]. Other widely used feature parameters, mel-frequency cepstral coefficients (MFCCs) [3], were calculated by using a filter-bank approach, in which the set of filters had equal bandwidths with respect to the mel-scale frequencies. This method is based on the fact that human perception of the frequency contents of sounds does not follow a linear scale. The above two most commonly used feature extraction techniques do not provide invariant parameterization of speech; the representation of the speech signal tends to change under various noise conditions. The performance of these speaker identification systems may be severely degraded when a mismatch between the training and testing environments occurs. Various types of speech enhancement and noise elimination techniques have been applied to feature extraction. Typically, the nonlinear spectral subtraction algorithms [4] have provided only minor performance gains after extensive parameter optimization. Furui [5] used the cepstral mean normalization (CMN) technique to eliminate channel bias by subtracting off the global average cepstral vector from each cepstral vector. Another way to minimize the channel filter effect is to use the time derivatives of cepstral coefficients [6]. Cepstral coefficients and their time derivatives are used as features in order to capture dynamic information and eliminate time-invariant spectral information that is generally attributed to the interposed communication channel.

Conventionally, feature extraction is carried out by computing acoustic feature vectors over the full band of the spectral representation of speech. The major drawback of this approach is that even partial band-limited noise corruption affects all feature vector components. The multiband approach deals with this problem by performing acoustic feature analysis independently on a set of frequency subbands [7]. Since the resulting coefficients are computed independently, a band-limited noise signal does not spread over the entire feature space. The major drawback of a pure subband-based approach may be that information about the correlation among various subbands is lost. Therefore, an approach that combines the information from the full band and subbands at the recognition stage was found to improve recognition performance [8]. It is not a trivial matter to decide at which temporal level the subband features should be combined. In the multiband approach [9], different classifiers for each band are used, and likelihood recombination is done at the hidden Markov model (HMM) state, phone, or word level. In another approach [10], the individual features of each subband are combined into a single feature vector prior to decoding. In our previous works [11], [12], we proposed a multiband linear predictive cepstral coefficient (MBLPCC) method in which the LPCCs from various subbands and the full band are combined to form a single feature vector. This feature extraction method was evaluated in a speaker identification system using vector quantization (VQ) and group vector quantization (GVQ) as identifiers. The experimental results showed that this multiband feature is more effective and robust than the full-band LPCC and MFCC features, particularly in noisy environments.

In past studies on recognition models, dynamic time warping (DTW) [13], HMM [14], [15], and GMM [16]-[19] were used to perform speaker recognition. The DTW technique is effective in the text-dependent speaker recognition, but it is not suitable for the text-independent speaker recognition. The HMM is widely used in speech recognition and it is also commonly used in text-dependent speaker verification. GMM [16] provides a probabilistic model of the underlying sounds of a person's voice. It is computationally more efficient than HMM and has been widely used in text-independent speaker recognition.

In this study, the MBLPCC features [11], [12] proposed previously are used as the front end of the speaker identification system. Then, cepstral mean normalization is applied to these multiband speech features to provide similar parameter statistics in all acoustic environments. In order to effectively utilize these multiband speech features, we use features recombination and likelihood recombination methods in the

GMM recognition models to evaluate the task of text-independent speaker identification. The experimental results show that the proposed multiband methods outperform GMM using full-band LPCC and MFCC features.

This paper is organized as follows. The proposed algorithm for extracting speech features is described in Sect. 2. Sect. 3 presents the multiband-based speaker recognition models. Experimental results and comparisons with the conventional full-band GMM are presented in Sect. 4. Concluding remarks are made in Sect. 5.

2 Multiresolution Features Based on Wavelet Transform

Based on time-frequency multiresolution analysis, the effective and robust MBLPCC features are used as the front end of the speaker identification system. First, the LPCCs are extracted from the full-band input signal. Then the wavelet transform is applied to decompose the input signal into two frequency subbands: a lower frequency subband and a higher frequency subband. To capture the characteristics of an individual speaker, the LPCCs of the lower frequency subband are calculated. There are two main reasons for using the LPCC parameters: their good representation of the envelope of the speech spectrum of vowels, and their simplicity. Based on this mechanism, we can easily extract the multiresolution features from all lower frequency subband signals simply by iteratively applying the wavelet transform to decompose the lower frequency subband signals, as depicted in Fig. 1. As shown in Fig. 1, the wavelet transform can be realized by using a pair of finite impulse response (FIR) filters, h and g, which are low-pass and high-pass filters, respectively, and by performing the down-sampling operation (↓2). The down-sampling operation is used to discard the odd-numbered samples in a sample sequence after filtering is performed.

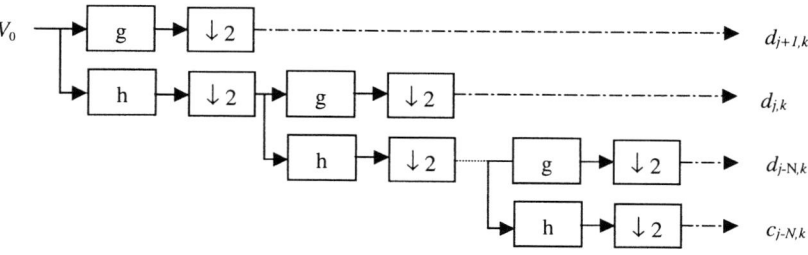

Fig. 1. Two-band analysis tree for a discrete wavelet transform

The schematic flow of the proposed feature extraction method is shown in Fig. 2. After the full-band LPCCs are extracted from the input speech signal, the discrete wavelet transform (DWT) is applied to decompose the input signal into a lower frequency subband and the subband LPCCs are extracted from this lower frequency subband. The recursive decomposition process enables us to easily acquire the multiband features of the speech signal. Based on the concept of the proposed method, the number of MBLPCCs depends on the level of decomposition process. If speech signals bandlimited from 0 to 4000 Hz are decomposed into two subbands, then three bands signals, (0-4000), (0-2000), and (0-1000) Hz, will be generated. Since the spectra of the three bands will overlap in the lower frequency region, the proposed

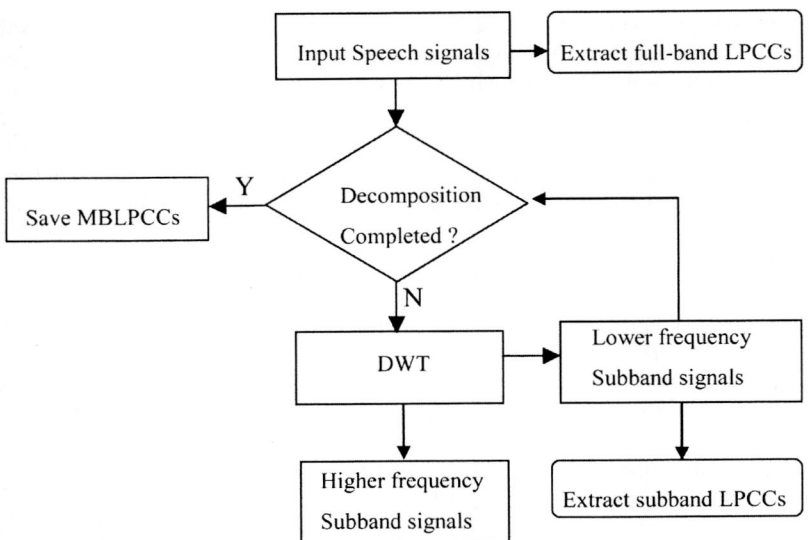

Fig. 2. Features extraction algorithm of MBLPCCs

multiband feature extraction method focuses on the spectrum of the speech signal in the low frequency region similar to extracting MFCC features.

Finally, cepstral mean normalization is applied to normalize the feature vectors so that their short-term means are normalized to zero as follows:

$$\hat{X}_k(t) = X_k(t) - \mu_k ,\qquad(1)$$

where $X_k(t)$ is the kth component of feature vector at time (frame) t, and μ_k is the mean of the kth component of the feature vectors of a specific speaker's utterance.

In this paper, the orthonormal basis of DWT is based on the 16 coefficients of the quadrature mirror filters (QMF) introduced by Daubechies [20] (see the Appendix).

3 Multiband Speaker Recognition Models

As described in Sect. 1, GMM is widely used to perform text-independent speaker recognition and achieves good performances. Here, we use GMM as the classifier. Our initial strategy for multiband speaker recognition is based on straightforward recombination of the cepstral coefficients from each subband (including the full band) to form a single feature vector, which is used to train GMM. We call this identifier model the feature combination Gaussian mixture model (FCGMM). The structure of FCGMM is shown in Fig. 3. First, the input signal is decomposed into L subbands. In the "extract LPCC" block, the LPCC features extracted from each band (including the full band) are further normalized to zero mean by using the cepstral mean normalization technique. Finally, the LPCCs from each subband (including the full band) are recombined to form a single feature vector that is used to train GMM. The advantages of this approach are that: (1) it is possible to model the correlation among the feature vectors of each band; (2) acoustic modeling is simpler.

Our next approach combines the likelihood scores of the independent GMM for each band, as illustrated in Fig. 4. We call this identifier model the likelihood combination Gaussian mixture model (LCGMM). First, the input signal is decomposed into L subbands. Then the LPCC features extracted from each band are further normalized to zero mean by using the cepstral mean normalization technique. Finally, different GMM classifiers are applied independently to each band, and the likelihood scores of all the GMM classifiers are combined to obtain the global likelihood scores and a global decision.

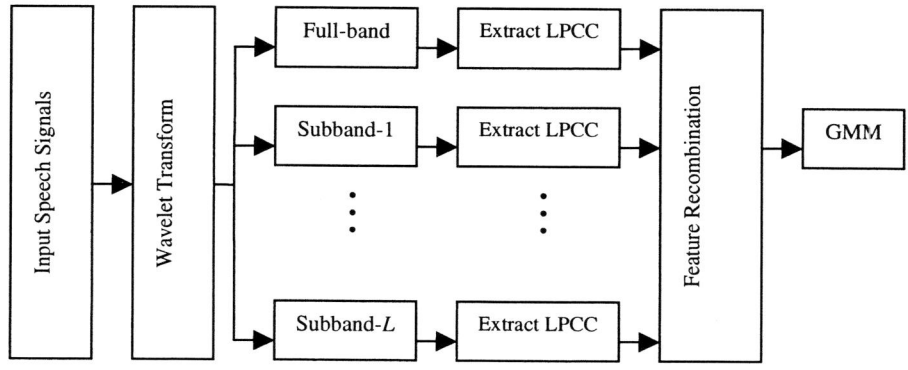

Fig. 3. Structure of FCGMM

For speaker identification, a group of S speakers is represented by LCGMMs, $\lambda_1, \lambda_2, ..., \lambda_S$. A given speech utterance X is decomposed into L subbands. Let X_i and λ_{ki} be the feature vector and the associated GMM for band i, respectively. After the logarithmic likelihood $\log P(X_i|\lambda_{ki})$ of band i for a specific speaker k is evaluated, the combined logarithmic likelihood $\log P(X|\lambda_k)$ for LCGMM of a specific speaker k is determined as the sum of the logarithmic likelihood $\log P(X_i|\lambda_{ki})$ for all bands as follows:

$$\log P(X|\lambda_k) = \sum_{i=0}^{L} \log P(X_i|\lambda_{ki}) , \qquad (2)$$

where L is the number of subbands. When $L = 0$, the functions of LCGMM and the conventional full-band GMM are identical. For a given speech utterance X, X is classified to belong to the speaker $\hat{S}$ who has the maximum logarithmic likelihood $\log P(X|\lambda_{\hat{S}})$:

$$\hat{S} = \arg \max_{1 \leq k \leq S} \log P(X|\lambda_k) . \qquad (3)$$

4 Experimental Results

This section presents experiments conducted to evaluate application of FCGMM and LCGMM to text-independent speaker identification. The first experiment studied the effect of the decomposition level. The next experiment compared the performance of FCGMM and LCGMM with that of the conventional GMM model using full-band LPCC and MFCC features.

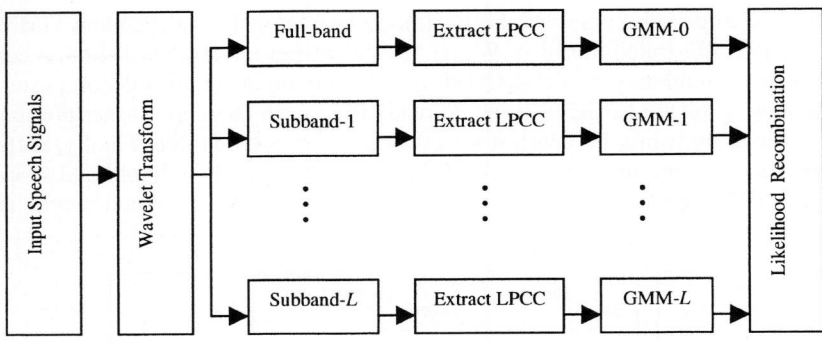

Fig. 4. Structure of LCGMM

4.1 Database Description and Parameters Setting

The proposed multiband approaches were evaluated using the KING speech database [21] for text-independent speaker identification. The KING database is a collection of conversational speech from 51 male speakers. For each speaker, there are 10 sections of conversational speech recorded at different time. Each section consists of about 30 seconds of actual speech. The speech from a section was recorded locally using a microphone and was transmitted over a long distance telephone link, thus providing a high-quality (clean) version and a telephone quality version of the speech. The speech signals were recorded at 8 kHz and 16 bits per sample. In our experiments, the noisy speech was generated by adding Gaussian noise to the clean version speech at the desired SNR. In order to eliminate silence segments from an utterance, simple segmentation based on the signal energy of each speech frame was performed. All the experiments were performed using five sections of speech from 20 speakers. For each speaker, 90 seconds of speech cut from three clean version sections provided the training utterances. The other two sections were divided into nonoverlapping segments 2 seconds in length and provided the testing utterances.

In both experiments conducted in this study, each frame of an analyzed utterance had 256 samples with 128 overlapping samples. Furthermore, 20 orders of LPCCs for each frequency band were calculated and the first order coefficient was discarded. For our multiband approach, we use 2, 3 and 4 bands as follows:

- 2 bands: (0-4000), (0-2000) Hz;
- 3 bands: (0-4000), (0-2000), (0-1000) Hz;
- 4 bands: (0-4000), (0-2000), (0-1000), (0-500) Hz.

4.2 Effect of the Decomposition Level

As explained in Sect. 2, the number of subbands depends on the decomposition level of the wavelet transform. The first experiment evaluated the effect of number of bands used in the FCGMM and LCGMM recognition models with 50 mixtures in both clean and noisy environments. The experimental results are shown in Table 1. One could see that the 3-band FCGMM achieved better performance under low SNR conditions (for example, 15 dB, 10 dB and 5 dB), but poorer performance under clean and 20 dB SNR conditions, compared with the 2-band FCGMM model.

Table 1. Effect of number of bands on the identification rate for FCGMM and LCGMM recognition models in both clean and noisy environments

Model	SNR	clean	20 dB	15 dB	10 dB	5 dB
FCGMM	2 bands	93.45%	85.55%	72.10%	50.25%	30.76%
	3 bands	91.09%	83.87%	76.64%	60.50%	46.22%
	4 bands	88.07%	81.18%	74.29%	63.03%	43.36%
LCGMM	2 bands	93.28%	86.39%	76.47%	53.78%	28.24%
	3 bands	94.96%	92.10%	86.89%	68.07%	43.53%
	4 bands	94.12%	89.41%	84.87%	71.76%	43.19%

The best identification rate of LCGMM could be achieved in both clean and noisy environments when the number of bands was set to be three. Since the features were extracted from (0-4000), (0-2000) and (0-1000) Hz subbands and the spectra of the subbands overlapped in the lower frequency region (below 1kHz), the success achieved using the MBLPCC features could be attributed to the emphasis on the spectrum of the signal in the low-frequency region.

It was found that increasing the number of bands to more than three for both models not only increased the computation time but also decreased the identification rate. In this case, the signals of the lowest frequency subband were located in the very low frequency region, which put too much emphasis on the lower frequency spectrum of speech. In addition, the number of samples within the lowest frequency subband was so small that the spectral characteristics of speech could not be estimated accurately. Consequently, the poor result in the lowest frequency subband degraded the system performance.

4.3 Comparison with Conventional GMM Models

In this experiment, the performance of the FCGMM and LCGMM models was compared with that of the conventional GMM model using full-band 20 orders LPCC and MFCC features under Gaussian noise corruption. For all the models, the number of mixtures was set to be 50.

Here, the parameters of FCGMM and LCGMM were the same as those discussed in Sect. 4.2 except that the number of bands was set to be three. The experimental results shown in Table 2 indicate that the performance of both GMM recognition models using full-band LPCC and MFCC features was seriously degraded by Gaussian noise corruption. On the other hand, LCGMM achieved the best performance among all the models in both clean and noisy environments, and maintained robustness under low SNR conditions. GMM using full-band MFCC features achieved better performance under clean and 20 dB SNR conditions, but poorer performance under lower SNR conditions, compared with 3-band FCGMM. GMM using full-band LPCC features achieved poorest performance among all the models. Based on these results, it can be concluded that LCGMM is effective in representing the characteristics of individual speaker and is robust under additive Gaussian noise conditions.

Table 2. Identification rates for GMM using full-band LPCC and MFCC features, FCGMM, and LCGMM with white noise corruption

Model \ SNR	Clean	20 dB	15 dB	10 dB	5 dB
GMM using full-band LPCC	88.40%	77.65%	61.68%	35.63%	19.50%
GMM using full-band MFCC	92.61%	85.88%	73.11%	51.60%	32.77%
3-band FCGMM	91.09%	83.87%	76.64%	60.50%	46.22%
3-band LCGMM	94.96%	92.10%	86.89%	68.07%	43.53%

5 Conclusions

In this study, the effective and robust MBLPCC features were used as the front end of a speaker identification system. In order to effectively utilize these multiband speech features, we examined two different approaches. FCGMM combines the cepstral coefficients from each band to form a single feature vector that is used to train GMM. LCGMM recombines the likelihood scores of the independent GMM for each band. The proposed multiband approaches were evaluated using the KING speech database for text-independent speaker identification. Experimental results show that both multiband schemes are more effective and robust than the conventional GMM using full-band LPCC and MFCC features. In addition, LCGMM is more effective than FCGMM.

Acknowledgements

This research was financially supported by the National Science Council (Taipei), under contract number NSC 92-2213-E032-026.

References

1. Atal, B.: Effectiveness of linear prediction characteristics of the speech wave for automatic speaker identification and verification. Acoust. Soc. Amer. J., Vol. 55, (1974) 1304-1312.
2. White, G. M., Neely, R. B.: Speech recognition experiments with linear prediction, bandpass filtering, and dynamic Programming. IEEE Trans. Acoustics, Speech, Signal Processing, Vol. 24, No. 2, (1976) 183-188.
3. Vergin, R., O'Shaughnessy, D., Farhat A.: Generalized mel frequency cepstral coefficients for large-vocabulary speaker-independent continuous-speech recognition. IEEE Trans. Speech and Audio Processing, Vol. 7, No. 5, (1999) 525-532.
4. Lockwood, P., Boudy, J.: Experiments with a nonlinear spectral subtractor (NSS), hidden Markov models and the projection, for robust speech recognition in cars. Speech Commun., Vol. 11, No. 2-3, (1992) 215–228.
5. Furui, S.: Cepstral analysis technique for automatic speaker verification. IEEE Trans. Acoust., Speech, Signal Processing, Vol. 29, No. 2, (1981) 254-272.
6. Soong, F. K., Rosenberg, A. E.: On the use of instantaneous and transitional spectral information in speaker recognition. IEEE Trans. Acoust., Speech, Signal Processing, Vol. 36, No. 6, (1988) 871-879.
7. Hermansky, H., Tibrewala, S., Pavel, M.: Toward ASR on partially corrupted speech. Proc. Int. Conf. Spoken Language Processing, Vol. 1, (1996) 462–465.
8. Mirghafori, N., Morgan, N.: Combining connectionist multi-band and full-band probability streams for speech recognition of natural numbers. Proc. Int. Conf. Spoken Language Processing, Vol. 3, (1998) 743–747.

9. Bourlard, H., Dupont, S.: A new ASR approach based on independent processing and recombination of partial frequency bands. Proc. Int. Conf. Spoken Language Processing, (1996) 426–429.
10. Okawa, S., Bocchieri, E., Potamianos, A.: Multi-band speech recognition in noisy environments. Proc. IEEE ICASSP-98, Vol. 2, (1998) 641–644.
11. Hsieh, C. T., Lai, E., Wang, Y. C.: A robust speaker identification system based on wavelet transform. IEICE Trans. Inf. & Syst., Vol. E84-D, No. 7, (2001) 839-846.
12. Hsieh, C. T., Lai, E., Wang, Y. C.: Robust speech features based on wavelet transform with application to speaker identification. IEE Proceedings – Vision, Image and Signal Processing, Vol. 149, No. 2, (2002) 108-114.
13. Furui, S.: Comparison of speaker recognition methods using statistical features and dynamic features. IEEE Trans. Acoust., Speech, Signal Processing, Vol. 29, No. 3, (1981) 342-350.
14. Poritz, A.: Linear predictive hidden markov models and the speech signal. Proc. IEEE ICASSP-82, Vol. 2, (1982) 1291-1294.
15. Tishby, N. Z.: On the application of mixture AR hidden Markov models to text independent speaker recognition. IEEE Trans. Signal Processing, Vol. 39, (1991) 563-570.
16. Reynolds, D. A., Rose, R. C.: Robust test-independent speaker identification using gaussian mixture speaker models. IEEE Trans. Speech Audio Processing, Vol. 3, No. 1, (1995) 72-83.
17. Miyajima, C., Hattori, Y., Tokuda, K., Masuko, T., Kobayashi, T., Kitamura, T.: Text-independent speaker identification using Gaussian mixture models based on multi-space probability distribution. IEICE Trans. Inf. & Syst., Vol. E84-D, No. 7, (2001) 847-855.
18. Alamo, C. M., Gil, F. J. C., Munilla, C. T., Gomez, L. H..: Discriminative training of GMM for speaker identification. Proc. IEEE ICASSP-96, (1996) 89-92.
19. Pellom, B. L., Hansen, J. H. L.: An effective scoring algorithm for Gaussian mixture model based speaker identification. IEEE Signal Processing Letters, Vol. 5, No. 11, (1998) 281-284.
20. Daubechies, I.: Orthonormal bases of compactly supported wavelets. Commun. Pure Appl. Math., Vol. 41, (1988) 909-996.
21. Godfrey, J., Graff, D., Martin, A.: Public databases for speaker recognition and verification. Proc. ESCA Workshop Automat. Speaker Recognition, Identification, Verification, (1994) 39-42.

Appendix

The low-pass QMF coefficients h_k used in this study are listed in Table 3. The coefficients of the high-pass filter g_k are calculated from h_k coefficients as follows:

$$g_k = (-1)^k h_{n-1-k}, \quad k = 0,1,\cdots,n, \tag{4}$$

where n is the number of QMF coefficients.

Table 3. The used QMF coefficients h_k

h_0	0.766130	h_4	0.032081	h_8	0.008685	h_{12}	0.002187
h_1	0.433923	h_5	0.042068	h_9	0.008201	h_{13}	0.001882
h_2	-0.050202	h_6	-0.017176	h_{10}	-0.004354	h_{14}	-0.001104
h_3	-0.110037	h_7	-0.017982	h_{11}	-0.003882	h_{15}	-0.000927

Selecting Prosody Parameters for Unit Selection Based Chinese TTS

Minghui Dong[1], Kim-Teng Lua[2], and Jun Xu[1]

[1] InfoTalk Technology, Synergy, #01-14, 1 International Business Park, Singapore 609917
{minghui.dong,jun.xu}@infotalkcorp.com
[2] Chinese and Oriental Language Information Processing Society, Incampus Education,
8 Jalan Kilang Timor, #01-02, Kewalram House, Singapore 159305
luakt@colips.org

Abstract. In unit selection text-to-speech approach, each unit is described by a set of parameters. However, which parameters effectively express prosody of speech is a problem. In this paper, we propose an approach to the determination of prosody parameters for unit selection-based speech synthesis. We are concerned about how prosody parameters can correctly describe tones and prosodic breaks in Chinese speech. First, we define and evaluate a set of parameters. Then, we cluster the parameters and select a representative parameter from each cluster. Finally, the parameters are evaluated in a real TTS system. Experiment shows that the selected parameters help to improve speech quality.

1 Introduction

The naturalness of synthesized speech is determined by the richness of prosody contained in the speech. To generate high quality speech, proper prosody should first be generated from input text.

In a text-to-speech (TTS) system, prosody is a set of parameters that describes rhythm, intonation, unit length, and loudness of speech. The main prosody parameters include pitch contour of an utterance, duration of units, and energy of speech of units.

Previous Chinese prosody models for TTS (e.g. chen et al, 1998) predict duration, energy value, and a curve to describe the pitch contour. The parameters are used in speech synthesis process by changing the speech signal. For example, in PSOLA synthesis, lengthening duration is done by inserting more pitch periods; lifting pitch value is done by reducing the offset between the signals to be added up; or changing volume is done by amplifying the amplitude.

Unit selection based synthesis approach (Black and Campbell 1995, Hunt and Black 1996) can generate good speech. However, in a unit selection-based approach, each unit has fixed prosody parameters. The prosody parameters of the unit do not cover the total prosody parameter space continuously. During selection of units, there is a problem on what parameters describe the desired unit.

Previous research (Liu, and Wang, 1998; Chu et al. 2001; Wang et al., 2000; Wu et al, 2001) usually dealt with prosody for unit selection TTS by using some symbolic representations or by defining some simple prosody parameters that describe duration, pitch contour and energy. However, it is unknown whether these parameters are effectively express main prosody properties of speech. In consideration of this, the parameters need to be specially designed for unit selection-based approach.

The main problems in prosody of current Chinese TTS systems include: rigid rhythm, inadequate pause, unclear tone, discontinuity in speech, sudden rising or lowering in pitch, too long or too short sound etc. The specific reasons for these problems are in the following aspects:

- General prosody parameter: Inappropriate pitch, duration, and energy values will lead to sudden rising or lowering in pitch, too long or too short sound, etc.
- Implementation or representation of breaks (prosodic breaks): Inappropriate implementation or inappropriate parametric representation of breaks may result in rigid rhythm, inadequate pause.
- Implementation or representation of tones: Inappropriate implementation or inappropriate parametric representation of tones may result in unclear tone and unclear sound.

Although the prosody parameters are intended to describe all prosody aspects, simply selecting some basic prosody values (duration, mean of pitch, energy) cannot effectively represent prosody. These parameters do not necessarily convey important perceptual information correctly. For example, it is unknown whether the tone and break information are correctly preserved in the parameters. We have to find an approach to the realization of these perceptual effects.

2 Methodology

Our approach to the problem includes the following steps: (1) We first define a set of candidate parameters, which are meant to describe the three aspects of the Chinese prosody problems (general prosody, break and tone). (2) Then we evaluate the parameters to find out whether they are sufficient to express prosody. (3) Next, we use clustering approach to select a set of representative parameters. (4) Finally, we apply the parameters into a real TTS system to evaluate the performance.

2.1 Candidate Prosody Parameters

A summary of all defined parameters for each syllable is as the following:
- Duration: The time length of the syllable.
- EnergyRMS, EnergyMax, EnergySum: RMS Average, Maximum, and Sum of energy of the voice part of the syllable.
- PitchMean: Mean value of pitch of the voiced part of syllable.
- PitchRange: The difference between maximal and minimal values of pitch contour in a syllable.
- PCon0, PCon1, PCon2, PCon3, PCon4, PCon5, PCon6, PCon7, PCon8: The 9 values are evenly sampled values of pitch contour of voiced part of a syllable. For the convenience of later use, we also represent PCon0, PCon4, PCon8 as PitchStart, PitchMiddle, PitchEnd respectively, which are just values of the start point, middle point and end point of the voiced part.
- EnergyStart, EnergyEnd: RMS energy values (with frame of 50 ms) at start and end points of each syllable.
- EnPer1, EnPer2, EnPer3, EnPer4, EnPer5: The values describe 5 percentage points within duration. The 5 points divide EnergySum equally into 6 segments.

Sum of energy for each segment is 1/6 of that of whole syllable. EnPer3 is also represented as EnergyHalfPoint for the convenience of later use.

Among the parameters we defined, each has its main concerns:

- Duration, Energy (EnergyRMS, EnergyMax, EnergySum), and PitchMean are general parameters that determine the global prosody of utterances (although they also have effects on local prosody).
- EnergyStart, EnergyEnd, EnPer1, EnPer2, EnPer3, EnPer4, and EnPer5 together with duration are mainly used to describe boundary effects (i.e. break).
- PCon0, PCon1, PCon2, PCon3, PCon4, PCon5, PCon6, PCon7, PCon8 together with PitchMean and PitchRange are mainly used to describe tones.

2.2 Parameter Evaluation

We have defined the parameters to describe prosody. However, are these parameters sufficient to describe important aspects of Chinese prosody? The two most important prosody properties of Chinese speech we are to realize in speech synthesis are tone and prosodic break. Therefore, we will examine whether the defined parameters are fit for describing them. To simplify the work, we only consider prosodic word break. Therefore, break means prosodic word break in this context. We investigate this by:

- Examining the distribution of the parameters for different tone types and boundary types. We use boxplots to see that the parameters have different distribution for different types of tone and boundary type. Using this way, we make sure that the parameters we will use are relevant parameters to the intended prosodic effects.
- Examining the ability of the parameters for describing tones and breaks from the view of recognition. If a computer can recognize the tones correctly, it is possible that human can easily perceive the tone based on the acoustic properties. We use CART approach for the recognition purpose in the work. Using this way, we make sure that the parameters we use are sufficient to describe the prosodic effects. Details will be described in experiment part.

2.3 Parameter Selection

We have listed all candidate prosody parameters in 2.1 and have confirmed that the defined parameters can describe tone and break in 2.2. However, with so many parameters, it is not efficient to predict all of them because many of them are highly correlated. Therefore, we should choose some representative parameters from all the candidates.

In this work, we use clustering approach to reduce the number of useful parameters. The distance between parameters is calculated based on correlation value between two parameters.

We use absolute correlation distance in the work. The distance is defined as:

$$d_{i,j} = 1 - |r_{i,j}| \qquad (1)$$

where $r_{i,j}$ is the Pearson product moment correlation between variables i and j.

The distance between two clusters is defined as the average distance between a variable in one cluster and a variable in the other cluster. The distance is defined as:

$$D_{k,l} = (\sum_{i=1}^{N_k} \sum_{j=1}^{N_l} d_{i,j})/(N_k N_l) \quad (2)$$

where N_k and N_l are the number of variables in clusters k and l.

Details of parameter selection will be described in experiment part.

3 Experiments

In this part, we first conduct experiments to evaluate the parameters for describing tones and breaks. Then we cluster parameters to select a set of useful parameters. Next, we will look at the properties of the selected parameters. Finally, we will evaluate the parameters in a real TTS system.

Our corpus consists of 31971 Chinese syllables in 3600 utterances, which are read by a professional Chinese speaker.

3.1 Parameters Describing Tone

The acoustic correlate of tone is pitch contour of a syllable in speech. Therefore, pitch related parameters describe tones. To further evaluate the parameters, we use the parameters together with other parameters to predict the tone category. In other words, we are trying to recognize tone type based on the parameters and other possible input. We use CART (Breiman et al, 1984) approach for the recognition. The features for the recognition of tone in this investigation is as the following:

- PitchMean;
- PitchRange;
- Nine sample values from pitch contour: PithchConP0, PitchConP1, PitchConP2, PitchConP3, PitchConP4, PitchConP5, PitchConP6, PitchConP7, PitchConP8;
- EnergyRMS;
- Duration.

Using CART with 10-fold cross validation, we conduct recognition experiments. We find the accuracy of training data is 82.0% and that of testing data is 76.4%. Excluding tone 5, the accuracy of training data is 82.3% and 78.2% respectively.

To understand the accuracy, we conduct a listening test for 200 syllables by 3 persons. Syllables are played one by one to listeners. Listeners are allowed to examine the sound repeatedly. Each person is asked to listen to the 200 syllables and to count the number of tones that can be clearly identified. The result shows that the average percentage of syllables with clear tone is 85.4%. This shows that the accuracy by tone recognition is close to the result of human perception. Therefore, the defined parameters can well describe tone.

3.2 Parameters Describing Break

We examine the parameters that are meant to account for the breaks. We know that at boundary of prosodic units, there are usually lengthen effects. This may lead to a longer duration for a syllable than at non-boundary positions. We define parameters

Duration, EnergyStart, EnergyEnd, EnergyPer1, EnergyPer2, EnergyPer3 (Energy-HalfPoint), EnergyPer4, and EnergyPer5 for boundary effects.

Like what we have done for tone, we also investigate the parameters from recognition view. We investigate the accuracy of predicting the end of prosodic word (EndOfPW) only. The reason is that end syllable (EndOfPW) and start syllable (StartOfPW) of prosodic word always appear as neighbors. The features for this recognition are as the following:

- Duration;
- EnergyMax, EnergySum, EnergyRMS;
- PitchMean, PitchRange;
- EnergyPer1, EnergyPer2, EnergyPer3, EnergyPer4, EnergyPer5.

We find the recognition accuracy for break is 82.0% for training data and 78.2% for testing data. We should note that we deliberately remove the syllable identity in the recognition input. This is to exclude the effect of text information. However, this reduces the accuracy also.

We conducted a listening test for syllables. Syllables are played one by one to listeners. Listeners are allowed to examine the sound repeatedly. Each listening is to judge whether the syllable is an end syllable of prosodic word. 3 persons listened to 200 syllables and achieved an accuracy of 72.1%. This result is even worse than that by break recognition. The reason for this result is that break is prominent only when multiple syllables are placed together, and many of the breaks between syllables sound between break and non-break. The result shows that our recognition rate is sufficiently good. Hence, the parameters help to describe break type.

3.3 Parameter Selection

Since there is redundancy in our candidate parameters, we conduct experiments to select representative parameters from the candidate parameter set. Using clustering approach, we select parameters that have less correlation values between each other. The procedure of clustering is an agglomerative hierarchical method that begins with all parameters separate, each forming its own cluster. In the first step, the two parameters closest together are joined. In the next step, either a third parameter joins the first two, or two other parameters join into a different cluster. This process will continue until all clusters are joined into one. At last, we need to decide the number of clusters.

The clustering process can be shown as in a dendrogram as shown in Figure 1. Figure 2 shows the similarity levels at each step of clustering. The similarity, $s(i,j)$, between two clusters i and j is given by:

$$s(i,j) = 100(1-D(i,j)) \qquad (3)$$

where $D(i,j)$ is the distance between two clusters.

In Figure 2, x-axis is the number of step. y-axis means, at this step, the parameters that have similarities above this value have been combined. In the figure, we can see that there is an abrupt change from similarity 81.4 to 65.7 at step 13. Therefore, we cut the dendrogram at similarity level 80.

Drawing a cutting line on the dendrogram at similarity value 80 in Figure 1, we get the final clusters. The final clusters are shown in Table 1. The table shows the parameters in each cluster. We select one parameter from each cluster as a representa-

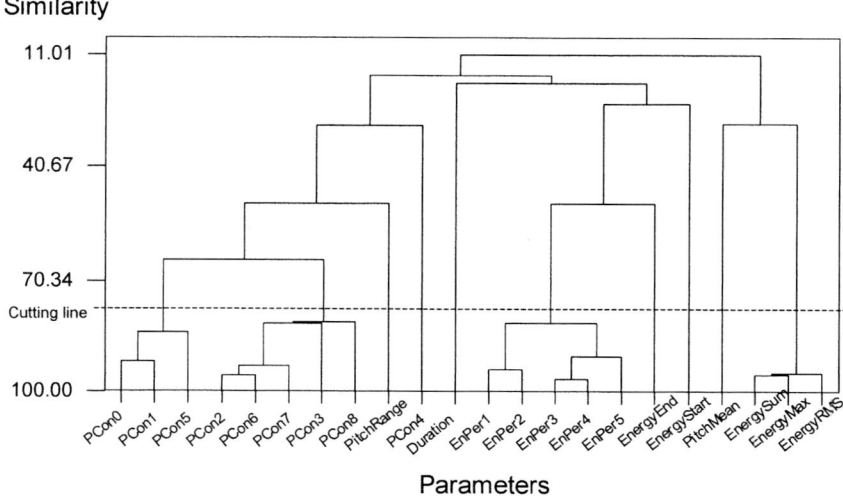

Fig. 1. Dendrogram for clustering parameters

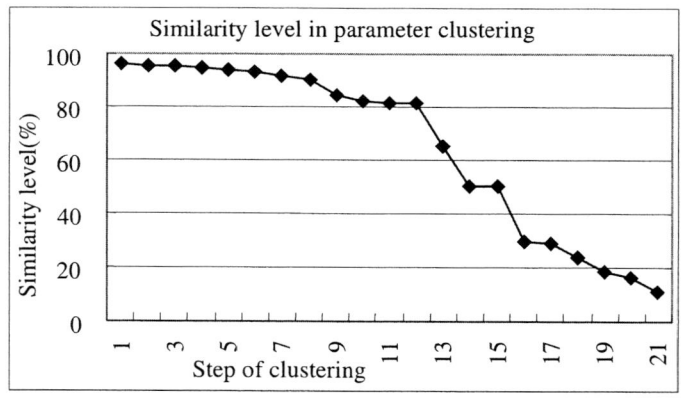

Fig. 2. Similarity level in paramter clustering step

tive of the cluster. The third column is the parameters we finally determined in TTS system.

In the table, we see that PCon0, PCon1 and PCon5 fall in one cluster. We choose Pcon0 (PitchStart) because it is the first value in the contour. Accurately determining this value will help to maintain the prosody smoothness between this syllable and previous syllable in utterance. Pcon4 constitutes a cluster itself. It is coincident that the value is actually the pitch value at the middle point of the contour. PCon2, Pcon3, Pcon6, Pcon7, and Pcon8 belong to one category. We choose Pcon8 (PitchEnd) as representative of this cluster. Selecting this parameter is also to maintain continuous in pitch between two syllables.

Table 1. Final clusters in parameter clustering

Cluster No.	Parameters in the cluster	Selected Parameter
1	Duration	Duration
2	PitchMean	PitchMean
3	PCon0 PCon1 PCon5	Pcon0
4	PCon2 PCon3 PCon6 PCon7 PCon8	Pcon8
5	PCon4	Pcon4
6	EnergySum EnergyMax EnergyRMS	EnergyRMS
7	EnPer1 EnPer2 EnPer3 EnPer4 EnPer5	EnergyHalfPoint
8	PitchRange	Pitchrange
9	EnergyStart	EnergyStart
10	EnergyEnd	EnergyEnd

Table 2. Correlation values between selected parameters

	Duration	PitchMean	PitchCon0	PitchCon4	PitchCon8	PitchRange	EnergyStart	EnergyEnd	EnergyRMS
PitchMean	-0.219								
PitchCon0	0.112	-0.217							
PitchCon4	-0.122	0.191	-0.378						
PitchCon8	-0.086	0.013	-0.572	-0.416					
PitchRange	0.171	-0.105	0.459	0.033	-0.523				
EnergyStart	0.022	-0.122	0.184	-0.087	-0.079	0.09			
EnergyEnd	-0.431	0.370	-0.198	0.016	0.235	-0.154	-0.075		
EnergyRMS	-0.109	0.328	-0.004	-0.006	-0.037	0.127	0.019	0.294	
EnergyPerHalf	-0.174	0.245	-0.235	0.087	0.213	-0.244	-0.262	0.506	-0.130

We also see that the three types of energy values fall into one cluster. We select the RMS energy as their representative.

Parameters EnPer1, EnPer2, EnPer3, EnPer4 and EnPer5 are clustered together. We select the middle value EnPer3 (EnergyHalfPoint) as representative.

We examine the correlation values between the selected parameters. The correlations are shown in Table 2. We see from the table that the highest correlation in absolute value is 0.572. Most correlation values are very low. Therefore, the selected parameters have little redundancy as we expected. These 10 parameters will be used in unit selection process.

3.4 Evaluation in TTS

Models for predicting the parameters are built using CART approach. The predicted parameters are used as part of cost function in a unit selection based TTS system.

To evaluate the accuracy of break and tone in the synthetic speech, we compare the synthesized speech by two kinds of cost functions, which are:

- Method 1: Symbolic representation of tone and break is used in cost function.
- Method 2: Parametric representation (the selected 10 parameters) is used in cost function.

We ask the 20 native speakers to listen to the synthetic speech of 100 utterances (1091 syllables), and count the breaks and tones that are correctly implemented. The accuracy is recorded for comparison. The result is shown in Table 3. From the table, we can see that the accuracies of breaks and tones obtained from the parameters are much better than using symbolic representation. This shows the parameters do help to improve speech quality of TTS.

Table 3. Accuracy of identified breaks and tones in synthesized speech

Method	Break	Tone
Symbolic Prosody	87.2%	86.1%
Prosody Parameter	93.4%	97.1%

4 Conclusion

In this work, we developed an approach to determining prosody parameters for unit selection based approach. First, we define a set of parameters that are useful for describing the perceptual prosody elements. Then, the parameters are evaluated to make sure they are factors to describe prosody. Next, we use clustering approach to cluster the parameters. Finally, the determined parameters are applied to a unit selection based TTS system. The experiment shows the determined parameters help to improve the speech quality for Chinese unit selection based TTS system.

References

1. Chen, S. H.; Hwang, S. H. and Wang, Y. R., An RNN-Based Prosodic Information Synthesizer For Mandarin Text-To-Speech. IEEE Trans. Speech Audio Processing. 6(3), 226-239. 1998.
2. Black, A. and Campbell, N. Optimizing Selection Of Units From Speech Databases For Concatenative Synthesis. In Proceedings of Eurospeech, pages 581–584, 1995.
3. Hunt, J. and Black, A. Unit selection in a concatenative speech synthesis system using a large speech database. In ICASSP-96, volume 1, pages 373–376, Atlanta, Georgia, 1996.
4. Chu, Min; Peng, Hu; Yang, Hongyun and Chang, Eric. Selecting Non-Uniform Units from a Very Large Corpus for Concatenative Speech Synthesizer. ICASSP2001, Salt Lake City, May 7-11, 2001.
5. Wang, Ren-Hua, Ma, Zhongke. Li, Wei, and Zhu, Donglai, A Corpus-Based Chinese Speech Synthesis with Contextual-Dependent Unit Selection. In Proceedings of the International Conference on Spoken Language Processing, (Beijing, China), ICSLP, 2000.
6. Wu, Chung-Hsien; Chen, Jau-Hung. Automatic generation of Synthesis Units and Prosodic Information for Chinese Concatenative Synthesis, Speech Communication, vol. 35, 219-237, 2001.
7. Breiman, L.; Friedman, J.; Olshen, R. and Stone, C. Classification and Regression Trees. Wadsworth and Brooks, Pacific Grove, CA., 1984.

Natural Language Database Access Using Semi-automatically Constructed Translation Knowledge

In-Su Kang[1], Jae-Hak J. Bae[2], and Jong-Hyeok Lee[1]

[1] Div. of Electrical and Computer Engineering, POSTECH and AITrc,
San 31, Hyojadong, Pohang, 790-784, R. of Korea
{dbaisk,jhlee}@postech.ac.kr
[2] School of Computer Engineering and Information Technology,
University of Ulsan, R. of Korea
jhjbae@ulsan.ac.kr

Abstract. In most natural language database interfaces (NLDBI), translation knowledge acquisition heavily depends on human specialties, consequently undermining domain portability. This paper attempts to semi-automatically construct translation knowledge by introducing a physical Entity-Relationship schema, and by simplifying translation knowledge structures. Based on this semi-automatically produced translation knowledge, a noun translation method is proposed in order to resolve NLDBI translation ambiguities.

1 Introduction

Natural language database interfaces (NLDBI) allow users to access database data, by converting natural language questions into formal database queries like SQL using translation knowledge, which defines mappings between natural language questions and target database structures.

Previous approaches can be classified according to the extent that translation knowledge is coupled with linguistic knowledge. Tightly coupled approaches hardwire translation knowledge into linguistic knowledge in the form of semantic grammars [7,12]. This approach severely suffers from the domain portability problem, since in adapting to other domains, new semantic grammars should be created with a considerable effort.

Loosely coupled approaches first analyze questions into a syntactic level [4,8] or logical forms [1,6,13]. In these approaches, translation knowledge is applied after analysis. Thus, transporting to new database domains does not need to change linguistic knowledge at all, only tailoring translation knowledge to new domains. Even in this case, however, it is nontrivial to describe mapping information [2]. In addition, creating such translation knowledge demands considerable human expertise in both NLP and DBMS, and also domain specialties.

In this paper, we try to semi-automatically construct translation knowledge by introducing an approximation of conceptual database schema and by simplifying translation knowledge structures. As far as we know, there were no semi-automatic attempts to obtain translation knowledge.

The remainder of this paper is as follows. Section 2 describes a conceptual schema used in this paper. Section 3 explains translation knowledge construction. Section 4 introduces translation ambiguity problem in NLDBI, and proposes a noun translation strategy as its solution. Experimental evaluation is given in Section 5, and related works and concluding remarks are given in Section 6. In this study, a *domain class* is used to indicate a table or a column in a database, and a *domain class instance* an individual column value.

2 Physical Entity-Relationship (pER) Schema

This paper extracts translation knowledge from a conceptual schema. However, a conceptual database schema is not always available. Moreover, even existing conceptual schemas often lack natural language descriptions. Thus, we define a *physical Entity-Relationship (pER) schema* as an approximation of real conceptual schema. A pER schema is composed of a pER graph and its linguistic descriptions. A pER graph is structurally equivalent to physical database structures, where a node corresponds to a table or a column, and an arc defines a relationship between two tables, or a property between a table and its column. Each node or arc contains linguistic descriptions that are called pER descriptions. There are three kinds of pER descriptions: linguistic name, linguistic definition, and relationship description.

A pER schema is created as follows. First, a physical database schema is automatically generated from a target database by reverse engineering within commercially available database modeling tools. Next, domain experts provide linguistic descriptions for each component of the physical schema according to the following guidelines.

- ✓ Provide a linguistic name in the form of a noun phrase
- ✓ Provide a linguistic definition in the form of a definitional sentence
- ✓ Provide a relationship description in a typical sentence including related domain classes and typical domain predicates

3 Construction of Translation Knowledge

3.1 Class-Referring Translation Knowledge

Definition
Figure 1 shows the whole automatic process of generating translation knowledge from database data and pER descriptions. Class-referring translation knowledge is defined as a set of pairs of C and D, where C is a domain class, and D is a document that contains terms referring to C. D has two types: class document and value document. For each domain class, a class document is obtained by class term extraction from pER descriptions of the domain class. In addition, for each domain class corresponding to a column, a value document is created by n-gram value indexing from column data of the domain class. Finally, these documents are then indexed to create a document collection to be retrieved by the later noun translation module.

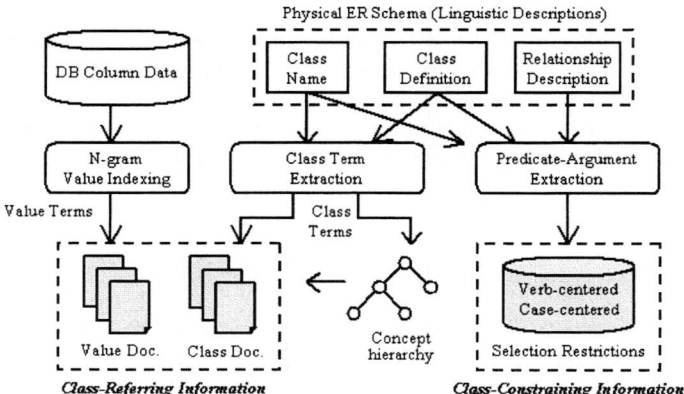

Fig. 1. Translation Knowledge Construction

Class Term Extraction

Ideally, a class document would contain all possible linguistic paraphrases referring to a domain class. However, it is nontrivial to create ideal class documents. So, currently, we rely on conceptual generalization. Each domain class is associated with its concept codes and genus terms, through which a question noun may be related to a domain class. Concept codes and genus terms are obtained from thesauri and machine readable dictionaries (MRD), respectively.

A class document D_c for a domain class C is created as follows. First, assume that an initial class document D_c contains class terms t_i that are extracted from a linguistic name NP_c of a domain class C. NP_c can be obtained from linguistic definitions of pER descriptions as well. A linguistic definition for the domain class C is a definitional sentence, which typically contains a genus term for the linguistic name of C. Genus terms can be easily detected from definitional sentences using a few pattern rules. Next, concept codes s_j of a head of NP_c are inserted into D_c. Then, from MRD, the head t'_k of each definition of each t_i is included into D_c, where t'_k is a genus term of t_i. Finally, the class document D_c is { $t_1, \ldots, t_p, s_1, \ldots, s_q, t'_1, \ldots, t'_r$ }.

Given NP_c, class terms t_i are extracted as follows. In Korean, NP_c is a compound noun, optionally having a Korean genitive case marker 'uy' ('of' in English). Its general form is $(N^+(uy)?\_)^*N^+$ in a regular expression, where _ is a word boundary and N is a simple noun. First, its genitive case markers are deleted, and each of the remaining compound nouns is segmented into a sequence of simple nouns. For example, $N_3N_2uy\_N_1$ is converted into $N_3+N_2+N_1$, where the last noun N_1 is a head of $N_3N_2uy\_N_1$. Then, all possible head-preserving class terms {$N_3N_2N_1, N_2N_1, N_1$} are generated from the simple nouns, since different combinations of the simple nouns may constitute different paraphrases referring to the same domain class.

Generally, when indexing documents in IR, each term is assigned a term weight based on TF (term frequency) and IDF (inversed document frequency) statistics [10]. In NLDBI, however, a set of all terms in class documents constitutes controlled vocabularies, since each term alone can stand for a document that the term belongs to. In addition, since each question noun corresponds to a single term IR query at retrieval in our approach, IDF factor does not influence ranking.

N-Gram Value Indexing
Unlike domain classes, paraphrases for domain class instances tend to occur in the forms of abbreviations, acronyms, or even substrings. For example, *JFK*, *Boeing*, and *MS* can be used in user questions to refer to the following domain class instances '*John F. Kennedy airport*', '*Boeing 737-300*', and '*Microsoft*', respectively. That is, we should support partial matching between question value terms and domain class instances, since question value terms may take different forms from domain class instances stored in a database.

This paper uses n-grams as indexing units of column data. For each column of a target database, n-grams of the column data is generated to create a value document. Among column data, linguistic value terms (e.g. '*John F. Kennedy airport*') are distinguished from alphanumeric value terms (e.g. '*Boeing 737-300*'). In Korean, for a linguistic value term of k syllables, all-length n-grams from bi-grams to k-grams are generated as index terms of a value document in order to prepare all substrings expected as question value terms. However, generating n-grams for alphanumeric terms causes a severe storage problem. The Damerau's method [4] reduces an open-ended set of alphanumeric terms into a closed set of patterns. Thus, it is adopted and slightly modified to include 2-byte characters like Korean. In the modified version, a canonical pattern *P* is defined as follows.

<P> ::= <U>{<U>}
<U> ::= [<C_1>|<C_2>|<N>|<S>][1|2|...|255]

where <C_k> is a sequence of k-byte characters,

<N> is a sequence of numbers,
<S> is a sequence of special characters.

For example, an alphanumeric database value *ST201A*, which is an example of a course identification number, is converted into a canonical pattern, $C_1 2N3C_1 1$. Next, in order to provide partial matching between patterns, a canonical pattern is decomposed into bi-grams. That is, bi-grams $C_1 2N3$ and $N3C_1 1$ are created and stored as index terms in a value document. These pattern-based n-grams may provide considerable storage reduction over storing canonical patterns, since canonical patterns are sliced into smaller n-grams that will have many duplicate n-grams.

3.2 Class-Constraining Translation Knowledge

We define class-constraining translation knowledge as follows.

$$K_v = \{\langle v, C_v \rangle\} \quad K_{cm} = \{\langle cm, C_{cm} \rangle\}$$

K_v is a set of selection restrictions between domain verbs and domain classes. K_{cm} is a set of selection restrictions between surface case markers and domain classes. *v* is a verb appearing in pER descriptions, and C_v is a set of domain classes corresponding to arguments that *v* governs. *cm* is a surface case marker appearing in pER descriptions, and C_{cm} is a set of domain classes corresponding to arguments that *cm* attaches.

K_v and K_{cm} are extracted from predicate-argument pairs that are acquired by parsing pER descriptions. First, each predicate-argument pair is expanded to a triple of <*verb, noun, case marker*>. The *case marker* means a surface case marker of the *noun*. Next, the second term of the triple is replaced by a *domain class* related to the noun, resulting in a new triple <*verb, domain class, case marker*>. The modified triple is further divided into <*verb, domain class*> and <*case marker, domain class*>. Then, by merging a set of <*verb, domain class*> having the same *verb*, K_v is produced. Similarly, K_{cm} is obtained by merging a set of <*case marker, domain class*> having the same *case marker*. K_{cm} will be useful for value terms that correspond to different domain classes according to its case marker.

4 Noun Translation

4.1 Translation Ambiguity

In NLDBI, two types of ambiguities occur when question nouns are translated into domain classes. Class term ambiguity occurs when a class term in a question refers to two or more domain classes. This ambiguity mostly results from general attributes that several domain entities share. For example, a question noun 'address' can refer to any 'address' attribute that the two entities 'customer' and 'employee' have at the same time.

Value term ambiguity occurs when a value term in a question refers to two or more domain class instances or its substrings. Hence, date or numeric expressions almost always cause value term ambiguity. In particular, in an air flight domain, country names or city names will be shared by many domain classes, such as the location of departure and the location of arrival. We try to resolve these two translation ambiguities through a noun translation scheme using the semi-automatically constructed translation knowledge. Noun translation is described in the following.

4.2 Class Retrieval

After question analysis, a user question is analyzed into a set of question nouns and a set of predicate-argument pairs. Noun translation utilizes an information retrieval (IR) framework to translate each question noun into a probable domain class. First, class retrieval converts each question noun into an IR query and retrieves relevant documents. Next, class disambiguation selects likely domain classes among the candidate domain classes retrieved by class retrieval using predicate-argument pairs of the user question.

A question noun may be a class term or a value term, and a value term may be a linguistic value term or an alphanumeric value term. We employ three types of query representations: a conceptual vector for a class term, an all-length n-gram vector for a linguistic value term, and a pattern-based n-gram vector for an alphanumeric value term. It is straightforward to distinguish whether a question noun is an alphanumeric term or not. However, it is nontrivial to distinguish between a class term and a linguistic value term, because many domain-dependent class terms are out-of-vocabulary words. Thus, for a question noun other than an alphanumeric term, class retrieval creates both a conceptual vector query and an all-length n-gram vector query, and retrieves documents for each vector query, and merges the retrieved documents.

For all-length or pattern-based n-gram vector queries, a query-document similarity is calculated using a Formula (1) where $Q = t_1, \ldots, t_i, \ldots, t_n$ is an ngram vector query, and t_i is the i-th ngram of Q, and $W(t_i)$ is a term weight of t_i on a document D.

$$Similarity(Q,D) = \Sigma\ W(t_i)$$

If we simply convert a class term into a single term lexical vector, it may cause a severe word mismatch problem [5]. Thus, the question noun is generalized to concept codes, which are then included in a lexical vector query. Unfortunately, this method may risk obtaining mistaken similarity values if the correct concepts of the two terms are not similar while incorrect concepts of the two terms are similar. However, considering that domain terminologies show marginal sense ambiguities [3], this concern will not be critical. For a conceptual vector query, a query-document similarity is computed using a Formula (2). Compared to the Formula (1), it simply selects the maximum value among weights of each matching term t_i, since each matching term t_i alone can stand for the domain class that t_i belongs to.

$$Similarity(Q,D) = \text{argmax}\ W(t_i)$$

4.3 Class Disambiguation Using Selection Restrictions

Class retrieval reduces the translation equivalents of each question noun to lexically or semantically equivalent domain classes. However, the above two ambiguities still remain after class retrieval. Class disambiguation resolves these ambiguities using class-constraining translation knowledge of K_v and K_{cm}. Disambiguation procedures proceed in two stages as shown in Figure 2.

In the first stage, for each question noun with two or more domain classes after class retrieval, K_v is searched to find a domain verb that is the most similar to the head verb of the question noun. The SIM value between two lexical words is the maximum of concept similarity values between all possible concept pairs of the two lexical words. Let B represent the set of domain classes associated with the domain

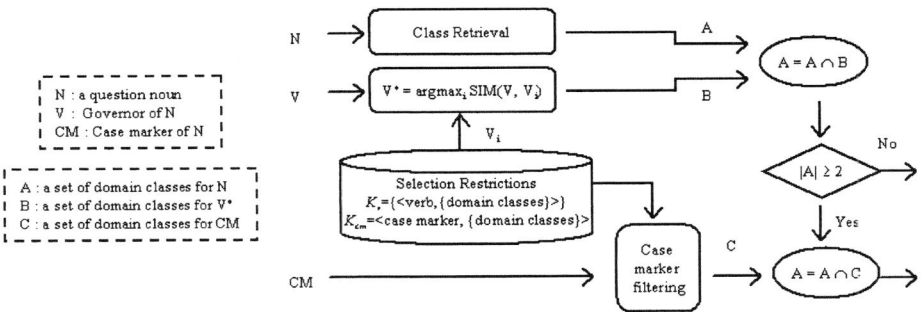

Fig. 2. Disambiguation using Selection Restrictions

verb, and let A be the set of domain classes retrieved by class retrieval for the ambiguous question noun. Then, A is replaced by A intersection B. The effect is to reduce ambiguities by removing from A inconsistent domain classes that is not expected by a governor of the question noun.

If ambiguities of a question noun remain after applying K_v, the second stage is fired, and K_{cm} is searched to find the same surface case marker as that of the question noun. Let C be the set of domain classes associated with the case marker. Then, A is further replaced by A intersection C. The effect is to select from A only the domain classes to which the case marker can attach.

4.4 Class Disambiguation Using Disambiguation Heuristic

Selection restrictions in the previous section cannot resolve all translation ambiguities because of incomplete class-constraining translation knowledge and inherent ambiguities. For example, suppose that an entity 'employee' has an attribute 'salary'. Then, given a question 'What is the salary of Lincoln ?', class retrieval may produce several domain classes for 'Lincoln', including 'customer' and 'employee'. Unfortunately, in this case, there are no selection restrictions to be applied from the predicate-argument information of the question. This section describes a heuristic to deal with the remaining ambiguities.

Generally, there are property-of relationships between an entity and its attributes in a conceptual schema. As a result, it is expected that question words corresponding to an entity and its attributes co-occur within certain restricted syntactic constructions. Hence, an *entity-attribute (EA) heuristic* says that if one of two words in a local context may refer to a set E of entities and the other to a set A of attributes, then the entities that do not have any of their attributes in A are deleted from E, and vice versa. In the above example, among the domain classes for 'Lincoln', an entity 'customer' is deleted, since 'salary' is not its attribute. The EA heuristic is similar to applicability restrictions [11] of NLDBI systems.

Currently, the local context includes a noun phrase and the case of sibling relations having the same governor such as '<u>salary</u> of <u>Lincoln</u>' and '<u>employee</u> who lives in <u>L.A.</u>'. In the last example, 'L.A.' may retrieve the 'address of the employee' and 'address of the customer'. However, the 'address of the customer' will be deleted by the entity-attribute heuristic.

5 Evaluation

Generally, the entire NLDBI system is difficult to evaluate, since it involves a wide range of subsystems. So, this paper focuses on noun translation to evaluate semi-automatically constructed translation knowledge using the following evaluation measures. *Translation ambiguity* is defined as the number of domain classes as translation equivalents for a question noun. *Noun translation precision* (NTP) means the number of correctly translated ones out of the total number of question nouns. *Question translation precision* (QTP) measures the number of questions with all nouns correctly translated out of the total number of questions.

For experiments, a sample database in Microsoft ® Access 2000 is used. This database models a customer-order-product-management domain, and is composed of 8 tables, 74 columns, 8 relationships, and 3211 tuples. A pER schema was created by one author of this paper using the ERwin® modeling tool. For this database, three graduate students were asked to create 60 questions. Ten of these were not used in experiments, since they either ask domain objects that do not exist in the database, or because certain application logics are required to ask the questions. Noun translation is applied to each of 127 question nouns contained in the 50 questions. In this experiment, we did not use MRD genus.

Table 1. Translation Ambiguity and Coverage

		ATA	Value ATA
Class	Lexical	2.42 (89%)	1.79 (100%)
Retrieval	Conceptual	2.39 (96%)	1.79 (100%)
Class disambiguation		1.72 (98%)	1.52 (100%)

Table 1 shows average translation ambiguity (ATA) and coverage after each stage of noun translation. Value ATA means the ATA calculated for only value terms. Specifically, translation ambiguities are averaged for only nouns that retrieve at least one domain class, because it is difficult to estimate the translation ambiguities of the nouns that do not retrieve any domain class. So, at each stage, translation ambiguities are averaged for different numbers of nouns.

The first two rows are the results after applying class retrieval using class-referring translation knowledge. Class-referring translation knowledge is similar to the translation dictionary in machine translation, since it defines a set of domain classes as translation equivalents for a lexical item. So, the figure 2.42 indicates initial translation ambiguity inherent in a translation dictionary for this database domain. Basic class retrieval based on lexical query vector representation covers 113 (89%) out of a total of 127 nouns. The second row corresponds to the performance of class retrieval using conceptual query vector representation. An additional 9 nouns retrieve some domain classes, and ATA reduces to 2.39. However, an initial value ATA is not influenced by conceptual generalization because most domain class instances are not registered in a general concept hierarchy we used.

Class disambiguation further decreases ATA to 1.72. This means that class-constraining translation knowledge has selection restriction capability on ambiguous domain classes of question nouns. Value term ambiguities are also resolved by class disambiguation.

For this experiment, the initial value term coverage is 100% whereas the traditional value dictionary method covers only 90% of question nouns. It shows that n-gram value indexing supports partial matching for database data.

Table 2. Translation Precision

	No Heuristic	Heuristic
NTP	66.13 %	86.29 %
QTP	38 %	72 %

For a user question to be successfully translated into a database query, every noun in a question should be translated into its correct domain class. Therefore, we investigate noun translation precision (NTP) and question translation precision (QTP). Without heuristic application, the results are disappointing, as shown in Table 2. However, when we apply the entity-attribute heuristic to 20 questions containing ambiguous question nouns after noun translation, the QTP performance improves significantly. Only 3 of 20 questions failed to generate the correct database query. So, the heuristic provides a promising post-processing of noun translation.

6 Related Work and Conclusion

Meng et al. [9] proposed a similar IR approach. However, our approach mainly differs from theirs in terms of the following three points. First, they do not address the n-gram value indexing that is critical for practical NLDBI systems. Second, our disambiguation strategy in noun translation relies on linguistically-motivated selection restrictions that are extracted from predicate-argument pairs of domain verbs. Instead, Meng and Chu [9] use neighboring words as disambiguation constraints, because their method does not perform any syntactic analysis. Finally, our IR model incorporates a lexical or conceptual match, but their model depends on a purely lexical match.

In this paper, we proposed a semi-automatic construction method of translation knowledge to deal with the domain portability problem. First, we defined a physical Entity-Relationship (pER) schema, which is manually created from a target database by domain experts. In addition, we simplified translation knowledge into two structures: class-referring documents and class constraining selection restrictions. These translation knowledge is automatically extracted from the natural language descriptions of the pER schema. Then, a noun translation strategy was proposed using class retrieval and class disambiguation. Experiments show the performance level that an NLDBI system can acquire through the automation of translation knowledge acquisition.

Acknowledgements

This work was supported by the KOSEF through the Advanced Information Technology Research Center (AITrc) and by the BK21 Project.

References

1. Androutsopoulos, I. 1993. Interfacing a Natural Language Front-End to Relational Database. *Master's thesis,* Technical Report 11, Department of Artificial Intelligence, University of Edinburgh.
2. Androutsopoulos, I., Ritchie, G.D., and Thanisch, P. 1995. Natural Language Interfaces to Databases – An Introduction. *Natural Language Engineering,* 1(1):29-81.
3. Copeck, T., Barker, K., Delisle, S., Szpakowicz, S., and Delannoy, J.F. 1997. What is Technical Text?. *Language Sciences* 19(4):391-424.

4. Damerau, F. 1985. Problems and Some Solutions in Customization of Natural Language Database Front Ends. *ACM Transactions on Office Information Systems* 3(2):165-184.
5. Furnas, G.W., Landauer, T.K., Gomez, L.M., and Dumais, S.T. 1987. The vocabulary problem in human-system communication. *Communications of the ACM* 30(11):964-971.
6. Grosz, B.J., Appelt, D.E., Martin, P.A., and Pereira, F.C.N. 1987. TEAM: An Experiment in the Design of Transportable Natural-Language Interfaces. *Artificial Intelligence* 32(2):173-243.
7. Hendrix, G.G., Sacerdoti, D., Sagalowicz, D., and Slocum, J. 1978. Developing a Natural Language Interface to Complex Data. *ACM Transactions on Database Systems* 3(2) 105-147.
8. Lee, H.D., and Park, J.C. 2002. Interpretation of Natural language Queries for Relational Database Access with Combinatory Categorial Grammar. *International Journal of Computer Processing of Oriental Languages* 15(3):281-304.
9. Meng, F., and Chu, W.W. 1999. Database Query Formation from Natural Language using Semantic Modeling and Statistical Keyword Meaning Disambiguation. *Technical Report,* CSD-TR 990003,University of California, Los Angeles.
10. Salton, G., and McGill, M.J. 1983. *An Introduction to Modern Information Retrieval*, McGraw-Hill.
11. Wallace, M. 1984. *Communicating with Databases in Natural Language.* Chichester, England:Ellis Horwood
12. Waltz, D.L. 1978. An English Language Question Answering System for a Large Relational Database. *Communications of the ACM* 21(7):526-539.
13. Warren, D., and Pereira, F. 1982. An Efficient Easily Adaptable System for Interpreting Natural Language Queries. *Computational Linguistics* 8(3-4):110-122.

Korean Stochastic Word-Spacing with Dynamic Expansion of Candidate Words List

Mi-young Kang, Sung-ja Choi, Ae-sun Yoon, and Hyuk-chul Kwon

Korean Language Processing Lab, School of Electrical & Computer Engineering,
Pusan National University, San 30, Jangjeon-dong, 609-735, Busan, Korea
{kmyoung,heya5,asyoon,hckwon}@pusan.ac.kr
http://klpl.re.pusan.ac.kr/

Abstract. The main aim of this work is to implement stochastic Korean Word-Spacing System which is equally robust for both inner-data and external-data. Word-spacing in Korean is influential in deciding semantic and syntactic scope. In order to cope with various problem yielded by word-spacing errors while processing Korean text, this study (a) presents a simple stochastic word-spacing system with only two parameters using relative word-unigram frequencies and odds favoring the inner-spacing probability of disyllables located at the boundary of stochastic-based words; (b) endeavors to diminish training-data-dependency by dynamically creating candidate words list with the longest-radix-selecting algorithm and (c) removes noise from the training-data by refining training procedure. The system thus becomes robust against unseen words and offers similar performance for both inner-data and external-data: it obtained 98.35% and 97.47% precision in word-unit correction from the inner test-data and the external test-data, respectively.

1 Introduction

When words are incorrectly spaced in Korean text, linguistic errors and ambiguities occurs. A word is defined in the present paper as a spacing unit not taking into account their linguistic function. Korean language processing is performed on a morpheme basis rather than that of a word because Korean shows predominance of agglutinative-morphology. This characteristic induces a higher difficulty of processing Korean language than a language that shows predominance of inflectional- or isolated-morphology, especially in implementing an automatic word-spacing. Word spacing in Korean is influential in deciding semantic and syntactic scope. Word-spacing rule is regularized in 'Revised Korean Spelling System and Korean Standard Language'[1]. Moreover, word-spacing can be optional in numerous cases in Korean, and this makes more intricate processing Korean text. The spacing error represents second majority of the erroneous words that we can encounter while processing Korean text: it takes up about 23.84 percent according to the statistic result of a previous work. [3]

---

[1] The regulation is announced by the Ministry of Education of Korea and came into effect in March, 1989.

This study presents a simple stochastic word-spacing system. An optimal stochastic model should know to provide a method for (a) diminishing data-dependency and (b) removing noise from the training-data in order to cope with training-data-dependency so that they do not create an overhead for the system. In this view, this paper proposes a stochastic model with only two parameters using syllable bigram and word frequencies. And it endeavors to (a) diminish data-dependency by creating candidate words to expend stochastic candidate words with the longest-radix-selecting algorithm and (b) remove noise from the training-data by refining training procedure. For this objective, this paper is composed of five sections. In section 2, we present studies related to the automatic Korean word-spacing method. Section 3 describes simple stochastic-word spacing model with syllable n-gram and word statistics for word-spacing-error correction. In section 4, the stochastic word-spacing system's performance will tested according training-data processing and candidate words list expansion. In the section 5, conclusions and suggestions for future studies will be made.

2 Word-Spacing in Korean and Related Studies

2.1 Word-Spacing in Korean

Word spacing in Korean defines part of speech and grammaticality of a sentence. The form *ba* can occupy the same syntactic position with other nouns and it can follow a verb with relative ending *-n*. The form *-nba* in the following sentence (s2) is a complex ending in which there is no space[2].

(s1) hwaginha-n # ba # eobs-da   to verify-Rel /thing /to not be-End "We haven't verified it"
(s2) hwaginha-nba # sasili-da   to verify-Cond /to be true-End "We have verified it and it is true"

The sentence (s3) shares the same verb *eobs-* with (s1). This verb needs an argument.

(s3) * hwaginha-nba # eobs-da   to verify-Cond /to not be-End

The sentence (s3) is judged as ungrammatical because of it does not provides an argument such as *ba*. Our previous rule-based approaches resolve this problem considering linguistic information of two constituents of a sentence.

2.2 Related Studies

A rule-based system can define the word-spacing correctness of the sentence such as (s1), (s2) and (s3) by examining the relation between a current word to be processed and another word. The system triggers parsing from current word under checking until its eventual dependent (i.e. an element selected by sub-categorization of the verb) on the left hand side. In the sentence (s3), the intransitive verb *eobs-* cannot find

---

[2] #: space (word boundary); -: morphological boundary; *: unacceptable sentence; Cond : condition ending; End : ending; Rel: relative ending.

a noun, which can be its argument. Thus the sentence to which they belong is judged as unacceptable. [3] This rule- and knowledge-based approach has shown a high precision ration of spacing-error correction (98.01% [2]) in processing word-spacing using linguistic knowledge. Nevertheless it is undeniable that rule- and knowledge-approaches reveals a disadvantage that considerable quantity of language has to be treated without the possibility of expanding this knowledge base. Furthermore, it requires a significant set-up time. In order to cover these disadvantages, several stochastic-based models have been proposed such as Kang et al. [5], Lee et al. [7], etc.

For the first, space insertion is estimated by considering left-, right- and inside-space probabilities extracted from the raw corpus. The experiment which has been performed with 156,487 disyllables using by space insertion probabilities shows a 97.7% syllable-unit accuracy. This study does not provide word-unit precision. Lee et al. [7] reconstitutes the model of Kang et al. [5] and obtain 76.71 and 67.80 word-unit precision and recall, respectively. Lee et al. [7] treated word-spacing problems such as POS tagging, using a hidden-Markov model. The probability of a current tag ti conditionally depends on the previous K spacing tags (space and no space) and the previous J syllables. The word-spacing model, this study thus propose, is denoted by $\wedge(T(K:J), S(L:I))$. The values of K, J, L, and I are tolerated until 2, as $0 \le K, J, L, I \le 2$, in order to avoid the data sparseness by considering enough context. Using the model $\wedge(T(2:2), S(1:2))$ which regards syllable tri-gram (current tag and previous two syllables), the study obtained the best results: 93.06% word-unit spacing precision.

The stochastic method is revealed to have a strong training-data-dependency and data sparseness. Especially in an agglutinative language as Korean, there is considerable risk in using syllabic statistics for the right-hand boundary of a word because of data sparseness. As we can see in Lee et al. [7], one of the method that a stochastic study can adopt to cope with the data sparseness, is to augment parameters for considering larger context. Nevertheless we cannot increase excessively parameters because of the system load. This study presents a simple stochastic word-spacing system. Therefore, this paper proposes a simple stochastic model with only two parameters using syllable bigram and word frequencies.

3 Simple Stochastic Word-Spacing Algorithm

A simple stochastic spacing algorithm finds a sentence composed of possible word set:

$$S = \{w_1, w_2, \cdots, w_k\} \quad (1)$$

S: sentence; W_k: word located between $k\text{-}1^{th}$ and k^{th} spacing locations.

Our system define the optimal word set using two parameters: (a) the probability of a kth word probability, $p(w_k)$, and (b) the odds favoring the inner-spacing (*OfI*) of a given disyllable (x,y), located both-side of the candidate k^{th} word boundary. The sentence with the most probable word spacing is estimated by using maximum likelihood estimator:

$$\arg\max_S \left[\prod_{k=1}^{n} P(w_k) \bullet OfI((x,y)_k) \right] \quad (2)$$

The computation of logarithms of equation (2) avoids underflow, and that multiplication of *OfI* by the exponent of a power *m* produces the best performance.

$$\arg\max_S \sum_{k=1}^{n} \{\log P(w_k) + m \log OfI((x,y)_k)\} \text{ where, } m = 2.42 \quad (3)$$

The kth word probability, which means the probability that a sequence of syllables could be a possible word, is obtained with relative frequencies of kth word in the training-data.

$$P(w_k) = \frac{freq(w_k)}{\sum_{k=1}^{n} freq(w_k)} \quad W_k: \text{ any word which is seen in the training-data} \quad (4)$$

The *OfI* of a given disyllable at both-side of the candidate k^{th} word boundary, that is $OfI((x,y)_k)$, is estimated by the rate of the inner-spacing probability of the disyllable, [i.e. $p((x\#y)_k)$], compared to the rate of no-inner-spacing probability [i.e. $1 - p((x\#y)_k)$, that is $p((xy)_k)$]:

$$OfI((x,y)_k) = \frac{P((x\#y)_k)}{1 - P((x\#y)_k)} \quad (5)$$

'#': the candidate k^{th} word boundary
$(x,y)_k$: adjacent disyllable at both-side of the candidate k^{th} word boundary.

We need a special-value assignment at the end of a sentence, as there is no right-side syllable of a possible word boundary *k*.

$$\arg\max_S \sum_{k=1}^{n} \left\{ \log P(w_k) + m \log \left[\frac{P((x\#y)_k)}{1 - P((x\#y)_k)} \right] \right\} \quad (6)$$

where, $m = 2.42$; if $k = n$, then $p((x\#y)_k) = 0.5$.

The Inner-spacing probability can be formulated as following using disyllable's relative frequency in the training-data (the frequency is sorted according to whether each syllable of the pair is spaced or not).

$$P((x\#y)) = \frac{freq(x\#y)}{freq(xy) + freq(x\#y)} \quad (7)$$

4 Trainings and Experiments

In the previous section we saw that our system define the optimal word set using two parameters: (a) the probability of a kth word probability, $p(w_k)$, and (b) the odds favoring the inner-spacing (*OfI*) of a given disyllable (*x,y*), located both-side of the candidate k^{th} word boundary. For the first experiment, the word probability and disyllable's statistic are extracted from the training-data made of a newspaper of 2 years' worth (CA). Disyllable frequencies are sorted according to whether it has inner space or not (i.e. (x#y), (xy)). And we have processed the data trough two steps. The following table shows the change of the total number of training corpus according to processing step.

Table 1. Corpus-A According to Processing Step

Training-data	Unit		N° of Type	N° of Token
Raw	Word unigram		1,654,088	18,996,289
	Syllable	x#y	382,784	17,226,420
	Bigram	xy	231,842	40,302,545
First Step	Correction		410,120	603,119
	Word unigram		1,564,071	18,961,913
	Syllable	x#y	390,689	17,569,271
	Bigram	xy	224,094	38,928,698
Second Step	Correction		740	849
	Word unigram		1,563,864	18,959,461
	Syllable	x#y	390,658	17,566,870
	Bigram	xy	224,059	38,921,512

For the test our word-spacing system's performance, we provide two test-data: (a) the inner test-data extracted from training-data, corpus-A, and (b) the external test-data extracted from Sejong Project's raw corpus.

Table 2. Test Data-1

Test Data	N° of Sentences	N° of Words	N° of Syllables
Inner	2,000	25,020	103,196
External	2,000	13,971	40,353

4.1 Experiment-1: Stochastic Words List

The system test is preceded by removing spaces from the input test-data and using following four kinds of evaluation measures: (a) syllable-unit precision, P_{syl}; (b) word-unit recall, R_w; (c) word-unit precision, P_w: and (c) Sentence-unit precision, P_S.

$$P_w = \frac{Correctly\ spaced\ words}{Total\ spaced\ words\ by\ the\ system} \times 100\ (\%) \quad R_w = \frac{Correctly\ spaced\ words}{Total\ words\ in\ test\ data} \times 100\ (\%)$$

$$P_{syl} = \frac{Correctly\ spaced\ syllables}{Total\ spaced\ syllables\ by\ the\ system} \times 100\ (\%) \quad P_S = \frac{Correctly\ spaced\ sentences}{Total\ spaced\ setences\ by\ the\ system} \times 100\ (\%)$$

The result of applying the equation (6) with stochastic information from the training-data is shown in the following table.

Table 3. Result with stochastic words list from Corpus-A (%)

Training-data	Test-data	R_w	P_w	P_{syl}	P_S
Raw	Inner	86.97	93.00	97.77	39.40
	External	89.22	86.88	96.62	59.65
1st Step	Inner	97.34	98.07	99.44	84.20
	External	91.74	88.91	97.17	65.70
2nd Step	Inner	97.38	98.09	99.45	84.40
	External	92.04	89.09	97.23	66.15

As shown in the Table 3, the performance changes dramatically according to the degree of training-data's edition. These changes are illustrated in the following Figure.

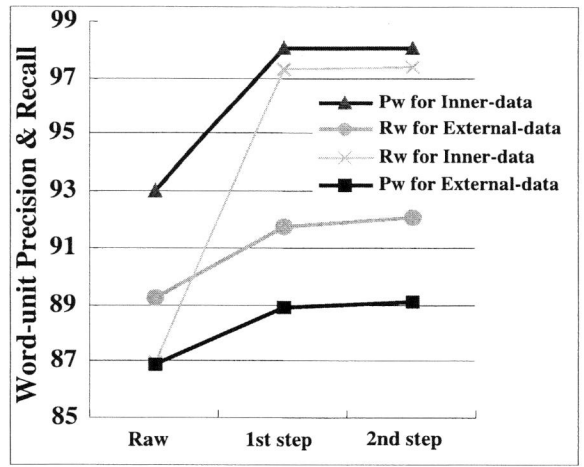

Fig. 1. Performance Change According to Training-data Edition

Nevertheless, the above results shows the stochastic method have a strong data sparseness and training-data-dependency. The system produces high precision for inner test-data (i.e. P_w = 98.09%), while the precision for external test-data becomes lower for the external test-data (i.e. P_w = 89.09%).

4.2 Experiment-2: Stochastic Words List Expansion

As the first attempt to overcome data sparseness, we have expanded stochastic words list from larger training-data. The word probability and disyllable's statistic are extracted from the training-data containing 33,643,884 word-tokens, made up of articles of two different newspaper companies ([A] newspaper - 2 years' worth; [B] newspaper - 1 year's worth) and TV news scripts ([C] news scripts of two broadcastings - 3 years' worth).

Table 4. Stochastic Words List Expansion

Training-data	Unit		N° of Type	N° of Token
A+B+ C	Word		1,949,866	33,641,511
	Syllable	x#y	474,495	31,195,735
		xy	253,935	66,062,670

For the test, provide two test-data are provided: (a) the inner test-data was extracted according to the same distribution ratio as a given corpus in the whole training-data (i.e. A [56%], B [28%], C [16%]), and (b) the external test-data from Sejong Project's raw corpus.

Table 5. Test Data-2

Test Data	N° of Sentences	N° of Words	N° of Syllables
Inner	2,000	17,396	65,483
External	2,000	13,971	40,353

Table 6. Result of Stochastic Words List Expansion (%)

Training-Data	Test-Data	R_w	P_w	P_{syl}	P_S
Stochastic-expansion	Inner	97.91	98.21	99.48	87.40
	External	93.70	90.96	97.78	71.00

The system's performance improved both data (their ameliorations of word-unit-correction precision are 0.12% and 1.87%, respectively) but the data sparseness is still remained with stochastic words list expansion: there is still a great discrepancy between the inner test-data's performance (i.e. P_w = 98.21%), and external data's (i.e. P_w = 90.96%).

4.3 Experiment-2: Dynamic Expansion with the Longest-Radix-Selecting Algorithm

As the second attempt to remove data-dependency, our present system expends dynamically stochastic words list with the longest-radix-selecting algorithm. This method dynamically searches the longest radix and aids it among possible k^{th} word with heuristic probability value (1.0/1billion). As the system dynamically provides candidate word, it does not burden system creating overhead.

Table 7. Result of Dynamic Expansion (%)

Training-Data	Test-Data	R_w	P_w	P_{syl}	P_S
Stochastic-expansion	Inner	97.90	98.35	99.50	88.00
	External	97.84	97.47	99.32	90.35

The Table 7 shows the performance improves significantly for the external data compared to the result of experiment with stochastic words list of Table 3 the amelioration of word-unit-correction precision for the external test-data was 6.51% with dynamic-expansion of candidate words list with the longest-radix-selecting algorithm. The encouraging effect is that the performance for the inner-data remains constant with this strategy. The Figure 2 shows performance changes between stochastic words list expansion (Table 6) and dynamic-expansion of candidate words list (Table 7).

The system thus becomes robust against unseen words. Similar performance is observed for the inner- and external-data. Sentence-unit precision is slightly lower for inner-data (88%) then external-data (90.35%). This is because the length of the sentences of the inner-data is longer then that of external-data. A word of one sentence incorrectly spaced influences sentence-unit precision. If the sentence is long, this incorrect spacing impacts performance with high relative importance.

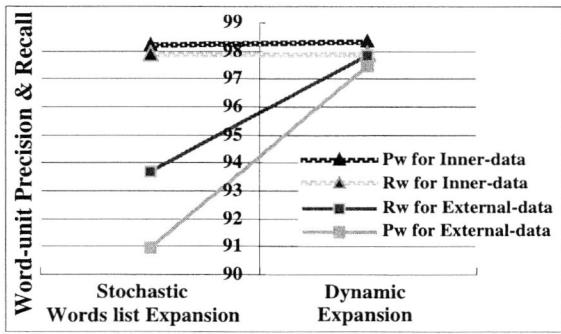

Fig. 2. Performance Change According to Dynamic Expansion

5 Conclusion and Further Studies

The word spacing-error represents second majority of the erroneous words in Korean text. Resolving word-spacing problem constitutes one of the main tasks for while processing Korean text. In order to cope with this problem, this paper presented a simple stochastic word-spacing system with only two parameters using syllable bigram and word frequencies. It (a) diminished training-data-dependency by dynamically expanding words list and (b) removed noise from the training-data by refining training procedure. The dynamic-extension of words list improves dramatically the system performance without creating overhead. The amelioration of word-unit-correction precision for the external test-data was 6.51% with dynamic-expansion of words list compared to the system with only stochastic words list. Similar performance guaranteed for both inner-data and external-data: it obtained 98.84% recall and 97.47% precision in word-unit correction from the external-data.

Though our system efficiently copes with data-sparseness proper to a stochastic mode and becomes thus robust against unseen words, we should investigate further for developing to deal effectively with the language productivity. This is especially true with Korean morphology, where various suffixes are commonly attached to the ends of lexical stems. Also there still remains a limit that a statistical method could never completely overcome. That is the statistic- and linguistic-ambiguities encountered while processing Korean text. The first consist in the fact that many words appear with the same probabilities. In that case, morpho-syntactic boundaries overlap each other, and the stochastic method would assign them the same value. The second, linguistic ambiguities, which produce doubtfulness or uncertainty in semantic- and syntactic-interpretation, can only be resolved by considering enough context of the word under checking. Therefore, we should investigate an efficient guessing-algorithm for unseen words, and develop the optimal combining algorithm between the statistical spacing method and the rule based spacing method in order to resolve stochastic- and linguistic-ambiguities.

Acknowledgements

This work was supported by National Research Laboratory Program (Contract Number: M10203000028-02J0000-01510).

References

1. Chung, Y.M. and Lee, J.Y.: Automatic Word-segmentation at Line-breaks for Korean Text Processing, *Proceedings of 6th Conference of Korean Society for Information Management* (1999) 21-24
2. Kang, M.Y. and Kwon, H.CH.: Improving Word Spacing Correction Methods for Efficient Text Processing, *Proceedings of the Korean Information Science Society*, (B) 30. 1 (2003) 486-488
3. Kang, M.Y., Park, S.H., Yoon, A.S. and Kwon, H.CH.: Potential Governing Relationship and a Korean Grammar Checker Using Partial Parsing. *Lecture Note in Computer Sience*, IEA/AIE (2002) 692-702
4. Kang, S.S.: Automatic Segmentation for Hangul Sentences, *Proceeding of the 10th Conference on Hangul and Korean Information Processing* (1998) 137-142
5. Kang, S.S. and Woo, C.W.: Automatic Segmentation of Words Using Syllable Bigram Statistics. *Proceedings of 6th Natural Language Processing Pacific Rim Symposium* (2001) 729-732
6. Kim, S.N., Nam, H.S. and Kwon, H.CH.: Correction Methods of Spacing Words for Improving the Korean Spelling and Grammar Checkers, *Proceedings of 5th Natural Language Processing Pacific Rim Symposium* (1999) 415-419
7. Lee, D.K., Lee, S.Z., Lim, H.S. and Rim, H.CH.: Two Statistical Models for Automatic Word Spacing of Korean Sentences, *Journal of KISS(B): Software and Applications*, 30. 4 (2003) 358~370
8. Manning, C.D. and Schütze H.: Foundations of Statistical Natural Language Processing, The MIT Press, Cambridge London (2001)
9. Sim, CH.M. and Kwon, H.CH.: Implementation of a Korean Spelling Checker Based on Collocation of Words, *Journal of KISS(B): Software and Applications*, 23. 7 (1996) 776-785
10. Sim, K.S.: Automated Word-Segmentation for Korean Using Mutual Information of Syllables, *Journal of KISS(B): Software and Applications*, 23. 9 (1996) 991-1000
11. Yoon, K.S., Kang, M.Y. and Kwon, H.C.: Improving Word Spacing Correction Methods Using Heuristic Clues, Proceedings of the EALPIIT2003 (2003) 5-11

You Don't Have to Think Twice if You Carefully Tokenize

Stefan Klatt and Bernd Bohnet

Institute for Intelligent Systems
University of Stuttgart
Universitätsstr. 38
70569 Stuttgart
{klatt,bohnet}@iis.uni-stuttgart.de

Abstract. Most of the currently used tokenizers only segment a text into tokens and combine them to sentences. But this is not the way, we think a tokenizer should work. We believe that a tokenizer should support the following analysis components in the best way it can.

We present a tokenizer with a high focus on transparency. First, the tokenizer decisions are encoded in such a way that the original text can be reconstructed. This supports the identification of typical errors and – as a consequence – a faster creation of better tokenizer versions. Second, all detected relevant information that might be important for subsequent analysis components are made transparent by XML-tags and special information codes for each token. Third, doubtful decisions are also marked by XML-tags. This is helpful for off-line applications like corpora building, where it seems to be more appropriate to check doubtful decisions in a few minutes manually than working with incorrect data over years.

1 Introduction

A tokenizer has two important properties. First, it is the only component that has to be used by every NLP application that involves an analysis task. Second, it is always used in the beginning of the analysis process.

Errors made by a tokenizer could rarely be corrected in the following analysis stages. Information that will be detected by a tokenizer and will not be made transparent could lead to repeated redundant processing of the same task. Sometimes it will make the decision more difficult as the following example shows.

In German texts, a comma has not always the reading of a comma. In (1), the first comma represents a beginning quotation mark (inside surrounding quotation marks). In English texts, the same problem occur with apostrophs as (2) shows. But a comma or an apostroph in such a context could also represent the usual reading due to spelling errors (cf. (3)).

(1) "Das Motto ‚One man, one vote' erschallte."
(2) "The motto 'One man, one vote' rang out."
(3) Madonna ,Kylie and Britney came to Hainan.

So, splitting up the comma from the rest of the token is not enough, if we do not want to create a very hard or even unsolvable disambiguation problem for later analysis stages like tagging or parsing as illustrated in (4).

(4)　Das Motto , One man , one vote ' erschallte .

In section 2, we consider the processing strategies and the output of most of the currently used tokenizers. We show the limitations of such systems for distinct text phenomena and present our solutions to solve these problems. In section 3, we describe the architecture of our tokenizer. In section 4, the results of our tokenizer tested on a small newspaper corpus are presented.

2　What Is and What Could Be

Most of the currently used tokenizers only segment a continuous text into discontinuous tokens and combine them to sentences. Very seldom, we find systems like the LT TTT tokenisation tool (Grover et al, 2000) that marks up a text with more information. LT TTT allows the pipelinig of tools that can add, modify or remove some piece of mark-up.

For a few tokenizers that only do a sentence boundary recognition, impressive high accuracy rates $\geq 99{,}5\%$ are reported in literature (e.g. (Mikheev, 2000), (Schmid, 2000)). Both systems consider the period disambiguation as a tagging problem and are statistically-based. On the other hand, we also find rule-based systems, where mostly a regular grammar is combined with word abbreviation lists like the *Alembic* Workbench with a reported accuracy rate of 99,1% (Aberdeen et. al, 1995). But, if we look at the text in (5), we see the limitations of such systems. Usual tokenizers split up this text into two sentences – each containing one quotation mark (cf. (6)), what is not very helpful for the following analysis tasks.

(5)　"Inflation expectations have fallen further. The external sector continues to perform well," Central Bank said.

(6)　`<s> " Inflation expectations have fallen further . </s>`
　　`<s> The external sector continues to perform well " ,`
　　`Central Bank said . </s>`

Looking more carefully at the punctuation mark constellation in (5), we are able to generate the output in (7). The two quotation marks can be analyzed as an utterance consisting of more than one sentence (tag `uts`)[1], in which the last sentence doesn't end with a sentence delimiter mark (tag `swpm`). The domain after the second quotation mark was annotated as a matrix clause – signalling that the missing sentential complement of the verb *say* must be the previous `uts`-unit. Finally, we combine the `uts`- and `mc`-unit to a `mcuts`-unit and annotate this domain with a corresponding tag (`mcuts`).

---

[1] At the moment, our annotated tags are not fully compatible with the recommendations of the *Text Encoding Initiative* (TEI) (Sperberg, 2003). The main reason for that is that the TEI tags only build a small subset of our tags. In the near future, we plan to substitute some of our tags with the corresponding TEI tags as far as possible.

(7)   `<mcuts> <uts> `` <s> Inflation expectations have fallen further . </s> <swpm> The external sector continues to perform well </swpm> '' </uts> , <mc> Central Bank said . </mc> </mcuts>`

In (7), we also modified two of the original tokens. Instead of using the given ambiguous quotation mark symbols, we substituted them by unambiguous symbols of the same kind, what is very helpful in the case of ill-formed sentences (cf. (30) and (31)). In a similar case – the occurences of quotation marks inside surrounding quotation marks in German – we prefer another solution. In (8) we have a comma representing a beginning quotation mark and an apostroph representing the corresponding ending quotation mark. Instead of substituting these tokens by an unambiguous representation, we mark these readings by assigning the tag `<sqm>` to it as shown in (9).

(8)   "Früher sagten sie nein zum Beitritt, heute sagen sie ‚Ja, aber'."
        "Earlier they said No to the joining, today they say 'Yes, but'."
(9)   `<ut> ,, <s> Früher sagten sie nein zum Beitritt , heute sagen sie <sqm> , Ja , aber ' </sqm> . </s> '' </ut>`

Another huge problem for usual tokenizers are constructions like the ones in (10). Most tokenizers separate the first quotation mark without considering the context of the corresponding quotation mark. This will usually lead to a representation like the one in (11). In (12), we see the output our tokenizer produces by annotating the relevant token forms by the tags `<bqm-in-word>` and `<bqm-in-mwe>`. The first one marks a compositum, the second one a multi word expression (MWE), where all parts except of the head noun are written in quotation marks.

(10)   "Top"-Hit, "Top 10"-Hit
(11)   " Top"-Hit , " Top 10"-Hit
(12)   `<bqm-in-word> ,, Top '' - Hit </bqm-in-word> ,`
        `<bqm-in-mwe> ,, Top 10 '' - Hit </bqm-in-mwe>`

The representation in (11) has also the disadvantage that we usually don't receive a reading for tokens like *10"-Hit* in a subsequent lexical lookup. A lexical lookup will be unproblematic for the six tokens *,, Top 10 " - Hit* in (12). After the lexical lookup, we can transform this representation to its original form, if we would do this. In (12), we also made a token separation triggered by an element, that wasn't positioned at one of the edges of a token. We do such a separation not only for special constellations with quotation marks, but also for other punctuation marks (e.g. periods (cf. (13)-(16)) and slashes (cf. (17)-(18))). This enables us to correct spelling errors due to a missing space after the punctuation marks (cf. (13)). Furthermore it allows an easier lexical lookup of typical slash constructions as the town/state-construction in (17).

(13)   arrived today.The weather
(14)   `arrived today . The weather`
(15)   www.aclweb.org
(16)   `www . aclweb . org`
(17)   in Lake Tahoo/Nevada
(18)   `in Lake Tahoo / Nevada`

Regarding (16), we have to take care that this separation must be transformed to its originally form. Therefore, we have to analyse the surrounding context in more detail. If a former token-medial period stands in some relation with a typical URL part like one of the tokens *http, www, com* etc., we decide to merge the period with its surrounding tokens and annotate the result by a more informative URL-tag like `<www>` or `<http>` (cf. (19)). Since we can't expect to receive a lexical reading for the token *www.aclweb.org*, we could make use of the `<www>`-tag for assigning the token its correct lexical reading very comfortably.

(19)   `<www> www.aclweb.org </www>`

If we identify problems for one of the following analysis components we're not able to repair, we prefer to mark the relevant tokens in some way for later manual checking instead of ignoring them as usual tokenizers do. In (20), we didn't find a corresponding quotation mark to the given one. Marking the relevant position by the tag `<qm-problem>` (cf. (21)) enables a fast manual correction of the relevant text passage, what we recommend if the text is used as a source for corpus linguistic analysis tasks. For the same reason, we mark unsure decisions. In (22), we assigned a possible enumeration of locations by the tag `<check-loc>`. If the tokenized texts are used for building text corpora as lexical resources, we believe that a manual checking that takes a few minutes or hours is better than work with ill-formed corpus data over years.

(20)   The " Boston Celtics are the best.
(21)   The `<qm-problem>` " `</qm-problem>` Boston Celtics are the best .
(22)   `<check-loc>` Genf / Scharm el Scheich / Nablus `</check-loc>` - President Hosny Mubarak

In the next section, we describe how our tokenizer assigns the above mentioned output structures.

3   System Architecture

The tokenizing process consists of two main stages. In the first stage, the input is separated into respective parts of tokens. In the second stage, these elements are merged into bigger units. This contains the annotation of linguistic structures such as sentence utterances as well as the annotation of problems and problematic decisions.

3.1   Separation into Possible Tokens

The first stage – the separation of a text into possible tokens – is also a bi-parted process. First, a *whitespace* separation is applied to the input text. After that, each punctuation character is separated from the front and the end of the so far received tokens. For a few punctuation marks (e.g. period, colon, quotation mark) in the middle of the so far separated token, we split up these tokens into three new tokens with the punctuation mark in the middle. After that, the separation of the left and right token parts is recursively repeated as described

Table 1. Output of the first tokenizer stage.

Token	mp	sp	rec	Token	mp	sp	rec	Token	mp	sp	rec	Token	mp	sp	rec
Die	-	+	0	.	+	m	2	haben	-	+	0	mit	-	+	0
Celtics	-	+	0	nba	-	+	4	ihr	-	+	0	90	-	+	1
(	+	b	0	.	+	m	3	1	-	+	0	:	+	m	0
http	-	+	1	com	-	+	4	.	+	e	0	97	-	+	1
:	+	e	1	/	+	m	1	Spiel	-	+	0	verloren	-	+	0
/	+	m	0	celtics	-	+	2	gegen	-	+	0	.	+	e	0
/	+	b	1	/	+	e	0	die	-	+	0				
www	-	+	3	)	+	e	0	Hornets	-	+	0				

before. All these informations are encoded for the merging decisions that have to be done in the next tokenizing stage (cf. section 3.2). In Table 1, we see the output of the first tokenizing stage for the sentence in (23).

(23) Die Celtics (http://www.nba.com/celtics/) haben ihr 1. Spiel gegen die Hornets mit 90:97 verloren.
The Celtics (http://www.nba.com/celtics/) have lost their first game against the Hornets by 90:97.

The first column contains the separated tokens. In the second column (mp), the sign - signals that the token only contains alphanumerical characters or dashes. Otherwise, we mark the token by the sign + to signal possible problems for the lexical lookup. In the third column (sp), we encode the separation process by marking tokens that were separated at the beginning (b), at the end (e) or in the middle (m) of the token form after the whitespace separation. In the fourth column (rec), we store the recursion level, in which the tokens were finally generated. The informations encoded in these four columns allow us (i) to reconstruct the original form of the text, (ii) to support the lexical analysis and (iii) to classify produced errors with the goal of building improved tokenizer versions in a fast way. All this is not possible with the usually used black-box systems mentioned before.

With these informations, we apply the second analysis stage that produces the final output shown in figure 1. It is a one-token-per-line-format, consisting of two colums. The first column represents the tokenized text, the second column contains the additional informations of Table 1 as a merged item. Structural attributes such as utterance (`ut`) and sentence borders (`s`) are marked by corresponding XML-tags as well as elements for which we identified a special reading (`colon-in-number` and `http-slash-end` for an URL starting with *http://* and ending with a slash). We also recommend a check of an identified ordinal number by the tag `<check-ord>`, since we're not absolutely sure to have done the correct decision. Furthermore, we mark the ordinal number by the information sequence `No+-0`[2] in the second column for a better tokenizer evaluation.

---

[2] The sequence `No+-0` encodes the information that the ordinal number is followed by an uppercase written noun, which wasn't lexically marked as a typical noun that often follows an ordinal number.

```
<s>                                    </check-ord>
Die        +-0                         Spiel      +-0
Celtics    +-0                         gegen      +-0
(          b+0                         die        +-0
<http-slash-end>                       Hornets    +-0
http://www.nba.com/celtics/   ++0      mit        +-0
</http-slash-end>                      <colon-in-number>
)          e+0                         90:97      ++0
haben      +-0                         </colon-in-number>
ihr        +-0                         verloren              +-0
<check-ord>                            .          e+0
1.         No+-0                       </s>
```

Fig. 1. Final Tokenizer Output.

3.2 Combining Tokens into Bigger Units

In the second processing stage, we make use of the analysis technique Pattern-matching Easy-First Planning, shortly PEP, (Klatt, 1997) for combining tokens into bigger units. PEP was originally developed with the goal of building parser and tagger components (cf. (Klatt, 2002)). But it may also be used for a lot of other NLP tasks like information extraction and – of course – tokenizing[3].

The analysis process of PEP is driven by traversing a transition network deterministically. A transition network is defined by several states (including an initial and a final state) that are linked by directed arcs. Every arc is associated with a so-called network function (NWF).

PEP has a lot of different NWFs, the most important ones are a pattern for finding adjacent elements in the input structure (the NWF nb) and a pattern for finding non-adjacent patterns with a left and right border element (the NWF seq). Transitions are tested in the given order of the network definition. A NWF always returns a boolean value. If it is TRUE, the goal state of the transition becomes the actual state. Otherwise the next transition with the same starting state is applied. PEP allows a bi-directional search of patterns from every token position inside the input text. There exist three different ways for the search of a pattern: a *categorial-driven* search, a *positional-driven* search and a *token-driven* search. The NWF (25) is an example of a categorial-driven search of a nb-pattern for parsing. Here, all adjacent determiners and nouns in (24) are detected and merged to a DP constituent (cf. (26)).

The NWF (27) is an example of a positional-driven search for parsing. Assuming that the word position pointer *s-top* is positioned at the beginning of the first word in (24), only the first determiner-noun-pair is detected (cf. (28)). In (27) the left context, which is associated with *s-top* (:LC *s-top*), is declared as the anchor point of the pattern (:AP LC). The anchor point is the

---

[3] Our tokenizer can be used as first component of a typical pipeline architecture. The irrelevants tags for subsequent components have to be filtered out by a postprocessing stage comparable to (Grover, 2000).

element, where the other elements of the pattern are searched from. In (27), we also make use of a *cover*-action. This means that the new built NP-structure covers its elements and makes them unavailable for the further analysis until this structure is probably uncovered. This is a very powerful mechanism for the ongoing analysis process as shown in some of the following examples.

(24) A dog saw a cat.
(25) (nb ((m-cat DET)) ((m-cat N)) :match-as ((m-cat NP)))
(26) | nb | DET A | N dog | saw | nb | DET a | N cat | .
(27) (nb ((m-cat DET)) ((m-cat N))
       :AP LC :LC *s-top* :cover surface :match-as ((m-cat NP)))
(28) | nb | DET A | N dog | saw a cat.

A token-driven search is marked by a network name in a lexical entry as shown in (29)[4].

(29) (",," ((((m-cat pm) (p (dual 1))))
              (*bqm-net* :stage tok :priority 900)))

Immediately after the lexicon lookup of the input tokens[5], this network (shown in Figure 2) is traversed at the beginning of the analysis process. Before this network is applied, the concerning word is surrounded by the word position pointers *z1* and *z2*.

```
initial node: 0      final node:    9
0->1: (nb ((cat pm) (token ",,")) :AP LC :LC *z1*))
0->9: (always-true))
1->2: (seq ((cat pm)) ((cat pm) (p _)) :AP LC :LC *z1*))
1->8: (always-true))
2->9: (prev-seq :right ((cat pm) (token "''")) :head left
                :cover surface :match-as ((cat dual-partners))))
2->3: (seq ((cat pm)) ((cat pm) (token (",," "''"))) :AP LC :LC *z1*))
2->8: (always-true))
3->9: (prev-seq :right ((cat pm) (token "''"))))
3->8: (always-true))
8->9: (nb ((cat pm)) :AP LC :LC *z2* :cover surface
                :match-as ((cat problem) (tag prob-dual-partners)))
```

Fig. 2. The token-driven net *bqm-net*.

---

[4] For tagging, parsing and information extraction applications in the PEP framework, we use some of the tokenizer tags as lexical entries connected with such a token-driven search. This enables us to guide the analysis process in a very comfortable way.

[5] Or a well-defined time later, which is defined by :stage and :priority – if we have to process more than one token-driven search action with the same :stage-value, then the values of :priority define in which order the corresponding networks are traversed.

In the transition 0->1, it is checked whether the beginning quotation mark (abbrev. as BQM) is still available and not covered by a former action. If it is covered, we go in the transition 0->9 to the final state, since the NWF `always-true` always returns the value TRUE. If it is not covered, we go to the next problematic punctuation mark (encoded as (p _) in the transition 1->2). As problematic punctuation marks are defined sentence delimiter elements (e.g. periods, question and exclamation marks) as well as punctuation marks that can surround sentence structures (e.g. quotation marks). If we don't find such an element to the right of the BQM (in fact, we hope to find the corresponding ending quotation mark), we mark the BQM as a kind of an ill-formed text by the tag `prob-dual-partners`.

If we found the next problematic token to the right, we test in the transition 2->9, whether we arrived by the corresponding quotation mark. If this is the case, we cover the whole domain by a cover-action, so that no quotation mark inside this domain is available for the further analysis process. If not, we check whether an ending quotation mark occurs somewhere else in the right context. If this is not the case, we mark the BQM mark as well by the tag `prob-dual-partners`. Otherwise we stop here and try to solve this problem later. If we apply this network for the two given beginning quotation marks in (30), we receive the output in (31). The box-notation illustrates the application of the cover mechanism. Since there is still one uncovered problematic punctuation mark in the input (a period), we have to continue to produce the final output shown in (32). How this is done, will be shown next.

(30)   "The Celtics" won against the "Indiana Pacers.

(31)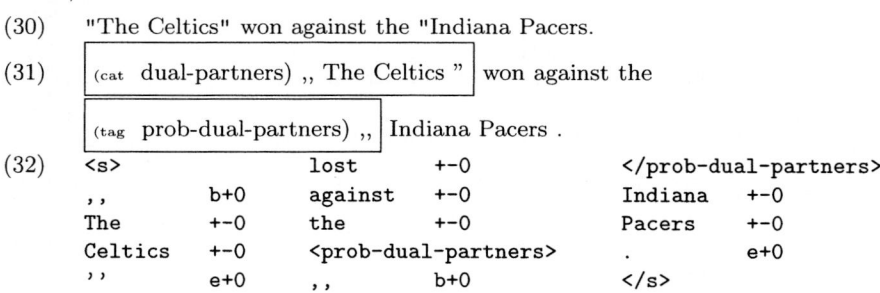

(32)
```
       <s>                lost         +-0        </prob-dual-partners>
       ,,                 b+0          against    +-0        Indiana              +-0
       The                +-0          the        +-0        Pacers               +-0
       Celtics            +-0          <prob-dual-partners>              .         e+0
       ,,                 e+0          ,,         b+0        </s>
```

After the application of the token-driven networks, we process the input from left to right iteratively, going to the next problematic punctuation mark and remembering the position we started our search from. Applying this strategy to the input in (30), we arrive by the period at the end of the input. Since this is the last token (and a sentence delimiter), we assign the whole sequence a sentence reading (tag `<s>`) and finish the tokenizing process.

Sometimes, this tasks is more complicated. As mentioned before, we also find periods surrounded by quotation marks in a text as indicated in (33). In such a context, we fix the inner domain of the quotation marks by two word position pointers and apply the above mentioned strategy to this inner domain. This leads to a detected sentence domain. Since it is immediately surrounded by the quotation marks, we mark this domain by an utterance-tag (`<ut>`).

(33)   "The Celtics won against the Indiana Pacers."

But this is a relatively easy task comparing to other punctuation mark constellations, we sometimes find in a text (like the one in (5)). Explaining the applied strategies for such constellations will go beyond the scope of this paper, so that we continue with the evaluation of the results our tokenizer produced, when it was applied on a small German newspaper corpus.

4 Evaluation

For the evaluation of our tokenizer, we annotated nearly 5800 German newspaper articles of three different text genres: international political news (au), economic news (wi) and soccer news (spfu). For the task of period disambiguation, we evaluated the first 1000 relevant tokens (periods as sentence delimiters and tokens with a period at the token end) for each subcorpus. The resulted recall quotes were inbetween 99.50%-100%, the resulted precision quotes inbetween 99.90%-100%. Comparing these results with the accuracy rates of the state-of-the-art tokenizers mentioned in section 2, we perform slightly better. But we don't want to claim that we outperform them, because the systems were tested on different corpora. Since this is another story, we continue with the evaluation of the other recognized structures that can support the later analysis stages.

Table 2 shows the frequency distribution of characteristic tags as well as of tags that are of importance for later analysis components that characterize the article structure. The tag `<source>` marks a news agency or the author of the text. In the latter case, we can extract unknown Christian names very easily. The tag `<loc>` marks a single location name at the beginning od a newspaper article in the context of a following dash. The tag `<loc-enum>` marks an enumeration of location names, the tag `<loc-mwl>` marks multi word location names as e.g. *New York* in the same context. Next, we see the occurences of usual sentences (`<s>`), sentences ending with no punctuation marks (`<swpm>`) utterances surrounding one (`<ut>`) and more sentences (`<uts>`), that can form with a matrix clause (`<mc>`) more complex textual structures (`<mcut>` and `<mcuts>`).

Table 2. A first selection of assigned tags.

tag	au	wi	spfu	tag	au	wi	spfu	tag	au	wi	spfu
article	1841	3506	406	loc-mwl	263	62	2	uts	782	521	680
source	1696	3095	335	s	48262	79067	11944	mc	1109	1123	1085
loc	1169	2242	292	swpm	176	183	165	mcut	558	705	498
loc-enum	148	391	26	ut	970	1393	615	mcuts	522	397	571

Due to the amount of the identified structures, it was only possible to proof the correctness for a few tags.

Table 3 shows the frequency distribution of a selection of tags that are very useful for a later determination of lexical readings. We introduced the meaning of the first four tags before. The tags `apo+number` and `apo+token` denote apostrophs that we placed at the token edges as in the original form (cf. (34)-(35)).

Table 3. A second selection of assigned tags.

Tag	au #	au f	wi #	wi f	spfu #	spfu f	Tag	au #	au f	wi #	wi f	spfu #	spfu f
bqm-in-word	125	-	76	-	20	-	sqm	45	-	18	-	1	-
bqm-in-mwe	76	-	23	-	4	-	apo+number	1	-	1	-	-	-
colon-in-number	10	-	13	-	728	-	apo+token	72	7	30	3	23	1

(34)   The season of <apo+number> '95 </apo+number>
(35)   <apo+token> hab' </apo+token> <apo+token> 'nen </apo+token>

We've evaluated for each subcorpus the total number of assigned tags (#) and how many of them were wrong (f). The eleven wrongly assigned tags are often the result of ill-formed sentences with single quotation marks inside surrounding quotation marks. Since we assigned most of these sentences a corresponding tag that marks a problem for the later analysis, we receive a recommendation to check these occurences manually. Looking at the frequency rates for the `colon-in-number`-tag, we also see that we can use our tokenizer as a kind of *text genre* classifier, especially for sports texts.

Finally, we regard the token-medial separations, we did for periods, slashes, colons and commas. But we made such an evaluation only for the `wi`-corpus. The results are listed in Table 4. Considering the number of cases due to a token-medial separation of a period, the result is surprisingly. More than 1600 sentences of all 79067 sentences of the `wi`-corpus were written with a spelling error in the original text, a very high rate, we didn't expect to find. So, we can conclude that it is worthwhile to do such token-medial separations. First, we can correct some ill-formed sentences in the original text. Second, we can identify tokens such as URLs that usually receive no readings in a following lexical lookup.

Table 4. Token-medial separations.

punctuation mark	#	false	accuracy	punctuation mark	#	false	accuracy
periods	1617	11	99.32	colons	47	2	95.74
slashes	1391	4	99.71	commas	11	3	72.72

5 Summary

We presented a tokenizer with a high focus on transparency. Instead of tokenizing a text in a black-box manner, it makes all its decisions transparent. Furthermore it annotates structures with all information it recognized during the tokenizing process that could be relevant for subsequent analysis components. It also mark unsure decisions or detected problematic text constellations for later manual checking what is highly recommendable if the produced text is used as a resource for corpus linguistic tasks. In a small experiment, in which we tokenized German newspaper texts, we were able to annotate a lot of such textual information and showed that our tokenizer is also very reliable for the task of sentence disambiguation.

References

Aberdeen, J., Burger, J., Day, D., Hirschman, L., Robinson, P., Vilain, C.: MITRE: Description of the Alembic System as Used for MUC-6. In *Proceedings of the Sixth Message Understanding Conference (MUC6)*, Columbia, Maryland (1995).

Grover, C., Matheson, C., Mikheev, A., Moens, M.: LT TTT –a flexible tokenisation tool. In *LREC 2000 – Proceedings of the Second International Conference on Language Resources and Evaluation*, Athens, Greece (2000).

Klatt, S.: Pattern-matching Easy-first Planning. In A. Drewery, G. Kruijff, and R. Zuber, editors, *The Proceedings of the Second ESSLLI Student Session*. Aix-en-Provence, France, 9th European Summer School in Logic, Language and Information (1997).

Klatt, S.: Combining a Rule-Based Tagger with a Statistical Tagger for Annotating German Texts. In Stephan Busemann, editor, *KONVENS 2002. 6. Konferenz zur Verarbeitung natürlicher Sprache*, Saarbrücken, Germany (2002).

Mikheev, A.: Tagging Sentence Boundaries. Technical report, University of Edinburgh (2000).

Schmid. H.: Unsupervised Learning of Period Disambiguation for Tokenisation. Technical report, University of Stuttgart (2000).

Sperberg-McQueen, C. M., Burnard, L.: *Guidelines for Electronic Text Encoding and Interchange: Volumes 1 and 2: P4*. University Press of Virginia (2003).

Automatic Genre Detection of Web Documents

Chul Su Lim[1], Kong Joo Lee[2], and Gil Chang Kim[3]

[1] Division of Computer Science, Department of EECS, KAIST, Taejon
cslim@csone.kaist.ac.kr
[2] School of Computer & Information Technology, KyungIn Women's College, Incheon
kjoolee@kic.ac.kr
[3] Division of Computer Science, Department of EECS, KAIST, Taejon
gckim@cs.kaist.ac.kr

Abstract. A genre or a style is another view of documents different from a subject or a topic. The genre is also a criterion to classify the documents. There have been several studies on detecting a genre of textual documents. However, only a few of them dealt with web documents. In this paper we suggest sets of features to detect genres of web documents. Web documents are different from textual documents in that they contain URL and HTML tags within the pages. We introduce the features specific to web documents, which are extracted from URL and HTML tags. Experimental results enable us to evaluate their characteristics and performances.

1 Introduction

Both automatic genre-classification and subject-classification for normal textual documents have been considered many times over the past years. With the rapid progress of WWW, extensive studies have been carried out on subject-classification of web documents in recent years. Although subject-classification for web documents has been extensively studied, genre-classification for those documents has not been recognized. More recently, however, the automatic genre-classification for web documents begins to attract considerable attention.

A genre or a style of documents is considered as another view of documents different from a subject. 'Sports', 'economics', 'tourism' and 'games' are the examples for the subject of documents while 'novel', 'poem', 'news article', and 'manual' are for the genre. A document related to 'sports' can be news or a novel. On the other hand, a document containing news articles deals with 'sports' or 'economics'. Classifying documents based on the genre should not be confused with identifying the subject of documents. For this reason, the results of classifying documents based on the genre would be totally different from those based on the subject.

From an information retrieval point of view, there is an increase in the approaches to organize retrieved documents according to a genre or a style as well as a subject of the documents. Annotating a document with genre information can help users find what they want much easier and faster.

In automatic genre detection, a document can be represented by the values of features that seem to express the attribute of a genre. A classifier can guess the genre of a new document based upon these values that it learned from a training corpus. Therefore, selecting features that can make a clear distinction among the genres is the core of automatic genre detection. Several previous studies have suggested useful features for identifying a genre of documents. Only a few studies, however, dealt with web documents and adopted the features specific to web documents. No detailed evaluation for them has been published.

Karlgren and Cutting in [1] have adopted twenty simple features for genre detection; lexical count (e.g. "therefore" or "which"), part-of-speech count (e.g. adverb, noun or present verb), and textual count (character count, long word count, or characters per word). Four years later, they proposed a genre category for web documents and built a balanced corpus based on this category[2]. They use lexical terms, part-of-speech tags and general textural count as the features. Additionally, the number of images and the number of HREF links used in a document are adopted as the features for web documents. They mentioned using about forty features, but there are no reports on their performance.

E. Stamatatos et al. has a series of studies on automatic genre detection. In [3], they represent a document by 4 main features - formality, elegance, syntactic complexity and verbal complexity, and then each main feature can be encoded as several style markers such as the number of words per sentence, verb-noun ratio, idiomatic expressions, and formal words. In [4], they implement a text genre detector using common word frequencies only. They collect 50 most frequent words from BNC (British National Corpus) that consists of written and spoken texts, and evaluate them on WSJ corpus. Also, they report that the most frequently used punctuation marks play an important role for discriminating a text genre remarkably. In [5], they employ language tools such as a syntactic parser for extracting features. Unlike the previous studies, they use phrasal level and analysis level features. They report that the result using these phrasal and analysis level features is better than the one using the most-frequently used words.

More recently, Lee and Myaeng in [6] present a method of automatic genre detection based on word statistics only. They use both genre-classified training corpus and subject-classified corpus in order to filter out the words from the feature set, which are more subject-dependent rather than genre-dependent.

Most previous works have been performed on general textual documents rather than web documents. Accordingly the features are chosen without consideration of web documents and web genres. The genre category they adopt is also suitable for general textual documents, not web documents.

In this paper, we will demonstrate the contribution of not only general textual features but also web-document specific features to automatic genre classification. First, we propose a genre category for web documents in the basis of the results obtained by [2]. Web documents are different from general textual documents in carrying URL and HTML tags, which are presumed to predict a style of a document. For instance, a document would be a type of homepage if the document has 'index.html' in its URL. We also suggest some features specific to web documents, discuss their characteristics and evaluate their performance in comparison with the features that have been proposed in the previous studies. Finally, we conclude what are the appropriate features for automatic genre detection for web documents.

2 Web Genres

2.1 Classes of Web Genre

It is not easy to find a well-established genre class for web documents. The only study available on this area is [7]. They classify web genres into two large categories - textual and non-textual - and then break them further into 11 categories: personal homepages, public/commercial homepages, interactive pages, link collections, other listings and tables, error messages for non-textual documents; journalistic materials, reports, other running texts, FAQs, and discussions for textual documents.

Their work is our basis for defining the classes for web genres. We refine their categories by adding new ones and subdividing some of them into more elaborate categories. Table 1 shows the class of the genres we employ in this work. The genres marked with asterisk in Table 1 are refined, and we will explain the marked only due to space limitation in this section.

Table 1. Web genre proposed in this paper.

	Web Genres	Samples	num doc.	num domain
non-text	(A) Personal homepages	resume	37	23
	(B)* Public homepages	Homepages of government, institution, organization, hospital	92	92
	(C)* Commercial homepages	Shopping mall sites	73	71
	(D)* Bulletin collection	BBS, complaint board, notice board	74	69
	(E) Link collection	Collection of links	61	54
	(F)* Image collection	Collection of images, pictures, sound	60	48
	(G) Simple table/lists	Simple yellow pages, mapping tables	32	28
	(H) Input pages	Login page, interactive pages, search page	48	46
text	(I) Journalistic materials	Press reportage, editorial, review	117	43
	(J)* Research report	Electronic journals, magazine thesis	97	41
	(K)* Official materials	corporation info., classified ad., legal info., copyright materials, contact info.	150	107
	(L)* Informative materials	recipes, lecture notes, encyclopedic info.	123	97
	(M) FAQs	faq	54	52
	(N) Discussions	pages in news group, various opinions	53	19
	(O)* Product Specification	Advertising pages for various products	114	62
	(P) Others (informal texts)	poem, private diary, memo, internet fiction	39	37
		total number of documents:	1,224	
		total number of unique domains:		729

As the number of commercial homepages such as online shopping malls continues to grow steadily, users sometimes might want to filter them out or selectively sort them from the pages retrieved by a search engine. Therefore, we subdivide public/commercial homepages of [7] into (B) public homepages and (C) commercial homepages separately even though a classifier cannot easily differentiate each other. The genre (D) is confined to the pages that include the collection of links pointing to the pages of various opinions, questions and answers. With the rapidly growing number of pages containing the collection of multimedia files such as image and sound, we newly define the genre (F). With respect to a textual genre, we subdivide "reports" of [7] into 3 classes (J), (K) and (L). The genre (J) is created for research papers with a fixed format. From a user's point of view, it looks very useful to differentiate between the two genres (K) and (L) even though their documents have many properties in common. The growth of on-line shopping requires a genre for product specifications (O).

2.2 Construction of Genre Corpus

A corpus is constructed by two graduate students in Computer Science. The total number of web documents collected is 1,224. Since URL of a document is one of the features adopted in this paper, not only the content of the document but also the domain that the document is fetched from are important. Hence, we guide the collectors not to gather the bulk of documents from a single domain. When we merge the documents collected by two collectors, we exclude a page if it already exists in the merged corpus. Besides, when more than five documents are fetched from the same domain and fall into the same genre, we randomly select and remove one of the documents one by one until their number does not exceed five.

A document sometimes consists of two or three frames that are separate pages with their own URLs. In our corpus, the documents consist of separate frames (pages) whose number varies from 1 to 4. Therefore, the total number of the documents is 1,224 while the total number of the pages that we gather is 1,328. Furthermore, 45 documents out of 1,224 are PDF/PS files and they are all included in the genre *research reports*. The rest are HTML files. The number of the documents and the number of source domains according to the genres are shown in the fourth and fifth columns in Table 1, respectively.

3 Set of Features for Detecting Web Genre

We use five distinct sets of features to classify genres. Each of them is extracted from URL, HTML tags, token information, lexical information, and structural information of documents, respectively. Among them, URL and HTML tags are the properties that only web documents contain. The others are common for both general textual documents and web documents. In order to extract the sets of features, we process the following steps shown in Figure 1.

We keep URL information with the original web page. After HTML parsing, we can extract a set of features related with HTML tags such as the number of links or the number of input text box. The token information such as the number of sentences and the average number of words per sentence can be gathered from an output of the sentence-boundary detector. In addition, the features related with the part-of-speech token should be extracted after the morphological analysis. In the case of Korean, a word is composed of a content word and

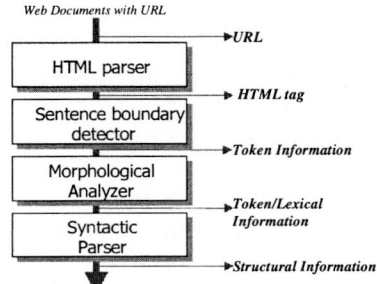

Fig. 1. Steps for extracting sets of features.

functional word(s) without delimiters such as space. A morphological analyzer can separate the content word from functional words. That is the reason why the features from the lexical information should be extracted after the morphological analysis. By using a syntactic parser, phrase and chunk information can be collected. In the following subsections, we will explain the sets of features in detail.

3.1 URL

HTTP URL defines the location of a document on the Web. It mainly consists of a name of the host (domain), a directory path and a filename. The general form of URL is as follows:

    http://<host>:<port>/<path>?<searchpart>

<port> can be omitted, and <path>, '?', <searchpart> are optional. We can define a depth of URL as the number of directories included in <path>. The URL can denote the characteristics of the documents. For example, the documents of entrance sites are often located right under the root host [8], so their URL depths are zero.

- **URL** features: (1) depth of URL, (2) file extension in URL (html, xml, asp, jsp, php, pdf ...), (3) whether or not using '~' in URL, (4) whether or not using main, index, default, home ... in URL filename, (5) domain area (com, edu, net, org, co.kr, ac.kr ...)
- **URL-L**exical features: We choose 35 lexical terms which occur more than three times in URL strings of training corpus; We adopt 35 lexical features – whether or not using them in URL string.

3.2 HTML Tags

HTML tags such as 'a' (anchor) and *img* can give us important clues on determining a genre of a web page. We can obtain 74 HTML tags from the training corpus, and all of them are used for the features in this work. How many times anchor tags are used in a page proportion to the number of characters is also introduced as a feature.

- **HTML** tag features : frequency of each tag / total frequency of HTML tags used in a doc; for 74 HTML tags (*col, a, img, area, frame, input, textarea* ...); frequency of anchor tag / total number of characters in a doc.

3.3 Token Information

Token information includes basic frequencies for the text token and the pos token, which most previous works employed. In general, letters, digits, punctuations, and symbols mingle in a document. Moreover, a Korean document consists of heterogeneous character sets such as *hangul* (Korean alphabets), *hanja* (Chinese letters), and alphabets. Two distinct styles of documents may differ in the ratio of usage of different character sets.

- **Text** token : (1) number of characters, (2) number of words, (3) number of candidate sentences, (4) number of detected sentences / number of candidate sentences, (5) average number of words per sentence, (6) average number of characters per word, (7) number of candidate sentences / number of characters, (8~13) number of type-words / total number of words; for 6 types - hangul, hanja, alphabet, digit, punctuation, and symbol.

After the morphological analysis, we can extract the features related with part-of-speech and dictionary information.

- **POS** token : (1~9) frequency of POS words / total number of words in a document; for 9 POS tags (noun, pronoun, adjective, verb ...), (10) average number of morphological results per word (morphological ambiguities), (11~15) frequency of dictinfo-words / total number of words; for 5 dictinfo words (sino-word, foreign-word, proper noun, onomatopoeic, title noun).

3.4 Lexical Information

Lexical information is the most commonly used feature for classifying genres in the previous studies. Since Korean has a great number of functional words, which play an important role in a sentence, we want to verify their performance in classifying genres. Thus, we separate the features of functional words from those of content words.

- **MC** : frequency of the content word / total number of words; for 50 most-frequently used content words
- **MF** : frequency of the functional word / total frequency of functional words; for 50 most-frequently used functional words
- **MP** : frequency of the punctuation / total frequency of punctuations; for 32 most-frequently used punctuations
- Usual/Unusual : (1) number of usual words / total number of words, (2) number of unusual words / total number of words; (usual words and unusual words are those whose frequencies in the training corpus are over 1,000 and only 1, respectively.)
- **Vocabulary** richness: size of vocabulary of doc / total number of words

3.5 Structural Information

Syntactic phrases of a sentence can be acquired from the results of a syntactic parser. We employ the features related with the phrases and the chunks as follows:

- **P**hrase-related features : (1~17) number of phrases / total number of phrases in a document; for 17 phrases such as NP, VP, AJP, AUXP ..., (18~34) average number of words per phrase for 17 phrases.
- Chunk-related features : count of multi-word expressions for 11 expressions such as date, time, postal address, telephone number, money, unit, copyright, e-mail, personal names, abbreviation, numerical expression.

4 Experiments and Discussion

4.1 Classifier and Experimental Environments

We use TiMBL version 4.0 [9] as a classifier in the experiments. TiMBL is based on memory-based learning, which is a direct descendant of the classical k-Nearest Neighbor approach. For evaluation, we adopt leave-one-out cross validation that TiMBL 4.0 supports.

Generally speaking, the textual representation of web documents consists of an anchor text and a body text. The title and Meta content are also useful texts as you can easily expect. In this paper, we divide the text of web documents into 3 separate segments; title & meta content, anchor text, and body text. Depending on which segment of a document is dealt with, the experiments are carried out on the 6 cases; T (Title and Meta content), A (Anchor text), B (Body text), and their 3 combinations - T+A, A+B, and T+A+B. The purpose of combining the segments is that we want to know which text segment is the most useful for automatic genre detection.

4.2 Experimental Results on Each Feature Set

The results summarized in Table 2 show the performance of each set of features under the given 6 combinations of textual segments. As URL and HTML tags are considered independent of the textual segment, their results remain equal to 6 different textual segments.

The first interesting finding in Table 2 is that the result of the segments including B (Body text) outperforms those without B for most sets of features except Usual/Unusual and VocRich. [10] reports that including body texts in the source of features deteriorates the accuracy of automatic classification. On the other hand, the overall text including the body is essential for genre classification because the statistics that are acquired by scanning a document from beginning to end can imply the property of a certain genre.

Comparing rows in Table 2, we find that the results of all sets of features except HTML tags are below 50% when used exclusively. The output of HTML

Table 2. The accuracy of each set of features.

Set of features	T	A	B	T+A	A+B	T+A+B
URL	39.8					
URL_lexical	43.5					
HTML	55.1					
TEXT token	38.3	43.4	46.4	44.5	43.2	43.1
POS token	31.6	44.6	36.9	36.1	38.4	39.1
MC	16.3	28.8	38.7	30	37.2	37.4
MF	21.6	29.5	42.9	31.3	44.2	44.2
MP	25.0	35.9	45.6	38.1	**46.9**	45.8
Usual/Unusual	15.0	18.1	17.4	18.6	16.4	16.4
VocRich	22.6	18.6	12.7	16.1	13.6	11.5
PHRASE	29.1	33.3	38.6	35	38.2	37.3
CHUNK	20.4	33.2	37	35	40.6	43.4

tags ranks the best, and MP is the second best. MP has already been known as one of the useful features for genre classification [5]. The result of MF is quite better than MC, which means the functional words play a more important role than content words do in identifying a genre.

The features URL-Lexical can identify the genre *FAQs* and *product specifications* very well because 36 documents out of 54 in *FAQs* include the term 'faq' in their URLs, which means many authors tend to name the faq page using the term 'faq'. In the case of *product specifications*, 47 documents out of 114 adopt 'detail', 'item', or 'product' in their URLs.

Here, we would like to know why the features of HTML tags perform outstandingly better than the others. When two documents included in the same genre are collected from the same domain, it is highly possible for their HTML tags to be almost identical even though other features such as the number of words or the most frequently used punctuations are quite different. In other words, the distance between the values of HTML tag feature of two documents in this case is far closer than that between other features. This leaves the features of HTML tags with the best accuracy. The performance of the features of HTML tags may be affected greatly by the relation between the domain and the genre.

4.3 Experimental Results on All Feature Sets

Table 3 shows the results of selective experiments, which we have done only on the text segments of A+B and T+A+B. When using all sets of features - the total number of features is 326 -, we can get 74% of accuracy. Applying the feature selection method, which is a forward sequential selection [11], we

Table 3. The results of selective experiments.

Used features	A+B	T+A+B
(1) All feature sets	73.9%	74.3%
(2) Best Combination of feature sets: URL+URL-Lexical+HTML tags+ POS token+MF+MP+Usual/Unusual+CHUNK	**75.7%**	75.6%

Table 4. The confusion matrix for the result of best combination in Table 3 (A+B).

	non-textual								textual							
	A	B	C	D	E	F	G	H	I	J	K	L	M	N	O	P
A	23	2	0	0	1	3	1	0	0	0	2	1	1	0	3	0
B	0	63	20	0	1	0	0	1	4	0	2	0	1	0	0	0
C	0	13	54	0	1	3	0	0	0	0	2	0	0	0	0	0
D	0	2	1	58	1	2	2	1	1	0	0	0	2	2	2	0
E	1	3	6	1	38	2	2	0	1	0	3	3	0	0	1	0
F	1	1	2	3	1	42	4	1	0	0	2	1	0	0	2	0
G	0	0	0	3	1	0	21	1	0	0	3	0	0	0	3	0
H	0	3	0	2	1	4	8	21	1	0	3	3	0	0	2	0
I	0	1	0	0	0	0	0	0	111	0	0	3	0	0	2	0
J	0	0	0	0	0	0	0	0	0	93	0	3	1	0	0	0
K	3	4	0	1	1	1	2	4	3	0	107	15	2	1	6	0
L	0	2	0	0	1	1	0	0	1	4	8	99	3	1	1	2
M	0	1	0	2	1	0	0	0	0	0	4	5	41	0	0	0
N	0	0	0	2	0	0	0	0	0	0	0	0	0	51	0	0
O	0	0	0	5	1	2	2	4	2	0	1	2	0	4	91	0
P	0	0	0	1	0	0	1	1	1	1	2	11	5	1	2	13
P/	82/	66/	65/	74/	78/	70/	49/	62/	89/	95/	77/	68/	73/	85/	79/	87/
R	62	68	74	78	62	70	66	44	95	96	71	81	76	96	80	33

A:personal homepages B:public homepages C:Commercial
D: bulletin collection E:link collection F: image collection
G:simple tables H:input pages I:journalistic J:research
K:official L:informative M:faq N:discussion O:product spec. P:others

can decide the best combination of feature sets. The excluded sets from this combination are TEXT token, PHRASE, MC and VocRich. The accuracy of the best combination can be improved up to 75.7% and its confusion matrix is depicted in Table 4.

The figures in the column 'A' in Table 4 indicate the number of documents guessed by a classifier as the genre 'A' while the figures in the row 'A' indicate the actual numbers of documents included in the genre 'A'. The last row of the table shows the precision and recall values for each category. The accuracies of textual genres are better than those of non-textual on the whole. The precisions/recalls of the genres (I), (J) and (N) rank the best. The documents in the genre research reports have distinctive values for most feature sets, so it is easy to detect them from the documents in other genres. Most news articles are of stereotyped format, henceforth, the documents in the genre journalistic materials can also be well classified. In the case of discussions, we found that many documents in this genre have accidentally very similar format with each other even though they are gathered from different domains. We reasoned that makes discussions one of the best genres to be well classified.

The genres (H), (G) and (P) occupy the lowest position. It means there are no distinguishable properties in the documents in these genres. Indeed many web documents contain tables, input window within their pages by default. As a consequence, we must look more carefully into whether or not these classes are indispensable for web genres.

As we expect, the genre (B) and (C) are very confusable, and so are the genre (K) and (L). Devising more elaborate features to be able to differentiate each other is left as a further study.

5 Conclusion

In this paper, we propose the sets of features for classifying the genres for web documents. Web documents are different from the textual documents in carrying URL and HTML tags. The features extracted from document's URL and HTML tags are appropriate for identifying the genres of documents. Through the experimental results, we have grasped the general idea of their contribution to genre classification. The features suggested in this paper are more or less language-independent. Therefore, we can apply these features into other languages without a little modification.

References

1. Karlgren, J., Cutting, D.: Recognizing text genres with simple metrics using discriminant analysis. In: Proc. of Computational Linguistics. (1994) 1071–1075
2. Karlgren, J., Bretan, I., Dewe, J., Hallberg, A., Wolkert, N.: Iterative information retrieval using fast clustering and usage-specific genres. In: Proc. of the DELOS Workshop on User Interfaces in Digital Libraries. (1998) 85–92
3. Michos, S., Stamatatos, E., , Kokkinakis, G.: An empirical text categorizing computational model based on stylistic aspects. In: Proc. of the Eighth Int. Conf. on Tools with Artificial Intelligence. (1996) 71–77
4. Stamatatos, E., Fakotakis, N., Kokkinakis, G.: Text genre detection using common word frequencies. In: COLING. (2000) 808–814
5. Stamatatos, E., Fakotakis, N., Kokkinakis, G.: Automatic text categorization in terms of genre and author. Computational Linguistics **26(4)** (2000) 471–495
6. Lee, Y.B., Myaeng, S.H.: Text genre classification with genre-revealing and subject-revealing features. In: ACM SIGIR. (2002) 145–150
7. Dewe, J., Bretan, I., Karlgren, J.: Assembling a balanced corpus from the internet. In: Nordic Computational Linguistics Conference. (1998) 100–107
8. Kraaij, W., Westerveld, T., Hiemstra, D.: The importance of prior probabilities for entry page search. In: ACM SIGIR. (2002) 27–34
9. Daelemans, W., Zavrel, J., van der Sloot, K.: Timbl: Tilburg memory based learner version 4.3 reference guide. Technical Report ILK-0210, Tilburg University (2002)
10. Pierre, J.: Practical issues for automated categorization of web pages. In: ECDL 2000 Workshop on the Semantic Web. (2000)
11. Caruana, R., Freitag, D.: Greedy attribute selection. In: Int. Conf. on Machine Learning. (1994) 28–36

Statistical Substring Reduction in Linear Time

Xueqiang Lü[1], Le Zhang[2], and Junfeng Hu[1]

[1] Institute of Computational Linguistics, Peking University, Beijing
{lxq,hujf}@pku.edu.cn
[2] Institute of Computer Software & Theory, Northeastern University, Shenyang
ejoy@xinhuanet.com

Abstract. We study the problem of efficiently removing equal frequency n-gram substrings from an n-gram set, formally called Statistical Substring Reduction (SSR). SSR is a useful operation in corpus based multi-word unit research and new word identification task of oriental language processing. We present a new SSR algorithm that has linear time ($O(n)$) complexity, and prove its equivalence with the traditional $O(n^2)$ algorithm. In particular, using experimental results from several corpora with different sizes, we show that it is possible to achieve performance close to that theoretically predicated for this task. Even in a small corpus the new algorithm is several orders of magnitude faster than the $O(n^2)$ one. These results show that our algorithm is reliable and efficient, and is therefore an appropriate choice for large scale corpus processing.

1 Introduction

Multi-word unit has received much attention in corpus oriented researches. Often the first step of multi-word unit processing is to acquire large n-gram set (word or character n-gram) from raw corpus. Then various linguistic and statistical methods can be employed to extract multi-word units from the initial n-grams . Chang [1] applied a two stage optimization scheme to improve the overall accuracy of an English Compound Word Extraction task. Merkel [2] used two simple statistical filters (frequency-based and entropy-based) to remove ill-formed multi-word units (MWUs) in a terminology extraction task. Moon [3] investigated the use of multi-word translation units in a Korean-to-Japanese MT system. These efforts, while varied in specifics, can all benefit from a procedure called n-gram *Statistical Substring Reduction*. The notation of "Statistical Substring Reduction" refers to the removal of equal frequency n-gram substrings from an n-gram set. For instance, if both n-grams "the people's republic" and "the people's republic of China" occur ten times in a corpus, the former should be removed from the n-gram set, for it is the substring of the latter n-gram with the same frequency. The same technique can be applied to some oriental languages (such as Chinese, Japanese, Korean etc.) of which the basic processing unit is single character rather than word. In the case of Chinese, say the two character n-grams "华人民共和国" and "中华人民共和国" have the same frequency in corpus, the former should be removed.

While there exists efficient algorithm to acquire arbitrary n-gram statistics from large corpus [4], no ideal algorithm for SSR has been proposed to date. When the initial

n-gram set contains n n-grams, traditional SSR algorithm has an $O(n^2)$ time complexity [5], and is actually intractable for large corpus. In this paper, we present a new linear time SSR algorithm.

The rest of this paper is organized as follows, Section 2 introduces basic definitions used in this paper. Section 3 presents two SSR algorithms, the latter has an $O(n)$ time complexity. This is followed in Section 4 with the mathematical proof of the equivalence of the two algorithms. Experimental results on three data sets with different sizes are reported in Section 5. We reach our conclusion in Section 6.

2 Preliminaries

In the rest of this paper, we shall denote by $\mathbb{N}$ the set of all integers larger than 0 and denote by $\mathbb{N}^*$ the set of all non-negative integers.

Definition 1. *The smallest counting unit in a corpus $\mathcal{C}$ is called a "statistical unit", denoted by lowercase letters. All other symbols in $\mathcal{C}$ are called "non-statistical unit". We denote by Φ the set of all statistical units in $\mathcal{C}$.*

Viewed in this way, a corpus $\mathcal{C}$ is just a finite sequence of statistical units and non-statistical units. When dealing with character n-grams, the statistical units are all characters occur in corpus $\mathcal{C}$; similarly, the statistical units of word n-grams are all words found in $\mathcal{C}$. In previous example "中", "人", "国" are statistical units for character n-grams and "the", "people's", "China" are statistical units for word n-grams. A particular application may include other symbols in a corpus as statistical units (such as numbers and punctuations).

Definition 2. *A string is a sequence of one or more statistical units, denoted by uppercase letters. The set of all strings is denoted by Ψ. If $X \in \Psi$, then there exists an integer $n \in \mathbb{N}$ such that $X = x_1 x_2 \ldots x_n$, where $x_i \in \Phi$, $(i = 1, 2, \ldots, n)$. We denote the ith statistical unit in X as* Char(X,i). *Then* Char(X,i) $= X_i$. *The length of X is defined to be the number of statistical units in X, denoted by* Len(X). *If* Len(X)$=n$, *then X is called an n-gram.*

Definition 3. *Let $Y \in \Psi$, and $Y = y_1 y_2 \ldots y_n$ ($n \in \mathbb{N}$, $n \geq 2$), then any p ($p \in \mathbb{N}$, $p < n$) consecutive statistical units of Y comprise a string X that is called the substring of Y. Equally, we call Y the super-string of X. We denote this relationship by $X \propto Y$. The left most p consecutive statistical units of Y make up of string X_{left} that is called the left substring of Y, denoted by $X_{left} \propto_L Y$. Similarly, the right most p consecutive statistical units of Y constitute string X_{right}, the right substring of Y, and is written as $X_{right} \propto_R Y$. We use* Left(Y,p) *and* Right(Y,p) *to denote Y's left substring with length p and right substring with length p respectively.*

Definition 4. *For $X \in \Psi$, $X = x_1 x_2 \ldots x_n$ ($n \in \mathbb{N}$), if X occurs at some position in the finite sequence of statistical units in $\mathcal{C}$, we say X occurs in $\mathcal{C}$ at that position, and call X a statistical string of $\mathcal{C}$. The set of all statistical strings in $\mathcal{C}$ is denoted by Ψ^C. Obviously we have $\Psi^C \subset \Psi$.*

Definition 5. *For $X \in \Psi^C$, the number of different positions where X occurs in $\mathcal{C}$ is called the frequency of X in $\mathcal{C}$, denoted by $f(x)$.*

Definition 6. *A high-frequency string is a statistical string in Ψ^C whose frequency is no less than f_0 ($f_0 \in \mathbb{N}$). We denote by $\Psi^C_{f_0}$ the set of all high-frequency strings in Ψ^C. The set of all strings in $\Psi^C_{f_0}$ such that $m_1 \leq \text{Len}(X) \leq m_2$, ($m_1, m_2 \in \mathbb{N}$ and $m_1 < m_2$) is written as $\Psi^C_{m_1 m_2 f_0}$. For convenience, we use Ω as a shorthand notation for $\Psi^C_{m_1 m_2 f_0}$. Obviously, we have $\Omega \subset \Psi^C_{f_0} \subset \Psi^C$.*

Definition 7. *For $X, Y \in \Omega$, if $X \propto Y$ and $f(X) = f(Y)$, then we say X can be reduced by Y, or equally, Y can reduce X. If X can be reduced by some Y then we say X can be reduced. Let $\Omega' = \{ X \in \Omega \mid \exists Y \in \Omega, X \text{ can be reduced by } Y \}$. $\Omega_0 = \Omega \setminus \Omega'$. Then Ω' denotes the set of strings in Ω that can be reduced, Ω_0 denotes the set of strings in Ω that can not be reduced. Obviously $\Omega_0 \subset \Omega$.*

Definition 8. *An algorithm that accepts Ω as input and outputs Ω_0 is a Statistical Substring Reduction algorithm.*

3 Two Statistical Substring Reduction Algorithms

3.1 An $O(n^2)$ SSR Algorithm

Suppose $|\Omega| = n$, then Ω has n statistical strings. The ith ($1 \leq i \leq n$) statistical string in Ω can be represented as a 3-tuple $< X_i, f_i, M_i >$, where X_i denote the ith statistical string, $f_i = f(X_i)$ is the frequency of X_i in corpus $\mathcal{C}$ and M_i is a merging flag. $M_i = 0$ means X_i is not reduced and $M_i = 1$ indicates X_i being reduced by its super-string. The initial value of all $\{M_i\}$'s are set to 0. The first SSR algorithm is given as Algorithm 1.

Algorithm 1 An $O(n^2)$ Statistical Substring Reduction Algorithm

---
1: Input: Ω
2: Output: Ω_0
3: **for** $i = 1$ to n **do**
4:    **for** $j = 1$ to n **do**
5:       **if** $X_i \propto X_j$ and $f_i = f_j$ **then**
6:          $M_i = 1$
7: **for** $i = 1$ to n **do**
8:    **if** $M_i = 0$ **then**
9:       output X_i

Obviously, this algorithm has an $O(n^2)$ time complexity, making it infeasible to handle large scale corpora.

3.2 An $O(n)$ SSR Algorithm

Algorithm 1 tries to find a string's super-strings by comparing it with all strings in Ω. Since only a small portion of strings in Ω can be potential super-strings of any given string, a great deal of time will be saved if we restrict the searching space to the possible super-string set. Based on this motivation we now describe a faster SSR algorithm.

To describe algorithm 2, we need to introduce the notation of reversed string first:

Definition 9. *Let* $X \in \Psi$, $X = x_1 x_2 \ldots x_n$ ($n \in \mathbb{N}$), *then* $X_R = x_n x_{n-1} \ldots x_1$ *is called the reversed string of* X. *All reversed strings of statistical units in* Ω *comprise the reversed string set* Ω_R. Reverse(X) *returns the reversed string of* X.

Algorithm 2 An $O(n)$ Statistical Substring Reduction Algorithm

---
1: Input: Ω
2: Output: Ω_0
3: sort all statistical strings in Ω in ascending order according to X_i's value
4: **for** $i = 1$ to $n - 1$ **do**
5:   **if** $X_i \propto_L X_{i+1}$ and $f_i = f_{i+1}$ **then**
6:     $M_i = 1$
7: **for** $i = 1$ to n **do**
8:   X_i=Reverse(X_i)
9: sort all statistical strings in Ω in ascending order according to X_i's value
10: **for** $i = 1$ to $n - 1$ **do**
11:   **if** $X_i \propto_L X_{i+1}$ and $f_i = f_{i+1}$ **then**
12:     $M_i = 1$
13: **for** $i = 1$ to n **do**
14:   X_i=Reverse(X_i)
15:   **if** $M_i = 0$ **then**
16:     output X_i

In this algorithm, all steps have a time complexity of $O(n)$ except step 3 and 9, which perform sorting on n statistical strings. It is worth mention that sorting can be implemented with `radix sort`, an $O(n)$ operation, therefore this algorithm has an ideal time complexity of $O(n)$. For instance, if the maximum length of statistical unit in Ω is m, we can perform a `radix sort` by an m-way statistical unit collection (padding all strings to length m with empty statistical unit). When special requirement on memory usage or speed is not very important, one can use `quick sort` to avoid additional space requirement imposed by `radix sort`. `quick sort` is an $O(n \log n)$ operation, so the overall time complexity of algorithm 2 is $O(n \log n)$.

In algorithm 2, only step 6 and 12 modify the merging flag, we call them *left reduction* and *right reduction* of algorithm 2. In algorithm 1, each string must be compared with all strings in Ω whereas in algorithm 2, each string is only required to be compared with two strings. This is why algorithm 2 reduces the number of comparison tremendously compared to algorithm 1.

4 The Equivalence of the Two Algorithms

While it is obvious to see that algorithm 1 is an SSR algorithm, it is unclear how can algorithm 2 have the same function, despite its lower time complexity. In this section we will give a mathematical proof of the equivalence of the two algorithms: they yield the same output given the same input set (not considering element order).

For a given corpus $\mathcal{C}$, Φ is a finite set, the finity of which is determined by the finity of $\mathcal{C}$. Since any two statistical units can be assigned an ordering (either by machine code representation or specified manually) such that the two statistical units are ordered from less to greater one. We can denote this ordering by $\preceq$. It is obvious that this ordering satisfies reflexivity, antisymmetry and transitivity. For any given $a, b \in \Phi$, either $a \preceq b$ or $b \preceq a$ holds, therefore $<\Phi, \preceq>$ is a finite well-ordered set. Here we introduce the symbol $\prec$ and write the condition $a \neq b$ and $a \preceq b$ as $a \prec b$.

Definition 10. *For $X, Y \in \Psi$, $X = x_1 x_2 \ldots x_n$ ($n \in \mathbb{N}$), $Y = y_1 y_2 \ldots y_m$ ($m \in \mathbb{N}$). If $m = n$ and for all i ($1 \leq i \leq m$) such that $x_i = y_i$, then we say X is equal to Y, denoted by $X = Y$. If $X \propto_L Y$, or there exists p ($1 \leq p \leq \min(n,m)$) such that $x_1 = y_1$, $x_2 = y_2$, ..., $x_{p-1} = y_{p-1}$ and $X_p \prec Y_p$, then we say X is less than Y. Whenever it is clear from context it is denoted by $X \prec Y$. If either $X = Y$ or $X \prec Y$ then we write $X \preceq Y$.*

Under these definitions it is easy to check that $<\Psi, \preceq>$, $<\Psi^C, \preceq>$, $<\Omega, \preceq>$ and $<\Omega_R, \preceq>$ are all well-ordered sets.

Definition 11. *Suppose $X, Y \in \Omega$ (or Ω_R), and $X \prec Y$, $\forall Z \in \Omega$ (or Ω_R) whenever $X \prec Z$ we have $Y \prec Z$. Then we say X is the proceeder of Y in Ω (or Ω_R) and Y is the successor of X in Ω (or Ω_R)*

Algorithm 1 compares current statistical string (X_i) to all statistical strings in Ω in order to decide whether the statistical string can be reduced or not. By comparison, algorithm 2 only compares X_i with its successors in Ω (or Ω_R) to find its super-strings.

The seemingly *in-equivalence* of the two algorithms can be illustrated by the following example: Suppose we have the following four statistical strings with f(X1) = f(X1) = f(X3) = f(X4) = f_0:

> X1="中华人民共和国" (the people's republic of China)
> X2="华人民共和国"   (people's republic of China)
> X3="中华人民共和"   (the people's republic of)
> X4="人民共"   (people's republic)

According to definition 7, X_2, X_3, X_4 will all be reduced by X_1 in algorithm 1. In algorithm2, X_2 is the right substring of X_1, it will be reduced by $X1$ in right reduction. Similarly, X_3 can be reduced by X_1 in left reduction for it is the left substring of X_1. However, X_4 is neither the left substring of X_1 nor X_1's right substring. It will not be reduced *directly* by X_1 in algorithm 2. As a matter of fact, X_4 will be reduced *indirectly* by X_1 in algorithm 2, the reason of which will be explained soon.

To prove the equivalence of algorithm 1 and 2, the following lemmas need to be used. Because of the space limitation, the proofs of some lemmas are omitted.

Lemma 1. *If $X \in \Psi$ and $X \propto Y \in \Psi^C$ then $X \in \Psi^C$ and $f(X) \geq f(Y)$.*

Explanation: a statistical string's substring is also a statistical string, whose frequency is no less than its super-string's.

Lemma 2. *For $X, Z \in \Omega$, $Y \in \Psi$. If $X \propto Y \propto Z$ and $f(X) = f(Z)$ then $f(Y) = f(X) = f(Z)$ and $Y \in \Omega$.*

Proof. Since $Y \in \Psi$, $Y \propto Z \in \Omega \subset \Psi^C$. by Lemma 1 we have $Y \in \Psi^C$ and $f(Y) \geq f(Z)$. Considering $X \in \Omega \subset \Psi$, $X \propto Y \in \Psi^C$, by Lemma 1 we get $f(X) \geq f(Y)$. Since $f(X) = f(Z)$ it follows that $f(Y) = f(X) = f(Z)$. Moreover $X, Z \in \Omega$, by definition 6 we get $m_1 \leq$ Len(X) $\leq m_2$, $m_1 \leq$ Len(Z) $\leq m_2$ and $f(X) \geq f_0$, $f(Y) \geq f_0$. Considering $X \propto Y \propto Z$, from definition 3, we conclude that Len(X) < Len(Y) < Len(Z). Therefore $m_1 <$ Len(Y) $< m_2$. Since $f(Y) = f(X) = f(Z) \geq f_0$. From definition 6 $Y \in \Omega$. □

Lemma 2 is the key to our proof. It states that the substring sandwiched between two equal frequency statistical strings must be a statistical string with the same frequency. In the above example both "中华人民共和国" and "人民共" occur f_0 times. By Lemma 2 "华人民共和国", "中华人民共和" and all other string sandwiched between X_1 and X_4 will occur in Ω with the frequency of f_0. Therefore $X_4 =$"人民共" can be reduced by $X_1=$"中华人民共和国" *indirectly* in algorithm 2.

Lemma 3. *If $X, Y, Z \in \Omega$. $X \prec Y \prec Z$ and $X \propto_L Z$ then $X \propto_L Y$.*

Lemma 4. *If $X, Y \in \Omega$ (or Ω_R), $X \propto_L Y$, Len(X)+1=Len(Y), $f(X) = f(Y)$; then Y is X's successor in Ω or (Ω_R).*

Lemma 5. *If $X, Y \in \Omega$ and $X \propto_R Y$ then $X_R, Y_R \in \Omega_R$ and $X_R \propto_L Y_R$.*

Lemma 6. *If $X, Y \in \Omega$, $X \propto Y$, Len(X)+1=Len(Y), $f(X) = f(Y)$ then X will be reduced in algorithm 2.*

Lemma 7. *If $X, Y \in \Omega$, $X \propto Y$, $f(X) = f(Y)$, then X will be reduced in algorithm 2.*

Proof. If Len(X)+1=Len(Y) the result follows immediately after applying Lemma 6. We now concentrate on the situation when Len(Y)>Len(X)+1. Let $X = x_1 x_2 \ldots x_n$ ($n \in \mathbb{N}$). Since $X \propto Y$, from definition 3 there exists $k, m \in \mathbb{N}^*$, which can not be zero at the same time, such that $Y = y_1 y_2 \ldots y_k x_1 x_2 \ldots x_n z_1 z_2 \ldots z_m$. If $k \neq 0$, let $M = y_k x_1 x_2 \ldots x_n$; if $m \neq 0$, let $M = x_1 x_2 \ldots x_n z_1$. In any case we have Len(X) + 1 = Len(M) <Len(Y). Considering $X, Y \in \Omega$, $X \propto M \propto Y$, $f(X) = f(Y)$, by Lemma 2 we have $M \in \Omega$ and $f(M) = f(X)$, therefore Len(X) + 1 = Len(M), by Lemma 6 X will be reduced in algorithm 2. □

Now we arrive the main result of this paper:

Theorem 1. *Algorithm 1 and 2 are equivalent, that is: given the same input Ω they both yield the same output Ω_0.*

Proof. Suppose $X \in \Omega$. If X can be reduced in algorithm 2, obviously X can also be reduced in algorithm 1. If X can be reduced in algorithm 1, then there exists a $Y \in \Omega$ such that $X \propto Y$, $f(X) = f(Y)$. By Lemma 7 X will be reduced in algorithm 2. So given the same Ω as input, the two algorithms will output the same Ω_0. □

Table 1. Summary of the three corpora

Label	Source	Domain	Size	Characters
corpus1	People Daily of Jan, 1998	News	3.5M	1.8 million
corpus2	People Daily of 2000	News	48M	25 million
corpus3	Web pages from internet	Various topics (novel, politics etc.)	1GB	520 million

Table 2. 2 – 20-gram statistical substring reduction results

Label	m_1	m_2	f_0	$|\Omega|$	$|\Omega_0|$	Algo 1	Algo 2
corpus1	2	20	6	110890	75526	19 min 20 sec	**0.82 sec**
corpus2	2	20	7	1397264	903335	40 hours	**14.87 sec**
corpus3	2	20	8	19737657	12888632	N/A	**185.87 sec**

5 Experiment

To measure the performances of the two SSR algorithms we conduct experiments on three Chinese corpora with different sizes (Table 1). We first extract 2-20 n-grams from these raw corpora using Nagao's algorithm. In our experiments, the high-frequency threshold is chosen to be $f_0 = \lfloor \log_{10} n \rfloor$, and n is the total number of characters in corpus, discarding all n-grams with frequency less than f_0. Then we run the two SSR algorithms on the initial n-gram set Ω and record their running times (not including I/O operation). All results reported in this paper are obtained on a PC with a single PIII 1GHz CPU running GNU/Linux. Table 2 summarizes the results we obtained. We did not run Algorithm 1 on corpus 3 for it is too large to be efficiently handled by Algorithm 1.

We can make several useful observations from Table 2. First, the SSR algorithm does reduce the size of n-gram set significantly: the reduced n-gram set Ω_0 is 30% – 35% smaller than Ω, conforming the hypothesis that a large amount of initial n-gram set are superfluous "garbage substrings". Second, the data in table 2 indicates that the newly proposed SSR algorithm is vastly superior to algorithm 1 in terms of speed: even on small corpus like corpus1 the speed of algorithm 2 is 1500 times faster. This difference is not surprising. Since algorithm 1 is an $O(n^2)$ algorithm, it is infeasible to handle even corpus of modest size, whereas the algorithm 2 has an ideal $O(n)$ time complexity, making even very large corpus tractable under current computational power: it takes less than five minutes to reduce a 2-20 n-gram set from corpus of 1 Giga bytes.

6 Conclusion

Ever since the proposal of Nagao's n-gram extraction algorithm, the acquisition of arbitrary n-gram statistics is no longer a problem for large scale corpus processing. However, the fact that no efficient SSR algorithm has been proposed to deal with redundant n-gram substrings in the initial n-gram set has prevented statistical substring reduction from being used widely. Actually, almost all researches involving large n-gram acquisition (statistical lexicon acquisition, multi-word unit research, lexicon-free word segmentation, to name just a few) can benefit from SSR operation. We have shown that a simple fast SSR algorithm can effectively remove up to 30% useless n-gram substrings. Furthermore, SSR algorithm can also combine with other filtering methods to improve filter accuracy. In a Chinese multi-word unit acquisition task, a combined filter with fast SSR operation and simple mutual information achieved good accuracy [6]. In the future, we would like to explore the use of SSR operation in bilingual multi-word translation unit extraction task.

In this paper, a linear time statistical substring reduction algorithm is presented. The new algorithm has an ideal $O(n)$ time complexity and can be used to rule out redundant n-gram substrings efficiently. Experimental result suggests the fast SSR algorithm can be used as an effective pre-processing step in corpus based multi-word research.

Acknowledgements

This research was funded by a grant from the National High Technology Research and Development Program (863 Program, Beijing, No. 2002AA117010-08), a grant from the National Natural Science Foundation (Beijing, No. 60083006) and a grant from the Major State Basic Research Development Program (973 Program, Beijing, No. G199803050111).

References

1. Chang, J.S.: Automatic Lexicon Acquisition and Precision-Recall Maximization for Untagged Text Corpora. PhD thesis, National Tsing-Hua University, National Tsing-Hua University Hsinchu, Taiwan 300, ROC. (1997)
2. Merkel, M., Andersson, M.: Knowledge-lite extraction of multi-word units with language filters and entropy thresholds. In: Proceedings of 2000 Conference on User-Oriented Content-Based Text and Image H andling, Paris, France (2000) 737–746
3. Moon, K., Lee, J.H.: Translation of discontinuous multi-word translation units in a korean-to-japanese machine translation system. International Journal of Computer Processing of Oriental Languages **15** (2002) 79–99
4. Nagao, M., Mori, S.: A new method of n-gram statistics for large number of n and automatic extraction of words and phrases from large text data of japanese. In: The 15th International Conference on Computational Linguistics. Volume 1. (1994) 611–615
5. Han, K., Wang, Y., Chen, G.: Research on fast high-frequency extracting and statistics algorithm with no thesaurs. Journal of Chinese Information Processing (in Chinese) **15** (2001) 23–30
6. Zhang, L., LÜ, X., Shen, Y., Yao, T.: A statistical approach to extract chinese chunk candidates from large corpora. In: Proceeding of 20th International Conference on Computer Processing of Oriental Languages (ICCPOL03). (2003) 109–117

Detecting Sentence Boundaries in Japanese Speech Transcriptions Using a Morphological Analyzer

Sachie Tajima[1], Hidetsugu Nanba[2], and Manabu Okumura[3]

[1] Interdisciplinary Graduate School of Science and Engineering,
Tokyo Institute of Technology
4259 Nagatsuta Midori-ku Yokohama, 226-8503, Japan
tajima@lr.pi.titech.ac.jp
http://lr-www.pi.titech.ac.jp/main_e.html
[2] Graduate School of Information Sciences Hiroshima City University
3-4-1 Ozukahigashi Asaminamiku Hiroshima, 731-3194, Japan
nanba@its.hiroshima-cu.ac.jp
[3] Precision and Intelligence Laboratory, Tokyo Institute of Technology
4259 Nagatsuta Midori-ku Yokohama, 226-8503, Japan
oku@pi.titech.ac.jp

Abstract. We present a method to automatically detect sentence boundaries(SBs) in Japanese speech transcriptions. Our method uses a Japanese morphological analyzer that is based on a cost calculation and selects as the best result the one with the minimum cost. The idea behind using a morphological analyzer to identify candidates for SBs is that the analyzer outputs lower costs for better sequences of morphemes. After the candidate SBs have been identified, the unsuitable candidates are deleted by using lexical information acquired from the training corpus. Our method had a 77.24% precision, 88.00% recall, and 0.8277 F-Measure, for a corpus consisting of lecture speech transcriptions in which the SBs are not given.

1 Introduction

Textual information is semi-permanent and is easier to use than speech information, which is only accessible sequentially when it is recorded. Therefore, for many purposes, it is convenient to transcribe speech information into textual information. Two methods are currently used for making transcriptions, manual transcription and automatic speech recognition (ASR).

Speech information is generally spoken language. Spoken language is quite different from written language used to describe textual information. For instance, in written language a 'sentence' can be a linguistic unit, but in spoken language, there exists no linguistic unit like 'sentence.' Consequently, SBs are not specified in manual or ASR speech transcriptions.

However, if SBs can be added to transcribed texts, the texts would be much more usable. Furthermore, SBs are required by many NLP technologies. For instance, Japanese morphological analyzers and syntactic analyzers typically regard their input as a sentence.

Since Japanese morphological analyzers regard their input as a sentence, they tend to output incorrect results when the input is a speech transcription without SBs. For instance, if the character string '...tokaitearimasushidekonomoji...' is inputted to the morphological analyzer Chasen [1], the output would be '... / to / kai / te / arima / sushi / de / kono / moji / ...' , where '/' indicates the word boundaries specified by the morphological analyzer. The correct one should be '... / to / kai / te / ari / masu / shi / de / kono / moji /...'. If a 'kuten' (period in English) is inserted between 'shi' and 'de', which is a correct SB, the output would be '... / to / kai / te / ari / masu / shi / . / de / kono / moji / ...', which is the correct result.

In this paper, we present a method to automatically detect SBs in Japanese speech transcriptions. Our method is solely based on the linguistic information in a transcription, and it can be integrated with the method that uses prosodic (pause) information mentioned in the next section.

The target of our system is manual transcriptions rather than ASR transcriptions, but we plan to apply it to ASR transcriptions in the future. In the present work, we have used the transcribed speeches of 50 lecturers whose age and sex are not biased [2, 3], and have constructed a corpus of 3499 sentences in which the SBs were manually inserted.

The next section discusses work related to SB detection. Section three describes the method of detecting SBs by using a morphological analyzer, and section four discusses the evaluation of our method.

2 Related Work

Despite the importance of a technology that could detect SBs, there has been little work on the topic.

In English, Stevenson and Gaizauskas [4] have addressed the SB detection problem by using lexical cues. In Japanese, Shitaoka et al. [5] and Nobata et al. [6] have done work on SB detection.

Shitaoka et al. [5] detected SBs by using the pause length in the speech and information about words that tend to appear just before and after SBs. Basically, the SBs are detected by using the probability $P(pause\ information|period)$. However, since pauses can occur in many places in speech [7], many incorrect insertions occurred when they inserted kutens in all of them. Therefore, they limited the places of kuten insertion to the places just before and after the words such as 'masu', 'masune', 'desu' that tend to appear at the SBs. Their method employs the following three pause lengths:

1. All pauses are used,
2. The pauses longer than the average length are used,
3. Assuming that the pause length differs depending on the expression, the pauses whose length exceeds a threshold for each expression are used.

Table 1. Results of experiment using different pause lengths.

	recall	precision	F-Measure
(1)	312/371(0.841)	312/451(0.691)	0.7589
(2)	254/371(0.685)	254/306(0.830)	0.7506
(3)	291/371(0.784)	291/342(0.851)	0.8161

The results of their method are shown in Table1. The best performance, 78.4% recall, 85.1% precision, and 0.816 F-Measure, was obtained for case 3.

Nobata et al. [6] proposed a similar method combining pause information with the manually created lexical patterns for detecting SBs in lecture speech transcriptions.

Our method, by contrast, detects SBs by using only linguistic information in the transcription, and it can be integrated with Shitaoka's prosodic method.

Although little work has been done on SB detection, there has been work in the related field of SB disambiguation and comma restoration. SB disambiguation is a problem where punctuation is provided, but the categorization of the punctuation as to whether or not it marks a SB is at issue [8,9]. Comma restoration is, as it indicates, the task of inserting intrasentential punctuation into ASR output [10–12].

3 Proposed Method

Our method to detect SBs consists of two steps:

1. identify candidate places for inserting SBs,
2. delete unsuitable candidate places.
    - delete unsuitable candidates by using information about words that seldom appear at a SB,
    - delete unsuitable candidates by using information about combinations of words that seldom appears at a SB.

The following subsections explain each step in detail.

3.1 Identifying Candidate SBs

To identify candidate places for inserting SBs, we use a Japanese morphological analyzer that is based on a cost calculation and selects as the best result the one with the minimum cost. The cost is determined by learning the suitable size corpus with a tag to the alternative trigram model which used bigram model as the base [13]. The idea behind using a morphological analyzer to identify candidates is that it outputs lower costs for better sequences of morphemes.

Therefore, by comparing the cost of inserting a SB with the cost of not inserting a SB, if the cost is lower for inserting a boundary, we can judge that the location is a likely candidate and the sequence of morphemes is more correctly analyzed by the morphological analyzer.

Next, we briefly describe the costs used in the Japanese morphological analyzer and illustrate the method of identifying candidate SBs.

Costs Used in the Morphological Analyzer. Cost is usually used for indicating the appropriateness of morphological analysis results, and lower cost results are preferred. A Japanese morphological analyzer usually uses a combination of morpheme cost (cost for words or POSs (Part of Speech)) and connection cost (cost for two adjacent words or POSs) to calculate the appropriateness of a sequence of morphemes. The Japanese morphological analyzer of Chasen [1], which we used in our work, analyzes the input string with the morpheme and connection costs statistically computed from the POS tagged corpus [14].

Consider, for example, the following two strings, 'oishii masu(delicious trout)' and 'itashi masu(I do)'. Although the end of both strings is 'masu', their POSs are different ('Noun-General'(NG) and 'Auxiliary Verb-Special MASU'(AVSM)), and their morpheme costs also differ as follows:

- The cost of the Noun- 'masu' is 4302,
- The cost of the Auxiliary Verb- 'masu' is 0.

Since 'oishii(the cost is 2545)' is an 'Adjective-Independence-Basic form' (AIB) and 'itashi(the cost is 3217)' is a 'Verb-Independence-Continuous form' (VIC), by using the following connection cost,

- The cost of AIB + NG is 404,
- There are no connection rules for AIB + AVSM,
- The cost of VIC + NG is 1567,
- The cost of VIC + AVSM is 1261.

the cost for each sequence of morphemes is calculated as follows:

- 'oishii(Adjective) + masu(Noun)': 2545 + 404 + 4302 = 7251,
- 'oishii(Adjective) + masu(Auxiliary Verb)': unacceptable.
  - Therefore, the analysis result is 'oishii(Adjective) + masu(Noun)'.
- 'itashi(Verb) + masu(Noun)': 3217 + 1567 + 4302 = 9086,
- 'itashi(Verb) + masu(Auxiliary Verb)': 3217 + 1261 + 0 = 4478.
  - Because 9086 > 4487, the analysis result is 'itashi(Verb) + masu (Auxiliary Verb)'.

Thus, by using costs, the morphological analyses will be grammatically correct.

Illustration of the Process of Identifying Candidate SBs. Whether the place between 'shi' and 'de' and the place between 'de' and 'kono' in a string 'kaitearimasu shi de kono' can be a SB is judged according the following procedure:

1. The morphological analysis result of 'kaitearimasushidekono' is 'kai(Verb) / te(Particle) / arima(Noun) / sushi(Noun) / de(Particle) / kono(Attribute)', and its cost is 16656. To compare it with the cost of the result including

a kuten, the morpheme cost of a kuten (200) and the minimum connection cost for a kuten (0) are added to the above cost; therefore, 16656 + 200 + 0 + 0 = 16856 is the total cost for the sequence of morphemes.
2. The morphological analysis result of 'kaitearimasushi. dekono' is 'kai(Verb) / te(Particle) / ari(Verb) / masu(Verb) / shi(Particle) / .(Sign) / de(Conjunction) / kono(Attribute)' , and its cost is 14245.
3. The morphological analysis result of 'kaitearimasushide. kono' is 'kai(Verb) / te(Particle) / arima(Noun) / sushi(Noun) / de(Particle) / .(Sign) / kono (Attribute)' , and its cost is 18018.
4. Because 16856 > 14245 from 1 and 2, the latter can be considered as the better sequence of morphemes. Therefore, the place between 'shi' and 'de' can be a candidate for a SB.
5. Because 16856 < 18018 from 1 and 3, the former can be considered as the better sequence of morphemes. Therefore, the place between 'de' and 'kono' cannot be a SB.

As illustrated above, by inserting a kuten between two morphemes in the input string, calculating the cost, and judging whether the place should be a candidate SB, we can enumerate all the candidate SBs.

3.2 Deleting Unsuitable Candidates

Deletion Using Words That Seldom Appear at a SB. Certain words tend to appear at the beginnings or ends of sentences. Therefore, the candidate places just before and after such words can be considered as suitable, whereas the other candidates may be unsuitable and should be deleted.

The words that tend to appear at a SB can be obtained by calculating for each word that appears just before and after the identified candidate SBs the following ratio in the training corpus: the number of occurrences in which a word appears at the correct SB to the number of occurrences in which the word appears at the candidate SB. The words with higher ratios tend to appear at SB. The sample words with higher ratios are shown in Table2.

Table 2. The sample words with which tend to appear before and after SBs.

the words which appear after SBs		
de	e	ee
(324/330)	(287/436)	(204/524)
the words which appear before SBs		
masu	ta	desu
(1015/1084)	(251/394)	(260/367)

By summing the values of the words just before and after each candidate SB, we can judge whether the candidate is suitable or not. If the sum of these values does not exceed a predetermined threshold, the candidate is judged as unsuitable and deleted. The threshold was empirically set to 0.7 in this work.

Deletion Using Combinations of Words That Seldom Appear at a SB.
Even if a word that tends to appear in a SB appears before or after the candidate SB, the candidate might still not be suitable, if the combination of the words seldom appears at a SB.

Consider the following example. In the training corpus, the string 'desuga'(no kuten insertion between 'desu' and 'ga') occurs, but the string 'desu. ga' never occurs, although 'desu' tends to appear at the end of a sentence, as shown in Table2.

Therefore, in case of the string 'kotodesugakono', the method in the last section cannot delete the unsuitable candidate SB between 'desu' and 'ga' because the value of 'desu' exceeds the threshold, as shown in Table2.

- The morphological analysis result of 'kotodesugakono' is 'koto(Noun) / desuga (Conjunction) / kono(Attribute)' . The total cost is 12730 + 200 + 0 + 0 = 12930.
- The morphological analysis result of 'kotodesu. gakono' is 'koto(Noun) / desu(Auxiliary verb) / .(Sign) / ga(Conjunction)/ kono(Attribute)'. The cost is 9938.
- Because 12930 > 9938, the place between 'desu' and 'ga' can be a candidate SB.
- The ratio in the last section for 'desu' is $260/367 = 0.7084 > 0.7$; therefore, whatever the value of 'ga' may be, the place between 'desu' and 'ga' will not be deleted as a result of using the method described in the last section.

To cope with the above problem, we need another method to delete unsuitable candidate places, i.e., one that uses the combination of words which seldom appears at a SB:

1. Identify in the corpus all the combination of words which tend to appear just before and after a SB,
2. If the occurrence of the combination of words without kuten insertion exceeds the preset threshold in the training corpus, select the combination as one that seldom appears in a SB. (The threshold was set to 10 in this work.) Furthermore, to prevent incorrect deletions, do not select the combination which occur once or more with kuten insertion in the training corpus.
3. If the combination of words just before or after the identified candidate SB is one that seldom appears at a SB, the candidate is deleted.

This method can cope with the above example; that is, it deletes the candidate SB between 'desu' and 'ga'.

4 Evaluation

4.1 Evaluation Measure

Precision, recall, and F-Measure were the measures used for the evaluation. They were defined as follows: Precision is the ratio of the number of correct SBs

identified by the method to the number of boundaries identified by the method. Recall is the ratio of the number of correct SBs identified by the method to the total number of correct boundaries. The F-Measure was calculated with following formula:
$$F - Measure = \frac{2 * Precision * Recall}{Precision + Recall}$$
The corpus, consisting of 3499 sentences for which kutens were manually inserted, was divided into five parts, and the experiments used a 5-fold cross validation.

4.2 Determining the Direction of Identifying the Candidate Boundaries

The identification of the candidate SBs using a morphological analyzer in section 3.1 can be performed in two directions: from the beginning to the end of the input string, or vice versa. If it is performed from the beginning, the place after the first morpheme in the string is tried first, and the place after the second is tried second, and so on[1].

We first conducted experiments in both directions. The F-Measures for either direction were equal 0.8215, but the places identified sometimes differed according to direction. Therefore, we calculated the intersection and union of the places for the two directions. F-Measure for the intersection is 0.8227 and the union is 0.8218.

From these results, we can conclude that the intersection of both directions yields the best performance; therefore, we will use the intersection result hereafter.

4.3 Evaluating the Effect of Each Method

Four experiments were conducted to investigate the effect of each method described in section 3:

1. Use only the method to identify candidate boundaries,
2. Use the method to identify the candidate boundaries and the deletion method using the words which seldom appear at a SB,
3. Use the method to identify the candidate boundaries and the deletion method using the combination of words which seldom appears at a SB,
4. Use all the methods.

The results are shown in Table 3. The recall of the identification method turns out to be about 82%. Since recall becomes lower by using the deletion methods, it is desirable that the identification method have a higher recall.

Comparing 1 and 2 of Table 3, the deletion of seldom appearing words can improve precision by about 40%, while lowering recall by about 4%. A similar result can be seen by comparing 3 and 4.

---
[1] [15] described the same problem, and tries to resolve it by multiplying the probability for the normal and opposite directions.

Table 3. The results for each experiment

	1	2	3	4
Recall	0.8184	0.7813	0.8182	0.7724
Precision	0.4602	0.8571	0.4719	0.8800
F-Measure	0.5889	0.8174	0.5982	0.8227

Comparing 1 and 3 of Table 3, the deletion of seldom appearing combinations of words can slightly improve precision with almost no lowering of recall. A similar result can be seen by comparing 2 and 4.

From these results, we can conclude that since both deletion methods can raise F-Measure, they can be considered as effective.

4.4 Error Analysis

The following are samples of errors caused by our method:

1. 'itashimashitadeeenettono'(FN; False Negatives)[2]
2. 'mierunda. keredomokoreha'(FP; False Positives)[3]

The reasons for the errors are as follows:

1. The SB between 'ta' and 'de' cannot be detected for 'itashimashi ta de ee nettono', because the string contains a filler 'ee'('ah' in English), and the morphological analyzer could not correctly analyze the string.
   When the input string contains fillers and repairs, the morphological analyzer sometimes analyzes the string incorrectly.
2. The place between 'da' and 'keredomo' was incorrectly detected as a SB for 'mierun da. keredomo koreha', because the combination of the words 'da' and 'keredomo' seldom appears at a SB but the number of occurrences is not zero; the combination was not selected as one that seldom appears at a SB.

5 Conclusion

In this paper, we presented a method that uses a Japanese morphological analyzer to automatically detect SBs in Japanese speech transcriptions.

Our method could yield a 77.24% precision, 88.00% recall, and 0.8277 F-Measure for a corpus consisting of lecture speech transcriptions in which SBs are not given. We found that by detecting SBs with our method, the morphological analysis could be performed more accurately and the error rate of the analyzer could be reduced, although the quantitative evaluation was not performed.

---

[2] Errors where the method misses the correct boundaries.
[3] Errors where the method incorrectly inserts boundaries.

Our method could outperform Shitaoka et al.'s method [5], which uses pause information and yields 78.4% precision, 85.1% recall, and 0.816 F-Measure, although this assessment is somewhat subjective as the corpus for their evaluations was different from ours. Our method can be integrated with the method that uses prosodic (pause) information, and such an integration would improve the overall performance.

As we mentioned in section 4.3, our method's recall was only 77.24%. A future work would therefore be to improve the recall, which would be possible if we had a larger training corpus in which SBs are manually tagged. Furthermore, we would like to apply our method to ASR speech transcriptions in the future.

We think our method can also be applied to English if a POS tagger is used in place of the Japanese morphological analyzer.

References

1. Matsumoto, Y., Kitauchi, A., Tatsuo Yamashita, Y.H., Matsuda, H., Takaoka, K., Asahara, M.: Morphological Analysis System ChaSen version2.2.9 Manual. (2002)
2. The National Institute for Japanese Language: 'The Corpus of Spontaneous Japanese(The monitor version 2001) Guidance of monitor public presentation. (2001) http://www.kokken.go.jp/public/monitor_kokai001.html.
3. The National Institute for Japanese Language: 'The Corpus of Spontaneous Japanese(The monitor version 2002) Guidance of monitor public presentation. (2002) http://www.kokken.go.jp/public/monitor_kokai002.html.
4. Stevenson, M., Gaizauskas, R.: Experiments on Sentence Boundary Detection. In: Proc. of ANLP-NAACL2000. (2000) 84–89
5. Shitaoka, K., Kawahara, T., Okuno, H.G.: Automatic Transformation of Lecture Transcription into Document Style using Statistical Framework. In: IPSJ SIG Notes on Spoken Language Processing, 41-3. (2002) in Japanese.
6. Nobata, C., Sekine, S., Uchimoto, K., Isahara, H.: Sentence Segmentation and Sentence Extraction. In: Proc. of the Second Spontaneous Speech Science and Technology Workshop. (2002) 527–534 in Japanese.
7. Seligman, M., Hosaka, J., Singer, H.: "Pause Units" and Analysis of Spontaneous Japanese Dialogues: Preliminary Studies. In: ECAI-96 workshop on "Dialogue Processing in Spoken Language Systems". (1996) 100–112
8. Palmer, D.D., Hearst, M.A.: Adaptive sentence boundary disambiguation. In: Proc. of the fourth Conference on Applied Natural Language Processing. (1994) 78–83
9. Reynar, J.C., Ratnaparkhi, A.: A maximum entropy approach to identifying sentence boundaries. In: Proc. of the fifth Conference on Applied Natural Language Processing. (1997) 16–19
10. Beeferman, D., Berger, A., Lafferty, J.: CYBERPUNC: A lightweight punctu IEEE International Conference on Acoustics, Speech and Signaation annotation system for speech. In: Proc. of the IEEE International Conference on Acoustics, Speech and Signal Processing. (1998) 689–692
11. Shieber, S.M., Tao, X.: Comma restoration using constituency information. In: Proc. of the Human Language Technology Conference of the North American Chapter of the Association for Computational Linguistics. (2003) 221–227

12. Tooyama, Y., Nagata, M.: Insertion methods of punctuation marks for speech recognition systems. In: Technical Report of IEICE, NLC2000-5. (2000) in Japanese.
13. Asahara, M., Matsumoto, Y.: Extended Hidden Markov Model for Japanese Morphological Analyzer. In: IPSJ SIG Notes on Spoken Language Processing, No.031. (2000) in Japanese.
14. Asahara, M., Matsumoto, Y.: IPADIC user's manual version 2.5. (2002)
15. Liu, D., Zong, C.: Utterance Segmentation Using Combined Approach Based on Bi-directional N-gram and Maximum Entropy. In: Proc. of ACL-2003 Workshop: The Second SIGHAN Workshop on ChineeseLanguage Processing. (2003) 16–23

Specification Retrieval – How to Find Attribute-Value Information on the Web

Minoru Yoshida[1,2] and Hiroshi Nakagawa[1,2]

[1] Information Technology Center, the University of Tokyo, 7-3-1 Hongo, Bunkyo-ku, Tokyo 113-0033
[2] CREST, JST

Abstract. This paper proposes a method for retrieving Web pages according to *objects* described in them. To achieve that goal, ontologies extracted from *HTML tables* are used as queries. The system retrieves Web pages containing the type of objects described by a given ontology. We propose a simple and efficient algorithm for this task and show its performance on real-world Web sites.

1 Introduction

This paper proposes a new type of document retrieval task to retrieve desired *type of objects* and algorithms required to perform it.

For this task, let us assume a situation wherein some people want information on other people on the Web. It is difficult to imagine efficient queries that satisfy their purpose. A query such as "about-me" is one possible answer, but obviously it overlooks many relevant Web pages because many "about-me" pages do not contain the term "about-me," and additionally, many "non-about-me" pages also contain information about profiles of people (*e.g.*, a site's top (home) page containing the author's information). On the contrary, even if a page contains the word "about-me," it does not always mean that the page presents a person's profile (*e.g.*, a sentence like "About-me pages are always boring"). This situation also holds for many other questions such as "What are the types of PCs currently owned by people?" or "List company profiles on the Web." In a situation, where users are only vaguely aware of what they want to know, they are unable to post relevant queries because they do not know answers.

However, the situation can be changed if the system has some *knowledge* about the type of target objects. For example, people can be characterized on the basis of *age*, *sex*, and *hobbies*. If you find such *attributes* or their typical *values* (*e.g.*, "29-years-old") on a Web page, you can confidently claim that the page provides a person's profile. Our aim is to give the system such knowledge in the form of *ontologies*[1] *extracted from HTML tables*. The task is to retrieve documents with a topic relevant to that of the HTML tables, from a set of unrestricted types of (*i.e.*, not limited to the ones that contain HTML tables) Web pages.

---

[1] Notice that the usage of the term "ontologies" in this paper is somewhat different from the standard one (which is mostly used to represent "concept hierarchies").

One proposed application of this research is to extract a set of people, a set of PC's specs, or a set of book information from a given Web site. By retrieving the desired pages and using some information extraction modules, a database of people, PCs, or books can be constructed from a Web site. Information extraction tasks usually assume some selected input ensured to contain the desired information. However, this is not the case for real-world Web documents. Our algorithm can be used to filter out useless documents that do not contain any desired information. Reducing the candidate set of documents to be investigated contributes to reducing the burden of information extraction modules and it will be possible to apply information extraction by some slow algorithms to a large set of documents.

Taking such applications into consideration, *recall* becomes more important than normal search engines, whose goal is often to retrieve only a few important Web pages that satisfy user needs.

The following sections of this paper are organized as follows. The related tasks and typical algorithms developed for them are mentioned in Section 2. The problem setting for our task is described in Section 3. Section 4 provides a detailed explanation of our algorithm, and section 5 shows the experimental results.

2 Related Work

In this section, we overview some topics related to our Web-page retrieval task. For the convenience of our readers, we also mention the commonly used methods for each task in order to comprehend the relationship between those methods and ours.

2.1 Document Categorization and Information Retrieval

Document categorization is the task of categorizing a given document into predetermined categories. Algorithms are provided with some *training data* to identify which features (*i.e.*, words, bigrams, etc.) are suggestive for each category. Several learning methods have been proposed, such as Bayesian classifiers [1], decision trees [2], K-Nearest Neighbor [3], Maximum Entropy [4], and Support Vector Machines [5].

On the other hand, Information retrieval is the task of searching documents that are required by users. Users present the system with a query, which is usually a set of words or sentences, and the system calculates the relevance of each document to the query. The relevance of documents is defined in many ways, including exact matches, Vector Space models [6] or Bayesian language models [7], etc.

It is not a straightforward procedure to build an algorithm for our retrieval task that directly uses the machine learning algorithms developed for the above tasks. Several machine learning algorithms assume that training data and test data can be modeled by the same set of features. However, this is not the case if the training data is a set of HTML tables or an ontology and the test data is a set of raw Web pages. The main problem in our task is that we have to develop one model for training data and another model for test data using common parameters. We propose the method of incorporating attribute-value structures of ontologies effectively into models for unstructured documents.

2.2 Search with Structures

Several reports about ontology-based searches have been described. Typically, they enhance query words by taking into account their related words such as synonyms, hyponyms, etc. [8] by using thesaurus, such as WordNet [9]. On the other hand, our ontologies contain *attribute-value* relations. This type of relations has different characteristics from synonyms or hyponyms, and it requires a new modeling strategy.

Research for searching unstructured documents by structured queries has also been established. For example, [10] proposed a method to retrieve unstructured documents by using queries with semantic tags such as named-entities, where unstructured target documents are annotated by a tagger. However, his approach assumes that query words (and structures) are given by users, making many relevant documents that contain not-exact but similar words to the query words unretrieved. Moreover, a fast and accurate tagger that annotates documents with *attribute-value tags* is needed for retrieval with attribute-value information by this method. However, there are no such taggers. On the other hand, our approach uses an ontology itself as a query, where each ontology is assumed to contain a lot of words about one topic in order to cover the topic as exhaustively as possible.

3 Problem Setting

In this section, we explain the overall architecture of our algorithm. The input and output of the algorithm are

Input: A set of Web pages P and an ontology o for a category C of current interest.
Output: A ranked list of Web pages in descending order of relevance to the category C.

Here, an *ontology* is a knowledge-base, describing attributes and their typical values of some type of objects such as humans, PCs, etc. As a straightforward approach can be used to output a ranked list if a score of each Web page is given, the problem is reduced to calculating a relevance score (defined as $P(C_+|p))^2$ for each Web page $p \in P$.

---

[2] The definition of C_+ is given in Section 4.3.

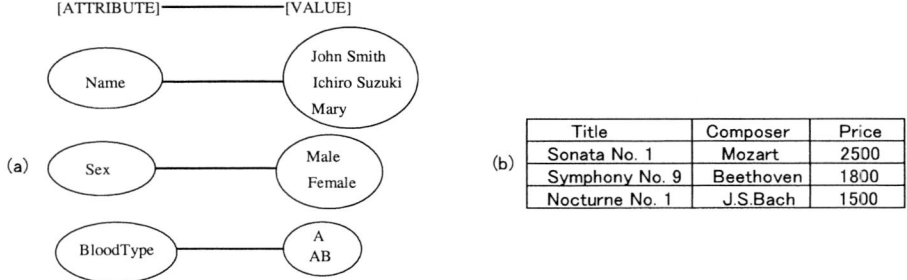

Fig. 1. (a) A Sample Ontology of Human and (b) A Table Describing CDs.

3.1 Ontologies Extracted from HTML Tables

In this paper, an *ontology* is a structured list of strings that describes one class of objects. It consists of *attributes* and their *values*, each of which is represented by a list of strings. Figure 1 (a) shows an example of the above. This ontology shows attributes of *human objects* and their typical values.

These ontologies can be obtained automatically from a set of *HTML tables*. Many HTML tables can be seen as structured documents that represent objects by stating their *attributes* and *values*. For example, the table in Fig. 1 (b) shows a set of CDs by providing the values of their title attributes, composer attributes, and price attributes. An algorithm proposed by [11] extracts a set of ontologies, each of which states the attributes of a class of objects and their typical values, from a set of HTML tables.

Attributes (and their corresponding values) are ranked in the order of the number of source HTML tables in which they appeared. We use top N attributes and their values for retrieval, ignoring the remaining parts of the ontologies. Currently, N is set to 10.

3.2 Web Pages

In Natural Language Processing (NLP) or Information Retrieval (IR) research areas, each document is usually modeled as *a bag of words*–that is, words and their frequencies contained in the document are used as features that specify it. One straightforward approach to Web page retrieval by HTML-table queries is to use *vector-space models* or some probabilistic models with bag-of-words statistics in both documents and queries.

However, we are confronted with some problems while trying to model Web pages relying on such methods. In this subsection, we cite some examples of the problems that emerge if we use vector-space-models or generative probabilistic modes to model Web pages when a human-ontology is used as an input.

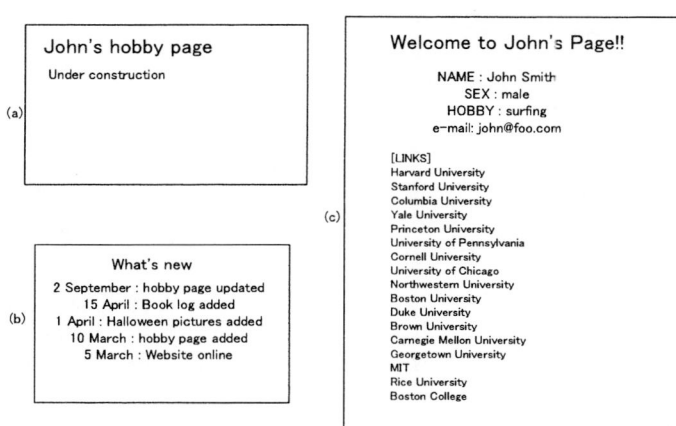

Fig. 2. (a) A too short page, (b) What's-new page with many up-date information, and (c) About-me page with large link lists.

Case 1: Too Short Pages See Fig. 2 (a). If we use standard vector-space models or generative probabilistic models, the page shown in Fig. 2 (a) will be assigned a high score because the word *hobby* or *John* frequently appears in the training data (which, in this case, is a human ontology) and this string occupies a large part of the page (two of five words).

Case 2: Too Long Values Even if the page length is not short, similar problems occur. See Fig. 2 (b). This page contains many strings related to date information. These strings make the relevance score of the page too large because date information appears frequently in the ontology (as birthdays). In other words, the fact that almost half of this page is dominated by human-related strings makes the relevance score of this page to a human topic erroneously high.

Case 3: Too Long Pages See Fig. 2 (c). Although this page contains a person's profile, but it also contains a long list of university names. This causes a problem because the list of university names is not related to the person's profile. The existence of several non-relevant strings makes dot-product or joint-probability inadequately low.

4 Algorithm

In order to cope with the three above-mentioned problematic cases, we propose an algorithm that avoids the case 3 problem by restricting the size of areas for processing and the case 1 and 2 problems by considering all over the attributes in the ontology.

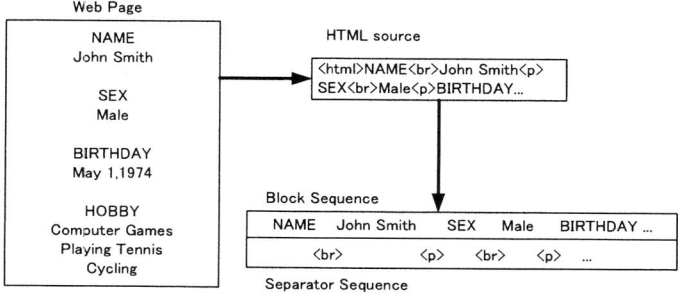

Fig. 3. Decomposition of a Web page into a block sequence.

The algorithm proceeds in the following manner.

Phase 1: Document Decomposition Given a Web page as an input, the process starts by decomposing it into a list of *blocks* whose definition is given in Section 4.1.

Phase 2: Area Selection Given a list of blocks, some sub-lists derived from it used in the following processes are selected.

Phase 3: Score Calculation The algorithm calculates a score of every selected sub-list and takes the highest score as the score of the whole list.

4.1 Document Decomposition Module: Making of Block Lists

The first phase of our system decomposes a given Web page into a *block sequence* as shown in Fig. 3. A block sequence for a Web page is obtained from its HTML source. In this decomposition, *HTML tags* are used as separators, *i.e.*, each area between one HTML tag and the next HTML tag is extracted as a block[3]. In a block sequence, blocks are listed in the same order as in the original HTML file.

We use such representation because a block is more appropriate to represent some information units as shown in the following example: Consider the sentences, "I am John Smith. I am 25 years old." The first sentence provides information about a name, and the next one provides information about an age. In this case, it is natural to think of a sentence as a unit of information and to separate documents by periods. However, there are often no periods in *non-sentential expressions* such as the lists shown in Fig. 3. HTML tags are important clues indicating boundaries of information for such non-sentential expressions.

4.2 Area Selection Module: Restricting Window Size

Now, we discuss the actual search process of Web pages using ontologies extracted from HTML tables. In some cases, searching all over the target page

---

[3] In addition, some special characters such as periods are also used as separators.

causes overestimation of relevance scores. Many Web documents contain parts unrelated to the current topics of search interest. Many Web documents containing profiles of people also contain some *unnecessary* information such as specifications of their PCs or links to their favorite Web pages. Searching for evidences all over the page causes some noises to be used as clues with high relevance scores and make searching results unreliable. (See Fig. 2 (c).) To avoid this problem, we set a limitation on the size of window in which evidences are searched. In other words, we use a type of passage retrieval technique [12] to select only the relevant parts of documents.

Currently the window size s is set at $2N$, where N is the number of attributes. This value represents the number of blocks when every attribute and value has a one-to-one correspondence to one block.

4.3 Score Calculation Module

Consider, for example, a situation where a user is looking for a set of about-me Web pages. If the user finds the word *hobby* appearing on some page, it is strong evidence that the page provides information about some person's profile, even without looking at any other part of the page. Taking such cases into account, we can approximate the probability that a given Web page p is relevant to the category C as $P(C_+|p) \approx \max_s P(C_+|s)$, where C_+ is an event that p is relevant to C, and s represents a word or a sequence of words appearing in p. This equation indicates that the most probable sequence s for the category C is sufficient as evidence to determine whether the given document belongs to category C.

In other words, the category C for the page p is determined by the *decision-list* [13] where p's n-grams are used as features[4] and decision-rules are ordered according to the value of the probability that "yes" values are returned.

However, the problem with this approach is its fragility. In the above example, all the pages that contain the word *hobby* will be categorized as about-me pages if the value of $P(C_+|s)$ is extremely high.

We solved this problem by *interpolating* several clues that suggest the target topic. The top N attributes and their values are selected for calculating the relevance of each page. The total relevance of a given page to the target topic is defined as the average of these N relevance scores in the following manner.

$$P(C_+|p) \approx \frac{1}{|A_N|} \sum_{a \in A_N} \max_s P(a_+|s)$$

where A_N is a set of the top N attributes and values in the ontology for the category C, and a_+ is an event that the page p is relevant to the attribute (or value) a.[5]

In other words, our algorithm searches the most *unique* strings to indicate attributes or their values in the target topic.

---

[4] Currently, only unigrams and bigrams are considered for the sake of efficiency.
[5] Note that we assume $\forall a \in A_N : a_+ \Leftrightarrow C_+$.

The next problem is how to estimate values of $P(a_+|s)$. Our approach is to use D_o, data from the outside of tables as negative examples while data from the inside of tables of the target topic as positive ones. Given n_a, the number of times s appears in the ontology representing the attribute a, and n_o, the number of times s appears in D_o (or in the ontology as attributes other than a), $P(a_+|s)$ is estimated by the following formula: $\hat{P}(a_+|s) = n_a/(n_a + n_o)$.

Currently, the input Web page set P is used as D_o. This has a good effect on the estimation because $n_o > 0$ holds for every s in P, which makes the estimation more reliable than using other sets as D_o.

Unlike the case of generative models, appearances of the same attribute or value in the same page is counted only once even if they appear many times. For example, even if many strings that seem to be birthday values appear many times in a page, the algorithm considers only one evidence that seems to be the most likely to indicate a birthday value.

The main reason we use this model is that it can naturally model the *uniqueness* and *diversity* of strings. Uniqueness means how exclusively a string s appears in specific topic and it is modeled as the parameter $P(C_+|s)$. Diversity means how many kinds of attributes of the target topic are presented. It is modeled as the interpolation of $P(C_+|s)$ over all attributes. In other words, our model can deal with attribute-value structures of ontologies and information outside of ontologies in a simple way. We think this simplicity makes the model robust and applicable to every kind of Web pages.

5 Preliminary Experiments

We chose two categories for experiments: people and PCs. An ontology for each category was extracted from HTML tables collected from the Web. A human ontology was extracted from 1327 tables, and a PC ontology was extracted from 68 tables.

Performance of the algorithms were measured on a set of 3,317 Web pages (written in Japanese) collected from the Web. Because this set is so large that it is hard to annotate all pages in it, we labeled only pages returned as top-30 results by each algorithm. We employed a *pooling method* [14] to calculate average precision and recall. Pooling is a method to select documents to be used for evaluation when a entire set of documents is too large to annotate all members of it. In pooling, every top N (=30, in this experiment,) results by each algorithm are *pooled* to a test collection.

We also implemented a standard vector-space-model based algorithm as a baseline. In this algorithm, unigram and bigram features[6] were used to model both ontologies and Web pages, and values for their features were set to the simple term frequencies. Relevance scores were calculated as dot-products of vectors. Note that we did not use IDF (Inversed Document Frequency) measure because it is not obvious how to define document frequency parameter relevant to both of unstructured Web pages and ontologies extracted from HTML tables.

---

[6] The same features as the ones used in our algorithm.

Table 1. Results in Average Precision.

Category	People			PC		
Features	AV	A	V	AV	A	V
Our method (Window)	**0.527**	0.374	0.215	**0.837**	0.461	0.746
Our method (Naive)	0.185	**0.231**	0.0995	0.488	0.351	0.481
Vector Space Model	0.0493	**0.139**	0.0158	0.208	**0.437**	0.282

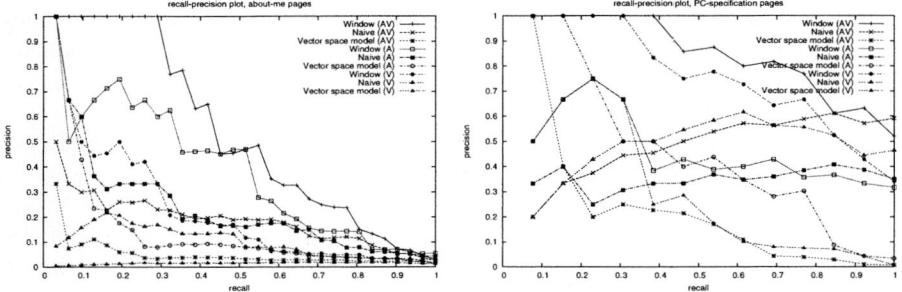

Fig. 4. Recall-precision plot for about-me pages and PC-specification pages.

To investigate the effect of attributes and values to the performance, we used three types of features: *AV*, *A* and *V*. *AV* represents that strings from both of attributes and values in an ontology were used, *A* represents that only strings in attributes were used, and *V* represents that only strings in values were used.

Table 1 shows the results in average-precision [15]. Average-precision is defined as $\{\sum_{1 \leq k \leq |D|} r_k \cdot precision(k)\}/|D_q|$ where D_q is a set of relevant documents, D is a set of all documents and r_k represents whether the k-th document is relevant (1) or not (0).

Here, *Window* means our algorithm when the area-selection module was used, *Naive* means our algorithm with no area-selection, and *Vector Space Model* means the standard vector-space-model based algorithm.

Improvement from *Naive* from *Vector Space Model* shows the effect of modeling uniqueness and diversity (*i.e.*, using information outside of ontologies and interpolating parameters all over the attributes and values).

We also observed dramatic improvement of the performance of our model when window-size restriction was used. This improvement was mainly caused by avoiding to retrieve very large pages where topic-related strings were scattered over whole parts of pages.

Figure 4 shows the result in recall-precision plot. We can see that the vector-space-model suffered from unrelevant documents especially for the human category. We think this was because words in the human ontology have more variety than those in the PC ontology, making more unrelevant documents retrieved.

6 Conclusion

This paper proposed an algorithm to retrieve specification information describing some attributes and their values of objects. The idea was to use ontologies extracted from HTML tables as queries. We also proposed the simple model for effectively detecting uniqueness and diversity of strings in Web pages. Experimental results showed that our proposed algorithm was effective in comparison with standard vector-space-model algorithm.

We are now working on making use of HTML tag information in target Web documents to achieve better retrieval results. Evaluation using more various kinds of topics and various kinds of ontologies are also interesting future work. We are especially interested in using very small ontologies extracted from one or a few HTML tables.

References

1. Lewis, D.D., Ringuette, M.: A comparison of two learning algorithms for text categorization. In: Proceedings of SDAIR-94, 3rd Annual Symposium on Document Analysis and Information Retrieval. (1994) 81–93
2. Quinlan, J.R.: C4.5: programs for machine learning. Morgan Kaufmann (1994)
3. Manning, C., Schütze, H.: Foundations of statistical natural language processing. MIT Press (1999)
4. Nigam, K., Lafferty, J., McCallum, A.: Using maximum entropy for text categorization. In: Proceedings of IJCAI-99 Workshop on Machine Learning for Information Filtering. (1999) 61–67
5. Cortes, C., Vapnik, V.: Support vector networks. Machine Learning **20** (1995) 273–297
6. Salton, G., Wang, A., Yang, C.: A vector space model for information retrieval. Journal of the American Society for Information Science **18** (1975) 613–620
7. Zaragoza, H., Hiemstra, D., Tipping, M.E.: Bayesian extension to the language model for ad hoc information retrieval. In: Proceedings of SIGIR 2003. (2003) 4–9
8. Sanderson, M.: Retrieving with good sense. Information Retrieval **2(1)** (2000) 49–69
9. Miller, G.A.: Wordnet: A lexical database for english. Communications of the ACM **38(11)** (1995) 39–41
10. Masuda, K.: A ranking model of proximal and structural text retrieval based on region algebra. In: Proceedings of the ACL 2003 Student Research Workshop. (2003) 50–57
11. Yoshida, M., Torisawa, K., Tsujii, J.: Extracting ontologies from World Wide Web via HTML tables. In: Proceedings of PACLING2001. (2001) 332–341
12. Salton, G., Allan, J., Buckley, C.: Approaches to passage retrieval in full text information systems. In: Proceedings of the 16th Annual International ACM SIGIR Conference on Research and Development in Information Retrieval. (1993) 49–58
13. Rivest, R.: Learning decision trees. Machine Learning **2** (1987) 229–246
14. Cormack, G.V., Palmer, C.R., Clarke, C.L.A.: Efficient construction of large test collections. In: Proceedings of the 21st International ACM SIGIR-98. (1998) 282–289
15. Chakrabarti, S.: Mining the Web: Discovering Knowledge from Hypertext Data. Morgan-Kaufmann Publishers (2002)

Conceptual Information-Based Sense Disambiguation

You-Jin Chung[1], Kyonghi Moon[2], and Jong-Hyeok Lee[1]

[1] Div. of Electrical and Computer Engineering, POSTECH and AITrc,
San 31, Hyojadong, Pohang, R. of Korea
{prizer,jhlee}@postech.ac.kr
[2] Div. of Computer and Information Engineering, Silla University,
San 1-1, Gwaebop-Dong, Sasang-Gu, Busan, R. of Korea
khmun@silla.ac.kr

Abstract. Most previous corpus-based approaches to word-sense disambiguation (WSD) collect salient words from the context of a target word. However, they suffer from the problem of data sparseness. To overcome the problem, this paper proposes a concept-based WSD method that uses an automatically generated sense-tagged corpus. Grammatical similarities between Korean and Japanese enable the construction of a sense-tagged Korean corpus through an existing high-quality Japanese-to-Korean machine translation system. The sense-tagged corpus can serve as a knowledge source to extract useful clues for word sense disambiguation, such as concept co-occurrence information. In an evaluation, a weighted voting model achieved the best average precision of 77.22%, with an improvement over the baseline by 14.47%, which shows that our proposed method is very promising for practical MT systems.

1 Introduction

Generally, a Korean homograph may be translated into a different Japanese equivalent depending on which sense is used in a given context. Thus, noun sense disambiguation is essential to the selection of an appropriate Japanese target word in Korean-to-Japanese translation.

Much research on word sense disambiguation (WSD) has revealed that several different types of information can contribute to the resolution of lexical ambiguity. These include surrounding words (an unordered set of words surrounding a target word), collocations (a co-occurrence of two words in some defined relation), syntactic relations (selectional restrictions), parts of speech, morphological forms, semantic context, etc [3], [8], [9]. Especially, collocations have been used as the most informative feature that provides important clues to WSD [9], [13]. To obtain collocations and surrounding words from corpora, most WSD systems collect root forms or surface forms of collocating words. However, the use of word-specific features suffers from the data sparseness problem and becomes the main reason for low system coverage.

Some researchers use conceptual information of the surrounding context to overcome the limitation of word-based approaches [6], [7], [12]. These concept-based models can correctly identify a word sense that occurs rarely or only once in the corpus. Also, they offer the additional advantage of smaller model storage requirements. However, like word-specific models, concept-based models have a fundamental obstacle: the difficulty of acquiring sense-tagged corpora. Thus, the previous concept-based approaches obtain domain information or conceptual co-occurrence data by using word definitions and subject codes in MRD instead of sense-tagged corpora. Such a method cannot guarantee the quality of the collected information.

In our WSD approach, we construct a sense-tagged corpus automatically by using linguistic similarities between Korean and Japanese. Our disambiguation model is based on the work of Li et al [5], especially focusing on the practicality of the method for application to real world systems. We alleviate the data sparseness problem by adopting a concept-based approach and reduce the number of features to a practical size by generalization processing.

This paper is organized as follows. Section 2 presents the overall system architecture. Section 3 explains the automatic construction of a sense-tagged Korean corpus and the extraction of features for word sense disambiguation. Section 4 describes the construction of feature set and the learning of disambiguation models. In Section 5, the experimental results are given, showing that the proposed method may be useful for WSD in a real text. In this paper, Yale Romanization is used to represent Korean expressions.

2 System Architecture

Our disambiguation method consists of two phases. The first phase is the extraction of features for WSD and the second phase is the construction of disambiguation models (see Figure 1).

Because our disambiguation model is designed for use in a machine translation system, the practicality of the method is important. To address the data sparseness problem, we adopt Li's method [5], based on concept co-occurrence information (CCI). CCI are concept codes of words that co-occur with the target word for a specific syntactic relation.

In accordance with Li's method, we automatically extract CCI from a corpus by constructing a sense-tagged Korean corpus. To accomplish this, we apply a Japanese-to-Korean MT system. Next, we extract CCI from the constructed corpus through partial parsing and pattern scanning. To increase coverage of the method, generalization processing is applied to the extracted CCI set. The generalized CCI are used as features for disambiguation models.

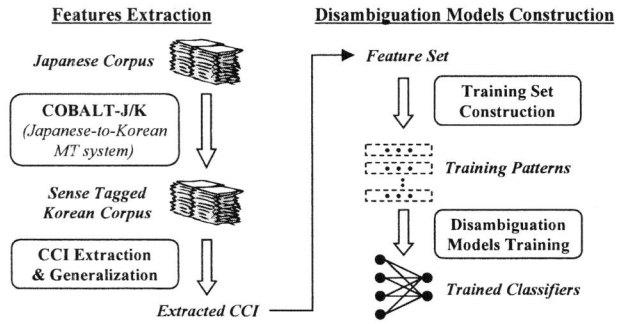

Fig. 1. System architecture

3 Feature Extracting for WSD

3.1 Automatic Construction of Sense-Tagged Corpus

Japanese and Korean are very similar in word order and lexical properties. Also, they have many nouns in common derived from Chinese characters. Because almost all Japanese common nouns represented by Chinese characters are monosemous, little transfer ambiguity is exhibited in Japanese-to-Korean translation of nouns, and we can obtain a sense-tagged Korean corpus of good quality by using those linguistic similarities between Korean and Japanese.

For automatic construction of the sense-tagged corpus, we used a Japanese-to-Korean MT system called COBALT-J/K[1]. In the transfer dictionary of COBALT-J/K, nominal and verbal words are annotated with the concept codes of the Kadokawa thesaurus [10], which has a 4-level hierarchy of about 1,100 semantic classes, as shown in Figure 2. Concept nodes in level L_1, L_2 and L_3 are further divided into 10 subclasses.

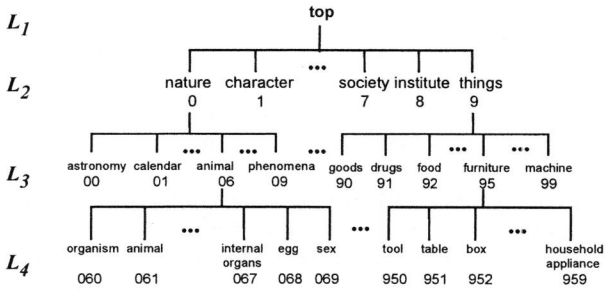

Fig. 2. Concept hierarchy of the Kadokawa thesaurus

We made a slight modification of COBALT-J/K to enable it to produce Korean translations from a Japanese text, with all content words tagged with specific concept codes at level L_4 of the Kadokawa thesaurus. As a result, a sense-tagged Korean corpus of 1,060,000 sentences can be obtained from the Japanese corpus (*Asahi Shinbun* (1994.11~1997.03), Japanese Newspaper of Economics (1993.09~1993.12), etc.).

The quality of the constructed sense-tagged corpus is a critical issue. To evaluate the quality, we collected 772 sample sentences (13,716 eojeols[2]) from the corpus and checked their precision. The total number of errors was 368, and included such errors as morphological analysis, sense ambiguity resolution, and unknown words. It corresponds to the accuracy of 97.32% (13,348/13,716 eojeols). Considering the fact that the overall accuracy of the constructed corpus exceeds 97%, we conclude that the generated sense-tagged corpus is highly reliable. Figure 3 shows an example of the sense-tagged corpus. Each Korean word is tagged with its original Japanese word and concept codes of the Kadokawa thesaurus.

---

[1] COBALT-J/K (Collocation-Based Language Translator from Japanese to Korean) is a high-quality practical MT system developed by POSTECH.

[2] An *eojeol* is a Korean syntactic unit consisting of a content word and one or more function words.

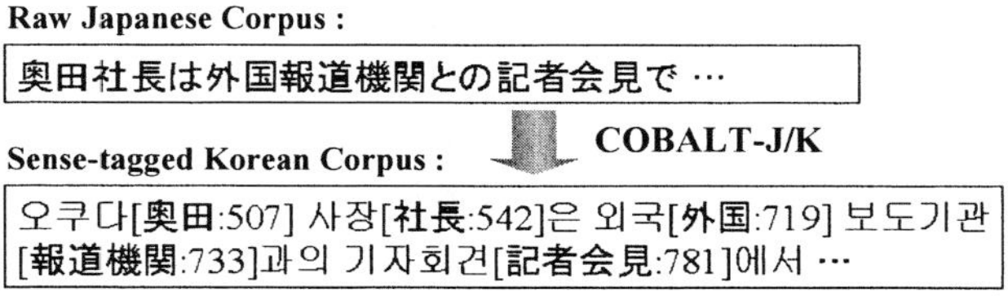

Raw Japanese Corpus:

奥田社長は外国報道機関との記者会見で …

Sense-tagged Korean Corpus:　COBALT-J/K

오쿠다[奧田:507] 사장[社長:542]은 외국[外國:719] 보도기관
[報道機關:733]과의 기자회견[記者會見:781]에서 …

Fig. 3. Construction of sense-tagged corpus

3.2 Extraction of CCI

Unlike English, Korean has almost no syntactic constraints on word order as long as the verb appears in the final position. The variable word order often results in discontinuous constituents. Instead of using local collocations by word order, Li defined 13 patterns of CCI for homographs using syntactically related words in a sentence [5]. Because we are concerned only with noun homographs, we adopt 11 patterns from them excluding verb patterns, as shown in Table 1. The words in bold indicate the target homograph and the words in italic indicate Korean particles.

We extract CCI of the target homograph from the sense-tagged corpus according to each pattern type defined in Table 1.

Table 1. Co-occurrence patterns for CCI extraction

type no.	Structure of pattern	type no.	Structure of pattern
co-type$_0$	unordered co-occurrence words	co-type$_1$	**noun** + noun or noun + **noun**
co-type$_2$	**noun** + other particles + noun	co-type$_3$	**noun** + *uy* + noun
co-type$_4$	**noun** + *lo/ulo* + verb	co-type$_5$	**noun** + *ey* + verb
co-type$_6$	**noun** + *eygey* + verb	co-type$_7$	**noun** + *eyse* + verb
co-type$_8$	**noun** + *ul/lul* + verb	co-type$_9$	**noun** + *i/ka* + verb
co-type$_{10}$	verb + relativizer + **noun**		

To select the most probable CCI which frequently co-occur with the target sense of a homograph, Li defined the discrimination value of a concept code using Shannon's entropy.

$$noise_k = -\sum_{i=1}^{n} \frac{p(C_k|S_i)}{\sum_{j=1}^{n} p(C_k|S_j)} \log_2 \frac{p(C_k|S_i)}{\sum_{j=1}^{n} p(C_k|S_j)} \quad (1)$$

$$DS_k = (\log_2 n - noise_k)/\log_2 n \quad (2)$$

In Equation 1, S_i represents the ith sense of the target homograph with n senses and C_k is the concept code of the co-occurring word. $noise_k$ is the noise value generated by the concept code C_k. If the discrimination value DS_k of C_k is larger than a threshold, C_k is selected as a useful CCI for deciding word sense S_i. Otherwise, C_k is discarded.

3.3 Generalization of Concept Codes

The extracted CCI are too numerous to be used in a practical system, and must be further selected. To perform code generalization, Li adopted Smadja's work [11] and defined the code strength using a code frequency and a standard deviation in each level of the concept hierarchy. The generalization filter selects the concept codes with a strength greater than a threshold. We perform this generalization processing on the Kadokawa thesaurus level L_4 and L_3. The more specific description of the CCI extraction and generalization is explained in [5].

4 Word Sense Disambiguation Models

4.1 Construction of Feature Set

To consider all features at the same time, we construct the feature set by integrating the extracted CCI into a single vector. In disambiguation processing, this feature integration gives each feature positive strength on the sense containing that feature and negative values on the other senses. Thus the discrimination power of a disambiguation model may be improved.

Figure 4[3] demonstrates a construction example of the feature set for the Korean homograph '*nwun*' with the sense 'snow' and 'eye'. The left side is the extracted CCI for each sense of '*nwun*' and the right is the constructed feature set. The resulting feature set is partitioned into several subgroups depending on their *co-types*, i.e., *co-type 0*, *co-type 1*, *co-type 2* and *co-type 8*. Since the extracted CCI set are different according to each word, each homograph has a feature set of its own.

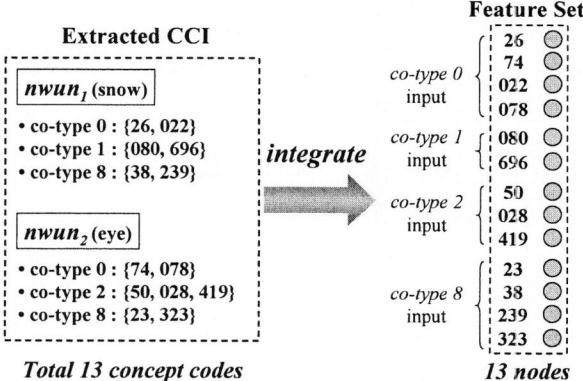

Fig. 4. Construction of feature set for '*nwun*'

---

[3] The concept codes in Figure 4 are simplified ones for the ease of illustration. In reality there are 78 concept codes for '*nwun*'.

4.2 Extraction of Training Patterns

After constructing the feature set for WSD, we extract training patterns for each homograph from the previously constructed sense-tagged corpus. The construction of training pattern is performed in the following 2 steps.

Step 1. Extract CCI from the context of the target homograph. The window size of the context is a single sentence. Consider, for example, the sentence in Figure 5 which means "Seeing her eyes filled with tears, ...". The target homograph is the word '*nwun*'. We extract its CCI from the sentence by partial parsing and pattern scanning. In Figure 5, the words '*nwun*' and '*kunye*(her)' with the concept code 503 have the relation of <noun + *uy* + noun>, which corresponds to '*co-type 2*' in Table 1. There is no syntactic relation between the words '*nwun*' and '*nwunmul*(tears)' with the concept code 078, so we assign '*co-type 0*' to the concept code 078.

Similarly, we can obtain all pairs of *co-types* and their concept codes appearing in the context. The extracted context CCI set is as follows: {<*co-type 0: 078, 274, 331, 503*>, <*co-type 2: 503*>, <*co-type 8: 331*>}.

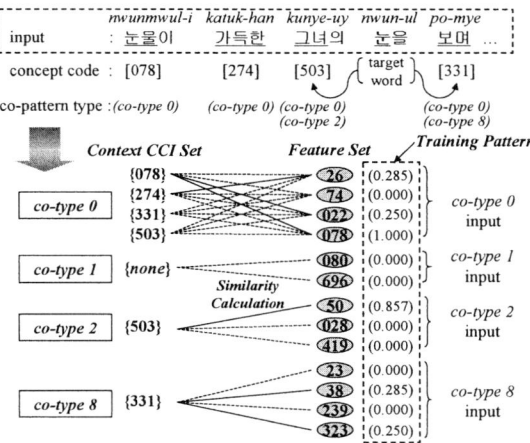

Fig. 5. Construction of training patterns by using concept similarity calculation

Step 2. Obtain the training pattern by calculating concept similarities between concept codes in the context CCI set and the feature set. Concept similarity calculation is performed only between the concept codes with the same CCI-type. This similarity value represents the extent of activation strength that each feature should receive. If the concept code in the feature set appears exactly in the context of the target homograph, it receives the highest strength of 1.0. But if the concept code does not appear in the input sentence exactly, it receives a strength value of less than 1.0, which is obtained by similarity calculation. The concept similarity score is assigned to each feature node as its activation strength, as shown in the right side of Figure 5. The use of this concept similarity scheme gives an advantage of broad system coverage. If we use an exact matching scheme instead of concept similarity-based matching, we may find only a few context CCI exactly matched with the concept codes in the feature set.

Equation 3 is the concept similarity calculation formula between the concept codes C_i and P_j.

$$Csim(C_i, P_j) = \frac{2 \times level(MSCA(C_i, P_j))}{level(C_i) + level(P_j)} \times weight \quad (3)$$

where $MSCA(C_i, P_j)$ is the most specific common ancestor of concept codes C_i and P_j, and *weight* is a weighting factor reflecting that C_i as a descendant of P_j is preferable to other cases. That is, if C_i is a descendant of P_j, we set *weight* to 1. Otherwise, we set the *weight* to 0.5 [4]. If more than two concept codes exist in one *co-type*, such as <co-type 0: 078, 274, 331, 503>, the maximum similarity value among them is assigned to the input node, as in Equation 4.

$$InputVal(P_j) = \max_{C_i}(Csim(C_i, P_j)) \quad (4)$$

In Equation 4, P_j is the concept code of the feature set, and C_i indicates the concept codes in the context CCI set which has the same *co-type*.

4.3 Learning of WSD Models

Using the obtained feature set and training patterns, we learned 5 types of individual classifiers, such as naïve Bayes (NB), neural network (NN), decision tree (DT), decision list (DL) and support vector machine (SVM). The neural network, decision tree and decision list often have been used in pattern recognition problems because of their strong capability in classification. Recently, the support vector machine has generated great interest in the machine learning community due to its excellent generalization performance in a wide variety of learning problems. Decision tree and SVM training were carried out with *C4.5* decision tree learner and *SVM light* package, respectively. Other classifiers were implemented on our own.

Also, we implemented 5 types of classifier combination systems introduced in [2]: probability summation, weighted probability summation, simple voting, weighted voting and rank-based combination. From a statistical point of view, if the size of the sample is small, generating different classifiers about the sample and combining them may result in a more accurate prediction of new patterns. On the other hand, based on a computational view, if the sample is large enough, the nature of the learning algorithm could lead to getting stuck in local optima. Therefore, a classifier combination is a way to expand the hypothesis space to represent the true function [1]. The following are the implemented models for classifier combination.

Probability Summation

$$PS\ score(S_i) = \sum_{k=1}^{N} P_k(S_i \mid x, D) \quad (5)$$

where N is the number of base classifiers and $P_k(S_i|x,D)$ is the probability distribution output of the k-th classifier for the sense S_i of the target word x on the given context D.

Weighted Probability Summation

$$WPS\ score(S_i) = \sum_{k=1}^{N} \lambda_k \cdot P_k(S_i \mid x, D) \tag{6}$$

where λ_k is the weight assigned to the k-th classifier. We used the average precision of each base classifier as λ_k. ($\lambda_{NN} > \lambda_{DL} > \lambda_{DT} > \lambda_{SVM} > \lambda_{NB}$)

Simple Voting

$$SV\ score(S_i) = \sum_{k=1}^{N} \delta(S_i, \hat{S}_k(x, D)) \tag{7}$$

where $\hat{S}_k(x,D)$ is the classification of the k-th classifier and δ is the Kronecker function: $\delta(x, y) = 1$ if x equals y, otherwise 0.

Weighted Voting

$$WV\ score(S_i) = \sum_{k=1}^{N} \lambda_k \cdot \delta(S_i, \hat{S}_k(x, D)) \tag{8}$$

Rank-Based Combination

$$RC\ score(S_i) = \sum_{k=1}^{N} \lambda_k \cdot rank_k(S_i \mid x, D) \tag{9}$$

where the rank of the sense S_i is inversely proportional to the number of senses that are more probable than S_i:

$$rank_k(S_i \mid x, D) = (|\{S_i' \mid P_k(S_i' \mid x, D) > P_k(S_i \mid x, D)\}| + 1)^{-1} \tag{10}$$

5 Experimental Evaluation

For an experimental evaluation, 15 Korean noun homographs were selected, along with a total of 1,200 test sentences in which one homograph appears (2 senses: 12 words, 3 senses: 2 words, 4 senses: 1 word). The test sentences were randomly selected from the KIBS (Korean Information Base System) corpus.

Table 2. Comparison results of machine learning classifiers

Individual Classifier	Precision	Combination Model	Precision
Most Frequent Sense (baseline)	62.75%	Probability Summation	76.22%
Naive Bayes	70.47%	Weighted Prob. Summation	76.38%
Decision List	75.05%	Simple Voting	76.47%
Neural Network (3-layer)	76.30%	Weighted Voting	77.22%
Decision Tree (pruning lvl. : 25%)	74.47%	Rank-based Combination	76.55%
SVM (RBF kernel)	73.55%		

The left side of Table 2 shows the comparison results of the system when each individual classifier is used. The baseline is the case when the most frequent sense

(MFS) was taken as the answer. Among the individual classifiers, 3-layer neural network model performs best. The neural network model performs significantly better than SVM and naïve Bayes at a significance level of 0.05, as measured by a McNemar test. However, the difference in performance between the neural network and the second best model (i.e. decision list) was not statistically significant.

To construct the classifier combination models, we selected the models with the best performing parameter in each individual classifier group. The right side of Table 2 shows the precision results of five classifier combination methods described in Section 4.3. As shown in Table 2, the weighted voting method showed the best performance above all other individual classifiers and the combination models. It performs significantly better than the best base classifier (i.e. neural network) at a significance level of 0.10. Also, it exceeds the baseline by 14.47%. This result indicates that sense disambiguation can be improved by classifier combination and also shows that our concept-based disambiguation model is promising for practical MT systems.

6 Conclusion

To resolve sense ambiguities of Korean nouns, this paper has proposed a practical word sense disambiguation method using concept co-occurrence information. We constructed a sense-tagged Korean corpus by using Japanese corpus and a machine translation system and extracted CCI features from it. We presented experiments comparing five different individual classifiers and also presented the evaluation results of five types of the classifier combination method. Although the source languages of the training and the test set were different, out conceptual information-based disambiguation models showed good performance. In an experimental evaluation, the weighted voting model achieved an average precision of 77.22% with an improvement over the baseline by 14.47%. This result indicates that the concept co-occurrence information-based approach is very promising.

Acknowledgements

This work was supported by the KOSEF through the Advanced Information Technology Research Center (AITrc) and by the BK21 Project in 2003.

References

1. Ardeshir, G.: Decision Tree Simplification for Classifier Ensembles. PHD Thesis, University of Surrey, U.K (2002)
2. Florian, R. and Yarowsky, D.: Modeling Consensus: Classifier Combination for Word Sense Disambiguation. In Proceedings of EMNLP, Philadelphia, PA, USA, pp.25-32 (2002)
3. Ide, N. and Veronis, J.: Introduction to the Special Issue on Word Sense Disambiguation: The State of the Art. Computational Linguistics, Vol.24, No.1, pp.1-40 (1998)
4. Kim, E. J. and Lee, J. H.: A Collocation-Based Transfer Model for Japanese-to-Korean Machine Translation. In Proceedings of the NLPRS, Fukuoka, Japan, pp.223-231 (1993)

5. Li, H. F., Heo, N. W., Moon, K. H., Lee, J. H. and Lee, G. B.: Lexical Transfer Ambiguity Resolution Using Automatically-Extracted Concept Co-occurrence Information. International Journal of Computer Processing of Oriental Languages, 13(1):53-68 (2000)
6. Luk, A. K.: Statistical Sense Disambiguation with Relatively Small Corpora Using Dictionary Definitions. In Proceedings of the 33rd Annual Meeting of the ACL, Columbus, Ohio, USA, pp.181-188 (1995)
7. Magnini, B., Strapparava, C., Pezzulo, G. and Gliozzo, A.: Using Domain Information for Word Sense Disambiguation. In Proceeding of SENSEVAL-2, Toulouse, France, pp.111-114 (2001)
8. McRoy, S.: Using Multiple Knowledge Sources for Word Sense Discrimination. Computational Linguistics, 18(1):1-30 (1992)
9. Ng, H. T. and Lee, H. B.: Integrating Multiple Knowledge Sources to Disambiguate Word Sense: An Exemplar-based Approach. In Proceedings of the 34th Annual Meeting of the ACL, Santa Cruz, CA, USA, pp.40-47 (1996)
10. Ohno, S. and Hamanishi, M.: New Synonym Dictionary. Kadokawa Shoten, Japan (1981)
11. Smadja, F.: Retrieving Collocations from Text: Xtract. Computational Linguistics, 19(1):143-177 (1993)
12. Yarowsky, D.: Word-Sense Disambiguation Using Statistical Models of Roget's Categories Trained on Large Corpora. In Proceedings of the COLING-92, Nantes, France, pp.454-460 (1992)
13. Yarowsky, D.: One Sense per Collocation. In Proceedings of the ARPA Human Language Technology Workshop, Princeton, NJ, USA, pp.266-271 (1993)

Influence of WSD
on Cross-Language Information Retrieval

In-Su Kang, Seung-Hoon Na, and Jong-Hyeok Lee

Div. of Electrical and Computer Engineering, POSTECH and AITrc,
San 31, Hyojadong, Pohang, 790-784, R. of Korea
{dbaisk,nsh1979,jhlee}@postech.ac.kr

Abstract. Translation ambiguity is a major problem in dictionary-based cross-language information retrieval. This paper proposes a statistical word sense disambiguation (WSD) approach for translation ambiguity resolution. Then, with respect to CLIR effectiveness, the pure effect of a disambiguation module will be explored on the following issues: contribution of disambiguation weight to target term weighting, influences of WSD performance on CLIR retrieval effectiveness. In our investigation, we do not use pre-translation or post-translation methods to exclude any mixing effects on CLIR.

1 Introduction

Cross-language information retrieval (CLIR) deals with the task of retrieving documents in one language using queries in another language. Since there are two different languages, a certain translation process is required to find a common representation through either query translation or document translation. Although large-scale document translation approaches [10] were reported, it has limitations: computational expensiveness and restricted document representation by incomplete MT systems. Compared with document translation, query translation is more flexible, and lightweight. However, it severely suffers from the translation ambiguity problem, resulting from insufficient linguistic context and noisy translation resources not designed for machine translation purposes.

Approaches for resolving translation ambiguity can be classified into direct and indirect methods, according to whether each target term is assigned a translation probability or not. Most indirect methods rely on query-structuring techniques such as a weighted Boolean model [6], sense-grouping [13], and Pirkola's pseudo term methods [4,11], and then disambiguation occurs implicitly by retrieval models. Direct methods [2,5,7,14] explicitly calculate translation probabilities of each target term using co-occurrence information from the assumption that correct translations tend to co-occur in target documents. Direct disambiguation is preferable, since it allows some term selection schemes such as selecting top n terms for each source language query term.

In this paper, we will study the net effect of translation ambiguity resolution on CLIR retrieval effectiveness in dictionary-based query translation. First, a statistical word sense disambiguation (WSD) approach for CLIR is developed to produce several disambiguation schemes that can explain most previous direct methods (Section 2). Then, the following issues are experimentally evaluated and discussed: disambiguation weight and collection weight (Section 4), relationships between WSD and CLIR performance (Section 5).

In our discussion, only dictionaries are considered as translation resources. Of course, other resources like corpora may influence disambiguation. For example, source language corpora can be used to obtain an additional context in order to resolve translation ambiguity in the form of pre-translation [1,8]. In addition, parallel or comparable corpora may provide translation likelihood values to existing translation pairs. However, normally, two-language corpora are not easily available, and source language corpora should be homogeneous to a target document collection for successful pre-translation.

For representing Korean expressions, the Yale Romanization is used in this paper.

2 Statistical WSD Approach for CLIR

From a statistical WSD perspective, translation ambiguity resolution is formulated as follows. An i-th source language query term s_i corresponds to a word to be disambiguated, and all possible translations of s_i correspond to a set of senses. Given a source language query $\mathbf{s} = s_1, \ldots, s_n$, and a target language query $\mathbf{t} = t_{11}, \ldots, t_{ij}, \ldots, t_{nm}$, where t_{ij} is the j-th translation of s_i, the probability of t_{ij} being the correct translation of s_i is defined by Formula (1). $s_i \rightarrow t_{ij}$ is reduced to t_{ij} since we always focus on disambiguation of a specific s_i. In addition, we discard $\mathbf{s}$ from the assumption that a likelihood of t_{ij} is not dependent on $\mathbf{s}$ if we already have $\mathbf{t}$ generated from $\mathbf{s}$. We call $\mathbf{t}$ a *disambiguation context*.

$$\Pr(s_i \rightarrow t_{ij} \mid \mathbf{s}, \mathbf{t}) = \Pr(t_{ij} \mid \mathbf{t}) \quad (1)$$

$$\Pr(t_{ij} \mid \mathbf{t}) \approx \Pr(t_{ij}) \Pr(\mathbf{t} \mid t_{ij}) \quad (2)$$

$$\approx \log \Pr(t_{ij}) + \sum \log \Pr(t \mid t_{ij}) \quad (3)$$

Formula (2) follows from the application of the Bayes formula, and from the deletion of a constant $\Pr(\mathbf{t})$ with respect to the ordering of the $\Pr(t_{ij} \mid \mathbf{t})$. Formula (3) is derived from the independence assumption between target terms t given a particular t_{ij}, and from the application of the monotonically increasing logarithmic function.

In this paper, $\Pr(t_{ij} \mid \mathbf{t})$ is called a *translation probability* that an i-th source language query term s_i is translated into its j-th translation t_{ij}. Precisely, it is not a probability in the above derivation, but translation strength. However, this paper uses a more common term *translation probability*.

In Formula (3), a priori probability $\Pr(t_{ij})$ can be estimated from a translation dictionary or a target document collection, or parallel corpora. In this paper, we assume uniformly distributed priors.

We interpret $\Pr(t \mid t_{ij})$ as the likelihood of a target term t being used in a sense context (e.g. a sentence or a document) where t_{ij} appears. In statistical WSD literatures, sense contexts are normally acquired by expensive manual sense tagging. For example, for one sense '$bank_1$' of a word '*bank*', one of its sense contexts will be a sentence where a word '*bank*' is used as the sense '*bank₁*'. However, a sense label in CLIR WSD corresponds to a surface word t_{ij}. Thus, we can easily obtain sense contexts from a target document collection itself. For example, for a Korean word '*unhaing(은행)*', sense contexts of '*bank*' (one of English translations of '*unhaing(은행)*') will be any sentence where '*bank*' appears in a target document collection. This paper does not address sense ambiguities from the perspective of the target language. Therefore, Pr($t \mid t_{ij}$) is obtained from maximum likelihood estimation, as in Formula (4), where m-estimate smoothing [9] is used to alleviate the data sparseness of word pairs.

$$\Pr(t \mid t_{ij}) = (n' + 1) / (n + |V|) \qquad (4)$$

In formula (4), n is the number of sense contexts of t_{ij}, and n' is the number of sense contexts of t_{ij} where t appears, and $|V|$ is the size of a dictionary vocabulary.

As far as we know, most previous CLIR direct disambiguation approaches [2,5,7,14] utilize mutual information (MI) instead of log Pr($t \mid t_{ij}$) in Formula (3) as follows.

$$\log \Pr(t \mid t_{ij}) = \mathrm{MI}(t, t_{ij}) \qquad (5)$$

Although the use of MI values lacks a theoretical foundation when applied to the CLIR WSD problem, the capability of MI to detect collocation words is known to support the assumption that correct target terms tend to co-occur in target documents. In this paper, these two estimation techniques (Formula (4), (5)) will be compared.

In the following, we investigate different interpretations of disambiguation context **t** with regard to the set of terms to be included.

- *T*(otal) : all translations of each s_j ($j \neq i$)
- *G*(roup) : the most likely translation of each s_j ($j \neq i$)
- *O*(ne) : the most likely context word among all translations of all s_j ($j \neq i$)

Table 1. Example of disambiguation contexts

Source Query	ca-tong-cha, sok-to, cey-han
Target Query	(*car*:0.7, *automobile*:0.5), (*speed*, *velocity*, *tempo*), (*restriction*:0.2, *limit*:0.8, *bound*:0.1)
Context Total	car, automobile, restriction, limit, bound
Context Group	car, limit
Context One	Limit

As indicated above, s_j applies to all query terms except the current query term s_i to be disambiguated. The first context option, *T*, simply uses all translations of all source language query terms. Hence, while *T* may include many incorrect noisy terms preventing normal operation of Pr($t_{ij} \mid$ **t**), synonyms of correct target terms in each translation group can have positive effects. The second option, *G*, uses only the most likely translation of each query term, by selecting a term that has the maximum value of Pr($t \mid t_{ij}$) among all terms within the same translation group. Context *G* is the most intuitive. The last context *O* uses only the best term that has maximum value of Pr($t \mid t_{ij}$) among all target terms. This option tries to exclude selection of any noisy terms.

Table 1 shows an example of different disambiguation context **t** to be used in order to calculate Pr(*speed* | **t**), given a Korean query "*ca-tong-cha(자동차) sok-to(속도) cey-han(제한)*" (car speed limit in English). In the second row, each figure denotes the likelihood of the corresponding context word given *speed*. For example, 0.7 attached to 'car' is obtained from Pr(car | *speed*).

3 Experimental Design

To evaluate the disambiguation effect on CLIR retrieval effectiveness, we created seven different disambiguation models, as described in Table 2. The first six models were derived from the statistical WSD formula using two estimation techniques and three disambiguation contexts discussed in Section 2. Additionally, a support vector machine (SVM) model was prepared to investigate the CLIR performance of a machine learning WSD approach. Among previous disambiguation works, Yibo et al. [14] used MI-T. Gao et al. [5] employed MI-G.

Table 2. WSD Models

Model	Estimation	Disambiguation Context
RF-T	MLE	Total
RF-G	MLE	Group
RF-O	MLE	One
MI-T	MI	Total
MI-G	MI	Group
MI-O	MI	One
SVM	MI	Total

An experimental evaluation of all WSD models was conducted on the NTCIR-3 Korean-to-English CLIR test collection [3] using a relaxed relevance judgment set. There are 32 topic files, which are comprised of four fields: Title, Description, Narrative, and Concept. The target document collection consists of 22,927 English newspaper articles published in 1998 and 1999. The total number of relevant documents is 741.

Before indexing each English document, stopwords were removed using our own stoplist of 374 words, and stemming is performed by the Porter's algorithm. For Korean queries, our laboratory's Korean Morphological Analyzer (KoMA) is used to extract nouns as query terms. In this experiment, we did not perform Korean stopword removal.

Our Korean-English translation dictionary is a general-purpose bilingual dictionary designed for human users. Table 3 and 4 shows dictionary statistics and query statistics, respectively. Surprisingly, degrees of our KE query ambiguity are very high. In most CLIR literatures including Korean as the query language, degrees of query ambiguity are reported to be less than 4, which is true for the degree of our dictionary ambiguity. In Table 4, 'word' and 'phrase' means that the number of translations was counted on the word and phrase basis, respectively.

Table 3. Statistics about K-E bilingual dictionary

# of Translation pairs	232,735
# of Korean unique terms	78,710
# of English unique terms	139,531
Dictionary ambiguity	2.96

Table 4. Query Statistics

		Title	Desc	Avg.
# of Korean query terms		152	320	
Dictionary coverage		0.68	0.75	0.73
KE Query Ambiguity	Word	8.83	11.81	10.32
	Phrase	8.35	11.33	9.84

Currently, we think that these high degrees of query ambiguity are due to the following points. We did not filter out words having parts-of-speech different from that of query terms when looking up a bilingual dictionary. In addition, we did not perform any dictionary preprocessing by human.

In addition, in order to investigate realistic CLIR WSD performances, we used only short queries, such as title and description fields, although WSD schemes are normally more effective with long queries. In all our experiments, the Okapi retrieval model approximated by Singhal [12] was used, and any feedback or query expansion was not performed to exclude any mixing effects in CLIR. All search results are reported in terms of the non-interpolated mean average precision.

Table 5 gives the baseline experimental results. KE baseline queries are obtained from expanding all dictionary translations of each source language query term. KE manual queries were created by manually selecting one correct target term for each source language query term from the KE baseline query.

Table 5. Mean average precision results of monolingual and cross-language baseline systems

	Title	Desc
E-E monolingual	0.2754	0.3514
K-E baseline	0.2174	0.1851
K-E manual	0.2989	0.2711

4 Disambiguation Weight vs. Collection Weight

From this section, we discuss two directions about how to utilize disambiguation results of a WSD module. One is to take only ordering of target terms. This will be handled in Section 5. The other is to incorporate disambiguation weights from a WSD module into target term weighting. For this, we designed a Formula (6), where $W(t)$ is a final target term weight. $W_{wsd}(t)$ is a disambiguation weight of a term t, and $W_{model}(t)$ is a collection term weight determined by a particular retrieval model, and α is a disambiguation importance. Notice that a disambiguation weight is obtained by applying a certain normalization technique to translation probabilities (Section 2.1) from a WSD module.

$$W(t) = ((1-\alpha) + \alpha \times W_{wsd}(t)) \times W_{model}(t) \tag{6}$$

If α equals 1, the disambiguation weight has an exclusive effect on the collection term weight. If α equals 0, the WSD module has no effect on target term weighting. The intermediate values of α control the contribution portion of a disambiguation weight on target term weight.

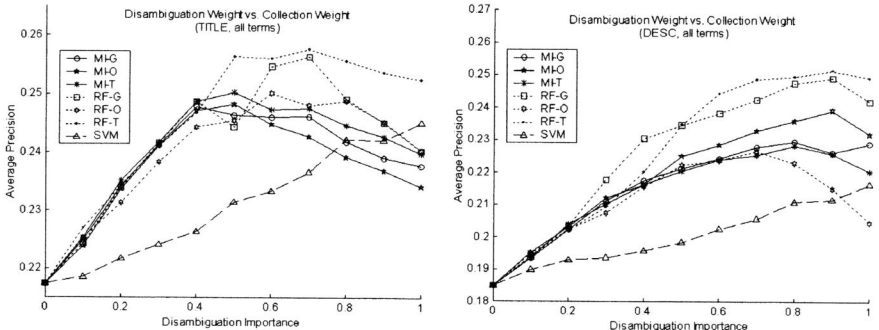

Fig. 1. Mean average precisions of different WSD models at varying disambiguation importance values

Figure 1 shows the non-interpolated mean average precision for each WSD model across disambiguation importance values for title and description queries, respectively. Solid lines depict MI estimation, and dotted lines, MLE estimation. Performances increase gradually. The reason is as follows. Within each translation group, most translations will be incorrect. Thus, larger disambiguation importance decreases the final term weight of the many noisy target terms a little more.

However, except for the SVM model that corresponds to a triangle, all models show the best performance at the intermediate α values between 0 and 1, and performance drops at $\alpha=1$. The performance difference at the optimal α value and 1.0 varies from 0.05 to 2.39 across models. We think the reason as follows. If exclusive disambiguation importance ($\alpha=1$) is used, the target term weight is completely dependent on the disambiguation weight from a WSD module. In that case, a WSD system dominates CLIR effectiveness. That is, incorrectly-disambiguated noisy terms may exhibit their full weights, resulting in undermining effectiveness.

Hence, the relative contribution of CLIR WSD module needs to be controlled through disambiguation importance, for example, as in Formula (6). Moreover, it would be better not to exclusively apply disambiguation weight to target term weight.

5 WSD vs. CLIR Retrieval Effectiveness

This section addresses the relationship between WSD performance and CLIR retrieval effectiveness. First, we calculated the WSD accuracy of each model across the varying number of top target terms. In calculating accuracies, if there is any correct translation among the top n terms from the WSD module, we considered the corresponding source query term to be correctly disambiguated. The results are shown in Figure 2. As the number n increases, the WSD performance increases.

As we expected, theoretically-sound WSD models using MLE estimation performed better in disambiguation than MI-based ad-hoc models. From the viewpoint of the disambiguation context discussed in Section 2.3, taking intuitive context G leads to better performance. Interestingly, the machine learning approach based on SVM performed well. Considering the high degrees of query ambiguity (8.83) of title queries used in this experiment, accuracy 61.9 for a top 1 term supports the application of SVM to CLIR WSD. However, the training phase of SVM requires large time and space complexity since we need a SVM model for each word. For this experiment, we created SVM models for only target query terms of NTCIR-3 Korean queries.

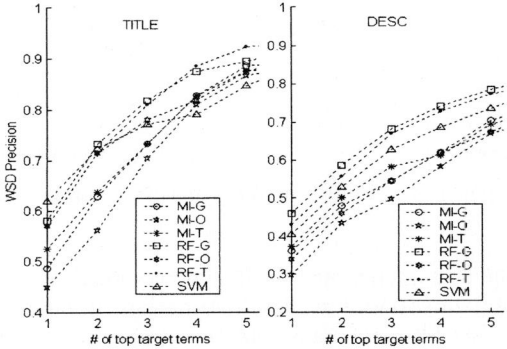

Fig. 2. WSD precision of different WSD models at varying number of top target terms

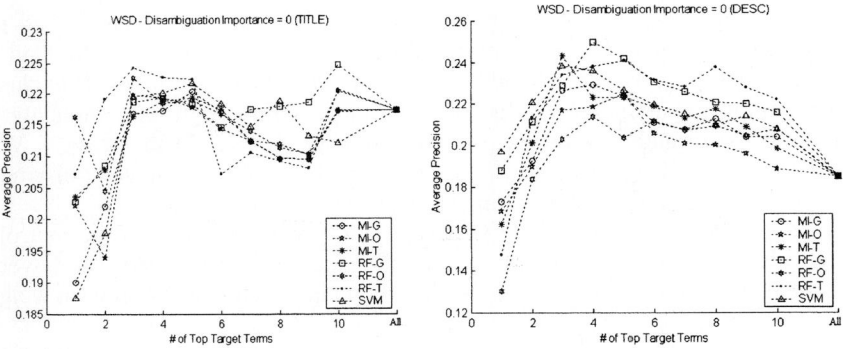

Fig. 3. Mean average precisions of different WSD models at varying number of top target terms with α set to 0

Next, we tested CLIR performances using the select-N method with the disambiguation importance set to 0. Select-N means that top n target terms from a WSD module are used in retrieval. As seen in Figure 3, performances sharply increase up to

4 top terms, then decrease gradually although some fluctuations occur for title queries. In the case of disambiguation importance set to 1 (Figure 4), performances similarly increase up to 4 top terms. However, when more than 4 top terms are taken, performances are nearly stable.

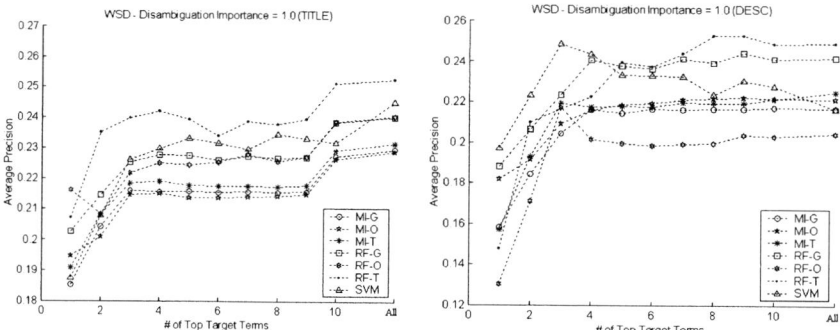

Fig. 4. Mean average precisions of different WSD models at varying number of top target terms with α set to 1

Therefore, when the select-N disambiguation scheme is used, it may be dangerous to use disambiguation importance set to 0. In other words, it is better to consider disambiguation importance α with the select-N scheme. In addition, in either case, it would be much safer to take at least 3 top terms.

Comparing Figure 2 with Figure 3 and 4, CLIR retrieval effectiveness does not rely on WSD performance for small number of top target terms, under the low WSD accuracy. In particular, this phenomenon is much severe for top 1 target term. We think the reason is that good WSD terms do not imply good keywords.

6 Conclusion

This paper presented a statistical WSD approach for a dictionary-based query translation in CLIR. From the viewpoint of translation ambiguity resolution, we explored the following issues: relative contribution of disambiguation weight in the final term weighting, and relationships between WSD and CLIR performance. From the empirical evaluations in a Korean-to-English CLIR, the following points were demonstrated or confirmed.

- It is recommended not to exclusively apply disambiguation weight to target term weight.
- It does not seem that CLIR retrieval effectiveness is directly related to WSD performance for a small number of top target terms, under the low WSD accuracy. For a large number of top target terms, a stable CLIR performance can be obtained by incorporating the disambiguation weight to the target term weight.
- Theoretically-sound WSD models are superior to previous ad-hoc MI-based models.

Acknowledgements

This work was supported by the KOSEF through the Advanced Information Technology Research Center (AITrc) and by the BK21 Project.

References

1. Ballesteros, L., and Croft, W.B. 1998. Resolving Ambiguity for Cross-language Retrieval. Proceedings of the 21st annual international ACM SIGIR Conference on Research and Development in Information Retrieval, pp.64-71
2. Chen, H.H., Bian, G.W., and Lin, W.C. 1999. Resolving Translation Ambiguity and Target Polysemy in Cross-Language Information Retrieval. Proceedings of the 37th Annual Meeting of the Association for Computational Linguistics, pp.215-222
3. Chen, K.H., Chen, H.H., Kando, N., Kuriyama, K., Lee, S.H., Myaeng, S.H., Kishida, K., Eguchi, K., and Kim, H. 2002. Overview of CLIR Task at the Third NTCIR Workshop. *Working Notes of the Third NTCIR Workshop Meeting*, pp.1-38
4. Darwish, K., and Oard, D. W. 2003. Probabilistic Structured Query Methods. Proceedings of the 26th annual international ACM SIGIR Conference on Research and Development in Information Retrieval, pp.338-344
5. Gao, J., Nie, J.Y., He, H., Chen, W., and Zhou, M. 2002. Resolving Query Translation Ambiguity using a Decaying Co-occurrence Model and Syntactic Dependence Relations. Proceedings of the 25th annual international ACM SIGIR Conference on Research and Development in Information Retrieval, pp.183-190
6. Hull, D. 1997. Using Structured Queries for Disambiguation in Cross-Language Information Retrieval. In AAAI Symposium on Cross-Language Text and Speech Retrieval
7. Jang, M.G., Myaeng, S.H., and Park, S.Y. 1999. Using Mutual Information to Resolve Query Translation Ambiguities and Query Term Weighting. Proceedings of the 37th Annual Meeting of the Association for Computational Linguistics, pp.223-229
8. McNamee, P., and Mayfield, J. 2002. Comparing Cross-Language Query Expansion Techniques by Degrading Translation Resources. Proceedings of the 25th annual international ACM SIGIR Conference on Research and Development in Information Retrieval, pp.159-166
9. Mitchell, T.M. 1997. Machine Learning. McGraw-Hill
10. Oard, D.W., and Hackett, P. 1998. Document translation for cross-language text retrieval at the University of Maryland. Proceedings of the 6th Text Retrieval Conference
11. Pirkola, A. 1998. The Effects of Query Structure and Dictionary Setups in Dictionary-Based Cross-language Information Retrieval. Proceedings of the 21st annual international ACM SIGIR Conference on Research and Development in Information Retrieval, pp.55-63
12. Singhal, A., Salton, G., Mitra, M., and Buckley, C. 1996. Document Length Normalization. Information Processing and Management, 32(5):619-633.
13. Sperer, R., and Oard, D.W. 2000. Structured Translation for Cross-Language Information Retrieval. Proceedings of the 23rd annual international ACM SIGIR Conference on Research and Development in Information Retrieval, pp.120-127
14. Yibo, Z., Le, S., Lin, D., and Yufang, S. 2000. Query Translation in Chinese-English Cross-Language Information Retrieval. Proceedings of the Joint SIGDAT Conference on Empirical Methods in Natural Language Processing and Very Large Corpora, pp.104-109

Resolution of Modifier-Head Relation Gaps Using Automatically Extracted Metonymic Expressions

Yoji Kiyota[1], Sadao Kurohashi[2], and Fuyuko Kido[3]

[1] PRESTO, JST
Academic Center for Computing and Media Studies, Kyoto University
Yoshida-Nihonmatsu-cho, Sakyo-ku, Kyoto 606-8501
kiyota@ar.media.kyoto-u.ac.jp
[2] Graduate School of Information Science and Technology, The University of Tokyo
7-3-1, Hongo, Bunkyo-ku, Tokyo 113-8656
kuro@kc.t.u-tokyo.ac.jp
[3] Microsoft Co., Ltd.
Odakyu Southern Tower, 2-2-1, Yoyogi, Shibuya-ku, Tokyo 151-8583
fkido@microsoft.com

Abstract. This paper proposes a method of extracting metonymic expressions and their interpretative expressions from corpora and its application for the full-parsing-based matching method of a QA system. An evaluation showed that 79% of the extracted interpretations were correct, and an experiment using testsets indicated that introducing the metonymic expressions significantly improved the performance.

1 Introduction

It is a critical issue for a text-based QA system to match a question with texts precisely, because of the following purposes:

- *Find exact answers.* The system not only has to retrieve relevant texts, but also has to detect exact answers from these texts.
- *Make appropriate asking-backs.* Users' questions are not always clear. Sometimes they make vague questions, and a lot of texts match with them. In such cases, the system has to give the users some asking-backs to make their questions more concrete. For example, Dialog Navigator [1] extracts the neighborhoods of the parts that match the question, because they often make the difference between matched texts more clear.

In order to achieve precise matching, recent systems for open-domain QA tasks, such as TREC QA track, are based on full-parsing of user questions and texts. Dialog Navigator also uses modifier-head relations of Japanese sentences.

In practice, however, when a user uses a metonymy in his/her question, the matching with texts based on full-parsing often fails. Metonymy is a figure of speech in which the name of one thing is substituted for that of something to which it is related [2].

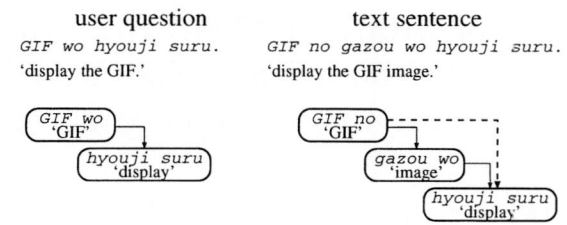

Fig. 1. A matching failure by a metonymy.

The ham sandwich is waiting for his check.

Fig. 1 shows an example of matching failure. In this example, the user seems to use *GIF* 'GIF' as the metonymy of *GIF no gazou* 'GIF image'. If the full-parsing based matching method is used, this matching score will be lower, because the direct relation between 'GIF' and 'display' in the user question does not exist in the text sentence. As this example shows, metonymic expressions could raise gaps of syntactic structures.

The above problem is so acute for QA systems for novice users, such as Dialog Navigator, because novice users often use metonymy in their question for the following reasons:

- their motivation for making short questions is relatively larger compared with that of experts, and
- they often use abrupt expressions that their neighbors do, because they are unfamiliar with accurate expressions used in manuals.

In this paper, we propose a method of resolving the syntactic structure gaps provoked by metonymy, based on automatic extraction of metonymic expressions from corpora.

Sect. 2 describes the outline of Dialog Navigator and its methods of matching user questions with texts. Sect. 3 gives an algorithm for extracting metonymic expressions from corpora and its application for the matching method. Sect. 4 gives criteria of the proposed method: evaluation of extracted metonymic expressions themselves, and testset-based evaluation. Finally, Sect. 5 compares our work to previous works on metonymy, and Sect. 6 concludes this paper.

2 Dialog Navigator

In this section, we show the outline of Dialog Navigator, and the text matching methods of the system.

2.1 Outline

Dialog Navigator is a dialog-based QA system about Microsoft products. We started its service in April 2002 at the web site of Microsoft Corporation. The features of the system are as follows:

Table 1. Text knowledge base.

text collection	# of texts	# of characters	matching target
Glossary	4,707	700,000	entries
Help texts	11,306	6,000,000	titles
Support KB	23,323	22,000,000	entire texts

[*yomu*]
yomu, yomikomu
'read', 'read .. into'
[*mēru*]
mēru, meiru, e-mail
'mail', 'mail', 'e-mail'
[*mēru wo yomu*]
mēru wo yomu, mēru wo jushin suru, message wo yomu, message wo jushin suru
'read a mail',   'receive a mail',   'read a message', 'receive a message'
[*pasokon wo kidou suru*]
pasokon wo kidou suru, Windows wo kidou suru, dengen wo ireru
'boot a PC',   'boot a Windows',   'switch on'
[*osoi*]
osoi, jikan ga kakaru
'slow', 'take a long time'

Fig. 2. Synonymous expression dictionary.

– *Large text knowledge base.* The system utilizes the large text collections provided by Microsoft Corporation. Table. 1 shows the text collections and their scales.
– *Precise text matching.* The system precisely matches user questions with texts, using question types, products, synonymous expressions, and parse results.
– *User navigation.* When a user asks a vague question such as "An error has occurred", the system navigates him/her to the desired answer, asking him/her back using both *dialog cards* and extraction of summaries that makes differences between retrieved texts more clear.

2.2 Text Matching Methods of Dialog Navigator

Dialog Navigator uses several methods to match a question with relevant texts precisely. First, it resolves expression gaps between the question and texts using *synonymous expression dictionary*. Secondly, the system matches a question with texts using syntactic information. Other methods are described in [1].

Expression Gap Resolution by Synonymous Expression Dictionary.
The expression gap between user questions and texts is a big problem. In addition

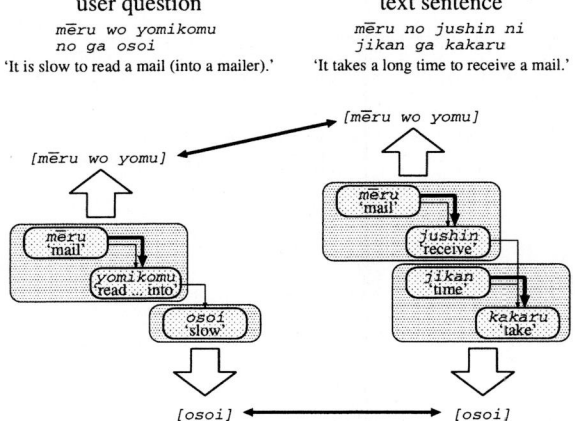

Fig. 3. Matching of synonymous expressions.

to synonyms, there are a great deal of synonymous phrases such as "boot a PC", "boot a Windows", and "switch on".

The system resolves such expression gaps using *synonymous expression dictionary* (Fig. 2). As shown in the figure, the dictionary groups both synonyms and synonymous phrases. The system matches synonymous expressions as shown in Fig. 3. In this figure, two synonymous expression groups are matched.

Score Calculation. The system calculates the score of each text as similarity between the question and a sentence in the text. To improve precision of text matching, it gives large points to modifier-head relations between *bunsetsu*[1] based on the parse results of KNP [3].

First, scores of all sentences in each text are calculated as shown in Fig. 4. Sentence score is the total points of matching keywords and modifier-head relations. We give 1.0 point to a matching of a keyword, and m points to a matching of a modifier-head relation (in Fig. 4, m is set to 1.0). Then sentence score is normalized by the maximum matching score (MMS) of both sentences as follows (the MMS is the sentence score with itself):

$$\frac{(\text{sentence score})^2}{\left(\begin{array}{c}\text{the MMS of a}\\ \text{user question}\end{array}\right) \times \left(\begin{array}{c}\text{the MMS of a}\\ \text{text sentence}\end{array}\right)} \qquad (1)$$

After that, the sentence that has the largest score in each text is selected as the representative sentence of the text. Then, the score of the sentence is regarded as the score of the text.

---

[1] *Bunsetsu* is a commonly used linguistic unit in Japanese, consisting of one or more adjoining content words and zero or more following functional words such as case-markers.

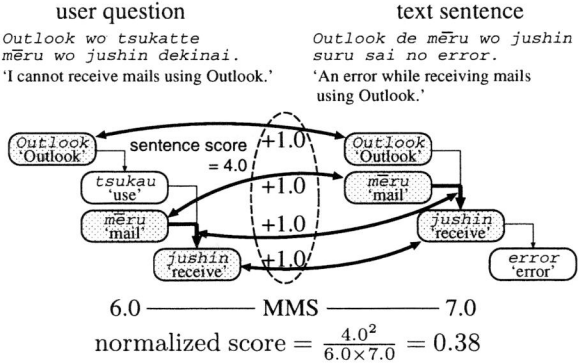

Fig. 4. Score calculation.

metonymic expressions				interpretative expressions					evaluation
A_α	P_α	V_α	f_α	A_β	B_β	P_β	V_β	f_β	
Excel	*wo*	*hiraku*	147	*Excel*	*file*	*wo*	*hiraku*	135	correct
'Excel'	obj-case	'open'		'Excel'	'file'	obj-case	'open'		
(open an Excel)				(open an Excel file)					
moto	*ni*	*modosu*	673	*moto*	*no size*	*ni*	*modosu*	103	correct
'original'	obj-case	'roll back'		'original'	'of' 'size'	obj-case	'roll back'		
(roll back)				(roll back to the original file)					
gamen	*ni*	*shitagau*	3	*gamen*	*no shiji*	*ni*	*shitagau*	96	correct
'screen'	obj-case	'follow'		'screen'	'of' 'instruction'	obj-case	'follow'		
(follow the screen)				(follow the instruction on the screen)					
address	*wo*	*hiraku*	4	*address*	*chou*	*wo*	*hiraku*	43	incorrect
'address'	obj-case	'open'		'address'	'book'	obj-case	'open'		
(open an address)				(open an address book)					
font	*wo*	*kaeru*	19	*font*	*no iro*	*wo*	*kaeru*	13	partly correct
'font'	obj-case	'change'		'font'	'of' 'color'	obj-case	'change'		
(change the font)				(change the color of the font)					

Fig. 5. Extracted metonymic expressions, their interpretations, and evaluation.

Finally, the system ranks the matched texts in order of their scores.

3 Processing Metonymic Expressions

To resolve the relation gaps as shown in Fig. 1, we propose a method of extracting metonymic expressions and their interpretative expressions from corpora, and its application for resolving the relation gaps.

3.1 Metonymic Expressions and Interpretative Expressions

In this paper, we target the combination of the following two expressions:

(α) ***A P V***
(β) ***A (no) B P V***

where A and B mean nouns, P means a case-marker, and V means a predicate[2]. For the example of Fig. 1, A='GIF', B='image', V='display', and $P=wo$ (object-case-marker). Namely, (α) is 'display the GIF', and (β) is 'display the GIF image'. In this case, it seems that (α) is a metonymy, and (β) is its interpretation.

We preliminarily extracted the combinations of (α) and (β) from corpora, and the result shows that most of the combinations are correct as metonymies and their interpretations. Therefore, we tried extraction of the combinations of (α) and (β), as an automatic extraction of metonymies and their interpretations.

In order to get a lot of metonymic expressions automatically, we use huge corpora: the text knowledge base provided by Microsoft Corporation, and a lot of user questions collected by Dialog Navigator. Most of the user questions are inputted by novice users, so they include plenty of metonymies.

In the following sections, we call (α) as *metonymic expression*, and (β) as *interpretative expression*.

3.2 Extraction of Metonymic Expressions and Their Interpretative Expressions

From parse results of all sentences in the corpora, pairs of metonymic expressions and their interpretative expressions are automatically extracted as follows:

1. Collect candidates of metonymic expressions (C_α): every phrase which matches the pattern "A_α P_α V_α" f_α times, where $f_\alpha \geq t_\alpha$.
2. Collect candidates of interpretative expressions (C_β): every phrase which matches the pattern " A_β *(no)* B_β P_β V_β" f_β times, where $f_\beta \geq t_\beta$.
3. For each expression of C_α, find its interpretative expressions in which $A_\beta = A_\alpha$, $P_\beta = P_\alpha$ and $V_\beta = V_\alpha$ from C_β.

where A_α, A_β and B_β mean nouns, P_α and P_β mean case-markers, and V_α and V_β mean predicates. We experimentally set the thresholds of frequency $t_\alpha = t_\beta = 3$.

We applied the method for 1,351,981 sentences, including 762,353 user questions and 589,628 sentences in the text knowledge base. As a result, we got 1,126 pairs of metonymic expressions and their interpretative expressions. Fig. 5 shows the examples.

3.3 Application for Matching

The system resolves the expression gaps by registering extracted metonymic expressions and their interpretative expressions in the synonymous expression dictionary. For example, by registering *GIF wo hyouji suru* 'display a GIF' and *GIF gazou wo hyouji suru* 'display a GIF image' as synonymous expressions, the matching score (Subsect. 2.2, $m = 1$) in Fig. 1 increases from 0.27 to 1.0.

---

[2] Japanese is a head-final language, and the arguments of each predicate are placed left to the predicate. "A *(no)* B" forms a noun phrase. *no* is similar to the English preposition 'of', but has more meanings.

Table 2. Evaluation on interpretations of extracted metonymic expressions.

Evaluation	# of expressions
Correct	158 (79%)
Partly correct	9 (5%)
Incorrect	33 (17%)
Total	200 (100%)

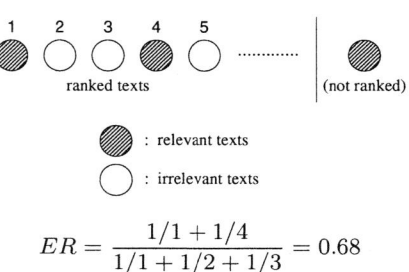

$$ER = \frac{1/1 + 1/4}{1/1 + 1/2 + 1/3} = 0.68$$

Fig. 6. Calculation of ER.

4 Evaluation and Discussion

In order to examine our method, we made two kinds of evaluations. One is a judgment whether extracted metonymic expressions are correctly interpreted, and another is an evaluation of the effect on the testsets of Dialog Navigator.

4.1 Evaluation on Interpretations of Extracted Metonymic Expressions

We selected 200 extracted interpretative expressions that occur the most frequently in the corpora. A subject evaluated each interpretative expression based on the following criteria:

Correct The interpretation is correct in any case.
Partly correct The interpretation is correct in particular case.
Incorrect The interpretation is incorrect, or the expression "$A_\alpha\ P_\alpha\ V_\alpha$" is not a metonymy.

Table. 2 shows the result, and the examples of the evaluations are shown in Fig. 5. 79% of the interpretative expressions were correct. The result shows a fairly successful performance of our method.

4.2 Performance on Testsets

To evaluate the performance of introducing metonymic expressions into Dialog Navigator, we prepared testsets, and defined a measure for evaluating the system output (ranked texts).

First, from the log of Dialog Navigator, we randomly selected user questions which contain the metonymic expressions or their interpretative expressions that the system extracted. Next, for each user question, a subject selected relevant texts in the text knowledge base[3]. As a result, 31 user questions were associated with Help texts as relevant ones, and 140 user questions were associated with texts of Support KB[4]. Finally, we got the following two testsets: the set of 31 user questions on Help texts, and the set of 140 user questions on Support KB.

We defined the evaluation rate (ER) of the system output (ranked texts) as follows:

$$ER = \frac{\sum_{i \in \mathcal{R}} \frac{1}{i}}{\sum_{j \in \{1,\cdots,n\}} \frac{1}{j}} \quad (2)$$

where n is the number of the relevant texts for an inputted user question, and $\mathcal{R}$ is the set of ranks of the relevant texts which the system outputted. Fig. 6 shows a calculation example of ER. Note that this measure is an extension of MRR (mean reciprocal rank) for evaluating open-domain QA systems. Usually, a question for an open-domain QA task has only one answer, but a question for Dialog Navigator often has several answers (relevant texts). Therefore, we introduced the normalization factor as shown in (2).

We experimented on the system using the testsets by the following methods:

baseline Using the methods described in Subsect. 2.2.

metonymy Using the methods described in Subsect. 2.2, and incorporated the extracted metonymic expressions and their interpretative expressions into *synonymous expression dictionary*.

We increased the weight on modifier-head relations m from 0 to 3.0, and calculated the average of ER for each condition.

Fig. 7 shows the result. It indicates that introducing metonymic expressions significantly improves the performance. In addition, it also shows the effectiveness of weighting on modifier-head relations.

(I1)~(I4) in Fig. 8 shows the examples of metonymic expressions that improved ER. For example, a metonymic expression (I1) was included in a user question, and the relevant text contained its interpretative expression. Due to the matching of these expressions, the score of this text overcame those of irrelevant texts. In contrast, (W1) and (W2) in Fig. 8 shows the examples of metonymic expressions that worsened ER. It is clear that these interpretations are incorrect.

---

[3] Some questions have no relevant texts.
[4] Some user questions were associated both Help texts and texts of Support KB.

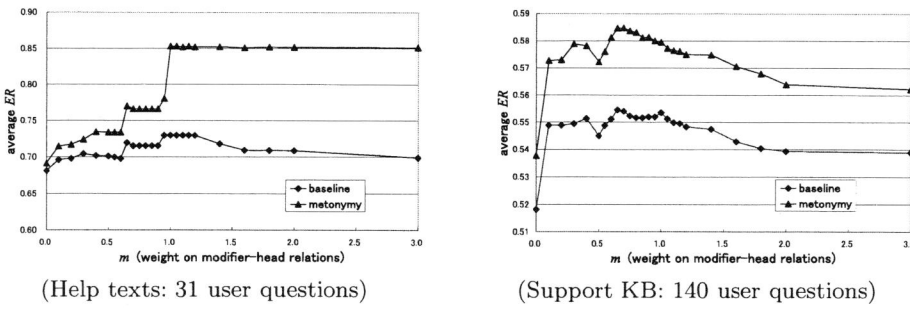

(Help texts: 31 user questions)   (Support KB: 140 user questions)

Fig. 7. Evaluation on the testsets.

	metonymic expressions $A_\alpha \quad P_\alpha \quad V_\alpha$	interpretative expressions $A_\beta \quad B_\beta \quad P_\beta \quad V_\beta$
(I1)	[user question] LAN de setsuzoku 'LAN' method-case 'connect' (connect by LAN)	[Help text] LAN keiyu de setsuzoku 'LAN' 'through' method-case 'connect' (connect through LAN)
(I2)	[user question] file ni kanrendukeru 'file' obj-case 'associate' (associate with files)	[Help text] file no shurui ni kanrendukeru 'file' 'of' 'type' obj-case 'associate' (associate with a file type)
(I3)	[user question] HTML de hozon 'HTML' method-case 'save' (save as an HTML)	[Support KB] HTML keishiki de hozon 'HTML' 'format' method-case 'save' (save in HTML format)
(I4)	[Support KB] application ga osoi 'application' subj-case 'slow' (an application is slow)	[user question] application no kidou ga osoi 'application' 'of' 'launch' subj-case 'slow' (a launch of an application is slow)
(W1)	[user question] page wo hyouji 'page' obj-case 'display' (display a page)	[Support KB] page no bangou wo hyouji 'page' 'of' 'number' obj-case 'display' (display page numbers)
(W2)	[Support KB] file wo insatsu 'file' obj-case 'print out' (print out a file)	[user question] file ichiran wo insatsu 'file' 'list' obj-case 'print out' (print out a list of files)

Fig. 8. Metonymic expressions that improved or worsened ER ($m = 1.0$).

5 Related Works

As we have mentioned in Introduction, processing metonymy is very important for QA systems. Moreover, it is vital for other NLP tasks such as machine translation [4].

In early 1990's, most of previous works on processing metonymy by computers were based on manually-constructed ontologies, semantic networks, or logical forms [5]. However, such knowledge structures require heavy cost of construction and maintenance, and makes scaling up quite difficult. Therefore, corpus-based approaches on processing metonymy were studied recently [6–8].

The type of metonymy we handled was studied by [7]. However, their works targeted only on the interpretation process of metonymy, and left the recognition process for a future work. Unlike them, our method treats both recognition and interpretation process of metonymy.

6 Conclusion

This paper proposed a method of extracting metonymic expressions and their interpretative expressions from the corpora, including a lot of questions of novice users collected by our system. Furthermore, we applied the extracted metonymic expressions into matching user questions with texts, and showed the effectiveness of our method.

Our method also extracts some wrong interpretations of metonymy, and sometimes they worsen the performance. Moreover, our method treated only a part of the metonymic world. To cope with such problem, we have to study a synthetic model of metonymy.

References

1. Yoji Kiyota, Sadao Kurohashi, and Fuyuko Kido. 2002. "Dialog Navigator" : A Question Answering System based on Large Text Knowledge Base. In *Proceedings of The 19th International Conference on Computational Linguistics (COLING 2002)*, pages 460–466.
2. George Lakoff and Mark Johnson. 1980. *Metaphors we live by*. University of Chicago Press.
3. Sadao Kurohashi and Makoto Nagao. 1994. A syntactic analysis method of long Japanese sentences based on the detection of conjunctive structures. *Computational Linguistics*, 20(4).
4. Shin'ichiro Kamei and Takahiro Wakao. 1992. Metonymy; reassessment, survey of acceptability, and its treatment in a machine translation system. In *Proceedings of 30th Annual Meeting of the Association for Computational Linguistics (ACL92)*, pages 309–311.
5. Dan Fass. 1991. met*: A method for discriminating metonymy and metaphor by computer. *Computational Linguistics*, 17(1):49–90.
6. Masaki Murata, Qing Ma, Atsumu Yamamoto, and Hitoshi Isahara. 2000. Metonymy interpretation using X NO Y examples. In *Proceedings of The 4th Symposium on Natural Language Processing 2000 (SNLP 2000)*.
7. Masao Utiyama, Masaki Murata, and Hitoshi Isahara. 2000. A statistical approach to the processing of metonymy. In *Proceedings of The 18th International Conference on Computational Linguistics (COLING 2000)*, pages 885–891.
8. Maria Lapata and Alex Lascarides. 2003. A probabilistic account of logical metonymy. *Computational Linguistics*, 29(2):261–315.

Word Sense Disambiguation Using Heterogeneous Language Resources

Kiyoaki Shirai and Takayuki Tamagaki

Japan Advanced Institute of Science and Technology
1-1, Asahidai, Tatsunokuchi, Ishikawa, 923-1292, Japan
kshirai@jaist.ac.jp

Abstract. This paper proposes a robust method for word sense disambiguation (WSD) of Japanese. Four classifiers were combined in order to improve recall and applicability: one used example sentences in a machine readable dictionary (MRD), one used grammatical information in an MRD, and two classifiers were obtained by supervised learning from a sense-tagged corpus. In other words, we combined several classifiers using heterogeneous language resources, an MRD and a word sense tagged corpus. According to our experimental results, the proposed method outperformed the best single classifier for recall and applicability.

1 Introduction

Word sense disambiguation (WSD) is the process of selecting the appropriate meaning or sense for a given word in a document. Obviously, WSD is one of the fundamental and important processes needed for many natural language processing (NLP) applications, such as machine translation systems. Over the past decade, many studies have been made on WSD of Japanese [1–3]. Most current research used machine learning techniques [4, 5], and achieved good performance. However, as supervised learning methods require word sense tagged corpora, they often suffer from data sparseness, i.e., words which do not occur frequently in a training corpus can not be disambiguated. Therefore, we cannot use supervised learning algorithms alone in practical NLP applications, especially when it is necessary to disambiguate both high frequency and low frequency words.

This paper aims at developing a robust WSD system for Japanese words, and proposes a method which combines several classifiers for WSD, classifiers learned from a sense-tagged corpus and those obtained from a machine readable dictionary (MRD). The main purpose of combining several classifiers derived from heterogeneous language resources (word sense tagged corpus and MRD) is to increase the recall and applicability of the overall WSD system. Even when a classifier obtained by supervised learning can not determine the correct meaning for a certain word due to lack of training data, the classifiers from an MRD may be able to determine the correct sense. Thus, the robustness of the WSD system is improved by using several classifiers simultaneously.

> **aisuru**
> 1) to have strong feelings of affection for someone/something
>   [*ko o **aisuru*** (He/She loves his/her child)] (**E1**)
>   [*kuni o **aisuru*** (He/She loves his/her nation)] (**E2**)
> 2) to have very strong feelings of affection for someone that you are sexually attracted to
> 3) to like or enjoy something very much
>   [*sake o **aisuru*** (He/She loves drinking)] (**E3**)

Fig. 1. Sense Set of *"aisuru"* (love).

2 Our Method

In this paper, word senses or meanings are defined according to the Japanese dictionary, the *Iwanami Kokugo Jiten* [6].

The basic idea of our method is to combine the following four classifiers.

- Classifiers using an MRD (the *Iwanami Kokugo Jiten*)
  1. Classifier using example sentences in an MRD
  2. Classifier using grammatical information in an MRD
- Classifier learned from a sense-tagged corpus
  3. SVM (Support Vector Machine) classifier
  4. Baseline classifier

Notice that classifiers 1 and 2 use an MRD (the *Iwanami Kokugo Jiten*), while 3 and 4 use a sense-tagged corpus. Thus two kinds of language resources are used for WSD.

2.1 Classifier Using Example Sentences in an MRD

Overview. In the Iwanami Kokugo Jiten, word definitions often contain example sentences. Figure 1 shows several such example sentences in the sense set of the Japanese verb *"aisuru"* (love). In Fig. 1, the sentences in square brackets are examples, in which the headword is indicated by boldface.

The WSD classifier described here measures the similarity between an input sentence containing a target word and example sentences in an MRD, selects the example sentence which has the highest similarity and outputs the word sense that contains it in its definition. For example, let us consider the case where the word sense of the verb *"aisuru"* in the sentence **S1** should be disambiguated.

S1 *kare* (he) *wa* (TOP) *musume* (daughter) *o* (ACC) *aisuru* (love)
(He loves his daughter.)

Notice that cases are indicated by case-markers in Japanese such as *"o"* (accusative case-marker) and *"wa"* (topical case-marker). The classifier measures the similarity between this sentence and the example sentences **E1**, **E2** and **E3** in Fig. 1[1]. Among them, **E1** may have the highest similarity with **S1**. Therefore, the classifier selects sense 1) in Fig. 1 as the correct meaning.

---
[1] Subjects (he/she) are omitted in these sentences.

> **shitau**
> 1) to follow someone/something with full of affection
>   [*haha o **shitau*** (He/She is attached to his/her mother)] (**E4**)
>   [*kokoku o **shitau*** (He/She is attached to his/her home country)] (**E5**)
>   [*kanojo ga hisoka ni **shitau** seinen* (Young man she loves in secret)] (**E6**)
> 2) to respect one's virtue, education or skills
>   [*toku o **shitau*** (He/She respects one's virtue)] (**E7**)

Fig. 2. Sense Set of "*shitau*" (be attached to).

Extraction of Example Sentences from Sense Descriptions of Hypernyms. One of the problems in using example sentences from the Iwanami Kokugo Jiten is that the number of example sentences in the dictionary is not large enough. This may cause a data sparseness problem, especially since not all definitions in the dictionary contain example sentences. For instance, there is no example sentence for definition 2) in Fig. 1. Such meanings will never be selected by the classifier. To overcome this problem, example sentences in the definitions of hypernyms are also used for WSD. We assume that the hypernym of a verb is the last verb of a definition sentence. For example, the following is the original definition of sense 2) of "*aisuru*" in Japanese.

aisuru

2) *isei* (opposite sex) *o* (ACC) *koi* (love) *shitau* (be attached to)

In this case, the last verb, "*shitau*" (be attached to) is assumed to be the hypernym of the verb "*aisuru*" (love). Therefore, the example sentences **E4**, **E5**, **E6** and **E7**, which are in the definition of "*shitau*" as shown in Fig. 2, are extracted as example sentences for sense 2) of "*aisuru*". In this way, we can obtain example sentences for those senses for which no example sentence is given.

Sentence Similarity. In this paper, instead of the similarity between an input sentence and an individual example sentence, the similarity between an input sentence s and a set of example sentences E for each sense, $sim(s, E)$, is considered.

$Sim(s, E)$ is defined according to the similarity between two case-filler nouns of the same case. First, NE_c and $NE_{c'}$ are extracted for each sense from an MRD. NE_c is the set of case-filler nouns extracted from example sentences, where c is a case-marker such as *o* (ACC) and *ga* (NOM). $NE_{c'}$ is the set of case-fillers extracted from example sentences in the definition of hypernyms. For example, for sense 1) of "*aisuru*" in Fig. 1, *ko* (child) and *kuni* (nation) are accusative case-fillers of the verb *aisuru* (love) in **E1** and **E2**, respectively. Thus NE_o for the sense 1) is $\{ko, kuni\}$. For sense 2) of "*aisuru*", *haha* (mother), *kokoku* (home country) and *toku* (virtue) are accusative case-fillers in **E4**, **E5**

1) NE_o = { ko (child), kuni (nation) }
2) $NE_{o'}$ = { haha (mother), kokoku (home country), toku (virtue) }
   $NE_{ga'}$ = { kanojo (she) }
3) NE_o = { sake (alcohol) }

Fig. 3. Extracted Case-fillers for "*aisuru*".

---
sarani
1) still more, further, furthermore
2) ⟨⟨with a negative expression⟩⟩ not in the least, not at all

---

Fig. 4. Sense Set of "*sarani*" (more).

and **E7**, respectively. As **E4**, **E5** and **E7** are example sentences of the hypernym of sense 2), these nouns are members of $NE_{o'}$ for sense 2). The case-fillers for the other cases are extracted in the same way. The extracted case-fillers for all senses of the verb *aisuru* (love) are summarized in Fig. 3.

Next, $Sim(s, E)$ is defined as follows:

$$Sim(s,e) = \sum_c w_c \cdot s_c(ns_c, NE_c) \qquad (1)$$

$$s_c(ns_c, NE_c) = \max_{ne_c \in NE_c} s(ns_c, ne_c) \qquad (2)$$

$$s(w_i, w_j) = \frac{2 \times d_k}{d_i + d_j}. \qquad (3)$$

In (1), $s_c(ns_c, NE_c)$ is the similarity between a case-filler ns_c of a case c in a sentence s and a set of case-fillers NE_c of the same case c extracted from example sentences in an MRD, which is given by (2). w_c in (1) is a weight parameter for the case c, which is defined empirically. We set weights $w_{c'}$ to be smaller than w_c, where case c' means that case-fillers are extracted from the example sentences of a hypernym of a verb, while c refers to the example sentences of the verb itself. In (2), $s_c(ns_c, ne_c)$ is the similarity between two nouns, ns_c and ne_c. It is defined by a thesaurus as (3). In (3), d_i and d_j are the depth of words w_i and w_j in a thesaurus, respectively, and d_k is the depth of the common superior class of w_i and w_j. For this study, we used the Japanese thesaurus *Nihongo Goi Taikei* [7] to calculate $s(w_i, w_j)$.

2.2 Classifier Using Grammatical Information in an MRD

The second classifier uses grammatical information in an MRD. In the Iwanami Kokugo Jiten, grammatical constraints for a certain word sense are sometimes described. For example, see Fig. 4, the sense set of the Japanese adverb "*sarani*" (more) in the Iwanami Kokugo Jiten. The description in double brackets ("⟨⟨" and "⟩⟩") is the grammatical information for sense 2), i.e., the adverb *sarani* whose meaning is sense 2) always appears with a negative expression.

Let us consider the sentence **S2**.

S2 *kôkai* (regret) *nado <u>sarani</u> si nai* (not)
(He/She doesn't regret it at all)

We can guess the correct sense of the adverb *"sarani"* in **S2** is sense 2) in Fig. 4, because there is the negative expression *nai* (not). In this way, grammatical information in an MRD can provide effective clues for WSD.

We developed the WSD classifier using grammatical information. First, we regard grammatical information as conditions that an input sentence should satisfy. The classifier checks whether an input sentence satisfies the conditions described by grammatical information for all meanings, and outputs all of those meanings which pass the check. Otherwise, the classifier outputs nothing, i.e., it can not determine the correct meaning.

As described earlier, grammatical information is described in double brackets in the Iwanami Kokugo Jiten. We extracted such descriptions, and developed a system which judges whether or not a sentence satisfies the conditions defined by the grammatical information. Followings are types of such conditions.

- Condition of inflection
- Condition of a headword, POS(part-of-speech) or conjugation form of the word just before or after the target word
- Condition of an idiom
- Condition of a negative expression
- Condition of a position of a word in a sentence

There are 973 definitions containing grammatical information in the Iwanami Kokugo Jiten. Out of the 973, our classifier can handle grammatical information for 582 senses. As the number of meanings of polysemous words in our dictionary is 37,908, the classifier using grammatical information can handle only 1.5% of them. The applicability of this classifier thus appears to be quite low. However, since many common words include grammatical information in the dictionary, we believe that the classifier is actually more applicable than expected. Furthermore, grammatical information is a reliable feature for WSD, and it appears that the correct word sense is mostly selected when this classifier is applied. For such reasons, when this classifier is combined with other classifiers, it makes a positive contribution to the performance of the overall WSD system.

2.3 SVM Classifier

The third classifier is the SVM classifier, one of the classifiers based on supervised learning. The features used in the model include POSs / surface forms of words just before and after the target word, base forms of content words found in $\pm n$ word window[2], and so on. We used the LIBSVM package[3] for training the

---
[2] Here we set n to 20.
[3] http://www.csie.ntu.edu.tw/%7Ecjlin/libsvm/

Table 1. Correctness of each classifier on the validation data.

	EXAM	GRAM	SVM	BL
C_{all}	0.329	0.816	0.797	0.796

SVM classifier. The SVM model is ν–SVM [8] with the linear kernel, where the parameter $\nu = 0.0001$. The pairwise method is used to apply SVM to multi classification.

The RWC corpus [9] is used as the training data. It is made up of 3,000 newspaper articles extracted from the 1994 Mainichi Shimbun, consisting of 888,000 words. Out of 3,000 newspaper articles, we use 2,400 articles for training. SVM classifiers are trained for 2,084 words which occur more than 10 times in the training data. No meaning is selected by the SVM classifier for the other words.

2.4 Baseline Classifier

The last classifier is the baseline classifier which always selects the most frequently used meaning. When there is more than one meaning with equally high frequency, the classifier chooses one of the meanings randomly. This is the typical baseline model when using only the word sense tagged corpus for WSD.

2.5 Combined Model

The combined model is the WSD system using the four classifiers described in 2.1, 2.2, 2.3 and 2.4. In this subsection, we will describe how to combine these classifiers.

First, we prepare validation data, a sense-tagged corpus, as common test data for the four classifiers. The performance of the classifiers for a word w is evaluated by *correctness* C_w defined by (4):

$$C_w = \frac{\text{\# of words in which one of meanings selected by a classifier is correct}}{\text{\# of words for which a classifier selects one or more meanings}} \quad (4)$$

As mentioned earlier, the main reason for combining several classifiers is to improve the recall and applicability of the WSD system. Note that a classifier which often outputs a correct meaning would achieve high correctness C_w, even though it also outputs wrong meanings. Thus, the higher the C_w of a classifier, the more it improves the recall of the combined model.

Combining the four classifiers is a simple process. The correctness, C_w, of each classifier for each word w is measured on the validation data. When more than two classifiers output meanings for a given word, their C_w scores are compared. Then, the word senses provided by the best classifier are selected as the final outputs.

When the number of words in the validation data is small, comparison of the classifiers' C_w is unreliable. For that reason, when the number of words in the

Table 2. Results.

	Precision	Recall	F-measure	Applicability
Combined	0.724	**0.772**	0.747	**0.944**
EXAM	0.466	0.080	0.137	0.115
GRAM	0.538	0.184	0.275	0.237
SVM	**0.797**	0.705	0.748	0.884
BL	0.794	0.748	**0.770**	0.942

validation data is less that a certain threshold O_h, the correctness for all words in validation data (C_{all}) is compared, rather than comparing the correctness for individual words w (C_w). In the experiment in Sect. 3, we set O_h to 10.

3 Evaluation

In this section, we will describe the experiment to evaluate our proposed method. Out of 3,000 newspaper articles in the RWC corpus, 300 articles was used as validation data, and other 300 articles as test data. They were mutually exclusive with the training data used for training the SVM and baseline classifier. Only polysemous words in the corpus were disambiguated. The number of such target instances in the validation and test data was 13,819 and 13,494, respectively.

Table 1 shows the correctness of each classifier for all words in validation data. "EXAM", "GRAM", "SVM" and "BL" represents the classifier using example sentences, the classifier using grammatical information, the SVM classifier, and the baseline classifier, respectively. The best classifiers according to C_{all} on the validation data is "GRAM".

Table 2 reveals the precision, recall, F-measure[4] and applicability of the combined model and the single classifiers (EXAM, GRAM, SVM and BL) on the test data. "Applicability" indicates the ratio of the number of instances disambiguated by a classifier to the total number of target instances.

Previous papers [10, 5] have reported that the SVM classifier performed well, but in our experiment its precision was almost same as that of the baseline classifier. We do not understand the precise reason for that, but will examine the effective features used for the SVM classifier to improve it in future.

The combined model outperformed any single classifier for recall and applicability. This indicates that our goal – to improve the recall and applicability of the WSD system by combining several classifiers – was accomplished to some degree. On the other hand, the precision and F-measure of the combined model was less than that of the SVM and baseline classifier, which were the best among single classifiers. This was because the precision of the classifiers using example sentences (EXAM) and grammatical information (GRAM) was low. To improve the precision of these classifiers using an MRD is an important future project.

In the combined model, 71.0% of target instances were disambiguated by the classifier trained on the sense-tagged corpus (52.6% by SVM and 18.4% by BL), while 23.4% were disambiguated by the classifier using an MRD (1.62% by

---

[4] $\frac{2PR}{P+R}$ where P and R represents the precision and recall, respectively.

EXAM and 21.8% by GRAM). This indicates that both a sense-tagged corpus and an MRD, i.e., the RWC corpus and the Iwanami Kokugo Jiten in this experiment, were useful for WSD.

4 Related Works

This paper proposes a method for combining several classifiers for Japanese WSD. In this section, some previous research using ensemble of two or more WSD classifiers will be compared with our proposed method.

Several research [5, 10–12] proposed combining several classifiers trained on the same training corpora with different feature sets. One of the characteristics of these methods was that only a word sense tagged corpus was used as a knowledge resource. Therefore, the ensemble of several classifiers appeared to improve the precision of the overall WSD system, but not its recall and applicability.

Methods that combined classifiers using sense-tagged corpora and other language resources were also proposed. For example, Agirre et al. proposed combining classifiers using machine learning techniques and classifiers based on the WordNet [13]. Instead of a thesaurus, this study used an MRD as a language resource in addition to a sense-tagged corpus.

Litkowski proposed the method combining classifiers trained on a sense-tagged corpus and an MRD [14]. However, his combination of two classifiers was indirect. Since the word sense definitions of the two classifiers were different, he converted the word senses produced by the MRD classifier to those defined by the classifier using the sense-tagged corpus. Such conversion is not always successful. Our approach, on the other hands, requires no sense conversion: all classifiers output word meanings according to the same definition.

Stevenson et al. also proposed a method using a sense-tagged corpus and an MRD for WSD [15]. Although they handled a large vocabulary in their experiment, target words for WSD were restricted to those which appeared in the sense-tagged corpus. Thus the usage of multiple knowledge resources contributed to improving the precision, but not the recall or applicability. Our approach aimed at the improvement of recall and applicability, as indicated in Tab. 2. Furthermore, the above three methods used different language resources aimed at English WSD, while this paper was concerned with Japanese WSD.

5 Conclusion

In this paper, we proposed a method that combines several classifiers, using different language resources, for Japanese WSD. Two classifiers using an MRD and two classifiers trained on a sense-tagged corpus were combined according to the performance of each classifier on the validation data set. The combined model outperformed the best single classifier for recall and applicability.

In future, we hope to increase the precision of the combined model. The classifiers using example sentences and grammatical information in an MRD should be improved to achieve higher precision. We will conduct an error analysis on these classifiers and investigate ways to improve them.

References

1. Fujii, A., Inui, K., Tokunaga, T., Tanaka, H.: To what extent does case contribute to verb sense disambiguation? In: Proceedings of the International Conference on Computational Linguistics. (1996) 59–64
2. Shinnou, H.: Learning of word sense disambiguation rules by co-training, checking co-occurrense of features. In: Proceedings of the International Conference on Language Resources and Evaluation. (2002) 1380–1384
3. Shinnou, H., Sasaki, M.: Unsupervised learning of word sense disambiguation rules by estimating an optimum iteration number in EM algorithm (in Japanese). In: SIG-NL, Information Processing Society of Japan. (2002) 51–58
4. Li, H., Takeuchi, J.: Using evidence that is both strong and reliable in Japanese homograph disambiguation. In: SIG-NL, Information Processing Society of Japan. (1997) 53–59
5. Murata, M., Utiyama, M., Uchimoto, K., Ma, Q., Isahara, H.: Japanese word sense disambiguation using the simple Bayes and support vector machine methods. In: Proceedings of the SENSEVAL-2. (2001) 135–138
6. Nishio, M., Iwabuchi, E., Mizutani, S.: Iwanami Kokugo Jiten Dai Go Han. Iwanami Publisher (1994) (in Japanese).
7. Ikehara, S., Miyazaki, M., Shirai, S., Yokoo, A., Nakaiwa, H., Ogura, K., Hiroshi, O., Hayashi, Y.: Nihongo Goi Taikei (in Japanese). Iwanami Shoten, Publishers (1997)
8. Schölkopf, B.: New support vector algorithms. Neural Computation **12** (2000) 1083–1121
9. Hasida, K., Isahara, H., Tokunaga, T., Hashimoto, M., Ogino, S., Kashino, W., Toyoura, J., Takahashi, H.: The RWC text databases. In: Proceedings of the International Conference on Language Resources and Evaluation. (1998) 457–462
10. Takamura, H., Yamada, H., Kudoh, T., Yamamoto, K., Matsumoto, Y.: Ensembling based on feature space restructuring with application to WSD. In: Proceedings of the Natural Language Processing Pacific Rim Symposium. (2001) 41–48
11. Pedersen, T.: A decision tree of bigrams is an accurate predictor of word sense. In: Proceedings of the Meeting of the North American Chapter of the Association for Computational Linguistics. (2001) 79–86
12. Klein, D., Toutanova, K., Ilhan, H.T., Kamvar, S.D., Manning, C.D.: Combining heterogeneous classifiers for word-sense disambiguation. In: Proceedings of the SIGLEX/SENSEVAL Workshop on Word Sense Disambiguation. (2002) 74–80
13. Agirre, E., Rigau, G., Padró, L., Atserias, J.: Combining supervised and unsupervised lexical knowledge methods for word sense disambiguation. Computers and the Humanities **34** (2000) 103–108
14. Litkowski, K.C.: Sense information for disambiguation: Confluence of supervised and unsupervised methods. In: Proceedings of the SIGLEX/SENSEVAL Workshop on Word Sense Disambiguation. (2002) 47–53
15. Stevenson, M., Wilks, Y.: The interaction of knowledge sources in word sense disambiguation. Computational Linguistics **27** (2001) 321–349

Improving Word Sense Disambiguation by Pseudo-samples

Xiaojie Wang[1,2] and Yuji Matsumoto[1]

[1] Graduate School of Information Science, Nara Institute of Science and Technology
8916-5 Takayama, Ikoma, Nara, Japan, 630-0192
[2] School of Information Engineering, Beijing University of Posts and Technology
Beijing, China, 100876
{xiaoji-w,matsu}@is.naist.jp

Abstract. Data sparseness is a major problem in word sense disambiguation. Automatic sample acquisition and smoothing are two ways that have been explored to alleviate the influence of data sparseness. In this paper, we consider a combination of these two methods. Firstly, we propose a pattern-based way to acquire pseudo samples, and then we estimate conditional probabilities for variables by combining pseudo data set with sense tagged data set. By using the combinational estimation, we build an appropriate leverage between the two different data sets, which is vital to achieve the best performance. Experiments show that our approach brings significant improvement for Chinese word sense disambiguation.

1 Introduction

Word sense disambiguation(WSD) has long been a central issue in Natural Language Processing(NLP). In many NLP tasks, such as Machine Translation, Information Retrieval etc., WSD plays a very important role in improving the quality of systems. Among different approaches for WSD, corpus-based supervised learning methods have been received increasing attention, and achieved state-of-the-art performance. But as pointed out by [5], two major obstacles often make supervised learning methods failure: unavailability of enough sense-tagged data and data sparseness. Some ways have been suggested to acquire large tagged samples automatically. [13] used a small size of seed words as clues for different senses of an ambiguous word to initiate a classifier and boosted them repeatedly. This method was extended to deal with parallel data based on a bilingual bootstrapping technique in [8]. [7] used monosemous lexical relatives of a word sense in WordNet to find training data. [10] extended this idea to other useful cue words, which was implemented in [1] to retrieve training data from the Web. [11] further enriched this method with a bootstrapping inspired by [13]. Translation correspondence in parallel text presents another way to avoid manual sense tagging. [2] presented a method to produce large quantities of sense annotated data, their technique takes advantage of the fact that a word with multiple senses in one language is often translated as distinct words in another language.

On the other hand, some methods that aim at alleviating the influence of data sparseness have been also employed to cope with zero-occurrence of features in training data for WSD. [4] interpolated conditional probabilities based on entire corpus,

[12] used a smoothing based on tagged data. Class-based models [9] and similarity-based methods [6] have also been used.

This paper proposes a method to alleviate the influence of data sparseness by combining sample acquisition and smoothing. We collect samples by using monosemous synonyms, which are named pseudo samples. In stead of using them directly as tagged samples like [7] and [10], we re-estimate conditional probabilities by a smoothing where pseudo samples are combined with the tagged samples in a more flexible and effectual way. In fact, since pseudo samples can be collected automatically, large quantities of pseudo samples can be available, while tagged samples are small, building an appropriate leverage between pseudo data and tagged data is vital to achieve the best performance. Experiments show a significant improvement is brought by our approach.

In this paper, we concentrate on WSD for Chinese one-character-word. In Chinese, a word composed of only one Chinese character is called one-character-word(OCW). Sense disambiguation for OCW is a major task in Chinese WSD. We propose a pattern-based way of collecting pseudo samples for OCWs in next section. In section 3, we present a new estimator for conditional probability, and compare it with other two estimators qualitatively. We implement several experiments in section 4, and give some evaluations in section 5. Finally, we draw some conclusions.

2   Pseudo-sample Acquisition

As well known, a sense-tagged sample for a word should have following two properties.

P1:the target word occurs in the sample.
P2:the target word is tagged with a certain sense.
P2 can be re-written as: P2$'$: a target sense occurs in the sample.

We define that a pseudo sample is a sample only satisfying P2$'$. That means a pseudo sample is for the target sense, no matter whether it includes the target word. For example, word "plane" has two different senses, one of which is for aircraft. We note it by s_1 and use it as the current target sense. Considering sentence S:

S: He was a passenger in an airplane.

Word "airplane" has only one sense that is just s_1. Although the target word "plane" does not occur in S, the target sense s_1 occurs in S. S is thus a pseudo sample for sense s_1.

This simple example offers us a two-step method to collect pseudo samples for a sense. The first step is to find some monosemous synonyms for the target sense, and then collect samples by searching occurrences of those words in corpora. The first step is the key for collection of pseudo samples. Since there is no machine-readable Chinese dictionary currently available for searching monosemous synonyms automatically, we here explore some linguistic phenomena to help us find some of them more efficiently.

We here concentrate on finding monosemous synonyms for OCWs. Sense disambiguation for OCW is a major part of Chinese WSD. In Chinese, besides OCWs, words composed of two Chinese characters are called two-character-words (TCWs). Words composed of more than one Chinese characters can be called multi-character-words(MCWs). Generally, MCWs become less ambiguous as the increase of the number of characters they include. According to HowNet Chinese Word List[3], among 6308 words which have two senses, 1302(more than 20%) are OCWs, among 461 words which have more than five senses, 444(more than 96%) are OCWs, the percentage of OCWs increases rapidly with the increase of number of senses. On the other hand, although the total number of OCWs is much less than that of MCWs (among 66037 words in HowNet, 7007 are OCWs), they usually occur in Chinese documents with high frequencies. According to a statistical result on Chinese People Daily from January 1995 to December 1996, 66 words are OCWs among top 100 high frequency words; 9 words are OCWs among top 10 high frequency words.

We return to introduce a linguistic phenomenon. In Chinese, some TCWs are composed of two different OCWs. If two OCWs have a common sense, the TCW composed of them usually has only one sense that is just the common sense of the two OCWs, so the TCW is a monosemous synonym of both OCWs.

For example, TCW 观看 (look at steadily) is composed of OCW 看 (look,see,etc.) and 观 (look,view,etc.). 观看 has only one sense that is just the common sense of 观 and 看. So 观看 is a monosemous synonym of both 看 and 观. We give a general description of this phenomenon as below.

Let s(w) be the set of senses of the word w, o_1 and o_2 be two OCWs, t be a TCW composed of them, then

$$s(t)=s(o_1) \cap s(o_2) . \qquad (2.1)$$

If o_1 and o_2 have only one common sense, for example, sense s_1, then TCW t has only one sense s_1, and thus is a monosemous synonyms for both o_1 and o_2. This phenomenon suggests us a way of finding monosemous synonyms for an OCW more efficiently. By using (2.1), we can identify if a TCW is a monosemous synonyms of a target OCW without looking it up in a dictionary. What we need to know is if the two OCWs(one of them is the target OCW) that compose the TCW have a common sense. Supposing the target sense is s_1 and target OCW is o_1. Firstly, we search an OCW dictionary to find if there is any OCW with sense of s_1. For each of these OCW, we combine it with o_1 to form two-character strings. The two strings are: o_1+OCW and OCW+ o_1. We then search these strings in a large corpus to see if they occur or not. Strings occurring with high frequency will be used as monosemous synonyms for target sense s_1 of o_1. For example, if o_1 is 看, 观 has the same target sense with 看, and then they can compose of two possible character strings: 看观 and 观看, where 观看 occurs in our corpus with high frequency, while 看观 does not. So we use 观看 as a monosemous synonym for common sense of both 看 and 观.

Above linguistic phenomenon gives us a pattern of how some monosemous synonyms for OCWs are generated. We have extracted some other patterns based on some other linguistic phenomena in Chinese. Each pattern suggests a way of finding some monosemous synonyms for OCWs.

Extracting synonyms in this kind of pattern-based way makes it possible to extract new words that are not in a dictionary and assign a sense to it. The results of synonym extraction in our experiments are reported in section 4.

After acquiring pseudo samples, we make use of these samples to expand variable space and re-estimate conditional probabilities of variables in the next section.

3   Conditional Probability Estimation

We present three estimators for conditional probability in sequence in this section. While only tagged samples are used in the first one, both tagged samples and pseudo samples are used in the second and third estimations. The second estimator treats pseudo samples directly as tagged samples; the third one is what we propose.

Let s_i be i-th sense of a target word w, F_t be a variable space brought by tagged training samples for sense s_i. A variable can be a word co-occurring with the target sense, part-of-speech of the target word or another kind of item which may be helpful for sense disambiguation task. For each $f \in F_t$, its conditional probability $P_t(f \mid s_i)$ can be estimated by (3.1) when only tagged samples are used.

$$P_t(f \mid s_i) = c(f, s_i) / c(s_i) \quad . \tag{3.1}$$

where $c(s_i)$ is total number of training samples for sense s_i, $c(f, s_i)$ is frequency of variable f occurring in these samples.

Let $w_1, w_2, ... w_n$ be n monosemous synonyms of sense s_i, each of them are used to collect some pseudo samples. Let F_j be a variable space brought by pseudo samples that are collected by using w_j. Let:

$$F_p = \bigcup_{j=1}^{n} F_j \quad .$$

Then we turn to disambiguate word w in a new variable space F where both tagged samples and pseudo samples are used.

$$F = F_p \cup F_t \quad .$$

Obviously, $F_t \subset F$, variable space used for disambiguating the target word w is expanded. Because pseudo samples can be collected automatically, by collecting larger quantities of pseudo samples, we can expand variable space to a large scale so that lots of variables unseen in tagged samples can be seen in the new variable space.

If a pseudo sample is directly used as a tagged sample, then one-occurrence in tagged samples is assigned with the same probability as that in pseudo samples. In this case, conditional probability is re-estimated by (3.2).

$$P(f \mid s_i) = (c(f, s_i) + \sum_{j=1}^{n} c(f, w_j)) / (c(s_i) + \sum_{j=1}^{n} c(w_j)) \quad . \tag{3.2}$$

where $c(w_j)$ is the total number of pseudo training samples collected by using w_j, $c(f,w_j)$ is the frequency of variable f occurring in these samples. In (3.2), one-occurrence in tagged samples and in tagged samples are both assigned with probability of $1/(c(s_i) + \sum c(w_j))$.

Because of $c(s_i) \ll c(w_j)$, (3.2) makes the contribution to conditional probability from tagged samples to suffer from a heavy drop. (It is clearer in the special case of $f \in F_t \setminus F_p$, we return to it in the end of this section.) We thus propose a more flexible combinational estimation to leverage these two different data sets.

For each variable $f \in F$, we use (3.3) to re-estimate its conditional probability.

$$P(f \mid s_i) = \lambda_0 P_t(f \mid s_i) + \sum_{j=1}^{n} \lambda_j P(f \mid w_j) \ . \tag{3.3}$$

where $\lambda_j \geq 0, (j = 0,1,..n)$, $\lambda_0 + \sum_{j=1}^{n} \lambda_j = 1$, $P(f \mid w_j)$ in (3.3) is estimated by (3.4).

$$P(f \mid w_j) = c(f, w_j) / c(w_j) \ . \tag{3.4}$$

Then, by synthesizing formulae (3.1), (3.3) and (3.4), we have:

$$P(f \mid s_i) = \lambda_0 (c(f, s_i) / c(s_i)) + \sum_{j=1}^{n} \lambda_j (c(f, w_j) / c(w_j)) \ . \tag{3.5}$$

By using (3.5), we assign each variable $f \in F$ a non-zero probability. Because F can be much larger than F_t, the amount of variables with zero probability can be lowered significantly. Especially, we assign unseen variables in tagged samples a non-zero probability according to their frequency in pseudo samples.

Besides of the expansion of non-zero variable space, (3.5) can give different weights to occurrences of variables in the two different data sets, which is unavailable in (3.2). The capability of assigning different weights to events in different data sets can help us build an appropriate leverage between them, and cause better performance. There are two ways of assigning different weights to different data sets in (3.5).

The first way is a more essential one. In (3.5), one-occurrence in tagged samples is assigned with a probability of $1/c(s_i)$, while one-occurrence in pseudo samples is assigned with a probability of $1/c(w_j)$. Because of $c(s_i) \ll c(w_j)$, one-occurrence of a variable in tagged samples contributes more gain for conditional probability than that in pseudo samples.

The second way can be achieved by adjusting coefficients λ_j, $j = 0,1,...n$ of each sub-estimations. Bigger λ_j means more weights are assigned.

At the end of this section, we give a qualitative comparison between (3.5) and (3.2) by using (3.1) as a baseline in the case of $f \in F_t \setminus F_p$.

When $f \in F_t \setminus F_p$, $c(f, w_j) = 0$, for $j = 1,...,n$. (3.5) is simplified to (3.6).

$$P(f \mid s_i) = \lambda_0 (c(f,s_i)/c(s_i)) \ . \tag{3.6}$$

If $\lambda_0 \to 1$, the probability decreases slightly comparing with (3.1) where only tagged samples are used to train classifiers. These decreases can be reserved for other variables.

At the same time, (3.2) is simplified to (3.7) when $f \in F_t \setminus F_p$.

$$P(f \mid s_i) = c(f,s_i)/(c(s_i) + \sum_{j=1}^{n} c(w_j)) \ . \tag{3.7}$$

Since $c(s_i) << c(w_j)$, the probability decreases heavily comparing with (3.1). This means that too many probabilities are reserved for other variables, while variables in $F_t \setminus F_p$ are diluted greatly.

In next section, we implement some experiments to show different results brought by above different estimates for conditional probability.

4 Experiments

Eight Chinese OCWs (target words) were used through all the experiments. All experimental data were extracted from People Daily from January 1995 to December 1996. Table 1 gives the detail of data used in experiments.

In Table 1, figures in brackets in 'Sense' column are numbers of sense tagged samples for each sense. These samples were tagged by a native speaker, and checked by another native speaker.

Table 1. Experimental data : TW:TargetWord, MW: Monosemous Words

TW	Sense	MW	TW	Sense	MW
看	s_1:see (25)	观看(300)	想	s_1:remind (24)	想起(300)
	s_2:treat (28)	看待(300)		s_2:think (33)	构想(261) 想方设法(39)
	S_3:visit (18)	看望(300)			
待	s_1:treat (68)	对待(300)	告	s_1:tell (31)	告诉(300)
	s_2:wait (73)	等待(300)		s_3:announce(64)	宣告(300)
	s_3:need (35)	有待(282) 亟待(18)		s_2:accuse (62)	控告(202) 告状(62) 状告(38)
存	s_1:exist (42)	存在(300)	穿	s_1:wear (40)	穿着(154) 穿戴(32)
	s_2:reserve (36)	保存(300)			
	s_3:exist in mind (31)	怀着(300)		s_2:across (36)	穿越(168) 横穿(50) 穿透(53)
	s_4:save money (28)	存款(300)			
换	s_1:exchange (43)	交换(300)	爱	s_1:love (22)	热爱(300)
	s_2:change (52)	更换(287) 改换(13)		s_2:cherish (22)	爱护(300)

All monosemous synonyms in 'MW' column were acquired by using patterns we described in section 2. Those patterns worked very well. Among 29 synonyms listed in Table 1, 25 are monosemous words in HowNet; 3 words have two senses in HowNet but being monosemous in Advanced Chinese Dictionary. There is one word(怀着) that occurs in neither of these two dictionaries, but it occurs in corpora frequently. Figures in brackets after monosemous words are numbers of pseudo samples for each sense used in our experiments. For some senses, since we cannot collect enough pseudo samples from our corpus using only one monosemous word, more than one monosemous words are used.

Pseudo samples were grouped into five increasing sets.

$DG5 \subset DG4 \subset DG3 \subset DG2 \subset DG1$

They include 20%, 40%, 60%, 80% and 100% of the entire data respectively.

In all experiments, ±20 words before or after the target words(or monosemous words) in the same sentence were used as variables. Naive Bayes was employed as the learning algorithm.

Three sets of 10-fold cross-validation experiments for sense tagged samples were implemented for each target word. Data division of tagged samples in each experiment is the same.

The difference among the three sets of experiments is on how to estimate conditional probabilities. We describe them respectively in what follows.

1. We note first experiment as T. In this experiment, conditional probabilities were estimated according to (3.1) where only tagged samples were used. The result of this experiment was used as the baseline in comparison with results from following two experiments where both tagged samples and pseudo samples were used for estimating conditional probabilities.
2. We note second experiment as TPS. In this experiment, conditional probabilities were estimated according to (3.2). This experiment was done on each pseudo data set, from DG5 to DG1.
3. We note third experiment as TPD. In this experiment, conditional probabilities were estimated according to (3.5). This experiment was also done on each pseudo data set, from DG5 to DG1.

Results from experiments T, TPS and TPD are shown in Table 2.

The first row of Table 2 identifies five different experimental data sets increasing from the left hand (DG5) to the right (DG1). The first column lists the target words to be disambiguated; the percentage in the bracket after each target word is the accuracy in experiment T. For each target word, there are two rows – TPS row and TPD row – for accuracies in experiments TPS and TPD respectively. The accuracy for experiment TPD is the best among 11 different settings of parameter λ_0. We will detail how the accuracy is changed with parameter λ_0 in the next section.

5 Evaluations

Comparing results in either TPS or TPD with their correspondences in T, we can find the accuracy in either TPS or TPD is better than that in T. Especially, results in TPD are significantly better than that in T when enough pseudo samples (more than those in

Table 2. Experimental results

Word (T)		DG5	DG4	DG3	DG2	DG1
看	TPS	76.9%	83.1%	79.0%	82.0%	79.4%
(72.0%)	TPD	79.4%	84.4%	83.1%	**85.0%**	82.8%
想	TPS	70.7%	68.3%	72.1%	72.1%	71.2%
(66.8%)	TPD	78.7%	76.1%	76.1%	75.5%	**80.3%**
爱	TPS	68.3%	65.5%	80.8%	73.3%	73.3%
(72.3%)	TPD	72.5%	77.5%	**80.8%**	75.0%	77.5%
待	TPS	77.1%	77.7%	76.6%	74.8%	75.1%
(72.9%)	TPD	79.1%	78.6%	79.6%	80.2%	**81.3%**
穿	TPS	85.5%	84.1%	84.1%	85.5%	85.7%
(85.4%)	TPD	92.0%	94.8%	92.3%	**96.1%**	**96.1%**
告	TPS	77.1%	78.3%	71.6%	77.3%	77.1%
(75.2%)	TPD	77.2%	79.3%	79.2%	81.4%	**82.1%**
存	TPS	55.2%	56.0%	54.4%	56.9%	55.7%
(53.9%)	TPD	57.6%	57.1%	58.6%	**62.2%**	60.9%
换	TPS	73.7%	72.5%	69.4%	70.7%	69.8%
(74.2%)	TPD	79.5%	78.4%	79.5%	80.5%	**80.5%**

DG3) are used. There is at least 6 points improvement for each target word; the best improvement is over 13 points. That means pseudo samples are very helpful in improving WSD.

Comparing each value in TPS rows with its correspondence in TPD rows, we can find all values of accuracy in TPD are better (only one equal) than those in TPS. For each target word, the classifier in TPD outperforms that in TPS significantly ($\alpha = 0.05$). That means the way of combining pseudo samples with tagged samples proposed by (3.5) is better than that in (3.2).

Comparing values in TPD on different data set, we can find more pseudo samples generally cause more improvement. This tendency does not appear in TPS. When there are more data available for us, we will make further investigation about if this tendency will continue in TPD.

There are some intermittent decreases of accuracy in TPD. For example, accuracy for word "爱" is 80.8% when DG3 is used, but decreases to 75.0% when DG2 is used. We implemented some new experiments. Let N0 note DG2\DG3(subtracting DG3 from DG2, i.e. DG2=DG3 ∪ N0). We recollected two pseudo samples sets(N1 and N2) for word "爱", where |N1| = |N2| = |N0|. Two new TPD experiments using DG3 ∪ N1 and DG3 ∪ N2 achieved accuracy of 81.2% and 79.1% respectively. The three different pseudo data sets brought very different results. The best one achieved by using N1 is 6.2 points higher than that using N0. This means sample selection is very helpful.

We further evaluate influences brought by pseudo samples more explicitly by checking relation between accuracy and coefficients $\lambda_j, j = 0,1,...n$ in (3.5). For the sake of simplification, in our experiments, pseudo samples collected by using different monosemous words for a same sense are treated as from a same word, so $n = 1$. For example, three different monosemous words (穿越, 横穿, 穿透) were used to collecting pseudo samples for the sense s_2 of the word 穿(as showed in Table 1), at this time,

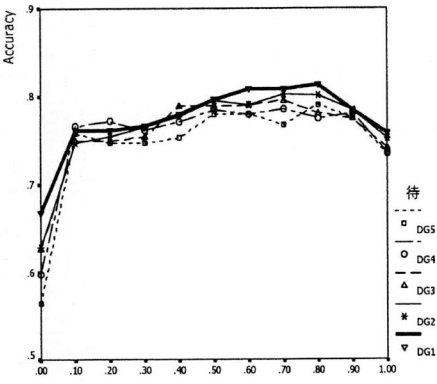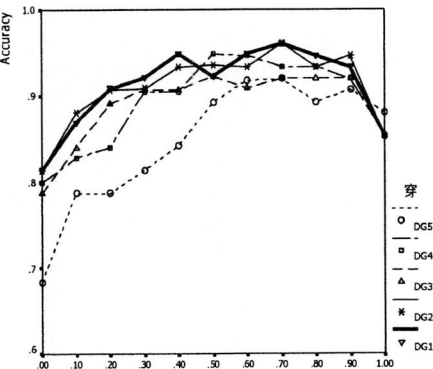

Fig. 1. λ_0-accuracy curve for word "待"   **Fig. 2.** λ_0-accuracy curve for word "穿".

$n=3$. For the sake of simplification, before we used these pseudo samples, we replaced all occurrences of 横穿 and 穿透 in these samples by 穿越, then the monosemous word in these samples is the same word 穿越, that is to say, $n=1$.

When $n=1$, (3.5) is simplified to (5.1).

$$P(f \mid s_i) = \lambda_0(c(f,s_i)/c(s_i)) + (1-\lambda_0)(c(f,w_1)/c(w_1)) \qquad (5.1)$$

There is only one parameter λ_0 in (5.1). We ranged λ_0 from 0 to 1 with an increase by 0.1 and implemented experiment TPD respectively.

Figures 1 and 2 give us λ_0-accuracy curves for two target words "待" and "穿" respectively, curves for other six target words have similar shapes. In both figures, x-axis is λ_0, y-axis is accuracy, and different marker style is for different pseudo data set.

From Figures 1 and 2, we can find the highest values of accuracy for all data sets are not achieved at neither $\lambda_0=0$ nor $\lambda_0=1$. In (5.1), $\lambda_0=0$ means that only pseudo samples are used to re-estimate conditional probability, while $\lambda_0=1$ means only tagged samples are used. That is to say, neither tagged samples nor tagged samples can achieve best performance by themselves; tagged samples and pseudo samples complement each other.

Best values of accuracy are always achieved in the interval (0.6,0.8). This means sense tagged samples received more weighs for high accuracy. Although pseudo samples are helpful, sense tagged samples are more informative than pseudo samples for WSD.

6 Conclusion

In this paper, we proposed a method for improving quality of WSD by combining automatic sample acquisition and smoothing. Firstly, we proposed a pattern-based method to acquire pseudo samples for Chinese OCWs, and then we estimated conditional probabilities for variables by combining pseudo data set with sense tagged data set. By using the combinational estimation, we built an appropriate leverage between the two different data sets, which is vital to achieve the best performance. Experiments show that our approach brings significant improvement for Chinese word sense disambiguation.

Although we concentrate on Chinese OCWs disambiguation in this paper, by combining with a way of acquiring monosemous synonyms, the method for re-estimating conditional probability can be used to improve quality of WSD for other kinds of words and for other languages. Because acquisition of pseudo samples and the smoothing are two independent components in our approach, the estimation just makes use of pseudo samples, but has no restriction on how to acquire pseudo samples.

Acknowledgements

We would like to thank anonymous reviewers for their useful suggestions.

References

1. Eneko Agirre and David Martinez. (2000) Exploring Automatic Word Sense Disambiguation With Decision Lists and the Web. In Proceedings of the Semantic Annotation And Intelligent Annotation workshop organized by COLING Luxembourg
2. Mona Diab and Philip Resnik.(2002) An Unsupervised Method for Word Sense Tagging using Parallel Corpora. In Proceedings of ACL-02, pp255-262
3. Zhendong Dong.(2000)http://www.keenage.com/
4. William W Gale, Kenneth W Church and David Yarowsky.(1992) A Method for Disambiguating Word Senses in a Large Corpus. Computers and Humanities, 26: 415-439
5. Nancy Ide and Jean Veronis.(1998) Introduction to the Special Issue on Word Sense Disambiguation: The State of the Art. Computational Linguistics, 24(1), 1-40
6. Yael Karov and Shimon Edelman.(1998) Similarity-based Word Sense Disambiguation. Computational Linguistics, 24(1),.pp.41-59
7. Claudia Leacook, Martin Chodorow and George A. Miller.(1998) Using Corpus Statistics and WordNet Relations for Sense Identification. Computational Linguistics, 24(1), 147-166
8. Cong Li and Hang Li.(2002) Word Translation Disambiguation Using Bilingual Bootstrapping. In Proceedings of ACL-02, pp343-351
9. Alpha K Luk.(1995) Statistical sense disambiguation with relatively small corpora using dictionary definition. In Proceedings of ACL-95, pp.181-188
10. Rada Mihalcea and Dan Moldovan.(1999) An Automatic Method for Generating Sense Tagged Corpora. In Proceedings of AAAI-99, pp.461-466, Orlando, FL, July
11. Rada Mihalcea.(2002) Bootstrapping Large Sense Tagged Corpora. In Proceedings of the 3rd International Conference on Languages Resources and Evaluations LREC 2002, Las Palmas, Spain, May
12. Ng, Hwee Tou.(1997) Exemplar-Based Word Sense Disambiguation: Some Recent Improvements. In Proceedings of the Second Conference on Empirical Methods in Natural Language Processing pp.208-213. Providence, Rhode Island, USA
13. David Yarowsky.(1995) Unsupervised Word Sense Disambiguation Rivaling Supervised Method. In Proceedings of ACL-95, pp.189-196

Long Distance Dependency in Language Modeling: An Empirical Study

Jianfeng Gao[1] and Hisami Suzuki[2]

[1] Microsoft Research, Asia, 49 Zhichun Road, Haidian District, Beijing 100080
jfgao@microsoft.com
[2] Microsoft Research, One Microsoft Way, Redmond WA 98052
hisamis@microsoft.com

Abstract. This paper presents an extensive empirical study on two language modeling techniques, linguistically-motivated word skipping and predictive clustering, both of which are used in capturing long distance word dependencies that are beyond the scope of a word trigram model. We compare the techniques to others that were proposed previously for the same purpose. We evaluate the resulting models on the task of Japanese Kana-Kanji conversion. We show that the two techniques, while simple, outperform existing methods studied in this paper, and lead to language models that perform significantly better than a word trigram model. We also investigate how factors such as training corpus size and genre affect the performance of the models.

1 Introduction

Long distance word dependency is a critical problem in language modeling. Classical language models are based on the trigram assumption, i.e. the next word is predicted based on the two immediately preceding words. However, the words relevant to predicting the next word may lay in any position beyond the scope of a word trigram. There are two critical questions in incorporating long distance word dependencies in language modeling: (1) How do we find the relevant words, i.e., how do we define long distance dependencies? Are they defined syntactically, semantically, or in any other way? (2) How can these dependencies be represented in a sound probabilistic model?

In this paper, we first describe two techniques which were originally introduced in [8]: the first is the method of skipping words in an *n*-gram language model in a linguistically meaningful way; the second is the use of clustering techniques in language modeling. We then present an extensive empirical comparison of these techniques with others that have been proposed previously for the same purpose, including those described in [2, 11, 15]. We re-implemented these methods (with some modifications as necessary) and generated language models using a large amount of Japanese newspaper corpus. We evaluated the resulting models on the task of Japanese Kana-Kanji conversion, which is a realistic application of a language model. While being relatively simple to implement, we show that the two techniques outperform existing methods studied in this paper, and lead to language models that are significantly better than a word trigram model. We also investigate how such factors as training corpus size and genre affect the performance of the language models.

2 Two Techniques

A trigram model predicts the next word w_i by estimating the conditional probability $P(w_i|w_{i-2}w_{i-1})$, where w_i is the word to be predicted, called the *predicted word*, and w_{i-2} and w_{i-1} are the context words used to predict w_i, called the *conditional words*.

A *skipping model* is an extension of a trigram model in that it predicts words based on two conditioning words that may not be adjacent to the predicted word (e.g. [16, 18, 19]). *Function word skipping* is a linguistically-motivated skipping model created by differentiating function words F from content words or *headwords H*. For example, in *Mary has bought a book in the store*, *Mary, bought, book* and *store* count as headwords, while *has, a, in, the* count as function words. Function word skipping incorporates two assumptions about language. First, we observe that headwords across phrase boundaries have dependency relations with each other. Therefore, we hypothesize (in the trigram context) that headwords may be conditioned not only by the two immediately preceding words, but also by two previous headwords. Second, we find that headword trigrams are also *permutable*, in the sense that they tend to capture order-neutral semantic dependency. For example, *Mary bought a book* and *the book Mary bought* can be expressed by the same headword trigram (*Mary~bought~book*) if we allow such permutations.

Clustering techniques attempt to make use of similarities between words to produce a better estimate of the probability of word strings [11]. In the context of computing the trigram probability $P(w_3|w_1w_2)$, either the predicted word w_3 or the conditional words, w_1 and w_2, can be clustered when building a cluster-based trigram model. [7] presents a thorough comparative study on various clustering models using the task of Japanese Kana-Kanji conversion, concluding that a model that uses clusters for predicted words, called the *predictive clustering model*, performed the best in most cases. In the current study, we used the predictive clustering technique in two different ways: first, we considered the distinction between two classes of words, H and F, as two pre-defined clusters. Secondly, we used the clustering technique to cluster similar words and headwords. We will now look at these in turn.

2.1 Permuted Headword Trigram Model

Assuming that each word token can uniquely be classified as a headword or a function word, the permuted headword trigram model (PHTM) can be considered as a cluster-based language model with two clusters, headword H and function word F. We then define the conditional probability of w_i based on its history as the product of two factors: the probability of the category (H or F), and the probability of w_i given its category. Let h_i or f_i be the actual headword or function word in a sentence, and let H_i or F_i be the category of the word w_i. The PHTM can then be formulated as follows:

$$P(w_i | \Phi(w_1...w_{i-1})) = P(H_i | \Phi(w_1...w_{i-1})) \times P(w_i | \Phi(w_1...w_{i-1})H_i) \\ + P(F_i | \Phi(w_1...w_{i-1})) \times P(w_i | \Phi(w_1...w_{i-1})F_i) \quad (1)$$

where Φ is a function that maps the word history ($w_1...w_{i-1}$) onto equivalence classes. $P(H_i|\Phi(w_1...w_{i-1}))$ and $P(F_i|\Phi(w_1...w_{i-1}))$ are the category probabilities, and $P(w_i|\Phi(w_1...w_{i-1})F_i)$ is the word probability given that the category of w_i is F. We used the unigram estimate for word category probabilities, i.e., $P(H_j|\Phi(w_1...w_{i-1})) \approx P(H_j)$ and $P(F_j|\Phi(w_1...w_{i-1})) \approx P(F_j)$.[1] We also used the standard trigram estimate for function word probability, i.e., $P(w_j|\Phi(w_1...w_{i-1}),F_j) \approx P(w_j|w_{j-2},w_{j-1},F_j)$, and approximated $P(F_j) \times P(w_j|w_{j-2},w_{j-1},F_j)$ by $P(w_j|w_{j-2},w_{j-1})$. The estimation of headword probability is slightly more elaborate, which incorporates the components for function word skipping and headword permutation:

$$P(w_i|\Phi(w_1...w_{i-1})H_i) = \lambda_1(\lambda_2 P(w_i|h_{i-2}h_{i-1}H_i) \\ +(1-\lambda_2)P(w_i|h_{i-1}h_{i-2}H_i)) + (1-\lambda_1)P(w_i|w_{i-2}w_{i-1}H_i). \quad (2)$$

This estimate is an interpolated probability of three probabilities: $P(w_i|h_{i-2}h_{i-1}H_i)$ and $P(w_i|h_{i-1}h_{i-2}H_i)$, which are the headword trigram probability with or without permutation, and $P(w_i|w_{i-2}w_{i-1}H_i)$, which is the probability of w_i given that it is a headword, where h_{i-1} and h_{i-2} denote the two preceding headwords, and $\lambda_1, \lambda_2 \in [0,1]$ are the interpolation weights optimized on held-out data. By separating the estimates for the probabilities of headwords and function words, we arrive at the final estimate below, where all probabilities are estimated using maximum likelihood estimation with Katz's backoff smoothing method, as described in [13], to deal with the sparse data problem: Predictive clustering model

$$P(w_i|\Phi(w_1...w_{i-1})) = \\ \begin{cases} \lambda_1(P(H_i|w_{i-2}w_{i-1}))(\lambda_2 P(w_i|h_{i-2}h_{i-1}) \\ + (1-\lambda_2)P(w_i|h_{i-1}h_{i-2})) \\ +(1-\lambda_1)P(w_i|w_{i-2}w_{i-1}) \quad w_i: \text{headword} \\ P(w_i|w_{i-2}w_{i-1}) \quad w_i: \text{function word} \end{cases} \quad (3)$$

Let $\overline{w_i}$ be the cluster which word w_i belongs to. In this study, we performed word clustering for words and headwords separately. As a result, we have the following two predictive clustering models, (4) for words and (5) for headwords:

$$P(w_i|w_{i-2}w_{i-1}) = P(\overline{w_i}|w_{i-2}w_{i-1}) \times P(w_i|w_{i-2}w_{i-1}\overline{w_i}) \quad (4)$$

$$P(w_i|h_{i-2}h_{i-1}) = P(\overline{w_i}|h_{i-2}h_{i-1}) \times P(w_i|h_{i-2}h_{i-1}\overline{w_i}) \quad w_i: \text{headword} \quad (5)$$

We computed these models following the method described in [8]. Substituting Equations (4) and (5) into Equation (3), we obtain the cluster-based PHTM, referred to as C-PHTM.

3 Main Results

We evaluated the language models on the task of Japanese Kana-Kanji conversion, which consists of converting a text string of syllabary-based Kana into an appropriate combination of Kanji and Kana. This is similar to the task of speech recognition, except that it does not include acoustic ambiguity. Performance on this task is measured in terms of the character error rate (CER), given by the number of characters wrongly converted from the phonetic string divided by the number of characters in the correct transcript.

---

[1] See [8] for a more detailed description of the model and its parameter estimation method.

For our experiments, we used two newspaper corpora, Nikkei and Yomiuri Newspapers, both of which have been pre-word-segmented. We built language models from a 36-million-word subset of the Nikkei Newspaper corpus, performed parameter optimization on a 100,000-word subset of the Yomiuri Newspaper (held-out data), and tested our models on another 100,000-word subset of the Yomiuri Newspaper corpus. The lexicon we used contains 167,107 entries.

Our evaluation was done using the N-best rescoring method (N=100), in which a list of hypotheses is generated by the baseline language model (a word trigram model in this study), which is then rescored using a more sophisticated language model. The main results are shown in Table 1, where the "oracle" result indicates the upper bound on performance. We see that both PHTM and C-PHTM outperform the baseline word trigram model, and the improvements are statistically significant according to the t test ($p<0.01$).

4 Comparative Study on Capturing Long Distance Word Dependency

Approaches to incorporating long distance word dependency in language modeling can be classified along the scale of how much linguistic structure they use. On one edge of the scale, there are higher order n-gram models and skipping models, which use no or very little linguistic information; on the other end of the spectrum, we have models that use sophisticated syntactic structure, such as dependency-based models (e.g. [3, 4, 9]) and constituency-based models (e.g. [1, 2, 17]). PHTM described in the previous sections fall between the two in the complexity of the linguistic structure it uses; in particular, it is similar to the models proposed by [15], but differs from their models in crucial details. In this section, we provide an extensive empirical comparison of PHTM with some of the previous approaches which we re-implemented and compared on the task of Japanese Kana-Kanji conversion.

4.1 Comparison with Higher-Order n-Gram Models

Goodman [11] showed that with a training corpus consisting of 280 million words and using Kneser-Ney smoothing [14], small improvements were observed even into 6-grams, suggesting the usefulness of larger context.

The PHTM can be thought of as a variation of a higher order n-gram model, in that the headword trigrams capture longer distance dependencies than trigram models. In order to see how far the dependency goes within our headword trigram models, we plotted the distribution of headword trigrams (y-axis) against the n of the word n-gram if it were to be captured by the word n-gram (x-axis) in Figure 1. For example, given a word sequence $w_1w_2w_3w_4w_5w_6$, and if w_1, w_3 and w_6 are headwords, then the headword trigram $P(w_6|w_3w_1)$ spans the same distance as the word 6-gram model.

From Figure 1, we can observe that approximately 95% of the headword trigrams can be captured by the higher-order n-gram model with the value of n smaller than 7. Based on this observation, we built word n-gram models with the values of $n=4$, 5 and 6, using the training data described in Section 3. For all n-gram models, we used the interpolated modified absolute discount smoothing method [6], which is a modified version of Kneser-Ney smoothing and achieved the best CER results in our

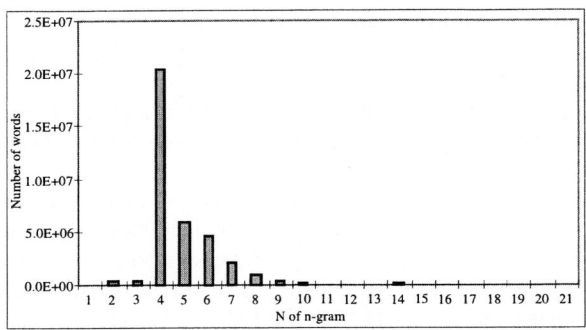

Fig. 1. Distribution of headword trigrams against the *n* of word *n*-gram

experiments. The CER results using higher-order *n*-gram models are presented in the third row of Table 1. They show that the performance of the higher order word *n*-gram models becomes quickly saturated as *n* grows: the best performance was achieved by the word 5-gram model, with the CER reduction of only 0.5% against the baseline trigram model. We increased the training data size to 180 million words, but obtained similar results. Following [11], we suspect that the poor performance of these models is attributed to the data sparseness problem. From these results, we conclude that simply extending the context window by brute-force can achieve little improvement; in contrast, the use of even the most modest form of structural information such as the identification of headwords and automatic clustering can improve the performance.

4.2 Comparison with ATR Models

Isotani and Matsunaga proposed two models that are based on the asymmetry between content and function words in [15]: the first model, referred to as ATR-I below, is an extension of word *n*-gram model: it is based on the assumption that the probability of each word in a sentence is determined by the preceding content and function word pair. Let f_i and c_i denote the last function word and the last content word in the substring $w_1,...,w_{i-1}$, relative to the word being predicted w_i. ATR-I can then be written as follows:

$$P(w_i) = \begin{cases} P(w_i \mid f_{i-1} w_{i-1}) & w_{i-1} : \text{content word} \\ P(w_i \mid c_{i-1} w_{i-1}) & w_{i-1} : \text{function word} \end{cases} \quad (6)$$

Isotani and Matsunaga used ATR-I alone without interpolating with another model, while [12] interpolated ATR-I with a conventional word trigram model.

The second model, referred to here as ATR-II, is an approximation of ATR-I in that it has fewer parameters than ATR-I. It assumes that the probability of each word is determined by the word immediately before it, and also by the preceding word of the same category (function word or content word) if the category of the word immediately before it is different from that of the word being predicted. In other words, ATR-II is of the form:

$$P(w_i) = \begin{cases} P(w_i \mid w_{i-1}) \times \dfrac{P(f_i \mid f_{i-1})}{P(f_i)} \\ \quad w_{i-1}: \text{content word}, w_i: \text{function word } (= f_i) \\ P(w_i \mid w_{i-1}) \times \dfrac{P(c_i \mid c_{i-1})}{P(c_i)} \\ \quad w_{i-1}: \text{function word}, w_i: \text{content word } (= c_i) \\ P(w_i \mid w_{i-1}) \quad \text{otherwise} \end{cases} \qquad (7)$$

We built these models using the training data described in Section 3, and performed experiments using (a) ATR-I, (b) a combined model where ATR-I was interpolated with a word trigram model, and (c) ATR-II. The results are presented in the fourth row of Table 1. Our results are consistent with those presented in [12, 15]. The CER using the ATR-I model alone is much higher than that of the baseline model. When interpolated with a word trigram model, the CER improves by 1.6%. Isotani and Matsunaga did not report error rate results of ATR-II in [15]; they only presented its perplexity, which was slightly higher than that of ATR-I. In contrast, our experiments show that ATR-II achieves lower CER than those either using ATR-I alone or using the combined model. We have two explanations for this: first, perplexity might not be a good criterion for evaluating combined language models. Second, ATR-II is a good approximation of ATR-I for practical purposes: both ATR models used the same set of information (i.e., the preceding content and function word pair) for word prediction, but ATR-II has the advantage of having many fewer parameters. Therefore, when the training data is not large enough, ATR-II might achieve better performance.

One significant difference between the ATR models and our own is that our models use separate probability estimates for headwords and function words as shown in Equation (3), which allows us to apply predictive clustering separately for these two submodels. In contrast, ATR models do not cluster words: the word categories are used only for the sake of finding the content and function word pair. In that sense, ATR models are conceptually more similar to skipping models (e.g. [16, 17, 19]), where only one probability estimate is applied for both content and function words. From the superior performance of PHTM to the ATR models, we believe that predictive clustering is a simple and effective technique in language modeling, and that the probability estimates for headword and function words should be done separately, as they play different semantic and syntactic roles in a sentence.

4.3 Comparison with Dependency Language Models

Chelba et al. [3] presents dependency language models (DLM) that capture linguistic constraints via a dependency structure, i.e., a set of probabilistic dependencies that express the relations between words in a sentence by an acyclic, planar, directed graph. Let W be a sentence, and D be its dependency structure. The DLM, in principle, recovers the probability of a sentence $P(W)$ over all possible D given W by estimating the joint probability $P(W, D)$: $P(W) = \sum_D P(W, D)$. In practice, they introduce two approximations to make the model feasible. First, they take $P(W) = \sum_D P(W, D) \approx P(W, D^*)$, where D^* is the most probable dependency structure of the sentence, which is discovered by maximizing $P(W, D)$: $D^* = \text{argmax } P(W, D)$. Below we simply use D to represent D^*. Second, they take $P(W, D) = P(W|D)P(D) \approx P(W|D)P(D|W)$, because it is very difficult to compute $P(D)$ directly, while $P(D|W)$ can be estimated through the parsing processing of generating D. Since this decomposition is statistically unwarranted, they only report word error rate results on the application of speech recognition: the best DLM achieves very small (less than 1%) yet statistically significant improvement ($p < 0.02$) over a bigram model.

The DLMs we implemented for our experiments are different from those in [3] in the following three aspects. First, we simply take $P(W) \approx P(W|D)$. We then decompose the value of $P(W|D)$ as the product of individual word probabilities: $P(W|D) = \prod_{i=1...n} P(w_i|\Phi(w_1...w_{i-1}, D))$. Here, D is determined using a modified version of Yuret's dependency parser [21][2]. The resulting D expresses the relations between headwords of each phrase in a sentence by an acyclic, planar, undirected graph where each headword (except the leftmost one) has exactly one related headword to its left. This is similar to link grammar described in [5].

Second, similar to PHTM, we differentiate the estimates for headword and function word probabilities (Equation (1)). We also used the unigram estimate for word category probabilities, and the standard trigram estimate for function word probability. For headword estimation, we chose a mapping function Φ that retains (a) two preceding words w_{j-1} and w_{j-2}, (b) two preceding headwords h_{j-1} and h_{j-2}, and (c) one linguistically related word w_d according to D. The final estimate is given below, where $\lambda_1, \lambda_2 \in [0,1]$ are the interpolation weights optimized on held-out data.

$$P(w_i|\Phi(w_1...w_{i-1}, D)) = \begin{cases} \lambda_1(P(H_i)(\lambda_2 P(w_i|h_{i-2}h_{i-1}) \\ + (1-\lambda_2)P(w_i|w_d, (i,d) \in D)) \\ + (1-\lambda_1)P(w_i|w_{i-2}, w_{i-1}) \\ \quad w_i: \text{headword} \\ P(w_i|w_{i-2}, w_{i-1}) \quad w_i: \text{function word} \end{cases} \quad (8)$$

Third, since a large Japanese training corpus annotated with D is not available, we used an unsupervised learning method that discovers D of a given sentence using a Viterbi iterative training procedure described in [9]. It consists of three steps: (a) we assumed that each headword pair within a headword trigram constitutes an initial dependency, e.g., given a headword trigram (h_1, h_2, h_3), there are 3 initial dependencies: d_{12}, d_{13}, and d_{23}. From the initial dependencies, we computed an initial dependency parsing model similar to [4]. (b) Given the parsing model, we used the Yuret's parser described above to select the most probable dependency structure for each sentence in the training data. This provides an updated set of dependencies. (c) We

---

[2] The parser reads a sentence from left to right; after reading each new word w_j, it tries to link w_j to each of its previous words w_i, and push the generated dependency d_{ij} into a stack. When a dependency crossing or a cycle is detected in the stack, the dependency with the lowest dependency probability in conflict is eliminated. We adopted this parser for detecting D in both testing and unsupervised training for its operating speed ($O(n^2)$) and reasonably good accuracy (see [21] for detail).

then re-estimated the parsing model parameters based on the updated dependency set. Steps (b) and (c) are iterated until the improvement in the probability of training data is less than a threshold.

The results are shown in the last row of Table 1. We can see that although DLM-1 (=DLM without using the headword trigram submodel) outperformed the baseline model by 6.4% in CER reduction, the result is slightly (but significantly according to t-test) worse than that of HTM. This can be explained by the fact that the headword-based component of DLM-1 is bigram-based, while it is trigram-based in HTM. In DLM-2, we linearly interpolated all three probabilities in Equation (8), and obtained a statistically significant ($p < 0.01$) improvement over HTM. The performance of DLM-2 (10.7% CER reduction) is quite similar to that of PHTM (10.5% CER reduction), which indicates an overlap in the data used in capturing long distance dependency: in fact, when we plotted the distribution of linguistically related word (w_d in Equation (8)) against the n of the headword n-gram, we discovered that about 83% of dependencies captured in DLM was also captured by the headword trigram model. The limited gain by incorporating the syntax-based dependency model might also be explained by the unreliable quality of the dependency annotation, which is generated in an unsupervised manner.

Table 1. Comparison of CER results

Model	Description	CER %	CER Reduction
Baseline	Word trigram model	3.73	---
Oracle	In the 100-best list with the minimum number of errors	1.51	59.5%
HTM	Equation (3) with λ_1=0.2 and λ_2=1	3.41	8.6%
PHTM	Equation (3) with λ_1=0.2 and λ_2=0.7	3.34	10.5%
C-PHTM	Equation (3) with λ_1=0.3 and λ_2=0.7	3.17	15.0%
4-gram	Higher-order n-gram model with a modified version of Kneser-Ney interpolation smoothing	3.71	0.5%
5-gram		3.71	0.5%
6-gram		3.73	0.1%
ATR-I	Equation (6)	4.75	−27.3%
ATR-I +	ATR-I interpolated with Baseline	3.67	1.6%
ATR-II	Equation (7)	3.65	2.1%
DLM-1	Equation (8) with λ_1=0.1 and λ_2=0	3.49	6.4%
DLM-2	Equation (8) with λ_1=0.3 and λ_2=0.7	3.33	10.7%

5 Conclusion

Linguistically-informed word skipping and predictive clustering are two simple techniques that work surprisingly well in language modeling. Using these techniques, our models achieved up to 15% CER reduction over a conventional word trigram model in a Japanese Kana-Kanji conversion task. Our models can effectively capture long distance dependencies among headwords up to the range of word 6-grams, while performing much better than a word 6-gram model. We attribute the success of our models to the use of linguistic structure in the form of headword identification and clustering, and to the fact that our models have many fewer parameters to train than higher-order n-gram models.

In the comparison with ATR models, we also showed that by clustering predictive words into head words and function words, we can optimize the probability estimates for these classes separately, leading to a superior performance of the proposed model.

We have also investigated the use of syntactic information in language modeling. One future challenge in this area is to find syntactically motivated dependencies that do not overlap with the dependencies that are already captured by headword-based n-gram models.

References

1. Charniak, Eugine. 2001. Immediate-head parsing for language models. In *ACL/EACL 2001*, pp.124-131.
2. Chelba, Ciprian and Frederick Jelinek. 2000. Structured language modeling. *Computer Speech and Language*, Vol. 14, No. 4. pp 283-332.
3. Chelba, C, D. Engle, F. Jelinek, V. Jimenez, S. Khudanpur, L. Mangu, H. Printz, E. S. Ristad, R. Rosenfeld, A. Stolcke and D. Wu. 1997. Structure and performance of a dependency language model. In *Processing of Eurospeech*, Vol. 5, pp 2775-2778.
4. Collins, Michael John. 1996. A new statistical parser based on bigram lexical dependencies. In *ACL-34:* 184-191.
5. Della Pietra, S., V. Della Pietra, J. Gillett, J. Lafferty, H. Printz and L. Ures. 1994. Inference and estimation of a long-range trigram model. Technical report CMU-CS- 94-188, Department of Computer Science, CMU.
6. Gao, Jianfeng, Joshua Goodman and Jiangbo Miao. 2001. The use of clustering techniques for language model – application to Asian language. *Computational Linguistics and Chinese Language Processing*. Vol. 6, No. 1, pp.27-60.
7. Gao, Jianfeng, Joshua Goodman, Guihong Cao and Hang Li. 2002a. Exploring asymmetric clustering for statistical language modeling. In *ACL 2002*, pp.183-190.
8. Gao, Jianfeng, Hisami Suzuki and Yang Wen. 2002b. Exploiting headword dependency and predictive clustering for language modeling. In *EMNLP 2002*, pp.248-256.
9. Gao, Jianfeng and Hisami Suzuki. 2003. Unsupervised learning of dependency structure for language modeling. In *ACL 2003*, pp.521-528.
10. Gao, Jianfeng and Hisami Suzuki. 2004. Capturing long distance dependency in language modeling: an empirical study. In *IJCNLP'04*. pp. 53-60.
11. Goodman, Joshua. 2001. A bit of progress in language modeling. *Computer Speech and Language*. October, 2001, pp 403-434.
12. Geutner, Petra. 1996. Introducing linguistic constraints into statistical language modeling. In *ICSLP96*, pp.402-405.
13. Katz, S. M. 1987. Estimation of probabilities from sparse data for other language component of a speech recognizer. *IEEE transactions on Acoustics, Speech and Signal Processing*, 35(3): 400-401.
14. Kneser, R and H. Ney. 1995. Improved backing-off for m-gram language modeling. In *ICASSP'95*: 181-184.
15. Isotani, R. and Matsunaga, S. 1994. A stochastic language model for speech recognition integrating local and global constraints. In *ICASSP-94*, pp. 5-8.
16. Ney, Hermann, Ute Essen and Reinhard Kneser. 1994. On structuring probabilistic dependences in stochastic language modeling. *Computer Speech and Language*, 8: 1-38.
17. Roark, Brian. 2001. Probabilistic top-down parsing and language modeling. *Computational Linguistics*, 17-2: 1-28.
18. Rosenfeld, Ronald. 1994. Adaptive statistical language modeling: a maximum entropy approach. Ph.D. thesis, Carnegie Mellon University.

19. Siu, Manhung, and Ostendorf, Mari. 2000. Variable n-grams and extensions for conversational speech language modeling. *IEEE Transactions on Speech and Audio Processing*, 8: 63-75.
20. Stolcke, A. 1998. Entropy-based pruning of backoff language models. In *Proceeding of DARPA News Transcription and Understanding Workshop*, Lansdowne, VA, pp.270-274.
21. Yuret, Deniz. 1998. Discovery of linguistic relations using lexical attraction. Ph.D. thesis, MIT.

Word Folding: Taking the Snapshot of Words Instead of the Whole

Jin-Dong Kim and Jun'ichi Tsujii

University of Tokyo
7-3-1 Hongo, Bunkyo-ku, Tokyo 113-0033 Japan
{jdkim,tsujii}@is.s.u-tokyo.ac.jp

Abstract. The snapshot of a word means the most informative fragment of the word. By taking the snapshot instead of the whole, the value space of lexical features can be significantly reduced. From the perspective of machine learning, a small space of feature values implies a loss of information but less data-spareness and less unseen data. The snapshot of words can be taken by using the word folding technique, the goal of which is to reduce the value space of lexical features while minimizing the loss of information.

1 Introduction

Natural Language Processing (NLP) techniques often treat text as the sequence of words. The words are read in and processed to make features that can provide important information. Usually, NLP techniques involve constructing a knowledge base that will be consulted to make certain decisions. The knowledge base can be rule-based [1], case-based [2], probability-based [3–5] or any other kind. In any case, the word plays a key role in constructing the knowledge base.

However, the use of words brings a couple of non-trivial problems. The huge variety of word forms will give rise to a model of huge size that eventually will restrict the use of various features. Spare data problem is also one of the well known problems that happens especially when a machine learning technique is employed.

There have been many works to reduce the space of words. Most of them are based on the notion that a word is divided into (zero or more) prefixes, a stem and (zero or more) suffixes. Stemming [6] is to reduce the space of the word by trimming relatively less important parts of words – most of them are suffixes – while leaving the important part of words (stems).

This paper presents a novel technique (word folding) that spots the most informative part (snapshot) of words. This seems similar to the stemming, but the results of the word folding can be any of the stem, prefix, suffix or even the whole word while the stemming yields the stem always.

2 The Tagging Model

Most of NLP tasks involve classification as the main problem. For example word sense disambiguation can be described as a classification problem where the sense

Table 1. Examples of Tagged Corpus. (a) Part-of-Speech Tagged Corpus (from Penn Treebank [7]). (b) Protein Tagged Corpus (from Genia Corpus [8]).

(a)		(b)	
Finmeccanica	NNP	IL-2	O
is	VBZ	gene	O
an	DT	expression	O
Italian	JJ	and	O
state-owned	JJ	NF-kappa	B
holding	VBZ	B	I
company	NN	activation	O
with	IN	through	O
interests	NNS	CD28	B
in	IN	requires	O
the	DT	reactive	O
mechanizal	JJ	oxygen	O
engineering	NN	production	O
industry	NN	by	O
.	.	5-lipoxygenase	B
		.	O

of a given word is the target feature to be classified, and the target word itself and the surrounding words may be exploited as the contextual features. Tagging can be also treated as the classification task where a sequence of associated classifications are involved.

In any case, a sequence of words is given as the input and a sequence of classification is made. Table 1 shows two examples of the tagged corpus each of which has the word sequence in the left column and the tags in the right. The tags are the result of classification of a certain target feature. (Part-of-speech of each word in the case of part-of-speech tagging and IOB tags [9] for protein in the case of Protein tagging)

The tagging model is probabilistically defined as finding the most probable tag sequence when a word sequence is given (equation (1)).

$$T(w_{1,k}) = arg \max_{t_{1,k}} P(t_{1,k}|w_{1,k}) \tag{1}$$

$$\approx arg \max_{t_{1,k}} \prod_{i=1}^{k} P(t_i|w_i) \tag{2}$$

$$\approx arg \max_{t_{1,k}} \prod_{i=1}^{k} P(t_i|t_{i-1}, w_i) \tag{3}$$

$$\approx arg \max_{t_{1,k}} \prod_{i=1}^{k} P(t_i|t_{i-1}) P(w_i|t_i) \tag{4}$$

$$\approx arg \max_{t_{1,k}} \prod_{i=1}^{k} P(t_i|\Phi(t_{1,i-1}, w_{1,k})) \tag{5}$$

Equation (2)~(5) represent simplified versions of the probabilistic model that make the computation tractable. Equation (2) represents the tagging model that selects the most probable tag for each word without considering the surrounding context. This model is considered as the simplest probabilistic tagging model and is often used as the baseline model. Equation (3) additionally takes account of the tag for previous word as contextual information. This model is used in this paper as the baseline model for the IOB tagging task. Equation (4) represents the well-known hidden Markov model (HMM). HMMs are widely used because they show fairly high performance while they have simple structure and are easy to implement. Equation (5) is very close to the original tagging model (equation (1)) except for the context classification function Φ, and the self-organizing Markov model[10] framework provides an effective way to induce the classification function from an annotated corpus. This model is used in this paper to demonstrate the effectiveness of the word folding technique.

3 Word Folding and the Snapshot of Words

The purpose of the **word folding** is to trim away the unnecessary parts of a word, leaving only an highly informative fragment of the word. The authors will call the fragment the **snapshot** of the word.

Potentially, a snapshot can be any part of a word. Considering the both edges, a word can be folded into one of four types of snapshots. First, a word can be folded into a prefix, where the rear part of the word is folded back and only the front part remains as the snapshot. A word can also be folded into a suffix with the front part being folded back. When both the front and rear parts are folded back, the internal substring remains as the snapshot. Even the whole word can remain as the snapshot without any part being folded. Table 2 lists the potential snapshots for recognizing proteins. In the table, the underscore sign('_') represents the edge of a word and the potential snapshots with the edge sign at the beginning, at the end and at the both sides present the prefix, suffix and whole word type of snapshots respectively. The potential snapshots without the edge sign present the substring type of snapshots.

Word folding involves decisions on which part of the word is the most informative. The decision can be made by consulting the **potential snapshot list (PSL)**. The PSL is a list of potential snapshots that is sorted in the descending order of the amount of information of each potential snapshots. When a word is

Table 2. Potential Snapshots for Protein Recognition.

_#-kin, _-kappa_, or-bet, r-beta_, ctor-be, _rs, _s#, s#k, ma-#, rsk_, ogenas, ehydrog, _peroxidase_, esA, sAr, _-AT, /c-R, b., -m, _sph, gomy, ngom, /RelA, elina, ion-#, linas, omyeli, S#K, r/C, RIIA, _-ki, NF-k, ctase, tyl-t, uctas, yl-tr, educta, _acetyl-, l-transf, ···

given, the PSL is consulted for finding the most highly ranked potential snapshot that matches one of the word's substrings. Then the potential snapshot is determined to be the snapshot of the word without ambiguity.

Actually, Table 2 is a PSL for protein recognition induced from the protein-annotated Genia corpus. With the list, for example, when the word *NF-kappa* is met in text, the substring *-kappa_* is determined to be the snapshot, because this is the most highly ranked potential snapshot in the PSL.

4 Building the Potential Snapshot List

The PSL can be induced from an annotated corpus. Since the building of the PSL is dependent on the annotation made into the corpus, the resulting PSL is task-oriented, and different PSLs have to be built for different tasks.

The potential snapshots can be extracted from the corpus, by collecting every possible substrings from the words in the corpus. A tagged corpus can be seen as a collection of examples which contains pairs of a word and the tag for it. Let E be a tagged corpus. Then the i'th example e_i in E is a pair of a word, w_i and the tag, t_i for it. From the word, w_i, a set of substrings, S_i can be extracted. Then the universal set of all the substrings, $\varsigma = \bigcup S_i$ becomes the set of potential snapshots. By ordering the potential snapshots according to the amount of information retained in each of them, the PSL for the task can be obtained.

The PSL can also be obtained in a position-dependent way. For example, a tagged corpus can be reorganized to be a collection of pairs of (w_{i-1}, t_i) instead of (w_i, t_i) to induce the PSL for the lexical feature of the word that immediately precedes the target feature.

4.1 Measures

Then the remaining problem is how to measure the amount of information of each potential snapshots. We examined several metrics including information gain (IG), entropy (H), relative entropy (RE) and binarized relative entropy (BRE).

The information gain [11] is one of the natural choices to measure the amount of information of a partition for a given task. For example, by a potential snapshot s, the whole example set E is partitioned into two subsets: the s-positive set of examples, $E_s = \{e_i | s \in S_i\}$ and the s-negative set of examples, $E_{\neg s} = \{e_i | s \notin S_i\}$. The amount of information of the partition is then measured by computing the difference of the entropy of the target feature in E and the average entropy of the target feature in each subset. The IG by the snapshot s is computed as follows[1]:

$$IG(T, s) = H_E(T) - (\frac{|E_s|}{|E|} H_{E_s}(T) + \frac{|E_{\neg s}|}{|E|} H_{E_{\neg s}}(T)) \qquad (6)$$

---
[1] To break the tie, high frequent substrings are preferred.

However, it has been turned out that the result is highly biased to substrings of high frequency and consequently, substrings in short length take the high rank. It is because IG considers not only the entropy of the s-positive set, E_s, but also the entropy of the s-negative set, $E_{\neg s}$. Since the s-negative set is much bigger than the s-positive set in most cases, the substring, s of low frequency can hardly have the chance to make big difference of information before and after knowing the partition.

To remove the bias, just the entropy (H) in the s-positive set is measured as follows:

$$H_{E_s}(T) = -\sum_{t \in T} p(t|s) log_2 p(t|s) \qquad (7)$$

It has been turned out that measuring just the entropy of the s-positive set makes a better ordering than the Information Gain (Experimental results on it will be shown later.). However, the entropy doesn't involve any notion of distance between the distributions of the target feature in the whole example set, E, and the s-positive set E_s. Consequently, the snapshots uniquely supporting the target feature value **O** are equally estimated to the snapshots uniquely supporting the target feature value **I**. However, since the **O** is the most prevailing target feature value, snapshots supporting **O** must be less important than that supporting **I** or **B**.

To take this observation into consideration, the relative entropy (RE) between E_s and E is measured as follows:

$$D(E_s||E) = \sum_{t \in T} p(t|s) log \frac{p(t|s)}{p(t)} \qquad (8)$$

Another measure named Binarized Relative Entropy (BRE) is also examined. It is based on the assumption that since the current task is tagging, only the most highly supported target feature value is important. In this method, for each target feature value, $t \in T$, the binarized target partition of E_t and $E_{\neg t}$ is assumed, and the relative entropy between the example set E and the s-positive example set is computed as follows:

$$D_t(E_s||E) = p(t|s) log \frac{p(t|s)}{p(t)} + p(\neg t|s) log \frac{p(\neg t|s)}{p(\neg t)} \qquad (9)$$

Then the largest $D_t, (t \in T)$ becomes the BRE of the snapshot. From experiments, it is found that BRE yields slightly different PSLs showing slightly better performance than RE.

4.2 Examples

Table 3 shows examples of snapshots taken by using the different PSLs that have been induced by using the four measures explained above. The example sentence is shown in the leftmost column, and the tag sequence for the sentence is in the rightmost column. The snapshots taken by using the measures information gain

(IG), entropy (H), relative entropy (RE) and binarized relative entropy (BRE) are shown in the second, third, fourth and fifth column respectively.

As is shown in the second column, the word folding by information gain yields quite short snapshots, while the word folding by the other three entropy-based measures yield more meaningful snapshots. The difference between the last three measures is roughly brought out on the snapshots for the second to the last word, *#-lipoxygenase*. The relative entropy yields longer snapshots than the entropy, and the binarized relative entropy yields longer snapshots than the relative entropy. This tendency occurs for the snapshots supporting the target feature value of low frequency. Note that the entropy yields longer snapshots then RE and BRE for the word *production* that is supporting **O**.

Table 3. Snapshots by Several Measures.

Word	IG	H	RE	BRE	Tag
IL-#	#_	_IL-#_	_IL-#_	_IL-#_	O
gene	e_	_gen	_gen	_gen	O
expression	re	xpressio	xpressio	xpressio	O
and	d_	_and_	_and_	_and_	O
NF-kappa	NF	_NF-ka	_NF-kappa_	_NF-kappa_	B
B	B_	_B_	_B_	_B_	I
activation	_a	atio	act	act	O
through	th	ugh	ugh	ugh	O
CD#	#_	_CD#_	_CD#_	_CD#_	B
requires	s_	req	req	req	O
reactive	e_	_rea	act	act	O
oxygen	_o	_oxy	gen_	yge	O
production	n_	oducti	_pro	_pro	O
by	y_	by	by	by	O
#-lipoxygenase	e_	e_	enas	ygenas	B
.	_._	_._	_._	_._	O

The snapshots can be taken differently depending on the relative position of the target word. Table 4 shows the snapshots differently taken according to the position, where W represents the word and S represents the snapshot, and they are detailed by the following singed numbers indicating the relative position from the current word. Note that the snapshots for the word, *examined* are taken differently according to the positions; The snapshot at the position -2 is taken most minutely because the meaning of the word is most significant at that position.

5 Experimental Setup

For the experimental task, the protein recognition task has been chosen. Protein recognition from biomedical literature is an emerging task which is receiv-

Table 4. Position-Dependent Snapshots by BRE.

W-0	S-2	S-1	S-0	S+1	S+2	Tag
we	$	$	we_	ls	xa	O
also	$	we_	so_	exa	e_	O
examined	we_	_als	ami	he_	N-gamma_	O
the	ls	amin	he_	N-g	in	O
IFN-gamma	_examined	_the_	N-gamma_	duction_	of_	B
induction	_the_	_I	nduct	_of	CII	O
of	-gamma_	nductio	_of	II	in	O
CIITA	induction_	_of_	CII	in	_RB_	O
in	_of_	IT	_in_	B_	-defe	O
RB	CI	_in_	RB_	_-def	lines	B
-defective	_in_	RB	_-d	lines	._	O
lines	_RB_	_-def	ines_	._	$	O
.	_-def	lines	_._	$	$	O

ing growing attention. GENIA corpus is a collection of abstracts from biomedical literature and has manually encoded annotations for biologically meaningful technical terms. Among the annotations, only the annotations for proteins (G#protein_XXX) have been taken. The XML-based format of GENIA corpus has been then converted into the vertical format with IOB tags, where *I* stands for inside of a protein, *O* stands for outside of proteins and *B* stands for the beginning of a protein. The resulting corpus is illustrated in Table 1(b).

The whole corpus was divided into exclusive training and test sets. For the test set, every 10'th abstract from the beginning was picked, and the remaining ones constituted the training set. Table 5 shows the size of each set of corpus.

Table 5. Size of the Corpus.

	Tokens	Sentences	Proteins
Train	450,674	16,726	28,679
Test	49,536	1,819	3,326
Total	500,210	18,545	32,005

The words are normalized by simple rules including decapitalizing the first letters of sentence-initial words and changing sequences of digits into pound signs ('#').

6 Experimental Results

Table 6 shows the baseline performance of protein recognition in five different setting of tasks. The second column shows the performance when the input is the sequence of words. The third, fourth, fifth and sixth columns show the

Table 6. Performance by Baseline Markov Models.

Model	Word	IG	H	RE	BRE
mm-w1-t1	.5386	.1556	.5181	.5453	.5470
(size)	1.4M	21K	614K	538K	552K
mm-w1-t2	.6360	.2336	.6138	.6384	.6372
(size)	2M	69K	965K	981K	985K

performance of protein recognition when the input is the sequence of snapshots taken by using the measures IG, H, RE and BRE respectively.

The model labeled with "mm-w1-t1" represents the Markov model considering the word feature and the target feature, and actually is the model that corresponds to the equation (2). The model labeled with "mm-w1-t2" represents the Markov model considering the word feature and the previous target feature as the contextual features to classify the current target feature, which corresponds to the equation (3). In any case, the performance by RE and BRE is better than others, and the difference between them is not significant. Note also that taking snapshots instead of words reduces the model size into less than half.

By using the self-organizing Markov model framework, the size of the baseline models can be reduced without significant loss of performance. Table 7 shows the performance of baseline models induced by using the SOMM framework. There are no or only very small amount of loss of performance while the size of models is reduced significantly. By using the self-organizing Markov models instead of the traditional uniform Markov models, various features can be exploited without suffering from the rapid increase of the model size.

Table 7. Performance by Baseline SOMMs.

Model	Word	IG	H	RE	BRE
somm-w1-t1	.5386	.1556	.5181	.5453	.5470
(size)	443K	16K	311K	302K	307K
somm-w1-t2	.6346	.2335	.6124	.6277	.6268
(size)	634K	48K	441K	475K	478K

Table 8 shows the overall performance of protein recognition by SOMM with various features. The models labeled with "somm-w3-XX" represent the self-organizing Markov model considering the word (or snapshot) features with window size 3, and the models labeled with "somm-w5-XX", with window size 5. With the models with window size of greater than 1 for word features, position-dependent snapshots have been taken as illustrated in the table 4.

Note that this is not such a work to get the state-of-the-art performance of the given task. Since the objective of the experiment is to prove the effectiveness of the word folding technique, only the word features and snapshots are exploited.

Table 8. Performance by SOMMs with Various Settings.

	# of correctly recognized proteins (recall/precision/f-score)		
Model	with Words	with snapshots by RE	with snapshots by BRE
somm-w1-t1	.4657 / .6385 / .5386	.4814 / .6288 / .5453	.4832 / .6302 / .5470
(size)	443K	302K	307K
somm-w3-t1	.6260 / .7187 / .6691	.6539 / .7039 / .6780	.6572 / .6995 / .6777
(size)	1,093K	957K	960K
somm-w5-t1	.6290 / .7189 / .6709	.6581 / .7073 / .6818	.6639 / .7093 / .6858
(size)	1,341K	1,216K	1,213K
somm-w1-t2	.5481 / .7536 / .6346	.5607 / .7392 / .6377	.5619 / .7347 / .6338
(size)	634K	475K	478K
somm-w3-t2	.6545 / .7453 / .6970	.6840 / .7386 / .7103	.6816 / .7348 / .7072
(size)	1,063K	927K	931K
somm-w5-t2	.6503 / .7370 / .6909	.6864 / .7303 / .7077	.6903 / .7326 / .7108
(size)	1,210K	1,079K	1,082K

The results is quite encouraging. Using the snapshots in place of the words always resulted in smaller models and yielded better results. Although the size reduction effect may not be so impressive[2], the improvement of performance is significant.

7 Conclusion

The word folding is a technique to reduce the value space of lexical features while minimizing the loss of information. This paper presents a novel technique to trim the unnecessary information while leaving important information. It is like filtering noisy data off to make beneficial information clearer. The idea of word folding came from the observation that even the human doesn't remember the complete form of words during reading text. Instead, only some impression of words remain in humans mind and are used to construct an idea. Word folding to take snapshots of words was an attempt to simulate the language processing mechanism occurring in human mind. Experimental results show the technique is quite promising. By using snapshots in place of the complete words, better performance by smaller models could be achieved.

For the future work, more experiments with other application may be crucial to prove the generality of this technique. Comparative experiments with other various features like part-of-speech, etc. is also required.

Acknowledgments

This research is partially supported by Information Mobility Project (CREST, JST) and Genome Information Science Project (MEXT).

---

[2] Note that this is also due to the feature of SOMM. SOMM has the feature of throwing away useless information.

References

1. Eric Brill. 1995. Transformation-Based Error-Driven Learning and Natural Language Processing: A Case Study in Part of Speech Tagging. *Computational Linguistics*, 21(4):543–565.
2. Walter Daelamans. 1999. Memory-Based Language Processing. Introduction to the Special Issue. *Journal of Experimental and Theoretical AI*, 11(3):287–292.
3. Eugene Charniak. 1993. Eauqtions for part-of-speech tagging. *Proceedings of the Eleventh National Conference on Artificial Intelligence*, 784–789.
4. Adam Berger, Stephen Della Pietra, and Vincent Della Pietra. 1996. A Maximum Entropy Approach to Natural Language Processing. *Computational Linguistics*, 22(1):39–71.
5. Vladimir Vapnik. 1998. *Statistical Learning Theory*. John Wiley and Sons Inc., New York, USA.
6. Martin Porter. 1980. An algorithm for suffix stripping *Program*, 14(3):130–137.
7. Mitchell Marcus, Beatrice Santorini, and Mary Ann Marcinkiewicz. 1993. Building a large annotated corpus of English: the Penn Treebank. *Computational Linguistics*, 19(2):310–330.
8. Jin-Dong Kim, Tomoko Ohta, Yuka Tateisi, and Jun'ichi Tsujii. 2003. GENIA corpus – a semantically annotated corpus for bio-textmining. *Bioinformatics*, 19(suppl.):i180–i182.
9. Erik F. Tjong Kim Sang. 1999. Representing Text Chunks. *Proceedings of 19th Conference of the European Chapter of the Association for Computational Linguistics*, 173–179.
10. Jin-Dong Kim, Hae-Chang Rim, and Jun'ichi Tsujii. 2003. Self-Organizing Markov Models and Their Application to Part-of-Speech Tagging. *Proceedings of the 41st Annual Meeting of the Association for Computational Linguistics*, 296–302.
11. Ross Quinlan. 1993. *C4.5: Programs for Machine Learning*. Morgan Kaufmann, San Mateo, USA.

Bilingual Chunk Alignment Based on Interactional Matching and Probabilistic Latent Semantic Indexing

Feifan Liu, Qianli Jin, Jun Zhao, and Bo Xu

National Laboratory of Pattern Recognition
Institute of Automation, Chinese Academy of Sciences
Beijing P.O. Box 2728, 100080
{ffliu,qljin,jzhao,bxu}@nlpr.ia.ac.cn

Abstract. An integrated method for bilingual chunk partition and alignment, called "Interactional Matching", is proposed in this paper. Different from former works, our method tries to get as necessary information as possible from the bilingual corpora themselves, and through bilingual constraint it can automatically build one-to-one chunk-pairs associated with the chunk-pair confidence coefficients. Also, our method partitions bilingual sentences entirely into chunks with no fragments left, different from collocation extracting methods. Furthermore, with the technology of Probabilistic Latent Semantic Indexing(PLSI), this method can deal with not only compositional chunks, but also non-compositional ones. The experiments show that, for overall process (including partition and alignment), our method can obtain 85% precision with 57% recall for the written language chunk-pairs and 78% precision with 53% recall for the spoken language chunk-pairs.

Keywords: Bilingual Chunking, Alignment, Interactional Matching, PLSI

1 Introduction

The knowledge granularity in natural language processing has four levels: text, sentence, chunk, and word. In these levels, chunk has its specific priority. As a kind of knowledge granularity between "sentence" and "word", "chunk" is much more unambiguous than "word", and more recurrent than "sentence". So, chunk is quite suitable for us to use in machine translation[10], word sense disambiguation, cross-lingual information retrieval system[11] and *etc.*

The popular alignment methods for chunk-level are commonly based on parsing technology[7] or length-based algorithm. But, it has been proven that these methods have poor performance when dealing with long sentences[2]. The more serious problem is that these methods can only deal with compositional chunk, such as "natural language – 自然 /natural 语言 /language", while they have no way to get non-compositional chunk-pairs, like "rain cats and dogs – 倾盆大雨". Furthermore, some methods([1],[3],[4]) can only extract chunks partly, and discard many fragments.

In this paper, an integrated method named "Interactional Matching" for Bilingual Chunk Alignment is proposed. Our aim is to get much enough information for recognizing one-to-one chunk-pairs from untagged corpora themselves, while using as less additional manually assignment as possible. The method involves two key technologies, namely Interactional Matching and Probabilistic Latent Semantic Indexing (PLSI). The former is used to conduct cross-lingual constraint in order to integrate the whole process including partition and alignment. And the latter is used to conduct chunk matching both for compositional chunk pairs and for non-compositional ones. Our method can output one-to-one chunk-pairs, together with their confidence coefficient, or called matching probabilities.

In this paper, we use Interactional Matching algorithm to deal with English-Chinese sentence-parallel corpora. Also, it's easy to extend this method to other bilingual pairs. We test this method in two types of corpora (English-Chinese Spoken Language and Written Language). The experiments show that our method can get overall 85% precision with 57% recall for written language chunk-pairs and 78% precision with 53% recall for spoken language chunk-pairs.

2 Related Work

Most of previous work of bilingual chunking and alignment are based on complex syntax information or focus on special kinds of phrases, such as V+NP, *etc.* Generally speaking, there are four representative methods, Xtract[1], Parsing([2],[7],[13],[14]), LocalMax([3],[4]), and Crossing Constraint[5]. Their characteristics are list in table 1, and we will analyze these four methods in detail.

Table 1. Comparison between different methods.

Algorithm	Xtract	Parsing	Local MAX	Crossing Constraint
Bilingual	N	Y	N	Y
Non-Compositional chunks	N	N	N	N
Having fragment	Y	N	Y	Y
Grammatical-based	N	Y	N	Y
Probabilistic-based	Y	N	Y	Y

(1) Frank Smadja (1993) proposed a probabi-listic method call Xtract, which is the first mature algorithm of extracting phrases from corpora. He defined two key measures for word sequence, cohesion degree and variance degree. Using this method, based on some central words, phrases and templates can be extracted from the single language corpora. However, he did not express how to deal with bilingual alignment.

(2) Syntax-parsing-based method is popular for structure alignment. Dekai Wu (1997) put forward inversion transduction grammar (ITG) for bilingual parsing. The stochastic ITG brings bilingual constraints to bear upon problematic corpus analysis tasks such as segmentation, bracketing, phrasal alignment and paring. This method got very good results for short and regular sentences. However, it is difficult to write a broad bilingual grammar to deal with long sentences in written lan-guage and irregular syntax in spoken language. Sun Le (2000) and Watanabe (2000) proposed methods based on parsing, bilingual lexicon and heuristic information, whereas these two methods can't treat with non-compositional chunks and can't also partition sentences completely.

(3) LocalMax was developed by Silva (1999), based on the Xtract method. He adopted two new association measures called Symmetric Conditional Probability and Mutual Expectation for extraction multiword lexical units. This idea produced a better result than Xtract, but still many fragments were discarded, and it can only deal with Monolingual corpora.

(4) Wei Wang and Ming Zhou (2001) proposed an integrated algorithm to do structure alignment, in which parsing and alignment are conducted together, and got good precision. However, this method needs quite a lot of prior knowledge, such as tree bank and word alignment information, *etc.* These knowledge, especially word alignment information, is very difficult to get.

In summary, the above methods have difficulties in complete chunking and alignment. In order to break the limitation, we propose an integrated algorithm of partition and alignment for the untagged bilingual corpora. Our method has the following characteristics:

a) Completely partition sentences into chunks (not extract collocations from corpora);
b) Independent on the syntax information, and grammatical rules;
c) Use bilingual constraint and integrate partition process and alignment process;
d) Can deal with compositional chunks as well as non-compositional chunks.

3 Interactional Matching Algorithm for Automatic Chunking and Alignment

3.1 Overview

We proposed a new integrated method for chunk partition and alignment, named "Interactional Matching". The purpose is to get one-to-one chunk-pairs from untagged bilingual corpora.

Input: Bilingual sentence-aligned corpora

Output: Chunk-pairs with confident coeffi-cients (compositional and non-compositional)

Technology: Bilingual constraint and PLSI

3.2 Interactional Matching Algorithm

Considering that our purpose is to find out one-to-one chunk-pairs from bilingual sentence pairs without fragments, we use the most general formula to represent the integrated algorithm.

Let i denote the number of one-to-one chunk-pairs partitioned from a sentence-pair; Let j denote the jth partition mode of English Sentence when partitioned into i chunks; Let k denote the kth partition mode of Chinese Sentence when partitioned into i chunks; (i^*, j^*, k^*) is the optimized result of partition and alignment. Then

$$(i^*, j^*, k^*) = \arg\max_{i,j,k}\{\alpha \times [K_e(i,j) + K_c(i,k)] + (1-\alpha) \times Align(i,j,k)\} \quad (1)$$

where $K_e(i,j)$ denotes the probability of partitioning the English sentence into i chunks, with the jth partition mode. $K_c(i,k)$ denotes the probability of partitioning the Chinese sentence into i chunks, with the kth partition mode. $Align(i,j,k)$ is the probability of aligning i one-to-one chunk pairs, based on the jth partition mode of English sentence and kth partition mode of Chinese sentence. And α is the coefficient, which can be adjusted based on the characteristics of the corpora.

For the N-words-long sentence, if it is partitioned into i chunks, there will be $[(N-1)!]/[(i-1)!(N-i)!]$ partition modes. So, for a sentence pair (N-words-long English sentence and M-words-long Chinese sentence), if both sentences are partitioned into i chunks, the total number of partition modes will be formalized as follows: $(N-1)!(M-1)!/\{[(i-1)!]^2(N-i)!(M-i)!\}$.

The meaning of formula (1) is to conduct any possible partition modes and to compare the integrated probabilities of all these situations to meet the optimization of partition and alignment. The coefficient α for written language is usually bigger than the one for spoken language, because the written language has more regular in syntax.

There are many ways to fulfill the functions $K_e(i,j)$, $K_c(i,k)$ and $Align(i,j,k)$. Here probabilistic-based method is adopted to design them as the following two parts, (A) and (B).

(A) We use the same model to design $K_e(i,j)$ and $K_c(i,k)$, and the formula can be written as follows:

$$K(i,j) = \Pr(i|language, length) \times \log[\theta + CohesionDegreeCluster(i,j)] \quad (2)$$

where $\Pr(i|language, length)$ is the prior distribution probability of number of chunks (NOC) related to the language type, and sentence length, which can be estimated by manually-chunked sentences. And the second logarithm item represents the weight of cohesion degree clustering, related to the number of chunks i and the partition mode j, where:

$$CohesionDegreeCluster(i,j) = [\sum_{q=1}^{N-i} Reserve(q)/(N-i) - \sum_{p=1}^{i-1} Cut(p)/(i-1)]$$

$$\div [\sum_{p_1=1}^{i-2}\sum_{p_2=p_1+1}^{i-1}(Cut(p_1) - Cut(p_2))^2 + \sum_{q_1=1}^{N-i-1}\sum_{q_2=q_1+1}^{N-i}(Reserve(q_1) - Reserve(q_2))^2] \quad (3)$$

Here N is the length of the sentence, p is an index for the partition points in mode j, q is an index for the non-partition points in mode j, $Cut(p)$ is cohesion degree of two words adjacent to the pth partition point in this sentence, $Reserve(p)$ is cohesion degree of two words adjacent to the pth non-partition point in this sentence. Also θ in formula (2) is a coefficient between 0 and 1. The cohesion degree of two words (w_1, w_2) is simply defined as:

$$D(w_1, w_2) = (1 - \beta) \times MI(w_1, w_2) + \beta \times Times(w_1, w_2) \qquad (4)$$

where MI is mutual information between two words. $Times(w_1, w_2)$ is just the co-occurrence times of word sequence (w_1, w_2), which is used to compensate irregular word sequence, such as some spoken expression. And β is a coefficient between 0 and 1, which is usually bigger for the spoken language than the one for the written language.

The value $K(i, j)$ indicates the possibility of partitioning the sentence into i chunks, with the jth partition mode. The formula (2) has two parts, first of which is the prior probability, and the second represents the weight of cohesion degree clustering, which indicates the characteristic of the sentence. Given the number of chunks i and partition mode j, all the values of cohesion degrees in a sentence are separated into two classes, $Cut(p)$ and $Reserve(q)$. $Cut(p)$ denotes the cohesion degree of pth partitioned point, and $Reserve(q)$ denotes the cohesion degree of qth reserved point. In order to give a effective weight to this classification result, we developed a self-clustering-based measurement algorithm, which is represented as formula (3). The numerator of formula (3) is the interactional distance between two classes of cohesion degrees, and the denominator is the internal distance of the two classes. So, $CohesionDegreeCluster(i, j)$ will be equal to a big value if the result of cohesion degree classification is reasonable; or it will be very small when the classification is unreasonable. And logarithm operator and θ are just used to adjust the dynamic range.

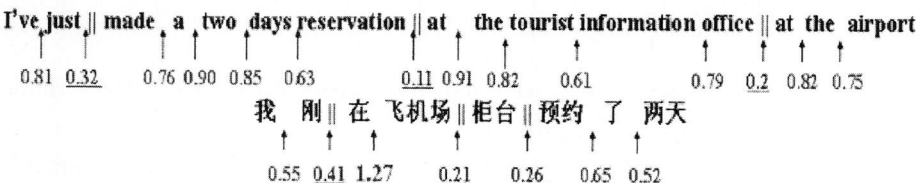

Fig. 1. Cohesion degrees under one partition mode with 4 chunks per sentence.

Figure 1 shows the example of chunking with above algorithm, which shows cohesion degrees between every two adjacent words in a sentence pair. Places marked with "$||$", are the partitioned points, which belong to the class $Cut(p)$. And other places are the reserved points, which belong to the class $Reserve(q)$. Use the formula (2) and (3), we can obtain the corresponding values such as $K_e(i = 4, j) = 0.32$ and $K_c(i = 4, k) = 0.29$, when the prior probabilities $Pr(4|Eng, 15) = 0.42$ $Pr(4|Chn, 8) = 0.30$, and coefficient $\theta = 0.5$.

(B) Different alignment has different matching measurement for one partition mode. Since every partitioned chunk can be represented as a word vector, we can get the matching value of one match mode by computing the similarity between vectors which can be realized using word similarity matrix $P(W,W)$. So we can choose one match mode of one-to-one chunk-pair by maximizing the matching degree which can be defined as follows:

$$Align(i,j,k) = \max_{m} \sum_{p=1}^{i} ScoreV(i,j,k,p,m) \tag{5}$$

$$= \max_{m} \sum_{p=1}^{i} [(wVectorE(i,j,p,m) \cdot P(W,W)) \cdot (wVectorC(i,k,p,m) \cdot P(W,W))^T]$$

where m denotes the mth match mode. $wVectorE(i,j,p,m)$ is the word vector, built from the pth chunk in mth match mode of English sentence partition result with i chunks at the jth partition mode. $wVectorC(i,k,p,m)$ is the word vector, built from the pth chunk in mth match mode of Chinese sentence partition result with i chunks at the kth partition mode. Note that here "pth chunk" denotes the sequence number of chunks in one match mode, not direct sequence number in original sentence. $P(W,W)$ is the word similarity matrix, with is built by probabilistic latent semantic indexing (PLSI). And $ScoreV(i,j,k,p,m)$ is the corresponding alignment probability between $wVectorE(i,j,p,m)$ and $wVectorC(i,k,p,m)$.

For the situation in Figure 1, the following table can be easily acquired.

Table 2. Aligning probabilities of matching mode.

ScoreV (10^{-3})	我刚	在飞机场	柜台	预约两天
I've just	**0.65**	0.16	0.07	0.21
made a two days reservation	0.13	0.19	0.09	**0.78**
at the tourist information office	0.12	0.34	**0.15**	0.20
at the airport	0.07	**0.75**	0.05	0.13

After comparing all the match modes, we select the maximal one as the value of $Align(i,j,k)$ which represents one optional alignment for the whole process. That is: $Align(i=4,j,k) = (0.65 + 0.78 + 0.15 + 0.75) \times 10^{-3}$.

We use PLSI[6] to estimate the word similarity matrix, because the traditional statistical method cannot associate the meanings between different words, while LSI can. For instance, "computer" and "software" appear together several times in the corpus, and the same as "software" and "hardware". Because of no co-occurrence between "computer" and "hardware", in the traditional method, the correlation degree between them is zero or a fixed small value. It's quite unreasonable. However, LSI can deal with this meaning clustering, and give a reasonable correlation degree between "computer" and "hardware". That's why LSI can deal with non-combinatorial chunks.

4 Experiment Results

First, we use roughly 3000 manually partitioned sentences to estimate the prior probabilities $\Pr(i|language, length)$ as Figure 2 shows.

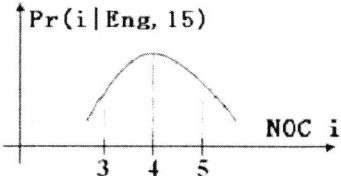

Fig. 2. Distribution of Number of Chunks(NOC) to sentence length and language.

Then we take two types of corpora as our testing data, which has been included in www.Chinese-LDC.org:

A) English-Chinese Spoken Language:
Travel Domain: 20000 Sentences Pairs (ECSL)

B) English-Chinese Written Language:
General Domain: 12000 Sentences Pairs (ECWL)

We try to get enough information from the testing data themselves for chunking and alignment without any additional annotated training corpora, so we need to preprocess the testing corpora by replacing some named entities with unified tag, which can be implemented automatically and easily by virtue of existing tools.

4.1 Overall Accuracy

Considering the whole process (partition and alignment), we can get the overall result. In this experiment, parameters in formula (1) (2) and (4) have been set and listed below:

Corpora	α	β	θ
ECSL	0.50	0.05	0.50
ECWL	0.60	0.045	0.50

A general concept of the precision-recall measure is used here to testify our algorithm, and the results are presented in table 3. Note that there is no manual interference in the whole process.

The column "No" indicates three threshold of confidence coefficient for correct chunk-pairs. Obviously, the performance on written language is much better by reason of its regular expressions.

And when adjusting the parameter α, we get the following Figure 3, which shows the best F measure of overall result related to the α. This result proves that the written language needs a bigger α than spoken language.

Table 3. Overall results of the experiments.

Corpora	No	Overall Accuracy		
		Precision (%)	Recall (%)	Standard F Mea-sure
ECSL	1	90	32	0.47
	2	**78**	**53**	**0.63**
	3	60	57	0.58
ECWL	1	90	40	0.55
	2	**85**	**57**	**0.68**
	3	60	66	0.63

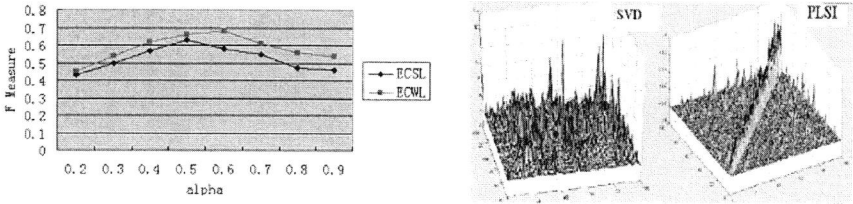

Fig. 3. The best F-measure related to α. **Fig. 4.** $P(W, W)$ sample of SVD and PLSI.

It is also proved by other experiments that the coefficient β is around the value of 0.05 and θ is around the value of 0.5, which are not sensitive to the overall result.

4.2 Partition Accuracy

In this section, the first part of formula (1) is used to do the partition experiment only. That is: $(i^*, j^*, k^*) = \arg\max_{i,j,k} \alpha \times [K_e(i,j) + K_c(i,k)]$

Table 4. Comparison between monolingual and bilingual partition accuracy.

Corpora	Language	Partition Precision (%)	
		Monolingual	Bilingual
ECSL	English	75	77
	Chinese	66	77
ECWL	English	81	86
	Chinese	74	86

Table 4 shows that bilingual chunking does much better than monolingual chunking because of the bilingual constraint implemented by our Interactional Matching algorithm. Also we can see English sentences have better performance, because they are less flexible in expressions.

4.3 Alignment Accuracy

Manually correcting the results of partition, we get 100% precision partition data, which was used to do alignment experiments (see the formula (5)).

Table 5. Alignment results using DMM and PLSI.

Corpora	DMM (%)		PLSI (%)	
	Precision	Recall	Precision	Recall
ECSL	82	75	91	80
ECWL	90	83	94	87

It is found from table 5 that PLSI outperforms the traditional Dictionary Matching Method (DMM), which just measures the matching similarity of chunks via a bilingual lexicon. It can be to some extent ascribed to the fact that meaning clustering has been realized in PLSI while DMM is only limited to morphological analysis. PSLI can therefore cope with most of non-compositional chunk pairs,such as "here and there – 各处 ", but DMM can't.

4.4 LSI Analysis

The accuracy of matrix $P(W,W)$ decides the precision of chunk alignment. Jin (2003) made effective improvements to the standard EM algorithm for PLSI[15], and calculated P matrix using 1000 bilingual texts. 100×100 matrix sample is shown in figure4. Note that in the Matrix P, there are no difference between English words and Chinese words. SVD and PLSI results are showed in Figure 4.The diagonal of matrix $P(W,W)$ represents the self-correlation values, which certainly should higher than cross-correlation values. So we can see that PLSI is better than SVD, not only on correlation, but also on the equilibrium of the matrix.

5 Conclusion

This paper presents an integrated method for bilingual chunk partition (not extraction) and alignment, called "Interactional Matching". Different from existing approaches, this method can automatically find out the one-to-one chunk-pairs through mining enough information from untagged bilingual corpora, without relying heavily on corpora which have been assigned with POS tags and syntax information. Furthermore, with the technology of PLSI, this algorithm is able to deal with both compositional and non-compositional chunks.

Experiment shows that this method gets good performance for partition and alignment on both written language and spoken language. And also this chunking technique can be applied to many tasks of natural language processing, such as machine translation and cross-lingual information retrieval.

Acknowledgments

This work was supported by the Natural Sciences Foundation under grant No. 60272041, 60372016, 60121302.

References

1. Frank Smadja: Retrieving Collocations from Text: Xtract. *Computational Linguistics*, 19(1), (1993) 143-177
2. Qiang Zhou: Automatically Bracket and Tag Chinese Phrase. *Journal of Chinese Information Processing*, 11(1), (1997) 1-10
3. Boxing Chen and Limin Du: Alignment of Single Source Words and Target Multi-word Units from Parallel Corpus. In: 1st *Students' Workshop on Computational Linguistics Proceedings*, August 20-23,(2002) 318-127
4. Silva J.F., Dias G., Guillor S. and Lopes J.G.P.: Using Localmaxs Algorithm for Extraction of Contiguous and Non-contiguous Multiword Lexical Units. In: 9th *Portuguese Conference in Artificial Intelligence*, Lecture Notes, Spring-Verlag, Universidade de Evora, Evora Portugal (1999)
5. Wei Wang, Ming Zhou, Jinxia Huang and Changning Huang: Structure Alignment Using Bilingual Chunking. In: *Proceedings of COLING 2002*, 24 August – 1 September, Taipei (2002)
6. Thomas Hofmann: Probabilistic Latent Semantic Indexing. In *Proceedings of the 22nd Annual ACM Conference on Research and Development in Information Retrieval*, Berkeley, Cali-fornia, August, (1999) 50-57
7. Dekai Wu: Stochastic Inversion Transduction Grammars and Bilingual Parsing of Parallel Corpora. *Computational Linguistics*, 23(3), (1997) 377-400
8. David Blei, Andrew Y. Ng and Michael Jordan: Latent Dirichlet Allocation. *Journal of Machine Learning Research*, (2003) 993-1022
9. Gene Golub, Knut Solna, and Paul Van Dooren: Computing the SVD of a General Matrix Product/Quotient, *SIAM Journal on Matrix Analysis and Applications*, 22(1), (2000) 1-19
10. Wei Cheng, Jun Zhao, Bo Xu and Feifan Liu: Bilingual Chunking for Chinese-English Spoken-language Translation. *Journal of Chinese Information Processing*, 17(2), (2003) 21-27
11. Jun Zhao: The Framework of Cross-lingual Information Retrieval. *Chinese-Japanese Natural Language Processing Proseminar (2nd)* (2002)
12. Cong Li and Hang Li: Word Translation Disambiguation Using Bilingual Bootstrapping. In *Proceedings of the Fortieth Annual Meeting of the Association for Computational Linguistics (ACL-2002)*, Philadelphia, July, (2002)
13. Watanabe H., Kurohashi S., Aramaki E.: Finding Structural Correspondences from Bilingual Parsed Corpus for Corpus-based Translation. *COLING 2000* (2000)
14. Le, S., Youbing, J., Lin, D. and Yufang, S.: Word Alignment of English-Chinese Bilingual Corpus Based on Chunks, *Proc. 2000 EMNLP and VLC* (2000) 110-116
15. Qianli Jin, Zhao, J., Xu, B.: Weakly-Supervised Probabilistic Latent Semantic Analysis and its Applications in Multilingual Information Retrieval. In: *Proceedings of 7th Joint Symposium on Computational Linguistics*, 9-11 August, (2003)

Learning to Filter Junk E-mail from Positive and Unlabeled Examples

Karl-Michael Schneider

Department of General Linguistics
University of Passau
schneide@phil.uni-passau.de

Abstract. We study the applicability of partially supervised text classification to junk mail filtering, where a given set of junk messages serve as positive examples while the messages received by a user are unlabeled examples, but there are no negative examples. Supplying a junk mail filter with a large set of junk mails could result in an algorithm that learns to filter junk mail without user intervention and thus would significantly improve the usability of an e-mail client. We study several learning algorithms that take care of the unlabeled examples in different ways and present experimental results.

1 Introduction

Junk mail filtering is the problem of detecting junk messages (spam, UCE, unrequested mass e-mailings of commercial, pornographic or otherwise inappropriate content) in a stream of e-mails received by a user and moving (or removing) the detected junk messages from her mail folder. Under the assumption that junk mail can be distinguished from legitimate (non junk) mail in terms of style and vocabulary, the problem can be rephrased as a text classification problem, and machine learning techniques can be employed to learn a classifier from examples [1–3].

A supervised learning algorithm needs examples of junk mail (positive examples) and legitimate mail (negative examples) in order to learn to distinguish between the two classes. While junk mail is unrelated to a particular user (junk messages are distributed to millions of users) and can be provided by a vendor of a junk filter, what constitutes legitimate mail depends very much on the individual user. Therefore, examples of legitimate mail cannot be provided by a software vendor but must be given to the junk filter by the user. From a user's perspective, however, it would be preferable to have a junk filter that requires as little intervention from the user as possible in order to learn to filter junk mail.

It is long known that unlabeled data can reduce the amount of labeled data that is required to learn a classifier [4], and recently it has been shown how unlabeled data can be exploited in text classification [5]. Moreover, one can even learn text classifiers from labeled examples of one class alone (positive examples), when these are augmented with unlabeled examples. This type of learning from positive and unlabeled examples is called *partially supervised text classification* [6, 7].

This paper considers junk mail filtering as partially supervised text classification, where junk mails are used as positive examples while the e-mails received by a user are unlabeled examples. Our intention is to reduce the effort of collecting training examples manually as much as possible, since junk e-mail can be collected automatically quite easily in large quantities and with high purity. An algorithm that learns to filter junk mail from a user's incoming e-mail when supplied with a large collection of junk mail, without user intervention, could significantly improve the usability of an e-mail client.

In typical applications of partially supervised text classification, the positive examples usually depend on the user, while there is a large set of unlabeled examples. For instance, in the identification of interesting websites for a user, the history of the user's activities and his bookmarks can serve as positive examples while arbitrary web pages, available in unlimited quantities from the world wide web, can be used as unlabeled examples. In contrast, in junk mail filtering, unlabeled examples (e-mails received by a user) are not available instantly and to anybody but must be accumulated over time by each user, while positive examples (junk e-mails) are not related to a particular user and are readily available in large quantities.

Unfortunately the number of unlabeled examples required to obtain a good classifier in partially supervised text classification is quite large. In this paper, we study the situation where a learning algorithm is initially given a sufficiently large set of positive examples (junk e-mails), and collects unlabeled examples during operation from the stream of messages received by the user. This means it has no unlabeled examples at all when it gets operational for the first time. Standard methods for incorporating unlabeled examples, like the EM algorithm [4, 5] may not work well in this situation. The question addressed in this paper is thus how good a learning algorithm can be when it has many positive examples but few unlabeled examples, and how fast it can improve as it collects more unlabeled examples. We study several learning methods and compare their learning success rates.

The paper proceeds as follows. In Sect. 2 we discuss related work, especially in the framework of partially supervised text classification. In Sect. 3 we review the statistical framework used in this paper. In Sect. 4 we describe the different learning strategies studied in this paper. Section 5 describes some experiments and discusses the results. Finally, in Sect. 6 we draw some conclusions.

2 Related Work

That learning from positive examples alone with the help of unlabeled examples is possible was shown by Denis [8] in a theoretical study in the context of PAC learning. Liu et al. [7] proved an upper bound on the expected error of a classifier that is selected such that all positive examples are classified correctly while the number of unlabeled examples classified as positive is minimized. In the case where the class labels are noisy or the hypotheses space is not powerful enough to learn the true classification, the expected error can still be bounded by choosing a classifier that correctly classifies a fraction r of the positive examples.

The key problem in partially supervised classification is to identify negative examples in the unlabeled data to train a classifier. Li and Liu [9] use the Rochio algorithm to find reliable negative examples among the unlabeled examples, and then apply a support vector machine (SVM) iteratively to find more negative examples, and to select a classifier. Yu et al. [10] remove positive examples from the unlabeled data by identifying strong positive features, and use the remaining data as negative examples to train an SVM.

A different method to obtain a classifier from positive and unlabeled examples was proposed by Denis et al. [6]. Instead of finding negative examples, the *positive Naive Bayes* algorithm estimates the distribution of words in the negative class from the distributions in the positive and unlabeled examples. We present this algorithm in Sect. 3.2.

Another problem closely related to partially supervised text classification is the problem of describing a class of objects when only examples of that class are given. This is sometimes called *one-class classification* or *novelty detection* [11]. The one-class SVM is a variant of the traditional two-class SVM that identifies outliers in the set of examples and then uses traditional SVM to estimate the support of the target class. One-class classification does not require unlabeled examples.

The problem of learning during operation is also related to online learning, where the parameters of a classifier are constantly updated as new labeled examples are received [12]. To the best of our knowledge, online classifiers have not been applied to the situation where only positive labeled examples are available. Whereas an online classifier is first trained from an initial training set and then updated during operation, this paper studies learning that begins when the first input message is received, with no prior training.

3 Bayesian Framework

3.1 Naive Bayes

We use a Naive Bayesian classifier to classify messages as junk or legitimate. The Naive Bayes classifier is based on a probabilistic model of text generation. It assumes that a message is generated by a mixture model by first choosing the category $c_j \in \mathcal{C} = \{junk, legit\}$ of the message according to a prior probability $P(c_j|\theta)$, where θ denotes the mixture parameters, and then generating the message according to some probabilistic model whose parameters depend on c_j. We use a multinomial model of text generation [13]. In this model, a document d_i is generated by choosing its length $|d_i|$ according to some distribution $P(|d_i|)$ and then drawing $|d_i|$ words independently from a fixed vocabulary V according to the distribution $P(w_t|c_j;\theta)$. The probability of d_i in c_j is given by the multinomial distribution:

$$P(d_i|c_j;\theta) = P(|d_i|)|d_i|! \prod_{t=1}^{|V|} \frac{P(w_t|c_j;\theta)^{N_{it}}}{N_{it}!} \qquad (1)$$

where N_{it} is the number of occurrences of w_t in d_i. The likelihood of d_i is

$$P(d_i|\theta) = \sum_{j=1}^{|\mathcal{C}|} P(c_j|\theta)P(d_i|c_j;\theta). \quad (2)$$

Using Bayes' rule, we can compute the posterior probability that d_i belongs to c_j:

$$P(c_j|d_i;\theta) = \frac{P(c_j|\theta)P(d_i|c_j;\theta)}{P(d_i|\theta)}. \quad (3)$$

For a given document d_i the Naive Bayes classifier selects the category c^* that maximizes (3).

Let $\mathcal{D} = \{d_1, \ldots, d_m\}$ be a set of labeled training documents. The learning algorithm must estimate the parameters $P(c_j|\theta)$ and $P(w_t|c_j;\theta)$ from $\mathcal{D}$. When $\mathcal{D}$ contains examples of both classes, this can be done using maximum likelihood estimates with Laplacean priors:

$$P(c_j|\hat{\theta}) = \frac{|c_j|}{|\mathcal{D}|} \quad (4)$$

and

$$P(w_t|c_j;\hat{\theta}) = \frac{1 + N(w_t, c_j)}{|V| + \sum_{s=1}^{|V|} N(w_s, c_j)} \quad (5)$$

where $|c_j|$ is the number of documents in c_j and $N(w_t, c_j)$ is the number of occurrences of w_t in c_j.

3.2 Positive Naive Bayes

When a learning algorithm has only labeled examples of one class, but has access to unlabeled examples, it must estimate the parameters for the other class from the combination of labeled and unlabeled examples. Let 0 and 1 denote the negative and positive class, respectively. Denis et al. [6] have shown how $P(0|\theta)$ and $P(w_t|0;\theta)$ can be estimated from positive and unlabeled examples when $P(1|\theta)$ is known.[1] We set $P(0|\hat{\theta}) = 1 - P(1|\theta)$. Let $\mathcal{P}$ and $\mathcal{U}$ denote the sets of positive and unlabeled examples, respectively. $P(w_t|0;\theta)$ will be estimated by projecting $\mathcal{U}$ to a set $\mathcal{P} \cup \mathcal{N}$ of positive and negative documents such that the positive and negative documents are distributed according to $P(c_j|\theta)$, and the distribution of words in $\mathcal{P} \cup \mathcal{N}$ is "most similar" to $\mathcal{U}$. Then $P(w_t|0;\theta)$ can be estimated by estimating the number of occurrences of w_t in $\mathcal{N}$.

The estimated number of negative documents is

$$|\mathcal{N}| = |\mathcal{P}| \cdot \frac{1 - P(1|\theta)}{P(1|\theta)}. \quad (6)$$

For a set $\mathcal{X}$ of documents, let $N(\mathcal{X})$, $N(w)$ and $N(w, \mathcal{X})$ denote the number of word occurrences in $\mathcal{X}$, the number of occurrences of w in $\mathcal{P} \cup \mathcal{N}$ and the

---
[1] Our presentation differs slightly from Denis et al. [6].

number of occurrences of w in $\mathcal{X}$, respectively. Assuming that documents in $\mathcal{U}$ are generated according to the distribution given by θ, the estimated number of word occurrences in $\mathcal{P} \cup \mathcal{N}$ is

$$\hat{N}(\mathcal{P} \cup \mathcal{N}) = \max\left\{ N(\mathcal{U}) \cdot \frac{|\mathcal{P}| + |\mathcal{N}|}{|\mathcal{U}|}, N(\mathcal{P}) \cdot \frac{2}{1 + P(1|\theta)} \right\}. \quad (7)$$

The second term is used as a lower bound to avoid documents of zero or negative length, especially when $\mathcal{U}$ is small [6]. The estimated number of word occurrences in $\mathcal{N}$ is

$$\hat{N}(\mathcal{N}) = \hat{N}(\mathcal{P} \cup \mathcal{N}) - N(\mathcal{P}). \quad (8)$$

Similarly, the estimated number of occurrences of w in $\mathcal{P} \cup \mathcal{N}$ is

$$\hat{N}(w) = \max\left\{ \hat{N}(\mathcal{P} \cup \mathcal{N}) \cdot \frac{N(w, \mathcal{U})}{N(\mathcal{U})}, N(w, \mathcal{P}) \right\}. \quad (9)$$

Then

$$\hat{N}(w, \mathcal{N}) = \min\{\hat{N}(w) - N(w, \mathcal{P}), \hat{N}(\mathcal{N})\} \quad (10)$$

is the estimated number of occurrences of w in $\mathcal{N}$.

4 Learning Strategies

We study the following scenario: A learner receives messages from a stream (called input messages), one at a time. Its task is to build a classifier and classify each input message when it is received. The category of the input message (junk or legitimate) is not known to the learner. The learner can build a new classifier for each new input message. To this end, it can memorize the input messages it has received. In addition, it has access to a fixed set of junk messages.

We study four different learning strategies. Each learner memorizes all the input messages it receives and employs a particular strategy to use the junk messages (positive examples) and the input messages (unlabeled examples) to build a Naive Bayes classifier. The *static NB learner* (SNB) simply considers each input message as a negative example (i.e. legitimate message) and uses the standard Naive Bayes parameter estimation as described in Sect. 3.1. The *static PNB learner* (SPNB) considers the stored input messages as mixed messages (i.e. junk and legitimate) and uses the positive Naive Bayes parameter estimation as described in Sect. 3.2. The *static EM learner* (SEM) uses the EM algorithm [4, 5] to build a classifier. It builds an initial model by considering the stored input messages as negative examples, and then uses this model to assign probabilistic labels to the stored messages and iterates until the model converges or a maximum number of iterations is reached. The *static PEM learner* (SPEM) is like the static EM learner except that for the initial model, it considers the stored input messages as mixed examples and uses the positive Naive Bayes parameter estimation. We expect the model built by the static learners to improve over time as the number of negative examples in the memory increases[2].

5 Experiments

We performed experiments with the four learning strategies described in Sect. 4 on two different e-mail corpora. The first corpus consists of 1397 junk messages and 500 mixed messages from the SpamAssassin public mail corpus.[3] We varied the amount of spam messages among the mixed messages between 15% and 50%. For the second corpus we used 2000 junk messages received by the author between January 22, 1998 and August 22, 2002, and 500 mixed e-mails received between October 16 and October 20, 2003 as input messages. 43% of the mixed messages were spam messages.

We extracted the text of each message and removed everything else, including all e-mail headers. The text was then tokenized, counting alphabetic sequences, numbers and all other characters as tokens. We did not perform stemming, case normalization, removal of stop words or other preprocessing.

Each input message was fed to the learner, and the predicted label (junk or legitimate) was recorded. In order to reduce the size of the model and to avoid overfitting, we performed feature selection using mutual information [13]. We used 5000 features for all learners except SNB, for which we found that varying the number of features linearly from 500 for the first input message to 5000 for the 500th input message increased the classification accuracy slightly.

For SEM and SPEM, the number of EM iterations was limited to 5. We found that allowing more iterations had no effect on the classification. For SPNB and SPEM, the parameter $P(1|\theta)$ was set to the fraction of positive examples in the unlabeled corpus used in the experiments.

We report precision and recall for each of the two classes, where legitimate precision is the percentage of legitimate messages among all messages that are classified as legitimate (i.e. pass the filter), and legitimate recall is the percentage of legitimate messages that are actually classified as legitimate. Similarly for spam.

Figures 1 and 2 show legitimate recall and spam recall for the SpamAssassin messages with a spam proportion of 40%, accumulated over the number of messages received, i.e. at any number of messages, the recall value for the messages received up to that point is shown. SNB and SEM have higher legitimate recall but much lower spam recall than SPNB and SPEM which consider the input messages as mixed messages for training.

In the next experiment, we investigated the effect of the spam proportion on the behaviour of the learners. Table 1 shows classification results for four different

---

[2] Note that the static learners do not store the labels assigned to the input messages by the classifier. In future experiments, we plan to consider dynamic learners that memorize the labels assigned to the input messages and use the input messages as labeled training examples.

[3] Available from http://spamassassin.org/publiccorpus/

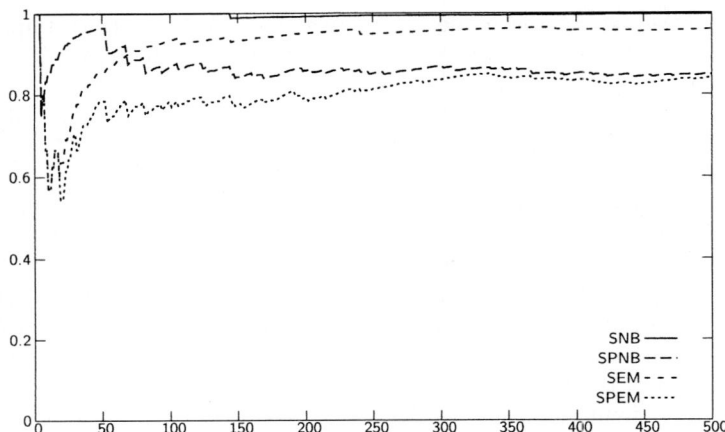

Fig. 1. Legitimate recall achieved by four learning strategies on the SpamAssassin corpus with 40% spam, accumulated over the number of messages received.

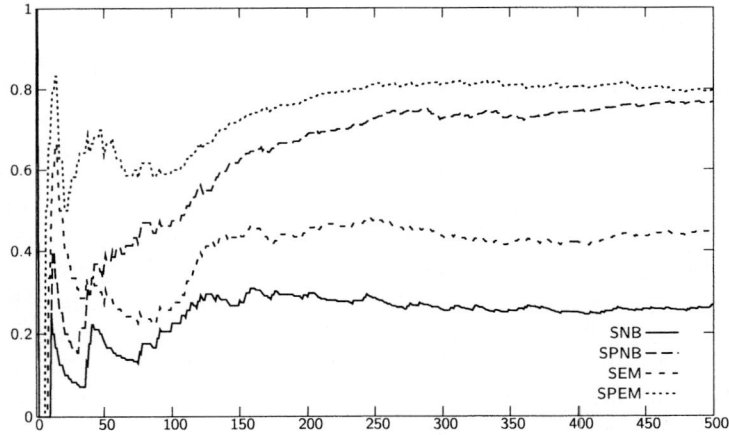

Fig. 2. Spam recall achieved by four learning strategies on the SpamAssassin corpus with 40% spam, accumulated over the number of messages received.

versions of the SpamAssassin (SA) corpus, where the spam proportion varies from 15% to 50%. In addition, the results for the private E-mail corpus is shown. In general, the learners that use the positive Naive Bayes parameter estimation have lower legitimate recall but higher spam recall, for all spam proportions, but the effect gets more pronounced for higher spam rates.

In another experiment, we varied the number of junk messages given to the learner. We show results for SNB and SPNB on the SpamAssassin corpus with 40% spam in Table 2. The number of junk messages varied from 30 to 1397.

Table 1. Legitimate recall and spam recall achieved by four learners on the SpamAssassin corpus with different spam proportions and on the author's E-mail corpus.

	SA/15%	SA/25%	SA/40%	SA/50%[4]	E-mail/43%
SNB	0.9977 0.4595	0.9945 0.3060	0.9966 0.2670	1.0000 0.2120	0.8550 0.6429
SPNB	0.9742 0.6486	0.9590 0.7313	0.8469 0.7670	0.8800 0.8200	0.6298 0.8193
SEM	0.9765 0.5000	0.9809 0.4701	0.9558 0.4515	0.9880 0.3800	0.9084 0.5882
SPEM	0.7277 0.7568	0.9016 0.8507	0.8367 0.7961	0.9600 0.6240	0.6298 0.8361

Table 2. Legitimate recall and spam recall achieved by SNB and SPNB on the SpamAssassin corpus with 40% spam, using different amounts of junk messages.

Junk	SNB	SPNB
30	0.9966 0.0146	0.7177 0.2816
60	0.9966 0.0194	0.6701 0.3010
125	0.9966 0.0291	0.5782 0.4466
500	0.9966 0.1408	0.6497 0.7282
1397	0.9966 0.2670	0.8469 0.7670

Both SNB and SPNB loose spam recall when provided with less junk messages, but for SNB the effect is much more pronounced.

6 Conclusions

We have considered junk mail filtering as a partially supervised text classification problem, where a large set of junk mails is used as positive examples and the e-mails received by a user are used as unlabeled examples. This setting requires no intervention of the user. We compared four different learning algorithms: A simple Naive Bayes algorithm that considers all messages received by the user as negative examples, and the positive Naive Bayes (PNB) algorithm of Denis et al. [6] that estimates the distribution of the negative examples from the positive and unlabeled examples; in addition, both algorithms were combined with the EM algorithm.

Our experiments show that the PNB algorithm achieves considerably higher spam recall, but at the cost of lower legitimate recall. While higher spam recall means better spam filtering, lower legitimate recall means more false positives (legitimate e-mails classified as spam). The latter may be acceptable in situations where false positives are associated with lower costs, but future work must aim at reducing the number of false positives when the PNB algorithm is used. One way could be to allow the PNB algorithm to take advantage of a small amount of negative examples supplied by the user, in addition to the positive and unlabeled examples.

---

[4] SPEM on the SpamAssassin corpus with 50% spam used only 500 junk messages, therefore the results are not directly comparable.

Another solution that would not require any modification of the learning algorithm is to allow the user to provide additional labeled (positive and negative) examples during operation by correcting misclassified examples. Although this strategy would be contrary to our goal of avoiding any user intervention, we would expect the PNB algorithm to require less intervention than the simple Naive Bayes algorithm.

Acknowledgements

The author would like to thank the anonymous reviewers for their helpful suggestions.

References

1. Sahami, M., Dumais, S., Heckerman, D., Horvitz, E.: A bayesian approach to filtering junk e-mail. In: Learning for Text Categorization: Papers from the AAAI Workshop, Madison Wisconsin, AAAI Press (1998) 55–62 Technical Report WS-98-05.
2. Drucker, H., Wu, D., Vapnik, V.N.: Support vector machines for spam categorization. IEEE Trans. on Neural Networks **10** (1999) 1048–1054
3. Androutsopoulos, I., Paliouras, G., Karkaletsis, V., Sakkis, G., Spyropoulos, C.D., Stamatopoulos, P.: Learning to filter spam e-mail: A comparison of a Naive Bayesian and a memory-based approach. In Zaragoza, H., Gallinari, P., Rajman, M., eds.: Proc. Workshop on Machine Learning and Textual Information Access, 4th European Conference on Principles and Practice of Knowledge Discovery in Databases (PKDD 2000), Lyon, France (2000) 1–13
4. Dempster, A.P., Laird, N.M., Rubin, D.B.: Maximum likelihood from incomplete data via the EM algorithm. Journal of the Royal Statistical Society, Series B **39** (1977) 1–38
5. Nigam, K., McCallum, A.K., Thrun, S., Mitchell, T.: Text classification from labeled and unlabeled documents using EM. Machine Learning **39** (2000) 103–134
6. Denis, F., Gilleron, R., Tommasi, M.: Text classification from positive and unlabeled examples. In: Proc. 9th International Conference on Information Processing and Management of Uncertainty in Knowledge-Based Systems (IPMU 2002). (2002) 1927–1934
7. Liu, B., Lee, W.S., Yu, P.S., Li, X.: Partially supervised classification of text documents. In: Proc. 19th International Conference on Machine Learning (ICML-2002). (2002) 387–394
8. Denis, F.: PAC learning from positive statistical queries. In: Proc. 9th International Workshop on Algorithmic Learning Theory (ALT'98). LNAI 1501, Springer-Verlag (1998) 112–126
9. Li, X., Liu, B.: Learning to classify texts using positive and unlabeled data. In: 18th International Joint Conference on Artificial Intelligence (IJCAI-03), Acapulco, Mexico (2003)
10. Yu, H., Han, J., Chang, K.C.C.: PEBL: Positive example based learning for web page classification using SVM. In: Proc. 8th ACM SIGKDD International Conference on Knowledge Discovery and Data Mining, New York, ACM Press (2002) 239–248

11. Manevitz, L.M., Yousef, M.: One-class SVMs for document classification. Journal of Machine Learning Research **2** (2001) 139–154
12. Chai, K.M.A., Ng, H.T., Chieu, H.L.: Bayesian online classifiers for text classification and filtering. In: Proc. 25th ACM SIGIR Conference on Research and Development in Information Retrieval (SIGIR 2002). (2002) 97–104
13. McCallum, A., Nigam, K.: A comparison of event models for Naive Bayes text classification. In: Learning for Text Categorization: Papers from the AAAI Workshop, AAAI Press (1998) 41–48 Technical Report WS-98-05.

A Collaborative Ability Measurement for Co-training

Dan Shen[1,2], Jie Zhang[1,2], Jian Su[1], Guodong Zhou[1], and Chew-Lim Tan[2]

[1] Institute for Infocomm Research, 21 Heng Mui Keng Terrace, Singapore, 119613
{shendan,zhangjie,sujian,zhougd}@i2r.a-star.edu.sg
[2] Department of Computer Science, National University of Singapore, Singapore, 117543
{shendan,zhangjie,tancl}@comp.nus.edu.sg

Abstract. This paper explores collaborative ability of co-training algorithm. We propose a new measurement (CA) for representing the collaborative ability of co-training classifiers based on the overlapping proportion between certain and uncertain instances. The CA measurement indicates whether two classifiers can co-train effectively. We make theoretical analysis for CA values in co-training with independent feature split, with random feature split and without feature split. The experiments justify our analysis. We also explore two variations of the general co-training algorithm and analyze them using the CA measurement.

1 Introduction

Co-training and several viable alternatives of co-training, such as Co-Boosting (Collins and Singer [1]), Co-Testing (Muslea et al. [2]) and Self-Training (Ng and Cardie [3]), have been successfully applied to a number of natural language processing (NLP) tasks. Most of the works follow the general co-training algorithm proposed by Blum and Mitchell [4] as shown in Fig. 1.

Given:
    a small labelled data set L
    a large unlabelled data set U
    two views V_1 and V_2 of a classification task
Loop for k iterations:
    Use L to train the classifier h_1 that considers V_1
    Use L to train the classifier h_2 that considers V_2
    Allow h_1, h_2 to label the data in U
    Select the labelled data from U and add them to L

Fig. 1. General co-training algorithm.

The performance of co-training relies on the *collaborative ability* of the two classifiers. With strong collaborative ability, each classifier can provide reliable and informative labelled data to the other iteratively and complement the other's predictions when labelling test data. On the contrary, they can not help each other with weak collaborative ability. In this paper, we propose a new measurement (CA) to represent the collaborative ability based on the overlapping proportion between the classifiers' certain and uncertain instances in test data set. We also make the theoretical analysis for the collaborative ability of classifiers with independent view split, with random view split and without view split. Experiments on text classification task justify our analysis. Based on the CA measurement, we are able to understand more about the learning behavior of co-training and give the suggestions that whether the two classifiers can be used for effective co-training. It will be useful for designing the co-training model in practice. In addition, we discuss the difference and relation between the CA measurement and the Uncertainty Correlation Coefficient (UCC) Measure proposed by Cao et al. [5]. Furthermore, we explore two variations of the general co-training algorithm when independent view split does not exist. Using the CA measurement, we analyze the collaborative abilities of the classifiers in these variations.

2 Collaborative Ability of Co-training

Collaborative ability of co-training can be considered from two aspects as follows:

- Can one classifier provide reliable and informative labelled data to the other iteratively?
- Can one classifier complement the other's prediction when labeling test data?

We estimate the collaborative ability based on the overlapping proportion between two classifiers' certain and uncertain instances in the test data set.

2.1 Collaborative Ability (CA) Measurement

We define the co-training model as follow:
X: a set of data Y: a set of class
Given a training data set, two co-training classifiers are to learn two functions h_1 and h_2, which map X to Y: $h_1 : X \rightarrow Y$ $h_2 : X \rightarrow Y$

Definition 1: The *Certainty Set* of classifier h on X is defined as:
$$CSet(h) = \{x | Conf(h(x)) \geq \alpha_1, x \in X\}$$

Definition 2: The *Uncertainty Set* of classifier h on X is defined as:
$$UCSet(h) = \{x | Conf(h(x)) < \alpha_2, x \in X\}$$

where α_1 and α_2 denotes a predefined threshold for certainty and uncertainty respectively ($\alpha_1 \geq \alpha_2$). $Conf(h(x))$ denotes the confidence score of $h(x)$.

Definition 3: The *collaborative ability of one classifier h_1 to the other classifier h_2* is defined as:
$$CA(h_2|h_1) = P(\{x | x \in CSet(h_1) \cap UCSet(h_2)\})$$

$CA(h_2|h_1)$ indicates the portion of the reliable and informative labelled data which h_1 can provide to h_2. If $CA(h_2|h_1)$ is high, there are a large portion of data which is very confident for h_1 and is not confident for h_2. In this case, h_1 can provide such data to h_2, and help h_2 to enhance the performance.

Similarly, we define the collaborative ability of the classifier h_2 to the classifier h_1 as follows:
$$CA(h_1|h_2) = P(\{x|x \in CSet(h_2) \cap UCSet(h_1)\})$$

Generally speaking, if $CA(h_2|h_1)$ is much higher than $CA(h_1|h_2)$, it is probably because h_2 is not sufficient enough for the learning task or the features h_2 used are too weak. In this case, the co-training process may benefit from h_1 rather than from both classifiers. Furthermore, when labelling test data, the predictions made by h1 will play the dominant role and the whole performance of the combined classifier may be close to the performance of h_1.

Definition 4: The *collaborative ability between the two classifiers h_1 and h_2* is defined as:
$$\begin{aligned}CA_{h_1h_2} &= CA(h_2|h_1) + CA(h_1|h_2) \\ &= P(\{x|x \in (CSet(h_1) \cap UCSet(h_2))\}) \\ &\quad + P(\{x|x \in (CSet(h_2) \cap UCSet(h_1))\})\end{aligned}$$

$CA_{h_1h_2}$ presents the degree of collaboration between h_1 and h_2. It can be used to determine whether the feature split is suitable for the learning task and the two classifiers are able to help each other.

If $CA_{h_1h_2}$ is low, it can be explained that the two classifiers' confidence degree for most of the data are consistent. There are two cases:

First, there is a large number of data of which both classifiers are very confident. These data are reliable but not informative. In the co-training, the occurrence of this case may indicate that the two classifiers have been bootstrapped successfully and the room for further improvement may not be large.

Second, there is a large number of data for which both classifiers cannot confidently predict. These data may be informative but not reliable. In the co-training, it indicates that the two classifiers are not effective enough, since one classifier can not provide reliable labelled data to the other.

Our CA measurement is different from the Uncertainty Correlation Coefficient (UCC) Measure proposed by Cao et al. [5]. UCC is defined as the portion of instances of which both classifiers are uncertain. The authors also state that the lower the UCC values are, the higher the performances can be achieved in co-training. The idea of our CA measurement is consistent with their statement. Furthermore, we consider not only the Uncertainty Correlation Coefficient (UCC) factor but also Certainty Correlation Coefficient (CCC) factor. As analyzed above, the lower the UCC and CCC values are, the stronger the collaborative ability of the classifiers is. In practice, we may compute the CA value as following:

$$\begin{aligned}N_{CUC1} &= |CSet(h_1) \cap UCSet(h_2)| \\ N_{CUC2} &= |UCSet(h_1) \cap CSet(h_2)| \\ N_{CC} &= |CSet(h_1) \cap CSet(h_2)| \\ N_{UCUC} &= |UCSet(h_1) \cap UCSet(h_2)| \\ CA_{h_1h_2} &= \frac{N_{CUC1} + N_{CUC2}}{N_{CUC1} + N_{CUC2} + N_{CC} + N_{UCUC}}\end{aligned}$$

2.2 Theoretical Analysis of CA Measurement

In order to make our theoretical analysis simpler, we set the threshold α_1 equal to α_2. Therefore, for all labelled data x,

$$P(\{x|x \in CSet(h)\}) + P(\{x|x \in UCSet(h)\}) = 1$$

Suppose: two events A and B, where A is the event that an instance belongs to $CSet$ of h_1 and B is the event that an instance belongs to $CSet$ of h_2.

$$P(A) = P(\{x|x \in CSet(h_1)\})$$
$$P(B) = P(\{x|x \in CSet(h_2)\})$$

Then:

$$P(\neg A) = P(\{x|x \in UCSet(h_1)\}) = 1 - P(A)$$
$$P(\neg B) = P(\{x|x \in UCSet(h_2)\}) = 1 - P(B)$$

Compute the CA value:

$$\begin{aligned} CA_{h_1 h_2} &= P(A, \neg B) + P(\neg A, B) \\ &= P(\neg B|A)P(A) + P(\neg A|B)P(B) \\ &= P(A) + P(B) - 2P(A, B) \end{aligned}$$

Let's consider the CA values in the co-training with independent view split, with random view split and without view split.

- **Independent View Split**
  In this case, the two classifiers have independent conditional probability for labelling the data with some confidence. That is, $P(A, B) = P(A)P(B)$. Therefore, the CA value will be:

  $$CA_{h_1 h_2}^{INDEP} = P(A) + P(B) - 2P(A)P(B)$$

- **Random View Split**
  If an independent view split is not available, the event A and B may be dependent on each other. That is, if one classifier is certain of an instance, the other classifier is more likely to be certain than uncertain of it and vice versa. That is,

  $$P(A|B) \geq P(A) \text{ and } P(B|A) \geq P(B)$$

Therefore,

$$P(A) + P(B) - 2P(A)P(B) \geq P(A) + P(B) - 2P(A, B)$$

$$CA_{h_1 h_2}^{INDEP} \geq CA_{h_1 h_2}$$

With the theoretical analysis above, we show that the CA value in the co-training with independent view split is higher than that in the co-training without independent feature split. It indicates that the classifiers with separate and redundant views will have the better collaborative ability. Our analysis has been supported by many previous research works (Blum and Mitchell [4]; Nigam and Ghani [6]), as they also stated that co-training with independent view split outperforms other co-training and variations. Furthermore, we find that the two classifiers may still be bootstrapped from each other given the acceptable collaborative ability even if there does not exist an independent view split. In most practical applications, we can use the CA measurement to estimate the collaborative ability and decide whether the two classifiers with certain feature split can be used for effective co-training.

- **Single View (Self-training)**
  We also evaluate the collaborative ability of the co-training without view split (self-training), which may be considered as a special case of general co-training algorithm. In this case,

$$P(A) = P(B) = P(A|B)$$

Therefore, the CA value of self-training is zero, i.e. one classifier can only be bootstrapped by itself.

2.3 Experiment Results

We choose text classification task to verify the effectiveness of CA measurement. Our experiment is similar to Nigam and Ghani [6] and Cao et al. [5]. We use four newsgroups from the 20 Newsgroups dataset to produce a new data set, as shown in Table 1. A preprocessing procedure is conducted on the texts in each group in order to remove newsgroup header and stop words, scale the length of text to the same, and eliminate some invalid texts, as in (Nigam and Ghani [6]).

Table 1. Data set with natural split feature set.

Class	Feature Set A	Feature Set B
Pos	comp.os.ms-windows.misc	talk.politics.misc
Neg	comp.sys.ibm.pc.hardware	talk.politics.guns

We produce three data sets as follows:

- **Data Set with Independent View Split**
  The two newsgroups in the first row of Table 1 constitute the positive class by joining together randomly selected documents from each of them. Similarly, the two newsgroups in the second row constitute the negative class. Thus, a two-class data set is produced. Since the vocabulary of the first column (Feature Set A) is different from the vocabulary of the second column (Feature Set B), the data set can be regarded as view independent. We denote this data set as *IndepViewSet*.
- **Data Set with Random View Split**
  We also produce a data set with random split view as in (Cao et al. [5]). In which, the whole feature set in the above data set is randomly split into two subsets, which may not be independent. We denote this data set as *RandViewSet*.

– **Data Set with Single View**
We use the whole feature set as a single view for this data set. It is produced for the purpose of self-training and two co-training variations which will be introduced in Section 4. We denote this data set as *SingleViewSet*.

In order to show the CA measurement in an empirical way, we conduct experiments based on the three data sets. We separate each data set into 3 positive and 3 negative instances as an initial training set, 500 positive and 500 negative instances as an unlabelled set and the rest about 900 instances as a test set. The separation made on the three data sets is identical. We use Naive Bayes classifiers as the learning algorithms in this co-training task. The certainty threshold α_1 is set to 0.8 and the uncertainty threshold α_2 is set to 0.6.

We train two Naive Bayes classifiers on the *IndepViewSet* for co-training, two naive Bayes classifiers on the *RandViewSet* for co-training and one naive Bayes classifier on the *SingleViewSet* for self-training. In each iteration, we select one most confident positive instance and one most confident negative instance of each classifier from the unlabelled set into the training set until the unlabelled set is empty.

Fig. 2 shows the three charts of experiment results. From the three charts, we can find that CA measurement of *IndepViewSet* co-training (around 0.5 0.6) is higher than those of *RandViewSet* co-training (around 0.3) and *SingleViewSet* self-training (zero). All of the findings above are consistent with our theoretical analysis.

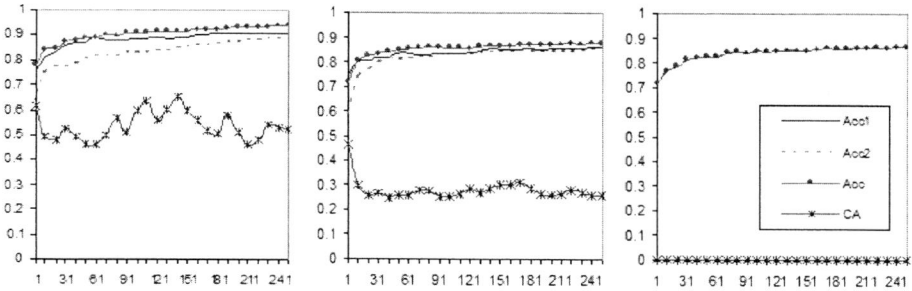

Fig. 2. Performance charts with CA measurement of three experiments. (Acc: accuracy of the combined classifier. Acc1/Acc2: accuracies of two co-training classifiers. 1st chart: co-training on *IndepViewSet*. 2nd chart: co-training on *RandViewSet*. 3rd chart: self-training on *SingleViewSet*.

Furthermore, from the first chart, we can find that the performances of two classifiers are constantly increasing during the whole process of co-training, and the performance of the combined classifier is much higher than that of the either co-training classifier. It shows that the classifiers have strong collaborative ability to help each other, which is presented by our CA measurement. We also find that the performance is still trending up at the end of 250 iterations, since CA is still at a high level. This suggests that more data may further improve the performance.

From the second chart, the classifiers can help each other improve the performance at the beginning iterations as CA is relatively high. While in later iterations, performance can only be improved slightly, as CA drops to a low level. The performance of the combined classifier is only slightly higher than that of the either co-training classifier. All these findings suggest that the collaborative ability on the *RandViewSet* is weaker than that on the *IndepViewSet*.

The third chart shows a special case for co-training which means no collaborative ability. Table 2 shows the summary of the final performances.

Table 2. Performance of three experiments in the 250 iteration. Acc: accuracy of the combined classifier. Acc1/Acc2: accuracies of two co-training classifiers.

	Acc	Acc1	Acc2	CA range
IndepViewSet	93.9	91.1	88.4	around 0.5 0.6
RandViewSet	89.8	87.6	86.0	around 0.3
SingleViewSet	86.5	86.5	86.5	0

3   Two Variations of Co-training

In this section, we study two alternatives of co-training when the independent view split is not available.

3.1   Co-training Using Two Learning Algorithms

We denote this variation as VCT-1 in Fig. 3. Actually, there are two different points between VCT-1 and the general co-training (bold in Fig. 3). VCT-1 uses two different learning algorithms to collaborate each other and both of them use a single feature set rather than two separate feature sets.

3.2   Co-training from Different Seed Sets

We denote this variation as VCT-2. Fig. 4 shows the VCT-2 algorithm and highlights the difference between VCT-2 and the general co-training algorithm in bold fonts. VCT-2 uses two different seed sets to start co-training. Furthermore, in the co-training iterations, the labelled data are transformed from the two unlabelled data sets U_1, U_2 to the two training data sets L_1, L_2 ($U_1 \rightarrow L_2$ and $U_2 \rightarrow L_1$) respectively. In VCT-2, two classifiers are based on the same learning algorithms and the single feature set.

In the next part, we will use CA measurement to estimate the effectiveness of VCT-1 and VCT-2.

3.3   Experiment Results

We also conduct experiments on the two variations of co-training above. For VCT-1, we use Naive Bayes and Support Vector Machine (SVM) as two learning algorithms C_1 and

Given:
    a small labelled data set L
    a large unlabelled data set U
    a single view V for a classification task
Loop until U is empty:
    Use L to train **classifier C_1 based on** V **using learning algorithm 1**
    Use L to train **classifier C_2 based on** V **using learning algorithm 2**
    Allow C_1, C_2 to label the data in U
    Select most confident p positive and n negative labelled data of C_1 from U and add them to L
    Select most confident p positive and n negative labelled data of C_2 from U and add them to L

Fig. 3. Co-training using two learning algorithms.

Given:
    two small labelled data sets L_1 and L_2
    a large unlabelled data set U
    a single view V for a classification task
Initialize:
    Divide U into **two unlabelled data set** U_1 and U_2
Loop until either U_1 or U_2 is empty:
    Use L_1 to train the classifier h_1 based on V
    Use L_2 to train the classifier h_2 based on V
    Allow h_1 to label the data in U_1
    Allow h_2 to label the data in U_2
    Select most confident p positive and n negative data labelled by h_1 **from U_1 and add them to L_2**
    Select most confident p positive and n negative data labelled by h_2 **from U_2 and add them to L_1**

Fig. 4. Co-training from different seed sets.

C_2. The Naive Bayes classifier is the same as used in the experiments of Section 3.3. SVM-light (Joachims 1999 [7]) with linear kernel function is used as C_2 in VCT-1. The certainty threshold α_1 is set to 1.0 and the uncertainty threshold α_2 is set to 0.8 in SVM. For VCT-2, the two classifiers we use are also the same Naive Bayes classifiers used in Section 3.3. Initial training sets and unlabelled data sets of the two classifiers are different.

The data set used in these experiments is the *SingleViewSet* as introduced in the Section 3.3. We also separate the *SingleViewSet* into 3 positive and 3 negative instances as an initial training set, 500 positive and 500 negative instances as an unlabelled set and the rest about 900 instances as a test set. In each iteration, we select one most confident positive and one most confident negative instance of each classifier from the unlabelled set into the training set until the unlabelled set is empty.

Fig. 5 shows the performance charts of VCT-1 and VCT-2. From the first chart (VCT-1), we can find that the CA measurement (around 0.3) is close to that of the *RandViewSet* co-training in the Section 3.3. We can also find that the two learning algo-

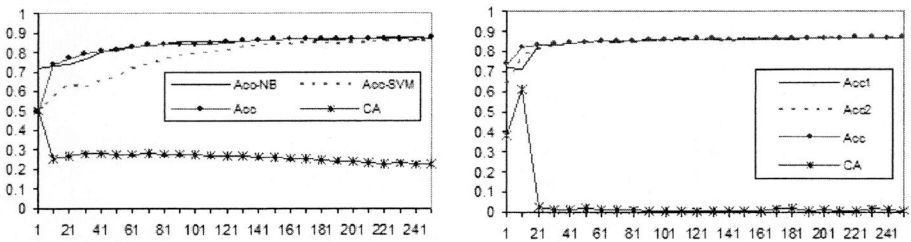

Fig. 5. Performance chart with CA measurement of VCT-1 and VCT-2.

rithms, Naive Bayes classifier and SVM classifier, can help each other slightly improve the performances. The final combined result (87.4) is also slightly higher than either of the co-training result and also higher than the result of self-training (86.5) shown in Section 3.3 which means it benefits from the collaboration of two learning algorithms. It is clear that VCT-1's collaborative ability is weaker than that of the *IndepViewSet* co-training. However, practically speaking, if we cannot split features into two views (view insufficiency) for certain task, we could consider VCT-1 by measuring its CA value. If CA is at an acceptable level, say above 0.3, the VCT-1 may be practical.

From the second chart (VCT-2), we can find that the CA value drops dramatically to nearly zero after iteration 21. In the first 20 iterations, the CA value is high which indicates that the two classifiers are collaborating well. Actually, from the accuracy curves, we can find that performances of the two co-training classifiers are improving fast and the combined performance is much higher than the performance of the either co-training classifier in the first 20 iterations. However, after the 21st iteration, the CA value is close to zero, which indicates that the classifiers do not have collaborative ability any more. In fact, the accuracy curves also show that the performances of the two co-training classifiers are too close to each other. In this case, it suggests that the two classifiers highly agree with each other and do not have ability to collaborate, which becomes a similar case to the self-training. Therefore, in this application, VCT-2 is not suitable for co-training. In addition, it also suggests that CA measurement can be used to determine when the co-training process can be stopped as well as the agreement value.

4 Conclusions

In the paper, we theoretically and empirically analyze the relation between CA measurement and collaborative ability in co-training algorithm. We show that the CA measurement can well represent the collaborative ability of two co-training classifiers. We use the CA value to compare three co-training settings and show that higher CA value leads to better co-training ability. Furthermore, we propose two variations of co-training and use CA measurement to evaluate them. The results on text classification task show that co-training with different learning algorithms is a viable alternative and co-training from different seed sets is not effective. The CA measurement enables us to understand more about the learning behavior of co-training and suggests whether the classifiers can be used for effective co-training. It will be useful for designing the co-training model in practice.

References

1. Collins, M., Singer, Y.: Unsupervised models for named entity classification. In: Proceedings of the 1999 Joint SIGDAT Conference on Empirical Methods in Natural Language Proceeding and Very Large Corpora. (1999)
2. I. Muslea, S.M., Knoblock, C.A.: Selective sampling with redundant views. In: Proceedings of the Seventeenth National Conference on Artificial Intelligence. (2000)
3. Ng, V., Cardie, C.: Weakly supervised natural language learning without redundant views. In: Proceedings of the Main Conference on HLT-NAACL 2003. (2002)
4. Blum, A., Mitchell, T.: Combining labeled data and unlabelled data with co-training. In: Proceedings of the 11th Annual Conference on Computational learning Theory. (1998)
5. Y. B. Cao, H.L., Lian, L.: Uncertainty reduction in collaborative bootstrapping: Measure and algorithm. In: Proceedings of the 41st Annual Meeting of the Association for Computational Linguistics. (2003)
6. Nigam, K., Ghani, R.: Analyzing the effectiveness and applicability of co-training. In: Proceedings of the 9th International Conference on Information and Knowledge Management. (2000)
7. Joachims, T.: Making large-scale svm learning practical. In: Advances in Kernel Methods - Support Vector Learning, B. Scholkopf and C. Burges and A. Smola (ed.), MIT-Press (1999)

Flexible Margin Selection for Reranking with Full Pairwise Samples

Libin Shen and Aravind K. Joshi

Department of Computer and Information Science
University of Pennsylvania
Philadelphia, PA 19104, USA
{libin,joshi}@linc.cis.upenn.edu

Abstract. Perceptron like large margin algorithms are introduced for the experiments with various margin selections. Compared to the previous perceptron reranking algorithms, the new algorithms use full pairwise samples and allow us to search for margins in a larger space. Our experimental results on the data set of [1] show that a perceptron like ordinal regression algorithm with uneven margins can achieve Recall/Precision of 89.5/90.0 on section 23 of Penn Treebank. Our result on margin selection can be employed in other large margin machine learning algorithms as well as in other NLP tasks.

1 Introduction

In recent years, the so-called *reranking* techniques [1] have been successfully used in parameter estimation in many applications which were previously modeled as generative models. A baseline generative model generates N-best candidates, and then these candidates are reranked by using a rich set of local and global features. Various machine learning algorithms have been adapted to the reranking tasks.

In the field of machine learning, a class of tasks, which are called *ranking* or *ordinal regression*, are similar to the reranking tasks in NLP. A primary motivation of the present paper is to apply ranking or ordinal regression algorithms to the reranking tasks in NLP, especially because we observe that there is no direct way to apply these ranking algorithms to reranking. More specifically, we will compare the existing reranking and ranking algorithms in the framework of *margin selection*. The goal then is to search for a desirable margin for the reranking tasks in NLP.

In order to experiment with various margins, we will introduce variants of the traditional perceptron algorithm [2, 3] for reranking, which allows the use of various margins; The training is also very fast. The basic idea of these perceptron like algorithms is that we dynamically search for pairs of inconsistent objects and use them to update the weight vector. Since the ranks are ordered, the dynamical search can be implemented efficiently.

Compared to previous work on perceptron for parse reranking [4], our new algorithms use full pairwise samples instead of partial pairwise samples. This allows us to search for margins desirable for reranking tasks in a larger space, which is unavailable in the previous work.

In this paper, we focus on the parse reranking task. However, the methods can, of course, be applied to other NLP reranking tasks. Our experimental results on the data set in [1] show that a perceptron like ordinal regression algorithm with uneven margins can achieve Recall/Precision of 89.5/90.0 on section 23 of WSJ PTB, which is comparable to 89.6/89.9 with the boosting algorithm in [1], although boosting is believed to have more generalization capability. Our results also show that the new margins introduced in this paper are superior to the margins used in the previous works on reranking. The results on margin selection can be employed in reranking systems based on other machine learning algorithms, such as Winnow, Boosting and SVMs, as well as other NLP tasks, e.g. machine translation reranking.

2   Previous Works

2.1   Reranking

In recent years, reranking has been successfully applied to some NLP problems, especially to the problem of parse reranking. Ratnaparkhi [5] noticed that by ranking the 20-best parsing results generated by his maximal entropy parser, the F-measure went to 93% from 87%, if the oracle parse was successfully detected. Charniak [6] reranked the N-best parses by reestimating a language model on a large number of features.

Collins [1] first used machine learning algorithms for parse reranking. Two approaches were proposed in that paper; one used Boosting Loss and the other used Log-Likelihood Loss. Boosting Loss achieved better results. The Boosting Loss model is as follows. Let $\mathbf{x}_{i,j}$ be the feature vector of the jth parse of the ith sentence. Let $\tilde{\mathbf{x}}_i$ be the feature vector of the best parse for the ith sentence. Let F_α be a score function

$$F_\alpha(\mathbf{x}_{i,j}) \equiv \alpha' \cdot \mathbf{x}_{i,j},$$

where α is a weight vector. The *margin* $M_{\alpha,i,j}$ on sample $\mathbf{x}_{i,j}$ is defined as

$$M_{\alpha,i,j} \equiv F_\alpha(\tilde{\mathbf{x}}_i) - F_\alpha(\mathbf{x}_{i,j})$$

Finally the Boost Loss function is defined as

$$BoostLoss(\alpha) \equiv \sum_i \sum_j e^{-(F_\alpha(\tilde{\mathbf{x}}_i) - F_\alpha(\mathbf{x}_{i,j}))} = \sum_i \sum_j e^{-M_{\alpha,i,j}}$$

The Boosting algorithm was used to search the weight vector α to minimize the Boost Loss.

We may rewrite the definition of the margin $M_{\alpha,i,j}$ by using pairwise samples as follows.

$$\mathbf{s}_{i,j} \equiv \tilde{\mathbf{x}}_i - \mathbf{x}_{i,j} \text{ , then}$$

$$M_{\alpha,i,j} = F_\alpha(\tilde{\mathbf{x}}_i) - F_\alpha(\mathbf{x}_{i,j}) = F_\alpha(\tilde{\mathbf{x}}_i - \mathbf{x}_{i,j}) = F_\alpha(\mathbf{s}_{i,j})$$

So the Boosting Loss approach in [1] is similar to maximizing the margin [7] between 0 and $F_\alpha(\mathbf{s}_{i,j})$, where $\mathbf{s}_{i,j}$ are pairwise samples as we have described above.

In [4], the voted perceptron and the Tree kernel were applied to parse reranking. Similar to [1], pairwise samples were used as training samples. The perceptron updating step was defined as

$$\mathbf{w}^{t+1} = \mathbf{w}^t + \tilde{\mathbf{x}}_i - \mathbf{x}_{i,j},$$

where $\mathbf{w}^t$ is the weight vector at the t th updating. This is equivalent to using pairwise sample $\mathbf{s}_{i,j}$ as we have defined above.

$$\mathbf{w}^{t+1} = \mathbf{w}^t + \mathbf{s}_{i,j}$$

In our previous work [8], we applied Support Vector Machines (SVMs) and Tree kernels to parse reranking. In that paper, pairwise samples were used explicitly through the Preference kernel. $\mathbf{u}_{i,j}^+$ and $\mathbf{u}_{i,j}^-$ defined as follows were used as positive samples and negative samples respectively.

$$\mathbf{u}_{i,j}^+ \equiv (\tilde{\mathbf{x}}_i, \mathbf{x}_{i,j}), \quad \mathbf{u}_{i,j}^- \equiv (\mathbf{x}_{i,j}, \tilde{\mathbf{x}}_i)$$

SVM is used to maximize the margin between positive samples and negative samples, which in turn is proportional to the margin between the best parse of each sentence and the rest of the N-best parses.

In the works on reranking, the margin is defined as the distance between the best candidate and the rest. The reranking problem is reduced to a classification problem by using pairwise samples implicitly or explicitly.

2.2 Ranking

In the previous works on ranking or ordinal regression, the margin is defined as the distance between two consecutive ranks. Two approaches have been used. One is *PRanking* that extends the perceptron algorithm by using multiple biases to represent the boundaries between every two consecutive ranks [9]. However, due to the introduction of a set of biases it is impossible to use PRanking in other ranking-like problems. The other approach is to reduce the ranking problem to a classification problem by using the trick of pairwise samples [10].

2.3 Large Margin Classifiers

There are quite a few linear classifiers[1] that can separate samples with large margin, such as SVMs [11], Boosting [7], Winnow [12] and Perceptron [13]. The performance of SVMs is superior to other linear classifiers because of their ability to maximize the margin, but SVMs are slow in training.

For margin selection, we do need an algorithm that runs fast for training, so that we can test various margins. Then the result of the margin selection can

---

[1] Here we do not consider kernels of infinite dimension.

be employed in other linear classifiers. For the purpose of margin selection we proposes perceptron like algorithms for the following two reasons. First, perceptron is fast in training which allows us to do experiments with various margin selections on real-world data. Furthermore, perceptron algorithms are simple in principle, which makes it easy to implement modification.

3 Ranks and Margins for Reranking

In the previous works on ranking, ranks are defined on the whole training and test data. Thus we can define boundaries between consecutive ranks on the whole data. In the reranking problem, ranks are *local*. They are defined over a sub set of the samples in the data set. For example, in the parse reranking problem, the rank of a parse is only defined as the rank among all the parses for the same sentence. The training data includes 36,000 sentence, with an average of about 27 parses per sentence [1].

As a result, we cannot use the PRank algorithm in the reranking task, since there are no *global* ranks or boundaries in reranking, as the PRank algorithm is designed to estimate the global rank boundaries over all the samples during the training. If we introduce auxiliary variables for the boundaries for each cluster, the number of the parameters will be as large as the number of samples. Obviously this is not a good idea. However, the approach of using pairwise samples works. By pairing up two samples, we actually compute the relative distance between these two samples in the scoring metric.

Let $\mathbf{r}_i$ be the candidate parse that ranks as the ith best for a sentence. The parses of the same sentence are ranked with respect to their *f-scores*, which measure the similarity to the gold standard parse. A parse with a large *f-score* is assigned a high rank. In reranking tasks, the margins between the best candidate and the rest are more useful. A hyperplane successfully separating $\mathbf{r}_1$ and $\mathbf{r}_2...\mathbf{r}_N$ is more predictive than a hyperplane successfully separating $\mathbf{r}_1...\mathbf{r}_{10}$ and $\mathbf{r}_{11}...\mathbf{r}_N$, if we are only interested in the topmost result in test. This is also how the existing reranking systems are designed. However there are some problems with this approach.

There is a practical problem for the definition of the *best* parse in a sentence. In parse reranking, we may find several best parses for each training sentence instead of one. In order to break the tie, usually one selects just one of them arbitrarily as the top ranked parse and discard all others.

Furthermore, if we only look for the hyperplane to separate the best one from the rest, we, in fact, discard the order information of $\mathbf{r}_2...\mathbf{r}_N$. For example, we did not employ the information that $\mathbf{r}_{10}$ is better than $\mathbf{r}_{11}$ in the training. Knowing $\mathbf{r}_{10}$ is better than $\mathbf{r}_{11}$ may be useless for training to some extent, but knowing $\mathbf{r}_2$ is better than $\mathbf{r}_{11}$ is useful.

On the other the hand, the resulting weight vector $\mathbf{w}$ is supposed to assign the highest score to $\mathbf{r}_1$. Should it not assign the second highest score to $\mathbf{r}_2$? Although we cannot give an affirmative answer at this time, it is at least reasonable to use more pairwise samples. This approach was avoided in the previous works on reranking, due to the problem of complexity of both the data size and the execution time. Thus we have provided a strong motivation for investigating some new reranking algorithms such that

- They utilize all the ordinal relations encoded in the ranked lists.
- The size of training data is the same as the original size of the ranked lists.
- The training time increases only moderately, although more information is used in training.

4 Perceptron for Ordinal Regression

4.1 Ordinal Regression

Let $\mathbf{x}_{i,j}, \mathbf{x}_{i,l}$ be the feature vectors of two parses for sentence i and $y_{i,j}, y_{i,l}$ be their ranks respectively, where $y_{i,j} + \epsilon < y_{i,l}$, and ϵ is a non-negative real number. It means that the rank of $\mathbf{x}_{i,j}$ of ϵ higher than the rank of $\mathbf{x}_{i,l}$. In this case, we say $\mathbf{x}_{i,j}$ is *significantly better* than $\mathbf{x}_{i,l}$. We are interested in finding a weight vector $\mathbf{w}$, such that

$$\mathbf{w} \cdot \mathbf{x}_{i,j} > \mathbf{w} \cdot \mathbf{x}_{i,l} + \tau, \text{ if } y_{i,j} + \epsilon < y_{i,l}$$

We ignore any pair of parses in which the difference in the ranks is $\leq \epsilon$. Hence, this problem is called ϵ-*insensitive ordinal regression*.

Let the training samples be

$$S = \{(\mathbf{x}_{i,j}, y_{i,j}) \mid 1 \leq i \leq m, \ 1 \leq j \leq k\},$$

where m is the number of sentences and k is the size of the N-best list. Let $f(\mathbf{x}) = \mathbf{w} \cdot \mathbf{x}$. We say the training data is ϵ-*distinguishable* by f if

$$\mathbf{w} \cdot \mathbf{x}_{i,j} > \mathbf{w} \cdot \mathbf{x}_{i,l}, \text{ if } y_{i,j} + \epsilon < y_{i,l},$$

for $1 \leq i \leq m, \ 1 \leq j, l \leq k$.

4.2 Dynamic Pairing

A straightforward method of using pairwise samples is to define positive and negative samples on the differences of vectors as in [10]. For each sentence i, $\mathbf{x}_{i,j} - \mathbf{x}_{i,l}$ is a positive sample if $y_{i,j} < y_{i,l}$, where $y_{i,j}$ is the rank of parse $\mathbf{x}_{i,j}$. Similarly, $\mathbf{x}_{i,j} - \mathbf{x}_{i,l}$ is a negative sample if $y_{i,l} < y_{i,j}$.

However, for real tasks, this greatly increases the data complexity from $O(mk)$ to $O(mk^2)$, where m is the number of training sentences, and k is the size of n-best list. For parse reranking k is about 27, and for machine translation reranking k is about 1000. Due to the limit of memory space we cannot define pairwise samples explicitly in this way.

The method to avoid this problem is to look up pairwise samples dynamically, as shown in **Algorithm 1**, a perceptron like algorithm. The basic idea is that, for each pair of parses for the same sentence, if

Algorithm 1 Ordinal regression.
Require: a positive learning margin τ.
1: $t \leftarrow 0$, initialize $\mathbf{w}^0$;
2: **repeat**
3:    **for** (sentence $i = 1, ..., m$) **do**
4:       **for** $(1 \leq j < l \leq k)$ **do**
5:          **if** $(y_{i,l} - y_{i,j} > \epsilon$ and $\mathbf{w}^t \cdot \mathbf{x}_{i,j} < \mathbf{w}^t \cdot \mathbf{x}_{i,l} + \tau)$ **then**
6:            $\mathbf{w}^{t+1} \leftarrow \mathbf{w}^t + \mathbf{x}_{i,j} - \mathbf{x}_{i,l}; t \leftarrow t + 1;$
7:         **else if** $(y_{i,j} - y_{i,l} > \epsilon$ and $\mathbf{w}^t \cdot \mathbf{x}_{i,l} < \mathbf{w}^t \cdot \mathbf{x}_{i,j} + \tau)$ **then**
8:            $\mathbf{w}^{t+1} \leftarrow \mathbf{w}^t + \mathbf{x}_{i,l} - \mathbf{x}_{i,j}; t \leftarrow t + 1;$
9:         **end if**
10:      **end for**
11:    **end for**
12: **until** no updates made in the outer **for** loop

Algorithm 2 Ordinal regression, sentence updating.
Require: a positive learning margin τ.
1: $t \leftarrow 0$, initialize $\mathbf{w}^0$;
2: **repeat**
3:    **for** (sentence $i = 1, ..., m$) **do**
4:       compute $\mathbf{w}^t \cdot \mathbf{x}_{i,j}$ and $u_j \leftarrow 0$ for all j;
5:       **for** $(1 \leq j < l \leq k)$ **do**
6:          **if** $(y_{i,l} - y_{i,j} > \epsilon$ and $\mathbf{w}^t \cdot \mathbf{x}_{i,j} < \mathbf{w}^t \cdot \mathbf{x}_{i,l} + \tau)$ **then**
7:            $u_j \leftarrow u_j + 1; u_l \leftarrow u_l - 1;$
8:          **else if** $(y_{i,j} - y_{i,l} > \epsilon$ and $\mathbf{w}^t \cdot \mathbf{x}_{i,l} < \mathbf{w}^t \cdot \mathbf{x}_{i,j} + \tau)$ **then**
9:            $u_j \leftarrow u_j - 1; u_l \leftarrow u_l + 1;$
10:         **end if**
11:      **end for**
12:      $\mathbf{w}^{t+1} \leftarrow \mathbf{w}^t + \sum_j u_j \mathbf{x}_{i,j}; t \leftarrow t + 1;$
13:    **end for**
14: **until** no updates made in the outer **for** loop

- the rank of $\mathbf{x}_{i,j}$ is significantly higher than the rank of $\mathbf{x}_{i,l}$, $y_{i,j} + \epsilon < y_{i,l}$
- the weight vector $\mathbf{w}$ can not successfully separate ($\mathbf{x}_{i,j}$ and $\mathbf{x}_{i,l}$) with a learning margin τ, $\mathbf{w} \cdot \mathbf{x}_{i,j} < \mathbf{w} \cdot \mathbf{x}_{i,l} + \tau$,

then we need to update $\mathbf{w}$ with the addition of $\mathbf{x}_{i,j} - \mathbf{x}_{i,l}$. It is not difficult to show Algorithm 1 is equivalent to using pairwise samples in training.

4.3 Sentence-Level Updating

In Algorithm 1, for each **repeat** iteration, the complexity is $O(mk^2d)$, where m and k are defined as above, and d is the average number of active features in a sample. We notice that the score of a parse $\mathbf{x}_{i,j}$ will be computed for k times in each **repeat** iteration. However, in many cases this is not necessary. In this section, we will revise Algorithm 1 to speed up the training phase.

Algorithm 2 is similar to Algorithm 1 except that the updating is not executed until all the inconsistent pairs for the same sentence are found. Therefore we only need to compute $\mathbf{w} \cdot \mathbf{x}_{i,j}$ for only once in each **repeat** iteration. So the complexity of each **repeat** iteration is $O(mk^2 + mkd)$.

4.4 Uneven Margins

For ϵ-insensitive ordinal regression, suppose $\epsilon = 10$ and our ordinal regression algorithm made two errors. One is on $(\mathbf{r}_1, \mathbf{r}_{11})$, and the other is on $(\mathbf{r}_{21}, \mathbf{r}_{31})$. The algorithm cannot recognize that the former is more serious than the latter. On the other hand, the algorithm does not try to distinguish $\mathbf{r}_1$ and $\mathbf{r}_{10}$, which is even worse.

Our solution is to apply *uneven margins* to the ϵ-insensitive ordinal regression. For example, we want to find a hyperplane for each sentence such that there is larger margin between $\mathbf{r}_1$ and $\mathbf{r}_{10}$, but a smaller margin between $\mathbf{r}_1$ and $\mathbf{r}_2$, where $\mathbf{r}_j$ is the parse that ranks j for a sentence. Similarly, we want a larger margin between $\mathbf{r}_1$ and $\mathbf{r}_2$, but a smaller margin between $\mathbf{r}_{10}$ and $\mathbf{r}_{11}$. Thus

$$margin(\mathbf{r}_1, \mathbf{r}_{10}) > margin(\mathbf{r}_1, \mathbf{r}_2) > margin(\mathbf{r}_{10}, \mathbf{r}_{11}) \quad (1)$$

So the solution is to search for a hyperplane such that

$$score(\mathbf{r}_p) - score(\mathbf{r}_q) > g(p, q)\tau$$

where $g(1, 10) > g(1, 2) > g(10, 11)$. Specifically, we replace one of the updating conditions

$$\mathbf{w} \cdot \mathbf{x}_{i,j} < \mathbf{w} \cdot \mathbf{x}_{i,l} + \tau$$

in line 6 of Algorithm 2 with

$$\frac{\mathbf{w} \cdot \mathbf{x}_{i,j} - \mathbf{w} \cdot \mathbf{x}_{i,l}}{g(y_{i,j}, y_{i,l})} < \tau, \quad (2)$$

and replace the updating condition

$$y_{i,l} - y_{i,j} > \epsilon \text{ with } g(y_{i,j}, y_{i,l}) > \epsilon, \quad (3)$$

which means that we ignore irrelevant inconsistent pairs with respect to g. We also replace the updating operation in line 7 with

$$u_j \leftarrow u_j + g(y_{i,j}, y_{i,l}), \ u_l \leftarrow u_l - g(y_{i,j}, y_{i,l}) \quad (4)$$

A similar modification is made in line 8 and 9.

It can be shown that modifying Algorithm 2 in this way is equivalent to using $(\mathbf{x}_{i,j} - \mathbf{x}_{i,l})/g(y_{i,j}, y_{i,l})$ as pairwise samples, so it is well defined. Due to the space limitation, we omit the proof of the equivalence in this paper.

There are many candidates for the function g. The following function is one of the simplest solutions.

$$g(p, q) \equiv \frac{1}{p} - \frac{1}{q}$$

We will use this function in our experiments on parse reranking.

5 Experimental Results

In this section, we will report the experimental results for parse reranking task. We use the same data set as described in [1]. Section 2-21 of the WSJ Penn Treebank (PTB)[14] are used as training data, and section 23 is used for test. The training data contains around 40,000 sentences, each of which has 27 distinct parses on average. Of the 40,000 training sentences, the first 36,000 are used to train perceptrons. The remaining 4,000 sentences are used as development data for parameter estimation, such as the number of rounds of iteration in training. The 36,000 training sentences contain 1,065,620 parses totally. We use the feature set generated by Collins [1].

In all of our experiments, we have employed the voted perceptron as in [15, 4]. The voted version makes the result on the test set more stable.

In the first set of experiments, Algorithm 2 and its uneven margin variants are used. In addition, we evaluate the performance of separating only the best parse from the rest in training by modifying the updating condition in Algorithm 2. Figure 1 shows the learning curves of different models on the test data, section 23 of Penn Treebank. Ordinal regression with uneven margins shows great advantage over the same algorithm using even margins. Its performance is also better than perceptron that is trained to separate the best parse from the rest.

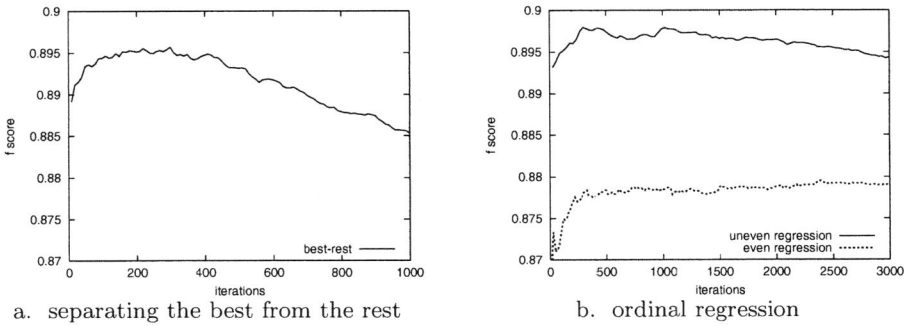

a. separating the best from the rest   b. ordinal regression

Fig. 1. Learning curves on PTB section 23.

By estimating the number of rounds of iterations on the development data, we get the results for the test data as shown in Table 1. Our ordinal regression algorithm with uneven margins achieves the best result in f-score. It verifies that using more pairs in training is helpful for the reranking problem. In addition, uneven margins are crucial to using ordinal regression to the reranking task.

In Algorithm 2, we update the weight vector on the sentence level so as to speed up the training, while in Algorithm 1 we update the weight vector for each pair of parses. Figure 2.a shows the comparison of the learning curves of the ordinal regression using parse level updating and the ordinal regression

Table 1. Experimental Results.

section 23, ≤100 words (2416 sentences)			
model	recall%	prec%	f-score%
baseline	88.1	88.3	88.2
best-rest	89.2	89.8	89.5
ordinal	88.1	87.8	88.0
uneven ordinal	89.5	90.0	89.8

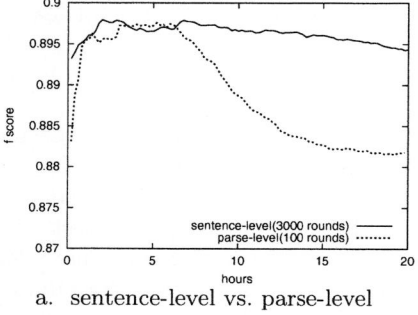
a. sentence-level vs. parse-level

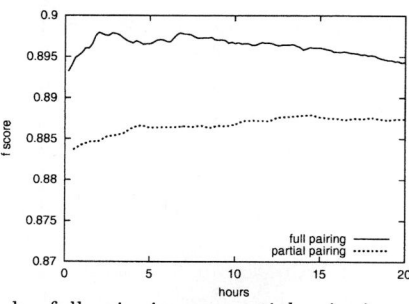
b. full pairwise vs. partial pairwise

Fig. 2. Learning curves on PTB section 23.

using sentence level updating. Algorithm 2 converges about 40% faster. The performance of Algorithm 2 is very good even within the first few rounds of iterations. Furthermore, the f-score on the test data remains at a high level although it is over-trained. Algorithm 1 easily leads to overfitting for the training data, while Algorithm 2 does not suffer from overfitting. This can be explained by an analog to the gradient methods. For Algorithm 1, we move in one direction at a time, so the result depends on the order of parses of a sentences, and it is easy to jump into a sub-optimum. For Algorithm 2, we move in multiple-directions at a time, so the result is more stable.

Our last set of experiments are about using all and partial pairwise samples. In order to theoretically justify Algorithm 2, we only use $k - 1$ pairwise parses for each sentence, e.g. pairs of parses with consecutive ranks. In Figure 3.b, we compare the results of using all pairs with the results when we use pairs of parses with consecutive ranks. Using only partial pairs makes the algorithm converge much slower.

6 Conclusions

In this paper, we have proposed a general framework for reranking. In this framework, we have proposed two new variants of perceptron. Compared to the previous perceptron reranking algorithms, the new algorithms use full pairwise samples and allow us to search for margins in a larger space, which are unavailable in the previous works on reranking. We also keep the data complexity unchanged and make the training efficient for these algorithms. Using the new perceptron like algorithms, we investigated the margin selection problem for the parse reranking task. By using uneven margin on ordinal regression, we achieves an f-score of 89.8% on sentences with ≤ 100 words in section 23 of Penn Treebank. The results on margin selection can be employed in reranking systems based on other machine learning algorithms, such as Winnow, Boosting and SVMs.

References

1. Collins, M.: Discriminative reranking for natural language parsing. In: ICML 2000. (2000)
2. Rosenblatt, F.: The perceptron: A probabilistic model for information storage and organization in the brain. Psychological Review **65** (1958) 386–408
3. Novikoff, A.B.J.: On convergence proofs on perceptrons. In: The Symposium on the Mathematical Theory of Automata. Volume 12. (1962)
4. Collins, M., Duffy, N.: New ranking algorithms for parsing and tagging: Kernels over discrete structures, and the voted perceptron. In: Proceedings of ACL 2002. (2002)
5. Ratnaparkhi, A.: A linear observed time statistical parser based on maximum entropy models. In: the Second Conference on Empirical Methods in Natural Language Processing. (1997)
6. Charniak, E.: A maximum-entropy-inspired parser. In: Proceedings of NAACL 2000. (2000)
7. Schapire, R.E., Freund, Y., Bartlett, P., Lee, W.S.: Boosting the margin: a new explanation for the effectiveness of voting methods. In: Proc. 14th International Conference on Machine Learning. (1997) 322–330
8. Shen, L., Joshi, A.K.: An SVM based voting algorithm with application to parse reranking. In: Proc. of CoNLL 2003. (2003)
9. Crammer, K., Singer, Y.: PRanking with Ranking. In: NIPS 2001. (2001)
10. Herbrich, R., Graepel, T., Obermayer, K.: Large margin rank boundaries for ordinal regression. In: Advances in Large Margin Classifiers. MIT Press (2000) 115–132
11. Vapnik, V.N.: Statistical Learning Theory. John Wiley and Sons, Inc. (1998)
12. Zhang, T.: Large Margin Winnow Methods for Text Categorization. In: KDD-2000 Workshop on Text Mining. (2000)
13. Krauth, W., Mezard, M.: Learning algorithms with optimal stability in neural networks. Journal of Physics A **20** (1987) 745–752
14. Marcus, M.P., Santorini, B., Marcinkiewicz, M.A.: Building a large annotated corpus of English: The Penn Treebank. Computational Linguistics **19** (1994) 313–330
15. Freund, Y., Schapire, R.E.: Large margin classification using the perceptron algorithm. Machine Learning **37** (1999) 277–296

A Comparative Study on the Use of Labeled and Unlabeled Data for Large Margin Classifiers

Hiroya Takamura and Manabu Okumura

Precision and Intelligence Laboratory, Tokyo Institute of Technology
4259 Nagatsuta Midori-ku Yokohama, 226-8503, Japan
{takamura,oku}@pi.titech.ac.jp
http://lr-www.pi.titech.ac.jp/main_e.html

Abstract. We propose to use both labeled and unlabeled data with the Expectation-Maximization (EM) algorithm in order to estimate the generative model and use this model to construct a Fisher kernel. The Naive Bayes generative probability is used to model a document. Through the experiments of text categorization, we empirically show that, (a) the Fisher kernel with labeled and unlabeled data outperforms Naive Bayes classifiers with EM and other methods for a sufficient amount of labeled data, (b) the value of additional unlabeled data diminishes when the labeled data size is large enough for estimating a reliable model, (c) the use of categories as latent variables is effective, and (d) larger unlabeled training datasets yield better results.

1 Introduction

One general trend in recent developments for statistical learning approaches in Natural Language Processing (NLP) is the incorporation of labeled and unlabeled data. For example, Naive Bayes (NB) classifiers can be enhanced with the Expectation-Maximization (EM) algorithm [12]. However, for large-margin classifiers [13] including Support Vector Machines (SVMs), which show a high categorization performance in many tasks of NLP and other fields [17, 6, 10], the question of how to combine labeled and unlabeled data for those classifiers has not been completely answered. In this paper, we propose a solution to this question. The high ability of SVMs makes this question worth to be tackled. Therefore we select SVMs as an example of a large-margin classifier in this research.

One possibility, which we focus on in this paper, is the use of the Fisher kernel [5]. This kernel function is based on a probabilistic generative model of data and the unlabeled data can be used to estimate the model. Since inputs to SVMs are only labeled data, this way of using unlabeled data is rather indirect. Although the estimation of models can be done with only unlabeled data, information from labeled data is too precious to be vainly discarded, as suggested by Tsuda [15]. For this reason, we propose to use both labeled and unlabeled data with the EM algorithm in order to estimate the generative model. Specifically, we take a generative model proposed by Nigam et al. [12] and conduct experiments of text categorization.

The objective of this research is to give answers to questions such as "in which situation does EM reinforce the effectiveness of the Fisher kernel?" and "the Fisher kernel using EM is better than NB with EM?"

Several methods have been proposed for the same or similar purpose. Transductive SVMs (TSVMs) proposed by Joachims [7] use unlabeled examples as labeled, by iteratively relabeling unlabeled examples. This method pursued the same purpose by adopting a different learning procedure from usual SVMs, while our method adopts a different feature representation. The Fisher kernel based on the Probabilistic Latent Semantic Indexing [4] is similar to ours in the sense that it is a combination of the Fisher kernel and the EM algorithm, but the information of labels is not used to estimate the model. Tsuda et al. [15] proposed, what they call, the Tangent vector Of Posterior log-odds (TOP) kernel. While Fisher kernels use generative probabilities, TOP kernels use posterior probabilities. Although TOP kernels yield high categorization performance, they are designed for binary classification tasks. Therefore we focus on the Fisher kernel here. However, as Tsuda et al [15] pointed out, if we take categories as latent variables as we do later in our model, the Fisher kernel becomes similar to the TOP kernel.

The rest of the paper is organized as follows. In Section 2, we explain Naive Bayes classifiers and its combination with the EM algorithm. They are used as the base model of our Fisher kernel. In Section 3, SVMs and the Fisher kernel are explained. SVMs are used as classifiers in the experiments. In Section 4, we propose a Fisher kernel constructed on the EM-enhanced Naive Bayes model. Experiments and conclusions are described respectively in Section 5 and Section 6.

2 Naive Bayes Classifiers and EM

This section introduces the multinomial NB model, which we later use as a generative model for the Fisher kernel because the multinomial model reportedly yields better results than other NB models [11].

2.1 Multinomial Model of NB Classifiers

This model has been successfully applied to text categorization and its generative probability of example $\mathbf{x}$ given a category c has the form:

$$P(\mathbf{x}|c,\theta) = P(|\mathbf{x}|)|\mathbf{x}|! \prod_w \frac{P(w|c)^{N(w,\mathbf{x})}}{N(w,\mathbf{x})!} , \qquad (1)$$

where $P(|\mathbf{x}|)$ denotes the probability that a text of length $|\mathbf{x}|$ occurs, and $N(w,\mathbf{x})$ denotes the number of occurrences of w in text $\mathbf{x}$. The occurrence of a text is modeled as a set of events, in which a word is drawn from the whole vocabulary.

2.2 Enhancing NB with EM

The EM algorithm is a method to estimate a model which has the maximal likelihood of the data, when some variables can not been observed (those variables are called *latent variables*) [1]. Nigam et al. [12] proposed a combination of Naive Bayes classifiers and the EM algorithm, which we use as a base for constructing a Fisher kernel.

First, we ignore the unrelated factors of Equation (1), and obtain the followings:

$$P(\mathbf{x}|c,\theta) \propto \prod_w P(w|c)^{N(w,\mathbf{X})}, \qquad (2)$$

$$P(\mathbf{x}|\theta) \propto \sum_c P(c) \prod_w P(w|c)^{N(w,\mathbf{X})}. \qquad (3)$$

In the following, we use θ to denote all the parameters of the model.

If we regard c as a latent variable and introduce a Dirichlet distribution as the prior distribution for the parameters, the Q-function (i.e., the expected log-likelihood) of this models is defined as:

$$Q(\theta|\bar{\theta}) = \log(P(\theta)) + \sum_{\mathbf{x} \in D} \sum_c P(c|\mathbf{x},\bar{\theta}) \times \log\left(P(c) \prod_w P(w|c)^{N(w,\mathbf{X})}\right), \qquad (4)$$

where $P(\theta) \propto \prod_c (P(c)^{\alpha-1} \prod_w (P(w|c)^{\alpha-1}))$; a Dirichlet distribution. α is a hyper-parameter and D is the set of examples used for model estimation.

Then we obtain the following EM steps:

E-step:

$$P(c|\mathbf{x},\bar{\theta}) = \frac{P(c|\bar{\theta})P(\mathbf{x}|c,\bar{\theta})}{\sum_c P(c|\bar{\theta})P(\mathbf{x}|c,\bar{\theta})}, \qquad (5)$$

M-step:

$$P(c) = \frac{(\alpha-1) + \sum_{\mathbf{x} \in D} P(c|\mathbf{x},\bar{\theta})}{(\alpha-1)|C| + |D|}, \qquad (6)$$

$$P(w|c) = \frac{(\alpha-1) + \sum_{\mathbf{x} \in D} P(c|\mathbf{x},\bar{\theta}) N(w,\mathbf{x})}{(\alpha-1)|W| + \sum_w \sum_{\mathbf{x} \in D} P(c|\mathbf{x},\bar{\theta}) N(w,\mathbf{x})}, \qquad (7)$$

where $|C|$ is the number of categories and $|W|$ is the number of words. For a labeled example, Equation (5) is not used. Instead of that, $P(c|\mathbf{x},\bar{\theta})$ is set as 1.0 if c is the category of example $\mathbf{x}$, otherwise 0.

As we can see from Equations (6) and (7), the larger α is, the more uniform the distribution becomes. In the actual application, α is treated as a user-given hyper-parameter.

3 Support Vector Machines and Fisher Kernel

In this section, we briefly explain SVMs and the Fisher kernel.

3.1 Support Vector Machines and Kernel Method

Suppose a set of ordered pairs consisting of a feature vector and its label $\{(\mathbf{x}_1, y_1), (\mathbf{x}_2, y_2), \cdots, (\mathbf{x}_l, y_l)\}$, $(\forall i, \mathbf{x}_i \in \mathbf{R}^d, y_i \in \{-1, 1\})$ is given. In SVMs, a separating hyperplane ($f(\mathbf{x}) = \mathbf{w} \cdot \mathbf{x} - b$) with the largest margin (the distance between the hyperplane and its nearest vectors) is constructed. Skipping the details of SVMs' formulation, here we just show the conclusion that, using some numbers β_i^* ($\forall i$) and b^*, the optimal hyperplane is expressed as follows:

$$f(\mathbf{x}) = \sum_i \beta_i^* y_i \mathbf{x}_i \cdot \mathbf{x} - b^* . \tag{8}$$

We should note that only dot-products of examples are used in the above expression.

Since SVMs are linear classifiers, their separating ability is limited. To compensate for this limitation, the *kernel method* is usually combined with SVMs [17].

In the kernel method, the dot-products in (8) are replaced with more general inner-products $K(\mathbf{x}_i, \mathbf{x})$ (kernel functions). The polynomial kernel $(\mathbf{x}_i \cdot \mathbf{x}_j + 1)^d$ ($d \in \mathbf{N}_+$) and the RBF kernel $\exp\{-\|\mathbf{x}_i - \mathbf{x}_j\|^2/2\sigma^2\}$ are often used. Using the kernel method means that feature vectors are mapped into a (higher dimensional) Hilbert space and linearly separated there. This mapping structure makes non-linear separation possible, although SVMs are basically linear classifiers.

3.2 Fisher Kernel

The above kernel functions are not dependent of data distribution. However, Jaakkola and Haussler [5] proposed a data-dependent kernel, which is based on the theory of information geometry.

Suppose we have a probabilistic generative model $P(\mathbf{x}|\theta)$ of the data (we denote a sample by $\mathbf{x}$). The Fisher score of $\mathbf{x}$ is defined as $\nabla_\theta \log P(\mathbf{x}|\theta)$, where ∇_θ means partial differentiation with respect to the parameters θ. The Fisher information matrix is denoted by $I(\theta)$ (this matrix defines the geometric structure of the model space). Then, the Fisher kernel $K(\mathbf{x}^1, \mathbf{x}^2)$ at an estimate $\hat{\theta}$ is given by:

$$(\nabla_\theta \log P(\mathbf{x}^1|\hat{\theta}))^t I^{-1}(\hat{\theta})(\nabla_\theta \log P(\mathbf{x}^2|\hat{\theta})) . \tag{9}$$

The Fisher score approximately indicates how the model will change if the sample is added to the training data used in the estimation of the model. That means, the Fisher kernel between two samples will be large, if the influences of the two samples are similar and large [14].

Matrix $I(\theta)$ is often approximated by the identity matrix to avoid large computational overhead.

4 Fisher Kernel on NB Model

Following the definition of the Fisher kernel, we construct our version of the Fisher kernel based on the NB model. In order to empirically investigate how the kernel works, we consider some variants with minor differences.

4.1 Derivation of the Fisher Kernel

As in the Fisher kernel proposed by Hofmann [4], we use *spherical parameterization* [8] $\rho_{wc} = 2\sqrt{P(w|c)}$ and $\rho_c = 2\sqrt{P(c)}$ instead of the original parameters $P(w|c)$ and $P(c)$, because this parameterization is supposed to provide a reasonable approximation of $I(\theta)$ by the identity matrix. The features for our Fisher kernel can be obtained by differentiating the Fisher score of each example with respect to each parameter:

$$\frac{\partial \log P(\mathbf{x}|\theta)}{\partial(\rho_{wc})} = \frac{P(c)N(w,\mathbf{x})\prod_w P(w|c)^{N(w,\mathbf{x})}}{P(\mathbf{x}|\theta)P(w|c)} \times \frac{\partial P(w|c)}{\partial \rho_{wc}}$$

$$= \frac{N(w,\mathbf{x})P(c|\mathbf{x},\theta)}{P(w|c)} \times \frac{\rho_{wc}}{2}$$

$$= \frac{N(w,\mathbf{x})P(c|\mathbf{x},\theta)}{\sqrt{P(w|c)}}, \tag{10}$$

$$\frac{\partial \log P(\mathbf{x}|\theta)}{\partial(\rho_c)} = \frac{P(c|\mathbf{x},\theta)}{P(c)}\frac{\partial P(c)}{\partial \rho_c}$$

$$= \frac{P(c|\mathbf{x},\theta)}{P(c)} \times \frac{\rho_c}{2}$$

$$= \frac{P(c|\mathbf{x})}{\sqrt{P(c)}}. \tag{11}$$

Matrix $I(\theta)$ is replaced by the identity matrix.

4.2 Some Variants to the Proposed Kernel

With slight changes, we can construct several variants to our Fisher kernel.

Sometimes we can use additional unlabeled examples other than labeled examples during the model estimation, but sometimes not. We also have an alternative to regard c as a given category or an unknown cluster. When unknown clusters are to be used, the initial values of the parameters are randomly set. The EM algorithm is supposed to form clusters consisting of similar examples.

We name each case to clarify the experimental settings to be described later:

        ul-cat : with unlabeled data, category for c,
        ul-cl : with unlabeled data, clusters for c,
        n-cat : without unlabeled data, category for c.

No EM computation was performed for n-cat in our experiments.

5 Experiments

To evaluate our methods, we conducted experiments of multiclass text categorization. The dataset we used is 20 Newsgroups[1], which has 20 categories and consists of 18828 newsgroup articles (we deleted invalid articles which have no text part). The size of each category is in the range of 600 to 1000 shown in Table 1. Each article has exactly one category label. The words that occur less than ten times in the whole dataset are not used as features in our experiments.

Table 1. The categories of 20-newsgroup.

Category	# articles
alt.atheism	799
comp.graphics	974
comp.os.ms-windows.misc	985
comp.sys.ibm.pc.hardware	982
comp.sys.mac.hardware	961
comp.windows.x	980
misc.forsale	972
rec.autos	990
rec.motorcycles	994
rec.sport.baseball	994
rec.sport.hockey	999
sci.crypt	991
sci.electronics	981
sci.med	990
sci.space	987
soc.religion.christian	999
talk.politics.guns	910
talk.politics.mideast	940
talk.politics.misc	775
talk.religion.misc	628

In this paper, *a labeled training dataset* means a dataset of labeled articles, and *a unlabeled training dataset* means a dataset of unlabeled articles that are used for model estimation with EM.

The whole dataset is split into a labeled training set consisting of 100 to 5000 articles, an unlabeled training set consisting of 10000 articles[2], and a test set consisting of 3765 articles. The two training sets are used to estimate the probabilistic model with the EM algorithm. The unlabeled training set is not

---

[1] Available from http://kdd.ics.uci.edu/.
Another frequently-used dataset is Reuters-21578, which is available from http://www.daviddlewis.com/resources/ . However, Reuters-21578 is mainly for the binary text categorization task, whereas 20 Newsgroups is for the multiclass task. This is why we use 20 Newsgroups here.

[2] Nigam et al. [12] also used 10000 additional unlabeled training samples.

used as input to SVMs. The test set is not used for the estimation of the model. We performed experiments with 5 different data-splits, which produce 5 non-overlapping test sets.

Hyper-parameter α for the Dirichlet prior of the parameters is set as 2.0, which is a frequently-used value. When unknown clusters are used as latent variables, the number of the unknown clusters is fixed to 20, which is the same as the number of the given categories.

We used SVMs for a classifier. Although soft-margin parameter C was fixed as 1.0 in our experiments, other values of this parameter did not produce any significant change in results. The one-versus-rest method [9] was employed for multiclass classification. All the feature vectors are normalized to the same length [2].

Deterministic annealing EM algorithm [16] is one standard way to avoid local maximum. We adopt this algorithm, which can be implemented with a slight change in Equation (5).

We evaluate results with classification accuracy, which is here defined as the number of correctly classified articles divided by the number of all the articles.

5.1 Comparison of the Methods

We compare the proposed methods (i.e., SVM (n-cat, ul-cat, ul-cl)), with the linear kernel SVMs and TSVMs[3], and the NB classifiers with or without a unlabeled training dataset. The linear kernel uses only labeled data for training. The result is summarized in Table 2.

Table 2. Categorization accuracy (%): comparison of the methods. This table compares several methods for text categorization. The numbers in the left-most column are the training data sizes. The other values are the categorization accuracies of the methods. SVMs (n-cat, ul-cat, ul-cl) are the result of SVM classification with the Fisher kernel. SVM (linear) and TSVM (linear) are the result of SVM classification with the linear kernel. The others are the result of NB methods with or without EM.

#labeled	SVM (n-cat)	SVM (ul-cat)	SVM (ul-cl)	SVM (linear)	TSVM (linear)	NB+EM (ul-cat)	NB
100	23.7	30.0	29.2	31.8	**33.5**	26.7	13.5
200	41.3	**46.9**	43.2	44.7	46.0	37.4	24.1
300	45.5	**53.3**	51.2	51.4	52.5	41.2	32.0
500	54.2	**61.1**	57.2	60.0	60.8	50.9	43.1
1000	68.0	**71.0**	67.8	68.9	69.3	65.0	59.3
2000	78.7	**79.0**	74.6	75.8	76.1	76.2	74.1
5000	85.1	**85.4**	82.0	82.1	82.0	83.6	82.8

For most of the labeled data sizes, SVM (ul-cat) yields the best accuracy. The exception is the labeled data size 100, where the linear kernel SVMs and TSVMs

---

[3] We use two packages:
TinySVM (http://cl.aist-nara.ac.jp/~taku-ku/software/TinySVM/),
SVM-light (http://svmlight.joachims.org/).

perform better. This is probably because the small labeled dataset cannot provide sufficient information enough for constructing a model which effectively represents the category structure. For large labeled data sizes, SVM (n-cat) is comparable to SVM (ul-cat), although the former is slightly worse than the latter. This fact shows that large labeled data can estimate a reliable model without help of unlabeled data. From these observations, we conclude that the Fisher kernel with labeled and unlabeled data works well for a sufficient amount of labeled data, although the value of using unlabeled data diminishes for very large labeled data.

The accuracies of SVM (n-cat) are worse than those of the linear kernel for up to 1000 labeled examples. This is presumably caused by the inaccurate estimation of the model, since the data size used in the model estimation is quite small for those cases. Similar phenomena are seen for NB with EM in the experiment by Nigam et al. [12], where they have drawn the same conclusion for the decrease of accuracy. The difference between SVM (ul-cat) and SVM (ul-cl) shows that the use of categories as latent variables is effective. On the other hand, the use of unknown clusters as latent variables only decreases the accuracy.

5.2 Different Sizes of Unlabeled Data

In the experiment above, we have shown that when the given categories are used as latent variables, the SVMs with EM-enhanced Fisher kernel perform well with 10000 unlabeled training examples.

A natural question that arises next is what happens if only fewer unlabeled training examples are available. To answer this question, we conduct experiments for different numbers of unlabeled training examples (from 1000 to 10000), while keeping the number of the labeled examples constant (we take 1000, 2000 and 5000).

The result is shown in Figure 1. For every number of labeled training examples, the accuracy monotonically increases as the number of unlabeled training examples increases. This result shows that larger unlabeled training datasets yield better results and that small unlabeled data only decrease accuracy.

The improvement for 5000 labeled examples is not so large as the ones for 1000 and 2000. One possible reason is that an accurate estimation has been done only with 5000 labeled examples and unlabeled training examples do not provide much additional information.

6 Conclusion

We proposed to use both labeled and unlabeled data with the EM algorithm in the estimation of the generative model, and construct the Fisher kernel on the model. We conducted several comparative experiments.

Our conclusions are, (a) SVMs using the Fisher kernel with labeled and unlabeled data work well for a sufficient amount of labeled and unlabeled data,

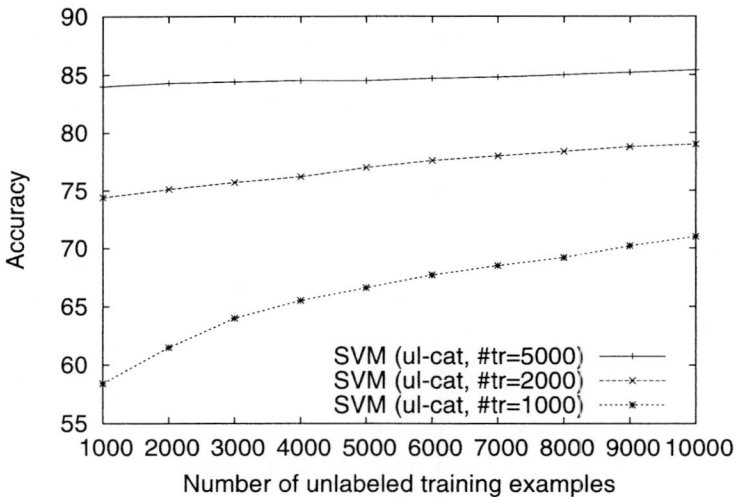

Fig. 1. Categorization accuracy (%): different sizes of unlabeled data, SVM (ul-cat). This figure shows the categorization accuracies of the proposed method (SVM (ul-cat)) for different sizes of unlabeled data. Three different lines correspond to the labeled training data sizes 5000, 2000 and 1000.

(b) the value of additional unlabeled data diminishes when the labeled data size is large enough for estimating a reliable model, (c) the use of categories as latent variables is effective, (d) larger unlabeled training datasets yield better results.

Future work includes the following.

All these conclusions are based on the NB model. To validate those conclusions in a more general level, experiments with other models and datasets will be required.

We can also adopt the model proposed by Nigam et al. [12], in which each category is separated into several smaller clusters.

In this paper, word clustering was not used. Hofmann and Puzicha [3] described a two-dimensional EM clustering, which can be used to model co-occurrence of word and document. Using such models for the Fisher kernel has the possibility of increasing accuracy for small labeled datasets, because features will be generalized in the model and the sparseness will be alleviated.

References

1. Arthur P. Dempster, Nan M. Laird, and Donald B. Rubin. 1977. Maximum likelihood from incomplete data via the EM algorithm. *Journal of the Royal Statistical Society Series B*, 39(1):1–38.
2. Ralf Herbrich and Thore Graepel. 2000. A PAC-bayesian margin bound for linear classifiers: Why SVMs work. In *Advances in Neural Information Processing Systems, 12*, pages 224–230.

3. Thomas Hofmann and Jan Puzicha. 1998. Statistical models for co-occurrence data. Technical Report AIM-1625, Artifical Intelligence Laboratory, Massachusetts Institute of Technology.
4. Thomas Hofmann. 2000. Learning the similarity of documents: An information geometric approach to document retrieval and categorization. In *Advances in Neural Information Processing Systems, 12*, pages 914–920.
5. Tommi Jaakkola and David Haussler. 1998. Exploiting generative models in discriminative classifiers. In *Advances in Neural Information Processing Systems 11*, pages 487–493.
6. Thorsten Joachims. 1998. Text categorization with support vector machines: Learning with many relevant features. In *Proceedings of the European Conference on Machine Learning*, pages 137–142.
7. Thorsten Joachims. 1999. Transductive inference for text classification using support vector machines. In *Proceedings of 16th International Conference on Machine Learning (ICML '99)*, pages 200–209.
8. Robert E. Kass and Paul W. Vos. 1997. *Geometrical foundations of asymptotic inference*. New York : Wiley.
9. Ulrich Kressel. 1999. Pairwise classication and support vector machines. In Bernhard Schölkopf, Christopher J. C. Burgesa, and Alexander J. Smola, editors, *Advances in Kernel Methods *Support Vector Learning*, pages 255–268. The MIT Press.
10. Taku Kudo and Yuji Matsumoto. 2001. Chunking with support vector machines. In *Proceedings of Second Meeting of the North American Chapter of the Association for Computational Linguistics (NAACL 2001)*, pages 192–199.
11. Andrew McCallum and Kamal Nigam. 1998. A comparison of event models for naive bayes text classification. In *Proceedings of AAAI-98 Workshop on Learning for Text Categorization*, pages 41–48.
12. Kamal Nigam, Andrew Mccallum, Sebastian Thrun, and Tom Mitchell. 2000. Text classification from labeled and unlabeled documents using EM. *Machine Learning*, 39(2/3):103–134.
13. Alexander J. Smola, Peter J. Bartlett, Bernhard Schölkopf, and Dale Schuurmans. 2000. *Advances in Large Margin Classifiers*. MIT Press.
14. Koji Tsuda and Motoaki Kawanabe. 2002. The leave-one-out kernel. In *Proceedings of International Conference on Artificial Neural Networks*, pages 727–732.
15. Koji Tsuda, Motoaki Kawanabe, Gunnar Rätsch, Sören Sonnenburg, and Klaus-Robert Müller. 2002. A new discriminative kernel from probabilistic models. *Neural Computation*, 14(10):2397–2414.
16. Naonori Ueda and Ryohei Nakano. 1998. Deterministic annealing EM algorithm. *Neural Networks*, 11(2):271–282.
17. Vladimir Vapnik. 1998. *Statistical Learning Theory*. John Wiley, New York.

Comparing Entropies Within the Chinese Language

Benjamin K. Tsou, Tom B.Y. Lai, and Ka-po Chow

Language Information Sciences Research Centre,
City University of Hong Kong, Tat Chee Avenue, Hong Kong
{rlbtsou,cttomlai,kapo.chow}@cityu.edu.hk

Abstract. Using a large synchronous Chinese corpus, we show how word and character entropy variations exhibit interesting differences in terms of time and space for different Chinese speech communities. We find that word entropy values are affected by the quality of the segmentation process. We also note that word entropies can be affected by proper nouns, which is the most volatile segment of the stable lexicon of the language. Our word and character entropy results provide interesting comparison with the earlier results and the average joint character entropies (a.k.a. entropy rates) of Chinese up to order 20 provided by us indicate that the limits of the conditional character entropies of Chinese for the different speech communities should be about 1 (or less). This invites questions on whether early convergence of character entropies would also entail word entropy convergence.

1 Introduction

Treating human language text or speech as an information source, character (or letter) and word entropies of human languages are useful reflections of inherent statistical properties of the languages concerned. Character (letter) and word entropies of English have been estimated to be 4.03 [5] and 11.47 [1]. Bigram and trigam conditional word entropies of English have been reported to be 6.06 and 2.01 [1]. Brown et al. [2] give an estimate of 1.75 for the limiting (infinite-length history) conditional entropy for the language. Character and word entropies of Chinese have been reported to be 9.7062 and 11.4559 [8]. As for high-order conditional entropies of Chinese, Tao [13] gives an estimated upper bound of 4.615 for characters and notes that characters and words conditional entropies in Chinese tend to equal limits. Using different methods, Shi et al. [11], Wu et al. [16] and Feng [5] give estimates of 4.1, 5.17 and 4.0462 for limiting conditional character entropies. Huang et al. [6] use n-gram probabilities obtained from training corpora with different techniques to account for data sparseness to calculate conditional character entropies of a test corpus. They report 1- to 4-gram values of 9.618, 6.088, 3.903 and 1.986 using maximum likelihood estimates, and 4-gram values of 13.11, 11.758, 10.179, 10.658, 10.036 and 6.585 using six other probability estimation methods.

This paper investigates the characteristics of entropy of Chinese with respect to characters and words, and also the effect of segmentation and proper nouns, which are some of the fundamental issues confronted by corpus processing.

We compute entropies from various sub-corpora of LIVAC [14], a synchronous corpus established by the Language Information Sciences Research Centre, City University of Hong Kong. We compare the results with respect to geographical and temporal variations. We also examine the effect of proper nouns on entropy variation. For fully verified segmented texts, proper nouns including personal, geographical and organizational names are tagged. This, therefore, enables such proper nouns to be extracted during entropy computation and results for both with and without proper nouns are compared. Next, we will consider the effect of different levels of segmentation on Chinese texts, from computer-segmentation only to fully verified segmentation. Finally, higher orders of average joint entropy (a.k.a. entropy rate) are studied.

2 Word Entropy

The sub-corpora of LIVAC being analyzed are designed along two dimensions: geographical and temporal variations.

Being a synchronous corpus, LIVAC (Linguistic Variations in Chinese Speech Communities) collects textual materials from news media every 4 days from 6 Chinese speech communities since July, 1995, and is planned to expand through 10 years until June, 2005. The news data are derived from a number of topics including editorials, cross-Formosan straits news, local news, sports, entertainment and finance. The present corpus size has reached over 140,000,000 characters and a dictionary of 650,000 words. Since the source materials of 6 places are collected on the same day, there is a purposeful overlap of materials in contrast to a balanced corpus which avoids such overlap, and thus offers a basis for rigorous comparison of language in actual use.

Table 1 shows the list of the sub-corpora constructed from LIVAC. 5 years of texts from three places including Beijing (A1), Taiwan (B1) and Hong Kong (C1) are first examined, followed by a combination of all three places (D1). Second, 1 year of texts from six places, namely Beijing (BJ), Taiwan (TW), Hong Kong (HK), Macau (MC), Shanghai (SH) and Singapore (SG), are examined (E1), followed by extension to 4 years (F1) and 5 years (G1) respectively. Last, another set of computations will be performed using the same sub-corpora, with the only exception that the proper nouns are excluded from calculation (A2, B2, ..., G2).

The entropy equation is:

$$H(X) = - \sum_{x_i \in V(X)} P(x_i) \log_2 P(x_i) \qquad (1)$$

where x_i = symbol, character or word types and $V(X)$ = the set of all x_i

Using a 64-bit computational platform, we have obtained well over six decimal places for the precision in our calculations. In the tables of results shown in this paper, only three to six decimal places are given for the sake of simplicity and yet which are sufficient for comparison and contrast.

Table 1. List of sub-corpora from LIVAC.

Sub-corpora	Description	Size
A1	BJ, 5 Years (1995-2000)	11M
A2	BJ, 5 Years (1995-2000) without Proper Nouns	-
B1	TW, 5 Years (1995-2000)	11M
B2	TW, 5 Years (1995-2000) without Proper Nouns	-
C1	HK, 5 Years (1995-2000)	11M
C2	HK, 5 Years (1995-2000) without Proper Nouns	-
D1	BJ, TW, HK, 5 Years (1995-2000)	33M
D2	BJ, TW, HK, 5 Years (1995-2000) without Proper Nouns	-
E1	Six Places: BJ, TW, HK, MC, SH, SG, 1 Year (1995-1996)	10M
E2	Six Places, 1 Year (1995-1996) without Proper Nouns	-
F1	Six Places, 4 Years (1995-1999)	45M
F2	Six Places, 4 Years (1995-1999) without Proper Nouns	-
G1	Six Places, 5 Years (1995-2000)	62M
G2	Six Places, 5 Years (1995-2000) without Proper Nouns	-

2.1 Geographical Variations

Table 2 shows word entropies computed from sub-corpora A1 to C1, and their combined collection as a whole (D1). H_0 is the zero-order word entropy, N the number of word types, and $H_{\max}$ the maximum word entropy achievable with size N of word types, equal to logarithm of N with base 2. H_q is called an entropy quotient which, under certain circumstances, is a measure of entropy disregarding the effect of different sizes of word types, and is suitable for comparison. It is defined as $H_q = \frac{H_0}{H_{\max}}$.

Table 2. Entropies of sub-corpora A1 to D2.

	A1	A2	B1	B2	C1	C2	D1	D2
H_0	11.47	11.13	11.69	11.37	11.96	11.64	11.97	11.61
N	120117	84789	111379	79694	123010	89906	245226	161796
$H_{\max}$	16.874	16.372	16.765	16.282	16.908	16.456	17.904	17.304
H_q	0.6797	0.6800	0.6971	0.6982	0.7071	0.7075	0.6684	0.6708
Corpus Size	11M	-	11M	-	11M	-	33M	-

The word entropy calculated from Beijing sub-corpus, A1, is 11.47, which is very close to the previous results, e.g. 11.46, obtained by Liu [8] using a balanced corpus which has a size of over 20,000,000 characters with a balanced distribution of source materials ranging from social sciences, literature and arts, and natural sciences. While Liu's result was based on a balanced corpus, the proximity of the result with that obtained from LIVAC, a synchronous corpus, is slightly surprising with regard to the different design philosophy and nature of the two corpora. This reflects the stability of Chinese word entropy particularly as used in Beijing.

On the other hand, the word entropy (11.69) for the Taiwan sub-corpus, B1, is obviously higher than Beijing's, and the figure for Hong Kong, C1, is even higher (11.96). This follows from the fact that the number of word types in Taiwan and Hong Kong is higher, and their usage distribution tends to be more even. This ordering holds true for H_q as well.

Sub-corpora D1 and D2 correspond to the results when Beijing, Taiwan and Hong Kong are considered together. It can be seen that the word entropy of D1 is higher than that of any one of the three constituent places. This is again a direct consequence of the higher N, the number of word types. However, H_q of D1 is smaller than that of all sub-corpora. The sizes of sub-corpora D1 and D2 are each about three times the already large sizes of the three one-place corpora, and it may not be reasonable to compare the H_q values of D1 and D2 with those of the one-place corpora. This needs further investigation. If it was nevertheless reasonable to make a comparison, this would mean that the unevenness of the vocabulary distributions did not cancel out, but accentuated one another.

2.2 Content Variations

Another dimension to look at the word entropy is the effect of proper nouns. Columns A2, B2 and C2 show the word entropies after proper nouns are extracted from the sub-corpora. Results show that the relative ordering remains the same among the three places. Besides, as N decreases due to a smaller size of word types, the entropy value also decreases.

The contrary is true for H_q, the entropy quotient, which demonstrates an increase in all cases. The slight rises seem to reflect that after proper nouns are extracted, the remaining corpus shows a more even distribution in word use. The result reveals that proper nouns play a significant role in everyday language use.

The effect of proper nouns is further discussed in Sect. 5.

2.3 Temporal Variations

Table 3 shows the entropy computation results of sub-corpora E1 to G2. It can be seen that as the corpus grows with time, the word entropy continues to increase, as a result of new words keep appearing across the years. H_q, however, exhibits a downward trend. This is analogous to the previous case of sub-corpora D1 and D2. We must also be careful about comparing the H_q values of corpora of very

Table 3. Entropies of sub-corpora E1 to G2.

	E1	E2	F1	F2	G1	G2
H_0	11.90	11.57	11.97	11.60	12.05	11.67
N	133090	95779	311735	195132	390990	236593
H_{max}	17.022	16.547	18.250	17.574	18.577	17.852
H_q	0.6991	0.6990	0.6560	0.6603	0.6488	0.6536
Corpus Size	10M	-	45M	-	62M	-

different (and large) sizes, but if comparison was nevertheless reasonable, we might conclude that not only the degree of unevenness will accumulate across places of the same period, but would also do so as the corpus size grew with time for the same place.

The change of H_q is illustrated in Fig. 1.

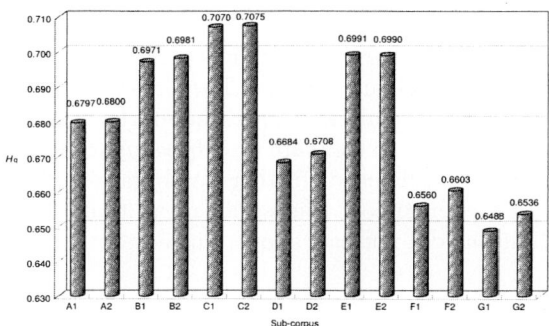

Fig. 1. Variations in H_q for sub-corpora A1 to G2.

3 Effect of Segmentation

When new data of Chinese text are collected and fed into the corpus, they are in form of a stream of characters with no boundary indications for words. This gives rise to the need for word segmentation.

For LIVAC, segmentation is performed progressively with computerized automation at the beginning and more human intervention introduced in later stages. We have performed the same set of word entropy computations to two other types of segmented corpus data, which are named as B-Segmented and C-Segmented sub-corpora while the previous one is named A-Segmented sub-corpus. Their differences are described in Table 4.

Table 4. Levels of segmentation.

Segmentation	Description
A-Segmented	computer-segmentation (backward maximum matching) and full human verification
B-Segmented	computer-segmentation and preliminary rule-based automatic verification
C-Segmented	computer-segmentation without any verification

The entropy computation results of B-Segmented and C-Segmented sub-corpora are shown in Table 5 and Table 6. They are illustrated together in Fig. 2.

Table 5. Entropies of B-Segmented sub-corpora.

	A1	A2	B1	B2	C1	C2	D1	D2	E1	E2	F1	F2	G1	G2
H_0	11.48	11.19	11.67	11.40	11.98	11.71	11.97	11.66	11.94	11.64	11.98	11.67	12.05	11.72
N	91460	70068	100272	76748	108386	82791	185916	131238	126798	96013	227786	157152	274008	177308
$H_{\max}$	16.48	16.10	16.61	16.23	16.73	16.34	17.50	17.00	16.95	16.55	17.80	17.26	18.06	17.44
H_q	0.696	0.695	0.703	0.703	0.717	0.717	0.684	0.686	0.705	0.703	0.673	0.676	0.667	0.672

Table 6. Entropies of C-Segmented sub-corpora.

	A1	A2	B1	B2	C1	C2	D1	D2	E1	E2	F1	F2	G1	G2
H_0	11.51	11.23	11.70	11.43	12.02	11.75	12.00	11.70	11.98	11.68	12.01	11.70	12.08	11.76
N	91473	70054	99815	76263	108035	82416	185028	130331	126511	95695	226902	156247	272675	175962
$H_{\max}$	16.48	16.10	16.61	16.22	16.72	16.33	17.50	16.99	16.95	16.55	17.79	17.25	18.06	17.42
H_q	0.699	0.698	0.705	0.705	0.719	0.719	0.686	0.688	0.707	0.706	0.675	0.678	0.669	0.675

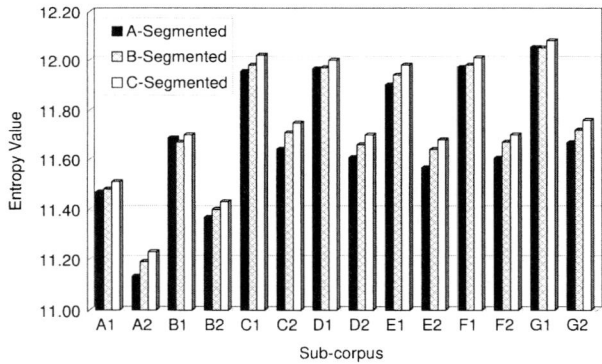

Fig. 2. Effect of segmentation to entropy.

We can observe from Fig. 2 that generally, as segmentation becomes more refined, the entropy values decrease. For example, in sub-corpus A1, the entropy decreases from 11.51 to 11.48, and further to 11.47 when the segmentation proceeds from C- to B- and then A-Segmented. Likewise, for larger sub-corpus G2, entropy decreases from 11.76 to 11.72, and further to 11.67. This suggests that finer segmentation may correct some unusual words arisen from mis-segmentation, and change them back to usual and common ones, thereby lowering the randomness and hence the overall word entropy. It draws attention to the significance of variation between properly segmented texts to relatively raw texts especially in terms of the drastic difference in the size of the relevant lexicon, e.g. N increases from 91,473 for C-Segmented texts to 120,117 for A-Segmented texts of sub-corpus A1. This also makes it possible that word entropy be considered a useful measure of segmentation effectiveness apart from precision and recall in natural language processing.

4 Entropies of Higher Order

In contrast to the zero-order entropy which gives an indication of information content from distribution of individual words, conditional entropy gives the same measure with respect to their positions in the text. The order of conditional entropy determines how many words preceding the word in question will be considered. The equation for conditional entropy is:

$$H_n(X) = - \sum_{V_{n+1}(X)} P(x[(i-n)..i]) \log_2 P(x_i | x[(i-n)..(i-1)]) \quad (2)$$

where $H_n(X)$ = the entropy of order n for corpus X, $x[a..b]$ = the tuple formed from ath to bth symbol in X, and $V_{n+1}(X)$ = the set of all $(n+1)$-tuples. Thus the summation is done over all $(n+1)$-tuples.

To lessen requirements on computation and memory resources, the average joint entropy (a.k.a. entropy rate), which does not involve conditional probability, can be used:

$$H'_n(X) = - \sum_{V_{n+1}(X)} P(x[(i-n)..i]) \log_2 \frac{1}{n+1} P(x[(i-n)..i]) \quad (3)$$

The Shannon-McMillan-Breiman theorem states that the limits of the conditional entropy and the average joint entropy are equal, assuming X to be a stationary and ergodic process. Theoretically, the value of average joint entropy is higher than conditional entropy of any order.

We have also managed to compute conditional entropies up to order 6 using limited computational resources. The results are comparable to Huang et al. [6].

The results of higher order average joint entropies for characters are shown in Fig. 3.

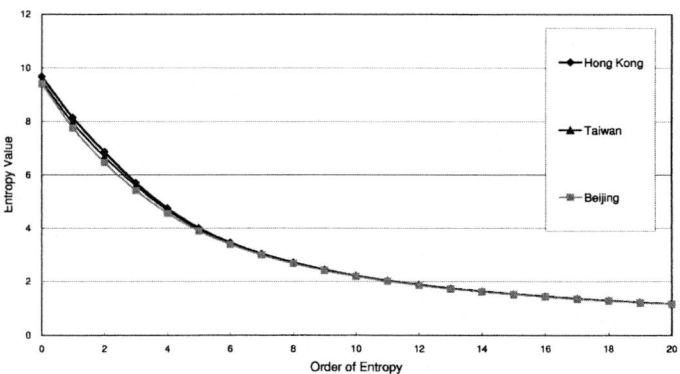

Fig. 3. Higher order average joint character entropy of Chinese.

The results were based on 8 years of LIVAC corpus data for Hong Kong, Taiwan and Beijing, each having a size of over 20,000,000 characters. Results show that the ordering of entropies is very stable with Hong Kong > Taiwan > Beijing for all orders of entropy. The differences diminish as the entropy order becomes higher. The differences do remain, however, no matter how small the differences become. The values of H_0 for Hong Kong, Taiwan and Beijing are 9.674, 9.496 and 9.411 respectively, while the values of H'_{20} are 1.1648, 1.159 and 1.157 respectively. From the graph, the character entropies for all three places tend to approach a limit, the true character entropy, which, as we estimated, should be about 1 or less. A larger corpus and higher computing power will be needed to more closely approach the limit.

Our preliminary results for higher order word entropy computation also show the tendency to approach a limit.

5 Effect of Proper Nouns

The effect of proper nouns can be further seen by considering sub-corpora G1 and G2. Higher order word entropies are obtained and the results are shown in Table 7.

Table 7. High-order entropies under the effect of proper nouns.

	G1		G2	
n	H_n	H_q	H_n	H_q
0	12.052	0.648784	11.668	<u>0.653619</u>
1	10.062	<u>0.436809</u>	9.887	0.433852
2	7.879	<u>0.322759</u>	7.823	0.322308
3	6.146	0.247986	6.118	<u>0.248013</u>
4	4.962	0.199419	4.940	<u>0.199463</u>
5	4.146	0.166421	4.127	<u>0.166446</u>
6	3.557	0.142723	3.541	<u>0.142736</u>
7	3.114	0.124914	3.100	<u>0.124921</u>
8	2.769	0.111050	2.756	<u>0.111054</u>
9	2.492	0.099954	2.481	<u>0.099956</u>
10	2.266	0.090873	2.256	<u>0.090874</u>
11	2.077	0.083303	2.068	<u>0.083305</u>
12	1.918	0.076898	1.909	<u>0.076899</u>
13	1.781	0.071407	1.773	<u>0.071408</u>
14	1.662	0.066648	1.655	<u>0.066649</u>
15	1.558	0.062484	1.551	<u>0.062484</u>

The larger H_q of the two sub-corpora is highlighted by an underline. To further demonstrate the effect of proper nouns, some 9-tuple examples for computing H'_8 are listed in Table 8.

For sub-corpus G1, it is very likely that the personal name "遲浩田" ("Chi Hao-tian") will appear after the 8-tuple "中央:軍委:副:主席:國務:委員:兼:國防部長" (the title of "the vice-chairman of PRC Central Military Commission; state councillor and minister of National Defense"). The combined 9-tuple has the highest

Table 8. Examples of 9-tuples from G1 and G2.

G1	Freq	G2	Freq
中央:軍委:副:主席:國務:委員:兼:國防部長:**遲浩田**	171	中央:副:主席:國務:委員:兼:國防部長:**今天**:在	15
兼:國防部長:**遲浩田**:上將:今天:上午:在:釣魚台:國賓館	6	國務:委員:兼:國防部長:**上將**:今天:上午:在:國賓館	6
國務:委員:兼:國防部長:**遲浩田**:今天:在:這裏	6	主席:國務:委員:兼:國防部長:**今天**:在:這裏:會見	6
主席:國務:委員:兼:國防部長:**遲浩田**:今天:在:這裏	8	國務:委員:兼:國防部長:**上將**:今天:在:這裏:會見	6
		委員:兼:國防部長:**上將**:今天:上午:在:人民:會見	9

frequency among the set of all 9-tuples, thus contributing significantly to the overall value. For G2, after proper nouns are extracted, there are more possibilities after the corresponding tuple, like "今天" ("today") and "上將" ("general"). On the whole, although the number of types will be reduced by eliminating proper nouns from the corpus data, the entropy quotient, H_q, will be higher.

It is also noteworthy that personalities represented by the proper nouns will change over time. To take personal names as an example, the person who holds a position or title may change, but the title itself may remain the same. In this connection, those tuples in sub-corpus G1 may likely change over time, but not for those in G2. These effects can also be captured by considering entropies of G1 and G2, and this will be an area to be further explored.

6 Conclusion

Our entropy computation results based on LIVAC sub-corpora have shown that entropy tends to vary significantly along geographical and temporal dimensions. We also show that proper word segmentation has an effect on entropy values. The more refined is the segmentation, the lower is the entropy. Besides, proper nouns play a significant role in language. When they are extracted, the actual entropy decreases while H_q, the *entropy quotient*, often becomes higher. We have suggested possible reasons and applications for these phenomena. We have also managed to compute average joint character entropy up to order 20. The results are indicative of an approximate value of the ultimate character and word entropies of Chinese language which remains to be determined. Further research is needed to obtain deeper properties of the Chinese language including those of word entropy.

References

1. Bell, T.C.: Text Compression. Prentice Hall, 1990
2. Brown P., Della Pietra, S., Della Pietra, V., Lai, Jennifer C., Mercer, Robert L.: An Estimate of an Upper Bound for the Entropy of English. Computational Linguistics, Vol.18, 1:31, 1992
3. Chen Yuan: Xiandai Hanyu Dingliang Fenxi (Quantitative Analysis of Modern Chinese). Shanghai Education Press, 1989
4. Cover T.M. and King R.: A Convergent Gambling Estimate of the Entropy of English. IEEE Trans. on Information Theory, IT-24(4), pp. 413–421, July 1978

5. Feng Zhiwei: Shuxue Yu Yuyan (Mathematics and Language). Hunan Education Press, February, 1991
6. Huang Xuanjing, Wu Lide, Guo Yikun, Liu Bingwei: Computation of the Entropy of Modern Chinese and the Probability Estimation of Sparse Event in Statistical Language Model. ACTA ELECTRONICA SINICA, 2000, Vol. 28, No.8, pp. 110–2
7. Jiang Di: An Entropy Value of Classical Tibetan Language and Some Other Questions. Proceedings of 1998 International Conference on Chinese Information Processing, 18–20 Nov., 1998
8. Liu Yuan, Wang Dejin, Zhang Sheying: The Probability Distribution and Entropy and Redundancy in Printed Chinese. Proceedings of International Conference on Chinese Information Processing, August, 1987, pp.505–509
9. Shannon C. E.: A Mathematical Theory of Communication. Bell System Technical Journal 27, 1948. pp. 379–423 and 623–656
10. Shannon C. E.: Prediction and Entropy of Printed English. Bell System Technical Journal 3, 1951. pp. 50–64
11. Shi Guiqing, Xu Bingzeng: Hanzi Zipin Fenbu, Zui Jia Bianma Yu Shuru Wenti (Character Frequency Distribution, Optimal Encoding and Input of Chinese). ACTA ELECTRONIC SINICA, Vol.12, No.4, 1984, pp. 94–96
12. Teahan W.J. and Cleary J.G.: The Entropy of English using PPM-based Models. Proceedings of Data Compression Conference (DCC'96), 1996, pp. 53–62
13. Tao Xiaopeng: The Design and Application of Language Model for the Minimum Entropy of Chinese Character. Manuscript, 2003
14. Tsou B. K., Tsoi W. F., Lai T. B. Y., Hu J., and Chan S.W.K.: LIVAC, A Chinese Synchronous Corpus, and Some Applications. Proceedings of the ICCLC International Conference on Chinese Language Computing, Chicago, 2000. pp. 233–238, http://livac.org
15. Weaver, W. and Shannon C. E.: The Mathematical Theory of Communication. University of Illinois Press, Urbana, Illinois. 1949
16. Wu Jun, Wang Zuoying: Hanyu Xinxi Shang He Yuyan Muxing De Fuzadu (Entropy and Complexity of Language Model of Chinese). ACTA ELECTRONICA SINICA, Vol.24, No.10, 1996, pp. 69–71

NTPC: N-Fold Templated Piped Correction

Dekai Wu[1,*], Grace Ngai[2,**], and Marine Carpuat[1]

[1] HKUST, Human Language Technology Center, Dept. of Computer Science
University of Science and Technology, Clear Water Bay, Hong Kong
{dekai,marine}@cs.ust.hk
[2] Hong Kong Polytechnic University, Dept. of Computing, Kowloon, Hong Kong
csgngai@polyu.edu.hk

Abstract. We describe a broadly-applicable conservative error correcting model, N-fold Templated Piped Correction or NTPC ("nitpick"), that consistently improves the accuracy of existing high-accuracy base models. Under circumstances where most obvious approaches actually reduce accuracy more than they improve it, NTPC nevertheless comes with little risk of accidentally degrading performance. NTPC is particularly well suited for natural language applications involving high-dimensional feature spaces, such as bracketing and disambiguation tasks, since its easily customizable template-driven learner allows efficient search over the kind of complex feature combinations that have typically eluded the base models. We show empirically that NTPC yields small but consistent accuracy gains on top of even high-performing models like boosting. We also give evidence that the various extreme design parameters in NTPC are indeed necessary for the intended operating range, even though they diverge from usual practice.

1 Introduction

In language processing tasks, situations frequently arise where (1) we have already trained a highly accurate model for classification and/or sequence recognition, (2) the model nevertheless cannot deal with some kinds of errors, because it does not consider complex conjunctions of many features (usually because the computational cost would be infeasible), and (3) we have some general idea as to what kinds of feature conjunctions might help. Such conditions are often found in tasks such as word sense disambiguation, phrase chunking, entity recognition, role labeling for understanding tasks, and the like.

We introduce a useful general technique called **N-fold Templated Piped Correction** or **NTPC** ("nitpick") for robustly improving the accuracy of existing base models under such circumstances. Given that the base accuracy is

---

[*] The author would like to thank the Hong Kong Research Grants Council (RGC) for supporting this research in part through research grants RGC6083/99E, RGC6256/00E, and DAG03/04.EG09.
[**] The author would like to thank the Hong Kong Polytechnic University for supporting this research in part through research grants A-PE37 and 4-Z03S.

already high, even small gains are desirable and difficult to achieve, particularly since it is difficult to correct the few remaining errors without also accidentally undoing correct classifications at the same time. NTPC has the virtues of consistently producing these small gains in accuracy, being straightforward to implement, and being applicable in a wide variety of situations.

To demonstrate the consistency and effectiveness of the method, we apply it to two tasks across four languages with very different characteristics, using an AdaBoost.MH base model already trained to high accuracy on named-entity datasets. This is typically representative of the kinds of language processing classification and sequence recognition tasks we are concerned with. Boosting was chosen for its superior reputation for error driven learning of ensemble models; along with maximum-entropy models and SVMs, it performs extremely well in language-independent named-entity recognition. Yet like all learning models, these base models can and do reach certain limits that other models are less susceptible to (despite which, boosting has typically been used for the final stage in NLP systems). This holds even after careful feature engineering to compensate is carried out. Error analysis for this task indicated that one of the major practical limitations of the model was that only a small number of conjunctions of features could be feasibly searched during boosting.

This type of phenomenon in fact occurs frequently, over a wide range of language processing tasks. Some systems attempt to compensate using *ad hoc* voting methods combining multiple base models, but this can lead to unpredictable results that often do not address the underlying causes of the remaining errors. The question is therefore how to systematically correct errors *after* a high-accuracy base model such as boosting has done its best.

NTPC combines a template-driven error correction learning mechanism with cross-validation style n-fold partitioning of datasets generated by the base model. The error correction mechanism possesses similarities in some theoretical respects to both decision lists and tranformation-based learning, but not with regard to their conventional uses. The n-fold partitioning setup is a form of stacking, but again not in a form typically used in NLP. We discuss the motivation and evidence for the necessity of the differences.

NTPC owes its leverage to (1) being able to explore a much wider range of conjunctive hypotheses than the base model, owing to its template-driven (and thus, template-constrained) hypothesis generator, (2) being able to observe right contexts not knowable to the base model, and (3) being extremely conservative via the combination of n-fold partitioning and zero error tolerance.

In the following sections, we first give the formal definition of the NTPC model. We then describe the experimental setup of the eight different tasks used to test NTPC, and discuss the relations to previous work. After presenting overall results, we identify and analyze some of the key theoretical characteristics that allow NTPC to perform better than other base models, and present the corresponding empirical confirmation to support these claims.

2 Error Correction in Extreme Operating Ranges

Several conditions must be true for an error correction model to be effective at its task. This is even more the case when the base model is state-of-the-art and already high-performing. The error correction model must be:

- *Biased differently*: The corrector must be able to capture phenomena which were not learned by the base model – therefore it must have characteristics that vary significantly from the base model.
- *Extremely risk-averse*: The goal of an error corrector is to achieve performance *gains* on a base learner. Therefore, one of the basic requirements is that it should only correct existing errors, and not introduce any new ones by miscorrecting accurate predictions.
- *Extremely reliable*: The error corrector works in ranges where errors are far and few in between. As a result, it needs to be able to identify valid error patterns, as opposed to noise-induced abberations.

NTPC is designed to fulfill the above requirements. The following will give a description of the model and discuss the various design issues with respect to the foregoing design requirements.

The inputs to NTPC are (1) a set of rule templates which describe the types of rules that it is allowed to hypothesize, (2) a single base learning model (the example in this paper being an AdaBoost.MH model), and (3) an annotated training set.

Figure 1 shows the architecture of NTPC. The training set is partitioned n times in order to train n base models. Each base model is evaluated on its corresponding held-out validation set, and the labelled n validation sets are then recombined to create the training set for *Error_Corrector_Leaner*. The Error Corrector learns a list of rules which are generated from a given set of templates:

$$\mathcal{R} = \{r | r \in \mathcal{H} \wedge \tau(r) > \tau_{\min} \wedge \epsilon(r) = 0\} \tag{1}$$

$$\tau(r) = \sum_{j=1}^{X} \sum_{r(x_j, \hat{y}_j) \neq \emptyset} \delta(r(x_j, \hat{y}_j), y_j) \tag{2}$$

$$\epsilon(r) = \sum_{j=1}^{X} \sum_{r(x_j, \hat{y}_j) \neq \emptyset} 1 - \delta(r(x_j, \hat{y}_j), y_j) \tag{3}$$

where $\mathcal{X}$ is a sequence of X training examples x_i, $\mathcal{Y}$ is a sequence of reference labels y_i for each example respectively, $\hat{\mathcal{Y}}$ is a sequence of labels $\hat{y}_i$ as predicted by the base model for each example respectively, $\mathcal{H}$ is the hypothesis space of valid rules implied by the templates, and $\tau_{\min}$ is a confidence threshold. $\tau_{\min}$ is set to a relatively high value (say 15), which implements the requirement of high reliability. $\mathcal{R}$ is subsequently sorted by the τ_i value of each rule r_i into an ordered list of rules $\mathcal{R}^* = (r_0^*, \ldots, r_{i-1}^*)$.

The evaluation phase is depicted in the lower portion of Figure 1. The test set is first labeled by the base model. The error corrector's rules r_i^* are then applied in the order of R^* to the evaluation set. The final classification of a sample is then the classification attained when all the rules have been applied. This differs from the similar-spirited decision list model (Rivest [1987]).

3 Experiments

To verify the hypotheses underlying the design of NTPC, we performed a series of experiments applying NTPC to eight different named entity recognition (NER) models, for various tasks and languages. The data used was from the shared tasks of the CoNLL 2002 and 2003 conferences (Tjong Kim Sang [2002]; Tjong Kim Sang and Meulder [2003]), which evaluated NER in Spanish, Dutch, English and German. The data consisted of two subsets in which named entities had been manually annotated.

3.1 Previous Work

Boosting (Freund and Schapire [1997]), at present one of the most popular machine learning techniques, is based on the idea that a set of many simple but moderately weak classifiers can be combined to create a single highly accurate strong classifier. It has the advantage of being able to handle large numbers of sparse features, many of which may be irrelevant or highly interdependent. This would make it appear to be well suited for NLP tasks which often exhibit these characteristics.

In our experiments, we construct a high-performance base model based on AdaBoost.MH (Schapire and Singer [2000]), the multi-class generalization of the original boosting algorithm, which implements boosting on top of decision stump classifiers (decision trees of depth one).

Boosting has been successfully applied to several NLP problems. In these NLP systems boosting is typically used as the ultimate stage in a learned system. For example, Schapire and Singer ([2000]) applied it to Text Categorization while Escudero et al. ([2000]) used it to obtain good results on Word Sense Disambiguation. More closely relevant to the experiments described here in, two of the best-performing three teams in the CoNLL-2002 Named Entity Recognition shared task evaluation used boosting as their base system (Carreras et al. [2002]; Wu et al. [2002]).

However, precedents for improving performance *after* boosting are few. At the CoNLL-2002 shared task session, Tjong Kim Sang (unpublished) described an experiment using voting to combine the NER outputs from the shared task participants which, predictably, produced better results than the individual systems. A couple of the individual systems were boosting models, so in some sense this could be regarded as an example. We began preliminary investigation of methods based on error correction for the CoNLL-2003 shared task (Wu et al. [2003]).

Tsukamoto et al. ([2002]) used piped AdaBoost.MH models for NER. Their experimental results were somewhat disappointing, but this could perhaps be attributable to various reasons including the feature engineering or not using cross-validation sampling in the stacking.

The AdaBoost.MH base model's high accuracy sets a high bar for error correction. Aside from brute-force *en masse* voting of the sort at CoNLL-2002 described above, we do not know of any existing post-boosting models that improve rather than degrade accuracy. We aim to further improve performance, and propose using a piped error corrector.

4 Results

Table 1 presents the results of the boosting-only base model versus the NTPC-enhanced models on the eight different named-entity recognition models, using different tasks and languages. For each task/language combination, the top row shows the base model (AdaBoost) result, and the bottom row shows the result of the piped system.

The evaluation uses the standard Precision/Recall/F-Measure metrics:

$$\text{Precision} = \frac{\text{num of correctly proposed NEs}}{\text{num of proposed NEs}}$$

$$\text{Recall} = \frac{\text{num of correct proposed NEs}}{\text{num of gold standard NEs}}$$

$$\text{F-measure}_\beta = \frac{(\beta^2 + 1) \times \text{Precision} \times \text{Recall}}{\beta^2 \times \text{Precision} + \text{Recall}}$$

The results in the table show that boosting already sets the bar very high for NTPC to improve upon. Nevertheless, NTPC manages to achieve a performance improvement on *every* task/language combination. This holds true across all languages – from English, on which the baseline accuracy is high to begin with; to German, on which the boosting model performs the worst.

We now identitfy and discuss some of the key characteristics of NTPC that contribute to its effectiveness.

4.1 Templated Hypothesis Generation

One of the inputs to NTPC is a set of pre-defined templates. These templates are formed from conjunctions of basic features such as part-of-speech, lexical identity and gazetteer membership, and may be as simple as "lexical identity of the current word AND the part-of-speech of the previous word", or as complex as "capitalization information of the previous, current and next words AND the lexicon and gazetteer membership statuses of the current word AND the current (i.e. most recent) class label of the current word." The rule hypotheses are generated according to these templates, as such, the templates are usually motivated by linguistically informed expectations.

The advantage of using hypotheses which are template-driven is that it allows the user to "tune" the system by writing templates which specifically target either the task at hand, or error patterns which are frequently committed by the base learner. They can also be used to prevent the error corrector from wasting time and memory by excluding rule templates which would be useless or overly trivial. In addition, these rule hypotheses are also often more complex and sophisticated than what the base models (in our case, decision stumps from AdaBoost.MH) can handle.

Table 1. NTPC consistently yields further F-measure gains on all eight different high-accuracy NER base models, across every combination of task and language.

Model	Task	Language	Experiment	Precision	Recall	F-Measure$_1$
M1	NE Bracketing	Dutch	M1	87.27	91.48	89.33
			M1 + NTPC	**87.44**	**92.04**	**89.68**
M2	NE Bracketing	English	M2	95.01	93.98	94.49
			M2 + NTPC	**95.23**	**94.05**	**94.64**
M3	NE Bracketing	German	M3	**83.44**	65.86	73.62
			M3 + NTPC	83.43	**65.91**	**73.64**
M4	NE Bracketing	Spanish	M4	89.46	87.57	88.50
			M4 + NTPC	**89.77**	**88.07**	**88.91**
M5	NE Classification + Bracketing	Dutch	M5	70.26	73.64	71.91
			M5 + NTPC	**70.27**	**73.97**	**72.07**
M6	NE Classification + Bracketing	English	M6	88.64	87.68	88.16
			M6 + NTPC	**88.93**	**87.83**	**88.37**
M7	NE Classification + Bracketing	German	M7	**75.20**	59.35	66.34
			M7 + NTPC	75.19	**59.41**	**66.37**
M8	NE Classification + Bracketing	Spanish	M8	74.11	72.54	73.32
			M8 + NTPC	**74.43**	**73.02**	**73.72**

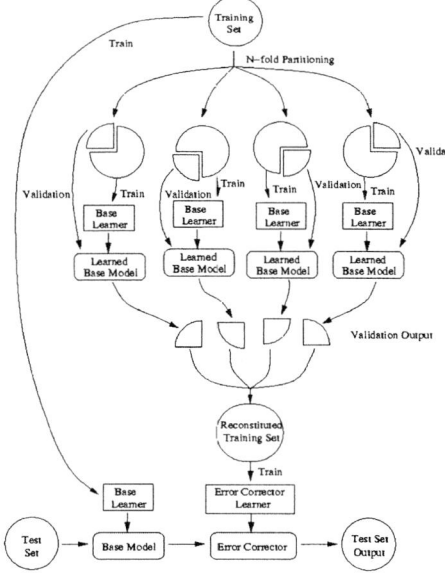

Fig. 1. Piped architecture with n-fold partitioning.

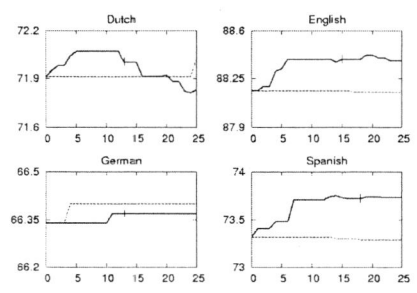

Fig. 2. Performance improvement is not reliably obtained without n-fold partitioning. (x-axis = number of rules learned, y-axis = F-Measure; bold = NTPC, dashed = without n-fold partitioning).

Empirical Confirmation. To judge the contribution of templated hypothesis generation, we examine the top rules learned for each language. The following shows several example rules which are representative of those learned by NTPC.

- *German rule 2*: (if the current word is currently labeled as part of a PERSON name, but the word "pradesh" follows in one of the succeeding three words, make it part of a LOCATION name)

```
        ne_0=I-PER
        word:[1,3]=pradesh
        => ne=I-LOC
```
- *Spanish rule 3*: (if the current word and the previous word are both uppercased but don't start a new sentence, and the following word is lowercased, and the current word is not in the lexicon nor in the gazetteer and is currently not part of a named entity, make it part of an ORGANIZATION name)
```
        wcaptype_0=noneed-firstupper
        wcaptype_-1=noneed-firstupper
        wcaptype_1=alllower
        captypeLex_0=not-inLex
        captypeGaz_0=not-inGaz
        ne_0=0
        => ne=I-ORG
```
- *Dutch rule 1*: (if the current word is "de", labeled as part of a PERSON's name and is uppercased but is the first word in a sentence, it should not be part of a named-entity)
```
        ne_0=I-PER
        word_0=de
        captype_0=need-firstupper
        => ne=0
```

The templates for these rules were all written with the base learner errors in mind, and thus contain highly complex conjunctions of features. It is a valid question to ask whether it is possible to add these conjunctive features to the base AdaBoost learner as additional decision stump features. This was indeed attempted, but AdaBoost was not able to handle the combinatorial explosion of feature-value pairs generated as a result.

4.2 Sensitivity to Right Context

One of NTPC's advantages over the base model is its ability to "look forward" to the right context. The problem for many NLP tagging and chunking models, where the unit of processing is a sentence, is that the text is processed from left-to-right, with the classifier deciding on the class label for each word before moving onto the next one. The result is that when features are extracted from the corpus for a particular word, the only class labels that can be extracted as features are those from the preceding (left-context) words. Since the words are labeled in order, the words that come later in the order (those in the right context) are not labeled yet, and as such, their labels cannot be used as features.

NTPC deals with this problem since the base model has already assigned a set of fairly accurate labels to all the words in the corpus. The error corrector has access to all these labels and can use them as word features as it deems necessary.

Empirical Confirmation. Our experiments confirmed that NTPC's ability to include right context features into its rules helped it outperform the base model. On average, 2-3 of the top ten rules learned for each language were right-context sensitive. The following shows an example of such a rule:

- *Dutch rule 6*: (if the current word is currently labeled as part of a PERSON's name, and the next word does not contain any uppercase characters and is currently not part of any named entity, take the current word out of the PERSON's name)
    ```
    ne_0=I-PER
    ne_1=0
    captype_0=alllower
    => ne=0
    ```

4.3 N-Fold Piping

The n-fold partitioning and "reconstitution" of the training set for NTPC's error corrector is a crucial step for NTPC's error corrector. The highly accurate labels generated by the base model are not as trivial and harmless as they appear – in fact, their presence results in very sparse data for the error corrector to learn from, and makes it very hard for the error corrector to generalize. If the n-fold partitioning step were omitted from the NTPC system, it would cause the error corrector to go astray easily. This is unlike the case of, say, transformation-based tagging, in which the training set is partitioned just once, as the poor initial state of the data actually serves to provide a strong bias that forces the learner to generalize across many examples. For this reason, it is important to correctly generate the n-fold cross validation partition sets with the base model. However, this is a time-consuming step, which may explain why it seems to be omitted from NLP models.

Empirical Confirmation. The n-fold piping is a complicated process and it is valid to ask whether this is actually necessary in practice. To test this, four experiments were performed, where the trained base model was used directly to relabel the training data. This data, together with the reference labels, was then provided to the error corrector as training data.

Figure 2 shows the results of the experiments. The stopping point for training (when $\tau(r) < \tau_{min}$) is denoted by the short vertical bar on each NTPC performance curve. The high performance of the base learner *on its own training data* creates a very small $\tau(r)$ at the start of training process – and as a result, *zero* error correcting rules are learned. It is possible to ignore the τ_{min} constraint and learn rules with very low $\tau(r)$ (the dashed lines show the performance of these rules). However, since these rules are mostly of dubious quality and also apply far and few in between, in most cases, they will not improve performance, and may even cause more errors to result – and it is not possible to reliably predict when a performance improvement will happen. In contrast, NTPC will *always* give a performance improvement.

4.4 Zero Error Tolerance

One of the most extreme decisions in the NTPC was the $\epsilon(r) = 0$ condition in *Error_Corrector_Learner*. In effect, this means that NTPC allows zero tolerance for noise and is overwhelmingly conservative about making any changes. The reason for this is, as an error *corrector*, NTPC has to be extremely careful not to introduce new errors. Since we have no information on the certainty of the base model's predictions, we assume that the training and testing corpora are drawn from the same distribution. This would mean that if a rule makes a mistake on the training corpus, it would be similarly likely to make one on the test corpus. Thus, to avoid over-eagerly miscorrecting the base model's predictions, the error corrector was designed to err on the side of caution and not make any corrections unless it has extremely high confidence that whatever it does will not cause any additional harm.

There are some structural similarities between NTPC and methods such as decision list learning (Rivest [1987]) and transformation-based learning (Brill [1995]), and some of the design decisions of NTPC may seem extreme when compared to them. However, these methods were not designed to be run on top of high-performing base models. A traditional rule list which is working on a very poorly labelled data set may be able to justify trading off some corrections with some mistakes, provided that the overall change in accuracy is positive. NTPC, on the other hand, is designed for situations in which the base accuracy of the initial data is already very high to begin with. With errors so few and far at hand, the sparse data problem is exacerbated. Furthermore, an error correction algorithm should, at the very least, not create more errors than it started out with, which is a valid argument on the side of being conservative. Overall, NTPC's approach and design decisions are well-justified when the details of the task at hand are considered.

Empirical Confirmation. The final issue behind NTPC's design is the $\epsilon(r) = 0$ condition in *Error_Corrector_Learner*. Considering that algorithms such as decision lists and transformation-based larning allow for some degree of error in their decisions, this seems like an overly extreme decision. Figure 3 shows results of experiments which compare NTPC against four other systems that allow relaxed $\epsilon(r) \leq \epsilon_{max}$ conditions for various $\epsilon_{max} \in \{1, 2, 3, 4, \infty\}$. The system that only considers net performance improvement – i.e. $\epsilon_{max} = \infty$, as transformation-based learning would have done – gets the worst performance in every case. Overall, the most accurate results are achieved by keeping $\epsilon(r) = 0$ – which also achieves the most consistent results over time (number of rules learned). This bears out our hypothesis for keeping a zero error tolerance design.

5 Conclusion

We have introduced a general conservative error-correcting model, **N-fold Templated Piped Correction** (NTPC) that, unlike other existing models, can reliably deliver small but consistent gains on the accuracy of even high-performing base models on high-dimensional tasks, with little risk of accidental degradation. We have given theoretical rationales and empirical evidence to show that the various design parameters underlying NTPC are essential, including (1) easily customizable template-driven hypothesis generation, (2) sensitivity to right

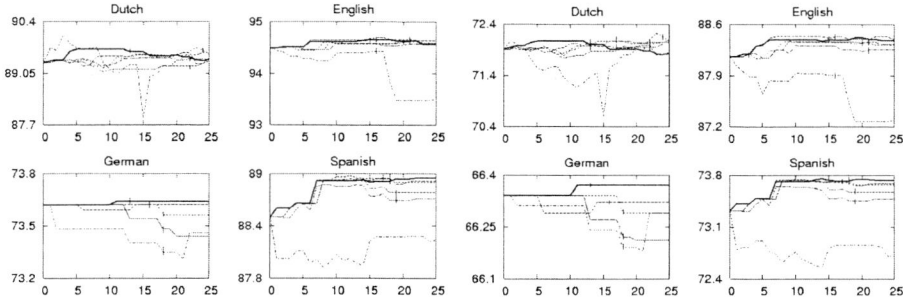

Fig. 3. NTPC's zero tolerance condition yields less fluctuation and generally higher accuracy than the relaxed tolerance variations, in bracketing experiments (left) as well as bracketing + classification experiments (right). (x-axis = number of rules learned, y-axis = F-Measure; bold = NTPC, dashed = relaxed tolerance).

context, (3) n-fold piping, and (4) zero error tolerance. The resulting method is robust and should be well suited for a broad range of sequential and classification NLP tasks such as bracketing and disambiguation.

The most frequently raised questions regarding NTPC concern whether its simplicity is justified, compared with more "sophisticated" models, particularly error correctors like TBL or decision lists. Yet in investigating these questions by explicit contrast against an earlier error corrector model, Stacked TBL (Wu et al. [2004]), we have assembled still further empirical confirmation bearing out the fact that the Occam's Razor assumptions underlying NTPC yield higher performance (Wu et al. [2004]).

References

[1995] Eric Brill. Transformation-based error-driven learning and natural language processing: A case study in part of speech tagging. *Computational Linguistics*, 21(4):543–565, 1995.

[2002] Xavier Carreras, Lluís Màrques, and Lluís Padró. Named entity extraction using AdaBoost. In Dan Roth and Antal van den Bosch, editors, *Proceedings of CoNLL-2002*, pages 167–170. Taipei, Taiwan, 2002.

[2000] Gerard Escudero, Lluis Marquez, and German Rigau. Boosting applied to word sense disambiguation. In *European Conference on Machine Learning*, pages 129–141, 2000.

[1997] Yoram Freund and Robert E. Schapire. A decision-theoretic generalization of on-line learning and an application to boosting. In *Journal of Computer and System Sciences, 55(1)*, pages 119–139, 1997.

[1987] Ronald L. Rivest. Learning decision lists. *Machine Learning*, 2(3):229–246, 1987.

[2000] Robert E. Schapire and Yoram Singer. Boostexter: A boosting-based system for text categorization. *Machine Learning*, 2(3):135–168, 2000.

[2003] Erik Tjong Kim Sang and Fien Meulder. Introduction to the CoNLL-2003 shared task: Language-independent named entity recognition. In Walter Daelemans and Miles Osborne, editors, *Proceedings of CoNLL-2003*. Edmonton, Canada, 2003.

[2002] Erik Tjong Kim Sang. Introduction to the CoNLL-2002 shared task: Language-independent named entity recognition. In Dan Roth and Antal van den Bosch, editors, *Proceedings of CoNLL-2002*, pages 155–158. Taipei, Taiwan, 2002.

[2002] Koji Tsukamoto, Yutaka Mitsuishi, and Manabu Sassano. Learning with multiple stacking for named entity recognition. In Dan Roth and Antal van den Bosch, editors, *Proceedings of CoNLL-2002*, pages 191–194. Taipei, Taiwan, 2002.

[2002] Dekai Wu, Grace Ngai, Marine Carpuat, Jeppe Larsen, and Yongsheng Yang. Boosting for named entity recognition. In Dan Roth and Antal van den Bosch, editors, *Proceedings of CoNLL-2002*, pages 195–198. Taipei, Taiwan, 2002.

[2003] Dekai Wu, Grace Ngai, and Marine Carpuat. A stacked, voted, stacked model for named entity recognition. In Walter Daelemans and Miles Osborne, editors, *Proceedings of CoNLL-2003*, pages 200–203. Edmonton, Canada, 2003.

[2004a] Dekai Wu, Grace Ngai, and Marine Carpuat. Raising the bar: Stacked conservative error correction beyond boosting. In *Fourth International Conference on Language Resources and Evaluation (LREC-2004)*. Lisbon, May 2004.

[2004b] Dekai Wu, Grace Ngai, and Marine Carpuat. Why nitpicking works: Evidence for Occam's Razor in error correctors. In *20th International Conference on Computational Linguistics (COLING 2004)*. Geneva, Aug 2004.

A Three Level Cache-Based Adaptive Chinese Language Model

Junlin Zhang, Le Sun, Weimin Qu, Lin Du, and Yufang Sun

Institute of Software, Chinese Academy of Sciences,
P.O.Box 8717,Beijing, 100080, P.R. China
Junlin01@iscas.cn

Abstract. Even if n-grams were proved to be very powerful and robust in various tasks involving language models, they have a certain handicap that the dependency is limited to very short local context because of the Markov assumption. This article presents an improved cache based approach to Chinese statistical language modeling. We extend this model by introducing the Chinese concept lexicon into it. The cache of the extended language model contains not only the words occurred recently but also the semantically related words. Experiments have shown that the performance of the adaptive model has been improved greatly.

1 Introduction

Statistical language models are core components of speech recognizers, optical character recognizers and even some machine translation systems. The most common language modeling paradigm used today is based on n-grams local word sequences. These models make a Markovian assumption on word dependencies; usually that word predictions depend on at most k previous words. Therefore they offer the following approximation for the computation of a word sequence probability:

$$P(w_i \mid h) \approx P(w_i \mid w_{i-n+1}^{i-1}) \ . \tag{1}$$

Even if n-grams were proved to be very powerful and robust in various tasks involving language models, they have a certain handicap: because of the Markov assumption, the dependency is limited to very short local context. Though cache language models [1] try to overcome this limitation by boosting the probability of the words already seen in the history, we think the method is still not good enough. In this paper we extend the classical cache language model into a three level cache based Chinese language model. The approach we present in this paper is based on the following observations: (1) author attempts to make use of the related words of previously used vocabulary to avoid the repetition of the same word. (2) A document always focuses on some specific topic, that is, many content words in the document relate to each other semantically. So we introduce the concept lexicon into the cache model. The extended cache contains not only the words history but also some semantically related words of vocabulary in the history. Experiments have shown that the performance of this adaptive model has been improved greatly.

In what follows, Section 2 discusses some of the related research. Section 3 describes our approach in detail. Section 4 is our evaluation about the improved cache based Chinese language model. Finally, Section 5 summarizes the work in this paper and discussed some of the future work.

2 Cache Based Language Model

It is commonly observed phenomena that words which have occurred recently are more likely to occur in future than would be predicted by a standard n-gram model. Cache-based language models are an attempt to exploit this fact. Typically a cache-based component is linearly interpolated with an n-gram language model:

$$P(w_i | w_1^{j-1}) = \lambda P_{cache}(w_i | w_1^{j-1}) + (1-\lambda) P_{n-gram}(w_i | w_{i-n+1}^{j-1}) . \tag{2}$$

The most common approach is that a cache of the previous K words is maintained, and a word's cache-based probability is computed as the relative frequency of the word within the cache. That is

$$P_{cache}(w_i | w_1^{i-1}) = \frac{1}{k} \sum_{j=i-k}^{i-1} I_{\{w_j = w_i\}} \quad I_\varepsilon = \begin{cases} 1, & \varepsilon = true \\ 0, & \varepsilon = false \end{cases} . \tag{3}$$

where I_ε is an indicator function which equals 1 if word in cache occurred, and 0 otherwise.

Such models were first proposed by Kuhn [1]. A cache-based component was added to a class-based n-gram model. A 200-word cache was maintained for each class, and the interpolation weight was chosen for each class separately. This model resulted in a decrease in perplexity over their baseline class-based language model [2].

Several researchers have built upon the work of Kuhn and De Mori. The obvious extension has been to add a cache-based component to a word-based n-gram, rather than a class-based model. Typically this has resulted in a reduction of perplexity [3].

The cache need not be limited to containing single words. Work has been conducted in which the probabilities of recently occurring bi-grams and tri-grams are also boosted [4]. This has met with fairly limited success in comparison to the results of the straightforward unigram cache, possibly because there are no enough information in the previous few hundred words to reliably estimate bi-gram and tri-gram probabilities.

Cache-based language models can be extended further by the use of decaying model[5]. In a regular cache model, the distance between the words has nothing to do with their mutual influence. While this assumption doesn't make sense in the decaying model, it takes into the distance of the words into account and thinks the influence will decrease with the enlargement of the distance between two words. Experiment shows that this method is effective.

3 Three Level Cache Based Chinese Language Modeling

3.1 Concept Lexicon

We use the "TongYiCi CiLin"[6] as the concept lexicon in this paper. "Ci Lin" is a Chinese concept lexicon which contains approximately 70 thousands of concepts. All the concepts are arranged into three-level categories according to their semantics. Top level of "CiLin" consists of 12 main classes which are labeled by English capital letters. The second level of 'CiLin" consists of 94 classes which are labeled by English lower case letters. In the third level, concepts are classified into 1428 classes using the number as the label. All the concepts in the same class of the third level category are regarded as synonym. For example, given the word "小时" (xiaoshi/Hour), We can find the synonyms such as "钟点"(zhongdian/Hour), "钟头" (zhongtou/Hour) and "时"(Shi/Time).

3.2 Chinese Bi-gram Language Model Training

Chinese has some special attributes and challenges. For example, there is no standard definition of a word and there are no spaces between characters in Chinese. However, statistical language models require word boundaries. Word-based language models work very well for Western languages where words are well defined, they are difficult to apply to Chinese. We might think that character language models could bypass the issue of word boundaries, but previous work found that a Chinese language model built on characters did not yield good results[7]. So our Chinese bi-gram language model is word-based, and thus requires a lexicon and a segmentation algorithm. Chinese language model training consists of several serial steps: Firstly, the training text is segmented on the basis of a predefined lexicon. The bi-gram language model is then trained on the segmented training set. To avoid the data sparse problem, we adopt the Witten-Bell smoothing approach in our static language model [8].

3.3 Three-Level Cache Based Chinese Language Model

The main problem in designing a cache based language model is to determine following factors: (1) which information should come from the cache; (2) which information should come from the static part of the model; (3) how these can be combined.

We extend the classical cache language model into a three level cache based Chinese language model. The approach we present in this paper is based on the following observations: (1) author attempts to make use of the related words of previously used vocabulary to avoid the repetition of the same word. (2) A document always focuses on some specific topic, that is, many content words in the document relate to each other semantically. So we introduce the concept lexicon into the cache model. The extended cache contains not only the words history but also some semantically related words of vocabulary in the history. In this model, the cache consists of the following three level sub-caches: original cache, synonym cache and semantic cache.

The original cache stores the recently occurred words in the document as classical cache language model does and the size of the cache is a fixed number. The language model of this level cache is a unigram language model of the recently occurred vocabulary in the document like this:

$$P_{orig-cache}(w_i | w_1^{i-1}) = \frac{1}{k} \sum_{j=i-k}^{i-1} I_{\{w_j = w_i\}} \quad I_\varepsilon = \begin{cases} 1, & \varepsilon = True \\ 0, & \varepsilon = False \end{cases} \quad (4)$$

where I_ε is an indicator function which equals 1 if word occurred, and 0 otherwise. k is the size of the first level cache.

Then we search the synonyms of the word occurred in the first level cache from "TongYiCi CiLin" and store them into the second level cache (synonym cache). We formally define the synonym cache as following:

$$SynCache = \{w_{i,j} \mid w_{i,j} \propto w_i \wedge w_i \in OrigCache\}$$

where $\propto$ denotes a synonym relationship derived from the "CiLin" and "OrigCache" denotes the vocabulary set of recently occurred word. Here the language model of synonym-cache is a unigram language model of the synonym related with the words in original cache. We compute this language model like this:

$$P_{syn-cache}(w_i \mid w_1^{i-1}) = \frac{1}{m} \sum_{j=(i-k)}^{i-1} \sum_{t=0}^{s} I_{\{w_{j,t}=w_i\}} \quad I_\varepsilon = \begin{cases} 1, & \varepsilon = True \\ 0, & \varepsilon = False \end{cases} \quad (5)$$

where I_ε is an indicator function which equals 1 if word occurred in synonym cache, and 0 otherwise. k is the size of the original cache. m is the size of the synonym cache $w_{t,j}$ belongs to synonym cache and denotes the number t synonym of the number j word in the original cache. s denotes the size of the synonym set for the number j word in the original cache.

What semantic cache stores are the semantically related vocabularies of the words in the original cache. We extract these words from "CiLin". An article always focuses on specific topic, so its content words expressing the meaning of the topic are semantically related with each other to some extent. We think the words which are more abstract than the synonym level in the concept tree of the "CiLin" can reflect this semantic relation. For example, we can derive the following semantically related vocabulary set from the concept lexicon:{阀门 (valve)/Bo030117, 火花塞 (spark plug)/Bo030115, 传动带 (driver) /Bo030111, 活塞 (piston)/Bo030118, 离合器 (clutch)/Bo030121, 螺钉 (bolt)/Bo030130}.It's not hard to observe the meaning cohesion of these words to express some topic. We can formally define the semantic cache as following:

$$SemanCache = \{w_{i,j} \mid w_{i,j} \perp w_i \wedge w_i \in OrigCache \wedge w_{i,j} \notin synCache\}$$

where $\perp$ denotes a "semantic relation" between words. Semantic cache language model is a unigram language model of the semantically related words of the vocabularies in the original cache. It can be computed as following:

$$P_{seman-cache}(w_i \mid w_1^{i-1}) = \frac{1}{m} \sum_{j=(i-k)}^{i-1} \sum_{t=0}^{s} I_{\{w_{j,t}=w_i\}} \quad I_\varepsilon = \begin{cases} 1, & \varepsilon = True \\ 0, & \varepsilon = False \end{cases} \quad (6)$$

where I_ε is an indicator function which equals 1 if word occurred in semantic cache, and 0 otherwise. k is the size of the original cache. m is the size of the semantic cache Here $w_{t,j}$ belongs to semantic cache and denotes the number t related word of the number j word in the original cache. s denotes the size of the related words set for the number j word in the original cache.

This way we have 4 language models now: a static language model, original cache language model, synonym cache language model and semantic cache language model. We interpolate the 4 language models into a three level cache based adaptive language model as equation (7). where λ、μ、ψ and δ are weight parameters. In actual computation, we can use EM approach to decide the value of them [9]. For example, equation 8 shows one computation step of the parameter λ:

$$P(w_i | w_1^{i-1}) = \lambda P_{orig\text{-}cache}(w_i | w_1^{i-1}) + \mu P_{syncache}(w_i | w_1^{i-1}) + \psi P_{seman\text{-}cache}(w_i | w_1^{i-1}) + \delta P_{n\text{-}gram}(w_i | w_{i-n+1}^{i-1}) \ . \quad (7)$$

$$\lambda_r = \frac{1}{n} \sum_d \frac{\lambda_{r-1} P_{orig\text{-}cache}(w_i | w_1^{i-1})}{\lambda_{r-1} P_{orig\text{-}cache}(w_i | w_1^{i-1}) + \mu_{r-1} P_{syncache}(w_i | w_1^{i-1}) + \psi_{r-1} P_{seman\text{-}cache}(w_i | w_1^{i-1}) + \delta_{r-1} P_{n\text{-}gram}(w_i | w_{i-n+1}^{i-1})} \ . \quad (8)$$

4 Experiments

The text corpus we used consists of approximately 50 million Chinese characters, containing documents with different domains, styles, and times. We randomly choose 80% of the documents in the corpus to train the Chinese bi-gram language model and the left documents in the corpus were used to evaluate the three-level cache based Chinese language model.

Three experiments were made on the corpus. The first one was designed to observe the influence of synonym factor after combining the classical cache based language model and the synonym cache language model. In this experiment, we regard the word number of the current document as the size of the cache and clear the cache after processing one document in order to make sure there is no influence between the different documents. The result can be seen in the table 1. From the result we know that the perplexity of the classical cache language model decrease 14.8% compared with the n-gram model. After combining the synonym cache language model, the perplexity of the new language model decrease 5.7% compared with classical cache model. So this indicates a better predicting ability of the synonym cache language model

Table 1. n-gram+original-cache+synonym -cache

	n-gram	n-gram+original-cache	n-gram+original-cache+synonym -cache
Perplexity	87.54	74.58	70.29

Table 2. n-gram□original-cache□semantic-cache

	n-gram+original-cache+semantic-cache
Perplexity	54.36

The second experiment was designed to observe the influence of semantically related words on the language model. We linearly interpolated the classical cache based language model with the semantic cache language model to form the new language model. Table 2 shows the experimental result. From the result we know that the perplexity of the new model decrease 27.1% compared with the classical cache language model. This indicates that the new model helps to find out those words describing topic of the document more precisely and greatly increases the performance of the language model.

In the third experiment we combine the synonym factor with the semantic cache model to see the total influence on the language model. Table 3 shows that the perplexity of the new model decrease 40.1% compared with the n-gram language model. This means the combination can produce a much better performance for the language model.

Table 3. n-gram+original-cache+synonym-cache+semantic-cache

	n-gram+original-cache+synonym -cache+semantic-cache
Perplexity	52.44

5 Conclusions and Future Work

We extend the classical cache language model into a three level cache based Chinese language model in this paper. The concept lexicon is introduced into the cache model and the extended cache contains not only the words history but also some semantically related words of vocabulary in the history. Experiments have shown that the performance of this adaptive model has been improved greatly. In the near future, we plan to explore the effect of combining current language model with decaying factor to find a better Chinese language model.

Acknowledgments

This work is supported by Beijing New Star Plan of Technology & Science (NO.H020820790130) and the National Science Fund of China under contact 60203007.

References

1. R. Kuhn, R. De Mori: A Cache-Based Natural Language Model for Speech Reproduction. IEEE Transactions on Pattern Analysis and Machine Intelligence(1990)
2. R. Kuhn, R. De Mori: Corrections to 'A Cache-Based Natural Language Model for Speech Reproduction'. IEEE Transactions on Pattern Analysis and Machine Intelligence (1992)
3. R. Iyer, M. Ostendorf: Modeling Long Distance Dependencies in Language: Topic Mixtures vs. Dynamic Cache Models. In Proceedings International Conference on Spoken Language Processing, Philadelphia, USA.(1996)
4. F. Jelinek, B. Merialdo, S. Roukos, M. Strauss: A Dynamic Language Model for Speech Recognition. In Proceedings of Speech and Natural Language DARPA Workshop (1991).
5. P. Clarkson, A. Robinson: Language model adaption using mixture and an exponentially decaying cache. In Boc. ICASSP-97 (1997)
6. Mei JiaJu, Zhu YiMing : TongYiCi Ci Lin. ShangHai‖ShangHai Dictionary Publication (1983)
7. K.C. Yang, T.H. Ho, L.F. Chien, L.S. Lee: Statistics-based segment pattern lexicon – a new direction for Chinese language modeling , in Proc. IEEE 1998 International Conference on Acoustic, Speech, Signal Processing, Seattle, WA. (1998) 169-172
8. I. Witten, T. Bell: The zero-frequency problem: Estimating the probabilities of Novel Events in adaptive text compression. In IEEE Transactions on Information theory. 37(4). (1991).
9. P. Dempster, N.M. Laivd, D.B. Rubin: Maximum likelihood from incomplete data via the EM algorithm. Journal of the Royal Statistical Society B,39:1-38 (1977)

Using a Smoothing Maximum Entropy Model for Chinese Nominal Entity Tagging

Jinying Chen, Nianwen Xue, and Martha Palmer

Department of Computer and Information Science
University of Pennsylvania, Philadelphia, PA, 19104, USA
{jinying,xueniwen,mpalmer}@linc.cis.upenn.edu

Abstract. This paper treats nominal entity tagging as a six-way (five categories plus non-entity) classification problem and applies a smoothing maximum entropy (ME) model with a Gaussian prior to a Chinese nominal entity tagging task. The experimental results show that the model performs consistently better than an ME model using a simple count cut-off. The results also suggest that simple semantic features extracted from an electronic dictionary improve the model's performance, especially when the training data is insufficient.

1 Introduction

Nominal entity tagging refers to the detection and classification of nominal entity mentions in textual data. The task is necessary to support higher-level NLP tasks such as co-reference resolution and relation detection, which is crucial for Information Extraction, Question-Answering and other NLP applications.

This paper treats nominal entity tagging as a classification problem and describes the results of applying a smoothing maximum entropy (ME) model with a Gaussian prior [1] to the Chinese nominal entity tagging task. The experimental results show that the model performs consistently better than an ME model using a simple count cut-off [2]. The results also suggest that simple semantic features extracted from an electronic dictionary improve the model's performance, especially when there is a severe sparse data problem.

In the next two sections, we briefly introduce the task of nominal entity tagging and the smoothing ME model with a Gaussian prior respectively. In Section 4, we describe the features we used in this task. We report our experimental results in Section 5 and conclude our discussion in Section 6.

2 Nominal Entity Tagging

It is generally the case that named entity mentions, nominal entity mentions and pronouns that refer to the same entity alternate in discourse. Nominal entity tagging, i.e., detecting and classifying the nominal entity mentions, is a first step towards resolving co-reference among different mentions of the same entity. Therefore, it is a crucial component to any Information Extraction or Question-Answering task that not only extracts entity mentions but also determines which entity mentions are co-referential and the relations between the entities.

Nominal entity tagging is a difficult problem because there is ambiguity involved in both nominal detection and classification. First, the same string can either be a nominal entity[1] or a non-nominal entity depending on the context. For example, "酒店/restaurant" is a nominal entity in "这/this 家/CL 酒店/restaurant", but it is part of a named entity in "五洲/Wuzhou 大/great 酒店/restaurant". In the classification task, the same string can belong to different categories based on the context. For example, "中心/center" is a facility in "康复/rehabilitation 中心/center" and a location in "广场/square 中心/center", depending on the local context of the current word (i.e., its pre-modifier in this case). A harder example involving global contextual information is shown in (1). Here, "港口/port" is a facility in (1a) but a geo-political entity in (1b).

(1) a. <u>广州/Guangzhou 的/DE 集装箱/container 港口/ **port**</u>，去年/last year 前9个月/the first nine months 的/DE 吞吐量/throughput 排名/rank 第5位/5th.
"The throughput of the container port in Guangzhou for the first 9 months of last year 5th."
b. 上海/Shanghai仍然/still是/is <u>中国/China 第一大/largest 的/DE集装箱/container 港口/ **port**</u>.
"Shanghai is still the largest container port in China."

Clearly, resolving these ambiguities is crucial to successful nominal entity detection and classification. Towards this end, we used a machine-learning approach, namely, a smoothing Maximum Entropy (ME) model with a Gaussian prior to solve this problem. Instead of treating detection and classification as two separate stages, we added a "non-entity" category to the five categories defined by LDC [3] and recast nominal entity tagging as a six-way classification problem. The five categories are Person (PER), Organization (ORG), Facility (FAC), Location (LOC) and Geo-political Entity[2] (GPE).

The LDC standard defines nominal entities over words as well as the phrases of which they are heads. The words are called **head words** and the phrases are called the **extents**. For example, in (1b), the GPE mention here includes both the head word "港口/port" and its extent "中国/China 第一大/largest的/DE集装箱/container 港口/port".

In our experiments, we segmented, POS-tagged and parsed the input text with an ME Segmenter [4], an ME POS-tagger [5] and a Chinese generative parser [6]. Since finding the head words is the most important part of the nominal entity tagging task, our focus in this paper is on detecting and classifying nominal words. We first used some heuristics to find the candidates. Briefly speaking, the candidates include all the common nouns as well as the words occurring in a nominal entity list extracted from the training data. We then ran the maximum entropy classifiers to decide which ones are nominal entities and what their categories are.

---

[1] In the rest of the paper, we do not explicitly distinguish between *nominal entities* and *nominal entity mentions*. The distinction can be made according to the context.
[2] GPE entities are geographical regions defined by political and/or social groups. A GPE entity subsumes and does not distinguish between a nation, its region, its government, or its people, e.g., 政府/government, 人民/people etc.

3   A Smoothing Maximum Entropy Model with a Gaussian Prior

Maximum Entropy (ME) modeling is a statistical approach that can be applied to any classification task [7]. The approach has been used to solve a wide range of NLP tasks, such as prepositional phrase attachment classification [8], part-of-speech tagging and parsing [2, 5] and word sense disambiguation [9] etc. An ME model combines evidence from different sources (features) without the independence assumption on its features.

In the nominal entity classification task, the ME model produces a probability for each category (PER, ORG, non-entity etc.) of a nominal entity candidate conditioned on the context in which the candidate occurs. The conditional probability is calculated by Equation (1),

$$p(l\,|\,c) = \frac{1}{Z(c)} \exp(\sum_{j=1}^{k} \lambda_j f_j(l,c)) \qquad (1)$$

where c represents the context containing the nominal candidate and l is the label for each entity category. $Z(c)$ is a normalization factor.

$f_j(l,c)$ represents the jth feature for the candidate and k is the total number of features used by the model. The features used in our model are all binary-valued feature functions (or indicator functions). A typical feature for training is shown in equation (2),

$$f_j(GPE, lastChar = 国)$$
$$= \begin{cases} 1 & \text{iff the candidate is labeled as} \\ & GPE\ \&\ its\ last\ character = 国 \\ 0 & otherwise \end{cases} \qquad (2)$$

Trained with labeled training data, an ME model can be regarded as a maximum likelihood model [7]. Like other maximum likelihood models, the ME model can suffer from overfitting. Several smoothing methods can be applied for ME models. Empirical evidence has shown that the smoothing ME model with a Gaussian prior performs better than the ME models with other smoothing methods and the basic idea of this approach is to use a zero-mean Gaussian prior with a diagonal covariance matrix to calculate the prior probability of the model [1].

In our experiments, we used Mallet, a Machine Learning for Language Toolkit that implements a smoothing ME model with a Gaussian prior[3] [10].

4   Features Used in the Model

The features used in our model include:
1. Simple features
   a. the current word w_0, and its part of speech tag p_0
   b. the words at positions −1 and +1, w_{-1} and w_{+1}, relative to w_0 and their part of speech tags p_{-1} and p_{+1}

---

[3] We choose the default value provided by Mallet, 1, as the value of the variance parameters after examining different values ranging from 0.1 to 10 with step value 0.1 by 10-fold cross-validation on the training data.

c. collocation features $p_{-1}w_0$, w_0p_{+1}
d. the last character lc of w_0
2. Syntactic features
   a. the word w'_{-1} preceding the minimal NP containing w_0, and its part of speech tag p'_{-1}
   b. the word w'_{+1} following the minimal NP containing w_0, and its part of speech tag p'_{+1}
3. Semantic features
   a. the semantic category s_0 of w_0 extracted from the Rocling dictionary, an electronic Chinese dictionary that assigns semantic categories to common nouns, such as *building* for "仓库/warehouse"
   b. collocation features $w_{-1}s_0$, $p_{-1}s_0$, s_0w_{+1}, s_0p_{+1}

The first three types of simple features (1a, b, c) are used to capture local contextual information about the current word. The features in (1d) are used to capture a particular property of many Chinese nouns, i.e., the last character of many Chinese nouns indicates their semantic categories. For example, "者/suffix" usually indicates the category of person, as in "记者/reporter", "作者/writer" and "读者/reader" etc.

The simple syntactic features are mainly used to capture the information contained in the pre-modifier or post-modifier of the NP containing the current word, as well as information from the main verb (with this NP as a subject or object) and punctuation information.

The simple semantic features are used to capture the semantic category of the current word. In our model, we use the current word and the surrounding words as lexical features. However, a model using only lexical information generally suffers from the problem of sparse data. In this case, the model needs to back off to more general features. The semantic features extracted from the Rocling dictionary and used here are more general than lexical features but still contain rich information about the word. Intuitively, this information should be very useful for deciding the category of a nominal entity. For example, a common noun representing a person usually has the semantic category *mankind*, and a word with the semantic category *region* is very likely to be a location. The Rocling dictionary contains 4474 entries and 110 semantic categories. It assigns one category to each Chinese noun without considering sense ambiguity. A rough count shows that about 30% of the candidates in the training and test data can be found in this dictionary.

5 Experimental Results

In our experiments, we trained and tested the model on the data set provided by LDC for the Automatic Content Extraction (ACE) research program, which contains a 110K-hanzi (Chinese characters) training data set and a 135K-hanzi evaluation data set. We compared our model's performance on the evaluation data set with a simple smoothing ME model that discards features occurring no more than 5 times in the training corpus. The experimental results are shown in Table 1. The precision is the number of correctly tagged nominal entities divided by the total number of nominal entities predicted by the nominal tagger for each category. The recall is the number of correctly tagged nominal entities divided by the total number of nominal entities in the evaluation data for each category. The scores are calculated based on the official ACE evaluation metric. According to this metric, a predicted nominal entity is correct when the overlap of its head and the head of the gold-standard nominal entity is over 1/3. The evaluation is performed on head words rather than the full extent of the nominal phrase since this is considered to be most important by this metric. Notice that the scores are calculated only for the five nominal categories. That is, non-entities are not considered.

The results in Table 1 clearly show that the ME model with a Gaussian prior is better than the ME model with a simple count cut-off, with a 6~7 percentage improvement for PER and GPE and a 10~20 percentage improvement for ORG and LOC.

We also investigated the effect of using simple semantic features discussed in Section 4. The experimental results, given in Table 2, indicate that the semantic features do improve the performance, boosting the performance by 2~3 percent for PER, GPE and ORG and over 15 percent for LOC and FAC.

The relatively low performance of the model on the last three categories (ORG, LOC and FAC) suggests that the training data may be insufficient. We did a rough count of the nominal entities in the training and evaluation data sets and found that the evaluation data set contains more entities than the training set. Furthermore, there are very few location and facility entities (fewer than 250) in the training set. Therefore, enlarging the training set should improve the model's performance further, especially for the last two categories.

Table 1. The performance of the two ME models on the evaluation data set

	The Smoothing ME Model with a Gaussian Prior (%)			The ME Model with Cut-off Threshold (%)		
	Prec.	Recall	F	Prec.	Recall	F
PER	88.13	72.26	79.41	89.38	60.97	72.49
GPE	80.47	67.95	73.68	74.76	61.54	67.51
ORG	69.83	45.83	55.34	64.98	33.50	44.21
LOC	70.10	46.13	55.64	67.96	22.58	33.90
FAC	66.88	28.31	39.78	68.21	27.25	38.94

Table 2. The performance of the smoothing ME model with a Gaussian prior with or without semantic features on the evaluation data set

	All Features (%)			W/o Semantic Features (%)		
	Prec.	Recall	F	Prec.	Recall	F
PER	88.13	72.26	79.41	89.35	67.95	77.19
GPE	80.47	67.95	73.68	82.14	61.14	70.10
ORG	69.83	45.83	55.34	75.00	40.35	52.47
LOC	70.10	46.13	55.64	70.40	28.39	40.46
FAC	66.88	28.31	39.78	79.10	14.02	23.82

To verify this, we randomly divided the evaluation data into two sets each of which has roughly an equal number of training files. One set is added to the official training data and the other set is used for testing. Now the training set contains roughly twice as many nominal entities as the test set. We retrained the ME model with a Gaussian prior and the results are shown in Table 3. In this table, we also give the model's performance with different feature sets (with or without semantic features). As we can see, the performance improves for all five categories and the improvement for the last two categories (LOC and FAC) are especially significant. Furthermore, the semantic features improve the model's performance consistently, although the improvement is not as dramatic as in the previous experiments with the smaller training set. This suggests that simple semantic features are especially useful when the training data is insufficient.

Finally, we give the performance of the two ME models trained on the enlarged training set in Table 4. The results show that the smoothing ME model with a Gaussian prior outperforms the simple smoothing ME model significantly, consistent with the results in the previous experiments.

Table 3. The performance of the ME model with a Gaussian Prior with or without semantic features trained on the enlarged training set

	All Features (%)			W/o Semantic Features (%)		
	Prec.	Recall	F	Prec.	Recall	F
PER	88.83	77.55	82.81	89.82	75.68	82.15
GPE	85.24	73.00	78.65	86.41	72.11	78.62
ORG	68.65	48.46	56.81	68.91	45.94	55.13
LOC	77.54	63.69	69.93	79.65	53.57	64.06
FAC	77.57	36.73	49.85	88.46	30.53	45.39

Table 4. The performance of the two ME models with semantic features trained on the enlarged training set

	The Smoothing ME Model with a Gaussian Prior (%)			The ME Model with Cut-off Threshold (%)		
	Prec.	Recall	F	Prec.	Recall	F
PER	88.83	77.55	82.81	91.31	65.32	76.16
GPE	85.24	73.00	78.65	83.45	65.72	73.53
ORG	68.65	48.46	56.81	66.17	37.25	47.67
LOC	77.54	63.69	69.93	81.13	51.19	62.77
FAC	77.57	36.73	49.85	80.72	29.65	43.37

An analysis of the tagging output shows that there are two major error types. The first error type comes from the preprocessing. In particular, segmentation errors often prevent the nominal tagger from finding the correct annotation candidates. For example, the nominal entity "发展中/developing 国家/country" was segmented as "发展/develop 中国/China 家/home". As a result, there is no easy way for the nominal tagger to get the correct candidate "国家/country", given that our tagger is word-based and relies on the segmentation output for finding the tagging candidates. The other major error type is due to the inability of the current model to capture global contextual information. For example, the word "港口/port" in the sentence shown in (1b) in section 2, repeated here as (2):

(2) 上海/Shanghai仍然/still是/is 中国/China 第一大/largest的/DE集装箱/container 港口/**port**.
"Shanghai is still the largest container port in China."

One useful piece of information that can help decide that "港口/port" is a GPE entity rather than a facility (as in (1a)) is the fact that "港口/port" refers to the same entity as "上海/Shanghai", a city in China. The features implemented in this model cannot capture such information.

6 Conclusion and Future Work

We have shown that a smoothing ME model with a Gaussian prior outperforms a simple smoothing ME model with a cut-off threshold in a Chinese nominal tagging task. The better performance remains consistent across training sets of different sizes, and different feature sets (with or without semantic features). We further showed that simple semantic features improve the model's performance, especially when the training data is insufficient. Given additional data, we expect that further improvement is possible.

For future work, we will explore using robust methods to incorporate more complicated features that encode co-reference. In addition, predicate-argument structure information might also help nominal entity tagging. For example, knowing the semantic role a noun plays with regard to a verb might help determine the nominal category of a noun. We will explore ways to extract such rich linguistic features using automatic methods [11, 12] and embed them into our model in a robust way in future work.

References

1. Chen, S.F., Rosenfeld, R.: A Gaussian Prior for Smoothing Maximum Entropy Modals. Technical Report CMU-CS-99-108, CMU (1999)
2. Ratnaparkhi, A.: Maximum Entropy Models for Natural Language Ambiguity Resolution. Ph.D. thesis, University of Pennsylvania (1998)
3. Mitchell, A., Huang, S.: Entity Detection and Tracking - Phase1: EDT and Metonymy Annotation Guidelines, Version 2.5 (2003)
4. Xue, N.: Chinese Word Segmentation as Character Tagging. International Journal of Compuational Linguistics and Chinese Language Processing, (2003) 8:1:29-48
5. Ratnaparkhi, A.: A Maximum Entropy Part-Of-Speech Tagger. In Proceedings of the Empirical Methods in Natural Language Processing Conference, University of Pennsylvania (1996)
6. Bikel, D.M.: Design of a Multi-lingual, Parallel-processing Statistical Parsing Engine. In Proceedings of HLT 2002, San Diego, CA, (2002) 24-27
7. Berger, A., Della Piertra, S., Della Pietra, V.: A maximum entropy approach to natural language processing. Compuational Linguistics, (1996) 22(1): 39-71
8. Ratnaparkhi, A., Reynar, J. and Roukos, S.: A Maximum Entropy Model for Prepositional Phrase Attachment. In Proceedings of the ARPA Human Language Technology Workshop, (1994) 250-255
9. Dang, H.T., Chia, C., Palmer, M., Chiou, F.: Simple Features for Chinese Word Sense Disambiguation. In Proceedings of COLING-2002 Nineteenth International Conference on Computational Linguistics, Taipei (2002)
10. McCallum, A.K.: "MALLET: A Machine Learning for Language Toolkit." http://www.cs.umass.edu/~mccallum/mallet (2002)
11. Gildea D., Jurafsky, D.: Automatic Labeling of Semantic Roles. Computational Linguistics (2002) 28:3, 245-288
12. Gildea, D., Palmer, M.S.: The Necessity of Parsing for Predicate Argument Recognition, In Proceedings of the 40th Meeting of the Association for Computational Linguistics, ACL-02, Philadelphia, PA (2002)

Deterministic Dependency Structure Analyzer for Chinese

Yuchang Cheng, Masayuki Asahara, and Yuji Matsumoto

Graduate School of Information Science
Nara Institute of Science and Technology, Nara 630-0192
{yuchan-c,masayu-a,matsu}@is.naist.jp

Abstract. We present a method of dependency structure analysis for Chinese. The method is a variant of Yamada's work (Yamada, 2003) originally proposed for English parsing. Our bottom-up parsing algorithm deterministically constructs a dependency structure for an input sentence. Support Vector Machines (SVMs) are utilized to determine the word dependency relations. Experimental evaluations on the CKIP Corpus show that the method is quite accurate on Chinese documents in several domains.

1 Introduction

Many syntactic analyzers for English have been implemented and have demonstrated good performance (Charniak, 2000; Collins, 1997; Ratnaparkhi, 1999). However, implementations of Chinese syntactic structure analyzers are still limited, since the structure of the Chinese language is quite different from other languages. We develop a Chinese syntactic structure analyzer. This paper presents our machine learning-based syntactic structure analyzer for Chinese.

The analyzer is a dependency structure analyzer. The reason the analyzer does not construct a phrase structure but a dependency structure is that dependency structures are simpler and more comprehensible than phrase structures. Construction of a word dependency annotated corpus is therefore easier than construction of a phrase structure annotated corpus which is used as training data. Consistency among annotators can also be more easily achieved by the simpler dependency structure.

We utilize a deterministic method for dependency relation construction. One approach to this problem is to use a generative dependency structure analysis consisting of two steps. First, a CYK-like dependency relation matrix is constructed, in which each element corresponds to a pair of tokens. The dependency relation between each pair is assigned a likelihood value. Second, the optimal dependency structure is estimated using the likelihood of the whole sentence, provided there is no crossing between dependencies. An alternative approach is to use a deterministic dependency structure analysis as proposed by (Kudo, 2002; Yamada, 2003). The dependency relations are composed by a bottom-up schema with machine learners. SVMs (Vapnik, 1998) estimate if there is a dependency relation between a pair of words deterministically in their methods (Kudo, 2002; Yamada, 2003). Our aim is to implement a variation of the latter deterministic method and to show how the method is applicable to Chinese dependency analysis.

Our analyzer is trained on the CKIP Chinese Treebank (K-J Chen et al, 1999), which is a phrase structure and head annotated corpus. The phrase structure is converted into a dependency structure according to the head information. We perform experimental evaluations in several settings on the corpus.

In the next section, we describe the CKIP Treebank used in our research. Section 3 shows our deterministic dependency analysis algorithm. Section 4 reports experimental evaluation and comparison with related work. Finally, we summarize our finding in the conclusion.

2 Corpus

2.1 CKIP Chinese Treebank

We use the CKIP Chinese Treebank Version 2.0 (K-J Chen et al, 1999) to train our analyzer. The corpus includes 54,902 phrase structure trees and 290,114 words in 23 files. The corpus has the following three properties:

(i) Word segmented, POS-tagged, parsed (phrase structure) and head annotated
(ii) Balanced corpus
(iii) Clause segmented by punctuation marks (commas and full stops)

These annotations are generated by a parser and are then manually revised.

The phrase structure is based on a lexical feature-based grammar formalism ICG – Information-based Case Grammar (Chen, 1996). The ICG representation includes thematic structures, phrasal structures and head-daughter dependency relations within brackets (K-J Chen et al, 1999; Lin, 1992; Chen and Huang, 1995).

The CKIP Treebank is a balanced corpus. Sentences in the corpus are selected from various media sources. The filenames in the corpus indicate the original source. We divide the corpus according to the sources, which is shown in section 4.1.

Since sentences in the CKIP Treebank are segmented into clauses by punctuation marks -- (, . ? !). The average word number of clauses is as short as 5.7 words.

2.2 Conversion of Treebank

The upper part of Table 1 shows a sample phrase structure in the CKIP Treebank. A bracketed token is a constituent in the phrase structure. Each token has the following structure: "Thematic role : POS-tag : word". The notation " | " means that the words on either side are siblings (K-J Chen et al, 1999). "Head" means that the constituent is the head word or phrase governing the siblings. We convert the phrase structures into the dependency structures based on the head information. The lower part of Table 1 shows the converted dependency structure. "Node ID" is the location of the word in the clause. "Parent node" identifies the parental node in the dependency structure. "Parent node -1" means that this word is the root node of the clause. Since the clauses in the corpus are chosen randomly, the corpus includes some corrupted clauses. (e.g. A clause with more than one root node.) We discard about 4,860 corrupted clauses to avoid confusion in SVM-training. Since these corrupted clauses don't compose complete tree structures. We use the remaining 50,002 clauses.

The number of the original POS-tags in the corpus is 289. The number of POS-tags is larger than the number of general purpose Chinese POS-tags. The reason for this is

Table 1. Tree structure conversion from phrase structure to dependency structure

NP(property:S的(head:S(agent:NP(Head:Nba:鄭成功)|
Head:VC31:收復|theme:NP(Head:Nca:臺灣))
|Head:DE:的)|property:VH11:偉大|Head:Nac:功業)
(*"The great triumph that Cheng Kheng-Koug recaptured Taiwan."*)

Word	POS	Node ID	Parent node
鄭成功	Nba	0	1
收復	VC31	1	3
臺灣	Nca	2	1
的	DE	3	5
偉大	VH11	4	5
功業	Nac	5	-1

Table 2. POS grouping

Grouped POS	Original POSs in the corpus
VA1	VA11, VA12, VA13
P	P1, P2,……,P60
Nha	Nhaa, Nhab, Nhac

that the POS-tags in this corpus are very fine-grained. For example, POS-tag "P31" and "P31 [+part]"[1] (CKIP, 1993) are regarded as two different tags. Fine-grained POS-tags are inefficiency for SVM-learning. According to (Chen and Huang, 1995), some POS have nearly the same function and can be generalized as one category. We group the 289 POS tags into 51 tags. Table 2 shows some examples of this POS grouping.

3 Parsing Methods

In this section, we describe our approach to Chinese dependency analysis. Our parsing algorithm is a variant of Yamada's work (Yamada, 2003). The dependency relations are composed by a bottom-up schem¹a. The algorithm has two major procedures:

(i) Extract the surrounding features for the current node
(ii) Estimate the dependency relation operation for the current node by SVMs (Vapnik, 1998)

First, we describe the algorithm. Second, we present the features for the SVMs. Third, we present an implementation issue – POS grouping.

3.1 Deterministic Dependency Analysis

Our dependency analysis is performed by a bottom-up schema. A dependency relation for each word position is represented by the following three operations: **shift**, **left** and

---

[1] The annotation "[ ]" means that the POS-tag has further semantic meaning, but the syntactic structure is the same as the POS-tag without "[ ]".

right. The operation is determined by a classifier – SVMs based on the surrounding features. The determination is iterated until the classifier cannot make any additional dependency relations on the whole sentence. The details of the three operations are as follows.

Shift means that there is no relation between the current node and the preceding (left adjacent) or the succeeding (right adjacent) node. In this case, the current node moves to the succeeding node. Figure 1 illustrates the shift operation. The current node is indicated by a square with thick lines in the figure. In this operation, no dependency relation is constructed.

Fig. 1. Shift operation

Right means that the current node becomes the child of the succeeding node. Figure 2 illustrates the right operation.

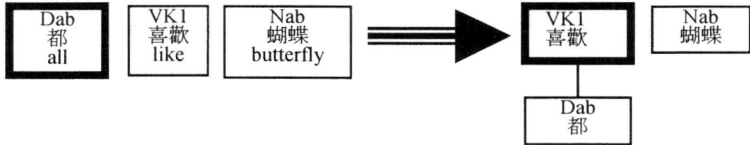

Fig. 2. Right operation

Left means that the current node becomes the child of the preceding node. Figure 3 illustrates the left operation.

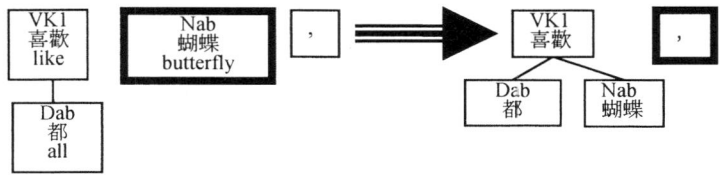

Fig. 3. Left operation

Note that before either the **left** or **right** operation is applicable to the current node, the current node should complete its child subtree. In other words, the current node cannot add any nodes to its child subtree. To check the subtree completion, the classifier utilizes surrounding features which are discussed in the next section.

The operation to apply is determined by SVMs (Vapnik, 1998). SVMs are a binary classifier based on a maximum margin strategy. Suppose we have a set of training data for a binary classification problem: $(x_1, y_1)...(x_n, y_n)$, where $x_i \in R^n$ is the feature vector of the i-th sample in the training data and $y_i \in \{+1,-1\}$ is the label of the sample. The goal is to find a decision function $f(x) = sign(\sum_{z_i \in SV} a_i y_i K(x,z_i) + b)$ for an input vector x. The vectors $z_i \in SV$ are called support vectors, which are representative examples. Support vectors and other constants are determined by solving a quadratic programming problem. $K(x,z)$ is a kernel function which maps vectors into a higher dimensional space. We use the polynomial kernel: $K(x,z) = (1 + x \cdot z)^d$. To extend binary classifiers to multi-class classifiers, we use a pair-wise method which utilizes $_nC_2$ binary classifiers between all pairs of the classes (Kreel, 1998).

This algorithm is shown in Figure 4. i is the index of the current node. T is a node sequence which consists of n elements $t_m (1 \leq m \leq n)$, each of which represents the root node of a sub-tree. Note: initially, all t_m are pairs of consisting a word and its POS tag $(w_i; p_i)$.

```
Input Sentence: (w_1, p_2), (w_2, p_2), ..., (w_n, p_n)
Initialize:
    i = 1 ; T = {(w_1, p_2), (w_2, p_2), ..., (w_n, p_n)}
    no construction = true ;
Start:
while |T| > 1 do begin
    if i == |T| then
        if no construction == true then break;
        no construction = true
        i = 1 ;
    else
        x = get contextual features(T; i) ; y = estimate action(model; x) ;
        construct subtree(T; i; y) ;
        if y == Left or Right then  no construction = false ;
    end;
    end;
end;
```

Fig. 4. Parsing algorithm

The algorithm contains the following three functions: *get contextual features, estimate action* and *construction*. *Get contextual features* extracts the contextual features surrounding i. *Estimate action* determines the appropriate dependency analysis operation -- namely **Right, Left,** or **Shift** – using SVMs. *Construct subtree* builds the subtree.

The variable *no construction* being *true* means that the model estimates **Shift** operations for all nodes in an iteration of the while loop. Because there is no further operation, the parser stops the analysis and outputs the subtrees in T. When the value of *no construction* is *false*, the current node moves to the beginning of the sentence, and the dependency analysis process is iterated until the size of T becomes 1. Sometime the classifier makes wrong decision and all nodes are subject to the shift operation. This situation means that the clauses cannot form a tree structure.

This algorithm is based on determination of classification procedures. Once a dependency relation is determined by SVMs, the relation cannot be rejected. In other words, the algorithm does not backtrack even if it cannot construct a complete dependency structure.

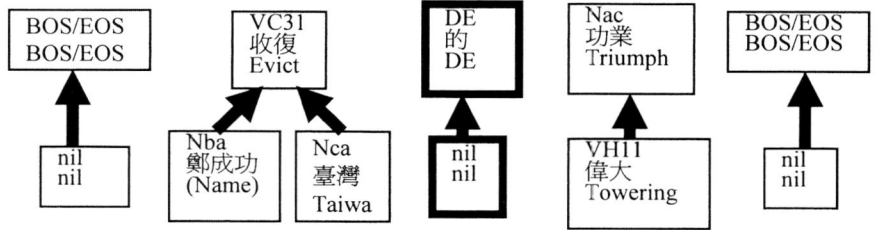

Fig. 5. An example of features used

3.2 Feature Extraction

The features for the current node are the words itself and the POS of 5 local nodes (the preceding 2 nodes, the current node, and the succeeding 2 nodes) and their child nodes. Figure 5 illustrates the features. The current node is "*DE*". All the information in the dashed box is extracted as the features. Note: our model uses only the immediate child nodes. We don't use grandchild nodes. The notation "*nil*" means there is no child for the node. The dummy node "*BOS/EOS*" represents the beginning or end of the sentence. Each word or POS in the context is represented as a pair "location-word" or "location-POS", and constitutes an element in the feature vector. The values of these elements are binary (1 (entity) or 0 (null)). SVMs use these binary feature vectors for analysis and classification.

3.3 Dividing the Training Data for Training Cost Reduction

The computational cost for training SVMs is higher than other statistical methods. If we use all the training data, it takes a long time for training. We therefore, divide the training data into smaller units of data according to the POS of the current node. The analyzer makes an SVM-model for each POS-tag and chooses the appropriate model during analysis. For instance, when the POS of the current node is "VC1", the analyzer uses the SVM-model trained using the data in which the current node is POS "VC1".

4 Experimental Evaluations

4.1 Experiments

We perform two experiments. First, in experiment (1) we investigate the influence of different data sources. Second, we investigate the influence of different data sizes in experiment (2). We use the polynomial Kernel function with degree d = 3 for SVMs through all settings.

Experiment (1) is aimed at comparing among the text categories. The files in the corpus are divided into four data sets according to the text categories. The data in each category are further divided into training and testing data. We use 80% of the data for training and 20% of the data for testing.

Experiment (2) aims to compare different training data sizes. We make 4 sets of training data of different sizes as shown in Table 4. We use the same test data as the experiment (1).

4.2 Results

The performance of our dependency structure analyzer is evaluated by the following three measures: Dependency Accuracy, Root Accuracy and Sentence Accuracy.

$$\text{Dependency Accuracy: } (Dep.\ Acc.) = \frac{\#\ of\ correctly\ analyzed\ dep.\ rel.}{\#\ of\ dep.\ rel.}$$

$$\text{Root Accuracy: } (Root.\ Acc.) = \frac{\#\ of\ correctly\ analyzed\ root\ nodes}{\#\ of\ clauses}$$

$$\text{Sentence Accuracy: } (Sent.\ Acc.) = \frac{\#\ of\ fully\ correctly\ analyzed\ clause}{\#\ of\ clauses}$$

The training data size in each of the four categories is approximately same. Table 3 shows the results of experiment (1). Though the training model "Anthology" is not the largest data, it achieves the best dep. accuracy when applied to the test data "Anthology", "Textbook", and "Magazine". The training model "Magazine" decreases the accuracy for the two test data "Anthology" and "Textbook". Whereas, all training data give better result in testing "Anthology" and "Textbook", but give worse result in testing "Magazine" and "News".

Table 4 shows the results of experiment (2). The results show that the accuracy of testing data "Anthology" and "Textbook" is almost saturated at the training data part (4), which has 64431 words. The other training data does not have clear saturation at part (4).

Table 3. Results : Comparisons among the categories

Experiment (1)		Accuracy (%)	Testing data			
			Anthology	Textbook	Magazine	News
Training data	Anthology	Dep. Acc.	**87.17**	**88.00**	**77.83**	73.63
		Root. Acc	94.05	93.51	88.64	85.36
		Sent. Acc.	**71.44**	74.42	**50.45**	49.21
	Textbook	Dep. Acc.	86.94	87.65	74.73	71.06
		Root. Acc	**94.44**	**93.63**	87.29	85.98
		Sent. Acc.	69.76	**74.71**	45.93	44.92
	Magazine	Dep. Acc.	79.51	82.88	76.62	74.07
		Root. Acc	89.92	92.47	**88.67**	**87.26**
		Sent. Acc.	51.80	61.69	48.33	48.63
	News	Dep. Acc.	85.32	86.94	75.24	**74.14**
		Root. Acc	93.28	92.76	88.23	86.89
		Sent. Acc	68.73	73.78	48.36	**50.16**

All these experiments are implemented on a Linux machine with XEON 2.4GHz dual CPUs and 4.0GB memory. The training time for part (4) was 34 minutes and 57 seconds, which was the longest in all experiments.

Table 4. Results: Comparisons among the training data sizes

Training data	Part(1)= KO10,11,12	Part(2)= All textbook	Part(3)= Part(2)+anthology	Part(4)= Part(3)+magazine 1.1
data size clauses/words	3770/ 17782	9920/ 44032	13036/ 64431	17213/ 89951
Textbook (test)	87.65 93.63 74.71	89.13 94.67 77.71	89.79 94.67 78.99	**90.75** **95.77** **81.19**
News (test)	71.06 85.98 44.92	73.24 86.10 48.39	75.24 86.85 51.97	**76.59** **88.16** **53.58**

4.3 Discussion

In experiment (1), the results show that the training model "Anthology" and the training model "Textbook" are better accuracy than the others. "Textbook" is used in elementary schools in Taiwan. "Anthology" is written using relatively simple expressions. Clauses in these categories have a more precise, shorter and simpler structure. Therefore the training models "Anthology" and "Textbook" include precise and fundamental Chinese dependency structure information. These models are more powerful than the models "Magazine" and "News". The models "Magazines" and "News" are based on many colloquial and elliptical expressions. Therefore, the models "Magazines" and "News" perform less well. For the same reasons, testing data "Magazine" and testing data "News" are harder to analyze than testing data "Anthology" and testing data "Textbook". All training models have better results when testing on "Anthology" and "Textbook", but worse when testing on "Magazine" and "News".

Zhou (2000) reports similar results to ours. In his experiments, the results for testing on texts from elementary schools in Singapore are better than testing on the "People's Daily" newspapers.

In experiment (2), when the training data is Part (3) or Part (4), the accuracy when testing on "Anthology" and "Textbook" increases slowly. This means that the accuracy is close to the models' limits. However in "Anthology" and "Textbook", the accuracy increases rapidly. We can be fairly confident that the efficiency when testing on "Magazine" and "News" can be further increase. To find the limits of accuracy for these categories, we need larger training data.

The average number of words in a clause is small. Some clauses include fewer than three words. These clauses are too short to represent a full syntactic structure. Such clauses make up less than 10% of words in the corpus. Clauses with more than 10 words make up 25% of words in the corpus. Although the average clauses length is small, the training data includes much longer clauses.

Here we note related work on parsing Chinese. Lai and Huang (2001) experimented on the Penn Chinese Treebank using a statistical method and achieved performance of about 86.1% for parent accuracy. Zhou (2000) experimented using elementary textbooks from Singapore and the newspapers "People's Daily" achieving precision of 90.4% and 67.7%. Since the experimental settings vary among researchers, we cannot compare accuracy directly. Considering dependency analysis of other languages, Kudo (2002) applied SVMs to Japanese dependency analysis with dependency accuracy of about 90%. Yamada, (2003) originally introduced the method used in this paper applied to English dependency analysis with results of about 90.1% (Dep. Acc.).

5 Conclusion

This paper presented a method for dependency structure analysis of Chinese based on Support Vector Machines. We evaluated our method on a dependency tagged corpus derived from the CKIP Treebank corpus. The method achieves 76%~91% accuracy on four different text types.

Future work includes two parts. First, since our experiment uses only 34% of training data, we will evaluate the accuracy again after increasing the training data. Second, as described in section 4.2, the average number of words in a clause is 5.7. We will evaluate our method on the Penn Chinese Treebank which contains longer sentences.

References

1. Eugene Charniak: A Maximum-Entropy-Inspired Parser. In Proc. of NAACL(2000)132–139
2. Keh-Jiann Chen, Chu-Ren Huang: 訊息為本的格位語法與其剖析方法. Technical report no. 95-03(1995)
3. Keh-Jiann Chen: A Model for Robust Chinese Parser. Computational Linguistics and Chinese Language Processing. vol. 1, no.1. (1996)183-204.
4. Keh-Jiann Chen, Chin-Ching Luo, Zhao-Ming Gao, Ming-Chung Chang, Feng-Yi Chen, Chao-Jan Chen: The CKIP Tree-bank: Guidelines for Annotation, Presented at ATALA Workshop (1999).
5. CKIP.: 中文詞類分析. Technical report no. 93-05(1993)
6. Michael Collins: Three Generative, Lexicalised Models for Statistical Parsing. In Proc.of ACL-EACL (1997) 16–23.
7. Ulrich. H.-G. Kreßel: Pairwise classification and support vector machines. In Advances in Kernel Methods, The MIT Press. (1998) 255–268.
8. Taku Kudo, Yuji Matsumoto: Japanese Dependency Analyisis using Cascaded Chunking, CONLL (2002)
9. Tom B. Y. Lai, C. N. Huang, Ming Zhou, Jiangbo Miao, T. K. C. Siun: Span-based Statistical Dependency Parsing of Chinese. NLPRS(2001)677–682
10. Fu-Wen Lin: Some reflections on the thematic system of Information-Based case Grammar. Technical report no. 92-01.(1992)
11. Adwait Ratnaparkhi: Learning to parse natural language with maximum entropy models. Machine Learning, 34(1-3)(1999)151–175
12. Vladimir N. Vapnik: Statistical Learning Theory. A Wiley-Interscience Publication.(1998)
13. Hiroyasu Yamada and Yuji Matsumoto: Statistical Dependency Analysis with Support Vector Machines, IWPT (2003)
14. Ming Zhou: A block-based robust dependency parser for unrestricted Chinese text, The second Chinese Language Processing Workshop attached to ACL (2000)

High Speed Unknown Word Prediction Using Support Vector Machine for Chinese Text-to-Speech Systems

Juhong Ha[1], Yu Zheng[1], Byeongchang Kim[2], Gary Geunbae Lee[1], and Yoon-Suk Seong[3]

[1] Department of Computer Science & Engineering,
Pohang University of Science & Technology,
Pohang, South Korea
{miracle,zhengyu,gblee}@postech.ac.kr

[2] Division of Computer and Multimedia Engineering, UIDUK University,
Gyeongju, South Korea
bckim@postech.ac.kr

[3] Division of the Japanese and Chinese Languages, UIDUK University,
Gyeongju, South Korea
seongys@empal.com

Abstract. One of the most significant problems in POS (Part-of-Speech) tagging of Chinese texts is an identification of words in a sentence, since there is no blank to delimit the words. Because it is impossible to pre-register all the words in a dictionary, the problem of unknown words inevitably occurs during this process. Therefore, the unknown word problem has remarkable effects on the accuracy of the sound in Chinese TTS (Text-to-Speech) system. In this paper, we present a SVM (support vector machine) based method that predicts the unknown words for the result of word segmentation and tagging. For high speed processing to be used in a TTS, we pre-detect the candidate boundary of the unknown words before starting actual prediction. Therefore we perform a two-phase unknown word prediction in the steps of detection and prediction. Results of the experiments are very promising by showing high precision and high recall with also high speed.

1 Introduction

In Chinese TTS, identification of words and assignment of correct POS (Part-of-Speech) tags for an input sentence are very important task. These steps have considerable effects on a Chinese-text-to-Pinyin conversion. Correctly converted pinyins are essential elements because they provide important information for selecting a synthesized unit in a speech database. But since there is no blank to delimit the words in Chinese sentences, we need a high quality word segmentation and POS tagging process for high quality pinyin conversion. However we can not include all the new words for segmentation and tagging in a dictionary even if we generate a word dictionary from very large amount of corpus. So, unknown word handling for correct pronunciation processing should be essential for more accurate and natural TTS sound.

Various kinds of pronunciation conversion methods for alphabet language including English have been proposed. For these methods, they used mainly statistical patterns and rules for unknown word pronunciation conversion. However, because most Chinese POS taggers split the unknown words into individual characters, unknown word processing method to group these individually splitted characters is naturally required for Chinese. Also, processing the words that include Chinese polyphonic characters is essential for correct pronunciation conversion. Piniyin conversion of Chinese polyphonic characters is a fairly complex problem, since there are no clear distinguished patterns.

We develop an unknown word processing method for Chinese person names, foreign transliterated names and location names among other proper nouns. For high speed and high performance processing to be useful in a TTS, we present a two-phase unknown word prediction method. At first, we pre-detect the candidate boundary of the unknown words from the result of segmentation and tagging. And then we predict unknown words using support vector machine which is one of the machine learning methods to exhibit the best performance.

Organization of this paper is as follows: First, section 2 examines some related methods on Chinese unknown word processing to compare with our method. Section 3 briefly introduces POSTAG/C[1] [4], which is a Chinese segmenter and POS tagger by automatic dictionary training from large corpus. In section 4, we explain a method to quickly choose the candidate boundaries of unknown words in a sentence for high speed processing. In section 5, we propose a classification method that predicts the unknown words and assigns the correct POS tags using Support Vector Machine. In section 6, we present some experiments and analysis results for person names and location names. Finally, in section 7, we make a conclusion and propose our future works.

2   Related Works

Word segmentation should be achieved as the first step for Chinese text processing. However, Chinese segmenter outputs a split into individual characters for the words that do not exist in a dictionary, and this splitting results in entirely wrong tags can be allocated in POS tagging step. Researches to solve the unknown word problems have been essential in Chinese text processing mainly to overcome the individual character splitting effects.

Chen and Ma proposed a statistical method for the problem[2]. They automatically generated morphological rules and statistical rules from Sinica corpus and try to predict the unknown words. Their results show a good precision of 89% but a marginal recall of 68% for Chinese person names, foreign transliterated names and compound nouns.

Zhang et al. presented a markov model based approach for Chinese unknown word recognition using a role tagging [6]. They defined a role set for every category of unknown words and recognized the unknown words by tagging with the role set using Viterbi algorithm. They only provide the recognition results

---
[1] POStech TAGger Chinese version.

of Chinese person and foreign transliteration names. They report a precision of 69.88% and a recall of 91.65% for Chinese person names and a precision of 77.52% and a recall of 93.97% for foreign transliteration names.

Goh et al. identified unknown words by a markov model based POS tagger and a SVM based chunker using character features [3]. Their experiments using one month news corpus from *the People's Daily* show a precision of 84.44% and a recall of 89.25% for Chinese person names and foreign transliteration names, a precision of 63.25% and a recall of 79.36% for organization names, and a precision of 58.43% and a recall of 63.82% for unknown words in general.

In this paper, we predict the unknown words using a SVM based method similar to Goh et al. [3]. However, we need a high-speed unknown word prediction method to be used in a real time voice synthesis system. Therefore, we first extract likely candidate boundaries where unknown words possibly occur in a sentence and then predict the words with these boundaries. So our method becomes a two-phase high speed processing method as shown in Fig. 1.

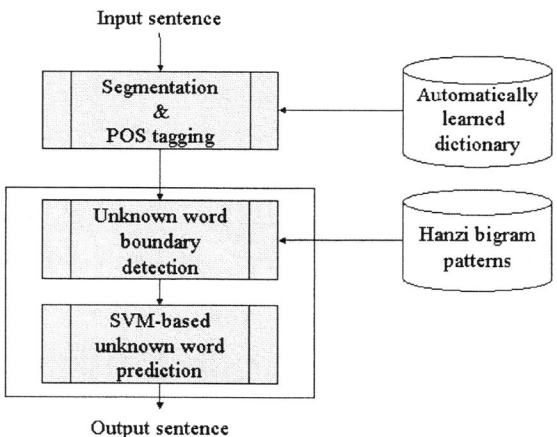

Fig. 1. Overall architecture of the proposed method.

3 Word Segmentation and POS Tagging

In our research, we used previously developed word segmentation and POS tagging system called POSTAG/C [4]. POSTAG/C is a system which combines word segmentation module based on rules and a dictionary with POS tagging module based on HMM (Hidden Markov Model). The word dictionary was fully automatically acquired by POS tagged corpus and the system has high portability to serve both GB texts as well as Big5 texts. Performance of the GB version achieves the precision and recall above 95%. The detail description will be outside of the paper's scope.

4 Detection of the Candidate Boundary

Each module which is a part of voice synthesis systems should be operated in real time. However, if we check all the texts to predict the unknown word from the beginning of input texts to the end, the speed may become very slow. Moreover, we need more efficient method if we take into account the slow speed of SVM which will be used in our research. SVM is one of the method to exhibit the best performance among all the machine learning methods, but slow learning and prediction time is its major shortcoming. To overcome the speed problems while not losing the accuracy, instead of examining the whole sentence, we detect the candidate boundaries where the occurrences of the unknown words are possible.

As a general Chinese word segmentation system, POSTAG/C also outputs a contiguous single Chinese character, hanzi, string for the unknown words. Therefore, we can use the boundary where single Chinese characters appear consecutively as the first candidates of the unknown words. Studies that show more than 90% of the unknown words are actually included in this boundary in Chinese theoretically support our approach [5]. Without stopping here, we extend our target boundary to increase the recall of the boundary detection by including 2-character words that exist around a single character and match to the hanzi bigram patterns with more than specified frequency. So, our system can cover the case such as in Fig. 2.

Fig. 2. Example of boundary detection including 2-character unknown words.

We can not use the sequence of all the single Chinese characters as the candidate boundaries because a single character very frequently can be used as a word. In our own statistics using the Chinese news paper, the number of total boundaries that are series of a single character in person names was 128,410 cases, but only 16,955 cases among them actually include the unknown words.

To cope with these spurious cases, we select the candidate boundaries for a series of single characters by matching to the pre-learned hanzi bigram patterns. These patterns are learned by person names and location names which are extracted from a training data. We generated the patterns by combining two characters which are adjacent in person names or location names. There are 34,662 person patterns and 15,958 location patterns used in our system. We select the boundaries where match with more than one bigram pattern.

5 SVM-Based Prediction of Unknown Word

We predict the unknown words from the output of the candidate boundary detection. We use a library for support vector machines, LIBSVM [1] for our experiments. Kernel function is a RBF which can achieve the best parameters for training in generating the final model.

5.1 SVM Features

We use 10 features for SVM training as in Table 1.

Table 1. Features for support vector machine (i: current position).

location	features
i-2	character and position tag
i-1	character and position tag
i	character and position tag
i+1	character and position tag
i+2	character and position tag

Each character in the boundary predicts its own position tag (see section 5.2) using lexical and position tag features of previous and next two characters. Moreover, we use additional features such as a possible character in a family name of Chinese person and foreign transliteration, and the last character of a location name. The number of features of a family name is taken from top 200, which are most frequently used in China, and the number of features of foreign trasliteration is 520. We also use high frequency 100 features of the last character of location names from in our corpus.

Using the individual characters as features for prediction is useful because we have to deal with the unknown words which are contiguous single characters. The character based features allow the system to predict the unknown words more effectivly in this case as shown in [3].

5.2 Candidate Boundary Prediction

We develop a SVM based unknown word prediction method for the output of the candidate boundary detection. We give a position tag for each character and create features which are used in training and testing.

The prediction first assigns the presumed position tags to the characters in a candidate boundary. Then we combine those characters according to the information of position tags, and finally identify the whole unknown word.

During the unknown word prediction step, we use 4 different classes of position tags to classify the characters. These classes are [**B-POS**], [**I-POS**], [**E-POS**] and [**O**], where POS is a POS tag of a word such as person name or location name, and **B**, **I** and **E** are the classes of characters according to positions in the word (**B**: Begin Position; **I**: Inside Position; **E**: End Position). **O** is the class of outside characters which are not classified into the previous three classes. After the prediction step, we combine these characters as a single word. Finally, we carry out some postprocessing using the error correction rules such as the following:

$$PT_i : [O], PT_{i-1} : [B - NR], PT_{i+1} : [E - NR] \rightarrow PT_i : [I - NR]$$

where PT_i is a current position tag, PT_{i-1} is a previous position tag, PT_{i+1} is a next position tag, and NR is a POS for a person name.

Fig. 3 shows an example of the final result of our unknown word prediction.

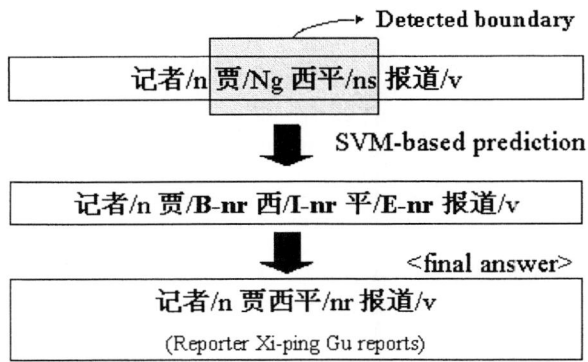

Fig. 3. Example of the SVM-based prediction.

6 Experiments

6.1 Corpus and Preprocessing

In this section, we show the prediction results of Chinese person names, foreign person transliterations and Chinese location names. The corpus in our experiments is one-month news articles from *the People's Daily*. We divide the corpus into 5 parts and conducted 5-cross validation. We delete all person names and location names from the dictionary to test the unknown word prediction performance. There are 17,620 person names and 24,992 location names. For more efficient experiments, we pre-processed the corpus; Chinese person names were originally splitted into the family name and the first name in the original *the People's Daily* corpus, and the compound words were also splitted into each component word. Therefore, we combined those splitted words into a single word. Then, dictionary was generated from the pre-processed corpus.

6.2 Experiments and the Results

The experiments can be divided into three parts. First experiment is to show how exactly our method selects the candidate boundary of an unknown word. The reduced amount of total boundaries to be recognized by SVM and the possible loss of unknown word candidates after applying our boundary detection step are shown in Table 2 and 3, for person and location, respectively.

Table 2. Reduction of the candidate boundaries (person).

	before	after	reduction rate
# of total boundary	128,410	20,434	84.09%
# of boundary including actual unknown words	16,955	14,712	13.23%

Table 3. Reduction of the candidate boundaries (location).

	before	after	reduction rate
# of total boundary	137,593	46,067	76.75%
# of boundary including actual unknown words	23,287	22,576	3.05%

As shown in the below tables, even if a few real person names and location names are excluded from the candidates (13,23% and 3.05%), the number of total boundaries for SVM to predict is drastically reduced by 84.09% and 76.75% respectively. We confirmed through our experiments that those missing candidates do not affect the overall performance for final SVM-based prediction.

Table 4. The gain of total prediction speed by using the candidate selection.

		candidate selection time (ms)	prediction time (ms)	total time (ms)
160 sentences	before		82,756	**82,756**
	after	140	2,930	**3,070**
300 sentences	before		171,942	**171,942**
	after	290	6,980	**7,270**

Secondly, Table 4 shows the speed gain according to the candidate selection method. For the target test data of 160 sentences and 300 sentences, we can get speed improvement over more than 25 times.

Finally, we tested the overall performance of the SVM-based unknown word prediction on the result of the candidate boundary selection. We divided the test corpus into 5 parts and evaluated them by 5-cross validation. Experiment results are measured in terms of precision, recall and F-measure, which are defined as equation (1), (2) and (3) below:

$$precision = \frac{\# \ of \ correctly \ predicted \ unknown \ words}{\# \ of \ total \ predicted \ unknown \ words} \quad (1)$$

$$recall = \frac{\# \ of \ correctly \ predicted \ unknown \ words}{\# \ of \ total \ unknown \ words} \quad (2)$$

$$F-meaure = \frac{2 \times precision \times recall}{precision + recall} \quad (3)$$

Table 5 shows the final results of the SVM based prediction for person names and location names.

Table 5. Prediction performance for person names and location names.

	precision	recall	F-measure
person name	88.06%	90.96%	89.49%
location name	90.93%	91.34%	91.14%

The result of the prediction is quite promising; Recall is very high as well as the precision compared with the previous results in similar environments. So, we can verify that SVM-based method using character features is a good approach for Chinese unknown word prediction. And the additional features such as Chinese family names, trainsliterated foreign names and the last characters of the location names, help to increase the performance of the prediction. Since our SVM was trained by somewhat unbalanced data, there were some over-predicted results in the output, where our postprocessing also plays a major role to increase the final performance.

7 Conclusion

The unknown word problem has remarkable effects on the accuracy and the naturalness of the sound in Chinese TTS systems. In this paper, we present a two-phase method for high speed unknown word prediction to be usable in a TTS system. We first pre-detect the candidate boundary of the unknown words from the result of Chinese segmentation and tagging. And then we predict the unknown words using the support vector machine. Experimental results are very promising by showing high precision and high recall with also high speed.

In the future, we would combine the proposed method with our automatic Text-to-Pinyin conversion module. Then we will be able to achieve more accurate conversion results. Also, to achieve better performance of uknown word prediction, we would apply our method to other classes such as organization names and more general compound nouns.

Acknowledgements

This research was supported by grant No. (R01-2003-000-10181-0) from the basic research program of the *KOSEF (Korea Science and Engineering Foundation)*.

References

1. Chih-Chung Chang and Chih-Jen Lin. 2003. *LIBSVM: a Library for Support Vector Machines. a guide of beginners*, http://www.csie.ntu.edu.tw/čjlin/libsvm.
2. Keh-Jiann Chen and Wei-Yun Ma. 2002. Unknown word extraction for chinese documents. *In Proceedings of COLING-2002*, pages 169-175.
3. Chooi-Ling Goh, Msasayuki Asahara, and Yuji Matsumono. 2003. Chinese unknown word identification using character-based tagging and chunking. *In Proceedings of the 41th ACL Conference*, pages 197-200.
4. Ju-Hong Ha, Yu Zheng, and Gary G. Lee. 2002. Chinese segmentation and postagging by automatic pos dictionary training. *In Proceedings of the 14th Conference of Korean and Korean Information Processing*, pages 33-39, (In Korean).
5. Ya-Jan Lv, Tie-Jun Zhao, Mu-Yun Yang, Hao Yu, and Sheng Li. 2000. Leveled unknown chinese word recognition by dynamic programming. *Journal of Chinese information*, Vol.15 No.1 (In Chinese).
6. Kevin Zhang, Qun Liu, Hao Zhang, and Xue-Qi Cheng. 2002. Automatic recognition of chinese unknown words based on roles tagging. *In Proceedings of the 1st SIGHAN Workshop on Chinese Language Processing*, COLING-2002.

Syntactic Analysis of Long Sentences Based on S-Clauses

Mi-Young Kim and Jong-Hyeok Lee

Div. of Electrical and Computer Engineering
Pohang University of Science and Technology (POSTECH) and
Advanced Information Technology Research Center(AITrc), R. of Korea
{colorful,jhlee}@postech.ac.kr

Abstract. In dependency parsing of long sentences with fewer subjects than predicates, it is difficult to recognize which predicate governs which subject. To handle such syntactic ambiguity between subjects and predicates, an "S(ubject)-clause" is defined as a group of words containing several predicates and their common subject, and then an automatic S-clause segmentation method is proposed using semantic features as well as morpheme features. We also propose a new dependency tree to reflect S-clauses. Trace information is used to indicate the omitted subject of each predicate. The S-clause information turned out to be very effective in analyzing long sentences, with an improved parsing performance of 4.5%. The precision in determining the governors of subjects in dependency parsing was improved by 32%.

1 Introduction

In most cases, a long sentence has fewer subjects than predicates. The reason is that several predicates can share one subject if they require the same word as their subject, or that the subject of a predicate is often omitted in a Korean sentence. So, in a long sentence, it is difficult to recognize the correct subject of some subjectless VPs. When we analyze the syntactic analysis errors of long sentences, we obtain the results as shown in Table 1. In the evaluation of our parser under MATEC'99[1] test corpus, subject errors form the second largest portion (24.26%) of syntactic parsing errors (See Table 1).

Although the dependency errors in NP form the largest error portion, these errors may not be so serious because many parser-based applications like MT deal with an NP structure as a single unit and do not analyze the syntactic relations within the NP.

So, this paper proposes a method of how to resolve the problem of subject dependency errors. To improve the performance of dependency parsing, we need to determine the correct dependency relations of subjects. This paper proposes an S(ubject)-clause segmentation method to reduce ambiguity in determining the governor of a subject in dependency parsing. S(ubject)-clause is defined as a group of words containing several predicates and their common subject. An S-clause includes one subject and several predicates that share the subject. The S-clause segmentation algorithm detects the boundary of predicates that share a common subjective word. We employ the C4.5 decision tree learning algorithm for this task and semantic features as well as morpheme features for learning.

---

[1] Morphological Analyzer and Tagger Evaluation Contest in 1999.

Table 1. Dependency tree errors for 12,000 test sentences (avg. 19.16 words/sentence)

Dependency tree errors	Error %	Dependency tree errors	Error %
Subject-predicate dependency errors	24.26%	Complement-predicate dependency errors	8.93%
Predicate-predicate dependency errors	14.18%	Dependency errors within NP	27.37%
Adjunct-predicate dependency errors	17.49%	Dependency errors resulting from POS-tag errors	7.77%

This paper also proposes a new dependency tree representation to reflect S-clauses. We need to represent the omitted subject in a dependency tree, since the semantic structure represents the omitted arguments in a semantic graph. So, if a syntactic structure represents the omitted arguments, semantic analysis procedure will be easier.

The next section presents the background of previous work on sentence segmentation and clause detection. Next, dependency analysis procedure using S-clauses in Korean and the dependency tree to reflect the S-clause results will be described. Afterwards, the features for learning decision tree will be explained, and some experimental results will show that the proposed S-clause segmentation method is effective in dependency parsing. Finally, a conclusion will be given..

2 Previous Work

A considerable number of studies have been conducted on the syntactic analysis of long sentences. First, conjunctive structure identification methods have been proposed [1], [6]. These methods are based on structural parallelism and the lexical similarity of coordinate structures. While they perform well in detecting the boundary of a coordinate structure, they cannot determine the boundary of predicates that share a common subject. Second, several studies have been made on clause segmentation (identification, splitting) [2], [9], [13]. The clause seems to be a natural structure above the chunk. Clause identification splits sentences that center around a verb. The major problem with clause identification concerns the sharing of the same subject by different clauses [7]. When a subject is omitted in a clause, Vilson [7] attached the features of the previous subject to the conjunctions. However, the subject of a clause is not always the nearest subject. Therefore, a new method is needed to detect the correct subject of a clause.

To determine the correct subject of some subjectless VPs, we define 'S(ubject)-clause' and propose an S-clause segmentation method. Unlike previous other researchers, who defined a clause to be a group of words that contain a verb and split a sentence into clauses centering on a verb, we did it centering on a subject. So the proposed segment is called 'S(ubject)-clause' to distinguish it from a traditional clause. We apply both semantic features and morpheme features to determine S-clauses and propose a new dependency tree formalism to reflect S-clauses.

3 Dependency Tree Representation for S-Clauses

To reflect the S-clause results, we use the following dependency tree formalism. Lombardo [8] uses non-lexical trace nodes to express the ellipsis of a node. In Fig. 1, ε_{u1} indicates the previous node u1 '*na-nun*(I)' was omitted in this position. In a similar way, we make non-lexical units for the omitted subjects of predicates.

In a new dependency tree, we make a dependency tree as follows: the subject in one S-clause is dependent on the farthest predicate of the S-clause. For other predicates except the farthest predicate in one S-clause, we make a non-lexical unit per predicate to indicate the omitted subject and regard the non-lexical unit is dependent on the predicate as its subject. We mark $\varepsilon_{(node\ id)}$ to indicate what the real subject is.

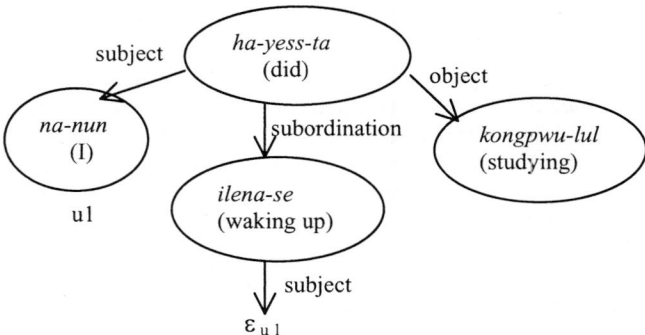

Fig. 1. Dependency tree example that uses non-lexical nodes

4 S-Clause Segmentation Based on Decision Tree Learning

4.1 The C4.5 Learning Algorithm

Decision tree induction algorithms have been successfully applied to NLP problems such as parsing [3], discourse analysis [10], sentence boundary disambiguation [11], and word segmentation [14]. We employed a C4.5 [12] decision tree induction program as the learning algorithm for S-clause segmentation.

4.2 Features

This section explains the concrete feature setting we used for learning. The S-clause is a broader concept than the clause. In order to determine the S-clauses, we must choose the clauses that are suitable for addition to the S-clause. Since the head word of a clause is the predicate in the clause, we merely use predicate information. The feature set focuses on the predicates. An S-clause can be embedded in another S-clause. Therefore, we should learn two methods to detect the left boundary and right boundary of an S-clause independently. We should include one subject between the left boundary and the right boundary of an S-clause. We call the subject to include in an S-clause the 'target subject'.

Table 2. Linguistic feature types used for learning

Feature	Description
1st feature	Type of a predicate
2nd feature	Surface form of the last ending of a predicate
3rd feature	Comma
4th feature	Similarity b/w subject concept that a predicate requires and 'target subject' concept
5th feature	Double subject possibility when the succeeding noun functions as a subject

Table 3. Values for each feature type

Feature type	Values
1st	adnominal, conjunctive, quotative, nominal, final
2nd	n, m, ki, um, ntey, ntul, ncuk, nci, lci, lcini, kena, keniwa, kenmanun, key, ko, na, nuntey, nunci, ni, nikka, taka, telato, tenci, tolok, tunka, tunci, tusi, la, lyeko, mye, myen, myense, mulo, a, ase, e, eto, ese, eya, una, uni, ulyeko, umye, umyen, umyense, umulo, ca, ci, cimanun... (all surface forms of Korean endings)
3rd	1, 0
4th	+, 0
5th	1, 0

Each predicate has 5 features, as shown in Table 2. The 1st feature concerns the type of a predicate. Next, the 2nd feature takes the value of the surface form of the last ending of a predicate. The 3rd feature deals with the information whether a predicate is followed by a comma or not. The use of a comma to insert a pause in a sentence is an important key to detect an S-clause boundary. The 4th feature deals with the semantic information that indicates the similarity between subject concept that a predicate requires and 'target subject' concept. We have a dictionary that describes the selectional restrictions of predicates and the concepts of nouns. We represent '+' if the similarity calculation result is larger than zero; otherwise, we represent '0'. We use Kadokawa thesaurus concept and apply the concept similarity method as presented in E.Kim [4]. Finally, we use double subject construction information. The information is for the adnominal predicates that modify the succeeding nouns. First, we should identify the relative clause gap. In other words, we should recognize if the succeeding noun functions as its subject or not. If the succeeding noun functions as its subject, we should not allow the predicate to have another word as its subject ('one argument per clause' rules). However, in Korean, double subject construction occurs very often. So, most of adnominal predicates can require another previous word as its subject although the succeeding noun functions as its subject, except some transitive verbs. So, the 5th feature indicates if an adnominal predicate can require another word as its subject or not, when the succeeding noun functions as its subject.

First, when we detect the left boundary of an S-clause, we consider the predicates between the 'target subject' and the nearest subject that precedes the 'target subject'. We use 15 features for left boundary detection: 3 predicates, and 5 features for each predicate as summarized in Table 2. The class set consists of 4 values (0~3) to indicate the position of the predicate that becomes a left boundary.

For right boundary detection, we consider the predicates between the 'target subject' and the next subject following the 'target subject'. We use 25 features for right boundary detection: 5 predicates, and the same 5 features for each predicate. Among the predicates between 'target subject' and the next subject following the 'target subject', we consider 4 predicates that appear near the 'target subject' and 1 predicate that locates last. The reason that 1 predicate that locates last is considered is as follows: If all the predicates between 'target subject' and the next subject following the 'target subject' require the 'target subject' as their common subject, the right boundary becomes the last predicate among them, since Korean is a head-final language. We cannot consider all the predicates between 'target subject' and the following subject of 'target subject' if the number of predicates is larger than 4. So, we consider the last predicate as a representative. Although the feature set is the same as that for right boundary detection, the window size for the right boundary is 5, which is larger than that for the left boundary. The reason is that Korean is a head-final language and the predicates of a subject appear after the subject. The detailed values of each feature type are summarized in Table 3.

We first detect the S-clause that includes the last subject of an input word set. If an S-clause is detected, we exclude the words that are included in the S-clause from the input word set. Then, we recursively detect the S-clause, including the last subject in the remaining word set until there are no subjects in the modified word set.

5 Experimental Evaluation

The S-clause segmentation method was evaluated under the Matec99' Test Set, focusing on the following two properties of the S-clause segmentation:
1. The size of training data vs. S-clause segmentation accuracy vs. parsing accuracy-1 (in a normal dependency tree) vs. parsing accuracy-2 (in a proposed dependency tree)
2. Significance of features

5.1 Training Data Size vs. S-Clause Segmentation Accuracy vs. Parsing Accuracies

A training set consists of 50,000 sentences whose average length is 14.63 words per sentence. A test set has 12,000 sentences that are different from the training sentences. The average length of the test sentences is 19.16 words per sentence, which is longer than that of training sentences because the S-clause segmentation method is mainly for improving the performance of syntactic analysis for long sentences.

Experiments were conducted with two parsing accuracies. The first one is for a normal dependency tree in which the number of nodes is equal to that of words in an input sentence. The second one is for a new dependency tree formalism that may have non-lexical units to indicate the omitted subjects.

To show the effectiveness of S-clauses, the parsers with and without S-clause segmentation are compared with each other. And also our parser is compared with other Korean and Japanese parsers. Here, we just compare their performance in terms of a normal dependency tree -- not a new dependency tree because other parsers do not detect the omitted subjects. The experiments of our parsers are summarized as follows:

1. The more accurate the S-clause segmentation, the better the parsing accuracy becomes (see Table 4).
2. The maximum S-clause accuracy is 84.77% (see Table 4).
3. The maximum parsing accuracy is 88.82% (accuracy-1) in a normal dependency tree and 83.58% (accuracy-2) in a proposed dependency tree (see Table 4).

In terms of the maximum parsing accuracy, let us compare our parser with the Japanese KN parser, which is known to achieve the best performance in Japanese dependency parsing. For performance evaluation of the KN parser with the same test set as in our parser, we constructed a bilingual test corpus by translating the Korean test set of 12,000 sentences using an existing high-quality Korean-to-Japanese MT system COBALT-K/J, and then by manually correcting the translation results. To detect the head of a subject, the KN parser uses only some heuristics [6]. As shown in Table 5, the performance of our parser without S-clause segmentation is worse than that of the KN parser. In our parser without S-clause segmentation, a word simply depends on the nearest head that does not lead to crossing links. However, after S-clause segmentation, the performance of our parser is similar to that of the KN parser. The accuracy of our parser in detecting the head of a subject is also better than that of the KN parser.

We also compare our parser with the Yon-sei dependency parser, as shown in Table 5. The parser using S-clauses outperforms the Yon-sei parser by one percent. Since the Yon-sei dependency parser is not a program that is open to the public, we simply compare the performance of our parser with that of Yon-sei parser written in Kim et al [5]. Therefore, the comparison of the performance between our parser and the Yon-sei dependency parser may be meaningless.

Table 4. The amount of training sentences vs. S-clause accuracy vs. Parsing accuracy for the 12,000 test sentences

Number of training sentences	5000	10000	20000	30000	40000	50000
S-clause Precision	83.02%	83.82%	83.90%	84.41%	84.47%	84.77%
S-clause Recall	81.99%	83.69%	83.72%	84.39%	84.42%	84.52%
Parsing Accuracy (in a normal dependency tree)	85.23%	86.36%	87.17%	88.03%	88.49%	88.82%
Parsing Accuracy (in a new dependency tree)	80.81%	81.68%	82.31%	82.94%	83.30%	83.58%

Table 5. Parsing accuracy comparison (avg 19.16 words/sentence)

	Our parser without S-clause segmentation procedure	Our parser with S-clause segmentation procedure	KN Parser	Korean Yon-sei parser
Accuracy in detecting the head of a subject	51.10%	83.28%	73.89%	Unknown
Parsing Accuracy (in a normal dependency tree)	84.19%	88.82%	88.93%	87.30%

Table 6. S-clause accuracy change when each attribute for left boundary removed

Feature	Accuracy change	Feature	Accuracy change
1st type	-5.46%	2nd concept similarity	-0.07%
1st surface form	-1.12%	2nd double subject	-0.00%
1st comma	-2.55%	3rd type	-0.79%
1st concept similarity	-0.13%	3rd surface form	-0.00%
1st double subject	-0.01%	3rd comma	-0.02%
2nd type	-1.36%	3rd concept similarity	-0.00%
2nd surface form	-0.22%	3rd double subject	-0.00%
2nd comma	-1.29%		

5.2 Significance of Features

Next, we will summarize the significance of each feature introduced in Section 4.2. Table 6 and Table 7 illustrate how the S-clause accuracy is reduced when each feature is removed. Table 6 clearly demonstrates that the most significant feature for the left boundary is the type of the previous 1st predicate – we obtain the information from the decision rules that, especially, the 'adnominal' type of the previous 1st predicate is a significant feature. As shown in Table 6, double subject features have less effect on the left boundary since double subject features are for the right boundary detection. Table 7 demonstrates that the most significant feature for the right boundary is comma information, since the S-clause accuracy without 1st, 2nd or 3rd comma information shows big decrease of accuracy. The double subject features for all the predicates are useful for right boundary detection. The 5th predicate information is more useful than the 4th predicate. In other words, the last predicate can be the head of a subject than the intermediate predicate. In Table 6 and 7, concept similarity features are not effective in detecting boundaries. The reason is that the dictionary information that describes the selectional restrictions of predicates is not so accurate.

Table 7. S-clause accuracy change when each attribute for right boundary removed

Feature	Accuracy change	Feature	Accuracy change
1st type	-2.90%	3rd concept similarity	-0.12%
1st surface form	-1.73%	3rd double subject	-0.73%
1st comma	-2.33%	4th type	-0.21%
1st concept similarity	-0.63%	4th surface form	-0.04%
1st double subject	-1.80%	4th comma	-0.00%
2nd type	-0.72%	4th concept similarity	-0.00%
2nd surface form	-1.32%	4th double subject	-0.03%
2nd comma	-1.83%	5th type	-0.81%
2nd concept similarity	-0.18%	5th surface form	-0.15%
2nd double subject	-1.44%	5th comma	-0.00%
3rd type	-0.66%	5th concept similarity	-0.05%
3rd surface form	-1.05%	5th double subject	-0.03%
3rd comma	-1.16%		

If we modify the dictionaries and increase the accuracy of selectional restriction descriptions, then the concept similarity features will be effective in S-clause detection.

This result may partially support heuristics; the left boundary would be an adnominal predicate since only adnominal predicates are *followed* by their subjects (other predicates are *preceded* by their subjects). Next, after the comma, a boundary mostly occurs. In particular, we need to concentrate on the types of predicates to attain a higher level of accuracy. To some extent, most features contribute to the parsing performance.

5.3 Discussion About S-Clause Errors

We classify the S-clause errors, as shown in Table 8. Table 8 shows that many S-clause errors are due to the Korean characteristics. Among the S-clause errors, subject detection errors rank first, which occupy 25.83%. So, the S-clause accuracy result is different from the S-clause recall result. Next, POS tagging errors result in the S-clause segmentation errors of 22.10 percent. These two errors occur before S-clause segmentation. So, this is another issue that remains for future work. Also, double subject errors are 7.28%. Some cases exist that a predicate requires double subjects in one sentence, but it requires only one subject in another sentence. We need to consider double subject constructions deeply. The errors of detecting right boundaries are greater in number than those of detecting left boundaries. It means that right boundary detection is more difficult. Many left and right boundary errors result in the selectional restriction errors. We should improve the accuracy of selectional restriction descriptions by updating dictionary information. Finally, to reduce S-clause errors, we should gather more non-predicates that function as predicates and include them into the boundary candidates.

Table 8. The type of S-clause errors

S-clause errors	Error %	S-clause errors	Error %
Subject detection errors	25.83%	Double subject errors	7.28%
Pos-tag errors	22.10%	Relative clause gap errors	6.70%
Selectional restriction errors	16.92%	Otherwise	...

6 Conclusion

This paper proposes an automatic S-clause segmentation method using both semantic features and morpheme features. We also propose a dependency tree representation formalism to reflect S-clauses. We use trace information to indicate the omitted subject of each predicate. The experimental results show that the parser using S-clauses outperforms that without S-clauses by 4.5% and also outperforms conventional Korean dependency parsers by 1.5 percent. To improve the S-clause accuracy, we should construct the dictionary that describes selectional restrictions more accurately, and consider double subject constructions deeply. Now, we use a non-lexical unit for the omitted subject node. However, in future work, we will use a non-lexical unit for all the omitted arguments and test the parsing result.

Acknowledgements

This work was supported by the KOSEF through the Advanced Information Technology Research Center(AITrc) and by the BK21 Project.

References

1. Rajeev Agarwal, Lois Boggess. A simple but useful approach to conjunct identification. In Proceedings of the 30th Annual Meeting of the Association for Computational Linguistics, Nantes, France (1992) 15-21
2. Xavier Carreras, Lluis Marquez, Vasin Punyakanok, and Dan Roth. Learning and Inference for Clause Identification. In Proceedings of European Conference on Machine Learning, Helsinki, Finland (2002) 35-47
3. Masahiko Haruno, Satoshi Shirai, and Yoshifumi Ooyama. Using Decision Trees to Construct a Practical Parser, In Proceedings of the 36th Annual Meeting of the Association for Computational Linguistics, Monteal, Quebec, Canada (1998) 505-511
4. E. Kim, J.H. Lee. A Collocation-Based Transfer Model for Japanese-to-Korean Machine Translation. In Proceedings of the Natural Language Processing Pacific Rim Symposium, Fukuoka, Japan (1993) 223-231,
5. Kwangbaek Kim, Euikyu Park, Dongryeol Ra and Juntae Yoon. A method of Korean parsing based on sentence segmentation *(written in Korean)*. In Proceedings of 14th Hangul and Korean Information Processing, Chung-ju, Korea (2002) 163-168,
6. Sadao Kurohashi and Makoto Nagao, A syntactic analysis method of long Japanese sentences based on the detection of conjunctive structures, Computational Linguistics, Vol. 20(4) (1994) 507-534
7. Vilson. J. Leffa. Clause processing in complex sentences. In Proceedings of the 1st International Conference on Language Resources and Evaluation, Granada, Spain (1998) 937-943
8. V. Lombardo, L. Lesmo, A formal theory of dependency syntax with non-lexical units. In Traitement Automatique des Langues, Mel'cuk I.: Dependency syntax: theory and practice, SUNY University Press (1988)
9. Antonio Molina and Ferran Pla. Clause Detection using HMM. In proceedings of the 5th Conference on Computational Natural Language Learning, Toulouse, France (2001) 70-72
10. Tadashi Nomoto and Yuji Matsumoto. Discourse Parsing: A Decision Tree Approach. In proceedings of the 6th Workshop on Very Large Corpora, Montreal, Quebec, Canada (1998) 216-224
11. David D. Palmer, Marti A. Hearst. Adaptive Multilingual Sentence Boundary Disambiguation, Computational Linguistics, Vol. 27. (1997) 241-261
12. J. Ross Quinlan. C4.5 Programs for Machine Learning. *Morgan Kaufmann Publishers.* (1993)
13. Erik F. Tjong Kim Sang and Herve Dejean. Introduction to the CoNLL-2001 Shared Task: Clause Identification. In proceedings of CoNLL-2001, Toulouse, France (2001) 53-57
14. Virach Sornertlamvanich, Tanapong Potipiti and Thatsanee Charoenporn. Automatic Corpus-Based Thai Word Extraction with the C4.5 Learning Algorithm, In Proceedings of the 18th International Conference on Computational Linguistics, Saarbrucken, Germany (2000) 802-807

Chinese Chunk Identification Using SVMs Plus Sigmoid

Yongmei Tan, Tianshun Yao, Qing Chen, and Jingbo Zhu

Natural Language Processing Lab
Northeastern University, Shenyang 110004
yongmeitan@21cn.com, tsyao@mail.neu.edu.cn,
Chen_flint@163.net, zhujingbo@mail.neu.edu.cn

Abstract. The paper presents a method of Chinese chunk recognition based on Support Vector Machines (SVMs) plus Sigmoid. It is well known that SVMs are binary classifiers which achieve the best performance in many tasks. However, directly applying binary classifiers in the task of Chinese chunking will face the dilemmas that either two or more different class labels are given to a single unlabeled constituent, or no class labels are given for some unlabeled constituents. Employing sigmoid functions is a method of extracting probabilities (class/input) from SVMs outputs, which is helpful to post-processing of classification. These probabilities are then used to resolve the dilemmas. We compare our method based on SVMs plus Sigmoid with methods based only on SVMs. The experiments show that significant improvements have been achieved.

1 Introduction

We study the problem of improving the performance of Chinese chunking when directly applying binary classifiers in Chinese chunking task.

Chunk recognition or chunking is a new research field in natural language processing, which identifies some special chunks of words without conducting deep parsing. As a preprocessing procedure, it can prominently decrease the complexity of further proceeding phrase recognition and phrase analysis, while it is beneficial to machine translation, information retrieval, information extraction, etc.

There are two main approaches to chunking. One is a rule-based method; the other is a statistical method. There is now a growing interest in applying machine-learning techniques to chunking, as they can avoid tedious manual work and are helpful for improving performance.

Much work has been done by researchers in this area. Zhang and Zhou [1] used the inner structure and lexical information of base phrases to disambiguate border and phrase type. Zhou et al., [2] introduced the Chinese chunk parsing scheme and separated constituent recognition from full syntactic parsing, by using words boundary and constituent group information. Zhao and Huang [3] systematically defined Chinese base noun phrase from the linguistic point of view and presented a model for recognizing Chinese base noun phrases. The model integrated Chinese base noun phrase structure templates and context features. These studies achieved promising results.

Using SVMs is an effective method for learning classifiers. This method has been successfully applied in many NLP fields, such as English chunking [4,5], POS tagging [6], Japanese Named Entity recognition [7] and text categorization [8].

The performance of the classifiers can be measured in terms of the generalization error.

Table 1. An example of Chinese chunk automatic recognition.

Input	小/h	刘/nhf	现在/nt	在/d	忙/v	着/u	开会/vi	呢/u	。/wp
Output	B-BNP	I-BNP	O	B-BVP	I-BVP	O	B-BVP	O	O
Chunk	BNP		O	BVP		O	BVP	O	O

We address the problem in this paper and use a method named SVM plus sigmoid to resolve it. To the best of our knowledge, this problem in chunking has not been studied previously.

In the process of using SVMs in recognizing Chinese chunks, we are often faced with in the dilemmas that either two or more different class labels are given to a single unlabeled constituent, or no class labels are given for some unlabeled constituents. We propose to train an additional sigmoid model to map the SVM outputs into probabilities after training the SVMs. These probabilities are then used to resolve the dilemmas.

We assume that employing sigmoid after using SVMs can classify samples more accurately than using SVMs only. More precisely, the generalization error of conducting classification using SVMs plus sigmoid is smaller than that using only SVMs.

The layout of this paper is as follows. Section 2 gives a description of related work. Section 3 presents our method: Chinese chunk recognition using SVMs plus Sigmoid and gives the experimental results of our method. Section 4 contains a discussion of our method. Our conclusion and future work can be found in section 5.

2 Related Work

2.1 Chinese Chunk

Chunks were first introduced by Abney [9], who used them for syntactic parsing. According to his definition, a chunk is the non-recursive core of an intra-clausal constituent, extending from the beginning of constituent to its head, but not including post-head dependents.

Like the definition of English chunk given by Abney, we define Chinese chunk as a single semantic and non-recursive core of an intra-clausal constituent, with the restriction that no chunks are included in another chunk. We define 7 types of Chinese chunk: BDP (base adverb phrase), BAP (base adjective phrase), BMP (base mount phrase), BTP (base temporal phrase), BNS (base locative phrase), BNP (base noun phrase), and BVP (base verb phrase).

1. BDP: the core word of the phrase is an adverb or the phrase is ended with Chinese de (4).
2. BAP: the core word of the phrase is an adjective.
3. BMP: the core word of the phrase is a non-time quantifier.
4. BTP: the core word of the phrase is a time quantifier.
5. BNS: the core word of the phrase is a locative noun.
6. BNP: the core word of the phrase is a common noun.
7. BVP: the core word of the phrase is a verb.

To represent Chinese chunks clearly, we define three types of chunk border tags in this paper.

1. B-XP XP ∈ {BDP, DAP, BMP, BTP, BNS, BNP, BVP} denotes that the current word is the first word of chunk XP.
2. I-XP XP ∈ {BDP, DAP, BMP, BTP, BNS, BNP, BVP} denotes that the current word is inside of chunk XP.
3. O denotes that the current word is outside any chunk.

Each chunk type XP has two border tags: B-XP and I-XP. There are 7 types of chunk. Together with the chunk border tag O, we have 15 different chunk border tags. Using these chunk border tags, we can consider the Chinese chunk recognition as a classification task.

Table 1 gives an example. Given a word sequence with part-of-speech tags, a chunk recognizer outputs a sequence of chunk border tags.

2.2 SVMs

SVM is a relatively new machine learning technique first presented by Vapnik [10,11]. Based on the structural risk minimization principle of computational learning theory, SVMs seek a decision boundary to separate the training examples into two classes and to make decisions based on the support vectors which are selected as the only effective examples in the training set.

Like other inductive learning approaches, SVMs take a set of training examples (e.g., feature vectors with binary values) as input, and find a classification function which maps them to classes. In this paper, a separating hyper-plane described by a weight vector w and a threshold b perfectly divides the training data x into 2 classes labeled as $y \in \{-1, +1\}$, each side containing data examples with the same class label only.

$$w \cdot x + b = 0 \quad w \in R^n, b \in R \tag{1}$$

Then SVMs learn linear decision rules:

$$y(\boldsymbol{x}) = sign(g(\boldsymbol{x})) = sign(\boldsymbol{w} \cdot \boldsymbol{x} + b) = \begin{cases} +1, & \text{if } (\boldsymbol{w} \cdot \boldsymbol{x} + b) > 0 \\ -1, & \text{otherwise} \end{cases} \quad (2)$$

The idea of structural risk minimization is to find a hypothesis for which one can guarantee the lowest probability bound for generalization error. This can be achieved by finding the optimal hyper-plane, i.e., the hyper-plane with the maximum margin. Margin is defined as the distance between the hyper-plane and the training samples which are most close to the hyper-plane.

Maximizing the margin means that the closest samples (support vectors) exist on both sides of the separating hyper-plane and the hyper-plane lies exactly in the middle of these support vectors. Computing this optimal hyper-plane is equivalent to solving the following optimization problem.

$$Minimize \quad \frac{1}{2}\|w\|^2 \quad (3)$$

$$subject\ to: \ y_i[(\boldsymbol{w} \cdot x_i) - b] \geq 1 \quad (i = 1, ... l)$$

For the non-linear separable data points, Boswell introduced the use of kernel functions [12]. There are 3 types kernel functions which are often used: polynomial function, radial basis function (RBF) and two-layered sigmoid neural nets.

In the chunking task of CoNLL-2000, Kudo and Matsumoto used SVMs in English text chunking and achieved the best performance among all the systems. However, this method has not been applied to Chinese chunking so far. So we use this method for recognizing Chinese chunks. In this paper, we employ linear classifiers described as formula (2).

3 SVMs Plus Sigmoid

A sentence containing n words can be represented as $W^T = w_1 w_2 \ldots w_n$, where $w_i (1 \leq i \leq n)$ is the i-th word in the sentence. The POS tag sequence of the sentence is $P^T = p_1 p_2 \ldots p_n$, where $p_i (1 \leq i \leq n)$ is the POS tag of word w_i. The sequence of chunk border tags of the sentence is $T^T = t_1 t_2 \ldots t_n$, where $t_i (1 \leq i \leq n)$ is the chunk border tag of i-th word. So Chinese chunk recognition can be considered as a classification problem where every word in the sentence should be assigned one of the 15 types of chunk border tags.

This task is a multi-class classification problem. As described above, the standard learning algorithm for SVMs constructs a binary classifier, so we employ multi-class SVMs to resolve it. If we use the pairwise method introduced by Kazama to extend multi-calss SVMs [13], then $\frac{15 \times (15-1)}{2} = 105$ classifiers should be produced and the cost is high. Therefore we used the alternative straightforward one-against-rest approach given by Kazama where 15 classifiers are produced [13].

3.1 Input Features

One remarkable advantage of SVMs is that their learning ability can be independent of the dimensionality of the feature space. SVMs measure the complexity of hypotheses based on the margin with which they separate the data, not the number of features. Another remarkable property is that SVMs can automatically focus on useful features as well as find appropriate combination of these features. Furthermore, it can achieve high generalization performance in very high dimensional feature spaces. So we use all the words w, all the part-of-speech p and all the chunk type border labels t of the training data as features. We take advantage of all the context information of each current position, so that every sample is represented as 13 features. In this paper, the classification process proceeds from left to right, which can be confirmed by the following definition of features.

$$x = (w_{-2}, p_{-2}, t_{-2}, w_{-1}, p_{-1}, t_{-1}, w_0, p_0, w_{+1}, p_{+1}, w_{+2}, p_{+2})$$

where w_0 denotes the current word, p_0 denotes the part-of-speech of the current word w_0, and t_0 denotes the chunk type border tag of the current word w_0, which is required to be classified into one of 15 classes;

w_{-i} denotes the word appearing at i-th word preceding the current word w_0, p_{-i} denotes the part-of-speech of w_{-i}, and t_{-i} denotes the chunk type border tag of w_{-i};

Likewise, w_{+i} denotes the word appearing at i-th word following the current word w_0 and p_{+i} denotes the part-of-speech of w_{+i}.

Binary SVM classifiers SVM^{light} [1] only accepts the numeric values as input, so we construct an inverse index table for all the features. In the table, every record is a binary array, i.e. $<feature, index>$. $feature$ is the feature and $index$ is the position of feature $feature$ in the feature list. e.g. $<w_{-2} =$ 美丽, $1001>$ represents that the feature $w_{-2} =$ 美丽 is the $1001st$ feature in the feature list. The inverse index table can be easily retrieved so that every sample can be transformed into its corresponding numeric value.

In experiment 1, we often in the dilemmas that different classes are assigned to a single unlabeled word by two or more classifiers, or no classes are assigned to an unlabeled word. In these cases, it is very difficult to decide which class the current chunk border tag t_0 belongs to. Hence we adopt a simple approach: for the first case, we randomly choose a class from the classes resulted from those classifiers, for the second case, we just tag it with the class O. This is our baseline method.

3.2 Sigmoid Function

That different classes are assigned to a single unlabeled word by two or more classifiers, or no classes are assigned to an unlabeled word are dilemmas. The

---
[1] SVMlight version 3.02.
http://www-ai.cs.uni-dortmund.ed/SOFTWARE/SVM_LIGHT/svm_light.eng.html.

baseline method described above is not reasonable enough, because when a classifier is only a sub component of a global model, the classification outputs must be integrated for the overall decision, i.e., we must use a uniform model to make decision.

To use a uniform model to make decision, we need to construct a classifier to produce a posterior probability $p(class/input)$, then choose the class based on the maximal posterior probability over all classes. However, a SVM produces an un-calibrated value that is not a probability. To map the SVMs outputs into probabilities, we train an additional sigmoid model [14]. In this approach, a parametric model is used to fit the posterior $p(y = 1/g)$, instead of estimating the class-conditional densities $p(g/y)$. The parameters of the model are adapted to give the best probability outputs. The Sigmoid model is as follows.

$$p(y = 1/g) = \frac{1}{1 + exp(Ag + B)} \quad (4)$$

The parameters A and B are fitted using maximum likelihood estimation from a training set (g_i, h_i), where $y = sign(g_i)$, $g_i = g(x_i)$. The definition of the target probability h_i is as follows:

$$h_i = \frac{y_i + 1}{2} \quad (5)$$

The parameters A and B are calculated by minimizing the negative log likelihood of the training data, i.e., cross-entropy error function:

$$Minimize \quad -\sum_i (h_i log(p_i) + (1 - h_i) log(1 - p_i)) \quad (6)$$

$$subject\ to: p_i = \frac{1}{(1 + exp(Ag_i + B))}$$

We use the union of all 15 sets of $g_i(x)$ as the training set of the sigmoid model. 10-fold Cross-validation produces large training sets and gives a lower variance estimate for A and B.

Even with cross-validation and unbiased training data, the sigmoid can still be overfitted. To avoid this problem, Platt uses an out-of-sample model: out-of-data is modeled with the same empirical density as the sigmoid training data, but with a finite probability of opposite label [14]. In other words, when a positive example is observed at a value g_i, we do not use $h_i = 1$, but assume that there is a finite chance of opposite label at the same g_i in the out-of-sample data. Therefore, for some ϵ_+, a value of $h_i = 1 - \epsilon_+$ will be used. Similarly, a negative example will use a target value of $h_i = \epsilon_-$.

We map the SVM outputs into probabilities by using the parameters given in Table 4, i.e.

$$p_i = 1/(1 + exp(A_i g_i + B_i)) \quad (0 \leq i \leq 14) \quad (7)$$

The SVM output $g_i = \boldsymbol{w} \cdot \boldsymbol{x}_i + b$ of a sample $\boldsymbol{x}_i$ is transformed into a probability $p_i (0 \leq p_i \leq 1)$ by using the formula (7).

Then we choose the class based on the maximal posterior probability overall classes, i.e.

$$f^* = argmax_{f_i} \ p_i = argmax_{f_i} \ \frac{1}{(1+exp(A_i g_i + B_i))} \quad (0 \leq i \leq 14) \quad (8)$$

Note that in our method, sigmoid models are trained by SVMs outputs.

3.3 Experimental Results

For comparison, we perform the following experiments on Chinese chunk identification based on methods described before. First, we do the experiment on Chinese chunk identification based on SVMs only, as described in Section 3.1. Second, we estimate the sigmoid parameters using 10-fold cross-validation, then do the experiment on Chinese chunk identification based on SVMs plus sigmoid as described in Section 3.2. The experimental results are shown in the Table 3.

In our experiments, we divide our 500KB Chinese tree-bank into 10 parts in advance and conduct 10-fold cross-validation. Each of the 15 SVMs is trained on permutations of 9 out of the 10 parts, and the remaining one is used for testing. All of the results presented in this paper are averaged over the 10 runs.

We measure the performance in terms of precision, recall and F-score, which are standard measures for the chunk recognition. These measures are given separately for the chunk types BAP, BDP, BMP, BNP, BNS, BTP and BVP.

Table 2 summarizes the information on the dataset. The format of the dataset follows that of CoNLL-2000 dataset.

Table 3 compares the results using SVMs (baseline method) or SVMs plus sigmoid in Chinese chunking. The experimental result of the baseline method is not satisfactory, because this way does not use a uniform model to make decision,

Table 2. The simple statistics on dataset.

Information	Value
The number of sentences	4386
The number of words	40778
The number of chunk types	7
The number of base phrases	3232

Table 3. The results based on SVMs and based on SVMs plus sigmoid.

Chunk type	SVMs			SVMs + sigmoid		
	Precision	Recall	FB1	Precision	Recall	FB1
BAP	76.60	83.72	80.00	83.33	83.33	83.33
BDP	100.00	100.00	100.00	100.00	100.00	100.00
BMP	94.74	97.30	96.00	94.74	97.30	96.00
BNP	87.30	88.00	87.65	88.19	89.60	88.89
BNS	83.33	83.33	83.33	86.11	89.86	87.94
BTP	77.78	77.78	77.78	77.78	77.78	77.78
BVP	87.33	89.73	88.51	88.67	91.10	89.86

Table 4. The parameters of sigmoid trained by cross-validation

f_i	Border tags	A_i	B_i	f_i	Border tags	A_i	B_i
0	B-BAP	-1.22345	3.54583	8	B-BNS	0	9.97511
1	I-BAP	-1.6878	2.52206	9	I-BNS	-2.80512	4.7527
2	B-BDP	-6.58168	0.204208	10	B-BTP	-5.01368	0.421334
3	I-BDP	-4.70771	1.77015	11	I-BTP	-4.86146	0.481041
4	B-BMP	-1.42426	1.58767	12	B-BVP	-1.50136	0.762406
5	I-BMP	-3.58818	-0.354963	13	I-BVP	-1.94256	-0.306017
6	B-BNP	-3.05942	0.0291156	14	O	-1.20067	-0.204161
7	I-BNP	-3.97426	1.6672				

then the predicted category is not confident, i.e., when a classifier is only a sub component of a global model, the classification outputs must be integrated for the overall decision.

Compared with the result of the baseline method, the result based on SVMs plus sigmoid shows choosing the category based on maximal posterior probability leads to an improved performance on most types of Chinese chunks, except BDP, BMP and BTP chunks. The recall of BAP is 0.39% lower than that of experiment 1 (as shown in Table 3), but the FB1 is higher than that of the experiment 1 (in Table 3), which proves the combination of SVMs plus sigmoid significantly outperforms SVMs.

Table 4 gives the sigmoid parameters estimated using 10-fold cross-validation.

From the above experimental results, we can see that the recognition results of each Chinese chunk type are notably different. The recognition results of BAP, BNS and BTP are most unsatisfactory. Looking through the errors in the results, we see that BAP internal structure is more flexible than another Chinese chunk type and BNS and BTP are subclasses of BNP. The ambiguities of these syntactic structures lead to their poor experimental results.

4 Discussion

We investigate the effects of directly using the outputs of SVMs to resolve the dilemmas that either two or more different class labels are given to a single unlabeled constituent, or no class labels are given for some unlabeled constituents.

The basic form of SVMs finds the hyper-plane which separates the training data and which has the smallest norm of the weight vector. This hyper-plane separates positive and negative training samples with the maximum margin. So we can assume that the larger the SVM's output, the more confident the classification result. To confirm it, we conduct the next experiment.

Given an unlabeled sample x, classifier f_i is the i-th classifier of the 15 classifiers, $g_i = \boldsymbol{w} \cdot \boldsymbol{x} + b$ is the output of the f_i. We assigned the tag to be the class label with the maximum SVM's output, i.e.

$$f^* = argmax_{f_i}\ g_i(x) = argmax_{f_i}\ (\boldsymbol{w} \cdot \boldsymbol{x} + b) \quad (0 \leq i \leq 14) \qquad (9)$$

Table 5. The results of voting by using SVMs outputs

Chunk type	Precision	Recall	FB1
BAP	80.00	83.33	81.63
BDP	100.00	100.00	100.00
BMP	94.74	97.30	96.00
BNP	83.78	86.11	84.93
BNS	85.54	81.99	83.73
BTP	77.78	77.78	77.78
BVP	87.33	89.73	88.51

Table 5 gives the experimental results of voting by SVMs outputs. Compared with the baseline system, Table 5 shows voting by SVMs outputs lead to an improved performance on the precision of BAP and BNS categories, but their score of recall falls. While the precision and the recall of BNP declines, the performance on other chunks does not vary. It can be concluded that classification by SVM's output is not likely to increase the performance on all categories, because voting by SVM's output cannot use a utility model to make decision, then the predicted category is not confident, i.e., when a classifier is only a sub component of a global model, the classification outputs must be integrated for the overall decision.

4.1 Conclusion and Future Work

In this paper, we propose a novel methodology for Chinese chunk identification, which combines SVMs with sigmoid. SVMs can automatically focus on useful features and robustly handle a large feature set to develop models that maximize their generalizability. A sigmoid function can map SVM output into posterior probabilities after the sigmoid parameters are estimated by the training data formed by 10-fold cross-validation. Over results show it is more reasonable to choose the class based on the maximal posterior probability over all classes than other methods when we are in the dilemmas that different classes are assigned to a single unlabeled word by two or more classifiers, or no classes are assigned to an unlabeled word. In particular, results show this method is better for Chinese chunk recognition than the method based on SVMs only.

In this paper we only use word information and part-of-speech information to recognize Chinese chunks. In the future work we will combine semantic information, collocation information and co-occurrence information into the Chinese recognition task to achieve better performance.

Acknowledgements

The authors would like to thank the anonymous reviewers for their helpful comments. This research was supported in part by National Natural Science Foundation (Beijing) (60083006), National 973 Project (Beijing) (G19980305011) and National Natural Science Foundation (Beijing) & Microsoft Research Asia (60203019).

References

1. Zhang, Y., Zhou, Q.: Automatic identification of chinese base phrases. Journal of Chinese Information Processing **16** (2002)
2. Zhou, Q., song Sun, M., ning Huang, C.: Chunking parsing scheme for chinese sentences. Chinese J.Computers **22** (1999) 1158–1165
3. Zhao, J., Huang, C.: A transformation-based model for chinese basenp recognition. Journal of Chinese Information Processing **13** (1998) 1–7
4. Kudo, T., Matsumoto, Y.: Use of support vector learning for chunk identification. In Proc. of CoNLL-2000 and LLL-2000 (2000)
5. Kudo, T., Matsumoto, Y.: Chunking with support vector machines. In NAACL-2001 (2001)
6. Nakagawa, T., Kudoh, T., Matsumoto, Y.: Unknown word guessig and part-of-speech tagging using support vector machines. In Proc. of the 6th NLPRS (2001) 325–331
7. Yamada, H., Kudoh, T., Matsumoto, Y.: Japanese named entity extraction using support vector machines. IPSJSIG (1999)
8. Joachims, T.: Learning to classify text using support vector machines, Kluwer (2002)
9. Abney, S.: Parsing by chunks. In Robert C. Berwick, Steven P. Abney, and Carol Tenny, editors, Principle-Based Parsing: Computation and Psycholinguistics, Kluwer Academic Publishers, Boston (1991) 257–278
10. Cortes, C., Vapnik, V.: Support-vector networks. Machine Learning **20** (1995) 273–297
11. N.Vapnik, V.: The nature of statistical learning theory. NY, USA: Springer-Verlag (1995)
12. Boswell, D.: Introduction to support vector machines. (2002)
13. Kazama, J., Makino, T., Ohta, Y., Tsujii, J.: Tuning support vector machines for biomedical named entity recognition (2002)
14. Platt, J.: Probabilistic outputs for support vector machines and comparison to regularized likelihood methods. (2000) 61–74

Tagging Complex NEs with MaxEnt Models: Layered Structures Versus Extended Tagset

Deyi Xiong[1,2], Hongkui Yu[1,4], and Qun Liu[1,3]

[1] Institute of Computing Technology, the Chinese Academy of Sciences, Beijing
dyxiong@ict.ac.cn
[2] Graduate School of the Chinese Academy of Sciences
[3] Inst. of Computational Linguistics, Peking University, Beijing
[4] Information Science & Technology College, Beijing University of Chemical Technology, Beijing

Abstract. The paper discusses two policies for recognizing NEs with complex structures by maximum entropy models. One policy is to develop cascaded MaxEnt models at different levels. The other is to design more detailed tags with human knowledge in order to represent complex structures. The experiments on Chinese organization names recognition indicate that layered structures result in more accurate models while extended tags can not lead to positive results as expected. We empirically prove that the $\{start, continue, end, unique, other\}$ tag set is the best tag set for NE recognition with MaxEnt models.

1 Introduction

In recent years, MaxEnt models (see [1]) or MaxEnt-based models are widely used for many NLP tasks especially for tagging sequential data (see [2] and [3]). These models have great advantages over traditional HMM models. One of these advantages, which is often emphasized, is that MaxEnt models can incorporate richer features in a well-founded fashion than HMMs do.

When tagging NEs with MaxEnt models, the common problem that NE taggers have to face is how to improve the performance of the recognition of NEs with complex structures. For many NE tagging models, good results are gained for recognizing NEs with simple structures (e.g. person names) while bad results for the recognition of those with complex structures (e.g. organization names). We think the key is to efficiently represent multilevel structures of complex NEs. To address this problem, we take special measures for complex NEs recognition from two different perspectives.

We find that complex NEs are often constituted with other simple NEs. This directly inspires us to build a multi-layer cascaded MaxEnt model as our first way to represent multilevel structures. We put simple NEs at lower levels and train a MaxEnt model for tagging them. And complex NEs are put at higher levels and another model is trained for them. Then we firstly run the model at lower levels and later the model at higher levels.

Multi-layer models, such as cascaded models, hierarchical models[1] are very popular in NLP because of their sound fitness for many hierarchically structured tasks. Many multi-layer models are developed, such as finite state cascades for partial parsing (see [10]), hierarchical HMMs for information extraction (see [6] and [14]). However, to our knowledge, this is the first attempt to use cascaded MaxEnt models for complex NEs tagging. The first reason for this may be that most other MaxEnt taggers (e.g. taggers in [2] and [3]) focus on designing complex features to gain rich knowledge since features can represent attributes at different levels of granularity of observations. However, too complex features will result in other problems such as model consistency and data sparseness (see [2]). In our cascaded MaxEnt models, features are kept simple at each level. The other reason is the error propagation existing in multi-layer models. However, in our experiments, even without any measures to control this error propagation, a significant performance improvement is gained compared with MaxEnt models without cascades.

The other method to represent hierarchical structures is to design detailed tags with human knowledge. For many tasks, such as part-of-speech tagging, parsing, fine-grained tags will lead to more accurate models (see [13]). We think traditional tagset for NEs tagging is coarse-grained to some extent, so we design more detailed tags for different classes of elements which occur in complex NEs. Our intuition was that we would see a performance gain from these extended tags. However, the results are quite the contrary. This lead to an extensive but empirical discussion of designing an appropriate tag set for a particular task which Yu et al. (see [9]) think is worthy of further investigation.

The paper is organized as follows. In Section 2 we simply introduce how a MaxEnt NE tagger works. In Section 3 we discuss the construction of muliti-layer MaxEnt models and their application in the complex NEs recognition. In Section 4 we introduce the extended tag set for Chinese organization names recognition. In the last section, we present our conclusions and future work.

2 Tagging NEs with Maximum Entropy Models

NE tagging is the problem of learning a function that maps a sequence of observations $o = (o_1, o_2, ..., o_T)$ to a NE tag sequence $t = (t_1, t_2, ...t_T)$, where each $t_i \in T$, the set of individual tags which constitute NEs or non-NEs. A MaxEnt NE tagger is constructed on the set of events $H \times T$, where H is the set of possible observation and tag contexts, or "histories", and T is the set of allowable tags. The probability of a tag t conditioned on a history h is given as follows by MaxEnt models.

$$P(t|h) = \frac{1}{Z(h)} exp(\sum_i \lambda_i f_i(h,t)) . \tag{1}$$

---

[1] Cascaded models and hierarchical models are two different typical styles of multi-layer models. The differences are discussed in Section 3.

where the functions $f_i \in \{0,1\}$ are model features and the λ_i are model parameters or weights of the model features, and the denominator $Z(h)$ is a normalization constant which is defined as:

$$Z(h) = \sum_t exp(\sum_i \lambda_i f_i(h,t)) \ . \quad (2)$$

This exponential form of MaxEnt models can be derived by choosing a unique model with maximum entropy which satisfies a set of constraints imposed by the empirical distribution q and the model distribution p with the following form:

$$E_p[f] = E_q[f] \ . \quad (3)$$

where E represents the expectation of f under a certain distribution.

Given training data $\Omega = \{h^i, t^i\}_{i=1}^N$, MaxEnt taggers are also trained to maximize the likelihood of the training data using the model distribution p:

$$L(p) = \prod_{i=1}^N P(t_i|h_i) \ . \quad (4)$$

The model parameters for the distribution p can be obtained by *Generalized Iterative Scaling* (see [4]) or *Improved Iterative Scaling* (see [7]). Given an observation sequence $(o_1, o_2, ..., o_T)$, a tag sequence candidate $(t_1, t_2, ..., t_T)$ has conditional probability:

$$P(o_1, o_2, ..., o_T | t_1, t_2, ..., t_T) = \prod_{i=1}^T P(t_i|h_i) \ . \quad (5)$$

The best tag sequence can be found by Viterbi search or beam search introduced by Ratnaparkni (see [2]).

3 Multi-layer MaxEnt Models

The fact that complex multilevel structures often appear in NLP tasks such as sequence labeling and parsing is the direct motivation for many different multi-layer models to be developed (see [10], [11] and [14]).

3.1 Cascaded Models vs. Hierarchical Models

There are two different methods frequently used to build multi-layer models. One way is to build models layer by layer, first simple structures of level one, then a little more complex structures of level two, and so forth. The models hypothesizing complex structures are cascaded on models for simple structures. We call multi-layer models constructed by this way cascaded models. The other way for the construction of multi-layer models is to build models recursively;

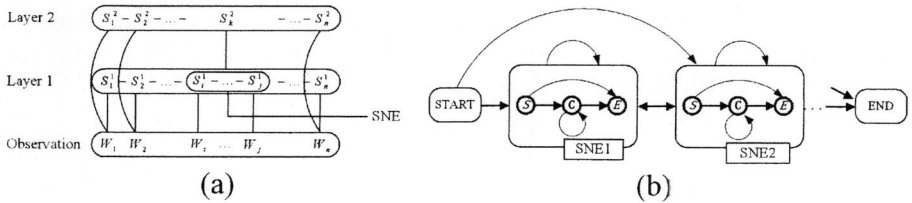

Fig. 1. Cascaded models (a) vs. hierarchical models (b). SNE means simple named entity predicted at the lower level.

bottom level models are embedded as sub-models in top level models. The multi-layer models built by this way have a hierarchical tree structure and therefore we name them hierarchical models.

Figure 1 gives a double-level cascaded model as well as a double-level hierarchical model for complex NEs recognition. The coupling between top levels and bottom levels in cascaded models is laxer than that of hierarchical models and this makes that cascaded models at different levels can be built separately and therefore flexible. Because of this flexibility, we choose cascaded MaxEnt models as our multi-layer models to represent multilevel structures in complex NEs.

3.2 Cascaded Double-Level MaxEnt Models for Chinese Organization Names Recognition

Chinese ORGs often include one or more PERs and/or LOCs on their left. For example, "中国长城工业总公司"(from MET-2 test corpus) is an organization name where "中国" and "长城" both are location names. We find that there are 698 different structures of ORG in six-month's China's People Daily (CPD) corpus(Figure 2). The most common structure is a location name followed by a noun, which accounts for 33.9% in CPD corpus. The statistical data indicate that ORGs should be recognized at a higher level than LOCs.

We design a cascaded double-level MaxEnt model (figure 1.a) for ORG recognition which has two MaxEnt models separately working at the bottom and top level. The bottom model predicts location and person names, and then the top model predicts organization names.

More specifically, Our cascaded double-level MaxEnt model works in the following steps:

1. Train a PER-LOC tagger as the bottom model with the training set where only PERs and LOCs are labeled.
2. Train a ORG tagger as the top model with the same training set where all PERs and LOCs are replaced by two tokens, separately, "未##人" and "未##地", and all ORGs are tagged.
3. When tested, the PER-LOC tagger firstly works and labels PERs as "未##人" and LOCs as "未##地".
4. Then the PER-LOC tagger takes as its input the output of the step 3 and labels ORGs in the test data.

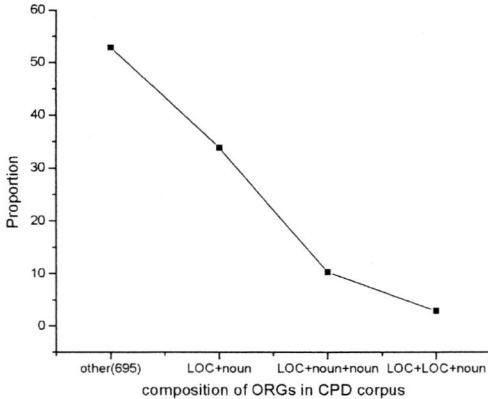

Fig. 2. Different Structures of ORG in CPD corpus and their proportions.

Of course, it is unrealistic to assume that true PER and LOC labels are provided by PER-LOC tagger, so there are some errors in the bottom model and they will be propagated to the top model. We think, however, multilevel structure knowledge represented by cascaded MaxEnt models has a greater positive effect on the performance than error propagation has the negative effect on it. Gao et al. (see [12]) used a similar approach to Chinese organization name recognition, but they didn't use Maxent models. And the other difference is that the way they treat the LOC level and ORG level is more like hierarchical models than cascaded models.

To compare our cascaded double-level MaxEnt model with the single-level MaxEnt model, we train them on one-month's (January, 1998) CPD news corpus (roughly 1,140,000 words) tagged with NER tags by Peking University, and test them on another month's (June, 1998) CPD news corpus (roughly 1,266,000 words). Both the training data and the test data are pre-segmented and converted to the annotation style used in [3]. We just use lexical features within a five-token context window and the *prevtag* features for both models so that the comparison can not be disturbed by introducing other factors. The *prevtag* features are binary functions on the previous tag and the current tag. An example of a *prevtag* feature is

$$f_j(t_i - 1, t_i) = \begin{cases} 1, \text{ if } t_{i-1} = start \text{ and } t_i = continue \\ 0, \quad\quad\quad\quad\quad\quad otherwise \end{cases}. \quad (6)$$

For both models, features that occur less than five times in the training data are not used, and the GIS algorithm is run for 1500 iterations. When having assigned the proper weight (λ value) to each of features, a beam search (see [2]) is used to find the best NE tag sequence for a new sentence.

The results of the two models are shown in Table 1. To assess the significance of the improvement according to F1, we use the paired samples t-test, and divide the test data into ten groups (each group contains three-day's CPD news). Each

Table 1. Performance of Single-Level Model and Double-Level Model When Tested on CPD Corpus.

Model	Total ORGs	Found ORGs	Correct ORGs	Prec.	Recall	F1
Single-Level Model	13453	8437	6893	0.817	0.512	63.0
Cascaded MaxEnt Model	13453	8808	7231	0.821	0.538	65.0

group is tested by both the single-level model and the double-level model. The p-value is less than 0.01. This indicates that layered structures are important for complex NEs tagging which are often neglected by MaxEnt taggers with a single level. Furthermore, the cascaded MaxEnt models are easy to be constructed. Taggers at higher levels can be trained on the output of lower taggers by rotated training used by [3], or directly trained on the corpus which is tagged with higher level tags.

4 Extended NE Tags

Traditional NE tags include *start*, *continue*, *end* and *unique* for each kind of NE and *other* for non-NE (see [3]). At the first, we doubt their ability to represent complex structures. Yu et al. (see [8]) design richer roles for Chinese organization names recognition with HMM-based models. In fact, these roles are special NE tags. Here we select some of Yu's roles as our extended ORG tags which are shown in Table 2.

Table 2. The extended tag set for ORG recognition.

Tags	Remarks	Examples
A	Prefix context	参与亚太经合组织的活动
C	Common tokens	北京电影学院
F	Translated terms	美国摩托罗拉公司
G	Location names	交通银行北京分行
I	Special tokens	中央电视台
J	Abbreviations	巴政府
D	Ends of ORGs	国务院侨务办公室
T	Unique ORGs	新华社
Z	Other (non-ORG)	

These tags are designed by incorporating human knowledge. For examples, the tag G indicates that its corresponding observation is a location name and the tag I shows that its observation is a token which is used to constitute ORGs very frequently. Therefore, in our intuition, we expect a performance gain from these extended tags designed with human knowledge.

We train two MaxEnt models; one is trained on the corpus labeled with traditional tag set, while the other is trained on the same corpus but labeled with the extended tag set. Both models just incorporate lexical features within a five-token context window. This time we train the two models on CPD news corpus in June and test them on CPD news corpus in January. The results are out of our expectation, which are shown in Table 3. After careful comparison of the two tag set, we find the five tags (C, F, G, I, and J) in ORG of the extended tag set can be equivalent to *start* and *continue* in the traditional tag set in a finite-state automata. That is to say, the extended tag set is redundant for ORG recognition and therefore the probability mass of a candidate tag sequence might be lessened across redundant state transitions. Although these tags are designed with human knowledge, they violate the second criterion of Yu et al. (see [9]), in other words, the extended tag set is not efficient compared with the traditional one.

Table 3. Performance of Traditional-Tagset Model, Extended-Tagset Model & Cut-Tagset Model When Tested on CPD Corpus.

Tagset	Prec.	Recall	F1
Traditional tagset	0.865	0.651	74.3
Extended tagset	0.867	0.625	72.6
Cut tagset	0.767	0.618	68.5

Then we check the efficiency of the traditional tag set. We combine *start* and *continue* states into one state – *not-end* state because we find there are a very few features indicating the start of ORGs. The results, however, show that the cut tag set is not sufficient for ORG recognition. Furthermore, we find insufficient tag set result in a larger accuracy decrease of taggers than inefficient tag set does. All of these show that designing an appropriate (efficient and sufficient) tag set is important enough for modelers to consider.

5 Conclusions and Further Work

We think the recognition of complex NEs is one of the most difficult problems of NE tagging. However, most MaxEnt taggers do not distinguish complex NEs from simple ones and thereby not take any special measures for the recognition of complex NEs. We have shown that MaxEnt taggers can greatly benefit from layered structures when tagging complex NEs and that the traditional tag set is sufficient and efficient even for the recognition of NEs with complicated structures. The experience for designing an appropriate NE tagset is also helpful for other tagging tasks. All of our experiments are made on a large-scale test corpus and this ensures that the improvement is important.

We plan to design more representative cascaded MaxEnt models for Chinese ORGs recognition by using the probabilities of PERs or LOCs predicted by the bottom model as features on the top model in order to control the error propagation. And we want to make choosing a tag set for particular tasks automatic by incorporating the choosing mechanism into taggers.

References

1. Adam Berger, Stephen Della Pietra, and Vincent Della Pietra. 1996. A maximum entropy approach to natural language processing. *Computational linguistics*, 22(1):39-71.
2. Adwait Ratnaparkhi. 1998. A maximum entropy part-of-speech tagger. In *Proceedings of the EMNLP Conference*, pages 133-142, Philadelphia, PA.
3. Andrew Borthwick. 1999. A Maximum Entropy Approach to Named Entity Recognition. Ph.D. thesis, Computer Science Department, New York University.
4. Darroch, J.N., & Ratcliff, D. 1972. Generalized iterative scaling for log-linear models. *The Annals of Mathematical Statistics*, 43(5), 1470–1480.
5. Daniel M. Bikel, Richard Schwartz, and Ralph M. Weischedel. 1999. An algorithm that learns what's in a name. *Machine Learning*, 34(1/2/3):211–231.
6. S. Fine, Y. Singer, and N. Tishby. 1998. The hierarchical hidden Markov model: Analysis and applications. *Machine learning*, 32:41-62, 1998.
7. Stephen Della Pietra, Vincent Della Pietra, and John Lafferty. 1997. *Inducing features of random fields. IEEE Transactions on Pattern Analysis and Machine Intelligence*, 19:380-393.
8. YU Hong-Kui, ZHANG Hua-Ping, LIU Qun. 2003. Recognition of Chinese Organization Name Based on Role Tagging, In *Proceedings of 20th International Conference on Computer Processing of Oriental Languages*, pages 79-87, ShenYang
9. Yu Shihong, Bai Shuanhu and Wu Paul. 1998. Description of the Kent Ridge Digital Labs System Used for MUC-7. *In Proceedings of the MUC-7*.
10. Steven Abney. 1996. Partial Parsing via Finite-state Cascades. In Proceedings of the ESSLLI '96 Robust Parsing Workshop.
11. Thorsten Brants. 1999. Cascaded Markov Models. In Proceedings of 9th Conference of the European Chapter of the Association for Computational Linguistics EACL-99. Bergen, Norway, 1999.
12. Jianfeng Gao, Mu Li and Chang-Ning Huang. 2003. Improved source-channel models for Chinese word segmentation. In *ACL-2003*. Sapporo, Japan, 7-12, July, 2003.
13. Dan Klein and Christopher D. Manning. 2003. Accurate Unlexicalized Parsing. ACL 2003, pp. 423-430.
14. M. Skounakis, M. Craven & S. Ray (2003). Hierarchical Hidden Markov Models for Information Extraction. Proceedings of the 18th International Joint Conference on Artificial Intelligence, Acapulco, Mexico. Morgan Kaufmann.

A Nearest-Neighbor Method for Resolving PP-Attachment Ambiguity

Shaojun Zhao and Dekang Lin

Department of Computing Science, University of Alberta, Edmonton, Alberta, T6G 2E8
{shaojun,lindek}@cs.ualberta.ca

Abstract. We present a nearest-neighbor algorithm for resolving prepositional phrase attachment ambiguities. Its performance is significantly higher than previous corpus-based methods for PP-attachment that do not rely on manually constructed knowledge bases. We will also show that the PP-attachment task provides a way to evaluate methods for computing distributional word similarities. Our experiments indicate that the cosine of pointwise mutual information vector is a significantly better similarity measure than several other commonly used similarity measures.

1 Introduction

Natural language sentences often contain various forms of attachment ambiguities. Consider the following examples:
(1) PP-attachment ambiguity:
  a. *Mary* [*ate* [*the salad*] [*with a fork*]]
  b. *Mary* [*ate* [*the salad* [*with croutons*]]]
(2) Relative clause attachment ambiguity:
  a. *They denied* [*the petition* [*for his release*] [*that was signed by over 10,000 people*]]
  b. *They denied* [*the petition for* [*his release* [*that would trigger an outrage*]]]
(3) Pre-nominal modifier ambiguity:
  a. [[*Child abuse*] *expert*]
  b. [*Child* [*computer expert*]]

Such ambiguities are a major source of parser errors (Lin 2003). In languages with little or no overt case marking, such as English and Chinese, syntactic information is insufficient to make attachment decisions (as demonstrated in the above examples). Many researchers have investigated the resolution of attachment ambiguities, especially for PP attachments.

As in previous work on PP-attachment (Hindle and Rooth 1993), we simplified the PP-Attachment problem by defining it as the following binary classification task. Given a 4-tuple of the form (V, N_1, P, N_2), where V is the head verb, N_1 is the head noun of the object of V, P is a preposition, and N_2 is the head noun of the prepositional complement, the goal is to classify the 4-tuple as either adverbial attachment (attaching to V) or adjectival attachment (attaching to N_1). For example, the 4-tuple (*eat, salad, with, fork*) is extracted from example (1a) and it has the target classification V; the 4-tuple (*eat, salad, with, croutons*) is extracted from example (1b) and it has the target classification N.

We present a nearest-neighbor algorithm for resolving PP-attachment ambiguities. The training examples are a set of 4-tuples with target classifications. Given a new 4-tuple to be classified, we search the training examples for its top-k nearest neighbors and determine its attachment based on the known classifications of the nearest neighbors. The similarity between two 4-tuples is determined by the distributional similarity between the corresponding words in the 4-tuples.

In the next section, we will briefly review the related work in PP-attachment. Section 3 presents several algorithms for computing distributional word similarity that are used in our experiments. The nearest-neighbor algorithm for resolving PP-attachment ambiguities is presented in Section 4. We then describe our experimental set up and results in Section 5 and conclude in Section 6.

2 Related Work

Altmann and Steedman (1988) showed that current discourse context is often required for disambiguating attachments. Recent work shows that it is generally sufficient to utilize lexical information (Brill and Resnik, 1994; Collins and Brooks, 1995; Hindle and Rooth, 1993; Ratnaparkhi et al., 1994).

One of the earliest corpus-based approaches to prepositional phrase attachment used lexical preference by computing co-occurrence frequencies (lexical associations) of verbs and nouns with prepositions (Hindle and Rooth, 1993). Training data was obtained by extracting all phrases of the form (V, N_1, P, N_2) from a large parsed corpus.

Supervised methods later improved attachment accuracy. Ratnaparkhi et al. (1994) used a maximum entropy model considering only lexical information within the verb phrase. They experimented with both word features and word class features. Their combination yielded 81.6% accuracy.

Collins and Brooks (1995) proposed a probabilistic model for PP-attachment, which employed a backed-off model to smooth the probabilities of unseen events. They discovered that P is the most informative lexical item for attachment disambiguation and keeping low frequency events increases performance. Their algorithm achieved 84.5% accuracy on the same data set as (Ratnaparkhi et al. 1994) and (Brill and Resnik 1994). This level of performance was also obtained by several methods proposed later. The boosting algorithm in (Abney *et al.* 1999) had an accuracy of 84.6%. The nearest-neighbor algorithm in (Zavrel *et al.* 1997) was 84.4% accurate.

The method in (Zavrel *et al.* 1997) is quite similar to ours. They construct a reduced-dimension feature vector for each word by applying the Principle Component Analysis (PCA). Each 4-tuple is represented by the concatenation of the feature vectors of the words in the 4-tuple. The distance between two 4-tuples is defined as the sum of the distances of each vector component.

A non-statistical supervised approach by Brill and Resnik (1994) yielded 81.8% accuracy using a transformation-based approach (Brill, 1995) and incorporating word-class information. They report that the top-20 transformations learned involved specific prepositions supporting Collins and Brooks' claim that the preposition is the most important lexical item for resolving the attachment ambiguity.

The algorithm in (Stetina and Nagao, 1997) employed a semantically tagged corpus. Each word in a labeled corpus is sense-tagged using an unsupervised word-sense disambiguation algorithm with WordNet (Miller, 1990). Testing examples are classified using a decision tree induced from the training examples. They report 88.1% attachment accuracy approaching the human accuracy of 88.2% (Ratnaparkhi et al., 1994). Li (2002) reported 88.2% accuracy. However, his result was obtained with a different corpus than (Ratnaparkhi *et al.*, 1994) and therefore is not directly comparable to ours.

3 Distributional Word Similarity

Words that tend to appear in the same contexts tend to have similar meanings. This is known as the Distributional Hypothesis in linguistics (Harris 1968). For example, the words *test* and *exam* are similar because both of them can be objects of verbs such as *administer, cancel, cheat on, conduct...* and both of them can be modified by adjectives such as *academic, comprehensive, diagnostic, difficult...*

Many methods have been proposed to compute distributional similarity between words, e.g., (Hindle, 1990), (Pereira *et al.* 1993), (Grefenstette 1994) and (Lin 1998). Almost all of the methods represent a word by a feature vector where each feature corresponds to a type of context in which the word appeared. They differ in how the feature vectors are constructed and how the similarity between two feature vectors is computed. The remainder of this section details the feature representation schemes and similarity formulas used in our experiments.

3.1 Syntax-Based Feature Representation

In syntax-based method, the corpus is first parsed and then features are defined in terms of the dependency relationships between words in a corpus. A dependency relationship (Hays, 1964; Hudson, 1984; Mel'čuk, 1987) is an asymmetric binary relationship between a word called *head*, and another word called *modifier*. The structure of a sentence can be represented by a set of dependency relationships that form a tree. A word in the sentence may have several modifiers, but each word may modify at most one word. The root of the dependency tree does not modify any word. It is also called the head of the sentence.

For example, the following diagram shows the dependency tree for the sentence "*John found a solution to the problem*".

John found a solution to the problem.

The links in the diagram represent dependency relationships. The direction of a link is from the head to the modifier in the relationship. Labels associated with the links represent types of dependency relations.

We define a feature of a word w to be (r, w') such that there is a dependency relationship r between w and w'. For example, the word *solution* in the above example has three features *(-obj, find)*, *(to, problem)* and *(det, a)*, where *-obj* is the inverse relation of the *obj* relation. The feature vectors of words are constructed by extracting all the features of all the words from the corpus. The value of each feature is the frequency count of the feature in the corpus. The following is a subset of the features and their values for the word *seminar*:

Features	Values
(-*subj, teach*)	3
(-*obj, sponsor*)	44
(-*obj, attend*)	81
(-*obj, teach*)	12
......	......

The features mean that *seminar* was used as the subject of *teach* 3 times, as the object of *sponsor* 44 times and as the object of *teach* 12 times.

3.2 Proximity-Based Feature Representation

The syntax-based method requires a parsed corpus, which is often unavailable. Since most dependency relationships involve words that are situated close to one another, the dependency relationships can often be approximated by co-occurrence relationships within a small window. In previous approaches, the size of the window varies from 1 to the size of a document. However, having window size larger than 1 often introduce confusion between word association and word similarity. For example, suppose the window is ±5 words and the corpus contains a sentence *He died in a horrific traffic accident,* the words *died, in, a*, and *horrific* all become common features of *traffic* and *accident*. As a result, *traffic* and *accident* have a high similarity simply because they tend to collocate with one another.

In (Turney 2001) and (Terra and Clarke 2003), only one word within a window around *w* is chosen as a feature of *w*. They chose the word that has the highest pointwise mutual information with *w*. We have taken a different approach. We define features of *w* to be the first non-stop word on either side of *w* and the intervening stop words (which we arbitrarily define as the top-20 most frequent words in the corpus). For example, suppose the corpus consist of a single sentence *John found a solution to the problem*, the features of *solution* will be

Features	Values
(*left, find*)	0.50
(*left, a*)	0.50
(*right, to*)	0.33
(*right, the*)	0.33
(*right, problem*)	0.33

3.3 Similarity Measures

Once the contexts of a word are represented as a feature vector, the similarity between two words can be computed using their context vectors. We use $(u_1, u_2, ... u_n)$ and $(v_1, v_2, ... v_n)$ to denote the feature vectors for the word *u* and *v* respectively, where *n* is the number of feature types extracted from a corpus. We use f_i to denote the *i*th feature. The remainder of this subsection explains the similarity measures used in our experiments.

Cosine Measure
The Cosine Similarity Measure between two words computes the cosine between their feature vectors.

$$sim_{Cos}(u,v) = \frac{\sum_{i=1}^{n} u_i \times v_i}{\sqrt{\sum_{i=1}^{n} u_i^2} \times \sqrt{\sum_{i=1}^{n} v_i^2}}$$

A serious problem with the cosine measure is that the contribution of a feature in the similarity function is weighted by its frequency count. Features involving frequent words, such as *the* or *of*, tend to be given much higher weight than words with more semantic content.

Cosine of Pointwise Mutual Information
The pointwise mutual information between a feature f_i and a word u measures the strength association between them. It is defined as follows:

$$pmi(f_i, u) = \log\left(\frac{P(f_i, u)}{P(f_i) \times P(u)}\right)$$

where $P(f_i,u)$ is the probability of f_i co-occurring with u; $P(f_i)$ is the probability of f_i co-occurring with any word; and $P(u)$ is the probability of any feature co-occurring with u. The Cosine of Pointwise Mutual Information is defined as:

$$sim_{CosPMI}(u,v) = \frac{\sum_{i=1}^{n} pmi(f_i, u) \times pmi(f_i, v)}{\sqrt{\sum_{i=1}^{n} pmi(f_i, u)^2} \times \sqrt{\sum_{i=1}^{n} pmi(f_i, v)^2}}$$

Dice Co-efficient
The Dice co-efficient is a particularly simple similarity measure. It only distinguishes between zero and non-zero frequency counts.

$$sim_{Dice}(u,v) = \frac{2 \times \sum_{i=1}^{n} s(u_i) \times s(v_i)}{\sum_{i=1}^{n} s(u_i) + \sum_{i=1}^{n} s(v_i)}$$

where $s(x)=1$ if $x>0$ and $s(x)=0$ otherwise.

Jensen-Shannon Divergence
The feature vectors can be converted into probability distributions by dividing each component with the sum of all components in the vector. The Jensen-Shannon divergence measures the distance between two probability distributions and their average distribution (Rao, 1982; Lin, 1991):

$$JS(q,r) = \frac{1}{2}\left[D(q \| avg_{q,r}) + D(r \| avg_{q,r})\right]$$

where the function $D(p_1(x)\|p_2(x))$ is the KL-Divergence:

$$D(p_1(x) \| p_2(x)) = \sum_x p_1(x) \log\left(\frac{p_1(x)}{p_2(x)}\right)$$

and $avg_{q,r}$ is the average distribution of q and r:

$$avg_{q,r}(x) = \frac{1}{2}[q(x) + r(x)]$$

The Jensen-Shannon divergence can be converted into a similarity measure by defining

$$sim_{JS}(u,v) = \frac{1}{1 + JS(u,v)}$$

When u and v are identical distributions, $JS(u,v)=0$ and $sim_{JS}(u,v)=1$.

4 Resolving PP-Attachment Ambiguity with Nearest Neighbors

Our algorithm for resolving PP-attachment ambiguity takes a 4-tuple (V, N_1, P, N_2) as input and classifies it as N or V. The class N means that the prepositional phrase modifies the noun N_1. The class V means that the prepositional phrase modifies the verb V. The classification process is comprised of 4 steps. Each step attempts to make a decision according to the weighted majority vote by the nearest neighbors of the input. The weight of a training example is the similarity between it and the input. Different steps have different definitions of what constitutes the nearest neighbors and use different formulas to compute the similarity between two 4-tuples. A step is taken only if the previous step fails to make a decision, which happens when the classes N and V received an equal vote (often due to an empty set of nearest neighbors).

In *Step 1*, the nearest neighbors consist of training examples that are identical to the input 4-tuple. The similarity between such an example and the input is 1.

In *Step 2*, the nearest neighbors consist of the top-k (k is determined using a development data set) most similar training examples that involve the same preposition as the input. The similarity between two 4-tuples t_1 and t_2 is computed as follows:

$$sim(t_1, t_2) = ab + bc + ca$$

where a, b and c are the distributional word similarities between the two verbs, the two N_1's and the two N_2's, respectively. The word similarity can be computed using any of the similarity measures discussed in the previous section. The 4-tuple similarity $sim(t_1, t_2)$ will be zero when any two of a, b and c are zeros.

Step 3 is identical to Step 2, except that the similarity between two 4-tuples t_1 and t_2 is defined as $sim(t_1, t_2) = a + b + c$, which has a zero value only when all of a, b and c are zeros.

In *Step 4*, the set of nearest neighbors includes all the training examples that involve the same preposition P as the input. The similarity between each of them and the input is considered to be a constant. If the votes for N and V are tied in this step, the default classification N is assigned to the input.

5 Experimental Results and Discussions

Data Sets

We computed the word similarities using the ACQUAINT Corpus, which consists of newswire text data in English, drawn from three sources: the *Xinhua News Service* (People's Republic of China), the *New York Times News Service*, and the *Associated Press Worldstream News Service*. It contains roughly 375 million words (about 3 GB of text). We computed the distributional word similarity using both syntax and proximity based methods. For the syntax-based methods, we parsed the corpus with Minipar (Lin 1994) and extracted dependency relationships. An evaluation with the Susanne corpus showed that 88.54% of the dependencies identified by Minipar are correct (Lin 2003).

The PP-attachment data set used in our experiments was extracted from the Penn Treebank WSJ corpus by Ratnaparkhi *et al* (1994). It includes a training set, a development set and a testing set, consisting of 20801, 4039 and 3097 elements respectively. We preprocessed the data to reduce all the words to their root forms. We replaced digits with @ signs. For example, 2003 becomes @@@@; $1.15 becomes $@.@@.

Parameter Tuning

For each feature type and similarity measure, we run the nearest neighbor algorithm on the development data set with different k. Figure 1 shows the results. We chose the k-values that produced the best performance on the development set and used them in the experiments with the test set.

Results on the Test Data Set

Table 1 shows the result of PP attachment accuracy using different methods for computing word similarity. Among different similarity measures, sim_{CosPMI} has the best performance, which is significantly higher than other similarity measures listed in this table with ≥95% confidence (assuming binomial distribution). It can also be seen that syntax-based features are better than proximity-based ones.

Despite the high performance of sim_{CosPMI}, the closely related sim_{Cos} measure performed rather poorly. The only difference between the two is that sim_{Cos} uses the frequency counts as feature values whereas sim_{CosPMI} uses the pointwise mutual information between a feature and the word. This suggests that frequency counts are inappropriate as feature values. In fact, the sim_{Dice} measure, which totally ignores all frequency counts, outperforms the measures that use them: sim_{Cos} and sim_{JS}.

The accuracies achieved by previous corpus-based methods that do not rely on manually constructed knowledge bases are shown in Table 2. The 86.5% accuracy by sim_{CosPMI} with syntax-based features is significantly higher than all of them with ≥98% confidence (assuming errors are binomially distributed).

For each of the steps in our algorithm, Table 3 gives its coverage (the number of decisions made in that step), the coverage % (the percentage of decisions made in that step) and the accuracy (the percentage of correct decisions in that step). It can be seen that over 99.8% of the coverage is provided by Steps 1 and 2 in which the preposition P and at least two of V, N_1 and N_2 are involved in the decisions. In contrast, only 40% of the decisions involve as many words in the method proposed in (Collins and Brooks 1994).

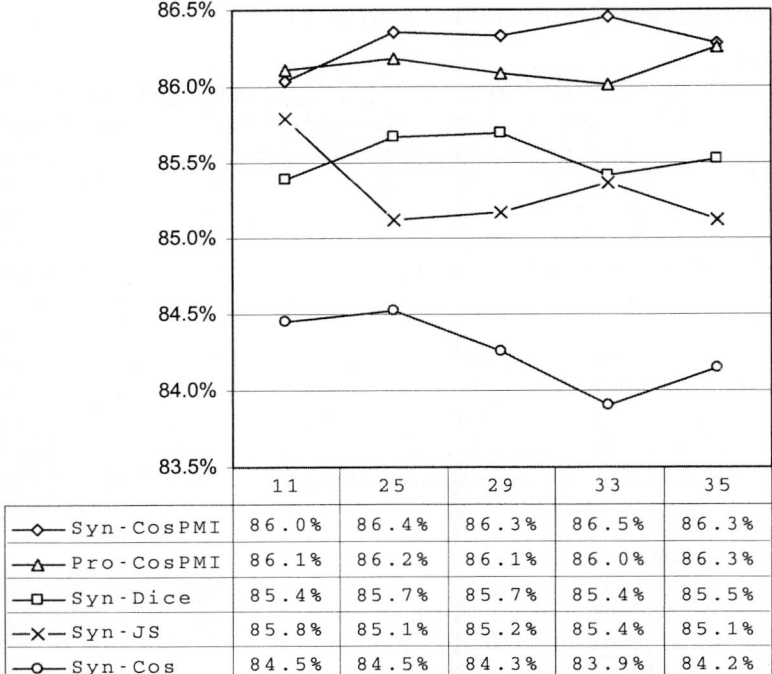

Fig. 1. Parameter Tuning on Development Set

Table 1. PP-Attachment Accuracy

Feature Type	Similarity	Accuracy	k
Syntax-based	sim_{CosPMI}	**86.5%**	33
Proximity-based	sim_{CosPMI}	85.6%	35
Syntax-based	sim_{Dice}	85.3%	29
Syntax-based	sim_{JS}	84.9%	11
Syntax-based	sim_{Cos}	83.1%	25

Table 2. Previous PP-Attachment Accuracies

Method	Accuracy
Ratnaparkhi, Reynar and Roukos 94	81.6%
Collins and Brooks 95	84.5%
Zavrel, Daelemans and Veenstra 97	84.4%
Abney, Schapire and Singer 99	84.6%
Our Result (using sim_{CosPMI})	86.5%

Table 3. Coverage and Accuracy of 4 Steps

Step	Coverage	Coverage %	Accuracy
1	244	7.88%	91.8%
2	2848	91.96%	86.0%
3	2	0.06%	100.0%
4	3	0.10%	100.0%
Overall	3097	100.00%	86.5%

6 Conclusion

We presented a nearest-neighbor algorithm for resolving prepositional phrase attachment ambiguities. Our algorithm achieved a significantly higher accuracy than other corpus-based methods that do not rely on manually constructed knowledge bases. We also demonstrated that the PP-attachment problem can also be used as an evaluation criterion for distributional word similarity. Our experiments showed that the cosine of pointwise mutual information is significantly better than several other commonly used similarity measures.

Acknowledgements

The authors wish to thank the anonymous reviewers for valuable inputs. This research is funded by NSERC Research Grant OGP121338 and by The *Alberta Ingenuity Centre for Machine Learning*.

References

1. Abney, S. and Schapire, R.E. and Singer, Y. 1999. Boosting Applied to Tagging and PP-attachment. In Proceedings of the Joint SIGDAT Conference on Empirical Methods in Natural Language Processing and Very Large Corpora, EMNLP-VLC, pages 38--45, College Park, MD.
2. Altmann, G. and Steedman, M. 1988. Interaction with Context During Human Sentence Processing. Cognition, 30:191-238.
3. Brill, E. 1995. Transformation-based Error-driven Learning and Natural Language Processing: A case study in part of speech tagging. Computational Linguistics, December.
4. Brill, E. and Resnik. P. 1994. A Rule-Based Approach to Prepositional Phrase Attachment Disambiguation. In Proceedings of COLING-94. pp.1198-1204. Kyoto, Japan
5. Collins, M. and Brooks, J. 1995. Prepositional Phrase Attachment through a Backed-off Model. In Proceedings of the Third Workshop on Very Large Corpora, pp. 27-38. Cambridge, Massachusetts.
6. Grefenstette, G. 1994. Explorations in Automatic Thesaurus Discovery, Kluwer Academic Publishers, Boston.
7. Harris, Z.S.1968. Mathematical Structures of Language. New York: Wiley.
8. Hays, D. 1964. Dependency Theory: a Formalism and Some Observations. Language, 40:511-525.
9. Hindle, D. 1990. Noun Classification from Predicate-Argument Structures. In Proceedings of ACL-90. pp. 268-275. Pittsburgh, Pennsylvania.
10. Hindle, D. and Rooth, M. 1993. Structural Ambiguity and Lexical Relations. Computational Linguistics, 19(1):103-120.
11. Hudson, R. 1984. Word Grammar. Basil Blackwell Publishers Limited. Oxford, England.
12. Li, H. 2002. Word Clustering and Disambiguation based on Co-occurrence Data. Natural Language Engineering, 8(1), 25-42.
13. Lin, D. 1998. Automatic Retrieval and Clustering of Similar Words. In Proceedings of COLING-ACL98. Montreal, Canada.
14. Lin, D. 1994. Principar - an Efficient, Broad-Coverage, Principle-Based Parser. In Proceedings of COLING-94. Kyoto, Japan.
15. Lin, D. 2003. Dependency-based evaluation of MINIPAR. In Building and using syntactically annotated corpora, Anne Abeille (editor), pp. 317-330. KLUWER, Dordrecht.

16. Lin, J. 1991. Divergence measures based on the Shannon entropy. IEEE Transactions on Information Theory, 37(1):145-151.
17. Mel'čuk, I. A. 1987. Dependency Syntax: theory and practice. State University of New York Press. Albany, NY.
18. Miller, G. 1990. WordNet: an On-Line Lexical Database. International Journal of Lexicography, 1990.
19. Pereira, F., Tishby, N., and Lee, L. 1993. Distributional Clustering of English Words. In Proceedings of ACL-93. pp. 183-190. Columbus, Ohio.
20. Rao, C.R. 1982. Diversity: Its measurement, decomposition, apportionment and analysis. Sankyha: The Indian Journal of Statistics, 44(A):1-22.
21. Ratnaparkhi, A., Reynar, J., and Roukos, S. 1994. A Maximum Entropy Model for Prepositional Phrase Attachment. In Proceedings of the ARPA Human Language Technology Workshop, pp. 250-255. Plainsboro, N.J.
22. Stetina, J. and Nagao, M. 1997. Corpus Based PP Attachment Ambiguity Resolution with a Semantic Dictionary. In Proceedings of the Fifth Workshop on Very Large Corpora, pp. 66-80. Beijing and Hong Kong.
23. Terra, E. L. and Clarke, C. 2003. Frequency Estimates for Statistical Word Similarity Measures. In the Proceedings of the 2003 Human Language Technology Conference, pp.244-251. Edmonton, Canada, May.
24. Turney, P.D. (2001), Mining the Web for synonyms: PMI-IR versus LSA on TOEFL, Proceedings of the Twelfth European Conference on Machine Learning (ECML-2001), Freiburg, Germany, pp. 491-502.
25. Zavrel, J. and Daelemans, W and Veenstra, J. 1997. Resolving PP attachment Ambiguities with Memory-Based Learning. In Proceedings of the Conference on Computational Natural Language Learning, CoNLL97, pages 136-144, Madrid, Spain.

Detection of Incorrect Case Assignments in Paraphrase Generation

Atsushi Fujita, Kentaro Inui, and Yuji Matsumoto

Graduate School of Information Science,
Nara Institute of Science and Technology
{atsush-f,inui,matsu}@is.naist.jp

Abstract. This paper addresses the issue of post-transfer process in paraphrasing. Our previous investigation into transfer errors revealed that case assignment tends to be incorrect, irrespective of the types of transfer in lexical and structural paraphrasing of Japanese sentences [3]. Motivated by this observation, we propose an empirical method to detect incorrect case assignments. Our error detection model combines two error detection models that are separately trained on a large collection of positive examples and a small collection of manually labeled negative examples. Experimental results show that our combined model significantly enhances the baseline model which is trained only on positive examples. We also propose a selective sampling scheme to reduce the cost of collecting negative examples, and confirm the effectiveness in the error detection task.

1 Introduction

Recently, automatic paraphrasing has been attracting increasing attention due to its potential in a wide range of natural language processing application [11, 1]. For example, paraphrasing has been applied to pre-editing and post-editing in machine translation [14], query expansion for question answering [13], and reading assistance [2, 6].

There are various levels of *lexical and structural paraphrasing* as the following examples demonstrate[1]:

(1) s. He *accomplished* the mission perfectly.
    t. He *achieved* the mission perfectly.
(2) s. *It was* a Honda *that* John *sold to* Tom.
    t. John *sold* a Honda *to* Tom.

In automating such paraphrasing, the difficulty of specifying the applicability conditions of each paraphrasing pattern is one of the major problems. For example, it is not easy to specify under what conditions "accomplish" can be paraphrased into "achieve." Paraphrasing patterns with wrong applicability conditions would produce various types of erroneous paraphrases from input, which we call *transfer errors*. We thus need to develop a robust method to detect and correct transfer errors in the post-transfer process by way of a safety net.

---
[1] For each example, 's' denotes an input and 't' denotes its paraphrase. A sentence with the mark '*' indicates it is incorrect. Note that our target language is Japanese. English examples are used here for an explanatory purpose.

Our previous investigation revealed that case assignment tends to be a major error source in paraphrasing of Japanese sentences [3]. Here is an example of incorrect case assignment: applying the *paraphrasing rule* "accomplish ⇒ achieve" (cf. (1)) to sentence (3s) generates (3t). But (3t) is incorrect, because the word "achieve" requires the words, such as "aim," "record" and "success," for its direct object.

(3) s. He *accomplished* the journey in an hour.
     t.*He *achieved* the journey in an hour.

One may suspect that incorrect case assignment can be detected simply by referring to a handcrafted case frame dictionary which describes allowable cases and their selectional restrictions for each verb. However, in existing case frame dictionaries of Japanese, selectional restrictions are generally specified based on coarse-grained semantic classes of noun. They are therefore not adequate for the purpose of the detection of incorrect case assignments (the detail will be given in Section 2).

To capture the difference between the usages of near-synonyms, we deal with words directly instead of relying on their semantic classes. Since a considerably large number of positive examples, namely, correct examples of case assignments, can be collected from existing corpora, one can construct a statistical language model and apply it to the error detection task [9, 7]. In this paper, to enhance such a statistical language model, we introduce the use of negative examples and address the following issues:

1. Unlike positive examples, negative examples are generally not available. A challenging issue is therefore how to effectively use a limited number of manually collected negative examples combining with a large number of positive examples.
2. Manual collection of negative examples is costly and time-consuming. Moreover, any such collection is sparse in the combinatorial space of words. Hence, we need an effective way to collect negative examples that truly contribute to error detection.

2 Incorrect Case Assignment

2.1 Characteristics

In [3], we investigated transfer errors in Japanese from two points of view: (i) what types of errors occur in lexical and structural paraphrasing of Japanese sentences, and (ii) which of them tend to be serious problem. We implemented about 28,000 paraphrasing rules[2] consisting of various levels of lexical and structural paraphrasing, and analyzed 630 automatically generated sentences. Through the investigation, we observed that case assignment tended to be incorrect, irrespective of the types of paraphrasing. A quarter of the paraphrased sentences (162/630) involved this type of errors. This ratio indicated the second most frequent errors[3].

---

[2] http://cl.naist.jp/lab/kura/KuraData/
[3] The most dominant type was inappropriate conjugation forms of verbs and adjectives (303/630), which could be easily corrected by changing their conjugation forms. The third most frequent error was incorrect functional word connections that occurred in 78 sentences. The other errors occurred in less than 40 sentences.

Case assignment can be incorrect at three different levels:

(i) Violation of syntactic constraints: Though both of the verbs *"tessuru"* and *"tsuranuku"* have the same meaning "devote", the paraphrased sentence (4t) is incorrect because *"tsuranuku"* cannot take the *"ni* (dative)" case.

(4) s. *Team play-ni tessuru.*
     team play-DAT devote-PRES
     He <u>devotes</u> himself to team play.
   t.*<i>Team play-ni tsuranuku.</i>
     team play-DAT devote-PRES

(ii) Violation of selectional restrictions: The verb *"katameru* (strengthen)" requires a concrete object for its *"o* (accusative)" case. Since the noun *"kontei* (basis)" in the paraphrased sentence (5t) does not satisfy constraint, (5t) becomes incorrect.

(5) s. *Building-no kiban-o katameta.*
     building-GEN foundation-ACC strengthen-PAST
     He strengthened the <u>foundation</u> of the building.
   t.*<i>Building-no kontei-o katameta.</i>
     building-GEN basis-ACC strengthen-PAST
     *He strengthened the <u>basis</u> of the building.

(iii) Semantic inconsistency between sibling cases: The nouns *"hyogen* (expressions)" and *"kakuchi* (every land)"* in the paraphrased sentence (6t) satisfy the semantic constraint for *"ga* (nominative)" and *"ni* (locative)" cases of the verb *"aru* (exist),"* respectively. Nevertheless, (6t) is incorrect, because of semantic discrepancy between the nouns of the nominative and locative cases.

(6) s. *Nankai-na hyogen-ga zuisho-ni aru.*
     crabbed-ADJ expressions-NOM many places-LOC exist-PRES
     There are crabbed expressions in <u>many places</u> (of the document).
   t.*<i>Nankai-na hyogen-ga kakuchi-ni aru.</i>
     crabbed-ADJ expressions-NOM every land-LOC exist-PRES
     *There are crabbed expressions in <u>every land</u>.

2.2 Task Setting

Supposing that the case assignments in input sentences into paraphrasing are all correct, the target of error detection is to detect anomalies yielded in the paraphrased case structures that consist of a verb, case particles, and case fillers (nouns).

As mentioned in Section 1, existing case frame dictionaries specify selectional restrictions relying on a coarse-grained semantic typology. For example, most of the dictionaries do not distinguish two near-synonyms *"kiban* (foundation)" and *"kontei* (basis)"*, and classifies them into the same semantic class "basis," although the difference between them is crucial in the context of example (5).

Instead, we deal with words directly. Let v, n and c be a verb, a noun and the case particle which relates n to v, respectively. We decompose the error detection task into the classification of triplet $\langle v, c, n \rangle$ into *correct* or *incorrect*. A given paraphrased sentence is judged to be incorrect if and only if any of the triplets included in the sentence is classified as incorrect. If we deal with $\langle v, c_1, n_1, c_2, n_2 \rangle$ to take into account the association between two sibling cases, as in [16], we might be able to detect semantic inconsistency. However, we have so far examined an error detection model taking only $\langle v, c, n \rangle$ into account, because the sibling cases can rarely be semantically inconsistent[4] and building a distribution model of $\langle v, c_1, n_1, c_2, n_2 \rangle$ is likely to cause a data sparseness problem.

3 Error Detection Models

In generative approaches, such as parsing and statistical machine translation, systems use statistics to estimate *relative likelihood* of output candidates. For the error detection in paraphrasing, however, we need a model for judging the *absolute correctness* of output candidates for the following reason. Paraphrasing systems are typically developed for a particular purpose such as simplifying text and controlling wording. In such systems, the variety of paraphrasing rules tends to be restricted; so the rule set may produce no appropriate paraphrase candidate for a given input sentence. An error detection model therefore needs an ability not only to compare candidates but also to give up producing output when none of the candidates is correct.

If error detection is defined as a discriminative task, i.e. classifying the candidates into *correct* or *incorrect*, one may want to use both positive and negative examples to train a classifier. However, any collection of negative examples is likely to be too small to represent the distribution of the negative class. Thus, it is probably not a good choice to input them together with a vast amount of positive examples into a single classifier induction algorithm such as support vector machines. We therefore separately train two models, the positive model (*Pos*) and the negative model (*Neg*), then combine them to create another model (*Com*) as shown in Figure 1. Since negative examples have to be collected by hand, we also investigate the effectiveness of a selective sampling scheme to reduce human labor.

3.1 Combining Separately Trained Models

Positive Model. Since a considerably large number of positive examples can be collected from existing corpora using a parser, one can estimate the probability $P(\langle v, c, n \rangle)$ with reasonable accuracy. On that account, we first construct a baseline model *Pos*, a statistical language model trained only on positive examples.

To calculate $P(\langle v, c, n \rangle)$ avoiding the data sparseness problem, one can use *Probabilistic Latent Semantic Indexing* (*PLSI*) [4] which bases itself on *distributional clustering* [12]. *PLSI* is a maximum likelihood estimation method. Dividing[5] $\langle v, c, n \rangle$ into $\langle v, c \rangle$ and n, one can estimate $P(\langle v, c, n \rangle)$ by:

---

[4] According to the analysis in [3], only 8 cases of the 162 incorrect case assignments had semantically inconsistent sibling cases.

[5] $P(\langle v, c, n \rangle)$ can be represented by the product of $P(\langle v, c \rangle)$ and $P(n|\langle v, c \rangle)$. Both of the marginal distributions corresponds existing linguistic concept; the former indicates the likelihood of a case structure, while the latter does the satisfaction degree of semantic constraint.

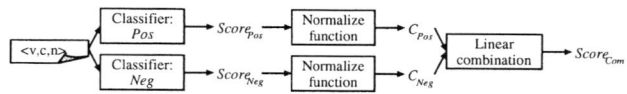

Fig. 1. Proposed model.

$$P(\langle v, c, n \rangle) = \sum_{z \in Z} P(\langle v, c \rangle | z) P(n|z) P(z),$$

where Z denotes a set of *latent classes* of co-occurrence, and probabilistic parameters $P(\langle v,c \rangle|z)$, $P(n|z)$, and $P(z)$ can be estimated by the EM algorithm.

Given $P(\langle v, c, n \rangle)$, we can use various co-occurrence measures to estimate the likelihood of a given pair of $\langle v, c \rangle$ and n. Well-known options are $P(\langle v, c, n \rangle)$ (*Prob*), *mutual information* (*MI*), and the *Dice coefficient* (*Dice*).

Negative Model. *Pos* might not be able to properly judge the *correctness* of $\langle v, c, n \rangle$ by setting a simple threshold, particularly in cases where $P(\langle v, c \rangle)$ or $P(n)$ is low. This defect is expected to be compensated for by the use of negative examples. However, we cannot incorporate negative examples into the statistical language model directly. We thus construct a negative model *Neg* separately from *Pos*.

One simple way of using negative examples is the k-nearest neighbor (k-NN) method. Assuming that the distance between an input triplet $\langle v, c, n \rangle$ and a labeled negative example $\langle v', c', n' \rangle$ depends on both the distance between $\langle v, c \rangle$ and $\langle v', c' \rangle$ and the distance between n and n', we formulate the following distance function:

$$Dist(\langle v, c, n \rangle, \langle v', c', n' \rangle) = DS\Big(P(Z|n), P(Z|n')\Big) \\ + DS\Big(P(Z|\langle v, c \rangle), P(Z|\langle v', c' \rangle)\Big).$$

Here, $P(Z|\langle v, c \rangle)$ and $P(Z|n)$ are the feature vectors for $\langle v, c \rangle$ and n. These probability distributions are obtained through the EM algorithm for *Pos*, and the function DS denotes *distributional similarity* between two probability distributions. We employ one of the popular measures of distributional similarity, *Jensen-Shannon divergence* (DS_{JS}) [9, 10]. Given the pair of probability distributions q and r, DS_{JS} is given by:

$$DS_{JS}(q, r) = \frac{1}{2}\left[D\left(q \,\Big\|\, \frac{q+r}{2}\right) + D\left(r \,\Big\|\, \frac{q+r}{2}\right)\right],$$

where the function D is the *Kullback-Leibler divergence*. DS_{JS} is always non-negative, and $DS_{JS} = 0$ iff $q = r$.

Given an input $\langle v, c, n \rangle$, *Neg* outputs the weighted average distance $Score_{Neg}$ between the input and its k nearest neighbors. Formally,

$$Score_{Neg} = \frac{1}{k}\sum_{i=1}^{k} \lambda_i \, Dist(\langle v, c, n \rangle, \langle v', c', n' \rangle_i),$$

where λ_i is the weight for $\langle v', c', n' \rangle_i$, the i-th nearest neighbor, larger value of $Score_{Neg}$ indicates the input is more likely to be correct.

Combined Model. Given the pair of scores output by *Pos* and *Neg*, our error detection model *Com* converts them into normalized confidence values C_{Pos} and C_{Neg} ($0 \leq C_{Pos}, C_{Neg} \leq 1$). Each normalization function can be derived using development data. *Com* then outputs the weighted average of C_{Pos} and C_{Neg} as the overall score:

$$Score_{Com} = \beta\, C_{Pos} + (1 - \beta)\, C_{Neg},$$

where $0 \leq \beta \leq 1$ determines the weights for the models, $Score_{Com}$ indicates the degree of correctness.

3.2 Selective Sampling of Negative Examples

We need negative examples that are expected to be useful in improving *Neg* and *Com*. For the current purpose, an example is not useful if it is positive, or if it is similar to any of the known negative examples. In other words, we prefer negative examples that are not similar to any existing labeled negative example. We henceforth refer to unlabeled instances as *samples*, and labeled ones as *examples*.

Our strategy for selecting samples can be implemented straightforwardly. We use *Pos* to estimate how likely a sample is negative. To compute the similarity between an unlabeled sample and labeled examples, we use *Neg*. Let p_x be the estimated probability of an unlabeled sample x, and s_x (> 0) be the similarity between x and its nearest negative example. The preference for a given sample x is given by, e.g., $Pref(x) = -s_x \log(p_x)$, which we use in the experiments.

Our selective sampling scheme is summarized as follows:

Step 1. Generate a set of paraphrases by applying paraphrasing rules to sentences sampled from documents in a given target domain.
Step 2. Extract a set of triplets from the set of paraphrases. We call it a *sample pool*.
Step 3. Sample a small number of triplets at random from the sample pool, and label them manually. Use only negative samples as the seed of the negative example set.
Step 4. For each sample x in the sample pool, calculate its preference by $Pref(x)$.
Step 5. Select the most preferred sample, and label it manually. If it is negative, add it into the negative example set.
Step 6. Repeat Steps 4 and 5 until a certain stopping condition is satisfied.

4 Experiments

4.1 Data and Evaluation Measures

We constructed data for training *Pos* and *Neg* in the following way (Also see Figure 2). During this process, paraphrase candidates were constructed for evaluation as well.

Step 1. 53 million tokens (8.0 million types) of triplets $\langle v, c, n \rangle$ were collected from the parsed[6] sentences of newspaper articles[7]. To handle case alteration properly, we dealt with active and passive forms of verbs separately.

---

[6] We used the statistical Japanese dependency parser CaboCha [8] for parsing. http://chasen.naist.jp/~taku/software/cabocha/
[7] Extracts from 9 years of the Mainichi Shinbun and 10 years of the Nihon Keizai Shinbun consisting of 25,061,504 sentences are used.

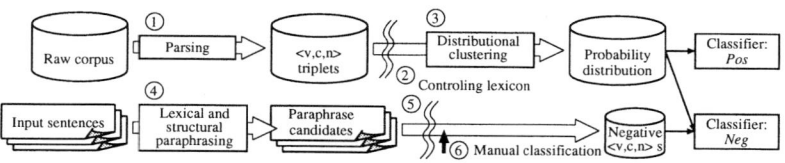

Fig. 2. Model construction scheme.

Step 2. Triplets occurring only once were filtered out. We also restricted c to be the most frequent seven case particles: "*ga* (NOM)," "*o* (ACC)," "*ni* (DAT)," "*de* (LOC)," "*e* (to)," "*kara* (from)," and "*yori* (from / than)." This procedure resulted in 3.1 million types of triplets consisting of 38,512 types of n and 66,484 of $\langle v, c \rangle$.

Step 3. We estimated the probabilistic parameters of *PLSI* by applying the EM algorithm[8] to the data, changing the number of latent classes $|Z|$ from 2 through 1,500.

Step 4. To develop a negative example set, we excerpted 90,000 sentences from the newspaper articles used in Step 1, input them into a paraphrasing system for Japanese[9], and obtained 7,167 paraphrase candidates by applying the same paraphrasing rules that were used for our previous investigation into transfer errors [3].

Step 5. We filtered out the generated candidates that contain no changed case structure and those that include either v or n with a frequency of less than 2,000 in the collection given in Step 1. Then, 3,166 candidates remained.

Step 6. Finally, we manually labeled the 3,166 candidates and their triplets. We obtained (i) 2,358 positive and 808 (25.5%) negative candidates[10], and (ii) 3,704 types of triplets consisting of 2,853 positive and 851 negative. The former set was used for evaluation, while the latter was used for training *Neg*.

For evaluation, we compare the performance of *Pos*, *Neg*, and *Com*. For each model, we set a threshold and used it so that a given input was classified as erroneous if and only if it received a lower score than the threshold. Given such a threshold, recall R and precision P can be calculated[11]. While we can estimate the optimal threshold for each model, in the experiments, we plot recall-precision (R-P) curves by varying the threshold. To summarize a R-P curve, we use 11-point average precision (*11-point precision*, hereafter) where the eleven points are $R = 0.0, 0.1, \ldots, 1.0$. To compare R-P curves, we conduct *Wilcoxon rank-sum test* using precision at eleven point above, assuming $p < 0.05$ as the significance level.

4.2 Results

Baseline. First, to illustrate the complexity of the task, we show the performance of the baseline models: a dictionary-based model, a word-based naive smoothing model, and

---

[8] http://chasen.naist.jp/~taku/software/plsi/
[9] We used KURA [15]. http://cl.naist.jp/lab/kura/doc/
[10] 41 out of 808 were incorrect due to semantic inconsistency between sibling cases.
[11] R = # of correctly detected erroneous candidates / # of erroneous candidates,
P = # of correctly detected erroneous candidates / # of candidates classified as incorrect.

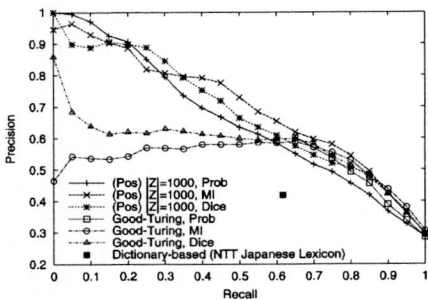
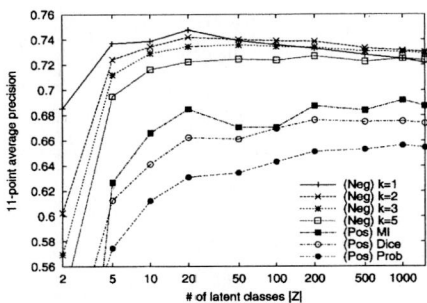

Fig. 3. R-P curves of baseline models.   **Fig. 4.** 11-point precision of models over $|Z|$.

our statistical language model *Pos*. We regard *Pos* as a baseline because our concern is to what extent *Pos* can be enhanced by introducing *Neg* and *Com*. For the case frame dictionary, we used the largest Japanese case frame dictionary, the NTT Japanese Lexicon [5] (*Dic*), and the Good-Turing estimation (*GT*) for the naive smoothing model.

As shown in Figure 3, *Pos* significantly outperforms both *Dic* and *GT*. *Prob*, *MI* and *Dice* with $|Z| = 1,000$ achieve 65.6%, 69.2% and 67.5% 11-point precision, while *Dic* achieves 41.9% precision under 61.6% recall[12], and *MI* and *Dice* based on *GT* achieve 51.9% and 58.0% 11-point precision[13]. Regarding *Pos*, there is no significant difference among the co-occurrence measures.

The performance of *Pos* is shown over the number of latent classes $|Z|$ in Figure 4. The larger $|Z|$ achieves higher 11-point precision. However, overly enlarging $|Z|$ presumably does not work well since the performance of *Pos* hits a ceiling. The optimal $|Z|$ relies on the lexicon but the performance distribution over $|Z|$ looks moderate. We therefore expect it can be estimated using development data with a reasonable cost.

Properties of Negative Model. *Neg* was evaluated by conducting 5-fold cross-validation over the labeled negative examples to keep training and test data exclusive. The weight λ_i for i-th nearest neighbor is set to $1/i$, the reciprocal of the similarity rank. The 11-point precision for combinations of parameters are shown in Figure 4. In contrast to *Pos*, the performance of *Neg* peaks at small $|Z|$. This is good news because a larger number of $|Z|$ obliges a higher computational cost for calculating each distance. Regarding the number of referring neighbors k, the 11-point precision peaks at $k = 1$. We speculate that the negative examples are so sparse against the combinatorial space that a larger k causes more noise. Hence, we can conclude that $k = 1$ is enough for this task.

The performance of *Neg* may seem too high given the number of negative examples we used. It is, however, not necessarily unlikely. We speculate the variety of triplets

---

[12] *Dic* classifies a given $\langle v, c, n \rangle$ as correct or not if and only if both v and n is described in the dictionary. In our experiment, since 338 paraphrase candidates (10.7%) are not judged, we calculated recall and precision using judged 2,828 candidates.

[13] Notice that *Prob* based on *GT* does not perform for a lower recall ($R \leq 0.66$, in our experiment) because it does not distinguish the triplets that have the same frequency.

involved in generated paraphrases is relatively small, because the set of paraphrasing rules we used was build for the purpose of text simplification. Since it is common property in applied paraphrasing systems as mentioned in Section 3, we can expect a limited number of negative examples are sufficient to cover the negative classes.

Combining Models with Selectively Sampled Examples. Using the 3,704 types of labeled triplets, we evaluated the effectiveness of (a) combining *Pos* with *Neg* and (b) selective sampling. We first sampled at random two sets of 100 samples from 3,704 labeled triplets. One involved 16 negative examples and the other 22. Using for each negative example set, we then simulated the selective sampling scheme, regarding the remaining 3,604 triplets as the sample pool. Parameters and metrics employed are *Prob* and $|Z| = 1{,}000$ for *Pos*, $|Z| = 20$ and $k = 1$ for *Neg*. In each stage of selective sampling (learning), we formed a combined model *Com*, employing the parameters and metrics on which each component model performed best, i.e., *MI* and $|Z| = 1{,}000$ for *Pos*, and $|Z| = 20$ and $k = 1$ for *Neg*. Combining ratio β was set to 0.5. We then evaluated *Com* by conducting 5-fold cross-validations as well as for *Neg*.

Figure 5 compares the performance of selective and random sampling, showing the averaged results for two seeds. In the figure, the horizontal axis denotes the number of sampled examples. The bars in the figure, which denote the number of obtained negative examples, designate that our preference function efficiently selects negative examples. The curves in the figure, which denote the performance curves, designate a remarkable advantage of selective sampling, particularly in the early stage of learning.

Figure 6 shows the $R\text{-}P$ curves of *Pos*, *Neg*, and *Com*. *Com* surpasses *Pos* and *Neg* over all ranges of recall. One can see that the models based on selective sampling exhibit $R\text{-}P$ curves as nicely as the model with the largest negative example set. It is therefore confirmed that even if the collection of negative examples are not sufficient to represent the distribution of the negative classes, we can enhance the baseline model *Pos* by combining with *Neg*. With the largest negative examples, *Com* achieved 81.3% 11-point precision, a 12.1 point improvement over *Pos*. Concerning the optimal β which depends on the set of negative examples, it can be easily estimated using development

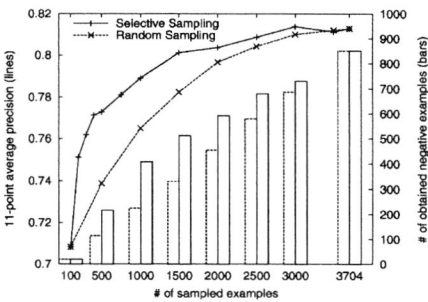

Fig. 5. Learning curves of *Com*. Lines: 11-point average precision, bars: # of obtained negative examples.

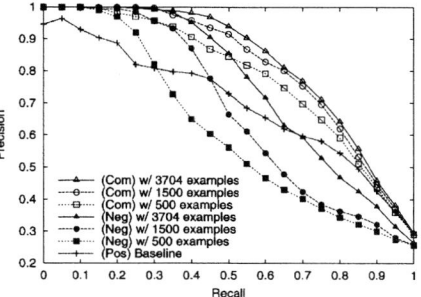

Fig. 6. $R\text{-}P$ curves of our models.

data. For the present settings, the performance peaks when a slightly greater weight is given to *Neg*, i.e., $\beta = 0.45$. However, we can use $\beta = 0.5$ as default, because there is no significant difference in performance between $\beta = 0.45$ and $\beta = 0.5$.

5 Conclusions

We presented the task of detecting incorrect case assignment, a major error source in paraphrasing of Japanese sentences. Our proposal are: (i) an empirical method to detect incorrect case assignments, where we enhanced a statistical language model by combining it with another model which was trained only on a small collection of negative examples, and (ii) a selective sampling scheme for effective collection of negative examples. Our methods were justified through empirical experiments.

Since our aim is to generate correct paraphrases, correcting the detected errors is another important issue. In [3], however, we observed that a only small part of incorrect case assignments (22/162) could be corrected by replacing the case markers, while the remaining large part could not be. Moreover, even if we could correct all incorrect case assignments, other types of frequent errors would still be in the paraphrased sentences. We thus think that coping with various type of errors should be given a preference.

References

1. ACL. *The 2nd International Workshop on Paraphrasing: Paraphrase Acquisition and Applications (IWP)*, 2003.
2. J. Carroll, G. Minnen, D. Pearce, Y. Canning, S. Devlin, and J. Tait. Simplifying text for language-impaired readers. In *Proc. of the 9th Conference of the European Chapter of the Association for Computational Linguistics (EACL)*, pages 269–270, 1999.
3. A. Fujita and K. Inui. Exploring transfer errors in lexical and structural paraphrasing. *Journal of Information Processing Society of Japan*, 44(11):2826–2838, 2003. (in Japanese).
4. T. Hofmann. Probabilistic latent semantic indexing. In *Proc. of the 22nd Annual International ACM SIGIR Conference on Research and Development in Information Retrieval (SIGIR)*, pages 50–57, 1999.
5. S. Ikehara, M. Miyazaki, S. Shirai, A. Yokoo, H. Nakaiwa, K. Ogura, Y. Ooyama, and Y. Hayashi, editors. *Nihongo Goi Taikei – A Japanese Lexicon*. Iwanami Shoten, 1997. (in Japanese).
6. K. Inui, A. Fujita, T. Takahashi, R. Iida, and T. Iwakura. Text simplification for reading assistance: a project note. In *Proc. of the 2nd International Workshop on Paraphrasing: Paraphrase Acquisition and Applications (IWP)*, pages 9–16, 2003.
7. F. Keller, M. Lapata, and O. Ourioupina. Using the Web to overcome data sparseness. In *Proc. of the 2002 Conference on Empirical Methods in Natural Language Processing (EMNLP)*, pages 230–237, 2002.
8. T. Kudo and Y. Matsumoto. Japanese dependency analysis using cascaded chunking. In *Proc. of 6th Conference on Natural Language Learning (CoNLL)*, pages 63–69, 2002.
9. M. Lapata, F. Keller, and S. McDonald. Evaluating smoothing algorithms against plausibility judgements. In *Proc. of the 39th Annual Meeting of the Association for Computational Linguistics (ACL)*, pages 346–353, 2001.
10. L. Lee. On the effectiveness of the skew divergence for statistical language analysis. In *Proc. of the 8th International Workshop on Artificial Intelligence and Statistics*, pages 65–72, 2001.

11. NLPRS. *Workshop on Automatic Paraphrasing: Theories and Applications*, 2001.
12. F. Pereira, N. Tishby, and L. Lee. Distributional clustering of English words. In *Proc. of the 31st Annual Meeting of the Association for Computational Linguistics (ACL)*, pages 183–190, 1993.
13. D. Ravichandran and E. Hovy. Learning surface text patterns for a question answering system. In *Proc. of the 40th Annual Meeting of the Association for Computational Linguistics (ACL)*, pages 215–222, 2002.
14. S. Shirai, S. Ikehara, and T. Kawaoka. Effects of automatic rewriting of source language within a Japanese to English MT system. In *Proc. of the 5th International Conference on Theoretical and Methodological Issues in Machine Translation (TMI)*, pages 226–239, 1993.
15. T. Takahashi, T. Iwakura, R. Iida, A. Fujita, and K. Inui. KURA: a transfer-based lexico-structural paraphrasing engine. In *Proc. of the 6th Natural Language Processing Pacific Rim Symposium (NLPRS) Workshop on Automatic Paraphrasing: Theories and Applications*, pages 37–46, 2001.
16. K. Torisawa. An unsupervised learning method for associative relationships between verb phrases. In *Proc. of the 19th International Conference on Computational Linguistics (COLING)*, pages 1009–1015, 2002.

Building a Pronominalization Model by Feature Selection and Machine Learning

Ji-Eun Roh and Jong-Hyeok Lee

Div. of Electrical and Computer Engineering POSTECH
and Advanced Information Technology Research Center (AITrc)
San 31, Hyoja-dong, Nam-gu, Pohang, R. of Korea
{jeroh,jhlee}@postech.ac.kr

Abstract. Pronominalization is an important component in generating a coherent text. In this paper, we identify features that influence pronominalization, and construct a pronoun generation model by using various machine learning techniques. The old entities, which are the target of pronominalization, are categorized into three types according to their tendency in attentional state: Cb and old-Cp derived from a Centering model, and the remaining old entities. We construct a pronoun generation model for each type. Eighty-seven texts are gathered from three genres for training and testing. Using this, we verify that our proposed features are well defined to explain pronominalization in Korean, and we also show that our model significantly outperforms previous ones with 99% confidence level by t-test. We also identify central features that have a strong influence on pronominalization across genres.

1 Introduction

Pronominalization is an important component in generating a coherent text. A redundantly prominent noun should be replaced by a pronoun; otherwise, the text becomes unnatural because of redundancy. Specifically, a redundant noun in Korean is frequently pronominalized as a zero pronoun[1], while a redundant noun in English is replaced by a (non-zero) pronoun. Korean is a highly context-dependent language, so any arguments recoverable from the context may be freely dropped off.

Our goal in this paper is identifying features that influence pronominalization, specifically the zero pronouns, and constructing a generation model by using various machine learning (ML) techniques. Old entities[2], which are the target of pronominalization, are categorized into three types according to their roles in the attentional state: Cb and oldCp derived from the Centering model [1], and the remaining old entities (oldE). A model for pronominalization is constructed for each of the three types.

This paper is organized as follows. In Section 2, we describe related works on pronominalization. In Section 3, we investigate several features that influence pronominalization, and in Section 4 we construct a model for pronominalization by using

---

[1] Generally, unexpressed argument of a verb is called a *zero pronoun, zero element, zero anaphor,* or *null element.* In this paper, we call the omitted element a *zero pronoun.*

[2] We defined an old entity as an entity of current sentence which is mentioned in the immediately previous sentence.

various ML techniques and provide a experimental. The conclusion is given in Section 5. In this paper, we assume that a Centering model, which is the main background knowledge of our proposed features, is familiar to readers.

2 Related Work

Recently, some studies attempted to use the centering model for pronominalization. Kibble [5] considered different strategies for choosing when to use a pronoun, and found the following to be the best: pronominalize the Cb only after Continue. Yamura-Takei et al. [13] also adopted the centering model to generate zero pronouns in Japanese[3]. He argued that all Cb can be generated as zero pronouns either in Continue or in Smooth-Shift transitions. The problem of the above two approaches will be discussed in Section 3, and it will be compared with our approach in Section 5.

Hashimoto et al [3] manually constructed a Japanese-oriented decision tree to select an appropriate pronoun, including the non-zero pronoun by analyzing newspapers, and exploring effective features. However, their decision tree was highly domain dependent, and the test set was too small to validate their manually evaluated algorithm. Yeh and Mellish [14] also tried to construct a Chinese-oriented simple decision tree which consists of five features: locality, syntactic constraints, discourse structure, topic continuity for the zero pronoun, and animacy. Locality and topic continuity are not novel in pronominalization. Moreover, the proposed syntactic constraints can be applied only to Chinese. This approach will be also compared with our model in Section 5. Finally, [8] and [12] investigated several features for English using labor-consuming corpus annotation, and proposed a probabilistic model for pronominalization, respectively. However, their features are not sufficient for Korean, because Korean and English have different characteristics in the usage of the pronoun.

3 Feature Selection

Almost all previous research [5], [13] based on centering model considers only Cb as the target of pronominalization, although many pronouns occur not only in Cb but also in old entities except for Cb in real texts. Otherwise, some previous research [3], [8], [14] handles the whole old entities by disregarding the fact that old entities have different tendencies in the attentional state.

In this paper, we regard all the old entities as the target of pronominalization, and then categorize them into three according to their characteristics in attentional state; Cb, Cp which is the old entity (oldCp), and the remnantal old entity except for Cb and oldCp (oldE). In the centering model that models the attentional state, Cb is generally closely related to *Cohesion* and Cp is closely related to *Salience*. Traditionally, the influence of each of these two, cohesion and salience, on pronominalization is open to discussion. Thus, we aim to investigate the influence of cohesion and salience from the viewpoint of pronominalization by using these three categories.

---

[3] Japanese is quite similar to Korean, in the sense that Japanese allows arguments to be freely omitted when they are recoverable from a given context.

Table 1. Overview of features for old entity e_i in S_i (S_i: i^{th} sentence)

Features	Description	Values
1. ppgr	grammatical role of e_i in the S_{i-2}	8 roles
2. pgr	grammatical role of e_i in the S_{i-1}	"
3. cgr	grammatical role of e_i in the S_i	"
4. modifeeF	whether e_i is modifee or not	yes, no
5. intraF	whether e_i places subordinated or matrix sentence	in, out
6. posF	the position of e_i in discourse segment	start, in
7. animacy	animacy of e_i	yes, no
8. pptrans	center transition of S_{i-2}, which includes e_i	10 transitions
9. ptrans	center transition of S_{i-1} which includes e_i	"
10. ctrans	center transition of S_i	"
11. cbcp	equality of $Cb(S_i)$ and $Cp(S_{i-1})$	same, diff
12. cost	inference cost between S_i and S_{i-1}	cheap, exp
13. cpcb	equality of $Cp(S_i)$ and $Cb(S_{i-1})$	same, diff

Table 1 shows our proposed features based on syntactic information, centering-derived information, and etc. Features 1 to 7 are equally applied to Cb, oldCp, and oldE. The others derived by centering model are applied to only Cb and oldCp, because oldE is not directly related to centering.

(1) Features for General Old Entities (Feature 1~7)

Kim [7] noted that zero objects in Korean cannot be explained by Centering, because many zero objects do not come from the Cb of the Continue transition. She clarified that almost all zero objects were used to remove redundancy in terms of a grammatical role, grounding that 60% of zero objects occurred when the object of the current sentence was the object of the previous sentence. Based on this result, the *histories of successive two grammatical role* of the old entity (feature 1 and 2) are employed. We assume that salience of entity is the most effectively perceived by its grammatical role, thus feature 3 is employed to catch the salience of the old entity.

Feature 4 represents a syntactic constraint which does not allow zero pronouns. If an entity is a *modifee*, the entity cannot be omitted.

Generally, a redundant entity between a subordinate sentence and a matrix sentence is obligatorily omitted when a complex sentence is constructed. Feature 5 aims to reflect this characteristic.

Feature 6 and feature 7 were already considered in pronominalization of Chinese [14]. These features can be applied to general languages. Especially, the relationship between animacy and pronoun is frequently mentioned regarding pronominalization.

(2) Features for Cb and OldCp (Feature 8~13)

The previous centering-based approaches on pronominalization are commonly very naïve, in that they only consider Cb of particular transitions without a serious consideration of the centering model. In this paper, we employ three successive center transitions[4] sequence (feature 8 ~ 10) and inference cost (feature 11 ~ 12) for Cb and oldCp.

From the interpretation (not generation) perspectives, most Korean linguists [6], [7], [10] agree that zero pronouns generally come from the Cb of Continue. However, what concern us here from the generation perspectives is whether all Cb in Continue transitions usually can be a zero pronoun, rather than whether zero pronoun comes from Cb in Continue transition. According to our analysis of raw data, only 46% Cb in all Continue transitions are pronominalized to the zero pronouns. If we follow the naive policy concerning of Cb in Continue, it will cause an excessive over-generation of zero pronouns. To resolve this problem, we adopt a *Cost-based Centering Model* that considers the inference cost. In this paper, the cost-based centering model refers to the revised centering model by [11], which extends the original 4 transition types to 6 types with respect to the cost for inferring. They assumed that the equality of $Cb(S_i)$ and $Cp(S_{i-1})$ can measure the cost between adjacent utterances, and separated Expensive-Continue and Expensive-Smooth-Shift from Continue and Smooth-Shift in accordance with the equality of $Cb(S_i)$ and $Cp(S_{i-1})$.

In this paper, we are certain that the Cb of Cheap-Continue is more redundantly prominent than the Cb of Expensive-Continue that follows Retain. The reason is that Retain intends to change the topic, and the prominence of Cb in Expensive-Continue decreases because of Retain. The following text was extracted from our corpus. It is a description of an exhibition 'Cakwi (a kind of Korean traditional farming tools)', and is a good example to illustrate this phenomenon.

(1) **Cakwi**-nun (Cakwi, topic) wuli-nala-uy (Korean) centhong-cekin (traditional) nong-kikwu-i-ta (farming tool is) (Cakwi is a Korean traditional farming tool.)
(2) **Cakwi**-uy (Cakwi, adnom) nal-un (edge, topic) celsaknal (celsaknal) ilako-hanta (is called). (Edge of Cakwi is called celsaknal.) ➔ **CP = nal (edge) CB = Cakwi, *Retain***
(3) **Cakwi**-nun (Cakwi, topic) hyengtay-ka (shape, subject) dokki-wa (axe) pisus-hata (is similar to). (Cakwi is similar to that of an axe.) ➔ **CP = CB = Cakwi, *Expensive-Continue***
(4) **Cakwi**-nun (Cakwi, topic) khuki-ey ttala (by its size) taycakwi (big-cakwi), socakwi-lo (small-cakwi) nanwin-ta (is categorized). (Cakwi is categorized as big-cakwi and small-cakwi by its size.) ➔ **CP = CB = Cakwi, *Cheap-Continue***

In the above text, the topic smoothly changes from 'Cakwi' to 'nal (edge of Cakwi)' in sentence (2), and Retain occurs. This implies that the topic of the next sentence is 'nal', and it decreases the prominence of Cb, 'Cakwi', in sentence (2). However, in sentence (3), the topic is returned to 'Cakwi' from 'nal', and Expensive-Continue occurs. In sentence (4), 'Cakwi' is maintained as a topic, and Cheap-Continue occurs. In this situation, it is natural that the Cb of sentence (3), 'Cakwi', is less prominent than the Cb of sentence (4), 'Cakwi', even though both 'Cakwi' are the same as the Cb of Continue transitions. If 'Cakwi' in sentence (3) is omitted, the topic (or subject) of 'pisus-hata (is similar to)' can be misinterpreted as 'nal', not 'Cakwi'. Therefore, it is reasonable to conclude that Cb of Expensive-Continue is less elliptical than that of Cheap-Continue. In addition, the ellipsis of Cb in Expensive-

---

[4] In this paper, we adopted the Cf-ranking and extended center transition types proposed by [9]. The extended transition types include 6 types proposed by [11].

Continue may cause ambiguity. The case of Smooth-Shift can also be explained in the same manner. For this reason, feature 11 must be taken into consideration.

Many researchers working on the centering model agree that considering adjacent transition pairs rather than a particular transition provides a more reliable picture about coherence and anaphora resolution [1], [4], [5], [11]. In this paper, we consider three successive transition sequences (feature 8 ~ 10) and inference cost proposed by [11] (feature 12) between adjacent sentences under the assumption that the cheaper the cost, the more elliptical the old entity.

Finally, in our investigation many people agree that the topic of discourse is continued in Continue, Retain and Rough-Shift transition sequence on the assumption that Cp of Rough-Shift is the same as Cb of Retain transition. Considering that topic-continuity is a necessary condition of pronominalization of topic, we employ feature 13 in order to investigate pronominalization in this particular topic-continuity situation.

4 Construction of Pronominalization Model

In this paper, we consider two classification problems: 2-class (NP: original noun, ZERO: zero pronoun) and 3-class classification (NP, PRO: non-zero pronoun, ZERO).

Table 2. Overview of collected texts

	DESC	NEWS	STORY	TOTAL
# of text	53	20	14	87
# of Cb	569	102	203	874
# of oldCp	55	3	25	83
# of oldE	744	166	240	1150

In order to construct a pronominalization model, we collect 87 texts from three genres, descriptive texts (DESC) from the on-line museum site, 'the national folk museum of Korea', news articles (NEWS), and Aesop's Fables (STORY). Then, we decomposed a complex sentence into simple sentences, recovered omitted elements, applied a centering model to get Cb, Cp, and center transition, and finally semi-automatically annotated the other features for each old entity. Table 2 shows the detailed information of the collected texts.

Almost all previous pronominalization models employ a decision tree as a classifier. In this paper, we adopt the following 6 classifiers and their small variants provided by WEKA 3.0[5]. The best classifier will be noted in the next Section.

- Decision tree (DT) using C4.5 and AltDT (Alternating Decision Tree learning)
- Instance-based learning: K-NN, K* (the best value K is selected by experiments)
- SVM using polynomial kernel function

---

[5] WEKA is machine learning s/w in Java and is developed by the University of Waikato. (http://www.cs.waikato.ac.nz/~ml/weka/index.html)

- Neural Network classifier (NN)
- Naïve-Bayes classifier (NB)
- Meta-learning: stacking and boosting – AdaBoosting (AB), LogitBoosting (LB)

4.1 Applying ML Techniques for Prediction of Pro-form

For an accurate evaluation, all experiments were performed by 10-fold cross-validation which was repeated ten times. Then the results were averaged.

First, we applied 11 ML techniques to the Korean texts of each genre and merged genres[6] (TOTAL) which was classified pro-forms into 2 and 3-class. The classification accuracy of pro-form according to each genre, target and machine learning is shown in Table 3. We know that the average precision is high in order of oldCp, Cb, and oldE with the respect to the target, and NEWS, DESC, TOTAL, and STORY with the respect to the domain. The average precision of 2-class classification is higher than that of 3-class classification.

Table 3. Average precision of each target/class/genre according to various ML techniques

unit: %

Target	Cb								oldCp								oldE							
Class	2				3				2				3				2				3			
Genre	D	N	S	T	D	N	S	T	D	N	S	T	D	N	S	T	D	N	S	T	D	N	S	T
NB	77	93	70	75	77	81	60	71	72		80	78	70		56	73	85	92	77	81	84	85	**68**	78
K-NN	74	87	65	77	75	80	48	73	80		68	81	81		32	69	79	89	70	80	78	77	59	73
LB+NN	83	89	66	81	84	85	51	76	83		68	85	81		28	73	85	87	74	82	81	78	58	76
SVM	82	90	66	80					76	N/A	76	75					83	92	79	83				
DT	81	**95**	71	80	81	**92**	47	78	78	N/A	88	72	76	N/A	72	75	84	**92**	76	84	83	88	67	79
K*	82	89	65	80	82	81	54	75	81	N/A	80	81	N/A		64	73	**86**	**92**	77	**85**	**85**	87	64	**81**
LB+DS	83	**95**	**75**	80	82	90	52	72	**85**		84	80	**87**		32	79	84	**93**	**80**	84	83	**89**	67	80
AB+DT	**85**	**95**	64	**82**	**85**	90	37	**79**	**85**		76	**87**	83		40	**79**	85	90	75	83	84	80	64	80
Stacking	81	**95**	70	**82**	82	91	60	78	81		76	83	72		60	73	84	**92**	73	84	82	85	64	80
AltDT	79	**95**	73	81					83		**92**	79					83	**92**	78	83				

D: DESC, N: NEWS, S: STORY, T: TOTAL

Table 4. Average precision of each pro-form of each genre

unit: %

Genre		DESC			NEWS			STORY			TOTAL		
	Target	Cb	oldCp	oldE	Cb	oldCp	OldE	Cb	oldCp	oldE	Cb	oldCp	oldE
2	NP	86	91	87	98		95	74	89	85	85	95	88
	ZERO	83	60	80	84	N/A	70	39	33	45	73	56	70
3	NP	84	87	86	95		88	68	49	78	85	84	85
	PRO	83	100	62	50		41	23		21	43	50	32
	ZERO	85	60	83	88		60	66	44	53	74	56	81

(We cannot obtain result from oldCp in NEWS genres, because the number of oldCp is too small.)

---

[6] In order to construct generation model across genres, we integrated texts of each genre, and made merged texts.

It is interesting that oldCp is more *predictable* than Cb. The oldCp is the most salient old entity in S_i, while Cb is the most coherent old entity between adjacent S_i and S_{i-1}. Therefore, it seems reasonable to conclude that salience with oldness is more influential on pronominalization than pure cohesion. However, this does not mean that oldCp is more frequently pronominalized than Cb.

Concerning domain kinds, the news article is the most predictable, and the story is the least predictable. Consider that a news article is a completely written text, while a story is a quasi-written text. In story, dialogues frequently occur, so context switch also frequently occurs. Additionally, pronouns which cannot directly access from adjacent sentences also frequently occur. So the centering model does not effectively apply to such texts, compared with other genres.

Concerning classifiers, AdaBoosting using DT and LogitBoosting using DS (decision stump, binary 1-level DT) are generally outperformed. Boosting uses voting and averaging but models are weighted according to their performance, and the new model is encouraged to become an expert for instances classified incorrectly by earlier models. It is natural that boosting is more powerful than stand-alone classifiers.

The average precision according to its pro-form of each genre was shown in Table 4. According to our expectation, the average precision of each target in each NP, PRO, and ZERO class is different. Concerning 2-class, generally, **(1)** oldCp is more predictable than Cb in NP class, **(2)** while Cb is more predictable than the others in the ZERO class. Concerning 3-class, **(3)** Cb is more predictable than oldCp in NP (except for DESC) and ZERO class, while oldCp is more predictable than Cb in PRO class. **(1)** can be interpreted to mean that the prediction that oldCp is not pronominalized is more accurate than the prediction that Cb is pronominalized. **(2)** means that the prediction that Cb is pronominalized to zero pronoun is more accurate that the prediction that oldE and oldCp are pronominalized to the zero pronoun.

Considering that Cp is closely related to salience and Cb is closely related to cohesion, these results lead us to the conclusion that salience has more influence on the prediction of NP, while cohesion has more influence on the prediction of the zero pronoun. This can explain Ryu's experimental result [10], ellipsis of Cb generally comes from in the order of Continue, Retain, in that cohesion is kept in both Continue and Retain.

Before we discuss **(3)**, we should notice that almost all PRO can be replaced by NP rather than ZERO; therefore it is natural that the accuracy of the NP in 2-class is lowered in 3-class. Consequently, the prediction of oldCp about NP is lowered, and the prediction which Cb is pronominalized is more accurate than the prediction where oldCp is not pronominalized.

In Korean written texts, the redundant noun has a tendency to be realized as the original one rather than as a pronoun when the zero pronoun is forbidden, unlike English. Thus, it is natural that the ZERO class is more predictable than PRO.

Roughly, in the **story** genre, oldE is more predictable than Cb and oldCp, because topic continuity cannot be well explained by the centering model in the story genre, so Cb and Cp related to the centering model are less influential compared with other genres.

4.2 Feature Analysis

In this paper, we proposed a total of 13 features that influence pronominalization. However, the contribution of each of these features is different. To identify strong features across genres, we adopt the correlation-based feature selection approach [2] as an evaluator and four search methods, best, genetic, random and exhaustive search. The results are averaged, and these results are similar to each three genres (Table 5). Feature 2, 3, 4, and 5 are commonly selected as central features for Cb, oldCp, and oldE in each class; in other words, the history of grammatical role of old entity and syntactic constraints succeed. The history of center transition also succeed, in that feature 9 is selected as a strong feature in oldCp.

Table 5. Central features across genres

target	2-class	3-class
Cb	11, 3, 4, 5, 1, 2	11, 3, 4, 5, 7, 2
oldCp	2, 3, 4, 5, 9	9, 3, 5, 4
oldE	2, 3, 4, 5	2, 3, 4, 5, 7

Feature 11, equality of $Cb(S_i)$ and $Cp(S_{i-1})$, is a central feature for the prediction of pro-form of $Cb(S_i)$. In our corpus of DESC texts, 61% zero pronouns come from Cb of Continue transition. 95% of 61% zero pronouns come from Cheap-Continue, and only 5 % come from Expensive-Continue. Additionally, we verified that in TOTAL 80% of zero pronouns come from under the situation that $Cb(S_i)$ is the same as Cp (S_{i-1}). This result clearly shows that our assumption – Cb of Expensive-Continue is less elliptical than that of Cheap-Continue – is correct.

Although feature 12 is not selected as the central feature, we can clarify that it is closely related to the zero pronouns, grounding that in TOTAL zero pronouns occur in 49% of transitions that associated with cheap-pair, while zero pronouns occur 24% of transitions that associated with expensive-pair. Thus, we conclude that the features derived from cost-based centering model succeed to predict the pro-form of Cb, specifically the zero pronouns. Concerning feature 6, in TOTAL only 11% of old entities that place in the first sentence of new paragraph are pronominalized to zero pronoun. However, total number of these old entities is only 16 cases, so the evidence for effectiveness of feature 6 is exiguous. Concerning feature 7, in TOTAL 29% of animate old entities are pronominalized to PRO, while only 1% of inanimate old entities are pronominalized to PRO. Compared with other texts, in story 'person' is frequently appears, so animate entities are plentiful. 71% old entities in PRO is animate in STORY, so the traditional assumption – most pronominal anaphors are animate – is roughly applied.

In our experiment, only 5 cases – Cp of Rough-Shift is same as Cb of Retain in Continue, Retain, and Rough-Shift sequence – occur. Among these 5 cases, 4 Cp of Rough-Shift transitions are pronominalized to the zero pronouns. However, test set is too small to validate the effectiveness of feature 13, like feature 6.

Finally, our model, which is constructed by AdaBoosting using DT, was compared with others'. The comparative three models could be completely implemented by our annotated texts. Yeh [14] considers all old entities, while [5] and [13] consider only Cb as the target of pronominalization. The comparison result was shown in Table 6. Except for Cb and OLD (OLD = oldE + Cb + oldCp) in 3-class of story genre, we statistically assure that our precision significantly outperforms the maximum precision of the previous approaches' at a 99% confidence level by T-test.

Table 6. Comparison of our model with previous works

unit: %

Genre	DESC				NEWS				STORY				TOTAL			
Target	Cb		OLD		Cb		OLD		Cb		OLD		Cb		OLD	
Class	2	3	2	3	2	3	2	3	2	3	2	3	2	3	2	3
Yeh [14]			77				68				68				74	
Kibble [5]	62	66			55	57			65	65			64	62		
Yamura-Takei [13]	62	62			59	56			59	53			61	59		
Our Model	**85**	**85**	**87**	**85**	**95**	**92**	**94**	**89**	**75**	**60**	**80**	**68**	**82**	**79**	**88**	**82**

5 Conclusion

In this paper, we propose several features derived from syntactic information and the cost-based centering model for pronominalization. We investigated strong features that influence pronominalization across genres, and found that our proposed features would be successful. Moreover, we found that equality of $Cb(S_i)$ and $Cp(S_{i-1})$ is effective for prediction of Cb, specifically zero pronouns. Based on these proposed features, we constructed a pronoun generation model by various ML techniques, and showed that our model outperformed previous approaches.

Classifying old entities into three types like Cb, oldCp, and oldE is very valuable because their own roles are different: cohesion, salience, and oldness, respectively. Our experimental result also shows that these three types have a different tendency toward pronominalization.

In this paper, we evaluate our model by comparing the pro-form generated by our model and the pro-form of collected texts. However, this comparison is too strict to evaluate the performance of our model, because some pro-form can be sufficiently natural, although it is completely different from the pro-form of original texts. To resolve the problem in future, our model will be manually evaluated by human readers with some agreement measures, such as Kappa statistics. Additionally, we will apply our model to different languages such as Japanese or Chinese. Finally, the practicality of the proposed method will also be verified in a real text generation system.

Acknowledgement

This work was supported by the KOSEF through the Advanced Information Technology Research Center (AITrc), and also partially by the BK 21 Project in 2003.

References

1. Grosz, B.J., Joshi, A.K. and Weinstein, S. 1995. *Centering: A Framework for Modeling the Local Coherence of Discourse*, Computational Linguistics 21(2), pp203-225
2. Hall, M. A. 1998. *Correlation-based Feature Subset Selection for Machine Learning*. Thesis submitted in partial fulfillment of the requirements of the degree of Doctor of Philosophy at the University of Waikato
3. Hashimoto Sachie, 2001. *Anaphoric Expression Selection in the Generation of Japanese*, Information Processing Society of Japan, No.143
4. Kibble, R. and Power, R. 1999. *Using centering theory to plan coherent texts*, In Proceedings of the 12th Amsterdam Colloquium.
5. Kibble, R. and Power, R. 2000. *An integrated framework for text planning and pronominalization* Proceedings of the 1st International Conference on Natural Language Generation (INLG-2000), Mitzpe Ramon, Israel, pp77-84
6. Kim, Mi Kyung, 1999. *Conditions on Deletion in Korean based on Information Packaging*, Discourse and Cognition 1(2), pp61-88
7. Kim, Mi Kyung, 2003. *Zero vs. Overt NPs in Korean Discourse: A Centering Analysis*. Korean Journal of Linguistics, 28-1, pp29-49
8. Poesio, M., Henschel, R., Hitzeman, J & Kibble, R. 1999. *Statistical NP generation: A first report*. In R. Kibble & K. van Deemter (Eds.), Proceedings of the Workshop on The Generation of Nominal Expressions, 11th European Summer School on Logic, Language, and Information, Utrecht, 9-13 August
9. Roh, J.E. and Lee, J.H. 2003. *Coherent Text Generation using Entity-based Coherence Measures*, ICCPOL, Shen-Yang, China, pp243-249
10. Ryu, Byung Ryul, 2001, *Centering and Zero Anaphora in the Korean Discourse,* Seoul National University, Ms Thesis
11. Strube, M. and Hahn, U. 1999. *Functional Centering: Grounding Referential Coherence in Information Structure* Computational Linguistics 25(3), pp309-344
12. Strube, M., Wolters, M. 2000. *A Probabilistic Genre-Independent Model of Pronominalization,* In Proceedings of the first Meeting of the North American Chapter of the Association for Computational Linguistics. Seattle, WA, USA, April 29 - May 4, pp18-25
13. Yamura-Takei , M., Fujiwara M., and Aizawa, T. 2001. *Centering as an Anaphora Generation Algorithm: A Language Learning Aid Perspective*, NLPRS 2001, Tokyo, Japan, pp557-562
14. Yeh, Ching-Long, Mellish, Chris, 1997. *An Empirical Study on the Generation of Anaphora in Chinese,* Computational Linguistics, 23-1, pp169-190

Categorizing Unknown Text Segments for Information Extraction Using a Search Result Mining Approach

Chien-Chung Huang[1], Shui-Lung Chuang[1], and Lee-Feng Chien[1,2]

[1] Institute of Information Science, Academia Sinica, Taiwan
{villars,slchuang,lfchien}@iis.sinica.edu.tw
[2] Department of Information Management, National Taiwan University, Taiwan

Abstract. An advanced information extraction system requires an effective text categorization technique to categorize extracted facts (text segments) into a hierarchy of domain-specific topic categories. Text segments are often short and their categorization is quite different from conventional document categorization. This paper proposes a Web mining approach that exploits Web resources to categorize unknown text segments with limited manual intervention. The feasibility and wide adaptability of the proposed approach has been shown with extensive experiments on categorizing different kinds of text segments including domain-specific terms, named entities, and even paper titles into Yahoo!'s taxonomy trees.

1 Introduction

Many Information extraction (IE) systems extract important facts [8], such as people names and event titles, from documents. However, given nowadays sentence analysis technology, it is not easy to understand the semantics of such word strings in a non-controlled subject domain. To extract more information from these extracted facts, a possible solution is to categorize the extracted facts into a well-organized topic taxonomy, and, based on the categories assigned, to find out their more semantically-deep meaning.

When applying text categorization techniques to complex domains with many categories, extremely large quantities of training documents are often necessary to ensure reasonable categorization accuracy [4]. Creating these sets of labeled data is tedious and expensive, since typically they must be labeled by a person. This leads us to consider an alterative approach that requires not much manual effort. Combining Web mining technique and text categorization technique, the proposed approach is efficient and highly accurate in categorization, and, most important of all, it can be easily adapted to different tasks and thus can be employed to design more advanced IE systems.

For general applications, an important fact extracted by an IE system is defined as a text pattern, which is a meaningful word string containing a key concept of a certain subject domain. More specifically, text segments can be domain-specific terms, named entities, natural language queries, or even paper title. Our task is to categorize these extracted text segments into appropriate categories.

Conventional text categorization techniques are often utilized to analyze relationships among documents, while both the aim and the skill of text pattern categorization

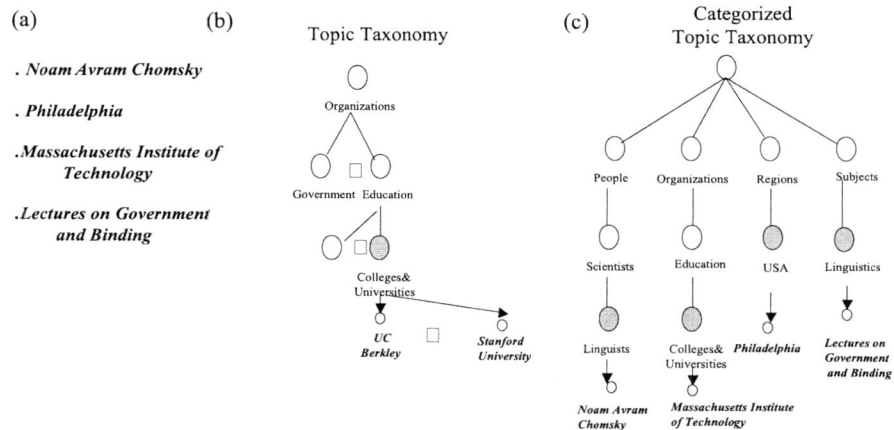

Fig. 1. A set of text segments and example topic taxonomy extracted from Yahoo!.

are quite different. Documents normally contain much more information than text segments. Therefore, the similarity between a document and a target class can be in some degree estimated with the difference of distribution of of words contained in the document itself and the training set of the class; on the contrary, the similarity between a short text pattern and a target class cannot be estimated in like manner. Obviously, if one wishes to categorize an unknown pattern, one has to use an external resource to give the unknown text pattern more features.

The Web is becoming the largest data repository in the world [11]. The rich Web corpus undoubtedly offers much possibilities for designing new applications. In this research, we intend to organize the text segments into a taxonomy, in which an overall topic structure of the extracted facts can be observed and deeper analysis performed. The taxonomy consists of two parts: keyword groups representing individual topic classes and a hierarchy of such topic classes. The topic taxonomy looks like a classification tree in which each node is associated with a keyword to represent a certain concept. Each non-leaf node (interior node) normally stands for a topic class, and its concept is composed of the concepts of its child classes in the hierarchy. For illustration, an example topic taxonomy extracted from Yahoo! is depicted in Figure 1, which includes (a) a set of example text segments, (b) a part of the topic taxonomy that can be used for categorizing the segments, and (c) the part of the taxonomy with segments categorized. From this figure, we could imagine that the concept of the Colleges & Universities class is composed of the concept of existing keywords such as "UC Berkeley" and "Stanford University." Suppose there is an unknown text pattern "Massachusetts Institute of Technology", it is expected that it is to be categorized into this class and offer more concept for it at the same time. For another example, the concept of the Education class is composed of the concept of the Colleges & Universities class along with the concepts of other sibling classes. Reserving the branches with segments categorized, a taxonomy tree as shown in (c) can provide another view for understating the unknown segments.

Normally, it is not too difficult for a human expert to construct a classification tree for a certain IE task, but there are unavoidably two challenge issues: (1) whether the constructed taxonomy is well-organized; (2) how to collect sufficient corpus to train a statistical model for each class. Our research is focused on dealing with the second issue. The proposed approach utilize real-world search engines to train our model. Our main idea is to employ highly ranked search result pages retrieved by the unknown segments and the keywords of the target classes as a source for feature extraction. This approach not only reduces manual labor but also supplements the insufficient information of unknown segments. The feasibility of the proposed approach has been shown with extensive experiments. We believe the proposed approach can serve as a basis toward the development of advanced Web information extraction systems. In the rest of this paper, we first review some related work and introduce the proposed approach; we then present the conducted experiments and their results; finally, we discuss some possible applications and draw conclusions.

2 Related Work

Word Clustering and Named Entity Identification. A number of approaches have been developed in computational linguistics for clustering functional-similar words and identifying named entities. These approaches relied on analysis of the considered objects' contextual information obtained from tagged corpus [3, 9]. Instead of using tagged corpus for categorizing word- or phrasal-level objects, the proposed approach is extended to fully exploit Web resources as a feature source to categorize text segments, which might be longer in length, into hierarchical topic classes. At the current stage of our research, we assume that the text segments are formed with a simple syntactic structure and containing some domains-specific or unknown words. Conventional syntactic sentence analysis might not be appropriate to be applied under such circumstances.

Complete grammatical sentence analysis is assumed inappropriate to be applied under this circumstance.

Web Mining. Our research is related to text mining [8], which concerns the discovery of knowledge in huge amounts of unstructured textual data from the Web. A variety of related studies have focused on different subjects, such as automatic extraction of terms or phrases [7, 2], the discovery of rules for the extraction of specific information segments [11], and ontology construction based on semi-structured data [1]. Different from these previous works, the proposed approach is to categorize text segments via mining of search result pages.

Text Categorization. As mentioned in Section 1, conventional text categorization techniques are often utilized to analyze relationships among documents [4], and there is much difference between document categorization and text pattern categorization. The latter seemed relatively little investigated in the literature. The work most closely related to ours in methodological aspect is [5], in which the named entities are categorized into three major types: *Organizations*, *Persons*, and *Locations*. Their work also use unlabel documents to help the process of categorization. Their idea is mainly like this: for the extracted text segments, the unlabeled data themselves offer useful contextual information, which, if properly exploited by statistical or machine-learning techniques, can ensure high accuracy of categorization. The difference between our work and theirs is not only that we use Web corpus while they do not, but also we use structural information of topic taxonomy rather than contextual information contained in unlabeled documents to train classifiers. Comparatively, in finding out the information about text segments, the information we extract are semantically deeper. Also, our approach, thanks to Web corpus, are more flexible and can be easily adapted to other applications.

3 The Proposed Approach

The diagram depicted in Figure 2 shows the overall concept of the proposed approach, which is composed of three computational modules: context extraction, model training and pattern categorization. The approach exploits the highly ranked search-result pages retrieved from online search engines as the effective feature sources for training the topic classes contained in the taxonomy and each unknown text pattern. The context extraction module collects features both for the topic classes and for the unknown text segments, the model training module utilizes the feature sources to train statistical model for the topic classes, and the pattern categorization module determines appropriate classes for the unknown text pattern.

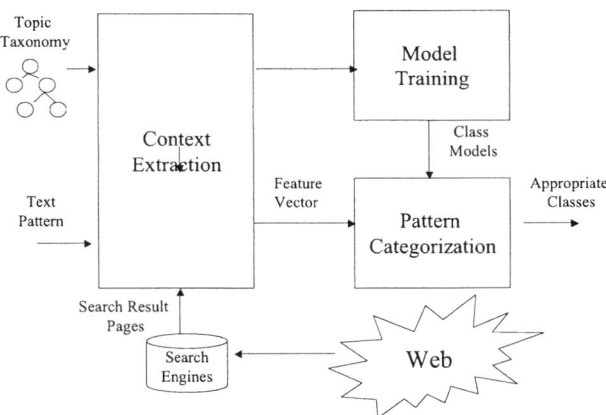

Fig. 2. An abstract diagram showing the concept of the proposed approach.

3.1 Context Extraction

We adopt the vector-space model as the data representation for both unknown text segments and target topic classes. The contexts of a text pattern are obtained from the highly ranked search-result pages (document snippets) returned by Web search engines, e.g., the titles and descriptions of search-result entries, and the texts surrounding the matched text segments. The features for a text pattern are then extracted from the returned snippets. The same procedure is used to collect document sets for training the topic classes in a predefined topic taxonomy.

Using Web search engines as information sources has both disadvantages and advantages. Web contents are usually heterogeneous and noisy, and need careful treatment. However, with the presentation schemes of most search engines, the neighboring contents surrounding a matched query (pattern) in Web pages are selectively shown in the returned snippets. Therefore, features are extracted from the corresponding text pattern's contexts instead of the whole Web page. Further, a huge amount of pages have been indexed, so most text segments can get sufficient results. As a result of recent advances in search technologies, highly ranked documents usually contain documents of interest and can be treated, at least in a certain amount of situations, as an approximation of the text segments' topic domains.

Representation Model. Suppose that, for each text pattern p, we collect up to N_{max} search-result entries, denoted as D_p. Each text pattern can then be converted into a bag of feature terms by applying normal text processing techniques, e.g., removing stop words and stemming, to the contents of D_p. Let T be the feature term vocabulary, and let t_i be the i-th term in T. With simple processing, a text pattern p can be represented as a term vector v_p in a $|T|$-dimensional space, where $v_{p,i}$ is the weight t_i in v_p. The term weights in this work are determined according to one of the conventional *tf-idf* term weighting schemes [10], in which each term weight $v_{p,i}$ is defined as

$$v_{p,i} = (1 + \log_2 f_{p,i}) \times \log_2(n/n_i),$$

where $f_{p,i}$ is the frequency t_i occurring in v_p's corresponding feature term bag, n is the total number of text segments, and n_i is the number of text segments that contain t_i in their corresponding bags of feature terms. The similarity between a pair of text segments is computed as the cosine of the angle between the corresponding vectors, i.e.,

$$sim(v_a, v_b) = \cos(v_a, v_b).$$

For the purpose of illustration, we define the average similarity between two sets of vectors, C_i and C_j, as the average of all pairwise similarities among the vectors in C_i and C_j:

$$sim_A(C_i, C_j) = \frac{1}{|C_i||C_j|} \sum_{v_a \in C_i} \sum_{v_b \in C_j} sim(v_a, v_b).$$

3.2 Model Training

In this research, we consider using a Yahoo!-like topic taxonomy for the problem of text-pattern categorization. A Yahoo!-like taxonomy is a natural hierarchy of topics, in which most of non-leaf classes contain an appropriate number of child classes. In most cases, manually constructing such a topic hierarchy for a certain IE task is not too difficult. For example, as will be shown in Section 4, based on the Yahoo! directory, we can easily construct a taxonomy tree composed of topic classes including People, Event, Time, and Place. For training a categorization model for each topic class, such a taxonomy tree is useful, as its child classes offer ample information to characterize its concept. For example, In the People class, there are 55 sub-classes at the second level, e.g., a Scientists class and a Politicians class; and there are about hundreds of sub-classes at the third level, nine of which, e.g., Mathematicians and Physicians, are the sub-classes of the Scientists class; these sub-classes enrich the concept of the scientists class.

In current stage of research, only non-leaf classes are considered as the target classes for categorization. For each non-leaf class, its training set is the union of the document snippets obtained by sending to search engines the class name and its child class names as queries. In our experiments, at most 100 document snippets could be extracted as the feature source for a specific query. Again, using the Scientists class as an example, there are totally 1000 (100+9*100) relevant document snippets that can be used to train its corresponding concept. Usually, it is not easy to obtain such amount of information from a corpus without extremely large sets of training documents.

On the other hand, the uniqueness and coverage of the child class names, however, might greatly affect the performance of the class model. If a class does not contain enough child classes or if many of its child class names are not meaningful, the features extracted from the retrieved document snippets might not be effective enough to characterize the concept of the class. Obviously, not all semantic classes can use this kind of approach to train their class models. Also, not every unknown text pattern can be categorized with the proposed approach. In fact, the proposed approach is more suitable to categorize the text segments that are more specific in their meaning and retrieve more contextual information from the Web. Therefore, the proposed approach prefers categorizing text segments into specific topic classes. It might not perform so well when categorizing common text segments into a broader class.

3.3 Pattern Categorization

Given a new candidate text pattern p, pattern categorization is to determine a set of categories C_p that are considered as p's related categories. With the same scenario stated previously, the candidate pattern p is represented as a feature vector v_p. For this categorization task, we here adopt a kNN approach.

kNN has been an effective classification approach to a broad range of pattern recognition and text classification problems [6]. By kNN approach, a relevance score between p and candidate cluster C_i is determined by the following formula:

$$r_{kNN}(p, C_i) = \sum_{v_j \in R_k(p) \cap C_i} sim(v_p, v_j)$$

where $R_k(p)$ are p's k most-similar objects, measured by sim function, in the whole collection.

The categories that a pattern is assigned to are determined by either a predefined number of most-relevant clusters or a threshold to pick those clusters with scores higher than the specified threshold value. Different threshold strategies have both advantages and disadvantages [12]. In this study, for evaluating the performance, we select the five most-relevant categories as candidates.

4 Experiment

To assess the performance of our approach, we have conducted several experiments. The Yahoo!'s taxonomy tree is used as our benchmark as it is readily available and well organized.

4.1 Domain-Specific Term Categorization

We first confined our attention to a specific domain, computer science, and conducted an experiment to observe how well our approach could be applied. In the Yahoo! Computer Science taxonomy tree, there are totally 36 first-level, 177 second-level, and 278 third-level classes. We used the first-level classes, e.g., "Artificial Intelligence" and "Linguistics," as the target classes and attempted to classify the class names at the third level, e.g., "Intelligent Software Agent," onto it. For each target class, we took its class name and child class names at the second level, e.g., "Machine Learning," "Expert System," and "Fuzzy Logic," as the seed instances for model training. These class names can be taken as a kind of domain-specific facts extracted in an IE task. Table 1 shows the result of the achieved top 1-5 inclusion rates, where top n inclusion rate is the rate of test segments whose highly ranked n candidate classes contain the correct class(es). To realize the effect of using second-level class names as seed instances in model training, the result is separated into two groups: with and without seed training instances.

Table 1. Top 1-5 inclusion rates for categorizing Yahoo!'s third-level CS category names.

Yahoo! (CS Class Names)	Top-1	2	3	4	5
KNN – With Seed Training Instances	.7185	.8841	.9238	.9437	.9636
KNN – Without Seed Training Instances	.4172	.6026	.6788	.7285	.7748

4.2 Paper Title Categorization

Besides using the third-level class names of the Yahoo!'s CS taxonomy tree, we also used another testing set. We collected a data set of the academic paper titles from four named computer science conferences in year 2002 and tried to categorize them into the 36 first-level CS classes again. Each conference was assigned to the Yahoo! category to which the conference was considered to belong, e.g., AAAI'02 was assigned to "Computer Science/Artificial Intelligence," and all the papers from that conference unconditionally belonged to that category. Table 2 lists the relevant information of this paper data set. Notice that this might not be an absolutely correct categorization strategy, as some papers in a conference may be even more related to other domains than the one we assigned them. However, to simplify our experiment, we make this straightforward assumption. Table 3 lists the experiment result. The purpose of this experiment is to examine the performance of categorizing longer text segments. Table 4 lists the categorization results of several miss-categorized paper titles. It can be observed that though these papers failed to be correctly categorized, they are conceptually related to

Table 2. The information of the paper data set.

Conference	# Papers	Assigned Category
AAAI'02	29	CS:Artificial Intelligence
ACL'02	65	CS:Linguistics
JCDL'02	69	CS:Lib. & Info. Sci.
SIGCOMM'02	25	CS:Networks

Table 3. Top 1-5 inclusion rates for categorizing paper titles.

Conference Paper	Top-1	2	3	4	5
KNN – With Seed Training Instances	.4628	.6277	.7181	.7713	.8085
KNN – Without Seed Training Instances	.2021	.2872	.3457	.3777	.4255

Table 4. Selected miss-categorized examples for categorizing paper titles.

Paper title	Conference	Target Cat.	Top-1	2	3	4	5
A New Algorithm for Optimal Bin Packing	AAAI	AI	ALG	AI	MOD	COLT	DNA
(Im)possibility of Safe Exchange Mechanism Design	AAAI	AI	NET	SC	LG	DB	MD
Performance Issues and Error Analysis in an Open-Domain Question Answering System	ACL	LG	AI	LG	ALG	DC	SC
Active Learning for Statistical Natural Language Parsing	ACL	LG	AI	LG	NN	COLT	ALG
Improving Machine Learning Approaches to Coreference Resolution	ACL	LG	AI	LG	ALG	FM	NN
A language modelling approach to relevance profiling for document browsing	JCDL	LIS	AI	UI	LG	LIS	ALG
Structuring keyword-based queries for web databases	JCDL	LIS	AI	LIS	DB	ALG	ARC
A multilingual, multimodal digital video library system	JCDL	LIS	LG	UI	LIS	ECAD	NET
SOS: Secure Overlay Services	SIGCOMM	NET	SC	NET	MC	OS	DC

Abbreviation List:
AI :Artificial Intelligence
ALG :Algorithms
ARC :Architecture
COLT:Computational Learning Theory
DB :Databases
DC :Distributed Computing
DNA :DNA-Based Computing
ECAD:Electronic Computer Aided Design
FM :Formal Methods
LG :Linguistics
LIS :Library and Information Science
MC :Mobile Computing
MOD:Modeling
NET :Networks
NN :Neural Network
OS :Operating Systems
SC :Security
UI :User Interface

those top-ranked categories to some degree. It is worthy of notice that the promising accuracy also shows the great potential of the proposed approach to classifying paper titles with Yahoo!'s taxonomy trees. From these tables, we can draw our preliminary conclusions: First, for very specific topic domains and text segments, our technique can obtain a rather high accuracy. Second, the seed instances used in model training have a crucial influence on the classification result. Without them, the performance drops significantly. Third, the result has shown that the proposed approach is also feasible for longer and specific text segments.

4.3 Named Entity Categorization

To observe how our technique performs in other circumstances, especially for named entities, we conducted another three experiments, i.e., using the sub-trees of "People" (People/Scientist), "Place" (Region/Europe), and "Time" (History-time Period) in Yahoo! as our testing beds. For these three cases, we randomly picked up 100, 100, and 93 class names, which can be considered as a kind of named entities, from the bottom-level and assigned them onto the top-level classes likewise. Tables 5 and 6 respectively list the relevant information of the sub-trees employed and some samples of the test named entities. It could be observed that in the "People" and "Place" cases, our technique got very satisfactory results, while in the "Time" case we did not get similar good result.

Table 5. The information of the three topic taxonomy trees extracted from Yahoo!.

Taxonomy Tree	# 1st-level Classes (Target Classes)	# 2nd-level Classes (Training Instances)	# 3rd-level Classes (Test Segments)
People (People/Scientist)	9	156	100
Place (Region/Europe)	44	N/A	100
Time (History-time Period)	8	274	93

Table 6. Top 1-5 inclusion rates for categorizing Yahoo!'s People, Place, and Time class names.

	Top-1	2	3	4	5
Yahoo! (People)	.8558	.9808	.9808	.9904	.9904
Yahoo! (Place)	.8700	.9500	.9700	.9700	.9800
Yahoo! (Time)	.3854	.5521	.6354	.6562	.6562

The reason of its degradation seems that the concept of a time period, such as "Renaissance" and "Middle Ages", is too broad and too much noise is contained in the returned snippets, thus lowering the precision of our categorization.

5 Information Extraction Applications

As we have shown in previous sections, as long as there exists a well-organized and reasonably-constructed taxonomy tree, we can categorize the unknown text segments onto it. Now suppose there is an article of unknown nature, we can extract some facts from it and classify them. Doing this, we may grasp their intended meaning and thereby have a clearer understanding of the whole article. We here use an example to illustrate our point. Randomly selecting several biography pages of scientist (these pages can be fetched from Yahoo!), we then extracted some facts (keywords) from them manually and attached them onto the taxonomy tree composed of the sub-trees of Computer Science, People, Place and Time that we have organized in Section 4. Note that a named entity may be categorized into multiple classes. After stemming the branches without attached facts, the taxonomy tree with the categorized facts can reflect a topic structure of the information contained in the facts. As shown in Figure 3, this kind of taxonomy tree offers a new perspective to understand the article.

Conventionally, when confronting a new document, one would try to classify the document and judge its content by the nature of the assigned class. In our case, we categorize its important facts. Although it is not fair to compare the effect of document categorization and that of text pattern categorization, we would like to point out that the benefit of text pattern categorization: (1) Text segments are more specific, giving a more concrete concept and are thus more suitable to be further exploited to develop advanced applications. (2) It is usually easier to categorize text segments than categorize the whole documents, since the latter often contains a lot of irrelevant information (features) and this may lead to poor performance in categorization.

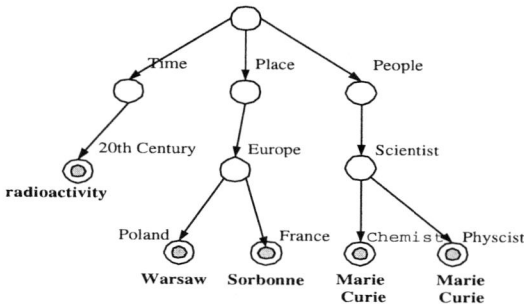

Fig. 3. A taxonomy tree with categorized facts.

6 Concluding Remarks

In this paper, we proposed a search result approach to categorizing unknown text segments for information extraction applications. Compared to conventional text categorization techniques, the proposed approach requires little manual effort and has few domain limitations. The feasibility of the proposed approach has been shown with extensive experiments. We believe the proposed approach can serve as a basis toward the development of more advanced Web information extraction systems.

References

1. E. Agirre, O. Ansa, E. Hovy, and D. Martinez. Enriching very large ontologies using the www. In *Proceedings of ECAI 2000 Workshop on Ontology Learning*, 2000.
2. H. Ahonen, O. Heinonen, M. Klemettinen, and A. Verkamo. Finding co-occurring text phrases by combining sequence and frequent set discovery. In *Proceedings of IJCAI'99 Workshop on Text Mining: Foundations, Techniques and Applications*, pages 1–9, 1999.
3. P. Brown, S. D. Pietra, V. D. Pietra, and R. Mercer. Word sense disambiguation using statistical methods. In *Proceedings of the 29th Annual Meeting of the Association for Computational Linguistics*, pages 264–270, 1991.
4. W. Cohen and Y. Singer. Context-sensitive learning methods for text categorization. In H.-P. Frei, D. Harman, P. Schäuble, and R. Wilkinson, editors, *Proceedings of the 19th Annual International ACM SIGIR Conference on Research and Development in Information Retrieval*, pages 307–315, Zürich, CH, 1996. ACM Press, New York, US.
5. M. Collins and Y. Singer. Unsupervised models for named entity classiffication, 1999.
6. B. V. Dasarathy. *Nearest Neighbor (NN) Norms: NN Pattern Classiffication Techniques*. McGraw-Hill Computer Science. IEEE Computer Society Press, Las Alamitos, California, 1991.
7. R. Feldman, Y. Aumann, A. Amir, W. Kloesgen, and A. Zilberstien. Maximal association rules: a new tool for mining for keyword co-occurrences in document collections. In *Proceedings of the Third International Conference on Knowledge Discovery and Data Mining*, pages 167–170, 1997.

8. M. Hearst. Untangling text data mining. In *Proceedings of the 37th Annual Meeting of the Association for Computational Linguistics*, 1999.
9. S. Johansson, E. Atwell, R. Garside, and G. Leech. THE TAGGED LOB CORPUS users' manual, 1986.
10. G. Salton and C. Buckley. Term weighting approaches in automatic text retrieval. *Information Processing and Management*, 24:513–523, 1988.
11. S. Soderland. Learning to extract text-based information from the world wide web. In *Proceedings of the 3rd International Conference on Knowledge Discovery and Data Mining*, pages 251–254, 1997.
12. Y. Yang. A study on thresholding strategies for text categorization. In *Proceedings of the 24th Annual International ACM SIGIR Conference on Research and Development in Information Retrieval*, pages 137–145, 2001.

Mining Table Information on the Internet*

Sung-won Jung, Gi-deuk Han, and Hyuk-chul Kwon

Korean Language Processing Lab. School of Electrical & Computer Engineering,
Pusan National University, Busan 609-735, Korea
{swjung,templer,hckwon}@pusan.ac.kr

Abstract. Making HTML documents, the authors use various methods for clearly conveying their intension. In those various methods, this paper pays special attention to tables because tables are commonly used within many documents to make the meanings clear, which are well recognized because web documents use tags for additional information. On the Internet, tables are used for the purpose of the knowledge structuring as well as design of documents. Thus, we are firstly interested in classifying tables into two types: meaningful tables and decorative tables. However, this is not easy because HTML does not separate presentation and structure. This paper proposes a method of extracting meaningful tables using a modified k-means and compares it with other methods. The experiment results show that classifying on web documents is promising.

1 Introduction

The ultimate goal of an information retrieval system is to offer the most suitable information to its users. Performance is measured by its ability to find documents with useful information for the user. The related works have, therefore, focused mainly on the method of improving recall and precision. Special attention was given to web documents where an increasingly large number of users produce un-verified documents. An efficient retrieval method is required to improve the accuracy of such systems.

To make a high precision system, we must analyze the semantics of html documents. However, it is very difficult with present technology to apply semantics to an internet retrieval system. Another method, by which we grasp the author's intention, is to analyze the structural information of html documents. For example, when an author creates a document, s/he appends the titles, make paragraphs and use indentations, numbers and symbols before the titles and tables.

This paper examines tables in several informational structures in html documents. The table form is more obvious than the plain text form, because we use a structured table in documents to convey our subject clearly. A performance improvement of an information retrieval system can be expected through the analysis of the tables because it is easy to find the tables and easy to extract the meanings in the web documents.

---

* This work was supported by National Research Laboratory Program (Contract Number: M10203000028-02J0000-01510) of KISTEP.

2 The Challenge

Current information retrieval systems rank related documents based on similarities between documents and the users' query[1]. Such systems place great importance on index words and have the following limitations.

Firstly, current systems do not draw the meaning from html documents. To retrieve information more accurately, semantics of html documents should be considered. These information retrieval systems measure the similarity between html documents and the users query based on the 'term frequency' and 'document frequency'. Furthermore, these systems accept the assumption that documents are related to the index word in proportion to the 'term frequency' of the documents. However, this assumption is only of limited validity.

Secondly, current systems do not distinguish relatively weighted indexes or keywords from general indexes in html documents. Because there can be more important keywords - even in the document, people tend to remember the important part when they read a certain document. If all keywords in a document are given the same weight, it is difficult to retrieve exactly what the users want. The systems consider the 'term frequency' and 'document frequency' of the indexes by an alternative method but it does not increase the matching accuracy sufficiently enough to satisfy all users.

Lastly, the current systems do not reflect structural information in html documents. We can grasp the writer's intention to some degree if we consider the structural information of the documents. As the writer uses titles for each paragraph, indentations and tabular forms to convey his intention clearly, they have significance in a document. These information retrieval systems, however, ignore the structural information when they extract index words from these documents.

In addressing these limitations the devised system aims to analyze and process tabular forms. For an author writing a document it may be more effective, therefore, to represent the document with a tabular form rather than to describe it in the usual methods. Related works, [3, 4, 5, 6, 7] that study the extraction of table information handle a special tabular form, and extract information using abstraction rules. Similarities exist with this and our previous research [8]. The defect of such methods, however, is that it is difficult to apply them to various web document formats. In order to address this problem a method of extracting meaningful tables using k-means algorithm and applying their results to an information retrieval system has been developed.

3 Characteristics of Table

Compared with other structural type of information, a table has various advantages as follows.

Firstly, a table tag is easy to be extracted from HTML documents. HTML has table tag contrary to plain text documents and we can recognize the tables from HTML document using table tag. This clue is served as the starting point for extracting table information from web documents.

Secondly, tables are a means of expressing semantic information structurally. A table is an arrangement of data, especially one in which the data are arranged in column and rows in an essentially rectangular form. Therefore, many authors are frequently using it in order to organize and transfer information.

Thirdly, presence of a table in a document can be a criterion to define whether this document is valuable. It is documents that the information retrieval system searches, thus it is the important factor to distinguish pages which contain useful information. Generally, if a document has a table, we judge that this document has meaningful information. This is the reason why an author makes a high level decision when s/he converts plain sentences to tables.

Despite all of the above advantages, it is difficult to extract table information from web documents as we discuss below.

Firstly, it is difficult to extract meaningful tables and meaningless ones, because of HTML's properties. HTML does not separate presentation and structure. Tables are used for aligning or ordering contents of documents than its origin use, i.e. structuring or conveying information.

We could understand by our recent stochastic experiment that the tables on the web are used more often for the design of the document than for our original goal. The statistics of the tables were researched manually on the web in relation to their classification. As Table 1 shows, the percentage of documents which include the <table> tags is about 77.78% - in total 86,475 documents. The <table> tags are used as frequently as was thought. The percentage of all investigated documents which included meaningful tables is 1.16%, which is less than was thought, and is about 1.5% if we consider only the documents which include tables.

Secondly the criterion between meaningful tables and meaningless ones is ambiguous in web page. Bulletins or hub pages such as Figure 1 are representative for this case. We should decide criteria in order to remove ambiguity that is produced while selecting meaningful tables and meaningless ones. Following these criteria, we could define efficient features for the extraction of meaningful tables.

Table 1. The statistic of the tables on the Internet

Item	Count
Total document number	86475
Number of documents with table	67259
Number of documents with meaningful table	1009
Rate of document including table in total documents	77.78%
Rate of document including meaningful table in total documents	1.167%
Rate of document including meaningful table in documents including table	1.500%

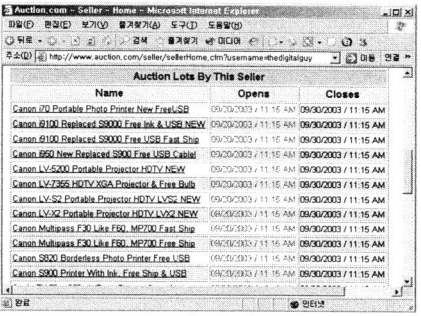 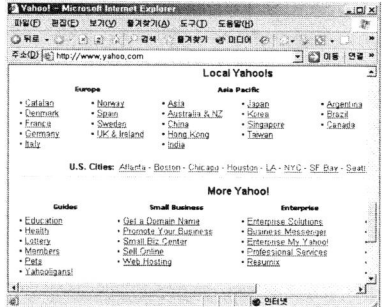

a. Bulletin page　　　　　　　　　b. Hub page

Fig. 1. Sample web pages

Thirdly, tables appear in various shapes. We assume that the meaningful tables have basically row index and column index. But the table defined as a single table by HTML, is often seen as several tables apparently (and vice versa). Also, web pages have frequently nested tables for improving visual effect.

4 Implementation

4.1 Classification of Tables

Various kinds of tables exist on the Internet. In general, a table is a printed or written collection of figures, facts, or information, arranged in orderly rows across and down the page which conveys an author's meaning more clearly. The <table> tag is supported in HTML for use on the web in a table. However, tables on the web are used not only for the purpose of the original goal but also to make the information clearer by lining it up. The task of deciding which tables are meaningful on the web is necessary before the information in a table can be extracted. To achieve this, the tables on the web have been classified into two types. We have generalized them in our previous research [9]. Following Table 2 and Figure 2 are a brief description of this generalization.

Table 2. Definition of meaningful and decorative tables

Meaningful Table	- The index of the table is located in the first row and the first column. - The contents of a cell extracted by a combination of rows and columns have specific information. - The term and document frequency cannot represent a relation between row index, column index and the content of a cell in a table.
Decorative Table	- The index of the table does not exist. - The table has no repeatability of cell form, and is not structural. - The contents of the table have complex contents such as long sentence, image, etc.

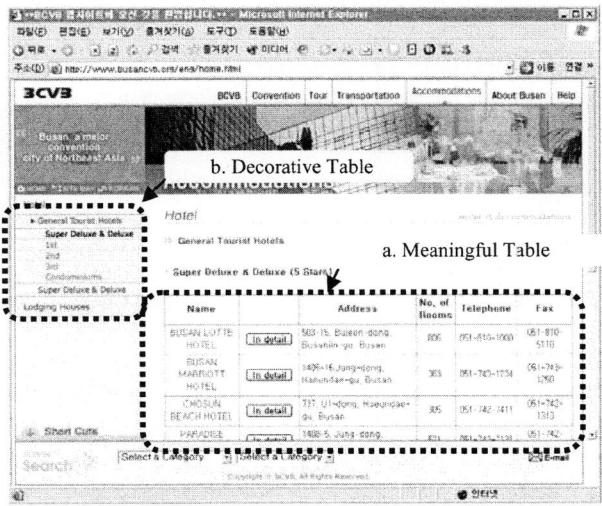

Fig. 2. The types of table on the Internet

4.2 Institution of Table Features

It is unusual to encounter a document which includes meaningful tables on the web - as the results show in Table 1. Nevertheless, the meaningful tables should be extracted from amongst the others for effective information retrieval; however, it is impossible to extract them manually due to the large number of internet documents. Therefore, the tables should be defined automatically, to identify if they are meaningful or not on the basis of the characteristics which were obtained previously by analyzing meaningful tables in the training data. For example, several characteristics could be acquired from Figure 2: presence of pictures, presence of background colors and the table size.

The whole features used in the devised system are as follows:

1. The presence of <caption> tag
2. The presence of <th> tag
3. The presence of <thead> tag
4. The classification of the cells on the first rows
5. The difference of the background color option between the row with the index and the next row, or the difference of the background color option between the column with the index and next column
6. The difference of the font color option between the row with the index and next, or the difference of the font color option between column with index and next column
7. The difference of the font face between the row with the index and next row, or the difference of the font face between column with the index and the next column
8. The presence of the border option
9. The ratio of empty cells
10. The ratio of cells including <a href> tag
11. The ratio of cells consisting of text only
12. The presence of rows or columns consisting of numeric data only
13. The ratio of cells consisting of only symbols
14. The presence of other tables in the table
15. The table size
16. The number of sentences with more than 40 characters in a cell
17. The type of table shape
18. The difference of the font size between the row with index and next row, or the difference of the font size between the column with the index and the next column
19. The index word type
20. The number of meaningful index column

4.3 Application of Learning Algorithm

We convert the features, which have been extracted from a table, to vector of 21 dimensions. These vectors are input data of machine learning algorithms. Our previous research [9] applies this data to ID3 algorism [2] using information gain. The limitation of our previous method is that it has nominal values as results. Thus, we were unable know which degree of ambiguity a table shows. Therefore, modified k-means

algorithm is used in this work because we need continuous value. Compared with decision tree algorithm, our new algorithm has following advantages:
1. This method can be used to determine the level of ambiguity existing in a table.
2. We can get representable types of tables
3. This method can apply to the extraction table information.
4. This method can easily combine other information retrieval methods.

Figure 3 illustrates our proposed method. Let's observe the process step by step. Firstly, each feature value is changed into its frequency ratio by numeric formula of step 1. This ratio means classification power of each feature. For the test we change our extract data from tables into a modified one with continues value. This modified learning data set, $\hat{S}$ is foundation data for proposed method. Secondly, data set $\hat{S}$ is divided into two subsets, meaningful tables and decorative tables. Each subset is clustered by k-means algorithm and we get centroids of clusters which are representable type of each subset.

The distance measure of k-means method uses cosine measure. We get an error rate from computing relationship between learning data and centroids of representable type using cosine measure. By using hill climbing method, coefficients modify. We obtain argmax by formula 2 of step 3 in order to what we obtain low error rate.

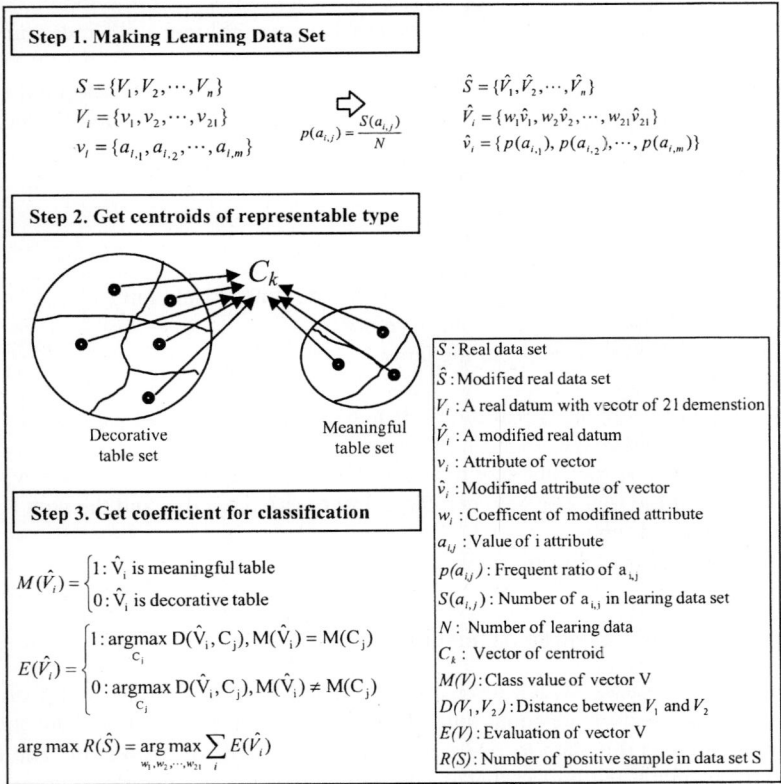

Fig. 3. Proposed Learning Algorithm

4.4 Extraction of Table Information

The system extracts the table information from the meaningful tables after filtering the tables on the web pages. For this, it is necessary to separate the table indexes and the contents of cells. It is not a simple problem to extract indexes from a table because tables on the Internet appear in various forms.

Besides, some tables can be interpreted as being part of several types. Figure 4 shows the evidence of this phenomenon. As the Figure 4-a shows, the first column is filled out with only sequences which is meaningless, while its second column is more meaningful.

And also, Figure 4-b has potentially two index columns, first column and second column. If a system cannot consider the user's intention, it is too hard to select an index row. In our previous work, we made table information with combination of three values: row index, column index, and content of the cell as Figure 5-a demonstrates. If we applied previous example to our previous work, extracted information would be many errors. Therefore, we design a new method that Figure 5-b illustrates.

First of all, we change the data structure of meaningful table information into two dimensional arrays. If system is received user's query, the system searches the table which has user's query. Index row and column of this table are row and column with user's query. In this case, system can extract two contents of cell like as Figure 5-b and he takes "6000" by common sense.

No.	Name	English	Korean	Mathematics
1	SungWon Jung	80	90	40
2	MiYoung Kang	90	85	65
3	WonHee Lee	75	85	80

a. Table with index in second column

Student ID	Name	Address	Tel. No.
200393174	SungWon Jung	YoungDo-Gu Pusan Korea	051-9554-2832
200393175	MiYoung Kang	GumJeong-Gu Pusan Korea	051-442-2983
200393176	WonHee Lee	GangSeo-Gu Seoul Korea	01-2983-2837

b. Table with two potential index columns

Fig. 4. Example of meaningful table from which it is difficult to extract information

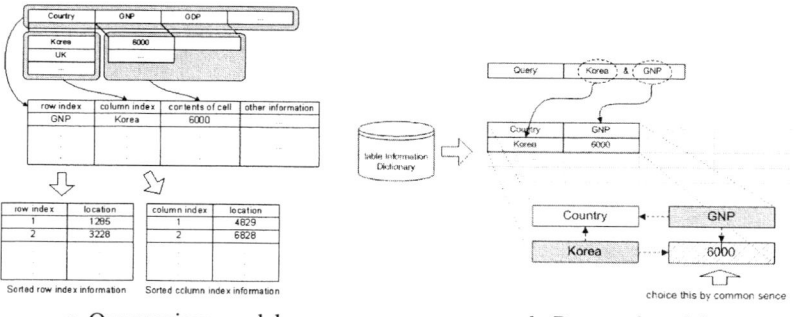

a. Our previous model   b. Proposed model

Fig. 5. Model of Information Extraction

5 Experimental Result

We implemented the system with an Intel Pentium IV that has a 2GHz CPU and 256 MBytes main memory. Sample data was extracted in about 50,000 internet documents and test data was chosen from about 5 millions internet documents that were collected in Artificial Intelligence Laboratory in Pusan National University.

Table 3 shows error rates according to variation of cluster number. The cluster number coincides with the number of representable type for each class. From Table 3, we set MN for 2 and DN for 3, because we judge one class with only one cluster to overfit.

Table 3. Error Rate for Number of Cluster

No. of Table: 9769		No. of Decorative Table Cluster(DN)				
		1	2	3	4	5
No. of Meaningful Table Cluster(MN)	1	247	106	60	40	48
	2	199	92	53	54	54
	3	131	113	98	71	54
	4	111	119	96	99	86

Table 4 is a result from the application of the modified k-means to test data. The data is 5,000 web documents collected on the Internet. For the results a recall of 84.58% and a precision of 75.52% were obtained.

Table 4. The application of the modified k-means

Number of tables	Decision Tree		Modified k-means	
	Recall	Precision	Recall	Precision
4283	81.54	55.21	86.92	79.58
8020	52.91	55.56	83.60	72.15
6341	67.47	39.72	78.31	62.50
9108	86.11	63.70	85.65	83.33
9769	95.83	38.33	91.67	68.75
37521	73.36	54.45	84.58	75.52

6 Conclusion

The devised information retrieval system requires making estimates to show correct information to the user. For the system to extract information from a table, it must classify whether it is a meaningful table or a decorative table. If a meaningful table is extracted, it is easy to process the information in the table to other data forms. For example, when a user inputs a query such as the "Temperature of Busan", the system should output the correct result using abstracted table information. This work can process data of a general information retrieval system or a specific domain that has many tables. The work needs a more accurate algorithm for classifying and learning a table thereafter.

Future work will seek to identify the correlation between documents and tables. The rationale behind this work will research the link between tables and documents i.e. if a table can supply the contents of a document, how relevant tables can affect the importance of a document.

References

1. Salton, G., McGill, M. J.: Introduction to Modern Information Retrieval, McGraw-Hill, New York (1983)
2. Mitchell, T. M.: Machine Learning, McGraw-Hill (1997), 53-79
3. Hammer, J., Garcia-Molina, H., Cho, J., Aranha, R., and A. Crespo.: Extracting Semistructured Information from the Web, SIGMOD Record, 26(2) (1997) 18-25
4. Huang Y., Qi G.Z., Zhang F.Y.: Constructing Semistructed information extractor from the Web document, Journal of Software 11(1) (2000) 73-75
5. Ashish., N., Knoblock, C.: Wrapper Generation for Semi-structed Internet Sources, SIGMOD Record, 26(4) (1997) 8-15
6. Smith, D., Lopez M.: Information Extraction for Semi-structed Documents, In Proceedings of the Workshop on Management of Semistructed Data, in conjunction with PODS/SIGMOD, Tucson, AZ, USA, May, 12 (1997)
7. Ning, G., Guowen, W., Xiaoyuan, W., Baile, S.: Extracting Web table information in cooperative learning activites based on abstract semantic model, Computer Supported Cooperative Work in Design, The Sixth International Conference on 2001 (2001) 492-497
8. Jung, S.W., Sung, K.H., Park, T.W., Kwon, H.C.: Effective Retrieval of Information in Tables on the Internet, IEA/AIE June (2002) 493-501
9. Jung, S.W., Lee, W.H., Park, S.K., Kwon, H.C.: Extraction of Meaningful Tables from the Internet Using Decision Trees, LNAI 2718, IEA/AIE (2003) 176-186

Collecting Evaluative Expressions
for Opinion Extraction

Nozomi Kobayashi[1], Kentaro Inui[1], Yuji Matsumoto[1],
Kenji Tateishi[2], and Toshikazu Fukushima[2]

[1] Nara Institute of Science and Technology,
Takayama, Ikoma, Nara, 630-0192, Nara
{nozomi-k,inui,matsu}@is.naist.jp
[2] Internet Systems Research Laboratories, NEC Corp.
Takayama, Ikoma, Nara, 630-0101, Nara
k-tateishi@bq.jp.nec.com, t-fukushima@cj.jp.nec.com

Abstract. Automatic extraction of human opinions from Web documents has been receiving increasing interest. To automate the process of opinion extraction, having a collection of evaluative expressions such as *"something* is confortable" would be useful. However, it can be costly to manually create an exhaustive list of such expressions for many domains, because they tend to be domain-dependent. Motivated by this, we explored ways to accelerate the process of collecting evaluative expressions by applying a text mining technique. This paper proposes a semi-automatic method that uses particular cooccurrence patterns of evaluated subjects, focused attributes and value expressions.

1 Introduction

There are explosively increasing number of Web documents that include human opinions, indicating dissatisfaction with products, complaints about services, and so on. Automatic extraction of such opinions has been receiving interest from the NLP and text mining communities [1–3].

The following is an excerpt from a message board on a car review site.

The seats are very comfortable and supportive.
But the back seat room is tight . . .

This example suggests that the core of an opinion typically consists of three elements: an evaluated subject, focused attribute and its value. One can extract the following triplets from above sentences:

⟨Product_X, seats, comfortable⟩
⟨Product_X, seats, supportive⟩
⟨Product_X, back seat room, tight⟩

Once opinions are obtained in the form as above, one can, for example, statistically analyze them and summarize the results as radar-charts in a fully automatic manner. In fact, our group has developed a prototype system that generates radar-charts of opinions extracted from review sites [4].

Motivated by this, we are aiming at the development of an automatic method to extract opinions, each of which is specified by a triplet ⟨evaluated subject, focused attribute, value⟩ from Web documents.

One approach to this goal is to use a list of expressions which possibly describe either evaluated subject, focused attribute or value (referred to subject expressions, attribute expressions, and value expressions, hereafter). Presumably, given a target domain, it is not difficult to obtain a list of expressions of subjects (product names, service names, etc.). However, it can be considerably expensive to manually create an exhaustive list of attribute and value expressions for many domains, because they tend to be domain-dependent. For example, *"gas mileage"* is an attribute expression in the car domain, but is not in the computer domain. The purpose of this paper is to explore how to reduce the cost of creating a list of evaluative expressions: attribute expressions and value expressions. We propose a semi-automatic method that uses particular cooccurrence patterns of subjects, attributes and values. We then report experimental results and show its efficiency compared to manual collection of those expressions.

2 Related Work

Pang et al. and Turney propose a method to classify reviews into *recommended* or *not recommended* [5, 6]. While their work focuses on document-wise classification, some other researchers approach sentence-wise classification. For example, Yu et al. address the task of discriminating opinion sentences from factual sentences and classifying opinion sentences into positive or negative[7]. Hatzivassiloglou et al. discuss the usefulness of gradable adjectives in determining the subjectivity of a sentence [8].

These research aim at the determination of the specific orientation (positive / negative) for sentence or document. In contrast, we aim not only at classifying opinions as positive or negative, but also at extracting the grounds why the opinion determined to be positive or negative. We will realize extracting the grounds by extraction of triplets.

There have also been several techniques developed for acquiring subjective words. For example, Hatzivassiloglou and MacKeown propose a method to identify the semantic orientation (positive / negative) of adjectives[9] . Riloff et al. apply bootstrapping algorithms to obtain subjective nouns[10]. These work intend to collect the words that are useful for determining subjectivity. As mentioned above, in order to extract triplets from opinions, we will collect expressions with the help of specific patterns that relates some of the elements in the triplets ⟨evaluated subject, focused attribute, value⟩.

3 Attribute and Value

Let us first discuss what sorts of expressions we should collect as attribute and value expressions for the sake of opinion extraction.

Consider one example, *"the leather seat (of some Product_X) is comfortable"*. This opinion can be considered to contain at least the following information:

- Subject: The subject of evaluation is *Product_X*.
- Attribute: The opinion focuses on a particular aspect of *Product_X*, *"the leather seat"*.

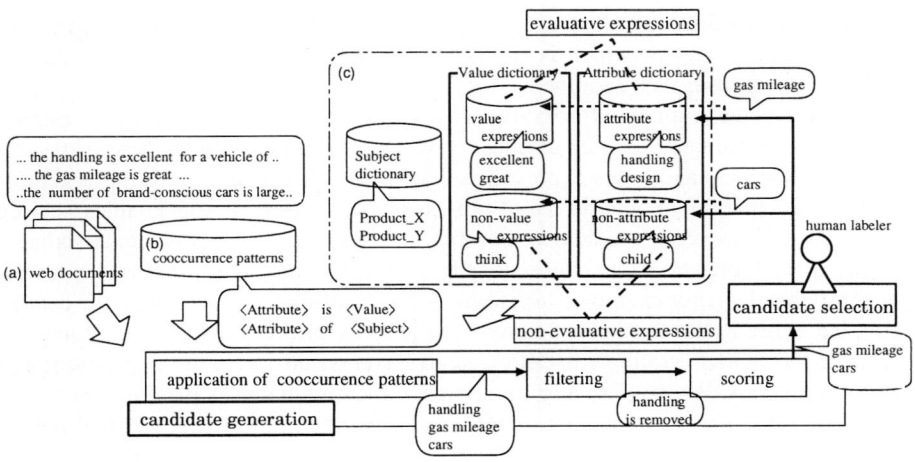

Fig. 1. Semi-automatic process of collecting attribute/value expressions.

- Value: The opinion says that the value of the attribute of *Product_X* is "*comfortable*".

To be more general, we consider an opinion as a chunk of information consisting of these three slots: ⟨*Subject, Attribute, Value*⟩. The attribute slot specifies which aspect of a subject is focused on. Attributes of a subject of evaluation include its qualitative and quantitative properties, its constituents, and services associated with it. The value slot specifies the quantity or quality of the corresponding aspect. The goal we pursue in this paper is to build a lexicon of linguistic expressions that can be used to realize attributes or values in the above sense.

Note that an opinion may also have a specific orientation (i.e. favorable or unfavorable). For example, "*I like the leather seats of Product_X*" expresses the writer's favorable orientation to the attribute "*the leather seats*". One may want to introduce the fourth slot and define an opinion as 4-tuple ⟨*Subject, Attribute, Value, Orientation*⟩. However, it is not necessarily worthwhile because the distinction between Value and Orientation is sometimes messy. We thus simply regard Orientation as a special type of Value.

4 Collecting Expressions Using Cooccurrence Patterns

Opinions can be linguistically realized in many ways. One of the typical forms would be:

⟨*Attribute*⟩ *of* ⟨*Subject*⟩ *is* ⟨*Value*⟩.

We use such typical patterns of textual fragments as clues for collecting attribute and value expressions. For example, applying the above coocurrence pattern to "*the leather seat of Product_X is comfortable*", we can learn that "*the leather seat*" may be an attribute expression and "*comfortable*" a value expression. If we have already known that "*comfortable*" is a value expression, we can reason that "*leather seat*" is more likely to be an attribute expression.

Figure 1 illustrates the process of collecting attribute/value expressions. The overall process consists of repeated cycles of *candidate generation* followed by *candidate selection*. In each cycle, the candidate generation step automatically produces an ordered list of candidates for either attribute or value expressions using coocurrence patterns and the current dictionaries of subject, attribute and value expressions. In the candidate selection step, a human judge selects correct attribute/value expressions from the list and add them to the dictionaries. Updates of the dictionaries may allow the candidate generation step to produce different candidates. Repeating this cycle makes both the attribute and value dictionaries richer gradually.

4.1 Candidate Generation

The candidate generation step uses three kinds of resources: (a) a collection of Web documents, (b) a set of coocurrence patterns, and (c) the latest version of the subject dictionary, the attribute dictionary and the value dictionary.

Suppose that we have the following coocurrence pattern:

$\underline{\langle Attribute \rangle}$ *is* $\langle Value \rangle$.

In this notation, we assume that $\langle Value \rangle$ corresponds to an already known value expression and the underlined slot $\underline{\langle Attribute \rangle}$ denotes an expression that can be taken as a candidate of an attribute expression. If our document collection includes sentences such as[1]:

... $\langle$*the handling*$\rangle_a$ *is* $\langle$*excellent*$\rangle_v$ *and* ...
... $\langle$*the gas mileage*$\rangle_a$ *is* $\langle$*great*$\rangle_v$ ...

We can obtain "*the handling*" and "*the gas mileage*" as candidates for attribute expressions.

Here we must note that such coocurrence patterns may also generate non-evaluative candidates as in the following case, from which a candidate expression "*cars*" is extracted:

... *the* $\langle$*cars*$\rangle_a$ *is* $\langle$*large*$\rangle_v$ *so that* ...

To reduce the labor of manual checking of such non-evaluative expressions, we first filter out candidates that have already been registered either in the attribute and value dictionaries. For this purpose, each dictionary is designed to keep expressions that have been judged as non-evaluative expressions in an earlier cycle as well as evaluative expressions. In case of Figure 1, "*handling*" is filtered out because it is already registered as an attribute expression. In addition to this simple filtering, we also use a statistics-based scoring function to rank extracted candidates and provide the human judge with only a limited number of highly ranked candidates. The details of the scoring function we used in the experiments will be given in Section 5.1.

---

[1] $\langle \rangle_a$ denotes the word sequence corresponding to the attribute slot of the coocurrence pattern. Likewise, we also use $\langle \rangle_v$ for the value slot and $\langle \rangle_s$ for the subject slot.

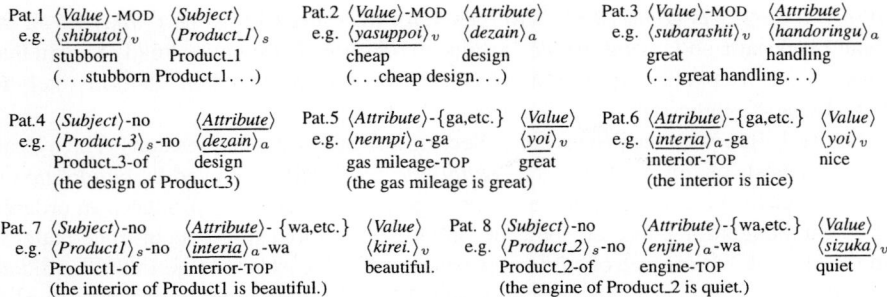

Fig. 2. The used cooccurrence patterns.

4.2 Candidate Selection

In the candidate selection step, a human judge labels an arbitrary number of highly ranked candidates and register them into the dictionaries. In Figure 1, given two candidates *"gas mileage"* and *"cars"*, the human labeler has judged the former as attributive expression and the latter as non-attributive expression.

5 Experiments

We conducted experiments with Japanese Web documents in two domains, cars and video games (simply game, hereafter), to empirically evaluate the effectiveness of our method compared to a manual collection method. In the experiments, we hired a person as the examiner who had no knowledge about the technical details of our method.

5.1 Semi-automatic Collection

Resources

Document collections: We collected 15 thousand reviews (230 thousand sentences) from several review sites on the Web for the car domain and 9.7 thousand reviews (90 thousand sentences) for the game domain.

Subject dictionaries: For subject expressions, we collected 389 expressions for car domain (e.g. *"BMW"*, *"TOYOTA"*) and 660 expressions for the game domain (e.g. *"Dark Chronicle"*, *"Seaman"*).

Initial attribute dictionary: For the seed set of attribute expressions, we manually chose the following 7 expressions for both domains that considered to be used across different domains:

> *nedan* (cost), *kakaku* (price), *sâbisu* (service), *seinou* (performance), *kinou* (function), *sapôto* (support), *dezain* (design).

Initial value dictionary: For the seed set of value expressions, we used an existing thesaurus and dictionaries to manually collect those that were considered domain-independent, obtaining 247 expressions, most of which were adjectives. The following are examples of them:

yoi (good), *kirei*(beautiful), *akarui* (bright), *kiniiru* (like / favorite), *takai* (high), *chiisai* (small)

Cooccurrence patterns: We preliminarily tested various cooccurrence patterns against another set of documents collected from the domain of mobile computers. We then selected eight patterns as shown in Figure 2 because they appeared relatively frequently and exhibited reasonable precisions. In addition to above patterns, we used another heuristic rule which indicate attribute and value expressions with suffixes. For example, we regard *"antei-sei"* (stability) as a candidate of attribute.

To reduce noise in the extraction, we specify the applicability condition of each pattern based on part-of-speech. For attributes, we extract unknown words, nouns (including compound nouns), except numerical expressions. For values, we extract only adjectives, verbs (including *sahen*-verbs), nominal adjectivals and noun phrases.

Scoring. With the above part-of-speech-based restrictions, Pat.4 to Pat.6 are still relatively underconstrained and tend to generate many non-evaluative expressions. We thus introduce a scoring function that accounts two scoring factors. One factor is the frequency of extracted expressions; namely, candidates with a high frequency in the target document collection have the preference. The other factor is the reliability of clues used for extraction. Suppose that we want to estimate the reliability of an instantiated cooccurrence pattern, say, "⟨Attribute⟩ *is low*". If this pattern has produced not only correct candidates such as "*cost*" and "*seat position*" but also many non-evaluative candidates such as "*body height*", we can learn from those results that the pattern is not so reliable, presumably less reliable than, say, "⟨Attribute⟩ *is comfortable*" which has produced very few non-evaluative candidates. Based on this consideration, we estimate the reliability of an instantiated pattern by the log-likelihood ratio between candidates and evaluative expressions.

5.2 Manual Collection

We conducted experiments comparing a manual method to our semi-automatic method. We had a human examiner tag attribute and value expressions using a tagging tool. Figure 3 shows an example of this process with the expressions that are tagged underlined. The examiner tagged expressions in 105 reviews (about 5,000 sentences) from the car domain and 280 reviews (about 2,000 sentences) from the game domain. Those reviews were taken from the same document collections that we used with our semi-automatic method. It is important to note that while the same person was responsible for both manual collection of evaluative expressions and judgment of our semi-automatic method, we avoided possible conflicts of interest by evaluating our method before manually collecting expressions.

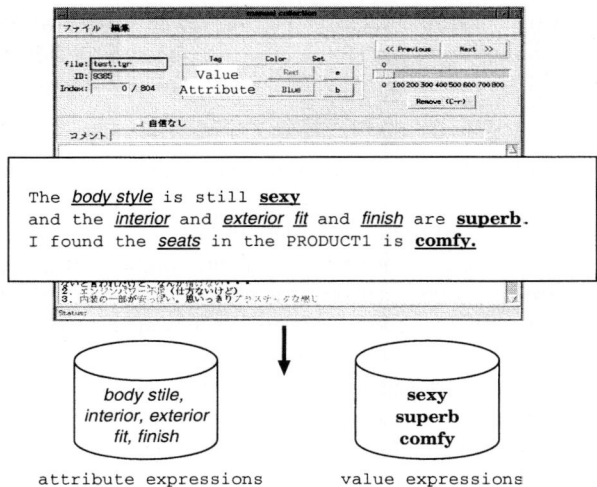

Fig. 3. Interface of the manual collection tool.

6 Results and Discussion

6.1 Collection Efficiency

Figures 4 and 5 show the plots of the number of collected expressions versus the required time. For the semi-automatic collection, we plot the cumulative number of expressions in each cycle of the collections process. For the manual collection, we plot the cumulative number of expressions collected from each 5 articles. The figures show that the semi-automatic method is significantly more efficient than the manual collection in collecting the same number of expressions. For example, the semi-automatic method takes only 0.6 hours to collect the first 500 attribute expressions while the manual extraction requires more than 5 hours. We also find that both domains exhibit quite similar

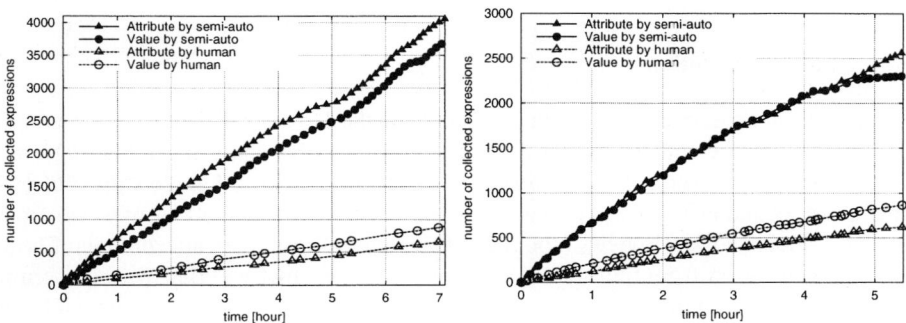

Fig. 4. Number of collected expressions (car).   **Fig. 5.** Number of collected expressions(game).

tendencies. This indicates that our method is likely to work well in a wide range of domains. Recall that, preliminary to the experiments, we used documents in the mobile computer domain, which was considerably different from the car and game domains, to tune the cooccurrence patterns. This suggest that the same set of patterns will work well in other domains.

One problem observed from the results is that the number of extracted expressions does not exhibit convergence. We think that this is due to the lack of proper treatment of compound expressions. For example, the examiner chose "engine" and "response" as attribute expressions in the car domain; however she also registered "engine response" into the attribute dictionary as a different entry. We are seeking more sophisticated ways for dealing with compound expressions that accounts their internal semantic structure. One simple option is to regard expressions comprised only with already known expressions as granted. The plausibility of such treatment should be examined in future experiments.

6.2 Coverage

It is also important to see to what extent the set of semi-automatically collected expressions cover the set of manually collected expressions. We investigated the overlap between the human extracted and semi-automatically collected expressions, finding that the semi-automatic collection covered 45% of manually collected expressions in the car domain and 35% in the game domain. Table 1 shows examples, where "common" indicates expressions collected commonly in both ways, and "semi-auto" and "manual" are expressions collected only by each method.

There are several reasons why the coverage of the semi-automatic method is not very high. One is that the current semi-automatic method does not generate candidates spanning beyond base-phrase (bunsetsu) boundaries. The human examiner does not suffer from this restriction and can collect complex phrases such as *"me kara uroko* (see the light)" and *"kaizen-no yochi ari* (there's room for improvement)" as well. This accounts for 30% of the total number of uncovered value expressions in the car and game domain.

In the attribute expressions, however, "*A no B*" ("B of A" in English) accounts for large share of uncovered attribute expressions (20% of the total number in the car domain and 27% for the game domain). "*A no B*" sometimes expresses a hierarchical relation between attributes, which are not recognized in our current setting. Consider "*engine no oto* (sound of the engine)" for example. This expression consists of "*engine*" and "*oto* (sound)", which are both attribute expressions. However, we should regard "*oto* (sound)" as an attribute of "*engine*". As this example shows, we should take into account hierarchical relations between attributes, deciding the range of attribute expressions.

6.3 Utility of Cooccurrence Patterns

Table 2 shows the usefulness of the patterns, where "number" indicates the number of expressions extracted by the patterns, and "correct/incorrect" indicates the number of value/non-value and attribute/non-attribute expressions.

Table 1. Examples of collected expression.

		common	semi-auto	manual
car	Attribute	sutairu(style) bodî karâ (body color)	shajû (weight) seijaku sei(quietness)	SOHC enjin(engine type) akarui sikichou (light in color tone)
	Value	good(good) jyouhin (elegant)	arai (gross) miwakuteki (alluring)	tekitô (appropriate) 100%
game	Attribute	oto (sound) ivento CG(event CG)	batoru supîdo(battle speed) kihon sousa (basic operation)	purei jikan (play time) chitekina senryaku (intelligent strategy)
	Value	yasuppoi (cheap) tsumaranai (boring)	soudai (magnificent) komikaru (comical)	sutoresu ga tamaru (stressful) ki ga nukenai (exciting)

Table 2. Performance of cooccurrence patterns.

		car			game		
		accuracy	number	correct/incorrect	accuracy	number	correct/incorrect
Value	pat.1,2	0.81	1362	1108/ 254	0.79	901	709/ 192
	pat.5	0.69	4917	3398/1519	0.82	2581	2119/ 462
	pat.8	0.67	239	159/ 80	0.93	15	14/ 1
Attribute	pat.3	0.42	895	372/ 523	0.24	894	214/ 680
	pat.4	0.46	726	331/ 395	0.63	40	25/ 15
	pat.6	0.76	5225	3965/1260	0.66	3975	2631/1344
	pat.7	0.58	273	159/ 114	0.56	23	13/ 10

Overall, the patterns that extract value expressions outperform the patterns that extract attribute. We speculate several reasons: one is that value expressions also cooccur with named entities (e.g. product names, company names, and so on) or general expressions such as *"mono* (thing)". Another reason is that it is difficult to decide the scope of attribute expressions. As mentioned above, there is a hierarchical relation between attributes. For example, while *"kyarakutâ*(character)" is an attribute, *"kyarakutâ"* may have its own attribute such as "*kao* (face)" or "*ugoki* (motion)". Presumably, whether this "attribute of attribute" is included in the attribute expression depends on the person making the judgment.

7 Conclusion

In this paper, we proposed a semi-automatic method to extract evaluative expressions based on particular cooccurrence patterns of evaluated subject, focused attribute and value. We reported the experimental results, which showed that our semi-automatic method was able to collect attribute and value expressions much more efficiently than manual collection and that the cooccurrence patterns we used in the experiments worked well across different domains. Our next step will be directed to the extraction of triplets ⟨*Subject, Attribute, Value*⟩ from the Web documents.

References

1. Dave, K., Lawrence, S., Pennock, D.M.: Mining the peanut gallery: Opinion extraction and semantic classification of product reviews. In: Proceedings of the 12th International World Wide Web Conference. (2003)

2. Murano, S., Sato, S.: Automatic extraction of subjective evaluative sentences using syntactic patterns. In: Proceedings of the 9th Annual Meeting of the Association for NLP. (2003) 67–70 (in Japanese).
3. Morinaga, S., Yamanishi, K., Tateishi, K., Fukushima, T.: Mining product reputations on the web. In: Proceedings of the Eighth ACM SIGKDD Internatinal Conference on Knowledge Discover and Data Mining. (2002) 341–349
4. Tateishi, K., Fukushima, T., Kobayashi, N., Wade, M., Takahashi, T., Inui, T., Fujita, A., Inui, K., Matsumoto, Y.: Web opinion extraction and summarization based on product's viewpoint. In: Proceedings of the 10th Annual Meeting of the Association for NLP. (2004) (in Japanese).
5. Tarney, P.D.: Thumbs up or thumbs down? semantic orientation applied to unsupervised classification of reviews. In: Proceedings of the 40th Annual Meeting of the Association for Computational Linguistics (ACL). (2002) 417–424
6. Pang, B., Lee, L., Vaithyanathan, S.: Thumbs up? sentiment classification using machine learning techniques. In: Proceedings of the Conference on Empirical Methods in Natural Language Processing (EMNLP). (2002) 79–86
7. Yu, H., Hatzivassiloglou, V.: Towards answering opinion questions: Separating facts from opinions and identifying the polarity of opinion sentences. In: Proceedings of the Conference on Empirical Methods in Natural Language Processing (EMNLP). (2003) 129–136
8. Hatzivassiloglou, V., Wiebe, J.M.: Effects of adjective orientation and gradability on sentence subjectivity. In: Proceedings of the 18th International Conference on Computational Linguistics (COLING). (2000) 299–305
9. Hatzivassiloglou, V., McKeown, K.R.: Predicting the semantic orientation of adjectives. In: Proceedings of the 35th Annual Meeting of the Association for Computational Linguistics and the 8th Conference of the European Chapter of the Association for Computational Linguistics (ACL-EACL). (1997) 174–181
10. Riloff, E., Wiebe, J., Wilson, T.: Learning subjective nouns using extraction pattern bootstrapping. In: Proceedings of the 7th Conference on Natural Language Learning (CoNLL). (2003) 25–32

A Study of Semi-discrete Matrix Decomposition for LSI in Automated Text Categorization*

Wang Qiang, Wang XiaoLong, and Guan Yi

School of Computer Science and Technology, Harbin Institute of Technology, Harbin
{qwang,wangxl,guanyi}@insun.hit.edu.cn

Abstract. This paper proposes the use of Latent Semantic Indexing (LSI) techniques, decomposed with semi-discrete matrix decomposition (SDD) method, for text categorization. The SDD algorithm is a recent solution to LSI, which can achieve similar performance at a much lower storage cost. In this paper, LSI is used for text categorization by constructing new features of category as combinations or transformations of the original features. In the experiments on data set of Chinese Library Classification we compare accuracy to a classifier based on k-Nearest Neighbor (k-NN) and the result shows that k-NN based on LSI is sometimes significantly better. Much future work remains, but the results indicate that LSI is a promising technique for text categorization.

1 Introduction

Text categorization, the assignment of free text documents to one or more predefined categories based on their content, is an important component in many information management tasks [1]. Now a variety of text categorization for supervised learning algorithms is based on vector space model (VSM). In this model documents are represented as a set of index terms that are weighted according to their importance for a particular document and for the general collection. But it can be misleading, because a document can be relevant for a test document without having any terms in common with it.

This paper explores the use of Latent Semantic Indexing (LSI) for text categorization as an improvement to VSM. The idea behind the LSI is to map each document and test vector into a lower dimensional space which is associated with concepts and compare the documents in this space [2]. We performed experiments using k-NN LSI, a new combination of the standard k-NN method on top of LSI, and applying a new matrix decomposition algorithm, Semi-Discrete Matrix Decomposition, to decompose the vector matrix. The Experimental results show that text categorization effectiveness in this space will be better and it will also be computationally less costly, because it needs a lower dimensional space.

This paper proceeds as follows. Section 2 presents the general framework for a recent LSI method, Semi-Discrete Matrix Decomposition (SDD). Then, the specific application of LSI to text classification is discussed in Section 3. Related work is presented in Section 4. Experimental result is shown in Section 5. Finally, Section 6 makes out plans for future work.

---

* This investigation was supported by the National Natural Science Foundation (Harbin 60175020) and The high Technology Research and Development Programme (Harbin 2002AA117010-09).

2 Latent Semantic Indexing

Current methods of VSM in indexing and retrieving documents from databases usually depend on a lexical match between query terms and keywords extracted from documents in a database. These methods can produce incomplete or irrelevant results due to the use of synonyms and polysemous words. In fact the association of terms with documents or implicit semantic structure can be derived using large sparse term by document matrices. So both terms and documents can be matched using representations in k-space derived from k of the largest approximate singular vectors of these terms by document matrices. This completely automated approach called Latent Semantic Indexing (LSI), which uses subspaces spanned by the approximate singular vectors to encode important associative relationships between terms and documents in k-space [3]. Using LSI, two or more documents may be close to each other in k-space yet share no common terms.

2.1 Singular Value Decomposition (SVD) for LSI

SVD is the most common method to LSI which decompose a term-by-document rectangular matrix X into the product of three other matrices: $A = U \sum V^T$, Where U (M × R) and V (R × N) have orthonormal columns and Σ (R×R) is the diagonal matrix of singular values. R ≤ min(M,N) is the rank of A. If the singular values of Σ are ordered by size, the K largest may be kept and the remaining smaller ones set to zero. The product of the resulting matrices is a matrix A_k which is an approximation to A with rank K:

$$A_k = U_k \sum_K V_k^T \qquad (1)$$

Where Σ k (K×K) is obtained by deleting the zero rows and columns of Σ, and U_k (M×K) and V_k (N × K) are obtained by deleting the corresponding rows and columns of U and V [4].

A_k in one sense captures most of the underlying structure in A, yet at the same time removes the noise or variability in word usage. Since the number of dimensions K is much smaller than the number of unique words M, minor differences in terminology will be ignored.

2.2 Semi-discrete Matrix Decomposition (SDD) for LSI

A semi-discrete decomposition (SDD) approximates a matrix as a weighted sum of outer products formed by vectors with entries constrained to be in the set S = {-1, 0, 1}. O'Leary and Peleg introduced the SDD in the context of image compression, and Kolda and O'Leary (1998, 1999) used the SDD for latent semantic indexing (LSI) in information retrieval. The primary advantage of the SDD over other types of matrix approximations such as the truncated singular value decomposition (SVD) is that, it typically provides a more accurate approximation for far less storage.

An SDD of an m×n matrix A is a decomposition of the form:

$$A_k = \underbrace{[u_1 u_2 \cdots u_k]}_{u_k} \cdot \underbrace{\begin{bmatrix} e_1 & 0 & \cdots & 0 \\ 0 & e_2 & \cdots & 0 \\ \vdots & \vdots & \ddots & \vdots \\ 0 & 0 & \cdots & e_k \end{bmatrix}}_{\Sigma_k} \underbrace{\begin{bmatrix} v_1^T \\ v_2^T \\ \vdots \\ v_k^T \end{bmatrix}}_{v_k^T} \qquad (2)$$

Here each u_i is an m-vector with entries from the set S = {-1, 0, 1}, each v_i is an n-vector with entries from the set S, and each e_i is a positive scalar. We call this a k-term SDD.

Although every matrix can be expressed as a mn-term SDD:

$$A = \sum_{i=1}^{m} \sum_{j=1}^{n} a_{ij} e_i e_j^T \qquad (3)$$

Where e_k is the k-th unit vector, the usefulness of the SDD is in developing approximations that have far fewer terms.

An SDD approximation can be formed iteratively via a greedy algorithm. Let A_k denote the k-term approximation ($A_0 \equiv 0$). Let R_k be the residual at the kth step, that is $R_k = A - A_{k-1}$. Then the optimal choice of the next triplet (d_k, x_k, y_k) is the solution to the sub problem:

$$\min F_k(d,x,y) \equiv \left\| R_k - dxy^T \right\|_F^2 \quad \text{s.t.} \; x \in S^m, y \in S^n, d > 0 \qquad (4)$$

This is a mixed integer programming problem. Assuming that a fixed number of inner iterations are set per step, the complexity of the algorithm is $O(k^2(m+n) + m\log m + n\log n)$. At the meanwhile, since the storage requirement for a k-term SDD is k floating point numbers plus k (m+n) entries from S, it is also inexpensive to store quite a large number of terms [5].

In evaluating queries, a document vector can be treated as

$$\tilde{A} = \Sigma_k^{1-\alpha} V_k^T \qquad (5)$$

This is a k-dimension vector. And the test vector is projected into the same k-dimensional space by:

$$\tilde{q} = \Sigma_k^{\alpha} U_k^T q \qquad (6)$$

The similarity between a document and test vector can be calculated by

$$S = \cos(\tilde{q}^T, \tilde{A}) = \frac{\left| \tilde{q}^T \cdot \tilde{A} \right|}{\sqrt{\sum_{i=1}^{k} (\tilde{q}^T)^2 (\tilde{A})^2}} \qquad (7)$$

In this study, the value of the splitting parameter α in equation has left at the default 0.

As in the Vector Model, documents can now be ranked according to their similarity to the test document, and the category of the query is the category of the most similar document.

3 LSI for Text Categorization

The k-NN method is a very simple approach that has previously shown very good performance on text categorization tasks [6][7]. Hence, we decided to use this method for classification. In this paper, we apply LSI model to the k-NN algorithm to verify the improvement on text categorization. To classify an unknown document vector d, the k-nearest neighbor (k-NN) algorithm ranks the document's neighbors among the training document vectors, and uses the class labels of the k most similar neighbors to predict the class of the input document. The classes of these neighbors are weighted by the similarity of each neighbor to d, where similarity may be measured by such as the Euclidean distance or the cosine between the two document vectors.

The k-NN LSI algorithm has four steps:

1. Index the training set
2. Use SDD to map each document vector into a lower dimensional space which is associated with concepts and process the documents in this space.
3. For each document $\vec{x}$ to be classified, retrieve its k most similar documents from the training set (where k is a parameter of the algorithm). Call this set $R_k(\vec{X})$.
4. For each category C, compute its relevance to $\vec{x}$ as:

$$S(c,\vec{x}) = \sum_{\vec{d} \in R_k(\vec{x},c)} sim(\vec{d},\vec{x}) \tag{8}$$

Where $R_k(\vec{x},C)$ is the subset of documents in $R_k(\vec{x})$ that are relevant to C.

There are many ways to transform the scores $S(c,\vec{x})$ for a particular category-document pair into a YES/NO decision on whether to assign that document to that category. In this paper, we use the methods called SCut. SCut assigns to each category a threshold t(C) and assigns a document $\vec{x}$ to category C if $S(c,\vec{x}) \geq$ t(C). The choice method of t(C) is explained in section 5.1.

4 Related Work

Another study has been performed using LSI for text classification. It is made by Ana Cardoso-Cachopo and Arlindo Limede Oliveira(2000). In a comparison between k-NN LSI and vector model, and using the Mean Reciprocal Rank (MRR) as a measure of overall performance, this study proved that k-NN LSI performed almost as well as the best performing methods, such as Support Vector Machine (SVM), for text categorization. But his study is confined to English corpus and SVD technique is adopted.

5 Experiments

This section provides some empirical evidence to show that LSI is a competitive solution to text classification. The results are examined on the data sets of Chinese Library Classification.

5.1 Data Sets and Protocol

The experiment operates Chinese text as processing object and uses the Chinese Library Classification 4 (Simplified Version) as criteria (Table 1), which is a comprehensive one in common use in China's most libraries, information institutes and centers. All the Data Sets are gathered from digital library and Internet. The web pages, all together containing 10,857 pages, are divided into thirty-seven categories.

Table 1. Chinese Library Classification

A Marxism, Leninism, Maoism & Deng Xiao ping's Theory	K History and Geography	TF Metallurgy Industry	TS Light industry and Handicraft industry
B Philosophy and Religion	N Natural Science	TG Metal and Metalworking Technology	TU Architecture Science
C Social Science	O Mathematics, Physics and Chemistry	TH Machine and Meter	TV Water Conservancy
D Politics and law	P Astronomy and Geosciences	TJ Weaponry	U Transportation
E Military Science	Q Bioscience	TK Kinetics Industry	V Aviation
F Economics	R Medicine and Hygiene	TL Atomic Energy	X Environmental Science and Security Science
G Culture, Science, Education and Athletics	S Agricultural Science	TM Electro technician	Z Comprehensive Books
H Linguistics	TB Industrial Technology	TN Radio electronics Tele-technology	
I Literature	TD Mining Engineering	TP Automation technology Computer Science	
J Art	TE Petroleum and Natural gas Industry	TQ Chemistry Industry	

The corpus is broken into words with Word-Lattice algorithm and after removing tokens that occur only once or are on a stoplist, a vocabulary of size 57,040 is left. We set 9,115 pages as the train set and others 1,742 as test set. In the stage of training, the Expected Cross Entropy (ECE) is used on train set for feature selection, which is defined as

$$ECE(T) = \sum_i p(c_i | T) \log \frac{p(c_i | T)}{p(c_i)} \qquad (9)$$

Where $p(c_i | T)$ is the probability of term T and category c_i co-occurrence and $p(c_i)$ is the probability of category c_i. In the process of turning documents into vectors, the term weights are computed using a variation of the Okapi term-weighting formula [8]:

$$w(t,\vec{d}) = \frac{tf(t,\vec{d})}{0.5 + 1.5 * \frac{len(\vec{d})}{avg\_len} + tf(t,\vec{d})} \times \log(\frac{0.5 + N - n(t)}{0.5 + n(t)}) \qquad (10)$$

Where $w(t,\vec{d})$ is the weight of term t in document $\vec{d}$; $tf(t,\vec{d})$ is the within-document frequency of term t; N is the number of documents in the training set; n(t) is the number of training documents in which t occurs; $len(\vec{d})$ is the number of tokens in document $\vec{d}$ after stop-word removal; avg_len is the average number of tokens per document in the training set. The values of N, n(t), and avg_len were computed from the entire training set.

Before the k-NN algorithm can be used, the value of k must be set. We used standard m-way cross-validation to set this value; the training data was split into m partitions, with documents assigned randomly to each partition. For each cross-validation run, m_{tr} of these partitions formed the training subset and m_{va} (= m - m_{tr}) partitions the validation subset. Partitions were rotated between the training and validation subsets so that each partition was used m_{tr} times for training and m_{va} times for validation. Performance was averaged over all m runs to produce a final value used for comparison between different values of k.

Setting the values of t(C) for the SCut method is through a Modified Leave-one-out Cross-validation Algorithm. For each document $\vec{d}$ in the training set, use every other document in the training set to assign scores $S(c,\vec{d})$ via the k-NN algorithm. Then set the values of t(C) to be those which produce optimal performance over this set of scores. This method has the advantage of deriving the values of t(C) from a data set that is as close as possible to the actual training data.

At last, we use the standard cosine-similarity metric to compute similarity between the training and test documents.

$$\text{e.g. } sim(\vec{d},\vec{x}) = \cos(\vec{d},\vec{x}) = \frac{\vec{d} \cdot \vec{x}}{\|\vec{d}\| \cdot \|\vec{x}\|} \quad (11)$$

5.2 Evaluation

In experiment, each document belongs to no more than two categories. But the evaluation only consults the first category with highest score.

For text categorization evaluation, the effectiveness measures of precision, recall and F1 are defined respectively. For $category_j$:

$$precision_j = \frac{l_j}{m_j} \times 100\%$$

$$recall_j = \frac{l_j}{n_j} \times 100\% \quad (12)$$

$$F1_j = \frac{recall_j \times precision_j \times 2}{recall_j + precision_j}$$

Where l_j is the number of test set category members assigned to $category_j$ and m_j is the total number of test set members assigned to $category_j$. Where n_j is the number of category members in test set.

Thus for all categories, Macro-recall, Macro-precision and Macro averaged F1 score are respectively defined.

In our experiment, different feature-set sizes were tested, and the size optimized by the global F1 score for classifier. Finally, 5362 features were selected for k-NN. And the k in k-NN was set to 50. Through the transformations of SDD, the 5362 feature terms become a lower dimensional space of rank-k approximation.

Affirmatively applying SDD in train phase upgrade a little training cost, but it is negligible to performance-promoting in test phase. The experiment shows that k-NN (SDD) promotes executive efficiency greatly with storage cost reduced from 96.6M to 5.62M and executive time condensed from 3437s to 435s.

The choice of k-value is an empirical method. The term-document matrix was fed into SDD transformation with a variety of k-values. The results of these levels are displayed in Figure 1. They showed the best average F1 with k=140.

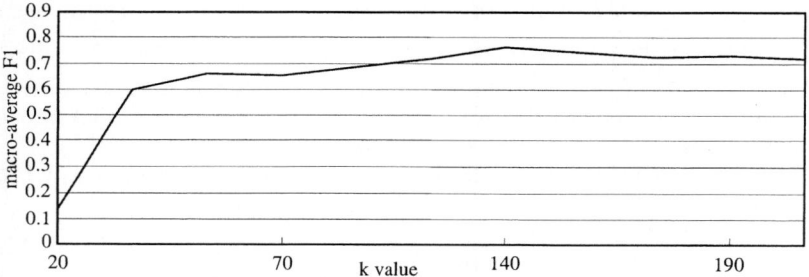

Fig. 1. Result of current LSI (SDD) system with various k-values

Table 2 shows the precision, recall and F1 score for each category on the full training set. Note that in all categories, k-NN LSI method made evaluation measure better in a different degree. Totally using k-NN LSI against k-NN VSM, 143 error documents are eliminated and F_1 score is 9.48 percent higher than before.

Figure 2 compare the performance curves of the improved and the original classifiers on F_1 score with respect to the 37 categories. These curves are obtained by regarding categories as the horizontal axis and plotting the per category F_1 scores for each classifier.

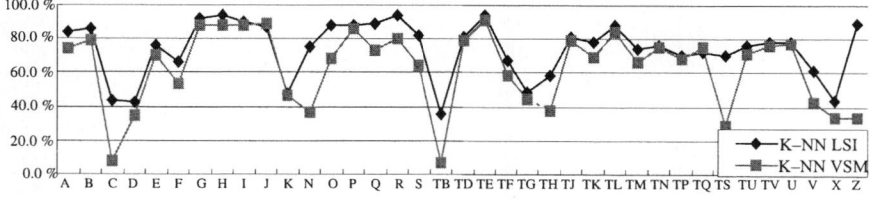

Fig. 2. The macro-averaged F_1 curves for each category using k-NN VSM versus k-NN LSI

A Study of Semi-discrete Matrix Decomposition for LSI 613

Table 2. Comparison of the results on P, R and F_1 between k-NN LSI and k-NN VSM

	n_j	k-NN LSI					k-NN VSM				
		m_j	l_j	Precsion$_j$	Recall$_j$	F_1	m_j	l_j	Precsion$_j$	Recall$_j$	F_1
A	49	49	41	83.67%	83.67%	0.8367	50	37	74.00%	75.51%	0.7475
B	41	47	38	80.85%	92.68%	0.8636	55	38	69.09%	92.68%	0.7917
C	48	16	14	87.50%	29.17%	0.4375	3	2	66.67%	4.17%	0.0784
D	50	72	26	36.11%	52.00%	0.4262	59	19	32.20%	38.00%	0.3486
E	50	39	34	87.18%	68.00%	0.7640	33	29	87.88%	58.00%	0.6988
F	50	95	48	50.53%	96.00%	0.6621	130	48	36.92%	96.00%	0.5333
G	94	101	90	89.11%	95.74%	0.9231	100	85	85.00%	90.43%	0.8763
H	50	48	46	95.83%	92.00%	0.9388	45	42	93.33%	84.00%	0.8842
I	50	59	49	83.05%	98.00%	0.8991	59	48	81.36%	96.00%	0.8807
J	50	49	43	87.76%	86.00%	0.8687	49	44	89.80%	88.00%	0.8889
K	50	17	16	94.12%	32.00%	0.4776	19	16	84.21%	32.00%	0.4638
N	8	8	6	75.00%	75.00%	0.7500	3	2	66.67%	25.00%	0.3636
O	24	19	19	100.00%	79.17%	0.8837	14	13	92.86%	54.17%	0.6842
P	50	59	48	81.36%	96.00%	0.8807	59	47	79.66%	94.00%	0.8624
Q	50	44	42	95.45%	84.00%	0.8936	32	30	93.75%	60.00%	0.7317
R	50	52	48	92.31%	96.00%	0.9412	45	38	84.44%	76.00%	0.8000
S	47	46	38	82.61%	80.85%	0.8172	59	34	57.63%	72.34%	0.6415
T	50	28	14	50.00%	28.00%	0.3590	9	2	22.22%	4.00%	0.0678
T	48	51	40	78.43%	83.33%	0.8081	48	38	79.17%	79.17%	0.7917
T	45	46	43	93.48%	95.56%	0.9451	47	42	89.36%	93.33%	0.9130
T	49	58	36	62.07%	73.47%	0.6729	54	30	55.56%	61.22%	0.5825
T	48	50	24	48.00%	50.00%	0.4898	78	28	35.90%	58.33%	0.4444
T	48	38	25	65.79%	52.08%	0.5814	37	16	43.24%	33.33%	0.3765
T	50	58	44	75.86%	88.00%	0.8148	63	45	71.43%	90.00%	0.7965
T	47	48	37	77.08%	78.72%	0.7789	45	32	71.11%	68.09%	0.6957
T	47	48	42	87.50%	89.36%	0.8842	51	41	80.39%	87.23%	0.8367
T	49	50	37	74.00%	75.51%	0.7475	51	33	64.71%	67.35%	0.660
T	46	46	35	76.09%	76.09%	0.7609	55	38	69.09%	82.61%	0.7525
TJ	50	83	47	56.63%	94.00%	0.7068	90	48	53.33%	96.00%	0.6857
T	48	55	37	67.27%	77.08%	0.7184	59	40	67.80%	83.33%	0.7477
T	48	32	28	87.50%	58.33%	0.7000	8	8	100.00%	16.67%	0.2857
T	50	47	37	78.72%	74.00%	0.7629	42	33	78.57%	66.00%	0.7174
T	50	62	44	70.97%	88.00%	0.7857	65	44	67.69%	88.00%	0.7652
U	49	58	42	72.41%	85.71%	0.7850	57	41	71.93%	83.67%	0.7736
V	50	32	25	78.13%	50.00%	0.6098	26	16	61.54%	32.00%	0.4211
X	50	23	16	69.57%	32.00%	0.4384	40	15	37.50%	30.00%	0.3333
Z	9	9	8	88.89%	88.89	0.88	3	2	66.67%	22.22%	0.33
M				77.32%	75.03%	0.76			69.26%	64.29%	0.6668

Through experiments we find that the efficiency of automated text categorization is dependent on train set quality seriously, therefore the parameter value presented in this paper should be adjusted to corpus in others application.

6 Conclusion

In this paper we presented a study with significance analyses on text categorization methods based on LSI (SDD). Our main conclusions are:

- LSI (SDD) can achieve similar or higher performance at a much lower storage cost and little executive time in automated text categorization. As the volume of information available on the Internet continues to increase, online text categorization is required seriously. So LSI (SDD) is a promising technique for text categorization.
- LSI (SDD) is a technique that warrants further investigation for text classification.

7 Future Work

Much work remains. Firstly, we can improve the method to compute the distance between two document vectors[9].With cosine computing documents similarity, the technique neglects the different among features and all index terms are of equal importance in the process of computing, which lead to the inexact results and drop down the precision of text categorization. Secondly, lexical analysis can be further studied by treating some phrases as terms. Thirdly, the reasons for the poor performance of a number of categorization should be investigated.

Acknowledgements

We would like to thank Sun ChenJie and Mao YongQuan for gathering web pages and system robust tests, which made the significant test carried out smoothly.

References

1. Kjersti Aas and Line Eikvil. June (1999). Text Categorisation: A Survey. Norwegian Computing Center.
2. Ana Cardoso-Cachopo and Arlindo Limede Oliveira, (2000). An Empirical Comparison of Text Categorization Methods, Instituto Superior T_ecnico Departamento de Engenharia Inform_atica Av. Rovisco Pais.
3. Michael W. Berry and Ricardo D.Fierro. (1996). Low_Rank Orthogonal Decompositions for Information Retrieval Applications. Numerical Linear Algebra with Applications, Vol1(1),1-72.
4. Scott C. Deerwester, Susan T. Dumais, Thomas K. Landauer, George W. Furnas, and Richard A. Harshman. (1990). Indexing by latent semantic analysis. Journal of the American Society for Information Science.
5. Kolda, T. G. and O'Leary, D. P. (2000). Algorithm 805: Computation and uses of the semidiscrete matrix decomposition, ACM Transactions on Mathematical Software 26(3): 415{435.
6. Yiming Yang and Xin Liu. August (1999). A re-examination of text categorization methods. Proceedings of the 22nd Annual International ACM SIGIR Conference on Research and Development in Information Retrieval, pages 42-49, Berkeley, CA, USA.

7. S. Dumais, J. Platt, D. Heckerman, and M. Sahami . (1998). Inductive Learning Algorithms and Representations for Text Categorization, Technical Report, Microsoft Research.
8. Tom Ault and Yiming Yang. (1999) kNN at TREC-9. Language Technologies Institute and Computer Science Department Newell Simon Hall 3612C, Carnegie Mellon University Pittsburgh, PA 15213?213, USA
9. Caron, J. (2000). Experiments with lsa scoring: Optimal rank and basis, Technical report,SIAM Computatio-nal IR Workshop.URL: citeseer.nj.nec.com

Systematic Construction of Hierarchical Classifier in SVM-Based Text Categorization

Yongwook Yoon, Changki Lee, and Gary Geunbae Lee

Department of Computer Science & Engineering,
Pohang University of Science & Technology,
Pohang 790-784, South Korea
{ywyoon,leeck,gblee}@postech.ac.kr

Abstract. In a text categorization task, classification on some hierarchy of classes shows better results than the case without the hierarchy. In current environments where large amount of documents are divided into several subgroups with a hierarchy between them, it is more natural and appropriate to use a hierarchical classification method. We introduce a new internal node evaluation scheme which is very helpful to the development process of a hierarchical classifier. We also show that the hierarchical classifier construction method using this measure yields a classifier with better classification performance especially when applied to the classification task with large depth of hierarchy.

1 Introduction

Text categorization is one of the key technologies which are useful to retrieve the information that a user wants to get. Currently, the researches on hierarchical classification of documents receive much concern among many others. It seems natural to derive some hierarchy from many different kinds of things in order to identify one thing from the other easily. Hence, an introduction of hierarchy into a large number of documents would help us to categorize those documents according to the theme of the document. In a hierarchy of documents, as the document gets closer to the root, it is assigned to a more comprehensive category. We can find an example at a commercial web portal site where the documents are divided into several categories which form a hierarchy as a whole. Most of the researches on hierarchical classification show that the hierarchical methods are superior to the flat methods which have no hierarchy between categories in text classification [5, 7, 2].

We need consider a hierarchy when we should construct a practical classifier that would be used at a web portal site. Occasionally, such hierarchy forms from tens to hundreds depth of height. Yang et al. [11] handled scalability problems in constructing such a large hierarchical classifier. In our paper, we want to develop a practical and effective method with which we can construct a high performance hierarchical classifier which would be applied to a large amount of documents with a big hierarchy of categories. In this environment the methods which were useful in the flat classification process are not applicable anymore due to the characteristics of a hierarchy of classes. We found that the internal node evaluation measure is very useful in the hierarchy construction process. We will show how this new evaluation measure can be used in the construction process for producing a more effective hierarchical classifier than the one without this measure. In addition, we will give a systematic process of classifier construction which may be applicable to the development of a hierarchical classifier in practice.

This paper is organized as follows. In section 2, we investigate some previous researches on hierarchical classification and compare those with our own method. In section 3, we introduce our new evaluation measure for hierarchical classification and give a detail description on the process of constructing an effective hierarchical classifier using Support Vector Machine (SVM). And in section 4, we describe some experiments of our hierarchical classification method on a well known experimental data and show the results and analyze the cause of performance increase. Finally in the section 5, we conclude with our suggestions and assertions, and discuss about some future works.

2 Related Works

Koller and Sahami [5] divided training documents into several thematically related subgroups, so that they could avoid the scalability problem that might occur in a system with a large number of documents. Koller and Sahami experimented with Reuters-22173. They showed the resulting hierarchical classifier outperforms the traditional flat classifier in the accuracy for the same set of leaf node classes.

Joachims [4] suggested the use of Support Vector Machines in the area of text categorization. He analyzed the characteristics of learning with text data and identified why SVM's are appropriate for this task. SVM's are widely used in the various learning tasks recently, and are well described in [10]. Bekkerman et al. [1] also showed the good performance of SVM's when they were used in the text categorization tasks with Reuters and 20 Newsgroups collection. They combined SVM's with a new feature selection method called information bottleneck.

Sun et al. [9] introduced many useful evaluation measures relevant to a hierarchical text classification. In their works, the classes are assumed to be dependant to each other. They proposed category similarity measure and distance-based measure which consider the contributions of misclassified documents. Those measures have the form of extending the Precision and Recall measure which were used in the traditional flat classification. They suggested another measure that might be more useful than the above two. It is a classifier-centric measure called blocking measure which is defined to examine the performance of sub-tree classifiers in a top-down level-based hierarchical classification method. At the next section we will introduce a new measure which is similar in concept to the blocking measure but takes on a different form and is derived from a different origin.

3 Systematic Construction of Hierarchical Classifier

There are four distinct category structures in a hierarchical text classification [9]. One of them is virtual category tree where each category can belong to at most one parent category and documents can be assigned to leaf categories only. In this paper, we only handle virtual category tree, because it is simple and its performance is easily compared with the flat classifier. In this section we describe an effective procedure for constructing a hierarchical classifier.

3.1 SVM's in Text Categorization

Assume we are given l learning samples of documents $\{(\mathbf{x}_1, y_1), (\mathbf{x}_2, y_2), \ldots, (\mathbf{x}_l, y_l)\}$ where each element consists of a pair, (document_vector, actual_class). Then, SVM training with this set of samples involves solving a quadratic programming to get the parameters, α and b. This optimal solution gives rise to a decision function which will be used at the prediction phase.

$$f(\mathbf{x}) = \text{sgn}\left[\sum_{i=1}^{l} y_i \alpha_i (\mathbf{x} \cdot \mathbf{x}_i) + b\right] \quad (1)$$

where α_i is the weight assigned to each training document. $\mathbf{x}_i$ such that α_i is not equal to zero is called *support vector* which performs an important role in classification.

3.2 Multi-labeled Text Classification

Although SVM provides only binary classification, by subsequently applying m binary classifications, it can do multi-labeled classification. As effectiveness measures of multi-labeled classification, the precision and recall have been used. To calculate the precision and recall for the classifier, we construct a contingency table as Table 1.

Table 1. Contingency Table for Category C_i.

Classifier C_i		Expert Judgments	
		Yes	No
Classifier Judgements	Yes	TP_i	FP_i
	No	FN_i	TN_i

In the table, TP_i denotes the number of samples correctly classified under C_i, FP_i denotes the number of samples incorrectly classified under C_i, and FN_i (TN_i) denotes the number of incorrectly (correctly) classified under $\neg C_i$. The performance of a classifier is usually represented with precision and recall. If we denote P_i and R_i as precision and recall of classifier C_i respectively, then these are defined as below:

$$P_i = \frac{TP_i}{TP_i + FP_i}, \quad R_i = \frac{TP_i}{TP_i + FN_i} \tag{2}$$

In the case of multi-labeled flat classification, the overall precision P and recall R of the classifier which classifies between m different classes are computed as follows:

$$P = \frac{\sum_{i=1}^{m} TP_i}{\sum_{i=1}^{m} TP_i + \sum_{i=1}^{m} FP_i}, \quad R = \frac{\sum_{i=1}^{m} TP_i}{\sum_{i=1}^{m} TP_i + \sum_{i=1}^{m} FN_i} \tag{3}$$

There also exist measures which combine the precision and recall into one measure. Such measures include Break-Even-Point (BEP) and F-measure. In this paper, we will use a micro-averaged Break-Even-Point as a combined measure, which is calculated, in a binary classification case, as $(P + R)/2$.

3.3 New Evaluation Measures

In classification task with a hierarchy of virtual category tree, we are only concerned with the performance of leaf node classifiers. The internal node classifiers just improve the final classification at the leaf node. However, we must not overlook their role in the classification, because the misclassifications in upper node classifiers exert bad effects on their direct sub-classifiers and are difficult to recover later.

We describe this situation in more detail. Assume we have four categories A, B, C, and D, and four corresponding binary classifiers. If we construct a flat classifier for this task and test with two documents Doc_1 and Doc_2, the result will be like Figure 1 (a). If we classify the same test documents using a hierarchical classification method, the situation is changed. Consider the hierarchy in (b) of Figure 1 where we have the same leaf node classifiers but an additional internal node classifier "BC". In this two-level hierarchical classification, we first classify the test documents at the level-1 classifiers A, BC, and D.

Next, with level-2 classifiers B and C, we subsequently classify the documents which the internal node classifier BC predicted as positive (whether it be TP or FP); at (b) of the Figure 1, the test document Doc_2 is the case. The final prediction on the membership to class B and C is delayed until the level-2 classifications are completed (delayed evaluation). Here, we obtain some merit of hierarchical classification. Consider the result of the flat classification with Doc_2 at (a) of Figure 1. For the class C, the result was FP. On the other hand, we find that the result of C at (b) is TN: a rise in performance. Though we failed in correct classification by flat method, we can expect a correct result at the narrower and thematically clustered group of classes.

By contrast, the test document Doc_1 is not further advanced to the level-2 classifiers, because the internal-node classifier BC has already predicted them as negative (whether it be TN or FN) (pre-expanded evaluation). The final leaf-level classification is determined now as either TN or FN to the classifier B and C according to the actual class of document Doc_1. This process of prediction follows the model of the top-down level-based classification called the "Pachinko-Machine."

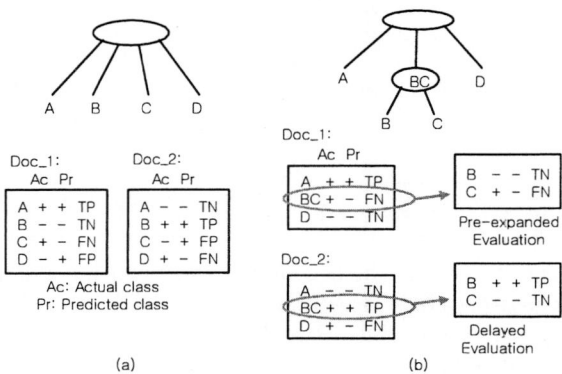

Fig. 1. Prediction Instances in the Flat and Hierarchical Classification.

At this point, we define a new evaluation measure for internal node classifiers, based on the above two observations: delayed evaluation and pre-expanded evaluation. When the internal node classifiers produce positive predictions, the final classifications are delayed until the leaf node classes of the documents are decided; so the predictions of internal node classifiers have no effect on the overall precision or recall of the classifier. When the internal classifiers produce negative predictions, however, the classification stops at the internal node and does not advance to the child classifiers. Therefore, we must take into account the count of negative predictions of all sub-classes of the internal node. This expansion process is based upon the actual classes of the test document. If the actual membership of the document to a sub-class of the internal node is negative, we determine the prediction as TN (the case of B); otherwise, we determine as FN (the case of C).

If we adopt micro-averaged measures, we can rearrange the traditional precision and recall into the intermediate precision P_j and recall R_j for an internal classifier C_j in a hierarchy tree as follows:

$$P_j = \frac{TP_j}{TP_j + FP_j}, \quad R_j = \frac{TP_j}{TP_j + EFN_j} \quad (where\ EFN_j = \sum_{j \in \text{Sub}_j} FN_j) \quad (4)$$

TP_j and FP_j in equation (4) are the same as in equation (2). EFN_j is the sum of the expanded false negatives of Sub$_j$, which is the set of all the sub-classifiers of internal classifier C_j. FN_i is the false negatives of sub-classifier C_j the value of FN_i is added by 1 only if the corresponding prediction of classifier C_j is false negative when the prediction of classifier C_j is expanded. In equation 4, P_j is the same as that of the flat classifier. However, in R_j, we take into account the expanded negative predictions of sub-classifiers. These intermediate precision and recall are directly used in our classifier selection algorithm in Figure 2. In the algorithm, they are used to select an optimal internal classifier that guarantees maximal overall performance of hierarchical classification system at the intermediate level.

Next, we consider the overall performance of a hierarchical classification system at the final leaf level. As for the overall precision P_h, it is the same as the flat case, since we only consider the leaf node predictions that are the same in both the flat and the hierarchical case. The overall recall in a hierarchical classification R_h is as follows:

$$P_h = P \quad \text{(as in equation (3))},$$

$$R_h = \frac{\sum\limits_{i \in Leaf} TP_i}{\sum\limits_{i \in Leaf} TP_j + \sum\limits_{i \in Leaf} FN_i + \sum\limits_{j \in Internal} EFN_j} \quad (5)$$

Leaf and *Internal* denotes the set of all leaf and internal node classifiers respectively. EFN_j denotes the expanded FN_j of the internal node classifier C$_j$ that is the same in the meaning as the one in equation (4). The sum of expanded FN's, reflects the accumulative misclassification errors from the root down to level $h-1$, if we take h as a hierarchy level. It is crucial to decrease this amount in order to acquire high performance at the final classification. Since this term does not exist in the flat classification, our new measure is totally compatible with the conventional precision and recall in equation (3); we can now obtain more fair comparison between the two different classification systems such as the flat and the hierarchical ones with the same target classes.

3.4 Classifier Construction Process

In the hierarchical classification task with a virtual category tree, it is important how to construct the internal node classifiers in order to guarantee maximum precision and recall at the leaf node classifiers. We would present a simple algorithm to perform this work using previously defined P_j and R_j measures in equation (4). A classifier construction process is, in essence, a training process for the classifier with learning samples.

First, with a set of training documents and their categories, we construct a taxonomy tree the categories. Often, this process is done manually, but it might require a certain automatic procedure such as a clustering algorithm if a more accurate result is required. Second, we divide the training documents into several subgroups according to the hierarchy structure. Finally, we train the internal node and the leaf node classifiers one by one using our new measures; this process is the most important one. Actually, the final procedure is repeated until we find the best classifier at each node; through a validation process of applying our new P_j and R_j measures, we can select a better performing classifier. In Figure 2 below, we present the algorithm of selecting the best classifiers from the root to the leaf nodes.

```
Algorithm Classifier-Selection
Input:
    C = (c₁, c₂, ..., cₘ)    // a set of categories
    T    // a virtual category tree
    D    // a set of validation documents
    A = (a₁, a₂, ..., aₜ)    // a set of SVM costs
Output:
    I    // a set of internal-node classifiers
    L    // a set of leaf-node classifiers, |L| = m
External Function:
    P(h)      // intermediate precision of classifier h
    R(h)      // intermediate recall of classifier h
Begin
    For k:= 0 to K-1 do    // from root down to leaf nodes
        For each internal and leaf node classifier h
            at the level-k of the tree T do
            For each cost a in A do
                Train the classifier h to the cost a;
                Test h for the appropriate data in D;
                Compute P(h) and R(h) and record results;
            End;
            Select the classifier h with the best P(h) and R(h)
                as the candidate classifier for the node;
        End;
    End;
End    // Algorithm
```

Fig. 2. Classifier Selection Algorithm.

4 Experiment

4.1 20 Newsgroups Collection

As dataset in our experiments, we used 20 newsgroup collections. Many of the previous works on TC have used this data as a test data [3, 8, 1, 6]. However, most of them, except [6], were for the flat classification. 20 Newsgroups collection is partially multi-labeled; 541 documents of the total 19,997 documents are posted to more than oneclass. And it has a natural thematic hierarchy in its each twenty newsgroup. We used the three-level hierarchy which can be directly derived from the USENET newsgroup hierarchy itself. Table 2 shows the hierarchy used in our experiments.

To represent a document as a suitable format for SVM training, we preprocessed the raw texts into a word vector format. For this process, we used BOW toolkit[1]. We removed general stop words, did no stemming, and did no feature selection because SVM can process a high-dimensional training data very well. An article of the USENET newsgroups consists of the header and the body part. For training, we include only the body part and the Subject line from the header of articles. We performed the two cases of experiments for the same dataset: the flat and the hierarchical classification. For each case, we applied two different classification methods: multi-labeled and uni-labeled. For a multi-labeled classification, a sequence of binary classifiers has been applied. For each case of

---
[1] http://www.cs.cmu.edu/~mccallum/bow

Table 2. Category Hierarchy of 20 Newsgroups in the experiments.

Level 1	Level 2	Level 3
alt.atheism misc.forsale soc.religion.christian		
comp	graphics os.ms-windows.misc windows.x	
comp	sys	ibm.pc.hardware mac.hardware
rec	autos motor-cycles	
rec	sport	baseball hockey
sci	crypt electronics med space	
talk	religion.misc	
talk	politics	guns mideast misc

experiment we performed 4-fold cross validation. As a toolkit for SVM training, we have used the one provided together with BOW toolkit.

4.2 Results and Analysis

Table 3 shows the result of the two methods, the flat and the hierarchical classification. The precision, the recall, and the micro-averaged BEP (using the P_h and R_h in equation (5)) are for the multi-labeled experiment, and the accuracy is for the uni-labeled experiment. Here the concept of the uni-labeled experiment is the same as the one described at [1]. The second row of the flat methods (SVM + IB-clustering) in Table 3 represents the state-of-the-art performance on the 20 Newsgroup collections so far [1].

Table 3. Comparison of the Flat and the Hierarchical Classification.

	Methods	BEP (Multi-label)	Accuracy (Uni-label)
Flat	Baseline (SVM)	75.9	89.2
Flat	SVM + IB-Clustering	88.6	91.0
Hierarchical	Without Evaluation	86.0	90.1
Hierarchical	With Evaluation	**89.0**	**94.3**
Hierarchical	Clustered Hierarchy	-	96.3 (Unfair)

The number of test documents is 5,000 and the total number of prediction instances is 100,000 same in both cases of the flat and the hierarchical method. We can see that the flat methods (Baseline SVM) show relatively lower precision and recall than the hierarchical methods (Without Evaluation). The second row of the hierarchical methods with evaluation represents the result when our classifier selection algorithm in Figure 2 was used in order to yield the maximum performance at leaf node classifications.

The result shows a great improvement over the case without the evaluation procedure; BEP has been increased by 3%. Moreover, it is higher than the Bekkerman et al.'s which is one of the best tuned flat classification results so far, even though our system doesn't get any explicit tuning. The third row is the result of [6], where only the single-labeled result was reported. But, their experimental setup makes a reasonable comparison difficult, because they have used additional inputs which were not used in our experiments: organization field of the header part of news articles. The Organization field provides excessive information to the classification.

5 Conclusion and Future Works

Hierarchical classification systems have better properties than flat classification systems. Their performance in classification accuracy is good, and due to the smaller number of training set, the training time is shorter that the flat case. But, when we are constructing a large hierarchical classifier for which virtual category tree is very huge in depth and in number of nodes, a more practical classifier-construction method is required. By using a reliable and practical construction method which adopts our new intermediate evaluation measures and algorithm, we could construct a high performance hierarchical classification system. Our experiments show a feasibility of our approaches to a very large classification system.

We are working on applying our new construction scheme to another text categorization dataset which includes Reuters news collection, WEB-KB, and some real-world data in the commercial web-portal sites. Instead of manually building a logical hierarchy, we may cluster automatically a logical hierarchy tree. The other interesting direction is on-line adaptive training of the documents. In practice, the documents are often augmented to the training set continuously, so we are doing researches on handling this situation combined with our hierarchical classification system.

Acknowledgements

This research was supported by grant No. (R01-2003-000-10181-0) form the basic research program of the KOSEF (Korea Science and Engineering Foundation).

References

1. Ron Bekkerman, Ran El-Yaniv, Naftali Tishby, and Yoad Winter. 2001. On Feature Distributional Clustering for Text Categoriztion. Proceedings of SIGIR 2001, 24th Annual International ACM SIGIR Conference on Research and Development in Information Retrieval, pp.146-153.
2. Susan Dumais and Hao Chen. 2000. Hierarchical classification of Web content. Proceedings of SIGIR-00, 23rd ACM International Conference on Research and Development in Information Retrieval, pp.256-263.
3. Thorsten Joachims. 1997. A probabilistic analysis of the Rocchio algorithm with TFIDF for text categorization. Proceedings of ICML-97, 14th International Conference on Machine Learning, pp.143-151.
4. Thorsten Joachims. 1998. Text categorization with supportvector machines: learning with many relevant features. Proceedings of ECML-98,10th European Conference on Machine Learning, pp.137-142.
5. Daphne Koller and Mehran Sahami. 1997. Hierarchically classifying documents using very few words. Proceedings of the Fourteenth International Conference on Machine Learning (ICML'97), pp.170-178.
6. Tao Li, Shenghuo Zho, and Mitsunori Orkhara. 2003. Topic Hierarchy Generation via Linear Discriminant Projection. Proceedings of SIGIR 2003, the 26th Annual International ACM SIGIR Conference on Research and Development in Information Retrieval, pp.421-422.
7. Andrew McCallum, Ronald Rosenfeld, Tom Mitchell, and Andrew Y. Ng, 1998. Improving Text Classification by Shrinkage in a Hierarchy of Classes. Proceedings of ICML-98, 15th International Conference on Machine Learning, pp.359-367.
8. Robert E. Schapire and Yoram Singer. 2000. BoosTexter: a boosting-based system for text categorization. Machine Learning, 39(2):135-168.
9. Aixin Sun, Ee-Peng Lim, and Wee-Keong Ng. 2003. Performance Measurement Framework for Hierarchical Text Classification. Journal of the American Society for Information Science and Technology, 54(11):1014-1028.
10. Vladimir Vapnik. 1995. The Nature of Statistical Learning Theory, Springer-Verlag.
11. Yiming Yang, Jian Zhang, and Bryan Kisiel. 2003. A Scalability Analysis of Classifiers in Text Categorization. Proceedings of SIGIR-03, 26th ACM International Conference on Research and Development in Information Retrieval, pp.96-103.

Implementing the Syntax of Japanese Numeral Classifiers

Emily M. Bender[1] and Melanie Siegel[2]

[1] University of Washington, Department of Linguistics,
Box 354340, Seattle WA 98195-4340
`ebender@u.washington.edu`
[2] Saarland University, Computational Linguistics,
PF 15 11 50, D-66041 Saarbrücken
`siegel@dfki.uni-sb.de`

Abstract. While the sortal constraints associated with Japanese numeral classifiers are well-studied, less attention has been paid to the details of their syntax. We describe an analysis implemented within a broad-coverage HPSG that handles an intricate set of numeral classifier construction types and compositionally relates each to an appropriate semantic representation, using Minimal Recursion Semantics.

1 Introduction

Much attention has been paid to the semantic aspects of Japanese numeral classifiers, in particular, the semantic constraints governing which classifiers co-occur with which nouns [1, 2]. Here, we focus on the syntax of numeral classifiers: How they combine with number names to create numeral classifier phrases, how they modify head nouns, and how they can occur as stand-alone NPs. We find that there is both broad similarity and differences in detail across different types of numeral classifiers in their syntactic and semantic behavior. We present semantic representations for two types and describe how they can be constructed compositionally in an implemented broad-coverage HPSG [3] for Japanese.

The grammar of Japanese in question is JACY[1], originally developed as part of the *Verbmobil* project [4] to handle spoken Japanese, and then extended to handle informal written Japanese (email text; [5]) and newspaper text. Recently, it has been adapted to be consistent with the LinGO Grammar Matrix [6].

2 Types of Numeral Classifiers

[7] divide Japanese numeral classifiers into five major classes: *sortal, event, mensural, group* and *taxanomic,* and several subclasses. The classes and subclasses can be differentiated according to the semantic relationship between the classifiers and the nouns they modify, on two levels: First, what properties of the

---

[1] http://www.dfki.uni-sb.de/~siegel/grammar-download/JACY-grammar.html

modified noun motivate the choice of the classifier, and second what properties
the classifiers predicate of the nouns. As we are concerned here with the syntax and compositional semantics of numeral classifiers, we will focus only on
the latter. Sortal classifiers, (*kind*, *shape*, and *complement* classifiers) serve to
individuate the nouns they modify. Event classifiers quantify events, characteristically modifying verbs rather than nouns. Mensural classifiers measure some
property of the entity denoted by the noun they modify (e.g., its length). NPs
containing group classifiers denote a group of individuals of the type denoted
by the noun. Finally, taxonomic classifiers force a kind or species reading on an
NP. In this paper, we will treat the syntax and compositional semantics of sortal
and mensural classifiers. However, we believe that our general analysis can be
extended to treat the full range of classifiers in Japanese and similar languages.

3 Data: Constructions

Internally, Japanese numeral classifier expressions consist of a number name and
a numeral classifier (1a,b,c). In this, they resemble date expressions (1d).

(1) a. juu mai   b. juu en   c. juu kagetsu d. juu gatsu
    10 NumCl   10 yen   10 month   10 month
                                 '10 months'   'October'

Externally, numeral classifier phrases (NumClPs) appear in at least four different contexts: alone, as anaphoric NPs (2a); preceding a head noun, linked by
the particle *no* (2b); immediately following a head noun (2c); and 'floated', right
after the associated noun's case particle or right before the verb (2d). These
constructions are distinguished pragmatically [8][2].

(2) a. ni hiki   wo   kau
    2 NumCl ACC raise
    '(I) am raising two (small animals).'
   b. ni hiki   no   neko wo   kau
    2 NumCl GEN cat   ACC raise
    '(I) am raising two cats.'
   c. neko ni hiki   wo   kau
    cat 2 NumCl ACC raise
    '(I) am raising two cats.'
   d. neko wo (ni hiki)   ie   de (ni hiki)   kau
    cat ACC (2 NumCl) house LOC (2 NumCl) raise
    '(I) am raising two cats in my house.'

NumClPs can be modified by elements such as *yaku* 'approximately' (before the
number name) or *mo* 'even' (after the floated numeral classifiers).

---

[2] Downing also notes instances of noun+*no*+NumClP. As this rare construction did
not appear in our data, it is not incorporated in our account.

The above examples illustrate the contexts with a sortal numeral classifier, but mensural numeral classifiers can also appear both as modifiers (3a) and as NPs in their own right (3b):

(3) a. ni kiro   no   ringo wo katta
       2 NumCl (kg) GEN apple ACC bought
       '(I) bought two kilograms of apples.'
    b. ni kiro   wo   katta
       2 NumCl (kg) ACC bought
       '(I) bought two kilograms.'

NumClPs serving as NPs can also appear as modifiers of other nouns:

(4) a. san nin   no deai   wa 80 nen haru
       3   NumCl GEN meeting TOP 80 year spring
       'The three's meeting was in the spring of '80.'

As a result, tokens following the syntactic pattern of (2b) and (3a) are systematically ambiguous, although the non-anaphoric reading tends to be preferred.

Certain mensural classifiers can be followed by the word *han* 'half':

(5) ni   kiro han
    two kg   half
    'two and a half kilograms'

In order to build their semantic representations compositionally, we make the numeral classifier (here, *kiro*) the head of the whole expression. *Kiro* can then orchestrate the semantic composition of the two dependents as well as the composition of the whole expression with the noun it modifies (see §6 below).

4 Data: Distribution

We used ChaSen [9] to segment and tag 10,000 paragraphs of the Mainichi Shinbun 2002 corpus. Of the resulting 490,202 words, 11,515 (2.35%) were tagged as numeral classifiers. 4,543 of those were potentially time/date expressions, leaving 6,972 numeral classifiers, or 1.42% of the words. 203 orthographically distinct numeral classifiers occur in the corpus. The most frequent is *nin* (the numeral classifier for people) which occurs 1,675 times.

We sampled 100 sentences tagged as containing numeral classifiers to examine the distribution of the constructions outlined in §3. These sentences contained a total of 159 numeral classifier phrases and the vast majority (128) were stand-alone NPs. This contrasts with Downing's study [8] of 500 examples from modern works of fiction and spoken texts, where most of the occurrences are not anaphoric. Furthermore, while our sample contains no examples of the floated variety, Downing's contains 96. The discrepancy probably arises because Downing only included sortal numeral classifiers, and not any other type. Another possible contributing factor is the effect of genre. In future work we hope to study the distribution of both the types of classifiers and the constructions involving them in the Hinoki treebank [10].

5 Semantic Representations

One of our main goals in implementing a syntactic analysis of numeral classifiers is to compositionally construct semantic representations, and in particular, Minimal Recursion Semantics (MRS) representations [11, 12]. Abstracting away from handle constraints (the representation of scope), illocutionary force, tense/aspect, and the unexpressed subject, the representation we build for (2b,c) is as in (6).

(6) _cat_n_rel(x), udef_rel(x), card_rel(x, "2"), _raise_v_rel(z,x)

This can be read as follows: A relation of raising holds between z (the unexpressed subject), and x. x denotes a cat entity, and is bound by an underspecified quantifier (**udef_rel**) as there is no explicit determiner. x is also an argument of a **card_rel** (short for 'cardinal_relation'), whose other argument is the constant value 2, meaning that there are in fact two cats being referred to.

For anaphoric numeral classifiers (2a), the representation contains an underspecified **noun_relation**, to be resolved in further processing.

(7) **noun_relation**(x), **udef_rel**(x), **card_rel**(x, "2"), **_raise_v_rel**(z,x)

Mensural classifiers have somewhat more elaborated semantic representations, which we treat as similar to English measure NPs [13]. On this analysis, the NumClP denotes the extent of some dimension or property of the modified N. This dimension or property is represented with an underspecified relation (**unspec_adj_rel**), and a **degree_rel** relates the measured amount to the underspecified adjective relation. The underspecified adjective relation modifies the N in the usual way. This is illustrated in (8), the semantic representation for (3a).

(8) _kilogram_n_rel(x), udef_rel(x), card_rel(x, "2"),
 degree_rel(unspec_adj_rel, x), unspec_adj_rel(y), _apple_n_rel(y),
 udef_rel(y), _buy_v_rel(z,y)

When mensural NumClPs are used anaphorically (3b), the element modified by the **_unspec_adj_rel** is an underspecified **noun_relation**, analogously to the case of sortal NumClPs used anaphorically:

(9) _kilogram_n_rel(x), udef_rel(x), card_rel(x, "2"),
 degree_rel(unspec_adj_rel, x), unspec_adj_rel(y), noun_relation(y),
 udef_rel(y), _buy_v_rel(z,y)

6 Implementing an Analysis

Our analysis consists of: (1) a lexical type hierarchy cross-classifying numeral classifiers along three dimensions (Fig. 1), (2) a special lexical entry for *no* for linking NumClPs with nouns, (3) a unary-branching phrase structure rules for promoting NumClPs to nominal constituents.

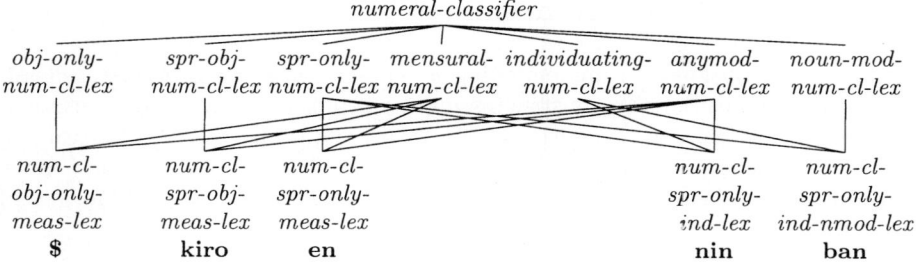

Fig. 1. Type hierarchy under *numeral-classifier*.

6.1 Lexical Types

Fig. 1 shows the lexical types for numeral classifiers, which are cross-classified along three dimensions: semantic relationship to the modified noun (*individuating* or *mensural*), modificational possibilities (NPs or PPs: *anymod*/NPs: *noun-mod*), and relationship to the number name (number name precedes: *spr-only*, number name precedes but may take *han*: *spr-obj*, number name follows: *obj-only*). Not all the possibilities in this space are instantiated (e.g., we have found no sortal classifiers which can take *han*), but we leave open the possibility that we may find in future work examples that fill in the range of possibilities. In this section, we treat each of the types in turn.

The constraint in (10) ensures that all numeral classifiers have the head type *num-cl_head*, as required by the unary phrase structure rule discussed in §6.3 below. Furthermore, it identifies two key pieces of semantic information made available for further composition, the INDEX and LTOP (local top handle) of the modified element, with the numeral classifier's own INDEX and LTOP, as these are intersective modifiers [6]. The constraints on the type *num-cl_head* (not shown here) ensure that numeral classifiers can modify only saturated NPs or PPs (i.e., NPs marked with a case postposition *wo* or *ga*), and that they only combine via intersective head-modifier rules.

(10) *numeral-classifier* :=
$$\begin{bmatrix} ...\text{CAT.HEAD} & \begin{bmatrix} num\text{-}cl\_head \\ \text{MOD} & \left\langle \begin{bmatrix} ...\text{INDEX} & \boxed{1} \\ ...\text{LTOP} & \boxed{2} \end{bmatrix} \right\rangle \end{bmatrix} \\ ..\text{CONT.HOOK} & \begin{bmatrix} \text{INDEX} & \boxed{1} \\ \text{LTOP} & \boxed{2} \end{bmatrix} \end{bmatrix}$$

The constraints on the types *spr-only-num-cl-lex*, *obj-only-num-cl-lex* and *spr-obj-num-cl-lex* account for the position of the numeral classifier with respect to the number name and for the potential presence of *han*. Both the number name (a phrase of head type *int_head*) and *han* (given the distinguished head value *han_head*) are treated as dependents of the numeral classifier expression, but variously as specifiers or complements according to the type of the numeral classifier. In the JACY grammar, specifiers immediately precede their heads, while complements are not required to do so and can even follow their heads (in rare cases). Given all this, in the ordinary case (*spr-only-num-cl-lex*), we treat the number name as the specifier of the numeral classifier. The other two cases involve numeral classifiers taking complements: with no specifier, in the case of pre-number unit expressions like the symbol $ (*obj-only-num-cl-lex*) and both a number-name specifier and the complement *han* in the case of unit expressions appearing with *han* (*spr-obj-num-cl-lex*). Finally, the type *spr-obj-num-cl-lex* does some semantic work as well, providing the **plus_rel** which relates the value of the number name to the "$\frac{1}{2}$" contributed by *han*, and identifying the ARG1 of the **plus_rel** with the XARG of the SPR and COMPS so that they will all share an index argument (eventually the index of the modified noun for sortal classifiers and of the measure noun relation for mensural classifiers).

(11) *spr-obj-num-cl-lex* :=

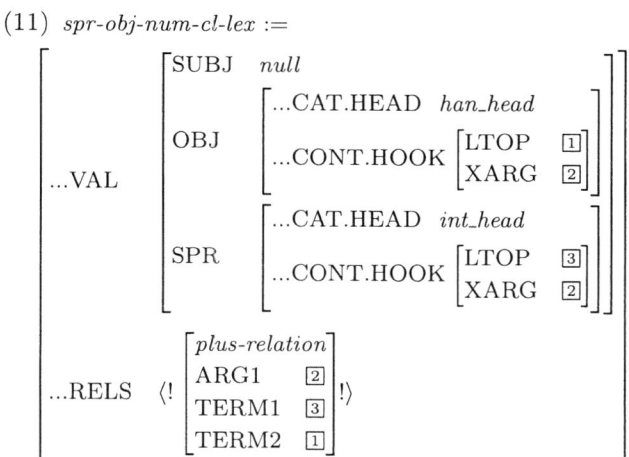

In the second dimension of the cross-classification, *anymod-num-cl-lex* and *noun-mod-num-cl-lex* constrain what the numeral classifier may modify, via the MOD value. Prenominal numeral classifiers are linked to the head noun with *no*, which mediates the modifier-modifiee relationship (see (2) and §6.2). However, numeral classifiers can appear after the noun (2c), modifying it directly. Some numeral classifiers can also 'float' outside the NP, either immediately after the case postposition or to the position before the verb (2d). While we leave the latter kind of float to future work (see §7), we handle the former by allowing most numeral classifiers to appear as post-head modifiers of PPs. Thus *noun-mod-num-cl-lex* further constrains the HEAD value of the element on the MOD list to be *noun_head*, but *anymod-num-cl-lex* leaves it as inherited (*noun-or-case-p_head*). This type does, however, constrain the modifier to show up after the head ([POSTHEAD *right*]), and further constrains the modified head to be [NUCL *nucl_plus*], in order to rule out vacuous attachment ambiguities between numeral classifiers attaching to the right left-attaching modifiers of the same NP.

The final dimension of the classification captures the semantic differences between sortal and mensural numeral classifiers. The sortal numeral classifiers contribute no semantic content of their own (represented with empty RELS and HCONS lists). In contrast, mensural numeral classifiers contribute quite a bit of semantic information, and therefore have quite rich RELS and HCONS values. As shown in (12), the *noun-relation* is identified with the lexical key relation value (LKEYS.KEYREL) so that specific lexical entries of this type can easily further specify it (e.g., *kiro* constrains its PRED to be **_kilogram_n_rel**). The type also makes reference to the HOOK value so that the INDEX and LTOP (also the INDEX and LTOP of the modified noun, see (10)) can be identified with the appropriate values inside the RELS list. The length of the RELS list is left unbounded, because some mensural classifiers also inherit from *spr-obj-num-cl-lex*, and therefore must be able to add the **plus_rel** to the list.

(12) *mensural-num-cl-lex* :=

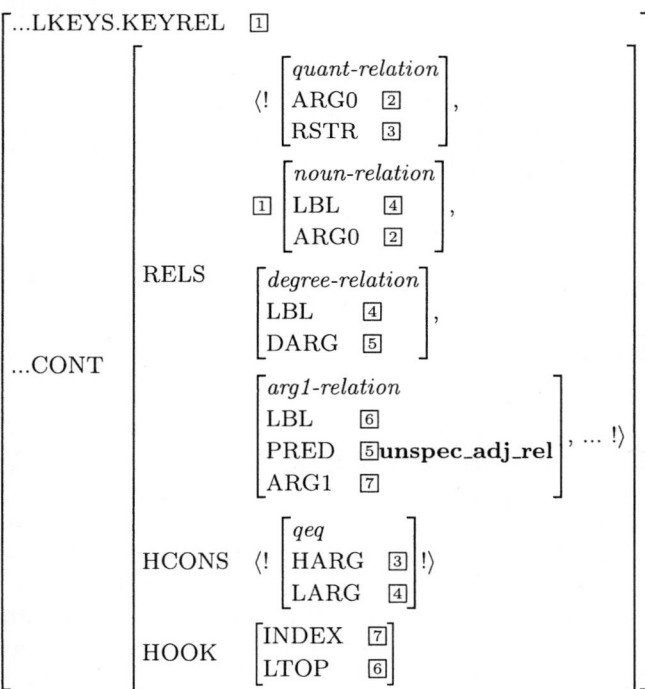

The types in the bottom part of the hierarchy in Fig. 1 join the dimensions of classification. They also do a little semantic work, making the INDEX and LTOP of the modified noun available to their number name argument, and, in the case of subtypes of *mensural-num-cl-lex*, they constrain the final length of the RELS list, as appropriate.

6.2 The Linker *no*

We posit a special lexical entry for *no* which mediates the relationship between NumClPs and the nouns they modify. In addition to the constraints that it shares with other entries for *no* and other modifier-heading postpositions, this special *no* is subject to constraints that specify that *no* makes no semantic contribution, that it takes a NumClP as a complement, and that the element on the MOD list of *no* shares its local top handle and index with the element on the MOD list of the NumClP (i.e., that *no* effectively inherits its complement's MOD possibility). Even though (most) numeral classifiers can either modify NPs or PPs, all entries for *no* are independently constrained to only modify NPs, and only as pre-head modifiers.

6.3 Unary-Branching Phrase Structure Rule

We treat NumClPs serving as nominal constituents by means of an exocentric unary-branching rule. This rule specifies that the mother is a noun subcategorized for a determiner specifier (these constraints are expressed on *noun_sc*), while the daughter is a numeral classifier phrase whose valence is saturated. Furthermore, it contributes (via its C-CONT, or constructional content feature) an underspecified *noun-relation* which serves as the thing (semantically) modified by the numeral classifier phrase. The reentrancies required to represent this modification are implemented via the LTOP and INDEX features.

(13) *nominal-numcl-rule-type* :=

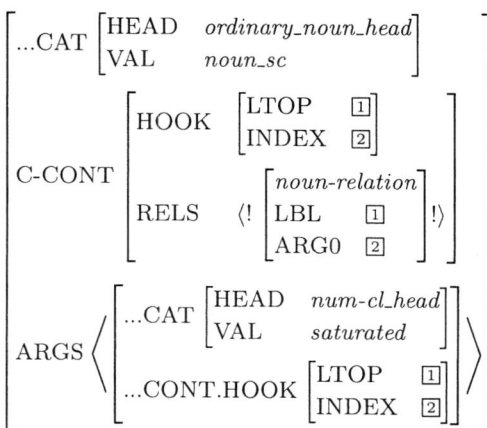

This rule works for both sortal and mensural NumClPs, as both are expecting to modify a noun.

7 Future Work

We have not yet implemented an analysis of pre-verbal floated NumClPs, but we sketch one here. The key is that NumClPs are treated as simple modifiers, not quantifiers. Therefore, they can attach syntactically to the verb, but semantically to one of its arguments. In our HPSG analysis, the verb will have unsaturated valence features, making the indices of its arguments 'visible' to any modifiers attaching to it.

There appear to be constraints on which arguments can 'launch' floated quantifiers, although their exact nature is as yet unclear. Proposals include: only nominals marked with the case particles *ga* or *wo* [14], only subjects or direct objects [15], or c-command-based constraints [16]. While there are exceptions to all of these generalizations, [8] notes that the vast majority of actually occurring cases satisfy all of them, and further that it is primarily *intransitive* subjects which participate in the construction.

These observations will help considerably in reducing the ambiguity inherent in introducing an analysis of floated NumClPs. We could constrain floated NumClPs to only modify intransitive verbs (semantically modifying the subject) or transitive verbs (semantically modifying the object). Some ambiguity will remain, however, as the pre-verbal and post-nominal positions often coincide.

Also missing from our analysis are the sortal constraints imposed by classifiers on the nouns they modify. In future work, we hope to merge this analysis with an implementation of the sortal constraints, such as that of [2]. We believe that such a merger would be extremely useful: First, the sortal constraints could be used to narrow down the possible referents of anaphoric uses of NumClPs. Second, sortal constraints could reduce ambiguity in NumClP+*no*+N strings, whenever they could rule out the ordinary numeral classifier use, leaving the anaphoric interpretation (see (4) above). Third, sortal constraints will be crucial in generation [2]. Without them, we would propose an additional string for each sortal classifier whenever a **card_rel** appears in the input semantics, most of which would in fact be unacceptable. Implementing sortal constraints could be simpler for generation than for parsing, since we wouldn't need to deal with varying inventories or metaphorical extensions.

8 Conclusion

Precision grammars require compositional semantics. We have described an approach to the syntax of Japanese numeral classifiers which allows us to build semantic representations for strings containing these prevalent elements — representations suitable for applications requiring natural language understanding, such as (semantic) machine translation and automated email response.

Acknowledgements

This research was carried out as part a joint R&D effort between YY Technologies and DFKI, and we are grateful to both for the opportunity. We would also like to thank Francis Bond, Dan Flickinger, Stephan Oepen, Atsuko Shimada and Tim Baldwin for helpful feedback in the process of developing and implementing this analysis and Setsuko Shirai for grammaticality judgments. This research was partly supported by the EU project DeepThought IST-2001-37836.

References

1. Matsumoto, Y.: Japanese numeral classifiers: A study of semantic categories and lexical organization. Linguistics **31** (1993) 667–713
2. Bond, F., Paik, K.H.: Reusing an ontology to generate numeral classifiers. In: Coling 2000, Saarbrücken, Germany (2000)
3. Pollard, C., Sag, I.A.: Head-Driven Phrase Structure Grammar. U of Chicago Press, Chicago (1994)
4. Siegel, M.: HPSG analysis of Japanese. In Wahlster, W., ed.: Verbmobil: Foundations of Speech-to-Speech Translation. Springer, Berlin (2000)
5. Siegel, M., Bender, E.M.: Efficient deep processing of Japanese. In: Proceedings of the 3rd Workshop on Asian Language Resources and Standardization, Coling 2002, Taipei (2002)
6. Bender, E.M., Flickinger, D., Oepen, S.: The Grammar Matrix: An open-source starter-kit for the rapid development of cross-linguistically consistent broad-coverage precision grammars. In: Proceedings of the Workshop on Grammar Engineering and Evaluation, Coling 2002, Taipei (2002) 8–14
7. Paik, K., Bond, F.: Spatial representation and shape classifiers in Japanese and Korean. In Beaver, D.I., Casillas Martínez, L.D., Clark, B.Z., Kaufmann, S., eds.: The Construction of Meaning. CSLI Publications, Stanford CA (2002) 163–180
8. Downing, P.: Numeral Classifier Systems: The Case of Japanese. John Benjamins, Philadelphia (1996)
9. Asahara, M., Matsumoto, Y.: Extended models and tools for high-performance part-of-speech tagger. In: Coling 2000, Saarbrücken, Germany (2000)
10. Bond, F., Fujita, S., Hashimoto, C., Kasahara, K., Nariyama, S., Nichols, E., Ohtani, A., Tanaka, T., Amano, S.: The Hinoki Treebank: A treebank for text understanding. In: Proceedings of the IJC-NLP-2004, Springer-Verlag (2004) this volume.
11. Copestake, A., Flickinger, D.P., Sag, I.A., Pollard, C.: Minimal Recursion Semantics. An introduction. Under review. (2003)
12. Copestake, A., Lascarides, A., Flickinger, D.: An algebra for semantic construction in constraint-based grammars. In: ACL 2001, Toulouse, France (2001)
13. Flickinger, D., Bond, F.: A two-rule analysis of measure noun phrases. In Müller, S., ed.: Proceedings of the 10th International Conference on Head-Driven Phrase Structure Grammar, Stanford CA, CSLI Publications (2003) 111–121
14. Shibatani, M.: Nihongo no Bunseki. Tasishuukan, Tokyo (1978)
15. Inoue, K.: Nihongo no Bunpou Housouku. Tasishuukan, Tokyo (1978)
16. Miyagawa, S.: Structure and Case Marking in Japanese. Academic Press, New York (1989)

A Graph Grammar Approach to Map Between Dependency Trees and Topological Models

Bernd Bohnet

Institute for Intelligent Systems
University of Stuttgart
Universitätsstr. 38
70569 Stuttgart
`Bernd.Bohnet@iis.uni-stuttgart.de`

Abstract. Determining the word order in free word order languages is deemed as a challenge for NLG. In this paper, we propose a simple approach in order to get the appropriate grammatically correct variants of a sentence using a dependency structure as input. We describe a linearization grammar based on a graph grammar that allows to retrieve a topological model using unordered constituent structures and precedence relations. The graph grammar formalism is totally language independent and only the grammar depends on the language. The grammar rules can be automatically acquired from a corpus that is annotated with phrase structures and dependency structures. The dependency structures annotation is retrieved by structure translation from the phrase structure annotation. We conclude with the description of a grammar and the evaluation of the formalism using a large corpus.

1 Introduction

In dependency grammar based Natural Language Generation, correct word sequences, have to be generated out of given dependency trees. This problem is especially difficult in free word order languages.

German, as a free word order language is a good example, because there are lot of topological models introduced by Kathol (1995), Bröker (1998), Duchier and Debusmann (2001), Gerdes and Kahane (2001), etc. They are all based on the German Field Model, cf. (Drach, 1937), (Bech, 1955), etc.

The so far introduced approaches use an additional structure between a sentence and the dependency tree, a so called topological model which represents the word order. We agree that a topological model is necessary. But we think that the introduced topolgical models are too complex and not language independent and that there is still a lack of procedures to map between dependency trees and topological models, and visa versa. Both the dependency trees and the topological models are structured objects. Graph grammars are best suited to map structured objects. Graph grammars are considered as an extension of string based processing to structured objects. They are intensively investigated in theoretical computer science and have therefore a strong theoretical foundation.

In this paper, first, we present a simple graph based topological model based on constituent structures and precedence relations; second, a graph grammar based approach to map between dependency structures and a topological model. Later on, we describe how rules can be automatically acquired, and we conclude with an evaluation of the formalism and grammars.

2 Topological Model

The topological model (TM) is based on two simple concepts: precedence units and precedence relations:

Definition 1. *[Precedence Unit]*
A precedence unit (PU) is a set of words or PUs that forms a continuous part of a sentence. The cardinality of an PU $|PU| >= 1$, i.e. no empty PUs are allowed.

Definition 2. *[Precedence Relation]*
A Precedence Relation (PR) holding between two different PUs or words λ_1 and λ_2 ($\lambda_1 \succ \lambda_2$) states that λ_1 is before λ_2.

Precedence units roughly represent constituent structures. Discontinous constituents are not allowed, because their function is to restrict the possible scrambling range onto the precedence unit, cf. definition 1.

The topological model called *precedence graph* is represented as a hierarchical graph *(HG)*. We have adapted the hierarchical graph definition of Busatto (2002), where he defined it as an underlying flat graph, on top of a directed acyclic graph *(DAG)* which are coupled by a *coupling graph*.

Definition 3. *[Attributed Labelled Directed Graph (ALG)]*
A directed labelled attributed graph is a tuple $\langle N, E, \Sigma_E, W, A, \alpha, s, t \rangle$ where N is a set of nodes, $E \subseteq N \times N \times \Sigma_E$ a set of edges, Σ_E a set of edge labels, W a set of values, A a set of attribute names, $\alpha : A \times 2^W \to N$ is a function that assigns attribues to nodes, and $s, t : E \to N$ are two functions that map each edge to its source and target node.

Definition 4. *[Directed Acyclic Graph (DAG)]*
A directed acyclic graph is a tuple $\langle P_D, E_D, s_D, t_D \rangle$ where P_D is a set of nodes, $E_D \subseteq P_D \times P_D$ a set of edges without cycles and parallel edges, and $s_D, t_D : E_D \to P_D$ are two functions that map each edge to its source and target node.

Definition 5. *[Coupling Graph (CG)]*
A Graph B is bipartite, if N_B can be partitioned into two sets of nodes X, Y, such that for all edges $e \in E_B$, either $s_B(e) \in X$ and $t_B(e) \in Y$ or $s_B(e) \in Y$ and $t_B(e) \in X$. We represent it as tuple $\langle X, Y, E, s, t \rangle$ where $E \subset (X \times Y) \cup (Y \times X)$. A coupling graph is a bipartite graph $B = (P_B, A_B, C_B, s_B, t_B)$ that satisfies the following conditions:

1. *Completeness condition: $\forall p \in P_B$ there exists an edge $e = (p, x) \in C_B$, i.e. every node in P_B is connected to at least one node in A_B.*

2. *Connection condition:* $\forall p \in P_B$, if there exists an edge $e = (p, x) \in C_B$, then $\forall e' = (p', x')$ with $e' \neq e \wedge p' = p \rightarrow x' \neq x$, i.e. every node in A_B is connected to at most one node in P_B

We call P_D the set of packages and A_B the set of atoms. For a coupling graph B, we define an association relation $\leftarrow_B = ((p, x) \in P_B \times A_B | (x, p) \in C_B)$ and if $p \leftarrow_B x$, then we say x is contained in p.

Definition 6. *[Hierarchical Graph (HG)]*
A hierarchical graph is a tuple $\langle G, D, B \rangle$, where G is a graph according to definition 3, D is a DAG, and B a coupling graph with $A_B = N_G$ and $P_B = P_D$.

Definition 7. *[Path]*
Let G be a directed graph. Then a path in G from u to v, for some $u, v \in N$, is a sequence of edges $e_1, ..., e_k$ $(k \geq 1)$ such that, $\forall i = 1, ..., k-1$, $t(e_i) = s(e_{i+1}), s(e_1) = u$, and $t(e_k) = v$.

Definition 8. *[Topological Sort]*
A topological sort is a permutation p of the nodes of a directed graph such that an edge i, j implies that i appears before j in p.

An example of a precedence graph represented as HG is shown in Figure 1.

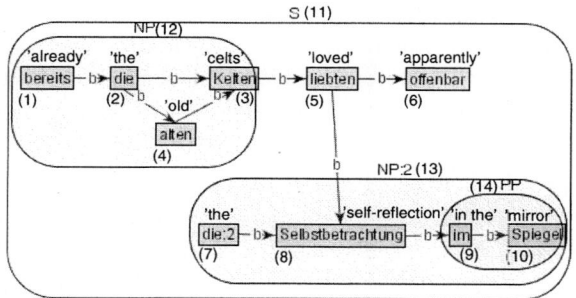

Fig. 1. Precedence graph. The numbers in the braces are the node number as used in the definition of the HG.

3 Dependency Structure

Dependency structures are attributed labelled directed trees, with nodes being labelled with the basic word form and edges being labelled with syntactic relations (e.g. *subjective, dobjective, iobjective,* etc.), cf. (Mel'čuk, 1988). Morphosyntactic features (e.g. *number, tense,* etc.) are represented as attributes, which are attached to the nodes. Unlike phrase structures, dependency structures do not store word order information. The dependency structures annotation is retrieved by structure translation from the phrase structure annotation which is described in detail in Bohnet (2003) An example of a dependency structure corresponding to the precedence graph of Figure 1 is shown in Figure 2.

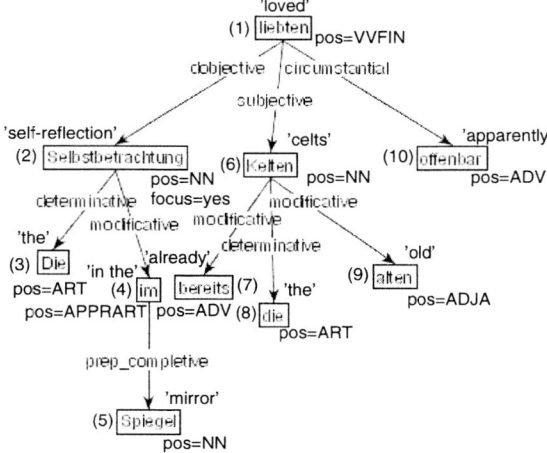

Fig. 2. A dependency structure.

4 Mapping of Dependency Structures to Precedence Graphs

In this section, we describe the implementation aspects of the mapping. As mentioned above, the mapping process is realized by a graph grammar. In what follows, we introduce the basic notion of graph mapping. A more detailed description is in Bohnet and Wanner (2001).

In the mapping procedure a compiler applies grammar rules to the input graphs. A graph rule is a tuple $R\langle G_l, G_r, C_D, C_R\rangle$. A rule consists of a left-hand side graph G_l, a right-hand side G_r, the set of conditions C_D which must hold in order for the rule to be applicable and the set C_R which specifies correspondences between parts of G_l and G_r.

If a fragment of the source graph matches the left-hand side of a rule, and the condition specified met, the fragment is mapped onto the subgraph specified in the right-hand side. An important point is that the source graph is not altered, but a completely new target graph is build up by the applied rules. Additionally, rules can contain context information both in the left-hand side and in the right-hand side. Left-hand side context means that a rule can share an input fragment with other rules; right-hand side context contains a target fragment that must have already been created by other rules. This sounds procedural but the rules are completely declarative. They only state that a part must be available. This means for the rule interpreter, the mapping of a source graph to a target graph is performed iteratively[1]. It consists of five steps that are applied to all rules in parallel:

---

[1] In the case of mapping of Dependency Structures to Precedence Graphs two iterations are necessary.

1. **Matching.** All occurrences of the left-hand side graph G_l of all rules are identified in the source structure. This procedure is efficient because the left-hand side graphs are small; the attributes and labels of nodes have a further restriction on the matching process.
2. **Evaluation.** The conditions are evaluated and the matches which do not fulfill the conditions are filtered out.
3. **Clustering.** During the clustering step, rules which are applicable together to the source structure are grouped into clusters.
4. **Application.** During the application step, the rules of each cluster are applied. For each applicable rule, an isolated elementary graph is created.
5. **Unification.** In the last step, the elementary structures are glued together. This is done by the unification of nodes that correspond to the same source node.

5 Linearization Grammar

In order to describe a simple grammar in our formalism, we will take the dependency structure in Figure 2 as a source for the sentence *Die Selbstbetrachtung im Spiegel liebten offenbar bereits die alten Kelten.* 'The old celts loved the self-reflection in the mirror apparently.' A linearization grammar shows two types of rules:

PU forming rules define sets of nodes that have to form a continuous sequence in the sentence. As PU we use flat unordered phrases similar to them in the German TIGER, and NEGRA corpora, but no discontinous phrases are created, because of phenomena displayed by languages like German such as scrambling, partial VP fronting, and partial VP extraposition, etc. The used procedure is similar to that introduced by Xia (2001) to retrieve phrase structures, but because of the free word order of German, it is only possible to retrieve unordered phrase structures, but that is what we need.

Precedence rules define the precedence relation $\succ$ between two PUs[2].

Furthermore, the precedence rules can be categorized in two distinct ways: with respect to the input structure, and with respect to the output structure. With respect to the input structure (the dependency trees) precedence rules fall into:

Vertical rules – linearizing a parent node to its descendant; The left-hand side of a rule consists of a path from a node p to d. In most cases the path consists of only one edge. (cf. example 3)

Horizontal rules – putting two descendant nodes in precedence relation to each other; Formally, the left-hand side of a rule consists of two paths starting at a node p and ending at the nodes v, w. (cf. example 2)

---

[2] In the rules, we write `b->` instead of $\succ$.

With respect to the output structures the precedence rules fall into three classes:

Clause level rules – define precedence relations between different PUs making use of the Topological Field Model and the information structure if available. The model is defined as the following total order: Vorfeld ('pre-field') ≻ Linke Klammer ('left bracket') ≻ Mittelfeld ('mid-field') ≻ Rechte Klammer ('right bracket') ≻ Nachfeld ('post-field').
This model is recursive, i.e., it is to be applied both on the matrix sentence and on all embedded clauses/infinitive constructions. Moreover, there are constraints on the number and type of constituents occupying different fields (e.g. there is at most one element in the left bracket either of type finite verb, subjunction or relative pronoun).

Example 1. [Vorfeld-Rule]

```
GL: ?X{ ?r-> ?Y }
GR: ?Ydm {b-> ?Xdm {VF_occ=yes } }
CD: ?X.pos=VVFIN|VAFIN|VMFIN; ?Y.focus=yes;
CR: ?X <=> ?Xdm; ?Y <=> ?Ydm;
```

Explanation: The left-hand side of the rule (GL – Graph Left) states that, if the input DS display two nodes tied by whatever edge together, then the specified right-hand side graph (GR – Graph Right) is created. It consists of two nodes which are connected by an edge labelled with b. To the node referenced by the variable ?Xdm the attribute VF_occ with the value yes is added; however, this can only happen if the conditions (CD – Condition) are evaluated to true. Two conditions are specified: the attribute pos should have one of the values of the given disjunction (VVFIN, VAFIN, or VMFIN)[3] and focus should have the value yes. Moreover, (CR – Correspondence) all attributes from X will be carried over to Xdm, and from Y to Ydm, respectively. In other words, this rule allows a part with focus to go before the finite verb and it remarks that the *Vorfeld* ('pre-field') is occupied, and because of that mark the standard rule is not applied, which normaly orders the subject into the *Vorfeld*. This rule is applicable once to the dependency structure that is shown in Figure 2.
G_l is matched in the source structure cf. Figure 2 and G_r is created in the target structure cf. Figure 1.

Field level rules – ordering PUs within a topological field if it contains more than one elements (e.g. Mittelfeld);

Phrase level rules – ordering PUs within a complex PU, e.g. within a PP, AP, NP, etc.

---

[3] These are STTS part of speech tags as defined in Thielen et al. (1999). VVFIN 'finite verb', VAFIN 'finite verb, aux', VMFIN, 'finite verb, modal'.

Example 2. [Determinative-H]
```
GL: ?X{ ?d->?Y
        ?q->?Z }
GR: ?Ydm { b-> ?Zdm }
CD: ?d = deteterminative; not ?Z.pos=ADV;
CR: ?X <=> ?Xdm; ?Z <=> ?Zdm;
```

Explanation: The rule above orders a determiner ahead of all other dependents, but not before adverbs (`ADV`). This rule is applicable twice to the dependency structure that is shown in Figure 2.

Example 3. [Determinative-V]
```
GL: ?X{ ?d->?Y }
GR: ?Ydm { b-> ?Xdm }
CD: ?d = deteterminative;
CR: ?X <=> ?Xdm; ?Y <=> ?Ydm;
```

Explanation: The rule above orders a determiner before its head, and this rule is two times applicable.

6 The Linearization of a PG

The linearization algorithm computes all correct linear variants of a sentence as defined in the precedence graph. It computes all topological sorts of each graph package and combines the results.

The linearization algorithm should be able to compute all combinations of the elements in a precedence graph. If there are no restrictions, then it has a complexity of $n!$. But if there are no conditions to introduce constraints then each solution is as good as each other and it is possible to take for instance the first one. The complexity to retrive one topological sort is $n * log(n)$.[4] The two possible topological sorts of the precedence graph of Figure 1 are shown below:

Die Selbstbetrachtung im Spiegel liebten offenbar bereits die alten Kelten.
Die Selbstbetrachtung im Spiegel liebten bereits die alten Kelten offenbar.

7 Automatic Rule Acquisition

In this section, we introduce an algorithm for the automatic acquisition of linearization rules. Therefore, it is necessary to acquire precedence rules (PR) and precedence unit rules (PUR). For the acquisition of the PUR, we use the algorithm of Xia (2001).

In order to learn precedence rules we use dependency structures and phrase structures as input. Therefore, we describe first the phrase structures that are represented as hierarchical graphs, and then the acquisition algorithm.

---
[4] It is easy to introduce an additional parameter to restrict the number of solutions. For practical use it is necessary, because the most frequent error implementing a linearization grammar is that the precedence graph is not restricted enough.

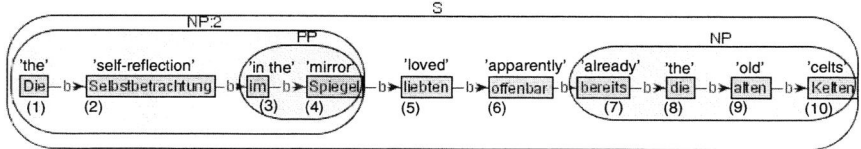

Fig. 3. Phrase structure represented as hierarchical graph.

7.1 Phrase Structures

For the acquisition of rules, we use the phrase structure annotation of the German NEGRA and TIGER Corpus which contain together about 60000 sentences of German newspapers. The phrase structures used in the corpora are supposed to be theory independent, cf. (Wojciech et al, 1997). Therefore, they are rather flat. In Figure 3 an example of a PS as an hierarchical graph is shown. The words of the corpora are annotated with syntactic categories (e.g. NN 'normal noun', KON 'coordinated conjunction', etc.), and the grammatical functions (e.g. SB 'subject' , OA 'accusative object', etc.) which are represented as attributes.

7.2 Acquisition of Linearization Rules

In this subsection, we describe the acquisition of linear precedence rules for packages. And later on, we describe the aquisition of a complete grammar.

Let $H^{PS} = (G^{PS}, D^{PS}, B^{PS})$ be a phrase structure, $H^{DS} = (G^{DS}, D^{DS}, B^{DS})$ a dependency structure, $f_{PS} : N_G^{DS} \to N_G^{PS}$ a function that maps nodes of dependency structures to nodes of a phrase structures, and $length(u, v)$ of a dependency structure the number of edge k on path from u to v. Then, a procedure for the acquistion of precedence rules is:

```
rules ← ∅
foreach package p ∈ P_D^{PS} create rules:
  s ← 1
  G_ts is a DAG, where E_ts ← ∅ and
    N_ts ← n is contained in p ∪ {f_PS(n)|e ∈ N^{DS} ∧ e(x, n) ∧ f_PS(x) contained in p}
  repeat
    // create vertical rules of path size s
    foreach path x with length(n, v) = s and n, v ∈ N^{DS}, where f_PS(s(e_i)), f_PS(t(e_i)) ∈ N_ts do
      if f_PS(n) ≻* f_PS(v) and adding an edge (f_PS(v), f_PS(n)) to E_ts
        restricts the graph G_ts more in respect to possible topological sorts then
        //it is not necessary to compute the sorts.
        rules ← rules+createVRule(v, n, H^{DS})
        E_ts ← E_ts ∪ (v, n)
      else if f_PS(v) ≻* f_PS(n) and adding an edge (f_PS(n), f_PS(v)) to E_ts
        restricts the graph G_ts more in respect to possible topological sorts then
        rules ← rules+createVRule(n, v, H^{DS})
        E_ts ← E_ts ∪ (n, v)
      end if
    end foreach
    // create horizontal rules of size s
    foreach paths x, y with length(n, v) + length(n, w) = s, where n, v, w ∈ N^{DS};
      x is a path from n to v, y is a path from n to w,
      and ∀e ∈ x, y, such that f_PS(s(e)) ∨ f_PS(t(e)) is contained in p do
      if f_PS(v) ≻* f_PS(w) and adding an edge (f_PS(v), f_PS(w)) to E_ts
        restricts the graph G_ts more in respect to possible topological sorts then
```

```
            rules ← rules+createHRule(n, v, w, H^{DS})
            E_{ts} ← E_{ts} ∪ (n, v)
        else if f_{PS}(w) ≻* f_{PS}(v) and adding an edge (f_{PS}(w), f_{PS}(v)) to E_{ts}
            restricts the graph G_{ts} more in respect to possible topological sorts then
            rules ← rules+createHRule(n, w, v, H^{DS})
            E_{ts} ← E_{ts} ∪ (n, v)
    end foreach
    s ← s +1
until (∀ n ∈ N_G^{PS} contained in p are total ordered or it is not possible to build further
rules)

// A vertical rule orders a parent to a child
function createVRule(n, v, H^{DS})
    create a rule r_i with the left hand side graph g_l that contains the path from n to v,
    where n, v ∈ N_G^{DS} and the lex-attributes are replaced with variable names.
    The right-hand side graph g_r contains two nodes n' = f_{DS}(n), v' = f_{DS}(v),
    the lex-attributes are replaced with variable names, and an edge: (n', v', b)
    The correspondence relation consists of (n, n'), (v, v').
end

// A horizontal rule orders two descendant in a DS
function createHRule(n, v, w, H^{DS})
    create a rule r_i with the left hand side graph g_l that contains the path from n to v and
    the path from n to w in the dependency tree H^{DS} and
    the lex-attributes are replaced with variable names.
    The right-hand side graph g_r contains two nodes n' = f_{DS}(v), v' = f_{DS}(w),
    the lex-attributes are replaced with variable names, and an edge (v', w', b).
    The correspondence relation consists of (v, v'), (w, w').
end
```

7.3 Statistic Based Grammar Acquistion

We use a statistical approach to learn a grammar, i.e. we count the frequency of the occurence of a rule during the acquistion step and if two rules contradict, then we take the most frequent.

A grammar is executed in two steps, first the clause level rules and phrase level rules are applied, cf. section 5. All phrase level rules are independent of all other rules, therefore they can be executed in the first step. For the learning procedure it is necessary to write the clause level rules manually, which are only a few rules. Further, the learning procedure must know the features of the clause level rules that are added, because the rules that are applied later make use of them. The learning procedure of the precedence rules consists of the following steps that are executed for each structure: 1. The clause level rules are applied. 2. The rules are acquired with the method described above. 3. It is checked, if the acquired rules are already learned in previous cycles, then only the counter of the rule is increased, else it is added to the set of rules. In subsequent steps, rules that contradict each other are determined and only the most frequent are kept. Finally similar rules are combined.

7.4 Problems of the Acquistion

In some cases, it is not possible to create rules for a package to achieve a total order, because the edge labels and attributes of the nodes are equal, e.g. if a verb has more than one circumstantial relation or adverbial relation, then it is not possible to create meaningful rules and the creation of such rules must be avoided.

7.5 Evaluation

In the evaluation step, we divide the corpus into two parts, which one of them is big and the other one is small. Then the learning procedure is applied to the bigger one, and from the smaller one we randomly select a sufficient number of dependency structures. And finally an independent evaluator checks the result.

We applied the learing procedure to 30000 structures and retrieved about 1550 precedence unit rules and 450 precedence rules. From the remaining, we selected randomly 100 structures and applied the rules on this structures. The evaluator rated 81 as correct and 19 as wrong.

8 Conclusion

We invented a simple topological model and a graph grammar based approach to map between dependency trees and the topological model. The formalism is language independent while all language dependent things are implemented in the grammar. We showed that it is possible to build (automatically) a grammar with a high coverage of 81%.

Therefore, our formalism seems best suited to map between a dependency structures and a topological model, and to overcome the lack of mapping procedures.

References

Kathol, A.: Linearization-Based German Syntax. PhD thesis, Ohio State University (1995)
Bröker, N.: Separating Surface Order and Syntactic Relations in a Dependency Grammar. In: COLING-ACL 98. (1998)
Duchier, D., Debusmann, R.: Topological dependency trees: A constraint-based account of linear precedence. In: Proceedings of the ACL. (2001)
Gerdes, K., Kahane, S.: Word order in german: A formal dependency grammar using a topological hierarchy. In: Proceedings of the ACL. (2001)
Drach, E.: Grundgedanken der deutschen Satzlehre. Diesterweg, Frankfurt (1937)
Bech, G.: Studium über das deutsche Verbum infinitum. Max Niemeyer Verlag, Tübingen (1955)
Busatto, G.: An Abstract Model of Hierarchical Graphs and Hierarchical Graph Transformation. PhD thesis, Universität Paderborn (2002)
Mel'čuk, I.: Dependency Syntax: Theory and Practice. State University of New York Press, Albany (1988)
Bohnet, B.: Mapping Phrase Structures to Dependency Structures in the Case of Free Word Order Languages. In: First International Conference on Meaning-Text Theory. (2003)
Bohnet, B., Wanner, L.: On Using a Parallel Graph Rewriting Formalism in Generation. In: Eight European Workshop on Natural Language Generation. (2001)
Xia, F., Palmer, M.: Converting Dependency Structures to Phrase Structures. In: The Proc. of the Human Language Technology Conference, San Diego (2001)
Thielen, C., Schiller, A., Teufel, S., Stöckert, C.: Guidelines für das Tagging deutscher Textkorpora mit STTS. Technical report (1999)
Wojciechl, S., Krenn, B., Brants, T., Uszkoreit, H.: An Annotation Scheme for Free Word Order Languages. In: Proceedings of the ANLP Conference. (1997)

The Automatic Acquisition of Verb Subcategorisations and Their Impact on the Performance of an HPSG Parser

John Carroll and Alex C. Fang

Department of Informatics, University of Sussex, Falmer, Brighton BN1 9RH, UK
{johnca,alexf}@sussex.ac.uk

Abstract. We describe the automatic acquisition of a lexicon of verb subcategorisations from a domain-specific corpus, and an evaluation of the impact this lexicon has on the performance of a "deep", HPSG parser of English. We conducted two experiments to determine whether the empirically extracted verb stems would enhance the lexical coverage of the grammar and to see whether the automatically extracted verb subcategorisations would result in enhanced parser coverage. In our experiments, the empirically extracted verbs enhance lexical coverage by 8.5%. The automatically extracted verb subcategorisations enhance the parse success rate by 15% in theoretical terms and by 4.5% in practice. This is a promising approach for improving the robustness of deep parsing.

1 Introduction

Typed unification-based grammatical frameworks such as head-driven phrase-structure grammars (HPSG; [1]) typically make use of two levels of lexical descriptions: a generic feature-based description for the word class in general and a set of lexical entries with specific features for each item. The grammar uses these lexical descriptions to assign precise syntactic and semantic analyses. Verb subcategorisation information, in particular, plays a vital role in the correct identification of complements of predicates. Consider:

> I'm thinking *of buying this software* too but the trial version doesn't seem to have the option to set priorities *on channels*.

The two prepositional phrases can only be attached correctly if the lexicon specifies that the verb *think* is complemented by the *of* phrase and that the complex transitive verb *set* can take a prepositional phrase headed by *on* as the object complement.

To date, verb subcategorisation lexicons have generally been constructed by hand. As with most handcrafted linguistic resources, they tend to excel in terms of precision of description but suffer from omissions and inconsistencies. A reason for this is that linguistically sophisticated descriptions of natural language are complex and expensive to construct and there is always some disparity between the computational grammarian's introspection and realistic input to the system. As an example, the LinGO English Resource Grammar (ERG; [2]) is a large HPSG grammar that contains around 2,000 lexical entries for over 1,100 verbs[1] selected to cover a number of

---

[1] We use version 1.4 (April 2003) of the LinGO ERG.

application-orientated corpora. When tested with 10,000 randomly selected sentences from a corpus of mobile phone-related discussions – a new domain for the ERG and containing many lexical items not present in standard dictionaries – it achieved a lexical coverage of only about 86% in terms of tokens and 42.3% in terms of types (see Section 4 below).

In this paper we describe research that aims to enhance the lexical coverage (and hence the parser success rate) of the LinGO ERG, using purely automatic techniques. We describe the construction and pre-processing of a domain-specific corpus, the extraction of verb subcategorisations from it using shallow processing, and experimental results on the impact of empirically extracted verb subcategorisations on the performance of the deep grammar/parser combination.

The approach we take is novel in that it combines unsupervised learning of language with manually constructed linguistic resources, working towards robust deep language processing.

2 Corpus Construction

We take as our domain and text type emails about models of mobile phones. In selecting a source for building a corpus of material of this type, practical considerations include:
- The source be unencumbered by copyright.
- The source be rich enough to allow for a sizable sample.
- The source be diversified enough to include a mixture of both spontaneous discussions and more formal prose (e.g. press releases).

As a result of these considerations, we decided to use the following mobile phone news groups, as archived by Google:
- alt.cell-phone.tech
- alt.cellular-phone-tech
- alt.cellular sub-groups:
- alltel, attws, bluetooth, cingular, clearnet, data, ericsson, fido, gsm, motorola, nextel, nokia, oki, rogersatt, sprintpcs, tech, telephones, umts, verizon

We downloaded 16,979 newsgroup postings, covering the period from 27 December 2002 to 4 April 2003.

2.1 Pre-processing

Each posting was automatically segmented into a header, quoted text, body text, and signature, based on the HTML markup and formatting clues. We made sure that only the body text was retained as part of the corpus, with the header, any quotation and signature automatically removed. Because of the planned evaluation of the subcategorisation lexicon, it was necessary to divide the corpus into training, development, and testing sections. From the corpus, 1,000 articles were set aside as the development set, 2,000 were held out for testing, and the rest (13,979 articles in all) were used for the training of the subcategorisation lexicon. Ten sets of 1,000 sentences were randomly selected from the testing section, to be used for evaluation purposes.

2.2 Language Processing

We next applied the RASP system [3] sentence boundary detector, tokeniser and part-of-speech (PoS) tagger to the training corpus. The 13,979 articles gave rise to 251,805 sentences. On this corpus we estimate sentence segmentation and tagging accuracy to both be around 95%, and the tagger's guessing of unknown words to be 80% accurate. The lexical component of the ERG is based around word stems rather than inflected word forms. We therefore applied the RASP morphological analyser [4] to reduce inflected verbs and nouns to their base forms.

We used the RASP parser to syntactically analyse the corpus. The parser uses a manually written "shallow" unification grammar of PoS tags and contains a statistical disambiguation model that selects the structurally most plausible syntactic analysis. The parser by default does not contain any word co-occurrence information, which makes it suitable for use in a system that acquires lexical information. The parser can recover from extra-grammaticality by returning partial analyses, which is essential for the processing of real-world data. The parser produces output that indicating the verb frame for each clause and the heads of the complements of the verb. Prepositional complements are also represented if they occur. After parsing, 165,852 of the 251,805 sentences in the training section of the corpus produced at least one verb pattern. This means that about 65.9% of the corpus was useful data for the extraction of verb subcategorisation patterns.

3 Lexicon Construction

This phase consists of two stages: extraction of subcategorisation frames, and then mapping them to the ERG scheme.

3.1 Extraction of Subcategorisation Frames

This stage involves the extraction of all the observed frames for any particular verb. For this purpose, we used the subcategorisation acquisition system of Briscoe and Carroll [5] as enhanced by Korhonen [6] and applied it to all the verbal pattern sets extracted from the training section of the parsed corpus. There are thus three subcategorisation representations: the RASP grammar subcategorisation values used in the parsed corpus, the Briscoe and Carroll (B&C) classes produced by the acquisition system, and the ERG lexical types for the target grammar.

From the training section of the corpus, a total of 16,371 such frames were extracted with 4,295 unique verb stems. On average, each verb has 3.8 different frames.

3.2 Mapping Between RASP and ERG

The final stage in constructing the new ERG verb subcategorisation lexicon is the mapping of subcategorisation frames from the B&C scheme to the ERG scheme. The B&C scheme comprises a total of 163 possible subcategorisations, and the ERG scheme, 216. A B&C-to-ERG translation map was manually drawn up[2] and automatically applied to the acquired subcategorisation lexicon. 145 of the B&C sub-

---

[2] We are grateful to Dan Flickinger for providing us with this mapping.

categorisation frames map to 70 unique ERG lexical types, indicating a considerable degree of many-to-one matching. In the current mapping, for example, 9 different B&C frames are mapped to v_empty_prep_trans_le, the ERG type for verbs complemented by a prepositional phrase:

NP-FOR-NP	She bought a book for him.
NP-P-ING-OC	She accused him of being lazy.
NP-P-ING-SC	She wasted time on combing her hair.
NP-P-ING-AC	She told him about going to the park.
NP-P-NP-ING	She blamed it on no one buying it.
NP-P-POSSING	She asked him about his missing the train.
NP-P-WH-S	She asked whether she should go.
NP-P-WHAT-S	She asked what she should do.
NP-PP	She added salt to the food.

Conversely, 48 ERG lexical types do not have a B&C counterpart. Both schemes encode syntactic and semantic distinctions but it is evident that they do this in different ways.

The eventual lexicon contains 5,608 entries for 3,864 verb stems, an average of 1.45 entries per verb. See Figure 1 for entries acquired for the verb *accept* (where the lexical type v_np_trans_le represents a transitive entry and v_unerg_le an intransitive one).

```
Accept_rasp_v_np_trans_le := v_np_trans_le &
        [ STEM < "accept" > ] .
Accept_rasp_v_unerg_le := v_unerg_le &
        [ STEM < "accept" > ] .
```

Fig. 1. Entries Acquired for *accept*.

4 Lexical Coverage

We carried out a number of experiments to measure the impact of the subcategorisation lexicon on the performance of the HPSG parser. First of all, we wanted to determine whether the empirically extracted verb stems would enhance the lexical coverage of the grammar. Secondly, we wanted to see whether the empirically extracted verb entries would result in better parsing success rate, i.e., more sentences receiving an analysis by the parser. A third possibility is that the use of empirically extracted verb subcategorisations, when applied to text of the same subject domain, would produce more accurate analyses. However, our experiments to date have been limited to the evaluation of the first two. In addition, we investigated the impact of the acquired lexicon on system performance, as measured by parsing time and space.

For the first experiment, we collected and unified all the verb stems from three machine-readable lexicons: 5,453 from the machine-readable Oxford Advanced Learner's Dictionary (OALD), 5,654 from ComLex [7], and 1,126 from the ERG lexicon. These three lexicons jointly yielded a total of 6,341 verbs. Comparing the 3,864 mobile phone verbs with this joint list, there are a number of items that are not represented which thus can be considered to be particular to the mobile phone domain. Manual inspection of the list indicates that there seem to be three groups of verbs. First of all, verbs like *recognise*, *realise*, and *patronise* may have crept into the list as a result of British English spelling not being represented in the three sources. Secondly, we observe some neologisms such as *txt* and *msg*, which are almost exclusively used within the mobile phone domain. Finally, we observe verbs that have been derived from free combinations of prefixes and verb stems such as *re-install* and *xtnd-connect*. These observations suggest the importance of the inclusion of variant spellings, and empirical corpus-based selection of lexical items.

To measure the lexical coverage of these verb stems, ten sets of 1,000 randomly selected sentences each were used as testing material. For comparison, all the verb stems (1,126 in all) were extracted from the manually coded ERG lexicon. The results show that the hand-selected verb stems have an average coverage of 85.9% for verb tokens and 42.3% for verb types in the 10 test sets. In comparison, the empirically selected list has a much higher coverage of 94.4% in terms of tokens and 62.9% in terms of types. The average token coverage of the lexicon that would be produced by taking the union of the verbs in OALD and Comlex is 91%. There is considerable variation in the coverage by ERG verb stems across the ten test sets (SD=1.1) while the empirically selected verbs have a much more consistent coverage with a standard deviation of only 0.34. The high level and consistency of coverage by the empirically selected verb stems demonstrate the advantages of a corpus-based approach to lexical selection.

5 Parse Success Rate

In order to achieve tangible results through comparison, we compared the original version of the ERG with an enhanced version that incorporates the empirically extracted verb subcategorisations. For these experiments we used the efficient HPSG parser PET [8], launched from [incr tsdb()], an integrated package for evaluating parser and grammar performance on test suites [9]. For all of the experiments described in the following sections, we set a resource limit on the parser, restricting it to produce at most 40,000 chart edges.

The evaluation aimed at two scenarios: theoretical enhancements from the empirically extracted verb subcategorisations and realistic improvements. The former was an attempt to ascertain an upper bound on parser coverage independent of practical limitations of parser timeouts as a result of the increase in lexical ambiguity in the grammar. The latter was performed in order to establish the real enhancements given practical constraints such as available parsing space and time. The following sections describe these two experiments.

5.1 Theoretical Enhancement

Deep grammars tend to require large amounts of memory when parsing to accommodate rich intermediate representations and their combination. High levels of lexical ambiguity often result in parser timeouts and thus could affect the correct estimate of the enhancements afforded by the extracted verb subcategorisations. Whether PET produces an analysis for a test item is decided by several factors. While the coverage of the grammar plays a central role, lexical complexities may cause the parser to run out of memory. We therefore attempted to factor out effects caused by increased lexical ambiguity in the acquired lexicon. For this purpose, a set of 1,133 sentences were specially selected from the test corpus with the condition that all the verbs were represented in the ERG grammar. We then manipulated this sub-corpus, replacing all of the nouns by *sense*, adjectives by *nice*, and adverbs by *nicely*. In doing so, it was guaranteed that failure to produce an analysis by the parser was not due to lexical combinatorial problems. Any observable improvements could be unambiguously attributed to the extracted verb subcategorisations.

The average parse success rate of the ERG for the test set is 48.5%, with sentences of fewer than 5 words receiving the highest percentage of analysis (60.8%). Lexical ambiguity is about 3.6 entries per word (33.71/9.32). In contrast, the enhanced ERG achieved a parse success rate of 63.5%, an increase of 15 basis points over that achieved by the original grammar. This time, 85.7% of the sentences of fewer than 5 words have at least one analysis, an almost 25% increase over the coverage of the same group by the original grammar. This improvement was achieved at a considerable increase in lexical ambiguity, 6.98 entries per word versus 3.6 for the original grammar. Parsing speed dropped from one second per sentence to about 4 seconds per sentence[3], and the average space requirement increased from 4.8 MB to 13.4 MB.

It should be noted that many 'sentences' in the original test set do not conform to standard English grammar; the version of PET that we used does not contain a robustness component, so such sentences failed to get a parse. In addition, lexical substitution was applied only to words tagged by RASP as either adverbs, adjectives, and nouns; there remain still a large number of ill-formed words (e.g. *that*, *dfgh*, *17c*) that eventually caused parse failures. Moreover, the words we used for lexical substitution are not grammatical in all contexts so in some cases substitution actually reduced parser coverage. Therefore, the absolute coverage figures should **not** be taken as definitive. However, since both setups used the same set of substituted sentences these failures do not affect our measurement of the difference in coverage, the subject of this experiment.

5.2 Realistic Enhancement

For the second experiment, we used a test set of 1,000 sentences randomly selected from the original test corpus. Unlike the previous experiment, the sentences were not lexically reduced. Since PET requires that every input token be known to the grammar, we supplemented the grammar with an openclass lexicon of nouns, adjectives and adverbs. These additional openclass items were extracted from the training section of the mobile phone corpus (as tagged by RASP) and consisted of 29,328 nouns, 7,492 adjectives, and 2,159 adverbs, totalling 38,797 stems. To cater for lexical items in the test set that are still not represented in the extended lexicon, the RASP tagging system was used as a PoS pre-processor for the test set. Each input sentence is thus annotated with PoS tags for all the tokens. For any lexical item unknown to the grammar, PET falls back to the PoS tag assigned automatically by RASP and applies an appropriate generic lexical description for the unknown word.

For this experiment, again, we have two grammars. The baseline statistics were obtained with the original handcrafted ERG grammar supplemented by the additional openclass items in the noun, adjective, and adverb classes. The enhanced grammar is additionally supplemented with the extracted verb subcategorisations. As indicated in

---

[3] There are 10 sentences which disproportionally increase the average. This appears to be due to errors in the subcategorisations for a few common words such as *ask*.

Table 1[4], the original ERG grammar scored an average parse success rate of 52.9% with the space limit of 40,000 edges. Four test items had to be deleted from the test set since they consistently caused the parser to crash. The actual success rate is 52.7%.

The same version of the ERG grammar was then integrated with the automatically extracted verb subcategorisations and the augmented version was applied to the same set of test sentences with the same system settings. As shown in Table 2, the enhanced grammar had 57.3% coverage, an increase of 4.4% over the original grammar without the automatically extracted verb subcategorisations.

We thus calculate the overall coverage enhancement as 4.4%. As in our previous experiment, we observed an expected increase in lexical ambiguity due to the increase of lexical items in the lexicon, up from 3.05 entries per word to 4.87. CPU time increased from 9.78 seconds per string for the original grammar to 21.78 for the enhanced grammar, with space requirements increasing from 45 MB to 55 MB.

Table 1. Realistic Coverage of the ERG.

Aggregate	total items #	positive items #	word string ø	lexical items ø	parser analyses ø	total results #	overall coverage %
l-length in [95 .. 100]	1	1	98.00	384.00	0.00	0	0.0
l-length in [75 .. 80]	2	2	79.00	0.00	0.00	0	0.0
l-length in [65 .. 70]	2	2	66.50	0.00	0.00	0	0.0
l-length in [60 .. 65]	2	2	61.00	226.00	0.00	0	0.0
l-length in [55 .. 60]	6	6	57.83	217.50	0.00	0	0.0
l-length in [50 .. 55]	6	6	52.50	168.33	0.00	0	0.0
l-length in [45 .. 50]	9	9	46.89	152.20	0.00	0	0.0
l-length in [40 .. 45]	12	12	41.50	152.00	0.00	0	0.0
l-length in [35 .. 40]	20	20	36.85	135.54	14450.67	3	15.0
l-length in [30 .. 35]	40	40	32.00	112.57	13822.00	4	10.0
l-length in [25 .. 30]	69	69	26.75	93.02	28522.00	16	23.2
l-length in [20 .. 25]	103	103	21.72	76.78	21720.29	35	34.0
l-length in [15 .. 20]	171	171	16.85	56.73	2009.83	81	47.4
l-length in [10 .. 15]	186	186	12.01	41.22	590.75	114	61.3
l-length in [5 .. 10]	243	243	7.09	21.71	87.99	172	70.8
l-length in [0 .. 5]	124	124	2.64	6.92	1.22	102	82.3
Total	996	996	15.42	47.04	2961.29	527	52.9

---

[4] The colums in Tables 2 and 3 contain the following information:
- Aggregate — sentence length breakdown
- Total items — number of sentences
- Positive items — sentences seen by the parser
- Word string — average number of words
- Lexical items — average number of lexical entries
- Parser analyses — average number of analyses
- Total results — total number of successfully parsed sentences
- Overall coverage — percentage of successfully parsed sentences

Table 2. Realistic Coverage of the Enhanced Grammar.

Aggregate	total items #	positive items #	word string ∅	lexical items ∅	parser analyses ∅	total results #	overall coverage %
i-length in [95 .. 100]	1	1	98.00	611.00	0.00	0	0.0
i-length in [75 .. 80]	2	2	79.00	407.00	0.00	0	0.0
i-length in [65 .. 70]	2	2	66.50	0.00	0.00	0	0.0
i-length in [60 .. 65]	2	2	61.00	341.00	0.00	0	0.0
i-length in [55 .. 60]	6	6	57.83	310.25	0.00	0	0.0
i-length in [50 .. 55]	6	6	52.50	265.50	0.00	0	0.0
i-length in [45 .. 50]	9	9	46.89	252.14	0.00	0	0.0
i-length in [40 .. 45]	12	12	41.50	236.56	52416.00	1	8.3
i-length in [35 .. 40]	22	22	36.86	200.67	220684.50	4	18.2
i-length in [30 .. 35]	40	40	32.00	161.66	22463.00	8	20.0
i-length in [25 .. 30]	70	70	26.76	140.51	12530.50	20	28.6
i-length in [20 .. 25]	103	103	21.72	112.88	11943.80	45	43.7
i-length in [15 .. 20]	171	171	16.85	86.07	1794.16	97	56.7
i-length in [10 .. 15]	186	186	12.01	59.87	413.61	126	67.7
i-length in [5 .. 10]	243	243	7.09	33.41	19.31	167	68.7
i-length in [0 .. 5]	124	124	2.64	10.49	1.19	104	83.9
Total	999	999	15.47	75.31	3728.04	572	57.3

6 Conclusion

We presented a novel approach to improving the robustness of deep parsing, through the unsupervised acquisition of a verb subcategorisation lexicon. The acquired information helps deep parsing to produce detailed logical form representations that shallow analysers are unable to.

We described the construction of a corpus in our target mobile phone domain, and the acquisition of verb subcategorisations from the corpus through shallow processing with the RASP system. The empirically selected verb stems show enhanced lexical coverage of 94.4% against the 85.9% achieved by an existing handcrafted list of verb stems.

We then reported experiments to establish theoretical and practical gains from the use of extracted verb subcategorisations. When tested with 1,133 lexically reduced sentences, we observed that the enhanced grammar had 15% better coverage than the original grammar. Under practical constraints of parsing space and time, the enhanced grammar had an overall parse success rate of 57.3%, a 4.4% increase over the original grammar.

In our experiments, we used a completely automatic process to augment an existing hand-crafted lexicon. If manual effort is available, a good strategy would be for a linguist to check the acquired entries before they are added to the lexicon.

In future work we will implement a process that intelligently filters verb entries for words that already have entries in the lexicon; this should lead to a smaller lexicon, higher parse success rates and reduced parsing time and space. We will also refine acquired entries that require the explicit declaration of the heads of prepositional phrase complements. We also intend to investigate whether automatically extracted verb subcategorisations are capable of improving the accuracy of analyses proposed by the parser, perhaps taking advantage of the frequency information that is also collected in the acquisition process.

Acknowledgements

This research was supported by EU project Deep Thought IST-2001-37836. We would like to thank the Deep Thought project team, and in particular Ann Copestake, Dan Flickinger and Stephan Oepen for helpful suggestions and comments on earlier drafts. We are also grateful to Stephan Oepen for technical assistance, and to Anna Korhonen for providing us with her subcategorisation acquisition system.

References

1. Pollard, C. and I. Sag. 1994. *Head-Driven Phrase Structure Grammar.* Chicago University Press.
2. Copestake, A. and D. Flickinger. 2000. An open-source grammar development environment and broad-coverage English grammar using HPSG. In *Proceedings of LREC 2000*, Athens, Greece.
3. Briscoe, E. and J. Carroll. 2002. Robust accurate statistical annotation of general text. In *Proceedings of the 3rd International Conference on Language Resources and Evaluation*, Las Palmas, Gran Canaria. 1499–1504.
4. Minnen, G., J. Carroll and D. Pearce. 2001. Applied morphological processing of English. *Natural Language Engineering,* 7(3). 207-223.
5. Briscoe, E. and J. Carroll. 1997. Automatic extraction of subcategorization from corpora. In *Proceedings of the 5th ACL Conference on Applied Natural Language Processing,* Washington, DC. 356–363.
6. Korhonen, A. 2002. *Subcategorization Acquisition.* PhD thesis published as *Techical Report UCAM-CL-TR-530.* Computer Laboratory, University of Cambridge.
7. Grishman, R., C. Macleod and A. Meyers. 1994. Comlex syntax: Building a computational lexicon. In *Proceedings of the 15th International Conference on Computational Linguistics,* Kyoto, Japan. 268–272.
8. Callmeier, U. 2000. PET – A platform for experimentation with efficient HPSG processing techniques. *Natural Language Engineering,* 6(1) (Special Issue on Efficient Processing with HPSG):99–108.
9. Oepen, S. 1999. *[incr tsdb()]: Competence and Performance Laboratory: User & Reference Manual,* Computational Linguistics, Saarland University, Saarbrücken, Germany.

Chinese Treebanks and Grammar Extraction

Keh-Jiann Chen and Yu-Ming Hsieh

Institute of Information Science, Academia Sinica, Nankang, Taipei
{kchen,morris}@iis.sinica.edu.tw

Abstract. Preparation of knowledge bank is a very difficult task. In this paper, we discuss the knowledge extraction from the manually examined Sinica Treebank. Categorical information, word-to-word relation, word collocations, new syntactic patterns and sentence structures are obtained. A searching system for Chinese sentence structure was developed in this study. By using pre-extracted data and SQL commands, the system replies the user's queries efficiently. We also analyze the extracted grammars to study the tradeoffs between the granularity of the grammar rules and their coverage as well as ambiguities. It provides the information of knowing how large a treebank is sufficient for the purpose of grammar extraction. Finally, we also analyze the tradeoffs between grammar coverage and ambiguity by parsing results from the grammar rules of different granularity.

Keywords: treebanks, knowledge extraction, grammar coverage, ambiguities, parsing.

1 Introduction

Parsing natural language sentences makes use of many different knowledge sources, such as lexical, syntax, semantic, and common sense knowledge [5, 14]. Preparation of knowledge bank is a very difficult task, since there are vast amount of knowledge and they are not well organized [15]. The Corpus-based approach provided a way of automatically extract different knowledge. From part-of-speech tagged corpora [3, 6, 8] to the syntactic structure annotated treebanks [12], each contributes explicit linguistic knowledge at different level for better automation on knowledge extraction. Treebanks provide an easy way for extracting grammar rules and their occurrence probability. In addition, word-to-word relations [2, 13] are also precisely associated. Hence it raises the following important issues. How will treebanks be used? How many annotated tree structures are sufficient in a treebank for the purpose of grammar generation? What are tradeoffs between grammar coverage and ambiguities? We will try to answer the above questions in the following sections.

1.1 Introduction to Sinica Treebank

Sinica Treebank has been developed and released to public since 2000 by Chinese Knowledge Information Processing (CKIP) group at Academia Sinica. Sinica Treebank version 1.1 (9 files) contains 38944 structural trees and 240,979 words in Chinese. Each structural tree is annotated with words, part-of-speech of words, syntactic structure brackets, and thematic roles. For conventional structural trees, only syntactic information was annotated. However, it is very important and yet difficult for Chinese

> 他叫李四撿球
> Ta jiao Li-si jian qiu.
> He ask Lisi pick ball.
> "He asked Lisi to pick up the ball."
>
> S(agent:NP(Head:Nhaa:Ta'He')|Head:VF2:jiao'ask'|goal:NP(Head:Nba:Li-si)|theme:VP(Head: VC2: jian 'pick'| goal:NP(Head:Nab:qui'ball')))

Fig. 1. An example

to identify word relations with purely syntactic constraints [16]. On the other hand, a purely semantic approach has never been attempted for theoretical and practical considerations [7]. Thus, partial semantic information was annotated in Chinese structural trees. That is, grammatical constraints are expressed in terms of linear order of thematic roles and their syntactic and semantic restrictions.

The representation of the dependency tree, as in Fig. 1, has the advantages of maintaining phrase structure rules as well as the syntactic and semantic dependency relations [6].

2 Uses of Treebanks and Grammar Extraction

Here we intend to find the useful information behind Sinica Treebank and transfer it into a formatted knowledge that the language analyzer can use.

2.1 Knowledge Extraction from Treebanks

From Sinica Treebank, four different types of information were extracted. They are a) Lexical and categorical information, b) Word-to-Word relations, c) Word Bi-grams, and d) Grammar rules.

A searching system of using the above four information has been developed. Users can use this searching system via a web browser at http://treebank.sinica.edu.tw/. The searching system architecture is shown in Fig. 2.

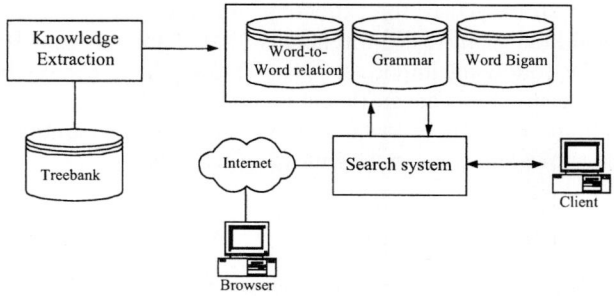

Fig. 2. The Tree-Searching system

The system provides the users with "Keyword Search" and "Sentence structure search" functions. The system can perform filtering and aggregating on the searching results.

By using the Treebank Searching System, we also found some annotation errors in the original treebank. Such information can be obtained from the statistical data of syntactic category and role. Therefore, the original content of the trees were corrected to improve the quality of the annotation.

2.2 Uses of the Extracted Information

Text annotation is for the purpose of making implicit knowledge in documents more explicit. Structure annotations, in particular, make the grammatical relations of a sentence explicit. The uses of each type of the extracted information from treebank are exemplified below.

Supposed that we want to know what grammatical functions of a syntactic category are, say VC2 (active transitive verb). We can search for the lexical/categorical data and get the results of Table 1. It shows that the active transitive verbs (VC2) will play the role of sentential head mostly. They occurred 8389 times in the treebank. The verb VC2 also functions as modifier of noun (property role), predication of a relative clause, and surprisingly adverbial manner role. The roles of DUMMY are conjuncts of conjunctive constructions.

Table 1. The thematic roles played by the verb type VC2

Role	Frequency	Role	Frequency
Head	8389	property	10
DUMMY1	27	Predication	10
DUMMY2	26	manner	10

The extracted word-to-word relations are mostly head-modifier and head-argument relations, which are also instances of world knowledge. For example, we can extract the knowledge of what entities are eatable from the argument of the verb 'eat'. Collocations are very useful information for lexicography and NLP. If we sort the extracted word-to-word relations, the most frequent relations are listed in Table 2. We also find some interesting linguistic patterns uniquely for Chinese language.

Table 2. Some common collocations found by word-to-word relations

Left word	Right word	Frequency
在 (zai)	中 (zhong)	348
在 (zai)	上 (shang)	318
是 (shi)	的 (de)	201
是 (shi)	就 (jiu)	183
...	...	...

Word bi-gram statistics is often the major information for constructing language model [11, 17]. Some other interesting information can also be extracted. For instance, to identify personal names in Chinese text their context information is very useful. Following table shows the collocations of proper names (PN) and most of them are titles of people.

Table 3. Words frequently co-occurred with PN.

Category	Word	Freq.	Category	Word	Freq.
DE	的 (de)	373	VE2	表示 (biao shi)	95
P21	在 (zai)	132	Nab	總統 (zong tong)	43
Cab	等 (deng)	86	Nab	教練 (jiao lian)	25
Caa	和 (he)	79	...	...	...

Grammar rule extraction is the major usage of Treebanks. Not only sentential/phrasal patterns but also their probabilities of usages can be derived as exemplified in Table 4. The probabilistic context-free grammars are proven to be very effective for parsing natural languages [10].

Table 4. The top 5 high frequency sentential patterns of the active transitive verb (VC2)

Rule	Freq.
Head-VC2 goal-NP	1713
Head-VC2	629
agent-NP Head-VC2 goal-NP	316
Head-VC2 goal-NP complement-VP	190
agent-NP Head-VC2	153

3 Grammar Coverage and Ambiguities

One of the major purposes of construction of treebanks is for grammar extraction. Probabilistic phrase structure rules can be derived from treebanks. However how many annotated tree structures are sufficient for the purpose of grammar generation? What are tradeoffs between the granularity of grammar representation and grammar coverage as well as ambiguities? We try to answer the above questions in this section.

3.1 Granularity vs. Grammar Coverage

In order to see how the size of treebank affects the quality of the grammar extraction, we use treebanks in different sizes and in different levels of granularities to extract grammars and then compare their coverage and ambiguous rates. The four levels of grammar representations are from fine-grain representation to coarse-grain representation. For example, the extracted lexical units and grammar rules of the tree in Fig. 1 are listed as follows. At fine-grain level each lexical unit is a thematic role constraint by the word and its phrasal category. Each rule is represented by a sequence of lexical/categorical units. At the three lower level representations, the lexical units are syntactic category based. The set of categories are from Case-2 fine-grain categories to Case-4 coarse-grain categories. Each lexical unit is a thematic role constraint by the lexical category and phrasal category.

Case-1: Fine-Grain Level (Word-Level)
S(agent:NP()|jiao|goal:NP()|theme:VP()), agent:NP(Ta),
goal:NP(Li-si),
theme:VP(jian|goal:NP()),
goal:NP(qiu)

Case-2: Category Level
S(agent:NP()|VF2|goal:NP()|theme:VP()), agent:NP(Nhaa),
goal:NP(Nba),
theme:VP(VC2|goal:NP()),
goal:NP(Nab)

Case-3: Simplified-Category Level
S(agent:NP()|VF|goal:NP()|theme:VP()), agent:NP(Nh),
goal:NP(Nb),
theme:VP(VC|goal:NP()),
goal:NP(Na)

Case-4: Coarse-Grain Level
S(agent:NP()|V|goal:NP()|theme:VP()), agent:NP(N),
goal:NP(N),
theme:VP(V|goal:NP()),
goal:NP(N)

It is clear that fine-grain grammar representation would have less grammar representational ambiguity, but with lower grammar coverage. On the other hand, the coarse-grain grammar representation is more ambiguous but with better coverage. The experiments were carried out to show the above-mentioned tradeoffs.

In order to answer the question of how many annotated tree structures are sufficient for the purpose of grammar generation, the grammar extraction processes were carried out on the treebanks of four different sizes, each with 10000, 20000, 30000, and 38725 trees. We exam the grammar coverage of each set of rules extracted from the treebanks of different sizes. For each treebank, we divide the treebank into ten equal parts. For example, we obtain $db_1^1...db_1^{10}$ from the treebank db_1 of size 10000 trees. Each part has 1000 trees. The grammar coverage was estimated as follows. For each part, we analyze its coverage rate by the grammar extracted from other 9 parts and average 10 coverage rates to be the coverage rate of the grammar derived from the experimental treebank. The grammar coverage experiments were carried out for all four different sizes of treebanks and for four different levels of granularities. The results are shown in Table 5 and depicted in Fig. 3.

The results indicate that as we expected the fine-grain rules have the least coverage rate, while the coarse-grain rules have the highest coverage rate. The coverage rate increases when the size of treebank increases. Since they are not in linear proportion, it is hard to predict exactly how large amount of trees are required in order to derive grammar rules with sufficient coverage. However, the result did show us that the size

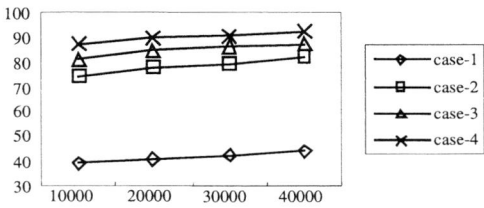

Fig. 3. Coverage rates vs. size of treebanks

Table 5. Grammar coverage rates

Level \ Size	10000	20000	30000	40000
Case-1	38.97%	40.67%	42.25%	43.95%
Case-2	74.28%	78.15%	80.08%	81.91%
Case-3	81.75%	84.56%	86.31%	87.71%
Case-4	87.67%	89.92%	91.14%	92.2%

of current treebank is not large enough to derive a fine-grain rule set with high coverage rate. Only the coarse-grain rules can reach up to 92.2% coverage rate, but the coarse-grain rules suffer from high ambiguity rates.

3.2 Granularity vs. Ambiguities

We intend to measure the ambiguity rate of a set of grammar rules from parsing point of view. A parsing process needs to decide the thematic role of each lexical token and decide which rules to apply. Therefore a simple way of measuring ambiguity of a grammar representation is to see how many possible thematic roles for each lexical item may played and how many different rules contains this token in the grammar representation. We consider four levels of granularities as defined in the above section. The lexical item for four levels of granularity are "Category:Word", "Category", "Simplified-Category", and "Coarse-grain Category" respectively. We use the grammar extracted from the whole treebank as the target of investigation. For four different levels of granularities, Table 6 shows the number of ambiguous roles in average played by each lexical item and the average number of grammatical rules partially matched a particular lexical item. The results did support the claim that fine-grain grammar representation would have less grammar representational ambiguity and the coarse-grain grammar representation is more ambiguous but with better coverage.

Table 6. Role ambiguities of the lexical item of the form Category:Word

Level \ Event	# of lexical items	Role ambiguities	# of grammatical rules	Rule ambiguities
*1	38,927	1.19	82,221	2.69
*2	190	3.08	24,111	132.47
*3	47	5.23	15,788	350.84
*4	12	9.06	10,024	835.30

*1: Category:Word, *2: Category, *3: Simplified-Category, *4: Coarse-grain Category

4 Parsing Results

The probabilistic context-free parsing strategies were used in our experiments [1, 9, 11]. Extraction of PCFG rules from a treebank is straightforward and we use maximum likelihood estimation to estimate the rule probabilities, as in [1]:

$$\hat{P}(N^i \rightarrow \xi^j) = \frac{C(N^i \rightarrow \xi^j)}{\sum_k C(N^i \rightarrow \xi^k)}$$

Based on the maximum likelihood estimation, we calculate the probabilities of rules in the four levels which are extracted form the 38,944 trees. The PCFG Parser uses these probabilities as its foundation. The standard evaluation and explanation of the parsing result is mentioned in [11]. The following table shows the result in terms of LP(Labeled Precision), LR(Labeled Recall), LF(Labeled F-measure), BP(Bracket Precision), BR(Bracket Recall), BF(Bracket F-measure), GC(Rule Coverage-rate). Note that a label contains not only syntactic category but also thematic role of a constituent. In addition, the evaluations restricted on the results for valid outputs only are also provided, i.e. without counting the sentences which have no valid parsing results. They are LF-1 and BF-1.

$$LP = \frac{\# \text{ correct constituents in parser's parse of S}}{\# \text{ constituents in treebank's parse of S}}$$

$$LR = \frac{\# \text{ correct constituents in parser's parse of S}}{\# \text{ constituents in parser's parse of S}}$$

$$F - measure = \frac{\text{Precision} * \text{Recall} * 2}{\text{Precision} + \text{Recall}}$$

The parser adopts a Earley's Algorithm. We modify the representation of the data in order to be applicable in our Sinica Treebank. Two testing data, EV-7 and EV-8, are randomly selected from newly developed Treebank outside of Sinica Treebank Version 1.1. Table 7 and 8 show results of the parsing evaluation respectively.

Table 7. EV-7 Result (38944 training, 842 testing)

Ev-7	Case-1	Case-2	Case-3	Case-4
GC	50.59	89.41	93.33	95.98
NP	*	10.33	0.71	0
LR	*	73.03	75.31	59.24
LP	*	71.29	74.53	60.92
LF	*	72.15	74.91	60.07
LF-1	*	80.46	75.45	60.21
BR	*	83.70	91.47	83.80
BP	*	80.48	89.70	85.74
BF	*	82.06	90.58	84.76
BF-1	*	91.51	91.23	84.96

Table 8. EV-8 Result (38944 training, 908 testing)

Ev-8	Case-1	Case-2	Case-3	Case-4
GC	48.59	88.26	93.07	95.74
NP	*	9.36	0.44	0
LR	*	71.75	75.79	60.78
LP	*	69.5	74.90	62.16
LF	*	70.73	75.34	61.46
LF-1	*	78.04	75.68	61.46
BR	*	83.97	91.83	84.02
BP	*	79.53	89.77	86.42
BF	*	81.69	90.79	85.20
BF-1	*	90.13	91.19	85.20

From Table 7 and 8, we can see that Case-4 has highest grammar coverage (GC), but lowest LF and BF due to higher rule-ambiguities. For the Case-2 model, LF-1 has the best result of 80.46%. However, 10.33% of the sentences are not able to be parsed due to the lower coverage of grammar rules. Case-3 model achieves the best overall performance for its balancing in rule coverage, rule precision and ambiguity. Therefore, the granularity of the rules contributes to the parser accuracy. In general, finer-grained models outperform coarser-grain models, but they also suffer the problem of low grammar coverage. The better parsing performance should be stretched by using more knowledge other than rule probabilities and by considering tradeoffs between grammar coverage and precision.

5 Conclusions and Future Work

Text annotation is for the purpose of making implicit knowledge in documents more explicit and thus the annotated documents will be easy for processing knowledge extraction. Treebanks provide an easy way of extracting grammar rules and their occurrence probability. In addition, head-modifier and head-argument relations provide the knowledge which is hardly acquired manually. However in our study we also show that for better grammar extraction, a much larger size treebank is required. To construct a very large manually edited treebank is time consuming. We suggest that the knowledge extraction process can be carried out iteratively. The parser can use the coarse-grain grammar and category-to-category relations, which are generalized from word-to-word relations, to produce large amount of automatically parsed trees. The category-to-category relations help to resolve ambiguity of coarse-grain grammar. The newly parsed trees would not produce any new grammar pattern, but they do provide lots of new word-to-word relations. The newly learned relations will increase the knowledge of the parser and hence increase the power of parsing. The whole iteration process can be viewed as a automatic knowledge learning system.

In this study, we also designed a Treebank Searching system. The system provides the users with "Keyword Search" and "Sentence structure search". Users can further process filtering and aggregating the results within a designated range. By using the Treebank Searching System, we also found some annotation errors in the original treebank. Such information can be discovered from the low frequency syntactic patterns. Therefore, the original treebank is improved after the discovered errors were corrected.

The grammar extraction experiments were carried out. The results indicate that the fine-grain rules have the least coverage rate, while the coarse-grain rules have the higher coverage rate. The coverage rate increases when the size of treebank increases. The fine-grain grammar has less representational ambiguity and the coarse-grain grammar is more ambiguous.

The parsing results reveal that there is plenty of room for exalting the tree bracketing. The relation-knowledge and function word characteristics may help to resolve the some construction ambiguity. We will aim at the individual word and category property and try to increase rule coverage rate by hybrid using Category Level and Simplified Category Level. Our future goal is to improve the parsing rate and maintain the high performance of the parser.

References

1. E. Charniak. 1996. *Treebank grammars.* Technical Report CS-96-02, Department of Computer Science, Brown University.
2. Keh-Jiann Chen. 1992. *Design Concepts for Chinese Parsers.* 3rd International Conference on Chinese Information Processing, pp.1-22.
3. Keh-Jiann Chen, Shing-Huan Liu, Li-ping Chang, and Yeh-Hao Chin. 1994a. *A Practical Tagger for Chinese Corpora.* Proceedings of ROCLING VII, pp.111-126.
4. Keh-Jiann Chen and Chu-Ren Huang. 1994b. *Features Constraints in Chinese Language Parsing.* Proceedings of ICCPOL '94, pp. 223-228.
5. Keh-Jiann Chen. 1996a. *A Model for Robust Chinese Parser.* Computational Linguistics and Chinese Language Processing, 1(1):13-204.
6. Keh-Jiann Chen, Chu-Ren Huang, Li-Ping Chang, Hui-Li Hsu. 1996b. *Sinica Corpus: Design Methodology for Balanced Corpra.* Proceedings of the 11th Pacific Asia Conference on Language, Information, and Computation (PACLIC II), Seoul Korea, pp.167-176.
7. Feng-Yi Chen, Pi-Fang Tsai, Keh-Jiann Chen, and Chu-Ren Huang. 2000. *Sinica Treebank. [in Chinese].* Computational Linguistics and Chinese Language Processing, 4(2):87-103.
8. CKIP (Chinese Knowledge Information Processing). 1993. *The Categorical Analysis of Chinese. [in Chinese].* CKIP Technical Report 93-05. Nankang: Academia Sinica.
9. M. Collins. 1999. *Head-Driven Statistical Models for Natural Language parsing.* Ph.D. thesis, Univ. of Pennsylvania.
10. G. Gazdar, E. Klein, G..K. Pullum, and I. A. Sag. 1985. *Generalized Phrase Structure Grammar.* Cambridge: Blackwell, and Cambridge, Mass: Harvard University Press.
11. Christopher D. Manning and Hinrich Schutze. 1999. *Foundations of Statistical Natural Language Processing.* the MIT Press, Cambridge, Massachusetts.
12. Mitchell Marcus, Beatrice Santorini, and Mary Ann Marcinkiewicz. 1993. *Building a large annotated corpus of English: The PENN Treebank.* Computational Linguistics, 19(2):313-330.
13. C. Pollard and I. A. Sag. 1994. *Head-Driven Phrase Structure Grammar.* Stanford: Center for the Study of Language and Information, Chicago Press.
14. J. Pustejovsky. 1995. *The Generative Lexicon.* MIT Press.
15. Shin-shyeng Tseng, Meng-yuan Chang, Chin-Chun Hsieh, and Keh-jiann Chen. 1988. *Approaches on An Experimental Chinese Electronic Dictionary.* Proceedings of 1988 International Conference on Computer Processing of Chinese and Oriental Languages, pp. 371-74.
16. Fei Xia, Martha Palmer, Nianwen Xue, Mary Ellen Okurowski, John Kovarik, Fu-Dong Chiou, Shizhe Huang, Tony Kroch, and Mitch Marcus. 2000. *Developing Guidelines and Ensuring Consistency for Chinese Text Annotation.* Proceedings of the second International Conference on Language Resources and Evaluation (LREC-2000), Athens, Greece.
17. Yao Yuan and Lua Kim Teng, 1997. *Mutual Information and Trigram Based Merging for Grammar Rule Induction and Sentence parsing.* Computer Processing of Oriental Languages, 11(2):177-190.

FML-Based SCF Predefinition Learning for Chinese Verbs

Xiwu Han, Tiejun Zhao, and Muyun Yang

Harbin Institute of Technology, Harbin City, Heilongjiang Province, 150001, China
{hxw,tjzhao,ymy}@mtlab.hit.edu.cn
http://mtlab.hit.edu.cn

Abstract. This paper describes the first attempt to acquire Chinese SCFs automatically and the application of Flexible Maximum Likelihood (FML), a variational filtering method of the simple maximum likelihood (ML) estimate from observed relative frequencies, to the task of predefining a basic SCF set for Chinese verb subcategorization acquisition. By setting a flexible threshold for SCF probability distributions over 1774 Chinese verbs, we obtained 141 basic SCFs with a reasonably practical coverage of 98.64% over 43,000 Chinese sentences. After complementation of 11 manually observed SCFs, a both linguistically and intuitively acceptable basic SCF set was predefined for future SCF acquisition work.

1 Introduction

Subcategorization is the process that further classifies a syntactic category into its subsets. Chomsky (1965) defines the function of strict subcategorization features as appointing a set of constraints that dominate the selection of verbs and other arguments in deep structure. Subcategorization of verbs, as well as categorization of all words in a language, is often implemented by means of their involved functional distributions, which constitute different environments accessible for a verb or word. Such a distribution or environment is called one subcategorization frame (SCF), usually integrated with both syntactic and semantic information. Since verbs are mostly the central pegs for various syntactic relations to hang on, lexicons with verb subcategory specified have always been one of the most desirable outcomes of traditional linguistics, and have become a research focus of NLP since Brent (1991).

One of the most important preconditions for SCF acquisition is the definition of a basic SCF set, which actually consists of and formally describes both the objects and results of the acquiring process. In this paper we refer to the process of defining a basic SCF set as SCF predefinition, and that of automatically or semi-automatically acquiring by means of statistics as SCF predefinition learning. Most researches on English verb subcategorization made SCF predefinition, but resources of previously predefined basic SCF sets are mainly syntactic dictionaries, or manually acquired data, or both. For example, Briscoe and Carroll (1997) and Korhonen (2001) manually combined SCFs in ANLT and COMLEX into their basic set, which in turn was complemented with a small part of observed unclassifiable syntactic patterns. And according to our knowledge no research on SCF predefinition learning has been presented till the time being.

As far as we know, this is the first attempt to acquire Chinese SCFs automatically. Relevant researches on Chinese verbs are generally limited to case grammar, valency, some semantic computation theories, and a few papers on manual acquisition or prescriptive designation of syntactic patterns. Due to irrelevant initial motivations, syntactic and semantic generalizabilities of the consequent outputs are not in such a harmony that satisfies the description granularity for SCF. For instances, Chinese sentence patterns provided by Lu (2000) and Lin (1998) are generally based on case information with comparatively too strong semantic while too weak syntactic generalization, and those of Zhan (2000) and Jin (2000) based on augmented valency features on the contrary are syntactically more generalized than required by the task.

Further more, it is difficult for subcategorization acquisition preconditioned with results of manual works to get rid of the consequent weak points, i.e. bad consistency, strong subjecttivity, small coverage, and uneasiness in modification or augmentation. Therefore, for the future task of Chinese verb subcategorization this paper brings forth an unsupervised method of statistically predefining a basic SCF set from a corpus of 43,000 comparatively simple Chinese sentences.

In the rest of this paper, we illustrate our verb syntactic frames for Chinese SCF in section 2. Section 3 simply describes the preparation for data and processing tools. Section 4 details our experiment on the filtering method of FML and section 5 presents the learned SCF predefinition. Section 6 gives conclusion for the results and prospects our future work.

2 Syntactic Frames for Chinese SCF

Early studies on modern Chinese grammar more often than not model from Aryan grammar templates, hence neglecting to some degree the lexical morphological differences between western and oriental languages, which has caused the dilemma in Chinese categorization. Recently both traditional and computational linguists have turned to functional distributions when specifying the classes of Chinese words (Bai, 1995), but words, such as "ai1zhe"(挨着),"ai2ma3"(挨骂), "song4gei3"(送给), "xing4zhang1"(姓张), and "zuo4lezuo4"(坐了坐), are regarded as verb phrases in some theories while as verbs in others. Therefore, verbs that will occur in our present SCF research consist only of those elemental ones, while excluding those derived or compound ones.

Chinese verb SCF, as generally defined, should formalize the external information of syntactic functions, i.e. observable syntactic features, which are summed up from linguistic theories as following items: 1) functioning as the predicate or head of the predicate phrase; 2) governing none or one or two objects; 3) when modified by adverbials often behaving variously yet regularly; 4) taking quantifiers, adjective phrases or/and prepositional phrases as complements; 5) realizing aspects often by "zhe" (着); "le"(了); and "guo4"(过), which are usually named as generalized syntactic functional morphemes; 6) taking "shang4"(上),

"qu4"(去), "chu1"(出), "xia4lai"(下来), etc. as complements, showing concrete or abstract tendency of the event concerned; 7) immediate repeating (vv) or interval repeating (v...v), often with information of aspect or mood; 8) being followed by other verbs with no lexical inflective transformation; 9) regularly alternating between normal patterns and passive, emphasized, or raised ones; 10) sometimes governing no nominal phrases as subjects; 11) sometimes segregated by external modifiers.

Consequently, SCF for Chinese verbs can be described as a quintuple grammar $< V, T_A, N_A, P_A, C_L >$, which is context-sensitive to some extent. Herein and below, for Chinese verbs i) V is a set of verbs capable of filling in the predicate slot; ii) T_A is a set of argument types, and T_A = {NP, VP, QP, BP, PP, BAP, BIP, TP, MP, JP, S} (See Table 1);iii) N_A is a set of numbers of argument slots; iv) P_A is the set of positions for argument slots; v) CL is the set of constant labels that may be added to some particular SCF, and CL = { "zhe"(着), "le"(了), "guo4"(过), "mei2"(没), "bu4"(不)}, where the first three furnish SCF aspects and the last two offer negation options.

Table 1. Argument Types.

T_A	Definition
NP	Nominal phrase
VP	Verbal phrase
QP	Tendency verbal complement
BP	Resulting verbal complement
PP	Positional phrase
BAP	Phrase headed by "ba3" (把)
BIP	Phrase headed by "bei4" (被) or other characters with passive sense
TP	Temporal phrase
MP	Quantifier complement
JP	Adjective or adverb or "de" (得) headed complement
S	Clause or sentence

For the reason of more maneuverability, four basic principles are established for the work of Chinese verb SCF formalization, i.e. a) in consistency with international SCF conventions as much as possible; b) with generality about Chinese verbs' syntactic behaviors as much as possible; c) of compatibility towards present criteria employed by NLP tools; d) arguments co-occur with the predicate in greater probability than adjuncts do. Besides, in conformance with our observation on linguistic behaviors of Chinese verbs, and in order to distinguish arguments from adjuncts, we prescribe some constraints or rules over the occurrence of each of the five tuples in an SCF, as shown in Table 2.

Table 2. Relative Rules SCF Description.

Tuples	Rules
V	Only one v ($v \in V$) except in repeating alternatives with one **v** but two slots.
NP	No more than two in a series and no more than three in one SCF.
VP, S	No serial occurrences.
QP, BP, JP	No serial occurrences and only occurring after v.
BAP, BIP	No more than one occurrence.
TP, PP	No co-occurrences with NP before v.
MP	No serial occurrences nor presence in adjacency before NP.
N_A and P_A	Shady elements without substantial presence in SCF.
CL	Notated as a binary vector, e.g. 01110^a.

[a] Here {01110} means that the given SCF takes perfect aspect "le" and experiential aspect "guo4", while doesn't take progressive aspect "zhe"; and can be negated with "mei2", while not with "bu4".

3 Data Preparation and Processing Tools

The task of predefining basic SCF set equals that of acquiring SCFs from corpora without predefinition, so it is important for high-precision SCF hypotheses generated from given corpus to ensure reasonable coverage or recall of predefined SCFs over actual lingual phenomena. In Chinese, the lack of strict lexical and syntactic inflection makes recognition of predicates and distinction between arguments and adjuncts two difficulties for NLP. Therefore, for the purpose of practicability, under the assistance of HMM tagger and parser (Zhao, 2000) we manually simplified the 1,774-verb-predicated 43,000 Chinese sentences, which were gathered from Modern Chinese Verb Syntactic Dictionary (Lin, 1998) and People Daily (January, 1998). We first determined the predicate verbs, and classified the sentences according to them, with one verb representing one class. The largest class is that of "da3" (打), containing 720 sentences, the smallest are "bai3jia4zi" (摆架子), "xiang1cha4" (相差), "cheng1zuo4" (称作), and "du2" (毒), containing only 2 sentences respectively, and on average each class contains 24.3 sentences. Then, we deleted or modified embedded clauses, other long and unrecognizable adjuncts, and most nominal attributives, but with the fundamental syntactic structure and pragmatic meaning unreformed. The processed sentences are of comparatively simple structures and more visible patterns, yet in close accordance with lingual competence of Chinese native speakers, and thus suitable for SCF recognizing. Hereafter, we'll refer to this manually processed corpus as Simple Sentence Corpus, and SSC for short.

Sentences in SSC are then segmented and tagged with the HMM tagger (Zhao, 2000), and the results are improved by an error-driven ameliorator based on lexical and syntactic knowledge. POS tags are in turn combined or generalized into phrase tags as in T_A, according to generalizing heuristic rules (a derived version of the base phrase recognizing rules in (Zhao, 2000)). From the phrase tag series we generate possible SCF hypotheses for given predicate verbs according to constraint heuristic rules as stated in Section 2. For example, assuming that one of the sentences in SSC is (a), the tagger and ameliorator returns (b), which is further generalized as (c), and the SCF generator returns hypothesis (d).

a. 老人把这孩子当自己的孙子抱回了家。
b. 老人/nc 把/p 这/r 孩子/nc 当/p 自己/r 的/usde 孙子/nc 抱/vg 回/vq 了/ut 家/ng 。/wj
c. [老人/nc]NP [把/p 这/r 孩子/nc]BAP [当/p 自己/r 的/usde 孙子/nc]PP [抱/vg]V [回/vq]QP [了/ut]LE [家/ng]NP 。/wj
d. NP BAP V QP NP

And we manually proofread the auto acquired SCF hypotheses from 13,500 sentences in SSC in order to make a training set for our FML, and the relevant performance is shown in Table 3. Using values in Table 3 to estimate the actual performance, we have token precision between 92.8%+/-0.44%, and type precision between 56.42%+/-5.31% with a confidence interval of 95%. Although large corpus and high token precision may roughly produce both token and type recall of 100, SCF predefinition, as the groundwork for practical acquisition, must be assured of a reasonable type precision. Thus, hypotheses generated here need further proof-testing.

Table 3. Performance Estimate for Hypothesis Generation.

Performance	Calculation Equations	Value
Token Precision	the number of correct SCF hypotheses /the number of all sentences	92.8%
Type Precision	the number of correct SCF types /the number of all generated SCF types	56.65%

4 FML Filtering Method

Previous filtering methods for SCF acquisition include binomial test, log likelihood ratio test, t-test, and maximum likelihood test etc. Though binomial test much far outperform log likelihood ratio and t-test, according to Korhonen (2001), without semantic back-off its F measure is by 11.9 lower than that of maximum likelihood, an outwardly much simpler method. Furthermore, different from SCF acquisition, predefinition of basic SCF is intended for the whole category of Chinese verbs, so semantic back-off doesn't fit for hypothesis testing. Besides, it is impossible to define $P(scf_i|V)$ for each SCF when the whole set of basic SCFs remains uncertain. Hence we decided to adopt the ML method, which first determines an empirical threshold that ensures the best overall performance on a training corpus, and then filters out with this threshold those low-frequency hypotheses generated from the actual corpus. However, linguistic phenomena of certain observations generally abide by Zipfian Law, so estimating the threshold for a large corpus with one learned from a small sample will definitely cause large estimation bias, especially when the available corpus doesn't reach such great capacity or when there are great differences of quantity and distribution between the training sample and the actual corpus. This bias can be overcome by flexibly setting the threshold, i.e. estimating it from the movement trend observed from a number of optimized thresholds for training sets of gradual quantities. We propose a new method of FML, which dynamically determines the filtering threshold according to the movement trend of hypothesis frequency expectations. The process is described step by step as follows.

i) The training corpus of 13,500 sentences was sampled into 5 training sets: S1, S2, S3, S4 and S5, containing 5,000, 7,000, 9,000, 11,000, and 13,500 sentences respectively, and satisfying S1∩S2∩S3∩S4∩S5 so that the linguistic feature distributions of the 5 sets were kept similar.

ii) SCF hypotheses from each set were generated and counted, showing general Zipfian distributions. See Figure 1.

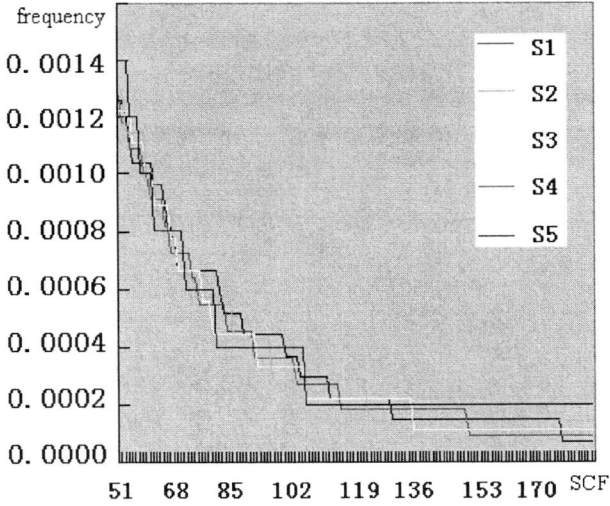

Fig. 1. Part of the SCF Frequency Distribution of the 5 Sets.

iii) The intervals of empirical thresholds were determined, while maximizing F measure of SCF hypotheses on S1, S2, S3 and S4. The expectations of hypothesis frequency for the 5 sets were also calculated. See Table 4[1]. For the tendency curves of these data with sampling quantity as the independent variable see Figure 2[2].

---

[1] In Table 4 those limits for S5 remain to be estimated according to data observed from the first 4 sets.
[2] In Figure 2 the part of broken line remains to be estimated.

Table 4. Intervals of Empirical Thresholds and Hypothesis Frequency Expectations.

Training Set	Upper Limit	Lower Limit	Expectation
S1	0.0004	0.0002	0.00467
S2	0.000286	0.000143	0.0041
S3	0.00022	0.00011	0.00366
S4	0.000182	0.000091	0.003268
S5	?	?	0.002985

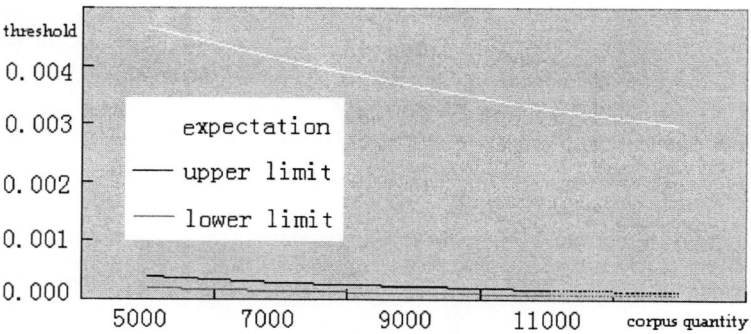

Fig. 2. Tendency Curves for Threshold Intervals and Hypothesis Frequency Expectations.

iv) For reasons that the SCF hypothesis frequency expectation is much more observable than an optimized empirical threshold, and sampling biases make both the hypothesis frequency and the empirical threshold out of literal harmony with the quantity of items sampled, but due to Zipfian Law samples with similar frequency expectations tend to have similar distributions, we use the hypothesis frequency expectation as independent variable to estimate the relative optimized empirical threshold. The functions that calculate a possible value θ for the optimized threshold from SCF hypothesis frequency expectation μ and sampling quantity s : $\theta = f(\mu, s)$, or simply from SCF hypothesis frequency expectation μ : $\theta = f(\mu)$, are illustrated in Figure 3.

v) By means of least square fitting, a possible function for Figure 3 (a) is worked out as $\theta \approx 37.42262\,\mu^2 - 0.17807\,\mu + 0.000315$, and in turn the optimized threshold for S5 is estimated as 0.00012, which locates within (0.000074, 0.000 148), the observed optimized interval for S5. Precision, recall and F measure for S5 are calculated on results with filtering methods of no filtering, S1 threshold, S3 threshold and the flexible threshold respectively, and are listed in Table 5[3].

---

[3] Equations used in Table 5 are: Token recall = Number of covered sentences with correct hypotheses / Number of all sentences with correct hypotheses; Type recall = Number of covered correct hypotheses / Number of all correct hypotheses.

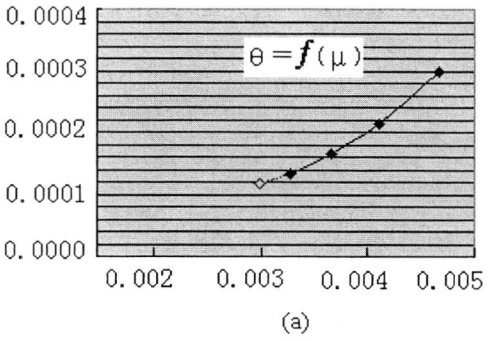 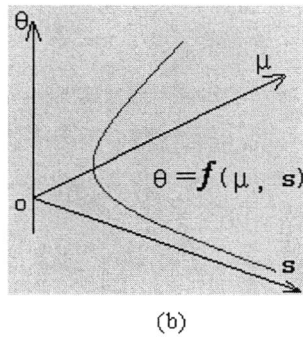

Fig. 3. Functions Fitted for Optimized Threshold, Hypothesis Frequency Expectation and Sampling Quantity. Notes: The part of broken line remains to be estimated. (b) shows a possible 3D curve. Note that (a) is the 2D projection of (b) along axis S.

Table 5. Performance of Four Filtering Methods

Method	Threshold value	Token precision	Token recall	Token F	Type precision	Type recall	Type F
zero θ	0	92.8%	100%	96.37	56.65%	100%	72.33
S1θ	0.0003	96.14%	97.45%	96.79	98.4%	44.3%	61.09
S3 θ	0.000165	95.89%	98.11%	96.99	85.92%	50.66%	63.73
Flexible θ	0.00012	95.6%	98.84%	97.2	84.43%	68.46%	75.61

By analysis of Table 5, it is clear that: first, filtering is better than no filtering because low type precision makes the latter method unpractical though the latter F measures are higher than the former ones; second, the overall performance of FML exceeds that of ML; third, the empirical threshold with a sampling quantity close to the quantity of actual corpus produces better results.

5 Predefined SCF Set

With data from S5 added, we can estimate the FML threshold for the whole corpus SSC from its SCF hypothesis frequency expectation μ=0.002482, and the result is θ=0.000104. Filtering hypotheses from SSC with the FML threshold, we got 141 basic SCFs, and the performance was estimated with relative data from S5. 95% confidence intervals are shown in Table 6.

The processed resources are rearranged according to knowledge of probability. When calculating prior probabilities for predefined basic SCFs, we added to the auto-acquired 141 SCFs 11 manually observed ones, and set their frequencies the same with those lowest auto-acquired. Thus, 152 basic SCFs are predefined altogether. P(SCF) and P(SCF|V) are calculated from frequencies distributed in the merged basic SCF set.

Table 6. Performance Estimation with Data from S5

Token precision	Token recall	Token F	Type precision	Type recall	Type F
95.6% +/-0.3%	98.84% +/-0.2%	96.94 to 97.44	84.43% +/-4.38%	68.46% +/-5.62%	70.41 to 80.78

6 Conclusion and Future Work

Resources acquired via our experiment as prior linguistic knowledge consist mainly of 3 parts, i.e. a predefined basic SCF set with $P(scf_i)$ distribution, a verb lexicon of 1,774 Chinese verbs with $P(scf_i|V_j)$ distribution, and an SCF labeled corpus of 42,528 Chinese sentences with precision of 95.3% or higher. $P(scf_i)$ and $P(scf_i|V_j)$ are indispensable for SCF auto acquisition on large scale, and SCF labeled corpus is much useful for developing supervised SCF acquisition methods. Meanwhile, type recall, the highest value of which is 68.16%, remains to be promoted though the 11 manually acquired SCFs obviously improves the total coverage. For such a problem, we have two solutions: a. Enlarge the coverage of basic SCF set by setting minimum probabilities for the 262 filtered out SCFs; b. When performing SCF acquisition on large scale, with help of some manual work, use the approach in this experiment to discover new basic SCFs.

Acknowledgement

This research has been supported by NNSFC (Grant No.60373 101), and HTRDPC863 (Grant No. 2002AA11701009).

References

1. Brent, M. R.: Automatic acquisition of subcategorization frames from untagged text. In Proceedings of the 29th Annual Meeting of the Association for Computational Linguistics, Berkeley, CA (1991) 209-214
2. Briscoe, T., Carroll,J.: Automatic extraction of subcategorization from corpora. In Proceedings of the 5th ACL Conference on Applied Natural Language Processing, Washington, DC (1997)
3. Chomsky, N.: Aspects of the Theory of Syntax. MIT Press, Cambridge (1965)
4. Dorr, B.J., Levow, G.A., Lin, D., Thomas, S.: Chinese-English Semantic Resource Construction, 2nd International Conference on Language Resources and Evaluation (LREC2000), Athens, Greece (2000) 757-760
5. Hu, Y., Fan, X.: Researches on Verbs. Henan University Press, Henan (1995) (in Chinese)
6. Jin, G.: Semantic Computations for Modern Chinese Verbs. Beijing University Press, Beijing (2001) (in Chinese)
7. Korhonen, A.: Subcategorization Acquistion, Dissertation for Ph.D, Trinity Hall University of Cambridge (2001)

8. Lin, X., et al: Modern Chinese Verb Dictionary. Beijing Language College Press, Beijing (1994) (in Chinese)
9. Lu, Ch., Hou, R., Dong, L.: Basic Syntactic Patterns for Modern Chinese, Chinese Education in the World, Volume 4 (2000) (in Chinese)
10. Shen, Y., Zheng, D.: Modern Chinese Valency Grammar. Beijing University Press, Beijing (1995) (in Chinese)
11. Zhan, W.: Valence Based Chinese Semantic Dictionary, Language and Character Applications, Volume 1 (2000) (in Chinese)
12. Zhao, T.: Knowledge Engineering Report for MTS2000. Machine Translation Laboratory, Harbin Institute of Technology. Harbin (2001)

Deep Analysis of Modern Greek

Valia Kordoni and Julia Neu

Department of Computational Linguistics, Saarland University
D-66041, Saarbrücken, Germany
{kordoni,neu}@coli.uni-sb.de

Abstract. We present a deep computational Modern Greek grammar. The grammar is written in HPSG and is being developed in a multilingual context with MRS semantics, contributing to an open-source collection of software and linguistic resources with wide usage in research, education, and application building.

1 Introduction

In this paper we describe the development of a large grammar fragment of Modern Greek in a multilingual context. The grammar is couched in the theoretical framework of HPSG (Head-Driven Phrase Structure Grammar; [1]) and benefits from an organization of semantics based on MRS (Minimal Recursion Semantics; [2], [3]).

MRS, a framework for computational semantics, in which the meaning of expressions is represented as a flat bag of Elementary Predications (EPs), combines naturally with typed feature structures, like the ones used in HPSG, and allows for structures which are underspecified for scopal information and can be compared across languages. HPSG itself is also suitable for multilingual grammar development, since the analyses in the extensive literature written in it can be shared across languages, but also parametrized accordingly, and its characteristic type hierarchy enables the writing of grammars that are easy to extend. Moreover, there are by now many useful open-source tools for writing, testing, and efficiently processing grammars written in HPSG and MRS: the LKB system for grammar development [4], [incr tsdb()] for testing grammars and tracking changes [5], and PET, a very efficient HPSG parser for processing [6].

The tool we use for the development, i.e., the writing and the testing of the Modern Greek grammar is the Grammar Matrix [7], an open source tool designed for the rapid development of multilingual broad coverage grammars couched in HPSG and MRS and based on LKB.

In the following we focus on some detailed examples from the deep Modern Greek grammar we have been developing since January 2003 using the Grammar Matrix, as part of the DELPHIN Collaboration (Deep Linguistic Processing with HPSG: An International Collaboration; for more see http://www.delph-in.net/), which currently involves research groups from DFKI in Saarbrücken, Saarland University, Stanford University, Tokyo University, the University of Sussex, Cambridge University, and the University of Trondheim, and whose main current research takes place in three areas: (i) robustness, disambiguation and specificity of HPSG processing, (ii) the application of HPSG processing to Information Extraction, and (iii) Multilingual Grammar Engineering, aiming mainly at the further promotion of the central role that robust and deep processing of natural language in a multilingual context based on HPSG plays nowadays in human language technology.

Our aim here is twofold: to present the deep computational grammar of Modern Greek, and to show the practical support we have drawn from the Grammar Matrix platform, which has enabled us to focus on the implementation of very demanding Modern Greek data right from the beginning of the project.

2 Modern Greek HPSG Syntax

The fundamental notion of an HPSG grammar is the sign, a complex feature structure which conveys phonological, syntactic, semantic, pragmatic and discourse information at the same time. The attribute-value matrix of a sign in the Modern Greek HPSG grammar is somewhat similar to a sign in the LinGO English Resource Grammar (ERG; [8]), as well as the HPSG Japanese Grammar (see [9]), with information about the orthographical realization of the lexical sign in STEM, syntactic and semantic information in SYNSEM, nonlocal information in NONLOC, head information that percolates up the tree structure via HEAD and subcategorization information in VAL(ENCE) (whose values are SUBJ, COMPS, SPEC, and SPR). These features, which are part of the sign geometry, as well as a large number of types which inherit from sign itself, are already defined in the Grammar Matrix.

For the implementation of the Modern Greek HPSG grammar we only needed to define further the parts of speech which are relevant to Modern Greek along with their specific head features. To these belong determiners, nouns, pronouns, affixes, prepositions and verbs, all of which inherit directly or indirectly from (the type) `sign` in the Grammar Matrix.

As far as the subcategorization patterns of verbal predicates in Modern Greek are concerned, it has turned out that for the best part these can be accounted for in the implementation of the Modern Greek grammar by relying on the material that the Grammar Matrix already provides for.

The grammar implementation is based on a system of types. Since the Modern Greek grammar is being developed for use in applications, it treats a wide range of constructions in Modern Greek, including valence alternations, cliticization phenomena, word order phenomena, subordinate clauses, unbounded dependency constructions (UDCs), raising and control, relative clause constructions, constructions headed by passives, and politeness constructions, among others. Due to space limitations, though, only some of these phenomena can be described here: we focus on cliticization and word order phenomena in Modern Greek. For a more detailed description of all the phenomena covered in the Modern Greek grammar see [10].

2.1 Cliticization Phenomena

Central to the efficient deep processing of Modern Greek is the implementation of clitics and clitic doubling phenomena (cf., [11]).

In general, Modern Greek distinguishes mainly between genitive and accusative clitics. Clitics in Modern Greek share a significant number of properties with what have been argued to be *pronominal affixes* in some Romance languages, such as French, and Italian (cf., [12], [13]). That is, they cannot be topicalized, they cannot be substituted by full pronouns, they cannot be coordinated, and they cannot be modified.

The implementation of Modern Greek pronominal affixes in the deep computational Modern Greek grammar described here draws on mainstream and well-established theoretical HPSG proposals, according to which in HPSG words may come along with an argument structure (ARG-ST/DEPS-ST), which is an attribute that determines the combinatorial potential of a word, including specific subcategorization restrictions (cf., [14]). The members of ARG-ST may be of sort *canonical* or of sort *noncanonical* (i.e., *gaps* or *affixes*; see also (1)). As shown in (1), *canon(ical-synsem)*: "is the type associated with all signs; *noncan(onical-synsem)* corresponds to an ARG-ST position that is not realized as a local syntactic dependent of the head. The latter subtype is in turn divided into the subtype *aff(ixal-synsem)* and *gap(-synsem)*. It is the presence of elements of type *aff* on a verb's ARG-ST list that triggers the morphological realization of the corresponding pronominal affixes. The type *non-aff* provides a cross-cutting classification, subsuming all types of *synsem* other than *aff*" [12].

(1)
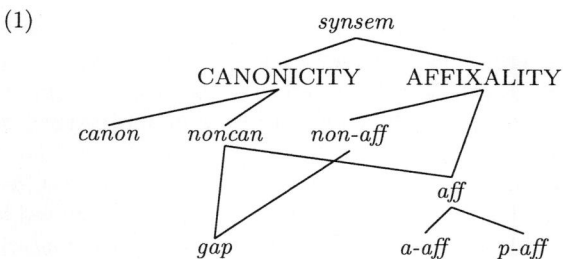

In the Modern Greek grammar pronominal affixes are defined as in Figure 1.

For the implementation of pronominal affixes in clitic doubling constructions in Modern Greek:

(2) O   Petros to   fonazei to koritsi.
     the Peter.N cl.A call.3S the girl.A
     "Peter is calling the girl".

we have introduced a new rule in the grammar, the *clitic doubling rule*.

The *clitic doubling rule*[1] inherits from the type `head-final` of the Grammar Matrix, and it enables a verb (the head) and an adjacent affix appearing on the left of the verb to combine (see Figure 2).

---

[1] Due to space limitations we do not show the *clitic doubling rule* here.

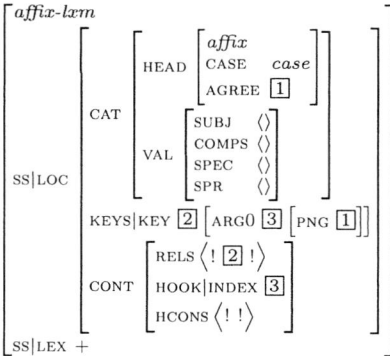

Fig. 1. Type for affixes in the Modern Greek grammar.

The verb comes along with a DEPS-ST list, whose lone element is token-identical to the synsem of the affix. After combining with the affix, the DEPS-ST list of the verb is empty. The COMPS list of the verb remains unchanged; it just gets fully copied to the projection V' (see Figure 2), since at this stage the verb still needs to combine with a direct object (i.e., the "clitic-doubled" NP *to koritsi* in example (2)), and potentially with more (optional) arguments. Finally, the values of the verb's SUBJ, SPR and SPEC are also copied to the projection V' (see Figure 2).

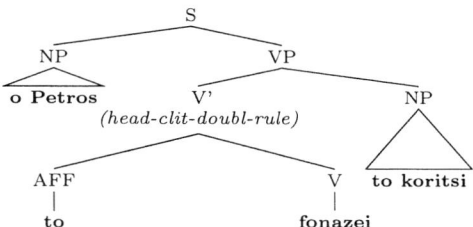

Fig. 2. Tree representation for the sentence "*O Petros to fonazei to koritsi*".

In order to restrict the agreement possibilities of the affix, we restrict the agreement features (person, number, and gender denoted as the value of an attribute AGREE) and CASE of the affix accordingly, so that the affix be coindexed with the first element of the COMPS list of the verb (i.e., coindexed with the direct object NP).

The information carried by the affix in the semantic representation of Modern Greek clitic doubling constructions in the Modern Greek grammar is already represented in the definition of transitive verbs. The value of the ARG0 of the affix is token-identical to the value of the corresponding AFFIX feature of the verb[2].

---

[2] The AFFIX feature of the verb has been introduced as part of a new relation *new-arg12-rel*, which inherits from the relation *arg12-rel* of the Grammar Matrix.

Thus, in the semantic representation of clitic doubling constructions in Modern Greek like the one in example (2), the verb is represented bearing a "slot" for an affix whose value is shared with the ARG0 value of the affix itself; that is, in the semantic representation the affix appears as a direct dependent of the verb (for more see next Section).

2.2 Word Order Phenomena

Central to the development of the Modern Greek grammar are also word order phenomena. The following examples represent the three most common word order constructions in Modern Greek.

- **Object-Verb-Subject Constructions**

(3) To koritsi fonazei o Petros.
    the girl.A call.3S the Petros.N
    "Peter is calling the girl".

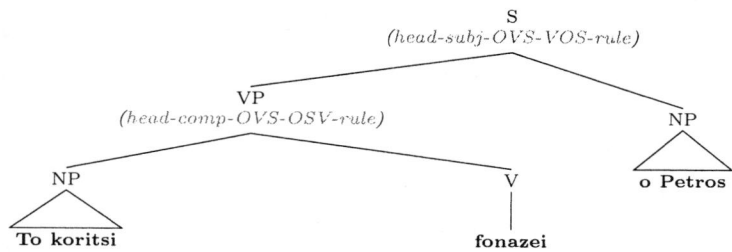

Fig. 3. Object-Verb-Subject construction.

For constructions like in (3) we implemented two phrase structure rules: the *head-comp-OVS-OSV-rule* (head-complement-**O**bject**V**erb**S**ubject-**O**bject**S**ub- ject**V**erb-rule) and the *head-subj-OVS-VOS-rule* (head-subject-**O**bject**V**erb**S**ub- ject-**V**erb**O**bject**S**ubject).

Figure 3 shows how the two rules work. First, the *head-comp-OVS-OSV-rule* combines the verb (*fonazei*) with its direct object (*to koritsi*) which appears on the left hand side of the verb. The resulting VP is combined with the subject (*o Petros*) via the *head-subj-OVS-VOS-rule*. Both rules inherit from supertypes of the Grammar Matrix; the *head-comp-OVS-OSV-rule* inherits from the type **head-final**, whereas the *head-subj-OVS-VOS-rule* is a subtype of the Matrix type **head-initial**. This is also the main point that differentiates the *head- comp-OVS-OSV-rule* and the *head-subj-OVS-VOS-rule* from the head-subject and head-complement schemas, because the order of the direct object and subject is simply switched.

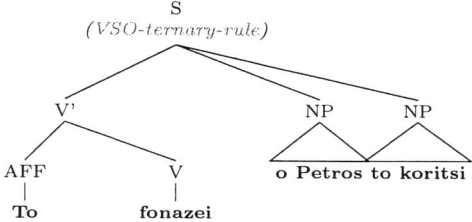

Fig. 4. Verb-Subject-Object construction.

– **Verb-Subject-Object Constructions**

(4) To fonazei o Petros to koritsi.
    cl.A call.3S the Petros.N the girl.A
    "Peter is calling the girl".

In (4) the word order is verb-subject-object and clitic doubling is obligatory. For constructions like these we use the *VSO-ternary-rule*. As shown in Figure 4, the rule combines three arguments in one step: the verb (*fonazei*), which already bears an affix (*to*), the subject (*o Petros*) and the direct (doubled) object (*to koritsi*).

– **CLLD: Clitic Left Dislocated Constructions**

(5) To koritsi o Petros to fonazei.
    the girl.A the Petros.N cl.A call.3S
    "Peter is calling the girl".

The sentence in (5) is an example for the so-called *clitic left dislocated constructions*, where the "doubled" element, i.e., the direct object, appears in the leftmost position of the sentence. The *CLLD-rule* combines the subject (*o Petros*) and the verb, which already bears the affix (*to*). In the next step, the *head-comp-OVS-OSV-rule* (see Figure 3) combines the resulting VP with the direct object (*to koritsi*) in order to form the sentence.

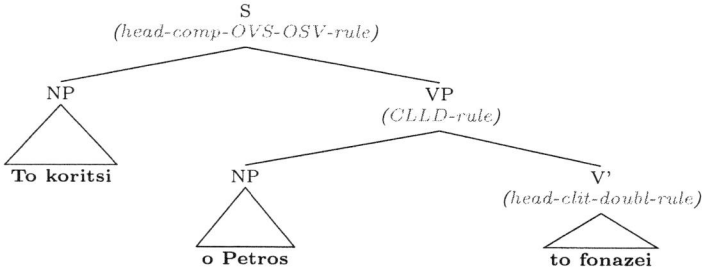

Fig. 5. CLLD construction.

3 MRS Semantics for Modern Greek

The deep computational grammar of Modern Greek, some important aspects of which we describe here, benefits from an organization of semantics based on MRS (Minimal Recursion Semantics; [2], [3]). Types associated with MRS are already included in the Grammar Matrix tool we use for the development of the Modern Greek grammar.

As already mentioned in Section (1), MRS, a framework for computational semantics, in which the meaning of expressions is represented as a flat bag of Elementary Predications (EPs) encoded as values of a RELS attribute, combines naturally with typed feature structures, like the ones used in HPSG, and allows for structures which are underspecified for scopal information and easily comparable across languages, thus being very appropriate for grammars, like the one we describe here, which are developed in a multilingual context, as part of an international initiative for multilingual deep linguistic processing based on HPSG (cf., Delphin Collaboration in Section (1)). Due to space limitations, here we discuss only the semantics related to the syntactic phenomena we have presented in Section (2.1), as well as the semantics of the Clitic Left Dislocated constructions in Section (2.2).

3.1 Clitic Doubling in Modern Greek

The analysis of Modern Greek clitic doubling constructions (see example (2) and Figure 2 in Section (2.1) above) has led us to innovations in the correspondence between semantic and syntactic structures in comparison to the Grammar Matrix.

In the MRS semantic representation of the sentence in (2) of Section (2.1) that we are showing in (6), *h1* is the ltop (local top) handle of the sentence, which appears again as handle of **prpstn** (proposition; this conveys that the sentence is a proposition, rather than a question, for instance). Each noun gets an instantiation variable x_n (see *x4*, *x11*, and so forth in (6)), which is bound to the respective determiners of the nouns. Each entry in the MRS semantic representation in (6) gets a handle which may be part of a QEQ-constraint of the HCONS list[3]. The verbal head in (6) comes along with three arguments: ARG0, ARG1 and ARG2. Except ARG0, which denotes the event variable of the verb itself, these arguments are denoted by variables which are shared with those of the corresponding noun entries in the RELS. The HCONS list includes the QEQ-constraints which hold between the nouns and their determiners, as well as between the MARG of the **prpstn** (*h16*) and the handle of the verb (*h10*). The verb in (6) also allows for an affix. Note that the affix entry bears a variable (*x9*), which is identical to the variable denoting the affix dependent of the verb. The handle of the affix, though, does not contribute to the QEQ-constraints. The affix has been combined with the verb by means of the clitic doubling rule (see Figure 2), and not by means of the head complement rule, a fact which is mirrored in the way this combination of the affix and the verb is denoted in the

---

[3] For more on QEQ-constraints and HCONS lists see [2] and [3].

semantic representation of the sentence in (2) shown in (6): the affix is not a "real argument" of the verb; it is part of the morphosyntactic features of the verb.

3.2 Clitic Left Dislocated Constructions

The MRS semantic representation of the sentence in (5) of Section (2.2) presented in (7) above captures the insights of both the syntactic analysis sketched in Figure 5 and of theoretical HPSG syntactic analyses of CLLDs in Modern Greek, like the ones of [15] and [11], who treat clitic duplicated phrases in Modern Greek CLLDs as adjuncts, following [16] in treating adjuncts as elements of COMPS and utilizing both ARG-ST for arguments and DEP(ENDENT)S-ST for all "dependents", both arguments and adjuncts.

(6) Semantic representation in MRS of the sentence in (2):

$$\begin{bmatrix} mrs \\ \text{HOOK} \begin{bmatrix} \text{LTOP} & h1 \\ \text{INDEX} & e2 \end{bmatrix} \\ \text{RELS} \left\langle \begin{bmatrix} o \\ \text{LBL} & h3 \\ \text{ARG0} & x4 \\ \text{BODY} & h6 \\ \text{RSTR} & h5 \end{bmatrix}, \begin{bmatrix} \text{Petros} \\ \text{LBL} & h7 \\ \text{ARG0} & x4 \end{bmatrix}, \begin{bmatrix} to \\ \text{LBL} & h8 \\ \text{ARG0} & x9 \end{bmatrix}, \begin{bmatrix} \text{fonazo} \\ \text{LBL} & h10 \\ \text{AFFIX} & x9 \\ \text{ARG0} & e2 \\ \text{ARG1} & x4 \\ \text{ARG2} & x11 \end{bmatrix}, \begin{bmatrix} to \\ \text{LBL} & h12 \\ \text{ARG0} & x11 \\ \text{BODY} & h14 \\ \text{RSTR} & h13 \end{bmatrix}, \begin{bmatrix} \text{koritsi} \\ \text{LBL} & h15 \\ \text{ARG0} & x11 \end{bmatrix}, \begin{bmatrix} \text{prpstn} \\ \text{LBL} & h1 \\ \text{MARG} & h16 \end{bmatrix} \right\rangle \\ \text{HCONS} \left\langle \begin{bmatrix} qeq \\ \text{HARG} & h5 \\ \text{LARG} & h7 \end{bmatrix}, \begin{bmatrix} qeq \\ \text{HARG} & h13 \\ \text{LARG} & h15 \end{bmatrix}, \begin{bmatrix} qeq \\ \text{HARG} & h16 \\ \text{LARG} & h10 \end{bmatrix} \right\rangle \end{bmatrix}$$

(7) Semantic representation in MRS of the sentence in (5):

$$\begin{bmatrix} mrs \\ \begin{bmatrix} \text{LTOP} & h1 \\ \text{INDEX} & e2 \end{bmatrix} \\ \text{RELS} \left\langle \begin{bmatrix} to \\ \text{LBL} & h3 \\ \text{ARG0} & x4 \\ \text{BODY} & h6 \\ \text{RSTR} & h5 \end{bmatrix}, \begin{bmatrix} \text{koritsi} \\ \text{LBL} & h7 \\ \text{ARG0} & x4 \end{bmatrix}, \begin{bmatrix} to \\ \text{LBL} & h8 \\ \text{ARG0} & x9 \end{bmatrix}, \begin{bmatrix} \text{fonazo} \\ \text{LBL} & h10 \\ \text{AFFIX} & x9 \\ \text{AFFIX2} & v11 \\ \text{ARG0} & e2 \\ \text{ARG1} & x12 \\ \text{ARG2} & x4 \end{bmatrix}, \begin{bmatrix} o \\ \text{LBL} & h13 \\ \text{ARG0} & x12 \\ \text{BODY} & h15 \\ \text{RSTR} & h14 \end{bmatrix}, \begin{bmatrix} \text{petros} \\ \text{LBL} & h16 \\ \text{ARG0} & x12 \end{bmatrix}, \begin{bmatrix} \text{prpstn} \\ \text{LBL} & h1 \\ \text{MARG} & h17 \end{bmatrix} \right\rangle \\ \text{HCONS} \left\langle \begin{bmatrix} qeq \\ \text{HARG} & h5 \\ \text{LARG} & h7 \end{bmatrix}, \begin{bmatrix} qeq \\ \text{HARG} & h14 \\ \text{LARG} & h16 \end{bmatrix}, \begin{bmatrix} qeq \\ \text{HARG} & h17 \\ \text{LARG} & h10 \end{bmatrix} \right\rangle \end{bmatrix}$$

4 Conclusion and Outlook

In this paper we have presented some important aspects of the deep computational grammar of Modern Greek we have been developing using the Grammar Matrix [7]. Our aim in this paper has been twofold: to present some interesting aspects of the HSPG grammar of Modern Greek, as well as to indicate which aspects of the Grammar Matrix as broad coverage grammar development platform are helpful and which have needed further development in the case of Modern Greek. In future work, the next immediate steps in the efficient deep analysis and processing of Modern Greek include the connection of the Modern Greek grammar system to a morphological analysis system, the incorporation of use of default entries for words unknown to the Modern Greek HPSG lexicon, the construction of a treebank, and the application to the grammar of stochastic disambiguation methods, like, for instance, the ones developed for the ERG by the Redwoods project at Stanford University (cf., [17]), in an effort to treat ambiguity, one of the most important performance issues for broad coverage grammars.

References

1. Pollard, C., Sag, I.A.: Head-Driven Phrase Structure Grammar. University of Chicago Press, Chicago (1994)
2. Copestake, A., Flickinger, D., Sag, I.A., Pollard, C.J.: Minimal Recursion Semantics: An Introduction (1999) Ms., Stanford University.
3. Copestake, A., Lascarides, A., Flickinger, D.: An Algebra for Semantic Construction in Constraint-based Grammars. In: Proceedings of the 39th Annual Meeting of the Association for Computational Linguistics (ACL 2001), Toulouse, France. (2001)
4. Copestake, A.: Implementing Typed Feature Structure Grammars. CSLI Lecture Notes, Number 110. Standord: CSLI Publications (2002)
5. Oepen, S., Carroll, J.: Performance Profiling for Parser Engineering. Journal of Natural Language Engineering 6(1): Special Issue on Efficient Processing with HPSG: Methods, Systems, Evaluation (2000) 81–97
6. Callmeier, U.: Pet – a platform for experimentation with efficient HPSG processing techniques. Journal of Natural Language Engineering 6(1): Special Issue on Efficient Processing with HPSG: Methods, Systems, Evaluation (2000) 99–108
7. Bender, E., Flickinger, D., Oepen, S.: The Grammar Matrix: An Open-Source Starter-Kit for the Rapid Development of Cross-Linguistically Consistent Broad-Coverage Precision Grammars. In Carroll, J., Oostdijk, N., Sutcliffe, R., eds.: Proceedings of the Workshop on Grammar Engineering and Evaluation at the 19th International Conference on Computational Linguistics. Taipei, Taiwan. (2002) 8–14
8. Flickinger, D.: On building a more efficient grammar by exploiting types. Journal of Natural Language Engineering 6(1): Special Issue on Efficient Processing with HPSG: Methods, Systems, Evaluation (2000) 15–28
9. Siegel, M., Bender, E.M.: Efficient Deep Processing of Japanese. In: Proceedings of the 3rd Workshop on Asian Language Resources and International Standardization, Coling 2002 Post-Conference Workshop, Taipei, Taiwan (2002)

10. Neu, J., Kordoni, V.: Implementation of a Modern Greek Grammar Fragment in HPSG. Technical report, Department of Computational Linguistics, University of Saarland (2003)
11. Kordoni, V.: Psych Verb Constructions in Modern Greek: a semantic analysis in the Hierarchical Lexicon. PhD thesis, University of Essex, Colchester, UK (2001)
12. Miller, P.H., Sag, I.A.: French clitic movement without clitics or movement. Natural Language and Linguistic Theory **15** (1997) 573–639
13. Monachesi, P.: The syntax of Italian clitics. PhD thesis, University of Tilburg, Tilburg (1996)
14. Manning, C.D., Sag, I.A.: Dissociations between Argument Structure and Grammatical Relations. In Webelhuth, G., Koenig, J.P., Kathol, A., eds.: Lexical And Constructional Aspects of Linguistic Explanation. CSLI Publications, Stanford, Calif. (1999) 63–78
15. Alexopoulou, T., Kolliakou, D.: On Linkhood, Topicalization and Clitic Left Dislocation. Journal of Linguistics **38.2** (2002)
16. Bouma, G., Malouf, R., Sag, I.A.: Satisfying constraints on extraction and adjunction. NLLT **19, Issue 1** (2001) 1–65
17. Oepen, S., Toutanova, K., Shieber, S., Manning, C., Flickinger, D., Brants, T.: The LinGO Redwoods Treebank. Motivation and Preliminary Applications. In: Proceedings of 19th International Conference on Computational Linguistics, Coling 2002. Taipei, Taiwan. (2002)

Corpus-Oriented Grammar Development for Acquiring a Head-Driven Phrase Structure Grammar from the Penn Treebank

Yusuke Miyao[1], Takashi Ninomiya[1,2], and Jun'ichi Tsujii[1,2]

[1] University of Tokyo, Hongo 7-3-1, Bunkyo-ku, Tokyo 113-0033
{yusuke,ninomi,tsujii}@is.s.u-tokyo.ac.jp
[2] JST CREST, Honcho 4-1-8, Kawaguchi-shi, Saitama 332-0012

Abstract. This paper describes a method of semi-automatically acquiring an English HPSG grammar from the Penn Treebank. First, heuristic rules are employed to annotate the treebank with *partially-specified derivation trees* of HPSG. Lexical entries are automatically extracted from the annotated corpus by inversely applying HPSG schemata to partially-specified derivation trees. Predefined HPSG schemata assure the acquired lexicon to conform to the theoretical formulation of HPSG. Experimental results revealed that this approach enabled us to develop an HPSG grammar with significant robustness at small cost.

1 Methodology

To date, manual writing has been the only way to develop grammars based on linguistic theories. Linguistics explains language phenomena as a symbolic system of metaphysical linguistic entities such as syntactic categories. Hence, grammar development has had to rely on the linguistic intuition of grammar writers to explicate a system of unobservable linguistic entities. However, manual writing is inherently impractical as a means of developing and maintaining a robust grammar. A large number of grammar rules or lexical entries require complicated implementations, and grammar writers face difficulties in maintaining the consistency of detailed constraints. Although a few studies could apply a hand-crafted grammar to a real-world corpus [1], these required considerable human effort that lasted for over a decade.

The new strategy outlined here is *corpus-oriented grammar development*, where a linguistics-based grammar is automatically acquired from an annotated corpus. Since the formulation of a grammar includes unobservable linguistic entities, we first *externalize* our linguistic intuition as *annotations* to a corpus. If unobservable linguistic entities were explicated as annotations, a system of linguistic entities, i.e., a grammar, would automatically be induced conforming to a linguistic theory that would explain the given annotations.

This idea is articulated within the context of *lexicalized grammar formalism*, including Lexicalized Tree Adjoining Grammar (LTAG) [2], Combinatory Categorial Grammar (CCG) [3], and Head-driven Phrase Structure Grammar (HPSG) [4]. Lexicalized grammars are formulated with a small number of grammar rules and a large lexicon. Hence, grammar rules can be manually written, while a lexicon should be automatically acquired.

To enable the acquisition of a lexicon in this situation, what must be externalized as annotations? Our previous work [5] suggests a solution: given grammar rules, lexical entries can be determined if each sentence is annotated with i) a history of rule applications, and ii) additional annotations to make the grammar rules be *pseudo-injective*. Lexical entries are then extracted by reverse-engineering the given annotations with the inverse application of grammar rules. In the acquisition of HPSG, these annotations are defined as *partially-specified derivation trees* of HPSG, which will be described in Section 3. Heuristics-based annotation will provide partially-specified derivation trees at low cost. The inverse application of HPSG schemata will integrate partially-specified constraints given as annotations and induce lexical entries.

Compared to manual development, our approach has the following advantages.

Inexpensive. The dominant cost in our approach is in maintaining annotation rules. Any heuristic rule and statistical method can be exploited, and a grammar writer is not hampered by having to maintain the consistency of the grammar. Development costs are therefore expected to be comparable to those for shallow analyzers, which utilize heuristic rules.

Wide-coverage. The acquired grammar can support various constructions in real-world texts. Lexical entries will be obtained even for constructions beyond the grammar developers' prospect.

Available for machine learning. An annotated corpus can be used as training data for the probabilistic modeling or machine learning of statistical parsing.

Organization of heuristic knowledge. Various types of knowledge implicitly represented by heuristic rules are externalized as the annotations to a corpus. Through grammar acquisition, such knowledge is automatically organized into a grammar conforming to a linguistic theory.

Studies on the extraction of LTAG [6–8] and CCG [9] proposed the acquisition of lexicalized grammars from the Penn Treebank. They invented a LTAG/CCG-specific procedure to extract lexical entries from a treebank with heuristic annotations. Our study further pursues this approach, and the extraction procedure exploits the inverse application of HPSG schemata. Compared to LTAG and CCG, constraints used by HPSG are more complicated and fine-grained. Although this seems to be an obstacle to grammar acquisition, we will demonstrate that heuristic annotation and inverse schemata allow the acquisition of a lexicon.

Several methods have been proposed to automatically acquire Lexical Functional Grammars (LFG) [10] from treebanks annotated using heuristic rules [11,12]. Their aim was to automate the process to annotate c-structures with *functional schemata*, which are unification-based grammatical rules in LFG. Since the consistency of resulting schemata depends directly on the design of annotation rules, these must carefully be arranged to conform to LFG. In our approach, however, grammar rules (schemata) are given and the target of annotation is partially-specified derivation trees, which are partial results of parsing. Since annotation is separated from the design of schemata, annotation rules are not responsible for the consistency of the grammar, and these are not

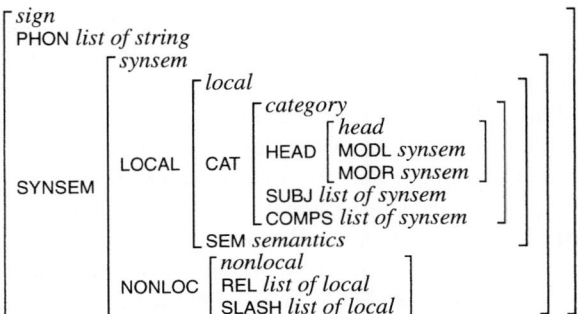

Fig. 1. HPSG sign.

necessarily systematically arranged. Predefined schemata organize partially-specified constraints into a lexicon, and guarantee its consistency.

Subcategorization acquisition has extensively been studied to extract a dictionary of subcategorization frames from annotated/unannotated corpora (surveyed by Korhonen [13]). The methods assumed that the classes of subcategorization frames were given, and words (in most cases, verbs) were classified into the given classes using heuristic patterns and/or corpus statistics. Our method does not require predefined subcategorization classes, and acquire lexical entries for all words in a corpus together with complete derivation structures. The method is intended to semi-automatically develop a grammar from scratch.

2 Head-Driven Phrase Structure Grammar

HPSG [4] is a linguistic theory based on lexicalized grammar formalism. A small number of schemata explain general grammatical constraints, while a large number of lexical entries express word-specific characteristics. Both schemata and lexical entries are represented by typed feature structures, and constraints represented by feature structures are checked with *unification* (for details, see Pollard and Sag [4]).

Figure 1 provides the definition of an HPSG sign, which represents the syntactic/semantic behavior of words/phrases. HEAD feature expresses the characteristics of the head word of a constituent, such as syntactic categories. MODL, MODR, SUBJ, and COMPS represent selectional constraints of left-modifiee, right-modifiee, left-argument, and right-argument. REL and SLASH features are used to explain relative expressions and unbounded dependencies. SEM feature represents the semantics of a constituent, and in this study it expresses a predicate-argument structure.

Figure 2 presents the Subject-Head Schema and the Head-Complement Schema[1] defined in Pollard and Sag [4]. In order to express general constraints, schemata only provide sharing of feature values, and no instantiated values.

---

[1] The value of *category* has been presented for simplicity, while the other portions of the sign have been omitted.

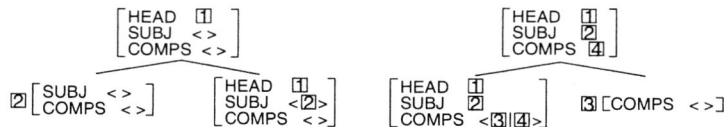

Fig. 2. Subject-Head Schema (left) and Head-Complement Schema (right).

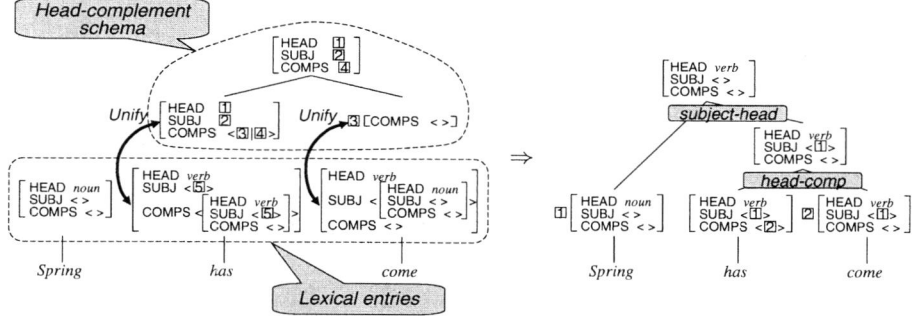

Fig. 3. HPSG parsing.

Figure 3 has an example of HPSG parsing of the sentence *"Spring has come."* First, each of the lexical entries for *"has"* and *"come"* are unified with a daughter feature structure of the Head-Complement Schema. Unification provides the phrasal sign of the mother. The sign of the larger constituent is obtained by repeatedly applying schemata to lexical/phrasal signs. Finally, the phrasal sign of the entire sentence is output on the top of the derivation tree.

3 Acquiring HPSG from the Penn Treebank

As discussed in Section 1, our grammar development requires each sentence to be annotated with i) a history of rule applications, and ii) additional annotations to make the grammar rules be *pseudo-injective*. In HPSG, a history of rule applications is represented by a tree annotated with schema names. Additional annotations are required because HPSG schemata are not injective, i.e., daughters' signs cannot be uniquely determined given the mother. The following annotations are at least required. First, the HEAD feature of each non-head daughter must be specified since this is not percolated to the mother sign. Second, SLASH/REL features are required as described in our previous study [5]. Finally, the SUBJ feature of the complement daughter in the Head-Complement Schema must be specified since this schema may subcategorize an unsaturated constituent, i.e., a constituent with a non-empty SUBJ feature. When the corpus is annotated with at least these features, the lexical entries required to explain the sentence are uniquely determined. In this study, we define *partially-specified derivation trees* as tree structures annotated with schema names and HPSG signs including the specifications of the above features.

We describe the process of grammar development in terms of the three phases: *specification, externalization, and extraction.*

3.1 Specification

General grammatical constraints are defined in this phase, and in HPSG, they are represented through the design of the sign and schemata. Figure 1 shows the definition for the typed feature structure of a sign used in this study. Some more features are defined for each syntactic category although they have been omitted from the figure: e.g., VFORM represents verbal forms.

Following Pollard and Sag [4], this study defines the following schemata: Subject-Head, Head-Complement, Head-Modifier, Modifier-Head, and Filler-Head Schema. In addition to these, two schemata are defined as supporting constructions that often occur in the Penn Treebank. The *Head-Relative Schema* is defined for relative expressions, while HPSG explains this construction with a null relativizer. The *Filler-Insertion Schema* is defined for the construction in which an inserted clause introduces a slash, which is filled by the entire sentence. For example, in the sentence "*Mr. Kuehn, the company said, will retain the rest of the current management team,*" the complement of the inserted clause is coindexed with the entire sentence.

3.2 Externalization

This phase annotates the Penn Treebank with partially-specified derivation trees. The following annotations are added to each node in a treebank tree: head/argument/modifier marks, SUBJ features, SLASH/REL features, HPSG categories, and schema names.

First, head/argument/modifier distinctions are annotated to each node in trees using *the head percolation table* [14, 15], and trees are converted to binary trees. Since this procedure is mostly the same as in existing studies [6, 9], the details are omitted here.

After this, we add annotations for constructions that require special treatment in the HPSG theory. Some of them are listed below.

Subject-control verbs. Subject-control verbs such as "*try*" take VP as its complement in HPSG analysis, and its subject is shared with the unfilled subject of the VP[2]. In the Penn Treebank, complements of control verbs are represented as S with the empty subject (the top of Figure 4). Such trees are annotated with the structure-sharings as shown in the bottom of Figure 4, where the SUBJ feature of to-infinitive is coindexed with NP-1 (represented by 1).

Slash & filler-head schema. Since Penn Treebank-style annotation represents unbounded dependencies with trace marker "*T*", this mark is exploited to detect unbounded dependencies. The algorithm is very similar to the marking of *forward arguments* described by Hockenmaier and Steedman [9]. The difference is that when the filler of the slash is found, i.e., the node with the same ID number, the corresponding construction is annotated with the Filler-Head Schema (or the Filler-Insertion Schema) (Figure 5).

---

[2] Strictly, this analysis is for *equi* verbs such as "*seem*", although these two classes of verbs have not been distinguished in our current implementation.

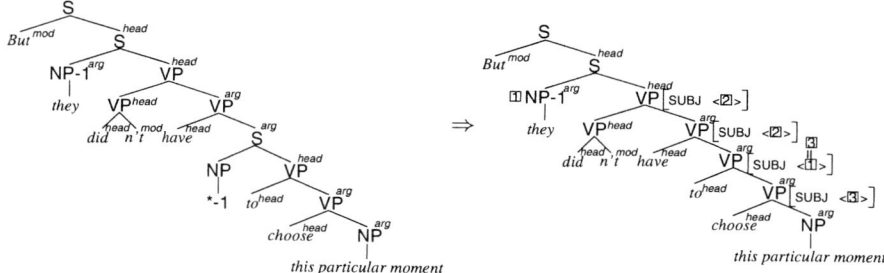

Fig. 4. Annotation of subject-control and auxiliary verbs.

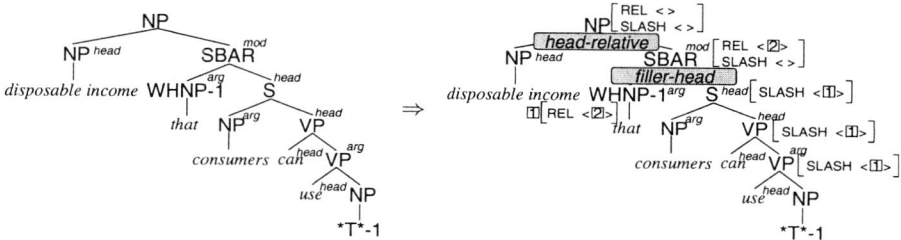

Fig. 5. Annotation of slashes and relative clauses.

Finally, each node is annotated with an HPSG category by mapping non-/preterminal symbols to HPSG categories. Because of the space limitation, mapping rules are omitted here.

The above procedure annotates the treebank with partially-specified derivation trees. For example, Figure 6 shows a partially-specified derivation tree corresponding to the treebank tree in Figure 4.

3.3 Extraction

In this phase, lexical entries are automatically extracted from partially-specified derivation trees given as the annotations to the treebank. *Inverse schemata* are applied to each phrasal sign in a partially-specified derivation tree. That is, given a mother as an input to a schema, daughters are computed. This procedure is considered to be the inverse of parsing described in Section 2. Figure 7 lists lexical entries for "*did*" and "*choose*", which are extracted from the partially-specified derivation tree shown in Figure 6.

Extracted lexical entries are then generalized to *lexical entry templates*. We manually listed features to be ignored for eliminating word-specific and context-specific constraints. For example, the TENSE features in the subcategorization list (SUBJ and COMPS) can be ignored because they are irrelevant to the syntactic constraints in English. Additionally, some lexical specifications can be added to lexical entry templates. Most important is the specification of lexical semantics. In the current implementation, predicate-argument structures are constructed using heuristic pattern rules on the structure of a lexical sign.

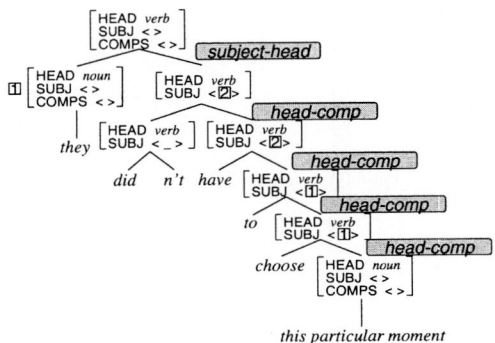

Fig. 6. Partially-specified derivation tree corresponding to Figure 4.

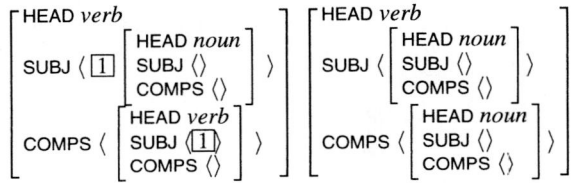

Fig. 7. Lexical entries for *"did"* (left) and *"choose"* (right) extracted from the partially-specified derivation tree in Figure 6.

4 Evaluation

The algorithm described in Section 3 was implemented to acquire an HPSG grammar from the Penn Treebank Section 02-21 (39,598 sentences).

Lexical entries were successfully extracted from 38,263 sentences. Table 1 lists the number of words/lexical entry templates in the obtained grammar[3]. Compared to the automatic extraction of LTAG [6], the number of lexical entry templates was significantly reduced. This implies that the HPSG grammar achieved a higher degree of abstraction. Compared to the automatic extraction of CCG [9], the number of templates increased. We assume that this was because CCG exploits grammar rules to explain syntactic variations (e.g. wh-extraction and relative clauses), while HPSG uses lexical entries. Hence, an HPSG grammar should have more lexical entries corresponding to various syntactic variations. This is substantiated by the results in Table 1, where the number of lexical entry templates for verbs is significantly higher than for the other parts of speech.

Table 2 shows lexical/sentential coverage against Section 23. Coverage was measured by comparing the acquired lexicon to lexical entries extracted from Section 23. In the table, G denotes the original grammar, and $\bar{G}$ a grammar modified to treat unknown words with a method similar to Hockenmaier and Steedman [9]; words occurring less

---

[3] The summation of the number of words is not equal to the total number because a word might be assigned more than one part of speech and be double-counted.

Table 1. Number of words/lexical entry templates in the grammar acquired from Section 02-21.

	noun	verb	adjective	adverb	preposition
words	24,947	10,634	8,126	1,300	184
templates	99	1,596	44	69	213
templates per word	1.33	2.05	1.31	2.90	9.89
	particle	determiner	conjunction	punctuation	total
words	60	44	36	15	42,669
templates	12	30	103	179	2,345
templates per word	1.48	4.84	11.72	27.27	1.70

Table 2. Lexical/sentential coverage (left) and parsing performance (right).

	seen	unseen				sentential	parsing			
	⟨sw,sc⟩	⟨sw,sc⟩	⟨sw,uc⟩	⟨uw,sc⟩	⟨uw,uc⟩		success	failure	error	time
G_0	94.99%	2.21%	0.10%	2.70%	0.00%	43.0%	51.9%	39.2%	8.9%	4.21
$\bar{G}_0$	98.48%	1.41%	0.10%	0.01%	0.00%	75.9%	85.4%	1.2%	13.4%	5.47
$\bar{G}_1$	98.46%	1.44%	0.10%	0.01%	0.00%	75.6%	88.9%	1.2%	9.9%	4.42
$\bar{G}_5$	98.38%	1.52%	0.10%	0.01%	0.00%	74.7%	93.1%	1.3%	5.6%	6.03
$\bar{G}_{10}$	98.25%	1.64%	0.10%	0.01%	0.00%	73.3%	96.1%	1.6%	2.3%	5.25

than 10 times in Section 02-21 were treated equally as unknown words. A suffix denotes the threshold of the frequency of lexical entry templates; a grammar includes a lexical entry template only if it occurred more than the threshold. The "seen" and "unseen" columns represent the lexical coverage, which is the same measure as the previous studies [6, 9]. The "seen" column has the ratio of the word/template pairs covered by the grammar. The results are comparable to the existing studies, despite the fine-grained constraints of HPSG. The "unseen" columns have the ratio of pairs not covered by the grammar, where "sw"/"uw" mean seen/unseen words, and "sc"/"uc" mean seen/unseen templates. In most cases, both word and template were in the grammar, but they were not related. This could have been improved by a more sophisticated method of treating unknown words. The "sentential" column indicates the sentential coverage, where a sentence was judged to be covered when the grammar included correct lexical entries for all words in the sentence. This measure can be considered to be the "ideal" accuracy attained by the grammar, i.e., sentential accuracy when a parser and a disambiguation model worked perfectly.

Table 2 also lists the results of parsing POS-tagged sentences in Section 23 containing less than or equal to 40 words (2,287 sentences). We conducted parsing experiments with an HPSG parser with CFG filtering [16]. The parser did an exhaustive search, and did not apply any heuristic techniques, such as beam-thresholding, to reduce the search space [1]. Without such techniques, however, predicate-argument structures (SEM features) cause an exponential explosion in the search space. The SEM feature was thus ignored in the parsing experiments. Another literature [17] described a technique to reduce the search space by beam-thresholding and reported the accuracy of predicate-argument relations attained with an automatically acquired HPSG grammar. The "success" column lists the ratio of successful parsing, i.e., at least one parse was output (not

Table 3. Reasons for the failures of grammar acquisition.

Shortcomings of annotation rules	Constructions currently unsupported	16
	Preprocessing failures	3
	Annotation failures	1
Errors in the Penn Treebank	Tree structure errors	6
	Nonterminal errors	4
	Preterminal errors	1
Constructions unsupported by HPSG	Argument clusters	13
	Head extraction	1
Total		45

necessarily including the correct answer). The "failure" column represents the ratio of failures i.e., no parses were output. The "error" indicates the ratio of sentences that exceeded the space limit (40,000 edges). The "time" shows the average parsing time for success/failure sentences. The results attest to the significant robustness of the grammar against real-world texts.

Grammar acquisition failed for 1,335 sentences, and the reasons for these failures were investigated for the sentences in Section 02 (45 failures). The results listed in Table 3 reveal that dominant reasons were the shortcomings in annotation rules and errors in the treebank. We intend to reduce both of these by enhancing annotation rules, which should lead to further improvements in the grammar. There were relatively fewer defects in the grammar theory than expected. The results indicate that the fragility of deep processing was not inherent to linguistic theory.

5 Concluding Remarks

The principal idea proposed here was to externalize linguistic intuition as annotations to a corpus, and a large lexicon was automatically extracted from the annotations by inversely applying grammar rules to the given annotations. This approach was applied to the acquisition of a robust HPSG grammar from the Penn Treebank, which was successfully obtained at low cost.

Our claim is that the fragility of deep linguistic analysis is the result of difficulties with the development of a robust grammar based on linguistics, as opposed to most researchers who believe in the inherent impossibility of deep analysis of real-world texts. This study enabled us to develop and maintain a robust grammar based on linguistics at low cost, and opened up the possibility of robust deep analysis of real-world texts.

References

1. Riezler, S., King, T.H., Kaplan, R.M., Crouch, R., III, J.T.M., Johnson, M.: Parsing the Wall Street Journal using a Lexical-Functional Grammar and discriminative estimation techniques. In: Proceedings of 40th ACL. (2002)
2. Schabes, Y., Abeillé, A., Joshi, A.K.: Parsing strategies with 'lexicalized' grammars: Application to tree adjoining grammars. In: Proceedings of 12th COLING. (1988) 578–583
3. Steedman, M.: The Syntactic Process. The MIT Press (2000)

4. Pollard, C., Sag, I.A.: Head-Driven Phrase Structure Grammar. University of Chicago Press (1994)
5. Miyao, Y., Ninomiya, T., Tsujii, J.: Lexicalized grammar acquisition. In: Proceedings of 10th EACL Companion Volume. (2003) 127–130
6. Xia, F.: Extracting tree adjoining grammars from bracketed corpora. In: Proceedings of 5th NLPRS. (1999)
7. Chen, J., Vijay-Shanker, K.: Automated extraction of TAGs from the Penn Treebank. In: Proceedings of 6th IWPT. (2000)
8. Chiang, D.: Statistical parsing with an automatically-extracted tree adjoining grammar. In: Proceedings of 38th ACL. (2000) 456–463
9. Hockenmaier, J., Steedman, M.: Acquiring compact lexicalized grammars from a cleaner treebank. In: Proceedings of 3rd LREC. (2002)
10. Bresnan, J., ed.: The Mental Representation of Grammatical Relations. MIT Press, Cambridge, MA (1982)
11. Cahill, A., McCarthy, M., van Genabith, J., Way, A.: Parsing with PCFGs and automatic f-structure annotation. In: Proceedings of 7th International Lexical-Functional Grammar Conference. (2002)
12. Frank, A., Sadler, L., van Genabith, J., Way, A.: From treebank resources to LFG f-structures: Automatic f-structure annotation of treebank trees and CFGs extracted from treebanks. In Abeille, A., ed.: Building and Using Syntactically Annotated Corpora. Kluwer Academic Publishers (2003) 367–389
13. Korhonen, A.: Subcategorization Acquisition. PhD thesis, Computer Laboratory, University of Cambridge (2002) Published as Techical Report UCAM-CL-TR-530.
14. Magerman, D.M.: Statistical decision-tree models for parsing. In: Proceedings of 33rd ACL. (1995) 276–283
15. Collins, M.: Three generative, lexicalised models for statistical parsing. In: Proceedings of 35th ACL. (1997) 16–23
16. Torisawa, K., Nishida, K., Miyao, Y., Tsujii, J.: An HPSG parser with CFG filtering. Natural Language Engineering Special Issue – Efficient Processing with HPSG: Methods, Systems, Evaluation **6** (2000) 63–80
17. Miyao, Y., Ninomiya, T., Tsujii, J.: Probabilistic modeling of argument structures including non-local dependencies. In: Proceedings of RANLP 2003. (2003) 285–291

Unsupervised Segmentation of Chinese Corpus Using Accessor Variety

Haodi Feng[1], Kang Chen[2], Chunyu Kit[3], and Xiaotie Deng[4]

[1] School of Computer Science and Technology, Shandong University, Jinan
fenghaodi@sdu.edu.cn
[2] Department of Computer Science and Technology, Tsinghua University, Beijing
ck99@mails.tsinghua.edu.cn
[3] Department of Chinese, Translation and Linguistics, City University of Hong Kong,
Kowloon, Hong Kong
ctckit@cityu.edu.hk
[4] Department of Computer Science, City University of Hong Kong, Kowloon,
Hong Kong
csdeng@cityu.edu.hk

Abstract. The lack of word delimiters such as spaces in Chinese texts makes word segmentation a special issue in Chinese text processing. As the volume of Chinese texts grows rapidly on the Internet, the number of unknown words increases accordingly. However, word segmentation approaches relying solely on existing dictionaries are helpless in handling unknown words. In this paper, we propose a novel unsupervised method to segment large Chinese corpora using contextual information. In particular, the number of characters preceding and following a string, known as the *accessors* of the string, is used to measure the independence of the string. The greater the independence, the more likely it is that the string is a word. The segmentation problem is then considered an optimization problem to maximize the target function of this number over all word candidates in an utterance. Our purpose here is to explore the best function in terms of segmentation performance. The performance is evaluated with the word token recall measure in addition to word type precision and word type recall. Among the three types of target functions that we have explored, polynomial functions turn out to outperform others. This simple method is effective in unsupervised segmentation of Chinese texts and its performance is highly comparable to other recently reported unsupervised segmentation methods.

1 Introduction

Chinese texts have no word delimiters such as spaces in English texts. A Chinese sentence is a continuous string of Chinese characters. The same sentence may have a number of possible segmentations that lead to different understandings and interpretations. Word segmentation is recognized as a critical initial step for many application tasks concerning Chinese text processing. Teahan *et al.* [15] state that interpreting a text as a sequence of words is beneficial for a number of information retrieval and text storage tasks, e.g., full-text search, word-based compression, and key-phrase extraction.

Existing word segmentation approaches can be categorized into three types: dictionary-based, statistics-based, and hybrid. For example, the forward and backward maximum matching methods, as discussed in [10], [9] and many others, are typical dictionary based methods that segment a sentence into words in terms of a given dictionary. Statistical methods make use of statistical information (e.g., n-gram frequencies) in various ways to facilitate word segmentation, as reported in [13], [5], [4] and [15]. Some statistical methods use pre-segmented corpora to train probabilistic models. Such supervised training requires a lot of human effort for preparing the training data. Since human knowledge is utilized, these systems usually outperform, to some extent, those with unsupervised training using an unsegmented corpus as training data. However, their adaptability and robustness are weak, in particular, in handling unseen words. In many applications, 100% accuracy is not necessary, e.g., as in clustering and abstraction. Instead, adaptability and robustness are strongly demanded.

Regarding unsupervised segmentation methods, Sun *et al.* [14] propose an approach based on various kinds of statistical information, e.g., mutual information and the difference of *t*-score between characters. For segmenting Japanese Kanji sequences, Ando and Lee [1] use a similar but robust statistical method to evaluate each possible boundary in the input text, and then determine which one is a suitable breaking point. Brent [2] has developed a model of how children segment utterances into words in the course of lexical development for learning their native language. Brent and Tao [3] extend this model to segmenting Chinese texts.

In this paper, we propose an unsupervised method to segment Chinese texts. We use a novel statistical criterion, called *accessor variety*, as measurement for how likely it is that a substring in a sentence is a word, and then find out the segmentation of the sentence that maximizes a target function with both the accessor variety and the length of the substring as variants. Each subtring (hence "string" for simplicity) in an input sentence is a possible word candidate for unsupervised segmentation.

We organize the rest of this paper as follows. Section 2 introduces the concept of accessor variety. Section 3 discusses our unsupervised segmentation method based on accessor variety and function optimization. Section 4 discusses various evaluation methods for word segmentation. Section 5 presents and analyzes experimental results. Finally, we conclude our work in Section 6.

2   Accessor Variety

The most important factor considered in our segmentation method is the *accessor variety* value of a string. The accessor variety criterion is used to judge how independent a string is from the rest of the text. This criterion is a straightforward formulation of Harris's [7] idea half century ago for determining a morpheme in an unfamiliar Indian language in terms of the number of contexts in which it can appear: the larger is the number, the more likely it is to be a morpheme. To illustrate this concept in a simple way, let us take a look at the following example. Suppose we have four Chinese sentences,

1. 门把手弄坏了 ("the door hurts the hand" or "the door handle is broken").
2. 小明修好了门把手 ("Xiao Ming fixed the door handle").
3. 这个门把手很漂亮 ("this door handle is very beautiful").
4. 这个门把手坏了 ("this door handle is broken").

Consider the string 门把手 in these four sentences. It has 3 distinct preceding characters, i.e., "S" (the start of a sentence), 了 and 个, and 4 distinct following characters, i.e., 弄, "E" (the end of a sentence), 很 and 坏. That is, it can be used in at least three different contexts, and therefore may carry some meanings that are independent of other words in these four sentences. In this case, its accessor variety value is min(3, 4)=3.

We use the accessor variety criterion, hence AV for short, to evaluate how independently a string is used in a corpus, and thus how likely it is that it should be segmented as a word. The AV of a string s is defined as:

$$AV(s) = \min(L_{av}(s), R_{av}(s))$$

Here, $L_{av}(s)$ is the *left* accessor variety of s, which is defined as the number of its distinct preceding characters (i.e., predecessors) except "S" that precedes s, plus the number of distinct sentences in which s appears at the beginning, and $R_{av}(s)$ is the *right* accessor variety of s, which is defined as the number of its distinct following characters (i.e., successors) except "E" that succeed s, plus the number of distinct sentences in which s appears at the end. In other words, "S" and "E" in different sentences are counted as distinct characters. The main reason for this is that there are words usually appearing at the beginning or the end of a sentence but rarely in the middle, e.g., 但是 (but) and 吗 (interrogative marker). They are meaningful words although there are not many other characters than "S" and "E" preceding or succeeding them.

From the definition of AV, it is clear that the AV value of a string should be able to reflect how independent the string is in a given corpus. Therefore, it is reasonable to segment a sentence into substrings with high AV values. In the next section, we will discuss how to use these values to automatically segment Chinese texts.

3 Unsupervised Segmentation Method

We regard the segmentation of a sentence as an optimization problem which intends to maximize a target function over all possible segmentations. In this paper, we only consider strings with lengths from one to not longer than six characters as word candidates, because longer words are rare in Chinese speech. The AV values of all strings from one to six characters can be extracted from a given corpus via automatic statistical procedures. No dictionaries or human efforts are needed.

In the following discussion, we use a *segmentation* to denote a segmented sentence, a *segment* to denote a continuous substring in the segmentation, and f to denote the target function. We use s to represent a string (e.g., a sentence),

S to represent a segmentation of s, n to represent the number of characters in s, and m to denote the number of segments in S. Then sentence s can be displayed as the concatenation of n characters, and S as the concatenation of m strings:

$$s = c_1 c_2 c_3 \cdots c_i \cdots c_n$$
$$S = w_1 w_2 w_3 \cdots w_i \cdots w_m$$

where c_i stands for a character and w_i stands for a segment.

In this paper, the target functions f have the following property:

$$f(S) = \sum_{i=1}^{m} f(w_i) \qquad (1)$$

Given a target function f and a particular sentence s, we choose the segmentation that maximizes the value of $f(S)$ over all possible segmentations.

We consider two factors in the formulation of $f(w)$. One is segment length, denoted as $|w|$, and the other is the AV value of a segment, denoted as $AV(w)$. Then, $f(w)$ can be formulated as a function of $|w|$ and $AV(w)$, i.e., $f(w) = f(|w|, AV(w))$. A target function like this can be regarded as a choice of normalization for the $AV(w)$ value to balance the segment length and the AV value for each segment. The consideration underlying this formulation is that although short segments usually have higher AV values, longer segments with high enough AV values are usually more preferable.

We consider three types of functions, namely, polynomial, exponential, and logarithmic functions. They are the most representative types of functions from the computational point of view. For each type, we try different functions by setting different powers or bases, and test their performance. Here are a number of typical types of target function.

$$f_1(w) = b^{|w|} \times \log AV(w)$$
$$f_2(w) = |w|^{|w|} \times AV^d(w)$$
$$f_3(w) = |w|^c \times AV^d(w)$$
$$f_4(w) = |w|^{|w|} \times \log AV(w)),$$

where b, c and d are integer parameters that are used to define the target functions. Notice that when $c = 1$ and $d = 1$, function $f_3(w) = |w| \times AV(w)$ becomes the normalized AV value of w if we consider its transfiguration $\frac{AV(w)}{\frac{n}{|w|}}$. Here, n is the number of characters in a sentence, which can be ignored since it is the common factor in each expression for each segment in each segmentation. When $b = 1$, $f_1(w) = \log AV(w)$ becomes the logarithm of AV value, in which case the value of a segmentation, which is the sum of the logarithms over all its segments, is equivalent to the multiplication of the AV values of its segments from the optimization point of view. Theoretically, we can assign any possible number to these parameters. However, numbers that are too large are meaningless in practice. Our experiments confirm this viewpoint by the fact that the segmentation reaches the peak of performance at small values for these parameters.

Suppose we have calculated the AV values for all substrings in a given corpus and decided the three parameters b, c, and d for a target function. Then, we can compute the value for each segmentation S of a sentence s following Equation (1). Since a substring with too small an AV value is usually multivocal and thus not a good candidate for a word, we do not want to segment a sentence into all substrings of this kind. For this purpose, we set an AV value threshold. For a string w with an AV value smaller than this threshold, we set its $f(w)$ value to a very small negative integer. With regard to the uniqueness of single characters, we try two different ways to deal with them in our experiments: in one way, they are handled in the same way as multi-character strings; in the other way, we always set their target function value $f(c) = 0$. The latter case means that when segmenting a sentence, we prefer multi-character segments with some good-enough AV values to single-character segments and prefer single-character segments (whose target function values have been set to 0) to multi-character segments with AV values that are too small (these values have been set to very small negative numbers).

Having all this information prepared, we are now ready to compute $f(S)$ for a given sentence s. Since the value of each segment can be computed independently from the other segments in S, $f(S)$ can be computed using a simple dynamic programming technique, for which the time complexity is linear to sentence length. Let us use f_i to denote the optimal target function value for the subsentence $c_1 c_2 \cdots c_i$, and $w_{j..i}$ to denote the segment $c_{j+1} c_{j+2} ... c_i$ (for $j \leq i$). Then we have the following dynamic equations:

$$f_0 = 0;$$
$$f_1 = f(w_{1..1} = c_1);$$
$$f_i = \max_{0 < i-j < 7} f_j + f(w_{j..i}), \text{ for } i > 1;$$
$$f(S) = f_n.$$

Notice that in each iteration, there are at most N (in our experiment $N = 6$) possible choices, where N is the maximum length of a word. Therefore, the time complexity of this dynamic programming is linear to sentence length.

4 Segmentation Evaluation

There are several segmentation evaluation methods, either based on word type or word boundary. Based on word type, the evaluation measures word type precision P_w and recall R_w are defined as follows, where the symbol # stands for "the number of".

$$P_w = \frac{\# \text{ correctly segmented words}}{\# \text{ all segmented words}}$$

$$R_w = \frac{\# \text{ correctly segmented words}}{\# \text{ all correct words in the corpus}}$$

Usually the correctness of a word is judged by humans in the evaluation.

The P_w and R_w measures are usually applied to evaluate how well a word segmentation procedure identifies words. However, they do not evaluate the segmentation directly, because they ignore whether the correct words are extracted from the correct places. The locations where the segmentation module puts spaces to mark the boundaries of words are another type of useful information for evaluating the segmentation performance [14]. Similarly, the word boundary precision P_b and recall R_b are defined as follows.

$$P_b = \frac{\text{\# word boundaries correctly marked}}{\text{\# all word boundaries marked}}$$

$$R_b = \frac{\text{\# word boundaries correctly marked}}{\text{\# all correct word boundaries}}$$

These word boundary measures overcome the defect of P_w and R_w. But they have their own problems. For example, consider the sentence 风是因为空气的流动产生的. Suppose 风是因为空气的流动产生的 is the correct segmentation, and the automatically generated segmentation is 风是因为空气的流动产生的. Here, the automatic segmentation method puts a space after 是, which will be considered as a correct word boundary by the word boundary evaluation since there is also a space at the same position in the hand-segmented result. However, the automatic method does not extract 是 correctly. The same problem happens at the position after the first 的. In other words, the word boundary evaluation method does not evaluate segmentation method precisely either.

We are interested in an evaluation method that can solve all these problems, i.e., word token recall, R_t for short. Word token recall can be defined in the following way: In an n-character sentence, there are totally n+1 positions where spaces might be inserted. We number these positions as 0, 1, ..., n-1, n, with 0 as the position before the first character and n as the position after the last character. Then each segment in a segmentation of this sentence corresponds to a pair of positions, i.e., the position directly before the segment and the position directly after the segment. Then the word token recall of a segmentation method is defined as the proportion of the automatically generated correct position pairs to all the position pairs in the correct segmentation, that is:

$$R_t = \frac{\text{\# correct pairs automatically gotten}}{\text{\# correct pairs}}.$$

A reason for us not to consider word token precision for the time being is that we only care how much of an input sentence is correctly segmented automatically, and not how many pieces the remaining part of the sentence is segmented, although this will influence the value of word token precision.

Let us use the previous example to show how R_t works. The sentence and possible word boundary positions in it are: (0)风(1)是(2)因(3)为(4)空(5)气(6)的(7)流(8)动(9)产(10)生(11)的(12). Suppose the position pairs in the correct segmentation (say, by hand) are (0,1)风(1,2)是(2,4)因为(4,6)空气(6,7)的(7,9)流动(9,11)产生(11,12)的, where there are eight pairs in total, and the position pairs in the automatic segmentation are (0,2)风是(2,4)因为(4,7)空气的(7,9)流动(9,12)产生的.

Comparing these two sets of position pairs, we find 2 correct position pairs in the automatic segmentation, i.e., {(2,4), (7,9)}. Then the R_t value of this automatic segmentation is 2/8. Given another automatic segmentation of this sentence as (0,2)风是(2,4)因为(4,5)空(5,6)气(6,7)的(7,9)流动(9,12)产生的, which carries 3 correct position pairs, i.e., {(2,4), (6,7), (7,9)}, its R_t value is 3/8.

Obviously, $R_t = 1$ means a perfect segmentation. Usually, $R_t < 1$. A higher R_t value means not only more correct locations but also more correct words extracted. Therefore, the R_t value is more rigorous than the evaluation based on word boundaries or word types. We use R_t as the criterion to evaluate our segmentation method. We will also compare it to P_w and R_w.

5 Experiments and Results

We have conducted a number of experiments on a 16.4M Chinese text corpus in BIG5 using our unsupervised segmentation methods. It is a collection of Hong Kong laws. We set the maximal segment length to 6. As discussed before, we consider three types of target functions, each of which carries one or two parameters to define an exact target function. In our experiments, we limit the values of these parameters b, c and d to the following ranges: $1 \leq b \leq 7$, $0 \leq c \leq 7$ and $d = 1$, or 2. In some experiments, we treat single-character strings in the same way as multi-character strings, while in other experiments, we define their target function values to be 0. We also consider different thresholds of AV value so that the values of the target functions on those substrings with AV values smaller than the thresholds would be set to a very small negative number. We compute and present the R_t values for all cases. For word type precision P_w and word type recall R_w, we only consider the cases where R_t is not too small.

For evaluation, we randomly choose 2000 sentences and then segment them by hand into standard segmentation, in order to obtain the correct position pairs in each sentence. Then, automatic segmentation results of these 2000 randomly chosen sentences are compared against the hand-segmented results for computing the values of R_t, R_w and P_w. These values can be automatically calculated once these 2000 testing sentences have been manually and automatically segmented. Notice, however, that the AV values of all substrings involved in the automatic segmentation are derived from the whole corpus, not merely from the testing corpus.

For each target function type, we assign different values to the parameters b, c and d, and evaluate the performance of the algorithm with the corresponding target functions. There are two ways that we handle the single-character strings. The way that we handle them in the same way as multi-character strings is denoted as Way I, and that we always set their target function value to 0 is denoted as Way II. Our experiments show that the algorithm performs much better in Way II than in Way I. Table 1 shows this effect clearly, where the R_t values for a number of target functions are listed in contrast to each other in terms of these two cases. The R_t, P_w and R_w values for a number of target functions that we have tested are listed in Table 2, Table 3, and Table 4, respectively, with Way II to handle single-character strings.

Table 1. R_t values: Way I vs. II.

Target Function	R_t (%) Way I	Way II	AV Threshold
$\|w\|^1 \times AV(w)$	45.1	65.2	2
$\|w\|^0 \times AV^2(w)$	47.9	66.0	2
$\|w\|^1 \times AV^2(w)$	45.7	66.0	2
$\|w\|^2 \times AV^2(w)$	42.7	65.0	2
$\|w\|^3 \times AV^2(w)$	42.6	64.9	2
$\|w\|^{\|w\|} \times AV(w)$	0.4	48.0	2
$\|w\|^{\|w\|} \times AV^2(w)$	22.7	60.9	2

Table 2. R_t of various target functions.

Target Function	R_t (%)	AV Threshold
$2^{\|w\|} \times \log AV(w)$	53.83	9
$\|w\|^1 \times \log AV(w)$	57.77	3
$\|w\|^0 \times AV(w)$	66.79	6
$\|w\|^1 \times AV(w)$	65.76	4
$\|w\|^0 \times AV^2(w)$	66.81	5
$\|w\|^1 \times AV^2(w)$	67.01	9
$\|w\|^2 \times AV^2(w)$	65.48	4
$\|w\|^{\|w\|} \times AV(w)$	50.28	3
$\|w\|^{\|w\|} \times AV^2(w)$	61.34	3

From these tables we can see that the R_t values are more consistent with P_w than with R_w, and that the polynomial target functions achieve, in general, higher R_t values than the exponential or logarithmic ones.

6 Conclusion

In this paper, we have attempted to tackle the unsupervised Chinese text segmentation problem by transforming it into an optimization problem with the aid of the novel criterion accessor variety that we have proposed for measuring the independence of each word candidate. We try to search for the best target function, in terms of segmentation performance, among the three types of function, i.e., polynomial, exponential and logarithmic. Each target function combines two types of information about a word candidate: its length and its AV value. The maximization problem for segmenting a sentence is then resolved by dynamic programming technique.

Our experiments show that the polynomial functions perform much better than the other two types of functions in terms of the word token recall (R_t) evaluation. Over all experiments, the best performance scores we have achieved for word token recall R_t, word type recall R_w, and word type precision P_w are as follows.

Table 3. Word type precision of various target functions.

Target Function	P_w (%) of Word Length 2-6, 2-4, 2, 3, 4, 5, 6	AV Thres.
$\|w\|^1 \times AV(w)$	75.54, 75.49, 83.99, 28.42, 63.33, 72.72, 100.00	3
$\|w\|^2 \times AV(w)$	73.54, 73.62, 84.33, 27.30, 50.65, 60.00, 70.00	3
$\|w\|^0 \times AV^2(w)$	74.00, 73.96, 82.51, 28.01, 68.18, 83.33, 100.00	3
$\|w\|^1 \times AV^2(w)$	72.25, 72.19, 79.42, 29.78, 52.94, 80.00, 100.00	3
$\|w\|^2 \times AV^2(w)$	76.55, 76.55, 85.58, 28.57, 66.67, 66.67, 100.00	3
$\|w\|^3 \times AV^2(w)$	72.60, 72.84, 81.49, 30.29, 60.94, 50.00, 66.67	3
$\|w\|^{\|w\|} \times AV(w)$	55.15, 65.12, 86.48, 31.20, 34.49, 18.82, 28.36	3
$\|w\|^{\|w\|} \times AV^2(w)$	71.60, 75.96, 86.38, 37.28, 51.88, 38.78, 29.36	3

Table 4. Word type recall of various target functions.

Target Function	R_w (%) of Word Length 2-6, 2-4, 2, 3, 4, 5, 6	AV Thres.
$\|w\|^1 \times AV(w)$	66.81, 70.00, 85.29, 32.61, 12.15, 12.77, 3.84	9
$\|w\|^0 \times AV^2(w)$	65.74, 68.93, 85.29, 26.63, 09.39, 12.77, 0.00	9
$\|w\|^1 \times AV^2(w)$	66.31, 69.53, 85.29, 28.80, 12.15, 12.77, 0.00	9
$\|w\|^2 \times AV^2(w)$	67.00, 70.13, 85.29, 32.61, 13.26, 14.89, 3.84	9
$\|w\|^3 \times AV^2(w)$	71.49, 74.67, 89.78, 38.59, 16.57, 17.02, 11.54	3
	67.95, 71.00, 85.29, 36.41, 16.57, 14.89, 11.54	9
$\|w\|^{\|w\|} \times AV(w)$	76.36, 78.13, 85.29, 57.61, 54.14, 55.32, 38.46	9
$\|w\|^{\|w\|} \times AV^2(w)$	75.28, 77.27, 89.69, 45.11, 32.04, 44.68, 42.31	3
	71.43, 73.40, 85.29, 42.39, 30.39, 40.43, 38.46	9

- R_t=67%, with R_w=69.5% and P_w=77.9%
- R_w=78%, with P_w=76% and R_t=61.3%
- P_w=79%, with R_w=70% and R_t=65.5%

These results are highly comparable to those achieved by recently published unsupervised segmentation methods, e.g., 75.1% word type precision and 74% word type recall in [11], 81.2% word type precision and 81.1% word type recall in [8]. Hence, our approach is a good choice for tackling the task of unsupervised Chinese text segmentation. It is also particularly suitable for processing large-scale data sets because of its simplicity in computation.

References

1. Rie Kubota Ando and Lillian Lee: Mostly-unsupervised statistical segmentation of Japanese: Applications to Kanji. NAACL-1(2000) 241–248
2. Michael R. Brent: An efficient, probabilistically sound algorithm for segmentation and word discovery. Machine Learning **34** (1999) 71–106
3. Michael R. Brent and Xiaopeng Tao: Chinese text segmentation with MBDP-1: Making the most of training corpora. ACL-EACL'01 (Toulouse, France, 2001) 82–89

4. Kwok-Shing Cheng, Gilbert H. Young, and Kam-Fai Wong: A study on word-based and integral-bit Chinese text compression algorithm. Journal of the American Society for Information Science **50** (1999) 218–228
5. Yubin Dai, Christopher Khoo, and Tech Ee Loh: A new statistical formula for Chinese text segmentation incorporating contextual information. SIGIR'99 (1999) 82–89
6. Beeferman Douglas, Adam Berger, and John D. Lafferty: Statistical models for text segmentation. Machine Learning **34**(1-3) (1999) 177–210
7. Zellig S. Harris: Papers in Structural and Transformational Linguistics. D. Reidel, Dordrecht (1970) 68–77
8. Jinhu Huang and David Powers: Experiments on unsupervised Chinese word segmentation and classification. First Student Workshop on Computational Linguistics (Peking University, 2002) 83–89
9. Chunyu Kit, Yuan Liu, and Nanyuan Liang: On methods of Chinese automatic word segmentation. Journal of Chinese Information Processing **3** (1) (1989) 1–32
10. Nanyuan Liang: CDWS – An automatic word segmentation system for written Chinese. Journal of Chinese Information Processing **1** (2) (1986) 44-52
11. Fuchun Peng and Dale Schuurmans: Self-supervised Chinese word segmentation. Advances in Intelligent Data Analysis (IDA-01)(Cascais, Portugal, 2001) 238–247
12. Jay M. Ponte and W. Croft Bruce: Useg: a retargetable word segmentation procedure for information retrieval. Technical Report TR96-2. University of Massachusetts (Amherst, MA, 1996)
13. Richard Sproat, Chilin Shih, William Gale, and Nancy Chang: A stochastic finite-state word-segmentation algorithm for Chinese. Computational Linguistics **22** (3) (1996) 377–404
14. Maosong Sun, Dayang Shen, and Benjamin K. Tsou: Chinese word segmentation without using lexicon and hand-crafted training data. COLING-ACL'98 (II)(Montreal, 1998) 1265–1271
15. William J. Teahan, Yingying Wen, Rodger J. McNab, and Ian H. Witten: A compression-based algorithm for Chinese word segmentation. Computational Linguistics **26** (3) (2000) 375–393
16. Yong-Heng Wang, Hai-Ju Su, and Yan Mo: Automatic processing of Chinese words. Journal of Chinese Information Processing **4** (4) (1990) 1–11
17. Zimin Wu and Gwyneth Tseng: Chinese text segmentation for text retrieval: Achievements and problems. Journal of the American Society for Information Sceince **44** (9) (1993) 532–542

Chinese Unknown Word Identification Using Class-Based LM

Guohong Fu and Kang-Kwong Luke

Department of Linguistics, The University of Hong Kong,
Pokfulam Road, Hong Kong
ghfu@hkucc.hku.hk, kkluke@hkusua.hku.hk

Abstract. This paper presents a modified class-based LM approach to Chinese unknown word identification. In this work, Chinese unknown word identification is viewed as a classification problem and the part-of-speech of each unknown word is defined as its class. Furthermore, three types of features, including contextual class feature, word juncture model and word formation patterns, are combined in a framework of class-based LM to perform correct unknown word identification on a sequence of known words. In addition to unknown word identification, the class-based LM approach also provides a solution for unknown word tagging. The results of our experiments show that most unknown words in Chinese texts can be resolved effectively by the proposed approach.

1 Introduction

Unknown word identification (UWI) plays an important role in developing a Chinese word segmentation system for practical applications. Most current word segmentation systems for Chinese need a dictionary to guide segmentation. However, no dictionary can be complete in practice. Although a dictionary may cover most words in use, there are many other words, such as proper nouns and domain-specific terms that cannot be collected exhaustively into it. Consequently, a robust word segmentation system for Chinese must be capable of identifying automatically these out-of-vocabulary words to avoid the sharp degradation of performance in open applications.

However, correct identification of unknown words is a big challenge for Chinese. On the one hand, Chinese unknown words are constructed dynamically and freely in practice. In theory, any combination of Chinese characters or known words may be a potential unknown word. On the other hand, there lack of enough explicit information in plain Chinese texts, such as capitalization in English for detecting unknown words.

Recently, a variety of techniques have been proposed for Chinese UWI, from rule-based methods to machine learning approaches. In particular, these techniques focused on how to explore or combine more features for the detection of unknown words. Wu and Jiang took word segmentation, including UWI as an integral part of full sentence analysis [1]. This mechanism uses a full sentence parsing to achieve the final disambiguation and identification of Chinese unknown words. However, the coverage of the parser may restrict its applications in practical systems. Zhang et al presented a novel method to Chinese UWI based on role tagging [2]. In order to recognize different types of unknown words, they defined different unknown word roles to varied internal components and contexts. However, their method needs a role-tagged corpus to learn role knowledge, which is not always available. Xue and Converse introduced position-of-character (POC) tags into Chinese word segmentation and proposed a supervised machine-learning approach [3]. Wang et al proposed the use of character-based formation patterns and juncture model for Chinese UWI [4]. However, these character-based methods may lose some more important word-level features for the correct identification of unknown words. To address this problem, Fu and Luke recently and incorporated word-juncture models and word-formation patterns with word bigram models and developed an integrated approach to Chinese word segmentation [5]. Their experiments showed that their method is effective for the segmenting of the complicated fragments mixed with ambiguities and unknown words.

In this paper, we present a modified class-based language model approach to Chinese UWI. In this work, Chinese UWI is taken as a classification problem and the part-of-speech of an unknown word is defined as its class. Furthermore, three groups of features, namely the contextual class information, the class-based word juncture models and the class-based word formation patterns, are statistically computed and combined in a class-based LM framework to perform UWI on a sequence of known words. In addition, the proposed method also provides a resolution for unknown word tagging. In this way, most unknown words can be identified and tagged effectively.

The rest of this paper is organized as follows: Section 2 presents a modified class-based LM for Chinese UWI. Section 3 describes in brief a two-stage decoding algorithm for word segmentation. Section 4 reports the experimental results of our system. In the final section we give our conclusions on this work.

2 Class-Based Language Modeling for Chinese UWI

2.1 POS as Class of Unknown Word

In this work, we specify the basic classes of unknown words in terms of their part-of-speech. There are a number of reasons for this hypothesis. Firstly, it is proved that part-of-speech is a very important feature for UWI [1][3]. In practice, there may exist certain relations between unknown words and their par-of-speech categorizations. Table 1 is a survey of the distribution of unknown words versus their par-of-speech tags on the training corpus (viz. Corpus A in Table 2). It shows the top nine frequent types of unknown words account for more than 91% of the total unknown words in the corpus, while unknown words have wide distributions in part-of-speech types. It is observed that unknown words in the training data are labeled with 30 different tags of the total 46 tags in Peking University tag set [7]. Secondly, a number of large part-of-speech tagged corpora are now available for Chinese, such as the Peking University corpus (PKU-Corpus for short; GB code) and the CKIP corpus (Big5 code), which makes it easier to learn the necessary class features for Chinese UWI.

More formally, we employ three rules to specify the classes for UWI: (1) For each unknown word, its part-of-speech is defined as its class; (2) For each known word whose part-of-speech tag is nr (personal name), ns (location), m (numeral), t (time), nt (organization name), nz (other proper nouns), j (abbreviation) or l (phrase), its part-of-speech category is used as its class; (3) For any other known words, they are defined as special individual classes by themselves.

Table 1. Distribution of unknown words versus their par-of-speech tags

Classes	POS-Tags	Number	Rates (%)	Accumulative rates (%)
Common noun	n	14391	20.77	20.77
Numeral	m	12600	18.18	38.95
Personal name	nr	12460	17.98	56.93
Time	t	9572	13.81	70.74
Location	ns	4740	6.84	77.58
Verb	v	3042	4.39	81.97
Abbreviation	j	2235	3.23	85.20
Phrase	l	2132	3.08	88.28
Other proper noun	nz	2121	3.06	91.34
Others	-	6000	8.66	100.00
Total	-	69290	100.00	100.00

2.2 Class-Based LM for Chinese UWI

The class-based LM is originally proposed to address the problem of data-sparseness and is now widely used for named entity recognition [6]. Here, we modify it for Chinese UWI by introducing word juncture models and word-formation patterns.

In practice, Chinese UWI can be also viewed as a problem of classification: Given a known word sequence $K_1^n = k_1 k_2 \cdots k_n$, Chinese UWI aims to find the best class sequence $\hat{T}_1^m = t_1 t_2 \cdots t_m (m \leq n)$ maximizing the conditional probability $P(T_1^m | K_1^n)$, i.e.

$$\hat{T}_1^m = \arg\max_T P(T_1^m | K_1^n) = \arg\max_T P(T_1^m) P(K_1^n | T_1^m). \tag{1}$$

Equation (1) is a general class-based LM, which consists of a contextual class model $P(T_1^m)$ and a word model $P(K_1^n | T_1^m)$, and is not computable in practice. Therefore, some approximate calculations are needed to make it applicable.

The contextual class model is usually approximated as a product of n-gram probabilities. With a view to the problem of data-sparseness, we employ the bigram model to approximate it as follows:

$$P(T_1^m) = P(t_1 t_2 \cdots t_m) \cong \prod_{i=1}^m P(t_i | t_{i-1}). \tag{2}$$

As for the approximate calculation of the word model, it is relative complicated. There are different ways of approximating in different applications. In view of the fact that most words take themselves as their word-classes in current work, here we simplify and approximate the word model $P(K_1^n | T_1^m)$ with the relevant class-based word juncture models and word-formation patterns as follows:

$$P(K_1^n | T_1^m) = P(J_{I1}^m J_{O1}^m W_1^m | T_1^m) \cong \prod_{i=1}^m P(J_O(w_{i-1} w_i, t_i)) P(J_I(w_i, t_i)) P_{WFP}(w_i, t_i). \tag{3}$$

Where, $W_1^m = w_1 w_2 \cdots w_m$ denotes a sequence of segmented word after UWI; $J_{O1}^m = J_{O1} J_{O2} \cdots J_{Om}$ denotes a sequence of word juncture types outside the segmented words; J_{Ii} denotes a sequence of word juncture types inside a segmented word $w_i (1 \leq i \leq m)$; $P(J_O(w_{i-1} w_i, t_i))$ is the outside class-based word juncture model, which estimates the probability of the juncture type between two segmented words w_{i-1} and (w_i, t_i); $P(J_I(w_i, t_i))$ is the inside class-based word-juncture model, which estimates the generative probability of the juncture type sequence inside a word w_i with a class t_i; $P_{WFP}(w_i, t_i)$ denotes the generative word-formation pattern probability of the components of the word w_i whose class is t_i. Note that a segmented word may be a known or unknown word after UWI while its components are always known words. The calculations of the class-based word juncture models and the word-formation patterns are presented in detail respectively in Section 2.3 and 2.4.

2.3 Class-Based Word Juncture Models

It has been proved that word juncture models (WJMs) are important for correct identification of Chinese unknown words [5]. In this section, we modify this model by introducing the classes defined in section 2.1.

Given a sequence of known words $k_1 k_2 \cdots k_l$, between each known word pair $k_{i-1} k_i (1 \le i \le l)$ is a *word juncture*. In general, there are two different types of junctures in Chinese UWI, namely *word boundary* (denoted by J_B) and *non-word boundary* (denoted by J_N). Let $J(k_{i-1} k_i, t_i)$ denote the type of a word juncture k_{i-1} and (k_i, t_i) (where k_i is included in a segmented word with a class t_i), then the juncture type probability can be defined as follows:

$$P(J(k_{i-1}k_i, t_i)) \stackrel{def}{=} \frac{Count(J(k_{i-1}k_i, t_i))}{Count(k_{i-1}k_i)}. \tag{4}$$

Where, $Count(k_{i-1}k_i)$ denotes the co-occurrence frequency of two known words k_{i-1} and k_i in the training data, and $Count(J(k_{i-1}k_i, t_i))$ refers to the frequency of a juncture type $J(k_{i-1}k_i, t_i)$ in the training data.

Obviously, a type of non-word boundary J_N should be assigned to each juncture inside an unknown word $w_i = k^i_{beg} k^i_{beg+1} \cdots k^i_{end}$. Thus, its inside word juncture model $P(J_I(w_i, t_i))$ can be simplified as a product of all inside juncture type probabilities $P(J_N(k^i_{l-1}k^i_l, t_i))$ based on the independent assumption of juncture type assignment. With respect to a known word candidate w_i, its inside word juncture probability $P(J_I(w_i, t_i))$ is one in that there is only one component word inside it, namely itself. Thus, the inside word juncture probability can be formulated as:

$$P(J_I(w_i, t_i)) = \begin{cases} \prod_{l=beg}^{end} P(J_N(k^i_{l-1}k^i_l, t_i)), & \text{if } w_i \text{ is an UW} \\ 1, & \text{if } w_i \text{ is a KW} \end{cases} \tag{5}$$

Where, $J_N(.)$ means the type of the word-juncture (.) is *non-word boundary* (viz. J_N); $k_l(beg \le l \le end)$ denotes a component of w_i, and t_i represents its class. UW and KW are the abbreviations respectively for *unknown word* and *known word*.

For each juncture between two adjacent segmented words $w_{i-1} = k_{beg}^{i-1} k_{beg+1}^{i-1} \cdots k_{end}^{i-1}$ and $w_i = k_{beg}^i k_{beg+1}^i \cdots k_{end}^i$, it should be assigned a type of word boundary J_B. Thus, the relevant outside word juncture probability can be formulated as follows:

$$P(J_O(w_{i-1}w_i,t_i)) = \begin{cases} P(J_B(w_{i-1}w_i,t_i)), \text{if both } w_{i-1} \text{ and } w_i \text{ are } KWs \\ P(J_B(k_{end}^{i-1}k_{beg}^i,t_i)), \text{ if both } w_{i-1} \text{ and } w_i \text{ are } UWs \\ P(J_B(k_{end}^{i-1}w_i,t_i)), \text{ if } w_{i-1} \text{ is } an\ UW \text{ and } w_i \text{ is } a\ KW \\ P(J_B(w_{i-1}k_{beg}^i,t_i)), \text{ if } w_{i-1} \text{ is } a\ KW \text{ and } w_i \text{ is } an\ UW \end{cases} \quad (6)$$

In a sense, the inside and outside word juncture models implicate the interactions of internal component words and the effect of contextual words respectively with respect to the forming of an unknown word w_i with a word-class t_i.

2.4 Class-Based Word-Formation Patterns

In addition to context information and word juncture features, the internal word-formation feature is another important cue for correct UWI [4][5]. In theory, a known word may be identified as an independent segmented word or a component of an unknown word during UWI. More formally, a known word k has four possible patterns to present itself after UWI: (1) k is an independent word by itself. (2) k is the beginning component of an unknown word. (3) k is one middle component of an unknown word. (4) k is at the end of an unknown word. For convenience, we use S, B, M and E to denote these four patterns respectively.

Let $pttn(k,t)$ denote a particular pattern of a known word k in a group of segmented words that are labeled with the same class t. Thus, the relevant formation pattern probability $P(pttn(k,t))$ can be defined as follows:

$$P(pttn(k,t_i)) \stackrel{def}{=} \frac{Count(pttn(k,t))}{Count(k)}. \quad (7)$$

Let t_i denote one candidate class of an unknown word $w_i = k_{beg}^i k_{beg+1}^i \cdots k_{end}^i$, then its word-formation pattern probability $P_{WFP}(w_i,t_i)$ is a product of the formation pattern probabilities $P(pttn(k_l^i,t_i))$ of its components, namely

$$P_{WFP}(w_i,t_i) = P(B(k_{beg}^i,t_i))P(E(k_{end}^i,t_i)) \prod_{l=beg+1}^{end-1} P(M(k_l^i,t_i)). \quad (8)$$

As for a known word w_i, its word-formation pattern probability $P_{WFP}(w_i,t_i)$ equals to its S-pattern probability, i.e. $P_{WFP}(w_i,t_i) = P(S(w_i,t_i))$.

In practice, the class-based word-formation patterns reflect different possibilities of a lexicon word in forming a special group of unknown words in different ways. For example, the word 化 (hua4, change) is usually used as a suffix of an unknown verb, while the word 性 (xing4, nature) is more likely to present itself at the end of an unknown common noun. Our survey on Corpus A shows that the word 化 occurs for 3, 0 and 122 times respectively at the beginning, middle and end of unknown verbs, and the relevant numbers are 2, 0, and 397 for the word 性 in common nouns.

3 Viterbi Decoding for Chinese UWI

3.1 Two-Stage Viterbi Decoding

In general, two main strategies are usually employed to perform word segmentation: the two-stage strategy and the integrated segmentation [5]. It is proved that the integrated segmentation is effective for different types of unknown words [5]. However, it is highly dependent on a complicated threshold-based lattice pruning procedure, which is very sensitive to the corpus for training. Furthermore, the integrated segmentation usually leads to the reduction of efficiency in segmentation. Accordingly, we still employ the two-stage strategy in current work. In order to yield correct segmentations for some complicated cases such as fragments mixed with ambiguities and unknown words in real texts, we use a pure known-word based n-gram to perform known word segmentation.

In practice, the proposed two-stage segmentation consists of two Viterbi decoding processes: (1) Known word decoding: In this process, all possible known word candidates for a input sentence are first generated by looking up the system dictionary and then, a Viterbi decoding algorithm is used to score these candidates with the known-word n-gram language models and find the best sequence of known-words that has the maximum score. (2) Unknown word decoding: This stage takes the output of the first step as its input. Unlike known word decoding, unknown word decoding consists of three main sub-steps: Firstly, all eligible unknown word candidates are generated for a sequence of known words. Note that each known word in input is kept as an eligible word candidate in this step. Secondly, all eligible class candidates are further constructed for each word candidate. All these candidates, including word candidates and class candidates, are stored in a lattice structure. Finally, the Viterbi algorithm is employed again to score all candidates using the class-based language models in Equation (2) and searches the best class sequence and word segmentation for the input. In this stage, a lattice-pruning algorithm shown in section 3.2 is also applied to block some ineligible unknown word or class candidates.

3.2 Lattice Pruning

Lattice pruning aims to prevent the improper candidates from entering the candidate lattice, which is crucial for Chinese UWI [1][5]. In order to achieve an effective lattice pruning, both word formation patterns and word juncture model are employed in our implementation to determine whether a possible candidate is really eligible.

In our decoder, there are actually two types of lattice pruning, namely the word pruning and the class pruning. The word pruning attempts to filter improper unknown word candidates based on three conditions, i.e. the maximum word-length condition, the minimum word-formation power condition and the minimum word-juncture condition (the details of these conditions are given in [5]), and the class pruning tries to prevent ineligible classes from becoming proper class candidates of the given word in terms of their class-based word-formation patterns. More formally, t is eligible class candidate of w, if and only if all the WFP probabilities of its components are greater than a threshold T_{CWFP}, namely $\min(P(pttn(k_{beg},t)),\cdots,P(pttn(k_{end},t))) > T_{CWFP}$.

In this paper, all thresholds for pruning are set as zero except the maximum word-length, which implies that any case observed in the training data is considered as an eligible candidate or an eligible component of a candidate.

4 Experiments

4.1 Experimental Data and Evaluation Measures

In evaluating our approaches, we conduct a number of experiments on the Peking University corpus (January 1998 of the *People's Daily*) and the PK-open test corpus for the First International Word Segmentation Bakeoff sponsored by SIGHAN [8]. As shown in Table 2, the Peking University corpus (PKU corpus for short) is a manually segmented and POS-tagged corpus [7], which is further labeled with the classes defined in section 2.1 and separated into two parts. The larger part (viz. the *Corpus A*) is used as the train data, and the smaller one (viz. the *Corpus B*) is for the closed-test. The SIGHAN-PK open-test data (viz. the *Corpus C*) is used here for the open test.

Table 2. Experimental corpora

Corpora	Number of words	Number of OOV words	OOV rate (%)
Corpus A	998085	69290	6.94
Corpus B	112373	7656	6.81
Corpus C	17605	1574	8.94

In addition, we use a lexicon of about 65, 000 words in our system. Based on this lexicon, the relevant out-of-vocabulary rates (OOV rate for short) of the three corpora are 6.94%, 6.81% and 8.94% respectively.

In our experiments, three measures, i.e. *recall* (R), *precision* (P) and the *balanced F-score* (F), are computed to evaluate our system. Here, recall (R) is defined as the number of correctly segmented words divided by the total number of words in the manually annotated corpus, and precision (P) is defined as the number of correctly segmented words divided by the total numbers of words segmented automatically by the system, and the balanced F-score (F) can be defined as follows:

$$F = \frac{2 \times P \times R}{P + R}. \tag{9}$$

4.2 Experimental Results

In order to examine the effectiveness of our system, we conducted three main experiments:

The first experiment aims to examine how the four sub-models of the proposed class-based LM contribute to the performance of our system, including the contextual class models, the inside/outside class-based word juncture models (I-CWJMs/O-CWJMs) and the class-based word-formation patterns (CWFPs). In this experiment, we turn off one component each time and evaluate the output of the rest components. The results are listed in Table 3.

Table 3. The results of the experiment on the contribution of each component

Models	F	R	P	F_{KW}	R_{KW}	P_{KW}	F_{UW}	R_{UW}	P_{UW}
Full system	96.8	97.0	96.6	97.6	97.9	97.3	85.5	84.6	86.4
Without UWI	87.5	92.4	83.2	90.5	99.1	83.2	0.0	0.0	0.0
Without pruning	95.9	95.6	96.2	97.0	96.5	97.5	81.6	84.3	79.0
Without class bigram	95.4	96.6	94.3	96.6	98.8	94.5	76.9	66.9	90.4
Without I-CWJMs	95.2	94.4	96.1	96.6	95.5	97.8	77.0	79.8	74.5
Without O-CWJMs	96.7	96.9	96.5	97.6	97.8	97.4	84.1	84.1	84.1
Without CWFPs	96.2	95.9	96.5	97.2	96.5	98.0	82.9	87.4	78.8

Table 3 reveals a number of observations. Firstly, UWI is very important for a high-performance Chinese word segmentation system. As shown in Table 3, if we turn off the UWI module, the system can achieve only an overall F-score of 87.5%, even though 99.1% of known words are segmented correctly in this case. Secondly, the combination of different features helps enhance the performance of segmentation. It is shown that the full system outperforms all other partial systems that some modules are turned off, while different features may offer different contributions to UWI. Thirdly, lattice pruning is very crucial for effective Chinese UWI. As can be seen in Table 3, the introduction of lattice pruning improves the F-score in UWI by 3.9 percents from 81.6% to 85.5% in comparison with the system without pruning and the relevant overall F-score in word segmentation jumps to 96.8% from 95.9%.

As mentioned above, the proposed method actually provides a unified solution to unknown word segmentation and tagging as well. The second experiment is thus designed to evaluate the performance of our system in unknown word tagging. In this experiment, the labeled F-score, the labeled recall and the labeled precision are calculated respectively. The results are summarized in Table 4.

As showed in Table 4, our system can achieve as a whole a labeled F-score of 81.8%, a labeled recall of 80.8% and a labeled precision of 82.5%, which indicates that most unknown words can be correctly identified and tagged by our system. The results also show that the system achieves different performances in tagging for different types of unknown words.

Table 4. The results of unknown word tagging

Class	Number	F	R	P
Common noun (n)	1,623	73.0	74.6	71.5
Numeral (m)	1,378	92.2	92.5	91.9
Personal name (nr)	1,405	86.4	91.2	82.1
Time (t)	1,035	95.6	95.4	95.7
Location (ns)	493	78.2	77.3	79.1
All classes	7,656	81.8	80.8	82.5

In practice, our third experiment is an open comparison test on the SIGHAN-PK open test data, which aims to compare our system with other public systems in the track. The details of the SIGHAN bakeoff can be seen in [8]. The results are summarized in Table 5.

As shown in Table 5, our system outperforms any other systems except the S10 system and the S01 system in terms of the overall F-score. Further analysis indicates that segmentation errors come from three main aspects, namely the inconsistent segmentations between the training data and the SIGHAN bakeoff data (e.g. 不一会儿, in a while), the cases that are unseen in the training corpus (e.g. 2003年, the year two thousand and three) and the complicated cases that are beyond our method (e.g. 2000年底, the end of two thousand).

Table 5. The comparison of our system with other systems for the SIGHAN-PK open test

Systems	R_{UW}	R_{KW}	R	P	F
S10	79.9	97.5	96.3	95.6	95.9
S01	74.3	98.0	96.3	94.3	95.3
S08	67.5	95.9	93.9	93.8	93.8
S04	71.2	94.9	93.3	94.2	93.7
S03	64.7	96.2	94.0	91.1	92.5
S11	50.3	93.4	90.5	86.9	88.6
Our system	**75.7**	**97.0**	**95.0**	**93.8**	**94.4**

5 Conclusions

In this paper, a modified class-based LM approach is presented to identify unknown words in Chinese texts. In this work, Chinese UWI is taken as a classification problem and part-of-speech is used to define the basic classes of unknown words. Furthermore, different types of features, including contextual class feature, class-based word juncture model and class-based word formation patterns, are combined in a class-based LM framework to perform correct unknown word identification on a sequence of known words. In addition to the identification of Chinese unknown words, this class-based LM approach also provides a resolution for Chinese unknown word tagging. Based on the proposed method, a word segmentation system is also implemented with a two-stage Viterbi decoding algorithm. The experimental results show that most Chinese unknown words can be effectively identified and tagged by this system. In future, we hope to apply the proposed approach in other NLP applications, such as part-of-speech tagging and named entity recognition.

Acknowledgement

We would like to thank the Institute of Computational Linguistics, Peking University for providing the experimental corpus. We especially thank the three anonymous reviewers for their valuable suggestions and comments.

References

1. Wu, Andi, and Zixin Jiang: Statistically-enhanced new word identification in a rule-based Chinese system. In: Proceedings of the Second Chinese Language Processing Workshop, Hong Kong (2000) 46-51
2. Zhang, Hua-Ping, Qun Liu, Hao Zhang, and Xue-Qi Cheng: Automatic recognition of Chinese unknown words based on roles tagging. In: Proceedings of The First SIGHAN Workshop on Chinese Language Processing, Taiwan (2002) 71-77

3. Xue, Nianwen, and Susan P. Converse: Combining classifier for Chinese word segmentation. In: Proceedings of the First SIGHAN Workshop on Chinese Language Processing, Taiwan (2002) 57-63
4. Wang, Xiaolong, Fu Guohong, Danial S.Yeung, James N.K.Liu, and Robert Luk: Models and algorithms of Chinese word segmentation. In: Proceedings of the International Conference on Artificial Intelligence, Las Vegas (2000) 1279-1284
5. Fu, Guohong, and Kang-Kwong Luke: An integrated approach to Chinese word segmentation. Journal of Chinese Language and Computing, Vol.13, No.3 (2003) 249-260
6. Sun, Jian, Ming Zhou, and Jianfeng Gao: A class-based language model approach to Chinese named entity identification. Computational Linguistics and Chinese Language Processing, Vol.8, No.2 (2003) 1-28
7. Yu, Shiwen, Huiming Duan, Suefeng Zhu, Bin Swen, and Baobao Chang: Specification for corpus processing at Peking University: Word segmentation, POS tagging and phonetic notation. Journal of Chinese Language and Computing, Vol. 13, No.2 (2003) 121-158
8. Sproat, Richard, and Thomas Emerson: The first international Chinese word segmentation bakeoff. In: Proceedings of the Second SIGHAN Workshop on Chinese Language Processing, Sapporo, Japan (2003) 133-143

An Example-Based Study on Chinese Word Segmentation Using Critical Fragments

Qinan Hu, Haihua Pan, and Chunyu Kit

Department of Chinese, Translation and Linguistics,
City University of Hong Kong, Hong Kong
qinan.hu@student.cityu.edu.hk, {cthpan,ctckit}@cityu.edu.hk

Abstract. In our study, sentences are represented as sequences of critical fragments, and critical fragments with more than one distinct resolution found in the training corpus are considered as being ambiguous. Different from other studies, the ambiguous critical fragments are disambiguated using an example-based system[1] in our study. The contexts, i.e. the adjacent characters, words and critical fragments, on either side of an ambiguous critical fragment, are used to measure the distance between training and testing examples. Two kinds of measures, overlap metric and chi-squared feature weighting, are employed, and our system achieves a precision of 93.65% and a recall of 96.56% in the open test.

1 Introduction

Generally speaking, the difficulties in Chinese word segmentation come from the following three aspects [Liu 2000]: lack of single accepted segmentation standard, unknown words, and ambiguity. Our study focuses on the third one, i.e. the ambiguity aspect. The ambiguities involved in Chinese word segmentation can be categorized into critical and hidden types [Guo 1997a], which are conventionally called overlapping and combinational ambiguities, respectively [Liang 1987]. A character sequence has critical ambiguity if it has more than one critical tokenization [Guo 1997a]. For example, the sequence "中國有" has critical ambiguity since it has two critical tokenizations, i.e. |中國|有| as in sentence (1) and |中|國有| as in sentence (2).

(1)|中國|有|世界|最|早|的|彗星|紀錄|，|
(2)|要|防止|民航|重組|中|國有|資產|的|流失|．|

A character sequence has hidden ambiguity if it has tokenization(s) other than those critical ones. For example, the sequence "學生會" has hidden ambiguity since it has two tokenizations, i.e. |學生會| as in (3) and |學生|會| as in (4). While the former is a critical tokenization, the latter is a true subtokenization of the former.

(1)|監督|學生會|各|部|工作|的|執行|，|
(2)|57.54%的|學生|會|主動|問好|打|招呼|．|

---

[1] An example-based system is similar in principle to a memory-based, similarity-based, exemplar-based, analogical, case-based, instance-based system and systems with the lazy learning technique [Daelemans et al. 2003].

2 Previous Studies

In this section, previous studies on ambiguity are reviewed from two aspects, i.e. ambiguity detection and resolution.

As for ambiguity detection, Yao et al. [1990] propose to detect critical ambiguities by looking for the discrepancies of the outputs from Forward Maximum Matching (FMM) and Backward Maximum Matching (BMM). This method is also used in some subsequent studies [Kit et al. 2002 inter alia]. However, not all critical ambiguities can be detected this way. For example, the sequence "從前所未有的" will be segmented identically as |從前|所|未|有的| as shown in (6) by both FMM and BMM, accordingly it will not be detected as having critical ambiguity. But in fact this sequence is critically ambiguous, since it has two critical tokenizations, |從|前所未有|的| and |從前|所|未|有的|, the former of which is the correct segmentation as shown in (5).

(5) |房地產|市場|也|逐漸|從|前所未有|的|低潮|中|恢復|正常|．|
(6) *|房地產|市場|也|逐漸|從前|所|未|有的|低潮|中|恢復|正常|．|
(7) *|房|地|產|市|場|也|逐漸|從|前|所|未|有|的|低|潮|中|恢復|正|常|．|

Sun et al. [1999] propose to make use of Longest Overlapping Ambiguous String (Longest OAS) to detect critical ambiguities. Longest OAS can detect a complete set of critical ambiguities from sentences. Some studies on the handling of critical ambiguities [Li 2003 inter alia] are based on this concept.

As for hidden ambiguity, Liu [2000] proposes to detect it by looking for the discrepancies of the outputs from FMM and Backward Minimum Matching. However, not all hidden ambiguities can be detected this way either. Take the same sequence "從前所未有的" as an example. It will be segmented as |從前|所|未|有的| by FMM, as shown in (6), and as |從|前|所|未|有|的| by Backward Minimum Matching, as shown in (7). Accordingly, two subsequences "從前" and "有的" will be detected as having hidden ambiguities. However, the algorithm fails to detect another subsequence "前所未有" as having hidden ambiguity. Other than the critical tokenization |前所未有|, this sequence has another tokenization |前|所|未|有| as in (7).

In summary, there are two problems in the previous studies on ambiguity detection. First, some ambiguous sequences are overlooked by their algorithms. Second, more often than not critical and hidden ambiguities co-occur as a mixture. But these previous detection algorithms consider them separately.

Guo's investigation on critical tokenization [1997a] provides a unified solution to the detection of the mixture of ambiguities. In Guo's study, the task of word segmentation is mathematically described as a selection process from a partially ordered set of all possible segmentations. In addition, critical points and critical fragments are defined. It proves that for any character string on a complete lexicon, critical points are all and only unambiguous word boundaries while critical fragments are the longest substrings with all inner positions critically/hidden ambiguous. It will be shown in the next section that the use of critical fragments avoids the problems mentioned above.

As for ambiguity resolution, various approaches have been employed to resolve ambiguities in word segmentation. Some approaches are based solely on lexicon, including FMM, BMM, Longest Matching [Wang et al. 1989; Guo 1997b], etc, while others are based on corpora, including Naive Bayesian Classifier [Li et al. 2003], Hidden Markov Model [Lai et al. 1992], Finite-State Model [Sproat 1996], Transformation-based Error Driven [Hockenmaier and Brew 1998], and Example-based approach [Kit et al. 2002]. The latter generally outperforms the former.

Guo [1998] also has a corpus-based study on disambiguation using critical fragments. In his study, the most frequent resolution to each critical fragment is learnt from a corpus and used as the disambiguation result. However, there has been no corpus-based study making use of the contextual information of critical fragments. Therefore, in our study, we adopt the example-based approach to make use of the contexts of critical fragments for disambiguation.

3 Using Critical Fragments in an Example-Based System

3.1 Critical Fragments

According to Guo [1997a], given a lexicon, critical points are those positions in a sentence at which there is always a word boundary, no matter how the sentence is segmented according to the lexicon. A critical fragment is the sequence between two adjacent critical points. The critical fragments in a sentence can be determined using the algorithm illustrated in Figure 1.

This algorithm can be exemplified in a slightly different way using sentence (5), repeated as (8) below. First, the algorithm looks for the longest matching word for each character according to a lexicon. The results are shown in (9). Second, the algorithm checks whether the longest words overlap with each other. Those overlapping words are aggregated together. For example, since the words "地產" and "產" are subsequences of the word "房地產", these three words are grouped into one. Since the words "從前, 前所未有, 所, 未, 有的, 的" overlap with one another, they are also grouped into one. After aggregation, the resulting fragments in (10) are the critical fragments for sentence (8).

Using this algorithm, a sentence is decomposed into a sequence of critical fragments on the following grounds. No ambiguous sequences will be overlooked by using critical fragments, since the sequence of critical fragments does not discard any parts of a sentence. In addition, the definition of critical fragments implies that the characters in different critical fragments are not related in the sense that no word will be formed across adjacent critical fragments. For example, the adjacent fragments "從前所未有的" and "低潮" in sentence (8) do not form a longer critical fragment, since there is always a word boundary between them. On the other hand, all closely related characters are within the same critical fragment. For example, the characters "恢" and "復" are within one critical fragment "恢復" because they form a word, and the characters in "從前所未有的" form one critical fragment due to a mixture of critical and hidden ambiguity. This decomposition guarantees that no critically/hidden ambiguous sequence will be separated into different critical fragments.

The results from using critical fragments can be compared with the results from those ambiguity detection algorithms in the previous studies. The FMM + BMM

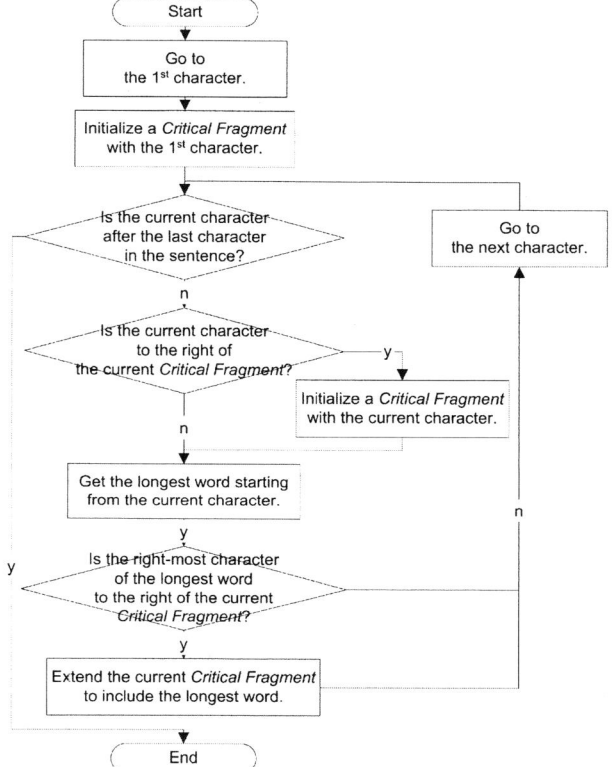

Fig. 1. Critical Fragment Detection Algorithm

algorithm will report that no critical ambiguity is found in sentence (8). The algorithm used to detect Longest OAS [Sun et al. 1997] will output one longest OAS as shown in (11). It does not deal with the sequences which only involve hidden ambiguities. The FMM + Backward Minimum Matching algorithm will output an incomplete set of sequences with hidden ambiguity, as shown in (12). However, no matter how these sequences are disambiguated, the segmentation results would be incorrect.

It is worth noting that not all critical fragments have more than one distinct resolution found in real texts. For those critical fragments having exactly one resolution empirically found, the resolution will be used as default. For others, relevant disambiguation is needed.

(8) 房地產市場也逐漸從前所未有的低潮中恢復正常。

			▼		▼	▼		▼		▼		
	低	潮	中	恢	復	正	常	·				

(10) 房 地 產 市 場 也 逐 漸 從 前 所 未 有 的

	低	潮	中	恢	復	正	常	·				

(11) 房 地 產 市 場 也 逐 漸 從 前 所 未 有 的

	低	潮	中	恢	復	正	常	·				

(12) 房 地 產 市 場 也 逐 漸 從 前 所 未 有 的

	低	潮	中	恢	復	正	常	·				

3.2 Example-Based Approaches

Based on the discussion in the previous sections, we know that the task of word segmentation can be achieved by disambiguating critical fragments. We implement an example-based system for this task. In our system, each occurrence of those critical fragments which have more than one distinct resolution found in the training corpus will have an entry in the example-base. Each training example is composed of three parts, i.e. the critical fragment, its manual segmentation and a vector of features describing its contexts of occurrence. The contexts here refer to the characters, words or critical fragments adjacent to both sides of the critical fragment in question.

To disambiguate a critical fragment, the system first finds the set of training examples which are of the same critical fragment. Then the features of the testing critical fragment will be compared with the features of each training example in that set. The manual segmentation of the training example which has the most similar features is proposed as the result.

To measure the distance between training and testing examples, two different metrics are explored.

Overlap Metric. The first metric used is the overlap metric. It is computed based on the following equation.

$$\Delta(X,Y) = \sum_{i=1}^{n} \delta(xi, yi) \quad (1)$$

where

$$\delta(xi, yi) = \begin{cases} 0 & if \quad xi = yi \\ 1 & if \quad xi \neq yi \end{cases} \quad (2)$$

X and Y are the feature vectors in training and testing examples respectively. Each feature vector is composed of n features. δ represents the distance between a pair of features. For any given critical fragment, $\Delta(X,Y)$ is the distance between the training and testing examples. It is the sum of mismatches between each pair of features.

For example, if we use the characters adjacent to both sides of a critical fragment as its features and set n to 6, then 3 characters on the left side and 3 characters on the right side in training and testing examples will be compared. For each pair of characters, if the characters are not identical, the distance between the training and testing examples will be increased by 1, otherwise there will be no change to the distance.

Chi-Squared Feature Weighting. Since different features may have different relevance to the predictions of the system, we assign different weights to features using chi-squared feature weighting [White and Liu 1994].

$$\Delta(X,Y) = \sum_{i=1}^{n} \chi_i^2 \delta(xi, yi) \tag{3}$$

For any given critical fragment, each pair of features corresponds to a weight χ^2. The χ^2 statistic is computed based on this formula.

$$\chi^2 = \sum_i \sum_j \frac{(Eij - Oij)^2}{Eij} \tag{4}$$

where Oij is the observed number of cases with the ith possible value of the current feature and the jth segmentation. Eij is the expected number of cases with the ith possible value of the current feature and the jth segmentation, if the null hypothesis (of no association between feature values and segmentations) is true. To calculate Eij, we need a contingency table to represent the cross-classification of segmentations and values of features. For example, a critical fragment has m possible segmentations and its adjacent characters are used as its features. Its ith feature has n possible values. Then the contingency table is constructed as follows.

Table 1. A Contingency Table

	Character 1	...	Character n	
Segment 1	n_{11}		n_{1n}	$n_{1.}$
...	...	...	...	...
Segment m	n_{m1}	...	n_{mn}	$n_{m.}$
	$n_{.1}$	...	$n_{.n}$	$n_{..}$

where n_{ij} (i = 1, m; j = 1, n) represents the observed frequency counts of cases with segmentation i and character j; and

$$n_{i.} = \sum_{j=1}^{n} n_{ij}, \quad n_{.j} = \sum_{i=1}^{m} n_{ij}, \quad n_{..} = \sum_{i=1}^{m} \sum_{j=1}^{n} n_{ij} \tag{5}$$

$$Eij = \frac{n_{.j} n_{i.}}{n_{ij}} \tag{6}$$

4 Experiments

Our system is examined using one month text of People's Daily, which is manually tagged by Peking University (PKU). This corpus is the same as the training corpus provided by Peking University in the 1st International Chinese Word Segmentation

Bake-off [Sproat and Emerson 2003]. We ran an open test on this corpus, that is, 90% of this corpus is randomly selected and used for training, while the remainder is used for testing. In addition, the lexicon is generated using words from the training data exclusively. Some properties of the corpus and the open test are listed in the table below.

Table 2. Open Test on the PKU Corpus

	Training Set	Testing Set
No. of Characters	1,658,452	183,205
No. of Words	1,009,491	111,956
No. of Distinct Words	52,705	16,882
No. of CFs	977,667	112,476
No. of Distinct CFs	62,287	16,304
No. of Distinct CFs Having Different Segmentations	1516	716

In our experiments, the FMM and BMM algorithms are implemented as the baseline. They are denoted by *FMM* and *BMM* respectively in the performance table. *OOV* denotes the number of characters which are out of vocabulary in an algorithm.

Several systems making use of critical fragments are implemented. Whether a critical fragment needs disambiguation in testing is empirically determined based on the training corpus. That is, if a critical fragment has more than one distinct segmentation found in the training corpus, it will be disambiguated. Otherwise, the unique segmentation is used as the result (denoted by *Unique*). In addition, to examine what kind of features is the most useful in the example-based system, we also compared the system performance when using characters, words and critical fragments (3 on either side) as the contexts. They are denoted by *Char*, *Word* and *CF* in the performance table, respectively. Each kind of contexts is measured using two distance metrics, i.e. the overlap metric and the chi-squared weighting, which are denoted by *Overlap* and *Chi*, respectively. In case more than one training example has the same minimum distance to a testing example, the segmentation with the highest frequency is used.

To examine the efficiency of the example-based approach to the disambiguation of critical fragments, we implement two other algorithms for comparison. The first is Guo's longest matching algorithm [1997b] and denoted by *Longest*. The second algorithm is on the basis of Guo's observation of "*one tokenization per source*" [1998]. That is, the same critical fragment in different sentences from the same source almost always has the same segmentation, although the fragment may have one or more possible segmentations. This approach is denoted by *Freq*.

In this performance table, except for the first four rows, others are based on critical fragments. A comparison of the performances of various algorithms reveals that systems making use of critical fragments generally outperform the FMM and BMM algorithms in terms of both precision and recall. Guo's *Freq* system outperforms his *Longest*. Moreover, the *Freq* system is exceeded by several example-based approaches, i.e. the two using characters as contexts, while other example-based systems present similar performances. The best performance in our study is given by the example-based system with characters as contexts (F=0.951).

Table 3. System Performance

	Word Count	Correct Word Count	Precision	Recall	F^a
FMM	114,195	105,988	92.49%#	94.73%#	0.9360#
OOV(FMM)	473	71			
BMM	114,155	106,206	92.71%^	94.93%^	0.9380^
OOV(BMM)	483	70			
Unique	110,779	104,349	93.87%*	93.27%*	0.9357*
Longest	3,521	2,720	93.36%*	95.70%*	0.9452*
Freq	4,130	3,602	93.63%*	96.49%*	0.9504*
Char_Overlap	4,204	3,688	93.65%*	96.56%*	0.9508*
Word_Overlap	4,214	3,638	93.59%*	96.52%*	0.9503*
CF_Overlap	4,217	3,631	93.59%*	96.51%*	0.9503*
Char_Chi	4,206	3,658	93.62%*	96.54%*	0.9505*
Word_Chi	4,216	3,618	93.57%*	96.50%*	0.9501*
CF_Chi	4,219	3,610	93.57%*	96.49%*	0.9501*
OOV(CF)	423	59			

\# The value is calculated together with those OOV words of FMM.
^ The value is calculated together with those OOV words of BMM.
* The value is calculated together with critical fragments with unique resolutions and OOV words.
^{a} We use a balanced F score, so that F = 2*Precision*Recall/(Precision+Recall).

5 Discussion

The errors in the results generally come from two sources. First, since this system does not have a new word recognition component, it is weak in handling OOV words. However, it is feasible to incorporate such a component into our system. Second, the inconsistency in the tagging also produced some errors.

Although chi-squared feature weighting is statistically plausible, experimental results show that the use of overlap metric and chi-squared weighting does not contribute differently. As recommended by Siegel [1956], χ^2 test can't be trusted if more than 20% of the expected frequencies (E_{ij}) are less than 5, or any expected frequency is less than 1. However, as we look closely at the computation of χ^2, we found that the features seldom meet this requirement.

A solution to this problem is to group the values of features together. That is, use classes of critical fragments as the values of features. Another solution is to make use of a larger training corpus.

6 Conclusion

In this study, we have implemented an example-based system which makes use of the concept of critical fragments. Experimental results show that this approach provides a satisfactory performance. In our further study, we will investigate the strategies mentioned in the discussion section.

Acknowledgment

Part of the results in this paper is derived from the research work of two Strategic Research Grants (#7001319, #7001397), City University of Hong Kong. We thank the University for its generous support. We would also like to thank Tom Lai for helpful comments and discussions.

References

1. Daelemans Walter, Jakub Zavrel, Ko van der Sloot and Antal van den Bosch. 2003. TiMBL: Tilburg Memory-Based Learner, Version 5.0, Reference Guide. http://ilk.uvt.nl/downloads/pub/papers/ilk0310.ps.gz.
2. Guo Jin. 1997a. Critical Tokenization and Its Properties. Computational Linguistics. Vol. 23, no. 4, pp. 569-596.
3. Guo Jin 1997b. Longest Tokenization. International Journal of Computational Linguistics & Chinese Language Processing. Vol. 2, no.2.
4. Guo Jin. 1998. One Tokenization per Source. Proceedings of the 36th Annual Meeting of the Association for Computational Linguistics. Montreal, Canada.
5. Hockenmaier, Julia and Chris Brew. 1998. Error-driven Learning of Chinese Word Segmentation. In Proceedings of the 12th Pacific Conference on Language and Information, Singapore. pp. 218-229.
6. Kit Chunyu, Haihua Pan and Hongbiao Chen. 2002. Learning Case-based Knowledge for Disambiguating Chinese Word Segmentation: A Preliminary Study. COLING2002 Workshop: First SigHAN, pp. 33-39.
7. Lai T.B.Y., S.C. Lun, C.F. Sun, and M.S. Sun. 1992. A Tagging-based First-order Markov Model Approach to Automatic Word Identification for Chinese Sentences. Proceedings of International Conference on Computer Processing of Chinese and Oriental Languages, Florida. pp. 17-23.
8. Li Mu, Jianfeng Gao, Chang-Ning Huang and Jianfeng Li. 2003. Unsupervised training for overlapping ambiguity resolution in Chinese word segmentation. In SIGHAN2002. Japan.
9. Liang Nanyuan (梁南元). 1987. An Automatic Word Segmentation System for Written Chinese – CDWS (書面漢語自動分詞系統 – CDWS). Journal of Chinese Information Processing. Issue 3. pp. 44-52.
10. Liu Kaiying (劉開瑛). 2000. Automatic Segmentation and Tagging of Chinese Texts (中文文本自動分詞和標注). Commercial Press, Beijing.
11. Siegel, S. 1956. Nonparametric Statistics. New York. McGraw-Hill.
12. Sproat Richard, William Gale, Chinlin Shih, and Nancy Chang. 1996. A Stochastic Finite-State Word-Segmentation Algorithm for Chinese. Computational Linguistics. Vol. 22, no. 3.
13. Sproat Richard and Thomas Emerson. 2003. The First International Chinese Word Segmentation Bakeoff. Proceedings of the *Second SIGHAN Workshop on Chinese Language Processing. Japan.*
14. Sun Maosong, Zhengping Zuo, Benjamin K Tsou. 1999. The Role of High Frequent Maximal Crossing Ambiguities in Chinese Word Segmentation (in Chinese). Journal of Chinese Information Processing. Issue 1, pp. 27-34.
15. Wang Xiaolong, Kaizhu Wang, Zhongrong Li and Xiaohua Bai (王曉龍, 王開鑄, 李仲榮, 白小華). 1989. The Problem of Least Word Segmentation and its Solution (最少分詞問題及其解法). Chinese Science Bulletin. Issue 13.
16. White Allan P. and WeiZhong Liu. 1994. Bias in Information-based Measures in Decision Tree Induction. Machine Learning, Vol. 15, Issue 3, pp. 321-329.
17. Yao Tianshun, Guiping Zhang and Yingming Wu. 1990. A Rule-based Chinese Automatic Segmentation System. Journal of Chinese Information Processing. Issue 1.

The Use of SVM for Chinese New Word Identification

Hongqiao Li[1], Chang-Ning Huang[2], Jianfeng Gao[2], and Xiaozhong Fan[1]

[1] Beijing Institute of Technology, Beijing 100081, China
{lhqtxm,fxz}@bit.edu.cn
[2] Microsoft Research Asia, Beijing 100080, China
{cnhuang,jfgao}@microsoft.com

Abstract. We present a study of new word identification (NWI) to improve the performance of a Chinese word segmenter. In this paper the distribution and types of new words are discussed empirically. In particular, we focus on the new words of two surface patterns, which account for more than 80% of new words in our data sets: NW11 (two-character new word) and NW21 (a bi-character word followed with a single character). NWI is defined as a problem of binary classification. A statistical learning approach based on a SVM classifier is used. Different features for NWI are explored, including in-word probability of a character (IWP), the analogy between new words and lexicon words, anti-word list, and frequency in documents. The experiments show that these features are useful for NWI. The F-scores of NWI we achieved are 64.4% and 54.7% for NW11 and NW21, respectively. The overall performance of the Chinese word segmenter could be improved by R_{oov} 24.5% and F-score 6.5% in PK-close test of the 1st SIGHAN bakeoff. This achieves the performance of state-of-the-art word segmenters[1].

1 Introduction

New word identification (NWI) is one of the most critical issues in Chinese word segmentation, a fundamental research problem in Chinese natural language processing (NLP). Recent studies (e.g. Sproat and Emerson, 2003; Chen, 2003) show that more than 60% of word segmentation errors result from new words that are not stored in a dictionary. Chinese NWI is challenging because of the two main reasons. First, new words appear constantly. Statistics show that more than 1000 new Chinese words appear every year (Thesaurus Research Center of Commercial Press, 2003). These words are mostly domain-specific technical terms (e.g. 视窗 'Windows') and time-sensitive political/social /cultural terms (e.g. 三个代表 'Three Represents Theory', 非典 'SARS', 海归 'oversea returned students'). Only a small amount of them will be stored as words in the dictionary, while most of them remain as OOV (out of vocabulary). Second, there are no word boundaries in Chinese text, so in most cases, NWI is better performed simultaneously with Chinese word segmentation which itself is a challenging task.

While previous approaches explore the use of one or two most promising linguistically-motivated features and detect new words heuristically, we believe it is better to

---

[1] This work was done while Hongqiao Li was visiting Microsoft Research Asia.

utilize all available features and to make a decision statistically: whether a character sequence in certain context is a new word or not. In this study, we define NWI as a binary classification problem, and use a statistical learning approach based on a SVM (Support Vector Machine) classifier. We then investigate various linguistic and statistical features that can be used in the classifier to improve the performance of NWI. In addition, other classifiers (e.g. Decision Tree, Naïve Bayes, kNN) are also suitable for NWI, but we don't attempt to compare these classifiers in this paper. These features include: in-word probability of a character, the analogy between new words and lexicon words, anti-word list and the frequency in documents. We evaluate the performance of NWI in terms of F-score (i.e. a balance of precision and recall, $\beta =1$) and R_{oov} (i.e. the recalling ratio of OOV words), using SIGHAN bakeoff corpus. Our models achieve F-score of 64.4% for NW11 (two-character new word) and 54.7% for NW21 (bi-character word followed with a single character). Enhancing a Chinese word segmenter by using NWI engine as a post procession, we improve the R_{oov} and F-score of the segmenter by 24.5% and 6.5% respectively

The rest of this paper is structured as follows. Section 2 presents previous work. Section 3 defines the new words in this study. Section 4 describes our approach in detail. Section 5 presents experimental results. Section 6 presents error analysis and discussion. Finally, we draw conclusions and propose future work in Section 7.

2 Previous Work

Previous approaches focus on the use of one or two linguistically-motivated features to detect new words heuristically. For example, Chen (2003) used only one feature for NWI: the probability of a character being inside a word, referred to as IWP afterwards. He then assumed that two adjacent characters form a new word if the product of their IWP is larger than a pre-set threshold. Chen reports that an improvement of 11% for Roov and 0.08% for F-score after his word segmenter has been enhanced by the NWI engine.

In addition to IWP, Wu (2002) used another feature: the likelihood score that represents, given a word as well as its part-of-speech tag and length, how likely a character appears in certain position within the word. Wu then reports an F-score of 56% for NWI. Wu also integrates it into a parser and it turns out that about 85% of the identified new words are real words. Other features explored previous include mutual information, context dependency, relative frequency and so on (e.g. Gao, 2002; Nie, 1995; Luo, 2003; Chiang, 1992).

We think that all of these features, either proposed previously or to be described below, are valuable for NWI and in many cases can complement each other. So in this study, we consequently define the NWI as a binary classification problem, and explore ways of combining various feature functions in a statistical classifier. We also notice that to make our method feasible, all features should be easily obtained from corpus or lexicon. Before we present our approach, we first define the scope of new words we will explore in this study.

3 Problem Statement

General speaking, a new word is any word that is not stored in a lexicon. But in this paper, we focus on identifying those words that cannot be detected by a certain Chinese word segmenter described in Gao et al. (2003). In Gao's segmenter, Chinese words are defined as one of the following four types: lexicon words (LW), morphologically derived words (MDW), factoids[2], and named entities (NE)[3]. Though the four types except the lexicon words have been considered as new words in previous research, they are not defined as new words in this study. We focus on new words (NW) that are mostly time-sensitive concepts and can be hardly grouped into any word type.

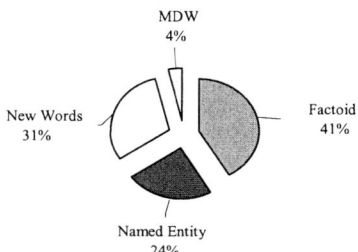

Fig. 1. The percentage of each OOV word type

We investigate the distribution of new words on PK corpus[4] (4.7MB training set and 89KB test set), which is a subset of the first SIGHAN bakeoff corpora. Fig. 1 shows the distributions of words that are not stored in the dictionary (OOV), including words of the type MDW, factoid, NE and NW. We see that NW amount to approximately 31% of OOV, which indicates a substantial improvement space of NWI to the performance of the word segmenter. These new words can be classified using two dimensions. First, from a semantic perspective, NW can be classified into (1) specific-domain concepts, such as 非典 'SARS', 抽射 'slap shot', 洞穿 'goal', 草菇 'straw mushroom', 牡丹花 'peony', and (2) abbreviations, such as 网协 'network association', 抗寒 'cold-proof', 执委 'council', 工价 'wage', 婚检 'health care for marriage'. From a surface pattern perspective, they can be classified into: (1) NW11 (two–character[5] new words, '1+1'), such as 下岗 'out of work', 旧债 'dead horse', 羊年 'year of the goat'. (2) NW21 (a bi-character word followed with a single character, '2+1'), such as 杜鹃花 'azalea', 黄金周 'golden week', 世纪坛 'century monument'; (3) NW12 (a single character followed with a bi-character word, '1+2'), such as 外资金 'foreign fund', 大世界 'the big world' ; (4) NW22 (two bi-character

---

[2] There are ten types of factoid in Gao's segmenter: date, time, percentage, money, number, measure, e-mail, phone number, and URL.
[3] There are three types of named entities: person name, location and organization.
[4] Available at http://www.sighan.org/bakeoff2003
[5] In this paper a character means a monosyllable morpheme.

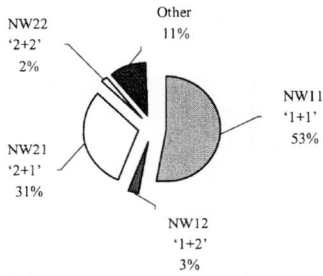

Fig. 2. The percentage of each type of NW

words, '2+2'), such as 卫生设备 'sanitary ware' and (5) others. Figure 2 shows the distribution of NW with different surface patterns and Table 1 shows some examples.

Since NW11 and NW21 amount most of new words (i.e. 84% of all new words in PK corpus), they are the focus of this study. We explore them in more detail below. We observe that each character of a NW11 is usually the abbreviated form of another word (or more precisely, lexicon word). For example, the NW11 解读 'unscramble' is composed by 解 'jie3' and 读 'du2', which are respectively the abbreviated forms of 解释 'explain' and 阅读 'read'. Other examples include 网协 'network association' as 网络 'network' and 协会 'association'; 执委 'executive council' as 执行 'executive' and 委员会 'council'. There are of course a few exceptions such as 羊年 'year of the goat', where both 羊 'yang2' and 年 'nian3' are one-character words. We also observed that NW21s are usually dominated by the last character, which had strong feature to use as a suffix, such as 花 'hua1' of 杜鹃花 , 牡丹花 ; 量 ' of 发电量 'power generation', 活动量 'quantity of activity'; 业 of 出租业 'taxi industry', 养殖业 'plant industry'.

Table 1. Some samples of new words in PK test

Types	Samples
NW11	解读,投射,养护,征召,脱销,喜迁,初审,修学,达政, 执委,冻鸡,旱船,旧俗,下岗,年味,羊年,海派,网协
NW21	杜鹃花,黄金周,家乡菜,太平鼓,文化村,住房梦,美食节,人情贷
NW12	外资金,大世界,踩高跷,全过程,总会长,荡秋千
NW22	卫生设备,劳动部长,交通部门,极端分子
Others	农牧渔业,县市区,亚冬会,党政军群,十六大,多云转晴,

There are in general two approaches to NWI. First is to **construct a live lexicon off-line**. That is, we extract new words from large corpus using statistical features such as the frequency of a character string. We then update the existing lexicon using the extracted new words for on-line applications. For example, Chiang(1992) uses statistical knowledge, Nie(1995) uses statistical and heuristic knowledge. The second approach is to **detect new words on-line.** That is, new words in a sentence or a document are identified on the fly. This is the approach we apply in this study.

4 A Binary Classifier for NWI

We define NWI as a binary classification problem. Of the great number of classifiers we experimented, including Perceptron, Naïve Bayes, kNN, SVM and so on, we choose SVM as our basic classifier due to its robustness, efficiency and high performance. Other classifiers maybe are also suitable for NWI, but we don't attempt to compare these classifiers in this paper. SVMs classify data by mapping it into a high (possibly infinite) dimensional *feature space* and constructing a maximum margin *hyperplane* to separate the classes in that space. We used SVM^{light} [6](Joachims, 1999), which is an implementation of the Support Vector Machine described in Vapnik (1995). We now consider the features for NWI.

4.1 IWP(c) and IWP(c, pos)

IWP(c) is the probability that a single character c is in a word. It is estimated using Equation 1, where * is a wild-card matching any Chinese character, and $C(.)$ represents the number of occurrence in a corpus given that the variable is a word.

$$\text{IWP}(c) = \frac{C(c*) + C(*c*) + C(*c)}{C(c) + C(c*) + C(*c*) + C(*c)} \quad (1)$$

IWP(c) is also used by Chen (2003) and Wu (2002) to detect NW11s: if the product of IWP values of two adjacent characters is larger than a pre-set threshold λ, the two characters form a NW11, as shown in Equation 2. We use this method as a baseline in this study.

$$\text{IF } \text{IWP}(a)\text{IWP}(b) > \lambda \quad \text{THEN } a \text{ and } b \text{ form a NW11} \quad (2)$$

We notice that some characters are more likely to occur in certain positions than in others within a word. For example, 性 'xing4' usually occurs in the last position of a word, while 老 'lao3' in the first position. Therefore, we take into account the position within a word in estimating IWP. The extended feature is IWP(c, pos), where pos is the position of the character c in a word, and can be assigned by three values: $pos = 1$, 2 and 0, indicating the first, middle and last positions, respectively. The values of IWP(c, pos) can be estimated by Equations 3 - 5.

$$\text{IWP}(c,1) = \frac{C(c*)}{C(c*) + C(*c*) + C(*c)} \quad (3)$$

$$\text{IWP}(c,2) = \frac{C(*c*)}{C(c*) + C(*c*) + C(*c)} \quad (4)$$

$$\text{IWP}(c,0) = \frac{C(*c)}{C(c*) + C(*c*) + C(*c)} \quad (5)$$

---

[6] Available at http://svmlight.joachims.org/

4.2 Analogy to New Words: F_{ANA}

We find that some characters can produce words with the same word patterns[7]. For example 上 'shang1' can produce: 上班 'go to work', 上午 'morning', 上面 'upside' et al.; 下 'xia4' can also produce following words by the former patterns: 下班 'knock off', 下午 'afternoon', 下面 'downside' et al. Other examples include 机 'ji1' and 车 'che1' with word patterns: 候__, 开__, 客__, 整__, et al.; 有 'you3' and 无 'wu2' with: __害, __理, __机 et al. We can learn all these word patterns between different characters in the lexicon. Using them we can make an analogy to new words, such as that the new word 上载 'upload' can be inferred from the lexicon word 下载 'download' by the pattern __载 and the analogy between 上 and 下, by the same token, 飞车 'flying car' from 飞机 'plane', 无方 'without means' from 有方 'with means'. In what follows, we will describe in detail how to value the analogy between new words and lexicon words. First, we give a hypothesis: the two characters can appear more times in the same word patterns, the analogy between them is more reliable. For example, according to our lexicon 下 has the most same word patterns with 上, and that there is a strong preference for them to produce analogous words. Equation 6 shows the valuating principle, where a, c, x, represent a Chinese character respectively, $C(.)$ is just the same as 4.1.

$$ANA(a,x) = \frac{\sum_c \{W(ac)W(xc) + W(ca)W(cx)\}}{\sum_c \{W(ac) + W(ca) + W(xc) + W(cx)\}} \quad W(ac) = \begin{cases} 1 \text{ or } C(ac), & ac \text{ is in lexicon} \\ 0, & \text{otherwise.} \end{cases} \quad (6)$$

A matrix of the analogy between all characters can be obtained. If $W(ac)$ is set as the indicator function, the matrix can be computed simply according to a lexicon or other segmented corpus, and there is no need to count the frequency of each lexicon word. If character position is taken into count, there are two values between different characters counted by (7).

$$ANA_0(a,x) = \frac{\sum_c W(ca)W(cx)}{\sum_c \{W(ca) + W(cx)\}} \quad ANA_1(a,x) = \frac{\sum_c W(ac)W(xc)}{\sum_c \{W(ac) + W(xc)\}} \quad (7)$$

Second, using the quantified analogy value between different characters we can draw an analogy to new word. Only the character that has the maximum value of the analogy with the character in new word is used. Equation 8 shows how to make the analogy to new word ab from lexicon word xb and ax apart. When the character position is taken into count, Equation 9 is used.

$$F_{ANA}^a(ab) = \max_x \{W(xb) ANA(a,x)\} \quad F_{ANA}^b(ab) = \max_x \{W(ax) ANA(x,b)\} \quad (8)$$

$$F_{ANA'}^a(ab) = \max_x \{W(xb) ANA_1(a,x)\} \quad F_{ANA'}^b(ab) = \max_x \{W(ax) ANA_0(x,b)\} \quad (9)$$

For example, a=下, b=岗 'gang3', when x=上 it gets the maximum value of the analogy and: $F_{ANA'}^a(ab) = 32/(134+91)$, if $W(ac)$ is an indicator function in Equation

---

[7] In this paper, word pattern is defined that one character in bi-character words is fixed and the remainder are variable. For example, __班 is a word pattern, some characters such as 上, 下, 早, 晚, 白, 夜 can fill the blank to form Chinese word 上班, 下班, 早班, 晚班, 白班, 夜班.

6; $F^a_{AN A'}(ab) = 1612/(1678+1603)$, if $W(ac) = C(ac)$. That means there are 32 common word patterns of 上 and 下 in the first position, such as ＿任, ＿游, ＿台, ＿车, ＿面, ＿午, ＿班 et al..

4.3 Anti-word List and Frequency

As an opposite of IWP, we collect a list of character pairs (called the anti-word list) where the two adjacent characters are most unlikely to form a word. Table 2 shows some examples in the last row. But if all these pairs were recorded, it would need a large amount of memory. In this paper, only when the IWP of one character in the pair is more than 0.5, it will be recorded. We then define a binary feature $F_A(ab)$. If ab are in the anti-word list, $F_A(ab) = 1$, otherwise $F_A(ab) = 0$.

Another important feature of new words is its replicability. A new word usually appears more than once in a document especially the new domain concept, such as 十六大 '16th NCCPC'. The number of times a new word w is repeated in the given document are named $F_F(w)$, for example F_F (十六大)=7 in PK test set. According to our statistic data, the average appearance times of new words, in PK test data is 1.79. $F_F(w)$ divided by the total number of word tokens in the text is used as the feature of new word frequency. We also notice that if the processing unit is a sentence this feature will be useless.

All the above features were used for NW11. For NW21, because there was no certain feature of bi-character Chinese words for new word identification, only IWP(b), IWP(b,0), F_A and F_F are used as features. The baseline model for NW21 simply used IWP(b) only and a threshold.

5 Experiments

We test our approach using a subset of the SIGHAN bake-off data: PK corpus (4.7MB training and 89KB test). The training text has been segmented, and contains news articles from People Daily of 1998. We divided the training set into 20 parts. At each step, we use one part as development set and the remainder as training. Because only the lexicon word with the maximum analogy value is used, so the number of features is not more than 8, training time for NWI models is not more than 2 minutes and testing time is not more than 1 second with a standard PC (PIII 800Mhz, 512MB).

We investigate the relative contribution of each feature by generating many versions of the SVM classifier. Precision (P), Recall (R) and F score (a balance of P and R, F=2PR/(P+R)) are used for evaluations in these and following experiments. The results are shown in Table 2.

From the table, we can see that:

- Using all described features together, the SVM achieves a very good performance of NWI. The best F score is about 7.1% better than that of the baseline model in detecting NW11 and about 15.6% better in detecting NW21.
- The use of IWP(c, pos) hurts the performance of NW11 identification, but it did work for NW21 identification. The reason is that the two characters of a NW11 do not have fix position property in common lexicon words, but the last character of

Table 2. The result of several NWI models. + means the feature is added into SVM, F_{ANA} means two features: F^a_{ANA} and F^b_{ANA}, $F_{ANA'}$ means the character position is concerned, $F^c_{ANA'}$ means the character position and word frequency are both concerned

Model		P	R	F
NW11	Baseline(λ =0.675)	0.5799	0.5657	0.5728
	IWP	0.5174	0.7056	0.5970
	IWP+pos	0.5048	0.6796	**0.5793**
	IWP+F_{ANA}	0.5154	0.6537	**0.5763**
	IWP+$F_{ANA'}$	0.5333	0.6926	0.6026
	IWP+$F^c_{ANA'}$	0.5331	0.6969	0.6041
	IWP+F_F	0.5271	0.7143	0.6066
	IWP+F_A	0.5489	0.7532	0.6350
	IWP+$F_{ANA'}$ +F_A + F_F	0.5635	0.7489	0.6431
	IWP+ $F^c_{ANA'}$ +F_A + F_F	0.5748	0.7316	**0.6438**
NW21	Baseline(λ =0.95)	0.4066	0.3776	0.3915
	IWP + F_A + F_F	0.3861	0.8243	0.5258
	IWP + F_A + F_F +pos	0.4094	0.8243	**0.5471**

NW21 doses have the strong feature to use as a suffix. For example, Though 读 is the last character of new word 解读, it is more often as the first character of words than the last, that is IWP(解,1)> IWP(解,0).

- F_{ANA} has no effect, but $F_{ANA'}$ is indeed effective for NWI. The reason may be that the analogy between different characters is related with its position inside words. For example 友 'you3' and 吧 'ba1' have product analogous words only when they are located at the finial character position in a word, such as 酒吧 'saloon', 酒友 'pot companion', 网吧 'internet bar', 网友 'net friend'; whereas in the first position 友 'you3' has the analogy of 喜 'xi3' with three common word patterns: __人, __爱, __好. The effects of $F_{ANA'}$ also proved that our hypothesis and valuating approach for the analogy to new words in section 4.3 are right.
- $F^c_{ANA'}$ has more effective than $F_{ANA'}$. It means that it is more reliable if word frequency is used to value the analogy to new word. The reason maybe is that the frequency of words has some effect on new word formation.
- F_A is very useful for NWI. Many interferential new word candidates could be filtered according to this feature.
- F_F is also useful for NWI. The reason is clear that frequency is an important property of words.

We perform another two experiments to find how NWI improves the performance of a Chinese segmenter. The first is based on PK-close test in SIGHAN and the other is based on PK open test. In these experiments the segmenter (Gao et al. 2003) is selected and NWI is used as post procession. But there are the different segmentation standards between this segmenter and PK corpus, such as in PK corpus surname is apart from the person name, for example 邓小平 'Deng Xiaoping' is segmented as 邓 'Deng' and 小平 'Xiaoping', but in this segmenter the whole name is a word. So some adjustment is in need to adapt this segmenter to PK corpus. Table 3 shows the results, where *Adjst* means the adjustment on the output of the segmenter.

Table 3. The result of the segmenter with NWI in PK corpus

PK-close	R	P	F	OOV	R_{oov}	R_{iv}
Gao's +Adjst	0.952	0.924	0.938	0.069	0.580	0.979
Gao's +Adjst +NWI	0.948	0.937	**0.942**	0.069	**0.683**	0.968
PK-open	R	P	F	OOV	R_{oov}	R_{iv}
Gao's +Adjst	0.959	0.942	0.950	0.069	0.696	0.978
Gao's +Adjst +NWI	0.953	0.947	**0.951**	0.069	**0.752**	0.968

The first line of the result table shows the performance of the segmenter without NWI and the second line is the result after NWI. We could see the R_{oov} is improved 24.5% and the F-score is improved about 6.5% in PK-close test; R_{oov} 13.5% and F-score 2.0% in PK open test. But the R_{iv} drops a little for the reason that some two neighboring single character words are incorrectly combined into a new word. If we integrated the NWI model into Gao's segmenter, it would drop less.

We also compare our approach with previous ones that described in Chen (2003), Wu (2003), and Zhang (2003). These segmenters have got excellent performance in 1st SIGHAN Chinese word segmentation bakeoff. Table 4 shows the results.

We find that: although there is not so much linguistic knowledge in Gao's segmenter and NWI, the performance of Gao's segmenter with NWI has reached the same level as these outstanding segmenters, especially R_{oov} is the best in PK-close test and the second in PK open test. So we conclude that the SVM provides a flexible statistical framework to effectively incorporate a wide variety of knowledge for NWI.

Table 4. The results of some segmenters in PK corpus. Wu's segmenter is S10 in the bakeoff, Chen's segmenter is S09 and ICTCAS is S01 in 1st SIGHAN bakeoff

PK-close	R	P	F	OOV	R_{oov}	R_{iv}
Wu's segmenter	0.955	0.938	0.947	0.069	0.680	0.976
Chen's segmenter	0.955	0.938	0.946	0.069	0.647	0.977
PK-open	R	P	F	OOV	R_{oov}	R_{iv}
Wu's segmenter	0.963	0.956	0.959	0.069	0.799	0.975
ICTCAS	0.963	0.943	0.953	0.069	0.743	0.980

6 Conclusion and Future Work

Our work includes several main contributions. First, the distribution and the formal types of new word in real text have been analyzed. NW11 and NW21 were found as the main surface patterns of new words; Second, several features were explored from the statistical and linguistic knowledge of new word, especially the feature of the analogy between new words and lexicon words; Third, our experiments have showed that the SVM based binary classification is useful for NWI.

Now we only concern the uni-gram of new word and NWI is as a post procession of Gao's segmenter. As future work, we would like to integrate NWI into the segmenter. For example, we can define NWI as a new word type, and the whole classifier as a feature function in the log-linear models that are used in Gao's segmenter.

Acknowledgements

We would like to thank the members of the Natural Language Computing Group at Microsoft Research Asia, especially to acknowledge Ming Zhou, John Chen, and the three anonymous reviewers for their insightful comments and suggestions.

References

1. Aitao Chen. Chinese Word Segmentation Using Minimal Linguistic Knowledge. In proceedings of *the Second SIGHAN Workshop*, July 11-12, 2003, Sapporo, Japan.
2. Andi Wu. Chinese Word Segmentation in MSR-NLP. In proceedings of *the Second SIGHAN Workshop*, July 11-12, 2003, Sapporo, Japan.
3. Andi Wu. Zixin Jiang. Statistically-Enhanced New Word Identification in a Rule-Based Chinese System. In proceedings of *the Second Chinese Language Processing Workshop*, Hong Kong, China (2000) 46-51
4. Geutner, Petra. Introducing linguistic constraints into statistical language modeling. In *ICSLP96*, Philadelphia, USA (1996) 402-405.
5. Huaping Zhang et al. HMM-based Chinese Lexical Analyzer ICTCLAS. In proceedings of *the Second SIGHAN Workshop*, July 11-12, 2003, Sapporo, Japan.
6. Jianfeng Gao, Mu Li and Chang-Ning Huang. Improved source-channel models for Chinese word segmentation. In *ACL-2003*. Sapporo, Japan, 7-12, July, 2003
7. Jianfeng Gao, Joshua Goodman, Mingjing Li, Kai-Fu Lee. Toward a unified approach to statistical language modeling for Chinese. *ACM Transactions on Asian Language Information Processing,* Vol. 1, No. 1, pp 3-33. 2002
8. Jian-Yun Nie, et al. Unknown Word Detection and Segmentation of Chinese using Statistical and Heuristic Knowledge, *Communications of COLIPS* (1995).
9. Richard Sproat and Tom Emerson. The First International Chinese Word Segmentation Bakeoff. In proceedings of *the Second SIGHAN Workshop*, 2003, Sapporo, Japan.
10. Shengfen Luo, Maosong Sun. Two-Character Chinese Word Extraction Based on Hybrid of Internal and Contextual Measures. In proceedings of *the Second SIGHAN Workshop*, July 11-12, 2003, Sapporo, Japan.
11. Thesaurus Research Center of Commercial Press. 2003. Xinhua Xin Ciyu Cidian. Commercial Press, Beijing, 2003.
12. T. H. Chiang, Y. C. Lin and K.Y. Su. Statisitical models for word segmentation and unknown word resolution, In proceedings of *the ROCLING*, Taiwan (1992) 121-146.
13. T. Joachims. Estimating the Generalization Performance of a SVM Efficiently. In proceedings of *the International Conference on Machine Learning*, Morgan Kaufman, 2000.
14. Vladimir N. Vapnik. 1995. The Nature of Statistical Learning Theory. Springer, 1995.

Chinese New Word Finding Using Character-Based Parsing Model

Yao Meng, Hao Yu, and Fumihito Nishino

FUJITSU R&D Center Co., Ltd. Room 1003, Eagle Run Plaza No.26 Xiaoyun Road Chaoyang District Beijing, 100016, P.R. China
{Mengyao,yu,nishino}@frdc.fujitsu.com

Abstract. The new word finding is a difficult and indispensable task in Chinese segmentation. The traditional methods used the string statistical information to identify the new words in the large-scale corpus. But it is neither convenient nor powerful enough to describe the words' internal and external structure laws. And it is even the less effective when the occurrence frequency of the new words is very low in the corpus. In this paper, we present a novel method of using parsing information to find the new words. A character level PCFG model is trained by People Daily corpus and Penn Chinese Treebank. The characters are inputted into the character parsing system, and the words are determined by the parsing tree automatically. Our method describes the word-building rules in the full sentences, and takes advantage of rich context to find the new words. This is especially effective in identifying the occasional words or rarely used words, which are usually in low frequency. The preliminary experiments indicate that our method can substantially improve the precision and recall of the new word finding process.

1 Introduction

New words are appearing continuously in various domains, especially with the rapid growth of the WEB text. The new word identification is therefore as the difficult and indispensable task in many Chinese processing fields.

Nowadays, many methods are presented to solve the new word identification such as rule-based methods[1][2], corpus-based methods[3][4], statistical methods [5–7], and so on. However, most of the methods focus only the unknown words with proper word-building rules, such as, personal name, place name, organization name, and other named entities. Few researchers pay attention to the newly generated words, occasionally words and other words that are not registered in the dictionary. The general methods for finding the new word are based on string's frequency[8][9]. An unsupervised statistical method is used to construct the candidate word list from large-scale corpus, then the new words are chosen by the human, and the new words are converted into the known words by adding them into the system dictionary. However, these methods are applicable only in very limited string context, and the suitable size of the candidate list is very difficult to decide. In most cases, they work only with the high-frequency words based on very large-scale corpus, but behave poorly if the word's frequency is very low. When an application needs to identify the new words just in a single sentence, most of the methods will fail.

In this paper, we present a novel new word finding method using character level Chinese parsing model to overcome the problems in the above methods. A statistical character parsing model is trained by People Daily corpus and the Penn Chinese Treebank. The character (Hanzi in Chinese), instead of the word, is inputted into our parser. The segmentation and phrase analyzing are integrated into the whole framework. The word will be determined at the last step in the parsing process. Consequently, the new word finding will be considered in the full sentence parsing. Comparing with the previous methods, several features in our methods can better meet the characteristics of Chinese grammar. First, the Chinese language hasn't clear borderline between word and phrase. The integral framework is helpful in providing the information about the full sentence for words identification; second, the context is especially useful to identify low frequent new words, such as occasional words and rarely used words. The character parsing model can take advantage of all kinds of information, including character to phrase and sentence; third, our model is strong enough to describe the word-building knowledge from word-internal structures to word's external relations. As a result, our method provides a convenient tool to update the change of Chinese words and identify new words.

In this paper, we test our method on Taiwan balance corpus (http://www.sinica.edu.tw) and a 1G Chinese Web text. The experimental results indicate our method is significantly better than the traditional statistical methods with 70.5% F-measure for Taiwan balance corpus.

2 Chinese New Word Identification Using Statistical Character-Based Parsing Model

2.1 Overview of Character Parsing Model

In general, the Chinese parsing model is separated into segmentation and phrase parsing. However Chinese grammar is so flexible that there isn't clear borderline from word and phrase in Chinese grammar. If the segmentation must depend on the information from phrase and sentence, the result is usually unsatisfying. In order to solve this problem, we present a character parsing model, which integrates segmentation and phrase parsing into one framework. The input of the parsing model is Hanzi, and the segmentation result will be determined by the final parsing result.

In a given Chinese sentence, each Hanzi has 4 possible positions: It is the left side of a word, the right side of a word, inside a word, or it is an individual word itself. If we consider the POS information on each word as well, each Hanzi will belong to one of a POS's left side, a POS's right side, inside a POS, and a word with a POS. We name this as Hanzi's POS feature. For example, there are 12 Hanzis and 8 words for the sentence, with the POS of each word in bold italics.

s: 另有/*v* 一/*m* 间/*q* 活动室/*n* 兼作/*v* 寝室/*n* 。/*w*
(There is a sports room, also used for bedroom.)

Where the POS feature of '另' is at the verb's left and the POS feature of '有' is at the verb's right, and so on. If the s is tagged by the Hanzi's POS feature, this is given by: *s'*: 另/*vl* 有/*vr* 一/*mo* 间/*qo* 活/*nl* 动/*ni* 室/*nr* 兼/*vl* 作/*vr* 寝/*nl* 室/*nr* 。/*wo*

We can get the POS feature for each Hanzi from the segmentation and POS tagging of the sentence. On the other hand, if we tag the POS feature for each Hanzi in the sentence, the word and its POS tagging can be produced by a combining process, which is similar to combining words into the phrase. For this reason, we can extend the sentence parsing to the Hanzi level. And the final parsing tree will give all the phrase structure, word's POS tagging and the segmentation of the sentence. For instance, when the parsing is inputted with words, the phrase structure for the above sentence is figure 1. If the input to the parsing is expended to Hanzi level, the analysis for the sentence will become figure 2. From the parsing result in Figure 2, the word segmentation and POS tagging can be produced naturally. The new word finding will be solved in the integral parsing process.

The figure 1 and figure 2 show that the character parsing model is essentially an extent of the word parsing model. The difference lies in whether to begin at word node or at Hanzi node.

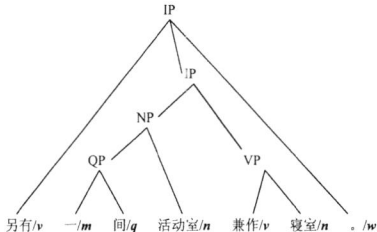

Fig. 1. Word level parsing tree   **Fig. 2.** Character level parsing tree

2.2 Statistical Character Parsing Model

Since the character parsing model need to consider the problems in the character's level, besides the general phrase structure rules, it should add the rules of Hanzi's POS feature and the rules of word internal structure. In our model, we treat the POS of a word as a special phrase label, and the Hanzi's POS feature as the special node label for Hanzi. By this way, all the statistical models using in the word level parsing can also be used in the character level. In this paper, we just adopt the standard PCFG to build our character parsing model.

In standard PCFG model, the probability of a parsing tree t for a sentence s is given by

$$p(t,s) = \prod_{i=1...m} p(R_i) \tag{1}$$

Where t is derived by m context-free re-write rules.

If the model changes from word to character, the probability of this tree will be estimated as:

$$p(t,s) = \prod_{i=1...m} p(R_i) \times \prod_{j=1...l} p(R'_j) \times \prod_{k=1...n} p(R''_k) \tag{2}$$

Where R_i is the same phrase re-write rule as it in equation (1); R' is the word internal structure rules(word-rules), the l words in the sentence are produced by l word-rules; R'' is the Hanzi's POS feature rules(Hanzi-rules), which tag the corresponding POS features for n Hanzis in the sentence. All the word-rules and Hanzi-rules are also context-free rules under the PCFG's independent assumption.

The word-rule is denoted by: $t \rightarrow o_l\{o_i\}o_r$ or $t \rightarrow o_o$

Where o_l, o_r, o_i, o_o is the left side of a certain POS, the right side of a certain POS, inside a certain POS, a certain POS, respectively, the t is a POS sign. The word-rule is used to combine the Hanzis into the word.

The Hanzi-rule is defined by $o \rightarrow c_i$, where o is a Hanzi's POS feature, c_i is the ith Hanzi in the current sentence.

For example, the part of Hanzi-rules and word-rules in the figure 2 are the following:

$R'_1 : v \rightarrow vl\ vr$, $R'_2 : n \rightarrow nl\ ni\ nr$ (word-rules)

$R''_1 : vl \rightarrow 另$, $R''_2 : vl \rightarrow 有$ and $R''_3 : ni \rightarrow 动$ (Hanzi-rules)

The best character parsing tree for a given Chinese sentence s is given by equation (3):

$$t^* = \arg\max_t p(t|s) = \arg\max_t p(t,s) = \arg\max_t (\prod_{i=1...m} p(R_i) \times \prod_{j=1...l} p(R'_j) \times \prod_{k=1...n} p(R''_k)) \quad (3)$$

The equation (3) is composed of three parts, which represent grammar features of different levels in Chinese parsing. The first part is the PCFG model, which expresses Chinese phrase structure rules. The second part describes word internal structure rules, and the third part defines the generating rules making character into word. The best parsing tree gives the best phrase structures and the segmentation result in the model. Finally, the equation (3) integrates word analysis and the phrase analysis into one framework.

2.3 Model Estimation

We use the maximum likelihood to calculate the probability of various rules in the model. We use the Penn Chinese Treebank[10] to train the probability of the phrase rules. The probability of word-rules and Hanzi-rules are trained by corpus of People Daily in 1998[11]. We retagged the POS of the words in the Penn Chinese Treebank using People Daily's POS scheme for the consistency of POS scheme in the two corpuses.

The first part of the equation (3) is the standard PCFG model. The probability of $R : A \rightarrow a$ is given by the relative frequency estimator.

$$p(A \rightarrow \alpha) = \frac{C(A \rightarrow \alpha)}{\sum_{\alpha' \in (N \cup T)^*} C(A \rightarrow \alpha')} \quad (4)$$

Here $C(A \rightarrow \alpha)$ is the number of times the production $A \rightarrow a$ in training corpus. The number of production in Penn Chinese Treebank and the detail estimation procedure can be seen in [10]

The probability of word-rules and Hanzi-rules are estimated from 300,000 sentences in People Daily in 1998 and 4000 Sentences in the Penn Chinese Treebank.

The probability of word-rule $R: t \to h$ is given by

$$p(t \to h) = \frac{C(t \to h)}{\sum_{h' \in (H)} C(t \to h')} \quad (5)$$

Where t is a POS tagging label, h is a Hanzi's POS feature, H is the set of all the Hanzi's POS features. And the size of the H is less than the 4 times of number of the POS tagging set (for every POS can have 4 options for Hanzi's POS features at the most).

The equation (6) is the probability of Hanzi-rule.

$$p(h \to c) = \frac{C(h \to c)}{\sum_{c' \in (\Delta)} C(h \to c')} \quad (6)$$

Where c is a Hanzi, Δ is Hanzi set. About 30,000 unique Hanzis are occurred in People Daily corpus. They are all the characters we used in the model.

Instead of the large number of the Chinese words, the Hanzi's set is very small. The number of often used Hanzi is less than 10 thousand. So estimation for the character parsing model don't pay more attention to the data sparse than the word parsing model. It is the merit of the character parsing model. The other merit in character parsing model is the training for phrase-rules and word-rules can use the different corpus. The POS-tagged corpus is already sufficient for the purpose to estimate the probability of word-rules and Hanzi-rules. So if you have the training data for segmentation and parsing, it isn't necessary to provide extra data for the character parsing modeling.

3 New Word Finding Using Character-Based Parsing Model

The character parsing model doesn't depend on the dictionary. Therefore, the *old* words and *new* words make no difference for our system. The parsing system will accept the Hanzi's string as a word, only if the string satisfies the rules in the model. The word-rules and character-rules can generate all the possible words. And the phrase parsing works like a filter for illegal words, it deletes some word candidates, which doesn't conform to the Chinese grammar in full sentence analysis. At last, combinations of Hanzi in the best parsing tree are accepted as the words.

For example, "兼作" is a possible word candidate in the sentence "另有活动室兼作寝室。". because there are some words in the training data whose first character is "兼", such as "兼职", "兼容", "兼顾", "兼具" and so on. And there also exist some words whose last character is "作". The character-rules about "兼" and the character-rules about "作" will be extracted form these words. And of course, the word-rule "$v \to vl\ vr$" also will be extracted from the two-character's verb in the training data. As the result, the "兼作" becomes a possible word using the word-rules and Hanzi-rules. It is certain that the word-rules and Hanzi-rules also generate some illegal words, such as the "动室", "有活" and so on. But this is the first step to build the words in our method. All the possible words will be checked by the phrase parsing. The upper phrase structure will delete those unsuitable words in the sentence. At last, only the words in the best parsing tree are saved. For the sentence "另有活动室兼作

寝室。", the best parsing is just the tree in figure 2. So the right segmentation "另有/ 活动室/ 兼作/ 寝室/ 。/" is given.

Finding new word in the corpus is very simple by our method: each sentence in the corpus is parsed by our character parser. All the words derived from the parsing trees are saved in a list. Comparing with the dictionary we already have, the new words will be extracted from the corpus.

4 Experimental Results

There is no authoritative Chinese dictionary yet. Sometimes, it is difficult to determine whether a string is a word or not. In this paper, we judge the word by the tagged corpus we have. In the first experiment, we test our method in the Taiwan balance corpus. We compare the word list, which is built with our method, with the words in the corpus. We consider a string as a word only if the string is tagged as a word in the corpus. In the second experiment, we test some words which occur in the People Daily corpus, but don't occur in the Taiwan corpus. These words are considered as the new words. We explore our method in identifying these new words.

The string frequency method and the method based on the character relation information[7] [9] are compared with our method. The test data are Taiwan balance corpus, and a 1G raw Web corpus.

4.1 New Word Finding with String Statistical Information

Finding new word with string's frequency is a base method. The main assumption is that the more times certain several characters co-occur, the higher the possibility that the several characters combine into a word. Therefore, this method counts the frequency of the strings from the large corpus, and extracts the possible words by the string-frequency sorting.

The weakness in this method is some random combination containing high-frequency Hanzi will be taken as the words. The noise combinations weaken the performance of this method. The method using the character's relation information solves the above problem partly. It considers both the string's frequency and the frequency of single character. If the two strings have the same frequency in corpus, the strings with characters of lower frequency are more likely to combine into word than the strings with the higher frequency of single character. This method can delete some high frequent random combination.

There are many methods to measure the degree of association among the characters, such as mutual information, t-score, ϕ^2 coefficient, and so on. The performance of these measures is similar. In this paper, we use the ϕ^2 coefficient for experiments.

Given a Chinese character string $c_i c_{i+1}$, we define the 4 parameters of a, b, c, d to calculate the ϕ^2 coefficient of string $c_i c_{i+1}$.

$a = freq(c_i, c_{i+1})$, $b = freq(c_i) - freq(c_i, c_{i+1})$,
$c = freq(c_{i+1}) - freq(c_i, c_{i+1})$, $d = N - a - b - c$.

Where $freq(c_i,c_{i+1})$ is the co-occurrence's time of the c_ic_{i+1} in the corpus, $freq(c_i)$ is the time that c_i is the first character in the two-character string. $freq(c_{i+1})$ is the time that c_{i+1} is the second character in the two-character string.

The ϕ^2 coefficient is defined as

$$\phi^2(c_i,c_{i+1}) = \frac{(ad-bc)^2}{(a+b)(a+c)(b+d)(c+d)} \tag{7}$$

The process of finding new words using ϕ^2 is very similar to the method using the word's frequency. The difference is just the measure prefers the ϕ^2 to the word's frequency.

4.2 Experimental Results and Discussion

4.2.1 Experiments in Taiwan Balance Corpus

We make experiments in Taiwan balance corpus firstly. The method based on string frequency, the method based on ϕ^2 coefficient, and our method, are tested in this corpus.

The Taiwan corpus has segmented and tagged the POS for each word. We extracted all 53,657 two-character words from this corpus. There are 538,867 two-character strings in the original sentences in the corpus. These strings include all *true* words and random two character strings happened in the corpus. The 250,601 strings in it just occur once in the corpus. We call them candidate word list. The different methods will extract the *true* words from the candidate word list, and the performance is evaluated by the number of the new words they found. The precision, recall and F-measure are given by:

Precision= $\frac{number\ of\ words\ in\ candidate\ list}{number\ of\ reported\ strings\ in\ candidate\ list}$ Recall= $\frac{number\ of\ words\ in candidate\ list}{number\ of\ words\ in\ corpus}$

F-measure= $\frac{2*precision*recall}{precision+recall}$

We sort the string list by frequency and the ϕ^2 measure to evaluate the frequency method and ϕ^2 method respectively. The performances of two methods in different threshold are shown in Table 1, and Table 2. For frequency method, the threshold changes form 1 time to 20 times each string occurs in the corpus. And For ϕ^2 method, the candidate word lists are separated into top 10,000, top 20,000, top 30,000 and all the strings in the corpus.

In order to test our character parsing method, we parse all 631,215 sentences in the corpus. 492,347 of those sentences get the parsing trees. Traveling the parsing tree, the possible words are extracted. They are the words found by our method in the corpus. Only traveling best parsing tree, we extract 40,348 possible words from the parsing trees. When we travel 3 best parsing trees for each sentence, the numbers of possible words will increase. 65,814 possible words are gotten from parsing trees. The precision and recall in this model are shown in table 3.

4.2.2 Experiments in Large-Scale Raw Corpus

The second experiment is to find the new words in 1G raw Chinese Web text using different methods. All the texts are collected by the web robot automatically in one

Table 1. Results in string frequency model

Occu. times	Precision	Recall	F-meas.
≥ 20	28.5%	23.5%	25.8%
≥ 10	26 %	36.2%	30.3%
≥ 5	21.5%	52.6%	30.5%
≥ 1	10 %	100%	18.2%

Table 2. Results in ϕ^2 method

ϕ^2 measure	Precision	Recall	F-meas.
Top 10,000	65.6%	12%	20.3%
Top 20,000	54.7%	20.4%	29.7%
Top 30,000	48.7%	27.2%	34.9%
All words	10%	100%	18.2%

Table 3. Results in character parsing model

Tree /Sent.	Precision	Recall	F-meas.
One best tree	74.5%	56%	63.9%
3 best trees	64 %	78.5%	70.5%

day. There are 3,246,691 two-character strings in the web corpus in sum. We measure ϕ^2 for each strings, and choose top 15,000 into candidate word list. Comparing with the Taiwan balance corpus and People Daily corpus, we find that there are 4519 words in Taiwan Balance corpus, other 10481 strings in top 15,000 don't occur in Taiwan balance corpus. And 616 of those possible words occur in People Daily. The remainder 616 words can be considered the new words we want to find in the WEB corpus, if we have had the dictionary extracted from Taiwan corpus. So if our method can find these words, we believe our method is able to find the new words.

For each string in 10481 strings, we parse two sentences which include this string. If the character parsing system indicates the string as a word, we accept it as a word. If the parsing system doesn't accept the string as a word after analyzing the full sentence, we don't consider it as a word either. We test 3 criterions to determine possible words in the experiment. The strongest criterions is that the string is a word only if both best parsing tree in parsed two sentences accept it as a word. In the table 4, the results in different criterions are shown:

Table 4. Results of new word finding in WEB corpus

Criterions	Precision	Recall	F-meas.
3-best trees in one sent	35.6 %	69.8 %	47.2%
1-best tree in one sent	54.4 %	43.2 %	48.2%
1-best tree in 2 sents	64.9 %	37.5 %	47.5%

'1-best tree in 2 sents.' means that the string is a word when both best parsing tree in both parsed sentences accept the string as a word. And the '3-best trees in one sent' means we consider 3-best trees in each sentence. That is, the possible string is regarded as a word, just one of parsing tree in a sentence consider it as a word.

The candidate word list is composed of top 15,000 in ϕ^2 measure. There are only 616 *new* words in this list (4519 words have been in Taiwan corpus, so we consider them as the *old* words). But the ϕ^2 method can't distinguish between a word and a not word from the remainder 10481 strings. That is, if someone wants to get the *true new* words in 10481 possible words, his method has no choice but to select new words by human. But the experiment reveals our method still finds the new words with rather high precision and recall. In the criterion using 3-best parsing trees in one of two sentences, the system gets 1207 candidate words from 3-best parsing trees. 69.8% of them are *true new* words. If we use the criterion of '1-best tree in 2 sents.', the candidate word list includes 356 strings, the precision will reach 64.9%. The result shows our method will refine the new words we want from the candidate list, where the ϕ^2 method can't work.

Both experiments indicate that our method is significantly better than using the string statistical methods in Chinese new words identification. These are reasonable results as our method uses more contextual information and supervised information than the methods based on string statistical information. Of course, our results benefit from the tagged training data and time spent parsing the sentence. Unlike the unsupervised methods, we need segmented corpus and middle-scale Tree bank. And, our time cost is much higher than the string statistical methods due to the parsing of the full sentences. However, some of segmented Chinese corpus and Treebank have been available along with the development of Chinese corpus. For example, all the data we used in this paper are open (http://www.sinica.edu.cn; http://www.icl.pku.edu.cn; http://www.ldc.upenn.edu). The time spent is the main week point in our method. In our experiments, the parser is implemented by CYK algorithm in C language on a work station (windows XP, 2.8GHz Xeon). The parsing speed is 150 sentences per minutes. But we think it is not a severe problem if the finding of the newly coined words from large-scale WEB information be done offline. On the other hand, for some application, it is worthy to spend some time finding out the occasional words and rarely used words in the sentence when the implementation devotes to get the elaborate information in the sentence.

5 Conclusions and Future Work

New word identification is a difficult and indispensable task in Chinese segmentation. In this paper, we present a novel Chinese new word finding method based on statistical character level parsing model. The model is trained by People Daily and Penn Chinese Treebank automatically. The character parsing model explores a new integral Chinese parsing method, including segmentation and phrase parsing. Unlike the previous methods, our method is strong enough to describe the word-building rules from internal structure to external relation. It works especially well in finding the occasional words or rarely used words in the sentence. The both experiments on Taiwan balance corpus and large-scale raw Web text show the substantial improvement of the performance in new word finding.

The favorable experimental results in new word finding encourage us to combine our method with existing new word finding methods, segmentation methods or parsing methods.

Our method can be regarded as a refining tool after extracting the candidate word list by string statistical information. It is possible to use string statistical method to produce a rough new word candidate list rapidly, and use our method to refine it further. The combination with existing new word finding methods can balance the more time cost in our method and the less performance in the method based on string statistical information. On the other hand, the dictionary is a very important linguistic knowledge base, the parsing with an appreciate dictionary is better than the parsing without dictionary. So we can detect the potential new words part in the sentence by the dictionary, and then use the character-level parser to get the final segmentation and parsing results. All these issues will be left for future research.

References

1. An-di Wu, Zi-xin Jiang. Word Segmentation in Sentence Analysis. In Proceedings of the 1998 International Conference on Chinese Information Processing, Beijing, pp.69~180,
2. Zhiying Liu 时间短语的分析与识别, 全国第7届计算语言学联合学术会议 pp.122~129, 2003
3. Rou Song, Hong Zhu. 基于语料库和规则库的人名识别法 《计算语言学研究与应用》 pp.150-154, 1993
4. Yan Sui, Pu Zhang. 基于"动态流通语料库"进行"有效字符串"提取的初步研究, 全国第6届计算语言学联合学术会议 pp.494~499, 2001
5. Maosong Sun, Dayang Shen, Benjiamin K Tsou. Chinese word segmentation without using lexicon and hand-crafted training data. In proceedings of the 36th ACL, pp.1265~1271, 1998
6. Wenliang Chen, Jingbo Zhu, Tiansun Yao et al. 基于BOOSTRAPPING 的领域词汇自动获取 全国第7届计算语言学联合学术会议 pp. 67~73, 2003
7. Xuanqing Huang, Lide Wu. 基于机器学习的无需人工编制词典的切词系统. 模式识别与人工智能, 1996(4), 297~303
8. Maosong Sun, Jiayan Zhou. 汉语自动分词研究评述 《当代语言学》第1期: pp.22~32, 2001
9. Ting Li, Yan Wu et al. 串频统计和词匹配相结合的汉语自动分词系统 《中文信息学报》第1期 pp.17~25, 1997
10. Nianwen Xue, Fei Xia. The Bracketing Guidelines for the Penn Chinese Treebank (3.0) IRCS Report 00-08, University of Pennsylvania, Oct 2000
11. Shiwen Yu, Huiming Duan, et al. 北京大学现代汉语语料库基本加工规范. 中文信息学报, No. 5, pp.49-64, pp.58-65, 2002

Thematic Session: Natural Language Technology in Mobile Information Retrieval and Text Processing User Interfaces

Introduction

One of the strongest impacts in recent information technology is the way mobility has changed computer applications. The rapid rate of handphone adoption, the ubiquitous PDA, and the low cost of wireless adoption has created new problems, new challenges, and new opportunities to researchers in many disciplines. One common thread through all these applications is the necessity for information retrieval and mobile text processing in one form or another. Another characteristic is the limited size of mobile devices and the consequent need for sophisticated methods of text input and output. Other applications with a similar need of language technology support under challenging conditions include e.g. communication aids and authoring tools.

The use of NLP plays an integral part in creating better user interfaces, more efficient text input technologies, authoring aids, summarization and analysis of output for precise display, and greater understanding in the interactive dialogue between user and applications working on text. We invited researchers focusing on

- text input and output technologies,
- language modeling,
- summarization,
- mobile database, information retrieval and management,
- speech and dialogue IR applications on mobile devices,

and HCI researchers on text retrieval and processing systems to explore user oriented and theoretical limits and characteristics of NLP for front-end and back-end solutions within the context of text retrieval and processing user interfaces.

As Chinese is not alphabetic and the input of Chinese characters into computer is still a difficult and unsolved problem, voice retrieval of information becomes apparently an important application area of mobile information retrieval (IR). It is intuitive to think that users would speak more words and require less time when issuing queries vocally to an IR system than forming queries in writing. The first paper presents some new findings derived from an experimental study on Mandarin Chinese to test this hypothesis and assesses the feasibility of spoken queries for search purposes.

Predictive text entry systems on computers like kana-to-kanji conversion provide a mechanism that enables users to select among possible words for a given input. Mistakes in selection are relatively common, and they introduce real-word errors. A proofreading system is thus needed to detect and correct real-word errors on a computer without imposing troublesome operations on users. To this end, a practical proofreading system for Japanese text is proposed in the second paper. The system automatically detects possible real-word homonym errors, and for each detected word, suggests substitution candidates of the same pronunciation. The user can either choose the most appropriate one or leave the original untouched. The system uses an algorithm based on the naive Bayesian method. Although the proofreading system was implemented for homonym errors in Japanese text, its design concept and algorithm are also applicable to other languages. The client program of the proofreading system is implemented on the Emacs text editor and works in real time.

In the third paper, we present a new *predictive pruning* algorithm for text entry and show empirically how it outperforms simple text prediction. Our tests are based on a new application domain for predictive entry: the input of Morse code. Our motivation for this work was to contribute to the development of efficient entry systems for the seriously disabled, but we found that the constraint of using a single key highlighted features of text prediction not previously closely scrutinised. In particular, our tests show how predictive text entry is affected by two factors: altering the rankings of completion candidates based on the difficulty of entering the remaining text with just the keyboard, and the number of candidates presented to the user.

In particular, we gratefully appreciate the support of the programme committee members in this special thematic session.

Michael Kuehn (University of Koblenz-Landau, Koblenz)
Mun-Kew Leong (Institute for Infocomm Research, Singapore)
Kumiko Tanaka-Ishii (University of Tokyo, Tokyo)

Reviewers

Hsin-Hsi Chen
Jean-Pierre Chevallet
Fabio Crestani
Yoshihiko Hayashi
Gareth Jones
Min-Yen Kan
Nils Klarlund

Gary Geunbae Lee
Mu Li
Kathleen McCoy
Sung Hyon Myaeng
Hwee Tou Ng
Manabu Okumura

Spoken Versus Written Queries for Mobile Information Access: An Experiment on Mandarin Chinese

Heather Du and Fabio Crestani

Department of Computer and Information Sciences
University of Strathclyde,
Glasgow,
Scotland, UK
{heather,fabioc}@cis.strath.ac.uk

Abstract. As Chinese is not alphabetic and the input of Chinese characters into computer is still a difficult and unsolved problem, voice retrieval of information becomes apparently an important application area of mobile information retrieval (IR). It is intuitive to think that users would speak more words and require less time when issuing queries vocally to an IR system than forming queries in writing. This paper presents some new findings derived from an experimental study on Mandarin Chinese to test this hypothesis and assesses the feasibility of spoken queries for search purposes.

1 Introduction

There is an increasing demand for mobile access to online information today. Mobile phone subscriptions are increasing faster than Internet connection rates. According to official figures released by The Chinese Ministry of Information Industries, the number of mobile phone subscribers in China reached 200 million at the end of November 2002, even though mobile phone calls cost about three times as much as calls made with fixed or "wired" telephones. The number of Chinese web pages is increasing rapidly. With the upcoming 3G wireless networks, it will enable this huge mobile user community to access information anywhere and anytime. Currently, the means of input user's information needs available are very much limited in keypad capability by either keying in or using a stylus on the mobile phone screen, and the speed is far from satisfaction. Moreover, such input style does not work well for those users who are moving around, using their hands or eyes for something else, or interacting with another person, not to mention those with visual impairment. In all those cases, given the difficulty of Chinese character input and the ubiquity of mobile phone access, speech enabled interface has come to the lime light of today's mobile IR research community which lets users access information solely via voice.

The transformation of user's information needs into a search expression, or query, is known as query formulation. It is widely regarded as one of the most challenging activities in information seeking [4]. Research on query formulation with speech is denoted as spoken query processing (SQP), which is the use of spoken queries to retrieve textual or spoken documents. While Chinese spoken document retrieval has been extensively studied over the years, especially supported by TREC-6 (Text REtrieval Conference) [10], little work has been devoted to Chinese SQP. Two groups of researchers have investigated the level of degradation of retrieval performance due to errors in the query terms introduced by the automatic speech recognition (ASR) system by carrying out experimental studies [1, 2]. These experiments claimed that despite the current limitations of the accuracy of speech recognition software, it is feasible to use speech as a means of posing questions to an IR system which will be able to maintain considerable effectiveness in performance. However, the query sets created in these experiments were dictated from existing queries in textual forms. Will people use same words, phrases or sentences when formulating their information needs via voice as typing onto a screen? If not, how different are their queries in written form from spoken form? Dictated speech is considerably different from spontaneous speech and easier to recognise [6]. It would be expected that spontaneous spoken queries to have higher levels of word error rate (WER) and different kinds of errors. Thus, the claim will not be valid until further empirical work to clarify the ways in which spontaneous queries differ in length and nature from dictated ones. We have carried out an experiment in English languages previously and derived some interesting findings which are reported in [5]. We are motivated by the comments from one of the reviewers for that paper to conduct a similar experiment in Mandarin language to see if we could obtain similar findings as the ones with English queries. From the experiment we conducted in English language, the results showed that using speech to formulate one's information needs not only provides a way to express naturally, but also encourages one to speak more semantically which resulted in longer queries than written text. Thus, we would expect, in the case of Mandarin Chinese, that spoken queries would be longer in length than written ones. Furthermore, the translation of thoughts to speech is faster than the transition of thoughts to writing. In order to test these two hypotheses on Mandarin queries, we repeated the same experiment with just some minor setup changes.

In this paper we present the results of an experimental study on the differences between Mandarin written and spoken queries. The paper is structured as follows. Section 2 describes our experimental environment of the study. The results of this study are reported in section 3. In section 4, the results are compared to the ones derived from the experiment on English queries. Conclusion with some remarks on the potential significance of the study is presented in section 5.

2 Experimental Study

Our view is that the best way to assess the differentiations in query formulation between spoken form and written form is to conduct an experimental analysis with a group of potential users in a setting as close as possible to a real world application [7]. We used a within-subjects experimental design and in total 10 subjects participated who are all native Mandarin-speaking students for a Master degree with good experience in using Chinese web search engines, but few have prior experience with vocal information retrieval. In the previous experiment, we recruited 12 native English speakers.

The topics we used for this experimental study was a subset of 10 topics extracted from TREC-5 Mandarin topic collection (topics 19-28). Each topic consists of four parts: id, title, description and narrative. The English parts of these topics were ignored and only the parts in Mandarin were presented to the participants. We used 10 TREC topics (topics 151-160) in the previous experiment on English language.

After we have experimented in English language, our aim now is to find out if we can derive the same results from an identical experiment in Mandarin Chinese. Therefore, the main experimental procedure and data collection methods remained the same as the English experiment which have been omitted for lacking of space here. A detailed description of the procedural can be found in [5].

3 Experimental Results and Analysis on Mandarin Queries

From this experiment, we collected 100 written queries and 100 spoken queries. We manually transcribed spoken queries into textual form. Each Chinese character has its own meanings, and it can form a compound word to give more complete and richer meaning with neighboring characters. In the context of a Chinese sentence, there are no spaces, or explicit separators between words to indicate boundaries, appearing as a linear sequence of equally spaced characters [8]. With the fact that a character may form a meaningful word with its previous or next neighboring character(s) in the context of a sentence, many different word combinations are possible. One mistaken word combination would lead to an incorrect segmentation for the rest of the sentence. Therefore, Chinese word segmentation has been a popular topic in the IR community. There are a number of segmentation approaches which have been proposed to tackle this problem [9]. The main approaches are statistical-based and dictionary-based methods. With the dictionary-based segmentation, words in Chinese text are segmented by comparing and matching the words in a dictionary. Such methods have a stronger accordance to the semantics and sentence structure of the Mandarin Chinese. As Chinese words can vary in length, the dictionary is flexible to change as the vocabulary can be updated and new words can be inserted manually. Therefore, we have chosen a dictionary-based method developed at the in2in research laboratory to segment the transcriptions of the spoken queries [3]. There were more than 58,000 entries in the dictionary adopted by this method. Some of the characteristics of written and spoken queries are reported in Table 1. This table pictures clearly that the average length of spoken queries is longer than written queries with a ratio rounded at 2.38 as we have hypothesised. After stopwords removal, the average length of spoken queries is reduced from 22.66 to 17.61with

Table 1. Characteristics of written and spoken queries.

Data set	Written queries	Spoken queries
Queries	100	100
Average length with stopwords	9.51	22.66
Average length without stopwords	8.29	17.61
Median length with stopwords	7.9	17.4
Average duration with stopwords	2m 33s	1m 36s

a 22% reduction rate and the average length of written queries is reduced from 9.51 to 8.29 with a reduction rate at 13%. These numbers indicate that spoken queries contain more stopwords than written ones. There is also a significant difference on durations for formulating queries in spoken and written forms.

3.1 Length of Queries Across Topics

The average length of spoken and written queries for each topic across all 10 participants is calculated and presented in Fig. 1. In Fig. 1, the scattered points for spoken queries are always above the ones for written queries, which suggests the spoken queries are lengthier than the written ones. This is the case for every topic persistently. This is exactly what we expected to see. When formulating queries verbally, the ease of speech encourages participates to speak more words. A typical user spoken query looks like the following:

"有关苏联在海湾战争中如何担任调停的角色，具体包括苏联与伊拉克的沟通，以及提出的停火协议还有要求多国部队从伊拉克撤出的和平建议"

Whereas its textual counterpart is much shorter:

"海湾战争，苏联，调停，沟通，停火，撤军"

3.2 Length of Queries Across Participants

We also summarise the average length of queries for all 10 topics across all participants and presented it in Fig. 2. We could observe from Fig. 2 that for 9 out

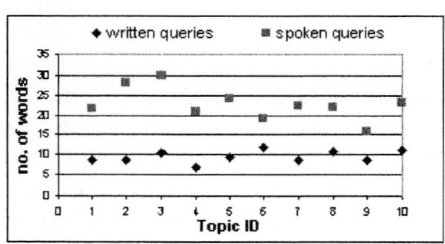

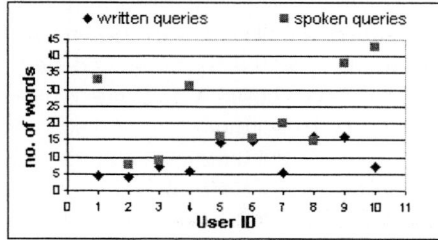

Fig. 1. Avg length of queries per topic. **Fig. 2.** Avg length of queries per user.

of 10 participants his/her spoken queries are longer than written ones. There is only one participant whose written queries are just slightly lengthier than spoken queries. However, the variations of the length between spoken and written queries for some participants are very timid. In fact, after we have studied the transcriptions of spoken queries, we observed that the spoken queries generated by these participants are very much identical to their written ones. The discrepancies of length within written queries are very insignificant and relatively stable. All participants used similar approach to formulate their written queries by specifying only keywords. The experience of using textual search engines influenced the participants' process of query formulations. For most popular textual search engines, the stopwords would be removed from a query before creating the query representation. Conversely, the length fluctuates rapidly within spoken queries among participants.

We didn't run a practice session prior to the experiment such as to give an example of how to formulate a written query and a spoken query for a topic, because we felt this would set up a template for participants to mimic later on during the course of experiment and we wouldn't be able to find out how participants would go about formulating their queries. Existing research also shows that people do not use the same language when talking to a computer as when talking to another human [11]. In this experiment, we observed that half of the participants adopted natural language to formulate their queries which were very much like conversational talk and the other half participants stuck to the traditional approach by only speaking keywords and/or broken phrases. They said they didn't "talk" to the computer was because they felt strange and uncomfortable to speak to a machine. This suggests that participants own personalities played a key role in the query formulation process.

3.3 Duration of Queries Across Topics

The time spent to formulate each query was measured. A maximum of 5 minutes was imposed on each topic and participants were not allowed to work past this. All participants felt that the time given was sufficient. The average time participants spent on each topic is shown in Fig. 3. Just as we would expect, it is the same case for every topic consistently that less time is required to form a spoken query than a written one. However, the discrepancies between the spoken queries and written queries for the first half topics are quite obvious whereas much less differences exist for the second half topics.

The variations of durations within written queries and within spoken queries were quite irregular, but nevertheless, we could observe that on average the written queries for the first half topics need more time to formulate than the second half topics, and for spoken queries, the second half topics require more time than the first half topics. This could be due to the way in which the tasks were assigned to the participants. They formulated written queries for the first half topics in session1 and the second half topics in session 2, while spoken queries were formulated for the second half topics in session 1 and the first half topics in session 2. Although we intentionally carried out the session 2 at least one week

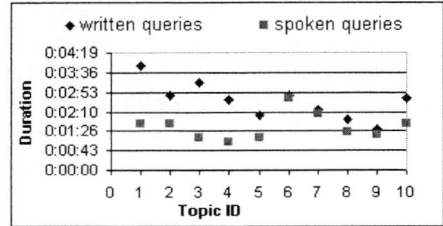 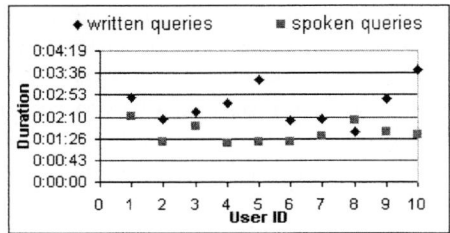

Fig. 3. Avg duration of queries per topic. **Fig. 4.** Avg duration of queries per user.

after the completion of session 1 to minimise the participants' memory jogging on these topics, some participants commented that they could still recall the topics very well, therefore, they could save time from comprehending the topics again in session 2. This trend is also reflected on the shifting of their ratings on task complexities which are reduced from session 1 to session 2. However, we couldn't neglect the fact that the cognitive load of participant to speak out their thoughts was also high. Some of them commented that they had to well-formulate their queries in head before speaking aloud with no mistakes. One could revise one's textual queries easily in a query field, but it would be difficult for the computer to understand if one alters one's words while speaking. Information retrieval via voice is a relatively new research area and there aren't many working systems available currently. Lacking of experience also pressurised the spoken query formulation process. We could claim that the complexity of the topics and the participants' knowledge about the topics also played a part in the query formulation process. We asked the participants to point out the most difficult and easiest topics during the interview. Their judgments conformed to Fig. 3, that is they spent longest time on the topics thought to be most difficult and least time on the ones deemed to be simple and straightforward.

3.4 Duration of Queries Across Participants

The duration of queries per participant is shown in Fig. 4. Every participant spent less time on spoken queries than written ones with only one exception. This strongly supports our claim that people would require less time to form spoken queries since that is the way they communicate to each other, furthermore, this means that it would be quicker to specify one's information needs via voice than key in or hand write into a mobile device. Since the mobile communication cost is still relatively expensive, the less the time needed to access information via a mobile device, the cheaper the cost incurs. The discrepancies between the written and spoken queries for some participants are significant and for other participants are minimal. The variations within spoken queries are relatively steady, but change rapidly among the written queries. Statistically, the quickest participant required only 01:44 on average for a written query whereas the slowest participant doubled that amount of time. This is because of the difficulty arisen from the input of Chinese using keyboards. In Chinese, there are two kinds of basic units: PinYin and Chinese character. PinYin represents the pronunciation of the character and usually consists of several alphabets. Chinese character is for expressing Chinese sentences and has several thousands kinds. Therefore, there are in general two kinds of technique for input Chinese into a computer: PinYin input method and character input method. The PinYin input method is most commonly used. The character input method is quite demanding as it requires memorising the keyboard distribution for the radicals of characters and it is difficult for a normal user. Therefore we have chosen the Microsoft Pin Yin input method in this experiment for participants to enter their written queries. To enter a Chinese character using a Pin Yin method, firstly, a user needs to input a PinYin string corresponding to twenty-six alphabets; then system presents the user a list of characters which have the same pronunciation; finally, the user selects the desired character from that list. This process is considerably slow as a Pin Yin for a Chinese character is often spelled by several alphabets and multiple characters have the same pronunciation, users need to browse through the list of candidate characters linearly to locate the correct one. Pin Yin as the standard pronunciation for Chinese characters is spoken among the population in the north of China, whereas people from different regions speak dialects which would pronounce same character differently. For those people, on top of the tedious character input process, it would be more difficult as they often make Pin Yin spelling mistakes. The participants we recruited for our experiment were from different parts of China, therefore their Pin Yin spelling skills were at different levels. Hence, whilst we can claim that people formulate their spoken queries more quickly we can't ignore the fact that the difficulty of Chinese character input also contributes to the extended written query formulation process.

3.5 Length of Spoken and Written Queries Without Stopwords Across Topics

From the previous analysis, we know that spoken queries as a whole are definitely lengthier than written queries. One would argue that people with natural tendency would speak more conversationally which results in lengthy sentences containing a great deal of words such as conjunctions, measurements or pronouns, that need to be linked to other words to form a complete expression, which have been referred as stopwords in information retrieval community, whereas the written queries are much terser but mainly contain content words such as nouns, adjectives and verbs, therefore, spoken queries would not contribute much than written queries semantically. However, after we removed the stopwords within both the spoken and written queries and plotted the average length of spoken and written queries against their original length in one graph, as shown in Fig. 5, which depicts a very different picture. A standard Chinese stopword list was adopted for this experiment.

In Fig. 5, the scattered points for spoken queries are consistently on top of the ones for the written queries; after stopword removal, each of them is also undoubtedly becoming shorter. Moreover, the points for spoken queries

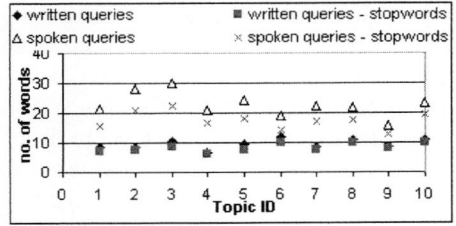
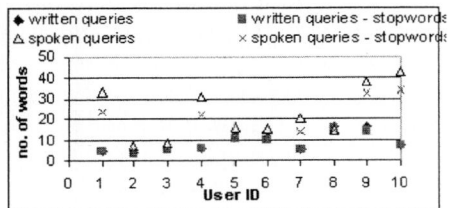

Fig. 5. Avg length of queries across topics.   **Fig. 6.** Avg length of queries per user.

without stopwords stay above the ones for written queries without stopwords consistently across every topic. Statistically, the average spoken query length without stopwords is 17.61 and for written query, that is 8.29, which shows the spoken queries have almost doubled the length of the written ones. This significant improvement in length indicates that the ease of speaking encourages people to express not only more conversationally, but also more semantically. From information retrieval point of view, more search words would improve the retrieval results. The accuracy of ASR systems is critical in SQP because IR engines try to find documents that contain words that match those in the query; therefore any errors in the query have the potential for derailing the retrieval of relevant documents. But the longer the query is, the higher the likelihood of an important word is repeated. If this word is not recognised one instance, it will probably be recognised from other occurrence. This redundancy provides some resilience to recognition errors. In the case in our experiment, even the recognition accuracy is only 50%, it would not cause greater degradations on the meanings for spoken queries than written queries. In other word, the spoken information clearly has the potential to be at least as valuable as written material.

3.6 Length of Spoken and Written Queries Without Stopwords Across Participants

The average length of spoken and written queries with and without stopwords across all 10 participants is shown in Fig. 6. This graph shows that very few stopwords are specified in the written queries. Statistically, on average a written query contains 1.5 stopword. This figure also demonstrates that half of our participants issued their spoken queries using natural language whereas the other half felt uncomfortable "talking" to a machine and only specified keywords in their spoken queries. This further sheds light on our claim that people's individual personality also influenced the spoken query formulation process.

4 Comparison with the Experimental Results of English Queries

We have conducted two experiments consecutively to analyze the differences between written and spoken queries in two different languages. The results of the first experiment in English language can be found in our paper [5]. The second one in Mandarin Chinese is presented in the previous section in this paper. We could observe some similarities between the results of these two experiments by comparing the data collected and figures generated. In both languages, people tend to speak more words for spoken queries than written ones. Spoken queries contain not only more stopwords but also more content words than written ones for both languages. Despite these two languages with completely different semantic structures, we have found that the number of words used to specify both written and spoken queries were extremely close. The discrepancy in the two experiment results exists in the durations of query formulation process. For the experiment in English language, we were unable to establish any strong claim because no significant differences existed between the two query forms in terms of duration. However, in this experiment reported here, we have observed that considerably less time is required to formulate spoken queries than written ones in Mandarin Chinese.

5 Conclusions

This paper reports on an experimental study on the differentiations between Mandarin written and spoken queries in terms of length and durations of the query formulation process, which can also contribute to the speech dialogue design for Chinese mobile information access systems. To the best of our knowledge there is no other similar study carried out in Mandarin Chinese for mobile IR. The results show that using speech to formulate one's information needs not only provides a way to express naturally, but also encourages one to speak more semantically. This indicates that spoken queries will have better quality than written ones in terms of information seeking since more search words will lead to better IR performance. Furthermore, as far as ASR systems are concerned, longer queries will have more context and redundancy which would potentially decease the impact of the ASR errors on retrieval effectiveness. One's individual personality is another factor influencing query-issuing approaches. In spite of the cognitive load, one can translate one's thoughts via voice more quickly than write them down in text form. Consequently, accessing information verbally on mobile devices will be more cost-effective and more affordable than conventional text input. This means that we can reach the conclusion that spoken queries as a means of formulating and inputting information needs on mobile devices are utterly feasible. Nevertheless, this empirical study was carried out with a small number of participants, further studies are required with larger user population to underpin these results.

References

1. Eric Chang, Frank Seide, Helen M. Meng, Zhouran Chen, Yu Shi, and Yuk-Chi Li. A system for spoken query information retrieval on mobile devices. *IEEE Transactions on Speech and Audio Processing*, 10:531–541, 2002.
2. Berlin Chen, Hsin min Wang, and Lin shan Lee. Retrieval of mandarin broadcast news using spoken queries. In *Proc. International Conference on Spoken Language Processing*, Beijing, 2000.
3. Hongbiao Chen. Clas: a general purpose system for chinese corpus processing. In *First International Conference on Formal Linguistics*, Changsha,China, 2001.
4. Colleen Cool, Soyeon Park, Nicholas Belkin, Jurgen Koenemann, and Kwong Bor Ng. Information seeking behavior in new searching environment. In *Second International Conference on Conceptions of Library and Information Science*, pages 403–416, Copenhagen, 1996.
5. Heather Du and Fabio Crestani. Spoken versus written queries for mobile information access. In *Proceedings of the MobileHCI03 workshop on Mobile and Ubiquitous Information Access*, Udine, Italy, 2003.
6. Eric Keller. *Fundamentals of Speech Synthesis and Speech Recognition*. John Wiley and Sons, 1994.
7. Steve Miller. *Experimental design and statistics*. Routledge, London, UK, second edition, 1994.
8. Doug Oard and Jianqiang Wang. Effects of term segmentation on chinese/english cross-language information retrieval. In *Proceedings of the Symposium on String Processing and Information Retrieval*, pages 149–157, Cancun, Mexico, 1999.
9. Maosong Sun, Dayang Shen, and Benjamin K. Tsou. Chinese word segmentation without using lexicon and hand-crafted training data. In *Proceedings of COLING-ACL-98*, pages 1265–1271, Montreal, Canada, 1998.
10. Ross Wilkinson. Chinese document retrieval at trec-6. In *Proc. 6th Text Retrieval Conference*, pages 25–30, 1998.
11. D William and Christine Cheepen. Just speak naturally: Designing for naturalness in automated spoken dialogues. In *Proceedings of Conference on Human Factors in Computing Systems*, pages 243–244, Los Angeles, 1998.

An Interactive Proofreading System for Inappropriately Selected Words on Using Predictive Text Entry

Hideya Iwasaki[1] and Kumiko Tanaka-Ishii[2]

[1] The University of Electro-Communications
Chofu-shi, Tokyo 182–8585
iwasaki@cs.uec.ac.jp
[2] The University of Tokyo
Bunkyo-ku, Tokyo 113-8658
kumiko@r.dl.itc.u-tokyo.ac.jp

Abstract. Predictive text entry systems on computers like kana-to-kanji conversion provide a mechanism that enables users to select among possible words for a given input. Mistakes in selection are relatively common, and they introduce real-word errors. A proofreading system is thus needed to detect and correct real-word errors on a computer without imposing troublesome operations on users. To this end, a practical proofreading system for Japanese text is proposed. The system automatically detects possible real-word homonym errors, and for each detected word, suggests substitution candidates of the same pronunciation. The user can either choose the most appropriate one or leave the original untouched. The system uses an algorithm based on the Naïve Bayesian method. Although the proofreading system was implemented for homonym errors in Japanese text, its design concept and algorithm are also applicable to other languages. The client program of the proofreading system is implemented on the Emacs text editor and works in real time.

1 Introduction

A predictive text entry system presents possible words as input candidates and lets the user select the most appropriate one. Such a system is especially effective for entering Asian language texts, such as Japanese and Chinese, because they have a large number of ideograms and consequently may require listing many words for the user's input. Example predictive entry systems are conversion entry systems, like *kana* to *kanji* in Japanese and *pinyin* to *hanzi* in Chinese. Another example is T9[1] [5], which uses nine keys ('0' – '9') and needs one key press per letter to enter text on a mobile device. For example, pressing "759" presents "sky", "sly", and "ply" as candidates.

In a predictive text entry system, a word is entered in two stages. First, the word is entered based on its input method, e.g. pronunciation in kana-to-kanji conversion or a sequence of digits in T9, and the system presents candidate words for the input. There is often more than one candidate because the relationship between the input and words is not one-to-one in most cases. We thus call the set of candidates for a given input a *confusion set*. Next, the desired word is selected from the confusion set. Mistakes

---

[1] http://www.t9.com/

made in the second stage can cause *real-word errors*. For example, real-word errors in kana-to-kanji conversion introduce incorrect homonyms.

Since the user's mistakes in selecting a word among the candidates are relatively common, a proofreading system without imposing troublesome operations on the user is indispensable to support the detection and correction of real-word errors. To this end, we have to solve two problems.

1. How to detect potential errors (suspicious words) and find appropriate alternatives for them.
2. How to design a system that makes it easy for users to correct the detected words.

In this paper, we propose a proofreading system that solves these problems and is practical to use. The targets of the system are homonym errors in Japanese text introduced in using kana-to-kanji conversion. Our main contributions are summarized as follows.

– A language-independent and entry system-independent algorithm based on the Naïve Bayesian method [2, 3] is presented for detecting and correcting most real-word errors.
– The results of experiments using Japanese text demonstrated that this algorithm has good proofreading ability with respect to the evaluation factors (recall, precision, and F-value). The algorithm can thus be used as the base for a practical proofreading system.
– An interactive proofreading system for Japanese text is presented that judges the likelihood of correctness of each homonymous content word, and, if necessary, suggests other candidates with the same pronunciation. Target words of the proofreading by the proposed system include both declinable words like verbs and adjectives and indeclinable words like nouns.

2 Proposed Proofreading System

The client (front-end) program of this system runs in Emacs, a widely used multilingual text editor. The user interface is quite similar to that of ispell, a conventional spell checker for English. The system is interactive; its response time is about the same as that of ispell, so it works in real time without imposing on the user.

Figure 1 shows example Emacs windows presented by the client to the user. The text is an article from a Japanese newspaper describing how an organization, which had been dissolved the previous year, had contributed 50 million yen in political donations to 112 members of the National Diet over the previous ten years, with the aim of buying influence. The errors in this article are as follows.

– On line 3, for the pronunciation "*giin*", "議院[Diet][2]" should be "議員[member of the Diet]".
– On line 4, for the pronunciation "*shuushi*", "終止[end]" should be "収支[income and expenditure]".

---

[2] The translations of Japanese words are shown in square brackets.

An Interactive Proofreading System for Inappropriately Selected Words   757

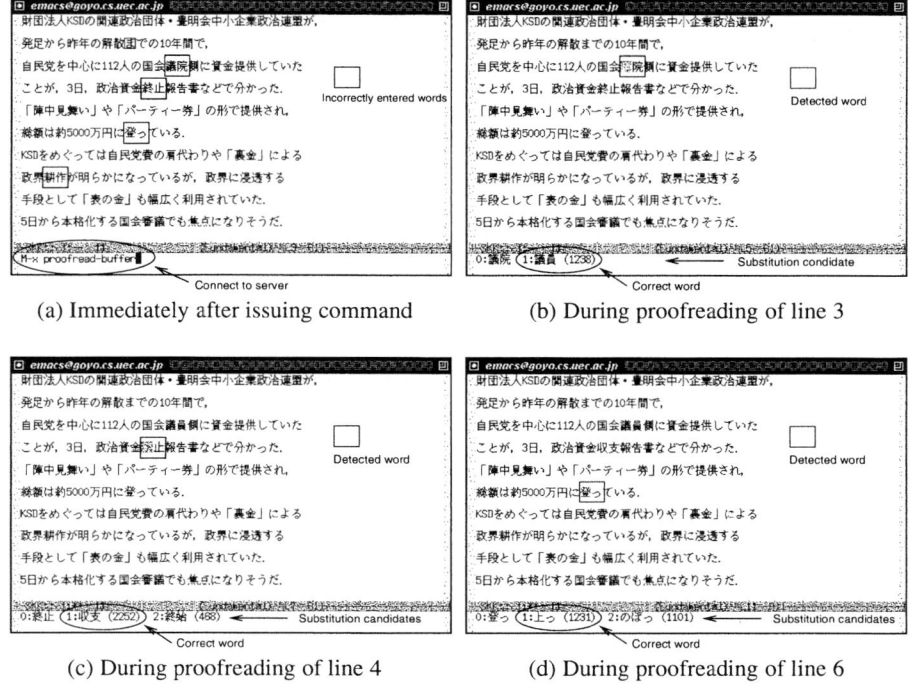

Fig. 1. Example windows of proofreading system.

- On line 6, for the pronunciation "*nobott*", "登っ[climb]" should be "上っ[amount to]".
- On line 8, for the pronunciation "*kousaku*", "耕作[farming]" should be "工作[maneuvering]".

The third error is a homonym error of declinable words; "上っ" is a conjugating form of the verb "上る", and similarly "登っ" is a conjugating form of "登る". The other errors are nouns, which are indeclinable words in Japanese.

To use the system, the user first specifies the region of text to be proofread and then issues the Emacs command to invoke proofreading. In Fig. 1 (a), all the text in the buffer has been specified by issuing the command "M-x proofread-buffer" (M-x means Meta-x). The client then sends the text within the specified region to the server and waits for the proofreading results.

The results include the detected (suspicious) words with their scores, and for each detected word, substitution candidates with their scores. The "score" is a measure of the likelihood of the appearance of the target word in the context. How this score is computed will be explained in Sect. 3. The client moves the Emacs cursor onto each detected word one by one and displays the substitution candidates in the minibuffer shown at the bottom of the window. For each candidate, the difference between the score of the candidate and that of the detected word is also shown. The user then interactively chooses the most appropriate candidate by entering its number or leaves the detected word unchanged by pressing '0'.

The example window in Fig. 1 (b) shows that the system has detected the first error ("議院" on line 3). It displays a single substitution candidate "議員" in the minibuffer and waits for the user's response. The difference in scores (1238) is displayed in parenthesis. To select the candidate, the user enters its number (in this case, '1'). The system then replaces the original word with the selected candidate and finds the next error, "終止", as shown in Fig. 1 (c). This time there are two substitution candidates: the correct word "収支" and another homonym "終始[from beginning to end]". Again the user selects the number of the appropriate candidate, and the text is modified based on the selection. Next, the system detects the third error (the verb "登っ" on line 6, whose plain form is "登る"). Since its homonyms, "上る" and "のぼる", are judged to be more appropriate than "登る", the system conjugates them into "上っ" and "のぼっ" and displays the conjugated forms as substitution candidates for "登っ" (Fig. 1 (d)).

The user can give the following special instructions during the proofreading process.

- The user can instruct the client to leave all occurrences of the currently detected word unchanged unconditionally hereafter without consulting the user, even though some may be detected as suspicious words.
- The user can instruct the client to apply the same change just made to all occurrences of the currently detected word unconditionally hereafter without consulting the user.
- The user can instruct the server to set the value of the "threshold" used in the detection of suspicious words to adjust the sensitivity of the detection of potential homonym errors. The threshold will be described in detail in Sect. 3.

The first and second features help the user maintain word usage consistency in the text. The first feature also eliminates unnecessary and bothersome user operations. This is because, in the course of proofreading, occurrences of the same (correct) word are apt to be detected as suspicious, especially when the word is used with a particular characteristic usage in the text.

As with most networked applications, the system consists of both a server program and client programs. The server program is implemented on the Unix operating system, and the clients run on the same computer as the server or elsewhere in the network. After accepting a connection from a client, the server receives Japanese text from the client and performs morphological analysis using Chasen[3] to split the text into a sequence of words. Then the server checks the correctness of each content word based on the proposed algorithm, which will be described in Sect. 3, and returns substitution candidates for words it judges incorrect. The client then prompts the user to either choose one of the candidates or leave the detected word untouched.

3 The Method

In this section, we describe the algorithm for calculating the likelihood of correctness of each target word and for enumerating the substitution candidates. The algorithm and

---
[3] http://chasen.aist-nara.ac.jp/

its mathematical model are not limited to a specific language or specific entry system; if an appropriate confusion set is defined for each target word, the algorithm can be used to proofread the text by any predictive text entry system.

3.1 Mathematical Model

Since each word has a context, clues for judging the correctness of usage can be gathered from the context [6]. From this observation, the mathematical model of the algorithm follows the Naïve Bayesian method [2]. We adopted this method due to its simplicity and good performance. In fact, as discussed in Sects. 4 and 5, our experimental results suggest that our method outperforms another simple method using the decision list.

Let the text be $w_1 w_2 \ldots w_L$, where w_i denotes a (content) word in a given text. We define *context* C_i of w_i as a sequence of words with a *hole*:

$$C_i = w_{i-N}, \ldots, w_{i-1}, \Box, w_{i+1}, \ldots, w_{i+N},$$

where $\Box$ indicates the hole, and N is an integer, called the *window size*, which determines the context range. If we put w_i into the hole, we have a subsequence of $2N+1$ words within the original text. If we place another word, v, into the hole, we get another sequence. If the second word (v) is "much" more plausible than the original, we conclude that w_i is suspicious and that v is more likely to be correct than w_i.

This idea is formulated in terms of $P(w \mid C_i)$, the conditional probability of word w appearing in context C_i. It can be calculated as

$$\frac{P(w) P(w_{i-N}, \ldots, w_{i-1}, w_{i+1}, \ldots, w_{i+N} \mid w)}{P(w_{i-N}, \ldots, w_{i-1}, w_{i+1}, \ldots, w_{i+N})}$$

using Bayes' rule. The denominator does not depend on w, so the denominator need not be taken into consideration when comparing values of $P(w \mid C_i)$ for various w's. To calculate the numerator (denoted $g(w, C_i)$), we make the following assumptions.

- Each word in C_i occurs independently of the other words in C_i, enabling approximate calculation.
- The co-occurrence probability, $P(w, w')$, of words w and w' followed by w within N (window size) words depends on the order of their appearance. Thus, in general, $P(w, w')$ is not equal to $P(w', w)$.

Consequently,

$$g(w, C_i) = P(w) \prod_{j=1}^{N} P(w_{i-j} \mid w) \prod_{j=1}^{N} P(w_{i+j} \mid w)$$

$$= P(w) \prod_{j=1}^{N} \frac{P(w_{i-j}, w)}{P(w)} \prod_{j=1}^{N} \frac{P(w, w_{i+j})}{P(w)}.$$

To sum up, the likelihood of the correctness of w in the hole position of C_i is estimated by computing $g(w, C_i)$. For some word v, if $g(v, C_i)$ is "much" greater than

$g(w_i, C_i)$, v is more likely to be correct than w_i and is a candidate to replace w_i. For practical calculation, we use $g'(w, C_i) = \log g(w, C_i)$ instead of $g(w, C_i)$, and set an appropriate threshold value to judge whether $g'(w, C_i)$ is "much" greater than $g'(w_i, C_i)$.

It is worth noting that, unlike the simple *bag of words* model where linear ordering of words within the context is ignored, the ordering of words is partially taken into consideration, in the sense that if w' is a word before the hole, then $P(w', w)$ is used; otherwise $P(w, w')$ is used.

3.2 The Algorithm

The algorithm based on the mathematical model in Sect. 3.1 needs "dictionaries" of the logarithmic values of the occurrence probabilities $P(w)$ for every possible word w and of the co-occurrence probabilities $P(w, w')$ for every possible pair of w and w' within the window size (N). These probabilities are computed beforehand from a large training corpus.

The algorithm is summarized as follows.

1. From a given text, extract only content words to get a sequence of words, $w_1 \ldots w_L$.
2. For every w_i, if w_i has confusion set (e.g. homonyms in a kana-to-kanji conversion entry system) $\{v_1, v_2, \ldots, v_{n_i}\}$, where n_i is the number of words in the set, then follow steps (a) – (d).
   (a) Compute $g'(w_i, C_i)$.
   (b) For every v_k, compute $d_k = g'(v_k, C_i) - g'(w_i, C_i)$.
   (c) Select all v_k's with $d_k \geq \theta$, where θ is a predefined threshold value.
   (d) If such v_k's do not exist, do not flag w_i as a possible error. Otherwise suggest those v_k's as substitution candidates for w_i. (Please note that if w_i is a declinable word, the v_k's have to be properly declined based on the context.)

The computed g' and the threshold correspond to the "score" and "threshold" introduced in Sect. 2. In this algorithm, window size N and threshold θ are adjustable parameters. The detection of possible errors can be finely controlled by adjusting θ. For example, setting θ to a greater value reduces the number of words identified as possibly incorrect. This is why the client of the proofreading system in Sect. 2 provides the mean for setting this threshold value.

In the algorithm, the greater the d_k, the more likely v_k is a candidate for replacing w_i. The algorithm could thus be set to automatically replace each word identified as possibly incorrect with the candidate with the highest score. However, this is risky because lack of user's selection could introduce other homonym errors. Therefore, as described in Sect. 2, our proofreading system presents substitution candidates in the order of likelihood and lets the user decide whether or not to replace the detected word.

There are two language-specific points in the application of the algorithm to a practical proofreading system. First, for text without word delimiters such as Japanese, morphological analysis has to be performed before step 1 of the algorithm. Second, the kinds of words dropped from the input text in step 1 depend on the language. For example, in Japanese, function words such as postpositional particles (e.g. "は" and "が") have no useful contextual information, so they have to be filtered out.

4 Experimental Results

To evaluate the effectiveness of the algorithm used in the proposed system, we conducted experiments using Japanese text. The morphological analyzer used was Chasen, the same one used in the proofreading system described in Sect. 2. Based on the results of a preliminary experiment, the window size was set to the optimal value, 5.

The $\log P(w)$ and $\log P(w, w')$ dictionaries were constructed from the Mainichi newspapers for 1998 (approximately 30 million words). About 82,000 distinct words and 875,000 pairs of co-occurrence relations were extracted within the window size. The test data sets (5,000 articles) were taken from the Mainichi newspapers for 1997.

4.1 Classification of Homonymous Words

Each homonymous word in the input text was classified into one of the following categories (Fig. 2 (a)) based on the results of the algorithm.

- *Detected word*: Word detected as homonym error; classified into one of three sub-categories depending on substitution candidate (alternative) of interest.
  IWCC: Incorrect word with correct candidate (Detected incorrect word with correct word as alterative)
  IWIC: Incorrect word with incorrect candidate (Detected incorrect word with incorrect word as alterative)
  CWD: Correct word detected
- *Undetected word*: Word not detected as homonym error; classified into one of two sub-categories.
  IWU: Incorrect word undetected
  CWU: Correct word undetected

The results were evaluated based on three factors (Fig. 2 (b)).

- Recall $R = \text{IWCC}/(\text{IWCC} + \text{IWIC} + \text{IWU})$
- Precision $P = \text{IWCC}/(\text{IWCC} + \text{IWIC} + \text{CWD})$
- F-value $F = 2PR/(P + R)$

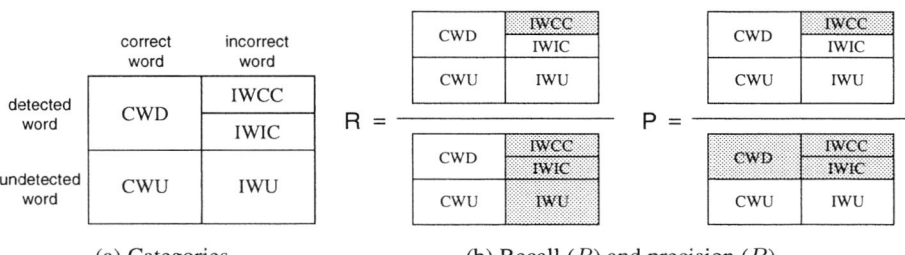

(a) Categories. (b) Recall (R) and precision (P).

Fig. 2. Categories of homonymous words and evaluation factors.

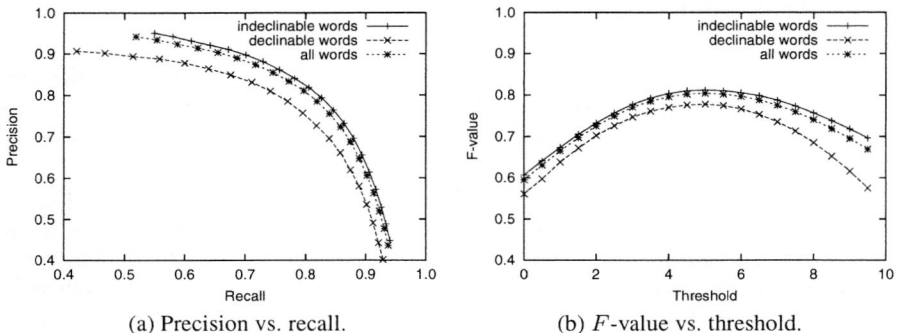

Fig. 3. Experimental results.

Recall (R) represents the ability to correct homonym errors in a given text, and precision (P) represents the reliability of the corrections. They are inversely correlated; making more detections raises the recall value but lowers the precision value. Conversely, detecting fewer errors improves precision at the expense of recall. It is therefore important to balance recall and precision by adjusting the degree of cautiousness. The F-value is the harmonious average of R and P, where the weights of R and P for contribution to F are set to equal. Since F represents the degree of the balance between R and P, a good strategy is to set the threshold so that F is maximized.

4.2 Results

To evaluate the ability of the algorithm, we set the substitution candidate with the highest calculated score as the alternative of each detected word. We assumed that for each occurrence of a homonymous word in the test data articles, a homonym error occurred with 5% probability. Each homonymous word was classified into one of the five categories above. After all words were classified, recall, precision, and F for the indeclinable words, the declinable words, and all words were calculated.

The recall and precision values for threshold values from 0 to 9.5 (intervals of 0.5) are plotted in Fig. 3 (a). The case of $\theta = 0$ is at the lower-right, and as θ is increased, the plot points move up and to the left. As the threshold was increased, the precision increased but the recall decreased. Figure 3 (b) represents the relationship between the threshold and F-value. The F-value first increased then decreased as the threshold was increased.

From these figures, we can see that recall, precision, and consequently F for declinable words were less than those for indeclinable words. This is because homonyms for declinable words are apt to have close or related meanings that makes them difficult to distinguish. Nevertheless, the maximum F-value for all words was good (0.804) when the threshold was 5.0. These results demonstrate that the quality of the substitution candidate with the highest score is sufficient for each detected word. The proposed algorithm is thus effective for practical proofreading.

5 Related Work and Discussion

Detecting and correcting real-word errors can be regarded as an instance of word sense disambiguation [1,4], and much work has been done on this problem.

For European languages, for example, Yarowsky [10] developed the decision list for accent restoration in Spanish and French, and Golding [3] applied a hybrid method to context-sensitive spelling correction. These approaches combine context information and local syntactic information on ambiguous words and produce good results. Golding, in particular, pointed out that a hybrid method based on the Bayesian method outperformed one based on decision lists. Our approach uses only context information and is based on the Naïve Bayesian method. It produced satisfactory results for detecting and correcting homonym errors in Japanese.

For Japanese, Oku and Matsuoka [7] used character n-gram ($n = 2, 3$) and reported 83% (2-gram) and 77% (3-gram) accuracies for correctly composed nouns. Their accuracy value corresponds to $(\text{IWCC} + \text{CWU})/(\text{IWCC} + \text{IWIC} + \text{CWD} + \text{IWU} + \text{CWU})$ here. It was 98.1% when the threshold was 5.0. Although the experimental conditions were different, our method showed higher accuracy.

Shinnou [8,9] made some improvements on the method based on the decision list [10,11] for the detection of homonym errors. He constructed a decision lists from the words immediately before and after the target word and from the independent words within three words of the target word. He reported that, when written words were incorporated as default evidence into the decision list, the F-value was 0.648 when the error rate was 5% [9]. Our experimental results suggest that our algorithm is potentially better than methods using a decision list. Another point to be noted is that his approach emphasized detecting homonym errors, but it remains unclear how to choose alternative words for the detected errors. Our integrated algorithm both detects homonym errors and presents substitution candidates at the same time.

Our method for detecting and correcting possible homonym errors can be further improved through customization. For example, we can customize the method to proofread text in a specific area, such as politics or economics by using dictionaries of occurrence and co-occurrence probabilities for that area. If the proofread text matches the area of the dictionaries, the proofreading should be more accurate than with generic dictionaries. Additionary, we can customize the method for personal use by preparing dictionaries constructed from text files (for example, files of mail text) written by the person. Since a person's vocabulary is generally limited, such customization would be especially effective.

6 Conclusion

We have described a proofreading system for detecting and correcting errors caused by mistakes in the selection of words in predictive text entry. The underlying algorithm is based on the Naïve Bayesian method and is independent of a specific predictive entry system or specific language. Experimental results for the proofreading of homonym errors in Japanese text showed that the algorithm performs better than methods in previous work.

We have implemented the proposed algorithm as an interactive system integrated into the Emacs text editor for proofreading homonym errors in Japanese. The Emacs client detects and suggests corrections for homonym errors in real time by communicating with the server. In the current implementation, the client shows only substitution candidates in the Emacs minibuffer. Enabling the user to consult online dictionaries with the meaning or usage of each candidate would be helpful when the user is unable to decide which candidate to choose. Such improvements to the user interface are left to future work.

References

1. P.F. Brown, S.A.D. Pietra, V.J.D. Pietra, and R.L. Mercer. Word-sense disambiguation using statistical methods. In *Proceedings of the 29th Annual Meeting of the Association of Computational Linguistics (ACL'91)*, pages 264–270, 1991.
2. W.A. Gale, K.W. Church, and D. Yarowsky. A method for disambiguating word sense in a large corpus. *Computers and the Humanities*, 26(5–6):415–439, 1992.
3. A.R. Golding. A Bayesian hybrid method for context-sensitive spelling correction. In *Proceedings of the 3rd Annual Workshop on Very Large Corpora*, pages 39–53, 1995.
4. N. Ide, and J. Veronis. Introduction to the special issue on word sense disambiguation: the state of the art. *Computational Linguistics*, 24(1):1–40, 1998.
5. C.L. James and K.M. Reischel. Text input for mobile devices: comparing model prediction to Actual Performance. In *Proceedings of the Annual SIGCHI Conference*, pages 365–371, 2001.
6. K. Kukich. Techniques for automatically correcting words in text. *Computing Surveys*, 24(4):377–439, 1992.
7. M. Oku, and K. Matsuoka. A method for detecting Japanese homophone errors in compound nouns based on character cooccurrence and its evaluation. *Natural Language Processing*, 4(3):83–99, 1997 (in Japanese).
8. H. Shinnou. Japanese homophone disambiguation using a decision list given added weight to evidences on compounds. *IPSJ Journal*, 39(12):3200–3206, 1998 (in Japanese).
9. H. Shinnou. Detection of Japanese homophone errors by a decision list including a written word as a default evidence. *IPSJ Journal*, 41(4):1046–1053, 2000 (in Japanese).
10. D. Yarowsky. Decision lists for lexical ambiguity resolution: application to accent restration in Spanish and French. In *Proceedings of the 32nd Annual Meeting of the Association of Computational Linguistics (ACL'94)*, pages 88–95, 1994.
11. D. Yarowsky. Unsupervised word sense disambiguation rivaling supervised methods. In *Proceedings of the 33rd Annual Meeting of the Association of Computational Linguistics (ACL'95)*, pages 189–196, 1995.

Dit4dah: Predictive Pruning for Morse Code Text Entry

Kumiko Tanaka-Ishii[1] and Ian Frank[2]

[1] The University of Tokyo
Bunkyo-ku, Tokyo, 113-8658
kumiko@r.dl.itc.u-tokyo.ac.jp
[2] Future University-Hakodate
Hakodate, Hokkaido
ianf@fun.ac.jp

Abstract. We present a new *predictive pruning* algorithm for text entry and show empirically how it outperforms simple text prediction. Our tests are based on a new application domain for predictive entry: the input of Morse code. Our motivation for this work was to contribute to the development of efficient entry systems for the seriously disabled, but we found that the constraint of using a single key highlighted features of text prediction not previously closely scrutinised. In particular, our tests show how predictive text entry is affected by two factors: altering the rankings of completion candidates based on the difficulty of entering the remaining text with just the keyboard, and the number of candidates presented to the user.

1 Introduction

The recent explosion in the use of mobile devices has encouraged work on predictive text entry systems for "constrained" domains with a restricted number of input keys. However, there has been no research on incorporating prediction at the farthest end of the constraint spectrum: devices with just one key.

Our contribution is to demonstrate empirically that prediction allows an entry speedup of up to 14.7% for one-key Morse code entry. Further, we introduce a new algorithm called *predictive pruning* that takes into account the difficulty of entering words with the keyboard (expressed via a function *type_diff*) when ranking completion candidates. With this algorithm, entry can be speeded up by 18.6%. Our experiments reveal subtle tradeoffs in the possible design choices, most notably with the choice of how many candidates to present to the user. To our knowledge, this is the first time that the notion of the difficulty of keyboard entry or the appropriate size for candidate lists have been investigated experimentally.

Our techniques are implemented in a system called Dit4dah (the name comes from the Morse code for the number 1: a *dit* then 4 *dahs*). By developing this system, we hope to contribute towards improving text entry systems for the severely disabled. Using Morse code in this context is not new. For instance, it is known that the disabled have difficulty maintaining a steady input speed, and adaptive methods have been advanced to facilitate automated recognition [1].

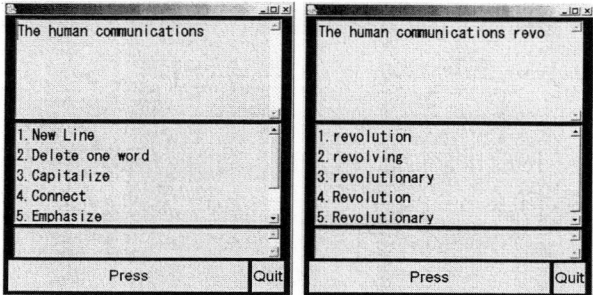

Fig. 1. Dit4dah Basic interface, in command selection mode and completion mode.

Also, a research group in the Japanese National Rehabilitation Center has developed a three-key device allowing users to enter text using Morse code [2]. Tests of this system on patients found it to be useful, but words must be input in full, requiring time and many key presses. It was in the hopes of finding an improved solution that we investigated the use of predictive methods with Morse code.

2 Dit4dah Overview

The primary design problem with single-key input is the efficient translation of keypresses into alphanumeric characters. We adopted Morse code because of its widespread use in the wireless community. Since most users will be faced with a learning curve no matter what system we select, a *de facto standard* language at least offers users the side-benefit of simultaneously increasing their ability to communicate using other existing technologies[1]. Our Java implementation of Dit4dah uses mouse-clicks to implement its single key, although many other options for facilitating input can be envisaged, such as breath control [3].

Figure 1 shows Dit4dah's basic interface. Morse code is entered by clicking on the key labelled "Press". In the left-hand image, a user has entered the string "The human communications" and the system is waiting for the next input. The user can enter further characters, or alternatively can select the menu items from 1 to 5 with an extended keypress.

During the actual process of entering an individual word, Dit4dah assists the user with possible completions. An example of this is shown in the right-hand image. Here, the user is entering the next word ("revolution"), and Dit4dah is offering possible completions that the user can select (again, with an extended keypress). The hope is that selecting words in this way can save time over inputting all the individual characters. Before we describe our predictive pruning technique for selecting and ordering these completions, we first give the necessary background on Morse code, and on the existing work on predictive text entry.

---

[1] There is also an appeal to basing a 21st century application on a 19th century input system.

Table 1. Interval semantics of Morse code.

Time	Entire duration of time interval has	
	key down	key up
unit	dot (•)	inter-pulse space
unit×3	dash (—)	inter-character space
unit×7	not assigned	inter-word space

3 Morse Code

Morse code was developed in the 1830s by Samuel Morse and his assistant Alfred Vail. It was designed to allow wire-based electronic communication by expressing characters as 'pulses' of different durations. Short pulses are called dots, or *dits*, and long pulses are called dashes or *dahs*[2]. The sound of Morse code is probably widely recognised (for example, it is sometimes used in film soundtracks to create atmosphere), but the formal definition needed to interpret key presses as dots and dashes is less well-known. If a single dot is defined as being one time unit, then Table 1 shows the semantics of the possible permitted key presses.

So, a dash is three times as long as a dot, and each dot or dash is separated by a single time unit. Alphanumeric characters are then defined as sequences of these dots and dashes.

Morse code is designed so that the most common characters can be input with the fewest time units[3]. Since text is a sequence of aplhanumeric characters (and not dots and dashes), there must also be a definition of the space between characters. In Morse code, this interval is allocated three time units. An even longer pause of seven time units with no key press is interpreted as an inter-word space.

Morse code presents a learning curve to the user, but in return can supply surprisingly fast text input. For example, during WWII, telegraph operators were expected to send at 25 words per minute (wpm). Morse is still a requirement for obtaining a Ham Radio license, and the US licence classes require input levels of 5wpm for 'Novice', 13wpm for 'General' and 20wpm for 'Amateur Extra'. However, the effort required to achieve such speeds should not be underestimated, and although the impressive manual by Pierpoint [3] claims that any normal person can reach 15-20wpm in a matter of weeks, the average casual user would be reluctant to make such an investment of time.

4 Predictive Text Entry

Predictive text entry assists text input by offering possible candidates for a user's incomplete or ambiguous entry. There are two types of prediction:

---

[2] To avoid possible confusion, throughout this paper, we will never refer to dots or dashes as "characters". They will always be "pulses". The term "character" will be reserved to describe traditional alphanumeric characters.

[3] We use the standard Morse code character set for English. Morse code alphabets for other languages have also been developed.

- by head word, and
- by disambiguation of abstracted characters.

An example of head word prediction would be to offer completions such as "chair" or "children" for the input "ch". The user can then choose between these completions, thus saving the time required to input the remaining characters.

Disambiguation of characters involves predicting the most likely word from keypresses of keys assigned more than one character. For example, mobile phones assign "ABC" to the key "2", "PQRS" to "7" and "WXYZ" to "9". So mobile phone prediction algorithms such as T9 [4] may disambiguate an input of "729" as "par" or "paw" or "saw". Disambiguation may also be combined with head word completion, for example predicting "saw" or "pays" from "72".

But, whichever system is being used, there are two basic tasks: obtaining candidates and showing them in the appropriate order. The basic approach for acquiring candidates is to use a corpus. As there are typically multiple candidates, the ranking of the possibilities becomes the crucial issue. It is common to use Bayes' Law to re-express the probability that some word W is the intended completion of the current input string S, so that the most likely W is:

$$\mathop{argmax}_{W} P(W|S) = \mathop{argmax}_{W} P(S|W)P(W). \qquad (1)$$

It is then assumed that the input has no error, so that prob$P(S|W)$ is 1, and the question becomes how to define P(W), the language model. Language models from basic unigram models to n-grams, HMM, and even models incorporating adaptation are common in the literature, e.g., [5]. In this initial work on Morse code, we used the simple language model described in the following section.

5 Dit4dah: Combining Morse Code and Predictive Text Entry

Implementing predictive text entry for Morse code presents an immediate problem: the user must be able to switch modes between normal text entry and candidate selection. In systems with multiple keys it is relatively simple to assign some keys for candidate selection and the rest for text entry. But Dit4dah has just a single key.

Fortunately, the interval semantics of Morse code offers a solution. We can see from Table 1 that a keypress lasting 7 time units is not assigned a meaning. This keypress can therefore be used to exit from text entry mode into candidate selection mode (or into a basic command-selection mode, if there is no text to complete). Once in a selection mode, returning to text entry mode is achieved by simply releasing the key, which also chooses a word for completion (or a command). Scrolling through the possible candidates (or commands) is achieved by keeping the key depressed for a further 3 time units.

For the candidate list itself, we use a 30Mbyte Wall Street Journal corpus. We restricted candidates to just words[4], giving us a dictionary of just under 90,000 entries. In this first implementation of Dit4dah, we used the simplest possible language model. For example, in addition to using only words (no n-grams), we ignore the effect of words already entered in partial input, and we do not bias the corpus with a user's frequently used words. Thus, any performance advantage of our algorithms for Morse entry indicates the benefits of prediction in general and not of some specific language model.

To rank our candidates, we first used the formula of Equation 1, but then pursued the insight that word frequency alone is not the only important factor affecting the best ordering. Especially for Morse code it is clear that the difficulty of input of the remaining characters in a word will be an important consideration. For example, consider the case where a user has entered the characters "sh". Possible completions for this include "she" and "shy". But a Morse code 'e' takes just a single time unit to enter, so a user would be unlikely to want a completion. On the other hand, a 'y' requires 13 time units to enter (— • — — is 9 units for the three dashes, 1 for the dot, and 3 for the inter-pulse pauses), so completion may be welcomed. Especially when the user is intending to input a longer word, completion will be important. For example, entering "should" would require these characters: o (— — —, 11 units), u (• • —, 7 units), l (— • —, 13 units), d (— • •, 7 units). Each character also has to be separated by an inter-character space, so the total input time is 11 + 7 + 13 + 7 + 9 = 47 units.

We define a function *type_diff* that takes as its argument a string of characters and returns the time in units required for entering the string. Dit4dah then uses *type_diff* to prioritize candidates that are harder to enter, thus making the best possible use of whatever space is available for displaying the candidates to the user. Since this is a significant topic in itself, we present Dit4dah's ranking algorithm in the next section.

6 Predictive Pruning

Our technique is based on pruning and is most easily explained with the aid of an example. We will use the abbreviation "PF" to denote the general approach of 'prediction based on frequency' described in §4. Imagine that a PF algorithm has generated the candidate list in the stage 1 of Table 2, where we simply number the words from 1 to 8. The second column shows *type_diff*, the number of time units required to complete the input using Morse, and the third column gives the selection difficulty, the time taken for completion, based on the actual settings of Dit4dah.

To prune a list, we simply process it from top to bottom, removing any word with a smaller value in the *type_diff* column than in the selection difficulty col-

---

[4] In English, it is natural to form candidates at word borders, which is not always true in languages without word border indications.

Table 2. Word3 and Word7 are pruned in three stages. The second column of each stage shows the *type_diff* and the third shows the selection difficulty.

stage 1			stage 2			stage 3		
Word1	20	7	Word1	20	7	Word1	20	7
Word2	22	10	Word2	22	10	Word2	22	10
Word3	12	13	Word4	15	13	Word4	15	13
Word4	15	16	Word5	30	16	Word5	30	16
Word5	30	19	Word6	25	19	Word6	25	19
Word6	25	22	Word7	8	22	Word8	23	22
Word7	8	25	Word8	23	25			
Word8	23	28						

umn. So, Word1 and Word2 survive (they are clearly time-saving completions), but Word3 is pruned, giving the list of stage 2.

In the initial completion list, Word4 would have been pruned, since its *type_diff* of 15 was less than its selection difficulty of 16. But now it has now moved up the list and no longer qualifies for removal. The next word to be pruned is therefore Word7 resulting in the list of stage 3.

No further pruning is possible, so we get a candidate list with six words, all of which have a *type_diff* greater than their selection difficulty. What is interesting here is that if the original ordering of the words had been different, we could have kept them all.

So, there is a subtle interplay between the use of frequency ranking and the use of *type_diff* that is not easy to capture in a single formula. Words that would be pruned if considered in isolation in the original candidate list can survive if enough words above them are pruned (eg, Word4 and Word8). However, if there is little difference between the word frequencies in the original ranked list, perhaps it is better to keep as many of them as possible by re-arranging them as we did in our example above. There are many other possibilities for incorporating *type_diff*. For instance, it is conceivable to directly modify the ranking function of Equation 1. In this paper, we concentrate on establishing the basic properties of the straightforward pruning algorithm described above, which we name *predictive pruning*, or PP. As we show in the following sections, its performance is both promising and subtle.

7 Theoretical Properties of PP: Horizon Effects

If we assume that both PF and PP always present the entire candidate list to the user, we can argue that PP never requires more time than PF for text input. A sketch of the proof considers the four possible cases of a user using the algorithms to input a `target` word:

1. `target` is not in PF or PP candidate lists.
2. `target` is in PF list, but pruned by PP.
3. `target` is in both lists, in the same position.
4. `target` is in both lists, but in different positions.

Table 3. An example horizon effect on PP.

Input	PF Candidates	PP Candidates
t	the, to, that	the, to, that
th	the, that, The	that, this, there
the	there, them, these	—

In cases 1 and 3 there is no difference in the speed of the algorithms. In case 2, the `target` is not present for PP, but in any case, entering it with completion took more time (by the definition of pruning) so PP is faster. In case 4, the only way that the `target` can move is if it is below a pruned candidate in the PP list. Since this results in `target` moving up the PP list, it requires less time to select `target` with PP than with PF. So, PP is always faster than PF.

In general, however, a text entry system cannot always show a user all the possible completions (e.g., there are a huge number of completions for any single-character input). Rather, the number of candidates presented to the user is typically limited to a fixed number, which we will call NthMax. What we now show is that the use of NthMax, in combination with the multi-step nature of text input, introduces a *horizon effect* that can result in PP suffering in comparison to PF.

With the introduction of NthMax, it may happen that `target` falls within the NthMax window of PP, but not the NthMax window of PF (since PP's candidates may be higher up the list, but never lower). In this case, PP will be less efficient than PF if it takes longer to select the `target` from far down the PP list than it takes for the user to input another character or more and then select the candidate from higher up in the PF list. As a concrete example of this, consider entering the word "there" with NthMax=3. Table 3 shows a possible set of candidates for both PP and PF as text entry proceeds.

After inputting "th", PP selects the third candidate for a cost of 13. However, the candidate list for PF after inputting "th" does not contain "there" so another character is input (an e, at cost 1), then an inter-character space (cost 3), before the first completion is selected (cost 7). This cost of 11 demonstrates that PF can win compared to PP when windowing hands it completions high up the list. Our results in the following section clearly show the exact nature of these horizon effects.

8 Empirical Tests

We used four different texts to compare the speed of straightforward Morse input against PP and PF at different values of NthMax. To cover a wide variety of writing styles, we used a technical paper from ACL 2003 (4287 words), the second author's email (6567 words), the US constitution (4973 words), and an extract from Tom Sawyer (the first 4714 words). Since Morse code itself has no protocol for capitalisation, we convert all these texts to lower case.

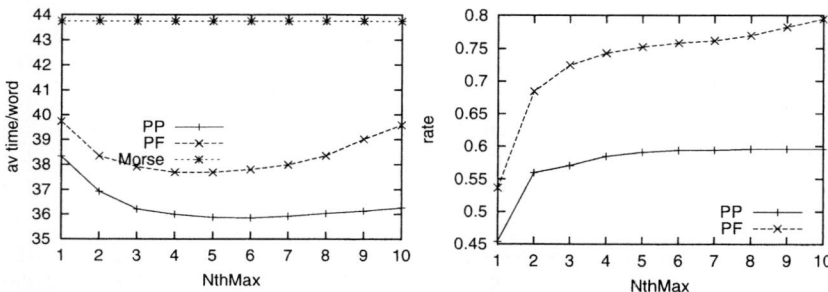

Fig. 2. Time units per word input for varying NthMax and rate of words entered using completion, plotted against NthMax, for second authors email.

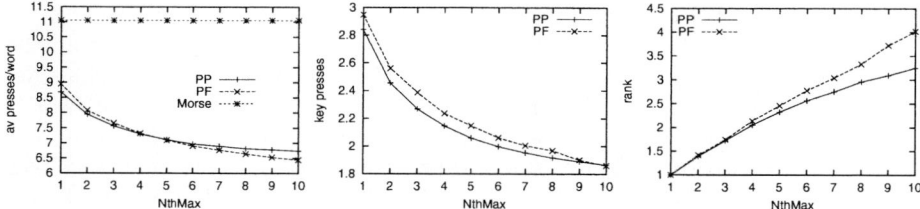

Fig. 3. Average key presses per word, number of Morse characters before completion, and average ranking of selected candidate, plotted against NthMax, for second authors email.

We establish a baseline for Dit4dah's performance using an entirely automated test regime that simply sums the time required for all keypresses. Such automated testing has been applied to other text entry systems [6], but the clear interval semantics of Morse code allows us to give an unequivocal measure in terms of the underlying Morse time units. For estimating the time required by PP and PF we assume that if a target word is present in a candidate list, it is selected at just the cost of the keypress that brings up and scans the list. This is a generous estimate in that a human user could be expected to spend time actually looking at the target list, but this is balanced by the likelihood that a human user would also be more prone to errors when using Morse code than when using completion. From the authors' personal use of the system, we found it feasible to be aware of the candidate lists while still entering text, as there is nowhere else to look (there is only one key).

The left figure of Figure 2 shows the results of the three input methods for the automated test on the file composed of the second author's email. This clearly illustrates that both prediction and pruning offer speed improvements over straightforward Morse entry, for all levels of NthMax. At best, PF offers a 14.67% speedup, whereas PP gives 18.60%. Note that the performance of PF is sensitive to the setting of NthMax, in that it suffers either if the value is too low or too high. PP, on the other hand, improves quickly with increasing NthMax at first and then shows little change.

One reason for this differing performance is illustrated by the right of Figure 2, which shows the percentage of words entered using completion as NthMax varies. This clearly shows that PP uses far fewer completions, which can only happen by finding many words that are more efficiently entered using Morse than with completions. The graph also shows that once NthMax reaches 5 the percentage of words for which PP uses completion changes very little, whereas for PF it continues to climb, thus degrading its time performance by choosing completions from low down the candidate list.

It may be surprising to also see that PP achieves its increases in speed without sacrificing number of key presses. Indeed, the leftmost graph of Figure 3 shows that when NthMax is less than or equal to 5, PP actually has fewer key presses. This can be partly explained by the middle graph of Figure 3. This shows the average number of characters in a word entered by PP and PF before completion takes place. PP encounters candidates sooner in the entry process, since the pruned candidate lists tend to lift targets into the NthMax window sooner. This helps to outweigh the disadvantage of actually entering far fewer words with completion.

Note that although fewer characters need to be entered by PP to find its completions, the final graph of Figure 3 shows that for low NthMax the average position of the candidates it selects from its lists is not significantly different from PF. This is the result of the horizon effect we described in §7, which can cause PP to make selections lower in the candidate list than PF. Only when NthMax becomes very large does the horizon effect decrease to the extent that PP's average candidate ranking is significantly lowered.

We are planning to tackle these horizon effects by incorporating lookahead into our pruning algorithm. Rather than pruning based on the just the current *type_diff* and selection difficulty, for each candidate in the list we can first calculate the *type_diff* and selection difficulty assuming that the user first inputs just one more character of the word using Morse. If this extra information decreases the selection difficulty by more than the cost of entering the extra character, then time can be saved. We also expect such lookaheads to remove the slight increase in word entry time shown as NthMax increases above 6 in Figure 2. This increase is exactly caused by words entering the candidate list at low positions, whereas for lower NthMax the user benefited from entering more text to bring them into the candidate list at a higher position.

Limitations of space prevent us from including graphs for our other data sets. However, they all display precisely the same trends as those for the email texts. Table 4 summarises the performance gains of PF and PP for each data set at NthMax=5.

9 Discussion and Future Work

The results above empirically demonstrate that both prediction and predictive pruning can significantly speed up Morse code text entry.

In terms of future algorithmic improvements, we intend to pursue ideas on lookahead and on incorporating *type_diff* into the ranking of Equation 1. It will

Table 4. Efficiency of Predictive Text Entry, at NthMax=5 for each data set.

	Number of words	Speed increase		Keypress reduction		Candidates selected	
		PP	PF	PP	PF	PP	PF
Technical	4287	18.60%	14.67%	34.8%	35.8%	59.51%	77.96%
Tom Sawyer	4714	13.60%	8.08%	28.76%	29.99%	50.36%	71.64%
US Constitution	4973	17.5%	13.59%	36.80%	37.35%	67.04%	82.99%
2nd author's e-mail	6567	18.04%	13.84%	35.68%	35.84%	59.08%	75.22%

also be important to repeat our tests with human users to see to what degree the results are replicated. Especially for human subjects, issues such as the severity of the pruning criterion may be important. For example, Word3 in our example of §6 was pruned by comparing a *type_diff* of 12 with a selection difficulty of 13. But actually, the candidate completion units are in many ways "easier" to input, and certainly have no chance of error. Indeed for human users, "estimated user error" could be a significant factor, especially for novices. Position in the candidate list and the length of candidates could also be important factors. For example, some users may prefer not to have the eighth candidate pruned (a selection difficulty of 26) if it takes as much as 25 time units to enter.

In fact, usability of Dit4dah is an issue that is close to our hearts, since this paper was actually inspired by the first author reading [7], which was written by a French teenager left unable to move or see, yet fully conscious, after a car accident. This entire book was painstakingly input with the help of Humbert's mother, who interpreted his only possible movement and spoke to him. Dit4dah would have been of no use in this situation as it requires both a mouse input and a visual feedback channel for viewing and selecting the candidates. However, we are interested in considering alternatives for both these modalities. Further, since many debilitative diseases are progressive in nature, there is the more high-level challenge of developing both the theory and the practice of smooth and minimal degradation of input speed without the need for users to re-learn a new system as their abilities change.

Finally, we believe that by tackling this highly constrained problem we have opened a window on the characteristics of predictive text entry in general. For example, to our knowledge this is the first research that considers the effects of varying NthMax. We are working on generalising our results further and investigating a range of parameters for systems with different numbers of keys. Although Morse code has exceptionally long character entry times, selection difficulty in Dit4dah is also relatively large and we expect that even for less constrained systems, pruning will still offer advantages.

10 Conclusion

We have introduced the new concept of pruning candidate lists and demonstrated how predictive pruning outperforms simple prediction both in theory and in practice.

Our techniques are implemented in a working system that we will now use with human users to further develop our ideas. We believe that our work can be applied to other text entry in less constrained environments, and also promises new possibilities in the development of input systems for users with serious physical impairments.

References

1. Wu, C., Luo, C.H.: Morse code recognition system with fuzzy algorithm for disabled persons. Journal of Medical Engineering & Technology 26 (2002) 202–207
2. Itoh, K.: Evaluation of display-based morse keyboard emulator. In: Proceedings of 12th Japanese Conference of Advancement of Rehabilitation Technology. Volume 12. (1997) 113–116
3. Pierpoint, W.G.: The Art and Skill of Radio Telegraphy: A Manual For Learning, Using, Mastering And Enjoying The International Morse Code As A Means Of Communication. Online book `http://www.qsl.net/n9bor/n0hff.htm` (2002)
4. Tegic 9: Internet home page of Tegic 9 (2000) `http://www.t9.com`
5. Tanaka-Ishii, K., Inutsuka, Y., Takeichi, M.: Personalization of text input systems for mobile phones. In: NLPRS. (2001)
6. James, C., Reischel, K.: Text input for mobile devices: Comparing model prediction to actual performance. In: Proceedings of the Annual SIGCHI Conference. (2001)
7. Humbert, V.: Je vous demande le droit de mourir. Michel Lafon (2003) ISBN: 2840989921.

Thematic Session: Text Mining in Biomedicine

Introduction

This thematic session follows a series of workshops and conferences recently dedicated to bio text mining in Biology. This interest is due to the overwhelming amount of biomedical literature, Medline alone contains over 14M abstracts, and the urgent need to discover and organise knowledge extracted from texts. Text mining techniques such as information extraction, named entity recognition etc. have been successfully applied to biomedical texts with varying results. A variety of approaches such as machine learning, SVMs, shallow, deep linguistic analyses have been applied to biomedical texts to extract, manage and organize information. There are over 300 databases containing crucial information on biological data. One of the main challenges is the integration of such heterogeneous information from factual databases to texts. One of the major knowledge bottlenecks in biomedicine is terminology. In such a dynamic domain, new terms are constantly created. In addition there is not always a mapping among terms found in databases, controlled vocabularies, ontologies and "actual" terms which are found in texts. Term variation and term ambiguity have been addressed in the past but more solutions are needed. The confusion of what is a descriptor, a term, an index term accentuates the problem. Solving the terminological problem is paramount to biotext mining, as relationships linking new genes, drugs, proteins (i.e. terms) are important for effective information extraction. Mining for relationships between terms and their automatic extraction is important for the semi-automatic updating and populating of ontologies and other resources needed in biomedicine. Text mining applications such as question-answering, automatic summarization, intelligent information retrieval are based on the existence of shared resources, such as annotated corpora (GENIA) and terminological resources. The field needs more concentrated and integrated efforts to build these shared resources. In addition, evaluation efforts such as BioCreaTive, Genomic Trec are important for biotext mining techniques and applications.

The aim of text mining in biology is to provide solutions to biologists, to aid curators in their task. We hope this thematic session addressed techniques and applications which aid the biologists in their research.

Sophia Ananiadou (National Centre for Text Mining, Manchester)
Jong C. Park (KAIST, Daejeon)

Reviewers

William Black
Christian Blaschke
Nigel Collier
Dietrich Rebholz-Schuhmann

Hae-Chang Rim
Jian Su
Alfonso Valencia
Pierre Zweigenbaum

Unsupervised Event Extraction from Biomedical Literature Using Co-occurrence Information and Basic Patterns

Hong-woo Chun, Young-sook Hwang, and Hae-Chang Rim

Natural Language Processing Lab., Dept. of CSE,
Korea University, Anam-dong 5-ga, Seongbuk-gu, 136-701, Seoul, Korea
{hwchun,yshwang,rim}@nlp.korea.ac.kr

Abstract. In this paper, we propose a new unsupervised method of extracting events from biomedical literature, which uses the score measures of events and patterns having reciprocal effects on each other. We, first, generate candidate events by performing linguistic preprocessing and utilizing basic event pattern information, and then extract reliable events based on the event score which is estimated by using co-occurrence information of candidate event's arguments and pattern score. Unlike the previous approaches, the proposed approach does not require a huge number of rules and manually constructed training corpora.
Experimental results on GENIA corpora show that the proposed method can achieve high recall (69.7%) as well as high precision (90.3%).

1 Introduction

Easier online access to large text data via the Internet offers lots of new challenges to the researchers trying to automatically extract information. Genomics is one of the fields that the information extraction researchers are interested in, since the number of electronic databases is increasing rapidly, while a vast amount of knowledge still resides in large collections of biomedical papers such as Medline. In order to extract meaningful information from these data, the primary study of interactions between genes and proteins is very important. These interactions form the basis of phenomena such as DNA replication and transcription, metabolic pathway, signaling pathway, and cell cycle control [3]. However, since information about interactions between proteins and genes still exist in the biomedical literature, we need a method of extracting meaningful information from the texts.

Recently, there were several studies for event extraction from biomedical literature. Proux (2000) extracted gene-gene interactions by scenarios of predicate patterns which were constructed manually. For example, 'gene product $acts$ as a modifier of gene' is a scenario of the predicate 'act', which can cover a sentence like: "Egl protein $acts$ as a repressor of BicD". Egl and $BicD$ are extracted as an argument of an event for predicate $acts$. Pustejovsky (2002) also used predicate patterns. However, they did not build these patterns manually, but trained patterns from the training corpora. For the training, they manually constructed the training corpora. After training, they tried to analyze the subject and the object relation for a main verb and to extract them as arguments for an event. When a sentence contains subordinate clauses, they also tried to extract an event in the same way. However, the above two researches have some problems. First, it is impossible for humans to define all of the patterns of event verbs. To make matters worse, there are also insufficient annotated corpora for training the patterns.

On the other hand, Jenssen (2001) tried to extract the biomedical information based on statistical method from over 10 million *Medline* which are unannotated corpora. They created a gene-to-gene network for 13,712 named human genes by linking two genes if they only occurred in the same article. At that time, *PubGene*, their system, gave each pair of genes a weight equal to the number of articles in which the pair was found. *PubGene* yields too many gene-gene interaction events, so it depreciates the reliability of events.

Currently, most of work for the event extraction from the biomedical literature usually considered only the pattern information or only the co-occurrence information.

In this paper, we propose a new unsupervised event extraction method from unannotated corpora. Our approach uses the shallow NLP techniques including a part-of-speech tagger, a chunker, and a dependency parser. Moreover, we use patterns which are generated automatically and statistical information of co-occurrence. The advantage of our approach is the minimal human intervention, namely it does not require a large number of patterns and manually constructed training corpora.

2 System Architecture

The ultimate goal of our research is to build a network of gene or protein interactions. As a primary work, we focus on extracting the events from biomedical literature. Generally, *Event Extraction* is to identify any instance of a particular class of events in a natural language text, to extract the relevant arguments of the event, and to represent the extracted information into a structured form [4]. In this paper, *Event* is defined as a binary relation between a subject entity and an object entity for special event verbs which are selected by biologists, and *Entity* is a biomedical entity such as protein, gene, cell, tissue, etc. Figure 1 illustrates the overall of the proposed method of event extraction.

As represented in Figure 1, our system has five modules. The input data of our system is raw corpus. First, the preprocessing procedure involves chunking, named entity tagging and dependency relation tagging. Chunking module transforms raw corpus into part-of-speech tagged and chunked corpus [7]. NE tagging module recognizes named entities - such as proteins, genes, cells, tissue, etc. - from part-of-speech tagged and chunked corpus. This module identifies each entity by a SVM classifier, classifies the semantic class of the identified entity by SVMs and then post-processes the recognized results by simple dictionary look-up [8]. Dependency relation tagging module is the result of the shallow parsing and analyzes dependency relations both between a subject and a verb, and between an object and a verb by SVMs [9].

Second, our system normalizes the sentence for the event extraction. Third, our system generates the candidate events and patterns from the normalized sentences and calculates their initial event scores by using the pre-constructed initial patterns. Fourth, our system iteratively updates the scores of events and patterns in a co-updating method.

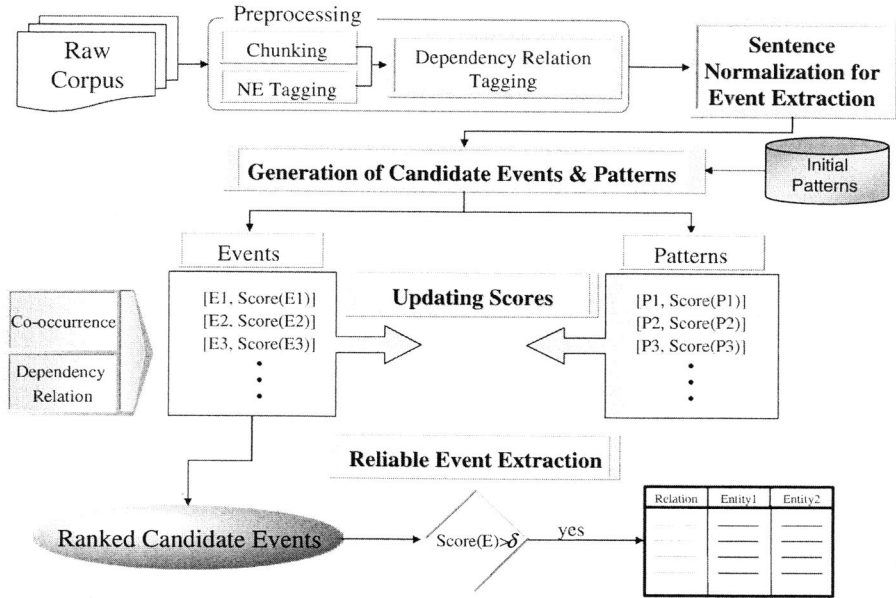

Fig. 1. System Architecture.

It is continued until the ranking of events by the event scores is no longer changed. Finally, our system extracts reliable events among the candidate events.

3 An Unsupervised Event Extraction Method

Some of the current approaches usually extracted events using patterns or statistical methods. In using patterns, it is impossible for humans to define all of the patterns of event verbs. Besides, there are also insufficient training corpora for learning, and constructing the training corpora is very expensive and time-consuming. In using statistical methods, this approach being dependent on the statistics from raw corpora tends to decrease the precision while increasing the recall. It was because it might extract unsuitable pairs of entities as an event if they occurred in the same article.

In our approach, we try to tackle the problems. That is, instead of using the insufficient annotated corpora, we use the co-occurrence information from raw corpora. Moreover, in order to complement the limitation of statistical approach for using raw corpora, we utilize the shallow NLP technique and pattern information. At the initial step, we use a small set of initial patterns which are the most simple patterns requiring the minimum human efforts. Co-occurrence information can be a candidate event if it satisfies the given constraints. Our approach automatically generates every possible pattern of the candidate events. We calculate the score of the events and their patterns by using three information which are the co-occurrence, the pattern information and the dependency relations among arguments and an event verb. These scores have reciprocal effects on each other, so each score updates, iteratively, other score until the ranking of candidate events remains unchanged. Finally, we extract reliable events based on the event score of the candidate events. Consequently, our approach minimizes the handwork and achieves high recall (69.7%) as well as high precision (90.3%).

From now on, we will describe our method by two steps. At first, we explain how to extract the candidate events. Next, we explain how to extract the reliable events from the candidates.

3.1 Candidate Event Extraction

Sentence Normalization for Event Extraction. After the preprocessing, we do not need the information of all words in a given sentence. In other words, since there are special items for event extraction, we just only take the items. At this point, sentence normalization means the reconstruction of sentences with the special items. During the normalization of the sentence, we consider the special items that are given in Table 1. They are replaced with the predefined form, such as the entity name, part-of-speech of a word, origin of an event verb, etc. Figure 2 shows an example of sentence normalization. In this example, there are four entities, two event verbs, one relative and one preposition. *Lipoxygenase metabolites* is an entity and it is classified by *Protein*. Therefore, it is substituted for *Protein*. *activate* is an event verb, so we attach $EV\_$ before *activate*. *which* is a relative, so we use its part-of-speech which are defined by PennTreebank. *via* is a preposition, so we attach $PP\_$ before *via*. Other special items in this example are applied by the normalization rules with the same manner. Note that the word 'then' is ignored during the normalization. The special items after sentence normalization are called the normalized items.

Table 1. Normalization Rules.

Normalization Items	Examples	Normalization Form
Entities	Protein, Gene, Cell, Other	Entity Name
Event verbs	Activate, Bind, Induce	EV_verb
Not event verbs	Be, Understand, Present	NEV_verb
Preposition	of, by, with, in	PP_preposition
Relative	Which, That	Part-of-Speech
Conjunctions	and, but, or	AND,BUT,OR
Symbols	'(',')',',',':',';'	'(',')',',',':',';'

Generation of Candidate Events and Patterns. Candidate events are extracted from the sentences that contain at least one event verb and two entities. This is a filtering. A candidate event consists of one event verb and one entity appearing before the event verb and another entity appearing after the event verb. In order to extract candidate events, we begin by finding all event verbs in a sentence, and then we couple all possible entity pairs for each event verb in the sentence. We also rely on common English grammar for choosing candidate events. In other words, we consider the agreement

... lipoxygenase metabolites activate ROI formation which then induce
IL-2 expression via NF-kappa B activation.

Protein EV-activate Other WDT EV-induce Protein PP-via Other

Fig. 2. An example of sentence normalization.

between a subject and the tense/number of a verb. At this time, we use the boundary words which are *Event verbs, Not event verbs, Colon*(:) and *Semi − colon*(;). Moreover, since some event verbs often co-occur with some particular preposition in an event, we also consider the relation between verbs and prepositions as important information for the event extraction. In addition, we automatically construct the pattern of each candidate event by arranging the normalized items both between entities of a candidate event.

Figure 3 shows an example of generation of candidate events and corresponding patterns. In the given sentence, there are two event verbs, *activate* and *induce*, and there are two entities before and after each event verb. Hence, our system extracts two candidate events. One candidate event is "*Lipoxygenase metabolites* activate *ROI formation*" and the other candidate is "*ROI formation* induce *IL − 2*". In this example, $NF − kappa\ B\ activation$ is an entity, but it is not extracted as an argument of the event. It is because the entity with the preposition 'via' is not allowed for an argument of an event. After generating the candidate events, we build patterns by arranging the normalized items between entities of candidate event. For the candidate events, pattern1 and pattern2 are built respectively. Table 2 shows some examples of the automatically constructed patterns.

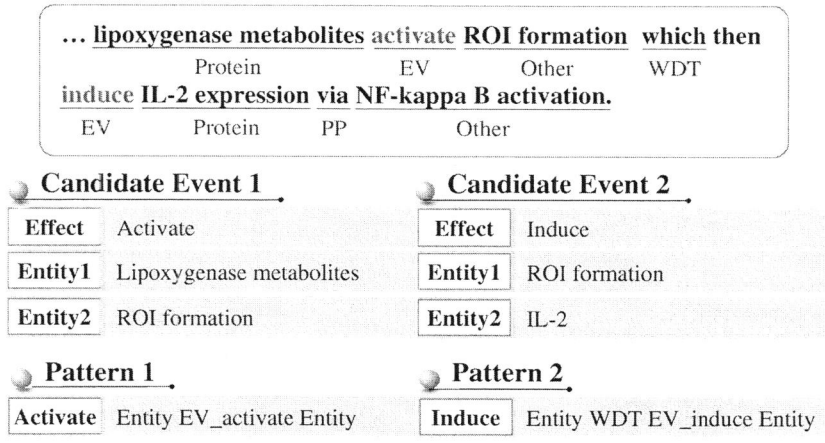

Fig. 3. An example of generation of candidate events and patterns.

Table 2. Examples of the patterns for the event verbs.

Event verbs	Patterns
Bind	Entity WDT EV_bind Entity
Activate	Entity EV_activate PP_with Entity
Induce	Entity EV_induce Entity AND Entity
Contain	Entity AND Entity EV_contain Entity
Phosphorylate	Entity EV_phosphorylate PP_to Entity

3.2 Reliable Event Extraction

Ranking Events and Patterns. After that, we have to choose reliable events from the candidates. We take an approach of ranking the candidate events by the event score. At the approach, we assume that an event can be extracted from one or more patterns in a whole document, vice versa; one pattern can be used for one or more events in a whole document. Thus, the pattern information may have an effect on the event score. Moreover, the event score also may have an effect on the pattern score. By taking the method of reciprocally co-updating each score, we expect that our system achieve high recall and precision.

In this section, we describe how to calculate the score of candidate events and patterns and how to complement each other's score in detail. Moreover, we explain how to extract reliable events by their scores.

Our ranking measure has two scores which are scores for each candidate event and each pattern. Event score means the reliability of each candidate event. To calculate score for events, we use two items. One is a particular value for each candidate event and the other is the average of the pattern score which are generated by the candidate event:

$$EventScore(E) = [InnateEventScore(E)] \times [Average\ of\ PatternScore(P^E)] \quad (1)$$

First, a particular value is called the *Innate EventScore* in this paper, and it is calculated by the co-occurrence scores among entities and an event verb and the dependency relation scores among entities and an event verb. In order to calculate co-occurrence, we deal with only main clause in sentences. It is because events in main clause are more reliable and we assume that one event can be described by one or more patterns in a whole document. The dependency relation uses shallow parser which tries to analyze the subject and object entities for an event verb in sentences. It is formulated as follows:

$$InnateEventScore(E) = [\alpha Co-occurrence + \beta Dependency\ Relation] \quad (2)$$

In this equation, α and β are the weight which are obtained by empirical experiments. We set 4 on α and 6 on β. The co-occurrence scores are calculated by the chi-square distribution:

$$\chi^2 = \sum_{i,j} \frac{(O_{ij} - E_{ij})^2}{E_{ij}} \quad (3)$$

where O_{ij} is the observed value and E_{ij} is the expected value. In our system, we count the frequency of all entities and event verbs in GENIA corpora and apply them to Equation 3. Moreover, the scores of the dependency relations are computed by the results of the dependency relation tagging. If a verb and an argument have a dependency relation, we give 1 point. Therefore, the maximum score in one candidate event is 2.

The second item is the average of the pattern score. At the initial step, we do not know the pattern score, so we figure it out using the initial patterns. We assume that the events which represented by the initial patterns are reliable, so we construct a set of initial patterns in the most general way which is attaching only entity before and after the event verb. These initial patterns restrict the length of events by 3 words. In our experiments, we consider the 162 event verbs and the number of the initial patterns is 162. Table 3 shows some examples of the initial patterns.

Table 3. Examples of the initial patterns.

Event verbs	Patterns
Bind	Entity EV_bind Entity
Activate	Entity EV_activate Entity
Induce	Entity EV_induce Entity
Contain	Entity EV_contain Entity
Phosphorylate	Entity EV_phosphorylate Entity

We give 1 point if the pattern of the event is in the initial pattern set, otherwise we give 0.5 point:

$$EventScore(E) = [InnateEventScore(E)] \times \begin{cases} 1 & if\ E\ is\ from\ initial\ patterns \\ 0.5 & otherwise \end{cases} \quad (4)$$

After the initial step, the average of the pattern score is calculated as follows:

$$Average\ of\ PattrnScore(P^E) = \frac{\sum_i PatternScore(P_i^E)}{\sum_j freq(P_j^E)} \quad (5)$$

where P^E means all patterns of an event E. The $freq(P_j^E)$ is the frequency of the pattern P_j^E which is generated by an event E. This equation implies that one event can be represented by one or more patterns.

The pattern score ($PatternScore(P)$) is equal to the reliability of each pattern. In other words, for each pattern, this equation means "how many events which are described by this pattern are reliable?". At this time, a reliable event is decided, not by humans, but by $EventScore$. When the $EventScore$ for a candidate is more than a given threshold, our system regards this event as a reliable one. The pattern score is calculated as follows:

$$PatternScore(P) = \frac{\sum_{EventScore(E_i^P) > \delta} freq(E_i^P)}{\sum_{E_j^P} freq(E_j^P)} \quad (6)$$

where δ is a current average score of events and E^p means all candidate events which are represented by a pattern p.

We can see that two equations – Equation 5 and Equation 6 – have reciprocal effects on each other. Thus, we can rerank the candidate events by recalculating the events' score and the patterns' score iteratively. This iteration continues until the ranking of candidate events no longer changes. As a result, the ranking of the reliable events become higher than that of the unreliable one.

In this experiment, we compare the results between initial event score and updating event score.

Extraction of Reliable Events. Our system extracts reliable events from candidates based on their scores. After updating the event score iteratively, we obtain the fine-tuned score and the events are ranked according to the score. As a result, the event of higher rank is more reliable than lower one. If an event score exceeds the given threshold, then our system will extract it as a reliable event. The threshold is determined through empirical experiments.

4 Experimental Results and Discussion

We experimented on the GENIA corpora [10] which consists of 18,544 sentences and contains the part-of-speech information and the named entity information. We considered the 162 event verbs that were selected by biologists, and we selected 500 sentences randomly and 372 sentences remained after filtering. Biologists checked all the remaining sentences and revealed that there were 241 events. From the events, total 335 patterns were generated.

The evaluation measures are Precision, Recall and F-measure which are commonly used [Equation 7, 8, 9].

$$Precision = \frac{\# \ of \ correct \ events}{\# \ of \ events \ selected \ by \ the \ system} \tag{7}$$

$$Recall = \frac{\# \ of \ correct \ events}{\# \ of \ answer \ events} \tag{8}$$

$$F-measure = \frac{2 \times Precision \times Recall}{Precision + Recall} \tag{9}$$

Figure 4 is a precision-recall graph for 241 events. Lower one is the result by initial event score and higher one is that by updating event score. According to the graph, the precision of the experiment considering initial event score is higher than the other over all recall range. These results show high recall while maintaining high precision. High precision is due to the pattern information as well as the information of dependency relation among arguments and an event verb. Moreover, high recall is due to the co-occurrence information between arguments in events. Even though the length of the pattern is long, if the co-occurrence score of the event is higher than the shorter one, then our system can regard the event of the longer pattern as more reliable. For reference, when we extracted event by using only the small initial patterns, the performance is 96.3% precision and 32.37% recall. From these results, we can see that the

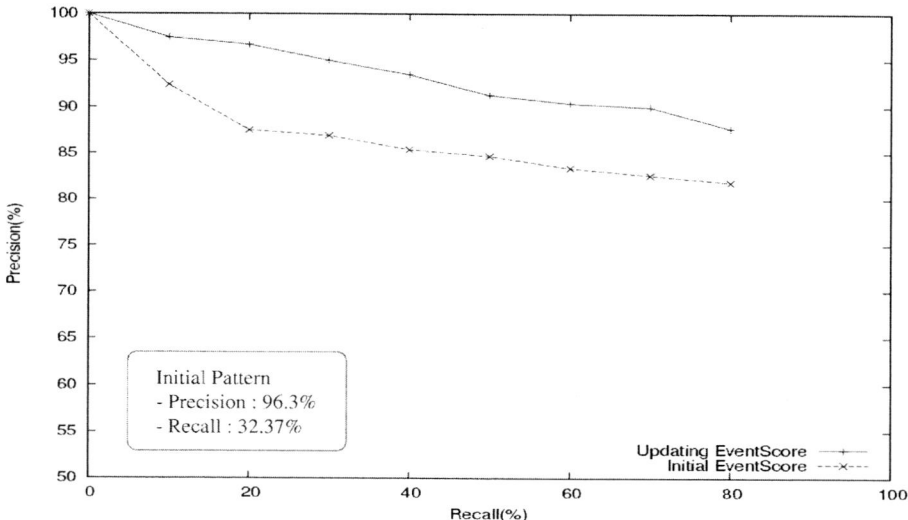

Fig. 4. Precision-Recall Graph for 241 Events.

co-occurrence, the dependency relations, and the pattern information take important roles in improving the performance.

However, there are several problems in our system. Our system limits the events as a binary relation between entities, so we cannot extract *process* as an event. For example, given a sentence "Mutational removal of the $JNK\ phosphorylation\ sites$ caused constitutive nuclear localization of $NFAT4$.", our system extracted "$JNK\ phosphory-lation\ sites$ cause $NFAT4$" as an event. However, the extracted event is unsuitable. We need to extract another information of the 'mutational removal' or 'constitutive nuclear localization' as an event, because they are meaningful information. Another problem in our system is that it highly depends on the named entity tagger. If an incorrect named entity tagging result is given as input, our system cannot extract the correct event.

5 Conclusions and Future Work

In this paper, we proposed a new unsupervised method of extracting events from biomedical literature, which uses the score measures of events and patterns having reciprocal effects on each other. Our research does not need a huge number of rules or annotated training corpora constructed manually. Our unsupervised event extraction is based on co-occurrence information, the analysis of the dependency relations and the patterns information. Our experimental results showed high recall (69.7%) while maintaining high precision (90.3%). By analyzing these results, we found that the co-occurrence information and the information of dependency relations as well as the pattern's score are very useful for extracting reliable events.

In the future, more experiments are required to do further analysis. Currently, the result of our event extraction system is the indirectional Entity-to-Entity network. Thus, I would like to exploit the voice information of verbs to generate directional relations between entities.

References

1. Douglas E. Appelt: Introduction to information extraction. Artificial Intelligence Communications, (1999) 12(3):161–172.
2. Denys Proux et al.: A pragmatic information extraction strategy for gathering data on genetic interactions. ISMB, (2000) 8:279–285.
3. Toshihide Ono et al.: Automated extraction of information on protein-protein interactions from the biological literature. Bioinformatics, (2001) 17(2):155–161.
4. Ralph Grishman: Information Extraction : Techniques and Challenges. Proceedings of the Seventh Message Understanding Conference(MUC-7), Columbia, (1998).
5. James Pustejovsky et al.: Medstract : Creating Large-scale Information Servers for biomedical libraries. Proceedings of the Workshop on Natural Language Processing in the Biomedical Domain, (2002) pp.85-92.
6. Tor-Kristian Jenssen et al.: A literature network of human genes for highthroughput analysis of gene expression. Nat Genet, (2001) 28(1):21–28.
7. Young-sook Hwang et al.: Weighted Probabilistic Sum Model based on Decision Tree Decomposition for Text Chunking. International Journal of Computer Processing of Oriental Languages, (2003) 16(1).
8. Ki-joong Lee, Young-sook Hwang, Hae-chang Rim: Two-Phase Biomedical NE Recognition based on SVMs. Proceedings of the ACL 2003 Workshop on Natural Language Processing in Biomedicine, (2003) pp33–40.
9. Kyung-mi Park, Young-sook Hwang, Hae-chang Rim: Grammatical Relation Analysis Using Support Vector Machine in Biotext. Proceedings of the 15th Conference of Hangul and Korean Information Processing, (2003) pp287–292.
10. GENIA Corpus 3.0p: http://www-tsujii.is.s.u-tokyo.ac.jp/genia/topics/Corpus/3.0/GENIA3.0p.intro.html (2003)

Annotation of Gene Products in the Literature with Gene Ontology Terms Using Syntactic Dependencies

Jung-jae Kim[1] and Jong C. Park[2]

[1] Korea Advanced Institute of Science and Technology, 373-1 Guseong-dong
Yuseong-gu, Daejeon 305-701, South Korea
jjkim@nlp.kaist.ac.kr
http://nlp.kaist.ac.kr/~jjkim

[2] Korea Advanced Institute of Science and Technology, 373-1 Guseong-dong
Yuseong-gu, Daejeon 305-701, South Korea
park@cs.kaist.ac.kr
http://nlp.kaist.ac.kr/~park

Abstract. We present a method for automatically annotating gene products in the literature with the terms of Gene Ontology (GO), which provides a dynamic but controlled vocabulary. Although GO is well-organized with such lexical relations as synonymy, 'is-a', and 'part-of' relations among its terms, GO terms show quite a high degree of morphological and syntactic variations in the literature. As opposed to the previous approaches that considered only restricted kinds of term variations, our method uncovers the syntactic dependencies between gene product names and ontological terms as well in order to deal with real-world syntactic variations, based on the observation that the component words in an ontological term usually appear in a sentence with established patterns of syntactic dependencies.

1 Introduction

As the proteomics research is turning to the task of uncovering novel pieces of knowledge about gene products (proteins), including protein-protein interactions [1, 15], subcellular localizations [6, 13], and their relationships with diseases [12], the need for consistently characterizing the functions of gene products is becoming well-recognized. Gene Ontology (GO) [5], which provides a common, controlled, and well-organized vocabulary that can be applied to all sorts of organisms, is under development in an answer to this need.

There are some attempts to assign GO terms to gene products both automatically and manually (cf. the GOA project [2]). Camon *et al.* (2003) presented an automated method of assigning GO terms to the entries of proteome databases, such as Swiss-Prot and InterPro [9], by utilizing the cross-references of GO with the classification systems of these proteome databases and Enzyme Commission (EC) numbers. At the same time, Swiss-Prot curators have manually assigned GO terms to the gene products which are not classified by any classification

Table 1. An example syntactic variation.

Protein	mAbs
GO term	*regulation of cell growth* (GO:0001558)
Sentence	To identify molecules regulating this interaction, we generated FDC-staining monoclonal antibodies (mAbs) and screened them for their ability to *block* FDC-mediated costimulation of *growth* and differentiation of CD40-stimulated B *cells*. (PMID:10727470)

systems, with the references in the literature. In this paper, we present an alternative method to automatically annotate gene products in the literature with GO terms by analyzing the sentences in the literature, which contain gene product names, with natural language processing techniques.

Some work has been done on the automatic annotation of gene products in the literature with the terms of Gene Ontology. Raychaudhuri *et al.* (2002) have utilized various document classification methods such as maximum entropy modeling in order to associate GO terms with literature abstracts, assuming that the GO terms associated with an abstract should be annotated to the genes that are associated with the abstract. Even though the method is reported to achieve an accuracy of 72% with maximum entropy modeling, we should note that the fact a GO term and a gene name occur together in the same abstract does not necessarily support the association between them.

Chiang and Yu (2003) have also developed a text mining system called MeKE, which extracts functions of gene products by utilizing the patterns that represent the syntactic relationships between gene products and their functions. The system employs a tokenization method in order to deal with variations of gene product names, for example alpha(1,3)-fucosyltransferase (GO:0017083), alpha (1,3)fucosyltransferase (PMID:9662332), and alpha-1,3-fucosyl-transferase (PMID:8207002), all of which refer to the same object. It is reported to show a relatively high accuracy of 68.9%~84.7%, but its tokenization method considers only restricted kinds of term variations, despite a rather high degree of morphological and syntactic term variations in the literature.

The degree of variations in the form of ontological terms in the literature is much higher than that of gene product names, so that the variations of ontological terms cannot be dealt only with a morphological treatment. For example, the ontological term *regulation of cell growth* may be represented with its syntactic variation as shown in the example of Table 1. The component words in the term, i.e. *regulation*, *cell*, and *growth*, are separated from, but syntactically related to each other in the example, where the action indicated by the verb *block* is regarded as a kind of regulating activities and the component word *cell* is pluralized.

Jacquemin (1999) has presented a method to deal with syntactic term variations. The method simplifies the problem of syntactic variations by focussing on binary terms only. The method utilizes patterns for syntactic variations, represented in regular expressions, including the variation 'verb-noun1' of 'noun1

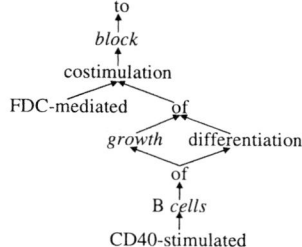

Fig. 1. A syntactic dependency structure.

(Modifier)-noun2(Head)' where 'verb' is a lexical variant of 'noun2'. The method is reported to achieve 91.1% precision, but it might not be straightforward for the regular-expressions utilized by the method to be extended to deal with the terms with more than two words or to deal with more complex linguistic phenomena such as relative clauses.

We adopted the notion of dependency from dependency parser (cf. Milward (1992)) in order to address these issues. For instance, the syntactic dependencies among the words in the substring of the example above, "to *block* FDC-mediated costimulation of *growth* and differentiation of CD40-stimulated B *cells*", can be depicted as the dependency graph in Figure 1. In a dependency graph, the arrow drawn from Word$_1$ to Word$_2$, as in the arrow from 'costimulation' to '*block*' in Figure 1, indicates the syntactic dependency between Word$_1$ and Word$_2$, denoted as (Word$_1$, Word$_2$). We extend the notion of syntactic dependency to exhibit transitivity as well, that is, the two dependencies, or (Word$_1$, Word$_2$) and (Word$_2$, Word$_3$), together imply (Word$_1$, Word$_3$). While the predicate-argument structures which can be identified by a sentential syntactic analysis can deal with the terms with more than two words and complex linguistic phenomena (cf. Friedman *et al.* (2001)), the extended notion of syntactic dependency can further deal with the phrases intervening component words in the literature. Therefore, the syntactic dependencies among the words, or *block*, *growth*, and *cells* in Figure 1, successfully represent the relationships among the component words in the ontological term *regulation of cell growth*.

The pre-specification of the syntactic and semantic relations between the component words in ontological terms would make it possible to recognize the syntactic variations of the ontological terms from the literature. The inter-relations among the ontological terms are specified in various ways including synonymy, 'is-a', and 'part-of' relations, but the intra-relations among the component words in GO terms may not be so clear. Based on the observation that the component words in an ontological term appear in a sentence with known patterns of syntactic dependencies as in Figure 1, we propose a method to annotate gene products in the literature with ontological terms by analyzing the syntactic dependencies of the sentences which contain the gene product names. In particular, the proposed method does not attempt to directly identify the semantic relations among the component words in GO terms, but to indirectly analyze the relationships among the basic terms according to the syntactic dependencies of sentences in order to overcome the overloaded representations of the semantics of all the GO terms (cf. Jacquemin (1999)).

2 Methods

In this section, we describe a method for the ontological annotation of gene products in the literature with three steps: first to locate the gene product names in the literature (§2.1), then to recognize the terms of Gene Ontology in the sentences containing the gene product names by analyzing the syntactic dependencies of the sentences (§2.2), and finally to annotate gene products with relevant ontological terms (§2.3).

2.1 Named Entity Recognition

We have collected the names of genes and gene products in the GN (gene name) and DE (description) fields of Swiss-Prot in order to locate them in the literature. In addition to their variations which require a process of tokenization as proposed by Chiang and Yu (2003), we have further dealt with other variations whose interpretations need domain knowledge. For example, the letter 'p' in Sla2p indicates 'protein', and therefore, Sla2p indicates the gene product (or protein) of the gene SLA2. Thus, if a term ends with 'p' and the rest is a gene name, then it is identified as the gene product name of the gene.

2.2 Ontological Term Recognition

We utilize the terms of Gene Ontology (GO) which provides a dynamic but controlled vocabulary that can be applied to all eukaryotes. Although GO provides three structured networks of defined terms to describe gene product attributes, we propose a grammar for the semantics of GO terms in Figure 2 with four primitives: **agent, phenomenon, event,** and **pathway**[1]. Agents indicate the objects in biological domain. Phenomena indicate individual biological phenomena, which do not necessarily require **agents**, such as *cell cycle* and *behavior*. We regard events as the biological events which require their targets, or objects, as in *binding* and *regulation*. A **pathway** is not an individual biological event, but a series of events. We have classified GO terms into the four primitive classes according to their headwords, where the primitive class into which the headword of a GO term is classified is regarded as the semantic type of the GO term.

The GO terms of each semantic type show different kinds of variations in the literature from those of other semantic types. The terms of **agent** and **phenomena** types mostly show only simple term variations in the literature when they do not involve modifying phrases which modify their headwords. The terms of **event**

---

[1] (A,B) indicates a binary relation in which A is the semantic parent of B, e.g. if A is an **event**, then B is the target of A, and if A is an **agent**, then B is the property of B.

```
GO TERM ::= AGENT              EVENT ::= event
         |  EVENT                    |  (event, agent)
         |  PATHWAY                  |  (event, phenomenon)
         |  phenomenon               |  (event, EVENT)
                                     |  (event, PATHWAY)

    AGENT ::= agent           PATHWAY ::= pathway
           |  (agent, EVENT)         |  (pathway, agent)
```

Fig. 2. Grammar for the semantics of GO terms.

Table 2. Verb-object relation.

Protein	RIP3
GO term	*inhibition of caspase activation* (GO:0001719)
Sentence	Overexpression of a dominant-negative mutant of RIP3 strongly *inhibited* the *caspase activation* but not the NFkappaB activation induced by TNFalpha. (PMID:10339433)

type further show syntactic and pragmatic variations in the literature, while the terms of **pathway** types can be represented in the literature in more complex ways. Tables 2 and 3 show the examples of syntactic variations, or a verb-noun relation and a noun-preposition-noun relation, respectively. In particular, the ontological term *regulation of cell differentiation* in Table 3 is of **event** type and the target of its headword, or *cell differentiation*, is also of **event** type, and therefore the semantic relations of the term are cascaded, as in (*regulation*, (*differentiation*, *cell*)). The headwords of the terms of **event** and **pathway** types can be expressed by their synonyms or hyponyms as in the example of Table 1. Furthermore, Table 4 shows the pragmatic variation of a GO term whose component words are expressed across several sentences, but describe the properties of the same protein, or Grap-2.

In this paper, we propose to recognize the syntactic variations of ontological terms by analyzing the syntactic dependencies of sentences. In particular, we utilize a parser for Combinatory Categorial Grammar [14] in order to deal primarily with complex coordinate phrases in the biological literature. For instance, the parser successfully identifies the coordination of *growth* and *differentiation*, without which the syntactic dependency between *growth* and *cells* cannot be identified.

2.3 Ontological Annotation

We have argued that the component words in ontological terms may show syntactic dependencies in the literature in §2.2, but we have also found that there are syntactic relations between gene product names and ontological terms which describe the functions of gene products. The simplest case is the one in which the gene product name is the ontological term itself. For example, the GO term

Table 3. Noun-preposition-noun relation.

Protein	E47
GO term	*regulation of cell differentiation* (GO:0045595)
Sentence	The E2A protein **E47** is known to be involved in the *regulation* of tissue-specific gene expression and *cell differentiation*. (PMID:10781029)

Table 4. Complex variation of ontological terms.

Protein	`Grap-2`
GO term	*SH3/SH2 adaptor protein activity* (GO:0005070)
Sentence	In this study, we report the molecular cloning of a novel *adaptor-like* protein, `Grap-2`, using the multisubstrate docking protein Gab-1 as bait in the yeast two-hybrid system. Sequence analysis revealed that `Grap-2` contains a *SH3-SH2-SH3* structure that has a high degree of sequence homology to those of the Grb-2 and Grap adaptor molecules. (PMID:9878555)

Table 5. Subject-object relation.

Protein	`h-warts/LATS1`
GO term	*protein serine/threonine kinase activity* (GO:0004674)
Sentence	A human homologue of the Drosophila warts tumor suppressor, `h-warts/LATS1`, <u>is</u> an evolutionarily conserved *serine/threonine kinase* and a dynamic component of the mitotic apparatus. (PMID:10207075)

Table 6. Complex syntactic relation between gene product name and ontological term.

Protein	`Mms19`
GO term	*transcription* (GO:0006350)
Sentence	An intriguing example is the Saccharomyces cerevisiae `Mms19` protein that <u>has</u> an unknown dual <u>function</u> in NER and RNA polymerase II *transcription* (PMID:11071939)

Xylulokinase activity in the molecular function category of Gene Ontology is assigned to the gene product name *Xylulokinase* in the literature, where the ending word 'activity' may be dispensed with in the annotation because many GO terms in the molecular function category are appended with the word 'activity' due to the possible confusion of gene products with their molecular functions.

In many cases, the ontological terms appear in the verb phrases whose subjects are the gene product names to which the terms are related. Tables 5 and 6 exemplify such cases, while the example in Table 6 shows quite a complex syntactic relation between the gene product name and the ontological term.

While the examples so far illustrate the syntactic relations between the gene product names and the ontological terms in the same sentences, they can also have a relationship via anaphoric expressions. Table 7 shows a relevant example in which the noun phrase 'the low-density lipoprotein receptor (LDLR)' is referred

Table 7. An example anaphoric expression.

Protein	LDLR
GO term	*lipid metabolism* (GO:0006629)
Sentences	The low-density lipoprotein receptor (LDLR) family is a group of related glycoprotein receptors that are bound to by a diverse array of ligands. These receptors play critical roles in the endocytotic processes of plasma apolipoproteins and therefore regulate cholesterol homeostasis and *lipid metabolism* (Krieger and Herz, 1994). (PMID:10049586)

Table 8. An example incorrect ontological annotation in subordinate clause.

Protein	Metaxin 2
GO term	*mitochondrial outer membrane* (GO:0005741)
Sentence	Metaxin 2 in intact mitochondrial was susceptible to digestion with proteinase K, indicating that metaxin 2 is located on the cytosolic face of the *mitochondrial outer membrane*. (PMID:10381257)

to by the anaphoric expression *these receptors* upon which the ontological term *lipid metabolism* is syntactically dependent.

Following the proposal in §2.2, we utilize the syntactic dependencies in the sentences, which contain gene product names, in the process of annotating gene product names in the literature with GO terms. We propose to annotate gene products in the literature with ontological terms in two cases: first, when the nearest common ancestor of both the gene product name and the ontological term in the dependency tree is a verb, whose subject and object contain the gene product name and the ontological term, respectively and vice versa, and second, when the gene product name is one of the ancestors of the ontological term in the syntactic dependency structures. In order to avoid incorrect annotation for the sentences which involve subordinate clauses such as *if*-clauses and *when*-clauses, as in Table 8[2], we apply the proposed method to main clauses and subordinate clauses individually, after separating them with such patterns as 'If SUBCLAUSE , MAINCLAUSE' and 'MAINCLAUSE , indicating that SUBCLAUSE' where MAINCLAUSE indicates the main clause of a sentence and SUBCLAUSE the subordinate clause.

3 Experimental Results

We have collected 211 abstracts into a corpus, which is utilized as the reference for GOA records. We have examined the GOA records related to the half of the

---

[2] The association of the ontological term *mitochondrial outer membrane* with the gene product name Metaxin 2 in the main clause of the example in Table 8 is incorrect, while the association of the ontological term with the same gene product name metaxin 2 in the matrix clause is correct.

Table 9. Experimental methods.

Baseline1	the gene product name and all the component words in the ontological term appear in the same sentence
Baseline2	the gene product name and the ontological term appear in the same sentence
Proposed method	the gene product name appear in the sentence where all the words in the ontological term have syntactic dependencies

Table 10. Experimental results.

	Baseline1	Baseline2	Proposed method
recognized GO terms	436	202	78
correct annotations	174	106	61
incorrect annotations	235	41	7
precision	42.5%	72.1%	89.7%

Table 11. An example incorrect term recognition.

Protein	PCNA
Incorrect GO term	*protein repair*
Sentence	Gadd45 was found to bind to **PCNA**, a normal component of Cdk complexes and a *protein* involved in DNA replication and *repair*. (PMID:7973727)

211 abstracts as the training corpus, and applied the proposed method to the other half as the test corpus.

In order to assess our proposal to utilize the syntactic dependencies in sentences, we have set baselines that do not utilize any relations between the component words in terms, but only recognize the terms whose component words occur in the same sentences (see Table 9).

Table 10 shows the experimental results of the baselines and proposed method. In order to focus on the syntactic relations among component words in terms, we considered only the terms with more than one component words. Furthermore, if two ontological terms extracted from the same sentence are in a synonymy, 'is-a' or 'part-of' relation in the GO hierarchy, then we ignored the more general one and utilized only the more specific term during the process of annotation. We have not calculated the recall, for which we would need a comprehensive understanding of the relevant gene products. We leave the task for future work.

The incorrect ontological term recognition in Table 11 can be dealt with only by utilizing biological knowledge so that, for instance, if *repair* is a kind of *DNA repair*, then it cannot be of the type *protein repair*, and by analyzing the coordinate string 'DNA replication and repair' properly (cf. Park and Cho (2000)).

Table 12. An example incorrect annotation.

Protein	SH3PX1
GO term	*intracellular transport* (GO:0046907)
Sentence	Since rat endophilin I is thought to play a role in synaptic vesicle endocytosis and SH3PX1 has sequence similarity to sorting nexins in yeast, we propose that endophilin I and SH3PX1 may have a role in regulating the function of MDC9 and MDC15 by influencing their intracellular processing, transport, or final subcellular localization. (PMID:7973727)

Table 12 shows an example of incorrect annotation in which the underlined possessive pronoun 'their' refers to MDC9 and MDC15, and thus, the ontological term *intracellular transport* is associated only with them, and not with SH3PX1. By contrast, the annotation of Cdc2 in the compound noun phrase 'Cdc2 kinase activity' with *kinase activity* is not correct, though the syntactic relation between 'their' and *intracellular transport* in Table 12 is very similar to the relation between Cdc2 and *kinase activity*. These problems may be addressed only on a case-by-case basis for compound noun phrases and with a grammar for the semantics of GO terms.

Notice that the present performance of 89.7% precision shows a marked improvement over Chiang and Yu (2003), without computing in advance all the patterns for the associations between gene product names and ontological terms.

4 Conclusion

We have described a method for automatic annotation of gene products in the literature with Gene Ontology terms. We utilize the syntactic dependencies of sentences in order to recognize the syntactic variations of ontological terms and to annotate gene products with them. By focussing on the syntactic dependencies, we have shown that it is possible to recognize a lot of syntactic variations of ontological terms. More importantly, we have shown that it is not necessary to compute in advance all the patterns for the associations between gene product names and ontological terms.

Our current method still cannot annotate gene products with ontological terms when they appear across multiple sentences. For this problem, we need to make use of the adjective or prepositional phrases which modify gene product names and also to resolve anaphoric expressions. We also need to raise the recall of the proposed method, by retrieving the hyponyms of the headwords of GO terms from the literature. A study towards this direction is on-going.

Acknowledgements

This work has been supported by the Korea Science and Engineering Foundation through Advanced IT Research Center.

References

1. Bader, G.D., Betel, D., Hogue, C.W.: BIND: the Biomolecular Interaction Network Database. Nucl. Acids. Res. **31**(1) (2003) 248–50
2. Camon, E., Barrell, B., Brooksbank, C., Magrane, M., Apweiler, R.: The Gene Ontology Annotation (GOA) Project: Application of GO in SWISS-PROT, TrEMBL and InterPro. Comp. Funct. Genom. **4** (2003) 71–74
3. Chiang, J.H., Yu, H.C.: MeKE: discovering the functions of gene products from biomedical literature via sentence alignment. Bioinformatics **19**(11) (2003) 1417–1422
4. Friedman, C., Kra, P., Yu, H., Krauthammer, M., Rzhetsky, A.: GENIES: a natural-language processing system for the extraction of molecular pathways from journal articles. Bioinformatics **17** Suppl. 1 (2001) S74–S82
5. The Gene Ontology Consortium: Gene Ontology: tool for the unification of biology. Nature Genet. **25** (2000) 25–29
6. Hua, S., Sun, Z.: Support vector machine approach for protein subcellular localization prediction. Bioinformatics **17**(8) (2001) 721–728
7. Jacquemin, C.: Syntagmatic and paradigmatic representations of term variation. Proc. ACL, University of Maryland (1999) 341–348
8. Milward, D.: Dynamics, dependency grammar and incremental interpretation. Proc. COLING (1992) 1095–1099
9. Mulder, N.J., *et al.*: The InterPro Database, 2003 brings increased coverage and new features. Nucl. Acids. Res. **31** (2003) 315–318
10. Park, J.C., Cho, H.J.: Informed parsing for coordination with Combinatory Categorial Grammar. Proc. COLING (2000) 593–599
11. Raychaudhuri, S., Chang, J.T., Sutphin, P.D., Altman, R.B.: Associating genes with Gene Ontology codes using a Maximum Entropy analysis of biomedical literature. Genome Research **12**(1) (2002) 203–214
12. Rindflesch, T.C., Tanabe, L., Weinstein, J.N., Hunter, L.: EDGAR: Extraction of drugs, genes and relations from the biomedical literature. Proc. Pacific Symposium on Biocomputing (2000) 517–528
13. Stapley, B.J., Kelley, L.A., Sternberg, M.J.E.: Predicting the subcellular location of proteins from text using support vector machines. Proc. Pacific Symposium on Biocomputing (2002) 374–385
14. Steedman, M.: The syntactic process. MIT Press (2000)
15. Xenarios, I., Salwinski, L., Duan, X.J., Higney, P., Kim, S., Eisenberg, D.: DIP: The Database of Interacting Proteins. A research tool for studying cellular networks of protein interactions. Nucl. Acids. Res. **30** (2002) 303–305

Mining Biomedical Abstracts: What's in a Term?

Goran Nenadic[1,4], Irena Spasic[2,4], and Sophia Ananiadou[3,4,*]

[1] Department of Computation, UMIST, Manchester M60 1QD, UK
G.Nenadic@co.umist.ac.uk
[2] Department of Chemistry, UMIST, Manchester M60 1QD, UK
I.Spasic@umist.ac.uk
[3] Computer Science, University of Salford, Salford M5 4WT, UK
S.Ananiadou@salford.ac.uk
[4] National Centre for Text Mining, Manchester, UK

Abstract. In this paper we present a study of the usage of terminology in the biomedical literature, with the main aim to indicate phenomena that can be helpful for automatic term recognition in the domain. Our analysis is based on the terminology appearing in the Genia corpus. We analyse the usage of biomedical terms and their variants (namely inflectional and orthographic alternatives, terms with prepositions, coordinated terms, etc.), showing the variability and dynamic nature of terms used in biomedical abstracts. Term coordination and terms containing prepositions are analysed in detail. We also show that there is a discrepancy between terms used in the literature and terms listed in controlled dictionaries. In addition, we briefly evaluate the effectiveness of incorporating treatment of different types of term variation into an automatic term recognition system.

1 Introduction

Biomedical information is crucial in research: details of clinical and/or basic research and experiments produce priceless resources for further development and applications [16]. The problem is, however, the huge volume of the biomedical literature, which is constantly expanding both in size and thematic coverage. For example, a query *"breast cancer treatment"* submitted to PubMed[1] returned nearly 70,000 abstracts in 2003 compared to 20,000 abstracts back in 2001. It is clear that it is indeed impossible for any domain specialist to manually examine such huge amount of documents.

An additional challenge is rapid change of the biomedical terminology and the diversity of its usage [6]. It is quite common that almost every biomedical text introduces new names and terms. Also, the problem is the extensive terminology variation and use of synonyms [5, 6, 11]. The main source of this "terminological confusion" is that the naming conventions are not completely clear or standardised, although some attempts in this direction are being made. Naming guidelines do exist for some types of biomedical concepts (e.g. the Guidelines for Human Gene Nomenclature [7]). Still, domain experts frequently introduce specific notations, acronyms, ad-hoc and/or in-

---

[*] This research has been partially supported by the JISC-funded National Centre for Text Mining (NaCTeM), Manchester, UK.
[1] http://www.ncbi.nlm.nih.gov/PubMed/

novative names for new concepts, which they use either locally (within a document) or within a wider community. Even when an established term exists, authors may prefer – e.g. for traditional reasons – to use alternative names, variants or synonyms.

In this paper we present a detailed analysis of the terminology usage performed mainly on a manually terminologically tagged corpus. We analyse the terminology that is used in the literature, rather than the terminology presented in controlled resources. After presenting the resources that we have used in our work in Section 2, in Section 3 we analyse the usage of "ordinary" term occurrences (i.e. term occurrences involving no structural variation), while in Section 4 we discuss more complex terminological variation (namely coordination and conjunctions of terms, terms with prepositions, acronyms, etc.). We also briefly evaluate the effectiveness of accounting for specific types of term variation in an automatic term recognition (ATR) system, and we conclude by summarising our experiments.

2 Resources

New names and terms (e.g. names of genes, proteins, gene products, drugs, relations, reactions, etc.) are introduced in the biomedical scientific vocabulary on a daily basis, and – given the number of names introduced around the world – it is practically impossible to have up-to-date terminologies [6]. Still, there are numerous manually curated terminological resources in the domain: it is estimated that over 280 databases are in use, containing an abundance of nomenclatures and ontologies [4]. Although some cross-references do exist, many problems still remain related to the communication and integration between them.

The characteristics of specific biomedical terminologies have been investigated by many researchers. For example, Ananiadou [1] analysed term formation patterns in immunology, while Maynard and Ananiadou [10] analysed the internal morphosyntactic properties of multi-word terms in ophthalmology. Ogren and colleagues [13] further considered compositional characteristics of the GO ontology[2] terms.

Previous studies are mainly focused on controlled vocabularies. However, controlled terms can be rarely found as on-the-fly (or "running") terms in domain literature. For example, we analysed a collection of 52,845 Medline abstracts (containing around 8 million words) related to baker's yeast (*S. cerevisiae*) and experimented with locating terms from the GO ontology (around 16,000 entries). Only around 8,000 occurrences corresponding to 739 different GO terms were spotted, with only 392 terms appearing in two or more abstracts[3]. Occurrences of controlled terms are more frequent in full text articles: for example, in a set of 621 articles (around 2 million words) from the Journal of Biomedical Chemistry[4] we have located around 70,000 occurrences with almost 2,500 different GO terms. This discrepancy is mainly due to the fact that abstracts tend to represent a summary using typically new and specific

---

[2] http://www.geneontology.org/
[3] Many GO ontology terms (i.e. entries) are rather "descriptions" than real terms (e.g. *ligase, forming phosporic ester bonds or oxidoreductase*), and therefore it is unlikely that they would appear in text frequently.
[4] http://www.jbc.org

terms, while full texts additionally relate presented work to existing knowledge using (widely known) controlled terms.

In this paper we focus on the terminology that is used in biomedical abstracts. To conduct the experiments, we have used the Genia resources [14] developed and maintained at the University of Tokyo, which include publicly available[5] manually tagged terminological resources in the domain of biomedicine. The resources consist of an ontology and an annotated corpus, which contains 2,000 abstracts obtained from PubMed by querying the database with the MeSH terms *human, blood cells* and *transcription factor*. All term occurrences in the corpus are manually tagged by domain experts, disambiguated and linked to the corresponding nodes of the Genia ontology. Also, "normalised" term forms (typically singular forms) are supplied, but apart from inflectional and some orthographic variations, the "normalisation" does not include other types of variation (e.g. acronyms). However, more complex phenomena (such as term coordinations) are annotated.

A total of 76,592 term occurrences with 29,781 distinct terms have been annotated by the Genia annotators in the version we have analysed. Three quarters of marked terms occur only once and they cover one third of term occurrences, while terms with frequencies of 5 or more cover almost half of all occurrences (see Figure 1 for the distribution).

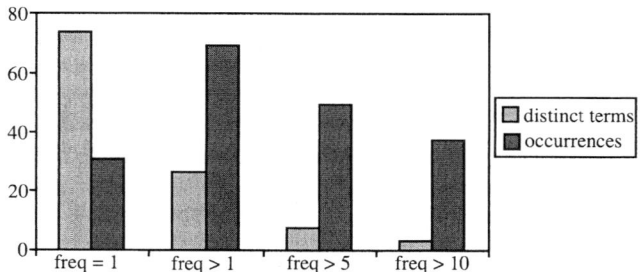

Fig. 1. Distributions (in %) of the Genia terms and their occurrences (coverage in the corpus)

3 Ordinary Term Occurrences

The vast majority of term occurrences (almost 98%) in the Genia corpus are "ordinary" term occurrences. An *ordinary occurrence* is a term occurrence associated with one term and is represented by a non-interrupted sequence of words (constituents), i.e. an occurrence that does not involve structural variation. Apart from ordinary occurrences, term constituents can be, for example, distributed within term coordination (e.g. *virus or tumor cells* encodes two terms, namely *virus cell* and *tumor cell*) and/or interrupted by acronym definitions (e.g. *progesterone (PR) and estrogen (ER) receptors*). However, only around 2% of Genia term occurrences are non-ordinary occurrences.

Ordinary terms are mostly multi-word units (terms containing at least one "white space"): 85.07% of all Genia terms are compounds, or almost 90% if we consider

---

[5] http://www-tsujii.is.s.u-tokyo.ac.jp/~genia/

terms with hyphens as multi-words (e.g. *BCR-cross-linking*, *DNA-binding*). The multi-word Genia terms typically contain two or three words (see Figure 2 for the distribution of the term lengths). Terms with more than six words are rare, although they do exist (e.g. *tumor necrosis factor alpha induced NF kappa B transcription*). Such terms are typically hapax legomena in the Genia corpus.

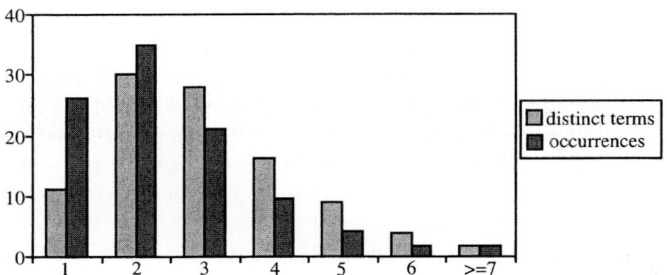

Fig. 2. Distributions (in %) of the Genia terms and their occurrences with respect to the length

Apart from using different orthographic styles, a range of specific lexical expressions characterise the common biomedical terminology. For example, neoclassical combining forms (e.g. *NF-kappa B*), adjectival and gerund expressions (e.g. *GTPase-activating protein*), as well as nominalizations and prepositional phrases (e.g. *activation of NF-kappaB by SRC-1*) are frequently used. Many terms in the domain incorporate complex relationships that are represented via nested terms. A nested term is an individual term that may occur within longer terms as well as independently [3, 13]. For example, the term *T cell* is nested within *nuclear factor of activated T cells family protein*. In the Genia corpus, nested terms appear in 18.55% of all term occurrences, with only 8.42% of all distinct Genia terms occurring as nested[6]. Almost a third of all nested terms appear more than once as nested, while more than a half of nested terms do not appear on their own elsewhere in the corpus. These facts suggest the recognition of inner structures of terms cannot rely only on spotting the occurrences of the corresponding sub-terms elsewhere in a corpus.

4 Terminological Variation

Terminological variation and usage of synonyms are extremely prolific in biomedicine. Here we discuss two types of term variation: one affecting only term candidate constituents (e.g. different orthographic and inflectional forms) and the other dealing with term structure (prepositional and coordinated terms). We also briefly examine how the integration of term variation into ATR influences the precision and recall performance (Subsection 4.4).

Variations affecting only term constituents are the simplest but the most prolific. For example, in Genia, a third of term occurrences are affected by inflectional variations, and – considering only distinct terms – almost half of the Genia terms had inflectional variants occurring in the corpus (i.e. almost half of occurrences are "nor-

---

[6] However, 2/3 of GO-ontology terms contain another GO-term as a proper substring [13].

malised" by the experts with respect to inflectional variation). Variations affecting term structure are less frequent, but more complex and ambiguous. Only around 7% of distinct Genia terms are affected exclusively by structural variation. We will examine in turn the most productive of these variations.

4.1 Terms Containing Prepositions

Terms containing prepositions are scarce: in the Genia corpus only 0.45% of all terms (or 0.5% of all multi-word terms) is constructed using a preposition[7]. Such terms are also extremely infrequent: 90% of the prepositional Genia terms appear only once in the corpus. The most frequent preposition is *of* (85% of prepositional terms) followed by only three other prepositions (*in, for* and *by*, see Table 1). In some cases terms can be "varied" by different prepositions (e.g. *nuclear factor of activated T-cells* and *nuclear factor for activated T cell*), and they can contain several prepositions (e.g. *linker of activation of T-cells*).

Table 1. Distribution and examples of the Genia terms containing prepositions

Preposition	Number of terms	Examples
of	113	*promoter of gene*
for	9	*binding site for AP1*
in	8	*increase in proliferation*
by	2	*latency by expression*

Interestingly, many potential term occurrences containing prepositions have not been marked as terms by the experts, unlike their semantically equivalent occurrences without prepositions. For example, in Genia, *HIV-1 replication* is marked as a term, while *replication of HIV-1* is not; similarly, *level of expression* is never marked as a term as opposed to *expression level*. Only in one case a prepositional term has been marked in an equivalent form without preposition elsewhere in the Genia corpus (*nuclear factor for activated T cell* appeared also as *activated T cell nuclear factor*). This analysis shows that biomedical experts seem to "prefer" nominal term forms, rather than prepositional expressions. Still, a number of terminologically significant expressions contain prepositions (e.g. *activation of PKC, NF kappa B activation in T-cells, expression of genes, production of cytokines, binding of NF kappa B, activation by NF kappa B*). These expressions – when individually presented to experts – are typically considered as terms. Therefore, the number of terminologically relevant prepositional expressions is much higher than the number of terms marked in the Genia corpus.

Still, the recognition of prepositional term expressions is difficult. Firstly, such expressions are extremely infrequent (for example, in the Genia corpus, only around 200 out of 60,000 preposition occurrences (i.e. 0.33%) have been marked as part of terms). Secondly, there are no clear morpho-syntactic clues that can help differentiate between terminologically relevant and irrelevant prepositional phrases.

---

[7] On the other hand, almost 12% of the GO-ontology terms contain prepositions (e.g. *regulation of R8 fate*), with prepositions frequently appearing in "description" parts (e.g. *oxidoreductase activity, acting on sulfur group of donors*).

4.2 Terms Encoded in Coordinations

Term coordination is a multi-word variation phenomenon where a lexical constituent(s) common for two or more terms is shared (appearing only once), while their distinct lexical parts are enumerated and coordinated with a coordination conjunction (CC). Consequently, term coordination encodes at least two terms. Apart from the pragmatic reasons of the language economy, stylistic motivations are also very important for the introduction of coordinations, as authors try to avoid recurrence of shared lexical units [5].

In the Genia corpus, term coordinations have been manually marked and they appear 1,585 times (1,423 distinct coordinations), out of 76,592 term occurrences, which is only 2.07% of all term occurrences. Still, a total of 2,791 terms are involved in coordinations, which makes 9.38% of all distinct Genia terms[8]. However, only one third of coordinated terms appear also as ordinary terms elsewhere in the corpus, which means that even 6.37% of all Genia terms appear exclusively as coordinated (i.e. they do not have any ordinary occurrence in the corpus, and can be extracted only from coordinations).

Coordinations containing conjunction *and* are by far the most frequent (87% of all term coordination occurrences), with *or*-coordinations contributing with more than 10% (see Table 2). Coordinated expressions encode different numbers of terms, but in the majority of cases (85-90%) only two terms are coordinated (see Table 3 for the detailed distributions for *and*- and *or*-coordinations).

In our analysis we distinguish between head coordinations of terms (where term heads are coordinated, e.g. *adrenal glands and gonads*) and argument coordinations (where term arguments (i.e. modifiers) are coordinated, e.g. *B and T cells*). In almost 90% of cases term arguments are coordinated, and as much as 94% of *or*-coordinations are argument coordinations.

Table 2. Distribution of term coordinations in the Genia corpus

CC	Number of occurrences	Examples
and	1381 (87.07%)	B-cell expansion **and** mutation
or	164 (10.34%)	natural **or** synthetic ligands
but not	20 (1.26%)	B- **but not** T-cell lines
and/or	8 (0.50%)	cytoplasmic **and/or** nuclear receptors
as well as	3 (0.19%)	PMA- **as well as** calcium-mediated activation
from to	3 (0.19%)	**from** memory **to** naive T cells
and not	2 (0.12%)	B **and not** T cells
than	2 (0.12%)	neonatal **than** adult T lymphocytes
not only but also	1 (0.07%)	**not only** PMA- **but also** TNF-induced HIV enhancer activity
versus	1 (0.07%)	beta **versus** alpha globin chain

---

[8] Only 1.4% of the GO-ontology terms contain CCs. However, these nodes mainly represent single concepts, and not coordinations of different terms.

Table 3. Number of terms in term coordinations in the Genia corpus

CC	Number of terms					
	2	3	4	5	6	7
and	1230 89.08%	101 7.31%	31 2.24%	14 1.01%	4 0.29%	1 0.07%
or	141 85.97%	19 11.59%	1 0.61%	2 1.22%	0 0.00%	0 0.00%

In order to further analyse the inner structure of coordinations occurring in the Genia corpus, we automatically extracted a set of regular expressions that described the morpho-syntactic patterns used for expressing term coordinations. Although the patterns were highly variable, the simplest ones[9] (such as $(N|A)^+ \ CC \ (N|A)^* \ N^+$) covered more than two thirds of term coordination occurrences.

Table 4. Ambiguities within coordinated structures

Example	adrenal glands and gonads
head coordination	[adrenal [glands and gonads]]
term conjunction	[adrenal glands] and [gonads]

Still, the structure of term coordinations is highly ambiguous in many aspects. Firstly, the majority of patterns cover both term coordinations and term conjunctions (where no term constituents are shared, see Table 4), and it is difficult (in particular in the case of head coordinations) to differentiate between the two. Furthermore, term conjunctions are more frequent: in the Genia corpus, term conjunctions appear 3.4 times more frequently than term coordinations.

In addition, some patterns cover both argument and head coordinations, which makes it difficult to extract coordinated constituents (i.e. terms). For example, the above-mentioned pattern describes both *chicken and mouse receptors* (an argument coordination) and *cell differentiation and proliferation* (a head coordination). Of course, this pattern also covers conjunction of terms (e.g. *ligands and target genes*). Therefore, the main problem is that coordination patterns have to be more specific, but there are no reliable morpho-terminological clues indicating genuine term coordinations and their subtypes. In some cases simple inflectional information can be used to identify an argument coordination expression more accurately. For example, head nouns are typically in plural (like in *Jun and Fos families*, or *mRNA and protein levels*), but this is by no means consistent: singular variants can also be found, even within the same abstract (e.g. *Jun and Fos family*, or *mRNA and protein level*, or *RA receptor alpha, beta and gamma*). Also, optional hyphens can be used as additional clues for argument coordinations (e.g. *alpha- and beta-isomorphs*). However, these clues are typically not applicable to head coordinations.

Not only recognition of term coordinations and their subtypes is ambiguous, but also internal boundaries of coordinated terms are blurred. For example, in the coordi-

---

[9] In these patterns, A and N denote an adjective and a noun respectively, while PCP denotes an *ing*-form of a verb.

nation *glucocorticoid and beta adrenergic receptors* it is not "clear" whether receptors involved are *glucocorticoid receptor* and *beta adrenergic receptor*, or *glucocorticoid adrenergic receptor* and *beta adrenergic receptor*. Furthermore, from *chicken and mouse stimulating factors* (a coordination following pattern N_1 *and* N_2 PCP N_3) one has to "generate" *chicken stimulating factor* (generated pattern N_1 PCP N_3) and *mouse stimulating factor* (pattern N_2 PCP N_3), while from *dimerization and DNA binding domains* (the same coordination pattern, N_1 *and* N_2 PCP N_3) terms *dimerization domain* (N_1 N_3) and *DNA binding domain* (N_2 PCP N_3) have to be extracted.

Therefore, we can conclude that significant background knowledge needs to be used to correctly interpret and decode term coordinations, and that morpho-syntactic features are not sufficient neither for the successful recognition of coordinations nor for the extraction of coordinated terms.

4.3 Terms and Acronyms

Acronyms are a very common term variation phenomenon as biomedical terms often appear in shortened or abbreviated forms [6]. Manually collected acronym dictionaries are widely available (e.g. BioABACUS [17] or acronyms within the UMLS thesaurus, etc.). However, many studies suggested that static acronym repositories cover only up to one third of acronyms appearing in documents [8].

In our experiments with acronyms we have found that each abstract introduces 1.7 acronyms on average: in a random subset of the Genia corpus (containing 50 abstracts) 85 acronyms have been defined. However, coining and introducing new acronyms is a huge topic on its own, and we will not discuss it here[10].

4.4 Term Variation and ATR

Although biomedical terminology is highly variable, only few methods for the incorporation of term variants into the ATR process have been suggested (e.g. [5, 11, 12]). In our experiments we evaluated the effectiveness of incorporating specific types of term variation (presented in 4.1– 4.3) into an ATR system (see [12] for details). We compared a baseline method (namely the C-value method [3]), which considered term variants as separate terms, with the same method enhanced by the incorporation and conflation of term variants [11, 12]. The baseline method suggests term candidates according to "termhoods" based on a corpus-dependent statistical measure, which mainly relies on the frequency of occurrence and the frequency of occurrence as a substring of other candidate terms (in order to tackle nested terms). When the baseline C-value method is applied without conflating variants, frequencies are distributed across different variants (of the same term) providing separate values for individual variants instead of a single frequency calculated for a term candidate unifying all of its variants. In the enhanced version [12], instead of individual term candidates we use the notion of *synterms*, i.e. sets of synonymous term candidate variants that share the same normalised, canonical form. For example, plural term occurrences are conflated with the corresponding singular forms, while prepositional term candidates are

---

[10] For more information on acronyms in the biomedical domain see [2, 6, 9, 11, 15].

mapped to equivalent forms without prepositions. Further, acronym occurrences are linked and "counted" along with the corresponding expanded forms. Then, statistical features of occurrences of normalised candidates from synterms are used for the calculation and estimation of termhoods.

The experiments with the Genia corpus have shown that the incorporation of the simplest variations (such as inflectional variants and acronyms) resulted in a significant improvement of performance: precision improved by 20-70%, while recall was generally improved by 2-25% (see [12] for further details). However, more complex structural phenomena had moderate positive influence on recall (5-12%), but, in general, the negative effect on precision. The main reason for such performance was structural and terminological ambiguity of these expressions, in addition to their extremely low frequency (compared to the total number of term occurrences).

5 Conclusion

In this paper we have analysed the terminology that is used in biomedical abstracts. The analysis has shown that the vast majority of terms are multi-words and they typically appear as ordinary terms, spanning from two to four words. Terms also frequently appear as nested in longer terminological expressions in text, while controlled dictionaries – having a more "complete world" of terms – have even higher proportion of nested terms than the literature. We also show other discrepancies (such as in prepositional and coordinated expressions) between variations occurring in literature and those found in dictionaries.

Regarding term variation, the biomedical terminology is mainly affected by simple term variations (such as orthographic and inflectional variation) and acronyms, which also have the most significant impact on ATR [12]. Only around 7% of terms involve more complex structural phenomena (such as term coordination or the usage of prepositional term forms). Although undoubtedly useful, attempts to recognise such variation in text may result in a number of false term candidates, as there are no reliable morpho-syntactic criteria that can guide the recognition process, and a knowledge-intensive and domain-specific tuning is needed (e.g. ontological information on adjectives and nouns that can be combined within coordination or with a given preposition). Still, the integration of term variation into an ATR system is not only important for boosting precision and recall, but also crucial for terminology management and linking synonymous term occurrences across documents, as well as for many text-mining tasks (such as information retrieval, information extraction, term or document clustering and classification, etc.).

References

1. Ananiadou, S.: A Methodology for Automatic Term Recognition. Proc. of COLING-94 1034-1038
2. Chang, J., Schutze, H., Altman, R.: Creating an Online Dictionary of Abbreviations from Medline. Journal of the American Medical Informatics Association. 9(6): 612-620, 2002
3. Frantzi, K., Ananiadou, S., Mima, H.: Automatic Recognition of Multi-word Terms: the C-value/NC-value Method. Int. J. on Digital Libraries. 3(2), 115-130, 2000

4. Hirschman, L., Friedman, C., McEntire, R., Wu, C.: Linking Biological Language Information and Knowledge. Proc. of PSB 2003 (the introduction to the BioNLP track)
5. Jacquemin, C.: Spotting and Discovering Terms through NLP. MIT Press, Cambridge MA (2001)
6. Krauthammer, M., Nenadic, G.: Term Identification in the Biomedical Literature. Journal of Biomedical Informatics. 2004 (*in press*)
7. Lander, ES, et al. (International Human Genome Sequencing Consortium): Initial sequencing and analysis of the human genome. Nature 409(6822), 860-921
8. Larkey, L., Ogilvie, P., Price, A., Tamilio, B.: Acrophile: An Automated Acronym Extractor and Server. Proc. of ACM Digital Libraries 2000, 205-214
9. Liu, H., Aronson, AR, Friedman, C.: A study of abbreviations in Medline abstracts. Proc. of AMIA Symposium 2002, 464-468
10. Maynard, D., Ananiadou, S.: TRUCKS: A Model for Automatic Multi-Word Term Recognition. Journal of Natural Language Processing. 8(1): 101-125, 2000
11. Nenadic, G., Spasic, I., Ananiadou, S.: Automatic Acronym Acquisition and Term Variation Management within Domain-Specific Texts. Proc. of LREC-3 (2002), 2155-2162
12. Nenadic, G., Ananiadou, S., McNaught, J.: Enhancing automatic term recognition through recognition of variation. Proc. of COLING-2004 (*in press*)
13. Ogren P., Cohen, K., Acquaah-Mensah, G., Eberlein, J., Hunter, L.: The Compositional Structure of Gene Ontology Terms. In: Proc. of PSB 2004, 214-225
14. Ohta T., Tateisi, Y., Kim, J., Mima, H., Tsujii, J.: Genia Corpus: an Annotated Research Abstract Corpus in Molecular Biology Domain. Proc. of HLT-2002, 73-77
15. Pustejovsky J., Castaño, J., Cochran, B., Kotecki, M., Morrell, M., Rumshisky, A.: Extraction and Disambiguation of Acronym-Meaning Pairs in Medline. Proc. of Medinfo, 2001
16. Pustejovsky J., Castaño, J., Zhang, J., Kotecki, M., Cochran, B.: Robust Relational Parsing Over Biomedical Literature: Extracting Inhibit Relations. Proc. of PSB 2002, 362-373
17. Rimer M., O'Connell, M.: BioABACUS: a database of abbreviations and acronyms in biotechnology and computer science. Bioinformatics. 14(10): 888-889, 1998

SVM-Based Biological Named Entity Recognition Using Minimum Edit-Distance Feature Boosted by Virtual Examples

Eunji Yi[1], Gary Geunbae Lee[1], Yu Song[1], and Soo-Jun Park[2]

[1] Department of CSE, POSTECH
Pohang, Korea 790-784
{juicy,gblee,songyu}@postech.ac.kr
[2] Bioinformatics Research Team
Computer and Software Research Lab. ETRI
Taejon, Korea 305-350
psj@etri.re.kr

Abstract. In this paper, we propose two independent solutions to the problems of spelling variants and the lack of annotated corpus, which are the main difficulties in SVM(Support-Vector Machine) and other machine-learning based biological named entity recognition. To resolve the problem of spelling variants, we propose the use of edit-distance as a feature for SVM. To resolve the lack-of-corpus problem, we propose the use of virtual examples, by which the annotated corpus can be automatically expanded in a fast, efficient and easy way. The experimental results show that the introduction of edit-distance produces some improvements. And the model, which is trained with the corpus expanded by virtual examples, outperforms the model trained with the original corpus. Finally, we achieved the high performance of 71.46 % in F-measure (64.03 % in precision, 80.84 % in recall) in the experiment of five categories named entity recognition on GENIA corpus (version 3.0).

1 Introduction

Recently, with the rapid growth in the number of published papers in biomedical domain, many NLP(Natural Language Processing) researchers have been interested in the task of automatic extraction of facts from biomedical articles. Since biomedical articles provide a wealth of information on proteins, genes, and their interactions, they can be used as a good information source. To extract useful information like interactions between several biological entities, we must firstly identify those entity names, e.g. protein names and gene names.

One of the main difficulties of biological named entity recognition is that there are many variant forms for each named entity in biomedical articles. So it is difficult to recognize them even if we meet a named entity already defined in the named entity dictionary. Edit distance, a useful metric to measure the similarity between two strings, has been used to help with those kinds of problems in fields such as computational biology, error correction, and pattern matching in large databases. To resolve this problem, we propose an SVM(Support Vector Machine)-based named entity recognition method, which uses the edit-distance metric as an additional feature.

Moreover, annotated corpus is essential to achieve good results of named entity recognition, especially for the machine learning based approaches, such as SVM, HMM, etc. But it is very difficult and time consuming to build such annotated corpora by human labor. So we propose an automatic corpus expansion method for SVM learning using virtual example idea.

The remaining part of this paper is organized as follows: First, we show some related works on biological NE(named-entity) recognition in section 2. In section 3, we describe the filtering stage to be used in SVM, and in section 4, we will explain our named entity recognition model based on SVM learning and using edit-distance. In section 5, we describe how to use virtual examples to automatically expand the training corpus. In section 6, we explain the experiments and their results to show the effectiveness of the proposed recognition model and the automatically expanded corpus. Finally, we will bring to a conclusion in section 7.

2 Related Works

To resolve the spelling variant problems in biomedical named entity recognition, Yi et al. [1] propose an HMM-based model combined with an edit-distance measure. They show that their edit-distance-combined model outperforms the basic model about 3%. Based on the idea that the edit-distance measure have some relation with observation probability, Yi et al. [1] modify the basic HMM model to incorporate with the edit-distance. But in the case of SVM-based recognition model, the modification of a model equation itself is difficult to be done in an intuitive way.

Another named entity recognition method using edit-distance is suggested by Tsuruoka and Tsujii [9]. They extract protein name candidates using edit-distance measure and filter the candidates to find the actual names. Their experimental result shows the recognition accuracy is 70.2% in F-measure. According to their method, edit-distance is calculated for every possible token sequence from the input token sequence. But their method possibly incurs some problem in recognition speed, since the biggest weak point of the edit-distance is that the complexity of computation is very high. Moreover, their method cannot easily extend the target recognition class to other categories like DNA, RNA, etc.

There are several SVM-based named entity recognition models. Lee et al. [3] proposes a two-phase recognition model. First, they identify each entity by an SVM classifier and post-process the identified entities. Then they classify the identified entities using another SVM. The identification performance is 79.9% and the recognition performance is 66.5%, both in F-measure. Since both phases use SVM classifiers, there method may suffer from slow speed both in training and in recognition. And the distinction between identification and classification can cause insufficient performance in recognition level, since the low coverage of the identification phase has a bad effect on the performance of the final recognition result. Yamamoto et al. [4] propose a SVM-based recognition method which uses various morphological information and input features such as base noun phrase information, head noun of the noun phrase, stemmed form of words, indicator terms, ontology features, etc. Their model attained F-measure 74.9% for protein name recognition. The performance is very high, but the model is only for one category recognition and needs various man-made dictionaries which are essential for the good performance.

3 Filtering of Outside Tokens

Named entity token is a compound token which can be a constituent of some named entity and all other tokens are outside tokens. In general, there are much more outside tokens than named entity tokens in a training data. Due to the characteristics of SVM, unbalanced distribution of training data can cause a drop-off of the classification coverage.

To resolve this problem, we filter out possible outside tokens in a training data by two filtering steps. First, we eliminate tokens which are not constituents of a base noun phrase. Since a named entity can be regarded as a complex noun, we assume that every named entity tokens should be inside of a base noun phrase boundary. Second, we exclude some tokens according to their part-of-speech tags. We build a part-of-speech tag list to be excluded by collecting the tags which have the small chances of being a named entity token, like predeterminer, determiner, etc.

After this two steps of filtering process, among 490,641 tokens of GENIA corpus [7] ver. 3.01p, about 40% of the possible outside tokens are filtered out and there are 280,228 tokens remained where about 35% of them turns out to be actual named entity tokens. Only 3.5% actual named entity tokens are filtered out.

Since the total number of tuples in a training data is also reduced during the filtering process, we can reduce the large portion of a training time which is in proportion to the square of the number of training data tuples. And there is another beneficial effect, i.e., reduction of recognition time, by reducing the number of support vectors which are the training results of SVM.

4 SVM-Based Recognition Using the Edit-Distance

Support Vector Machine (SVM) is a powerful machine learning method introduced by Vapnik [8], and it has been applied to various tasks in NLP such as chunking, part-of-speech tagging and unknown word guessing and achieves very good performance. It is also well-known that SVM is outstanding in its ability of generalization in a high dimensional feature space and high level of feature redundancy. We define a named entity recognition problem as a classification problem assigning an appropriate classification tag for each token in the input sentence. We use BIO representation for the classification tag.

4.1 Basic Features of SVM-Based Recognition

As an input to the SVM, we use bit-vector representation, each dimension of which indicates whether the input matches with the corresponding feature. The followings are the basic input features:

- surface word
  - only in the case that the previous/current/next words are in the surface word dictionary
- word feature
  - word feature of the previous/current/next words
- prefix / suffix
  - prefixes/suffixes which are contained in the current word among the entries in the prefix/suffix dictionary
- part-of-speech tag
  - POS tag of the previous/current/next words
- previous named entity tag
  - named entity tag which is assigned for previous word

The surface word dictionary is constructed by 12,000 words which occur more than one time in the training part of the corpus. The prefix/suffix dictionary is constructed by collecting the overlapped character sequences longer than two characters which occur more than two times in the named entity token collection.

4.2 Use of Edit-Distance

Edit distance is a measure for the similarity of two strings [6]. Consider two strings X and Y over a finite alphabet whose length are m and n respectively with $m \geq n$. The edit distance between X and Y is defined as the weight of all sequences of edit operations (insertions, deletions, and substitutions of characters) which transform X into Y. Since the edit distance is a useful metric to measure the similarity between two strings, it has been used in various fields including comparison of DNA sequences and amino-acid sequences, written-character recognition, and spelling correction.

To incorporate the effect of the edit-distance with SVM-based recognition method, we adopt edit-distance features as additive input features. Each token has N edit-distance features where N is the number of named entity category. To calculate the value of each edit-distance features, we define candidate tokens CT_i for each $i = 1, \cdots, N$ and initialize them as empty string, and then do the followings for each tokens in the input sentence.

- For each $i = 1, \cdots, N$, do the followings:
  1. (a) If the previous token was begin or inside of the named entity category NE_i, then concatenate current word to CT_i.
     (b) Otherwise, copy current word to CT_i.
  2. Calculate the minimum value among the edit-distances from CT_i, to each entry of the named entity dictionary for category NE_i, and store it as MED_i.

3. Calculate $medScore_i$ dividing MED_i by the length of CT_i (for normalization).
4. Set the ith edit-distance feature value for the current token same to $medScore_i$.

In the calculation of the edit-distance, we use cost function suggested by Tsurouka and Tsujii [9]. The cost function has consideration for different lexical variations such as about hyphen, lower-case and upper-case letter, etc., which is appropriate to the biomedical named entity recognition.

5 Automatic Corpus Expansion by Virtual Examples

To achieve good results in machine learning based classification, it is important to use a training data which is sufficient not only the quality but also in the quantity. But making the training data by hand needs a lot of man power and usually takes long time.

There can be various attempts to expand the amount of training data automatically [1] [2]. Expanding the training data using virtual example idea, which has been used in various fields such as written character recognition and document classification [5], is a new attempt of corpus expansion in biomedical domain. In this method, the training data is expanded by augmenting the set of virtual examples which are generated using some prior knowledge on the training data. So it is the key point to find and apply suitable prior information to generate good virtual examples.

To make virtual examples for biological named entity recognition, we use the fact that the syntactic role of a named entity is a noun and the basic syntactic structure of a sentence is preserved if we replace a noun with another noun in the sentence. Based on this paradigmatic relation, we generate a new sentence by replacing each named entity in the given sentence by another named entity which is in the named entity dictionary of the corresponding class and then augment the sentence into the original training data. If we apply this replacement process n times for each sentence in the original corpus, then we can get a virtual corpus about $n+1$ times bigger than the original one. Since the virtual corpus contains more context information which is not in the original corpus, it is helpful to extend the coverage of a recognition model and also helpful to improve the recognition performance.

Our corpus expansion method has two beneficial aspects. First, since the whole process is automatic and very simple, we can achieve a large amount of training data in a fast and an easy way. Second, if we build the named entity dictionary only by collecting the named entities in the training corpus, all we need to expand the corpus is an original annotated training corpus.

6 Experiments and Results

We use 1,600 abstracts as training data which are selected at random from 2,000 abstracts of GENIA corpus ver. 3.01p, and use remained 400 abstracts in test.

Table 1. Effect of edit-distance features.

feature type	category	precision	recall	F-measure
basic	protein	72.34	76.28	74.26
	DNA	52.75	53.96	53.35
	RNA	35.04	35.29	35.16
	cell type	71.69	75.49	73.54
	cell line	63.85	63.76	63.80
	Total	**66.92**	**69.76**	**68.31**
basic+ED	protein	73.52	77.61	75.03
	DNA	52.87	56.77	54.75
	RNA	36.03	32.47	34.16
	cell type	73.15	75.61	74.36
	cell line	63.66	63.66	63.66
	Total	**67.90**	**70.57**	**69.21**

Table 2. Effect of virtual examples: using basic features.

corpus type	category	precision	recall	F-measure
original	protein	72.34	76.28	74.26
	DNA	52.75	53.96	53.35
	RNA	35.04	35.29	35.16
	cell type	71.69	75.49	73.54
	cell line	63.85	63.76	63.80
	Total	**66.92**	**69.76**	**68.31**
original +virtual	protein	69.19	81.48	74.83
	DNA	55.35	65.31	59.92
	RNA	33.12	38.97	35.81
	cell type	70.06	79.29	74.39
	cell line	65.36	70.60	67.88
	Total	**65.44**	**76.21**	**70.42**

We set five categories, protein, DNA, RNA, cell type, and cell line, as for the target categories of the recognition among the categories of GENIA ontology.

To show the effect of edit-distance features in SVM-based recognition model, we compare the performance of recognition between the model which uses only the basic features and the model which uses edit-distance features additively to the basic features (see table 1). The model which uses edit-distance features outperforms the basic model not only in overall performance but also in the most of individual category performance. Even for the categories with some decrease in the category performance, the amount of decreases is very small.

To show the usefulness of virtual examples, we train each model, one is only with basic features and the other with additive edit-distance features, both using the original corpus and using the original corpus augmented by virtual corpus. Original corpus is same to the training corpus of the previous experiment, and virtual corpus is the collection of virtual examples which are generated according

Table 3. Effect of virtual examples: using basic features plus edit-distance features.

corpus type	category	precision	recall	F-measure
original (basic+ED)	protein	73.52	77.61	75.03
	DNA	52.87	56.77	69.87
	RNA	38.03	30.47	33.83
	cell type	73.15	76.61	74.84
	cell line	61.61	62.66	62.13
	Total	**67.36**	**70.87**	**69.07**
original +virtual (basic+ED)	protein	69.03	84.34	75.92
	DNA	53.94	75.05	62.77
	RNA	42.60	52.94	47.21
	cell type	64.53	81.24	71.93
	cell line	62.87	76.42	68.99
	Total	**64.03**	**80.84**	**71.46**

Table 4. Summary of table 1-3. Only the overall performance is shown.

corpus	feature	precision	recall	F-measure
original	basic	66.92	69.76	68.31
	basic+ED	67.36	70.87	69.07
original +virtual	basic	65.44	76.21	70.42
	basic+ED	64.03	80.84	71.46

to the method in section 5. We generate four virtual example sentences for each sentence in the original corpus. Table 2 demonstrates the result of the virtual example model which only uses basic features and table 3 shows the corresponding result of the model which uses edit-distance features additively. In both cases, the model using virtual corpus in the training outperforms the original model in F-measure, since the performance in recall is largely increased even though sometimes there are slight performance decrease in precision. Table 4 shows a summary of the overall performance for every combination on feature type and corpus type.

7 Conclusion

In this paper, we propose a method for named entity recognition in biomedical domain which adopts edit-distance measure to resolve the spelling variant problem. Our model uses the edit-distance metric as additive input features of SVM which is a well-known machine learning technique showing good performance in several classification problems. Moreover, to expand the training corpus which is always scarce, in an automatic and effective way, we propose an expansion method using virtual examples. Experimental results show that the introduction of edit-distance features to SVM-based recognition model increases the overall performance and also show that the automatically expanded corpus using virtual examples is helpful to improve the recognition performance especially in recall.

Now we are searching for other features for further performance improvement, since recognition precision on some classes, such as DNA or RNA, is relatively low compared to the protein on protein class, although the overall performance is remarkably increased compared to the basic model. Also, we are working on the compensation method which can minimize the precision drops in the corpus expansion method using virtual examples.

Acknowledgements

This research is funded by ETRI.

References

1. E.Yi, G.G.Lee, and S.Park: HMM-based protein name recognition with edit-distance using automatically annotated corpus. Proceedings of the workshop on BioLINK text data mining SIG: Biology literature information and knowledge, ISMB 2003
2. J.An, S.Lee, G.Lee: Automatic acquisition of named entity tagged corpus from World Wide Web. Preceeding of ACL 2003.
3. K.Lee, Y.Hwang, H.Rim: Two-phase biomedical NE recognition based on SVMs. Proceedings of ACL 2003 Workshop on Natural Language Processing in Biomedicine.
4. K.Yamamoto, T,Kudo, A.Konagaya, Y.Matusmoto: Protein name tagging for biomedical annotation in text. Proceedings of ACL 2003 Workshop on Natural Language Processing in Biomedicine.
5. P.Niyogi, F.Girosi, T.Poggio: Incorporating prior information in machine learning by creating virtual examples. Proceedings of IEEE, vol. 86, page 2196-2207 (1998).
6. R.A.Wagner, M.J.Fisher. The string-to-string correction problem. Journal of the Association for Computer Machinery, 21(1)(1974).
7. T.Ohta, Y.Tateisi, J.Kim, H.Mima, J.Tsujii: The genia corpus: An annotated research abstract corpus in molecular biology domain. Proceedings of HLT 2002.
8. V.Vapnik: The Nature of Statistical Learning Theory. Springer Verlag(1995).
9. Y.Tsuruoka, J.Tsujii: Boosting precision and recall of dictionary-based protein name recognition. Proceeding of ACL 2003 Workshop on Natural Language Processing in Biomedicine.

Author Index

Amano, Shigeaki 158
Ananiadou, Sophia 776, 797
Aramaki, Eiji 206
Asahara, Masayuki 500

Bae, Jae-Hak J. 280
Bai, Shuo 71
Bender, Emily M. 626
Bilac, Slaven 216
Bohnet, Bernd 299, 636
Bond, Francis 158
Bruza, Peter 100

Carpuat, Marine 476
Carroll, John 646
Chang, Du-Seong 61
Chang, Jason S. 224
Chang, Yi 71
Chen, Jinying 493
Chen, Kang 694
Chen, Keh-Jiann 655
Chen, Qing 527
Chen, Wan-Chen 263
Cheng, Yuchang 500
Cheong, Paulo 100
Chien, Lee-Feng 576
Choi, Key-Sun 61
Choi, Sung-ja 290
Chow, Ka-po 466
Chuang, Shui-Lung 576
Chuang, Thomas C. 224
Chun, Hong-woo 777
Chung, You-Jin 348
Čmejrek, Martin 168
Crestani, Fabio 745
Curín, Jan 168

Denecke, Matthias 1
Deng, Xiaotie 694
Ding, Yuan 233
Dohsaka, Kohji 1
Dong, Minghui 272
Du, Heather 745
Du, Lin 487
Du, Yongping 81, 139

Fan, Xiaozhong 723
Fang, Alex C. 646
Faruquie, Tanveer A. 254
Feng, Haodi 694
Frank, Ian 765
Fu, Guohong 704
Fujita, Atsushi 555
Fujita, Sanae 158
Fukushima, Toshikazu 596
Fukusima, Takahiro 177

Gao, Jianfeng 396, 723
Gao, Wei 110
Ge, Jiayin 139
Guo, Honglei 90

Ha, Juhong 509
Han, Gi-deuk 587
Han, Xiwu 664
Hashimoto, Chikara 158
Havelka, Jiří 168
Hsieh, Ching-Tang 263
Hsieh, Yu-Ming 655
Hu, Gang 90
Hu, Junfeng 320
Hu, Qinan 714
Huang, Chang-Ning 723
Huang, Chien-Chung 576
Huang, Xuanjing 81, 139
Hwang, Young-sook 777

Inui, Kentaro 555, 596
Iwasaki, Hideya 755

Jiang, Jianmin 90
Jin, Qianli 120, 416
Joshi, Aravind K. 446
Jung, Sung-won 587

Kang, In-Su 130, 280, 358
Kang, Mi-young 290
Kasahara, Kaname 158
Kashioka, Hideki 177, 206
Kawahara, Daisuke 12
Kido, Fuyuko 367
Kim, Byeongchang 509

Kim, Gil Chang   310
Kim, Jin-Dong   406
Kim, Jong-Bok   42
Kim, Jung-jae   787
Kim, Mi-Young   518
Kit, Chunyu   694, 714
Kitamura, Mihoko   244
Kiyota, Yoji   367
Klatt, Stefan   299
Kobayashi, Nozomi   596
Kordoni, Valia   674
Kuboň, Vladislav   168
Kuehn, Michael   743
Kumano, Tadashi   177
Kurohashi, Sadao   12, 206, 367
Kwon, Hyuk-chul   290, 587

Lai, Eugene   263
Lai, Tom B.Y.   466
Lam, Wai   110
Lee, Changki   616
Lee, Gary Geunbae   509, 616, 807
Lee, Jong-Hyeok   130, 280, 348, 358, 518, 566
Lee, Kong Joo   310
Leong, Mun-Kew   743
Li, Hongqiao   723
Li, Xin   81
Lim, Chul Su   310
Lin, Chuan   149
Lin, Dekang   545
Lin, Tracy   224
Liu, Feifan   416
Liu, Qun   537
Lua, Kim-Teng   272
Lü, Xueqiang   320
Luke, Kang-Kwong   704

Ma, Minhua   187
Ma, Shaoping   149
Matsumoto, Yuji   244, 386, 500, 555, 596
Mc Kevitt, Paul   187
Meng, Yao   733
Miyao, Yusuke   197, 684
Moon, Kyonghi   348

Na, Seung-Hoon   130, 358
Nakagawa, Hiroshi   338
Nakano, Mikio   1
Nanba, Hidetsugu   328

Nariyama, Shigeko   158
Nenadic, Goran   797
Neu, Julia   674
Ngai, Grace   476
Nichols, Eric   158
Ninomiya, Takashi   197, 684
Nishino, Fumihito   733

Ohtani, Akira   158
Okumura, Manabu   328, 456

Palmer, Martha   233, 493
Pan, Haihua   714
Park, Jong C.   776, 787
Park, Soo-Jun   807

Qiang, Wang   606
Qu, Weimin   487

Radev, Dragomir   32
Rim, Hae-Chang   777
Roh, Ji-Eun   566

Schneider, Karl-Michael   426
Seong, Yoon-Suk   509
Shei, Wen-Chie   224
Shen, Dan   436
Shen, Libin   446
Shirai, Kiyoaki   377
Siegel, Melanie   626
Song, Dawei   100
Song, Yu   807
Spasic, Irena   797
Su, Jian   22, 436
Sun, Le   487
Sun, Yufang   487
Suzuki, Hisami   396

Tajima, Sachie   328
Takamura, Hiroya   456
Tamagaki, Takayuki   377
Tan, Chew Lim   22, 436
Tan, Yongmei   527
Tanaka, Hideki   177, 206
Tanaka, Hozumi   216
Tanaka, Takaaki   158
Tanaka-Ishii, Kumiko   743, 755, 765
Tateishi, Kenji   596
Tsou, Benjamin K.   466
Tsujii, Jun'ichi   52, 197, 406, 684
Tsuruoka, Yoshimasa   52

Udupa U., Raghavendra 254

Wang, Xiaojie 386
Wong, Kam-Fai 100, 110
Wu, Dekai 476
Wu, Jian-Cheng 224
Wu, Lide 81, 139

XiaoLong, Wang 606
Xiong, Deyi 537
Xu, Bo 120, 416
Xu, Hongbo 71
Xu, Jun 272
Xue, Nianwen 493

Yang, Jaehyung 42
Yang, Muyun 664
Yang, Xiaofeng 22
Yao, Tianshun 527
Yi, Eunji 807

Yi, Guan 606
Yoon, Ae-sun 290
Yoon, Yongwook 616
Yoshida, Minoru 338
You, Lan 139
Yu, Hao 733
Yu, Hongkui 537

Zhang, Jie 436
Zhang, Junlin 487
Zhang, Le 320
Zhang, Min 149
Zhang, Tong 90
Zhang, Zhu 32
Zhao, Jun 120, 416
Zhao, Shaojun 545
Zhao, Tiejun 664
Zheng, Yu 509
Zhou, Guodong 22, 436
Zhu, Jingbo 527

Lecture Notes in Artificial Intelligence (LNAI)

Vol. 3345: Y. Cai (Ed.), Ambient Intelligence for Scientific Discovery. XII, 311 pages. 2005.

Vol. 3339: G.I. Webb, X. Yu (Eds.), AI 2004: Advances in Artificial Intelligence. XXII, 1272 pages. 2004.

Vol. 3336: D. Karagiannis, U. Reimer (Eds.), Practical Aspects of Knowledge Management. X, 523 pages. 2004.

Vol. 3327: Y. Shi, W. Xu, Z. Chen (Eds.), Data Mining and Knowledge Management. XIII, 263 pages. 2004.

Vol. 3315: C. Lemaître, C.A. Reyes, J.A. González (Eds.), Advances in Artificial Intelligence – IBERAMIA 2004. XX, 987 pages. 2004.

Vol. 3303: J.A. López, E. Benfenati, W. Dubitzky (Eds.), Knowledge Exploration in Life Science Informatics. X, 249 pages. 2004.

Vol. 3275: P. Perner (Ed.), Advances in Data Mining. VIII, 173 pages. 2004.

Vol. 3265: R.E. Frederking, K.B. Taylor (Eds.), Machine Translation: From Real Users to Research. XI, 392 pages. 2004.

Vol. 3264: G. Paliouras, Y. Sakakibara (Eds.), Grammatical Inference: Algorithms and Applications. XI, 291 pages. 2004.

Vol. 3259: J. Dix, J. Leite (Eds.), Computational Logic in Multi-Agent Systems. XII, 251 pages. 2004.

Vol. 3257: E. Motta, N.R. Shadbolt, A. Stutt, N. Gibbins (Eds.), Engineering Knowledge in the Age of the Semantic Web. XVII, 517 pages. 2004.

Vol. 3249: B. Buchberger, J.A. Campbell (Eds.), Artificial Intelligence and Symbolic Computation. X, 285 pages. 2004.

Vol. 3248: K.-Y. Su, J.'i. Tsujii, J.-H. Lee, O.Y. Kwong (Eds.), Natural Language Processing – IJCNLP 2004. XVIII, 817 pages. 2005.

Vol. 3245: E. Suzuki, S. Arikawa (Eds.), Discovery Science. XIV, 430 pages. 2004.

Vol. 3244: S. Ben-David, J. Case, A. Maruoka (Eds.), Algorithmic Learning Theory. XIV, 505 pages. 2004.

Vol. 3238: S. Biundo, T. Frühwirth, G. Palm (Eds.), KI 2004: Advances in Artificial Intelligence. XI, 467 pages. 2004.

Vol. 3230: J.L. Vicedo, P. Martínez-Barco, R. Muñoz, M. Saiz Noeda (Eds.), Advances in Natural Language Processing. XII, 488 pages. 2004.

Vol. 3229: J.J. Alferes, J. Leite (Eds.), Logics in Artificial Intelligence. XIV, 744 pages. 2004.

Vol. 3228: M.G. Hinchey, J.L. Rash, W.F. Truszkowski, C.A. Rouff (Eds.), Formal Approaches to Agent-Based Systems. VIII, 290 pages. 2004.

Vol. 3215: M.G.. Negoita, R.J. Howlett, L.C. Jain (Eds.), Knowledge-Based Intelligent Information and Engineering Systems, Part III. LVII, 906 pages. 2004.

Vol. 3214: M.G.. Negoita, R.J. Howlett, L.C. Jain (Eds.), Knowledge-Based Intelligent Information and Engineering Systems, Part II. LVIII, 1302 pages. 2004.

Vol. 3213: M.G.. Negoita, R.J. Howlett, L.C. Jain (Eds.), Knowledge-Based Intelligent Information and Engineering Systems, Part I. LVIII, 1280 pages. 2004.

Vol. 3209: B. Berendt, A. Hotho, D. Mladenic, M. van Someren, M. Spiliopoulou, G. Stumme (Eds.), Web Mining: From Web to Semantic Web. IX, 201 pages. 2004.

Vol. 3206: P. Sojka, I. Kopecek, K. Pala (Eds.), Text, Speech and Dialogue. XIII, 667 pages. 2004.

Vol. 3202: J.-F. Boulicaut, F. Esposito, F. Giannotti, D. Pedreschi (Eds.), Knowledge Discovery in Databases: PKDD 2004. XIX, 560 pages. 2004.

Vol. 3201: J.-F. Boulicaut, F. Esposito, F. Giannotti, D. Pedreschi (Eds.), Machine Learning: ECML 2004. XVIII, 580 pages. 2004.

Vol. 3194: R. Camacho, R. King, A. Srinivasan (Eds.), Inductive Logic Programming. XI, 361 pages. 2004.

Vol. 3192: C. Bussler, D. Fensel (Eds.), Artificial Intelligence: Methodology, Systems, and Applications. XIII, 522 pages. 2004.

Vol. 3191: M. Klusch, S. Ossowski, V. Kashyap, R. Unland (Eds.), Cooperative Information Agents VIII. XI, 303 pages. 2004.

Vol. 3187: G. Lindemann, J. Denzinger, I.J. Timm, R. Unland (Eds.), Multiagent System Technologies. XIII, 341 pages. 2004.

Vol. 3176: O. Bousquet, U. von Luxburg, G. Rätsch (Eds.), Advanced Lectures on Machine Learning. IX, 241 pages. 2004.

Vol. 3171: A.L.C. Bazzan, S. Labidi (Eds.), Advances in Artificial Intelligence – SBIA 2004. XVII, 548 pages. 2004.

Vol. 3159: U. Visser, Intelligent Information Integration for the Semantic Web. XIV, 150 pages. 2004.

Vol. 3157: C. Zhang, H. W. Guesgen, W.K. Yeap (Eds.), PRICAI 2004: Trends in Artificial Intelligence. XX, 1023 pages. 2004.

Vol. 3155: P. Funk, P.A. González Calero (Eds.), Advances in Case-Based Reasoning. XIII, 822 pages. 2004.

Vol. 3139: F. Iida, R. Pfeifer, L. Steels, Y. Kuniyoshi (Eds.), Embodied Artificial Intelligence. IX, 331 pages. 2004.

Vol. 3131: V. Torra, Y. Narukawa (Eds.), Modeling Decisions for Artificial Intelligence. XI, 327 pages. 2004.

Vol. 3127: K.E. Wolff, H.D. Pfeiffer, H.S. Delugach (Eds.), Conceptual Structures at Work. XI, 403 pages. 2004.

Vol. 3123: A. Belz, R. Evans, P. Piwek (Eds.), Natural Language Generation. X, 219 pages. 2004.

Vol. 3120: J. Shawe-Taylor, Y. Singer (Eds.), Learning Theory. X, 648 pages. 2004.

Vol. 3097: D. Basin, M. Rusinowitch (Eds.), Automated Reasoning. XII, 493 pages. 2004.

Vol. 3071: A. Omicini, P. Petta, J. Pitt (Eds.), Engineering Societies in the Agents World. XIII, 409 pages. 2004.

Vol. 3070: L. Rutkowski, J. Siekmann, R. Tadeusiewicz, L.A. Zadeh (Eds.), Artificial Intelligence and Soft Computing - ICAISC 2004. XXV, 1208 pages. 2004.

Vol. 3068: E. André, L. Dybkjær, W. Minker, P. Heisterkamp (Eds.), Affective Dialogue Systems. XII, 324 pages. 2004.

Vol. 3067: M. Dastani, J. Dix, A. El Fallah-Seghrouchni (Eds.), Programming Multi-Agent Systems. X, 221 pages. 2004.

Vol. 3066: S. Tsumoto, R. Słowiński, J. Komorowski, J.W. Grzymała-Busse (Eds.), Rough Sets and Current Trends in Computing. XX, 853 pages. 2004.

Vol. 3065: A. Lomuscio, D. Nute (Eds.), Deontic Logic in Computer Science. X, 275 pages. 2004.

Vol. 3060: A.Y. Tawfik, S.D. Goodwin (Eds.), Advances in Artificial Intelligence. XIII, 582 pages. 2004.

Vol. 3056: H. Dai, R. Srikant, C. Zhang (Eds.), Advances in Knowledge Discovery and Data Mining. XIX, 713 pages. 2004.

Vol. 3055: H. Christiansen, M.-S. Hacid, T. Andreasen, H.L. Larsen (Eds.), Flexible Query Answering Systems. X, 500 pages. 2004.

Vol. 3048: P. Faratin, D.C. Parkes, J.A. Rodríguez-Aguilar, W.E. Walsh (Eds.), Agent-Mediated Electronic Commerce V. XI, 155 pages. 2004.

Vol. 3040: R. Conejo, M. Urretavizcaya, J.-L. Pérez-de-la-Cruz (Eds.), Current Topics in Artificial Intelligence. XIV, 689 pages. 2004.

Vol. 3035: M.A. Wimmer (Ed.), Knowledge Management in Electronic Government. XII, 326 pages. 2004.

Vol. 3034: J. Favela, E. Menasalvas, E. Chávez (Eds.), Advances in Web Intelligence. XIII, 227 pages. 2004.

Vol. 3030: P. Giorgini, B. Henderson-Sellers, M. Winikoff (Eds.), Agent-Oriented Information Systems. XIV, 207 pages. 2004.

Vol. 3029: B. Orchard, C. Yang, M. Ali (Eds.), Innovations in Applied Artificial Intelligence. XXI, 1272 pages. 2004.

Vol. 3025: G.A. Vouros, T. Panayiotopoulos (Eds.), Methods and Applications of Artificial Intelligence. XV, 546 pages. 2004.

Vol. 3020: D. Polani, B. Browning, A. Bonarini, K. Yoshida (Eds.), RoboCup 2003: Robot Soccer World Cup VII. XVI, 767 pages. 2004.

Vol. 3012: K. Kurumatani, S.-H. Chen, A. Ohuchi (Eds.), Multi-Agents for Mass User Support. X, 217 pages. 2004.

Vol. 3010: K.R. Apt, F. Fages, F. Rossi, P. Szeredi, J. Váncza (Eds.), Recent Advances in Constraints. VIII, 285 pages. 2004.

Vol. 2990: J. Leite, A. Omicini, L. Sterling, P. Torroni (Eds.), Declarative Agent Languages and Technologies. XII, 281 pages. 2004.

Vol. 2980: A. Blackwell, K. Marriott, A. Shimojima (Eds.), Diagrammatic Representation and Inference. XV, 448 pages. 2004.

Vol. 2977: G. Di Marzo Serugendo, A. Karageorgos, O.F. Rana, F. Zambonelli (Eds.), Engineering Self-Organising Systems. X, 299 pages. 2004.

Vol. 2972: R. Monroy, G. Arroyo-Figueroa, L.E. Sucar, H. Sossa (Eds.), MICAI 2004: Advances in Artificial Intelligence. XVII, 923 pages. 2004.

Vol. 2969: M. Nickles, M. Rovatsos, G. Weiss (Eds.), Agents and Computational Autonomy. X, 275 pages. 2004.

Vol. 2961: P. Eklund (Ed.), Concept Lattices. IX, 411 pages. 2004.

Vol. 2953: K. Konrad, Model Generation for Natural Language Interpretation and Analysis. XIII, 166 pages. 2004.

Vol. 2934: G. Lindemann, D. Moldt, M. Paolucci (Eds.), Regulated Agent-Based Social Systems. X, 301 pages. 2004.

Vol. 2930: F. Winkler (Ed.), Automated Deduction in Geometry. VII, 231 pages. 2004.

Vol. 2926: L. van Elst, V. Dignum, A. Abecker (Eds.), Agent-Mediated Knowledge Management. XI, 428 pages. 2004.

Vol. 2923: V. Lifschitz, I. Niemelä (Eds.), Logic Programming and Nonmonotonic Reasoning. IX, 365 pages. 2003.

Vol. 2915: A. Camurri, G. Volpe (Eds.), Gesture-Based Communication in Human-Computer Interaction. XIII, 558 pages. 2004.

Vol. 2913: T.M. Pinkston, V.K. Prasanna (Eds.), High Performance Computing - HiPC 2003. XX, 512 pages. 2003.

Vol. 2903: T.D. Gedeon, L.C.C. Fung (Eds.), AI 2003: Advances in Artificial Intelligence. XVI, 1075 pages. 2003.

Vol. 2902: F.M. Pires, S.P. Abreu (Eds.), Progress in Artificial Intelligence. XV, 504 pages. 2003.

Vol. 2892: F. Dau, The Logic System of Concept Graphs with Negation. XI, 213 pages. 2003.

Vol. 2891: J. Lee, M. Barley (Eds.), Intelligent Agents and Multi-Agent Systems. X, 215 pages. 2003.

Vol. 2882: D. Veit, Matchmaking in Electronic Markets. XV, 180 pages. 2003.

Vol. 2872: G. Moro, C. Sartori, M.P. Singh (Eds.), Agents and Peer-to-Peer Computing. XII, 205 pages. 2004.

Vol. 2871: N. Zhong, Z.W. Raś, S. Tsumoto, E. Suzuki (Eds.), Foundations of Intelligent Systems. XV, 697 pages. 2003.

Vol. 2854: J. Hoffmann, Utilizing Problem Structure in Planing. XIII, 251 pages. 2003.

Vol. 2843: G. Grieser, Y. Tanaka, A. Yamamoto (Eds.), Discovery Science. XII, 504 pages. 2003.

Vol. 2842: R. Gavaldá, K.P. Jantke, E. Takimoto (Eds.), Algorithmic Learning Theory. XI, 313 pages. 2003.

Vol. 2838: N. Lavrač, D. Gamberger, L. Todorovski, H. Blockeel (Eds.), Knowledge Discovery in Databases: PKDD 2003. XVI, 508 pages. 2003.

Vol. 2837: N. Lavrač, D. Gamberger, L. Todorovski, H. Blockeel (Eds.), Machine Learning: ECML 2003. XVI, 504 pages. 2003.